FROM
ARISTOTELIAN
TO
REAGANOMICS

FROM ARISTOTELIAN TO REAGANOMICS

A Dictionary of Eponyms with Biographies
in the Social Sciences

RICHARD C. S. TRAHAIR

GREENWOOD PRESS

Westport, Connecticut • London

Library of Congress Cataloging-in-Publication Data

Trahair, R. C. S.
    From Aristotelian to Reaganomics : a dictionary of eponyms with
biographies in the social sciences / Richard C. S. Trahair.
        p.   cm.
    Includes bibliographical references and index.
    ISBN 0–313–27961–6
    1. Social sciences—Dictionaries. 2. Eponyms—Dictionaries.
3. Biography—Dictionaries.   I. Title.
    H49.5.T73   1994
    300'.3—dc20   93–37503   ‡ 2903058b

British Library Cataloguing in Publication Data is available.

Library of Congress Catalog Card Number: 93–37503
ISBN: 0–313–27961–6

First published in 1994

Greenwood Press, 88 Post Road West, Westport, CT 06881
An imprint of Greenwood Publishing Group, Inc.

Printed in the United States of America

The paper used in this book complies with the
Permanent Paper Standard issued by the National
Information Standards Organization (Z39.48–1984).

10 9 8 7 6 5 4 3 2 1

Contents

Introduction

This dictionary and sourcebook provides information about individuals whose names have been given to the language used by social scientists and those in related occupations and professions. This dictionary assumes that social science is a broad field rather than an academic discipline, and it includes events, ideas, and activities of professionals in such fields as anthropology, archaeology, economics, econometrics, economic history, political economy, education, criminology, legal studies, demography, human geography, journalism, ancient and contemporary history, management, business administration and industrial relations, social philosophy, politics, international relations, political science, popular culture, mass behavior, social psychology, sociology, and religious studies. It also includes problems and issues that center on gender, class, and social stratification. Such people use a specialized technical language, they draw on ideas in the humanities as well as the natural sciences, and they use literary images and characters as well as precise concepts from the research laboratory. Therefore, in this work the social sciences are considered as broadly as possible, and the entries for the dictionary and sourcebook are drawn from the periphery as well as the center of the social sciences.

The book includes close to a thousand eponyms; each one includes a definition, the period when the term was used, the name of individuals whose names attach to the term, and a short sketch of the lives involved. Each item is followed by a list of sources that the reader might expect to find in a good public library or with help from a reference librarian.

At the end of the dictionary the entries have been classified according to their relevance to various fields of social science (see Appendix): anthropology and archaeology; economics; education; gender; human geography; journalism; language and linguistics; legal studies; management, administration, industry, and business; philosophy and early social theory; politics and political science; popular culture and mass behavior; psychology and social psychology; religion; and sociology. With few exceptions, the individuals appear only once in the classification.

We compiled the entries for students and teachers, for people with an interest in social science generally, and for those who are simply curious about the individual whose name attaches to the information or idea in question.

Many people helped in this work. From the United States we acknowledge help from Robert F. Bales, James D. Barber, Arthur G. Bedeian, Warren Bennis, Patricia Brandt, Steven Brown, Fred E. Fiedler, R. D. Ford of the U.S. Navy, Eugene Garfield, Laelia Gilborn, Paul Glick, David Hawkins, Frederick Herzberg, Barbara J. Hill, Stanley C. Hollander, Ole Holsti, George F. F. Lombard, Melvin L. Kohn, Sandra J. Krizmanich, Walter T. Martin, Bruce Mazlish, William S. Robinson, Carmi Schooler, Herbert A. Simon, Woodman Taylor, Mark W. Tomkins, J. Whelan, and David G. Winter. In Europe the following were most helpful: G. Dekerk, Mieke van den Berghe, Antony Jay, and Les Wilkinson. In Australia we are indebted to Isabel Mouthino who graciously translated various European languages for the work. Valuable contributions also came from Richard Gillespie, M.A.K. Halliday, Leon Mann, John A.T. Morgan, Chris Puplick, and L. Teirlinch. At La Trobe University my colleagues who helped considerably were Peter Beilharz, Bill Breen, Andrew Dawson, David De Vaus, Ken Dempsey, Ray Juredini, Allan Kellehear, Beryl Langer, Brian Graetz, Martha MacIntyre, Angus McIntyre, John Morton, Glenn Mulligan, Rudolph Plewhe, John Salmond, Nonie Sharp, and Yoshio Sugimoto.

At the Borchardt Library, La Trobe University, we were very fortunate to benefit from the professional expertise and amazing patience of the reference librarians as a group, and in particular from Christine Maher, Margot Hyslop, Eva Fisch, Val Forbes, Ann Miller, and Julie Marshall. From the School of Social Sciences' research budget, Dean Talis Polis was able to provide funds to support this work during 1991–1993. We are also grateful to Beth Robertson and her helpers in the Department of Sociology at the university.

For several years Beatrice Meadowcroft has worked with the author on the subject of eponyms; this work owes much to her diligence and tenacity in researching the eponyms. I am very grateful for her efforts and advice. Toward the end of the project, she was joined by Faye Wilson who was an enormous help indeed. And the work began, long ago, with the question from Marion Glanville, "Who really were Boycott and Bowdler?"

Errors of fact, opinion, omission, presentation, and interpretation are our responsibility; we would be pleased to learn of any errors in the work and of any eponyms that ought to have been included. Details will be acknowledged with gratitude and used in the hope that the work can be improved.

What are eponyms? Eponyms begin with a name, and the name is usually that of a person. In the social sciences, many eponymous events are associated with the names not of people but of important places. So we have introduced some toponyms, for example, Dumbarton Oaks, the Gleneagles Agreement, Masada, the Potsdam Conference, Jonestown, and Sharpeville.

Where do eponyms come from? What purpose do they serve? Eponyms arise in many ways and serve different purposes, and although this is not the place to discuss their origins, we will note some of their features. Sometimes people give their own name to an item, and sometimes others do it in their honor. Most eponyms come from people who are still living or lived some time ago, but others are based on a fictional character, a legendary hero, or even a monster. Because in social science we call upon names in novels and stories, several fictional characters appear—for example, Fagin, Pickwick, Podsnap, Taper, and Tadpole. Each has a special meaning for daily social life and interpersonal relations, although they are not at the core of social science. Such eponyms are used to identify or summarize a social or political type, or the attributes of an occupation, for example, Tartuffe and Gradgrind. Some begin life in a cartoon like Mickey Mouse; others are slang, like ratfink; and still others are the modern inventions of political commentators, for example, Mary factor, Madonna connection, Mae West factor, Perotians, Darmanesque, Capraesque, and Clinton Republican. Others are born in secret or by accident, for instance, Maud Committee.

Some eponyms, like Rodhamism and the Kennedy Round, are modern and topical; others are old, some perhaps being of interest only to students of the English Civil War—for example, Pride's Purge and Barebones Parliament. Others are quite abstract and refer to a vast range of social thought and theorizing; these include Hegelian, the Halévy Thesis, Marxian, the Merton Thesis, and Meadian. Some refer specifically to only one item, for instance, Kinsey Report and Onassis Prize.

Usually eponyms in social science serve many purposes and have a life course of their own. In the natural sciences an eponym is primarily restricted to or reserved for a tribute to individuals who have made important contributions to their field. The same applies in the social sciences, especially in economics, where sophisticated theories and highly technical contributions appear; examples are Leontief curve, Kondratieff cycles, and Hicksian equilibrium. The same applies in modern psychology (Zusne, 1987). But in the social sciences eponyms have also been used to chide and vilify people, to destroy their reputation, and to identify them as villains. And often the eponym will mean one thing at one time and something quite different at another. In recent memory Reaganomics, Thatcherism, and Rogernomics were favorable terms that summarized ideas underlying the great economic and business growth in the United States, England, and New Zealand. Rogernomics held great promise for South American economies, as well as for those in Eastern Europe. But now we are not so sure.

In the social sciences, particularly psychology, many scales and measurement techniques are eponymous, and the interested reader will find them referred to in Zusne (1987) and in Miller (1991). We chose technical scales that are used frequently by authorities in the social sciences, for example, the Likert and Guttman scales. Well-known measures of social stratification, values, power and leadership, and responses to social conditions are also included, such as the Allport-Vernon-Lindzey Scale of Values, the Bogardus Scale of Social Distance, the Burgess Marriage Adjustment Scale, the Edwards Social-Economic Grouping of Occupations, the Holmes-Rahe Scale of Stress, the North-Hatt Scale, Rokeach's Dogmatism Scale, Seashore's Group Cohesiveness Index, and Srole's Anomie Scale.

The eponyms for this book were chosen from general reading and by scanning the dictionaries and encyclopedias in social sciences, textbooks, Ruffner et al. (1977), and professional journals, magazines, and newspapers. We decided on eponyms that told us of the times when they were used, the ideas they helped to refine, clarify, and extend, great social changes they related to, sacrifices that were endured, challenges, and fascinating ideas and curious activities. Some of my colleagues wanted only eponyms that had a secure place in academic social sciences, whereas others were keen on new eponyms from a wider world; some thought their colleagues' eponyms were ephemeral, too unusual, rarely used, esoteric, or too distant from what they believed was the core of social science, and others disagreed. All these criteria were considered; some were used with vigor and others not. Of course, the final criterion was the author's personal interest. So the list includes eponymous terms that are old as well as recent; at the core of the field and on its periphery; serious, refined, and intellectual, as well as lighthearted, earthy, and practical; theoretical and abstract as well as empirical and concrete.

A few observations about eponyms are worth making because they seem to indicate the future directions of research in this field of social science language. First, why do some fields of interest have more eponyms than others? Most eponyms come from politics; economics yields many technical and theoretical eponyms; and religion provides a vast source. But anthropology yields very few eponyms. Second, new eponyms originate every day in the newspapers, magazines, and even on television. For example, in his debate with Al Gore during the 1992 presidential election, Dan Quayle invented the expression a ''Clinton.'' Because they are being made daily, eponyms provide excellent data for the analysis of a society and tell how a culture promotes and destroys its notables, guilty or innocent, produces and manufactures the famous, and praises and dishonors those who leave a mark on our lives.

The most notable social research on eponyms was made by the American sociologist, Robert K. Merton (1973), who concluded that eponyms provide one of the most significant institutional rewards that a scientist can enjoy. To become eponymous, he suggests, is a powerful force, and forms the point at which the psychological motives of the scientist meet the demands and rewards of scientific work. He ranks eponyms for scientists and places first those people after whom an era is named; these include Newtonian epoch, Darwinian era, and the Freudian age. At the next rank are those people who established a new science.

Here belong Johann Friedrich Herbart, father of pedagogy, and Wilhelm Wundt, father of experimental psychology. Among such people are those in a subclass of science—Aristotelian logic and Keynesian economics. At the third level are the theorems and the laws, the technical instruments and the hypotheses, the constants and the curves. In Merton's list a few social scientists appear—for example, Lorenz curve, Zeeman effect, Spearman rank-correlation coefficient, the Rorschach ink-blot test, the Bogardus Social Distance Scale and the Thurstone Scaling technique, Bales classification for the study of social interaction, and Guttman's scalogram analysis. Merton uses medicine to illustrate his conclusion that eponymy is a prize, a token that is allowed to only a few. The Nobel Prize, an eponym in itself, is probably the most outstanding token of recognition.

Far from being anonymous in their work, Merton states, scientists have labored to achieve recognition as first in their field. In science, eponyms are terms in the international language that perpetuate an original thinker, a creative genius. As Merton remarks, the eponym is one of the most prestigious kinds of recognition in institutionalized science, as well as the most enduring. In discussions of the ambivalence that accompanies the creation of an eponym, Merton identifies a process by which fame and eponyms are linked, "the Matthew Effect."

The process of becoming eponymous also attracted the attention of Stephen M. Stigler (1980). According to Stigler's law of eponymy, eponyms are never named after their original discoverer. He illustrates his point with the scientific units named after those people who were not their originators, for example, watt, volt, and ohm. Stigler's law holds because eponyms in the natural sciences are named only after a long time, or at least at a great distance from the original event by those who generally are not well informed as to the origin of the phenomenon and who seek to recognize an individual's general merit rather than a particular achievement. Stigler extends his law to other fields and wonders what has an effect on the awarding of an eponym. The time lag between the discovery and the award? The importance of the discovery? The nation or culture in which the discovery has been made? The institutions associated with the discovery?

In the social sciences, eponyms are also used to bestow political recognition on those who are close to the center of power. In the United States, names are attached to laws and acts to celebrate the effort that has been put into getting them passed; in Britain eponyms appear less often in this regard. In Britain eponyms are used to reward notables who chair a court of inquiry or a royal commission, especially in matters relating to social conflict, justice, or welfare, for example, industrial relations and education, and national health. This occurs in the United States, too (e.g., the Kerner Commission), but it does not seem to be as common as naming laws after those who worked to get them through Congress.

Sometimes it is neither the chairperson nor the dominant character who earns the eponym; rather, it is the victim. In one legal case, a rule is named after a victim, not those who thought about it or uncovered it, and considered its ramifications. An example is the McNaughton rule in Britain for deciding when a person is not responsible for a crime due to insanity. The same holds in the United States for the Durham Rule. Another well-known victim was Roe of *Roe v. Wade,* and once, in Florence, Italy, a whole family was the victim for its part in the Pazzi Conspiracy.

Whatever rules, guidelines, or conclusions emerge in the study of eponyms, there are exceptions, special cases, theses and antitheses, as the Hegelian dialectic would tell us, and this suggests an interesting field of synthesis for eponym research. Meanwhile, in the social sciences eponyms will continue to indicate the labors of serious scholars and critics. They will always proceed to give immortality to both the virtuous and the wicked, and in everyday language they will never cease telling of the complexity of ideas. For this reason, they are useful to teachers and students who prefer to approach a search with title, author, subject, and citation indexes (Garfield, 1984).

REFERENCES

Garfield, Eugene. 1984. Current comments: what's in a name? The eponymic route to immortality. *Essays of an information scientist* 7:384–395.

Merton, Robert K. 1973. *The sociology of science: theoretical and empirical investigations.* Chicago: University of Chicago Press.

Miller, Delbert M. 1991. *Handbook of social research methods and research design.* 5th ed. New York: David McKay.

Ruffner, James A., et al., eds. 1977. *Eponyms dictionaries index.* Detroit: Gale Research.

Stigler, Stephen M. 1980. Stigler's law of eponymy. In Thomas F. Gieryn, ed. *Science and social structure: a festschrift for Robert K. Merton.* New York: New York Academy of Sciences:147–157.

Zusne, Leonard. 1987. *Eponyms in psychology: a dictionary and sourcebook.* Westport, Conn.: Greenwood Press.

A

ABRAHAM'S BOSOM, ABRAHAMIC COVENANT, ABRAHAM-MAN.
Abraham's Bosom is of Rabbinic origin and is used in the parable of the Dives and Lazarus, which appears in Luke 16:22. It signifies a place of repose where Abraham rests. In Roman Catholicism it is a place where saintly souls of the Old Covenant enjoy peace, or is heaven itself. The Covenant is the agreement between God and Abraham that the Messiah would be a descendant of his family because Abraham left his own home and country to live in the Promised Land, Canaan, as God wished; also the rite of circumcision. In Tudor and Stuart England an Abraham-man was one who would fake insanity while begging for a livelihood.

Abraham (early 2d millennium B.C.), a legendary figure, was the first Hebrew patriarch. At 15 months of age, Abraham had the body of a 15-year-old lad and wisdom so great that his father introduced him to King Nimrod. He was always ready to obey God's commands. At the age of about 75, he left Ur of Chaldees to migrate to the land of Canaan with his wife Sarai and his nephew Lot. He settled there and lived a prosperous life in the faith of Jehovah (Genesis 12–13). He had one son, Ishmael, by Hagar, his wife's maid; he and Ishmael built the Kaaba over the sacred stone at Mecca. He destroyed the idols made and worshiped by his father, Terah. At age 100, Abraham had Isaac by Sarai. Jehovah tested Abraham by demanding the life of his son Isaac, but just as Abraham was about to put the boy to death a ram was put in his son's place. When Sarai died, Abraham purchased a cave as a family burial place, Machpetah, the first piece of the Promised Land owned by Abraham. He died at age 175 and was buried beside Sarai.

See also NIMROD.

Sources

Cross, Frank L. 1974. *The Oxford dictionary of the Christian church.* 2d ed. New York: Oxford University Press.

Douglas, James D., ed. 1974. *The new international dictionary of the Christian church.* Exeter: The Paternoster Press.

Meagher, Paul K.; O'Brien, Thomas C.; and Aherne, Marie, eds. 1979. *Encyclopedic dictionary of religion.* Washington, D.C.: Corpus Publications.

McHenry, Robert, ed. 1992. *The new encyclopedia Britannica.* Chicago: Encyclopedia Britannica, Inc.

Thompson, Thomas L. 1974. *The historicity of the patriarchal narratives: the quest for the historical Abraham.* New York: W. de Gruyter.

Roth, Cecil E., ed. 1971. *Encyclopedia Judaica.* New York: Macmillan.

ACHESON-LILIENTHAL REPORT. A report on international control of atomic energy (May 1946). The plan stated that since the United States possessed the world's only atomic bombs, the nation should remain in control of its atomic capability; other nations would have to agree to inspection by the international agency connected with the United Nations. The report was scrapped in favor of a plan devised by Bernard Baruch (1870–1965), the U.S. delegate to the United Nations Atomic Energy Commission, but the plan was unacceptable to the Russians.

Dean Gooderham Acheson (1893–1971) was born in Middletown, Connecticut, and graduated from Yale and Harvard Law School (1918). After service in the navy during World War I, he was admitted to the bar (1921). In 1933 he became undersecretary of the Treasury and in 1944 assistant secretary to the State Department where he specialized in international economic matters and helped to establish the Lend-Lease Program. He succeeded George C. Marshall (1880–1959) as secretary of state in 1949. Acheson wrote several important books on foreign affairs as well as his memoirs, *Present at the Creation* (1967).

David Eli Lilienthal (1899–1981), a U.S. government official and a lawyer, served as director in charge of the power program of the Tennessee Valley Authority (TVA) during 1933–41. During World War II he expanded the TVA, making it the largest producer of electricity in the United States by 1944. In 1945 he joined the State Department to establish plans for atomic energy control, and was chairman of the U.S. Atomic Energy Commission (1947–50). He sought to advance the U.S. lead in the production of atomic energy and weapons. During 1953–79, he was chairman of the Development and Research Corporation for dam and power projects.

Sources

Commager, Henry S., ed. 1968. *Documents of American history.* 8th ed. New York: Appleton-Century-Crofts.

Findling, John E. 1980. *Dictionary of American diplomatic history.* Westport, Conn.: Greenwood Press.

Graebner, N. 1961. *American secretaries of state in the 20th century.* New York: McGraw-Hill.

Moritz, Charles, ed. 1981. *Current biography yearbook.* New York: H. W. Wilson.

ACKERMAN FORMULA. A formula about the size of a country's population in terms of its area's resource endowment and related economic characteristics. The formula is expressed as

$$P = \frac{RQ(TAS_t) + E_s + T_r \pm F - W}{S}$$

where P = population; R = amount of resources; Q = factor measuring natural quality of resources; T = physical technology factor; A = administrative techniques; S = standard of living; S_t = resource stability; E_s = scale economies element; T_r = resources added through trade; F = institutional element and friction loss subsequent upon institutional characteristics of society; and W = frugality element (wastage or intensity of use).

Edward Augustus Ackerman (1911–73) was born in Post Falls, Idaho, and educated in Coeur d'Alene. He joined the U.S. Forest Service and worked for a local newspaper until he entered Harvard to study geography (Ph.D. 1939). He became a political geographer, taught at Harvard (1940–48), published *New England's Fishing Industry* (1941), and in World War II served in the Office of Strategic Services (1941–43) and, later, in the U.S. Supreme Command in Japan. While a faculty member at the University of Chicago (1948–55), he served on the Water Resources Policy Commission (1950–51), was assistant general manager of the TVA (1952–54), and later joined the Carnegie Institute of Washington (1960–73). He wrote *Japan's Natural Resources and Their Relation to Japan's Economic Future* (1953), ''Population and Natural Resources'' and ''Geography and Demography'' in P. M. Hauser and O. D. Duncan, eds., *The Study of Population: An Inventory and Appraisal* (1959). He adopted an interdisciplinary approach in his many papers on the problems of natural resources and population. He was president of the Association of American Geographers, served many private and public agencies, and helped establish a systematic, scientific approach to geography. He co-authored *American Resources: Their Management and Conservation* (1951) and *Technology in American Water Development* (1959).

Sources

Goodall, Brian. 1987. *The Penguin dictionary of human geography.* Harmondsworth, Middlesex: Penguin.

Petersen, William, and Petersen, Renee. 1985. *Dictionary of demography.* Westport, Conn.: Greenwood Press.

White, Gilbert F. 1974. Edward A. Ackerman, 1911–1973 [with bibliography]. *Annals of the Association of American Geographers* 64:297–309.

ACKOFF'S FABLES. A collection of short stories with a very sharp moral point about bureaucracies or systems—stories that may not be true but ought to be. The fables are irreverent, witty reminders of flaws and obstructions in bureaucracies. Each fable contains a moral, a general law, or a warning—for example, no system is as smart as some of the people it serves; there is no such thing as a new trick to an old dog; the right information cannot be extracted from the wrong data; learning begins with questions we cannot answer, and learning ends with questions we can answer.

Russell Lincoln Ackoff (b. 1919) studied at the University of Pennsylvania. (Ph.D., Philosophy of Science, 1947). During World War II he served in the U.S. Army, after which he taught philosophy and mathematics at Wayne University (1947–51), and was a professor of operations research at Case Institute of Technology (1951–64). After a visiting professorship at the University of Birmingham (U.K.), Ackoff returned to the University of Pennsylvania where he was a professor of management science and prominent in the study of social systems research (1964–86). He has written or co-authored nineteen books and over 150 articles for academic journals. Among his published works are *The Design of Social Research* (1953), *Scientific Method* (1962), *Redesigning the Future* (1974), *The Art of Problem Solving* (1978), and *Creating the Corporate Future (1981)*. He serves on the editorial boards of many professional journals, holds memberships in prominent professional societies of management education and operations research, and has conducted research for over 300 corporations and government agencies. He is chairman of the board of INTERACT, the Institute for Interactive Management, Inc.; Anheuser-Busch Professor Emeritus of Management Science, the Wharton School, University of Pennsylvania; and August A. Busch, Jr., Visiting Professor of Marketing, John M. Olin School of Business, Washington University, Saint Louis, Missouri.

Sources

Ackoff, Russell L. 1991. *Ackoff's fables: irreverent reflections on business and bureaucracy.* New York: John Wiley.

Personal Communication.

ACTON'S LAW. In a letter to Mandell Creighton (1843–1901) in April 1887, Lord Acton wrote:

> I cannot accept . . . that we are to judge Pope and King unlike other men, with a favored presumption that they did no wrong. If there is any presumption, it is the other way, against holders of power, increasing as the power increases. Historic responsibility has to make up for the want of legal responsibility. *Power tends to corrupt, and absolute power corrupts absolutely.* Great men are almost always bad men, even when they exercise influence and not authority: still more when you superadd the tendency or the certainty of corruption by authority.

John Emerich Edward Dalberg Acton, first Baron Acton of Alderham (1834–1902), a moralist and historian, was born at Naples, educated in Paris and Edinburgh, and spent six years studying in Munich where he acquired his outlook on history. He became an austere liberal who lived to pursue truth and uphold the rights of the individual. In the 1850s he visited the United States, attended the coronation of the czar, toured Italy, and after settling in England became M.P. for Carlow, but found politics uncongenial. In 1865 he married a Bavarian countess. He edited and wrote for a Catholic liberal publication and became a noted critic of the Roman Catholic Church, although his soul belonged to the church. Between 1868 and 1872 he helped found and contribute to the *North British Review*. In the 1860s Acton became a close friend of William Gladstone (1809–98), who made him a peer in 1869. In 1892 Acton was lord-in-waiting to Queen Victoria. He helped establish the *English Historical Review* in 1886, and because of his exalted reputation among Britain's intellectuals, he became a professor of modern history at Cambridge and an honorary fellow at All Souls and Trinity Colleges. At Cambridge he delivered his famous lectures on the French Revolution and began the project "Cambridge Modern History." His *Lectures in Modern History* (1906), *Historical Essays and Studies* (1907), and *Lectures on the French Revolution* (1910) appeared after his death.

Sources

Butterfield, Herbert. 1948. *Lord Acton*. London: Historical Association.

Creighton, Louise von Glehn. 1904. *Life and letters of Mandell Creighton, D.D. Oxon and Cam.: sometime bishop of London*. London: Longmans, Green.

Lee, Sidney, ed. 1920. *Dictionary of national biography: supplement 1901–1911*. London: Oxford University Press.

Tulloch, Hugh. 1988. *Acton*. London: Weidenfeld and Nicolson.

ADAM SMITH'S INVISIBLE HAND. The market forces that control the processes of economic production and distribution, traditionally managed by small enterprises. The theory assumes that perfect competition exists between single-unit enterprises and that this is the most efficient way to coordinate all economic activities and resources. Today some economic historians argue that, with the establishment of modern business enterprises (1840–1920) and their administrative coordination of economic activities, competition has become imperfect and economic resources have been misapplied.

Adam Smith (1723–90) was born in Kirkcaldy, near Edinburgh after the death of his father, a customs clerk. Educated at the local high school and Glasgow University, Smith matriculated in 1737 at age 14 and, with an M.A. went to Balliol College, Oxford for six years. In 1751 on his return to Glasgow, Smith became an outstanding lecturer and was appointed a professor of logic at the university, where he later occupied a chair of moral philosophy. The concept of the "invisible hand" appeared in his *Theory of Moral Sentiments* (1759) which relates economics to a social philosophy that assumes business aims to serve society rather than an individual's greed. After some years in Paris, Smith returned to Glasgow where he wrote *An Inquiry into the Nature and Causes of the Wealth of Nations* (1776). The work was well received and became a classic in economics. Smith revised it and republished it, and in the sixth edition, 1790, he added a new part that stated the social psychology behind economic aspirations. Smith's *Wealth of Nations* helped found the new science of political economy. He belonged to the London Literary Club among whose members were Dr. Samuel Johnson (1709–84), David Garrick (1716–79), and Joshua Reynolds (1723–92).

Sources
Campbell, Roy, and Skinner, Andrew. 1982. *Adam Smith.* London: Croom Helm.
Chandler, Alfred D., Jr. 1977. *The visible hand: the managerial revolution in American business.* Cambridge, Mass.: Belknap / Harvard University Press.
Eatwell, John; Milgate, Murray; and Newman, Peter. 1987. *The new Palgrave: a dictionary of economics.* London: Macmillan.
McHenry, Robert, ed. 1992. *The new encyclopedia Britannica.* Chicago: Encyclopedia Britannica, Inc.
Raphael, Davis D. 1985. *Adam Smith.* Oxford: Oxford University Press.
Sills, David L., ed. 1968. *International encyclopedia of the social sciences.* New York: Macmillan and Free Press.
Stephen, Leslie, and Lee, Sydney, eds. 1917. *The dictionary of national biography.* London: Oxford University Press.

ADLERIAN. Relating to or a follower of the Austrian psychologist and his theory.

Alfred Adler (1870–1937), a Viennese physician, was educated at the University of Vienna and began private practice in 1898 as an eye specialist. After continuous studies in philosophy and neurology, psychology, and social science, he joined the circle of Freud's followers in 1902, but by 1911 he had defected from it after much disagreement with Freud over the basic tenets of psychoanalysis. Adler saw human actions as motivated by future expectations and neurosis as due to a sense of inferiority; he also stressed the significance of society and culture. Adler's *Practice and Theory of Individual Psychology* (1927) became popular in the United States and spread to many Western countries where he gave public lectures and worked in universities and treated patients. He died on the street in Aberdeen.

Sources
Bottome, Phyllis. 1939. *Alfred Adler: apostle of freedom.* London: Faber and Faber.
Orgler, Hertha. 1963. *Alfred Adler: the man and his work.* New York: Liveright.
Sills, David L., ed. 1968. *International encyclopedia of the social sciences.* New York: Macmillan and Free Press.
Zusne, Leonard. 1984. *Biographical dictionary of psychology.* Westport, Conn.: Greenwood Press.

AGNEWISM. Ideas and views of President Richard Nixon's vice-president, especially his emphasis on law and order, his debauching of the U.S. Supreme Court, his attack on dissent, and his fake issues and false choices of the U.S. administration.

Spiro Theodore Agnew (b. 1918) was born in Baltimore, Maryland, into an immigrant family from Greece. He attended public schools and entered Johns Hopkins University to study chemistry, but transferred to Baltimore Law School, studying at night while working as a clerk. He served in the U.S. Army in France and Germany during World War II and afterward graduated in law (1947). Specializing in labor cases, he became a member of the Zoning Board of Appeals, Baltimore County, and eventually, in 1966, governor of Maryland. He was U.S. vice-president (1969–73) and resigned when charged with bribery while he was governor of Maryland; he pleaded "no contest" in the Federal District Court, Baltimore, to a charge of income tax evasion. The presiding judge called the case a "tragic event"; he fined Agnew $10,000 and put him on probation for three years.

Sources

Agnew, Spiro T. 1980. *Go quietly . . . or else.* New York: William Morrow.

Barnhart, Clarence; Steinholz, Sol; and Barnhart, Robert. 1973. *Dictionary of new English, 1963–73.* London: Longman.

Cohen, Richard M., and Witcover, Jules. 1974. *A heartbeat away: the investigation and resignation of vice-president Spiro T. Agnew.* New York: Viking Press.

Harper, John F., and Allen, Louis. 1988. *Political scandals and causes célèbres since 1945.* Harlow: Longman Current Affairs.

Jacob, Kathryn A., and Ragsdale, Bruce A. 1989. *Biographical directory of the United States Congress: 1774–1989.* Bicentennial ed. Washington, D.C.: U.S. Government Printing Office.

Lippman, Theo. 1972. *Spiro Agnew's America.* New York: W. W. Norton.

Moritz, Charles, ed. 1968. *Current biography yearbook.* New York: H. W. Wilson.

ALDINGTON-JONES REPORT. A British report of a joint special committee of the Port Authority (1972). The committee was established to deal with employment problems on the docks resulting from containerization and the running down of dock facilities. The pool of dock workers for whom there was no regular work was replaced first by a special voluntary severance scheme and later by a register of names.

Toby (Austin Richard William) Low, first Baron Aldington (b. 1914), was educated at Winchester and New College, Oxford, called to the bar in 1939, and during World War II received honors for service from Britain, France, and the United States. As M.P. for Blackpool (1945–62), he became parliamentary secretary in the Ministry of Supply (1951–54) and minister of state, Board of Trade (1954–57). He was chairman of the Port of London Authority (1971–77), a director of Lloyds Bank (1967–85), and since 1984 has been chairman of Leeds Castle Foundation.

Jack L. Jones (b. 1913) was born in Liverpool and worked both on the docks and in the engineering industry. He became a notable trade union leader and was elected general secretary of the Transport and General Workers' Union (1968–77). He was also deputy chairman of the National Ports Council (1967–79) and joint chairman on the special committee on ports in 1972. He received the Order of the Companion in 1978 and became an associate fellow of the London School of Economics.

Sources

Jones, Jack, and Morris, Max. 1982. *A–Z of trade unionism and industrial relations.* London: Heinemann.

Marsh, Arthur. 1979. *Concise encyclopedia of industrial relations.* Westmead, Farnborough, Hants: Gower.
Who's who, 1991. London: Adam and Charles Black.

ALGER COMPLEX. A moralist delusion or fallacy among administrators concerning the effect of subordinates' push for their promotion. The delusion or
fantasy comprises, first, the obsessive feeling that a subordinate who pushes
harder than average deserves to advance farther and faster than average, and,
second, the power of pushing seems greater if the subordinate suffers, for example, from peptic ulcer, nervous breakdown, or insomnia (Peter and Hull,
1969).

Horatio Alger Jr. (1832–99), son of a clergyman, was born in Revere, Massachusetts, and was raised in a strict and puritanical manner. He studied at Gates
Academy, and he taught journalism before taking up religious studies at Harvard
Divinity School in 1860. After graduating he went to Paris where he lived a
Bohemian life, before returning to America to become a Unitarian minister. In
1866 he quit the pulpit and went to New York to write, and stayed there except
for a brief visit to the Pacific Coast and Paris. In New York he was chaplain
and philanthropist to the Newsboy's Lodging House. He published 119 works
that extolled the view that struggling against both poverty and temptation would
lead a lad to fame and riches. His noted central hero was in the Ragged Dick
series beginning in 1877. His *Luck and Pluck* (1869) and *Tattered Tom* (1871)
series were not as popular. He also wrote biographies of statesmen who rose
from rural poverty to wealth in the city. Approximately two million copies of
his novels were published, and he became rich. A spendthrift, and excessively
generous with money, he saw his wealth diminish sharply, and in 1896 he settled
with his sister in Natick, Massachusetts.

See also HORATIO ALGER STORY.

Sources

Alger, Horatio, Jr. 1890. *Struggling upward: or Luke Larkin's luck.* [Orig. New York:
Hurst, Alger Series for Boys, no date.] Philadelphia: H. T. Coates.
Gardner, Ralph D. 1978. *Horatio Alger: or, the American hero era.* New York: Arco.
Johnson, Allen, ed. 1927. *Dictionary of American biography.* Vol. I. New York: Charles
Scribner's Sons.
Peter, Laurence J., and Hull, Raymond. 1969. *The Peter principle: why things always
go wrong.* New York: William Morrow.

ALLPORT-VERNON-LINDZEY SCALE OF VALUES. A social psychological measure of the strength of interest in six areas of human interest—
theoretical, economic, aesthetic, social, political, and religious.

Gordon Willard Allport (1897–1967) was born in Montezuma, Indiana; his
father was a physician and his mother a schoolteacher. After graduating from
high school in Cleveland, Ohio, he completed his Ph.D. in psychology at Har-

vard (1924). He began teaching at Harvard in 1924 and became chairman of the Department of Psychology in 1938. Although he contributed to psychological theory, Allport claimed leadership of no particular school or limited system of psychology. He is generally recognized as a pioneer in the development of the psychology of personality that emerged in the United States after World War I.

Philip Ewart Vernon (1905–87) was born in Oxford, the son of an Oxford University lecturer in physiology, and pioneered the field of industrial psychology. Encouraged by his father, Philip studied psychology and graduated from Cambridge University with honors in science. A Rockefeller fellowship brought him to America to pursue his interest in measurement of personality. In 1933 he returned to London as a psychologist in the Maudsley Hospital Child Guidance Clinic. While head of the Department of Psychology at Glasgow University (1938–47) he served as psychological research adviser to the War Office and Admiralty, devising selection tests and training methods. Following his tenure as the chair of educational psychology, University of London (1949–68), he immigrated to Canada where he was a professor of educational psychology at the University of Calgary until 1978. Vernon wrote fourteen books and over 200 articles.

Gardner Lindzey (b. 1920) was born in Wilmington, Delaware, and studied at Pennsylvania State University. Under Gordon Allport at Harvard University, he completed his Ph.D. in 1949, and he was chairman of the Harvard Psychological Clinic until 1956. His research centered on the use of Murray's Thematic Apperception Test, on prejudice and scapegoating, and on the revision of the Allport-Vernon Scale. As editor, writer, and teacher, Lindzey influenced research on aspects of personality and social psychology, especially in the fields of homosexuality, prejudice, and genetics. He became director of the Center for Advanced Study in the Behavioral Sciences at Stanford in 1975 and retired in 1989.

Sources

Allport, Gordon W.; Vernon, Philip E.; and Lindzey, Gardner. 1950. *Study of values.* Boston: Houghton Mifflin.

Corsini, Raymond J. 1984. *Encyclopedia of psychology.* New York: John Wiley.

Costa, Paul, and Maddi, Salvatore. 1970. *Humanism in personology; Allport, Maslow and Murray.* Chicago: Aldine Atherton.

Devine, Elizabeth; Held, Michael; Vinson, James; and Walsh, George, eds. 1983. *Thinkers of the twentieth century: a biographical, bibliographical and critical dictionary.* London: Macmillan.

Evans, Richard I. 1971. *Gordon Allport: the man and his ideas* New York: E. P. Dutton.

Jensen, Arthur. 1989. Philip Ewart Vernon (1905–87): Obituary. *American Psychologist* 44, 5:844.

Sills, David L., ed. 1968. *International encyclopedia of the social sciences.* New York: Macmillan and Free Press.

VandenBos, Gary R., ed. 1989. Contribution by a psychologist in the public interest. Gold Medal Award: Gardner Lindzey. *American Psychologist* 44:662–64.

Who's who in America, 1991. Chicago: Marquis.
Zusne, Leonard. 1987. *Eponyms in psychology*. Westport, Conn.: Greenwood Press.

ALMON LAG. A concept used by economists in the study of time series. The Almon distributed lag estimates the weights of a distributed lag using polynomial specifications.

Shirley Montag Almon (1935–75) was born in Saxonburg, Pennsylvania, and graduated from Goucher College, Baltimore and Harvard (Ph.D., 1964). She introduced the concept in 1963 at the September meeting of the Econometric Society. In 1965 the main point of her dissertation, "The Distributed Lag between Capital Appropriations and Expenditures," was published in *Econometrica* 33:178–196. Afterward she worked as an economist for the Women's Bureau in Washington, the National Bureau of Economic Research, the Federal Reserve Bank of San Francisco, and the Federal Reserve Board in Washington. Before joining the staff of the U.S. President's Council of Economic Advisers in 1966, she taught at Harvard and Wellesley College.

Sources

Blaug, Mark. 1985. *Great economists since Keynes*. Brighton, England: Harvester Press.
Eatwell, John; Milgate, Murray; and Newman, Peter. 1987. *The new Palgrave: a dictionary of economics*. London: Macmillan.

ALONSO MODEL. A model of intraurban spatial variations in land values, land use, and land use intensity that centers on accessibility and associated transport costs. The model shows that all workplaces are concentrated close to the city center. Consequently, the further a household is from this center, the greater its commuting costs. If a fixed amount of money is available, the model shows that less can be spent on property, dwellings, and land. The model assumes that all households want as much land or space as possible; land is more plentiful on the edge of the city; and land is cheaper at the edge of the city. So it is the rich who choose to live in the lower density outer areas, while the poor are confined to inner city districts.

William Alonso (b. 1933) was born in Buenos Aires, Argentina, and studied demography and economics at Harvard University and the University of Pennsylvania (Ph.D., 1959). At Harvard he taught regional planning and directed the Center for Urban Studies (1963–66). At the University of California, Berkeley, he taught regional planning and was a member of the Institute of Urban and Regional Development. He also taught at Yale (1966) and advised on urban development matters in Cuba and for the Ford Foundation, as well as various city and regional development schemes. His research focuses on urban and regional development. He published "Urban Zero Population" in *Daedalus* 102 (1973); *City Sizes and Quality of Life: Some Observations* (1975); and *The Mature Metropolis* (1977).

Sources
Evory, Ann, ed. 1982. *Contemporary authors.* Vol. 6. Detroit: Gale Research.
Jaques Cattell Press, ed. 1978. *American men and women of science: the social and behavioral sciences.* New York: Jaques Cattell and R. R. Bowker.
Johnston, Ronald J. 1981. *The dictionary of human geography.* Oxford: Basil Blackwell.
Peterson, William, and Peterson, Renee. 1985. *Dictionary of demography.* Westport, Conn.: Greenwood Press.

ALTHUSSERIANISM. Contemporary Marxist thinking that suggests that after the 1840s Karl Marx was not as greatly dominated by Hegel's ideas as he had been earlier, and, putting aside ideals of his youth, he now pursued scientific sociology; that economic determinism did not dominate the ideas of the older Marx; that he argued that social life and politics interact with, rather than react to, the economy in a society; that different aspects of a society enjoy their own autonomy; and that the thesis of economic determinism attributed to Marx is both questionable and of limited value.

Louis Althusser (1918–90) was born in Birmandries, near Algiers in Algeria and was educated at Algiers, Marseilles, Lyons, and the Ecole Normale Supérieure in Paris. He served in the French Army and spent World War II as a prisoner of war. Afterward he returned to work at the Ecole Normale Supérieure and joined the French Communist party (1948). In 1981 he was manic-depressive, strangled his wife, and was committed to a mental institution. He died in Paris. His early major articles of the 1960s appeared in *La Pensée* and *La Nouvelle Critique.* In Europe he was an influential social philosopher and became the center of a cult of contemporary Marxists. His theory, central to the 1960s, was further developed in the 1970s.

Sources
Althusser, Louis. 1969. *For Marx.* Harmondsworth: Penguin.
Althusser, Louis. 1971. *Lenin and philosophy, and other essays.* New York: Monthly Review.
Althusser, Louis. 1976. *Essays in self-criticism [with bibliography].* London: New Left Books.
Beilharz, Peter, ed. 1992. *Social theory: a guide to central thinkers.* Sydney: Allen and Unwin.
Bullock, Alan, and Woodings, R. B., eds. 1983. *The Fontana biographical companion to modern thought.* London: Collins.
Clarke, Simon, et al. 1980. *One-dimensional Marxism: Althusser and the politics of culture.* London: Allison and Busby.
Elliott, Gregory. 1987. *Althusser—the detour of theory.* London: Verso.
Obituary: *New York Times Biographical Service* 21:989, October 1990; *New York Times,* October 24 1990.
Turner, Roland. 1987. *Thinkers of the twentieth century.* 2d ed. London: St. James Press.

AMULREE REPORT. A British report (Holidays with Pay Act 1938, Command Paper 5724, April 6, 1938) on holidays with pay, which found that out of a total of 18.5 million employees 10.75 million did not have paid holidays. The committee recommended that all industries without paid holiday agreements give at least one week's holiday with pay. To encourage the voluntary acceptance of the principle of an annual holiday with pay, the committee also recommended that the statute should not be introduced until the parliamentary session of 1940–41.

William Warrender Mackenzie, first Baron Amulree (1860–1942), was educated at Perth Academy, Edinburgh University and University College, London. He was called to the bar, Lincoln's Inn (1886) and received the Freedom of the City of Perth (1938). He was created a baron in 1939. In the early 1930s he was secretary of state for air and president of the Air Council, and chairman of many committees including the committee to inquire into the claims of men dismissed from police and prison services due to the 1919 Police Strike. He was on a departmental committee on the Shop Hours Act of 1937, the Building Industry Council of Review (1928–33), the Royal Commission of Licensing Laws (1929–31), a court of inquiry into Panel Doctors' Fees (1937), and the Committee on Holidays with Pay (1937–38). He was also on the Committee for Highway Law Consolidation (1938–41). Among his publications were Pratt and Mackenzie's *Law of Highways,* which went through sixteen editions, and Patterson's *Licensing Act.* He was one of the editors of Lord Halsbury's *Laws of England.*

Sources

Cameron, Gordon C. 1965. The growth of holidays with pay in Britain. In Graham L. Reid and Donald J. Robertson, eds. *Fringe benefits, labor costs and social security.* London: Allen and Unwin, Chapter 10.

Keesings contemporary archives: weekly diary of world events. 1937–40:3045. London: Keesings Publications.

Marsh, Arthur. 1979. *Concise encyclopedia of industrial relations.* Westmead, Farnborough, Hants: Gower.

Who was who, 1952. London: Adam and Charles Black.

ANANIAS, ANANIAS CLUB. A liar; newspapermen and women who publish lies or information they promised to keep in confidence.

In the New Testament (Acts 5:1–10) Ananias and his wife Sapphira are said to have kept money to themselves from the sale of land belonging to the church. For this offense Ananias was struck dead when Peter the Apostle declared that, in attempting to cheat the church, Ananias had in fact lied to none other than God. Later that day, Sapphira died similarly after she uttered the same falsehood. Although he did not coin the terms, Theodore Roosevelt, U.S. president (1901–9), often spoke of people who deceived others as "Ananias," and he referred to the "Ananias Club," a hypothetical institution, when remarking on newspapermen and women who printed what they had promised not to make public. Lillard (1896) and Mathews (1951) trace the use of the term in politics and social life in the United States.

Sources
Benet, William R. 1948. *The reader's encyclopedia.* London: Harrap.
Hendrickson, Robert. 1988. *The dictionary of eponyms: names that became words.* New York: Dorset.
Lillard, John F. B. 1896. *Poker stories: as told by statesmen, soldiers, lawyers, commercial travelers, bankers, actors, editors, millionaires, members of the Ananias Club and the talent embracing the most remarkable games 1845–95.* New York: Harper.
Mathews, Mitford M. 1951. *A dictionary of Americanism: on historical principles.* Chicago: University of Chicago Press.
Swanberg, W. A. 1961. *Citizen Hearst: a biography of William Randolph Hearst.* New York: Charles Scribner's Sons.

ANDERSONIAN. Pertaining to or an adherent of the twentieth-century Australian philosopher who advocated a form of liberal pluralism that strongly supported freedom of thought and speech and assumed that social relations were based on the interaction of competition and collaboration and on an incomplete knowledge and understanding of human experience and ideals.

John Anderson (1893–1962) was born in Lanarkshire, Scotland. He studied at the University of Glasgow, won academic prizes, and taught in the universities at Cardiff, Glasgow, and Edinburgh before taking the Challis Chair in Philosophy at the University of Sydney in Australia (1926–58). He was a persuasive, controversial, and creative philosopher who became a democrat and was drawn a little to communism. He did not accept any theory of ultimates or totalities of knowledge, believing that sound knowledge was based on an intimate familiarity with complex matters. He advocated a thoroughly critical approach to all issues. Although he was a poor speaker, in his university he became an effective leader who demanded extensive discussion before making decisions. He insisted on high academic standards, abjured all interest in using universities to train professionals. In support of the freedom of speech, he once distributed James Joyce's banned *Ulysses* as a prayerbook.

Source
Nairn, Bede, and Serle, Geoffrey, eds. 1979. *The Australian dictionary of biography.* Vol. 7. Melbourne: Melbourne University Press.

ARDREY'S LAWS. Three amusing laws of administration that center on primitive conflict among animals and relate to human conflict. First, territorial animals—individual or social—live in incessant hostility with their neighbors (Ardrey, 1961); second, warfare emerges only when the defensive instinct of a determined territorial proprietor is challenged by the compulsion of an equally determined territorial neighbor (Ardrey, 1961); and third, natural selection encourages social mechanisms that exist for no other reason than to provide the conditions for antagonism, conflict, and excitement (Ardrey, 1966). Thomas Martin (1973) adapted these laws to the pathology of management.

Robert Ardrey (1908–80) was born in Chicago and died in Kalk Bay, South

Africa. He was a playwright and screenwriter who studied science at the University of Chicago, but under the influence of Thornton Wilder decided to be a dramatist. He wrote several plays, among them *Casey Jones* (1938), and became a Hollywood screenwriter in 1938. His play *Thunder Rock* was a hit in London during World War II. In 1955 he turned to anthropology in an effort to better his understanding of human motivation. In his books he argued that human beings are born aggressive and are bent on protecting property and dominating other people. Although Ardrey was not a professional anthropologist, he did much to popularize the discipline. For the screen he wrote *The Four Horseman of the Apocalypse* and *Khartoum.*

Sources

Ardrey, Robert. 1961. *African genesis: a personal investigation into the animal origins and nature of man.* London: Collins.

Ardrey, Robert. 1966. *The territorial imperative: a personal inquiry into the animal origins of property and nations.* London: Collins.

Locher, Frances, C., ed. 1980. *Contemporary authors,* Vols. 93–96. Detroit: Gale Research.

Martin, Thomas L., Jr. 1973. *Malice in blunderland.* New York: McGraw-Hill.

Moritz, Charles, ed. 1973. *Current biography yearbook.* New York: H. W. Wilson.

ARIAN DOCTRINE. An heretical doctrine arising from the following statement attributed to Arius: "If the Father begat the Son, he that was begotten had a beginning of existence; and from this it is evident, that there was a time when the Son was not. It therefore necessarily follows, that he had his substance from nothing" (Douglas, 1974). From this it can be argued that the Son and Father are not of the same substance; that the Son is not equal to the Father; that although the Son never emerged from eternity he did exist before he appeared on earth; that the Messiah was a divine with the flesh of a man. Since the doctrine accepts that God is not only uncreated but also unbegotten, unoriginated, absolutely incommunicable and unique, then the doctrine leads one to assume the Scriptures are false; and that Christ is the adopted Son of God, and merely participates in God's grace. The doctrine was in direct opposition to the Athanasian Creed.

Arius (c. 256–336) was born in Libya and studied theology with Lucian of Antioch. After his ordination in Alexandria, Arius asserted that the Son of God was an Intermediate Being, above all other creation, but not of divine origin. This doctrine was delivered in his sermons, became popular in songs, and was taken up by others trained in Antioch. Such teachings were condemned at the first Ecumenical Council, Nicaea (318) whose bishops stated that the Son of God was begotten, not made. Around 321, Bishop Alexander of Alexandrina excommunicated Arius, and he was forced to flee to Asia Minor. In 325 Emperor Constantine banished Arius, and the Council of Nicaea formally anathematised the heresy. Nevertheless, the Sect was not fully destroyed. After the death of Constantine in 337, further conflict grew between the followers of Arius and the orthodox Athanasian creed. During the next twenty years, the Arians split into three main groups, each one advancing its own view on the divinity of Jesus. By late 381, Arianism had been so discredited that the Arians were driven from the empire; they gained some support among the Teutonic tribes, but when the Franks were converted to Catholicism about 496, the Arian doctrine began to disappear from even the religion of the Teutonic tribes.

See also ATHANASIAN CREED.

Sources

Brown, Harold O.J. 1984. *Heresies: the image of Christ in the mirror of heresy and orthodoxy from the apostles to the present.* Garden City, NY: Doubleday.

Cross, Frank L. 1974. *The Oxford dictionary of the Christian church.* 2d ed. New York: Oxford University Press.

Douglas, James D., ed. 1974. *The new international dictionary of the Christian church.* Exeter: The Paternoster Press.

Hanson, Richard P.C. 1989. *The search for the Christian doctrine of God: the Arian controversy, 318–381.* Edinburgh: T. and T. Clark.

McDonald, William, ed. 1967. *New Catholic encyclopedia.* New York: McGraw-Hill.

ARISTIDES. Embodiment of justice.

Aristides (530–468 B.C.), an Athenian statesman and general, was one of ten Greek leaders who helped defeat Persia's King Darius I at the battle of Marathon (490 B.C.). Aristides was made chief archon, but because he opposed Themistocles' naval policies, he was exiled from Athens in 482 B.C. But in 479 B.C., at the battle of Plataea, he again led a victorious Athenian Army against the Persians, and in the next year he helped Themistocles refortify Athens. Aristides assessed the fair share of finance and ships for member states of the Greek confederacy—the Delian League; this example of honesty and probity gave him the title ''Aristides the Just.''

Sources

Dryden, John, trans. 1683–86. *Plutarch: the lives of the noble Grecians and Romans.* Rev. Arthur H. Cough, 1864. New York: Modern Library, Random House.

Sansome, David, ed. 1989. *The Lives of Aristides and Cato/Plutarch.* Warminster, Wiltshire: Aris and Phillips.

ARISTOTELIAN AND GALILEAN MODES OF THOUGHT. A distinction made by Kurt Lewin (1890–1947) in a paper in which he identified urgent problems in current experimental and theoretical psychology by describing several differences between modes of thought that determined the research of medieval Aristotelian and post–Galilean physicists. In Lewin's own work the mode was Galilean and characteristic of the Gestalt school of social psychology; the theories were systemic rather than developmental. Because they were often expressed mathematically, they encouraged careful definition of concepts; Lewin sought to explain the constancies in social relations through genotypical rather than phenotypical laws or elements and essences of a situation. Concepts would be applied beyond eras, cultures, and territories, and would be used in all social and psychological sciences. For social psychology Lewin sought exception-free laws rather than statistical, probabilistic propositions; advocated the close study of concrete cases; and argued that experiments should simply illustrate the relations in a pure case. Lewinian "field theory" used concepts of life-space and social field. Lewin founded the study of group dynamics and classical experiments in frustration, aggression, and autocratic and democratic leadership. His aim was ever to go beyond the laboratory and to change the world for the better.

Kurt Lewin. See LEWINIAN FIELD THEORY.

Aristotle. See ARISTOTELIAN.

Galileo (Galileo Galilei, 1564–1642) was born at Pisa and died at Arcetri near Florence. He was descended from a noble, though impoverished, Florentine family and studied at the University of Pisa without taking a degree (1581–86). He discovered the isochronism of the pendulum in 1583 and the hydrostatic balance in 1586. Galileo was a professor of mathematics at Pisa from 1589 to 1591 and at Padua from 1592 to 1610. In 1609 he constructed a telescope and discovered Jupiter's satellites. In 1633 he was summoned to Rome where his doctrines were condemned by the pope and he was forced by the Inquisition to renounce the Copernican theory of the universe. His main works were *Dialogue on the Two Chief Systems* (1633) and *Dialogue of the New Science* (1638). On October 31, 1992, after thirteen years of study by a Vatican commission, Pope John II rehabilitated Galileo. The commission decided that the judges, who at the time believed the earth to be fixed, had acted in good faith, but that in 1633 they had been unable to separate their good faith from ancient cosmology.

Sources

Devine, Elizabeth; Held, Michael; Vinson, James; and Walsh, George, eds. 1983. *Thinkers of the twentieth century: a biographical, bibliographical and critical dictionary.* London: Macmillan.

Finocchiaru, Maurice A. 1989. *The Galileo affair: a documentary history.* Berkeley: University of California Press.

Keesings contemporary archives: record of world events. November 1992:39219. London: Keesings Publications.

Lewin, Kurt. 1931. The conflict between Aristotelian and Galileian modes of thought in contemporary psychology. *Journal for General Psychology* 5:141–147.

McHenry, Robert, ed. 1992. *The new encyclopedia Britannica.* Chicago: Encyclopedia Britannica, Inc.

Seegar, Raymond J., ed. 1966. *Men of physics: Galileo Galilei: his life and his work.* Oxford: Pergamon Press.

ARISTOTELIAN, ARISTOTELIANISM.

ARISTOTELIAN, ARISTOTELIANISM. A follower or student of the Greek philosopher Aristotle; logical and deductive. A system of belief upholding the views of Aristotle especially in the use of syllogisms in logic, the establishment of the essence of a subject under observation and the theorems derived from its properties.

Aristotle (384–322 B.C.), the son of a physician, was born at Stagira in Chalcidice and died at Chalcis in Euboea. At age 18 he went to Athens and became a pupil of Plato for twenty years. From 342 to 336 B.C. he helped educate the 13-year-old Alexander (afterward "The Great") In c. 335 Aristotle returned to Athens where he produced the greater part of his scientific works. He was one of the most influential of Greek philosophers and the founder of the Peripatetic school. When Alexander died in 323 B.C., Aristotle was caught in a tide of anti-Macedonian feeling and was charged with impiety. He fled from Athens to Chalcis, Euboea, where he died of a stomach illness. For many years after his death Aristotle's reputation was blackened: his appearance was rumoured to be ugly and he was alleged to have had a lisp, to have been ungrateful and disloyal to Plato, and to have died of drinking poison. Aristotle's existing works, imperfectly preserved, fall into four groups: the logical; the metaphysical and those relating to natural science; the ethical; and the "Poetics" and "Rhetoric." His ideas relate to methodology in social science; ethics and politics; economics; law; and education. His *Politics* greatly influenced Western social thought from the thirteenth to the nineteenth century. His views on law separated the corrective from the distributive theories of justice; and his views on education emphasized character development, citizenship and cultural interests, and the value of rational ability and critical judgment.

Sources

Cross, Frank L. 1974. *The Oxford dictionary of the Christian church.* 2d ed. New York: Oxford University Press.

Douglas, James D., ed. 1974. *The new international dictionary of the Christian church.* Exeter: The Paternoster Press.

McDonald, William, ed. 1967. *New Catholic encyclopedia.* New York: McGraw-Hill.

Ross, William D. 1923. *Aristotle.* 5th ed. rev. 1960. London: Methuen.

Ross, William D. 1908–52. *Aristotle's works.* Oxford: Clarendon Press.

Sills, David L., ed. 1968. *International encyclopedia of the social sciences.* New York: Macmillan and Free Press.

Zusne, Leonard. 1984. *Biographical dictionary of psychology.* Westport, Conn.: Greenwood Press.

ARMAGNACS. A group of Orleans princes who supported the Comte d'Armagnac after Louis, duke of Orleans, was murdered by John of Burgundy (1407). Open warfare between the Burgundians and the Armagnacs began in 1410. The Armagnacs held the South and the south coast of France, comprised of powerful noblemen, and supported an anti-English war policy. They led the resistance to the young English king Henry V's invasion of France and were defeated at the battle of Agincourt in 1415. Paris mobs who opposed them captured their leaders and killed about 3,500 of them, including the Comte d'Armagnac in 1418.

Bernard, the seventh Comte d'Armagnac (?–1418), was a French partisan and leader of the Armagnacs during the French civil war against the Burgundians. He was a constable and chief minister of France (1415) and was murdered in prison by a Paris mob after the Burgundians captured Paris. Armagnac, a southern district of France, was made a countship in the tenth century and was united to the French Crown in the sixteenth. It was the name given to mercenaries from the region who trained in the civil war. After the massacre of 1418 the Armagnacs lost much of their influence, especially as the new king, Charles VII, was reconciled with the Duke of Burgundy. However, in 1444, because the Armagnacs were still a potential danger to the unity of France they were sent by Charles VII to support his ally Emperor Frederick III in a dispute he had at the time with the Swiss. Late in the fifteenth century, the territories of the counts of Armagnac were confiscated by the king of France, Louis X, and the Armangacs were later joined with the French crown under Henry IV.

See also CABOCHIENS.

Sources

Cook, Chris. 1983. *Dictionary of historical terms.* London: Macmillan.

Howatt, Gerald, M.D. 1973. *Dictionary of world history.* London: Thomas Nelson.

McHenry, Robert, ed. 1992. *The new encyclopedia Britannica.* Chicago: Encyclopedia Britannica, Inc.

Smith, Benjamin. 1903. *The Century cyclopedia of names.* London: The Times.

ARNOLDISTS. A religious movement in Italy during the twelfth century which aimed to impose poverty on the Church; although they were condemned and much weakened in influence at the Synod of Verona (1184), they remained an expression of discontent within the Church well into the thirteenth century. In modern times poets, dramatists, and Italian politicians have drawn upon the ideas of the Arnoldists, and in doing so, have much distorted Arnold's character by failing to see clearly that he was a religious reformer who was forced by circumstance into the role of a political revolutionary.

Arnold of Brescia (c. 1100–1155) was an Italian reformer in religion and politics whose life was spent in opposition to the temporal authority and power of the popes. In 1137, as a prior in Brescia's monastery, Arnold revolted against Bishop Manfred. Two years later, Pope Innocent II banished Arnold to France where he joined forces with Peter Abelhard (1079–1142), the French theological revisionist. In time both were declared heretics. In 1141, after his outspoken attack on orthodoxy, Arnold was exiled by the French king to Switzerland and later to Germany. In 1146 he returned to Rome, where he supported those citizens who sought independence from ecclesiastical domination by the pope and his cardinals. As first his move to support republicanism was reasonably successful, but in July 1148 Arnold was excommunicated. Quickly, the revolt against the pope's temporal authority rose again, and Arnold helped to consolidate the gains already made by those seeking independence. In response, Rome was put under interdict, the independence movement collapsed, and Arnold fled. He was caught by Frederick I Barbarossa who was on his way to Rome to be crowned emperor of the Holy Roman Empire. Arnold was tried, found guilty, and given over to Frederick I for execution.

Sources

Cook, Chris. 1983. *Dictionary of historical terms.* London: Macmillan.

Douglas, James D., ed. 1974. *The new international dictionary of the Christian church.* Exeter: Paternoster Press.

Greenaway, George W. 1931. *Arnold of Brescia.* Cambridge: Cambridge University Press.

McHenry, Robert, ed. 1992. *The new encyclopedia Britannica.* Chicago: Encyclopedia Britannica, Inc.

Preece, Warren E., ed. 1965. *Encyclopedia Britannica.* Chicago: Encyclopedia Britannica, Inc., William Benton.

ARROW-DEBREU MODEL OF GENERAL EQUILIBRIUM. A modern economic theory about the efficiency and viability of the market system. It follows neoclassical assumptions concerning individual rationality, market clearing, and rational expectations, and it uses the techniques of fixed point theory and convexity. In 1951 Arrow and Debreu published their papers, and in 1954 their joint work appeared. Debreu was awarded the Noble Prize for Economics (1983) largely because the theory was such an effective model for more than thirty years after it first appeared.

Kenneth Joseph Arrow. See ARROW'S THEOREM.

Gerard Debreu (b. 1921), a professor of economics and marketing at the University of California (Berkeley), was born in Calais, France, and educated at the University of Paris (1946–56). He received honorary degrees from the universities of Bonn, Lausanne, Northwestern, and Toulouse, and was awarded fellowships from major American foundations, including the Guggenheim and Rockefeller, as well as from European universities and governments. He won the Nobel Prize for Economics in 1983 for contributing to general equilibrium theory in economics and to microeconomic theories of welfare. His books have been translated from English into three European languages and Japanese, and he has helped edit major international journals in economics and applied mathematics.

Sources

Arrow, Kenneth J. 1951. An extension of the basic theorems of classical welfare economics. In J. Neyman, ed., *Proceedings of the second Berkeley symposium on mathematical statistics and probability.* Berkeley: University of California Press.

Arrow, Kenneth J., and Debreu, Gerard. 1954. Existence of an equilibrium for a competitive society. *Econometrica* 22:265–290.

Blaug, Mark, ed. 1986. *Who's who in economics: a biographical dictionary of major economists, 1700–1986.* 2d ed. Cambridge, Mass.: MIT Press.

Debreu, Gerard. 1951. The coefficient of resource allocation, *Econometrica* 19:273–292.

ARROW'S THEOREM. ''Arrow's Theorem, or the Impossibility theorem, states that there is no social choice mechanism which satisfies a number of reasonable conditions . . . and which will be applicable to any arbitrary set of individual criteria'' (Arrow, K. J. In Eatwell et al., 1987:124). It was introduced by Arrow in 1950. In an election for a leader, the voters can never get one leader if they are allowed to choose any person whom they feel they want. Reasonable conditions must be agreed to by all voters; for example, every candidate for the leader position must accept nomination and be endorsed by a registered party.

Kenneth Joseph Arrow (b. 1921), a New Yorker, completed his Ph.D. at Columbia University in 1951. During his outstanding career as an economist, he received honorary degrees in Jerusalem, Vienna, Helsinki, as well as from Harvard and Yale. Among his many distinctions are the Nobel Prize for Economics (1972) and the Order of the Rising Sun, Japan. His contributions lie in the theory of social choice, general equilibrium theory in economics, welfare economics, business, and public administration. He published seven books, and his papers appear in six volumes.

Sources

Arrow, Kenneth J. 1950. A difficulty in the concept of social welfare. *Journal of Political Economy* 58:328–346.

Blaug, Mark, ed. 1986. *Who's who in economics: a biographical dictionary of major economists, 1700–1986.* 2d ed. Cambridge, Mass.: MIT Press.

Devine, Elizabeth; Held, Michael; Vinson, James; and Walsh, George, eds. 1983. *Thinkers of the twentieth century: a biographical, bibliographical and critical dictionary.* London: Macmillan.

Eatwell, John; Milgate, Murray; and Newman, Peter. 1987. *The new Palgrave: a dictionary of economics.* London: Macmillan.

Von Weizacher, Cal C. 1972. *Kenneth Arrow's contribution to economic science.* Rheda, Germany: Institut für Mathematische Wirtshaftforschung and der Universität Bielefeld.

ASCH EXPERIMENT. An experiment in social psychology that advanced understanding of social conformity. To answer the question, Would a person yield to group consensus when it was evident the consensus was wrong? In an experimental group, individuals were asked to judge the length of lines which the experimenter's confederates, unknown to the individual in this role, judged falsely. The first results showed that over 25 percent of the time individuals yielded to the pressure of false judgments of the majority. The experimental design became the standard for early conformity research.

Solomon Elliot Asch (b. 1907) was born in Warsaw, Poland, and brought to the United States at age 13. He studied at the City College of New York and Columbia University (Ph.D., 1932). He started teaching at Brooklyn College. In 1936 under Max Wertheimer's influence, his interest turned to psychology. He was drawn to Gestalt psychology and in 1944, on Wertheimer's death, was appointed to his mentor's position at the New School for Social Research. In 1947 Asch joined Wolfgang Köhler and W.C.H. Prentice at Swarthmore College where he completed his noted experimental studies in conformity. In 1966 he became director of the Institute for Cognitive Studies at Rutgers University, and in 1972 he was a professor of psychology at the University of Pennsylvania. He was honored by fellowships from several foundations, and by awards from Columbia University and the American Psychological Association. His contributions to social psychology centered on prestige suggestion, impression formation, conformity, and association.

Sources

Asch, Solomon E. 1951. Effects of group pressure on the modification and distortion of judgments. In Harold Guetzkow, ed. *Groups, leadership, and men.* Pittsburgh, Pa.: Carnegie Press.

Asch, Solomon E. 1952. *Social psychology.* Englewood Cliffs, N.J.: Prentice-Hall.

Asch, Solomon E. 1955. Opinions and social pressure. *Scientific American* 193:31–35.

Asch, Solomon E. 1956. Studies in independence and conformity I. A minority of one against a unanimous majority. *Psychological Monographs: General and Applied* 70, 9, whole no. 416.

Mausner, Bernard. 1979. Solomon E. Asch. In David L. Sills, ed. *International encyclopedia of the social sciences.* Biographical Supplement. Vol. 18. New York: Macmillan and Free Press.

Rock, Irvin. 1990. *The legacy of Solomon Asch: essays in cognition and social psychology.* Hillsdale, N.J.: Erlbaum Associates.

ASHBY'S LAW. The Law of Requisite Variety, also known as ''Ashby's Law,'' asserts that only variety can absorb variety, and only variety can destroy variety; more specifically, that the capacity of any physical device as a regulator cannot exceed its capacity as a channel of communication, and to force desirable outcomes in a situation over which it has only partial control, any regulator is limited by the information it has available. In a theory about the design of the brain, Ashby says that the law indicates that if a certain quantity of disturbance is prevented by a regulator from reacting to some essential variables, then that regulator must be capable of exerting at least that quantity of selection (Ashby, 1960: 229). In modern theories about social systems, the law states that a regulatory body must be competent to produce as many states as can the social system that it regulates, and that the capacity of a regulator is limited by its capacity as an information channel. The concept is used in theories that assume that social systems are much like the open systems of biology, and it has been applied to modern theories of management and organizational control. As Beer (1967: 50) contends in his description of a management control system, only with variety in the control mechanisms can one deal successfully with variety in the system being controlled.

William Ross Ashby (1903–72) was born in London and educated at the Edinburgh Academy, Cambridge University, and Saint Bart's Hospital. In 1932 he was honored by the Royal Medico-Psychological Association, completed research at Saint Andrew's Mental Hospital, Northampton, and at Barnwood House Hospital, Gloucester, where he became its director of research. In the 1960s he was director of the Burden Neurological Institute, Bristol and a professor of cybernetics at the University of Illinois, and in 1971 he became a fellow of the Royal College of Psychiatry. His chief contributions were to studies of psychiatry and the brain, but he pioneered the study of the organization and control of complex systems generally.

Sources

Ashby, William R. 1956. *An introduction to cybernetics.* New York: John Wiley.

Ashby, William R. 1960. *Design for brain: the origin of adaptive behavior.* 2d ed. New York: John Wiley.

Beer, Stafford. 1967. *Cybernetics and management.* 2d ed. London: English Universities Press.
Conant, Roger, ed. 1981. *Mechanisms of intelligence: Ashby's writings on cybernetics.* Seaside, Calif.: Intersystems.
Obituary: William Ross Ashby. 1973. *Operational Research Quarterly* 24:1–2.
Obituary: William Ross Ashby. 1973. In Michel Silva, ed. *Britannica book of the year.* Chicago: William Benton.

ATHANASIAN CREED. An elaborate and precise statement on the Trinity and the Incarnation. The dogma of redemption is central to the creed, as is the belief that if Christ were not truly God, he could never have been given divine life and resemblance to mankind. This view was in direct opposition to the Arian doctrine. While the Arians argued that Christ was not the son of God, but rather a subordinate human being, the Athanasians said the scriptures teach that Christ is the eternal son of God, God's direct creation of the world by God, and the redemption of the world and humankind by God through Christ.

Saint Athanasius (c. 297–373) was an Alexandrian patriarch (328–373) and doctor of the church who strongly supported orthodoxy during the conflict between followers of the Arian doctrine and the Athanasian creed in the fourth century. In his youth he struggled for the acceptance of the Nicene orthodoxy, and in 325 he defended the belief that Jesus Christ was made of the same substance as the Father. This was in direct contradiction to the Arian doctrine. He succeeded his superior, Bishop Alexander, when he died in 328 and shortly after, Athanasius was found guilty of sacrilege, murder, commercial fraud, and magic. Between 335 and 346 he was frequently sent into exile. Afterward he reigned in Egypt for ten years, but in 357 he was exiled once again. During this exile he wrote his famous *Discourses against Arians.* In 362 he was restored to his position, exiled twice more, and in 366 reinstated as a spokesman for orthodoxy until his death. By 381 Nicene orthodoxy had triumphed. His feast day is May 2. The term *Athanasian Creed* cannot be definitively credited to Athanasius; today it is attributed to an unknown Western author of the sixth century.

Sources

Cross, Frank L. 1945. *The study of Saint Athanasius.* Oxford: Clarendon Press.
Cross, Frank L. 1974. *The Oxford dictionary of the Christian church.* 2d ed. New York: Oxford University Press.
Douglas, James D., ed. 1974. *The new international dictionary of the Christian church.* Exeter: Paternoster Press.
Eliade, Mircea, ed. 1987. *Encyclopedia of religion.* New York: Macmillan.
Grillmeier, Aloys. 1975. *Christ in Christian tradition.* 2d ed., revised. Atlanta: John Knox Press.
Kannengiesser, Charles. 1991. *Arius and Athanasius: two Alexandrian theologians.* Aldershot: Gower Publishing.
McDonald, William, ed. 1967. *New Catholic encyclopedia.* New York: McGraw-Hill.
Quastern, Johannes. 1960. *Patrology.* Vol. 3. Westminister, MD: Christian Classics.

ATTILAISMS. Leadership qualities or secrets that advance success in modern business.

Attila the Hun (406–53), king of the Huns (445–53), wreaked havoc on the Roman Empire. Although he received tributes and concessions, he took more when he found his past enemies in the Roman Empire were at disadvantage. When his demand for half the Western Empire was rejected, he invaded and ravaged Gaul (451) before being defeated by the Roman warrior, Aetius. Attila withdrew to Hungary, but in 452 invaded Italy and destroyed Aquileia, Patavium (Padua), Verona, Brixia (Brescia) and Mediolanum (Milan). Pope Leo I met Attila and persuaded him to withdraw beyond the Danube and make peace with the Romans. Attila, who ruled with his brother until Attila murdered him (445), was short, squat, barrel-chested, almost a dwarf, with a disproportionately large head, flat nose, and bulging eyes. He did not die in battle but from a bleeding nose or heart attack while consummating his marriage in Hungary. So that his grave would never be known and desecrated, those who buried him were murdered by the Huns. His sons succeeded him and divided his empire among themselves. Recently, his savage approach to war has been applied to the traditional view in management that business is a savage activity that only the fittest—like Attila—ought to enter and can survive (Roberts, 1989).
Sources

Gordon, Colin D. 1960. *The age of Attila: fifth century Byzantium and the barbarians.* Ann Arbor: University of Michigan Press.

Maechen-Helfen, Otto. 1973. *The world of the Huns: studies in their history and culture.* Edited by Max Knight. Berkeley: University of California Press.

Roberts, Wess. 1989. *Leadership secrets of Attila the Hun.* New York. Warner Books.

Thompson, Edward A. 1948. *A history of Attila and the Huns.* Oxford: Clarendon Press.

Webb, Robert N. 1965. *Attila, king of the Huns.* New York: F. Watts.

AUGUSTAN. Relating to the reign of the first Roman emperor, or an outstanding period of Latin literature, and, more recently, to any period of great literary achievement.

Augustus (63 B.C.–A.D. 14) was born Gaius Octavianus, grandnephew of Julius Caesar. He gained supreme power by his defeat of Mark Antony at the battle of Actium in 31 B.C. In 27 B.C. he was given the title Augustus, Latin for "Venerable." A wise, able, but ruthless power seeker, he pursued peace, law, and order for Rome. His rule was notable for its military campaigns abroad and its moral reform at home. He cultivated religion, restored and built temples, inaugurated the worship of the emperor, disapproved of divorce, and encouraged marriage. He changed Rome from a city of brick buildings to one of marble, and he patronized the arts and the literature of his reign. The Augustan Age, a fine period of Roman classicism, produced Horace in satire and lyric, Virgil in epic, Livy in history, and Ovid in poetry. The term is applied to any period of brilliant literature—for example, Queen Anne's reign in England (1702–14) and Louis XIV's in France (1643–1715)—and has come to mean classic and refined in literary terms.

Sources

McHenry, Robert, ed. 1992. *The new encyclopedia Britannica.* Chicago: Encyclopedia
    Britannica, Inc.
Morris, William, ed. 1965–66. *Grolier universal encyclopedia.* 10 vols. New York:
    American Book-Stratford Press, Inc.
Ousby, Ian, ed. 1988. *The Cambridge guide to literature in English.* Cambridge: Cam-
    bridge University Press, Hamlyn Publishing Group Ltd.
Smith, Benjamin. 1903. *The Century cyclopedia of names.* London: The Times.

AUGUSTINE. One who believes in predestination and irresistible grace and in
the teachings of Saint Augustine.

Saint Augustine (354–430) was born in Tagaste, Algeria. His father was pa-
gan, and his mother a Christian. At age 16 Augustine went to Carthage to study
the humanities but became a promiscuous pleasure-seeker and followed Mani-
chaeism. In 386, after hearing sermons by Bishop Ambrose, Augustine became
a Christian and returned to Tagaste. He was so capable a speaker that he was
soon appointed to assist the elderly bishop at Hippo Regius (now Bona) in 395.
Augustine's *Confessions* chronicling his spiritual development is regarded as
literature's first genuine self-analysis. He systematized the philosophy and
dogma of Christianity and became known as the ''Christian Aristotle.'' In his
Christian philosophy of society, he raised the political problems of church and
state; he also distinguished the secular and religious ''spheres'' of societies, and
the earthly or profane city of self-love from the heavenly city of love for God
in *De civitate dei (The City of God)* (413–26). His doctrines argued that the
scriptures can guide all beings in their quest for knowledge; that God's principles, evident to all, should be established in philosophical science, for example,
ethics and politics; that humankind need give no support to the earthly society
but only to the divine order; and that holy laws and the example of Jesus are
the true guides for all humankind in all things. With the saints Ambrose, Gregory, and Jerome, Augustine is placed among the Fathers of the church.

Sources

Augustine, Saint. 413–426. *The city of god.* Translated by Demetrius B. Zema. Reprinted
    from the 1950–54 ed. Washington: Catholic University of America Press (1981–
    90).
Brown, Peter R. L. 1967. *Augustine of Hippo.* London: Faber and Faber.
Deane, Herbert A. 1963. *The political and social ideas of St. Augustine.* New York:
    Columbia University Press.
McHenry, Robert, ed. 1992. *The new encyclopedia Britannica.* Chicago: Encyclopedia
    Britannica, Inc.
Oates, Whitney J. 1948. *Basic writings of Saint Augustine.* 2 vols. New York: Random
    House.
Sills, David L., ed. 1968. *International encyclopedia of the social sciences.* New York:
    Macmillan and Free Press.
Smith, Warren T. 1980. *Augustine: his life and work.* Atlanta: John Knox Press.
Zusne, Leonard. 1984. *Biographical dictionary of psychology.* Westport, Conn.: Green-
    wood Press.

AUSTINIAN. Relating to a theory of law that assumes that a command is vital to understanding a law; consequently, human law is a command of a sovereign to whom most people are regularly obedient. Also, relating to the imperative aspect of the theory and how it separates the law from morals, even though they may be related to the law.

John Austin (1790–1859) was born in Suffolk, England, and at age sixteen served briefly in the army. He sold his commission, studied law, and was called to the bar in 1818. Later, he read law with John Stuart Mill and was a close associate of James Mill and Jeremy Bentham, whose ideas he later clarified and made readily understandable. He gave up the law and in 1826 took the chair of jurisprudence, University of London, but was not a success, so he resigned in 1832, the year his lectures were published. He undertook a government investigation of the British administration of Malta; afterward he spent some years in Germany and wrote articles on the flaws in protectionism and the value of centralizing the laws. The Revolution of 1848 in Paris drove him back to England where he retired and published his *Plea for Constitution,* which warned of the dangers of extending the franchise and the dread of democracy. He revolutionized jurisprudence by bringing to it clarity of mind and more precise definitions for legal terms, by distinguishing the law from the metaphors commonly used, and by demanding the codification of law.

Sources

Austin, John. 1832. *The province of jurisprudence determined.* London: J. Murray.
Campbell, Enid M. 1959. *John Austin and jurisprudence in nineteenth-century England.* Ann Arbor: University Microfilms.
Eastwood, Reginald A., and Captain, George W. 1929. *The Austinian theories of law and sovereignty.* London: Methuen.
Rumble, Wilfred E. 1985. *The thoughts of John Austin: jurisprudence, colonial reform, and the British constitution.* London: Athlone Press.
Sills, David L., ed. 1968. *International encyclopedia of the social sciences.* New York: Macmillan and Free Press.
Stephen, Leslie, and Lee, Sydney, eds. 1917. *The dictionary of national biography.* London: Oxford University Press.

AUSTRIAN SCHOOL OF ECONOMICS. A school of economic thought founded with the publication of Carl Menger's *Grundsätze der Volkwirthschaftslehre* (1871). The school became prominent for its opposition to prevailing thought in economics through its exposition of the subjective theory of value based on marginal utility. It aimed to deal with essences of value rather than with quantities, and it did not follow the use of mathematics. The followers assumed that economic laws were based on elemental, invariable human needs and satisfaction. They were not interested in the conditions under which the needs appeared, were expressed, limited, or gratified.

Carl Menger (1840–1921) was born in Neu-Sandez, Galizieu, a part of Austria that later became Poland. He came from a family of civil servants and army officers, and his father was a lawyer. Carl studied at the University of Vienna and then Prague (1860–63). After his doctorate he became a journalist, worked in Lemberg and Vienna, and published his first book, *Principles of Economics* (1871). As a result, he was appointed to the faculty of the University of Vienna. He was a tutor and traveling companion to Crown Prince Rudolph, after which he was made a professor. With support from two young economists, Eugen von Böhm-Bawerk (1851–1914) and Friedrich von Wieser (1851–1926), Menger's writings drew much attention from the international community and gave recognition to the Austrian school of economics.

Sources

Eatwell, John; Milgate, Murray; and Newman, Peter. 1987. *The new Palgrave: a dictionary of economics.* London: Macmillan.
Rutherford, Donald. 1992. *Dictionary of economics.* London: Routledge.

AVERCH-JOHNSON MODEL AND THE AVERCH-JOHNSON EFFECT. The model of a firm operating to secure a fair return. The model shows that a profit-maximizing firm will operate inefficiently because its social cost is not minimized at the output it selects and because it adjusts to regulations by substituting capital for labor. The result, the Averch-Johnson effect, examines unintended consequences of the fair-rate-of-return regulation; for example, such regulation may cause the firm to select capital-intensive technologies that produce its output at too high a social cost. The main Averch-Johnson effect is that the capital–labor ratio selected by a profit-maximizing, regulated firm will be greater than that consistent with a cost-minimizing one for any output it chooses to produce.

Harvey Allen Averch (b. 1935), a government official, studied at the universities of Colorado and North Carolina (Ph.D., 1962), and became a senior staff economist at the Rand Corporation (1961–71). He directed the Division of Social Systems and Human Resources Research Application Directorate (National Science Foundation) in Washington (1971–74), and received awards for distinguished and meritorious service to the foundation in 1973 and 1977. He wrote *Strategic Ambiguity, Asymmetry and Arms Control: Some Basic Considerations* (1963), published many articles, and became a professor of policy and economics at the University of Maryland (1985).

Leland Leroy Johnson (b. 1930) was born in Oklahoma and educated at the University of Oregon, received a Standard Oil fellowship, and completed his Ph.D. at Yale (1957). Afterward he taught at Yale and then worked at the Rand Corporation (1957–67). Next, he was director of the President's Task Force on Community Policy in the U.S. State Department a member of the Rand Corporation's senior staff (1967–73), and thereafter director of the corporation's community policies. Among his publications are studies of the behavior of the firm and technological advances in telecommunications.

Sources

Averch, Harvey A., and Johnson, Leland L. 1962. Behavior of the firm under regulatory constraints. *American Economic Review* 52:1053–1069.

Eatwell, John; Milgate, Murray; and Newman, Peter. 1987. *The new Palgrave: a dictionary of economics.* London: Macmillan.

Jaques Cattell Press, ed. 1973. *American men and women of science: the social and behavioral sciences.* New York: Jaques Cattell and R. R. Bowker.

Pearce, David W., ed. 1986. *Macmillan dictionary of modern economics.* New York: Macmillan.

Who's who in America 1990–91. Chicago: Marquis.

B

BAADER-MEINHOF GROUP. A terrorist group formed in 1968 that supported itself with robbery and used arson, kidnapping, and assassinations especially against West German businessmen and their firms, and politicians. In 1976 the gang hijacked an Air France flight, an event that led ultimately to the Entebbe Airport Raid. By 1972 most gang members were in prison. In 1989–90, after the Berlin Wall had been dismantled, it was found that during the communist regime the secret police had given gang members sanctuary.

Andreas Baader (1943–77) was the son of an archivist and historian who had disappeared after being taken prisoner by the Russians in 1945. Andreas, a difficult child, was raised by his grandmother, mother, and an aunt. He disliked school, entered a private school to study art, later tried copywriting, and left home to lead a Bohemian life. At age 20, he went to Berlin and developed a reputation as a violent and rebellious character. In April 1968 he helped set fire to a Frankfurt department store to protest the oppression, exploitation, and injustice of a society that had tolerated Nazi rule. He was sentenced to prison for three years. He escaped with help from Ulrike Meinhof, was recaptured after many exploits (1976), and was found shot dead in his cell in 1977.

Ulrike Meinhof (1934–76) was born in Oldenberg into a family that aligned itself politically and religiously against the Nazis. At age 6, after her father died, she was raised and educated in a Catholic school and later a grammar school in Weilburg. She studied at university, became politically active, joined the Europa movement, the socialist German Student Union, and the illegal Communist party (1958), and strongly opposed nuclear arms and the rearmament of Germany. She was a journalist for *konkret* until it became too counterrevolutionary for her. She became a popular and notable young journalist, and a television commentator and producer; she also wrote many articles on class struggle and violence. She became acquainted with Baader in 1968 and at the time wrote an article on arson in department stores. In 1970 Baader was imprisoned, and she helped him escape, thereby leaving journalism and going underground and herself becoming a member of the terrorist group and active in its exploits. She was caught and found hanged in her cell in 1976.

Sources

Aust, Stefan. 1987. *The Baader-Meinhof group: the inside story of the phenomenon.* London: Bodley Head.

Becher, Jillian. 1971. *Hitler's children: the story of the Baader-Meinhof terrorist gang.* Philadelphia: Lippincott.

McHenry, Robert, ed. 1992. *The new encyclopedia Britannica.* Chicago: Encyclopedia Britannica, Inc.

BABBITT. A narrow-minded, materialistic, self-important, and complacent businessman of the 1920s.

George F. Babbitt is the central character in *Babbitt* (1922) by Harry Sinclair Lewis (1885–1951). The novel revolves around a group of businessmen and their families living in the imaginary city of Zenith, in the United States in the 1920s during Prohibition. George Babbitt is a successful realtor and regards himself as a prominent citizen. He belongs to numerous lodges and clubs, behaves in a hearty manner, and displays sound morals and a deep regard for the U.S. Constitution. In middle age George is confronted with enlightened ideas in politics, culture, love, and a refined way of life. This draws him from his basic values for a time. But with relief and some repentance he reverts to type, and takes up his familiar round again for fear of losing his friends.

Sinclair Lewis graduated from Yale (1908), went into publishing, and wrote under the name of "Tom Graham." An established writer by 1926, he refused a Pulitzer Prize for his *Arrowsmith* in retribution for not having been awarded it for his earlier work. He received the Nobel Prize for literature in 1930. His character Babbitt remains a symbol of middle-class standards for the typical American middle-class businessman.

Sources

Garraty, John A., ed. 1977. *Dictionary of American biography.* Supplement 5. New York: Charles Scribner's Sons.

Lewis, Sinclair. 1922. *Babbitt.* 1950 ed. New York: Brace and Co.

Schorer, Mark. 1961. *Sinclair Lewis: An American life.* New York: McGraw-Hill.

BABOUVISM. Egalitarianism, particularly relating to the universal equality of incomes, that gives a basis to the growth of socialist and communist ideas.

François Noël (Gracchus) Babeuf (1760–97) was born in Saint Quentin, France. His father was a tax farmer, and François became a surveyor. At age twenty-five he had a well paid job and high social standing, but he disliked his work and turned to political journalism. After becoming acquainted with the Academy Arras, a literary society, he befriended Dubois de Fosseux, its secretary. In 1787 Babeuf had Fosseux distribute a revolutionary brochure "La Constitution de Corps-militare,'' a critique of the aristocratic caste system in the French Army. It advocated a people's assembly to which the king of France should be responsible for his actions, and which would act as an ultimate court of appeal. In Paris in 1789 he founded a journal, and for his political activities was imprisoned. In prison he set down his plans for an ideal society, arguing that it would be best achieved through revolution. He further spread revolutionary principles, demanding social equality and communal ownership of lands and goods. His *Manifesto of Equals* (1790) maintained that ownership and inequality created evil in society. The answer lay in an agrarian society—achieved through revolution—in which property was owned by the community. All members of the community would work to enjoy a frugal but abundant life. Babeuf argued that because all people had similar needs and faculties, they should have the same diet and education. He was given the name ''Gracchus'' because his land reforms were similar to those of the second-century Roman statesman. In 1792 he worked as an archivist outside Paris; two years later he returned to Paris to found another journal which criticized the rightists in power, and again he was arrested. In prison he formulated his doctrines more clearly and began work as a professional revolutionary. On his release from prison he formed a secret society of six members and planned insurrection. Later he met with Jacobins and military insurgents who aimed to raise a 17,000 strong militia to have the popular Constitution of 1793 reinstated in France. His opponents saw his ideas as a conspiracy of equals. Informants betrayed him, and eventually he was arrested, tried, found guilty, and sent to the guillotine. His strategies served as a model for future politico-social movements of the nineteenth century in Europe.

Sources

Bax, Ernest B. 1911. *The last episode of the French Revolution: being a history of Gracchus Babeuf.* London: Grant Richards.

Miller, David ed. 1987. *The Blackwell encyclopedia of political thought.* Oxford: Basil Blackwell.

Rose, R. B. 1978. *Gracchus Babeuf: the first revolutionary Communist.* Stanford: Stanford University Press.

Scott, John A. 1972. *The defense of Gracchus Babeuf before the high court of Vendom.* With essay by Herbert Marcuse. New York: Schocken Books.

Seligman, Edwin R.A., ed. 1930. *Encyclopedia of the social sciences.* New York: Macmillan.

Thomson, David. 1947. *The Babeuf plot: the making of a republican legend.* London: K. Paul, Trench, Trubner.

BACONIAN (a). Relating to or a follower of the seventeenth-century English philosopher or his ideas; one who believes that he was the author of Shakespeare's plays.

Francis Bacon (1561–1626) was born in London, son of Sir Nicholas Bacon, and became a celebrated English philosopher, jurist, and statesman. Bacon studied at Cambridge, was admitted to the bar in 1582, and was elected to Parliament in 1584, serving until 1614. He wrote several papers on statecraft—particularly on relations between the Crown and the Commons—and was created baron of Verulam (1618) and viscount St. Albans (1621). Bacon became lord chancellor, and in 1620 his *Novum Organum* was published. Its second book contains the principles of his inductive philosophy. Shortly afterward he was tried for bribery, condemned, fined, and removed from office. Thereafter he worked on his literary and philosophical writings. Some—among them J. C. Hart (1848), Delia Bacon (1857), and Nathaniel Holmes (1866; 1888)—have suggested that Bacon was the true author of Shakespeare's works. About 500 works have appeared on this question, but today the claim carries little credit.

Sources

McHenry, Robert, ed. 1992. *The new encyclopedia Britannica.* Chicago: Encyclopedia Britannica, Inc.

Overton-Fuller, Jean. 1981. *Francis Bacon: a biography.* London: East-West Publications.

Sills, David L., ed. 1968. *International encyclopedia of the social sciences.* New York: Macmillan and Free Press.

Stephen, Leslie, and Lee, Sydney, eds. 1917. *The dictionary of national biography.* London: Oxford University Press.

Zusne, Leonard. 1984. *Biographical dictionary of psychology.* Westport, Conn.: Greenwood Press.

BACONIAN (b). Pertaining to the thirteenth-century English philosopher.

Roger Bacon (1214–94) was born in Somersetshire, England, and educated at Oxford and Paris universities. He knew the classics and claimed an acquaintance with Aristotle's works. He joined the Franciscan order in 1250, was sent to Paris in 1257, and, after some years, Bacon was asked by Pope Clement IV to write a general treatise on the sciences, which resulted in his major work *Opus Majus* (1266–68). This work showed his attitude to reform in the existing methods of philosophical and scientific ideas. Notably, he rejected authority and verbal subtleties as grounds for knowledge, and he identified obstacles to the achievement of true knowledge. The work was an encyclopedic account of grammar, logic, mathematics, physics, experimental research, and moral philosophy. A Franciscan council condemned his later writings as heretical, and consequently he was placed in confinement (1278). After being freed in 1292, he died in obscurity.

Sources

McHenry, Robert, ed. 1992. *The new encyclopedia Britannica.* Chicago: Encyclopedia Britannica, Inc.

Seligman, Edwin R.A., ed. 1930. *Encyclopedia of the social sciences.* New York: Macmillan.

Stephen, Leslie, and Lee, Sydney, eds. 1917. *The dictionary of national biography.* London: Oxford University Press.

Zusne, Leonard. 1984. *Biographical dictionary of psychology.* Westport, Conn.: Greenwood Press.

BACONISTS. A group of rebels in the colony of Virginia (1676), and later the name adopted by liberals in Maryland (1678).

Nathanial Bacon (1647–76) was born in Suffolk and educated in Cambridge University and Gray's Inn. He immigrated to Virginia and was noted for his siding with those who suffered under colonialism. In 1676 he led a rebellion against the Indians, and he also wanted to reform all colonial law in order to remove the social inequalities he had readily observed in Virginia. Without permission he led a small army against an Indian tribe and later forced Governor Berkeley to call a new assembly to institute political reforms. Before this was done, Bacon led two further attacks on Indians and dispersed the tribes. He was chosen to be a member of the new reform assembly, but he was captured with his associates, reproached for his illegal actions, pardoned, and readmitted to the ruling council from which he had been excluded. Still angry with the governor and suspecting a plot against his life, Bacon gathered his followers and demanded permission to march against the Indians. The governor raised a band to put down Bacon and his followers but failed. Bacon declared himself ruler of the colony, but shortly afterward fell ill and died, leaving a reputation as one of the more notable of the rebellious colonial leaders.

Source

Johnson, Allen, ed. 1927. *Dictionary of American biography.* Vol. I. New York: Charles Scribner's Sons.

BAKHTINIAN. An approach to cultural history that concerns itself with unofficial and popular elements in a great writer's works, for example, carnivalization, a means of subversion or uncrowning, and heteroglossia, the interaction of dialogue between different viewpoints or languages.

Mikhail Mikhailovich Bakhtin (1895–1975) was born in Orel, Russia, and studied at Odessa University in Saint Petersburg. In the 1920s he was active in Lenin's literary circles and was upholding Formalism. He published books under the names of his associates on Marxism, Freud, and Formalism. After he published *Problems of Dostoyevsky's Poetics* (1929), he was arrested and exiled to Kazakhstan for six years. In 1936 he was appointed to the Teachers' College, Kimr, near Moscow, and during 1937–45 he participated in the activities of the Literary Institute at Moscow's Academy of Sciences and was at Saransk Teachers' College until he retired. Until the reissue of his Dostoyevsky study in 1963, Bakhtin was in the mainstream of academic writing. He was known mainly for his work in linguistic and literary studies, and he enjoyed a reputation as one of the finest literary theoreticians of the twentieth century. Much of his thinking was influenced by the Formalists, and he centered his attention on the structural aspects of fiction.

Sources

Clark, Katrina, and Holquist, Michael. 1984. *Mikhail Bakhtin.* Cambridge, Mass.: Harvard University Press.

Nordquist, Joan. 1988. *Mikhail Bakhtin.* Santa Cruz, Calif.: Reference and Research Services.

Turner, Roland, ed. 1987. *Thinkers of the twentieth century.* 2d ed. Chicago: St. James
    Press.
Vernoff, Edward, and Shore, Rima, eds. 1987. *International dictionary of 20th century
    biography.* New York: New American Library.

BAKKE **DECISION.** A U.S. Supreme Court decision that favored a white
man's claim that he had been denied equal protection under law. When refused
entry to medical school, University of California (Davis), which had set aside
16 of 100 available places for minority applicants, Allan Bakke sued, arguing
that his application was better than that of some of the minority applicants who
had been accepted. Although the school was within its rights to take into account
race when selecting applicants, the Court decided that Bakke should be admitted
to Davis Medical School.

Allan Bakke (b. 1940) was born in Minnesota, son of a mail delivery man
and a teacher. He studied engineering at the University of Minnesota and supported himself by serving in the Naval Reserve Officers Training Corps; he was
a marine who saw combat in Vietnam. He became a captain, and in 1967 he
was a research engineer at Ames Research Center for the National Aeronautical
and Space Administration. Determined to become a medical doctor, in 1972 he
applied to the Davis Medical Center, University of California. Rejected twice,
Bakke sued the university, claiming racial prejudice excluded him from a medical education, and this violated state and federal laws. He graduated and now
practices medicine.

Sources

Regents of the University of California v. Allan Bakke, 435 S.S. 265 (1978).
Schwarz, Bernard. 1988. *Behind Bakke: affirmative action and the Supreme Court.* New
    York: New York University Press.
Shafritz, Jay M. 1988. *The Dorsey dictionary of American government and politics.*
    Chicago: Dorsey.
Sindler, Allan P. 1978. *Bakke, Defunis, and the minority admissions: the quest for equal
    opportunity.* New York: Longman.
Wilkinson, J. Harvie. 1979. *From Brown to Bakke: the Supreme Court and school in-
    tegration, 1954–1978.* New York: Oxford University Press.

BALES'S INTERACTION PROCESS ANALYSIS. The first theoretically
oriented general-purpose system of categories for the direct observation and
classification of interpersonal behavior in groups: asks for and gives information,
opinion, and suggestion; shows agreement, disagreement, tension, tension release, solidarity, and antagonism.

Robert Freed Bales (b. 1916) was born in Ellington, Missouri, and studied
sociology and psychology at the University of Oregon and Harvard (Ph.D.,
1945). He researched into alcoholism with Alcoholics Anonymous, studied clinical psychology at Henry Murray's Psychological Clinic at Harvard, and was
influenced by Kurt Lewin's Research Center for Group Dynamics at MIT. In
the early 1950s he completed a didactic analysis in psychoanalytic training, and

taught sociology at Harvard where he directed the Laboratory in Social Relations (1960–67). He became chairman of the social psychology program in 1970 and a consultant to the Harvard University Health Services. He was visiting lecturer in social sciences at the universities of Michigan, Columbia, and Salzburg, and served on boards for the National Institute of Mental Health (1957–60) and several professional associations. He is a member of the American Academy of Arts and Sciences and an affiliate of the Boston Psychoanalytic Society. Among his publications are contributions to many texts in social psychology; he co-authored *Working Papers in the Theory of Action* (1953), *Family Socialization, and Interaction Process* (1955), and co-edited *Social Groups: Studies in Social Interaction* (1955). He also co-authored *SYMLOG: A System for the Multiple Level Observation of Groups* (1979). Today Bales is professor of social relations, emeritus, at Harvard University, and researches and develops computerized expert programs for assessment and training with the SYMLOG consulting group in leadership, education, therapy, personality and group dynamics, managerial teams, work teams, and problem-solving groups. He has recently helped develop courses at the Harvard Business School. He has received many awards and honors from professional associations of psychologists and sociologists, and has served as editor of journals in both fields.

Sources

Bales, Robert F. 1950. *Interaction process analysis: a method for the study of small groups.* Cambridge, Mass.: Addison-Wesley.

Bales, Robert F. 1970. *Personality and interpersonal behavior.* New York: Holt, Rinehart and Winston.

Who's who in America, 1990–91. Chicago: Marquis.

Personal Communication.

BALFOUR DECLARATION. A letter dated November 2, 1917, from Britain's foreign secretary to Lord Rothschild, declaring sympathy for the Zionist ideal to establish a national home in Palestine for the Jewish people, but asserting that in achieving the ideal in Palestine the non-Jewish communities should lose none of their civil and religious rights.

Arthur James Balfour, first Earl Balfour (1848–1930) was born at Whittinghame, East Lothian. He went to Eton and Trinity College, Cambridge, and studied the moral sciences. He was a Conservative M.P. for Hertford during 1874–85, and was helped in his career by his uncle, the third marquess of Salisbury. While enjoying great social status and entertaining lavishly in his Scottish home, Balfour was secretary for Scotland, chief secretary for Ireland, and Conservative leader in the House of Commons and first lord of the Treasury. When Lord Salisbury resigned in 1902, Balfour became prime minister, and three years later he in turn resigned in favor of Sir Henry Campbell-Bannerman. Shortly after losing his seat in the 1906 election, Balfour was returned as M.P. for the city of London. In the coalition government of 1915, Balfour became first lord of the Admiralty under Herbert Henry Asquith's prime ministership. He issued his declaration after overcoming much opposition from within as well as outside the cabinet, and in 1919 he resigned as foreign secretary but stayed in the cabinet as lord president of the Council. He accepted an earldom in 1922. His philosophical view that science was no sounder a base for knowledge than theology appeared in his *A Defence of Philosophical Doubt* (1879) and *Foundations of Belief* (1895).

Sources

Egremont, Max. 1980. *Balfour: a life of Arthur James Balfour.* London: Collins.
Oxbury, Harold. 1985. *Great Britons: 20th century lives.* Oxford: Oxford University Press.
Stein, Leonard J. 1961. *The Balfour Declaration.* London: Vallentine, Mitchell.
Weaver, J.B.H., ed. 1937. *Dictionary of national biography 1922–1930.* London: Oxford University Press.
Zebel, Sydney H. 1973. *Balfour: a political biography.* Cambridge: Cambridge University Press.

BALLINGER-PINCHOT CONTROVERSY. A controversy beginning in 1909 over conservation and the sale of public lands and eventually involving U.S. President William Howard Taft.

Richard Achilles Ballinger (1858–1922) was born at Boonesboro, Iowa, into a prominent American family. He graduated from Williams College, was admitted to the bar in 1886, and specialized in mining law. He became a notable figure in Seattle, and its reform mayor during 1904–6. Under President Theodore Roosevelt he was appointed commissioner of the General Land Office (1907) and secretary of the interior under President Taft (1909). He entered a conflict with Gifford Pinchot; land, timber, mineral, and water rights were at stake, and so, on advice from Pinchot and others, President Roosevelt had established a conservation policy. Ballinger seemed to have little sympathy for the policy, and he interpreted the law in the interests of those who sought to develop the resources, not conserve them. When a field man in the Land Office complained to the president that Ballinger had held up investigations into fraudulent coal land claims in Alaska, the president authorized Ballinger to fire him. With support from conservationists, the man began a newspaper trial of Ballinger's policies that was brought into the U.S. Congress. A congressional committee exonerated Ballinger, but his critics forced his resignation in 1911. He returned to his law practice.

Gifford Pinchot (1865–1946) was born in Simsburg, Connecticut, into a prosperous merchant family and was named after the U.S. landscape painter, Sanford Gifford. He was tutored in French and studied at private schools. He was educated at Yale and later studied forestry in France, founded the Yale School of Forestry (1903–36), and became chairman of the National Conservation Association (1910–25). He was the first professional forester in the United States and a leading conservationist, and he was appointed chief of the Division of Forestry in the U.S. Department of Agriculture. A friend of President Roosevelt

(1901–9), Pinchot became most influential in making over millions of acres of land to reserves and coined the term *conservation*. He also helped found the Progressive party in 1912. Twice he served as reform governor of Pennsylvania (1923 and 1935), and he believed strongly that government should curb the influence of big business.

Sources

Garraty, John A., and James, Edward T., eds. 1974. *Dictionary of American biography.* Supplement 4. New York: Charles Scribner's Sons.

Johnson, Allen, ed. 1927. *Dictionary of American biography.* Vol. I. New York: Charles Scribner's Sons.

Smith, Edward C., and Zurcher, Arnold J. 1968. *Dictionary of American politics.* 2d ed. New York: Barnes and Noble.

Vernoff, Edward, and Shore, Rima, eds. 1987. *International dictionary of 20th century biography.* New York: New American Library.

BARBAROSSA. The German Supreme command's code-name for the German invasion of Russia in 1941. At the time of the invasion, Russia and Germany had a nonaggression agreement, the Molotov-Ribbentrop, or Hitler-Stalin Pact. On December 10, 1940, the invasion, initially named "Fritz," was renamed and approved by Hitler and planned for May 1941. Delayed until troops fighting in Greece became available, Operation Barbarossa began on June 22, with support from Romanian and Finnish forces, and seventy-nine German divisions invaded Russia.

Barbarossa, an Italian name meaning "Red beard," was given to the German hero and Holy Roman emperor, Frederick I (1123–90). He was the son of the duke of Swabia and was elected German king and Holy Roman emperor in 1152 in Frankfurt. Immediately, he began to challenge papal authority in Europe by violating the Concord of Worms of 1122, refusing to honor previous treaties and alliances, making new concessions and treaties, refusing inducements to gain power through a strategic marriage, and seeking to restore his imperial rights in Italy. To this end he conquered Milan and levied taxes on the Italians. While on the Third Crusade through Asia Minor, Frederick I was drowned. German legend states that he continued to live, awaiting his country's call to service, in a cave among the Kyffhäuser Mountains at Germany's geographical center.

Sources

McHenry, Robert, ed. 1992. *The new encyclopedia Britannica.* Chicago: Encyclopedia Britannica, Inc.

Snyder, Louis L. 1976. *Encyclopedia of the Third Reich.* New York: McGraw-Hill.

BARBER'S MODEL. A fourfold classification of U.S. presidents that shows how character affects administrative style while in office. The presidents are active or passive in the energy they bring to their work, and positive or negative in their attitude to the work itself. The best presidents seem to be active-positive types who are confident in themselves, like politics, and watch their results keenly, for example, Franklin D. Roosevelt, Truman and Kennedy. The poor-est—the active-negative types—are compulsively driven to have power, for example, Wilson, Johnson, and Nixon. The predictive value of the classification has grown since the early 1970s.

James David Barber (b. 1930) was born and educated in Charleston, West Virginia, and graduated from Greenbriar Military School and the University of Chicago. He served in the U.S. Army Counter-intelligence Corps during 1953–55 and taught at Stetson University from 1955 to 1957. He studied at Yale (1960, Ph.D., Political Science) and taught there for twelve years and became director of the Office for Advanced Political Studies in 1967. In the 1960s he was a fellow of the National Science Foundation and the Center for Advanced Study in Behavioral Sciences. In 1972 he was made a professor of political science and public policy at Duke University and served as chair of the Political Science Department. He has published widely on leadership, citizenship, law-making, and women in politics, and has researched and lectured in Great Britain, Europe, the Far East, and Central and South America. He has served on the advisory boards of many professional journals, worked for Amnesty International, and served as a consultant to several publishers and research foundations.
Sources

Barber, James D. 1992. Prediction as a test for hypothesis: application to the psychology of presidents. *Political Psychology* 13:543–552.

Barber, James D. 1993. *The presidential character: predicting performance in the White House.* 4th ed. Englewood Cliffs, N.J.: Prentice-Hall.

Evory, Ann, ed. 1982. *Contemporary authors.* New Revision Series. Vol. 6. Detroit: Gale Research.

Personal Communication.

BAREBONES PARLIAMENT. The Parliament of Nominees, or the "Little Parliament," summoned on July 4, 1653 by Oliver Cromwell after he dismissed the Long Parliament. It was named after one of its members, a devout Puritan. The Parliament took the name of the Commonwealth of England and was ridiculed for its reforming zeal; it established civil marriage and a register of births and burials. Amidst debate on church organization, it became so deadlocked that it unwittingly dismissed itself by resigning its powers to Lord General Cromwell on December 12, 1653.

Praise-God Barebones, or Barbon or Barebone (?1596–1679) was an anabaptist, leather-seller, and politician. His origins are obscure, but in 1642 he published a defense of baptizing children. After establishing a reputation as a preacher, Praise-God was asked by Oliver Cromwell to be member for the city of London in the Little Parliament. Enemies of the Little Parliament ridiculed it by quickly christening it "Barebones." Although his name attaches to the parliament, Barebones did not speak in the house; it seems that all he did was leave to the house as instructed to see some petitioners at the door on August 2, 1653, and return to the house with a petition given him by Lieutenant-Colonel

John Lilburne. Praise-God did not become an M.P. After the Little Parliament was disbanded, he continued his zealous preaching, worked to prevent the return of Charles II to the throne, and was imprisoned for over six months after the Restoration (1661–62).

Sources

Stephen, Leslie, and Lee, Sidney, eds. 1917. *The dictionary of national biography.* London: Oxford University Press.

Wilding, Norman, and Laundy, Philip. 1971. *An encyclopaedia of Parliament.* Rev. 4th ed. London: Cassell.

BARLOW REPORT, 1940. A report of a British Royal Commission established in 1938, titled *Distribution of the Industrial Population* (1940). It found that two-fifths of the population lived in seven urban areas described as ''sprawling agglomerations of humanity.'' It stated that the distribution was detrimental to the economic and social life of the people, and it recommended a more even distribution of industry and population to reduce inhuman congestion, improve economic conditions in poor areas, and have a strategic military benefit.

Sir Clement Anderson Montague-Barlow (1866–1951) was educated at Repton and King's College, Cambridge, and called to the bar, Lincoln's Inn, in 1895. He practiced primarily in education and charity cases, lectured for the Law Society and the London School of Economics, and examined in law at London University. He was on the London County Council (1907–10), director/chairman of Sotheby & Company (1909–28) and served in the Salford Brigade (1914–16) during World War I. He was elected M.P. for South Salford (1910–23), was parliamentary secretary to the minister of labor (1922–24), and served on several select committees regarding soldiers' welfare. In addition, he represented the government at the International Labor Offices in Genoa and Geneva (1920–22). In 1938 he chaired the Royal Commission on the Location of Industry. He was chairman of the council of Malvern Girls' College during 1932–45, and published essays on church reform and education.

Sources

Hanson J. L. 1974. *A dictionary of economics and commerce.* Suffolk: Richard Clay.

Pearce, David W., ed. 1986. *Macmillan dictionary of modern economics.* New York: Macmillan.

Who was who, 1951–60. London: Adam and Charles Black.

BARLOW REPORT, 1946. A British educational report (1946) that recommended that universities should double the output of science graduates. It greatly influenced the policies of both universities and grammar schools in the years after World War II.

Sir James Alan Noel Barlow (1881–1968), second Baronet, attended Marlborough and Corpus Christi College, Oxford, and became a notable public servant. He began as a clerk in the House of Commons (1906) and became undersecretary at the Treasury (1934), remaining there until retirement. He

chaired the Barlow Committee, which proposed to establish a policy on the use of Britain's scientific personnel resources for the ten years after World War II.
Sources
Blishen, Edward. 1969. *Blond's encyclopaedia of education.* London: Blond Educational.
Deighton, Lee, ed. 1971. *The encyclopedia of education.* New York: Macmillan and Free Press.
Williams, E. T., and Nichols, C. S., eds. 1981. *Dictionary of national biography 1961–1970.* Oxford: Oxford University Press.

BARNARD'S EXECUTIVE FUNCTIONS, BARNARD'S ZONE OF IN-DIFFERENCE. Three functions of an executive are to provide a communication system; to promote the securing of essential personal efforts; and to formulate and define purpose. For authority in an organization to function effectively there is a zone of indifference for each member within which he or she accepts orders without question and voluntarily obeys them.

Chester Irving Barnard (1886–1961) was born in Massachusetts, worked on a farm, and studied economics at Harvard University while he earned money tuning pianos and operating a dance band. On a technicality he was not eligible for a bachelor's degree at Harvard, but eventually, through his experience in organizations he received honorary doctorates from many universities. In 1909 he joined the American Telephone & Telegraph Company, and by 1927 he was the president of New Jersey Bell. As a self-educated scholar, he applied the sociological ideas of Max Weber (1864–1920), Kurt Lewin (1890–1947), and Vilfredo Pareto (1848–1923) to organizations, seeing them as cooperative rather than competitive systems. With an idea that was antithetical to most management beliefs about controlling subordinates, Barnard stated that authority in an organization had two features: the personal or subjective acceptance of a directive; and the objective, formal character of the directive. Consequently, authority in an organization resided not in a person who gave orders, but in the extent to which subordinates accepted orders.
Sources
Barnard, Chester I. 1938. *The functions of the executive.* Cambridge, Mass.: Harvard University Press.
Scott, William G. 1992. *Chester I. Barnard and the guardians of the management state.* Lawrence: University of Kansas Press.
Wolf, William B. 1974. *The basic Barnard: an introduction to Chester I. Barnard and his theories of organization and management.* Ithaca, N.Y.: New York State School of Industrial Relations.

BARNARDOS, BARNARDO BOY, BARNARDO'S CHILDREN, BAR-NARDO'S HOME. Destitute British children; a home in London for destitute children.

Thomas John Barnardo (1845–1905) was born in Dublin to a furrier of Spanish and German origins. At age 14, Thomas became a clerk for a wine merchant and saw the effects of alcoholism at first hand. In 1862 he experienced a religious conversion, was called to be a missionary in China, and went to London for training in medicine (1866). While studying, he found destitute boys sleeping in alleys or on roofs. To help them he became superintendent of the Ernest Street ragged school—a school for destitute boys—gave up the call to China (1867), and founded the East End Juvenile Mission. Under Lord Shaftsbury's patronage, he received money to establish the first refuge for destitute boys in Stepney Causeway (1870). He bought two pubs and converted them to refuges (1873), and in 1874 he established the Girls Village Home and later, in 1887, opened an office in Toronto. The refuges, known as ''Dr. Barnardo's Homes,'' were Protestant; Dr. Barnardo frequently came into conflict with Catholic authorities over the care of children who had been born to Catholic parents. In 1899 the refuges were given over in trust to the National Incorporated Association for the Reclamation of Destitute Waif Children, and in 1903 Queen Alexandra agreed to be patron of the association.

Sources

Chapman, Jennifer. 1991. *Barnardo today: who will still love me?* London: Virgin.

Lee, Sidney, ed. 1912. *Dictionary of national biography: supplement 1901–1911.* London: Oxford University Press.

Preece, Warren E., ed. 1965. *Encyclopedia Britannica.* Chicago: Encyclopedia Britannica, Inc., William Benton.

Rose, June. 1987. *For the sake of the children: inside Dr. Barnardo's: 120 years of caring for children.* London: Hodder and Stoughton.

Williams, Arthur E. 1943. *Barnardo of Stepney, the father of nobody's children.* 2d ed. 1954. London: Allen and Unwin.

BARROWISTS. A British religious sect similar to the Brownists and Separatists in the 1590s.

Henry Barrow (c. 1550–93) was born in Norfolk and educated at Clare College, Cambridge, where he studied law. A dissolute student, he was suddenly converted on hearing a sermon, and he became a strict Puritan (1580). At first, he followed the Brownists and the Separatists who advocated the separation of the authority of church and state. He wrote *A True Description of the Word of God, of the Visible Church* (1589) and *A Brief Discovery of the False God* (1590). With the Separatist John Greenwood, Barrow was jailed for refusing to recant, and in 1592 he established his own Christian church, which he defined as ''a company of faithful people, separated from the unbelievers and heathens of the land.'' In his church the laity and the clergy were one in their autonomy over the congregation. Barrow and Greenwood were imprisoned, tried, found guilty of seditious writings, and put to death.

Sources

Cook, Chris, and Wroughton, John. 1980. *English historical facts: 1603–1688.* London: Macmillan.

Cross, Frank L. 1974. *The Oxford dictionary of the Christian Church.* 2d ed. New York: Oxford University Press.

McHenry, Robert, ed. 1992. *The new encyclopedia Britannica.* Chicago: Encyclopedia
    Britannica, Inc.

BARTHIAN. A variety of Christian theology that rejects higher criticism and
deduces all doctrines from the Bible but does not go to the extremes of fundamentalism.

Karl Barth (1886–1968) was a professor at Bonn and Basle and a Protestant
who had been disillusioned by the failure of theologians to examine properly
the social and political problems early in the twentieth century. Immediately
after World War I, he published his *The Epistle to the Romans.* This stressed
"the wholly otherness of God," and shocked the Protestant theologians whose
rationalist, psychological, and historicist views of God had prevailed for over a
hundred years. As a result, he was appointed to a chair of theology at Göttingen
(1921), and later to Münster (1925) and Bonn (1930). He attacked liberals in
the Protestant church, believing that man could reach religious understanding
by his own reason. Barth emphasized the corrupting influences of sin and developed a dogmatic theory emphasizing joy in the transcendence and gracious-
ness of God as it was revealed in Jesus Christ. He helped established the Barmen
Declaration (1934) against the pseudo-religious views of the Nazis. Because he
refused to accept Nazi interference in the churches of Germany and refused to
swear allegiance to Hitler, he was expelled from Germany in 1935 and was
made a professor of systematic theology at the University of Basle until he
retired in 1961. The ecumenical significance of his work gave him a secure
reputation in Europe; he was honored in the United States in 1962, and in Britain
was awarded the Medal for Service in the Cause of Freedom. By emphasizing
the complete "otherness" of God, in contrast to anthropomorphic images of
God in the nineteenth century, Barth became the most influential of radical,
modern Protestant theologians in the twentieth century.
Sources
Busch, Eberhard. 1976. *Karl Barth: his life from letters and autobiographical texts.*
    Trans. by John Bowden. London: S.C.M. Press.
Devine, Elizabeth; Held, Michael; Vinson, James; and Walsh, George, eds. 1983. *Think-
    ers of the twentieth century: a biographical, bibliographical and critical
    dictionary.* London: Macmillan.
Green, Clifford. 1989. *Karl Barth: theologian of freedom.* San Francisco, CA: Collins.

BARUCH PLAN. A plan to neutralize the international use of atomic power
(1946). It proposed that the United States would stop production of the atomic
bomb after the establishment of a World Atomic Authority to control production
and that, in this regard, the United Nations Security Council would limit the use
of its members' veto. Russia rejected the plan in the United Nations Security
Council largely because of the veto issue.

Bernard Mannes Baruch (1870–1965) was born in Camden, South Carolina,
and at age 10 was taken to New York where his father was a medical practi-

tioner. Bernard was educated in public schools, graduated from the City College of New York, joined a broker's firm (1891), and speculated successfully in sugar, railroad, and tobacco stocks by selling short on a falling market. A millionaire at 30, he established his own firm and with the Guggenheim brothers speculated in metals and rubber in the United States and abroad. As a Democrat on Wall Street, he used his wealth to enter politics, befriending presidents from Woodrow Wilson to Kennedy. He began a notable political career by becoming chairman of the Advisory Commission of the Council for National Defense (1916) and chairman of the War Industries Board (1918). He established a master plan for the U.S. industrial mobilization and made excellent suggestions regarding the economic issues of the Treaty of Versailles in 1919. After World War II, Truman appointed him ambassador to the United Nations Atomic Energy Commission (1946) where he helped shape the U.S. policy to become the major controller of atomic energy.

Sources

Baruch, Bernard M. 1957–1960. *Baruch.* 2 vols. New York: Holt, Rinehart and Winston.

Coit, Margaret L. 1957. *Mr. Baruch.* Boston: Houghton Mifflin.

Garraty, John A., ed. 1974. *Encyclopedia of American biography.* New York: Harper and Row.

Malone, Dumas, ed. 1934. *Dictionary of American biography.* Vol. VII. New York: Charles Scribner's Sons.

Plano, Jack C., and Olton, Roy. 1988. *The international relations dictionary.* 4th ed. Santa Barbara, Calif.: ABC-CLIO.

Schwarz, Jordan A. 1981. *The speculator: Bernard Baruch in Washington 1917–1965.* Chapel Hill: University of North Carolina Press.

Vernoff, Edward, and Shore, Rima, eds. 1987. *International dictionary of 20th century biography.* New York: New American Library.

BARZUN'S LAW. In an indictment of Western education, Jacques Barzun argued that the power of the intellect was being emasculated by claims to authority and power which are based on art, science, and philanthropy. As a result, intellectuals claimed they were powerless in modern times; this claim was then used by intellectuals to justify why they should no longer attempt rigorous work with their minds. This led to a law formulated by Barzun (1959: 77): "Abdicating power generates the taste for organized inaction and the pursuit of pseudowork." He noticed it appearing in "broody sittings of committees, and proliferating plans and reports fore and aft to nonexisting accomplishments." Under these circumstances, especially in universities, such committees ensure that intellectual rigor and order is forbidden by insisting on committee members saying nice things to each other and expressing good fellowship all the time.

Jacques Martin Barzun (b. 1907) was born in Creteil, France, and immigrated to the United States in 1920. He studied at Columbia University (Ph.D., 1933) and became an American citizen in 1933. At Columbia he became a professor of history (1938) and one of America's notable educators, critics, literary consultants, a literary adviser to Charles Scribner's Sons, and a prolific author. He is an authority on art and music. His controversial *House of Intellect* (1959) criticized modern intellectuals for the wholesale adoption of science, art, and philanthropy. He advocated an education policy for broadly based study in liberal arts rather than for training in a vocation or profession. Among his writings are *A Study in Modern Superstition* (1937), *Of Human Freedom* (1939), *Teacher in America* (1945), *God's Country and Mine* (1954), *Music in American Life* and *The Energies of Art: Studies of Authors, Classic and Modern* (1956), *The Modern Researcher* (1957), *Classic, Romantic and Modern* (1961), and *The American University* (1968). Many of his works are being reprinted.

Sources

Barzun, Jacques. 1959. *The house of intellect.* New York: Harper and Row.
The international who's who, 1992–93. London: Europa Publications.
Vernoff, Edward, and Shore, Rima, eds. 1987. *International dictionary of 20th century biography.* New York: New American Library.
Who's who in America, 1992–93. Chicago: Marquis.

BASILIAN. A monk or nun who follows the rule of Saint Basil.

Saint Basil ("Basil the Great," 329–79) was born at Causerie in Cappadocia. He was the brother of Saint Gregory of Nyssa and was converted to religion by his sister, Saint Macrina. He studied at Constantinople under Libanius and at Athens in the schools of philosophy and rhetoric, and later returned to Causerie as a rhetorician. He strongly supported the orthodox faith in the struggle against Arianism and was a distinguished preacher. At about 36 years of age, he retired to Pontus and entered a monastic life, and, as one of the Fathers of the Greek church, became bishop of Causerie and metropolitan of Cappadocia (370–79). He wrote much of *The Longer Rule* and the *Shorter Rule,* and it is on these that the Basilian monkhood is based. His works *On the Holy Ghost* and *Against Eunomius* are strong defenses of the Catholic religious system.

Sources

Cross, Frank L. 1974. *The Oxford dictionary of the Christian Church.* 2d ed. New York: Oxford University Press.
Deferrari, Roy J. 1926. *Saint Basil: the letters.* 4 vols. Reprinted 1961. London: Heinemann.
Douglas, James D., ed. 1974. *The new international dictionary of the Christian Church.* Exeter: Paternoster Press.
McHenry, Robert, ed. 1992. *The new encyclopedia Britannica.* Chicago: Encyclopedia Britannica, Inc.

BATMANIA. Commentators' term for the enthusiasm created for selling the U.S. movie *Batman* in June 1989 and the sequel in 1992.

Batman (b. 1939), a comic strip character, was created by Bob Kane (b. 1916) and Bill Finger (1917–74) as a counter to "Superman," a popular comic of the day. Finger thought the ears of a bat and the cowl would distinguish Batman from Superman. Many writers worked on the successful comic book, but only Kane's name appeared until 1964 when the comic was changed. Called "Batman,'' the character first appeared in *Detective Comics,* Volume 27, and established itself as ''Batman'' in a comic of the same name in April 1940. He was 6' 2", square-jawed, and wealthy. His real name was Bruce Wayne (1918?–). At age 9, Wayne witnessed the murder of his rich parents in crime-ridden Gotham City and pledged his life to a war against evil. A millionaire philanthropist in everyday life, he was known in his secret work as the ''Caped Crusader'' and was assisted by a young lad, Robin. In the fight against crime in Gotham city, their major task was to defeat the Joker, a wicked, curious character, who was a transformation of Jack Napier, the murderer of Wayne's parents. The characters were born again on television (1966–68). Adam West appeared as Batman; because the television characterization and plots were played for high camp, not all Batman fans accepted this version. The $40 million movie of 1989 starred Michael Keaton as Batman and Jack Nicholson as the Joker. But the characterization of the hero had changed. He became 5' 10", had receding hair, and had lost his square jaw. Brooding and depressed by the death of his parents, he was lonely and isolated, and had no assistant. Bob Kane was hired to change the character from a teenager's hero to the complex character that would attract a mature audience. In 1989 many businesses leased the name of Batman and attached it to hundreds of items for sale, for example, Batshirts, Batshorts, Batmugs, and Batwatches. Eventually, newspaper writers coined ''Batwhatever, Batphernaila, Batstuff and Bat-hype.'' This followed a successful campaign to increase the distribution of the Batman Comic by 100,000 copies in 1986 and to dispense with the image of Batman as portrayed on television.

Sources

Morrock, Richard. 1989. Birth symbolism and Batmania. *The Journal of Psychohistory* 17:208–214.

Vernoff, Edward, and Shore, Rima, eds. 1987. *International dictionary of 20th century biography.* New York: New American Library.

BAVELAS EXPERIMENT. A social psychology experiment using five-person groups with four communication networks—a wheel, chain, Y-formation, and a circle. In the wheel, messages are sent to a central position where information is relayed to other members. Results show that the centralized form is more productive for routine decision making and the decentralized forms take longer to reach decisions, but the quality of the decisions is better, especially for performing complex tasks. Many variations on this experiment have appeared, and the work itself is regularly cited in discussions of group dynamics.

Alex Bavelas (b. 1913), born in Chicopee, Massachusetts, was educated at Springfield College, the University of Iowa, and MIT (Ph.D., Psychology, 1948). He was appointed a professor of psychology at MIT in 1945 serving until 1956, after which he taught at Stanford University (1958–70) and the University of Victoria in Canada.

Sources

Bavelas, Alex. 1950. Communication patterns in task-oriented groups. *Journal of the Acoustical Society of America* 22:725–730.

Jaques Cattell Press, ed. 1978. *American men and women of science: the social and behavioral sciences.* New York: Jaques Cattell and R. R. Bowker.

Sills, David L., ed. 1968. *International encyclopedia of the social sciences.* New York: Macmillan and Free Press.

BAYESIAN INFERENCE, BAYESIAN METHODS. Statistical analysis in which prior information is combined with sample data to estimate outcomes or test hypotheses. It is a technique of inductive reasoning used in economics. A useful formula in the social sciences is:

$$P(P/D) = P(D/P)*P(P)/P(D)$$

where $P(P/D)$ is the posterior probability of the event P given the occurrence of the event D; $P(D/P)$ is the likelihood of the event D occurring when the event P is seen; $P(P)$ is the prior probability of the event P knowing nothing about the event D; and $P(D)$ is the overall likelihood of event D in some basic population. The method has been applied to real-world problems in the last thirty years—for example, expert witness testimony, item-response theory, and test validation. It is based on the quantification of a prior probability for a phenomenon under study, such as the consensus of experts on the outcome of a research study. But Bayesian statistics have been criticized because they involve the quantification of subjective judgments by researchers and do not appear to rely on tests of statistical significance, known sampling distributions, and tests of the null hypothesis.

Reverend Thomas Bayes (1702–61) was born in England, educated privately, and helped his father, a dissenting theologian, at Holborn. Thomas may have learned his mathematics from Abraham de Moive (1667–1754), a founder of probability theory. After ordination, Bayes became the Presbyterian minister at Tunbridge Wells and published a religious work, *Divine Benevolence* (1731), as well as *Introduction to the Doctrine of Fluxions* (1736), which defended mathematicians and the usefulness of mathematics. In 1742 he was elected a fellow of the Royal Society for his work on fluxions and his defense of mathematicians. Bayesian methods originated from the solution of the "inverse" or "converse" probability problem, which was published in his posthumous *An Essay Towards Solving a Problem in the Doctrine of Chances* (1763).

Sources

Berger, J. O. 1984. The robust Bayesian viewpoint. In J. B. Kadane, ed. *Robustness of Bayesian analysis.* Amsterdam: Elsevier, pp. 63–124.

Eatwell, John; Milgate, Murray; and Newman, Peter. 1987. *The new Palgrave: a dictionary of economics.* London: Macmillan.

Gillespie, Charles C., ed. 1973. *Dictionary of scientific biography.* New York: Charles Scribner's Sons.

Griffiths, William E. 1987. *Models, estimators, tests and the Reverend Thomas Bayes.* Sydney: University of New South Wales.

McHenry, Robert, ed. 1992. *The new encyclopedia Britannica.* Chicago: Encyclopedia Britannica, Inc.

Pollard, W. E. 1986. *Bayesian statistics for evaluation research: an introduction.* Beverly Hills, Calif.: Sage Publications.

Sills, David L., ed. 1968. *International encyclopedia of the social sciences.* New York: Macmillan and Free Press.

Svyantek, Daniel; O'Connell, Matthew; and Baumgardner, Terri L. 1992. Applications of Bayesian methods to OD evaluation and decision-making. *Human Relations* 45:621–636.

BEDAUX SYSTEM. A popular wage incentive system from the 1920s that was intended to raise the incentive to work by giving each worker a bonus on time saved in excess of the set time for a given task; the bonus would be reduced if it went above a certain level. "B" was used by "Bedaux Engineers" to specify the unit of measurement for the system. A "B" was equal to a minute, and there were 60 Bs in a standard task which was to be done in one hour. So the system appeared to allow a comparison of unit costs for different operations since the work was reduced to a common denominator, the B standard.

Charles Eugene Bedaux (1887–1944) was born in Charenton-le-pont, France and immigrated to America in 1906 where he became interested in efficiency of work. He became familiar with the scientific principles of Frederick W. Taylor (1856–1915) and his followers, and believed that they had established schedules for labor without taking adequate account of fatigue and rest in their calculations. Bedaux devised an efficiency system while working in St. Louis, but found that it provoked so much controversy that no firm would adopt it. In 1911, after a short visit to France, Bedaux returned to America to work, occasionally making trips to Europe. In 1914, he was in Brussels when World War I erupted and volunteered immediately for training as a sniper in the French Foreign legion. On active duty he was supervising the movement of weapons and supplies when a crate fell on his foot, crushing it: he was compulsorily retired from service. While recovering, the solution to efficiency problems came to him, and he saw that he could incorporate the rest and fatigue factors into the system that was later to become the Bedaux system. In the 1930s, he worked chiefly in the United States, Britain, and France, and he developed close relations with people of high office in Nazi Germany. He moved in the same circles as English royalty and offered his home as the place for the wedding of the Duke of Windsor and Mrs. Simpson. When France was occupied by Germany in 1940, Bedaux served as an intermediary between the Nazis in Berlin and the Vichy French. Upon the liberation of France, he was arrested on suspicion of treason and committed suicide in 1944.

Sources

Christy, Jim. 1984. *The price of power: a biography of Charles Eugene Bedaux.* Toronto: Doubleday.

Magnussen, Magnus; Goring, Rosemary; and Thorn, John O., eds. 1990. *Chambers biographical dictionary.* Edinburgh: Chambers Ltd.

Marsh, Arthur. 1979. *Concise encyclopedia of industrial relations.* Westmead, Farnborough, Hants: Gower.

Roberts, Harold R. 1966. *Robert's dictionary of industrial relations.* Washington, D.C.:
    BNA.

BEHRENS-FISHER PROBLEM, BEHRENS-FISHER DISTRIBUTION. A
technical problem for data analysis in social sciences that centers on the appro-
priateness of testing the equality of means of two distributions when it is clear
their variances are quite different or unknown; a sampling distribution for sample numbers under 30. Confusion and controversy arose regarding the test of
the significance of the difference between observed means which was first given
by Behrens (1929). According to Fisher (1941), not only a simple hypothetical
variance but also the ratio of two such variances was required to be estimated
by means of the fiducial distribution. Behrens's original solution produced analytic problems which Fisher solved by using the asymptotic approach, published in 1926. When the results are inverted, Behrens's distribution corresponds
to normal (Fisher, 1941).

W.-V. Behrens (fl. 1920s) was a German statistician at the University of
Königsberg who, in his last published paper, attempted to solve the problem in
1929. A solution was developed by the British statistician Ronald A. Fisher in
1941.

Ronald Alymer Fisher (1890–1962) was born in London and studied mathematics and physics at Cambridge (D.Sc., 1926). He worked at Rothamsted
Experimental Agricultural Station (1919–1933), where he made his contributions
to experimental design, statistics, and genetics. He became professor of genetics
at University College, London (1938–43) and at Cambridge (1943–57), and
retired to the University of Adelaide. The Royal Society awarded him its Royal
Medal in 1938, its Darwin Medal in 1948, and its highest honor, the Copely
Medal, in 1956. He was knighted in 1952.

Sources

Behrens, W.-V. 1964. The comparisons of means of independent normal distributions
    with different variances. *Biometrics,* 20:16–27.
Box, Joan Fisher. 1978. *R. A. Fisher: the life of a scientist.* New York: John Wiley.
Fisher, Ronald A. 1935. The fiducial argument in statistical inference. *Annals of Eugen-
    ics,* 6:341–348. Reprinted in J. H. Bennett, ed. 1972. *Collected papers of R.A.
    Fisher.* Vol III: 1932–36:317–324. Adelaide: The University of South Australia.
Fisher, Ronald A. 1941. The asymptotic approach to Behrens's integral with further tables
    for the d test of significance. *Annals of Eugenics,* 11:141–172. Reprinted in J. H.
    Bennett ed. 1974. *Collected papers of R.A. Fisher.* Vol IV: 1937–47:323–354.
    Adelaide: The Univeristy of South Australia.
Sills, David L., ed. 1968. *International encyclopedia of the social sciences.* New York:
    Macmillan and Free Press.
Williams, E. T., and Nichols, C. S., eds. 1981. *Dictionary of national biography 1961–
    1970.* Oxford: Oxford University Press.
Zusne, Leonard. 1987. *Eponyms in psychology: a dictionary and sourcebook.* Westport,
    Conn.: Greenwood Press.
Zusne, Leonard. 1984. *Biographical dictionary of psychology.* Westport, Conn.: Green-
    wood Press.

BENEDICT ARNOLD. A traitor.

Benedict Arnold (1741–1801) was born into a distinguished Rhode Island family. He ran away from home to fight in the French and Indian War before completing his apprenticeship as a druggist. In 1762, on the death of his parents, he moved to New Haven and established himself as a druggist and bookseller. He became captain in the Connecticut militia (1775) and rose to colonel. With the planned invasion of Canada, Arnold made an historic march through the Maine wilderness under George Washington's command. The reputation of this hero of the military was destroyed when, as a general, he was found to have plotted to deliver the garrison at West Point to Britain's Major John André for £20,000 in 1780. The plot failed, and Arnold fled to England with his family in 1781; his name became synonymous with that of a traitor in the United States. In England, too, he found his reputation under attack, attempted commercial ventures, and failed. Altogether he recovered only £6,000 for his treason. Later he sought more; although he was given 13,400 acres in Canada, it afforded him little. He tried and failed to enter British military service in the Napoleonic Wars and died in London.

Sources

Dudley, Lavinia P. 1963. *The encyclopedia Americana.* International ed. New York: Americana Corp.

Flexner, James T. 1953. *The traitor and the spy: Benedict Arnold and John André.* 1975 ed. Boston: Little, Brown.

Johnson, Allen, ed. 1927. *Dictionary of American biography.* Vol. I. New York: Charles Scribner's Sons.

Morpurgo, J. E. 1975. *Treason at West Point: the Arnold-André conspiracy.* New York: Mason-Charter.

Randall, Willard S. 1991. *Benedict Arnold: patriot and traitor.* London: The Bodley Head.

Stephen, Leslie, and Lee, Sydney, eds. 1917. *The dictionary of national biography.* London: Oxford University Press.

BENEDICT'S PATTERNS OF CULTURE. A theory used by American anthropologists to describe and explain cultural differences between tribes.

Ruth Fulton Benedict (1887–1948) established the configural approach to anthropology. She studied English at Vassar College (1905–9); with a humanities background she studied under Alex Goldenweiser and Elsie C. Parsons at the New School for Social Research (1919–21), then under Franz Boas at Columbia University, and did a Ph.D. on North American Indian religion (1923). In 1929 she published *The Science of Custom* which showed how to use human understanding in the study of culture. In 1928 she reported a major insight that brought some order to the contrast she had observed between Pueblo and Pima cultures. The organizing principle was that the cultures draw differently on the inherent potentialities of humankind, emphasizing some in later generations and ignoring others. Consequently, the heritors of each culture elaborated one personality style at the expense of another. She developed the insight by using Nietzsche's classical distinction in his work on Greek tragedy. She named the Pueblo culture Apollonian and the North American Indians a Dionysian in her *Patterns of Culture* (1934). Thereafter, Benedict's emphasis on the open system approach to human culture had a strong influence on cultural anthropology.

Sources

Benedict, Ruth. 1934. *Patterns of culture.* 1959 edition with a new preface by Margaret Mead. Boston: Houghton Mifflin.

Devine, Elizabeth; Held, Michael; Vinson, James; and Walsh, George, eds. 1983. *Thinkers of the twentieth century: a biographical, bibliographical and critical dictionary.* London: Macmillan.

Mead, Margaret. 1959. *An anthropologist at work: writings of Ruth Benedict.* Boston: Houghton Mifflin.

Modell, Judith Schacter. 1983. *Ruth Benedict: pattern of life.* Philadelphia: University of Pennsylvania Press.

Sills, David L., ed. 1968. *International encyclopedia of the social sciences.* New York: Macmillan and Free Press.

Zusne, Leonard. 1984. *Biographical dictionary of psychology.* Westport, Conn.: Greenwood Press.

BENEDICTINE. Pertaining to the sixth-century Italian monk or his order; a nun following the rules of the order.

Saint Benedict (c. 480–c. 550) was a hermit. From the information given to Pope Gregory I by four disciples of Saint Benedict, he was known as the Patriarch of Western Monasticism and was a compiler of a monastic rule, chiefly at Monte Cassino in Italy. He destroyed the remains of paganism in Cassino and brought its population to Christianity. He does not seem to have been ordained or to have contemplated founding the order that was established in Italy in about 530. He was buried at Monte Cassino in the same grave as his sister, Saint Scholastica. The rule of Saint Benedict was gradually adopted by most Western monastic houses, though sometimes with their own modifications.

Sources

Cross, Frank L. 1974. *The Oxford dictionary of the Christian Church.* 2d ed. New York: Oxford University Press.

Douglas, James D. 1974. *The new international dictionary of the Christian Church.* Exeter: Paternoster Press.

McCann, Justin. 1937. *Saint Benedict.* 1979 ed. London: Sheed and Ward.

McHenry, Robert, ed. 1992. *The new encyclopedia Britannica.* Chicago: Encyclopedia Britannica, Inc.

Martin, John S., ed. 1981. *A man with an idea: St. Benedict of Nursia.* Melbourne: University of Melbourne Publications.

Richards, Jeffrey. 1980. *Consul of God: the life and times of Gregory the Great.* Boston: Routledge and Kegan Paul.

BENJAMIN. An old term used by Australian aborigines to refer to a favored man, especially a husband.

Benjamin is the youngest son of the patriarch, Jacob (Genesis 42–46). Be-

cause of the local famine, Jacob sent his older sons to Egypt for corn. While there, they were suspected of being spies; to prove they were not, they had to go home and return with their little brother, Benjamin. Jacob was reluctant to allow this but finally relented. Benjamin was recognized as a brother—by Joseph, the elder son of Jacob, whom his brother had envied and tried to murder—and at Joseph's table Benjamin was favored five times as much as the others.
Sources
Metford, J.C.J. 1983. *Dictionary of Christian lore and legend.* London: Thames and Hudson.
Ramson, William S., ed. 1988. *The Australian national dictionary.* Melbourne: Oxford University Press.

BENNINGTON STUDY. A renowned longitudinal study in American scientific social psychology conducted at Bennington College for Women. The study was done in the fourth year of the college's establishment and was conducted by Theodore M. Newcomb (1903–84), a faculty member of the college during 1934–41. The problem was to see how conservatively reared women students would react to an innovative education taught by progressive, liberal, and even left-wing faculty. Begun in 1935–39 and followed up in 1959–60 and 1984, the study showed that political orientations can be readily molded in late adolescence and in early adulthood, but once established, political attitudes may remain firm throughout the person's life. A self-contained community, at the time the college was on a hilltop four miles south of Bennington, Vermont. Bennington was given its name by Governor Benning Wentworth in connection with a New Hampshire grant (1749).
Sources
Alwin, Duane F.; Cohen, Ronald L.; and Newcombe, Theodore M. 1991. *Political attitudes over the life span: the Bennington women after fifty years.* Madison: University of Wisconsin Press.
Newcombe, Theodore M. 1943. *Personality and social change: attitude formation in a student community.* New York: Holt, Rinehart and Winston.
Newcombe, Theodore M. 1946. The influence of attitude climate upon some determinants of information. *Journal of Abnormal Social Psychology* 51:291–302.
Newcombe, Theodore M.; Koenig, Kathryn E.; Flacks, Richard; and Warwick, Donald P. 1967. *Persistence and change: Bennington College and its students after twenty-five years.* New York: John Wiley.
Stewart, George R. 1970. *American place-names: a concise and selective dictionary for the continental United States of America.* New York: Oxford University Press.

BENNIS'S PRINCIPLE. Routine work drives out nonroutine work.
Warren Bennis (b. 1925), born in New York, was the youngest infantry officer serving the Allied forces in World War II in Europe. He became a captain and received the Bronze Star and Purple Heart. He studied at Antioch, the London School of Economics (1952), and the Massachusetts Institute of Technology (Ph.D., 1955). After teaching at MIT's Sloan School of Management, he taught

at Harvard and Boston universities, and became provost and executive vice-president, State University of New York, Buffalo (1967–71); he was president of the University of Cincinnati (1971–77). He has written eighteen books and published over 750 articles, mainly on the application of humanistic psychology to various problems, especially leadership, in organizations. He has taught in many countries, consulted with major firms throughout the world, and served many university research centers as well as advised several government agencies. He has eight honorary degrees and is noted for outstanding contributions to education in colleges and industry. Bennis's principle first appeared in his *Why Leaders Can't Lead: The Unconscious Conspiracy Continues* (1976), reprinted in 1989. At present, Bennis is a university and distinguished professor of business administration, University of Southern California.

Sources

Bennis, Warren. 1991. Autobiography—part I: an invented life: shoe polish, Milli Vanilli, and sapiential circles. *Journal of Applied Behavioral Science* 27:413–424.

Bennis, Warren. 1992. Autobiography—part II: Bethal, Boston and sapiential circles, 1955–67. *Journal of Applied Behavioral Science* 28:318–330.

Evory, Ann, ed. 1982. *Contemporary authors.* Vol. 6. New Revision Series. Detroit: Gale Research.

Who's who in America, 1988–89. Wilmette, Ill.: Marquis Who's Who. Macmillan.

Personal Communication.

BENNITE. British Labor left-wing supporter who follows Tony Benn's lead. Benn advocates public investment in and ownership of industry and the democratization of authority at work. He wants Britain to quit Ireland, and he once recommanded that Britain leave the European Community and North Atlantic Treaty Organization. In 1992 Benn argued for constitutional reform that would end the role of the Crown and the House of Lords, and abolish patronage. He supported the devolution of power from London to Northern Ireland, equal representation for women in Parliament, the disestablishment of the church, and the vote for people aged 16. He also sought to establish confirmation procedures for judges before their appointment. In 1993, Benn failed to win re-election to Britian's Labour Party National Executive after thirty-four years of membership.

Anthony Neil Wedgewood Benn (b. 1925), second Viscount Stansgate of Stansgate, joined the British Labor party in 1943, studied at New College Oxford, and entered Parliament in 1950. In July 1963 he renounced his viscountancy and took the name, Tony Benn. He was postmaster general in Harold Wilson's government (1964), minister of technology (1966–70), secretary of state for industry, and minister for posts and telecommunications (1974–75), and minister of state for energy (1975–79). In 1975–1979, when he was on the Labor Party Executive Committee, he supported party democracy and more socialism in the party's policy. After losing his seat in 1983, he won a by-election in 1984. In the party he has always led the left wing, and his ideas appear in *Arguments for Socialism* (1979).

Sources
Adams, Jab. 1992. *Tony Benn.* London: Macmillan.
Benn, Tony. 1992. Britain as a republic? *Guardian Weekly,* June 14:12.
The international who's who, 1992–93. London: Europa Publications.
McHenry, Robert, ed. 1992. *The new encyclopedia Britannica.* Chicago: Encyclopedia
    Britannica, Inc.

BENTHAMISM. Utilitarian philosophy based largely on the principle of the greatest happiness for the greatest number.

Jeremy Bentham (1748–1832) was educated at Oxford and trained as a barrister but gave up practice for the study and reform of political and legal institutions. He worked with James Mill on political and moral philosophy, jurisprudence, and prison reform. He made plans for a model prison which were taken seriously but never put into practice. As the first major proponent of utilitarianism, he assumed that pain and pleasure were the primary human motives, and that political interests were founded on them. Since human beings are selfish, he asserted, an adequate political system would be one where pleasure dominated its outcome. To him natural science showed this outcome could be measured. He advocated the organization of society to secure "the greatest happiness for the greatest number." He had a decisive influence on nineteenth-century British political thought, especially through his *Introduction to the Principles of Morals and Legislation* (1789). He argued that psychological hedonism may be integrated with ethical hedonism by applying both sanctions and reason. Consequently, a nation's citizens would be both rewarded and punished by the law's application of penalties or sanctions in a reasoned manner. His reputation was made secure in Europe when he was given French citizenship in 1792. Since World War II, Bentham's reputation has grown with the publication of previously unknown writings, and more recent scholars have suggested that his work is far more valuable than earlier writers and critics had thought.

Sources
Atkinson, Charles M. 1909. *Jeremy Bentham: his life and work.* Reprinted 1969. New
    York: A. M. Kelley.
Dinwiddy, John R. 1989. *Bentham.* Oxford: Oxford University Press.
Harrison, Ross. 1983. *Bentham.* London: Routledge and Keegan Paul.
Hart, Herbert L. A. 1982. *Essays on Bentham: studies in jurisprudence and political
    theory.* Oxford: Oxford University Press.
McHenry, Robert, ed. 1992. *The new encyclopedia Britannica.* Chicago: Encyclopedia
    Britannica, Inc.
Mack, Mary P. 1962. *Jeremy Bentham: an odyssey of ideas.* New York: Columbia University Press.
Manning, David J. 1968. *The mind of Jeremy Bentham.* London: Longmans.
Steintrager, James. 1977. *Bentham.* London: Allen and Unwin.
Stephen, Leslie, and Lee, Sydney, eds. 1917. *The dictionary of national biography.* London: Oxford University Press.
Zusne, Leonard. 1984. *Biographical dictionary of psychology.* Westport, Conn.: Greenwood Press.

BERGOFF TECHNIQUE. Methods of strikebreaking perfected by the "King of Strikebreakers" in the United States: the methods included espionage, murder, intimidation, and beating of strikers; importing train- or boatloads of workers to the strike site to beat up strikers and then do their work; impersonation of government agents; and creation of "back-to-work" movements supported by apparently "loyal" workers in a local community to undermine strikers' solidarity.

Pearl Louis Bergoff (1876–1947) was born in Michigan, son of a wandering Jewish fish-trader and land speculator. The boy was raised in Allendale and Centerville, Dakota Territory, and also in Canada, and at age 13 was abandoned with $50 by his father. Pearl worked on various railroads and became a company spy for railroad management. He established his own Vigilant Detective Agency in New York in 1906 and worked as a bodyguard. In 1907 he was hired to break a strike of New York City streetcleaners, then one on the waterfront, and a telegraphers' strike, and in 1909 he helped break the streetcar drivers' strike in Philadelphia. He worked on the hotel employees strike in New York in 1912, and at the peak of his success he had thousands of men on his books, who came to be known as "Bergoff's army." He achieved his greatest recognition during 1920–22. Although Bergoff was known to use violence and illegal practices, businessmen with industrial relations problems still sought him out. In 1923 when business declined he went to Florida and lost most of his money in land deals. On returning to New York he tried to build houses, but failed, and got little strikebreaking work until 1932. During this period he also established the Bergoff Detective Service. He became the most notable professional American strikebreaker during the mid-1930s. In 1934 in Akron, Ohio, he proposed building back-to-work movements; to organize, direct, and control these apparently "local" movements, he supplied labor spies and strikebreakers. In 1935 he sold the idea to Remington-Rand, and in the strike at that company the technique became a distinct method in strikebreaking. The National Association of Manufacturers listed its several parts and popularized it as the "Mohawk Valley Formula."

Sources

Levinson, Edward. 1935. *I break strikes! The techniques of Pearl L. Bergoff.* New York: McBride.
Obituary, *New York Times,* August 13, 1947:5.
Roberts, Harold S. 1966. *Roberts' dictionary of industrial relations.* Washington, D.C.: BNA.
Time, 50, August 25, 1947:60.

BERGSONISM. A philosophy of creative evolution.

Henri Louis Bergson (1859–1941) was born in Paris, son of a Jewish musician and a British mother. He was educated at the Ecole Normale Supérieure and the University of Paris, and became professor at the College de France (1900–24). In the 1920s he resigned from the college to attend to international affairs, politics, moral problems, and religion. In this period he was converted to Roman Catholicism. In 1927 he won a Nobel Prize for Literature. Bergson advanced a theory of evolution, based on the spiritual dimension of human life, arguing that the creative urge, not natural selection, was the prime force in evolution. His approach to problems was more poetic than philosophical, and he would use analogy in place of the conventions of rigorous reasoning.

Sources

Grogin, R. C. 1988. *The Bergson controversy in France, 1900–1914.* Calgary: University of Calgary Press.

McHenry, Robert, ed. 1992. *The new encyclopedia Britannica.* Chicago: Encyclopedia Britannica, Inc.

Magnussen, Magnus; Goring, Rosemary; and Thorn, John O., eds. 1990. *Chambers biographical dictionary.* Edinburgh: Chambers Ltd.

Zusne, Leonard. 1984. *Biographical dictionary of psychology.* Westport, Conn.: Greenwood Press.

BERKELEIAN. Relating to the sixteenth-century philosopher who denied the objective existence of the material world and asserted that it exists only through the senses.

George Berkeley (1685–1753) was born at Dysert Castle, Kilkenny, and educated at Kilkenny and Trinity colleges, Dublin. He became a fellow and tutor at Trinity until 1713. He published *A Treatise Concerning the Principles of Human Knowledge* (1710), an expansion of his *Essay Towards a New Theory of Vision* (1709). When it failed to convince people of his theory—with its notable claim "to be is to be perceived"—he published a more popular version, *The Three Dialogues Between Hylas and Philonous* (1713). His contemporaries thought his ideas were foolish. Berkeley's philosophical system originated in criticism of John Locke's ideas (1632–1704). Berkeley denied the existence of matter, asserting that only minds and mental events exist, and he gave ingenious arguments that maintained material objects exist only by being perceived. After travels in England, France, and Italy, he returned to Ireland in 1721 and, becoming concerned with corruption and decadence, he published, anonymously, *Essay Towards Preventing the Ruin of Great Britain.* He was made dean of Derry in 1724. In 1728 he went to Rhode Island, and for three years he waited for funds to establish a college in Bermuda to promote the gospel among the "American savages." Although the mission failed, he had considerable influence on higher education in America. He returned to England where he was appointed bishop of Cloyne in Cork. Jonathan Swift (1667–1745) presented him at court, and he became an associate of Joseph Addison (1672–1719) and Alexander Pope (1688–1774). He retired to Oxford in 1752.

Sources

Boylan, Henry. 1978. *A dictionary of Irish biography.* New York: Harper and Row.

McHenry, Robert, ed. 1992. *The new encyclopedia Britannica.* Chicago: Encyclopedia Britannica, Inc.

Warnock, Geoffrey J. 1982. *Berkeley.* Oxford: Basil Blackwell.

Zusne, Leonard. 1984. *Biographical dictionary of psychology.* Westport, Conn.: Green-
        wood Press.

BERKELEY SCHOOL OF GEOGRAPHY. A school of geographers led by
Carl Ortwin Sauer (1889–1975).

Sauer was born at Warrenton, Missouri, and educated at Northwestern and
the University of Chicago. He was a professor of geography at the University
of California at Berkeley from 1923 to 1954. With John B. Leighly (1895–
1986), Sauer had a major impact on the growth of American studies in geography. The school was comprised mainly of Sauer's own Ph.D. students, for
example, Marvin Mikesell, Dan Stanislawski, and Frederick Simoons. The
school had a definite cultural focus but presented no unswerving view on methods or subject. The Berkeley school was noted for its resistance to fashions and
its disinterest in the economic geography of advanced industrial society; a sense
of identity based on Carl Sauer's personality; and a shared interest in humankind's role in creating the cultural landscape.

Berkeley, formerly Oceanview, is a city on the eastern side of San Francisco
Bay, and since 1873 it has been the site of the main campus of the University
of California. Originally, the site was a grant from the Spanish Crown to the
Peralta family (1820), and it was named Rancho San Antonio. In 1853 a group
of American citizens purchased the property, calling it Oceanview; the trustees
changed it to Berkeley (1866) after considering the poem by George Berkeley
(1685–1753), Irish bishop and philosopher, ''On the Foundation of an Institution
of Learning in America.''

See also BERKELEIAN.

Sources
Dudley, Lavinia P. 1963. *The encyclopedia Americana.* International ed. New York:
        Americana Corp.
Johnston, Ronald J. 1981. *The dictionary of human geography.* Oxford: Basil Blackwell.
Leighly, John B., and Parsons, James J. 1979. Berkeley: drifting into geography in the
        late 20s and the later Sauer years. *Annals of the Association of American Geog-
        raphers* 69:4–15.
Magnussen, Magnus; Goring, Rosemary; and Thorn, John O., eds. 1990. *Chambers bi-
        ographical dictionary.* Edinburgh: Chambers Ltd.
Stanislawski, Dan. 1975. Carl Ortwin Sauer: 1889–1975. *Journal of Geography* 47:548–
        554.

BERNARDINE. A Cistercian.

Saint Bernard of Clairvaux (1090–1153) was born into a noble family at
Fontaines, near Dijon, Burgundy, entered the Cistercian monastery of Citeaux
in 1113, and became the first abbot of the newly founded monastery of Clairvaux
in Champagne in 1115. A studious, ascetic life combined with stirring eloquence
made Bernard's reputation as an oracle in the Christian church. He wrote more
than 400 epistles, 340 sermons, a biography of Saint Malachy, and twelve theological treatises. He founded over seventy monasteries, and the Catholic Church

considers him as the last of its Fathers. He was canonized in 1174 and nominated a doctor of the church (1830). In 1953 Pope Pius XII extolled him as *mellifluus doctor,* a scholarly title that required both sanctity and eminent learning from its recipient (McDonald, 1967). His feast day is August 20.

Sources

Cross, Frank L. 1974. *The Oxford dictionary of the Christian Church.* 2d ed. New York: Oxford University Press.

Douglas, James D., ed. 1974. *The new international dictionary of the Christian Church.* Exeter: Paternoster Press.

Farmer, David H. 1978. *The Oxford dictionary of saints.* Oxford: Clarendon Press.

McDonald, William, ed. 1967. *New catholic encyclopedia.* New York: McGraw-Hill.

McHenry, Robert, ed. 1992. *The new encyclopedia Britannica.* Chicago: Encyclopedia Britannica, Inc.

Merton, Thomas. 1954. *The last of the fathers: Saint Bernard of Clairvaux and the encyclical letter, Doctor Mellifluus.* New York: Harcourt Brace.

BERNOULLI HYPOTHESIS. The marginal utility of money income is inversely proportional to the level of income. The hypothesis explains the "Saint Petersburg paradox," so named because the original paper on the problem in 1738—Specimen Theoriae Novae de Mensura Sortis—appeared in the *Papers of the Imperial Academy of Sciences in Petersburg.* The problem is: Why don't gamblers put large sums on a game when the expected value of winning approaches infinity? Answer: They are less interested in the money than the value of its utility. This contributes to theories of maximizing utility under moral conditions rather than simply a monetary goal.

Daniel Bernoulli (1700–1782) was born in Gröningen, a member of a family that reared eight mathematicians over three generations. After studies in medicine (1717) at the University of Basel, Bernoulli completed a doctorate on the lung's actions in 1721. Thereafter he became interested in mathematics and became a professor of mathematics at St. Petersburg (1725). On returning to Basel in 1732, he was appointed a professor of anatomy, botany, and physics. His work covered trigonometrics, mechanics, vibrating systems, and hydrodynamics. He solved the differential equations stated by Jacopo Riccati, now called Bernoulli's Equation. His masterpiece was *Hydrodynamica* (1738) which includes the Bernoulli equation, the earliest account of a kinetic theory of gases. The hypothesis relates to a game that Daniel's cousin Nicholas suggested: Toss a coin n times until it comes up heads, and pay out 2^n in ducats. The mathematical expectation of gain has no limit; common experience, however, indicates the fair price to pay out should have a limit. Bernoulli argued that the paradox could be resolved by replacing moral for mathematical expectations, and multiplying probabilities by personal and not by monetary values. He thought incremental utility to be inversely proportional to the gambler's fortune at the time. A similar approach had been suggested by the mathematician Gabriel Cramer (1704–52) to Nicholas in 1728: If the utility were limited, then the moral expectations would be finite. An English translation of the paper was published by Louise Sommer in *Econometrica* in 1954.

Sources

Abbott, David. 1985. *The biographical dictionary of scientists: mathematicians.* London: Blond Educational.

Bernoulli, Daniel. 1738. Exposition of a new theory on the measurement of risk. Translated from the Latin by Louise Sommer. *Econometrica,* 22, 1954:23–36.

Eatwell, John; Milgate, Murray; and Newman, Peter. 1987. *The new Palgrave: a dictionary of economics.* London: Macmillan.

Gillespie, Charles C., ed. 1973. *Dictionary of scientific biography.* New York: Charles Scribner's Sons.

Magnussen, Magnus; Goring, Rosemary; and Thorn, John O., eds. 1990. *Chambers biographical dictionary* Edinburgh: Chambers Ltd.

Pearce, David W., ed. 1986. *Macmillan dictionary of modern economics.* New York: Macmillan.

BERNREUTER PERSONALITY OR PERSONAL ADJUSTMENT INVENTORY. A questionnaire that measures six human traits: neurotic tendency; self-sufficiency; introversion-extroversion; dominance-submission; confidence; and sociability.

Robert Gibbon Bernreuter (b. 1901) was born in Tampico, Illinois, and completed a Ph.D. in general psychology (1931) at Stanford University. He was a teacher and became director of the Pennsylvania State College Psychological Clinic (1931–56), during which time he published his personality inventory. He retired in 1966, and became emeritus and vice-president of student affairs and the university.

Sources

Bernreuter, Robert G. 1931. *The personality inventory.* Stanford, Calif.: Stanford University Press.

Bernreuter, Robert G. 1935. *Manual for the personality inventory.* Stanford, Calif.: Stanford University Press.

Jaques Cattell Press, ed. 1973. *American men and women of science: the social and behavioral sciences.* New York: Jaques Cattell and R. R. Bowker.

Zusne, Leonard. 1987. *Eponyms in psychology: a dictionary and sourcebook.* Westport, Conn.: Greenwood Press.

BERRY BLIGHT, BERRYISM, BERRYITE. The deep economic depression in the colony of Victoria that followed "Black Wednesday" (January 8, 1878). Liberalism in the colony and protectionist policy. A conservative follower of the colonial treasurer.

Sir Graham Berry (1822–1904) was born near London, apprenticed to a Chelsea draper, and in 1852 sailed to Victoria where he established a prosperous wine and spirits store. In Melbourne he became a political radical, and by 1871 he was the colony's leading protectionist, entered the Legislative Assembly, and became treasurer. He resigned amid charges of nepotism, but later polarized politics in the colony; he won the 1877 election and became treasurer again and chief secretary. After the Legislative Council had rejected an essential bill, Berry dismissed large numbers of public servants on January 8, 1878, in revenge, but rationalized the decision to conserve public funds. After he left the colony, it went into deep economic depression—''Berry Blight''—as evidenced in high unemployment and a movement of capital from Victoria to New South Wales. In 1880 Berry's ministry was defeated.

Source

Pike, Douglas, et al., eds. 1960–90. *Australian dictionary of biography.* Vol. 3. Melbourne: Melbourne University Press.

BERTILLONAGE, BERTILLON SYSTEM. A measurement system for identifying criminals.

Alphonse Bertillon (1853–1914) was born in Paris and studied anthrometry, the comparative study of dimensions of the body. He was head of the Department of Identification in the Préfecture of Police of the Seine (1879). Devised in 1882, the system includes precise measurement of the body, data on movements of the body, estimates of moral attributes and mental abilities, and unusual physical features, such as scars and tattoos. Even though the system was dropped with the advent of fingerprinting, many features of it are still used internationally, for example, body measurements, physical descriptions of the body, and unique behavioral features to help investigators find their suspects. Bertillon published *L'Anthropométrie judicaire* (1890) and *Identification Anthropométrique* (1893).

Sources

Law, M. D., and Dixon, M. Vibart, eds. 1966. *Chambers encyclopedia.* London: Pergamon Press.

McHenry, Robert, ed. 1992. *The new encyclopedia Britannica.* Chicago: Encyclopedia Britannica, Inc.

Prevost, M., and Roman-D'Amat, J. 1954. *Dictionnaire de biographie Française.* Paris: Librairie Letouzey et Ané.

Rhodes, Henry T.F. 1956. *Alphonse Bertillon, father of scientific detection.* London: Harrop.

BERTRAND'S DUOPOLY MODEL. A model of duopolistic competition in which each producer assumes the other will not change his or her price—already fixed—and that if one of them then lowers his or her own price, that person can marginally capture the whole market. A weakness in the model is that it assumes producers set prices and not quantities.

Joseph Louis Francois Bertrand (1822–1900) was born in Paris and was raised largely by his uncle, a noted professor of mathematics at the École Polytechnique. At age 11 Bertrand took his B.A. and B.Sc., and at 17 he was awarded a D.Sc. He officially entered the École Polytechnique in 1839 and the Ecole des Mines in 1842. He was a professor of elementary mathematics at the College Saint-Louis from 1841 to 1848. During the 1848 Revolution he served as a captain in the National Guard. Before being appointed a professor of special mathematics at the Lycee Henry IV (1852), he published many works on mathematics. He became a professor of mathematical analysis at the École Polytechnique (1856–1895) and then at the College de France until his death. In the Franco-Prussian War, after the surrender of Paris to German forces (1871), the republican government of France was threatened by an insurrection in Paris. Houses were set alight as radicals established the Paris Commune; many of Bertrand's manuscripts were lost during the public disturbances when his house was burned, but he rewrote two on thermodynamics and calculus. His ideas on the theory of errors and his studies on curves, surfaces, and probability were widely read.

Sources

Eatwell, John; Milgate, Murray; and Newman, Peter. 1987. *The new Palgrave: a dictionary of economics.* London: Macmillan.

Gillespie, Charles C., ed. 1973. *Dictionary of scientific biography.* New York: Charles Scribner's Sons.

Pearce, David W., ed. 1986. *Macmillan dictionary of modern economics.* New York: Macmillan.

BEVANITE. Supporters of the British minister for health in protest of the Labor cabinet's decision in April 1951 to impose National Health prescription charges to meet the costs of defense.

Aneurin Bevan (1897–1960) was born at Tredegas, Monmouthshire, son of a miner, and early in his life worked in the mines but left due to an eye disease. He studied for two years at Central Labor College and entered politics in 1929 as a Labor member for Ebbw Vale. During World War II he was a strong critic of his own party and the Churchill government. He edited the *Tribune* (1940–45), an independent socialist paper. After the war, Bevan became minister for health in Clement Attlee government and established the National Health scheme. He became minister for labor in 1951 but resigned in May 1952 when he and his supporters opposed Labor party policy on defense, the rearmament of Germany, and the building of the hydrogen bomb. Bevan was defeated for party leadership by Hugh Gaitskill in 1955 and was made shadow foreign secretary in 1957.

See also BUTSKELLISM.

Sources

Bevan, Aneurin. 1952. *In place of fear.* 2d ed. 1978. London: Quartet.

Campbell, John. 1987. *Nye Bevan and the mirage of British socialism.* London: Weidenfeld and Nicolson.

Foot, Michael. 1963–1974. *Aneurin Bevan: a biography.* 2 vols. New York: Atheneum.

Krug, Mark M. 1961. *Aneurin Bevan: cautious rebel.* New York: T. Yoseloff.

McHenry, Robert, ed. 1992. *The new encyclopedia Britannica.* Chicago: Encyclopedia Britannica, Inc.

Townsend, Sue. 1989. *Mr. Bevan's dream.* London: Chatto and Windus.

Williams, E. T., and Palmer, Helen M., eds. 1971. *Dictionary of national biography 1951–1960.* London: Oxford University Press.

BEVERIDGE REPORT, BEVERIDGE SYSTEM. A report, *Social Insurance and Allied Services* (1942), that provided the basis for Britain's social security system after World War II. Arguing that old age, ill-health, and unemployment led to poverty, the report proposed establishing a system to pay benefits to such disadvantaged people with national insurance contributions. The system was broadly adopted, but unexpected income-related benefits became very important, when it produced the effect of a poverty tax as rising incomes led to a loss of system benefits among those who needed them.

William Henry Beveridge (1879–1963) was born in Rangpur, Bengal, son of a judge in the Indian Civil Service; he was educated at a boarding school in Worcester and at Charterhouse (1882), and studied at Balliol and University colleges, Oxford (1879–1902). A lawyer, he became a subwarden at Toynbee Hall in East London, and thereafter he was an active social and economic reformer among progressive liberals and Fabians, as well as associates of Sidney and Beatrice Webb. He wrote *Unemployment: A Problem of Industry* (1909) and established the London Unemployment fund (1904–5). He turned to journalism with the *Morning Post,* publishing over 1,000 articles on social and economic reforms. While serving the government during World War I, he came into conflict with trade unions over restrictions on their power to negotiate work conditions in the war industry, and he was later excluded from the Ministry of Labor and put in the Ministry for Food. In 1919 he was knighted. Thereafter he helped raise funds for expanding the London School of Economics and the social sciences in Britain generally. In time, his autocratic administrative style and his relations with the school's academic secretary limited his influence, and he took the mastership of University College at Oxford. In June 1941 he began his inquiry into poverty in Britain and reported his recommendations; to eradicate society's ignorance, idleness, disease, and squalor, he advanced a scheme of national health services, family allowances, a policy of full employment, and subsistence-level social insurance. In 1944 he published *Full Employment and Free Society* to show ways to promote full employment. He became an M.P. in 1945, was made a baron, and entered the House of Lords. He published his autobiography *Power and Influence* (1953), a family history *India Called Them* (1947), and *Voluntary Action* (1948). He was honored by universities in Britain, the United States, Canada, New Zealand, Australia, and Europe.

Sources

Beveridge, Janet P. 1954. *Beveridge and his plan.* London: Hodder and Stoughton.

Harris, José. 1977. *William Beveridge: a biography.* Oxford: Clarendon Press.

Hanson, J. L. 1974. *A dictionary of economics and commerce.* Suffolk: Richard Clay.

McHenry, Robert, ed. 1992. *The new encyclopedia Britannica.* Chicago: Encyclopedia Britannica, Inc.

Williams, E. T., and Nichols, C. S., eds. 1981. *Dictionary of national biography 1961–1970.* Oxford: Oxford University Press.

BEVIN BOYS. During World War II the young men who were conscripted at random to be coal miners in Britain.

Ernest Bevin (1881–1951) was born in Winsford, Somerset, and his impoverished parents died before he was 7. At age 13 he went to Bristol and worked as a van-boy and later a driver, educated himself, and became a Baptist lay preacher. In 1905 he worked without pay for the Bristol Right to Work Committee, and in 1910 he formed the carter's branch of the Docker's Union, eventually becoming a full-time official of the union. Bevin defended waterside workers in court during an inquiry into activities on the waterfront, and he became general secretary of the Transport and General Workers' Union (1921–40). In Churchill's wartime cabinet he was minister for labor and national service, when his name was attached to the manpower policy for the coal mines; after the 1945 election Bevin was made secretary of state for foreign affairs in Prime Minister Attlee's government. Believing that peace in the world depended on close relations between the United States and Russia, he avoided a policy of separate alliances and supported United Nations moves to contain conflict. But as the cold war developed, Bevin supported the North Atlantic Treaty Organization (1949) and the Brussels Pact (1948).

Sources

Bullock, Alan L.C. 1960–83. *The life and times of Ernest Bevin.* 3 vols. London: Heinemann.

Bullock, Alan L.C. 1985. *The humanist tradition in the West.* New York: W. W. Norton.

Evans, Trevor. 1946. *Bevin.* London: Allen and Unwin.

Law, M. D., and Dixon, M. Vibart, eds. 1966. *Chambers encyclopedia.* London: Pergamon Press.

McHenry, Robert, ed. 1992. *The new encyclopedia Britannica.* Chicago: Encyclopedia Britannica, Inc.

BIG BROTHER. A black moustached face of a nonperson with ultimate power in a totalitarian state described by George Orwell in his novel *1984* (1949). The face appeared on a poster above or associated with the phrase "Big Brother Is Watching You." The term also stands for an artificial form of familial protection, for example, the Big Brother Association, a charity that offers alternative parenting.

See also ORWELLIAN.

Sources

Beauchamp, Gorman. 1984. Big Brother in America. *Social Theory and Practice* 10: 247–260.

Orwell, George. 1949. *Nineteen eighty four.* With critical introduction and annotation by Bernard R. Crick. 1984. Oxford: Clarendon Press.

Shafritz, Jay M. 1988. *The Dorsey dictionary of American government and politics.* Chicago: Dorsey.

BINFORDIAN THESIS. In archaeology the assertion that "data relevant to most, if not all, the components of the past sociocultural systems are preserved in the archeological record" (Binford, 1968). Consequently, human cultures in archaeology are assumed to be sociocultural systems in which social and religious factors regulate cultural change; as such, nonmaterial factors may be reconstructed partly from the patterns of artifacts and the changes noted in cultural style.

Lewis R. Binford (b. 1930) developed this radical approach to archaeology in the 1960s. He was a graduate student at the University of Michigan, where he studied descriptive archaeology and artifact typology and, under the influence of Leslie White (1900–75), he aspired to become the T. H. Huxley of archaeology. In opposition to the view that archaeology provides merely the material information on a culture, Binford challenged the assumption of incompleteness in archaeological records, advanced the scientific method in his discipline, followed a functionalist approach to explanation by adopting the open system approach, and sought to integrate archaeology with anthropology. He wrote on the importance of sound research designs and the use of statistics (e.g., regression analysis) to test propositions, and argued that analogies, inductions, and inferences were insufficient in theory building for archaeology. He worked in Australia and among the Nunamuit Eskimo and the Navajo. His prominent associates were William Longacre (b. 1937) and Paul S. Martin (b. 1928).

Sources

Binford, Lewis R. 1962. Archaeology and anthropology. *American Antiquity* 28:217–221.

Binford, Lewis R. 1964. A consideration of archeological research design. *American Antiquity* 29:425–441.

Binford, Lewis R. 1968. Archeological perspectives. In Sally R. Binford and Lewis R. Binford, eds. *New perspectives in archaeology.* Chicago: Aldine.

Binford, Lewis R. 1972. *An archeological perspective.* New York: Seminar Press.

Martin, Paul S. 1971. The revolution in archaeology. *American Antiquity* 36:1–8.

BING BOYS. Canadian forces in World War I.

Julian Hedworth George Byng, Viscount Byng of Vimy (1862–1935), was born at Barnet, England, into a distinguished military family. He went to Eton and afterward joined the 10th Hussars. He fought in the Sudan in 1884, and later became a captain and a major. In the South African war he commanded the Light Horse (1900–1) and became a colonel. Before World War I he held various cavalry commands in Britain and was sent to Egypt. When war began he was recalled and sent to Gallipoli (1915), and in May 1916 he took command of the Canadian forces. He was greatly liked, especially in April 1917 when he brought fame to the Canadians with their capture of Vimy Ridge. He became a general (1917), led the first large-scale tank attack of the war, was raised to the peerage (1919), and received an honorary doctorate at Cambridge (1919). He was a popular appointment as governor-general to Canada, but fell from favor when he refused to dissolve Parliament during the "King-Byng Affair." Back in Britain, he became chief commissioner for the metropolitan police (1928), reorganized it, retired, and shortly before he died was promoted to field marshall (1932).

See also KING-BYNG AFFAIR.

Sources
Legg, Leopold G.W., ed. 1949. *Dictionary of national biography 1931–1940*. London: Oxford University Press.
Marsh, James H., ed. 1988. *The Canadian encyclopedia*. 2d ed. Edmonton: Hurtig.
Wallace, W. Stewart, and McKay, William A. 1978. *The Macmillan dictionary of Canadian biography*. 4th ed. Toronto: Macmillan.

BION-TYPE GROUP. A technique of group psychotherapy.

Wilfred Ruprecht Bion (1897–1979) was born in Muttra, India, and sent to Bishop's Stortford College for his education. In World War I he served in the Royal Tank Corps, and afterward at Oxford he studied modern history. On graduating he returned to his old school to teach French and history, but in 1924 he left to study medicine at University College Hospital (1930) and received a gold medal for surgery. His interest turned to the treatment of delinquents through psychotherapy, and by 1933 he had joined the Tavistock Clinic, London, and started his training in psychoanalysis under John Rickman and later under Melanie Klein at the British Institute of Psycho-Analysis. Bion's work with groups began during wartime with studies of intragroup tension. He helped establish the War Office Selection Boards and Community Therapy organizations. His papers on groups appeared first in *Human Relations* (1945–51) and later in his book, *Experiences with Groups* (1961). Bion's ideas were taken up by British psychiatrists and those in the helping professions who found the cost of individual therapy too high. Bion remained a psychoanalyst, left the Tavistock Clinic in 1948, and established his own psychiatric practice, no longer using group therapy. He became director and, later, president of the clinic, the British Psycho-Analytical Society (1955–65). He developed a complex theory of thinking, and he published three books on the topic in the early 1960s. Bion left England in 1968 to settle in California and travel in Brazil. He practiced in Los Angeles, gave seminars, and published a three-volume autobiography.

Sources
Bion, Wilfred R. 1989. *A memoir of the future*. Rev. ed. London: Karnac.
Bion, Wilfred R. 1987. *The long week-end 1897–1919*. 2d ed. by Francesca Bion. London: Free Association.
Bion, Francesca. 1982. Letter to the Editor. *International Journal of Psycho-Analysis* 63: 261.
Lyth, Oliver. 1980. Obituary [with bibliography]: Wilfred Ruprecht Bion (1897–1979). *International Journal of Psycho-Analysis* 61:269–273.

BIRCHER. A member of the John Birch Society, a secret, ultraconservative, anticommunist organization in the United States.

John Morrison Birch (1918–1945) was born in India to missionary parents and graduated from a Baptist university. He was a clergyman in Macon, Georgia, before being made an officer. Being fluent in Chinese, he was given intelligence work in China. During World War II he served under General Claire Chennault, and in May 1945 he was transferred to the Office of Strategic Services. On a mission to collect intelligence 150 miles south of Yenan in south China, an area occupied by both communist and Nationalist Chinese forces, Birch was shot and killed when passing a communist road block. In 1958–59 Robert Henty Winborne Welch, Jr. (1899–1985) launched the John Birch Society, naming it after John Birch whom, it was alleged, was the first victim of the cold war. Birch also became known as the last soldier to be killed in World War II. The aim of the society was to rid the United States of federal welfare, end its role in NATO, have the United States quit the United Nations, and impeach Chief Justice Earl Warren. The Society pursued its ends by establishing local chapters, publishing *American Opinion* as well as *The Blue Book of the John Birch Society,* and a monthly bulletin for its members encouraging them to enter into local politics. Its central headquarters is in Belmont, Massachusetts. At one time the Society had over 100,000 members. It is still active but attracts diminishing attention (Barrett, 1990).

Sources

Barrett, T. 1990. Once a red always a red. *Newsweek,* 116, 17 September: 36.

Griffin, G. Edward. 1975. *The life and words of Robert Welch.* Westlake Village, Calif.: American Media.

Maolain, Ciaron O., comp. 1987. *The radical right: a world directory.* Essex: Longman.

O'Toole, George J. 1988. *The encyclopedia of American intelligence and espionage.* New York: Facts on File.

Rees, Philip. 1990. *Biographical dictionary of the extreme right since 1890.* New York: Harvester Wheatsheaf.

Schapsmeier, Edward L., and Schapsmeier, Frederick H. 1981. *Political parties and civic action groups.* Westport, Conn.: Greenwood Press.

Stone, Barbara S. 1974. The John Birch Society: a profile. *Journal of Politics* 36:184–197.

Vernoff, Edward, and Shore, Rima, eds. 1987. *International dictionary of 20th century biography.* New York: New American Library.

BIRMINGHAM SCHOOL OF ECONOMICS. A school of economic thought which advocated high prices maintained by inflation of the currency.

The school was led by Thomas Attwood (1783–1856), a banker, whose political influence was advanced when he founded the Birmingham Political Union for the Protection of Public Rights (1830) and sought reform of Parliament by aligning his interests with those of the Chartists. The economic depression following the Napoleonic Wars (1815) had alarmed him, and he became interested in currency questions. He published *The Remedy* (1816). He wanted to drop the use of metal as a standard for currency and replace it with a managed currency in the belief that this would lead to full employment. He was also interested in the equitable representation of the middle and lower classes in government. Accordingly, he worked for the Reform Bill of 1832 and was elected a member of Parliament for Birmingham during 1832–39. In time, his ideas were thought too unorthodox, and his speeches on political and economic matters, given through the Birmingham Union, attracted diminishing attention.

Sources

Blaug, Mark, ed. 1986. *Who's who in economics: a biographical dictionary of major economists, 1700–1986.* 2d ed. Cambridge, Mass.: MIT Press.

Eatwell, John; Milgate, Murray; and Newman, Peter. 1987. *The new Palgrave: a dictionary of economics.* London: Macmillan.

Stephen, Leslie, and Lee, Sydney, eds. 1917. *The dictionary of national biography.* Supplement. London: Oxford University Press.

BIRRELISM, BIRRELIGION. Shrewd comments on the human condition. The political significance of the British Education Bill (1906).

Augustine Birrell (1850–1933) was born in Wavertree, Liverpool, and educated at Amersham Hall School, Reading, Trinity Hall, and Cambridge. He became a barrister (1875; Q.C. 1895) and a professor of law at London University. In 1889 he entered the British Parliament and became president of the National Board of Education (1906) and chief secretary for Ireland (1907–16). He published *Obiter Dicta* (2 vols., 1884; 1887), which was noted for its unobtrusive scholarship and shrewd and sensitive approach to human life. From this work came the term *Birrelism.* In 1906 he became president of the Board of Education and introduced the Education Bill, which was designed to redress the religious grievances of nonconformists and to give equality of treatment in single school regions. The term *Birreligion* was coined to indicate the importance of his education bill. It was defeated in the House of Lords. When he became chief secretary of Ireland, he founded the Roman Catholic National University of Ireland, but he failed to evaluate the circumstances leading to the 1916 Easter Rebellion and Irish separatism. Therefore, he resigned and left public life in 1918, returned to writing, and published *More obiter dicta* (1924). The term *Birreling* was coined to refer to his agreeable but not masterly discussions of literature.

Sources

Aldrich, Richard, and Gordon, Peter. 1987. *Dictionary of British educationists.* London: Woburn Press.

Hendrickson, Robert. 1988. *The dictionary of eponyms: names that became words.* New York: Dorset.

Legg, Leopold G.W., ed. 1949. *Dictionary of national biography 1931–1940.* London: Oxford University Press.

BISMARCKIAN. An aggressive policy or style in politics, especially foreign affairs.

Prince Otto Eduard Leopold Von Bismarck Schönhausen, duke of Lauenburg (1815–1898), was born on the ancestral estate at Schönhausen in the Kurmark into a Junker family that had given many generations of service to the Prussian state. He studied at the universities of Göttingen and Berlin; entered the United Landtag of Prussia in 1847; and in 1849–50, as a member of the second chamber of the Prussian Diet, became known as an outspoken advocate of reactionary ideas and practices. He was appointed Prussian premier and minister of foreign affairs in 1862. That same year, during a conflict with the Landtag over raising military expenditures, he made his famous statement: "It is not by speeches and majorities that the great questions of the day are settled. . . . It is by iron and blood." These words spread through Prussia, and the phrase changed to "blood to iron": Bismarck was criticized but never took back what he had said. In 1871, after the Franco-Prussian war, he founded the German Reich, and became chancellor (1871–1890). In November 1886 he again sought an increase in military spending from the Reichstag. Furious when it demanded an annual instead of a three-year review of military funding, Bismarck echoed the 1862 "iron and blood" speech, saying, "The Germany army is an institution which cannot depend on transient Reichstag majorities." He became known as the "Iron Chancellor." He lost his influence in 1890 and spent his final years in retirement bitterly attacking those who succeeded him in ruling Germany.

Sources

Carr, William. 1969. *A history of Germany 1815–1945.* London: Edward Arnold.

Crankshaw, Edward. 1981 *Bismarck.* London: Macmillan.

Partridge, Eric. 1984. *A dictionary of slang and unconventional English.* London: Routledge and Kegan Paul.

Richter, Werner. 1964. *Bismarck.* Trans. Brian Battershaw. London: Macdonald.

Semple, Charlotte. 1972. *Otto Von Bismarck.* New York: Twayne Publishers.

Snyder, Louis L. 1967. *The blood and iron chancellor: a documentary biography of Otto von Bismarck.* Princeton, N.J.: Van Nostrand.

Waller, Bruce. 1985. *Bismarck.* Oxford: Basil Blackwell.

BLACK MARIA. A prison van.

Maria Lee (fl. 1798) is a legendary character, a black woman who owned a boarding house in Boston. She had been a teamster and became an American heroine when she delivered guns to Alexander Hamilton (1798). Her delivery was performed under great natural hazards; furthermore, she was ambushed by smugglers as she headed for the cutter, *Scammel.* Afterward she opened a respectable boarding house for sailors on the Boston waterfront. She was immensely strong and once rescued a policeman who had been attacked by criminals. In time, when troubled by an offender the police would say: "Call for the black, Maria!" Sometimes she would help escort prisoners all the way from the waterfront to jail, thereby ensuring the respectability of her boarding house. In 1835, when the first of the British police horse vans were used, they were black and may have been named in her honor.

Sources

Dudley, Lavinia P. 1963. *The encyclopedia Americana.* International ed. New York: Americana Corp.

Hendrickson, Robert. 1988. *The dictionary of eponyms: names that became words.* New York: Dorset.

BLACKETT'S CIRCUS. A British operations research team comprising three physiologists, two mathematical physicists, one astrophysicist, an army officer, a surveyor, two mathematicians, and a general physicist. The team helped solve complex logistical problems of warfare in World War II.

Patrick Maynard Stuart Blackett (1897–1974), only son of a London stockbroker, served as a navy lieutenant in World War I, studied physics at Cambridge, and became a fellow at Kings College in 1925. In 1933 he became a professor of physics at Birkbeck College; and at the Victoria University of Manchester in 1937 he established an international research laboratory. During World War II he was an adviser to the Royal Air Force, and with his ''Circus'' revolutionized operational research on the use of radar in antiaircraft defense and the search for enemy submarines. For ten years after publishing his dissenting view on Britain's atomic energy policy in *Military and Political Consequences of Atomic Energy* (1948), he was dropped as a government adviser. Meanwhile, he helped expand the role of physics research and the growth of universities in Britain, sat on many government committees, and finally was taken up by Harold Wilson in 1963. Consequently, Blackett made a great impact on British science and technology. He received many civil and professional distinctions, the Nobel Prize for Physics (1948), several honorary degrees from universities around the world, and became a life peer in 1969.

Sources

Lord Blake, and Nicholls, C.S., eds. 1986. *The dictionary of national biography: 1971–
    80.* Oxford: Oxford University Press.
Trefethen, Florence N. 1954. A history of operations research. In Joseph F. McCloskey
    and Florence N. Trefethen, eds. *Operations research for management.* Baltimore,
    Md.: Johns Hopkins University Press.

BLAKE AND MOUTON'S MANAGERIAL GRID. A technique for describing, analyzing, and teaching management styles to improve organized life. It is a framework for studying a wide range of people and production problems simultaneously, and for suggesting alternative solutions to them. The technique has been used in various settings, particularly in the United States, but also in Canada, Europe, and Asia.

Robert Rogers Blake (b. 1918) was born in Providence, Rhode Island, and educated at Berea College and the University of Virginia. During World War II, he served in the U.S. Army Air Force. He received his doctorate at the University of Texas (Ph.D., 1947), after which he was appointed a professor of psychology at the University of Texas in Austin, lectured at the universities of Reading and Harvard, and on a Fulbright scholarship was a clinician at the Tavistock Clinic. In 1961 he became the president of Scientific Methods Inc., a behavioral science firm that specialized in educational and organizational development. He is a fellow of the American Psychological Association, various academic fraternities in the United States, and the American Board of Professional Psychology. In 1964 he and Jane S. Mouton published their book on the Managerial Grid. It was widely publicized and became a popular technique in management training in many fields, winning several book awards.

Jane Srygley Mouton (b. 1930) was born in Port Arthur, Texas, educated at the University of Texas in Austin and Florida State University, and was awarded a Ph.D. from the University of Texas (1957). She became a professor of psychology in 1959 and helped found Scientific Methods Inc., where she became the president in 1982. She belongs to the American Psychological Association, the American Board of Professional Psychology, various university societies, and the American Association for the Advancement of Science. She and Blake co-authored the original work on the managerial grid, revised it, and published *Synergogy: A New Strategy of Education, Training and Development* (1984), as well as many books that apply their original idea to various administrative jobs, for example, secretary and academic administrator.

Sources

Bedeian, Arthur, ed. 1992–93. *Management laureates: a collection of autobiographical essays.* Vol. I. Greenwich, Conn.: JAI Press.

Blake, Robert R., and Mouton, Jane S. 1964. *The managerial grid.* Houston, Tex.: Gulf. Revised 1978, 1984.

Blake, Robert R., and Mouton, Jane S. 1985. *Solving costly organizational conflicts.* San Francisco: Jossey-Bass.

Metzger, Linda, ed. 1984. *Contemporary authors.* New Revision Series. Vol. 13. Detroit: Gale Research.

May, Hal, and Trosky, Susan M. 1988. *Contemporary authors.* Vol. 123. Detroit: Gale Research.

BLAND-ALLISON ACT. A United States currency act (1877), with an amendment, that served the interests of those who advocated "free silver" and their opponents who supported "sound money." The act aimed to rid the United States of currency deflation, which had plagued its economy since the end of the Civil War, without raising problems of currency inflation.

Richard Parks Bland (1835–99) was born near Hartford, Ohio County, in Kentucky. After one year's study at Harford Academy, he taught school in Kentucky, and them moved to Missouri and continued teaching (1855). For the next ten years he prospected and mined in California, Colorado, and Nevada. He was admitted to the bar and became treasurer of Carson County in Utah Territory before returning to Missouri in 1866. He served as a Democrat for Missouri in the U.S. Congress between 1872 and 1899. As chairman of the Committee on Mines and Mining (1875–77), he saw the evils of a flat-paper money inflation and the importance of an international agreement on bimetallism. He led the "free silver" wing of the Democratic party and strongly opposed monopolies, protection, and imperialism. Named "Silver Dick" by his opponents, he fought for a "free silver" coinage, and when the act was passed in 1878 he became a national figure.

William Boyd Allison (1829–1908) was born in Perry, Ohio, raised on a farm, studied at Wooster Academy, Allegheny College, and then taught school briefly before graduating from Western Reserve and being admitted to the bar in 1849.

From 1862 to 1870, he served in the U.S. Congress for Iowa and developed a moderatist's approach to the currency problem. As a senator (1872–1908), he declined offers to be in the cabinet, preferring to work for harmony in party matters and to make politically advantageous deals. His name attaches to the act because he was responsible for the amendment that limited the silver purchase for coinage each month.

Sources

Jacob, Kathryn A., and Ragsdale, Bruce A. 1989. *Biographical directory of the United States Congress: 1774–1989.* Bicentennial ed. Washington, D.C.: U.S. Government Printing Office.

Johnson, Allen, ed. 1927. *Dictionary of American biography.* Vol. I. New York: Charles Scribner's Sons.

Myers, Margaret A. 1970. *A financial history of the United States.* New York: Columbia University Press.

Sage, Leland. 1956. *William Boyd Allison: a study in practical politics.* Iowa City: State Historical Society.

BLIMP, BLIMPISH. A political type of conservative elderly military officer.

Colonel Blimp (b. 1934), a cartoon character, seen first in a Turkish bath, was the invention of David Alexander Low (1891–1963), a New Zealand-born cartoonist whose most notable work first appeared in *The Bulletin* (Australia) and the *Evening Standard,* London. In 1934 Low created a character who was dogmatic and befuddled, and captured him with self-contradictory aphorisms. Colonel Blimp lived quietly for a year on such ideas as: "We need better relations between Capital and Labor. If the trades unions won't accept our terms, crush em." The Spanish Civil War changed Colonel Blimp into a symbol of military incompetence, and the character became defined, discussed, and widely misapprehended. Eventually, he came to represent British inertia, all that was stupid and dull in Britain, an excuse for deriding authority, an assault on aristocratic tradition, a symbol of patriotic humbug, a contemptuous military fool. His critics gave him a life-history: he was alleged to have been born in England, well connected, gone to Sandhurst, served in the Indian Army, lived in South Kensington, and married the daughter of the bishop of Bath and Wells. Although Low conceived of Colonel Blimp as merely a stupid man, others projected this stupidity onto a figure who contradicted himself, loathed democracy, decried education, preferred isolationism, was anti-Semitic, anticolonialist, violent, and warlike, opposed to economic reorganization, in favor of rearmament, sabotaged peace, excused totalitarianism, objected to trade sanctions, and favored appeasement. The film, *The Life and Death of Colonel Blimp,* made British military officers appear worldwide as stupid, complacent, self-satisfied, and ridiculous. During World War II Colonel Blimp appeared intermittently in the *Evening Standard* and gradually faded; in 1954 "blimpish" appeared as a synonym for military and administrative incompetence.

Sources
Low, David, 1956. *Low's autobiography.* London: Michael Joseph.
McHenry, Robert, ed. 1992. *The new encyclopedia Britannica.* Chicago: Encyclopedia
    Britannica, Inc.

BLOOM'S TAXONOMY. An educational classification of mind into three areas: cognitive knowledge and its application; affective feelings and their values; and the psychomotor skills.

Benjamin Samuel Bloom (b. 1913) was born in the United States, received an M.A. from Pennsylvania State University, and studied at the University of Chicago (Ph.D., 1942) where he became a professor of education. He assisted the university examiner and later filled the position; in that job he decided to move university education from the teaching of information to how information could be used to solve problems. Bloom found that some students were unable to solve problems and that success in problem-solving came to those who were systematic and analytic, while others simply tried to recall an answer they had memorized. The approaches were known as active and passive, respectively. The work was important in education when first published by Bloom and Lois Broder (1950), and later became the basis of Bloom's taxonomy of those things students are expected to learn. In 1956 he published his *Taxonomy of Educational Objectives.* Later he published *Stability and Change in Human Characteristics* (1964) and his *Handbook on Formative and Summative Evaluation of Student Learning* (1971). Later, he developed a mastery learning system that assumes that, although students differ, what one person can learn, nearly all can learn. He seriously questioned traditional teaching methods and what students learn while teachers are teaching.

Sources
Chance, Paul. 1987. Master of mastery. *Psychology Today* 21, no. 42:42–46.
Page, G. Terry; Thomas, John. B.; and Marshall, Alan R. 1977. *International dictionary
    of education.* London: Kogan Page.
Rowntree, Derek. 1981. *Dictionary of education.* London: Harper and Row.
Sutherland, Stuart. 1989. *Macmillan dictionary of psychology.* Worcester, U.K.: Billing
    and Sons.

BLOOMFIELDIAN. Relating an approach to the scientific study of language that was developed between the mid-1930s and 1950s in the United States, and that affected structural linguistics. It emphasized behavioristic principles for the study of meaning and rigorous scientific procedures to establish the role of language in human interaction. Although some critics considered Bloomfieldianism a fashion, its methods are still used in field studies of language today.

Leonard Bloomfield (1887–1949) was born in Chicago and studied German at the University of Wisconsin. Influenced by Eduard Prokosch, Bloomfield went to the University of Chicago (Ph.D., 1909), and taught German at the universities of Cincinnati and Illinois before publishing his *An Introduction to the*

Study of Language (1914). Using an inductive method in place of the standard techniques for the study of a new language, Bloomfield published work on Tagalog grammar. Later, he studied Algonquian for its regularity of sound changes. In 1924 he helped establish the Linguistic Society of America and the journal, *Language.* In 1927 he worked with E. Sapir at the University of Chicago and wrote his noted book, *Language* (1933). In this work he integrated the field of linguistics and formulated a model of languages beginning with phonemes and progressing to morphemes, then words, phrases and clauses, and finally sentences. Later, he turned to teaching the fundamentals of language to children, succeeded Sapir at Yale University (1940), and during World War II helped produce foreign language manuals for the military.

Sources

Devine, Elizabeth; Held, Michael; Vinson, James; and Walsh, George, eds. 1983. *Thinkers of the twentieth century: a biographical, bibliographical and critical dictionary.* London: Macmillan.

Esper, Erwin A. 1968. *Mentalism and objectivism in linguistics: the sources of Leonard Bloomfield's psychology of language.* New York: Elsevier.

Garraty, John A., and James, Edward T., eds. 1974. *Dictionary of American biography.* Supplement 4. New York: Charles Scribner's Sons.

Sills, David L., ed. 1968. *International encyclopedia of the social sciences.* New York: Macmillan and Free Press.

BOB'S YOUR UNCLE. Political arrangements have been made, so everything will go as planned.

Robert Arthur Talbot Gascoyne-Cecil, third Marquess of Salisbury (1830–1903), was born at Hatfield House, educated at Eton and Oxford, and elected a fellow of All Souls. After a tour to Australia, in 1853 he became the Conservative member for Stamford. He was elected chancellor of Oxford University in 1869. He opposed the disestablishment of the Irish church and the Irish Land Act, and he supported the Peace Preservation Bill. In Disraeli's government he was successively secretary of state for India and foreign secretary (1878–80). On Disraeli's death in 1881, Salisbury became the Conservative leader in the House of Lords and prime minister in 1885. His nephew, Arthur James Balfour, first earl of Balfour (1848–1930) entered Parliament in 1874 and became chief secretary for Ireland in 1887 in his uncle's government. When his uncle resigned in 1902, Balfour became prime minister. Because Salisbury arranged for his nephew to hold high positions, thereby advancing the young man's political career, the phrase ''Bob's your uncle'' was coined with the idea that with such political influence nothing could go wrong and one could get a political post merely by mentioning one's interest in it. While serving under Lloyd George as foreign secretary, Balfour was noted for the Balfour Declaration (1917) that promised a home in Palestine for Zionists.

See also BALFOUR DECLARATION.

Sources
Lee, Sidney, ed. 1920. *The dictionary of national biography: supplement 1901–1911.* London: Oxford University Press.
Magnussen, Magnus; Goring, Rosemary; and Thorn, John O., eds. 1990. *Chambers biographical dictionary.* Edinburgh: Chambers Ltd.
Morris, William, ed. 1965–1966. *Grolier universal encyclopedia.* 10 vols. New York: American Book-Stratford Press, Inc.

BOBBY, PEELER. A British policeman.

Sir Robert Peel (1788–1850) was born near Bury in Lancashire, son of Sir Robert Peel, who, after making a fortune in cotton printing, entered the House of Commons. Young Robert was educated at Harrow and then at Christ Church, Oxford, where he took a double first in classics and mathematics. He entered the House of Commons in 1809 and at the age of 24 became chief secretary for Ireland. There he established the Irish police force, the ''Peelers.'' He returned from Ireland in 1818 and in 1822 became home secretary in Lord Liverpool's government. With the duke of Wellington Peel stood aside from the administration that succeeded that of Lord Liverpool in 1827, for they were opposed to conciliation toward Roman Catholics in Ireland. As home secretary, Peel reluctantly supported the Catholic Emancipation Act (1829); his notable achievement was the establishment of the Metropolitan Police, the ''Bobbies,'' as a regular force in 1829. He also reorganized the legal system by abolishing many needlessly severe laws. He attempted to reform the early Corn Laws to allow for a complex system of resting-places for the price at which corn could be brought into Britain. In this regard his followers were ''Peelites.'' His plan met opposition from landholders in Parliament who had long benefited from protection, and from Richard Cobden's and John Bright's Anti-Corn Law League which sought abolition, not alteration, of the Corn Laws.

Sources
Evans, Eric J. 1991. *Sir Robert Peel: statesmanship, power and party.* London: Routledge.
Evans, Ivor H. 1989. *Brewer's dictionary of phrase and fable.* 14th ed. London: Cassell.
Fay, Charles R. 1932. *The Corn Laws and social England.* Cambridge: Cambridge University Press.
Longmate, Norman. 1984. *The bread stealers: the fight against the Corn Laws, 1839–1846.* Hounslow: Maurice Temple Smith.
Magnussen, Magnus; Goring, Rosemary; and Thorn, John O., eds. 1990. *Chambers biographical dictionary.* Edinburgh: Chambers Ltd.
Ramsay, Anna, and Augusta, W. 1971. *Sir Robert Peel.* London: Constable.
Stephen, Leslie, and Lee, Sidney, eds. 1917. *The dictionary of national biography.* London: Oxford University Press.

BOGARDUS SCALE OF SOCIAL DISTANCE. A rating scale (1933) that asks respondents to indicate how close they feel they are or would be willing to be to a person who represents a particular social group.

Emory Stephen Bogardus (1882–1973) was born near Belvidere, Illinois, and educated at Northwestern University. He studied economics and sociology at the University of Chicago (Ph.D., Sociology, 1911) and became a professor of sociology at the University of Southern California (1911–49) where he organized, founded, and was the first chairman of the Department of Sociology. He was also the director of the Division of Social Work (1920–37) and dean of the Graduate School (1945–49). He received a D.Litt. from the University of Southern California (1945) and the University of Arizona (1960), and an LL.D. from the University of Boston (1950), as well as other honors. He edited the *Journal of Sociology and Social Research* and various other publications in the social sciences. He was a prolific author, and among his works were *Fundamentals of Social Psychology* (1924; 1950; 1976) which went through several editions, as did *Principles of Cooperation* (1952; 1963); *The Development of Social Thought* (1940); and *Toward a World Community* (1964). Among other works were *Sociology* (1934) and *Social Distance* (1959). He also wrote a book of poems, *The Traveler* (1956).

Sources

Bogardus, Emory S. 1959. *Social distance.* Yellow Springs, Ohio: Antioch.
Bogardus, Emory S. 1960. *The development of social thought.* 4th ed. New York: David McKay.
May, Hal, ed. 1986. *Contemporary authors.* Vol. 116. Detroit: Gale Research.
Miller, Delbert C. 1991. *Handbook of research design and social measurement.* 5th ed. Newbury Park, Calif.: Sage Publications.
Sills, David L., ed. 1968. *International encyclopedia of the social sciences.* New York: Macmillan and Free Press.
Who was who in America, 1974–76. Vol 6. Chicago: Marquis.
Zusne, Leonard. 1987. *Eponyms in psychology: a dictionary and sourcebook.* Westport, Conn.: Greenwood Press.

BOLÍVAR. Monetary unit of Venezuela.

Simón Bolívar (1783–1830), a South American revolutionary leader, was the noted liberator of South America from Spanish domination. He was born in Caracas, of a noble family, studied law at Madrid, and was in Paris during the French Revolution. After Venezuela declared its independence in 1811, he was given command of an army and, in 1813, entering Caracas as conqueror, he proclaimed himself dictator of western Venezuela. He led revolutions against the Spanish in New Granada (named Colombia or Grand Colombia in 1819, which included Venezuela, Ecuador, and Colombia), Peru, and Upper Peru (later known as Bolivia). He was driven out but made repeated attacks on Venezuela from the West Indies and eventually rid the land of royalist troops by 1824. In 1821 Bolívar was chosen president of Colombia, which then comprised Venezuela, Colombia, and New Granada. Bolivia was named in his honor.

Sources

McHenry, Robert, ed. 1992. *The new encyclopedia Britannica.* Chicago: Encyclopedia Britannica, Inc.

Masur, Gerhard. 1969. *Simón Bolívar.* 2d ed. Albuquerque: University of New Mexico Press.
Moron, Guillermo. 1964. *A history of Venezuela.* London: Allen and Unwin.
Salcedo-Bastardo, J. L. 1977. *Bolívar: a continent and its destiny.* Ed. and trans. Annella McDermott. Richmond, Surrey: Richmond Publishing.
Wepman, Denis. 1985. *Simón Bolívar.* New York: Chelsea House.

BOLLANDIST. Any of the Jesuit writers who continued to work on *Acta Sanctorum.*

John van Bolland (1596–1665), also known as Jean de Bolland, was born in Tirlemont, Brabant, and died at Antwerp. He became a Jesuit. In 1643 he founded and was first editor of *Acta Sanctorum,* a collection of biographies and legends of the saints, with allied documents, edited in original languages and arranged according to their feast days in calendar order. Heribert Rosweyde, a Jesuit hagiographer, had planned to publish the lives of the saints in Latin. Bolland continued to collect material after Rosweyde's death in 1629. It now comprises over sixty volumes. His name was given to those who collaborated in the work and to his successors. After 1882 modern historical methods were applied to the work.

Sources

Knowles, David. 1963. *Great historical perspectives: problems in monastic history.* London: Thomas Nelson.
McHenry, Robert, ed. 1992. *The new encyclopedia Britannica.* Chicago: Encyclopedia Britannica, Inc.
Meagher, Paul K.; O'Brien, Thomas C.; and Aherne, Marie, eds. 1979. *Encyclopedic dictionary of religion.* Washington, D.C.: Corpus Publications.

BOLO. Traitor, spy, or underground political worker for Germany during World War I.

Paul-Marie Bolo, ''Bolo Pasha'' (1867–1918), was born in Marseilles and was a dentist until he became a trader, failed, and had to leave the country. He lived in Spain and returned to France to enter business in 1892. He was prosecuted for breach of trust and sentenced by default. He turned up in Argentina and married a singer who kept him. He was arrested for theft in Valparaiso, released on bail, and fled to Paris, where he married, bigamously, the widow of a wealthy wine merchant. With her power of attorney, he became rich and created banks in South America and founded the Swiss White Cross. Well connected, he lived lavishly and came close to financial ruin. In 1914 he met the khedive of Egypt, who conferred the title ''pasha'' on Bola and made him his financial agent in Paris. After the khedive was expelled from Egypt for aiding the Germans, he fled to Switzerland where Pasha Bolo served his interests. Bolo tried to buy French newspapers in order to influence public opinion. Money for this effort came from Germany and was traced through many banks including the Morgan Bank. Bolo was court-martialed in 1916 on charges of giving intelligence to Count Johann von Bernstorff, the German ambassador to the United

States, and of making financial deals with Americans. No witness he nominated to support his not-guilty plea came to speak for him; most were in prison, abroad, or were criminal suspects. Only his brother, with a moving courtroom address, came to Bolo's support. Bolo was found guilty of all charges and executed in 1918.

Sources

Hendrickson, Robert. 1988. *The dictionary of eponyms: names that became words.* New York: Dorset.

Prevost, M., and Roman-D'Amat, J. 1954. *Dictionnaire de biographie Française.* Paris: Librairie Letouzey et Ané.

BONAPARTEAN, BONAPARTISM, BONAPARTIST. After the nineteenth-century emperor of France. Dictatorial and imperialistic policies found in a military dictatorship that invokes, manipulatively, the sovereign power of the people. Supporter of the descendants of Napoleon.

Napoleon Bonaparte I (1769–1821) was born in Ajaccio, Corsica, and educated at the military academy in Paris. He became an army officer in 1785, fought during the French Revolution, and was promoted to brigadier general in 1793. The threat of revolt brought him in command of the army of the interior in 1795. He then commanded the army of Italy in several victories, but the English defeated him in Syria (1798) and he returned to France. A coup of 1799 gave him supreme power in a military dictatorship. In 1804 he was crowned hereditary emperor of the French. For his family he reintroduced princely titles, and for his followers he created an imperial nobility. His downfall came after he invaded Russia in 1812. He was exiled to Elba, returned to France briefly, but spent his remaining years on Saint Helena Island.

Sources

Barnett, Corelli. 1978. *Bonaparte.* London: Allen and Unwin.

Harris, Nathaniel. 1988. *Napoleon.* London: Batesford.

McHenry, Robert, ed. 1992. *The new encyclopedia Britannica.* Chicago: Encyclopedia Britannica, Inc.

Tames, Richard. 1974. *Napoleon.* London: Harrap.

Thompson, James M. 1951. *Napoleon Bonaparte: his rise and fall.* Oxford: Basil Blackwell.

Tulard, Jean. 1985. *Napoleon: the myth of the saviour.* Trans. Teresa Waugh. London: Weidenfeld and Nicolson.

Wright, Gordon. 1962. *France in modern times: 1760–present.* London: J. Murray.

BONDOMANIA. Excitement surrounding the popular character and adventures of the secret agent 007, during the 1960s–1980s.

James Bond (1900–90) was an American ornithologist whose book, *Birds of the West Indies* (1936), was on Ian Fleming's breakfast table when he wrote *Casino Royale* (1953), the first of the 007 adventures. Fleming is reported to have said, '' . . . this name, brief, unromantic, and yet very masculine was just what I needed.'' The fictional James Bond was ''born'' in about 1924, the only child of a Scot, Andrew Bond, and a Swiss, Monique Delacroix. Andrew represented the Vickers armament firm on the European continent. James lived in Europe for eleven years until his parents died in a mountaineering accident. He was raised by an aunt at Pett Bottom, near Canterbury in Kent, sent to Eton, but was removed and finished his education at Fettes, his father's old school. He entered the Ministry of Defence, and for service to his country was made C.M.G. He declined a knighthood. Fleming's books have been filmed regularly since the early 1960s when *Dr No* appeared. The term *Bondomania* was coined to describe the following that the character attracted at the height of the cold war (1947–90), especially after the filming of *From Russia with Love.*

Sources

Amis, Kingsley. 1965. *The James Bond dossier.* London: Jonathan Cape.

Holbrook, David. 1972. *The masks of hate: the problem of false solutions in the culture of the acquisitive society.* Oxford: Pergamon Press.

Obituary of James Bond. 1900–90. *ISIS,* 132:130.

Pearson, John. 1966. *The life of Ian Fleming.* London: Jonathan Cape.

Tanner, William. 1965. *The book of Bond, or Everyman his own 007.* London: Jonathan Cape.

BONE UP ON, TO. To study a subject because it will be needed shortly for examination or for some other pressing purpose.

Henry George Bohn (1796–1884) was a scholar and a London publisher. His father was a German bookbinder and second-hand bookseller. Young Bohn entered the business in 1831, and after amassing a vast range of books, issued his famous "Guinea Catalogue" listing over 23,000 entries. In 1846 he began publishing inexpensively a vast range of books—over 600 volumes of valuable works in literature, science, philosophy, and theology—in his "Classical Library." He edited *Bibliotheca Parrianna* and Lowndes's *Bibliographers' Manual,* and translations of many works. The term first appeared in the 1860s and was used by students of Bohn's translations of the classics, or "trots" as they called them.

Sources

Findlater, Andrew, ed. 1895. *Chambers encyclopedia.* New ed. London and Edinburgh: William and Robert Chambers Ltd. Philadelphia: J. B. Lippincott Co.

Hendrickson, Robert. 1987. *The Facts on File encyclopedia of word and phrase origins.* New York: Facts on File.

Partridge, Eric. 1984. *A dictionary of slang and unconventional English.* Ed. Paul Beale. London: Routledge and Kegan Paul.

Smith, Benjamin. 1903. *The Century cyclopedia of names.* London: The Times.

BORDA COUNT. A system of collective choice whereby voters rank candidates; the candidate is allocated marks corresponding to the ranks, and the marks are summed; the candidate with the highest total wins.

Jean-Charles de Borda (1733–99) was born in Dax, near Bordeaux. He studied at a Jesuit college but soon scorned religion. He became a naval captain, cavalry officer, physics scholar, and inventor of scientific instruments. Over the years he was elected to the Paris Academy of Sciences, the Academy of Bordeaux, the Marine Academy and the Bureau des Longtitudes. He made important contributions to fluid mechanics, geodesy, and the determination of weights and measures. He showed that Newton's theory of fluid resistance was false, developed the use of surveying instruments, and was noted generally for bringing precision into French physics of the eighteenth century. Concerned that the single-vote system might select the wrong candidate, Borda read his *Sur la forme des elections* (1770) at the Academy of Sciences. The paper was not noted; in 1784 he read another that again repeated his earlier points. Shortly afterward the Academy adopted his method to admit members.

Sources

Eatwell, John; Milgate, Murray; and Newman, Peter. 1987. *The new Palgrave: a dictionary of economics.* London: Macmillan.

Gillespie, Charles C., ed. 1973. *Dictionary of scientific biography.* New York: Charles Scribner's Sons.

Pearce, David W., ed. 1986. *Macmillan dictionary of modern economics.* New York: Macmillan.

Prevost, M., and Roman-D'Amat, J. 1954. *Dictionnaire de biographie Française.* Paris: Librairie Letouzey et Ané.

BOSWELLIAN. Tirelessly observant and devoted style of biography or life-history.

James Boswell (1740–95) was educated both privately and at Edinburgh University. He studied civil law at Glasgow and at 18 began an intimate, frank, and personal journal. He ran away to London in 1760, studied law, and came to love London's urban life. For a time he practiced law in England and Scotland, and then turned to literature and politics. A visit to Corsica in 1765 led him to support the cause of Corsican liberty and to his first substantial work, *An Account of Corsica* (1768). In 1769 he returned to London and became a Catholic. He met Samuel Johnson in London (1762–63) and described their travels together in 1773 in *Journal of a Tour to the Hebrides* (1785). His *The Life of Samuel Johnson* (1791) gives an excellent view of the period and many of its notables, and with its enthusiasm for the subject and its worldly and balanced perspective on the context of the life set the tone for biographies and life-histories. Boswell's manuscripts were discovered in Malahide Castle, Ireland (1927), and in Fettercairn House, Scotland (1930), and were collected at Yale University.

Sources

Brady, Frank. 1984. *James Boswell: the later years, 1769–1795.* London: Heinemann.

Daiches, David. 1976. *James Boswell and his world.* London: Thames and Hudson.

McHenry, Robert, ed. 1992. *The new encyclopedia Britannica.* Chicago: Encyclopedia Britannica, Inc.

Magnussen, Magnus; Goring, Rosemary; and Thorn, John O., eds. 1990. *Chambers biographical Dictionary.* Edinburgh: Chambers Ltd.

Pottle, Frederick A. 1929. *The literary career of James Boswell.* Reprinted 1965. Oxford: Clarendon Press.

Pottle, Frederick A. 1966. *James Boswell: the earlier years, 1740–1769.* Reprinted 1985. London: Heinemann.

Stephen, Leslie, and Lee, Sydney, eds. 1917. *The dictionary of national biography.* London: Oxford University Press.

BOULANGISM. The French political movement (1886–90) that advocated military revenge on Germany after France's defeat in the Franco-Prussian War.

General Georges Ernest Jean Marie Boulanger (1837–91) was born in Rennes, France, and educated at Saint Cyr. In the French Army he fought in Italy, China, and in the Franco-Prussian War; he also helped suppress the 1871 Paris commune. He was a French military hero. In 1886, as minister for war, he introduced many reforms for soldiers—especially pay and living conditions—and he would often argue that France should win back its lost honor by adopting a strong militarist position toward Germany. He advanced this cause by appearing in Parisian crowds mounted on his horse, and he became known as ''The Man on Horseback.'' His movement failed, and he lost his position in 1887; nevertheless, ''Boulanger fever'' continued to rise. The army exiled him to a post at Clermont-Ferrand, and in 1888 he was deprived of his command. He was elected a deputy for Dordogne and Nord, and demanded the constitution be revised. The government prosecuted him when a coup d'etat seemed imminent. In 1889 after failing to win enough support he fled France, and he shot himself in Brussels on his mistress's grave.

Sources

Gorman, Herbert S. 1942. *Brave general.* New York: Farrar and Rinehart.

Harding, James. 1971. *The astonishing adventure of General Boulanger.* New York: Charles Scribner's Sons.

Magnussen, Magnus; Goring, Rosemary; and Thorn, John O., eds. 1990. *Chambers biographical dictionary.* Edinburgh: Chambers Ltd.

Seager, Frederich H. 1969. *The Boulanger affair: political crossroads of France, 1866–1889.* Ithaca, N.Y.: Cornell University Press.

BOULWARISM. In collective bargaining, a practice whereby a firm makes an offer to a union and refuses to bargain thereafter. The practice was begun in the United States by the General Electric Company and was named after its former vice-president. Today the practice is regarded as contrary to the legal requirement of parties to bargain in good faith. Although General Electric has abandoned the practice, it still may be found in some American industries.

Lemuel Ricketts Boulware (1895–1990) was born in Springfield, Kentucky, and studied at the University of Wisconsin. He served as a captain in the U.S. Army during 1917–19 and won a Medal of Merit for war service. He worked for the General Electric Company as a marketing consultant and was responsible for employee, community, and union relations (1945–47), and later became vice-president for public and employee relations. He received a Distinguished American Citizen Award from Harding College in 1963. He published *The Truth about Boulwarism: Trying to Do the Right Thing Voluntarily* (1969) and *What You Can Do about Inflation, Unemployment, Productivity, Profit and Collective Bargaining* (1972).

Sources

Marsh, Arthur. 1979. *Concise encyclopedia of industrial relations.* Westmead, Farnborough, Hants: Gower.

Pearce, David W., ed. 1986. *Macmillan dictionary of modern economics.* New York: Macmillan.

Roberts, Harold S. 1966. *Roberts' dictionary of industrial relations.* Washington, D.C.: BNA.

Who's who in America, 1990–91. Chicago: Marquis.

BOURBON. One who learns nothing by experience; a political diehard; the name given to the American Democratic party by its opponents and used to refer to a conservative in American politics, especially to identify southern Democrats of old-fashioned views (Mathews, 1951). The terms was used in the mid-1860s through the late 1940s.

The Bourbons were two lines of royal descent in Europe, one in France and the other in Spain and Italy. In France the more prominent Bourbon dynasty (1589–1792) comprised Henry IV (1553–1610), Louis XIII (1601–43), Louis XIV (1638–1715), Louis XV (1710–74), and Louis XVI (1754–93). The name is taken from Bourbon l'Archambault, the major town of a tenth-century lordship in the French kingdom. Near the end of the ninth century, the first line of Bourbons was established with Adhémar, the first baron, but this line of descent ended in 1488. The fourth line of Bourbon descent, and the most noted, came through Antoine de Bourbon whose son became Henry VI, king of France. Louis VI's younger son, Philip, duke of Anjou (1683–1746), became Philip V, king of Spain, and established the Spanish and Italian Bourbons. The famous French dynasty ended with Louis XVI's death on the scaffold. Thus, as legend tells, the Bourbons, for all their royal attributes, learned nothing and forgot nothing, and for this reason their name denotes one who fails to learn from experience.

Sources

Chisholm, Hugh, ed. 1910–11. *Encyclopedia Britannica.* 11th ed. New York: Encyclopedia Britannica Co.

Mathews, Milford M. 1951. *A dictionary of Americanisms: on historical principles.* Chicago: University of Chicago Press.

McHenry, Robert, ed. 1992. *The new encyclopedia Britannica.* Chicago: Encyclopedia Britannica, Inc.

Rowen, Herbert H. 1980. *The king's state.* New Brunswick, N.J.: Rutgers University Press.

BOURIGNONIST. One who holds that the Christian religion comprises nothing but an inner feeling and a divine impulse rather than any knowledge or practice.

Antoinette Bourignon (1616–80) was born at Lille in France and died at Francker, Netherlands. She wore the Augustinian habit and traveled in France, Holland, England, and Scotland. She became convinced that she was directly illuminated by God for the reforming of things temporal and spiritual, and in this belief she attacked all forms of religious organization. She became the founder of the Bourignonist sect, which maintained that Christianity does not consist in faith and practice but in inner feelings and supernatural impulses. Her works were published in nineteen volumes by her disciple, Peter Poiret, a Calvinist minister, in *Toutes les Oeuvres de Mile A. Bourignon* (1679–84).

Sources

Cross, Frank L. 1974. *The Oxford dictionary of the Christian Church.* 2d ed. New York: Oxford University Press.

Douglas, James D., ed. 1974. *The new international dictionary of the Christian Church.* Exeter: Paternoster Press.

Hastings, James, ed. 1920. *Encyclopedia of religion and ethics.* New York: T. and T. Clark.

Law, M. D., and Dixon, M. Vibart, eds. 1966. *Chambers encyclopedia.* London: Pergamon Press.

McHenry, Robert, ed. 1992. *The new encyclopedia Britannica.* Chicago: Encyclopedia Britannica, Inc.

Magnussen, Magnus; Goring, Rosemary; and Thorn, John O., eds. 1990. *Chambers biographical dictionary.* Edinburgh: Chambers Ltd.

BOWLBY CHILD. A phrase indicating emotional distress and a sense of loss in adults as largely due to painful and long periods of maternal deprivation during childhood. The deprivation leads to low self-esteem, lack of trust in others, and the fear of being abandoned. The longer the deprivation, the more devoted is the care needed to manage the distress and loss.

Edward John Mostyn Bowlby (1907–90) was born in London, educated at the Royal Naval College, Dartmouth, and at Trinity College, Cambridge (M.D., 1939). In 1946 he published *Forty Four Juvenile Thieves, Their Characters and Home Life.* From 1946 he worked at London's Tavistock Clinic and directed the Department for Children and Parents. He was also a consultant for the World Heath Organization (WHO) after 1950. His WHO publication, *Maternal Care and Mental Health,* appeared in 1951. His ideas on child rearing and on the importance of observing a child in its natural environs met much resistance. The theoretical model of child rearing that is based on maternal feeding combined with infantile fantasies has given over to his views on a child's experiences of attachment and loss of parental care. This work began in the 1930s when he left Cambridge University to observe at close hand maladjusted children in Norfolk. He found, first, that a child needs security and love from a caregiver and, second, that happy, healthy children come from stable homes that stay put, with two parents who give love, time, and attention in a community or neighborhood of families and friends. He published *A Secure Base* (1989) and *Charles Darwin: A New Biography* (1990).

Sources
Ainsworth, Mary D. Salter. 1992. John Bowlby (1907–90). *American Psychologist* 47: 648.
Bowlby, John. 1969–1980. *Attachment and loss*. 3 vols. New York: Basic Books.
Devine, Elizabeth; Held, Michael; Vinson, James; and Walsh, George, eds. 1983. *Thinkers of the twentieth century: a biographical, bibliographical and critical dictionary*. London: Macmillan.

BOYCOTT. To coerce people by uniting in a refusal to do no trade with them; nonviolent intimidation.

Charles Cunningham Boycott (1832–97) was born in Burgh Saint Peter, Norfolk, served in the army, and on retirement as a captain in 1873 became an agent for the earl of Erne's estates in County Mayo, Ireland. When the Land League, founded in 1879 in Ireland, demanded a rent cut of 25 percent because of poor harvests, Boycott refused. He tried to evict tenants. Then Charles Stewart Parnell, president of the Land League suggested that tenants avoid all commerce with anyone who failed to cut rents, and so the tenants refused to work or to speak with him. Consequently, Boycott had to use labor from outside the county to harvest his crops. This intimidation led him to quit Ireland to manage estates in Suffolk and resulted in the Land Act of 1881, with the establishment of fair rent tribunals.

See also PARNELLISM.

Sources
McHenry, Robert, ed. 1992. *The new encyclopedia Britannica*. Chicago: Encyclopedia Britannica, Inc.
Marlowe, Joyce. 1973. *Captain Boycott and the Irish*. London: Deutsch.
Nielson, William A. 1964. *Webster's biographical dictionary*. Springfield, Mass.: Merriam.
Stephen, Leslie, and Lee, Sydney, eds. 1917. *The dictionary of national biography*. London: Oxford University Press.

BRADDON'S BLOT. A clause in Australia's constitution which states that for the first ten years after federation the Commonwealth government would have one-fourth of the customs and excise revenue, and the balance would go to the states.

Edward Nicholas Coventry Braddon (1829–1904) was born at Saint Kew, Cornwall, and educated in London and at University College. In 1847 he went to Calcutta, India, as a clerk in his cousin's firm, and later he went to an indigo factory, Krishnagar. After an administrator's career and military service in India, Braddon settled in northwest Tasmania and used his administrative skills to advance himself in local politics. In 1877 he was appointed minister of lands and later was Tasmania's agent-general in London, where he induced investors to support railways and mining ventures in Tasmania. He was knighted in 1891 and returned to the colony in 1893 to support opposition policies in government. From 1894 to 1899 he was the colony's premier, restored Tasmania's economy, and introduced proportional representation in elections. He introduced section 87 of the Australian constitution, so that three-quarters of the revenue from customs and excise taxes would be returned to the states for ten years. Immediately, this was called "Braddon's blot" on the Australian constitution.

Source

Pike, Douglas, et al., eds. 1966–90. *Australian dictionary of biography.* Melbourne: Melbourne University Press.

BRADLEYAN. Relating to the ideas of the nineteenth-century British idealist philosopher.

Francis Herbert Bradley (1846–1924) was one of the twenty-two children of the Reverend Charles Bradley, an Evangelical preacher. Francis was born in London and educated at Oxford, and he became a fellow of Merton College in 1870. He drew on the ideas of Hegel (1770–1831), and disagreed with the utilitarians and Herbert Spencer (1820–1903) in the belief that to realize oneself an individual should integrate his or her works with the context in which they are done. In metaphysics he thought nature was an imperfect representation of the Absolute, a self-sufficient spirit that needed nothing for its sense of completeness. His ethics and logic made him a leading figure in the idealist school of philosophy; his system greatly influenced the early Bertrand Russell (1872–1970) and, indirectly, Ludwig Wittgenstein (1889–1951). Bradley was determined "to let nothing stand in the way of an honest enquiry into truth." Among his most noted works are *Ethical Studies* (1876), *The Principles of Logic* (1883), *The Appearance of Reality* (1893), and *Essays on Truth and Reality* (1914).

Sources

Law, M. D., and Dixon, M. Vibart, eds. 1966. *Chambers encyclopedia.* London: Pergamon Press.

Magnussen, Magnus; Goring, Rosemary; and Thorn, John O., eds. 1990. *Chambers biographical dictionary.* Edinburgh: Chambers Ltd.

Wollheim, Richard. 1959. *F. H. Bradley.* Harmondsworth: Penguin.

BRADY BILL. A gun control measure in the United States that was introduced after the attempted assassination of President Ronald Reagan in 1981.

James Scott Brady (b. 1940) was born in Centralia, Illinois, and graduated from the local high school and the University of Illinois. In 1962 he joined the Young Republicans and worked for Everett M. Dirksen (R-Ill.). He studied briefly at law school and turned to teaching and accounting, before taking up a career in public relations and politics for the Illinois State Medical Society (1966). Eventually, he went to Washington as a communications consultant to the House of Representatives and served notables like Richard Nixon and Gerald Ford (1973–77). In 1980 he joined President Reagan's team and became his press secretary, but on March 30, 1981, he was wounded in an assassination attempt on the president. After extensive surgery, he slowly improved but did not fully recover. In 1985 his wife became interested in gun control laws, but

Brady, still a White House employee, was not able to join her due to the powerful gun lobby that the Republicans supported. In 1988 he began supporting limits on access to the "Saturday Night Special," a readily concealed handgun commonly used in urban crimes. In September 1988 when the Brady Hand Gun Violence Protection Act was defeated, Brady went to Capitol Hill to have the vote reversed. The Judiciary House Committee approved the bill in 1990, and to generally great surprise Ronald Reagan endorsed it personally (1991). President Bush was obliged to give it only limited support in the face of the opposition of the gun lobby.

In late November 1993 debate on the Brady Bill ended and it went to a conference committee to be reconciled with a version passed by the House. The bill proposed a waiting period of five days before a gun may be bought by a purchaser. To some people the bill is an achievement, but to others it is a mere symbol because it does nothing about the 100 million handguns now in circulation in the United States. The bill became law in 1994. Today Brady works for the National Organization on Disability and for Handgun Control Inc. in Washington.

Sources

Dickensen, Mollie. 1987. *Thumbs up: the life and courageous comeback of White House press secretary, Jim Brady.* New York: William Morrow.

Gibbs, Nancy. 1993. Bill Clinton's watchwords: law and order. *Time,* August 23: 44–45.

The international who's who, 1992–93. London: Europa Publications.

Moritz, Charles, ed. 1991. *Current biography yearbook.* New York: H. W. Wilson.

BRADY COMMISSION, BRADY PLAN. A U.S. commission, established in the wake of the October 1987 stock market crash, which recommended that only one institution, the U.S. Federal Reserve system, should coordinate financial regulation: clearing systems should be unified to cut financial risks; information on trade, time of trade, and the final communications in each market should be improved; rules on margins should be integrated; and across markets the circuit breakers—price limits or halting of trade—should be coordinated. The plan was intended to overcome the United States' imbalance of international trade in the late 1980s.

Nicholas Frederick Brady (b. 1930), a Wall Street investment banker, a pragmatic and moderate Republican, and a friend of President Bush, was born in New York. He was educated at an exclusive private school, studied at Yale, and completed an M.B.A. at Harvard Business School (1954). He became a vice-president of Dillon, Read & Company after financing a new company in the technology for recycling newsprint. By 1971 he was the president of the reorganized Dillon, Read. He became an active Republican, worked for George Bush's campaign in 1980, and was appointed to the U.S. Senate to take the vacancy of the Democrat, Harrison A. Williams. In his first speech, Brady called for cuts in Social Security. In December 1982 he resigned from the Senate—

an organization whose members he said he admired but whose counterproductiveness he found frustrating—to give a newly elected Democrat senator, Frank R. Lautenberg, an advantage in seniority over other freshman senators. President Reagan appointed him to the National Bi-partisan Commission on Central America. Brady came to public attention when, at Bush's suggestion, after the stock market crash of October 1987, he was appointed by James A. Baker, secretary of the Treasury, to President Reagan's Task Force on Market Mechanisms. The committee comprised Robert R. Glauber, James C. Cotting, Robert G. Kirby, John R. Opel, and Howard S. Stein. It found that the crash was caused primarily by two recently developed computerized trading techniques used by large firms: (1) portfolio insurance trading, which was a hedge against losses when large amounts of stock were sold quickly, and (2) stock index arbitrage, which exploited small differences between real (actual) and anticipated (future) stock prices. The report was received cooly by most of the president's administration, the Federal Reserve Bank, and investors who did not like too much regulation of markets. Brady succeeded Baker as secretary of the Treasury in August 1988. The Brady Plan assumed that a balance in America's international trade could be achieved through sound investments that would yield good returns in the long run; accordingly, Brady aimed to wean managers away from attempting to make quick profits and to seek sound, long term investments (Brady, 1989). Upon President Bush's defeat in the 1992 presidential election, Brady's plans folded.

Sources

Brady, Nicholas F. 1989. Dealing with the international debt crisis. *Department of State Bulletin,* 89, May: 53–56.

The international who's who, 1992–93. London: Europa Publications.

Moritz, Charles, ed. 1988. *Current biography yearbook.* New York: H. W. Wilson.

Rutherford, Donald. 1992. *Dictionary of economics.* London: Routledge.

Who's who in America, 1992–93. Chicago: Marquis.

BRANDT REPORT. A report of the Independent Commission on International Development Issues (1980) in West Germany. The commission, opened in December 1977, was chaired by Willy Brandt and included distinguished men and women from noncommunist countries. The commission's aim was to consider worldwide problems raised by the inequitable distribution of economic and social opportunities and poverty.

Willy (Herbert Frahm) Brandt (1913–92), German chancellor, Nobel Peace Prize winner, was educated at Lübeck and established himself as a socialist propagandist. After Hitler came to power, Brandt went to Norway, became a citizen, and during the German occupation in World War II worked with the Norwegian underground. After the war, he returned to German politics and became a member of the Bundestag (1949). In 1957 he became Oberbürgermeister of West Berlin and in 1960 he succeeded Eric Ollenhauer as leader of the West German Social Democratic party. He was chancellor during 1969–72 and resigned following the arrest of one of his secretaries as a communist spy. Among his writings are *The Ordeal of Co-existence* (1963) and *Reflections and Letters* (1971).

Sources

Boleesch, Hermann O., and Leicht, Hans D. 1971. *Willy Brandt, a portrait of the German chancellor.* Trans. Alice Denes. Tübingen: Erdman.

Harpprecht, Klaus. 1972. *Brandt: portrait and self-portrait.* London: Abelard-Schuman.

Prittie, Terence C.F. 1974. *Willy Brandt: portrait of a statesman.* London: Weidenfeld and Nicolson.

BRETTON WOODS SYSTEM. In July 1944, at Bretton Woods, New Hampshire, an international agreement was reached to secure world trade and settle international payments. Among the economic problems raised between 1919 and 1939 had been nonpayment of First World War debts, the economic Depression, trade wars, gold and silver currency standards, and volatility of export earnings. Two schemes were offered—one based on the work of the British economist John Maynard Keynes, and the other from Harry White of the U.S. Treasury. White's scheme was favored. To secure world trade and international payments after World War II, the International Monetary Fund was created, and the International Bank for Reconstruction and Development was established. In addition, the U.S. dollar became the international currency, and gold was set at US$35 per ounce. The system was effective until about 1973 when it ended due to uneven growth of world income and the differing money policies of the fast-growing industrial nations.

In 1769 Bretton Woods was established in Strafford County, New Hampshire, and named after the English seat of the earls of Strafford. The county, as well as a town in Vermont so named (1761), were given their titles because the earl of Strafford in the 1760s was a kinsman of Benning and John Wentworth, governors of New Hampshire.

Sources

Eatwell, John; Milgate, Murray; and Newman, Peter. 1987. *The new Palgrave: a dictionary of economics.* London: Macmillan.

Greenwald, D., ed. 1982. *Encyclopedia of economics.* New York: McGraw-Hill.

Stewart, George R. 1970. *American place-names: a concise and selective dictionary for the continental United States of America.* New York: Oxford University Press.

BREZHNEV DOCTRINE. A doctrine stated by the first secretary of the Soviet Communist party on November 12, 1968, which asserted the right of the Soviet Union and its allies to control any territory of one of its members that came under attack by hostile forces from both inside and outside the territory. Western commentators coined the term in response to Soviet repression in Czechoslovakia earlier in 1968.

Leonid Il'ch Brezhnev (1906–82) was born in Kamenskoe (now Dneprodzerzhinks) and began work as a surveyor and agricultural administrator. He joined the Communist party in 1931, graduated in metallurgy in 1939, and became a senior political officer in the Russian Army in World War II. He was first secretary of the Central Committee of the party in Moldavia (1950) and a member of the party's Central Committee in 1952. On Stalin's death he was appointed deputy head of the political administration of the armed forces (1953). After serving under Nikita Khrushchev, he became a member of the Presidium and head of state in 1960. He succeeded Khrushchev as party leader in 1964 until his death in 1982. He is best remembered for the doctrine that arose from the invasion of Czechoslovakia where Soviet domination seemed under threat. However, his eighteen years were noted generally for their stagnation and corruption, and in particular for the use of the KGB to ensure that the Helsinki Agreement was never properly met and that psychiatric techniques and procedures were used to control dissidents.

See also HELSINKI ACCORD.

Sources

Dornberg, John. 1974. *Brezhnev: the masks of power.* London: Deutsch.

Edmonds, Robin. 1983. *Soviet foreign policy: the Brezhnev years.* Oxford: Oxford University Press.

Mitchell, R. Judson. 1978. A new Brezhnev doctrine: the restructuring of international relations. *World Politics* 30:366–390.

Shafritz, Jay M. 1988. *The Dorsey dictionary of American government and politics.* Chicago: Dorsey.

Vronskaya, Jeanne. 1989. *A biographical dictionary of the Soviet Union 1917–1988.* London: K. G. Saur.

BROCARD. A brief maxim or proverb in philosophy, an elementary law, a canon, or a jibe or biting speech.

Bishop Burchard (French: Brocard) of Worms (965–1025) was educated at the Benedictine Abbey, Lobbes, and was ordained in Mainz where he was its first judge and chamberlain. He was made the bishop of Worms by Emperor Otto III in 1000. He helped to build Worms and to restore the morale of its people after the many attacks by the Hungarians. As a civil and ecclesiastical leader, he pursued a balanced view in the preparation of canon law. He developed a code of laws for feudal subjects in Worms, sat on several councils, helped establish several sees, and advocated important reforms. His major work, *Decretum collectorium* or *Brocardus (Brocardia),* summarized canon law and directives in twenty volumes. They were written in brief and sententious prose, and his name became associated with brief statements in law and philosophy.

Sources

Hendrickson, Robert. 1988. *The dictionary of eponyms: names that became words.* New York: Dorset.

Meagher, Paul K.; O'Brien, Thomas C.; and Aherne, Marie, eds. 1979. *Encyclopedic dictionary of religion.* Washington, D.C.: Corpus Publications.

BROKAW HAZARD. An error of judgment that may arise when following the notable U.S. television interviewer's advice: "Most of the clues I get from people are verbal, not physical. I don't look at a person's face for signs he is lying. What I'm after are convoluted answers or sophisticated evasion." The hazard involves failing to take account of individual differences in emotional expression; some people are habitually convoluted and evasive in their discussions. The error was made in a publicity interview by John Weisman (1977), and the hazard was noted in a social psychological study of lies by Paul Ekman (1985).

Thomas John Brokaw (b. 1940) was born in Webster, South Dakota, and attended public schools. He became interested in politics at an early age, as well as the NBC-TV Huntley–Brinkley Report in the late 1950s and 1960s. At the University of South Dakota he studied political science and became a news journalist on KMTV, part of the NBC network. By 1973 he had become a White House correspondent in Washington, by 1974 was noted as a popular young news interviewer, and spent much time on the Watergate scandals. In his characteristically forthright style, Brokaw interviewed such luminaries as Gerald Ford and by 1976 became the sole host on NBC's "Today" show, when the network agreed that he need not read commercials. Although Brokaw was sometimes tough with interviewees on the show, his intelligent, informed, relaxed interviewing style earned him a fine reputation.

Sources

Ekman, Paul. 1985. *Telling lies: clues to deceit in the market place, politics and marriage.* New York: W. W. Norton.
Moritz, Charles, ed. 1981. *Current biography yearbook.* New York: H. W. Wilson.
Weisman, John. 1977. The truth will out. *TV guide.* September 3:13.

BROTHER JONATHAN. An early, legendary name for America and its inhabitants.

Jonathan Trumbull (1710–85) was born in Lebanon, Connecticut, and graduated from Harvard in 1727. For thirty-five years he was a successful merchant, but in 1766 his business failed and he was almost bankrupt. He was a member of the Governor's Council (1740–54) and deputy governor of Connecticut (1766) for almost four years, a chief justice of the Superior Court, and then governor (1769–84). A strong supporter of colonial rights, he took a radical position—the only state governor to do so—on hostilities with Britain. He was an adviser to and close friend of George Washington. According to legend, once, when Washington needed ammunition and his advisers could not help him, he said: "We must consult Brother Jonathan." Because Trumbull had the answer to the problem, Washington said in reference to his services that he was justly entitled to "first place among patriots." In time the phrase "to consult Brother Jonathan" became a proverb, and by 1816 "Brother Jonathan" came to mean an American.

Sources

Malone, Dumas, ed. 1932. *Dictionary of American biography.* Vol. V. New York: Charles Scribner's Sons.

Preston, Wheeler. 1974. *American biographies.* New York: Harper and Brothers. Detroit: Gale Research.

BROWNIST. One who holds church principles similar to those of the Independents or Congregationalists of England.

Robert Browne (c. 1550–c. 1633), was born at Tolethorp, Rutlandshire, in England. He was educated at Cambridge and subsequently preached at Cambridge and elsewhere. In about 1580 at Norwich, he organized a congregation of dissenters who became known as Brownists. Finding themselves persecuted by ecclesiastical authorities, they followed Browne's leadership to Middleburg, Holland, in 1581. Following dissension among his followers in 1583, Browne left Holland and in three years was master of Stamford Grammar School; in 1591, after becoming reconciled to the church, he was appointed a rector in Northamptonshire. When he was over 80 years of age, he was jailed for assaulting a constable; in his cell he became ill and died.

Sources

Cross, Frank L. 1974. *The Oxford dictionary of the Christian Church.* 2d ed. New York: Oxford University Press.

Douglas, James D., ed. 1974. *The new international dictionary of the Christian Church.* Exeter: Paternoster Press.

Eliade, Mircea, ed. 1987. *Encyclopedia of religion.* New York: Macmillan.

Hastings, James, ed. 1920. *Encyclopedia of religion and ethics.* New York: T. and T. Clark.

McHenry, Robert, ed. 1992. *The new encyclopedia Britannica.* Chicago: Encyclopedia Britannica, Inc.

Stephen, Leslie, and Lee, Sydney, eds. 1917. *The dictionary of national biography.* London: Oxford University Press.

BROWNLOW COMMITTEE. A committee of three men—Charles E. Merriam (1874–1953), Luther Gulick (b. 1892), and Louis Brownlow (1879–1963)—appointed by President Franklin D. Roosevelt to analyze and recommend the staffing requirements of the executive branch of the U.S. presidency in 1936. The committee recommended that the president needed helpers who were prepared to work anonymously and not receive immediate public recognition. In 1939 the U.S. Congress gave the president permission to restructure the executive branch agencies. The executive office of the president was created with six assistants; today it has over 100 assistants.

Louis Brownlow was born in Buffalo, Missouri, and was educated at home because of a childhood illness. He became a newspaperman in Tennessee and later Washington, and then for the Haskin Syndicate, worldwide (1906–15). Between 1915 and 1920 he was commissioner of the District of Columbia, then city manager of Petersburg, Virginia (1920–23), Knoxville, Tennessee (1924–26), and the experimental community at Radburn, New Jersey (1927–31). In 1931 he taught political science at the University of Chicago and later was appointed director of the Public Administration Clearing House in Chicago

(1931–45). He served various organizations of professional government administrators. One of these was the chairmanship of the President's Committee on Administrative Management (1936–37).

Sources

Brownlow, Louis. 1955. *A passion for anonymity: the autobiography of Louis Brownlow: first half.* Chicago: University of Chicago Press.

Brownlow, Louis. 1958. *A passion for politics: the autobiography of Louis Brownlow: second half.* Chicago: University of Chicago Press.

Fesler, James W. 1987. The Brownlow Committee fifty years later. *Public Administration Review* 47:291–296.

Karl, Barry D. 1963. *Executive reorganization and reform in the New Deal.* Cambridge, Mass.: Harvard University Press.

Karl, Barry D. 1979. Louis Brownlow. *Public Administration Review* 39:511–516.

Shafritz, Jay M. 1988. *The Dorsey dictionary of American government and politics.* Chicago: Dorsey.

Who's who in America, 1961–68. Chicago: Marquis.

BRUTUS. A treacherous person.

Marcus Junius Brutus (85–42 B.C.), also known as Quintus Caepio Brutus after his adoptive father Quintus Servilius Caepio, the descendant of Lucius Brutus, took the side of Pompey in the civil war between Pompey and Caesar. He was pardoned by Caesar and given high office, but later he led the conspiracy to murder Caesar and replace him with Lucius and thereby restore the republic. After Caesar's death, Brutus fled to Greece and later committed suicide. Brutus is also remembered as a political idealist; in Shakespeare's *Julius Caesar* he was "the noblest Roman of all." The same image appears in Michelangelo's bust of Brutus.

Sources

Brunt, Peter A. 1988. *The fall of the Roman republic and related essays.* Oxford: Oxford University Press.

Grant, Michael. 1978. *History of Rome.* London: Weidenfeld and Nicolson.

McHenry, Robert, ed. 1992. *The new encyclopedia Britannica.* Chicago: Encyclopedia Britannica, Inc.

BRYCE REPORT (1895). A British Royal Commission on secondary education (1895), which recommended a central authority be established for secondary education, the extension of local authorities' responsibilities for elementary and secondary education, and provision of scholarships for elementary school pupils. The report is noted for finding that few places were available for girls in secondary schools.

James Bryce (1838–1922). See BRYCE REPORT (1915).

Sources

Aldrich, Richard, and Gordon, Peter. 1987. *Dictionary of British educationists.* London: Woburn Press.

Blishen, Edward. 1969. *Blond's encyclopaedia of education.* London: Blond Educational.

Law, M. D., and Dixon, M. Vibart, eds. 1966. *Chambers encyclopedia.* London: Pergamon Press.

Magnussen, Magnus; Goring, Rosemary; and Thorn, John O., eds. 1990. *Chambers biographical dictionary.* Edinburgh: Chambers Ltd.

Oxbury, Harold. 1985. *Great Britons.* Oxford: Oxford University Press.

Weaver, John R.H., ed. 1937. *Dictionary of national biography 1922–1930.* London: Oxford University Press.

BRYCE REPORT (1915). A British report on German military actions in Belgium during World War I. When the report was issued, British and U.S. newspapers condemned Germany for its atrocities. In truth, much of the information had been invented, and little effort went into its evaluation. Today the report is regarded as official propaganda that paraded as a legal investigation.

James Bryce, Viscount Bryce (1838–1922), was born in Belfast, but at age 8 he was taken by the family to Glasgow where he went to school. Six years later he returned to Belfast and was raised by his uncle, attended Belfast Academy, and went to Glasgow University. He studied law and history at Trinity College, Oxford, and became a fellow of Oriel College. He studied and traveled in Europe, and was at the bar (1867–82). As assistant commissioner of the Schools Inquiry Commission (1865–67), he advocated coordinating education at three levels—elementary, secondary, and university—and strongly supported the education of women. He taught law at Owens College, Manchester, until 1874, was elected to Parliament (1880–1906); was chancellor of the Duchy of Lancaster (1892–94) and president of the Board of Trade (1894–95); and later, in 1907, was made Britain's ambassador to Washington. Many universities honored him, and although he had refused a peerage in 1907, he was created a viscount in 1914. He wrote *Studies in Contemporary Biography* (1903) and *Modern Democracies* (1921). He was one of a small group responsible for the formation of the League of Nations. In September 1915 he presided over the commission established to consider breaches of law and of established uses of war that Germany was alleged to have committed, especially in Belgium. The report concluded that the Germans had been excessively violent so as to terrorize the civilians and lower morale in Belgium's army.

Sources

Ker, Philip, ed. 1990. *The Penguin book of lies.* London: Viking Press.

Weaver, John R.H., ed. 1937. *Dictionary of national biography 1922–1930.* London: Oxford University Press.

BUCHMANISM. Beliefs held by members of the Oxford Group movement that life changes can produce changes in the world. To do this, the Oxford Group members described their religious experiences and sought guidance from God.

Frank Nathan Daniel Buchman (1878–1961) was born in Pennsburg, Pennsylvania. After visits to the Near and Far East, he believed that most civilizations were about to end. In 1921, on a visit to Oxford, he lectured and founded Oxford

Groups. Later he led groups around the world to extend the influence of his idea that the world needed to be morally rearmed under a dictatorship of God and absolute moral standards. In the 1930s he supported appeasement of Nazi Germany, praising Hitler for his defense against "the anti-Christ of Communism." He introduced the "Moral Re-Armament" movement to the United States in 1938, and that year published his *Moral Re-armament.* During World War II his influence waned. Later he published *Remaking the World* (1949) and *The World Rebuilt* (1951).

Sources

Burke, William J., and Howe, Will D., eds. 1962. *American authors and books.* New York: Crown.

Moritz, Charles, ed. 1961. *Current biography yearbook.* New York: H. W. Wilson.

Van Doren, Charles, ed. 1974. *Webster's American biographies.* Springfield, Mass.: Merriam.

Vernoff, Edward, and Shore, Rima, eds. 1987. *International dictionary of 20th century biography.* New York: New American Library.

BUDDHISM. An Asian religion whose followers believe that pain is an essential part of their life and that only with moral and mental purification can one be free of suffering.

Siddhartha Gautama, a Rajput prince (c. 560–440 B.C.), was early in his youth interested in all living things, especially their distress and sufferings. He gave up all his material world—wealth, marriage, family—and wandered as a monk. All humans will suffer, he believed, because of their hostility to one another, ignorance, and self-centered existence. Through contemplation, these shortcomings could be rectified, and life's miseries excised. He taught that he was one of a line of Buddhas who appear at intervals in the world and speak the same doctrine of enlightenment, which is the meaning of the name. After the death of each Buddha, the religion he espouses flourishes, is forgotten and decays, and reappears with the next Buddha and the lost truth or dharma. These teachings spread through the East and eventually to Europe. Like his contemporary, Confucius, Buddha left no written word.

Sources

Carrithers, Michael. 1983. *The Buddha.* Oxford: Oxford University Press.

Carrithers, Michael. 1989. *Founders of faith.* Oxford: Oxford University Press.

McHenry, Robert, ed. 1992. *The new encyclopedia Britannica.* Chicago: Encyclopedia Britannica, Inc.

Malalasekera, George P. 1961–77. *Encyclopedia of Buddhism.* 3 vols. Sri Lanka: Government Printing.

Meagher, Paul K.; O'Brien, Thomas C.; and Aherne, Marie, eds. 1979. *Encyclopedic dictionary of religion.* Washington, D.C.: Corpus Publications.

BULLOCK REPORTS. Two reports by British Committees of Inquiry. The first, *A Language for Life (1975),* inquired into the teaching of English and recommended 333 improvements, most of which were largely ignored by the government, but many had a major impact on teaching practices and the education of teachers. The second report, *Industrial Democracy (1977),* inquired into the best means of establishing industrial democracy using employee representation on the Board of Directors, which was Labor government policy. The recommendations suggested that employees be appointed to the boards of all companies with more than 2,000 workers, but industrialist members of the committee rejected this proposal and much controversy ensued. James Callaghan, the Labor prime minister, established a committee that made recommendations and proposals slightly different from the Bullock Report. Industrial democracy was no longer acceptable in Britain after the 1979 election, although both the Labor party and the SDP-Liberal alliance were committed to worker participation in their policies.

Alan Louis Charles Bullock, Baron, a life peer (b. 1914), was educated at Bradford Grammar School and Wadham College, Oxford (D.Litt., 1969). He was a fellow, dean, and tutor in modern history at New College (1945–52), and censor of Saint Catherine's Society, Oxford (1952–62). He chaired a research committee of the Royal Institute of International Affairs (1954–78) and was on the National Advisory Council on the training and supply of teachers (1963–65) and the Schools' Council (1966–69). He was also on the Committee on Reading and Other Uses of the English Language and the Committee of Inquiry on Industrial Democracy (1976), as well as on the Organizing Committee of the British Library (1971–72) in addition to many other appointments. Among his publications are *Hitler: A Study of Tyranny* (1952; rev. 1964); *The Liberal Tradition* (1956); and *The Life and Times of Ernest Bevin* (1960–83). He helped edit *The 20th Century* (1971) and the *Dictionary of Modern Thought* (1977; 1988), the *Fontana Dictionary of Modern Thinkers* (1983), and *Hitler and Stalin: Parallel Lives* (1991).

Sources

Elliott, John. 1978. *Conflict or cooperation? The growth of industrial democracy.* 2d ed., 1984. London: Kogan Page.

Who's who, 1991. London: Adam and Charles Black.

BUMBLEDOM. Bumptious conceit and official arrogance of minor authority or petty official.

Charles Dickens's *Oliver Twist* (1836) featured a high and mighty beadle named Mr. Bumble. He was a stout, hard-hearted, self-important, and fussy official. After marrying Mrs. Corney, Mr. Bumble was much reduced in his personal authority, and eventually he ended his working life in the workhouse where he once ruled.

Sources

Benét, William R. 1988. *The readers' encyclopedia: an encyclopedia of world literature and arts, with supplement.* New York: Thomas Y. Crowell.

Drabble, Margaret, ed. 1985. *Oxford companion to English literature.* 5th ed. London: Oxford University Press.

BURCHETT INTERVIEW, BURCHETT DECLARATION. An interview conducted by the controversial Australian journalist with Vietnam's foreign minister, Nguyen Duy Trinh (1967), in which Nguyen challenged the U.S. president Lyndon Johnson to peace talks on Vietnam. On a visit to London in 1967, Alexei Kosygin, the Russian leader, used the interview as an outline for peace negotiations, while the Hanoi government, through Mai Van Bo, called the interview the Burchett Declaration.

Wilfred Graham Burchett (1911–83), son of a builder in Australia, left home in 1936 and joined the Society for Cultural Relations with Russia in England, and worked for Intourist and for the release of Jews from Germany, before returning to Australia in 1939 to become a war correspondent in the Pacific and Asia. His personal scoop was a fine eyewitness account of Hiroshima in 1945. Back in London, and later as a Berlin correspondent for *The Times,* he made enduring contacts with the KGB. He returned to Australia in 1950 to lecture against the banning of the Australian Communist party and nuclear armament, and he went on to report on cease-fire talks in the Korean War. He is alleged to have used POWs for propaganda interviews against the West. He reported on the Vietnam War, supported the Viet Cong cause, and in 1967 arranged for a leading New York journalist to visit Hanoi, and subsequently planned the interview that bears his name. As a well-known agent of influence, he visited President Nixon and Secretary of State Henry Kissinger in 1971 to tell them Hanoi would not negotiate peace terms; he also arranged for Jane Fonda to visit Hanoi and scripted her talks (1972). Later he went on a fund-raising lecture tour of the United States, defending all aspects of communist rule in many lands (1977).

Sources

Burchett, Wilfred G. 1969. *Passport: an autobiography.* Melbourne: Thomas Nelson.

Burchett, Wilfred G. 1981. *Memoirs of rebel journalist: at the barricades.* South Melbourne: Macmillan.

Manne, Robert. 1989. *Agent of influence: the life and times of Wilfred Burchett.* Toronto: Mackenzie Institute.

Perry, Roland. 1988. *The exile: Burchett, reporter of conflict.* Richmond, Victoria: Heinemann, Australia.

Perry, Roland. 1993. How the KGB used Wilfred Burchett. *The Age,* March 6: Extra 5.

Wilde, William H.; Hooton, Joy; and Andrew, Barry. 1985. *The Oxford companion to Australian literature.* Melbourne: Oxford University Press.

BURGESS MARRIAGE ADJUSTMENT SCALE. A scale of marriage adjustment that includes questions on the couples' degree of agreement and critical issues; common interests and joint activities; frequency of overt demonstrations of affection and mutual confidence; complaints; feelings of loneliness, misery, and irritability (Miller, 1991).

Ernest Watson Burgess (1886–1966) was born in Ontario, Canada, and raised in Oklahoma. He studied at Kingfisher College, Kingfisher, and at the University of Chicago (Ph.D., 1913). He taught at the universities of Toledo, Kansas, and Ohio State, after beginning his career at the University of Chicago (1916–51). He was an urban sociologist with a strong interest in the family and aging. He considered the family in real terms—"unity of interacting personalities"— rather than as an idealized institution. After studies on the success and failure of parole systems, he turned to the study of success and failure in marriage. He saw engaged couples after three to five years of marriage and concluded that homogeneity of attitudes among partners contributed greatly to the stability of marriage. He also studied the changing economic roles in families as the parents aged. In general, he raised the status of family studies in sociological research. He was president of the American Sociological Association and a member of the Sociological Research Association, the National Conference on Family Relations, and the Gerontological Society. He co-authored works on urban sociology, the family, delinquency, engagement, and marriage.

Sources

Burgess, Ernest W., and Cottrell, Leonard S. 1939. *Predicting success or failure in marriage.* Englewood, Cliffs, N.J.: Prentice-Hall.

Burgess, Ernest W., and Locke, Harvey J. 1960. *The family.* 2d ed. New York: American Books.

Miller, Delbert C. 1991. *Handbook of research design and social measurement.* 5th ed. Newbury Park, Calif.: Sage Publications.

Sills, David L., ed. 1968. *International encyclopedia of the social sciences.* New York: Macmillan and Free Press.

BURIDAN'S ASS. A widely known philosophical sophism, of dubious origin, concerning the choice given to a hungry animal—a dog, not an ass—between equidistant sources of food.

Jean Buridan, Joannes or John Buridanus (fl. c. 1295–1366), was born at Bethune, Artois. After studying under William of Occam, he gave philosophy lectures and became a notable logician at the University of Paris, where eventually he was appointed rector (1328). The story of "Buridan's Ass" helped schoolmen show the failure of the will to take action when subject to equally powerful motives. The story tells of a hungry ass placed between two equidistant bundles of hay and how it starves to death because it cannot make the choice between the two bundles. Some sources record that in his commentary on Aristotle's *De caelo* Buridan used the example of a dog, not an ass; other sources state that Buridan is incorrectly regarded as the author of the sophism; and still others suggest that the sophism was from an opponent of Buridan who intended to ridicule his ideas on determinism. Both Aristotle and Dante mention the sophism.

Sources

Cross, Frank L. 1974. *The Oxford dictionary of the Christian Church.* 2d ed. New York: Oxford University Press.

Law, M. D., and Dixon, M. Vibart, eds. 1966. *Chambers encyclopedia.* London: Pergamon Press.

McHenry, Robert, ed. 1992. *The new encyclopedia Britannica.* Chicago: Encyclopedia
      Britannica, Inc.
Smith, Benjamin. 1903. *The Century cyclopedia of names.* London: The Times.

BURKE MODEL. A form of commercial collaboration between government
and business based on cronyism, the abuse of fiscal responsibility, and denial
of public accountability. This was a political development characteristic of the
1980s Australian Labor party with its pragmatism, corporatism, and the "rich
mates" syndrome. The Burke Model refers to the former West Australian premier who helped rescue Rothwell's Bank after the October 19, 1987 market
crash. He would make deals with businessmen outside the state cabinet and seal
them with issues of government credit. The policy was intended to restore confidence in the West Australian economy.

Honorable Brian Thomas Burke (b. 1947) was educated at Marist Brothers
College in Subiaco, Western Australia, and at the University of Western Australia. He became a journalist on local newspapers and television before entering
Parliament as a member of the Australian Labor party. He became a shadow
minister in 1976 and later, during 1981–83, the leader of the opposition. When
in government, he was minister of women's interests, tourism and forests, and
premier, treasurer, and minister for public sector management. He was a justice
of the peace, and in 1988–91 he was Australian ambassador to the Republic of
Ireland and the Holy See. On June 16, 1992, he was charged on five counts of
misusing public money, misappropriating about $17,500 during 1983–86, and
making false claims on expense accounts.

Sources

Hamilton, John. 1988. *Burkie: a biography of Brian Burke.* Perth, Western Australia: St.
      George Books.
O'Brien, Patrick, and Webb, Martyn J., eds. 1991. *The executive state: WA Inc and the
      constitution.* Perth, Western Australia: Constitutional Press.
Who's who in Australia, 1988. Melbourne: Herald and Weekly Times.
Who's who in Australia, 1991. London: Adam and Charles Black.

BURKE'S PEERAGE. An alphabetical catalogue of the British aristocracy.

John Burke (1787–1848) was born in Tipperary and undertook literary work
in London, but he became interested in genealogical research instead. He published *A Genealogical and Heraldic History of the Peerage and Baronetage of
the United Kingdom* (1826). It was issued again in 1847 and ever since has
appeared annually. It was the first time such a compilation had been arranged
alphabetically, and it included peers and baronets together. Burke's son, Sir John
Bernard, a barrister, assisted Burke and began annual re-editing. Burke also
published *Burke's London Gentry* (1833–38).

Sources

McHenry, Robert, ed. 1992. *The new encyclopedia Britannica.* Chicago: Encyclopedia
      Britannica, Inc.

Stephen, Leslie, and Lee, Sydney, eds. 1917. *The dictionary of national biography.* London: Oxford University Press.

BURNHAM COMMITTEES. British standing joint committees appointed to review and make recommendations on teachers' remuneration. The first Burnham Committee was established in 1919, but in time three committees were chosen, one each for elementary, secondary, and technical schools.

Harry Lawson Webster Levy Burnham, first Viscount (1862–1933), was born in London, the eldest son of the first Baron Burnham, and educated at Eton and Balliol College, Oxford. He studied modern history and became a barrister, Inner Temple (1889). He was a member of the Royal Commission on Civil Establishments (1889–94) and the Speaker's Conference on Electoral Reform (1916), and attended the joint conference on the reform of the House of Lords under Lord Bryce in 1918. Meanwhile, he was managing proprietor of the *Daily Telegraph* (1902–28) and succeeded his father as Baron Burnham in 1916, was made a Companion of Honor in 1917, and was created Viscount Burnham in 1919. He is best remembered for his work as chairman of the Standing Joint Committee, consisting of teachers and local education authority representatives, to establish pay scales for teachers in state schools.

Sources

Aldrich, R., and Gordon, P. 1987. *Dictionary of British educationists.* London: Woburn Press.

Legg, Leopold G.W., ed. 1949. *Dictionary of national biography 1931–1940.* London: Oxford University Press.

Magnussen, Magnus; Goring, Rosemary; and Thorn, John O., eds. 1990. *Chambers biographical dictionary.* Edinburgh: Chambers Ltd.

Marsh, Arthur. 1979. *Concise encyclopedia of industrial relations.* Westmead, Farnborough, Hants: Gower.

BURT AFFAIR. The controversy surrounding the research of the twentieth-century British psychologist and educationist.

Sir Cyril Burt (1883–1971) was born in London, the son of a doctor who also kept a chemist shop. Cyril was educated at a Board School and at King's School, Warwick. He won a scholarship to Christ's Hospital, London (1895–1902), read widely, went on a scholarship to Jesus College, Oxford (1902–6), and studied briefly at the University of Würzburg (1908). He taught at the University of Liverpool during 1908–12, was psychologist to the London County Council during 1913–32, and became a professor of psychology at University College, London. He published *The Young Delinquent* (1925), *The Backward Child* (1937), and *The Factors of the Mind* (1940), and edited the *British Journal of Statistical Psychology* until 1963. Although he thought the roots of delinquency lay in the environment, to him intelligence was largely inherited, as he claimed his research showed. However, in 1974 he was accused of fraud after two scholars—one an environmentalist and the other an hereditarian—

conflicted over the reporting of his correlations. In 1976 the *Sunday Times* (London) medical correspondent accused Burt of fraud. Burt's official biographer, Leslie Hearnshaw (1979), argued that Burt's later work was unsound because Burt had Ménière's disease. By 1984 Burt was portrayed as a dishonest schemer, but recent research suggests his critics overstated their case.

Sources

Fletcher, Ronald. 1991. *Science, ideology, and the media: the Cyril Burt scandal.* New Brunswick, N.J.: Transaction Books.

Green, Bert F. 1992. Expose or smear? The Burt affair. *Psychological Science* 3:328–331.

Hearnshaw, Leslie S. 1979. *Cyril Burt: psychologist.* London: Hodder and Stoughton.

Joyson, Robert B. 1989. *The Burt affair.* London: Routledge and Kegan Paul.

Zusne, Leonard. 1984. *Biographical dictionary of psychology.* Westport, Conn.: Greenwood Press.

BUSH PLAN, BUSHSPEAK, BUSHUSURU. The Bush Plan was a list of weapons cuts in excess of the 30 percent reduction in long-range nuclear weapons agreed to in the Strategic Arms Reduction Treaty signed in Moscow in 1991; the plan sought to have Russia reduce its nuclear arsenal by as much. Bushspeak is the standing of English on its head with banalities and corny touches. During a U.S. president's first 100 days in office, press reporters often collect irrationalities in the new president's public addresses and publish them. Examples of ''Bushspeak'' are:

> Life its own self, as Dan Jenkin said. Life its own self. Figure that out Norm. But what it means is, I have a lot more to learn from President Reagan. . . . Now, like, I'm president. It would be pretty hard for some drug guy to come into the White House and start offering it up, you know? . . . I bet if they did, I hope I would say ''Hey, get lost. We don't want any of that.''

> So my argument is with the argument. My argument is with the argument that when I say, you know, I'd like to see Noriega out, that means *carte blanche* commitment on my part of the American force. I am not going to do that. Yeah. (*Guardian Weekly,* January 27, 1991:28)

Bushusuru refers to the Japanese prime minister's banquet in early 1992 where before a television audience President Bush vomited and fainted. In sections of Tokyo, Japanese men normally drank alcohol for relief from the rigidity of their stylized social relations and would vomit on the way home; this came to be called bushusuru after the illness of the U.S. president.

George Herbert Walker Bush (b. 1924), raised in Connecticut, son of a U.S. senator, was the forty-first president of the United States. He was educated in Massachussetts and at Yale (1948), served in World War II, and founded an oil company in Texas. He failed twice to enter the Senate, but became a member of the U.S. House of Representatives (1967–70), was ambassador to the United Nations (1970–73), head of the U.S. Liaison Office in Peking (1974–75), and director of the C.I.A. (1975–76). Under Ronald Reagan, Bush became U.S. vice-

president (1981–89) and in 1988 was elected president, defeating Governor
Michael Dukakis (D-Mass.). He served only one term and was defeated by
Governor Bill Clinton (D-Ark.) in November 1992.

Sources

Anon. 1989. *President Bush: the challenge ahead.* Washington, D.C.: Congressional
    Quarterly, Inc.
King, Nicholas. 1980. *George Bush: a biography.* New York: Dodd, Mead.
Muller, David. 1991. *The seven heads of George Bush: behind the architect of the New
    World Order.* Bundoora, Victoria, Australia: South Publications.
Shafritz, Jay M. 1988. *The Dorsey dictionary of American government and politics.*
    Chicago: Dorsey.
Vernoff, Edward, and Shore, Rima, eds. 1987. *International dictionary of 20th century
    biography.* New York: New American Library.
Woodruff, John. 1992. Bush mishap throws up a new verb. *The Age [Melbourne],* Feb-
    ruary 2:11.

BUTSKELLISM. A portmanteau term for policies of both Britain's first Conservative government (1951–55) and its Labor politicians in the earlier government. Political commentators combined the names of the previous Labor
chancellor of the Exchequer, Hugh Gaitskell, with that of Richard Butler, the
Conservatives' chancellor. The policies had broad popular support across party
lines, for example, economy of mixed public and private ownership, limited
selective economic intervention by government, and the promotion and maintenance of a welfare state. When it became clear that the Conservatives and
Labor did not differ in economic policies, "Butskellism" became a term of
abuse about the economy to which the moderates of each party gave their support. In Butskellism the Labor politicians saw insufficient government intervention, whereas right-wing Conservatives objected that Butskellism failed to move
Britain into a free market economy. Butskellism gave over to monetarist policies
in the late 1970s.

Richard Austen "RAB" Butler, Baron Butler of Saffron Waldon (1902–82),
was born in Attock Serai in India. He was educated at Marlborough and Cambridge; was president of the University Union and fellow of Corpus Christie
(1925–29); and became M.P. for Saffron Waldon in Essex in 1929. His name
was associated with the Education Act (1944), which reorganized secondary
schooling and introduced the "11+" system for selecting grammar school pupils. In Churchill's government (1951), Butler was chancellor of the Exchequer,
and he introduced the emergency "credit squeeze" budget, his last. He retired
in 1965 with the reputation of a progressive, thoughtful, and dedicated Tory
leader, became master of Trinity College (1965–78), and published his memoirs,
The Art of the Impossible (1971), and his autobiography, *The Art of Memory*
(1982).

Hugh Todd Naylor Gaitskell (1906–63) was born in London, educated at
Winchester and New College, Oxford, and went to London University College
as a lecturer, becoming department head in 1938. Earlier, he had become a

socialist during the 1926 General Strike, and afterward he went to Nottingham to tutor with the Workers' Educational Association. He was elected M.P. for Leeds in 1945 and became parliamentary secretary to the Ministry of Fuel and Power, and its minister, in 1947. He was chancellor of the Exchequer during 1950–51. He introduced the National Health Service charges, which caused Aneurin Bevan, the Health minister, to resign. This led Gaitskell into a long feud with Bevan and the hostile left wing of the Labor party. He was the party leader in 1955. When the 1960 party conference supported unilateral nuclear disarmament, he so firmly opposed the policy that in 1961 the party reversed the decision. In 1962 he was opposed to Britain's entry into the European Common market.

See also BEVANITE.

Sources

Blake (Lord), and Nicholls, C. S., eds. 1990. *Dictionary of national biography 1981–1985*. New York: Oxford University Press.

McHenry, Robert, ed. 1992. *The new encyclopedia Britannica*. Chicago: Encyclopedia Britannica, Inc.

Magnussen, Magnus; Goring, Rosemary; and Thorn, John O., eds. 1990. *Chambers biographical dictionary*. Edinburgh: Chambers Ltd.

Middlemas, Keith. 1979. *Politics in an industrial society*. London: Deutsch.

Robertson, David. 1985. *The Penguin dictionary of politics*. Harmondsworth: Penguin.

Vernoff, Edward, and Shore, Rima, eds. 1987. *International dictionary of 20th century biography*. New York: New American Library.

Williams, E. T., and Nichols, C. S., eds. 1981. *Dictionary of national biography 1961–1970*. Oxford: Oxford University Press.

BUTTERWORTH REPORT. A British report (1972) of an inquiry into the work and pay of probation officers and social workers. It recommended that the pay of probation officers and hospital social workers should be related to the existing salary structure in the local authority service.

John Blackstock Butterworth (b. 1918) was educated at Queen Elizabeth's Grammar School, Mansfield, and the Queen's College, Oxford. He served in the Royal Artillery during 1938–46 and was called to the bar, Lincoln's Inn in 1947. He held several university appointments, and in 1964 he was chairman of the Inter-University Council for Higher Education overseas. He chaired the inquiry into the work of probation officers and social workers in 1971 and was a member of the royal commission on the working of the tribunals of inquiry, a governor of the Royal Shakespeare Theater (1964), and a trustee of the Shakespeare Birthplace Trust (1966). He was created a baron in 1985.

Sources

Marsh, Arthur. 1979. *Concise encyclopedia of industrial relations*. Westmead, Farnborough, Hants: Gower.

Who's who, 1992–93. London: Adam and Charles Black.

C

CABAL. A group of secret plotters.

Originally, the term referred to all and later only part of what Moses learned at Sinai, coming from the Jewish *qubbalah* and the Latin *cabala* or *cahbala*. It means "tradition" in Hebrew. Its early form referred to an esoteric method for interpreting the scriptures based on tradition that claimed to have been handed down by word of mouth from Abraham. In Jewish tradition the method became so valued that it connoted magical, sophisticated ideas for the elite only. In English it came to mean not the ideas and information so much as those who held them. This meaning was reinforced during the reign of England's Charles II (1660–85) whose Privy Council included five members who connived to remain in power: *C*[lifford], *A*[rlington], *B*[uckingham], *A*[shley], and *L*[auderdale]. This group controlled the court's foreign policy for England (1667–73).

Thomas Clifford, first Lord Clifford of Chudleigh (1630–73), was born at Ugbrooke, Exeter, the son of Hugh Clifford, commander of a regiment of foot soldiers in King Charles I's campaign against the Scots (1639). He was educated at Exeter College, Oxford, and traveled after further studies at the Middle Temple. He was elected to the Convention and to the Pensionary parliaments (1661); a Catholic, he joined Lord Arlington to ensure the influence of the "King's Friends" in the Commons. In 1672 he was made a noble, and was appointed lord high treasurer and treasurer of the Exchequer. He gave up these posts when the cabal was scattered in 1673, and he may have committed suicide.

Henry Bennet Arlington, first earl of Arlington (1618–85), was born in Arlington, Middlesex, educated at Westminister School and Christ Church, Oxford, and spent time in Spain before returning to England after the Civil War. He was created Lord Arlington in 1663 and Earl Arlington in 1672, and in 1674

was impeached unsuccessfully for popery and self-aggrandisement. He retired
to Suffolk after serving as lord chamberlain.

George Villiers Buckingham, second duke of Buckingham (1627–87), son of
the first duke, was born in Wallingford House, London. After his father's assassination, he was raised with the children of Charles I, and when the Civil
War began, he joined the royalists and served under Prince Rupert. He barely
escaped with his life in 1648 when he joined the uprising by Lord Holland in
Surrey. He went with Charles II to Scotland and returned for a secret marriage
to the daughter of Lord Fairfax in 1657. At the Restoration, he became a privy
councillor and acquired a reputation for wit and debauchery among the courtiers.
He killed the earl of Shrewsbury in a duel (1667), lost influence to Aldington,
and was dismissed in 1674.

Anthony Ashley Cooper, first earl of Shaftesbury (1621–83), was born in
Wimborne Saint Giles, Dorset, and, after ten months' service with the royalists
in the Civil War, joined the parliamentarians and Cromwell's Council of State.
However, he was always suspected of royalist sympathies. He came under royal
favor at the Restoration because he had joined the commissioners who went to
France to invite Charles II home. He became Baron Ashley in 1661 and earl of
Shaftesbury in 1672, and led the group that sought to exclude the Roman Catholic Duke of York (James II) from the throne, to change the way parliament
was dissolved and summoned, to get rid of guards and mercenaries, and to
prevent any further government support for popery and arbitrary use of power.
Because he was so opposed to Charles II on the question of who should be
Britain's next king, he was arrested for treason in July 1681, tried in November,
and acquitted. He continued to undermine the king. Warned he could be re-
strained again, he fled to Amsterdam in December 1682 and died of gout a
month later.

John Maitland, duke of Lauderdale (1616–82), was born near Haddington and
succeeded his father as second earl of Lauderdale in 1645. At Worcester in
1651, he was taken prisoner and jailed for nine years. He became Scottish
secretary of state at the Restoration and aimed to ensure the absolute power of
the Crown in church and state. As a member of the Privy Council, he sat in the
"Cabal Ministry" and was made duke in 1672. Having attracted many enemies,
he was nearly removed from the royal presence by request of the Commons
which, curiously, failed by one vote in 1678.

Sources

Harris, William H., and Levey, Judith S., eds. 1978–79. *The new illustrated Columbia
    encyclopedia.* New York: Rockville House and Columbia University.

Magnussen, Magnus; Goring, Rosemary; and Thorn, John O., eds. 1990. *Chambers bi-
    ographical dictionary.* Edinburgh: Chambers Ltd.

Stephen, Leslie, and Lee, Sydney, eds. 1917. *The dictionary of national biography.* Lon-
    don: Oxford University Press.

CABOCHIENS. A guild of butchers who terrorized the Armagnacs in early
fifteenth-century Paris. They were dissolved in 1416.

Simon de Coustellier ["the Cutler"] Caboche (fl. 1407–13) led a group of terrorists (1407) with support from the duke of Burgundy during the civil war between the Armagnacs and the Burgundians. The Cabochiens popular revolt (1413) began in Paris and opposed the extravagances of the Court of Charles VI, the greed of royal officials, and the demoralization of the people in struggles between Orleanist and Burgundian factions. In April 1413 the butchers and skinners besieged the Bastille and threatened the nobles. Caboche was a skinner; he and his followers were guilty of frightful atrocities. In May a list of grievances was presented, but because there was no effective government, none could be carried out. In time, political interests in Paris turned to the Orleanist or Armagnac cause against the Burgundians, and with the English invasion in 1415 order was restored and in 1416 the Cabochiens were dissolved.

See also ARMAGNACS.

Sources

Harbottle, Thomas B. 1973. *Dictionary of historical allusions.* Detroit: Gale Research.

Howatt, Gerald M.D. 1973. *Dictionary of world history.* London: Thomas Nelson.

McHenry, Robert, ed. 1992. *The new encyclopedia Britannica.* Chicago: Encyclopedia Britannica, Inc.

Smith, Benjamin. 1903. *The Century cyclopedia of names.* London: The Times.

CADMEAN VICTORY. A costly victory.

In Greek legend Cadmus was the son of Agenor, king of Phoenicia and Telephassa. Cadmus was sent by his father in search of his sister, Europa, whom Zeus had abducted. Cadmus's companions were eaten by a dragon, which he attacked and beat with help from Athene; in the plain Cadmus sowed the dragon's teeth, which came up as armed men. Into their midst he threw a stone, whereupon they fought one another until all died except five who helped Cadmus to found Thebes. He ruled the city with great wisdom. Later, Cadmus married Harmonia, daughter of Aphrodite. Because of their children's misfortune (they were persecuted by Hera), Cadmus and Harmonia begged the gods to relieve them of life's miseries, and the two were turned into serpents. Later Greek mythology credits Cadmus with introducing the alphabet.

Sources

Graves, Robert. 1978. *New Larousse encyclopedia of mythology.* London: Hamlyn.

Hamilton, Edith. 1940. *Mythology: timeless tales of gods and heroes.* Boston: Little, Brown.

Harris, William H., and Levey, Judith S., eds. 1978–79. *The new illustrated Columbia encyclopedia.* New York: Rockville House and Columbia University.

Mercatante, Anthony S. 1988. *The Facts on File encyclopedia of world mythology and legend.* New York: Facts on File.

Patrick, Richard. 1974. *Greek mythology.* London: Octopus.

CAESAR, CAESARESQUE, CAESAR CIPHER, CAESAROPAPISM. An absolute monarch, autocrat, emperor. Arrogant and autocratic. A code that substitutes the third letter following the one that is intended. Control of the church by a secular ruler or by the state.

Gaius Julius Caesar (100–44 B.C.) was raised in an ancient patrician family. His outstanding achievements in war, scholarship, and statecraft earned him his reputation of greatness. When young he served the military in Asia and then returned to a political career in Rome. In 59 B.C. he was elected consul, and the next year he was sent to Gaul where he established a well-trained army. He sometimes fought with his men and endured much hardship. In 45 B.C. he returned to Rome and proclaimed himself its dictator. He took the title of imperator, assuming the powers of an autocrat by becoming head of all offices of state, deeply believing that supreme power should rest in the hands of only one capable man. He devised the simple code for secret communications. Many senators objected to a dictatorship and plotted his death. Eventually, his friends assassinated him.

Sources

Bradford, Ernle D.S. 1984. *Julius Caesar: the pursuit of power.* London: Hamish Hamilton.

Fuller, John F.C. 1965. *Julius Caesar: man, soldier, and tyrant.* London: Eyre and Spottiswoode.

McHenry, Robert, ed. 1992. *The new encyclopedia Britannica.* Chicago: Encyclopedia Britannica, Inc.

Peskett, A. G., trans. 1961. *Caesar: the civil wars.* Cambridge, Mass., and London: Loeb Classical Library, Harvard University Press and William Heinemann.

CAESAR'S WIFE PRINCIPLE. The principle, in politics, that any public figure, especially an elected representative, must never be suspected of crime.

Pompeia, Caesar's third wife, was preparing a special feast for Caesar when Publius Clodius, a wealthy, eloquent, insolent, impudent, and fresh-faced nobleman who had fallen in love with her, attempted to get her attentions. She did not dislike him, but she was so firmly under her mother Aurelia's daily surveillance that Clodius could never hope to meet Pompeia without difficulty. Disguised as a young woman singer, he got into Pompeia's sleeping quarters with help from one of her maids and waited while the maid went to fetch her mistress. Tired of waiting, Clodius searched through the house for himself and was eventually discovered by Aurelia's women and thrown out of the house. The women told their husbands, and throughout the city the rumor spread quickly that Clodius was a villain, had slandered the gods and committed incest with his sister, and was guilty of high treason. The people of Rome flew to his defense, and the judges were not inclined to condemn him for fear of the people's reaction. Caesar immediately put his wife away, even though he had no evidence of what had happened. When asked why he had done this, he said, ''Because I will not that my wife be so much suspected.'' Some say he put her away to please the people, and others that he had little time for her anyway. In their confusion the judges discharged all accusations against Clodius.

See also CAESAR.

Source
Spencer, T.J.B., ed. 1964. *Shakespeare's Plutarch.* Harmondsworth: Penguin.

CAESAREAN TRANSFERENCE. An irrational prejudice, established by Laurence Peter and Raymond Hull (1969), against subordinates and colleagues based on physical attributes unrelated to work performance. In their witty analysis of organizations the authors of *The Peter Principle* regarded this as indicating an irrational prejudice rather than a real danger. Shakespeare had Caesar draw attention to the apparent danger of lean and hungry men. In *Julius Caesar* Act I, Scene 2, Caesar states:

> Let me have men about me that are fat,
> Sleek-headed men, and such as sleep a-nights.
> Yon Cassius has a lean and hungry look;
> He thinks too much: such men are dangerous.

Sources
Humphreys, Arthur, ed. 1984. *Julius Caesar: the Oxford Shakespeare.* Oxford: Clarendon Press.
Peter, Laurence J., and Hull, Raymond. 1969. *The Peter principle: why things always go wrong.* New York: William Morrow.

CAINITE. A descendant of Cain; a member of the second-century sect of Gnostics who revered both Cain and Judas.

Cain was the first child of Adam and Eve. He murdered his brother, Abel, out of jealousy because Jehovah valued Abel's sacrifice more than Cain's. In A.D. 130 a sect of Ophite Gnostics called themselves Cainites and devised an explanation for Cain's alleged crime. They claimed that it sprang from two principles; it was assumed first that Cain was the product of intercourse between Eve and a superior power; and second, that the characters of Cain and Abel symbolized their parentage, so that in slaying Abel, the superior rose over the inferior. The Cainites renounced the New Testament and favored "The Gospel of Judas." This justified the false disciple, the subsequent crucifixion of Jesus, the view that heaven and earth were the product of some evil principle, and the idea that Cain and his descendants had been wronged.

Sources
Brewer, Ebenezer Cobham. 1970. *Brewer's dictionary of phrase and fable.* Centenary ed. Rev. by Ivor H. Evans. New York: Harper and Row.
Dudley, Lavinia P. 1963. *The encyclopedia Americana.* International ed. New York: Americana Corp.
Ferguson, Everett, ed. 1990. *The encyclopedia of early Christianity.* New York: Garland Publishing.
McHenry, Robert, ed. 1992. *The new encyclopedia Britannica.* Chicago: Encyclopedia Britannica, Inc.

CALIXTIN(E). A follower of the sixteenth-century syncretist divine.

Georg Calixtus (1586–1656) was born at Medelby in Schleswig-Holstein and became an eminent theologian of the Lutheran Church. After studies in philosophy and theology at Helmstedt (1603–19), he traveled in Germany, Belgium, England, and France, and became a professor of theology at Helmstedt University in 1614. He held conciliatory views and gave the impression that his great knowledge and experience of the world made him tolerant toward everyone regardless of their religious opinions, providing they held those views with an honest conviction. He argued that the oldest fundamentals of Christian faith—the facts contained in the Apostles' Creed—were evident to all Christian sects. When he was accused of apostasy, his friends supported him and he was able to keep his academic post until he died in Helmstedt.

Sources

McDonald, William J., ed. 1967. *New Catholic encyclopedia.* New York: McGraw-Hill.
McHenry, Robert, ed. 1992. *The new encyclopedia Britannica.* Chicago: Encyclopedia
    Britannica, Inc.

CALVINISM. Christian beliefs on predestination, natural man's inability to have true faith or to repent, true grace, election, and the continuity of a saintly state of grace until the true moment of divine of glory; an extremely moral, strict, and severe attitude to everyday life.

Jean Chauvin or John Calvin (1509–64) was born at Noyon, Picardy, in France. He studied at Paris, Orleans, and Bourges where under the influence of several Protestants he broke with the Roman Catholic Church and became a great Protestant reformer and theologian. Driven from Paris during the Reformation, Calvin published his *Institutes of the Christian Religion* (1536) at Basel. In Geneva he became a preacher and professor of theology, but his deep interest in radical reforms led to his expulsion, and he spent years lecturing at Strasburg before finally returning to found the Academy of Geneva (1559). His reforms were adopted in the church system he upheld whereby the congregation chose the church presbyters. The religious practices of Calvinism were characteristically bleak, dancing and music were seen as sinful, and the constraints on material pleasures left an impression that Calvinistic acts lacked all sense of worldly enjoyment.

Sources

McDonald, William J., ed. 1967. *New Catholic encyclopedia.* New York: McGraw-Hill.
McHenry, Robert, ed. 1992. *The new encyclopedia Britannica.* Chicago: Encyclopedia
    Britannica, Inc.
Miller, David, ed. 1987. *The Blackwell encyclopedia of political thought.* Oxford: Basil
    Blackwell.
Mullett, Michael. 1989. *Calvin.* London: Routledge.

CAMERON REPORT. A British report of many industrial relations inquiries which arose from complaints by bank union employees, electricians, railwaymen, and workers at Briggs Motor Bodies and Webber Offset. The complaints were directed to the Committee on Freedom Association of the International Labor Organization in 1963.

Honorable Lord John Cameron (b. 1900), was educated at Edinburgh Academy University and became a queen's counselor in Scotland in 1936. He served in the Royal Naval Voluntary Reserve in both world wars. After World War II, he became dean of the Faculty of Advocates (1946–48), and a member of a Committee of Law of Contempt of Court (1948–55); he served on many industrial relations inquiries and was on the Royal Commission on Civil Liability and Compensation for Personal Injury (1970; 1973–78); and was a senator of the College of Justice in Scotland and Board of Sessions (1955–85). He was knighted in 1951 and 1978, and in 1983 was made an honorary member of the fellow of the Royal Society of Edinburgh and the British Academy as well as a doctor of the University of Edinburgh.

Sources

Marsh, Arthur. 1979. *Concise encyclopedia of industrial relations.* Westmead, Farnborough, Hants: Gower.

Who's who, 1993. London: Adam and Charles Black.

CAMERONIAN. A supporter of Richard Cameron, the main preacher of dissenting Covenanters, who would not accept the Revolution Settlement of the Church of Scotland (1689–90). His supporters believed that the settlement failed to recognize the perpetual obligation that Scotland had incurred in the National Covenant in 1638 and by all of Great Britain in the Solemn League and Covenant in 1643; a Cameronian is also a soldier of the Cameronian regiment, which was formed in 1689 by a band of Richard Cameron's followers.

Richard Cameron (1648–80), a Scottish Covenanter, was born in Falkland, Fife, where he became a schoolmaster. He may have been a tutor in Sir William Scott's household. In 1673 he preached under the influence of John Welsh, the Covenanter. Cameron was exiled to Holland after being defeated at Bothwell Bridge in 1679. In Holland he helped publish the first Sanquhar Declaration, which disowned the royal authority of Charles II and affixed the Declaration to the market cross in Sanquhar, a small burgh of Dumfriesshire 58 miles northwest of Edinburgh, in 1680. Then with sixty armed comrades he fled to the hills and evaded capture for a month, but in July 1680 the rebels were attacked by a body of dragoons, and Cameron was killed at Aird's Moss, Ayrshire. Some of his followers survived, and James Renwick affixed the second Sanquhar Declaration to the market cross in 1685.

Sources

McDonald, William, ed. 1967. *New Catholic encyclopedia.* New York: McGraw-Hill.

McHenry, Robert, ed. 1992. *The new encyclopedia Britannica.* Chicago: Encyclopedia Britannica, Inc.

CAMP DAVID ACCORDS, CAMP DAVID SPIRIT. When Egypt's President Sadat (1918–81) visited Jerusalem in November 1977, President Jimmy

Carter (b. 1924) thought that Egypt and Israel—at war since 1948—could be brought to discuss their differences in a place that both respected. In March 1979 the thirty-year war ended with the signing of the Camp David Accords. The Camp David Spirit is the amicable attitude toward world problems that was thought to have arisen after President Eisenhower's meetings at Camp David with Soviet Chairman Nikita Khrushchev (1894–1971) in 1959. Today it refers to the general feeling for Israeli-Arab relations. The spirit is anathema to those Arabs who allege that the peace made by Egypt sacrificed the Palestinians and made possible the Israeli invasion of Lebanon in 1982.

Camp David is the U.S. presidential conference center for informal international negotiations. In July 1942 President Franklin D. Roosevelt (1882–1945) established a retreat, ''Shangri La,'' in Catoctin Mountain Park in Maryland, a 10,000-acre tract originally purchased as a national park. In 1942 it was declared a security area, maintained by the Office of Strategic Services and the Marines. Secret wartime conferences and secret visits with Winston Churchill (1874–1965) were held there. President Truman (1884–1972) did not use it as much as Roosevelt, although it was in constant use throughout the Truman administration. In 1953 President Dwight D. Eisenhower (1890–1969) renamed it Camp David to honor his grandson, David Eisenhower (b. 1948). Presidents Kennedy (1917–63) and Johnson (1908–73) used Camp David as a retreat; President Nixon (1913–94) had Secretary Brezhnev (1906–82) visit in June 1973; President Ford (b. 1913) visited with President Suharto (b. 1921) in July 1975; President Reagan (b. 1913) saw many heads of state and government at Camp David, including those from Mexico (1981), Britain (1984; 1986), and Japan (1986); while President Bush conferred with leaders from Mexico, Australia, West Germany, Britain, Turkey, and the Soviet Union at Camp David. The center covers 200 acres and includes Aspen Lodge, the residence, and an office and conference hall. Since it is a naval installation, it is permanently staffed by naval personnel, U.S. Marines, and members of the White House communications staff.

Sources

McHenry, Robert, ed. 1992. *The new encyclopedia Britannica.* Chicago: Encyclopedia Britannica, Inc.

Pauling, Linus, ed. 1986. *World encyclopedia of peace.* Vol. 1. Oxford: Pergamon Press.

Quandt, William B. 1986. *Camp David: peacemaking and politics.* Washington, D.C.: Brookings Institution.

Telhami, Shibley. 1990 *Power and leadership in international bargaining: the path to the Camp David Accords.* New York: Columbia University Press.

Telhami, Shibley. 1992. Evaluating bargaining performance: the case of Camp David. *Political Science Quarterly* 107:629–653.

Personal Communication.

CAMPBELL'S ACT. In the United States the Campbell's Act refers to the British Fatal Accident Act (1846) or Lord Campbell's Act, which enables executors or administrators of people who have been killed due to negligence to bring action for the benefit of the wife, parent, or children for the deceased against the party guilty of the negligence. For the first time the act permitted action for wrongful death, which had previously been unknown in common law. Both federal and state statutes in the United States provide for such action. Other ''Lord Campbell Acts'' known as such in Britain include the British Libel Act (1843), which amends the law regarding defamatory words and libel; the Obscene Publications Act (1857), which authorizes magistrates to issue a warrant for the seizure of obscene books and other publications.

John Campbell, first Baron Campbell (1779–1861) was born in Cupar, Fife, in Scotland, and educated at Cupar Grammar School. He studied for the church at Saint Andrews, turned to law in 1800 and journalism, and was called to the bar in 1806. He reported cases until 1816 when his legal work filled his time. He reported on and headed the Real Property Commission in 1829 which examined the registration of deeds relating to landownership and tenure. He was a Whig M.P. (1830–49), knighted, and appointed solicitor-general (1832) and attorney-general (1834). He sponsored several reform acts. He was made a baron in 1841, became the chancellor of the Duchy of Lancaster in 1846, chief justice of the Queen's Bench in 1850, and lord chancellor in 1859.

Sources

Bysiewicz, Shirley R. 1983. *Monarch's dictionary of legal terms for home, office and school use.* New York: Monarch–Simon and Schuster.

Ivamy, E.R. Hardy. 1988. *Mozely and Whiteley's law dictionary.* London: Butterworth.

James, John S. 1971. *Stroud's judicial dictionary.* London: Sweet and Maxwell Ltd.

Simpson, Alfred W.B. 1984. *Biographical dictionary of the common law.* London: Butterworth.

Stephen, Leslie, and Lee, Sydney, eds. 1917. *The dictionary of national biography.* London: Oxford University Press.

Walker, David M. 1980. *The Oxford companion to law.* Oxford: Clarendon Press.

CAMPBELLITE. A nickname for a member of the organization the Disciples of Christ.

Alexander Campbell (1788–1866) was born near Ballymena in County Antrim, Ireland, and immigrated to America in 1807. The son of Reverand Thomas Campbell, a Presbyterian minister, Alexander was educated in his father's school. After attending Glasgow University in Scotland, he joined his father's Christian Association of Washington, Pennsylvania, and was ordained in 1812. Although he was Presbyterian, he joined the Baptists in 1812 and worked as an itinerant preacher in western Pennsylvania, West Virginia, and Ohio. He protested against the creeds that proclaimed the Bible to be the sole authority on religious matters. In 1826 he published a translation of the New Testament in which the words ''baptist'' and ''baptism'' were replaced with ''immerser'' and ''immersion.'' In 1832 Campbell's followers, the Disciples of Christ, known popularly as Christians or Campbellites, joined the Kentucky Christians of Barton W. Stone (1772–1844) to establish the Disciples of Christ (Christians). By

1881 the sect had 5,100 churches and over a half-million members. The Disciples of Christ (Christians) began a program of unity of Christian religion based on a common faith in Christ and participated in the World Council of Churches. In 1985 the Disciples of Christ joined with the United Church of Christ in an ecumenical partnership.

Sources

Dunnavant, Anthony L. 1991. *Restructure: four historical ideals in the Campbell-Stone movement and the development of the polity of the Christian Church (Disciples of Christ).* New York: P. Lang.

Garrison, Winfred E., and Degroot, Alfred T. 1958. *The Disciples of Christ: a history.* Saint Louis: Bethany Press.

Harrell, David E. 1966–73. *A social history of the Disciples of Christ.* 2 vols. Nashville: Disciples of Christ Historical Society (Vol. 1); Atlanta, Ga.: Publishing System Inc. (Vol. 2).

Johnson, Allen, and Malone, Dumas, eds. 1929. *Dictionary of American biography.* Vol. II. New York: Charles Scribner's Sons.

McAllister, Lester G., and Tucker, William E. 1975. *Journey into faith: a history of the Christian Church (Disciples of Christ).* Saint Louis: Bethany Press.

McDonald, William, ed. 1967. *New Catholic encyclopedia.* New York: McGraw-Hill.

McHenry, Robert, ed. 1992. *The new encyclopedia Britannica.* Chicago: Encyclopedia Britannica, Inc.

CAMPBELLMANIA. Frenetic support for the rising woman politician to lead the ruling Progressive Conservatives in Canada after the resignation of Prime Minister Brian Mulroney in March 1993.

Avril Campbell (b. 1947) changed her name to "Kim" at age 12 and was raised in British Columbia. She was an outstanding student at Vancouver High School; at the University of British Columbia she studied political science and began Soviet Studies at the London School of Economics. She lectured in science and history, Vancouver Community College, and in political science at the University of British Columbia. In 1980 she was elected to the Vancouver School Board. As a local Social Credit party supporter, she failed to gain a senior political post until 1988 when she turned to the Conservatives and won a Vancouver seat for them. Quickly, she was made minister for justice and then for defense in Mulroney's administration; she was also named minister of state for Indian Affairs and Northern Development in 1989 and made attorney-general in the cabinet reshuffle in 1990. When Mulroney resigned in March 1993, she was considered to be the next leader of the Progressive Conservative party. At the time of rising support for her, "Campbellmania," she called for "Campbell rationality"; her views included the "politics of inclusion" and a progressive view on homosexual rights, abortion, and gun control. Twice divorced, she is known as a tough-minded person who seeks to avoid polarization in politics. She did not want to be identified with other politically powerful women: Margaret Thatcher, Golda Meier, Indira Gandhi, or Benazir Bhutto. Her support within the Progressive Conservative party was achieved through her fund-raising ability and considerable support from Quebec. She became leader in June 1993. In October she led the party to defeat and lost her seat.

Sources
Keesings contemporary archives: record of world events. 1989:36426; 1990:37242; 1991:38140. London: Keesings Publications.
Scott, Gavin. 1993. Life—and hope—of the party. *Time* (Australia), April 12:46.
Who's who in the world, 1992–93. Chicago: Marquis.

CANNONISM. A policy followed in the U.S. legislature that stipulates that the speaker of the House holds the authority to determine what legislation would be put before the House. In 1909 the House of Representatives rejected a resolution to limit the speaker's power, but in 1910 George William Norris (1861–1944) led a revolt against Speaker Joseph Cannon by trying to reintroduce a similar resolution; Cannon tried to prohibit debate and the House overruled him. After a twenty-nine hour debate, the House favored the resolution. Cannon offered to resign, but because he was so popular he remained speaker for another year.

Joseph Gurney Cannon (1836–1926) was born at New Garden, Guilford County, North Carolina, and was raised and educated in Bloomington, Indiana. He studied at Cincinnati Law School, and was admitted to the bar and began practice in Terre Haute, Indiana, in 1858. In 1859 he moved to Tuscola, Illinois, and became the state's attorney for the twenty-seventh judicial district of Illinois (1861–68). As a Republican, he was elected to the U.S. Congress, serving from 1873 to 1891, 1893 to 1913, and 1915 to 1923. He was the last autocratic speaker; he had dominated the House of Representatives at the end of the nineteenth century and from 1903 to 1910. During this period, he determined the fate of much legislation from his position as chairman on the Rules Committee where he used his office to stop legislation from entering the House. His autocratic use of power was cut when new rules prohibited the speaker from serving on that committee and assigning people to it, and, when in the House, he could no longer deny recognition to members during debates. He never supported any particular legislation, although he did oppose the progressive policies of President Theodore Roosevelt.

Sources
Bolles, Blair. 1951. *Tyrant from Illinois: Uncle Joe Cannon's experiment with personal power.* New York: W. W. Norton.
Jacob, Kathryn A., and Ragsdale, Bruce A. 1989. *Biographical directory of the United States Congress: 1774–1989.* Bicentennial ed. Washington, D.C.: U.S. Government Printing Office.
James, Edward T. 1973. *Dictionary of American biography.* Supplement 3. New York: Charles Scribner's Sons.
Johnson, Allen, and Malone, Dumas, eds. 1929. *Dictionary of American biography.* Vol. II. New York: Charles Scribner's Sons.
Norris, George W. 1945. *Fighting liberal: the autobiography of George W. Norris.* New York: Macmillan.

CAPETIAN. A member or supporter of the Capetian dynasty (987–1328) in France. Notable Capetians were the founder of the dynasty, Hugh Capet (d. 996), Philip II Augustus (1165–1223), and Louis IX (1214–70) who was king of France from 1226 and canonized as Saint Louis (1297). The Capetians are known from descriptions in monastic chronicles, and their lives appear to have been dominated by extremes of piety and sexual excess. Until the rule of Louis VI (1108–37) and Louis VII (1137–80), the Capetians had little impact on France as a whole. Thereafter, especially through the efforts of Phillip II Augustus (1180–1223), the Capetian influence was marked in the creation and maintenance of the distinctive local administrative systems that lasted until the decline of the *ancien regime.* The dynasty ended through a lack of male heirs, and in 1328, on the death of Charles IV, the house of Valois became France's rulers. In 1589 Henry IV founded the Bourbon dynasty in France, which ruled until 1848, except during the French Revolution and the Napoleonic era.

Hugh Capet (d. 996) was elected king of France in 987 and ruled until his death. Capet, the son of Hugh the Great, had succeeded his father as the count of Paris and the duke of France in 956. With the end of the direct line of Charles the Great, he was elected king. His domain was bounded by the Somme, the Loire, Normandy, Anjou, and Champagne; he had insufficient military forces to control the dukes of Normandy, Brittany, Burgundy, and Vermandous and possess their lands.

Sources

Cantor, Norman F. 1963. *Medieval history: the life and death of civilization.* New York: Macmillan.

Halphen, Louis. 1922. France, the last Carolingians and the accession of Hugh Capet, and France in the eleventh century. In A. M. Gwatkin, D. D. Whitney, J. R. Tanner, and M. A. Previté-Orton. *The Cambridge medieval history.* Vol. III. Cambridge: Cambridge University Press, pp. 82–103.

Jones, Barry, ed. 1989. *The Macmillan dictionary of biography.* Melbourne: Macmillan.

McHenry, Robert, ed. 1992. *The new encyclopedia Britannica.* Chicago: Encyclopedia Britannica, Inc.

Smith, Benjamin. 1903. *The Century cyclopedia of names.* London: The Times.

CAPRAESQUE. A term derived from the New Deal films in which sentimental social comedies glorified the little, decent man fighting for what was right against powerful, corrupt institutions that perverted democratic values.

Frank Capra (1897–1991) immigrated with his parents from Sicily to California in 1903, worked his way through college, and in the 1930s was a leading director for Columbia Studios. His films depicted America as a land of opportunity for honest, patriotic, clean-living people who could overcome all of life's problems. His sanctimonious, demagogic movies were sometimes called "Capracorn." After making silent movies, he became a success with *Rain and Shine* (1930), *Platinum Blonde* (1931, Jean Harlow) and the Oscar winner, *It Happened One Night* (1934, Clark Gable and Claudette Colbert). After a long illness, he felt driven by God to make films that were not as sensuous and suggestive. He therefore decided to present Americans with their wholesome dreams, for example, *Mr Deeds Goes to Town* (1936), *You Can't Take It with You* (1938), and *Mr. Smith Goes to Washington* (1939). During the 1960s his films were thought to be reactionary, and his last movie was *Pocketful of Dreams* (1961), a remake of the 1933 success, *Lady for a Day*.

Sources

Bergan, Ronald. 1991. Obituary: Frank Capra, pedlar of the American dream. *Guardian Weekly,* September 15.

Bullock, Alan, and Woodings, Robert B., eds. 1983. *The Fontana biographical companion to modern thought.* London: Collins.

Capra, Frank. 1971. *The name above the title: an autobiography.* New York: Macmillan.

Wakeman, John, ed. 1987. *World film directors.* Vol. 1. 1890–1945. New York: H. W. Wilson.

CARLIST. A supporter of the claims of the nineteenth-century Spanish pretender.

Carlos Maria Isidro de Borbón (1788–1855) was the second son of Charles IV of Spain and the first Carlist pretender. After his father abdicated in 1808, he was held prisoner with the rest of his family in France until 1814. He was a devout, conservative Catholic; the clerical party supported him when he refused to recognize Isabella, the daughter of his brother Ferdinand VII, as successor to the throne of Spain. When his niece became queen in 1833, Don Carlos took up arms and was defeated in the first Carlist War in 1839. He escaped to France and renounced the claim to the Spanish throne, in favor of his son. In the late 1840s the Carlists waged the second Carlist War, attempted a military coup d'etat in 1860, and fought another war during 1872–76. In the Spanish Civil War (1936–39), the Carlists supported General Francisco Franco. Their claim to the throne was maintained until 1957 when forty-six Carlist leaders swore their allegiance to Don Juan—the third son of Alfonso XIII (1886–1941)—who was a critic of Franco. Franco named his close supporter, Juan Carlos, son of Don Juan, his heir; when Franco died, Juan Carlos was king.

Sources

Magnussen, Magnus; Goring, Rosemary; and Thorn, John O., eds. 1990. *Chambers biographical dictionary.* Edinburgh: Chambers Ltd.

McHenry, Robert, ed. 1992. *The new encyclopedia Britannica.* Chicago: Encyclopedia Britannica, Inc.

CARLYLISM (ALSO CARLYLESE, CARLYLESQUE, CARLYLEAN). The vigorous and irregular phraseology and vocabulary of the nineteenth-century British social critic and historian.

Thomas Carlyle (1795–1881) was born in Scotland, son of a stonemason. At first educated to become a religious, he instead turned to mathematics and became tutor to the son of a rich man. In 1826 he married Jane Welsh, and from 1828 to 1834 he lived in a lonely farmhouse at Craigenputtock. Many find his writing style difficult, filled with strange, distorted, rugged phrases, passionate outbreaks and much fury. He used tricks of punctuation and grammar which reflected the undisciplined nature of his personality. His best known works are *The French Revolution* (1837), *Heroes and Hero Worship* (1841), *Past and Present* (1843), and *Life of John Stirling* (1851).

Sources

Cazamian, Louis. 1932. *Carlyle.* Reprinted 1966. Hamden, Conn.: Archon Books.

Le Quesne, A. Laurence. 1982. *Carlyle.* Oxford: Oxford University Press.

McHenry, Robert, ed. 1992. *The new encyclopedia Britannica.* Chicago: Encyclopedia Britannica, Inc.

Miller, David, ed. 1987. *The Blackwell encyclopedia of political thought.* Oxford: Basil Blackwell.

Stephen, Leslie, and Lee, Sydney, eds. 1917. *The dictionary of national biography.* London: Oxford University Press.

CAROLINE, CAROLEAN. Relating to the seventeenth-century English kings, Charles I and Charles II.

Charles I (1600–49), king of England, Scotland, and Ireland (1625–49), was the second son of James I, king of England, and Anne of Denmark. Charles became heir to the British throne on the death of his older brother Henry in 1612. Charles was partly responsible for provoking the Puritan Revolution in England, which, although largely a religious revolution, involved social and economic issues. In the first four years of his reign, Charles dissolved four parliaments because they challenged his assumption of the divine right to rule England; this was specifically related to his right to raise taxes not authorized by the House of Commons. In 1642 civil war erupted, and in 1649 the victor, Oliver Cromwell, agreed that Charles be tried for treason; he was found guilty and beheaded.

Charles II (1630–85) was the second son of Charles I and Henrietta Maria, sister of Louis XIII of France. When his father was beheaded, Charles, then 18 years of age, was in France. His royalist supporters in Scotland and Ireland proclaimed him king of England. In 1651 he was crowned king of Scotland and marched into England, but he was defeated by Cromwell and had to escape to France. In 1660 the English monarchy was finally restored, and Charles II returned to England. He was regarded as a skillful politician. During his reign, the British Parliament's powers gradually increased, and two powerful political parties, the Whigs and Tories, emerged. In addition, Charles II saw the beginning of British colonization, the growth of the India trade as well as trade with the Americas, and the development of England as a great power at sea. He was called the "Merry Monarch" because of his many mistresses and extravagant way of life.

Sources

Haigh, Christopher, ed. 1985. *The Cambridge historical encyclopedia of Great Britain and Ireland.* Cambridge: Cambridge University Press.

Stephen, Leslie, and Lee, Sydney, eds. 1917. *The dictionary of national biography.* London: Oxford University Press.
Wroughton, John, and Cook, Chris. 1980. *English historical facts: 1603–1688.* London: Macmillan.

CAROLINGIAN, CARLOVINGIAN. Relating to the dynasty of Frankish kings.

Charlemagne, Charles the Great (742–814), was king of the Franks (768–814) and emperor of the West (800–14). He was probably born at Aix-la-Chapelle, and he was the elder son of Pepin III (d. 768). Before he died, Pepin divided his kingdom: Austrasia, Neustria, and half of Aquitania went to Charles, and the remaining half of Aquitania, Burgundy, Provence, Gothia, Alsace, and Alemannia went to Charles's brother, Carlomen. In 768 the respective kings were enthroned; three years later on the death of Carlomen, Charles took his dead brother's domain, despite the claims of Carlomen's son, Pepin. With the pope's blessing, on Christmas Day, 800, Charles became emperor of the Holy Roman Empire, an attempt to unite Western Europe as it had once been under Roman rule 300 years before. Charles fought wars on many fronts, and from his great successes he earned the title "The Great." To his kingdom he added north and central Italy and Bavaria; he conquered the Saxons and captured Barcelona. Traditionally, his coronation is seen as a turning point in European history where the Dark Ages gave way to the Middle Ages, and centuries of barbaric war were followed by the establishment of politically stable kingdoms.

Sources

Bullough, Donald A. 1992. *Carolingian renewal: sources and heritage.* Manchester: Manchester University Press.
Gwatkin, Henry M., and Whitney, James P. 1913. *The Cambridge medieval history.* Vol. II. Cambridge: Cambridge University Press.
Hussey, Joan M., ed. 1966. *The Cambridge medieval history.* Vol. IV. Cambridge: Cambridge University Press.
McHenry, Robert, ed. 1992. *The new encyclopedia Britannica.* Chicago: Encyclopedia Britannica, Inc.

CARR REPORT. A British report (1958) on industrial training. It examined the adequacy of existing institutions to cope with the large increase in school leavers expected in the labor market in the early 1960s. The committee recommended increasing the number of apprenticeships for school leavers.

Leonard Robert Carr, Baron Carr of Hadley (b. 1916), was educated at Westminster School, London, and Cambridge University. He spent World War II overseeing the production of aluminium sheeting for aircraft at John Dale Ltd. where in 1948 he was appointed director of research and development. He was elected to Parliament as a Conservative in 1950 and 1951, and was parliamentary private secretary to Anthony Eden. When Eden became prime minister, Carr was promoted to parliamentary secretary to the Ministry of Labor and National Service. He took a cabinet position in Heath's government (1970) and left the

Ministry of Labor in 1972 to become a majority leader of the House of Commons, at the same time that he was appointed lord president of the Privy Council. He was home secretary during 1972–74, and in 1975 he was made a life peer. After serving as chairman of the Education and Training committee in 1977–82, he was appointed advisory board member of P. A. Partners (1985–87) and chairman of Business in the Community (1984–87).
Sources
Marsh, Arthur. 1979. *Concise encyclopedia of industrial relations.* Westmead, Farnborough, Hants: Gower.
Who's who, 1991. London: Adam and Charles Black.

CARRY NATION. An intemperate temperance agitator.

Carry Amelia Nation, née Moore (1846–1911), was born in Garrard County, Kentucky, attended the Missouri State Normal School, and in 1867 married Dr. Charles Gloyd, an alcoholic, who died six months after the marriage. Next, she married David Nation, a lawyer and minister. She became a schoolteacher and was so deeply affected by her unhappy first marriage that she believed she had been called by a divine power to bring an end to saloons and drinking alcohol. In 1899 she began her career in Kansas trying to close liquor saloons by axing them to pieces ("hatchetation") for which she was jailed. Her magazine was called the *Battleaxe,* and soon the term came to mean "overbearing, dominating woman." To join her movement, one had to renounce the bottle and sign a pledge to give up spirituous liquors. Later, in the 1880s, the pledge was extended to all alcoholic drinks. Because the first pledge mentioned only spirits, one could sign it "OP," meaning the "Old Pledge." But if one wanted to sign for total abstinence, then one initialed the pledge with a "T"—hence the term "teetotaler." Her second husband of twenty-three years divorced her on the grounds of desertion.
Sources
Ashbury, Herbert. 1929. *Carry Nation.* New York: Alfred A. Knopf.
Dudley, Lavinia P. 1963. *The encyclopedia Americana.* International ed. New York: Americana Corp.
Hendrickson, Robert. 1988. *The dictionary of eponyms: names that became words.* New York: Dorset.
Nation, Carry A. 1904. *The use and need of the life of Carry A. Nation.* Topeka: F. M. Stevens.

CARTER DOCTRINE. In his final State of the Union Address on January 23, 1980, President Jimmy Carter announced that any attempt by a foreign power to obtain control of the Persian Gulf would be regarded as an attack on America's vital interests and could be resisted with military force.

James Earl "Jimmy" Carter, Jr. (b. 1924) was born in Plains, Georgia, raised in Archery, and studied at Georgia South Western College and the Georgia Institute of Technology. In 1943 he began a military career and was a commissioned officer in 1953 when he left the U.S. Navy to manage his late father's peanut business in Plains. In 1962 he ran successfully for the Georgia State Senate, and served from 1963 to 1966; in 1967 after he lost the 1966 Democratic nomination for state governor, he had a deep religious experience and became a born again Christian. He was state governor in 1971–74. Immediately, he aimed for the U.S. presidency, gained the Democratic nomination in 1976, and defeated Gerald Ford to become the first U.S. president from the Deep South since Andrew Jackson. Remarkably, Carter had overcome the disadvantage of being relatively unknown in U.S. politics. In 1980, despite the dramatic decline in his popularity, he was renominated to the presidential office, but he was defeated by Ronald Reagan. He retired from politics and now works for international peace.

Sources

Carter, Jimmy. 1982. *Keeping the faith: memoirs of a president.* New York: Bantam.

Fink, Gary. 1980. *Prelude to the presidency; the political character and leadership style of Governor Jimmy Carter.* Westport, Conn.: Greenwood Press.

Kucharsky, David. 1976. *The man from Plains: the mind and spirit of Jimmy Carter.* New York: Harper and Row.

Kuniholm, Bruce R. 1986. The Carter Doctrine, the Reagan corollary, and prospects for United States policy in Southwest Asia. *International Journal* 41:342–361.

Phillips, Robert S., ed. 1983. *Funk and Wagnall's new encyclopedia.* New York: Funk and Wagnall, Inc.

Thompson, Kenneth W., ed. 1990. *The Carter presidency: fourteen intimate perspectives of Jimmy Carter.* Lanham, Md.: University Press of America; Charlottesville: Miller Center, University of Virginia.

CARTESIAN, CARTESIAN LINGUISTICS. Relating to the seventeenth-century French philosopher. Linguistics using theories or methods influenced by Descartes.

René Descartes (1596–1650) was born near Tours, France. At age 8 he was sent to a Jesuit College at La Fleche where his remarkable intellect was soon noticed; quickly he learned astronomy, languages, and mathematics. Much of his life was spent in Holland; he was invited to live in Sweden by Queen Christina and died there shortly after arrival. Reason was more important to him as the source of truth than philosophical tradition or noted authorities. He conceived of the universe as space, matter, and motion in a mechanical system, governed by mathematical laws. Even though some of his central ideas found no support from Newton's work, Descartes was a major influence on philosophy and science. His chief work was *Traite des Passions* (1649).

Sources

Cottingham, John. 1986. *Descartes.* New York: Basil Blackwell.

Grene, Marjorie. 1985. *Descartes.* Brighton: Harvester Press.

McHenry, Robert, ed. 1992. *The new encyclopedia Britannica.* Chicago: Encyclopedia Britannica, Inc.

Magnussen, Magnus; Goring, Rosemary; and Thorn, John O., eds. 1990. *Chambers biographical dictionary.* Edinburgh: Chambers Ltd.

CASTROISM, FIDELISM. The beliefs and actions of the twentieth-century Cuban revolutionary leader, who aligned Cuba with Russian communism and opposed the United States.

Fidel Castro Ruz (b. 1927), son of a Spanish sugar planter in Oriente Province, Cuba, worked on the family's 23,000 acre sugarcane estate when he was a youth. At a Jesuit preparatory school in Havana, Fidel excelled in Spanish, history, and agriculture, and he was the school's best athlete in 1944. After graduating from the University of Havana in 1958 as a lawyer, he championed the poor and disadvantaged. Following the establishment of a military dictatorship by General Fulgencis Batista, Castro helped organize a rebel force of young idealists dedicated to democracy and social justice. In 1953 Castro led an attack on Batista, proclaiming total war against the regime in 1958. Castro's guerillas won, and in February 1959 Castro was sworn in as premier of Cuba; by the end of the year the real power in Cuba lay in his hands and those of his immediate associates. In his 1961 May Day speech, Castro declared that Cuba was a socialist country and that instead of holding elections, the government would depend on the direct support of the people at massed rallies. That year the United States broke diplomatic relations with Cuba. Castro wanted to reform Cuba's agriculture, industry, and education, and was successful enough to strengthen his regime. His opposition to the United States was balanced by the country's dependence on the Soviet Union. Castro's domination of Cuban government and the society is total. He is committed to a disciplined society, and he is determined to remake the Cuban national character, creating work-oriented, socially concerned individuals. The creation of a statesman-like image gained him growing acceptance in the Third World.

Sources

Bonsal, Philip W. 1971. *Cuba, Castro, and the United States.* Pittsburgh: University of Pittsburgh Press.

Bourne, Peter. 1987. *Castro.* London: Macmillan.

Halperin, Maurice. 1981. *The taming of Fidel Castro.* Berkeley: University of California Press.

Harnecker, Marta. 1987. *Fidel Castro's political strategy: from Moncada to victory.* Trans. M. Zimmerman. New York: Pathfinders.

Moritz, Charles, ed. 1970. *Current biography yearbook.* New York: H. W. Wilson.

Szulc, Tad. 1986. *Fidel: a critical portrait.* New York: William Morrow.

CATILINE, CATILINARIAN. A reckless and daring conspirator.

Lucius Sergius Catiline (c. 108–62 B.C.) was a lieutenant of Sulla and a governor of Africa; but his ambitions to become consul were frustrated because he was charged with poor government and was suspected of extortion as well as with the murder of his own brother. Afterward he and others plotted to kill the new consuls; the plot was uncovered, but he was acquitted after the trial. When his frequent attempts to become consul failed, he organized a conspiracy to murder Cicero, kill the consuls, rob the Treasury, burn Rome, and seize power.

Cicero discovered the plot, announced it in his Catilinarian oration, and thus the plot was foiled. Catiline fled to Etruria and was killed in battle against Rome's forces.

Sources

Chisholm, Kitty, and Ferguson, John. 1981. *Rome: the Augustan age.* London: Oxford University Press.

Harris, William H., and Levey, Judith S., eds. 1978–79. *The new illustrated Columbia encyclopedia.* New York: Rockville House and Columbia University.

McHenry, Robert, ed. 1992. *The new encyclopedia Britannica.* Chicago: Encyclopedia Britannica, Inc.

CEAUSESCA ORPHAN. A child taken from its parents, raised in a Romanian institution, and then either put out for adoption to another country for a high price or used as labor.

Nicolae Ceausesca (1918–89) was born in Scorniscesti into a peasant family and joined the Communist party in the late 1930s, gaining appointment to secretary of the Bucharest branch in 1945. He was a politician in 1947 when the first communist government was established in Romania. He became minister for agriculture until 1950, minister for the armed forces (1950–54), and in 1965, on the death of the Stalinist Gheorghe Gheorghiv-Dej, he became leader of the Communist party and president and head of state. Although he followed Stalin's repressive rule in his domestic policy, he was popular for his nationalist policies and for refusing to allow Russia to control Romania's internal affairs. He had good relations with China and Western nations, and he often criticized the Soviet Union. When Gorbachev's reforms led to a popular uprising, Ceausesca was isolated and condemned for violations of human rights. He and his wife, Elena, tried before a military tribunal in December 1989, were charged with genocide, corruption, and destruction of the Romanian economy. Both were found guilty and executed by firing squad.

Sources

Behr, Edward. 1991. *Kiss the hand you cannot bite: the rise and fall of Ceausescus.* London: Hamish Hamilton.

Keesings contemporary archives: record of world events. 1989:366320; 366321; 367047; 377104. London: Keesings Publications.

CELESTINE. A monk of an order founded in 1264 by Peter of Morrone, who later became pope.

Pietro Del Murrone, Pope Celestine V (1215–96), was successor to Pope Nicholas IV. An ascetic, he was formerly a Benedictine, became a hermit, and lived in the Abruzzi Mountains. He attracted followers, who became known as Celestines, and later he brought them into the Benedictine order. He was elected pope on July 5, 1294, thereby ending a two-year dispute among the cardinals over who should succeed Nicholas IV. Charles II, king of Naples, dominated Celestine by keeping the pope in Naples; Celestine granted privileges to all who asked and gave the cardinals all the duties of his papal office while he lived in

his cell. Because his reign was so chaotic and he was victim to so many op-
portunists, he abdicated after five months and in December ordered a new election for pope. Dante thought him a coward for his decision and placed him at
the entrance to hell in his *Inferno.*

See also BENEDICTINE.

Sources

McDonald, William, ed. 1967. *New Catholic encyclopedia.* New York: McGraw-Hill.
McHenry, Robert, ed. 1992. *The new encyclopedia Britannica.* Chicago: Encyclopedia
    Britannica, Inc.

CHAMBERLAIN LETTER. A letter delivered to Adolf Hitler by Sir Horace
Wilson from Prime Minister Neville Chamberlain on September 26, 1938, suggesting that German and Czech representatives together consider how to hand
over the ceded territory of Sudetenland, Czechoslovakia. On September 30 Hitler and Chamberlain signed the Munich Agreement, prepared by Chamberlain
in advance, indicating that Britons and Germans never wanted to go to war
again and that their future differences would always be solved by consultation.
On his return to England that evening, the newspapers proclaimed Chamberlain
the savior of peace.

Arthur Neville Chamberlain (1869–1940) was born in Birmingham, attended
Rugby, managed the family's banana and sisal plantation in the Bahamas (1890–
97), and then returned to Birmingham where he became a leading industrialist
and local councillor. Elected a Conservative M.P. for the Ladywood division of
Birmingham in 1918, Chamberlain rose rapidly in British politics in the 1920s
to become minister for health and chancellor of the Exchequer, and succeeded
Prime Minister Stanley Baldwin in May 1937. His government followed a policy
of appeasement toward Hitler. The British and German delegation met on September 15, 1938 and agreed in principle on the self-determination for Sudeten
Germans, but when they met again on September 22, in a fury Hitler demanded
different terms. The Czech government found the new terms anathema and war
seemed certain. To avoid war, Chamberlain sent his letter and followed it with
the Munich Agreement. It was Chamberlain who was held to be primarily responsible for appeasing Hitler, although the policy had broad support in Britain.
After the Munich Agreement, Hitler's treatment of the Jews and others became
better known, and Chamberlain prepared for war, which he declared on Germany
in September 1939 when Germany did not withdraw its troops from Poland.
Lacking the inspirational leadership needed from a politician in wartime, Chamberlain stepped down in May 1940, replaced by Winston Churchill. He died of
cancer in November that year.

Sources

Charmley, John. 1989. *Chamberlain and the lost peace.* London: Hodder and Stoughton.
Cockett, Richard. 1989. *Twilight of truth: Chamberlain, appeasement and the manipu-
    lation of the press.* London: Weidenfeld and Nicolson.
Dilks, David. 1984. *Neville Chamberlain.* Cambridge: Cambridge University Press.

Legg, L.G. Wickham, ed. 1949. *The dictionary of national biography. 1931–40.* London: Oxford University Press.

Oxbury, Harold. 1985. *Great Britons: twentieth-century lives.* Oxford: Oxford University Press.

CHAPIN'S LIVING ROOM SCALE. A multiple-item index of social class or socioeconomic status based on symbols, activities, and possessions. Chapin defined socioeconomic status as the position that an individual or family occupies by reference to the prevailing average standards of cultural positions, effective income, material possessions, and participation in the group activities of community. After ten years of research, the scale was shortened to a Social Status Scale of seventeen items of living room equipment—radio, newspapers, fireplaces, hardwood floors—and its state of repair. The scale was found to relate to both income and occupation, and since it did not correlate closely with other measures of socioeconomic position, it is regarded as a measure of lifestyle rather than social class.

Francis Stuart Chapin (1888–1974) was born in Brooklyn, New York, and educated at Columbia University (Ph.D., Sociology, 1911). He was a member of the U.S. Army General Staff School, held many academic positions, including instructor of economics at Wellesley College, and was a professor of sociology and director of social work, University of Minnesota from 1922 to 1953, and then became emeritus. He was a consultant to the League of Nations and a postwar government adviser. In 1920 he published his highly regarded *Field Work and Social Research* at which time he was professor of economics and sociology at Smith College and director of the Smith College Training School for Social Work. His research centered on the application of statistical methods and experimental designs to sociological research on housing, and social and cultural change.

Sources

Barber, Bernard. 1957. *Social stratification.* New York: Harcourt, Brace and World, Inc.

Chapin, Francis S. 1935. *Contemporary American institutions: a sociological analysis.* New York: Harper.

Jaques Cattell Press, ed. 1973. *American men and women of science: the social and behavioral sciences.* New York: Jaques Cattell and R. R. Bowker.

Sills, David L., ed. 1968. *International encyclopedia of the social sciences.* New York: Macmillan and Free Press.

Trattner, Walter, ed. 1986. *Biographical dictionary of social welfare in America.* Westport, Conn.: Greenwood Press.

CHAUVINISM. Extreme devotion to and blind fanaticism for one's national origins, jingoism, and rejection of foreigners; recently, an expression of the attitude held by men who appear to oppose the principle of equal civil and economic rights for women.

Nicolas Chauvin (c. 1770–1820), from Rochefort, was one of Napoleon's often wounded veterans who retired on a small pension. After Napoleon's defeat,

Chauvin continued to publicly support the deposed emperor, thereby making Chauvin a laughable zealot in his home village. His excessive and misplaced patriotism made him an object of constant ridicule. The name was made popular in Charles and Jean Cogniard's famous vaudeville comedy, "La Cocarde Tricolore" (1831), where the extremely patriotic character uttered "Je suis français, je suis Chauvin." The patriotic Chauvin was characterized in *Le Soldat Laboureur* by Scribe and other French publications.

Sources

Hendrickson, Robert. 1988. *The dictionary of eponyms: names that became words.* New York: Dorset.

Jones, Barry. 1989. *The Macmillan dictionary of biography.* Melbourne: Macmillan.

Plano, Jack C., and Olton, Roy. 1988. *The international relations dictionary.* 4th ed. Santa Barbara, Calif.: ABC-CLIO.

CHESHIRE HOMES. An international organization established to care for the sick and disabled. In the early 1990s 267 such homes flourished in forty-nine countries.

Geoffrey Leonard Cheshire (1917–92), a life peer (1991), was the son of an Oxford law lecturer, and educated at the Dragon and Stowe, and at Merton College, Oxford, where he studied law. He became a fine tennis player, racing driver, and pilot. During World War II he commanded No. 617, "Dambusters," the RAF bomber squadron that dropped the bouncing-bombs used to blow up German dams during World War II. He became Britain's most decorated pilot and at age 24 was the RAF's youngest captain; he was an official observer at the bombing of Nagasaki in 1945. After the war he established a commune on a farm in Hampshire for disabled war veterans; it failed. He suffered mental ill-health, considered becoming a monk, went to British Columbia as a lumberjack, and eventually returned to a solitary life on his farm in England. There he helped a former commune member who was dying from cancer. In the early 1950s he toured England seeking money for the disabled and ill, and opened homes for their welfare. He married in 1955, raised two children, and helped establish the Cheshire Foundation which gained support from many prominent public figures. He published *Bomber Pilot* (1943), *Pilgrimage to the Shroud* (1956), *Face of Victory* (1961), *The Hidden World* (1981), and *The Light of Many Suns: The Meaning of the Bomb* (1985). Later he traveled to Moscow and the Middle East where he carried his work forward, and he published an autobiography, *Where Is God in All This?* (1990).

Sources

Barker, Dennis. 1992. Obituary: Lord Cheshire—a struggle to selflessness. *Guardian Weekly,* August 8:23.

The international who's who, 1992–93. London: Europa Publications.

Who's who, 1992–93. London: Adam and Charles Black.

CHICAGO SCHOOL OF ECONOMICS, CHICAGO SCHOOL OF POLITICS, CHICAGO SCHOOL OF SOCIOLOGY. A group of economists at the University of Chicago who supported individual freedom as a primary goal, laissez-faire capitalism, privatization of government functions, and government deregulation of monetary controls. The founder was Frank Knight (1885–1973), who was appointed a professor of economics in 1928, and contributed to the ethics and methodology of economics as well as the definition and interpretation of the concept of "social cost." He published *Risk and Uncertainty* (1921), *The Economic Organization* (1933), *The Ethics of Competition* (1935), and *Freedom and Reform* (1947). Milton Friedman (b. 1912), who became a professor of economics at Chicago in 1948, greatly influenced the government of Western economies and was awarded the Nobel Prize for Economics in 1976. Another member of the group, Oscar Lange (1904–65), a Polish socialist, taught at several American universities before going to Chicago (1938–45).

A group of political scientists advocated that politics would be advanced best through the scientific, empirical, and quantitative study of individual's activities in political situations rather than through study of merely political institutions and policies and their impact on individuals. Among them was Charles E. Merriam (1874–1953), a founding member of the school, a practicing politician, and a major leader among the progressives of his day. They advocated a form of behavioralism in political science and attracted such followers as Harold D. Lasswell (1902–78), David B. Truman (b. 1913), and Valdimer O. Key (1908–63).

The University of Chicago established the first graduate department in sociology, and it is regarded as one of the world's most important centers for the study of sociology. It was founded in 1892 by Albion Small (1854–1926), who in 1895 also founded the *American Journal of Sociology*. Robert E. Park (1864–1944) and Ernest W. Burgess (1886–1966) developed research on the city and urban life. Charles H. Cooley (1864–1929), George H. Mead (1863–1931), and William I. Thomas (1863–1947) developed a notable analysis of the self in society and helped establish the new field of social psychology. The school was later represented by symbolic interactionism and the work of Erving Goffman (1922–82) in modern sociology.

Sources

Eatwell, John; Milgate, Murray; and Newman, Peter. 1987. *The new Palgrave: a dictionary of economics*. London: Macmillan.

Greenwald, Douglas, ed. 1982. *Encyclopedia of economics*. New York: McGraw-Hill.

Hinkle, R. C., and Hinkle, G. J. 1954. *The development of modern sociology*. New York: Random House.

Shafritz, Jay M. 1988. *The Dorsey dictionary of American government and politics*. Chicago: Dorsey.

Sills, David L., ed. 1968. *International encyclopedia of the social sciences*. New York: Macmillan and Free Press.

CHOMSKYAN. A follower of or pertaining to the work of the modern American linguist who revolutionized the study of language; relating to his critical politics.

Noam Chomsky (b. 1928) was born in Philadelphia and educated at the University of Pennsylvania; during 1951–55 he was a member of the Society of Fellows, Harvard University, and in 1955 he was appointed a professor of linguistics at the Massachusetts Institute of Technology. He has been at prestigious universities and research centers as a prominent linguist ever since; thousands of university teachers and students have attended his lectures on the philosophy of language and mind. His fame extended beyond linguistics when he spoke openly against U.S. politics in Vietnam; he became a hero of the young left and risked jail by refusing to pay taxes that could support war. Today his politics comprise an attack on the United States and its abuse of its global power since World War II, for example, in Indochina (1960s and 1970s), the Middle East, and Central America (1980s). He writes stinging attacks against U.S. elites for their abuse of power, self-delusion, lying, hypocrisy, and political cynicism. Among his victims have been U.S. presidents Reagan and Bush, the *New York Times,* U.S. foreign policy in Latin America, its antidemocratic policies, plutocracy, and denial of freedom to the masses in the Third World. Chomsky's great contribution was to establish transformational-generative grammar, a complex system that revolutionized the science of linguistics. His linguistics are found in *The Logical Structure of Linguistic Theory* (1975), *Syntactic Structures* (1957), and *Language and the Mind* (1968). His politico-historical themes may be found in *American Power and the New Mandarins* (1969), *Peace in the Middle East?* (1975), *The Political Economy of Human Rights* (1979), and many other books, especially *Deterring Democracy* (1991).

Sources

Bullock, Alan, and Woodings, Robert B., eds. 1983. *The Fontana biographical companion to modern thought.* London: Collins.

Chomsky, Noam. 1976. *Reflections on language.* London: Fontana.

Devine, Elizabeth; Held, Michael; Vinson, James; and Walsh, George, eds. 1983. *Thinkers of the twentieth century: a biographical, bibliographical and critical dictionary.* London: Macmillan.

Lyons, John. 1978. *Chomsky.* London: Fontana.

May, Hal, and Lezniak, James G. 1990. *Contemporary authors.* Vol. 28. New Revision Series. Detroit: Gale Research.

CHRISTIAN, CHRISTIANITY. Pertaining to the religion based on the teachings of the religious leader from Nazareth and appearing in Protestant, Roman Catholic, Orthodox, and Eastern forms.

According to the teachings of Christianity, Jesus Christ (c. 4–33) was born of the Virgin Mary, wife of Joseph of Nazareth, in Galilee. He may have been a carpenter. At the age of about 28, after the imprisonment of John the Baptist, Jesus, whom John had baptized, began teaching. Most of his work was done in Galilee, north Palestine, and Jerusalem. He preached about the imminent approach of the kingdom of God and spoke in parables, and he performed miracles to illustrate his meaning and his accreditation from God. He chose twelve disciples, the Apostles, who spread his word. One of these disciples, Judas, betrayed him to the authorities, and Jesus was crucified. Jesus interpreted his imminent death as a covenant sacrifice, and he prophesied that a new, godly community would emerge after he died. "Christ," meaning "the anointed one," was the Greek term for the Hebrew "Messiah." It was first used in Antioch (Acts 11:26) to refer to his followers after he had risen from the dead, and it indicated he was their Lord. Thereafter they became known as Christians. According to recent historical research, Jesus was pretender to the throne of King David, raised in a strict dynastic order, and became a crown prince. When he found he could not be king, he gathered a circle of friends and began his own politico-religious mission (Thiering, 1992).

Sources

Cross, Frank L. 1974. *The Oxford dictionary of the Christian church.* 2d ed. New York: Oxford University Press.

Ferguson, Everett, ed. 1990. *The encyclopedia of early Christianity.* New York: Garland Publishing.

Hastings, J., ed. 1912. *Dictionary of Christ and the Gospels.* New York: Charles Scribner's Sons.

McDonald, William, ed. 1967. *New Catholic encyclopedia.* New York: McGraw-Hill.

McHenry, Robert, ed. 1992. *The new encyclopedia Britannica.* Chicago: Encyclopedia Britannica, Inc.

Thiering, Barbara. 1992. *Jesus the man.* New York: Doubleday.

CHRISTIAN DEMOCRACY, CHRISTIAN EXISTENTIALISM, CHRISTIAN SCIENCE, CHRISTIAN SOCIALISM. Christian Democracy is a political ideology, often associated with the Catholic Church, which expects its adherents to uphold liberal, anticommunist, and antifascist policies, a social market economy, and the integration of a society and of nations, especially in Europe. Political parties that upheld these views were found in West Germany and Italy.

Christian Existentialism is a modern ideology that takes much from the work of Søren Kierkegaard (1813–55), especially the belief that human experience is the best test of religious doctrine and that metaphysical speculations and reasoning are largely inadequate.

Christian Science is a healing religion upheld by the followers of Mary Baker Eddy (1821–1910) and the only one in America to have survived the nineteenth-century rise of medicine as a science. See also EDDYISM.

Christian Socialism comprises movements that unite the ethics in Christian teachings with the collectivism found in socialist beliefs. The movement began with Frederick D. Maurice (1805–72) and Edward Carpenter (1844–1929) in nineteenth-century England, and later in various refinements by the Protestant church it appeared in France, Germany, the United States, and Scandinavia. In Switzerland it was founded by Leonhard Ragaz (1868–1945), who taught that the core of socialism was not materialistic but idealist, while Marxism was merely a religion and Christianity was a set of ethics upholding pacifism.

Jesus Christ. See CHRISTIAN.

Sources

Bullock, Alan; Stallybrass, Oliver; and Trombley, Stephen, eds. 1988. *The Fontana dictionary of modern thought.* 2d ed. London: Fontana.

Gottschalk, S. 1973. *The emergence of Christian Science in American religious life.* Berkeley: University of California Press.

Lueker, Erwin L. 1975. *Lutheran cyclopedia.* St. Louis: Concordia.

Rowland, C. 1987. *Radical Christianity.* New York: Orbis Books.

CHURCH COMMITTEE. A U.S. Select Committee (1975–76) that was authorized to investigate the extent, if any, to which any agency of the federal government engaged in illegal, improper, or unethical activities. Investigation assembled a large collection of classified intelligence documents. Some CIA officials considered the committee a mechanism Senator Church was using to further his plans to win the Democratic nomination for the U.S. presidency in 1976; others saw it an inquisition. Serious internal problems for the CIA ensued, leading in January 1976 to President Ford appointing George Bush to succeed William Colby as head of the CIA. The committee's recommendations strengthened control over the CIA and the U.S. intelligence community (1978).

Frank (Forrester) Church (1924–84), born in Boise, Idaho, was educated in public schools and joined the United States Army in 1942. He became a commissioned infantry officer in 1944 and was assigned to military intelligence. He was discharged in 1946 after seeing service in India, Burma, China, and California. Following graduation from Stanford University (1947), he studied law. In 1950, after being admitted to the bar, he began practice in Boise, Idaho. He became a U.S. Democratic senator from Idaho (1956) and was chosen as the U.S. delegate to the twenty-first General Assembly of the United Nations. He was reelected to the Senate from 1957 to 1981. During his political career he was a member and chairman (1979–81) of the U.S. Senate Foreign Relations Committee, was committed to the banning of nuclear tests, and supported liberal legislation on civil and equal rights and conservation. After he left the Senate, he practiced international law until his death in 1984.

Sources

Jacob, Kathryn A., and Ragsdale, Bruce A. 1989. *Biographical directory of the United States Congress: 1774–1989.* Bicentennial ed. Washington, D.C.: U.S. Government Printing Office.

Moritz, Charles. 1978; 1984. *Current biography yearbook.* New York: H. W. Wilson.

O'Toole, G.S.A. 1988. *The encyclopedia of American intelligence and espionage.* New York: Facts on File.

CHURCHILLIAN. Of influence and stature like that of the great twentieth-century British statesman, the modern British symbol of the defense of freedom;

sombre in tone of speech especially when referring to the trials ahead and in appealing to national unity, elegant in expression and witty.

Sir Winston Leonard Spencer Churchill (1874–1965) was born at Blenheim Palace, Oxfordshire. He was sent to Harrow, passed into Sandhurst, and became an officer in the 4th Hussars in 1894. He entered Parliament as a Conservative in 1900. Later he switched to the Liberal party. He was secretary of state for war during World War I and for air during 1918–21, and colonial secretary from 1921 to 1922. Having been many years out of power in Britain, he returned in 1940, when Prime Minister Chamberlain was forced to resign. Churchill seemed to arrive at the right time, God-given, to raise the spirits of those who believed in a political system that had everywhere been reviled, duped, and corrupted by totalitarianism and dictatorship. Britain's national identity became linked with Churchill during World War II. He is remembered in his speeches by such utterances as: "Never in the field of human conflict was so much owed by so many to so few. . . . I have nothing to offer but blood, toil, sweat and tears." When Graham Sutherland painted Churchill after the war, the artist so clearly depicted the bulldog spirit associated with the tenacity of the wartime Churchill that Churchill's wife had it destroyed. He has been the subject of many biographies, some laudatory and others seriously questioning his leadership in wartime.

Sources

Blake, Robert, and Louis, W. Roger, eds. 1993. *A major new assessment of his life in peace and war.* Oxford: Oxford University Press.

Gilbert, Martin. 1991. *Churchill: A life.* London: Heinemann.

Lamb, Richard. 1992 *Churchill as war leader—right or wrong?* London: Allen and Unwin.

Williams, E. T., and Nichols, C. S., eds. 1981. *Dictionary of national biography 1961–1970.* Oxford: Oxford University Press.

CICERONE, CICERONIAN. A person who shows strangers the curiosities of a place, a guide; to act as a guide; the name given by the Italians to the guides who show visitors the antiquities of their country. Cicerones vary in degrees of knowledge and respectability; some are noted archaeologists, while others are thieves who live dishonestly from tourists. Ciceronian means relating to or after the manner of the Roman orator, writer, and statesman, especially in his Latinity.

Marcus Tullius Cicero (106–43 B.C.) was born at Arpinum (now Arpino) in Italy. It is said that he was so-named because of a wart on the end of his nose (in Latin, "cicer"). He studied law, oratory, literature, and philosophy in Rome and later in Greece and Asia. His rich prose style combined clarity with eloquence and became the model for all other Latin prose. He enriched his own language and wrote on many subjects of intellectual interest. In 51 B.C. Cicero accepted the governorship of the Roman province of Cilicia. When he came back to Rome a year later, he joined Pompey, a bitter enemy of Caesar. After Caesar's assassination, Cicero entered Roman politics and gave his Philippic orations attacking Mark Antony, only to be executed as an enemy of the state.

Sources
Chisholm, Kitty, and Ferguson, John. 1981. *Rome: the Augustan age.* Oxford: Oxford University Press.
McHenry, Robert, ed. 1992. *The new encyclopedia Britannica.* Chicago: Encyclopedia Britannica, Inc.
Miller, David, ed. 1987. *The Blackwell encyclopedia of political thought.* Oxford: Basil Blackwell.

CLARENDON CODE. Four acts passed in the English Parliament (1661–65) after the restoration of Charles II to the throne (1660). The acts sought to destroy the influence of the Protestant Dissenters by excluding them from secular office and limiting their religious freedom. They were the Municipal Corporation Act (1661) which required town government members to join the Church of England, renounce the Solemn League Covenant, and swear allegiance to the Crown; the Act of Uniformity (1662) demanding that all church and educational officials accept the Book of Prayer; the Conventicle Act (1664) which severely punished groups of five or more who met for Nonconformist meetings; and the Five Mile Act (1665) which required all Nonconformist preachers and teachers who came within five miles (8 km) of a parish to swear never to resist the king.

Edward Hyde Clarendon (1609–74), first earl of Clarendon, was born in Dinton, educated at Oxford, became a lawyer, and entered Parliament in 1640. As a representative of Charles I, Hyde's negotiations failed to end the first English Civil War; then he became an adviser to Charles II, going into exile with him until the monarchy was restored after Cromwell's rule. He was made an earl in 1661 and served as lord chancellor from 1660 to 1690. After the unpopular Treaty of Breda, at the end of the Anglo-Dutch War, Clarendon was dismissed, left for France, and wrote his *History of the Rebellion* (1702–4).

Sources
Harris, R. W. 1983. *Clarendon and the English revolution.* London: Chatto and Windus, Hogarth Press.
Ollard, Richard. 1987. *Clarendon and his friends.* London: Hamilton.
Stephen, Leslie, and Lee, Sydney, eds. 1917. *The dictionary of national biography.* London: Oxford University Press.

CLAUSEWITZ. A formidable strategist and tactician.

Karl von Clausewitz (1780–1831) was a Prussian general and writer on military strategy. He served in the Rhine campaigns in 1793–94 and fought against Napoleon Bonaparte (1812–14). For Russia he helped negotiate the Convention of Tauroggen, which prepared for the alliance of Prussia, Russia, and Great Britain against Napoleon. On rejoining the Prussian forces, he fought at Waterloo, and in 1818 he became director of the Prussian War College. His main work, *On War,* was unfinished and published posthumously. It outlines "total war," the idea that all citizens, territory, and property of an enemy should be the subject of all varieties of attack. To Clausewitz war was a political act, a continuation of diplomacy by alternative means, in which political leaders of a state should determine the scope of a war, its aims, and the control of its direction. These views had a considerable impact on modern military practices and greatly enhanced the role of the military in international relations.

Sources

Clausewitz, Karl von. 1966. *On war.* 3 vols. Trans J. J. Graham, revised ed. Introduction and notes by F. N. Maude. London: Routledge and Kegan Paul.

Greene, Joseph I. 1945. *The living thoughts of Clausewitz.* London: Living Thoughts Library.

Harris, William H., and Levey, Judith S., eds. 1978–79. *The new illustrated Columbia encyclopedia.* New York: Rockville House and Columbia University.

Howard, Michael, and Paret, Peter, eds. and trans. 1984. *On War: Karl von Clausewitz.* Princeton, N.J.: Princeton University Press.

Sills, David L., ed. 1968. *International encyclopedia of the social sciences.* New York: Macmillan and Free Press.

CLAWSON METHOD. A method of measuring and predicting recreation demand that centers on the price people are prepared to pay. The notional price is used as a measure of the benefit they derive from their recreational experience. Demand schedules include the distribution of population around a recreational facility and the transport costs incurred in using it.

Marion Clawson (b. 1905) was born in Elko, Nevada, graduated in Agriculture from the University of Nevada, and studied at the University of California and Harvard (Ph.D., 1943). After working in Washington and in Berkeley, he joined the U.S. Department of Agricultural Research and Planning Studies on the Columbia Basin Irrigation Project (1940–42). Afterward, from 1942 to 1945, he worked on the Central Valley Irrigation Project in California and in 1947–78 he was regional administrator, Bureau of Land Management, at the U.S. Department of the Interior in San Francisco. He directed the Bureau of Land Management in Washington (1948–53), advised Israel on its economy (1953–55), and directed a land use and management program on Resources for the Future (1953). Among his many publications are *Farm Management* (1947), *Western Range Livestock Industry* (1949), *Uncle Sam's Acres* (1951), *Man and Land in the United States* (1964), and *Forests for Whom and for What?* (1975).

Sources

Blaug, Mark, ed. 1986. *Who's who in economics: a biographical dictionary of major economists, 1700–1986.* 2d ed. Cambridge, Mass.: MIT Press.

Clawson, Marion. 1987. *From sagebrush to sage: the making of a natural resources economist.* Kalamazoo, Mich.: Ana Publications.

Goodall, Brian 1987. *The Penguin dictionary of human geography.* Harmondsworth, Middlesex: Penguin.

Jaques Cattell Press, ed. 1973. *American men and women of science: the social and behavioral sciences.* New York: Jaques Cattell and R. R. Bowker.

Healy, Robert G., and Shands, William E. A. 1989. A conversation with Marion Clawson. *Journal of Forestry* 87:18–24.

Who's who in America, 1980–81. Chicago: Marquis.

CLEMENTINE. Relating to or a follower of any of the popes named Clement, but especially Clement I and Clement V.

Clement I, Saint Clement, Clement of Rome (d. c. 101) was pope from about 92 to 101. He was the first ecclesiastical writer or "Apostolic Father," and the third bishop of Rome. He was personally acquainted with the saints, Peter and Paul. His two "Epistles to the Corinthians" (c. 96) were regarded as a canonical book of the Bible until the fourth century. They are a source of information about the early life, beliefs, and organization of the Christian Church. They were lost until rediscovered by Patrick Young (1584–1652), librarian to James I and Charles I.

Clement V, originally named Bertrand de Got (c. 1260–1314), was born in Gascony, France, and studied canon law in Orleans and Bologna. He was bishop of Comminges (1295–99) and archbishop of Bordeaux (1299–1305), and he became Pope Clement V (1305–14) with the help of King Philip of France. To repay King Philip, Clement V called the Council of Vienne to put down the Knight Templars, a military and religious order whom the king wished he controlled (1311). Clement V founded the University of Perugia in 1307 and established the study of Asia at the University of Paris and Oxford. He contributed to the development of canon law with his *Constitutiones Clementinae,* which were letters including authoritative decisions and disciplinary matters.

Sources
Cross, Frank L. 1974. *The Oxford dictionary of the Christian church.* 2d ed. New York: Oxford University Press.

Douglas, James D., ed. 1974. *The new international dictionary of the Christian church.* Exeter: Paternoster Press.

Ferguson, Everett, ed. 1990. *The encyclopedia of early Christianity.* New York: Garland Publishing.

McDonald, William J., ed. 1967. *New Catholic encyclopedia.* New York: McGraw-Hill.

McHenry, Robert, ed. 1992. *The new encyclopedia Britannica.* Chicago: Encyclopedia Britannica, Inc.

Myers, Allen C., ed. 1987. *The Eerdman's Bible dictionary.* Grand Rapids, Mich.: William B. Eerdman's.

Phillips, Robert S., ed. 1983. *Funk and Wagnall's new encyclopedia.* New York: Funk and Wagnall, Inc.

CLIFFORD-ELSEY REPORT. A secret 26,000-word memorandum (1946), written at the request of President Truman, on Soviet violations of treaty pledges. It became the germ of U.S. foreign policy for Europe after World War II.

Clark McAdams Clifford (b. 1906) was born at Fort Scott, Kansas, and educated at Washington University, Saint Louis (LL.B., 1928). He was a distinguished lawyer and adviser to Democratic presidents Truman and Johnson. Truman employed Clifford in 1945 to create the CIA, the Defense Department, and the Joint Chiefs of Staff; Clifford advocated racial integration of the armed forces and the Truman Loyalty Program, which was intended to protect the U.S. public service from infiltration by communists. The secret memorandum, the

Clifford-Elsey report, was so explosive that Truman confiscated all copies; the memo was first published in 1968 in the memoirs of Arthur Krock (1886–1974). The document summarizes the views of George Kennan (b. 1904), Dean Acheson (1893–1971), and others, and is reputed to have shaped the Truman Doctrine and the Marshall Plan. In 1965 Clifford failed to persuade President Johnson that the Vietnam War could not be won; as secretary of defense in 1968, however, his advice on Vietnam was heeded. In a sad post-note to his distinguished career, in 1993 he and his partner, Robert Altman, were accused of a $20 billion fraud involving the Bank of Credit and Commerce International. Thus, at the age of 86 Clifford lost his illustrious reputation, and his wealth was frozen pending possible seizure. He underwent heart surgery and was so weak he could not stand trial for the alleged fraud. Altman was found not guilty in August 1993.

George McKee Elsey (b. 1918) was born in California and educated at Princeton, Harvard, and the American International College. He was a member of the White House staff during the Truman years.

Sources

Beaty, Jonathan, and Gwynne, S. C. 1993. BCCI: The trial. *Time* (Australia) April 12: 56–57.

Clifford, Clark, with Holbrooke, Richard. 1991. *Counsel to the President.* New York: Random House.

Gwynne, S. C. 1993. Innocent as charged. *Time* (Australia) August 30: 51.

Krock, Arthur. 1968. *Memoirs: sixty years in the firing line.* New York: Funk and Wagnalls.

Sobel, Robert, ed. 1971. *Biographical dictionary of the United States executive branch 1774–1971.* Westport, Conn.: Greenwood Press.

Who's who in America, 1990–91. Chicago: Marquis.

Who's who in America, 1991–92. Chicago: Marquis.

The international who's who, 1992–93. London: Europa Publications.

CLINTON, CLINTON REPUBLICANS, CLINTONISM, CLINTON DOCTRINE.

To have it both ways, especially in giving different replies to the same question. Younger, more moderate supporters of the Republican party who favored abortion rights during the 1992 U.S. presidential election campaign. "A rather traditional form of social democracy tinged with American populism, Keynesian policies plus the electric chair, public investment plus a hundred thousand more cops on the streets" (Walker, 1992). The first term was coined by Dan Quayle in the debate between the vice-presidential candidates on October 14, 1992; the second appeared in the *Los Angeles Times* on August 16, 1992; and the third was used by a British reporter, Martin Walker in 1992. The Clinton Doctrine is an early statement of foreign policy that emerged from President Clinton's inauguration and stated that there would always be "American leadership of a world we did so much to make." The policy can be traced back at least to President Woodrow Wilson (Walker, 1993).

William Jefferson Clinton (b. 1946) was born in Hope, Arkansas. His natural father died before William was born, and he was adopted at age 4 by his mother's second husband, Roger Clinton. William was raised and received his early education in Hot Springs, Arkansas, and completed a degree in international affairs at Georgetown University in 1968. He was a Rhodes Scholar and graduated from Yale Law School in 1973. At 16 he had already chosen politics as a career. In 1972 he worked for George McGovern and the House Judiciary Committee, taught at the University of Arkansas Law School in 1973, directed Jimmy Carter's successful campaign for the presidency in Arkansas and at age 32, in 1978, became the youngest governor in Arkansas history. In the 1980s he lost and then regained the governorship, nominated Michael S. Dukakis at the presidential convention in 1988, and defeated the incumbent George Bush for the U.S. presidency in 1992.

Sources

Allen, Charles, and Portis, Jonathan. 1992. *The comeback kid: the life and career of Bill Clinton.* New York: Birch Lane Press.

Moritz, Charles, ed. 1988. *Current biography yearbook.* New York: H. W. Wilson.

Walker, Martin. 1992. The America-firster, keeps the world waiting. *The Guardian Weekly,* November 15:7–8.

Walker, Martin. 1993. A new generation and a new beginning. *The Guardian Weekly,* January 31:1.

CLIOMETRICS. A method of historical research based largely on statistical information.

Clio, one of the nine Muses, sits beside an open box of books or examines a scroll of paper in her role as the Muse of history. Some relate her to musicians and say she was the lover of Pierus, and by him, the mother of Hyacinthus; others claim that Aphrodite inspired Clio with passion to punish her because she had derided the goddess's own love for the handsome Adonis. She was said to have invented historical and heroic poetry.

Sources

Bell, Robert E. 1982. *Dictionary of classical mythology.* Santa Barbara, Calif.: ABC-CLIO.

Bell, Robert E. 1991. *Women of classical mythology.* Santa Barbara, Calif.: ABC-CLIO.

Benét, William R. 1990. *The reader's encyclopedia of world literature and arts, with supplement.* New York: Thomas Y. Crowell.

Grimal, Pierre. 1986. *The dictionary of classical mythology.* Oxford: Basil Blackwell.

COASE THEOREM. An economic theorem that assumes external factors do not lead to the misallocation of resources if there are no transaction costs and if property rights are both enforceable and defined clearly. As a rule, both producer and consumer would negotiate for a mutually satisfying outcome in the market, thereby internalizing the external factor. According to the neutrality theorem, the result of such trading would be the same no matter whether it was the consumer or the producer of the externality who held property rights of veto over the resource's use. The theorem came from a series of examples in 1960.

Ronald Harry Coase (b. 1910) was born in Willesden, England. He studied economics and business law relating to business at the London School of Economics. He taught at the Dundee School of Economics, and in 1951 went to the United States where he taught and researched at the universities of Buffalo, Virginia, and Chicago. In 1964 he was made editor of the *Journal of Law and Economics,* in which he published many of his contributions. His work clearly altered the economic theory of business, externalities, and public goods, as well as the argument that an economy is organized by market exchanges. In 1937 he wrote his article about "transaction costs" which cost a company money. In addition, one of his major articles explains why there is a McDonald's rather than 100,000 little entrepreneurs selling hamburgers. He won the Nobel Prize for Economics in 1991 for his 1960 and 1937 articles on companies, production, and marketplace transactions. He retired emeritus and became a senior fellow in the Chicago Law School in 1979.

Sources

Blaug, Mark, ed. 1986. *Who's who in economics: a biographical dictionary of major economists, 1700–1986.* 2d ed. Cambridge, Mass.: MIT Press.

Eatwell, John; Milgate, Murray; and Newman, Peter. 1987. *The New Palgrave: a dictionary of economics.* London: Macmillan.

Pearce, David W., ed. 1986. *Macmillan dictionary of modern economics.* New York: Macmillan.

Sills, David L., ed. 1968. *International encyclopedia of the social sciences.* New York: Macmillan and Free Press.

COBB-DOUGLAS PRODUCTION FUNCTION. A single measure of the production processes for an entire economy. It became popular because it is easy to use and has the minimal properties that economists desire. It appeared prior to 1916, notably in the theory of distribution, and it has often been applied econometrically because it can explain the data so well.

Charles Wiggins Cobb (1875–1949) was a mathematician and economist at Amherst College in Amherst, Massachusetts. He wrote *Plane Analytic Geometry* (1913), *The Asymptotic Development for a Certain Function of Zero Order* (1913), *Manufacturing in Ten States: 1921–1931* (1935), *Notes on Massachusetts Manufacturing* (1939), and *Notes on United States Manufacturing* (1940–47).

Paul Douglas (1892–1976) was born in Salem, Massachusetts, raised in Maine, and graduated from Bowdoin College in 1913. After postgraduate studies at Columbia University, he began teaching at the University of Chicago (1920), and apart from wartime service in the Marines, he remained there until 1948 when he became a member of the U.S. Senate, serving from 1948 to 1966. His economic fame was based on his rediscovery of the Cobb-Douglas Production Function in 1928. During a leave of absence from Amherst College (1924–27), Douglas met Charles W. Cobb and began work on the production function. Capitalizing on the early work of his colleague, Cobb, a fellow mathematician and economist, Douglas succeeded in estimating a statistical equation expressing the physical output of the manufacturing sector as a function of its labor and capital inputs. However, it was only in the 1950s with the rise of the theory of economic growth, that the Cobb-Douglas Production Function became a single expression for the production processes of an entire economy. In 1930 Douglas published his *Real Wages in the United States: 1890–1926,* and in 1934 his notable *The Theory of Wages.*

Sources

Blaug, Mark. 1985. *Great economists since Keynes.* Brighton, England: Harvester Press.

Douglas, Paul. 1934. *The theory of wages.* New York: Macmillan.

Eatwell, John; Milgate, Murray; and Newman, Peter. 1987. *The new Palgrave: a dictionary of economics.* London: Macmillan.

Ruffner, James A., et al., eds. 1977. *Eponyms dictionaries index.* Detroit: Gale Research.

COBBETT'S PARLIAMENTARY DEBATES. The first records of British parliamentary debates in modern times, later known as Hansard.

William Cobbett (1763–1835), British journalist and reformer, was born at Farnham, Surrey, son of a small farmer. He started work as a ploughboy, but at age 14 ran away from home and, after working for a time in London and Chatham, where he is said to have mastered Lowth's *English Grammar,* he enlisted in the British Army (1783). He resigned in 1792 to expose abuses in the military forces, but, being unable to prove his accusations, he fled to France and later America to avoid prosecution. In America he taught English to French refugees, and as "Peter Porcupine" he wrote fierce attacks on American democracy in his Philadelphia newspaper, *Porcupine's Gazette.* On his return to England in 1802, he began *Cobbett's Parliamentary Debates,* and in the same year he started the Tory journal, *Cobbett's Weekly Political Register,* which became the basic reading of the literate working class. Following his criticism of the flogging of militia men by German mercenaries, Cobbett was jailed at Newgate in 1810–12 for libel. He championed parliamentary reform and became M.P. for Oldham in the first Parliament elected under the 1832 reform bill.

Sources

Aldrich, Richard, and Gordon, Peter. 1987. *Dictionary of British educationists.* London: Woburn Press.

Cole, George D.H. 1947. *The life of William Cobbett.* 3 vols. Rev. ed. London: Home Van Thal.

Magnussen, Magnus; Goring, Rosemary; and Thorn, John O., eds. 1990. *Chambers biographical dictionary* Edinburgh: Chambers Ltd.

Osborne, John W. 1966. *William Cobbett: his thought and his times.* New Brunswick, N.J.: Rutgers University Press.

Stephen, Leslie, and Lee, Sydney, eds. 1917. *The dictionary of national biography.* London: Oxford University Press.

COBDENISM, COBDENITE, COBDEN TREATY. An English economic policy of 1840–60 that opposed the Corn Laws and upheld free trade. One who

supported such views on free trade and related British foreign policies. An Anglo-French commercial treaty for reciprocal tariffs, 1859–60.

Richard Cobden (1804–65), was born in Sussex, England. At age 15 he went
to London to work for his uncle, a calico merchant, and in 1828 he established
an independent firm and mill in Manchester, employed 2,000 workers, and by
35 was very rich. His philosophy of free trade was first expressed in two pamphlets, *England, Ireland, and America* (1835) and *Russia* (1836). In 1838 he
and John Bright joined with five other merchants to found the Anti-Corn Law
League. To decrease living costs, the league agitated for the repeal of duties on
corn and other grain imports. Strong resistance to the policy came from landed
interests. Cobden believed free trade would break down national barriers and
give everyone a material interest in avoiding war. Cobden entered Parliament
in 1841, worked for the repeal of the Corn Laws, and after 1849 concerned
himself mainly with foreign policy, advocating nonintervention in Europe and
an end to imperial expansion. He believed that battles are won by the cheapest
goods, nonintervention in foreign lands, and a policy of laissez faire in industry.
He became unpopular for his opposition to the Crimean War (1854–56), lost
his seat in 1857, was reelected in 1859, and negotiated the Cobden Treaty.
Sources

Eatwell, John; Milgate, Murray; and Newman, Peter. 1987. *The new Palgrave: a
    dictionary of economics.* London: Macmillan.
Filler, Louis. 1963. *A dictionary of American economic reform.* New York: Philosophical
    Library.
Morely, John. 1905. *The life of Richard Cobden.* 12th ed. London: T. F. Unwin.
Stephen, Leslie, and Lee, Sydney, eds. 1917. *The dictionary of national biography.* Lon-
    don: Oxford University Press.

COCCEIANS. Followers of the seventeenth-century Dutch theologian.

Johannes Cocceius (1603–69) was born and raised in Bremen. As a notable
Dutch Hebraist and theologian, he became a professor of biblical philology at
the Academy of Bremen in 1629 and at the University of Francker in 1636, and
a professor of dogmatics at Leyden in 1650. He published several learned works
including a dictionary of Hebrew (1669). His theory of life was based on the
Bible, and the biblical covenant between the individual and God was central to
his ideas. In the Old Testament he found Jesus Christ prefigured throughout,
and he asserted that the Old Testament foreshadowed both Christ's history and
his church. In the older Protestant theology, his contributions are valued for
their contribution to the historical development of revelation.
Sources

Cross, Frank L. 1974. *The Oxford dictionary of the Christian Church.* 2d ed. New York:
    Oxford University Press.
Douglas, James D., ed. 1974. *The new international dictionary of the Christian Church.*
    Exeter: Paternoster Press.
Dudley, Lavinia P. 1963. *The encyclopedia Americana.* International ed. New York:
    Americana Corp.

McHenry, Robert, ed. 1992. *The new encyclopedia Britannica.* Chicago: Encyclopedia
    Britannica, Inc.
Smith, Benjamin. 1903. *The Century cyclopedia of names.* London: The Times.

COCHISE. Relating to a prehistoric Indian culture of southeast Arizona adjacent to New Mexico. It is characterized by an abundance of flat milling slabs
and, in the early stage, by a lack of defensive weapons. In later stages there is
evidence of change from a seed-gathering to a hunting economy.

Cochise (c. 1815–74) was chief of the Chiricahua group, among Apache Indians in Arizona. Until 1861 he was friendly with whites. But when his family
was hanged by American soldiers for crimes they did not commit, Cochise
warred relentlessly against the American Army, becoming noted for his integrity,
courage, and military skill. A close friendship with Thomas J. Jeffords (1832–
1914) was the basis for a peace, and it was agreed that Cochise would live on
a reservation that had been created from the chief's native territory. In 1869
Jeffords was appointed Indian trader for the Southern Apaches and gained Cochise's good-will probably while he supervised the mail route that went through
Cochise's encampment. However, after Cochise died his people were moved to
another reservation.

Sources

Gove, Philip B., ed. 1966. *Webster's third international dictionary,* Springfield, Mass.:
    G. and C. Merriam.
Harris, William H., and Levey, Judith S., eds. 1978–1979. *The new illustrated Columbia
    encyclopedia.* New York: Rockville House and Columbia University.
Magnussen, Magnus; Goring, Rosemary; and Thorn, John O., eds. 1990. *Chambers bi-
    ographical dictionary.* Edinburgh: Chambers Ltd.
Sweeney, Edwin R. 1991. *Cochise: Chiricahua Apache chief.* Norman: University of
    Oklahoma Press.
Van Doren, Charles, ed. 1974. *Webster's American biographies.* Springfield, Mass.: G.
    and C. Merriam.

COCKBURN COMMISSION. A British royal commission on labor laws
which considered the question of common law conspiracy in trade disputes that
arose largely from the Criminal Law Amendment Act of 1871. As a consequence, the Masters and Servants Act of 1867 and the Criminal Law Amendment Act were repealed, thereby making it legal for people to enter a trade
dispute, such as a strike, especially regarding their working conditions. The law
was changed in 1971 with the Industrial Relations Act.

Sir Alexander James Edmund Cockburn (1802–80), a noted British jurist, was
called to the bar in 1829, and with many election cases he became a prominent
trial lawyer. He was recorder of Southampton in 1841 and entered Parliament
in 1847. His most famous success was the acquittal of Daniel McNaughten
(1843) who was found insane when he killed the prime minister's secretary.
Cockburn was attorney-general (1851–56), chief justice of Common Pleas

(1856–59), and during the royal commission which he chaired he was lord chief justice (1859–80).

See also McNAUGHTON RULES.

Sources

Marsh, Arthur. 1979. *Concise encyclopedia of industrial relations.* Westmead, Farnborough, Hants: Gower.

Stephen, Leslie, and Lee, Sydney, eds. 1917. *The dictionary of national biography.* London: Oxford University Press.

CODE OF HAMMURABI. The most complete monument of Babylonian law. The Sumerians developed this code partly because they accepted the idea of a hierarchy, operating under a god of the city and his earthly representative. One of their earliest rulers outlined his efforts to impose respect for traditional customs and to limit the priests and officials in the city from oppressing the poor (c. 2370 B.C.). Centuries later, the first known code of laws, of which only a fragment remains, was issued (c. 2130 B.C.). The main source of the Code of Hammurabi is a monument in black stone. Under M. J. de Morgan, a French expedition discovered at the acropolis of Susa the black diorite stone in three pieces, which is now assembled in the Louvre. The code was first translated in 1902 by the French Assyriologist, Jean Vincent Scheil, in the official report of the expedition.

Hammurabi, first king of Babylonia (c. 2287–2232 B.C.), ruled in the city of Babylon and proved a great warrior and a fine ruler in peacetime. He drove out the Elamitic invaders, united the northern and southern parts of Babylonia, established the city, and is known as the founder of the Babylonian Empire. Apart from erecting many temples, one of his greatest works was the nahr-Hammurabi, an enormous waterway that became known as the Royal Canal of Babylon.

Sources

Bromiley, Geoffrey W., ed. 1979–88. *The international standard Bible encyclopedia.* Grand Rapids, Mich.: William B. Eerdman's.

McHenry, Robert, ed. 1992. *The new encyclopedia Britannica.* Chicago: Encyclopedia Britannica, Inc.

Smith, Benjamin, ed. 1903. *The Century cyclopedia of names.* London: The Times.

CODE NAPOLEON. Before the French Revolution France had two kinds of laws—written law and customary law. Even though several attempts were made to unite them, none succeeded, and in 1789 the Constituent Assembly demanded a common code for the whole kingdom but one was not forthcoming. Napoleon ordered the code be drawn up. Parts were subject to public discussion, but Napoleon withdrew them, expelled those who were in opposition to them, and formed committees of those remaining. By 1804 the promulgation of a code had begun. Known as the Civil Code, it comprises thirty-six laws; they were passed in 1803–4 and brought together in one body of law the Code Civil des

Francais, and final promulgation came in 1810. The name is sometimes used to cover all of Napoleon's legislation.

See also NAPOLEONIC.

Sources

Bysiewicz, Shirley R. 1983. *Monarch's dictionary of legal terms for home, office and school use.* New York: Monarch–Simon and Shuster.

Higgs, Henry. 1925–26. *Palgrave's dictionary of political economy.* Rev. ed. Reprint 1963. New York: Augustus M. Kelley.

Ivamy, E.R. Hardy. 1988. *Mozley and Whiteley's law dictionary.* London: Butterworth.

COKE (UP)ON LITTLETON. The suggestion that, with respect to the matter at hand, subtleties of the law may be involved.

Sir Edward Coke (1552–1634), a judge and law writer, was commonly known as Lord Coke. The only son of an old Norfolk family, he was educated at Cambridge and after being admitted to the bar (1578) rose rapidly from recorder of Coventry (1585), member for Adelburgh (1589), and solicitor general (1592) to speaker of the House of Commons (1593). In 1613 he became chief justice of the King's Bench and a privy councillor. On trivial grounds he was removed from the bench but later reinstated; he became alienated from the court when he led a popular party that was opposed to Spain and to monopolies. In 1621–22 he was imprisoned in the Tower of London. He carried forward his opposition to the next reign and was largely responsible for the Petition of Rights (1628). He published the first text on modern common law, *Institutes of the Laws of England* (1628–44), which dealt with tenures, statutes, criminal law, and jurisdiction of law courts. "Coke upon Littleton" is a commentary with considerable value.

Sir Thomas Littleton (1422–81), was born Thomas Westcote, at Frankley House, in Worcestershire; as heir to his mother, he was baptized in her name. In 1450 he was the recorder of Coventry, became king's sergeant (1455), and a judge of common pleas in 1466. In 1475 he was knight of Bath. He is noted for his *Tenures* (1481), written in Law French and the main subject of Sir Edward Coke's commentary "Coke upon Littleton."

Sources

Magnussen, Magnus; Goring, Rosemary; and Thorn, John O., eds. 1990. *Chambers biographical dictionary.* Edinburgh: Chambers Ltd.

Miller, David, ed. 1987. *The Blackwell encyclopedia of political thought.* Oxford: Basil Blackwell.

Radin, Max. 1955. *Law dictionary.* Dobbs Ferry, N.Y.: Oceana Publications.

Simpson, Alfred W.B. 1984. *Biographical dictionary of the common law.* London: Butterworth.

Stephen, Leslie, and Lee, Sydney, eds. 1917. *The dictionary of national biography.* London: Oxford University Press.

COLBERTISM. Economic policies that center on the circulation of money and are attributed to the powerful seventeenth-century French statesman.

Jean Baptiste Colbert (1619–83) was born at Reims, son of a draper, trained in business by a mercantile family that held public offices. He served Cardinal Mazarin (1651) under whom he learned economic administration. In 1661, on Mazarin's death, Colbert rose rapidly to power and held many official posts in finance, commerce, buildings, the navy, all serving the absolute monarch, King Louis XIV (1665). For almost twenty years Colbert was the most powerful of the king's men. He reduced the public debt by repudiating some obligations, reducing the value of others, and fashioning a system of accounts that kept the government's spending within its income. Powerful traditions and local interests prevented him from making taxes more equitable. With subsidies and tariffs, he protected and encouraged industrial growth and regulated the quality and prices of agricultural and industrial products. He also helped found the Academy of Sciences, the French Academy, and the Paris Observatory. In time, his efforts to establish the French economy were undermined by the extravagance of the king and his war policies. Colbert's primary aim was to keep money circulating, not because money was equated with wealth, but because it helped pay taxes and promote economic activities. Colbert died rich and a nobleman, the marquis de Seignelay. His policies, based as they were on no training in economics, relied on entirely businesslike decisions, tenacity, honesty, and shrewdness.

Sources

Eatwell, John; Milgate, Murray; and Newman, Peter. 1987. *The new Palgrave: a dictionary of economics.* London: Macmillan.

Magnussen, Magnus; Goring, Rosemary; and Thorn, John O., eds. 1990. *Chambers biographical dictionary.* Edinburgh: Chambers Ltd.

COLBY HYPOTHESIS. An explanation for urban development based on centrifugal and centripetal forces. Centrifugal forces drive households and businesses away from congested, polluted, expensive inner-city areas toward the suburbs. This promotes decentralization and sprawl. Centripetal forces attract such establishments to a center for benefits of access. The balance between the forces determines the evolution of urban morphology. The explanation owes much to physics.

Charles Carlyle Colby (1884–1965) was born in Romeo, Michigan. After graduating from Michigan State Normal College in 1898, he studied at the University of Chicago (Ph.D., 1910). He was head of the Department of Geography, State Normal School, Winona, Minnesota, from 1910 to 1913 and taught in the Geography Department at the universities of Chicago and California. He advised the War Shipping Administration during the war, was a member of the Land Commission and the National Resources Planning Board, and chaired the Subcommittee on Regional Approaches to Employment Stabilization in 1940. Among his publications are *Source Book for the Economic Geography of North America* (1921), *Economic Geography for the Secondary Schools* (1931), and *Changing Currents of Geographic Thought in America* (1936). He edited *Ge-*

ographical Aspects of International Relations (1937), *Pilot Study of Southern Illinois* (1956), and *Water Transport: Component of Civilization* (1965).
Sources
Colby, Charles. C. 1932. Centripetal and centrifugal forces in urban geography. *Annals of the Association of American Geographers* 23:1–20.
Johnston, Ronald J. 1981. *The dictionary of human geography.* Oxford: Basil Blackwell.
Who was who in America, 1961–68. London: Adam and Charles Black.

COMSTOCKERY. Prudery appearing as licensed bigotry in the pursuit of conventional morality.

Anthony Comstock (1844–1915), an obese stamp collector with a love of children, crusaded for morals in the United States. He was born in New Canaan, Connecticut, served on the Union side in the Civil War, and worked as a shipping clerk and salesman in New York until 1873. He campaigned against obscene literature for the Young Men's Christian Association. He married in 1871 and adopted a daughter after their only child died in December 1871. He wrote the New York State statute in 1868 which forbade immoral works; in 1873 he lobbied for stricter federal legislation against obscene matter, known as the Comstock Act or Laws. The bill brought under tight control the distribution of all literature regarding contraception and obscenity. He organized the New York Society for the Suppression of Vice. As its secretary, a post he held for life, Comstock arranged the destruction of much literature and many pictures and paintings in which people appeared nude. His supporting argument centered on the possible harm of obscenity to children; to his opposition he was a symbol of licensed bigotry, and to his followers he was a strong protector of conventional morality. He had over 2,500 people convicted on morals charges, and his direct methods led, he believed to his credit, to no fewer than fifteen suicides. Among his writings were *Frauds Exposed* (1880) and *Traps for the Young* (1883). He objected strongly to the play *Mrs. Warren's Profession,* calling it "one of Bernard Shaw's filthy productions," and proceeded against it. In retaliation, Shaw coined the term *comstockery,* which first appeared in the United States in the *New York Times* in 1905. By 1915 Comstock had become an amusing symbol of prudery. Nevertheless, that year President Wilson had him represent the United States at the International Purity Congress in San Francisco.
Sources
Broun, Heywood C., and Leech, Margaret. 1927. *Anthony Comstock, roundsman of the Lord.* New York: A and C. Boni.
Craig, Alec. 1962. *The banned books of England and other countries: a study of the conception of literary obscenity.* London: Allen and Unwin.
Johnson, Allen, and Malone, Dumas, eds. 1929. *Dictionary of American biography.* Vol. II. New York: Charles Scribner's Sons.
Van Doren, Charles, ed. 1974. *Webster's American biographies.* Springfield, Mass.: G. and C. Merriam.

COMTISM. A philosophical system of positivism that advocated a minimum of invariable laws for the study of society and a set of definite relations between knowledge and predictions of social action.

Auguste Comte (1798–1857), a French philosopher and mathematician and reputed founder of positivism, placed sociology—his term—at the peak of his hierarchy of the sciences. He was born at Montpellier and educated in Paris, and was an associate of Henri de Saint-Simon (1760–1825), serving as his secretary in 1817. Primarily a social reformer, Comte sought to eliminate moral anarchy following Napoleon's regime and to produce a form of social regeneration by establishing a society where people and nations would live in comfort and harmony. In his lectures of 1820, *Cours de philosophie de positive* (1834–42), he presented his ideas for achieving such a society. He devised three states of knowledge: theological, metaphysical, and positive, and he classed the sciences according to their decreasing generality and increasing complexity: mathematics, astronomy, physics, chemistry, biology, and sociology. In his *Systeme de politique positive* (1851–54), he set down a positive religion that seemed to parody Roman Catholicism with its sacraments, prayers, and other rituals. It was religion with no metaphysics and one that put forth humanity as the main object of worship without the inside knowledge that people have of one another and themselves.

Sources

Coser, Lewis A. 1977. *Masters of sociological thought.* New York: Harcourt Brace Jovanovich.

Miller, David, ed. 1987. *The Blackwell encyclopedia of political thought.* Oxford: Basil Blackwell.

Ralson, Timothy, ed. 1963. *The founding fathers of social science.* Harmondsworth: Penguin.

Sills, David L., ed. 1968. *International encyclopedia of the social sciences.* New York: Macmillan and Free Press.

Zusne, Leonard. 1984. *Biographical dictionary of psychology.* Westport, Conn.: Greenwood Press.

Zusne, Leonard. 1987. *Eponyms in psychology: a dictionary and sourcebook.* Westport Conn.: Greenwood Press.

CONDORCET'S PARADOX. When transitory preferences are aggregated, an intransitive preference may be obtained; for example, a majority of voters prefer candidate A to B, B to C, and C to A! At an individual level it is hard to conceive of such an outcome because none of the candidates is collectively preferred to others.

Marie Jean Antoine Nicolas de Caritat, marquis de Condorcet (1743–94), was born in Ribemont, educated by Jesuits, and studied philosophy and mathematics at the Collége de Navarre, Paris. He was appointed secretary of the Académie des Sciences in 1777 and elected to the French Academy in 1782. His theory of probability was published in 1785, while his two biographies, one of Turgot (1786) the other of Voltaire (1789), established his literary reputation. He entered politics as a supporter of the French Revolution and was elected to the Legislative Assembly, over which he briefly presided in 1792. He fled the Reign of Terror and in hiding produced his *Sketch of the Intellectual Progress of Man Kind* (1795), a theory of the nine stages of progress in human civilization. The tenth stage was to be the achievement of perfection through education. He was found in a village near Paris, imprisoned, and was dead a day later in his cell. Condorcet believed that humankind was reasonably decent and that it could well use the results of science and industry and commerce. He advocated women's suffrage, intellectual equality of the sexes—except in higher education—equality at law of husband and wife, civil marriage, birth control, a national system of education, co-education, special schools for the gifted, and schools for adults. He influenced the course of United States democracy with his belief that inequalities in education produced tyranny. He thought social progress depended on a well educated populace at two levels: the lower classes needed technical education and the ruling class needed an education that developed their critical faculties as citizens.

Sources

Badinter, Elisabeth, and Badinter, Robert. 1988. *Condorcet, 1743–1794: un intellectuel en politique.* Paris: Fayard.

Baker, Keith. 1975. *Condorcet, from natural philosophy to social mathematics.* Chicago: University of Chicago Press.

Boudon, Raymond, and Bourricaud, François. 1982. *A critical dictionary of sociology.* Trans. Peter Hamilton, 1989. London: Routledge.

Miller, David, ed. 1987. *The Blackwell encyclopedia of political thought.* Oxford: Basil Blackwell.

Phillips, Robert S., ed. 1983. *Funk and Wagnall's new encyclopedia.* New York: Funk and Wagnall, Inc.

Sills, David L., ed. 1968. *International encyclopedia of the social sciences.* New York: Macmillan and Free Press.

Zusne, Leonard. 1984. *Biographical dictionary of psychology.* Westport, Conn.: Greenwood Press.

CONFUCIAN. Relating to the ideas of the great Chinese philosopher.

Confucius (551–479 B.C.) is the Latinized form of Kung Fu-Tzu, meaning "Master Kung" or "the philosopher." Born in Lu (now Shantung) Province, he was raised in humble circumstances. At 15 he pursued a career as a state official; at 22 he was a storekeeper; and later he became supervisor of royal lands. He studied the ideas and customs of the ancients, attracted pupils, and at 50 years of age he was a minister of justice. To solve China's political and moral difficulties at the time, he thought Chinese culture would be best preserved by teachings from the wisdom of the Chou Dynasty (1030–256 B.C.). Since the elite of his day, did not accept this notion, Confucius began to teach young Chinese the political and moral wisdom of that dynasty himself. Forced into exile, he traveled throughout the provinces hoping to find favor for his moral and political reforms, which he believed could renew the world. At age 67 he returned home and died. Tradition holds that at the end of his life he wrote works that were considered the classic teachings of Confucianism. During the Ha Dynasty (220–206 B.C.), Confucius's ideas were set down coherently, and in the face of the competing philosophies, Taoism and Buddhism, Confucianism dominated Chinese politics and morals until 1911. Confucius and his beliefs are as reactionary in China today as they were in his day.

Sources

Cleary, Thomas. 1992. *The essential Confucius.* London: HarperCollins.

Crim, Keith, ed. 1981. *Abingdon dictionary of living religions.* Nashville, Tenn.: Abingdon Press.

McHenry, Robert, ed. 1992. *The new encyclopedia Britannica.* Chicago: Encyclopedia Britannica, Inc.

Schumacher, Stephan, and Woerner, Gert, eds. 1986. *The Rider encyclopedia of Eastern philosophy and religion.* London: Rider Books.

Sills, David L., ed. 1968. *International encyclopedia of the social sciences.* New York: Macmillan and Free Press.

CONNALLY AMENDMENT. A reservation attached by the United States to its acceptance in 1946 of the compulsory jurisdiction of the Statute of the International Court of Justice. The amendment denies that the court has compulsory jurisdiction in "disputes with regard to matters which are essentially within the domestic jurisdiction of the United States of America as determined by the United States of America." Consequently, the amendment leaves the United States free to determine whatever it thinks is a domestic matter and what is beyond the purview of the court.

Thomas Terry Connally (1877–1963) was born in Texas, attended public schools, graduated from Baylor University, and studied law at the University of Texas. A Democrat, he was elected to the U.S. Senate (1929–53) and had great impact on U.S. foreign policy as chairman of the Senate Foreign Relations Committee (1941–53). He helped plan the United Nations and was a member of the International Court of Justice. He persuaded the Senate to accept membership in the court. He lost the chairmanship of the Foreign Relations Committee in 1947 when the Republicans gained power; he obtained Senate approval for the Marshall Plan; and on regaining the chairmanship two years later he strongly supported the North Atlantic Treaty Organization.

Sources

Cohen, Mary, ed. 1988. *Congress A to Z.* Washington, D.C.: CQ's Ready Reference Encyclopedia Quarterly, Inc.

Jacob, Kathryn A., and Ragsdale, Bruce A. 1989. *Biographical dictionary of the United States Congress: 1774–1989.* Bicentennial ed. Washington, D.C.: U.S. Government Printing Office.

Plano, Jack. 1988. *The international relations dictionary.* 4th ed. Santa Barbara, Calif.: ABC-CLIO.

CONSTANTINIAN. Relating to the first-century emperor of Rome and his period of rule. The main feature of the period was the acceptance of Christianity and the many religious rivalries of the time.

Flavius Valerius Constantinus (c. 288–337) became Constantine I, "Constantine the Great." Born at Naissus (today Nis, Yugoslavia), he was the eldest son of Constantus and his first wife Helena, and was educated at the courts of Galerius and Diocletian in the East. In about 306, on his father's death, the boy was appointed Caesar; two years later he was recognized as Augustus by Augustus Maximian. He married Fausta, his second wife, Maximian's daughter, and two years later he put Maximian to death for plotting to incite a popular uprising. In 323 Constantine became the sole Augustus and made Christianity acceptable within the state. In 325 he converted the Nice Council; in 330 he made Constantinople the capital of the Roman Empire. To protect his rule he may have had his eldest son, Crispus, the child by his first wife Minervina, killed for treason; he also put his wife Fausta to death for no clear reason. In the last fourteen years of his rule peace came to his regime, and the question of religion was taken up. Constantine was drawn personally and politically to the Christians; he handled the problem of the church's relations with the state well; Christians became loyal to him, and the bishops appeared to become part of the state. During his final illness, Constantine declared himself a Christian and asked to be baptized.

Sources

Bowder, Diana. 1978. *The age of Constantine and Julian.* London: Paul Elek.

Gwatkin, Henry M., and Whitney, Jeanne P. 1911. *The Cambridge mediaeval history.* Vol. I. The Christian empire. Cambridge: Cambridge University Press.

CORDOBA. Monetary unit of Nicaragua.

Francisco Hernández de Cordoba (Cordova) (c. 1475–1526) was a Spanish soldier and explorer. He went to the Isthmus of Panama with Pedrarias—Pedro Arias de Avila, the Spaniard who founded Panama in 1519—and in 1524 was sent by him to take possession of Nicaragua against the rights of the discoverer, Gil Gonzales de Avila. Cordoba established Granada, Leon, and other towns, and found the outlet to the lake. He sent his lieutenant, Hernando de Soto (1496?–1542), against Gil Gonzales in Honduras. But when Hernán Cortés (1485–1547) came to Honduras, Cordoba defected from Pedrarias, gave allegiance to Cortés, and later tried to establish an independent government. When he heard of this development, Pedrarias came to Nicaragua, captured and decapitated Cordoba, and became governor of Nicaragua (1526).

Sources

Smith, Benjamin. 1903. *The Century cyclopedia of names.* London: The Times.

Van Doren, Charles, ed. 1974. *Webster's American biographies.* Springfield, Mass.: G. and C. Merriam.

COURNOT'S DUOPOLY MODEL. An economic theory based on the behavioral assumption that each of two rival firms will maximize profits, providing that its competitor's output remains constant.

Antoine Augustin Cournot (1801–77), a French mathematician, philosopher, economist, and university administrator, was the first to define and draw a demand curve, and to make serious use of calculus in the resolution of a maximization problem in economics. He helped found modern mathematical economics. He was born in central France and educated first locally and then at the Ecole Normale Supérieure in Paris. In 1823 he entered the household of Maréchél Saint-Cyr as literary adviser and tutor to his son for ten years. After obtaining a doctorate in science (1829), he was briefly a professor of mathematics at the University of Lyons, and later a high-level administrator at the universities of Grenoble and Dijon. In 1838 he was made a knight of the Legion of Honor and an officer (1845). In his last years he was blind. He retired from public life in 1862 to continue private research until he died.

Sources

Blaug, Mark. 1986. *Great economists before Keynes.* Brighton, England: Harvester Press.

Eatwell, John; Milgate, Murray; and Newman, Peter. 1987. *The new Palgrave: a dictionary of economics.* London: Macmillan.

Pearce, David W., ed. 1986. *Macmillan dictionary of modern economics.* New York: Macmillan.

COWPER-TEMPLE CLAUSE. A clause in the British Education Act of 1870 which states that "no religious catechism or religious formulary, which is distinctive of any particular denomination shall be taught" in the board schools set up under that act. Disraeli described it as "inventing and establishing a new sacerdotal class . . . which will in the future exercise an extraordinary influence upon the conduct of Englishmen." The principle was reaffirmed in 1902, with changes made in 1944.

William Francis Cowper-Temple, Baron Mount-Temple (1811–88), was born at Brockett Hall, Hertfordshire, educated at Eton, and in 1827 entered the army. He became private secretary to his uncle, Lord Melbourne, and in 1835 the Liberal M.P. for Hertford (1835–68) and for South Hampshire (1860–80). In 1880 he was created Baron Mount-Temple. He was lord of the Admiralty, 1846–52 and 1852–55, and president of the Board of Health, 1855–57. He was the first vice-president of the Committee of the Council on Education and became chairman of the National Education Union (1860–66). In this position he was a spokesman for nondenominational education and designed the act to allay suspicions that board schools would be subject to the influence of clerics.

Sources

Aldrich, Richard, and Gordon, Peter. 1987. *Dictionary of British educationists.* London: Woburn Press.

Blishen, Edward. 1969. *Blond's encyclopaedia of education.* London: Blond Educational.

COXEY'S ARMY. An American group of protesters who marched on Washington, D.C. in 1894.

Jacob Sechler Coxey (1854–1951) was born in Selinsgrove, Pennsylvania, and attended public schools in Danville. After graduation, he worked for eight years in the local iron mill, rose to become stationary engineer, and then began his own scrap iron business. After three years he left for Massillon, Ohio, where he established a successful sandstone quarry (1881–1929). In the financial panic of 1893 he sacked forty men from his quarries. He deplored unemployment and proposed two ways to reduce it: he advocated federal funding for road construction that would put men to work and thought that work could be created if the state could borrow funds with non-interest bonds for public works. He was also a strong supporter of greenbacks to replace metal-based currency. To draw attention to his ideas he adopted a scheme suggested by Carl Browne, a Greenbacker and a one-time circus barker. The scheme was to send a petition of jobless men to the U.S. Congress by having them march from Massillon to Washington. In March 1894 a hundred men and forty journalists began on a fifteen-mile-a-day march to the capital; five hundred arrived on May 1. The U.S. Congress was not much impressed by what became known as "Coxey's Army." That Fall, Coxey ran for Congress and drew 21 percent of the vote. Thereafter he often ran for office to promote his idea of using the non-interest bearing bonds to fund public works. After he retired from his firm he was elected Republican mayor of Massillon (1931), and for two years he worked to have his plan adopted. He failed, however, to get sufficient support.

Sources

Coxey, Jacob S. 1914. *Coxey: his own story. Why the march to Washington in 1894. Why the march to Washington in 1914.* Massillon, Ohio: J. S. Coxey.

Garraty, John A., ed. 1977. *Dictionary of American biography.* Supplement 5. New York: Charles Scribner's Sons.

Hendrickson, Robert. 1988. *The dictionary of eponyms: names that became words.* New York: Dorset.

Van Doren, Charles, ed. 1974. *Webster's American biographies.* Springfield, Mass.: G. and C. Merriam.

CRAMER'S RULE. A method for solving linear simultaneous equations. It assumes that all terms in such equations, except coefficients of regression, are known numbers. The coefficient of regression may be solved by using Cramer's rule for the ratio of two determinants that each yield unknown values. The determinants are always square, and the numerical values can be determined. The rule is applied in economics.

Gabriel Cramer (1704–52) was born and educated in Geneva, Switzerland, and at age 20 was given the chair of mathematics at the Academie de Calvin in Geneva. He shared the chair with Giovanni Calandrini. The two mathematicians took turns at the post: while one traveled to enhance his knowledge, the other stayed behind to perform the duties attaching to the post. Cramer also became a professor of philosophy and was made a member of the Royal Society (London), and the academies of Berlin, Lyons, Montpellier, and the Institute of Bologna. Cramer died while traveling in France. He is noted for his work on the Cramer curve and for the value of his concept of utility for connecting the theory of probability with mathematical economics.

Sources

Abbott, David, ed. 1985. *The biographical dictionary of scientists: mathematicians.* London: Blond Educational.

Gillespie, Charles C., ed. 1971. *Dictionary of scientific biography.* New York: Charles Scribner's Sons.

Hazewinkel, Michael, ed. 1988. *Encyclopedia of mathematics.* Dordrecht, Netherlands: Kluwer Academic Publisher.

CREANSPEAK. Relating to the habit of the federal Australian Labor party (ALP) parliamentarian to string together combinations of phrases to circumvent difficult questions; to find a convoluted way of expressing a simple question; to answer to a simple question with long, evasive phrases and conditional comments; to use long skeins of sentences, great overarching loops of words and leave hapless subordinate clauses desperately searching for subjects or verbs; to stud one's speeches with jargon like "wage outcomes," "sectorial policies," "cross sectorial reforms," "pro-active roles," "structural adjustments" (Ward, 1991).

Simon Findlay Crean (b. 1949) was born in Melbourne, Victoria, and in the mid-1950s went with his family to live in Canberra where his father was a politician. In Melbourne he attended Melbourne High School, joined the ALP, Albert Park Branch, helped his father in the federal election campaigns, and became the branch secretary. After studying economics at Monash University, Crean took up a career in industrial relations with the Federated Storemen and Packer's Union. He moved from research officer (1970–74) to assistant general secretary (1974–79) to general secretary (1979–85); he was junior vice-president of the Australian Council of Trade Unions (1981–83), and then senior vice-president until 1985, when he was elected president. He was also on the National Labor Consultative Council (1984–90) and a member of the prime minister's Economic Planning Advisory Council. In March 1990 he was elected to the federal Parliament, was sworn into the ministry without actually taking his seat, and was quickly given the Science and Technology portfolio. A year later he became the minister for primary industries and energy.

Sources

International who's who, 1991–92. 55th ed. London: Europa Publications.

Ward, Peter. 1991. Fast track to the top. *The Australian Magazine,* December 7–8:17–27.

CROCKFORD. A British directory of clerical matters; the official directory of the Church of England and the Anglican communion.

John Crockford (1823–65) was born at Taunton and at age 20, in 1843, was made the publisher of *The Law Times,* which he saved from bankruptcy. Gradually, he established himself as a publisher of nonlegal works on commission, and by 1849 he had two registered presses in his own name. He also published *The Critic* (1844–63) and was manager of *The Field* (1854) until his death. He published *The Clerical Journal,* a supplement to the *Clerical Directory* in weekly parts (1855–57): it was a biographical and statistical book of reference for facts relating to the clergy and the church, and appeared in one volume (1858). The second edition, *Crockford's Clerical Directory* (1860), included 18,555 memoirs. The *Directory* was highly profitable for its owner, Edward W. Cox (1809–79), and it made Crockford prosperous enough to purchase a fine home at Saint John's Park shortly before he died.

Sources

Altholz, Josef L. 1984. Mister Serjeant Cox, John Crockford and the origins of Crockford's Clerical Dictionary. *Victorian Periodicals Review* 17, 4:153–158.
Boase, Frederic. 1965. *Modern English biography.* London: Frank Cass.

CROMWELLIAN. A follower of England's seventeenth-century lord protector; dictatorial.

Oliver Cromwell (1599–1659) was born at Huntingdon and educated at Huntingdon Grammar School and Sydney-Sussex College, Cambridge. He studied law at London. He inherited a small estate (1617) and married the daughter of a London merchant (1620). He supported Puritanism enthusiastically and as M.P. for Huntingdon was a strong critic of Charles I in the divided Parliament of 1628–1629. After Parliament was dissolved, he went back to farming but again sat for Cambridge in the Short Parliament and the Long Parliament (1640). When the Civil War began, he gathered a calvary troop, formed his Ironsides regiment, supported the Roundheads, and eventually led his Model Army to victory over Charles I. He had Charles I executed in 1649, and in 1653 he became England's lord protector after rejecting an offer of the Crown. He ruled as a dictator. His name became synonymous with absolute control, a form of domination that he had once found anathema under the rule of Charles I. Before dying, he named his son lord protector and was buried at Westminster. In 1660, when the royalists returned to power, Cromwell's body was exhumed, hanged, and beheaded.

Sources

Fraser, Antonia. 1973. *Cromwell: our chief of men.* London: Weidenfeld and Nicolson.
Hill, Christopher. 1970. *God's Englishman: Oliver Cromwell and the English revolution.* London: Weidenfeld and Nicolson.
Magnussen, Magnus; Goring, Rosemary; and Thorn, John O., eds. 1990. *Chambers biographical dictionary.* Edinburgh: Chambers Ltd.
Stephen, Leslie, and Lee, Sydney, eds. 1917. *The dictionary of national biography.* London: Oxford University Press.

CROWE MEMORANDUM. A British review of German policies and intentions. It seemed to favor Germany, for example: " . . . it would be neither just or politic to ignore the claims to a healthy expansion which a vigorous and growing country like Germany has a natural right to assert in the field of legitimate endeavour . . . nor is it for the British Government to oppose Germany's building as large a fleet as she may consider necessary or desirable for the defence of her national interests" (Crowe, 1907).

Sir Eyre Alexander Barby Wichart Crowe (1864–1925) was born in Leipzig, educated in Germany, and in 1885 entered the British Foreign Office. He submitted his memorandum to Sir Edward (later Viscount) Grey, who considered it both "interesting and suggestive" concerning the state of relations between Britain, Germany, and France in 1907. Eyre was secretary to the British delegation at the second peace conference at The Hague in 1907 and was a British delegate at the London International Maritime Conference which drew up the unsuccessful Declaration of London in 1908–9. He was an agent for the British in the Savarkar Case (1911), which involved treason and assassination by terrorists working secretly for the revolutionary Free India Society in London (1906–11); later he became assistant under-secretary for foreign affairs in 1912, and believed that Britain must support the French in 1914. He served Britain at the peace conference at Versailles and became permanent undersecretary for foreign affairs (1920–25).

Sources

Crowe, Eyre A. 1907. Memorandum on the present state of British relations with France and Germany, 1 January 1907. In George P. Gooch and Harold W.V. Temperley, eds. 1928. *British documents on the origins of the war 1889–1914*. Vol. 3. London: H.M.S.O.

McHenry, Robert, ed. 1992. *The new encyclopedia Britannica.* Chicago: Encyclopedia Britannica, Inc.

Weaver, J.B.H., ed. 1937. *Dictionary of national biography 1922–1930.* London: Oxford University Press.

CURIEL APPARATUS. An organization used to advance left-wing causes, especially communism, and a rapprochement between Arab states and Israel in the 1970s.

Henri Curiel (1913–78), the youngest son of Daniel and Zephirah Curiel, was born into a well-established banking family in Cairo. He attended the French Jesuit College in Cairo and studied law at Cairo University. He would visit the peasants on his family's estates and bring them medicine for the treatment of eye diseases. Henri was distressed by the poverty and misery he witnessed in Egypt and by the contrast between the peasant life and the comfort in which he had been raised. His brother, Raoul, a social democrat, introduced Henri to the ideas of Marx and Lenin, and he developed a strong interest in left-wing politics. He turned to communism, spread its influence in Egypt, and helped found the Egyptian Communist party in the 1940s. When expelled from Egypt, he went to France where he supported the Algerian war of liberation and tried to ameliorate conflicts between the Palestine Liberation Organization and the Israelis. He was murdered by right-wing terrorists in Paris.

Sources

Blake, George. 1990. *No other choice; a biography.* London: Jonathan Cape.

Johnson, William R. 1988. The elephants and the gorillas. *The International Journal of Intelligence and Counterintelligence* 1:42–56.

CURZON LINE. The border between Poland and the Soviet Union confirmed at the 1945 Yalta Conference.

George Nathaniel, first Marquis Curzon of Kedleston (1859–1925), was born at Kedleston Hall, Derbyshire, and educated at Eton and Oxford. He was M.P. in 1886 and after travels in Europe became undersecretary for India (1891–92) and for Foreign Affairs (1895). He was appointed viceroy of India in 1898 and received his Irish barony. He partitioned Bengal and introduced many reforms as well as establishing the North West Frontier Province. In 1905, after conflicting with Lord Kitchener, he resigned, reentered politics in England as Lord Privy Seal in 1915, was foreign secretary from 1919 to 1924, and was made a marquis in 1921. While he was foreign secretary, the problem arose regarding the border between Poland and Russia. In the 1919–20 Russo-Polish War, the Poles invaded Russia, and Curzon suggested that while waiting for peace negotiations the Poles should retreat to what was known as the Curzon Line. Poland rejected it and gained more territory and the line was settled. Like the Curzon Line, a boundary was established in 1939 between Soviet-occupied Poland and Nazi Germany. In 1945 it was accepted as the Soviet-Polish border.

Sources

Crystal, David, ed. 1990. *The Cambridge encyclopedia.* Cambridge: Cambridge University Press.

McHenry, Robert, ed. 1992. *The new encyclopedia Britannica.* Chicago: Encyclopedia Britannica, Inc.

Magnussen, Magnus; Goring, Rosemary; and Thorn, John O., eds. 1990. *Chambers biographical dictionary.* Edinburgh: Chambers Ltd.

Nicolson, Harold G. 1937. *Curzon: the last phase, 1919–1925: a study in past war diplomacy.* New ed. London: Constable.

Rose, Keith. 1985. *Curzon: a most superior person.* London: Macmillan.

Weaver, John R.H., ed. 1937. *Dictionary of national biography 1922–1930.* London: Oxford University Press.

CUSTER'S LAST STAND. A great and heroic effort that ends in defeat. The idea is taken from accounts of conflicts between American Indians and whites. It depicts an American leader as dying a hero's death against insuperable odds. Recent research shows the accounts to be based more on legend than on historical evidence (Fox, 1993).

George Armstrong Custer (1839–76) was born in New Rumley, Harrison County, Ohio, son of a farmer and blacksmith. He went to local schools until he was 10, and then was raised by his parents and half-sister who lived in Michigan. He graduated from West Point in 1861 and shortly afterward was court-martialed for failing to stop a brawl between two cadets. Proceedings were put aside in Washington. He served in several campaigns, notably at Gettysburg and Virginia, and as a cavalry commander distinguished himself by defeating hostile Indians. At the battle of Little Bighorn, Montana, on June 25, 1876, Custer and 264 troops were ambushed and shot, some say because the American Indians, led by Crazy Horse under directions from Sitting Bull, had long-range Winchester repeater rifles, while Custer's troops had only Springfield carbines. The U.S. government had issued the Indians the repeating rifle to hunt animals.

One story says that Sitting Bull ordered that Custer, Sitting Bull's "half-brother," be spared and that later Custer committed suicide. Others say he died with a wound in his left side and his temple pierced; however Custer died, his men's corpses were allegedly found scalped and mutilated.

Sources

Carroll, John M., comp. ed. 1977. *Custer in the Civil War: his unfinished memoirs.* San Rafael: Presidio Press.

Custer, George A. 1963. *My life in the plains: or personal experiences with Indians.* Kenneth Fenwick, ed. London: Folio.

Dippie, Brian, ed. 1980. *Nomad: George A. Custer in turf, field and farm.* Austin: University of Texas Press.

Fox, Richard A. 1993. *Archaeology, history and Custer's last battle.* New York: Oxford University Press.

Johnson, Allen, and Malone, Dumas, eds. 1930. *Dictionary of American biography.* Vol. III. New York: Charles Scribner's Sons.

Merrington, Marguerite, ed. 1950. *The Custer story: the life and intimate letters of George A. Custer and his wife Elizabeth.* Reprint 1987. Lincoln: University of Nebraska Press.

Van Doren, Charles, ed. 1974. *Webster's American biographies.* Springfield, Mass.: G. and C. Merriam.

CYRENAIC. Relating to the philosophy of Aristippus of Cyrene who asserted that pleasure is the purpose of living and who followed the doctrine of practical hedonism.

Aristippus of Cyrene (elder and younger) were both philosophers, of the same name, one a grandson to the other; they were connected with the school of philosophy at Cyrene in North Africa, founded in the fourth century B.C. There is some confusion between them. The elder Aristippus went to Athens as a follower of Socrates; he is said to have led a life of luxury. The younger Aristippus probably contributed more to the philosophy of the school, whose main tenet was that a person's aim in life should be the pursuit of his or her immediate bodily pleasure. The Cyrenaics also held that knowledge is limited to what is perceived at any particular moment; this is an extreme form of skepticism.

Sources

Bowder, Diana, ed. 1982. *Who was who in the Greek world.* Oxford: Phaidon.

Findlater, Andrew, ed. 1895. *Chambers encyclopedia.* New ed. London and Edinburgh: William and Robert Chambers Ltd. Philadelphia: J. B. Lippincott Co.

McHenry, Robert, ed. 1992. *The new encyclopedia Britannica.* Chicago: Encyclopedia Britannica, Inc.

Smith, Benjamin. 1903. *The Century cyclopedia of names.* London: The Times.

CZAR, TSAR, TSARINA, TSAREVITCH, TSAREVNA. A ruler or tyrannical despot.

When Julius Caesar died in 44 B.C., his name was adopted by the Roman emperors beginning with Augustus (27–14 B.C.) and retained until the fall of the Holy Roman Empire (800–1806). With minor alterations in spelling, the word was taken over by the rulers of many European countries in the belief that they were rulers by divine appointment, and that state and church were interdependent. The word "czar" is traceable to the slavic "cesare," deriving from "Caesar" in the fifteenth century. After Ivan IV Vasilievich (the Terrible, 1530–84) assumed the role of "tsear" to describe his rule as king of Poland, the term was applied to all Russian rulers. The Russian tsar was regarded as God's appointee as head of both church and state. His wife was tsarina, his son tsarevitch, and his daughter tsarevna.

See also CAESAR.

Sources

Hendrickson, Robert. 1988. *The dictionary of eponyms: names that became words.* New York: Dorset.

Simpson, J. A., and Weiner, E.S.C., eds. 1989. *The Oxford dictionary.* 2d ed. Oxford: Clarendon Press.

D

D'HONDT SYSTEM. An election procedure using the method of the "largest average." Voting is done by proportional representation and is used in some European countries, including Spain and Belgium, and in the Australian Capital Territory until 1992. The ballot papers are made out so that a voter may endorse a party or individuals. To vote he places a "1" in any box on the ballot paper and may indicate preferences if he wants. So the voting is simple, but the counting is time consuming and complicated. The method favors the largest party and lowers the threshold in little constituencies that elect few members and choose among few competing party lists. So the smallest number of votes required for representation will be a function of the constituency's size, share of seats, and number of parties.

Victor d'Hondt (1841–1901) was born in Gand, Belgium, and died there. He was a professor of common law at Gand University and dedicated much of his energy to a campaign for proportional representation. He provided the complex mathematical formula for proportional representation known as the D'Hondt System, and it was adopted after 1899 outside Belgium.

Sources

Carstairs, Andrew McLaren. 1980. *A short history of electoral systems in Western Europe.* London: Allen and Unwin.

D'Hondt, Victor. 1885. *Exposé du système pratique de représentation proportionnelle adopté par le Comité de l'Association réformiste belge.* Gand Eug.: Vanderhaegen.

Grofman, Bernard, and Lijphart, Arend, eds. 1986. *Electoral laws and their political consequences.* New York: Agathon Press.

Hasquin, Hervé. 1988. *Dictionnaire d'histoire de Belgique.* Brussels: Didier Hatier.

Lakeman, Enid, and Lambert, James D. 1964. *Voting in democracies: a study of majority and proportional electoral systems.* 2d rev. ed. London: Faber and Faber.

Legrain, Paul. 1981. *Le Dictionnaire des Belges.* Brussels: Legrain.
Robertson, David. 1985. *The Penguin dictionary of politics.* Harmondsworth: Penguin.
Weiner, Myron; Ozbudn, Ergun; and Kearney, Robert N., eds. 1987. *Compet Ozbudeun-lections [Competitive elections] in developing countries.* Durham, N.C.: Duke University Press.

DAMOCLEAN. Relating to the "sword of Damocles," a symbol of impending political calamity.

Damocles, who lived in the first half of the fourth century B.C., was a courtier and sycophant of Dionysius the Elder, a tyrant of Syracuse. A charming flatterer, Damocles was fond of saying that the life of any prince must certainly be occupied in pursuing nothing but his own happiness. Dionysius decided to show how happy the life of a prince was. So Damocles was dressed like a prince and entertained with a great banquet, but above him, suspended by a single horse hair, was a sword. Should he move, the hair would break and down would fall the sword. Consequently, Damocles learned that at any moment a prince must remember that his life is always in danger. The phrase "the sword of Damocles" was used in the mid–eighteenth century; in his *Vanity Fair* (1848) William Makepeace Thackeray (1811–63) used it to infer an ever present evil; today in political commentary it frequently refers to a possible threat to those in power.
Sources

Crystal, David, ed. 1990. *The Cambridge encyclopedia.* Cambridge: Cambridge University Press.
Hammond, Nicholas G.L., and Scullard, Howard H., eds. 1970. *The Oxford classical dictionary.* Oxford: Clarendon Press.
Lemprière, John, and Wright, F. A., eds. 1972. *Lemprière's classical dictionary of proper names mentioned in ancient authors.* London: Routledge and Kegan Paul.

DARBYITE. A member of the Plymouth Brethren, a religious group, who, though disagreeing on some issues, all supported the view that every Christian had the right to preach the Gospel and administer sacraments. They sought to revive the practices of the New Testament, and they rejected creeds, payments to ministers, church titles, and denominationalism.

John Nelson Darby (1800–82) was the principal founder of the Plymouth Brethren. He was born in London and educated at Westminister School and Trinty College, Dublin. Although he was called to the bar, he put the law aside and was ordained in about 1825, and until he resigned with doubts about the establishment of the church, he served as a curate at Wichlow (1825–27). In 1825 Darby had joined with A. N. Groves and others in a group calling themselves The Brethren, and published their first pamphlet "The Nature and the Unity of the Church of Christ." They rejected denominational distinctions and all ecclesiastical forms of organization. In 1836 the group members fell out, and in 1845 a separate assembly was formed; the division spread to Bristol, London, and other cities, and Darbyism itself was established. Groups formed in Dublin and congregations in France, Germany, and Switzerland; from 1859 to 1874

Darby often visited the United States and Canada. In Europe his followers were known as Darbyites or Exclusive Brethren. Most of Darby's prolific writing comprised doctrinal and controversial points of religion, practical and devotional treatises, and many hymns.

Sources

Cross, Frank L. 1974. *The Oxford dictionary of the Christian Church.* 2d ed. New York: Oxford University Press.

McDonald, William, ed. 1967. *New Catholic encyclopedia.* New York: McGraw-Hill.

McHenry, Robert, ed. 1992. *The new encyclopedia Britannica.* Chicago: Encyclopedia Britannica, Inc.

Stephen, Leslie, and Lee, Sydney, eds. 1917. *The dictionary of national biography.* London: Oxford University Press.

DARLING CASE. In medical sociology, a case (1960) noted for the change it brought to doctor-administrator relations in hospital. The case involved a suit for damages sought for alleged medical and administrative negligence.

Dorrence Kenneth Darling II (fl. 1960) lived in Collinsville, Illinois, where his father was a school superintendent, and studied at Eastern Illinois University in Charleston. On November 5, 1960, while playing defensive halfback for his university football team, his right leg suffered a multiple fracture when an opponent blocked him. Immediately, he received emergency care and was taken to Charleston Community Memorial Hospital where the leg was put in a cast. By November 19 he was in such pain he was taken to Barnes Hospital in Saint Louis. On January 23, 1961, the right leg was amputated below the knee. Through his father Darling sued both the physician and the administrators for negligence. While the physician settled out of court, the administrators argued that they were not required to provide anything more than the conditions necessary for medical practice to be executed. But the court found the administration was negligent for not consulting with another physician as hospital bylaws provided. The case indicated that administrators have a responsibility for the patient's treatment. It seriously altered traditional doctor–administrator relations in hospital by leading the administrators to demand, and be granted, greater control over what had traditionally been the professional domain and activities of medical doctors.

Sources

Cockerham, William C. 1978. *Medical sociology.* 3d ed. 1986. Englewood Cliffs, N.J.: Prentice-Hall.

North Eastern Reporter, 2d Series. Vol. 200 N.E. 2d. (1964):149–191. Saint Paul, Minn.: West Publishing.

DARMAN DOCTRINE, DARMANESQUE. If the numbers are inconvenient, let someone else add them up; too clever by half in politics.

Richard Gordon Darman (b. 1943) was born in Charlotte, North Carolina, the eldest son of a wealthy textile manufacturer. He was educated at Rivers County Day School in Weston, Massachusetts, studied at Harvard (M.B.A. 1967), and entered the Nixon administration (1971–72). He became an assistant to the secretary of defense in 1973 and was a scholar at the Woodrow Wilson International Center in 1974. He directed a consulting firm before returning to politics as an assistant secretary for policy in the Commerce Department in 1976. Darman lectured at Harvard's Kennedy School (1977–80), and was an executive director of the White House transition team in 1980–81 and an assistant to President Reagan from 1981 to 1985. After being deputy treasury secretary (1985–87), he resigned in 1987 to direct a merchant bank, but returned to politics in 1989 to control the Office of Management and Budget. As budget director, he earned a reputation for his vanity and his withering arrogance toward his peers. During the 1988 presidential campaign, he was told to accept the advice "be nice or be gone." When he saw the great change in Darman's personal manner, Vice-President Bush decided Darman would continue as the budget director. Darman attributed his sudden change in character to growing up, his wife's influence, and the moral dictum: Never again say anything negative about people. After Bush came to power, Darman's political stratagems were followed behind the scenes in Washington, and were so successful and "darmanesque," that by June 1989 he had become President Bush's de facto domestic policy adviser.

Sources

Dowd, Maureen. 1992. A primer: how the White House budget czar not only survives, but thrives. *New York Times,* September 22: L+ A25.
Moritz, Charles, ed. 1989. *Current biography yearbook.* New York: H. W. Wilson.
Who's who in American politics. 1989–90. 12th ed. New York: R. R. Bowker.

DARWINIAN. One who follows Charles Darwin's theory on the origins of the human species.

Charles Robert Darwin (1809–82), the English naturalist, was born in Shrewsbury, England. In his youth he was interested in chemistry experiments and specimen collecting. His father, a leading medical man, sent Charles at age 16 to study medicine at the University of Edinburgh. Charles found surgery performed without anaesthetic repugnant and turned to the study of marine life. Next, his father sent him to study divinity at the University, Cambridge (1827). There Charles met John S. Henslow (1776–1861), a cleric interested in botany. Darwin's interest in science redeveloped, and with a growing confidence in his judgement and support from Henslow, he left Cambridge in spring 1831 for a geological expedition in North Wales. Later, again with Henslow's help, Darwin was encouraged to sail as official naturalist on the journey of the H.M.S. *Beagle* (1831–36). This expedition journey marked the beginning of Darwin's work collecting data that gave rise to his concept of natural evolution. He published the theory, *Origin of the Species* (1859), which attracted scientists but repelled those with conservative, religious opinions. Later he extended the ideas in his *Descent of Man* (1871) and other works.

See also SPENCERIAN.

Sources

Bowler, Peter J. 1990. *Charles Darwin: the man and his influence.* London: Basil Black-
    well.
Crystal, David, ed. 1990. *The Cambridge encyclopedia.* Cambridge: Cambridge Univer-
    sity Press.
Desmond, Adrian, and Moore, James. 1991 *Darwin.* London: Michael Joseph.
Stephen, Leslie, and Lee, Sydney, eds. 1917. *The dictionary of national biography.* Vol.
    5. London: Oxford University Press.
Zusne, Leonard. 1984. *Biographical dictionary of psychology.* Westport, Conn.: Green-
    wood Press.
Zusne, Leonard. 1987. *Eponyms in psychology: a dictionary and sourcebook.* Westport,
    Conn.: Greenwood Press.

DAVIS-BACON ACT. A federal U.S. statute passed in 1931; it provided a
basic eight-hour day on public construction projects and the payment of prevailing wages—union wages—as set down by the U.S. Department of Labor.
The act was amended in 1935, 1940, and 1964 requiring contractors on a construction site to maintain the pay and additional benefits that are obtainable in
the local area.

James John Davis (1873–1947) was born in Tredegar, Wales, and immigrated
to the United States in 1881, attended public schools in Sharon, Pennsylvania,
and became a puddler's apprentice (1884) in a steelmaking firm. By 1893, after
work in several steel firms, he was employed in the tin mills of Elwood, Indiana,
and then held office in the Amalgamated Association of Iron, Steel, and Tin
Workers of America. He campaigned for William McKinley in 1896, was
elected city clerk of Elwood in 1898, and later was elected recorder of Madison
County (1902–7). He read law, and in 1907 he went to Pittsburgh to organize
for the Loyal Order of Moose, and chaired its war relief commission in 1918.
He established a jewelry firm and undertook real estate ventures. Under presidents Harding, Coolidge, and Hoover he was secretary for labor (1921–30),
advocated conservative unionism, and then became a Republican senator from
Pennsylvania (1930–45). Afterward he returned to work for the Loyal Order of
Moose.

Robert Low Bacon (1884–1938) was born in Jamaica Plains, Boston, graduated from Harvard Law School (1910), and worked briefly at the United States
Treasury Department before entering the banking industry in New York (1911–
22). He served in the U.S. armed forces during World War I, received a Distinguished Service Medal, and rose to the rank of colonel. Elected a Republican
senator from New York (1923), he served in seven consecutive congresses.

Sources

Allen, Steven G. 1983. Much ado about Davis–Bacon: a critical review and new evi-
    dence. *Journal of Law and Economics* 26:707–736.
Garraty, John A., and James, Edward T., eds. 1974. *Dictionary of American biography.*
    Supplement 4. New York: Charles Scribner's Sons.
Jacob, Kathryn A., and Ragsdale, Bruce A. 1989. *Biographical dictionary of the United*

States Congress: 1774–1989. Bicentennial ed. Washington, D.C.: U.S. Government Printing Office.

Morris, Dan, and Morris, Inez. 1974. *Who was who in American politics.* New York: Hawthorn.

Roberts, Harold S. 1966. *Roberts' dictionary of industrial relations.* Washington, D.C.: BNA.

Shafritz, Jay M. 1988. *The Dorsey dictionary of American government and politics.* Chicago: Dorsey.

DAWES PLAN. A plan to restructure Germany's finances after World War I. In April 1924 a committee recommended reorganizing the German currency and proposed a schedule of reparation payments beginning at £5 million per year and after the fifth year rising to £125 million. The sums would be guaranteed by railway and industrial bonds, and by taxes on alcohol, sugar, and tobacco. In addition, the occupation of the Ruhr was to end so that Germany had control of its own territory. Finally, Germany was to receive a loan for use as a currency reserve and for payment of the first annuity. The plan failed to set a total amount of borrowing on the part of Germany and was replaced by the Young Plan (1929).

Charles Gates Dawes (1865–1951), Republican U.S. vice-president (1924–29), was born in Marietta, Ohio, and graduated from Marietta College and Cincinnati Law School, was admitted to the bar in 1886, and practiced in Lincoln and Evanston. Dawes managed McKinley's campaign in Illinois in 1896, and in President McKinley's administration he became comptroller of the currency (1897–1902). During World War I he was made a brigadier-general and afterward a member of the Liquidation Commission of the Allied Expeditionary Force and of the Liquidation Board of the War Department. In 1921 the Republican administration of President Harding named Dawes the first director of the budget. Three years later as chairman of the Committee of Experts of the Allied Reparations Commission, he produced the Dawes Plan. Meanwhile, he was a president of the Central Trust Company (1902–21) and chairman of its board (1922–26). He was an ambassador to Great Britain (1929–32). Among his books were some on banking, and his memoirs comprise *A Journal of the Great War* (1921), *Notes as Vice President* (1935), *Journal as Ambassador to Great Britain* (1939), *Journal of Reparations* (1939), and *Journal of the McKinley Years* (1950).

See also YOUNG PLAN.

Sources
Findling, John E. 1980. *Dictionary of American diplomatic history.* Westport, Conn.: Greenwood Press.

Garraty, John A., ed. 1977. *Dictionary of American biography.* Supplement 5. New York: Charles Scribner's Sons.

Jacob, Kathryn A., and Ragsdale, Bruce A. 1989. *Biographical directory of the United States Congress: 1774–1989.* Bicentennial ed. Washington, D.C.: U.S. Government Printing Office.

Shafritz, Jay M. 1988. *The Dorsey dictionary of American government and politics.* Chicago: Dorsey.

Timmons, Bascom N. 1953. *Portrait of an American: Charles G. Dawes.* New York: Holt.

Van Doren, Charles, ed. 1974. *Webster's American biographies.* Springfield, Mass.: G. and C. Merriam.

DE CONCINI RESERVATION. Attached to the Panama Canal Neutrality Treaty of 1978 is a reservation that asserts the United States and the Republic of Panama may independently use the military to stop the closing of the canal. So the United States is allowed to use military force against future Panamanian governments should they prevent it from using the canal.

Dennis De Concini (b. 1937) was born in Tucson, Arizona, educated in the public schools of Tucson and Phoenix, and studied political science at the University of Arizona. He was determined to enter politics and in 1958, at only 21 years of age, he was elected precinct committee man for Pima county. After serving in the U.S. Army in 1959–60, he completed a law degree at the University of Arizona (LL.B. 1963). In Tucson he practiced law (1963–76) and became a member of Arizona governor's staff (1965–67) and attorney for Pima county (1973–76) before being elected Democrat senator for Arizona in 1976 and again in 1982. In 1988 he sought a third term. In his first term, even though he was a freshman senator, De Concini was controversial. He was concerned that the Panama Treaty, whereby the United States would turn over the control of the canal to Panama at the end of 1999, might leave America without the right to intervene militarily if the canal's operations were threatened. He wanted any anticipated threat to include not only those from outside forces but also labor unrest and other internal strife. On the eve of the vote, De Concini required from President Carter a "reservation" that would allow the United States to use its military in Panama to keep the canal open. The president agreed reluctantly, and the bill was passed in March 1978. De Concini then voiced a second reservation, one that would cover the period through 31 December 1999. Panama protested. The president convinced De Concini to support the view that the United States did not wish to claim the right to interfere in Panama's internal affairs. As amended, the De Concini reservation was approved in April 1978. Since then, De Concini has maintained his reputation as a gadfly among conservative Democrats and has held great respect until his name was associated with that of Charles Keating and the collapse of the Lincoln Savings and Loan company. In 1991, the U.S. Senate Ethics committee found him guilty of poor judgment and apparent impropriety, but not actual wrongdoing. De Concini considered himself exonerated.

Sources

Graham, Judith, ed. 1992. *Current biography yearbook.* New York: H. W. Wilson.

Jacob, Kathryn A., and Ragsdale, Bruce A. 1989. *Biographical directory of the United States Congress: 1774–1989.* Bicentennial ed. Washington, D.C.: U.S. Government Printing Office.

Shafritz, Jay M. 1988. *The Dorsey dictionary of American government and politics.*
    Chicago: Dorsey.
Who's who in America, 1990–91. Chicago: Marquis.

DE JONGE CASE. A U.S. Supreme Court decision of 1937 that stated that
"peaceable assembly for lawful discussion" was no crime; the decision has a
secure place in the history of American industrial relations law.

In July 1934 Dirk De Jonge was the second speaker at a meeting arranged
by the Portland Section of the Communist party to protest against raids on
workers' homes and the shooting of striking longshoremen by Portland police.
The police had taken action in regard to a maritime strike—allegedly caused by
the communists—that was in progress in Portland at the time. At the meeting,
De Jonge protested against the conditions in the county jail. He was indicted
for criminal syndicalism, that is, a doctrine that advocates crime, physical violence, and sabotage to accomplish industrial or political change. An Oregon
statute held that to advocate the doctrine of criminal syndicalism and teach it at
a meeting attracted a penalty of one to ten years in prison and a fine of $1,000.
The state of Oregon indicted him, and his defense was that the meeting had
been public, orderly, and held for lawful purposes, even though it had been
called by the Portland section of the Communist Party. He was found guilty
and sentenced to seven years in prison. On appeal to the United States Supreme
Court the Oregon statute was found repugnant to the Fourteenth Amendment.
The U.S. Supreme Court, led by Chief Justice Charles Evans Hughes, declared
that peaceful assembly was cognate with free speech, and freedom of the press,
and that citizens of a republic could meet peaceably to consult on public matters
and petition for redress of grievances.

Sources

Commager, Henry S., ed. 1968. *Documents of American history.* 8th ed. New York:
    Appleton-Century-Crofts.
De Jonge v. Oregon 299 US 33 (1937).
Levy, Leonard W. 1986. *Encyclopedia of American Constitution.* New York: Macmillan.
Roberts, Harold S. 1966. *Roberts' dictionary of industrial relations.* Washington, D.C.:
    BNA.

DEBRETT, TO BE IN DEBRETT. A guide to the British aristocracy; to be
of noble birth.

John Field Debrett (c. 1750–1822) was publisher and editor in London. John
Almon (1737–1805), Debrett's predecessor, had already published lists of the
peers. Almon gave his business over to Debrett in 1781, having resigned with
a moderate fortune. Debrett published *Debrett's Peerage of England, Scotland
and Ireland* in two volumes in 1802; it was the first listing of its kind. New
editions regularly appeared, with the fiftieth edition published shortly after John
Debrett's death. Debrett's name became so closely associated with this catalogue

of the aristocracy and the names of the British elite that later editions used his name in the title. In 1808 he published *Baronetage of England.*
Source
Stephen, Leslie, and Lee, Sydney, eds. 1917. *The dictionary of national biography.* London: Oxford University Press.

DEMAUSE HYPOTHESIS. The hypothesis that the United States' participation in the Gulf War was the result of a temporary mental disorder. The hypothesis is part of a general theory of war as a group-psychotic episode characterized by thinking patterns, imagery, and defensive mental processes of splitting and projection that are only found in limited psychotic episodes among individuals (DeMause, 1991; DeMause, 1982:92; Goetzel, 1993).

Lloyd DeMause (b. 1931) was born in Detroit, son of an engineer and a teacher. He was educated at General Motors Institute (1948–52) and served in the U.S. Army (1952–54). At Columbia University he studied political science (B.A. 1957), where he also did graduate study and further post-graduate work at the National Association for Psychoanalysis (1957–60). He applied ideas of psychoanalysis to politics. In 1959 he established his publishing company, Atcom Inc., and in 1974 founded and became director of New York's Institute for Psychohistory. In 1975 he taught at Boston College, the Center for Family Studies, and the New York Center for Psychoanalytic Training. He founded the International Psychohistorical Association and is a member of the American Historical Association, the American Anthropological Association, and the Medieval Academy of America. He publishes regularly in the *Journal of Psychohistory,* and in 1984 published *Reagan's America.*
Sources
Bowden, Jane A., ed. 1977. *Contemporary authors.* Vols. 65–68. Detroit, Michigan: Gale Research.
DeMause, Lloyd. 1982. *Foundations of psychohistory.* New York: Creative Roots.
DeMause, Lloyd. 1988. On writing childhood history. *Journal of Psychohistory.* 16: 136–176.
DeMause, Lloyd. 1991. The Gulf War as mental disorder. *Journal of Psychohistory,* 19: 1–20.
Goetzel, Ted. 1993. The Gulf War as a mental disorder? A statistical test of DeMause's hypothesis. *Political Psychology,* 14: 711–12.
Personal Communication.

DEMOSTHENIC. As oratorical and eloquent a public speaker as the notable Athenian orator.

Demosthenes (c. 383–322 B.C.) was an Athenian orator, born in the Attic deme (township) of Paeania. He studied under Isaeus. He may have had to overcome a poor delivery in speeches; according to legend, to do this he put pebbles in his mouth to improve his voice by excessive practice. After long periods of practice at law, he became an orator (351 B.C.). He became famous for orations that were intended to alert the listeners to the danger of Greece being subject to domination by Philip of Macedon. His cause was lost when Philip won at the battle of Chaeronea (338 B.C.). Demosthenes tried to rebuild the strength of Greece and rid the land of Macedonian influence but failed; he then fled and poisoned himself before he could be captured.

See also PHILIPPIC.

Sources

Hornblower, Simon. 1983. *The Greek world: 479–323 B.C.* London: Methuen.

McHenry, Robert, ed. 1992. *The new encyclopedia Britannica.* Chicago: Encyclopedia Britannica, Inc.

Saunders, A.N.W., trans. and intro. 1970. *Greek political oratory.* Middlesex, England: Penguin.

Smith, Benjamin. 1903. *The Century cyclopedia of names.* London: The Times.

DENGISM. Policies adopted in China after September 1978 when Deng Xiaoping established his power. The policy moved away from central planning, accepted market forces, decentralized decision making in production, and tended toward capitalism, which was referred to as ''socialism with Chinese characteristics.'' Controls over literature and freedom of speech were relaxed, but anyone important who advocated democracy would be arrested. In 1985 a play, *WM,* which showed the Chinese Communist party's control over society as being merely curtailed and not removed, was banned. Dengism refers to post–1978 policies, includes many variations, and appears to be a policy based largely on pragmatism.

Deng Xiaoping or Teng Hsiao-p'ing (b. 1904) was born in Szechwan Province in China and studied in France (1921–24) where he joined the communist movement, and later, in 1925, he visited the Soviet Union. On returning to China, he established himself as a political and military leader and organizer in Kiangsi Soviet, an autonomous area that had been established by Mao Zedong in southwest China. After the communists rose to power in China (1952), Deng became a vice-premier, and in 1954 he was named secretary-general of the Chinese Communist party and a year later, a member of the politburo, the ruling body of the country. In the late 1960s, during the Cultural Revolution, radical supporters of Mao attacked Deng; by 1973 he had been reinstated and was made deputy premier. Although he retired in 1989, he retained absolute authority in the party.

Sources

Goodman, David S.G., et al. 1986. *The China challenge.* London: Cardinal.

Goodman, David S.G. 1990. *Deng Xiaoping.* London: Cardinal.

McHenry, Robert, ed. 1992. *The new encyclopedia Britannica.* Chicago: Encyclopedia Britannica, Inc.

Uli, Franz. 1988. *Deng Xiaoping.* Trans. Tom Artin. Boston: Harcourt Brace Jovanovich.

DEVONSHIRE COMMISSION. The British Royal Commission on Scientific Instruction and Advancement of Science (1870–75).

William Cavendish, seventh duke of Devonshire (1808–91), scientist, industrialist, and educationist, was born in London, educated at Eton and Trinity College, Cambridge, in 1829. He was a staunch Whig M.P. for Cambridge University, Malden, Yorkshire, and Derbyshire. In 1858, after succeeding to the dukedom, Cavendish gave up politics to advance science and industry. He helped develop iron and steel manufacture and harbor facilities. He also became the chancellor of the University of London (1836–56), the University of Cambridge (1860–81), and Victoria University (1881–91). He chaired the royal commission named after him; it recommended that the schools devote six hours a week to science and that to receive a degree individuals should study science, languages, and mathematics.

Sources

Aldrich, Richard, and Gordon, Peter. 1987. *Dictionary of British educationists.* London: Woburn Press.

Stephen, Leslie, and Lee, Sydney, eds. 1921–22. *The dictionary of national biography.* Supplement. London: Oxford University Press.

DEWEYAN, DEWEY COMMISSION. Relating to the ideas and practices of the influential American educationist. A Commission of Inquiry at Coyoacan, Mexico, that looked into charges against Leon Trotsky at the Moscow Trials in 1937.

John Dewey (1859–1952), an American philosopher, psychologist, and practicing educator, was born at Burlington, Vermont. After graduating from the University of Vermont and Johns Hopkins University (Ph.D., 1884), he taught philosophy at the University of Michigan (1884–88) and later, in 1889, became head of the Department of Philosophy and Education at the University of Chicago. In Chicago he initiated his reform movements in educational theory and practice, testing them in the University High School. From 1901 to 1930 he was professor of philosophy at Columbia University. At Columbia he published many articles and books; his last major work, *Experience in Education* (1938), states Dewey's basic philosophy of education and criticizes the excesses of the progressive education movement. He supported a method of teaching which began with the everyday experience of the child, and he maintained that unless a connection was made early between school activities and life experiences, genuine learning and growth were impossible. His work had a deep, lasting effect on American education and in many countries of the Western world. In 1937 he headed an inquiry into the charges of espionage and sabotage against Leon Trotsky and his son made by Stalin's regime; the Dewey Commission report found that the Moscow trials were a frameup.

Sources

Deighton, Lee, ed. 1971. *The encyclopedia of education.* New York: Macmillan and Free Press.

Devine, Elizabeth; Held, Michael; Vinson, James; and Walsh, George, eds. 1983. *Thinkers of the twentieth century: a biographical, bibliographical and critical dictionary.* London: Macmillan.

Dykhuizen, George. 1973. *The life and mind of John Dewey.* Carbondale: Southern Il-
    linois University Press.
Ohles, John F., ed. 1978. *Biographical dictionary of American educators.* Westport,
    Conn.: Greenwood Press.
Wald, Alan. 1977. Memories of the John Dewey Commission: Forty years later. *Antioch
    Review* 35:438–451.
Zusne, Leonard. 1984. *Biographical dictionary of psychology.* Westport, Conn.: Green-
    wood Press.

DE WITT. To lynch.

Jan (c. 1625–72) and Cornelius (1623–72) De Witt were born at Dort, Netherlands. Jan, a Dutch statesman, became grand pensionary of Holland in 1653
and a year later ended Holland's war with England by treaty with Oliver Cromwell. Between 1665 and 1668 he helped, first, to conduct war with England,
and later to negotiate the "Triple Alliance" with England and Sweden, thereby
frustrating Louis XIV's plans to annex the Spanish Netherlands. In 1672 he was
overthrown by the Orange party, arrested, and tortured in prison at the Hague.
When his brother came to visit him, a chauvinist mob broke in, hacked them
to pieces, and hanged their remains on posts.

Sources

Edmundson, George. 1908. The administrations of John De Witt and William of Orange.
    In A. W. Ward, G. W. Prothero, and Stanley Leathes, eds. *The Cambridge modern
    history.* Vol. V. The Age of Louis XIV. Cambridge: Cambridge University Press,
    pp. 137–167.
Lord Macaulay. 1913. *Macaulay's history of England.* London: Macmillan.
Smith, Benjamin. 1903. *The Century cyclopedia of names.* London: The Times.

DICKENSIAN. Relating to the British nineteenth-century novelist's fictional
accounts of sordid employment and living conditions and the generally brutal
features of industrialization.

Charles John Huffman Dickens (1812–70) was born at Portsmouth, had little
education, and when his father, a government clerk, was jailed for debt, Charles
went to work in a blacking warehouse. In 1824 he attended the Wellington
House Academy for two years, studied at another school briefly, and worked as
a lawyer's clerk (1828). He learned shorthand and became a journalist on the
Morning Chronicle and other papers, was a reporter of House of Commons
debates, and wrote for magazines (1835). After some of his articles appeared in
"Sketches by 'Boz'" (1834), Dickens was commissioned to write humorous
pieces on sport, which led to his *Pickwick Papers* (1836–37), a work that made
him famous. He was a prolific writer, and he became a popular novelist (by
1841). On travels in the United States and Canada in 1842, he acted as a missionary for international copyright and spoke against slavery and restriction of
free speech. He visited Italy and Switzerland during 1843–45. In the late 1850s
and through the 1860s he toured, giving public readings of his work. His social
and political views—presented with pathos, sentiment, and drama—indicate a

strong belief in the application of reason to the conditions that create injustices in life. His works depicted both the low and the high life of London, its culture and social norms, and often emphasized the oppressiveness and poverty of workhouses and industrial life and their effect on the family.

Sources

Ackroyd, Peter. 1990. *Charles Dickens.* London: Sinclair-Stevenson.

Giddings, Robert. 1983. *The changing world of Charles Dickens.* London: Vision

Kaplan, Fred. 1988. *Dickens: a biography.* London: Hodder and Stoughton.

Mackenzie, Norman, and MacKenzie, Jeanne. 1979. *Dickens: a life.* Oxford: Oxford University Press.

Stephen, Leslie, and Lee, Sydney, eds. 1917. *The dictionary of national biography.* London: Oxford University Press.

Williams, Raymond. 1970. Dickens and social ideas. In M. Slater, ed. *Dickens 1970.* London: Chapman and Hall, pp. 77–98.

DICKSON'S CURSE. At federal election time in Australia when a candidate dies during the campaign it is said that a curse has been put on the relevant electorate; according to electoral law, it means the voters in that electorate have to vote one month after the rest of the nation.

James Robert Dickson (1832–1901) was born at Plymouth in Devon; he was educated and began work in Glasgow before migrating to Victoria in 1854. After working in his cousin's bank, he moved to Queensland (1862) and by the early 1870s had established his own firm of auctioneers and estate agents. He grew rich and became chairman of several banks by 1893, a layman in the Church of England, a justice of the peace, and a fellow of the Royal Geographical Society. In addition, he entered politics in 1873 and became colonial treasurer but quit in 1887 over a dispute on the land tax. He retired from business to travel in Europe for four years, but on returning in 1892 reentered politics as a supporter of the use of South Sea Islanders as labor in the Queensland tropics. His political career included a brief spell as state premier. He was in the Australian delegation to England for the passing of the Commonwealth bill through the Imperial Parliament. After being knighted in 1901, he was appointed minister of defense in the first federal administration. But at the Commonwealth inaugural ceremonies he fell ill and died before the election of members for the first federal Parliament. Hence, his name is given to the curse of having to postpone voting for a month at federal elections when a candidate dies during the campaign.

Source

Pike, Douglas, et al. 1966–90. *Australian dictionary of biography.* 12 vols. Carlton, Victoria: University of Melbourne Press.

DIDDLE. To cheat, swindle, or victimize.

The term *diddle* has an obscure origin, but its criminal sense was established in early nineteenth-century English with the invention of Jeremy Diddler, leading character in James Kenney's (1780–1849) highly successful farce *Raising the Wind* (1803). Jeremy continually borrowed small sums of money that he did

not pay back, and he sponged in other ways on many people. The character also appears in William Makepeace Thackeray's *The Kickleburys on Rhine* (1850).
Sources
Freeman, William. 1973. *Everyman's dictionary of fictional characters.* London: J. M. Dent and Sons.
Smith, Benjamin. 1903. *The Century cyclopedia of names.* London: The Times.
Stephen, Leslie, and Lee, Sydney, eds. 1971. *The dictionary of national biography.* [See Kenney.] London: Oxford University Press.

DIGGLEISM. A British educational philosophy, so named by the Progressive party, in protest against the domination of the London School Board by the leader of its Moderate party.

Joseph Robert Diggle (1840–1917) was born at Astley, Lancashire, and educated at Manchester Grammar School and Wadham College, Oxford. As curate, he served Saint Mary's Bryanston Square in London from 1876 to 1879. To see if the clergy could enter political life, he stood as a parliamentary candidate in 1885 but failed. He joined the London School Board, Marylebone Division, and as chairman (1879–94) dominated its proceedings. While he was leader of the Moderate party, he had many of the board's committee positions filled by his followers. Such influence led the Progressive party to coin the word "Diggleism" and to distribute articles in a pamphlet called *The Case Against Diggleism* (1894). The argument was that to save voluntary schools from competition with the London School Board, teachers, accommodation, and school equipment had been let go. A sincere, dedicated worker for the cause of education, Diggle retired from the board in 1894. He tried to enter politics again as a Unionist, but a school board candidate opposed him and again he was defeated. His ideas had appeared in *The School Board for London: A Plea for Better Administration* (1881).
Source
Aldrich, Richard, and Gordon, Peter. 1987. *Dictionary of British educationists.* London: Woburn Press.

DILLON'S RULE. Legal criteria that strictly limit the power of U.S. municipal corporations; the corporations have only those powers that are stated in the city charter, powers necessarily or fairly implied by or incidental to formally expressed powers, and powers essential to the stated aims of the corporation.

John Forrest Dillon (1831–1914) was born in Montgomery County, New York, of Irish parents and spent his boyhood in Davenport, Iowa. He completed an M.D. at the University of Iowa (1850), and when illness prevented him from practicing medicine he ran a drugstore and studied law. He was admitted to the bar in 1852, was elected prosecuting attorney and later a judge (1858), and in 1862 became a Republican supreme court judge, and eventually a chief justice of Iowa. In Iowa's supreme court he introduced the Rule, which in 1868 was adopted by the courts of all U.S. states. He spent ten years as a U.S. circuit judge (1869–79) and lectured in jurisprudence at the University of Iowa until 1879 when he was appointed a professor of law at Columbia College (1879–82). Later he practiced in New York. He was a particularly shrewd corporation lawyer, often acted for the railroads, and became rich. His politics were Republican, and he was opposed to slavery before the Civil War. Among his writings, the best remembered is *Municipal Corporations* (1872), which established the field as a separate area of law. In its final edition (1911) Dillon dedicated the work to the American Bar Association, whose president he had been in 1891–92.

Sources

Dillon, John F. 1911. *Commentaries on the law of municipal corporations.* Boston: Little, Brown.

Johnson, Allen, and Malone, Dumas, eds. 1930. *Dictionary of American biography.* Vol. III. New York: Charles Scribner's Sons.

Shafritz, Jay M. 1988. *The Dorsey dictionary of American government and politics.* Chicago: Dorsey.

Smith, Edward C., and Zurcher, Arnold J. 1944. *Dictionary of American politics.* 2d ed. New York: Barnes and Noble.

DINGLEY ACT. A U.S. protective tariff act, effective 1897–1909.

Nelson Dingley (1832–99) was born in Durham, Maine, and educated in Waterville College (now Colby University) and Dartmouth College. A diarist, debater, and advocate of temperance, he taught Sunday School. After being admitted to the bar in 1856, he became half owner of the *Lewiston Evening Journal* and used it to develop his interest in journalism, temperance, and politics. He helped establish the new Republican party, became a member, was elected to the state legislature in 1861, and became governor of Maine in 1874. He advocated free education, prohibition, and taxes on the railroads. In 1881 he entered the U.S. House of Representatives and remained until his death. He supported a protective tariff, was chairman of the Committee of Ways and Means, which prepared the act bearing his name, and replaced the Wilson-Gorman Act of the Democrats. Poor health forced him to refuse President McKinley's offer of secretary of the Treasury, but in 1898 he served on the commission on the Alaskan boundary.

Sources

Jacob, Kathryn A., and Ragsdale, Bruce A. 1989. *Biographical directory of the United States Congress: 1774–1989.* Bicentennial ed. Washington, D.C.: U.S. Government Printing Office.

Johnson, Allen, and Malone, Dumas, eds. 1930. *Dictionary of American biography.* Vol. III. New York: Charles Scribner's Sons.

DIOGENIC, DIOGENES COMPLEX. Relating to the Cynic philosopher, cynical. In administration, a mosaic of standoffish eccentricity that creates enough suspicion and distrust to disqualify a subordinate for promotion (Peter and Hull, 1969).

Diogenes (c. 412–323 B.C.) was probably born and raised in Sinope on the Black Sea, and he went to study the philosophy of the Cynics in Athens. The path to wisdom lay in mastery of the self, and this achievement required giving up pleasures that stood in the way. He imposed an austere life on himself, and learned to tolerate extremes; he is said to have searched with a lantern through the streets of Athens in daylight in hopes of finding an honest man.

Sources

Boardman, John; Griffin, Jasper; and Murray, Oswyn, eds. 1986. *The Oxford history of the classical world.* Oxford: Oxford University Press.

McHenry, Robert, ed. 1992. *The new encyclopedia Britannica.* Chicago: Encyclopedia Britannica, Inc.

Peter, Laurence J., and Hull, Raymond. 1969. *The Peter principle: why things always go wrong.* New York: William Morrow.

Smith, Benjamin. 1903. *The Century cyclopedia of names.* London: The Times.

DIONYSIAN AND APOLLONIAN TEMPERAMENTS. Two temperaments identified in anthropological studies of American Indians by Ruth Benedict (1887–1948) in her *Patterns of Culture* (1934). Taking the distinction from Nietzsche's study of Greek tragedy (1872), Benedict contrasted the Pueblos and other cultures of North America. The Dionysian was a character type that annihilated ordinary limits to existence and, in drunkenness and frenzy, pressed to excess the belief that by these means wisdom would be attained. The Apollonian, distrusting excesses, kept to the middle road and avoided meddling in disruptive psychological states. The Southwest Pueblos were partly Apollonian; the American Indians, including those in Mexico, were Dionysian, valued violent experiences and broke through the usual sensory routines by using visions and dreams to attain supernatural power.

Dionysus was the son of Zeus and Semele, and had the task of supervising the growth of all natural things, especially vegetation. As the god of wine—one of his seven names was Bacchus—he was expected to bring rest and freedom from care to the weary. This he did with festivals of processions, dances, and choruses from which developed Greek drama. In Rome Bacchus's festivals were celebrated so vigorously that they had to be banned in 186 B.C. One story tells that when pirates captured Dionysus he was bound to the ship's mast. Quickly his bonds fell and twisted themselves into vines while Dionysus himself turned into a lion. In fear, the pirates flung themselves overboard and became dolphins.

Apollo, son of the God Zeus and Leto, was one of the most powerful gods of ancient Greece. He was god of light, lifegiving and destroying, and like the sun; in art he represented the perfect young man; he was also the god of music, song, and poetry; and as god of the art of healing he bestowed this power on his son, Aesculapius. Apollo's chief concern was with law and order; he presided over the establishment of cities, constitutions, and law codes and had particular jurisdiction over homicide cases. Apollo was more often represented in ancient art than any other deity. Sculptors usually portrayed him as a beautiful youth with flowing hair tied in a knot above his forehead, which was bound with a wreath of laurel. He usually carried either a lyre or a bow.

Sources

Benedict, Ruth. 1934. *Patterns of culture.* Boston: Houghton Mifflin.

Jobes, Gertrude. 1962. *Dictionary of mythology, folklore and symbols.* New York: Scarecrow Press.

Pinset, John. 1969. *Greek mythology.* London: Hamlyn.

Sills, David L., ed. 1968. *International encyclopedia of the social sciences.* New York: Macmillan and Free Press.

DISNEYISM, DISNEY PIONEERS, DISNEY EXPERIENCE. A growing international obsession that drives people to visit America's Disneylands. Those who search evermore for new places to establish a Disneyland. The experience of attending a Disneyland and finding it costly. Since 1956 310 million people have visited California's Disneyland, 300 million have been attracted to Florida's Disneyworld; in ten years 100 million have visited Japan's Disney-Nippon. The rising attendance rates and the relationship between population size and attendance rates indicates that, internationally, as some commentators believe, Disneyland has outgrown its host. The Disney pioneers are searching Kiev, Warsaw, Stockholm, and Moscow for sites for Disney-Mir, and by 2000 the growth rate in attendance will probably exceed the growth rate of the human race. The Disney experience suggests that in 1991 a family visit to Florida's Disneyworld costs $2,000, and the price of some thrilling 5-minute rides was $1 a second for the ride itself, with 50 minutes waiting for the ride.

Walter Elias Disney (1901–66) was born in Chicago and moved to Kansas at age 10. Later he returned to Chicago to study at McKinley High School where his talent for drawing was apparent. During World War I he served in the Voluntary Ambulance Unit in France, and after the war he returned to Kansas to work in the Pesman-Rubin Art studio as a commercial artist. He became a cartoonist in 1920. He and Ub Iwerks joined forces to begin a film animation company in Disney's garage. In 1922 Laugh-O-Gram films was incorporated, and after initial problems Disney went to Hollywood, established himself, and in 1928, with help from Iwerks, Walt Disney Productions made *Mickey Mouse* which secured Disney's career. He brought the animated cartoon to perfection. During World War II he made training films and, later, True-Life Adventure films. In the early 1950s he got funds from television to build the amusement park "Disneyland" in California. In 1955 the Mickey Mouse Club began its television career. Disney won thirty-nine awards from the Academy of Motion Picture Arts and Sciences, four Emmy awards, and over 800 awards and decorations for his work. Among his most noted animated motion pictures were his *Snow White and the Seven Dwarfs, Bambi, Fantasia, Dumbo, Pinocchio,* and *Cinderella.* On his death the Disney empire was taken over by Walt Disney's brother, Roy.

Sources
Holliss, Richard, and Sibley, Brian. 1988. *The Disney studio story.* New York: Crown.
Leebron, Elizabeth, and Gartley, Lynn. 1979. *Walt Disney: a guide to references and resources.* Boston: G. K. Hall.
Mosley, Leonard. 1986. *The real Walt Disney: a biography.* London: Grafton.
Who was who in America, 1961–68. Chicago: Marquis.

DIVISIA INDEX. A continuous-time statistical index number devised in 1925–26 and widely used in theoretical discussions of data aggregation and the measurement of technical change.

François Divisia (1889–1964) was born in Tizi-Ouzo, a department of Algiers, and studied at the Algiers grammar school and Bordeaux University, graduating in law. He joined the École Polytechnique (Military Academy of Artillery and Engineering) in 1909, but mobilization interrupted his education. In World War I he was awarded the Military Cross and a knighthood of the Legion of Honor. In 1919 he joined the Department of Civil Engineering and was a government engineer (1938–59). He taught industrial economy at the National School of Arts and Crafts and political and social economy at the École Polytechnique. He became president of the International Society of Econometrics and of the Paris Society of Statistics, and was a fellow of the American Statistical Association and the American Society for the Advancement of Science. He belonged to the Society of Political Economy, the International Institute of Statistics, the French Association of Economic Science, and many other international learned societies. He published seven books; the first was *Economie ratioannelle* (1927) and the last *Technique et Production* (1951).

Sources
Eatwell, John; Milgate, Murray; and Newman, Peter. 1987. *The new Palgrave: a dictionary of economics.* London: Macmillan.
Katz, Samuel, and Johnson, Norman, eds. 1982. *Encyclopedia of statistical sciences.* New York: John Wiley.
Roman-D'Amat, J., and Limouzin-Lamothe, R. 1967. *Dictionnaire de biographie Française.* Vol. 11. Paris: Librairie Letouzey et Ané.
Who's who in France, 1964–65. Paris: Jacques Lafitte.

DIX-MANN FORMULA. A nineteenth-century plan to improve U.S. mental health treatment in hospitals. The legislation passed both houses of Congress, was vetoed by President Franklin Pierce (1854), but the formula was applied for almost 100 years.

Dorothea Lynde Dix (1802–87) was born in Hampden, Maine, and in her grandparents' Boston home founded Dix Mansion, a girls' school (1821–35). She produced many children's textbooks (1824–33), and traveled to the West Indies and London. Later she began teaching Sunday School in a house of correction and, appalled by the cruelty toward the insane (1841), began a private investigation of jails, almshouses, and houses of correction in many states. She started a national campaign to ensure the mentally ill were treated differently from criminals, and to establish legislation that would set aside funds from the sale of national land for the care of the insane and raise taxes to care for them. She traveled in Europe (1845–57) advising on the establishment and administration of hospitals, and in 1861 she was appointed superintendent of women nurses. After the U.S. Civil War, she continued her humanitarian work.

Horace Mann (1796–1859) was born in Franklin, Massachusetts, and raised in rural poverty, but with help from a schoolteacher was prepared for entry to Brown University, and later graduated in law and was admitted to the bar in 1823. He entered the Massachusetts State Legislature (1827–33), and the Senate (1833–37) and saw important laws passed on public education. He established and edited *Common School Journal* (1834–38) and raised the quality of teaching and the breadth of education in public schools. He studied European education (1843) and by 1848 was an antislavery Whig in the U.S. House of Representatives. When defeated in 1852, he became the president of Antioch College, Ohio. In addition to his public education efforts, he supported the establishment of state hospitals for the insane with Dorothea Dix, and restrictions on slavery, lotteries, and liquor sales. His motto was: ''Be ashamed to die until you have won some victory for humanity.''

Sources

Downs, Robert B. 1974. *Horace Mann: champion of public schools.* New York: Twayne
    Publishers.

Garraty, John A., and Sternstein, Jerome L. 1974. *Encyclopedia of American biography.*
    New York: Harper and Row.

Johnson, Allen, and Malone, Dumas, eds. 1930. *Dictionary of American biography.* Vol.
    III. New York: Charles Scribner's Sons.

Johnson, Ann B. 1990. *Out of Bedlam: the truth about deinstitutionalization.* New York:
    Basic Books.

Marshall, Helen E. 1937. *Dorothea Dix: forgotten Samaritan.* Chapel Hill.: University
    of North Carolina Press.

Messerli, Jonathan. 1972. *Horace Mann: a biography.* New York: Alfred A. Knopf.

Zusne, Leonard. 1984. *Biographical dictionary of psychology.* Westport, Conn.: Greenwood Press.

DODGE-MARTIN THESIS. ''[D]iseases which are very characteristic of our times, namely the chronic diseases, are etiologically linked with excessive stress and in turn this stress is the product of specific socially structured situations inherent in the organization of modern technological societies'' (Dodge and Martin, 1970:3).

David Laurence Dodge (1931–88) was born and raised in Concord, New Hampshire, and served in the U.S. Navy in Korea during the early 1950s. He was educated at Louisiana State College and San Diego State University, and the University of Oregon (Ph.D., 1963). He taught there as well as at San Francisco State College (now University) and San Diego State College (now University). In 1967 he joined the faculty of the Department of Sociology and Anthropology at the University of Notre Dame in Illinois where he specialized in deviant behavior and medical sociology. He researched marital status and social stress, as well as drug and alcohol use among students, and he worked on a theory of deviance to account for its positive forms. For twenty-one years he directed and supervised undergraduate and graduate studies, and became an enormously popular teacher.

Walter Tilford Martin (b. 1917) studied at the University of Washington (Ph.D., 1949) and joined the Department of Sociology at the University of Oregon in 1947. During World War II he was in the U.S. Army. He was a Social Science Research Council scholar, and from 1957 to 1968 he was chairperson of the Department of Sociology, University of Oregon. In addition, he was visiting professor at the universities of Kansas (1956–57), Wisconsin (1958), and New England, Australia (1973–74). He also researched in Niarobi, Kenya (1968–69). He was a member of several professional societies and associations, and among his publications are *The Rural Fringe* (1953) and, with J. P. Gibbs, *Status Integration and Suicide* (1963).

Sources

Dodge, David L., and Martin, Walter T. 1970. *Social stress and illness: mortality patterns in industrial society.* Notre Dame, Ind.: University of Notre Dame Press.

May, Hal, ed. 1985. *Contemporary authors.* Vol. 112. Detroit: Gale Research.

Who's who in America, 1982–83. Chicago: Marquis.

Personal Communication.

DOMINICAN. Relating to Saint Dominic or to the Dominicans, Black Friars.

Domingo De Guezman (c. 1170–1221) was born at Calahorra, Old Castle, Spain, studied at the University of Palencia, and became a canon and later, in 1199, prior of canons at Osma Cathedral. In about 1203 he and the bishop traveled to Rome for permission to evangelize among the Tartars. Instead, Pope Innocent III sent them to southern France to preach to the Albigenses. In poverty the two wandered and preached until 1216 when Domingo was given a house and church at Toulouse for his followers. Pope Honorius III gave him permission to establish a new order, the Dominicans (1216). Saint Dominic began the widespread use of the rosary. He died at Bologna in Italy. The Dominicans appeared in England in 1221 and were known as Black Friars because of their clothing— a black mantle over a white habit. At first they lived in Holborn, and in 1285 they moved to Montfichett Tower, which was given to them as a monastery.

Sources

Cross, Frank L. 1974. *The Oxford dictionary of the Christian Church.* 2d ed. New York: Oxford University Press.

Douglas, James D., ed. 1974. *The new international dictionary of the Christian Church.* Exeter: Paternoster Press.

Eliade, Mircea, ed. 1987. *Encyclopedia of religion.* New York: Macmillan.

McHenry, Robert, ed. 1992. *The new encyclopedia Britannica.* Chicago: Encyclopedia Britannica, Inc.

DONAT OR DONET. A primer or a grammar.

Aelius Donatus (fl. 333) was a Roman grammarian who taught at Rome in the fourth century and had Saint Jerome as a pupil. In about 358 he wrote *Ars grammatica,* known as the "Donat," which became the foundation of later grammatical works. Donat's writings constitute almost a complete course in Latin grammar. In the Middle Ages it was the only textbook used in schools, so that in Western Europe Donat became synonymous with grammar. The book was one of the first on which printing by means of letters cut on wooden blocks was attempted. Today copies are bibliographic curiosities. Donatus also wrote commentaries on Virgil and Terence.

Sources

Kenney, E. J., and Clausen, Wendell V., eds. 1982. *Latin literature.* New York: Cambridge University Press.

McHenry, Robert, ed. 1992. *The new encyclopedia Britannica.* Chicago: Encyclopedia Britannica, Inc.

DONATIST. A member of an African Christian sect in the fourth and fifth centuries who protested against any lessening of the extreme reverence given to martyrs.

Donatus of Casae Nigrae (d. c. 355) was bishop of Carthage in 315, and headed a body of priests who held that the church must include only holy members and that the true church was comprised only of saints. This sect had begun in North Africa in 311 as a result of a dispute over the election of the bishop of Carthage. The Donatists maintained that their own party was the only true and pure church; they treated the lapsed very severely, and since they believed that baptisms were invalid, rebaptized converts from the Catholic Church. Although they were persecuted (317–21), the Donatists were the majority party among North African Christians. They were threatened when Emperor Constans (347–48) exiled Donatus; but he returned under Emperor Julian. After Donatus's death, his followers were led by a cleric, Parmenian. The Donatists were politically astute and gained a following because they supported the cause of both slaves and oppressed natives against the Roman landlords.

Sources

Eliade, Mircea, ed. 1987. *Encyclopedia of religion.* New York: Macmillan.

Frend, William H.C. 1985. *The Donatist church: a movement of protest in Roman North Africa.* Oxford: Clarendon Press.

McHenry, Robert, ed. 1992. *The new encyclopedia Britannica.* Chicago: Encyclopedia Britannica, Inc.

Meagher, Thomas C.; O'Brien, Thomas C.; and Aherne, Consuleo M., eds. 1979. *Encyclopedic dictionary of religion.* Washington, D.C.: Corpus Publications.

DONOVAN COMMISSION. A British Royal Commission on Trade Unions and Employer's Associations (1965–68) which considered mainly the postwar growth of short unofficial strikes at work. The commission found that problems in Britain's industrial relations were arising from the managers and shop stewards who were undermining traditional industrywide systems of collective bargaining with informal and disorderly negotiations on working conditions and pay.

Sir Terence Norbert Donovan, Baron Donovan (1898–1971), served in World War I with the Bedfordshire Regiment in France and the Royal Air Force in France and Germany, after which, in 1920, he entered the Civil Service, the Revenue Department. He was a barrister at the Middle Temple (1924), became King's Counsel (1944–45), and was elected M.P. for the Eastern Division of Leicester (1945–50). He became judge of the high court of justice (King's Bench Division) in 1959–60, lord justice of appeal in 1960–64, and chaired the Royal Commission on Trade Unions and Employer's Organizations in 1965. He was knighted in 1950 and became a life peer, Baron Donovan of Winchester, in 1964.

Sources

Blake (Lord), and Nicholls, C. S., eds. 1986. *Dictionary of national biography 1971–1980.* Oxford: Oxford University Press.

Marsh, Arthur. 1979. *Concise encyclopedia of industrial relations.* Westmead, Farnborough, Hants: Gower.

Roberts, Frank C., comp. 1978. *Obituaries from the Times 1971–1975.* Reading: Newspaper Archive Developments.

Townsend, P., ed. 1970. *Burke's Peerage.* 105th ed. London: Burke's Peerage Ltd.

Who's who, 1970. London: Adam and Charles Black.

Who was who, 1971–80. London: Adam and Charles Black.

DOOLITTLE REPORT. A U.S. intelligence report in 1954, commissioned by President Eisenhower, dealing with the clandestine services of the Central Intelligence Agency. Its main recommendations were that if the United States was to survive, longstanding concepts of fair play had to be reconsidered; the United States had to develop effective espionage and counterespionage services and learn to subvert, sabotage, and destroy its enemies through more clever, more sophisticated, and more effective methods than those used against the United States.

James Harold Doolittle (1896–1993) was born in California and raised in Nome, Alaska, before returning to California in 1908. Early in life, he was an amateur boxer and flyweight champion (1912) and became deeply interested in flying. He studied engineering at the Los Angeles Junior College of the University of California and in World War I enlisted in the aviation section of the U.S. Army. Trained as a pilot, he became a pioneer in aviation by setting a transcontinental record in 1922. He graduated from Massachusetts Institute of Technology in aeronautical engineering, won the Schneider Cup seaplane race in 1925, and made the first instrument flight across America in 1929. He worked for Shell Oil during 1929–40 and returned to the U.S. Army Air Corps in World War II to lead the first air raid on Tokyo in April 1942. A general, he served in Africa and led the Eighth Air Force in attacks on the German oil industry. When he returned to Shell in 1946, he became a director but also held many government advisory posts relating to aeronautics and space, sat on the President's Science Advisory Committee, and chaired the commission that inquired into the clandestine services of the Central Intelligence Agency. Afterward, in 1955, he was appointed to President Eisenhower's Board on Foreign Intelligence. He served similarly under Presidents Kennedy and Johnson until 1965.

Sources

Candee, Marjorie D., ed. 1957, *Current biography yearbook.* New York: H. W. Wilson.

Cox, J. A. 1992. Tokyo bomber. Doolittle do'od it. *Smithsonian* 23:112–114.

Doolittle, James H., and Glines, Carroll V. 1991. *I could never be so lucky again: an autobiography.* New York: Bantam Books.

Garrison, P. 1988. Jimmy Doolittle. *Flying,* October, 115:74–76.

Glines, Carroll V. 1964. *Doolittle's raiders.* Princeton, N.J.: Van Nostrand.

O'Toole, George, J.A. 1988. *The encyclopedia of American intelligence and espionage.* New York: Facts on File.

Reynolds, Quentin. 1953. *The amazing Mr. Doolittle: a biography of Lieutenant General James H. Doolittle.* New York: Appleton-Century-Crofts.

Thomas, Lowell, and Jablonski, Edward. 1976. *Doolittle: a biography.* Garden City, N.Y.: Doubleday.

Who's who in America, 1988–89. Chicago: Marquis.

DOROTHY DIX. A question put to a government minister by a member of the party in power to give the minister an opportunity to deliver a prepared speech.

Elizabeth Meriwether (1870–1951) was born near Woodstock, Tennessee, into a southern aristocratic family that lost its slaves after the Confederacy surrendered. She was educated at a genteel school and married George O. Gilmer in 1888. His serious mental illness forced her to work, and to prevent her own mental breakdown she began writing sketches from her life. A neighbor helped her get them published in the New Orleans *Picayune* (1896–1902), whereupon she established a writing career. Because no respected woman could use her own name as a writer, she chose her nom-de-plume because she liked "Dorothy," and "Dix" was the name of a slave in her old family. She wrote a column for those in love. In 1901 she joined the staff of the New York *Journal,* and worked for the Wheeler Syndicate (1917) and Ledger Syndicate (1923). In time 2,000 letters came daily in reply to her column of advice and replies to personal questions. Because the lovelorn wrote with similar questions and a limited range of problems, her answers became familiar and developed a pattern of their own. Consequently, her answers had the air of prepared statements. Among her books were *Mirandy* (1914) and *Dorothy Dix, Her Book* (1922), and she learned enough from writing the column to publish *How to Win and Hold a Husband* (1939). In Australia in 1941 "Dorothy Dix" referred to the censor; in 1963 it had established itself as part of Australian parliamentary jargon.

Sources

Garraty, John A., ed. 1977. *Dictionary of American biography.* Supplement 5. New York: Charles Scribner's Sons.

Ramson, William S., ed. 1988. *The Australian national dictionary.* Melbourne: Oxford University Press.

DORRITE. A political activist in the May 1842 Rhode Island rebellion for the extension of suffrage in that state.

Thomas Wilson Dorr (1805–54) was born in Providence, Rhode Island, educated at Phillip Exeter Academy, and graduated from Harvard in 1823. He studied law in New York, was admitted to the bar in 1827 and practiced in Providence. He entered the Rhode Island Assembly in 1834, and in 1840, with the formation of the Rhode Island Suffrage Association, Dorr became a leader in a lifetime struggle to reform Rhode Island's constitution and liberalize voting regulations. A People's party was formed, and the state had two ruling groups, one legal and the other headed by ''Governor Dorr.'' His followers clashed with the legitimate government, and hostilities culminated in the Dorr Rebellion (1842), a march on the Providence Arsenal, and the firing of an ancient cannon at its establishment-oriented defenders. Dorr's followers deserted him, and he gave himself up. He was imprisoned on charges of treason promulgated by the state's establishment. Ultimate pardon and restoration of all his civil rights in 1851 came only when he was a broken man.

Sources

Johnson, Allen, and Malone, Dumas, eds. 1930. *Dictionary of American biography.* Vol. III. New York: Charles Scribner's Sons.

Morris, Dan, and Morris, Inez. 1974. *Who was who in American politics.* New York: Hawthorn Books.

Sperber, Hans, and Trittschuh, Travis. 1962. *American political terms.* Detroit: Wayne State University Press.

DOW-JONES AVERAGE OR INDEX, THE DOW. An indicator of the relative prices of stocks and shares on the New York Stock Exchange.

Charles Henry Dow (1851–1902) was born in Connecticut and worked on several newspapers in New England before becoming a reporter for *Mail and Express* (New York) and the Kiernan News Agency in 1880. He established Dow, Jones & Company in 1882 and published security market indices. The index uses three trends in the movement of stocks: primary (long-term) trend, secondary (short-term) trend, and daily fluctuations. Over the years the calculation of the Dow-Jones index has been modified and refined.

Edward Davis Jones (1856–1920) was born in Worcester, Massachusetts, and studied briefly at Brown University. He became a reporter for the *Providence Evening Press* and later editor of the *Sunday Despatch.* He and Dow were friends and became partners in establishing a New York newspaper for businessmen. Dow seemed to have the ideas, while Jones analyzed information with much skill in the news agency, Dow, Jones & Company (1882). The comma between their names was dropped, and in 1889 they published their *Wall Street Journal* with Dow as editor (1889–91). Jones retired in 1899.

Sources

McHenry, Robert, ed. 1992. *The new encyclopedia Britannica.* Chicago: Encyclopedia Britannica, Inc.

Rosenberg, Jerry M. 1982. *Inside the Wall Street Journal: the history and the power of Dow Jones & Co. and America's most influential newspaper.* New York: Macmillan.

Wendt, Lloyd. 1982. *The Wall Street Journal: the story of Dow Jones and the nation's business newspaper.* Chicago: Rand McNally.

DOWNING, GEORGE DOWNING. A treacherous man from seventeenth-century England.

Sir George Downing (1624–84) was born in Dublin, and his family immigrated to New England (1638), settling in Salem. Downing became a tutor after graduating from Harvard but soon returned to England in the role of a ship's chaplain. In England he supported both Oliver Cromwell and Charles II. He served Cromwell's army in Scotland in 1650, was a member of both of Cromwell's parliaments, and tried to have Cromwell crowned king. By 1659 Downing was in Holland making his peace with Charles, admitting to the errors of his ways under Cromwell and promising allegiance to the next king. In 1663 he was made a baronet, and during the war with the Dutch managed the Treasury, and was clearly a favorite of Charles II. A selfish character, treacherous and ungrateful, a false man who betrayed trust, Downing became an early model for a traitor.

See also CROMWELLIAN.

Sources

Hendrickson, Robert. 1988. *The dictionary of eponyms: names that became words.* New York: Dorset.

Johnson, Allen, and Malone, Dumas, eds. 1930. *Dictionary of American biography.* Vol. III. New York: Charles Scribner's Sons.

Stephen, Leslie, and Lee, Sydney, eds. 1917. *The dictionary of national biography.* London: Oxford University Press.

DRACONIAN. Extremely severe; especially referring to laws or their implementation.

Draco or Dracon (fl. 621 B.C.), a celebrated politician, lawgiver, and Archon of Athens, drew up the first code of written law, procedures, and sanctions (621 B.C.). Because the laws and penalties were so harsh—death was the penalty for even trivial offenses—they were repealed or changed by Solon. Only Draco's law on homicide remained. A ''Draconian Law'' is therefore synonymous with harshness and excessive severity.

Sources

Boardman, John; Griffin, Jasper; and Murray, Oswyn, eds. 1986. *The Oxford history of the classical world.* Oxford: Oxford University Press.

McHenry, Robert, ed. 1992. *The new encyclopedia Britannica.* Chicago: Encyclopedia Britannica, Inc.

DRAGO DOCTRINE. On December 29, 1902, a note sent to the Argentine minister in Washington, D.C., protested the blockade of Venezuelan ports by Great Britain, Italy, and Germany to enforce their demands for payment of monies owing to them. The note, based on the doctrine of the Argentinian, Carlos Calvo (1868), stated that no debt claims by other nations against any sovereign Latin American state should be collected by force or occupation.

Luis Maria Drago (1859–1921), an Argentine diplomat and jurist, was born in Buenos Aires, son of a distinguished Argentine family. He studied law at the University of Buenos Aires, went into practice, and was later appointed a judge of the Court of Appeals, serving until his election to Congress. He became minister for foreign affairs in the cabinet of General Julio Roca, and it was during that ministry that his note embodying the Drago Doctrine was sent. In 1907 he represented Argentina at the Second Hague Conference and also served on the Permanent Court of Arbitration.

Sources

Calvo, Carlos. 1868. *International law of America and Europe in theory and practice.* Paris: Guillaumin.

Commager, Henry S., ed. 1968. *Documents of American history.* 8th ed. New York: Appleton-Century-Crofts.

Delpar, Helen, ed. 1974. *Encyclopedia of Latin America.* New York: McGraw-Hill.

Dudley, Lavinia P. 1963. *The encyclopedia Americana.* International ed. New York: Americana Corp.

McHenry, Robert, ed. 1992. *The new encyclopedia Britannica.* Chicago: Encyclopedia Britannica, Inc.

Plano, Jack C., and Greenberg, Milton. 1989. *The American political dictionary.* New York: Holt, Rinehart and Winston.

DREYFUSARD. A defender of the French soldier who was convicted, and later acquitted, of treason between 1894 and 1906.

Alfred Dreyfus (c. 1859–1935) was born at Mulhausen, Alsace, the son of a rich Jewish manufacturer. He came to Paris in 1874, and on the General Staff of the French Army rose to the rank of artillery captain. In 1893–94 he was falsely charged with delivering documents connected with national defense to a foreign government. He was court-martialed, degraded, and transported to the Cayenne Ile du Diable (Devil's Island). The efforts of his wife and friends to prove him an innocent victim of injustice, forgery, and malice led to a frenzy of militarism and anti-Semitism in France. The novelist Emile Zola (1840–1902) attacked the government in his *J'accuse* (1898). Following the suicide of Colonel Henry, who had falsified evidence at the original trial, the case was reopened and Dreyfus was found guilty but pardoned in 1899. In 1906, when anti-Semitism in France had become less intense, the verdict was reversed. During World War I Dreyfus was awarded the Legion of Honor (1919). The atmosphere surrounding the case was captured well by Marcel Proust (1871–1922).

Sources
McHenry, Robert, ed. 1992. *The new encyclopedia Britannica.* Chicago: Encyclopedia Britannica, Inc.
Magnussen, Magnus; Goring, Rosemary; and Thorn, John O., eds. 1990. *Chambers biographical dictionary.* Edinburgh: Chambers Ltd.
Proust, Marcel. 1913–28. *Remembrance of things past.* Trans. C. K. Scott Moncrieff and Terence Kilmartin, 1981. London: Chatto and Windus.
Snyder, Louis L. 1973. *The Dreyfus case: a documentary history.* New Brunswick, N.J.: Rutgers University Press.

DROOP QUOTA. A method of assessing the results of an election which requires a quota. The quota is the minimum number of votes a candidate needs at any stage, except the last, to qualify for election. Normally, this is the smallest whole number that is larger than the number of ballot papers returned/number of seats competed for + 1. Thus, if 20,000 people vote and three seats are to be filled, the Droop quota set will be 5,001; it will be 3,334 if five seats are to be filled.

Henry Richmond Droop (c. 1831–84), son of John Abraham Droop of Middlesex, was educated at Marlborough and Trinity College, Cambridge, became a fellow of his college (1855), and a lecturer in mathematics. He was a barrister at Lincoln's Inn in 1859 and the author of several books, including *Proportional Representation as Applied to the Election of Local Governing Bodies* (1871).

Sources
Allibone, Samual A. 1891. *A supplement to Allibone's critical dictionary of English literature and British and American authors.* 2 vols. Philadelphia: John Kirk. Reprint, 1965; Detroit: Gale Research.
Boase, Frederic. 1965. *Modern English biography.* London: Frank Cass.
Dummett, Michael. 1984. *Voting procedures.* Oxford: Clarendon Press.

DRUZE. A member of a closed Arabic-speaking religious sect found primarily in southern Syria and Lebanon, whose beliefs draw on the Koran, the Holy Bible, and Gnosticism. Some live in Israel and Jordan, and a few in the United States, Canada, and Latin America.

Muhammad ibn Isma-'i-al Darazi- (fl. 1017–20), from whose name Druze (Arabian, Duru-z) is derived, was part Turkish. An Isma-'i-li- teacher who came from Bukhara to Egypt (1017–18), he was one of three who established the sect and died within three years of its founding. He led 200,000 people from persecution in Egypt to settle in Syria between Djebail and Saide. He claimed that the divine spirit in Adam had been sent to Hamzah ibn 'Ali, a Persian feltmaker, the major founder of the sect; then the spirit was transmitted, by way of imams, to al-Hakim, the Fatimid caliph of Egypt. Darazi- was probably a disciple of Hamzah. In conflict with each other, both founders sought favors of al-Hakim, the third founder and divine figure of the sect. Darazi- may have been executed by order of the caliph (1019–20) after having been denounced by Hamzah, or he may have simply departed secretly to Syria. In 1021 both al-

Hakim and Hamzah died. The death of all three founders gave rise to the Druze belief that their founders are merely absent and will return. When their founders return, the Druze believe they will conquer all enemies, uphold justice, and rule the world. Today the Druze demand self-determination and consider all outsiders enemies; they have fought fiercely for their aims since the civil war began in Lebanon in the mid-1970s.

Sources

Betts, Robert B. 1988. *The Druze.* New Haven, Conn.: Yale University Press.

Eliade, Mircea, ed. 1987. *Encyclopedia of religion.* New York: Macmillan.

Meagher, Paul K.; O'Brien, Thomas C.; and Aherne, Consuleo M., eds. 1979. *Encyclopedic dictionary of religion.* Washington, D.C.: Corpus Publications.

DULLESIAN BRINKMANSHIP. With "If you are scared to go to the brink you are lost" (*Life,* January 16, 1956), John Foster Dulles introduced brinkmanship to international relations, that is, the deliberate creation of a recognizable risk of war, not completely under one's control; a tactic whereby one lets the situation get out of hand, because being out of hand is intolerable to the opposition and will rein them in. Thomas Schelling (1963) coined the term, but the concept of "-manship" comes from the popular books of the British author, Stephen Potter (1900–69) on *Gamesmanship* (1947) and *One-upmanship* (1952) which recommended humorous and unfair tactics in taking advantage of others.

John Foster Dulles (1888–1959) was raised in Watertown, New York, educated at public schools and at Princeton (1904–8), and studied law at George Washington University. He specialized in international law. During World War I, he worked to ensure Central American government support of the United States; he was on the World Trade Board and became counsel to the U.S. delegation at the repatriations commission in Versailles. Between the wars, he became an expert in foreign financial and industrial interests, and published *War, Peace and Change* (1939). After World War II, he was the foreign policy adviser to the 1948 Republican presidential candidate, Governor Thomas E. Dewey; he was also adviser to the U.S. delegation at the San Francisco conference of the United Nations Organization. Briefly, he was a U.S. senator (1949) and helped negotiate the peace treaty with Japan. He became President Eisenhower's secretary of state (1953–59) and in strong opposition to Russian communism developed the "brinkmanship" policy. He published *War or Peace* (1950), a criticism of U.S. foreign policy. He coined the term *massive retaliation* for the West's planned nuclear response to foreign (Russian) aggression.

Sources

Garraty, John A., ed. 1980. *Dictionary of American biography.* Supplement 6. New York: Charles Scribner's Sons.

Immerman, Richard H., ed. 1989. *John Foster Dulles and the diplomacy of the cold war.* Princeton, N.J.: Princeton University Press.

McHenry, Robert, ed. 1992. *The new encyclopedia Britannica.* Chicago: Encyclopedia Britannica, Inc.

Pruessen, Ronald W. 1982. *John Foster Dulles: the road to power.* New York: Free Press.

Schelling, Thomas C. 1963. *The strategy of conflict.* Cambridge, Mass.: Harvard University Press.

Weintal, Edward, and Bartlett, Charles. 1967. *Facing the brink.* New York: Charles Scribner's Sons.

Wintle, Justin. 1989. *The dictionary of war quotations.* London: Hodder and Stoughton.

DUMBARTON OAKS. A conference between the United States, the USSR, Great Britain, and China (1944) to discuss the creation of an international organization for peace. It was agreed that the "Big Five" (including France) would be permanent members of the United Nations Security Council charged with maintaining international peace after World War II. The conference was in two parts; the first produced the Dumbarton Proposals for a general international organization. China was excluded from this part because Russia was still neutral in the war with Japan. At the second part Britain and the United States met with the Chinese who endorsed the proposals. Russia had raised two problems: it insisted that each member of the Security Council have the power to veto its majority decisions, and that all sixteen of the Russian republics in the USSR should have a seat in the U.N. General Assembly. The decisions were discussed and partly confirmed at the Yalta Conference in February 1945.

Dumbarton Oaks is a mansion in Georgetown, Washington, D.C. It was built in 1801 and was originally the home of William Hammond Dorsey. In 1920 the U.S. diplomat, Robert Bliss, acquired the property. It housed a collection of Byzantine art of the fourth and fifth centuries, Columbian art, a library for each of the art collections, and another specializing in landscape gardening. In 1940 Mrs. Bliss presented Dumbarton Oaks to Harvard University as well as the funds needed to maintain the mansion and the collections.

See also YALTA AGREEMENT.

Sources

Canby, Courtlandt. 1984. *The encyclopedia of historic places.* London: Mansell Publishing.

Hilderbrand, Robert C. 1990. *Dumbarton Oaks: the origins of the United Nations and the search for post-war security.* Chapel Hill: University of North Carolina Press.

Laquer, Walter. 1973. *A dictionary of politics.* Rev. ed. New York: Free Press.

McHenry, Robert, ed. 1992. *The new encyclopedia Britannica.* Chicago: Encyclopedia Britannica, Inc.

DUNCE. One slow at learning.

Johannes Duns Scotus (c. 1265–1308) was a native of Maxton in Roxburgshire, or of Dunse in Berwickshire, Scotland. He was a fellow of Merton College, Oxford, studied in Paris, and joined the Franciscan order of Friars Minor in 1293. He became a professor of theology at Oxford in 1301 and also taught at Cologne. In 1304 he went to Paris, where his ingenious arguments on the Immaculate Conception earned him the soubriquet of Doctor Subtilis, the "Subtle Doctor.'' In the belief that human will was superior to intellect and that love was more important than knowledge, he argued that the essence of the idea of heaven lay in love rather than in any vision of God. So he was a great opponent to the method of Thomas Aquinas in preferring speculation instead of practice in the foundation of Christian theology. Because Scotus supported the papal party, Philip the Fair banished him from Paris. The Scotists, a scholastic sect, followed him, until reformers attacked the belief system. In the sixteenth century, the church reformers were greatly opposed to his ideas because they gave such strong support to the papacy against those who upheld the divinity of monarchs. His followers became known as Dunsmen or Dunses and were distinguished by their objection to the new ideas about the divinity of monarchs. In time, the name ''Duns'' or ''Dunce'' became synonymous with resistance to all new ideas, and to learning, and later meant ''unable to learn.''

See also SCOTISM.

Sources

Bettoni, Efrem. 1961. *Duns Scotus: the basic principles of his philosophy.* Trans. and ed. Bernadino Bonansea. Washington, D.C.: Catholic University of America Press.

Cross, Frank L. 1974. *The Oxford dictionary of the Christian Church.* 2d ed. New York: Oxford University Press.

Effler, Roy R. 1962. *John Duns Scotus and the principle ''omne quod movetur ab alio movetur.''* St. Bonaventur, N.Y.: Franciscan Institute.

Harris, Charles R.S. 1959. *Duns Scotus.* New York: Humanities Press.

McHenry, Robert, ed. 1992. *The new encyclopedia Britannica.* Chicago: Encyclopedia Britannica, Inc.

Magnussen, Magnus; Goring, Rosemary; and Thorn, John O., eds. 1990. *Chambers biographical dictionary.* Edinburgh: Chambers Ltd.

Ryan, John K., and Bonansea, Bernadino M.V. 1965. *John Duns Scotus 1265–1965.* Washington, D.C.: Catholic University of America Press.

Wolter, Allan B., and McCord Adams, Marilyn. 1990. *The philosophical theology of John Duns Scotus.* Ithaca, N.Y.: Cornell University Press.

DURHAM RULE. A U.S. ruling that states an accused person is not criminally responsible if the unlawful act was the product of a mental disease or mental defect. It was introduced to the District of Columbia and raised problems of interpretation. The law also required that an evil-meaning mind be the cause of an unlawful act. Since this concept of mind had no place in psychiatry, pleas of insanity became problematic at law and the rule is no longer the guideline it once was.

Monte Durham (b. 1928) was discharged from the U.S. Navy in 1945 as psychologically unfit for service. In 1947 he pleaded guilty to auto theft and was put on one to three years probation; later he attempted suicide and was hospitalized for two months. In January 1948 he was convicted for passing bad checks and imprisoned. Meanwhile, he was found to be of unsound mind and diagnosed as psychotic with a psychopathic personality. After fifteen months of treatment, he was conditionally released, violated his parole, was caught, and again found to be of unsound mind. He was discharged in May 1951, began to hallucinate, and on July 13 was caught breaking into a house. He was convicted after a trial without jury. On appeal, the court adopted a new test of criminal responsibility, which meant that Durham was not criminally responsible for his actions. He was remanded for a new trial. The case raised many problems in the definition of mental defect, disease, the motives for a criminal act, and how they were related.

Sources

Durham v. *U.S. Federal Reporter.* 2d Series. Vol. 214 F 2d. 1954. St. Paul, Minn.: West
    Publishing.

Maeder, Thomas. 1985. *Crime and madness: the origins and evolution of the insanity
    defense.* New York: Harper and Row.

Mason, John K., and McCall-Smith, R. A. 1987. *Butterworth's medico-legal encyclo-
    pedia.* London: Butterworth.

Stone, Alan A. 1976. *Mental health and the law: a system in transition.* New York:
    Jason Aronson.

DURHAM-McDONALD TEST. Much control for defining mental health in the United States was placed in the hands of psychiatrists (see Durham Rule, 1945). But in 1962 a decision was taken in the case of Ernest McDonald, which took control from psychiatrists and returned it to the jury. This decision stated that what psychiatrists consider a mental disease for clinical reasons may not be the same disease for a jury who must decide criminal responsibility. Ever since, tests of mental disease and disorder have been debated in U.S. courts.

Ernest McDonald (n.d.) had been convicted of manslaughter and sentenced to five to fifteen years in prison. At work he had shot a person during an altercation, and there was some reason to believe that he did so at the behest of his employer. He appealed against the decision on the grounds of mental disease or defect, being unable to distinguish right from wrong in a complex situation, high impulsiveness under stress, and being easily influenced by a person on whom he was dependent. Psychiatric evidence showed that he had an IQ of 68, had not gone beyond sixth grade, and was so impulsive that, unlike a normal person, he would probably be unable to see the consequences of his actions.

Sources

McDonald v. *U.S. Federal Reporter.* 2d Series. Vol. 312 2d. 1962. St. Paul, Minn.: West
    Publishing.

Maeder, Thomas. 1985. *Crime and madness: the origins and evolution of the insanity
    defense.* New York: Harper and Row.

DURKHEIMIAN, DURKHEIM'S LAW OF SUICIDE, DURKHEIM'S LAW OF SOCIAL DEVELOPMENT. Relating to the prominent French sociologist, especially his delineation of the field of sociology as being the study of social facts concerning a society's structure and process. The law of suicide states that a society's suicide rate varies inversely with the degree of integration and solidarity of the groups to which people belong. Two stages of societal development are mechanical solidarity, and organic and voluntary solidarity, which relate to the functional organization of society.

Emile Durkheim (1858–1917), an Alsatian Jew, was a teacher of philosophy in schools near Paris (1882–87); he became a professor of social science in Bordeaux (1887) and in the University of Paris (1902) where he taught philosophy of education and sociology. From the biological and psychological facts of human behavior he distinguished the social facts—customs, laws, duties, obligations, and contracts—in his *Rules of Sociological Method* (1895; English trans. 1938). His two empirical studies of social facts, *The Division of Labor in Society* (1893; trans. 1933) and *Suicide* (1897; trans. 1951), illustrate the thesis that there is more to human action than the individual propensity to form social units. For example, the degree of social order determines the extent to which people are well integrated in themselves. Durkheim believed that empirical study could guide humankind to happiness. Finally, in his lectures on education, *The Elementary Forms of the Religious Life* (1912; trans. 1915), Durkheim outlined how the individual personality relates to the social system. His influence in France lasted over seventy years; his insights were not used extensively outside France until the 1920s in British anthropology by B. Malinowski and A.R. Radcliffe-Brown, and in American sociology by Robert Merton and Talcott Parsons. With Karl Marx, Vilfredo Pareto, and Max Weber, Durkheim is one of the founders of modern social inquiry.

Sources

Coser, Lewis A. 1971. *Masters of sociological thought.* New York: Harcourt Brace Jovanovich.

Devine, Elizabeth; Held, Michael; Vinson, James; and Walsh, George, eds. 1983. *Thinkers of the twentieth century: a biographical, bibliographical and critical dictionary.* London: Macmillan.

Langer, Beryl. 1992. Emile Durkheim. In Peter Beilharz, ed. *Social theory: a guide to central thinkers.* Sydney: Allen and Unwin.

Miller, David, ed. 1987. *The Blackwell encyclopedia of political thought.* Oxford: Basil Blackwell.

Sills, David L., ed. 1968. *International encyclopedia of the social sciences.* New York: Macmillan and Free Press.

Zusne, Leonard. 1984. *Biographical dictionary of psychology.* Westport, Conn.: Greenwood Press.

DUVERGER'S LAW. Analysis of voting shows that a simple majority single-ballot system favors the two-party system. There is a near perfect correlation between a voting system that uses simple-majority/winner-takes-all and the establishment of a two-party system. Proportional representation weakens a two-party system.

Maurice Duverger (b. 1917), a French political scientist, was born at Angoulême, educated at Bordeaux University, and lives in Paris. He was a professor of political science at the University of Paris (1955–85) and became emeritus in 1985. He established and directed the Center d'Analyse comparative des systèmes politique, Sorbonne, was elected to the European Parliament in 1989, and became a member of the American Academy of Arts and Sciences. He stated the law in his book, *Political Parties* (1952).

Sources

Duverger, Maurice. 1951. *Political parties: their organization and activity in the modern state.* New York: John Wiley.

International who's who, 1991–92. London: Europa Publications.

Riker, William H. 1986. Duverger's law revisited. In Bernard Grofman and Arend Lijphart, eds. *Electoral laws and their political consequences.* New York: Agathon.

Who's who in France, 1990–91. Paris: Jacques Lafitte.

E

ÉCOLE NATIONALE DES PONTS DE CHAUSSÉES. A venerated French academic institution of education in economics. The School of Engineering in Paris, which was established in 1747 by Daniel Trudaine, the finance minister to Louis XV (1715–74) has traditionally produced talented economists in France. At the school no formal course in economics was established until 1847; but beginning in 1792 engineering students were expected to study economics. With the great changes in higher education in France after the French Revolution, the school was raised to a graduate institution. It developed a fine reputation during the nineteenth century by improving the quality of teaching and research and by promoting the study of new subjects such as modern languages, geology, mineralogy, administrative law, political economy, thermodynamics, and applied chemistry. Today the school is one of the most notable educational institutions in France. With its rigid, highly centralized organization, it attracts the nation's intellectual elite who require a highly valued education in economics.
Source
Eatwell, John; Milgate, Murray; and Newman, Peter. 1987. *The new Palgrave: a dictionary of economics.* London: Macmillan.

EDDYISM. Eddyism, later called "Christian Science," is the only American healing movement that survived the rise of scientific medicine in the nineteenth century and became an international religion. Its main precepts center on the belief that illness is sinful and unnecessary. Curing illness involves a person yielding to God along the lines suggested in the daily reading program laid down in *Science and Health* (1875).

Mary Morse Baker Eddy (1821–1910) was born on a farm in Bow, New Hampshire, and as a child she was delicate and subject to seizures. After a desultory education, she studied under her brother's guidance. She married twice before her marriage at 55 to A. Gilbert Eddy. In 1866 she slipped on the ice and recovered so quickly that she thought divine influence had mended her, and was much taken with the story of Jesus healing a paralyzed man. Turning to the Bible, and with the ideas of Portland's faith healer, Phinias P. Quimby (1802–66), she developed a healing technique. In time, she established a church whose religious authority lay not in Jesus but in her book, *Science and Health,* on how to interpret the Bible. Because a book and not a divine person was the authority of the church, Christian Science enjoyed the organizational stability that other faith-healing religions did not. Throughout most of her life Mrs. Eddy was ill and depressed; nevertheless, she established and skillfully maintained a church organization with its center—the First Church of Christ, Scientist, "the Mother Church"—in Boston (1890s), and the prestigious newspaper *The Christian Science Monitor.*

Sources

Bates, Ernest, and Dittemore, John V. 1932. *Mary Baker Eddy: the truth and tradition.* New York: Knopf.

Johnson, Allen, and Malone, Dumas, eds. 1930. *Dictionary of American biography.* Vol. III. New York: Charles Scribner's Sons.

Peel, Robert. 1966–77. *Mary Baker Eddy.* 3 vols. New York: Holt, Rinehart and Winston.

Silberger, Julius, Jr. 1980. *Mary Baker Eddy: an interpretative biography of the founder of Christian Science.* Boston: Little, Brown.

EDSEL. A synonym for failure in business, especially because of poor marketing. The term comes from Edsel, an automobile, intended to celebrate the late Edsel Ford, only son of Henry Ford I and father of Henry Ford II who was president of the company when the automobile was launched on "Edsel Day," September 4, 1957. Only 84,000 were sold, at a net loss of $350 million, and so the model was discontinued in 1959. Market research had shown a demand for a relatively expensive automobile, but public requirements combined with economic circumstances dissipated that demand by the time the vehicle became available.

Edsel Bryant Ford (1893–1943) was born in Detroit, Michigan, the only son of Henry and Clara (Bryant) Ford, and educated in Detroit public schools and the Detroit University School. Edsel grew up with the automobile industry. Henry's first successful automobile was tested in the year of Edsel's birth, he drove the original Model A at the age of 10, and at 14 he owned a Model M. Edsel began work at the Ford plant in 1912, and although interested in mechanics, he soon showed a preference for administration. At 22 he became company secretary and several years later, treasurer. In 1915 Edsel took a leading role in the firm and was appointed president, but Henry Ford often humiliated his son by canceling projects on which Edsel had made considerable progress. Although it cost him dearly in emotional strain, Edsel never questioned his father's right to determine policy. He married, had three sons and one daughter, and died of cancer at 49 years of age.

Sources

Brooks, John N. 1963. *The fate of Edsel and other business ventures.* London: Gollancz.

Collier, Peter, and Horowitz, David. 1988. *The Fords.* London: Collins.

Deutch, Jan G., ed. 1976. *Selling the people's Cadillac: the Edsel and corporate responsibility.* New Haven, Conn.: Yale University Press.

James, Edward T. 1973. *Dictionary of American biography.* Supplement 3. New York: Charles Scribner's Sons.

McHenry, Robert, ed. 1992. *The new encyclopedia Britannica.* Chicago: Encyclopedia Britannica, Inc.

Shapiro, Karl. 1971. *Edsel.* New York: B. Geis Associates.

EDWARDIAN. Relating to the reign of any King Edward, but especially Edward VII.

Edward VII (1841–1910), king of England (1901–10), was born in London at Buckingham Palace, second child and eldest son of Queen Victoria (1819–1901) and Prince Albert (1819–1861). At birth he was the duke of Cornwall and at one month the prince of Wales. Educated by private tutors, he later traveled in Germany and the Mediterranean, attended lectures at Edinburgh University, and was admitted to Oxford (1859). He married Alexandra of Denmark (1844–1925). During King Edward's reign, British literature and architecture upheld the values of the English middle class. The ornate and reputedly stuffy Victorian and late Victorian styles and character gave over to modern features, and later sharp differences developed between the two periods, Victorian and Edwardian. In King Edward's time, sudden changes took place in the technology of medicine, art, and industrial and domestic technology. For example, electricity was put into kitchens and the theater, and Edward was one of the first royal figures to undergo an appendix operation. An indulgent father, he had little time for the highly disciplined education he had had to tolerate; he followed a relaxed regime at home, and he maintained a high-spirited and affectionate family life. He was punctilious and eager to carry out the duties that his mother permitted him to take on; critics disapproved of his interest in sport, with its attendant evils, gambling and gluttony. Unlike his mother's supporters, Edward tolerated the moral, intellectual, and artistic deviations—both lasting and superficial—that followed the turn of the century.

Sources

Cowles, Virginia S. 1956. *Edward VII and his circle.* London: Hamilton.

Preece, Warren E., ed. 1965. *Encyclopedia Britannica.* Chicago: Encyclopedia Britannica, Inc., William Benton.

Read, Donald, ed. 1982. *Edwardian England.* London: Croom Helm and the Historical Association.

EDWARDS SOCIAL-ECONOMIC GROUPINGS OF OCCUPATIONS. A socioeconomic measure performed by classifying occupations into six major groups, each with a distinct standard of life and showing similar intellectual and social attributes: the classification is based on education and income. Briefly, the categories are professional and technical workers; business managers, officials, and proprietors; clerical sales workers; craftsmen and foremen; operative workers; unskilled service and domestic workers.

Alba M. Edwards (fl. 1872–1969) was born in Savannah, Missouri and studied at the University of Oklahoma and Yale (Ph.D. 1906). He was special agent at the Carnegie Institution in Washington (1906–7) and an acting professor at Bowdoin College (1907–9), and became a statistician at the U.S. Bureau of the Census (1909–43). He published *Labor Legislation of Connecticut* (1907), as well as many census reports and articles in statistics. He was a member of the American Statistical Association.

Sources

Edwards, Alba M. 1934. *Comparative occupational statistics for the United States.* Washington, D.C.: U.S. Government Printing Office.
Miller, Delbert C. 1991. *Handbook of research design and social measurement.* 5th ed. Newbury Park, Calif.: Sage Publications.
U.S. Bureau of Census. 1960. *1960 Census of population: classified index of occupations and industries.* Washington, D.C.: U.S. Government Printing Office.
Who was who in America, 1969–73. Vol. 5. Chicago: Marquis.

EISENHOWER DOCTRINE. A U.S. diplomatic policy that authorized the president to use military force to defend Middle East nations that request aid to overcome overt communist-inspired aggression (Public Law No. 7, 85th U.S. Congress). A consequence of the Suez Crisis (1956), this doctrine was formulated by Secretary of State John Foster Dulles (1888–1859) and found favor with the Baghdad Pact nations and others nearby. In April 1957 the threat of its implementation helped King Hussein during a period of political and economic instability in Jordan.

Dwight David Eisenhower (1890–1969), thirty-fourth president of the United States, was born in Denison, Texas, and moved to Abilene, Kansas, where he grew up in modest circumstances. In 1911 he was appointed to West Point; after graduation he served in the U.S. Army around the world, rising steadily in rank and responsibility. Soon after the Japanese attack on Pearl Harbor (December 1941), he became commander of the U.S. forces in Europe and helped plan the Allied invasion of Europe. Promoted to lieutenant general, he became Allied commander in chief for the invasion of North Africa (1942) and planned the invasions of Sicily and Italy in 1943. In June 1944 he oversaw the D-Day landing and was promoted to five-star general in December. Eisenhower accepted the Republican presidential nomination in 1952 and won the election by an overwhelming margin. His first term was dominated by foreign affairs problems. He proposed radical new plans for world disarmament, "Atoms for Peace," but he failed to win world support. He was reelected in 1956 by an even greater margin than before. In retirement he published *Mandate for Change* (1963), a volume of memoirs, and his autobiography, *At Ease* (1968).

Sources

Ambrose, Stephen E. 1983. *Eisenhower: soldier, general of the army, president elect.* New York: Simon and Schuster.

Ambrose, Stephen E. 1984. *Eisenhower: president and elder statesman.* New York: Simon and Schuster.

Commager, Henry S., ed. 1968. *Documents of American history.* 8th ed. New York: Appleton-Century-Crofts.

Findling, John E. 1980. *Dictionary of American diplomatic history.* Westport, Conn.: Greenwood Press.

McHenry, Robert, ed. 1992. *The new encyclopedia Britannica.* Chicago: Encyclopedia Britannica, Inc.

ELECTRA COMPLEX. A psychoanalytic term for a daughter's pattern of unconscious affection for her father and hostility toward her mother. It was introduced by Carl G. Jung (1875–1961) in 1913 but rejected by Sigmund Freud (1856–1939) because he thought female sexuality was more complicated than Jung's idea implied.

In Greek mythology, Electra was the daughter of Agamemnon and Clytemnestra and sister of Orestes. On discovering that her mother and Aegisthus had murdered her father, Electra sought revenge. Electra also longed for the return of her brother; she saved Orestes' life by sending him away when their father was murdered. When he matured, she helped him slay their mother and her lover. Sophocles, Aeschylus, and Euripedes dramatized the reunion and revenge, but only in Euripedes's play did Electra help kill her mother. According to some legends, she married Orestes's friend, Pylades, and had two sons. In psychoanalytic psychology the young girl's Electra Complex is parallel to the young boy's Oedipus Complex, but in theory the resolution of each complex and its problems are quite different.

See also OEDIPUS COMPLEX.

Sources

Bell, Robert E. 1982. *Dictionary of classical mythology.* Santa Barbara, Calif.: ABC-CLIO.

Freud, Sigmund. 1920. The psychogenesis of a case of homosexuality in a woman. *The standard edition of the complete psychological works of Sigmund Freud.* Trans. James Strachey. Vol. 18. London: Hogarth Press and Institute of Psychoanalysis.

Freud, Sigmund. 1931. Female sexuality. *The standard edition of the complete psychological works of Sigmund Freud.* Trans. James Strachey. Vol. 21. London: Hogarth Press and the Institute of Psychoanalysis.

Hamilton, Edith. 1940. *Mythology: timeless tales of gods and heroes.* Boston: Little, Brown.

Jung, Carl G. 1913. *The collected works: Freud and psychoanalysis.* Vol. 4. Trans. R.F.C. Hull. Bolligen Series XX, 1970 ed. Princeton, N.J.: Princeton University Press.

ELIZABETHAN. Relating to the reign of the Virgin Queen of England (1558–1603), especially the spirit of the times, with its vivid, adventurous, artistic brilliance—and the remarkable achievements in architecture, commerce, exploration, literature, and war.

Elizabeth I (1533–1603), daughter of Henry VIII (1491–1547) and Anne Boleyn (?1507–36), was declared illegitimate shortly before her mother was beheaded for alleged adultery. In 1544 Parliament legitimated Elizabeth in the royal succession. She was well educated, and because she could have been a center of the Protestant cause she was imprisoned. When she appeared to conform to Roman Catholicism, however, she received some measure of her original freedom. At 26, Elizabeth was enthroned. At that time, England was in debt, torn by religious strife, and had lost wars with France. By the time of her death forty-five years later, England was united, a major European power, and had enjoyed an outstanding development in literature, learning, commerce, and colonization. Elizabeth established Protestantism and harsh penalties for Roman Catholics. She had many suitors, and for personal and political motives she used the lure of marriage to further England's diplomatic ends. Her foreign policy kept England free of war for thirty years, and in 1588, at the peak of her popularity, Elizabeth saw her naval chiefs repel the Spanish Armada. During the Elizabethan period, England saw great voyages of discovery across the Atlantic, colonial adventures, outstanding developments in theater (William Shakespeare, 1564–1616 Christopher Marlowe, 1564–93), poetry (Edmund Spenser, 1552–99) and music (William Byrd, 1543–1623, John Bull, c. 1563–1628, and John Dowland, c. 1563–c. 1626).

Sources

McHenry, Robert, ed. 1992. *The new encyclopedia Britannica.* Chicago: Encyclopedia Britannica, Inc.

Routh, Charles R.N., ed. 1989. *Who's who in Tudor England.* 2d ed. Rev. by Peter Holmes. London: Shepheard-Walwyn.

Stephen, Leslie, and Lee, Sydney, eds. 1917. *The dictionary of national biography.* London: Oxford University Press.

ENGELS' CURVE, ENGELS' LAW. In economics a curve showing that the percentage of income spent on food decreases as income increases. An empirical law of consumption that states that the proportion of a nation's income spent on food indicates its welfare, so, the lower that proportion, the higher the welfare of the nation.

Ernst Engels (1821–96) was born in Dresden and, in his early years, associated with the French sociologist Frederic le Play, whose interest in the family led him to conduct household surveys. The expenditure data convinced Engels of a relationship between household income and the allocation of household expenditures between food and other items. Engels was director of the Prussian Statistical Bureau in Berlin (1860–82) where he expanded and strengthened official statistics. However, Engels resigned in opposition to Bismarck's protectionist policies. In his own research Engels put much value on human life, which he regarded from the cost side. His influence on official statistics went beyond

Germany, and in 1885 he was among the founders of the International Statistical Institute.

Sources

Eatwell, John; Milgate, Murray; and Newman, Peter. 1987. *The new Palgrave: a dictionary of economics.* London: Macmillan.

Pearce, David W., ed. 1986. *Macmillan dictionary of modern economics.* New York: Macmillan.

Preece, Warren E., ed. 1965. *Encyclopedia Britannica.* Chicago: Encyclopedia Britannica Inc., William Benton.

EONISM. The adoption by a man of women's dress and manners, cross-dressing, transvestism; a modern issue in debates about gender that points to the value of a third term or concept for the analysis of an allegedly phallo-centric patriarchal society that characteristically recognizes only male and female.

Charles, Geneviève, Louis, Auguste, André, Timothée D'Eon De Beaumont (1728–1810) was a chevalier (knight) whose family came from the minor nobility. He was born at Tonnerre in Burgundy. Although baptized as a boy, there was doubt about his sex. When young he was dressed as a girl, and at 3 years of age was dedicated to the Virgin Mary under a woman's name. He was educated as a boy and became a doctor of law, but did not practice. As the king's secret agent, he was sent to Saint Petersburg where he resumed women's clothing, and Empress Elizabeth received him as such. In 1756 he spent four years as a man at the French embassy in Russia. After a brief spell in the French Army, he was sent to England as the secretary to a special ambassador with whom he quarreled; afterward, because he refused to be recalled to France, the king ordered him to resume women's dress. In 1778 when war with England broke out, D'Eon appealed to be allowed to resume men's clothing and to serve in the army. His request was refused. Later he earned a living as a fencing instructor. On his death an examination of his body confirmed that he had been male. Havelock Ellis coined the term *eonism* in 1928 in *Studies in the Psychology of Sex.*

Sources

Ellis, Havelock. 1928. *Studies in the psychology of sex.* 1936 ed. New York: Random House.

Ellis, Havelock. 1938. *Psychology of sex: a manual for students.* 2d ed. New York: Emerson Books.

Garber, Marjorie. 1992. *Vested interests.* New York: Routledge.

Homberg, Octave M.J., and Jousselin, Fernand. 1911. *D'Eon de Beaumont: his life and times.* London: G. Bell.

McHenry, Robert, ed. 1992. *The new encyclopedia Britannica.* Chicago: Encyclopedia Britannica, Inc.

ERASTIANISM. The belief that all punitive control should be held by civil authorities, a view that today implies the complete dominance of the state over the church in ecclesiastical matters.

Thomas Erastus—grecized from Lüber, Lieber, or Liebler (1524–83)—was born at Baden and died near Basel, Switzerland. He studied theology at Basel and philosophy and medicine in Italy, and became professor of medicine at Heidelberg (1558) and professor of ethics at Basel (1580). He was a follower of Huldreich Zwingli (1484–1531). As a skilled physician, Erastus strongly opposed Paracelsus, the belief in astrology, the transmutation of metal, and other popular superstitions. As a Protestant controversialist, his chief work, *Explicato* (1568), published in 1589, was a collection of theses arguing against the church's right to inflict excommunication and related disciplinary penalties. In 1574 he was excommunicated for his vigorous opposition to Calvinism, but a year later the edict was removed. The full expression of Erastianism appeared in Thomas Hobbes's *Leviathan*. In seventeenth-century England "Erastian" was used during the debates (1643) in the Westminster assembly as a term of abuse by Presbyterians for the party of those who denied the right of autonomy to the church, a right that Erastus himself neither denied nor maintained. His theses were translated into English as *The Nullity of Church Censures* (1682) and *A Treatise of Excommunication* (1682).

Sources

Cross, Frank L. 1974. *The Oxford dictionary of the Christian Church.* 2d ed. New York: Oxford University Press.

Douglas, James D., ed. 1974. *The new international dictionary of the Christian Church.* Exeter: Paternoster Press.

Harris, William H., and Levey, Judith S., eds. 1978–79. *The new illustrated Columbia encyclopedia.* New York: Rockville House.

McHenry, Robert, ed. 1992. *The new encyclopedia Britannica.* Chicago: Encyclopedia Britannica, Inc.

Wesel-Roth, Ruth. 1954. *Thomas Erastus.* Baden: Schauneberg.

ERIKSONIAN. Relating to the psychosocial studies and theory of the twentieth-century American social scientist, especially on the growth and crises in the individual's sense of identity and life-history.

Erik Homburger Erikson (b. 1902) was born of Danish parents in Frankfurt, Germany, where his mother was deserted before the child was born. She married Dr. Theodore Homburger, and Erik was given his name but did not learn of his real father for many years. He regarded the secret as "loving deceit." At age 37 when he became an American citizen, he changed his name to Erikson. He was Jewish and, despite his Aryan appearance, suffered much rejection in Germany. Later he became a Christian. In 1927 he went to Vienna to teach at a school for Freud's patients and friends; there he trained in psychoanalysis with a special interest in children. Afterward he studied the Montessori method of education. He fled Nazi Germany in 1933 going first to Denmark and later to the United States, settled in Boston, and worked with Henry Murray (1893–1988) at Harvard. Later, he went to the Yale Institute of Human Relations, joined in anthropological studies of the Sioux in South Dakota, and developed his interest in the impact of culture on childhood. He moved to San Francisco, began a psychological practice, joined the staff of the Institute of Child Welfare at Berkeley in 1939 and later studied the Yurok Indians of northern California (1943). From his studies of Indians and veterans of World War II, he concluded that distressed people suffered not from repressed conflicts, but rather from confusion of identity due to being torn from their cultural traditions. In 1950 he returned to Massachusetts and worked at the Austen Riggs Center, and later at Harvard (1960–70) where he taught courses in the human life cycle. Among his notable studies are *Childhood and Society* (1950), *Young Man Luther* (1958), *Insight and Responsibility* (1964), *Identity: Youth and Crises* (1968), *Gandhi's Truth* (1970), a Pulitzer Prize winner, *Life History and the Historical Moment* (1975), *Identity and the Life Cycle* (1980), and *The Life Cycle Completed* (1982). He has been honored by many professional societies and universities in the United States and Europe.

Sources

Coles, Robert. 1970. *Erik H. Erikson: the growth of his work.* Boston: Little, Brown.

Devine, Elizabeth; Held, Michael; Vinson, James; and Walsh, George, eds. 1983. *Thinkers of the twentieth century: a biographical, bibliographical and critical dictionary.* London: Macmillan.

Ryan, Bryan, ed. 1990. *Major twentieth-century writers: a selection of sketches from contemporary authors.* Detroit: Gale Research.

Turner, Roland, ed. 1987. *Thinkers of the twentieth century.* 2d ed. London: St. James Press.

Who's who in America, 1990–91. Chicago: Marquis.

EROSTRATUS OR IIEROSTRATUS. An utterly wicked and godless person.

Erostratus was a mad Ephesian who set fire to the Temple of Diana (or Artemis) in 356 B.C. on the day that Alexander the Great happened to be born. He did this to make himself a celebrity and to immortalize his name; but the Ephesians forbade his name ever to be mentioned.

Source

Benét, William R. 1948. *The reader's encyclopedia: an encyclopedia of world literature and the arts.* London: Harrap.

EROTIC. Tender, romantic, supportive, physical passion; the loving side of psychoanalytic libido.

In Greek religion Eros was the god of love and its personification. As one of the oldest of the gods, he was born from Chaos, and he signified harmony and power. Other stories report that Aphrodite and Ares were his parents, and, armed with bow and arrows, he appears as a youth with wings. In Greek poems he seems unsympathetic and caring little in love's unhappy moments. Sometimes he is the god of fertility and may be worshiped as such. In Roman myths he is Amor or Cupid, and he appears naked as a child with wings, son of Venus and her companion. Anteros, Eros's brother, sometimes accompanies him as love's enemy or the avenger of unrequited love. After World War I, Sigmund Freud

(1856–1939) wrote on the dual instincts, Eros and the Death Instinct (Thanatos), and the means by which they were fused in his *Beyond the Pleasure Principle* (1920) and *The Ego and the Id* (1923).

Sources

Aldington, Richard, and Ames, Delano, trans. 1978. *New Larousse encyclopedia of mythology.* London: Hamlyn.

Eidelberg, Ludwig. 1968. *Encyclopedia of psychoanalysis.* London: Collier-Macmillan.

Grimàl, Pierre. 1986. *The concise dictionary of classical mythology.* Oxford: Basil Blackwell.

Zusne, Leonard. 1987. *Eponyms in psychology: a dictionary and sourcebook.* Westport, Conn.: Greenwood Press.

ESPERANTO. The most successful of the artificial universal languages devised in the nineteenth century; today it has over 8 million supporters.

"Doktoro Esperanto," meaning "Doctor Hopeful," is the pseudonym of Dr. Lazarus Ludwig Zamenhof (1859–1917) who was born in Bialystok, in Russian Poland. His father taught languages in an effort to integrate Jews and Gentiles in a community of Russians, Poles, and Germans. The family moved to Warsaw where Lazarus studied languages and sciences and took a medical degree in 1885. He studied ophthalmology in Vienna in 1886. However, his major interest lay in the belief that national and racial hatred was made worse by language differences, and he concluded that a language of the world would help promote understanding and peace. He advocated his system in 1887 with the publication in Russian of *Lingvo Internacia de la Doktoro Esperanto* (An International Language by Doctor Esperanto). The system is based on common words in most tongues which have a basis in Latin grammar. It is easy to learn and master quickly. It spread first in Russia and later to Germany and the United States. It was regarded as a clear language (1924) for telegraphy and is used at international conferences, in commerce, and on radio. Over 30,000 items of original or translated literature are in the language as well as some scientific journals.

Sources

Barnhardt, Robert, ed. 1988. *The Barnhardt dictionary of etymology.* New York: H. W. Wilson.

Boulton, Marjorie. 1960. *Zamenhof, creator of Esperanto.* London: Routledge and Kegan Paul.

McHenry, Robert, ed. 1992. *The new encyclopedia Britannica.* Chicago: Encyclopedia Britannica, Inc.

EUHEMERISM. The belief that explains mythology as growing out of actual historical events.

Euhemerus (fl. 300 B.C.), a Greek mythographer and philosopher, was born at Messina, Sicily, and probably lived in the second half of the fourth century, B.C. He was in the service of Cassandra of Macedonia (311–298 B.C.) and wrote *Sacred History,* which gave an anthropomorphic explanation of current mythology. In the fragments that remain of this work, Euhemerus stated that he sailed to No-man's-land, Panchaea, an imaginary isle, where he found that the truth about mythical times had been engraved on pillars of bronze. His work rationalized the fables, declaring that the gods had been kings or heroes, were later deified by their subjects, and that the myths were exaggerated and distorted records of true events. He held to Cyrenaic philosophy, and many ancient philosophers considered him an atheist. His work was translated by Quintus Ennuis into Latin, but only a few fragments of the translation survived. His theory fitted well with the contemporary theory that religious beliefs could be explained in terms of naturalism.

See also CYRENAIC.

Sources

Dudley, Lavinia P. 1963. *The encyclopedia Americana.* International ed. New York: Americana Corp.

McHenry, Robert, ed. 1992. *The new encyclopedia Britannica.* Chicago: Encyclopedia Britannica, Inc.

Partridge, Eric. 1970. *Name into word.* Plainview, N.Y.: Books for Libraries Press.

Smith, Benjamin. 1903. *The Century cyclopedia of names.* London: The Times.

EULER'S THEOREM. In economics a proposition that if a production function involves constant returns to scale, then the sum of the marginal products will equal the total product. The theorem was important in the development of the marginal-productivity theory of distribution.

Leon(h)ard Euler (1707–83) was born and educated at Basel, Switzerland, and studied under Johann Bernoulli (1667–1748). A brilliant mathematician at 16, Euler was awarded an M.A. in 1723. He was invited to the Naval College at Saint Petersburg for three years and was made a professor of physics at the Academy of Sciences; in 1733 he took Daniel Bernoulli's position as a professor of mathematics. Studying the sun made him blind in the right eye. In 1741 Frederick the Great invited him to Berlin, where he was appointed the director of the Berlin Academy of Sciences (1744–66) until his return to Saint Petersburg where he was made its director of the Academy of Sciences. Cataracts now made him blind in the left eye. Euler's works on mathematics comprise over seventy volumes and relate to pure and applied mathematics in many mathematical fields. He was one of the original contributors to calculus. In his last years he was unable to see at all, but he could still calculate with great skill. A differential equation was named after him, which related the number of faces, edges, and vertices of a polyhedron, and his name was given to the equation connecting five fundamental numbers in mathematics.

Sources

Abbott, David. 1985. *The biographical dictionary of scientists: mathematicians.* London: Blond Educational.

Eatwell, John; Milgate, Murray; and Newman, Peter. 1987. *The new Palgrave: a dictionary of economics.* London: Macmillan.

Greenwald, Douglas, ed. 1982. *Encyclopedia of economics.* New York: McGraw-Hill.

Harris, William H., and Levey, Judith S., eds. 1978–79. *The new illustrated Columbia encyclopedia.* New York: Rockville House.

McHenry, Robert, ed. 1992. *The new encyclopedia Britannica.* Chicago: Encyclopedia Britannica, Inc.

Pearce, David W., ed. 1986. *Macmillan dictionary of modern economics.* New York: Macmillan.

EUTYCHIAN. Relating to the doctrine that Christ's human nature was merged in the divine.

Eutyches (c. 378–c. 452) was a heresiarch of the Eastern Church and founded the sect of Eutychians. He was an archimandrite and, in Constantinople, a leader of strong opponents of Nestorianism. His opponents believed Christ had two natures, but Eutyches thought that Christ's humanity was part of his divinity and that Christ had only a divine nature. This made it accurate to state that ''God had been crucified for us.'' Eutyches was accused of heresy and deposed by a local synod called by Saint Flavian, a patriarch of Constantinople (448). But owing to the manipulation of the membership of the Robber Synod, he was reinstated, declared orthodox, and his opposition was deposed. After much conflict, the Council of Chalcedon reversed the Robber Synod's wrongs, Eutyches was finally deposed in 451, exiled, and Eutychianism ended.

Sources

Cross, Frank L. 1974. *The Oxford dictionary of the Christian Church.* 2d ed. New York: Oxford University Press.

Harris, William H., and Levey, Judith S., eds. 1978–79. *The new illustrated Columbia encyclopedia.* New York: Rockville House.

McHenry, Robert, ed. 1992. *The new encyclopedia Britannica.* Chicago: Encyclopedia Britannica, Inc.

Magnussen, Magnus; Goring, Rosemary; and Thorn, John O., eds. 1990. *Chambers biographical dictionary.* Edinburgh: Chambers Ltd.

F

FABIAN. Relating to the cautious and dilatory use of a delaying strategy in battle so as to wear down the enemy; a member of, or sympathizer with the Fabian Society, a group of socialists who aim at gradual social change.

Fabius Maximus Verrucosus Quintus was surnamed Cunctator, "The Delayer" (d. 203 B.C.). He was born into a notable family from the fifth century B.C. and became an outstanding general. After Hannibal defeated Rome's consul, Flaminius, in 217 B.C., Fabius was appointed Dictator at Rome. He carried on a defensive campaign against Hannibal, avoiding any direct engagement and harassing the enemy, eventually weakening the Carthaginians by numerous skirmishes. In Rome dissatisfaction with this way of conducting war arose, and Fabius was replaced by Minucius who adopted a more aggressive policy. The Fabian Society was founded in 1884 and advocated the use of tactics like those of Fabius; it rejected revolutionary change and relied on propaganda, education, and discussion. Among its members was George Bernard Shaw (1856–1950).

See also SHAVIAN.

Sources

Hammond, Nicholas G.L., and Scullard, Hayes H., eds. 1970. *The Oxford classical dictionary*. Oxford: Clarendon Press.

MacKenzie, Norman, and Mackenzie, Jeanne. 1977. *The Fabians*. New York: Simon and Schuster.

Miller, David, ed. 1987. *The Blackwell encyclopedia of political thought*. Oxford: Basil Blackwell.

Pèase, Edward R. 1963. *The history of the Fabian Society*. London: F. Cass.

FAGIN. A person who trains young thieves, receives stolen goods.

Fagin, an old Jew in Charles Dickens's *Oliver Twist* (1837), lived in a den in the London slums with a group of homeless boys. He taught them to pick pockets and pilfer with great skill. His associates were the burglar, Bill Sykes, and the prostitute, Nancy. Oliver met Fagin through the Artful Dodger, and Fagin accepted bribes to corrupt the boy. Beneath a suave and fawning manner Fagin was malicious, grasping, and cruel. In the end he was arrested, tried, and hanged.

Sources

Hammond, Nicholas G.L., and Scullard, Howard H. 1985. *The Oxford companion to English literature.* Oxford: Clarendon Press.
Ousby, Ian, ed. 1988. *The Cambridge guide to literature in English.* Cambridge: Cambridge University Press.

FATHER DAMIEN. A man of God, selfless and heroic.

Joseph De Veuster (1840–89) was born in Tremelo, Belgium, son of a small farmer. He studied with the Fathers of the Society of the Sacred Heart of Jesus and Mary and in 1859 took the name of Damien. He was sent to the Sandwich Isles in 1863 and in 1864 was ordained. In 1874 he volunteered alone to help the 700 lepers on Molokai where conditions appalled him morally and physically, and where the government had not provided permanent medical staff. He supplied basic medical care, built shelters, dug graves, and developed a new water supply. In 1885 he contracted leprosy but continued his work. Joseph Dutton joined him as a helper and friend. In his last year Joseph had three priests and three Franciscan sisters help him in the colony. On his death an international campaign began to establish proper care for lepers. His body was taken to Belgium for burial in 1936.

Sources

Daws, Gavan. 1973. *Holy man: Father Damien of Molokai.* New York: Harper and Row.
Douglas, James D., ed. 1974. *The new international dictionary of the Christian Church.* Exeter: Paternoster Press.
Farrow, John. 1937. *Damien the leper.* London: Burns, Oates and Washbourne.
Meagher, Paul K.; O'Brien, Thomas C.; and Aherne, Marie, eds. 1979. *Encyclopedic dictionary of religion.* Washington, D.C.: Corpus Publications.

FATHER MATHEW. A temperance reformer.

Theobald Mathew (1790–1856) was born at Thomastown Castle, Chashel County, Tipperary. In 1807 he entered the Maynooth seminary in Dublin but quit to join the Capuchins, Dublin. He was ordained in 1814, opened a free school for the poor in Cork city, and formed a group of young men to alleviate Cork's poverty. After working for twenty-five years, he was asked to join the temperance cause. He took the pledge of abstinence in 1838, saying "Here goes in the name of the Lord." Within six years half the population supported him, and the crime rate fell dramatically; also, the taxes on spirits fell by half. In Britain he was a success, and in 1849 in the United States, as the "Apostle of Temperance," he drew many converts to the cause of total abstinence. His name became a synonym for temperance reformer, and Queen Victoria awarded him a pension for his good works. Ill-health prevented him from accepting Rome's proposal that he become a bishop.

Sources

Boylan, Henry. 1978. *A dictionary of Irish biography.* New York: Barnes and Noble.

Malcolm, Elizabeth. 1986. *Ireland sober, Ireland free: drink and temperance in nineteenth-century Ireland.* Dublin: Gill and Macmillan.

Meagher, Paul K.; O'Brien, Thomas C.; and Aherne, Marie, eds. 1979. *Encyclopedic dictionary of religion.* Washington, D.C.: Corpus Publications.

FATIMID. A descendant of Mohammed's daughter; a modern Islamic symbol used to encourage nascent Muslim feminism.

Fatima—Fatima Bint Mohammed, The Prophet (c. 606–32)—was born in Mecca, the daughter of the prophet Mohammed by his first wife, Khadija. With her sisters Aisa, Khadijah, and Mary, she was one of the four perfect women. She wed her cousin, Ali Ibn Abi Talib, endured a stormy marriage, and their sons Hasan and Husayn became the only male perpetuators of Mohammed's line. A third son died in infancy. Details of her death and gravesite are a mystery: however, on her father's death, a year before hers, she was drawn into a political conflict with the first caliph, Abu Baka, over both her inheritance and her husband's blood right to leadership in the community. In Islamic legend her place was secured by her familial relation with Mohammed; according to tradition, she is a virgin, bright, blooming, and never menstruates. At its peak of influence, the Fatimid Caliphate extended from North Africa to Iraq; its members believed their leaders were the true descendants of the fourth Caliph Ali and his wife Fatima, and that the Fatimids were destined to replace the orthodox Abbasid Caliphate. The dynasty began to decline in the second half of the eleventh century and was finally suppressed in 1177. Today some people present Fatimid as an authentic symbol of Muslim female liberation.

Sources

Eliade, Mircea, ed. 1987. *Encyclopedia of religion.* New York: Macmillan.

McHenry, Robert, ed. 1992. *The new encyclopedia Britannica.* Chicago: Encyclopedia Britannica, Inc.

Preece, Warren E., ed. 1965. *Encyclopedia Britannica.* Chicago: Encyclopedia Britannica, Inc., William Benton.

FAYOL'S GANGPLANK. A means of preventing delays in communication in an administrative hierarchy whereby employees may cross formal lines of communication if all parties agree and superiors are informed. Consequently, communications laterally become swift, communications are not overloaded, and, at the same time, the principle of unity in command is preserved.

Henri Fayol (1841–1925), a graduate of the National School of Mines, Saint Etienne, France, spent almost sixty years working in the Commentary-Fourchambault Company. He was promoted to high office in the organization, and for his contributions to the theory and practice of administration and management was awarded the Delasse Prize in 1893, the Legion of Honor, and a

Gold Medal of the Society for the Encouragement of Industry. In 1908 he set down his famous principles of administration which were published in *Administration industrielle et générale* (1916). From his own experience he stated several principles of management: division of work, authority, discipline, unity of command, unity of direction, subordination of interests to the organization, remuneration, centralization, scalar chain of authority, order, equity, and stability of tenure. The scalar chain linked superiors from the top authority to the lowest level; across the parallel lines of command, Fayol postulated the "gangplank" to help increase the efficiency of communications. Although Fayol's ideas did not extend beyond France until after 1945, today he is recognized as one of the founders of administrative theory.

Sources

Fayol, Henri. 1916. *Industrial and general administration*. Trans. J. A. Coubrough, 1930. Geneva: International Management Institute.

Roman-D'Amat, J., ed. 1975. *Dictionnaire de biographie Francais*. Paris: Librairie Letouzey et Ané.

Storrs, Constance, trans. 1949; 1967. *General and industrial management*. London: Pitmans.

Wren, Daniel A. 1987. *The evolution of management thought*. 3d ed. New York: John Wiley.

FEBRONIANISM. Relating to a doctrine that grew out of the Enlightenment and was antagonistic to the claims of the pope in asserting the independence of national churches.

Justinus Febronius was the pseudonym of Johann Nikolaus von Hontheim (1701–90). He was born at Trier, Prussia, and he died at Montquintin, Luxembourg. He studied at Louvain under Z. B. van Espen and at Leiden. He was influenced by J. von Spangenberg and was his assistant at the electoral diet at Frankfurt in 1742. Febronius published his views in *De statu ecclesiae et legitima potestate Romani pontifici* (1763). It appeared in French, Italian, Spanish, and Portuguese. The book recognized that the pope was the head of the church and supervisor of its administration, faith, and morals, but it attacked medieval extensions of temporal power. It argued that as far as possible all church affairs should be placed and kept in episcopal and civil hands, and that all papal claims based on the "False Decretals" should be annulled. Clement XIII ordered the German bishops to outlaw the work, and although the response was delayed, the elector of Trier complied. Maria Theresa had the Latin and German editions suppressed, but the prohibition was withdrawn by 1769. Febronianism was taught at Austrian universities and became popular where Roman centralism and the ultramontane principle were disliked, for example, in Portugal, Spain, and Venice. But Clement XIII sent encouraging letters to the many Catholic theologians who answered Febronius. The influence of Febronianism extended beyond the French Revolution and Napoleonic Wars, as efforts were made to establish a German national church. But Rome did not forget Febronianism and its political threat to the traditions of the Roman Catholic Church. Eventually, poor support from German bishops caused the collapse of the movement.

Sources

Cross, Frank L. 1974. *The Oxford dictionary of the Christian Church.* 2d ed. New York: Oxford University Press.

Douglas, James D., ed. 1974. *The new international dictionary of the Christian Church.* Exeter: Paternoster Press.

McDonald, William, ed. 1967. *New Catholic encyclopedia.* New York: McGraw-Hill.

FELDENKRAIS METHOD. A program of reeducation that requires students to change their habitual movement patterns through simple, gentle movements in a noncompetitive environment. The method helps the student understand how to achieve and maintain accurate alignment, dispense with effort and unnecessary muscular stress, maintain balance and movement, and relate to movement an interrupted pattern of breathing. The method helps singers, actors and musicians, athletes, and people with neuromuscular disorders. It is particularly useful for dancers studying the New Dance and helps them become aware through the movement techniques that the method provides.

Moshe Feldenkrais (1904–84), was born in Russia and as a youth became interested in athletics, martial arts, jujitsu, hypnosis, and psychology. Under the influence of Georges Ivanovitch Gurdjieff (1872–1949), he developed a theory of personal development. After completing a doctorate in applied physics at the Sorbonne, he immigrated to England. During the 1940s an old soccer injury flared up and led him to explore his body through its movements. This experience and knowledge of various fields he had studied formed the basis for his method; he spent the remaining years in Israel and United States teaching his ideas. He is reputed to have introduced judo to the West. He directed the Feldenkrais Institute in Tel Aviv until he died. His first publication appeared in 1972, and later he published *Body and Mature Behavior* (1973), *The Case of Nora* (1977), and *The Elusive Obvious* (1981). He assumed that since the body reflected attitudes, improving the body's functioning would improve the state of mind, make attitudes more flexible, and restore the individual's human dignity.

Sources

Feldenkrais, Moshe. 1972. *Awareness through movement: health exercises for personal growth.* New York: Harper and Row.

Keller, J., and Freer, B. 1981. Body. *People (U.S.)* 16 (September 7):87–88.

Rosenfeld, A. 1981. Teaching the body how to program the brain is Moshe's miracle. *Smithsonian* 11 (January):52–56 ff.

FENIAN SOCIETY. An Irish secret society active in Ireland, Britain, and the United States in the 1860s. An association of Irishmen, the Fenian Brotherhood, was founded in New York by John O'Mahony in 1857 and in Ireland by James Stephens (1824–1901). It planned an unsuccessful revolt against Britain's domination of Ireland. Between 1863 and 1872 it held eleven "national congresses" in the United States after which it continued in existence as a secret society.

The American Fenians raided British Canada during 1866–71 and caused much conflict between the British and U.S. governments.

Fenian, a modern English name for the Irish Fiann or Fianna, is applied in Irish tradition to members of tribes who formed a militia of the Ardrigh king of Eire or Erin, champions of Erin. The original, principal figure in the Fenian legends is Finn or Fionn MacCumhaill and his warrior band, the Fianna Éireann, who were skilled in war and poetry. Legends date from the third century and form the Fenian Cycle of tales and ballads which are central to Irish folklore and early literature.

Sources

McHenry, Robert, ed. 1992. *The new encyclopedia Britannica.* Chicago: Encyclopedia Britannica, Inc.

Ryan, Desmond. 1967. *The Fenian chief: a biography of James Stephens.* Dublin: Gill and Son.

Smith, Benjamin, ed. 1903. *The Century cyclopedia of names.* London: The Times.

FERRER MOVEMENT, FERRER COLONY. A movement and a colony established on the basis of an experimental and an evening school at a cultural center in New York City in 1915. It was founded by an anarchist community led by Harry Kelly (1871–1953), Joseph Cohen (1881–1953), and Leonard Abbott (1878–1953). The students came from the families of radical workers in the New York City garment industry. For five years the school maintained itself despite internal disputes in the movement and the colony. By 1918 the colony had stabilized itself by moving to a new site, building dwellings for twenty families, and maintaining the Modern School as the center of the colony. However, between 1940 and 1946 the community was riven with so much conflict that it broke up.

Guardia Francisco Ferrer (1859–1909) was born in Allela, near Barcelona, and was self-educated. He was a railway worker, a freethinker, and a republican. He went to Paris in 1886, taught Spanish, and was much taken with socialism. In 1901 he was bequeathed a legacy to found a school, and he returned to Barcelona to establish a Modern School (Escuela Moderna), an anticlerical institution. In 1906, after he was accused of conspiring with others to assassinate Spain's king and queen, his school was closed, and for a year he was put in prison. While visiting England in 1909, he heard of the Republican uprising in Barcelona and he immediately returned home. He was arrested, charged with complicity in the uprising, tried, convicted, and shot the same day, October 13. In Spain and abroad, his death led to much criticism. Afterward the Spanish ministry fell, and Ferrer earned the reputation of an anarchist and martyr.

Sources

Abbott, Leonard, ed. 1910. *Francisco Ferrer, his life work and martyrdom.* 1987 Microfiche. Alexandria, Va.: Chadwyck-Healey.

Dudley, Lavinia P. 1963. *The encyclopedia Americana.* International ed. New York: Americana Corp.

Fogarty, Robert S. 1980. *Dictionary of American communal and utopian history.* West-
    port, Conn.: Greenwood Press.
Grossman, Rudolf, 1987. *Francisco Ferrer: sein Leben und sein Werk.* By Pierre Ramus.
    [Originally *Die Freie Generation.*] Paris, 1910. Microfilm. Alexandria, Va.: Chad-
    wyck-Healey.
McCabe, Joseph. 1987. *The martyrdom of Ferrer.* Alexandria, Va.: Chadwyck-Healey.
Veysey, Lawrence. 1973. *The communal experience.* New York: Harper and Row.

FESTINGER'S THEORY OF COGNITIVE DISSONANCE. A social psychological theory that predicts conditions under which attitudes and opinions
change. When the cognitions of a person are discrepant, tension is created, and
the person reduces it by making the cognitions consistent. The tension is "cognitive dissonance" and appears to have the motivational characteristics of a
drive, although not all theorists accept this notion. The theory provoked 1,000
studies in twenty-five years. It faced many challenges, endured refinements and
limitations, but remained valuable in theory and useful in the practice of attitude
change and personality, social cognition, and self-perception.

Leon Festinger (1919–89) was born in New York and educated at City College. He worked with Kurt Lewin (1890–1947) at the University of Iowa, where,
as a research associate, he was awarded higher degrees (Ph.D., 1942). He went
with Lewin to the Massachusetts Institute of Technology in 1945 when the
Research Center for Group Dynamics was founded. After Lewin's death, Festinger became director of the center when it moved to the University of Michigan. He taught at the University of Minnesota in 1951 and Stanford in 1955
as a professor of psychology. From 1968 until he died, he was an outstanding
scholar at the New School for Social Research, New York. Among his social
psychological studies, the best known centered on his cognitive dissonance theory, which provided predictions based on the potential conflict affecting individuals in their decision making and attitudes. A festschrift of his work appeared
in 1990.

Sources

Chapanis, Natasha P., and Chapanis, Alphonse. 1964. Cognitive dissonance: five years
    later. *Psychological Bulletin* 61:1–22.
Cialdini, Robert B. 1981. Attitude and attitude change. In Mark R. Rosenzweig and
    Lyman W. Porter, eds. *Annual Review of Psychology* 32:377–383.
Cooper, Joel, and Croyle, Robert T. 1984. Attitudes and attitude change. In Mark R.
    Rosenzweig and Lyman W. Porter, eds. *Annual Review of Psychology* 55:404–
    412.
Festinger, Leon. 1957. *A theory of cognitive dissonance.* Evanston, Ill.: Row, Peterson.
Sarason, Irwin G., and Smith, Ronald E. 1971. Personality. In Paul H. Mussen and Mark
    R. Rosenzweig. *Annual Review of Psychology* 22:424–426.
Schacter, Stanley, and Gazzanigna, Michael S., eds. 1990. *Extending psychological fron-
    tiers: selected works of Leon Festinger.* New York: Russell Sage Foundation.
Zajonc, Robert B. 1990. Leon Festinger (1919–89). *American Psychologist* 45:661.

FIEDLER'S CONTINGENCY MODEL. A theory of organizational leadership based on leader-member relations (liking and trusting in a group), task structure (clarity in definition of tasks), and position power (authority of the position, not the person). Fiedler stated that the pattern of leadership that was appropriate for maximizing a group performance was contingent on the situation of the group and its task.

Fred E. Fiedler (b. 1922) immigrated to the United States from Vienna in 1938, became a U.S. citizen in 1943, and served in the U.S. Army during 1942–45. He studied psychology at the University of Chicago (Ph.D., 1949), became director of the Group Effectiveness Laboratory at the University of Illinois (1959–69) and later was professor of psychology and management, University of Washington, where he has directed organizational research since 1969. He is a fellow of American professional societies in psychology and in management; he has also been consulting editor for many professional and scientific journals that publish on organizations, administration, social psychology, and military psychology. Fiedler has received many awards and honors for contributions to naval and military services, and studies in leadership. He advises many U.S. government departments and institutes in the United States, Europe, and Asia. According to his theory, the belief that there is one best way to be a leader is a false guide to managers and administrators; he therefore emphasizes the value of flexibility in fitting the appropriate actions of a leader to a situation. His work has contributed to recent theories which include more conditions appropriate for maximizing group effectiveness, for example, interaction patterns in groups and personal aspirations.

Sources

Bedeian, Arthur G., ed. 1992–93. *Management laureates: a collection of autobiographical essays.* Vol. I. Greenwich, Conn.: JAI Press.

Fiedler, Fred E. 1967. *A theory of leadership effectiveness.* New York: McGraw-Hill.

Fiedler, Fred E., and Chemers, Martin M. 1974. *Leadership and effective management.* Glenview, Ill.: Scott, Foresman.

Fiedler, Fred E., and Garcia, J. E. 1987. *New approaches to effective leadership: cognitive resources and organizational performance.* New York: John Wiley.

Wren, Daniel A. 1987. *The evolution of management thought.* 3d ed. New York: John Wiley.

Personal Communication.

FINK, RATFINK. Scab, blackleg, a worker hired to break strikes.

Albert Fink (1827–97) was born in Lauterback, Germany, and studied architecture and engineering in Darmstadt in 1848. He immigrated to the United States and worked for the Baltimore and Ohio Railroad, and in 1857 joined the Louisville and National Railroad, becoming its chief engineer in 1860. Some sources say he was a detective for the line. He rose to vice-president and general superintendent in 1869, published on the economics of rail transport and financing, and helped found the study of railroad economics. He retired in 1875, but then became a director of the Southern Railway and Steamship Association and helped suppress the destructive competition between its members. Later, he organized and was a commissioner of the Trunk Line Association, New York City (c. 1877–89). He was not in railroad disputes, but his operatives may have policed the rates charged on the lines, and some were probably management spies, known as "Finks." Alternatively, the term may have come by transformation from "Pinkerton Men" or "Pinks" to "Finks" who were hired in 1892 to stop the Homestead steel strikes. There were synonymous with the British "scabs" or "blacklegs."

Allan Pinkerton (1819–84) was born in Glasgow, immigrated to the United States in 1842, and opened a cooper's business in Dundee, Illinois in 1843. He helped capture counterfeiters and other criminals, which led him to be elected a sheriff of Kane County. When he moved to Chicago, he was appointed a deputy sheriff of Cook County and then, in 1850, joined the Chicago police force as its first railway detective. That same year, following several railway robberies, he opened his own firm, the Pinkerton National Detective Agency, and helped solve many crimes on the railroads. In 1861 he discovered a plot to assassinate President-elect Lincoln. His detective agency became noted for its work against labor unions and their movements, and his name became synonymous with employers' strikebreaking. James McParlan was a "Pinkerton" noted for his work in crushing the Molly Maguires in the Pennsylvania coal fields.

See also MOLLY MAGUIRES.

Sources

Johnson, Allen, and Malone, Dumas, eds. 1930. *Dictionary of American biography.* Vol. III. New York: Charles Scribner's Sons.

Malone, Dumas, ed. 1934. *Dictionary of American biography.* Vol. VII. New York: Charles Scribner's Sons.

Morn, Frank. 1982. *The eye that never sleeps: a history of the Pinkerton National Detective Agency.* Bloomington: Indiana University Press.

Van Doren, Charles, ed. 1974. *Webster's American biographies.* Springfield, Mass.: G. and C. Merriam.

Weiss, Robert. 1978. The emergence and transformation of private detective industrial policing in the United States, 1850–1940. *Crime and Social Justice* 9:35–48.

FIRTHIAN. Pertaining to the principles of the twentieth-century British linguist who assumed that in a theory of linguistics language patterns cannot be understood with only one system of analytic principles. Little of Firth's teaching was published, but a neo-Firthian group of scholars at University College London, 1965–70, used many of his ideas.

John Rupert Firth (1890–1960) studied history at Leeds University and became a history lecturer. He served in the British Army during World War I; went to Lahore, India, as a professor of English at the University of Punjab (1920–28), taught at the University of London (1928–37), and was made a professor of general linguistics (1944–56). He established linguistics as a separate academic discipline and founded the British approach known as the London School. He was interested in phonological and semantic theory. In contributing to phonological analysis, Firth emphasized that a linear model of phonology did not help understand spoken languages that have no written alphabet. He argued that the sound of a word was directly related to its meaning. This view was developed during his friendship with Bronislaw Kaspar Malinowski (1884–1942), the anthropologist; the view is not generally accepted by those who attribute the meaning of words not only to their context but also to their pretheoretical use. He published *Speech* (1930), *The Tongues of Men* (1937), and his collected papers (1957).

Source
Bazell, Charles E., ed. 1966. *In memory of J. R. Firth.* London: Longmans.
Bright, William, ed. 1992. *International encyclopedia of linguistics.* New York: Oxford University Press.
Devine, Elizabeth; Held, Michael; Vinson, James; and Walsh, George, eds. 1983. *Thinkers of the twentieth century: a biographical, bibliographical and critical dictionary.* London: Macmillan.
Firth, John R. 1957. *Papers in linguistics, 1934–1951.* London: Oxford University Press.
Mitchell, T. F. 1975. *Principles of Firthian linguistics.* London: Longmans.

FISHER EQUATION. In monetary theory the equation is $PT = MV$, where P is the general price level, T is the total volume of transactions, V is the transactions velocity of money, and M is the quantity of money.

Irving Fisher (1867–1947), a New Yorker, was the son of a Congregational minister and is regarded as one of the United States' outstanding economists. He was educated at Yale where he taught mathematics before joining the Economics Department in 1895. He established an international reputation with his Ph.D. thesis, "Mathematical Investigations in the Theory of Value and Prices" (1891/92). The work contained the design of a machine to illustrate general equilibrium in a multimarket economy. He remained at Yale until he retired in 1935. Fisher helped found, and was first president of, the Econometric Society in 1930; he was also a director of Remington Rand (now the Rand Corporation) and a founder and president of the Eugenics Research Association, the Stable Money League, and the American Statistical Association, as well as many other companies and agencies. He made a private fortune from the invention of a visible card-index filing system and spent most of it in later life campaigning for many causes, including world peace and prohibition.

Sources
Blaug, Mark. 1986. *Great economists before Keynes.* Brighton, England: Harvester Press, Wheatsheaf Books.
Eatwell, John; Milgate, Murray; and Newman, Peter. 1987. *The new Palgrave: a dictionary of economics.* London: Macmillan.
Nemmers, E. E. 1977. *Dictionary of economics and business.* Totowa, N.J.: Rowman and Littlefield.

FLAMINIAN. Pertaining to the Roman censor and to the public works he constructed while in office.

Gaius Flaminius (d. 217 B.C.) was born into a plebeian family and became a popular leader in Rome by challenging the Senate's authority. For example, he helped distribute recently acquired land to the plebeians against the opposition of the Senate, and later disobeyed a senatorial order, crossed the Po, and defeated the Insubres. He became censor (220 B.C.) and had the Circus Flaminius built on the Campus Martius and constructed the Via Flaminia to Ariminum. He supported a law that helped ensure that senators were debarred from commerce (218 B.C.). He was reelected consul in 217, which showed popular dissatisfaction with the Senate's approach to the war against Hannibal. Eventually, Hannibal ambushed Flaminius, and he perished.

Source
McHenry, Robert, ed. 1992. *The new encyclopedia Britannica.* Chicago: Encyclopedia
    Britannica, Inc.

FLEUR-DE-LUCE. The French emblem, "the flower of Louis," adopted with the shield of France by Louis VIII; "fleur-de-lys," flower of the lily.

This stylized device in heraldry, similar to the fleur-de-lis, is often found in early art and may not necessarily signify a flower. Its principal importance lies in its significance in the French royal arms. According to legend, the lily, a symbol of purity, came from heaven to Clovis when he was baptized, and "fleur-de-lis" is a play on words on "fleur-de-Louis," that is, Louis Clovis (466–511). Louis VI (1081–1137) used it on his seal and coins; at his consecration Louis VIII (1187–1226) wore blue vestments on which were embroidered golden lilies, and afterward a blue shield of golden fleur-de-lis became the royal arms. In honor of the Holy Trinity, Charles V of France reduced the number of fleur-de-lis to three in 1376.

Sources
McHenry, Robert, ed. 1992. *The new encyclopedia Britannica.* Chicago: Encyclopedia
    Britannica, Inc.
Partridge, Eric. 1970. *Name into word.* New York: Books for Libraries.

FLEXNER REPORT. A report on the quality of U.S. medical education (1910) which found that only Harvard, Western Reserve, and Johns Hopkins had acceptable standards. The report recommended full-time faculty in medical schools, laboratory and hospital facilities for medical students, higher admission standards to medical school, integration of medical teaching and research, higher medical school qualifications, and graduate-level medical education in universities.

Abraham Flexner (1866–1959) was born at Louisville, Kentucky, and studied at Johns Hopkins University. He taught for four years before establishing his own school to prepare pupils for college. He studied psychology at Harvard and in Berlin. In Germany he saw what he believed was the best education system.

He published *The American College* (1908), which called for fewer extracurricular activities and more intellectual study from students. He joined the Carnegie Foundation for the Advancement of Teaching where he was commissioned to study medical education in 1910 and issued his report, *Medical Education in the United States and Canada.* The resulting publicity culminated in the closing of about 120 medical schools and revolutionized the training of the medical profession. The report was followed by his *Medical Education in Europe* (1912), which led to his appointment on John D. Rockefeller, Jr.'s General Education Board. He reported on prostitution in Europe (1914) and made many studies of the school systems in the United States (1916–25). In 1928 he gave the Rhodes Trust Memorial Lectures at Oxford and published his *Universities—American, English and German* (1930). That year he organized and established the Institute for Advanced Study at Princeton and was its director until 1939 when he retired.

Sources

Chapman, Carlton C. 1974. The Flexner report. *Daedalus* 103:105–117.

Flexner, Abraham. 1940. *I remember: the autobiography of Abraham Flexner.* Revised in 1960 and titled *Abraham Flexner: an autobiography.* New York: Simon and Schuster.

Harris, Michael R. 1970. *Five counter revolutionaries in higher education: Irving Babbitt, Albert Jay Nock, Abraham Flexner, Robert Maynard Hutchins, Alexander Meikeljohn.* Corvallis: Oregon State University Press.

Malone, Dumas, ed. 1933. *Dictionary of American biography.* Vol. VI. New York: Charles Scribner's Sons.

Parker, Franklin. 1962. Abraham Flexner 1866–1959. *History of Education Quarterly* 32:119–209.

FOLLETT'S CIRCULAR RESPONSE. In complex organizations a process whereby one party, through open interaction with another, has the opportunity to influence the other and achieve power with them rather than over them. The process requires revealing private information to the other, preferring to share control rather than wresting it from the other, and giving up the illusion that resolving conflict can be achieved by resort to a final authority or arbitration.

Mary Parker Follett (1868–1933) was born in Boston, educated at the Thayer Academy and the Harvard Annex (later Radcliffe College), studied philosophy and politics, and became an expert in vocational guidance, adult education, and the new social psychology. Her philosophy, based on ideas of the German, Johann Fichte (1762–1814), assumed that a person's freedom was best achieved through commitment to group membership and one's interpersonal network. She published *The New State: Group Organization and the Solution of Popular Government* (1918) in which she advocated the principle that an individual's potential development would be best realized through their group membership. Her *Creative Experience* (1924) presented the same theme. As a philosopher for business, she applied her thinking to the management of conflict and advocated the "circular response" as the most appropriate approach to its resolution.

Sources
Follett, M. P. 1918. *The new state: group organization and the solution of popular government.* London: Longmans.
Follett, M. P. 1924. *Creative experience.* London: Longmans.
Follett, M. P. 1926. The illusion of final authority. *Bulletin of the Taylor Society* 5:243.
Metcalf, Henry C., and Urwick, Lyndall, eds. 1940. *Dynamic administration: the collected papers of Mary Parker Follett.* New York: Harper and Row.
Wren, Daniel A. 1987. *The evolution of management thought.* 3d. ed. New York: John Wiley.

FORDISM. A system of mass production that spread in the United States from 1900 to 1940, and dominated the postwar reconstruction of many European and Asian countries; the system is controlled by large corporations, which also control mass markets and the purchasing power of the working class. In the 1970s Fordism entered a crisis that gave rise to neo-Fordism and post-Fordism.

Henry Ford (1863–1947) was born at Greenfield, Michigan, son of Irish immigrants, raised on his father's farm, and educated at the local school. At 16 he left farming and became an apprentice machinist. Afterward he joined the Detroit Dry Dock Company where he learned about power plants and serviced steam traction engines for farmers. He produced his first petrol-driven motor car in 1893; in 1899 he founded his own company in Detroit, designed his own cars, and in 1903 the Ford Motor Company was formed. Ford pioneered the mass production assembly line for his famous T-model automobile (1908–9) and produced 15 million by 1928. Although his son Edsel was appointed company president in 1918, Ford dominated the firm. Later, Henry's hostility to unions in the automobile industry led the National Labor Relations Board to condemn Ford's labor policies. Ford's eldest son Henry Ford II took control of the company in 1945, and the production methods were used abroad in postwar reconstruction developments.

See also EDSEL.

Sources
Braverman, Harry. 1974. *Labor and monopoly capital: the degradation of work in the twentieth century.* New York: Monthly Review Press.
Bryan, Ford R. 1990. *Beyond the Model-T: the other ventures of Henry Ford.* Detroit: Wayne State University Press.
Gelderman, Carole W. 1982. *Henry Ford: the wayward capitalist.* New York: St. Martin's Press.
Jardim, Anne. 1970. *The first Henry Ford: a study in personality and business leadership.* Cambridge, Mass.: MIT Press.
Kern, Horst, and Schumann, Michael. 1985. *Das ende der arbeitsteilung? Rationalisierung in der industrielle produktion.* Munich: Verlag C.H. Beck.
Lewis, David L. 1976. *The public image of Henry Ford: an American folk hero and his company.* Detroit: Wayne State University Press.
Nevins, Allan, and Hill, Frank. 1954–63. *Ford: the times, the man and the company.* 3 vols. New York: Charles Scribner's Sons.

Piore, Michael J., and Sabel, Charles F. 1984. *The second industrial divide: possibilities for prosperity.* New York: Basic Books.
Sabel, Charles F. 1982. *Work and politics: the division of labor in industry.* Cambridge: Cambridge University Press.
Sward, Keith. 1948. *The legend of Henry Ford.* New York: Rinehart.

FORDIZATION. Freezing of facial features that occurred among Ford employees whenever Henry Ford I tried to prevent the inroads of unionism in his company. Because Ford employed an army of men to spy on workers and listen for evidence of conspiracy, workers learned to communicate without moving their lips in what became known as a "Ford whisper." Their frozen features were called "Fordization of the Face."

See also FORDISM.

Source
Collier, Peter, and Horowitz, David. 1988. *The Fords.* London: Collins.

FOURIERISM. A socialist system that reorganizes society into small cooperative communities or phalanges that allow development of people's talents and expression of feelings.

François Marie Charles Fourier (1772–1837) was born into a family of French merchants of Besançon. The family forced him into commerce, and in 1789 he went to Lyon to study banking. He pursued commerce throughout Europe; he also found he was inventive: he devised a musical notation and a railway with passenger carriages. While serving in the military (1794–96), he planned an administrative reform that met with approval; later he researched urban architecture to find improvements. In 1798 information about overpriced fruit led him to suspect basic disorder in industrial organization, and he turned to the study of society. When working as a clerk, he published his *The Theory of Four Movements* (1808), which stated that parallel to the natural order in the universe was a social order among humankind, and that human identity developed through eight stages. At the highest stage humankind lived in harmony and expressed emotions freely. In 1812 he received an annuity from his mother's estate and thereafter had sufficient leisure to study and write. He published *A Treatise on Domestic Agricultural Association* (1822) and *The New Industrial Worker* (1830). In condemning society for its competitiveness and waste, he advocated a utopian socialism. The basic unit of the utopian community was the phalanx, a group of 1,620 people living in common buildings or phalanstery, using about 5,000 acres, and dividing work according to individual abilities. Phalanges would eventually link and form one federation. He advocated a world language and government. His converts appeared in France and the United States where the noted examples were Brook Farm in Massachusetts (1841–46) and the North American Phalanx in Red Bank, New Jersey. Albert Brisbane (1809–90) introduced and popularized Fourierism in the United States beginning in

1839. The societies flourished but later failed when people lost interest in associationism.

Sources

Beecher, Jonathan. 1987. *Charles Fourier: the visionary and his world.* Berkeley: University of California Press.

Fourier, Francois M. C. 1851. *The passions of the human soul and their influence on society and civilization.* Trans. by Hugh Doherty. 1968 edition. New York: A. M. Kelly.

Guarneri, Carl J. 1991. *The utopian alternative: Fourierism in nineteenth-century America.* Ithaca, N.Y.: Cornell University Press.

McHenry, Robert, ed. 1992. *The new encyclopedia Britannica.* Chicago: Encyclopedia Britannica, Inc.

Prevost, M., and Roman-D'Amat, J. 1986. *Dictionnaire de biographie Francaise.* Paris: Librairie Letouzey et Ané.

Riasanovsky, Nicholas. 1969. *The teachings of Charles Fourier.* Berkeley: University of California Press.

Spencer, Michael C. 1981. *Charles Fourier.* Boston: Twayne Publishers.

FRANCISCAN. A lay brother, friar, or novice of the mendicant order of the Roman Catholic Church. Franciscans are bound to poverty, may carry no money with them, and are known as Minors or Minorites by virtue of their humility and as Greyfriars from the original color of their habit. The "Conventual Franciscans," a branch of the order (1230), wear black and are permitted to have some income.

Saint Francis of Assisi (1181/82–1226), the "Seraphic" saint, was born in Umbria, Italy, the son of a cloth merchant of Assisi. His father hoped that Francis would follow him into the business, but Francis chose to be a soldier instead. In 1202 he fought in a war against Perugia, was imprisoned, fell ill on his escape, recovered, and served papal forces under Count Gentile (1205). A series of visions and revelations formed his religious conversion. He returned to Assisi and was drawn to poverty, solitary prayer, and the helping of lepers. He renounced his father and his material interests and broke with the family; he worked to restore several chapels, and traveled and preached simple rules for living. In 1209 twelve mendicant friars sought approval of the Franciscan rules from Pope Innocent III. According to tradition, it was given on April 16, the foundation day of the Franciscan order. Their basic rule was to follow Christ's beliefs and do as he had done; nevertheless, a view developed that Francis was one who primarily loved nature, poverty, and practiced social work while he wandered and preached. In 1212 he began a second order, for women, the Poor Clares, named after Saint Clare (Clara) of Assisi, and later a third, the Order of Brothers and Sisters of Penance, which brought Franciscan ideas to the world generally. Shipwreck prevented his going to the Holy Land in 1212, and illness stopped him from visiting Spain. He visited Egypt in 1219, where he impressed the sultan and was allowed to visit holy places in Palestine. His order grew rapidly in Italy, and many ensuing organizational problems required his attention. By 1224 he had withdrawn from the external matters of the order to La Verna where he is said to have had a vision of a seraph with six wings, and endured the stigmata of crucifixion on his hands, feet, and side. For two years he lived in pain, blind from an eye disease that he had contracted in the East. He died in Assisi and was canonized on July 16, 1228. Francis's love of nature was later regarded as his major characteristic, and many artists painted him preaching to birds and other animals.

Sources

Cross, Frank L. 1974. *The Oxford dictionary of the Christian Church.* 2d ed. New York: Oxford University Press.

McHenry, Robert, ed. 1992. *The new encyclopedia Britannica.* Chicago: Encyclopedia Britannica, Inc.

FRANKFURT SCHOOL. In 1923, under Carl Grünberg, the Institute for Social Research was established at the University of Frankfurt. During the Nazi regime, the institute was exiled to New York and did not return to Germany until 1949. Its major thinkers were Max Horkheimer (1895–1973), who was director from 1930 to 1958, Walter Benjamin (1892–1940), Theodore Adorno (1903–69), and Herbert Marcuse (1898–1979). The school provided a critical theory of Marxism which opposed all forms of positivism, especially the idea of value freedom in social science and all interpretations of Marxism afflicted with materialism and an immutable dogma, for example, Stalinism. The school advocated an open-ended, continuously self-critical approach; it avoided dogmatic theory and dogmatic social changes. The school believed that greater appreciation of Marx's early writings was necessary, and it encouraged the realization of Marx's debt to Hegel and the belief that consciousness rather than economic determinism molded the world. The school devoted great attention to the aesthetics of mass society and rescued Marxist cultural criticism from its repression. The school's major modern figure is Jürgen Habermas (b. 1929), a professor of philosophy, von Goethe University, Frankfurt, who related conditions of rationality to the social structure of language use. The school has promoted the libertarian aspect of Marx's thought and has influenced radical movements—for example, the New Left and the rejection of modern technocratic society whether capitalist or noncapitalist, with a conviction that a satisfactory clear alternative can emerge only during the actual practice of revolution.

Frankfurt-am-Main (50 07N 8 40E) is a manufacturing and commercial city in Darmstadt district in western Germany. Most German emperors were crowned there, and it was the birthplace of Goethe and the meeting place of the German National Assemblies (1848–49). Today it is an international center of road, rail, and air traffic in Europe where engineering, pharmacy, telecommunications, and domestic appliance firms operate.

Sources

Arato, Andrew, and Gebhardt, Eike, eds. 1978. *The essential Frankfurt School reader.* Oxford: Basil Blackwell.

Bottomore, Thomas B. 1984. *The Frankfurt School.* Chichester: Ellis Horwood.

Connerton, Paul. 1980. *The tragedy of enlightenment: an essay on the Frankfurt School.* Cambridge: Cambridge University Press.

Crozier, Michael. 1992. The Frankfurt School. In Peter Beilharz, ed. *Social theory: a guide to central thinkers.* Sydney: Allen and Unwin.

Crystal, David, ed. 1990. *The Cambridge encyclopedia.* Cambridge: Cambridge University Press.

Miller, David, ed. 1987. *The Blackwell encyclopedia of political thought.* Oxford: Basil Blackwell.

Turner, Roland, ed. 1987. *Thinkers of the twentieth century.* 2d ed. London: St. James Press.

FRAZERIAN HERO. A type of hero taken largely from the work of James Frazer; the type is characterized by the ritual murder of a king or royal figure for the welfare of the community, and is based on the hero Aeneas, in Virgil's *Aeneid.* After many trials, Aeneas kills Prince Turnus so that he can wed Lavinia and then succeed her father to the throne of Italy, Aeneas's homeland.

James George Frazer (1854–1941) was born in Glasgow and educated at the University of Glasgow. A fellow of Trinity College, Cambridge (1879), he was called to the bar but never practiced. Influenced by Sir E. B. Tylor and William Robertson Smith, Frazer studied the history of religion. He published *Totemism* (1887) and *The Golden Bough* (1890–1915), a vast study in myths, comparative folklore, and religion. The title of the second book refers to the branch that Aeneas broke from a tree before entering the underworld, and the work seeks to explain the rule of an ancient Italian priesthood. Frazer helped establish the *Cambridge Review* (1879), lectured at Trinity College (1905), and published *Letters of William Cowper* (1912). At the University of Liverpool, he was appointed a professor of social anthropology (1907–22) and later returned to Cambridge. He published on superstitions and exogamy (1910) and was the Gifford Lecturer (1911–12; 1922–23). He wrote *The Fear of the Dead in Primitive Religion* (1933); he was also a classicist and contributed to biblical studies. He was knighted in 1924 and awarded honorary degrees from universities in Britain, Paris, Strasbourg, and Athens. He was elected to the Royal Society, was an original member of the British Academy, and was honored in France, Germany, and Holland.

Sources

Downie, R. Angus. 1940. *James George Frazer, the portrait of a scholar.* London: Watts.

Fraser, Robert L. 1990. *The making of "The Golden Bough": the origin and growth of an argument.* London: Macmillan.

Legg, Leopold G.W., and Williams, E. T., eds. 1959. *Dictionary of national biography 1941–1950.* London: Oxford University Press.

Segal, Robert A., intro. 1990. *In quest of the hero: The myth of the birth of the hero; The hero; The hero pattern in the life of Jesus.* Princeton, N.J.: Princeton University Press.

FREUDIAN. Pertaining to the theory of the libido and the knowledge and method of psychoanalysis.

Sigmund Freud (1856–1939), a Jewish neurologist, was born in Moravia. He spent most of his life in Vienna, and made visits to England, Rome, and the United States. In 1938 the Nazis allowed him to leave Austria for England. After his early medical studies, he went to study under the Parisian neurologist, Charcot. Freud developed a deep interest in the unconscious mental processes of both neurotic and normal people. In 1896, on the death of his father, Freud began his personal psychoanalysis and quickly developed the idea of the Oedipus Complex to account for the unconscious emotional relations between family members. He also developed a theory of mind and therapeutic practice that helped to reveal to individuals their unconscious mental functioning. In 1905, when he put great emphasis on the sexual wishes of children and deviant sexual behavior, he became the center of a lifelong controversy and was often condemned by medical and academic authorities. In time, he attracted a devoted group of followers, some of whom held to his ideas while others developed their own psychological schools. Today several schools of such thought are among Western psychological theories, and Freud's original ideas and practices have come under considerable scrutiny.

Sources

Clarke, Ronald W. 1980. *Freud: the man and the cause.* New York: Random House.

Gay, Peter. 1988. *Freud: a life for our time.* New York: Doubleday.

Isbister, J. N. 1985. *Freud: an introduction to his life and work.* Cambridge: Polity.

Jones, Ernest. 1953–57. *The life and work of Sigmund Freud.* 3 vols. New York: Basic Books.

Kirsner, Douglas. 1992. Sigmund Freud. In Peter Beilharz, ed. *Social theory: a guide to central thinkers.* Sydney: Allen and Unwin.

Kurzweil, Edith. 1989. *The Freudians: a comparative perspective.* New Haven, Conn.: Yale University Press.

Macmillan, Malcolm B. 1991. *Freud evaluated: the completed arc.* Amsterdam: Elsevier Science.

Sulloway, Frank J. 1979. *Freud: biologist of the mind.* London: Burnett.

FROEBELIAN. Pertaining to a system of kindergarten schools.

Friedrich Froebel (1782–1852) was born at Oberweissbach, a village in the Thuringian forest in Germany. A slow learner, introspective and moody in childhood, he developed considerable skill in observing nature around him. He was apprenticed to a forester and later was a student of architecture. He studied at the universities of Jena, Göttingen, and Berlin. In 1806 he was a tutor to the children of a baron whose attitude of neglect toward his offspring persuaded Froebel to the belief that parents ought to be more involved in the education of their children. He went to Burgdorf, Switzerland, to study education with Johann Heinrich Pestalozzi (1742–1827). In 1813–14 he served in campaigns against the French. In 1816 he established what he called the "Universal German Educational Institution" at Griesham, a Thuringian village (1816). It flourished until 1828 when it was suspected of comprising dangerous demagogues and their rabble. In 1832 he lost control of it, and went to Switzerland for five years. In 1837 he returned and founded the first kindergarten and boarding school for its teachers in Blankenburg in Thuringia. His system advocates the encouragement of learning rather than firm instruction; as a result, games are taught and combined with instruction in skills, the value of family life, and the study of nature. His ideas and work met with much resistance at the time and were even forbidden by state law in Prussia. During the early 1850s his ideas won international support for the kindergarten system, and despite resistance to them in Prussia, his work was encouraged by Baroness Marenholtz-Bülow, who helped establish kindergartens in England and Europe. His theory and practice of education for preschool appeared in his *Die Menschenerziehung (The Education of Man)* in 1826.

Sources

Fröbel, Friedrich W. A. 1889. *Autobiography of Friederich Froebel.* Reprinted 1971. Ann Arbor, Michigan: University Microfilms International, 1981.

Husen, Torsten, and Postlethwaite, T. Neville. 1985. *The international encyclopedia of education research and studies.* Oxford: Pergamon Press.

Lilley, Irene M. 1967. *Friederich Froebel: a selection from his writings.* Cambridge: Cambridge University Press.

McHenry, Robert, ed. 1992. *The new encyclopedia Britannica.* Chicago: Encyclopedia Britannica, Inc.

Shapiro, Michael S. 1983. *Child's garden: the kindergarten movement from Froebel to Dewey.* University Park: Pennsylvania State University Press.

Snider, Denton J. 1900. *The life of Friedrich Froebel: founder of the kindergarten.* Chicago: Sigma Publishing. Ann Arbor, Michigan: University Microfilms International, 1981.

Zusne, Leonard. 1984. *Biographical dictionary of psychology.* Westport, Conn.: Greenwood Press.

FULBRIGHT, FULBRIGHT ACT. A prestigious scholarship, usually awarded to an academic, to enable travel abroad for research and teaching. An act, including an amendment to the Surplus Property Act of 1944, which was based on the proposal that the money received from the sale of millions of dollars of surplus war material in Allied countries should be used to finance a cultural and educational exchange.

James William Fulbright (b. 1905) was born in Sumner, Missouri. He became a Rhodes Scholar, studied law, and was admitted to the bar in 1934. For a year he served in the antitrust division of the U.S. Justice Department before teaching law at George Washington University (1935–36) and the University of Arkansas (1936–39). After being elected to the House of Representatives in 1942, he became a senator in 1944. In 1946 with the worldwide acclaim for the Fulbright Act in the Seventy-ninth U.S. Congress, his name earned international recognition. The act allowed the exchange of students between the United States and other nations. Fulbright was chairman of the Senate Foreign Relations Committee (1959–74) and in this position spoke firmly for growth in public education and the extension of the U.S. Senate's role in America's long-term policy-making. In 1961, as an opponent of America's interference in the policies of other countries, he stood firmly against the Bay of Pigs invasion, the invasion of the Dominican Republic in 1965, and the United States' growing intervention in Vietnam. He published *Old Myths and New Realities* (1965) and *The Arrogance of Power* (1967). In 1974 he was defeated as Democratic candidate from Arkansas for the U.S. Senate. In 1989 he received the Onassis Foundation prize of $100,000 for his contributions to education and peace.

Sources

Commager, Henry S., ed. 1968. *Documents of American history.* 8th ed. New York: Appleton-Century-Crofts.

Findling, John E. 1980. *Dictionary of American diplomatic history.* 2d ed. 1989. Westport, Conn.: Greenwood Press.

Jacob, Kathryn A., and Ragsdale, Bruce A. 1989. *Biographical dictionary of the United States Congress: 1774–1989.* Bicentennial ed. Washington, D.C.: U.S. Government Printing Office.

Smith, G. 1989. Reflections of a conservative optimist. *New York Times Book Review,* February 19:7.

G

GADSDEN PURCHASE. The U.S. purchase of approximately 45,000 square miles, comprising present-day southern Arizona and New Mexico, through which ran the best route for a southern transcontinental railroad. The Mexican government of Santa Anna sold the territory for $10 million, and the treaty purchasing it was negotiated by the U.S. minister for Mexico (1853). Today the U.S.-Mexican border is defined by the purchase.

James Gadsden (1788–1858) was born in Charleston, South Carolina. After graduating from Yale in 1806 and serving in the army (1811–21), he became president of the Louisville, Cincinnati, and Charleston Railroad (1835) for ten years. He supported plans for a transcontinental railroad along the southern route from New Orleans to California. In 1853, helped by his friendship with Jefferson Davis, secretary of war, Gadsden was appointed minister to Mexico. His principal mission was to purchase land for the southern rail route, and he received authority to buy as much territory as he could for $50 million. He remained in Mexico until 1856.

Sources

Dudley, Lavinia P. 1963. *The encyclopedia Americana.* International ed. New York: Americana Corp.

Findling, John E. 1980. *Dictionary of American diplomatic history.* Westport, Conn.: Greenwood Press.

Jacob, Kathryn A., and Ragsdale, Bruce A. 1989. *Biographical directory of the United States Congress: 1774–1989.* Bicentennial ed. Washington, D.C.: U.S. Government Printing Office.

Johnson, Allen, and Malone, Dumas, eds. 1931. *Dictionary of American biography.* Vol. IV. New York: Charles Scribner's Sons.

McHenry, Robert, ed. 1992. *The new encyclopedia Britannica.* Chicago: Encyclopedia Britannica, Inc.

Van Doren, Charles, ed. 1974. *Webster's American biographies.* Springfield, Mass.: G. and C. Merriam.

GAIA HYPOTHESIS, GAIA THEORY. An hypothesis that states that conditions on earth are made congenial for life by the presence of life itself. A theory that assumes the planet Earth is an enormous organism in which all things interact and thereby maintain all aspects of life; a metaphysical expression of the spirituality of science; an ideology of the New Age movements that expresses views on environmentalism and the maintenance of Mother Earth or Earth Mother. The term was chosen by James Ephriam Lovelock (b. 1919), an independent British scientist, to advance his views on the origins of life. Originally, the British writer William Golding (1911–93) suggested the name.

Gaia, in Greek mythology, is the Earth Goddess. She is sometimes the Earth itself as well as a goddess resident in the Earth. At Delphi she originally held the oracular shrine, and her original role was to be the "fixed and firm one," not an abstraction; she was also the witness to all oaths in the belief that she must know everything that occurs on her surface. She was born of Chaos; her child and her husband are one—Heaven; her offspring comprise such natural events as seas, rivers, mountains, and figures, for example, the Titans, Cyclopes. Following her separation from Uranus she gave birth to the Giants and Erinyes, and afterward to Typhon. As a goddess, she was the cult of the Earth, and for this reason the Romans would place their newly born on the ground to absorb its life.

Sources

Hammond, Nicholas G.L., and Scullard, Howard H., eds. 1970. *The Oxford classical dictionary.* Oxford: Clarendon Press.

Lovelock, James E. 1979. *Gaia: a new look at life on earth.* Oxford: Oxford University Press.

May, Hal, and Trotsky, Susan M., eds. 1988. *Contemporary authors.* Vol. 123. Detroit: Gale Research.

Tulloch, Sara. 1991. *The Oxford dictionary of new words.* Oxford: Oxford University Press.

GALBRAITHIAN, GALBRAITHIAN THESIS. In the critical and irreverent style of the Harvard economist and political commentator. A modern thesis in political economy which states there is a political constituency of contentment, comprising the rich and the secure, who need little except lower taxes, less state intervention, the chance for quick profits, and support for laissez-faire economics. Consequently, liberal ideology is marginalized. This contentment explains the rise in public squalor and private affluence, and makes hypocrites of the economists of the New Right. The new aspect of the thesis is that now—unlike the situation in Victorian Britain and in early nineteenth-century America—the contented are the majority and therefore electorally powerful (Galbraith, 1992).

John Kenneth Galbraith (b. 1908) was born in Iona Station, Ontario, Canada, and immigrated to the United States in 1931 and was naturalized in 1937. He studied at Ontario Agricultural College, the University of California, Berkeley (Ph.D., 1934), and Cambridge University in England (1937–38). He became a professor at Harvard in 1949 and is now emeritus. He was the U.S. ambassador to India during 1961–63. Among his many books are *The Great Crash, 1929* (1954), *The Affluent Society* (1958), *The New Industrial State* (1967), and his autobiography, *A Life in Our Times* (1980).

Sources

Blaug, Mark. 1985. *Great economists since Keynes.* Brighton, England: Harvester Press.

Blaug, Mark, ed. 1986. *Who's who in economics: a biographical dictionary of major economists, 1700–1986.* 2d ed. Cambridge, Mass.: MIT Press.

Devine, Elizabeth; Held, Michael; Vinson, James; and Walsh, George, eds. 1983. *Thinkers of the twentieth century: a biographical, bibliographical and critical dictionary.* London: Macmillan.

Friedman, Milton. 1977. *From Galbraith to economic freedom.* London: Institute of Economic Affairs.

Galbraith, John K. 1980. *The Galbraith reader: from works of John Kenneth Galbraith.* Harmondsworth: Penguin.

Galbraith, John K. 1992. *The culture of contentment.* London: Sinclair-Stevenson.

McHenry, Robert, ed. 1992. *The new encyclopedia Britannica.* Chicago: Encyclopedia Britannica, Inc.

Metzger, Linda, ed. 1985. *Contemporary authors.* Vol. 14. Detroit: Gale Research.

Riesman, David. 1982. *State and welfare: Tawney, Galbraith and Adam Smith.* London: Macmillan.

Sharpe, Myron E. 1974. *John Kenneth Galbraith and the lower economics.* White Plains, N.Y.: International Arts and Sciences.

GALLUP POLL. A method of establishing public opinion taken by questioning a representative sample of the population; an instrument used to check public opinion on a politician's images and political issues, especially during an election campaign.

George Horace Gallup (1901–84), an American public opinion statistician, was born at Jefferson, Iowa, and educated at the State University and studied psychology and journalism (Ph.D., 1928). His Ph.D. thesis, "A New Technique for Objective Methods for Measuring Reader Interest in Newspapers," had the seed of what would later become the Gallup Poll. He taught journalism at Drake University and at Northwestern University, and in 1935 he founded the American Institute of Public Opinion and was director of the Audience Research Institute (1939–84) in Princeton, New Jersey. In 1936 the results of the U.S. presidential election brought attention to his poll because he accurately predicted the election outcome as well as the error in the outcome of other estimates that had been based on telephone interviews. He published his *Guide to Public Opinion Polls* (1944). In 1948 the Gallup Poll falsely predicted that Governor Thomas E. Dewey would beat Harry S Truman in the U.S. presidential election. Most democracies now use the Gallup Poll or a variation of it; it has become an essential part of the political process and has been used as a marketing tool for many years. He became chief executive and chairman of the board of Gallup Organization Inc. at Princeton (1958–84), was president of the International Association of Public Opinion Institutes (1947–84), and president of the National Municipal League (1953–56). He died in Switzerland.

Sources

Gallup, George H. 1972. *The sophisticated poll watcher's guide.* Princeton, N.J.: Princeton Opinion Press.

McHenry, Robert, ed. 1992. *The new encyclopedia Britannica.* Chicago: Encyclopedia Britannica, Inc.

Metzger, Linda, ed. 1984. *Contemporary authors.* Vol. 13. Detroit: Gale Research.

Roth, Anna, ed. 1952. *Current biography yearbook.* New York: H. W. Wilson.

Who's who in America, 1986–87. Chicago: Marquis.

GALTON'S PROBLEM. A problem in anthropology concerning sets of associated traits and relating to cross-cultural comparisons. Francis Galton required that traits selected for comparison be both equivalent and independently selected. The problem was that Sir Edwin Burnett Tylor (1832–1917) had not shown how units of population were identified and differentiated and how different traits were to be distinguished from those independently arrived at when he was making his comparisons.

Sir Francis Galton (1822–1911) was born in Birmingham, England, and after being educated at several small schools he studied locally at King Edward's School (1836–38). He was apprenticed to doctors in the city, and entered medical school, King's College, London in 1939. After one year's travel abroad, he returned to study at Trinity College, Cambridge, and completed his medical studies in 1844. His father's death that year gave him enough money to travel as an explorer in Southwest Africa. His interests turned to meteorology, and he made one of the first attempts at weather maps, discovering the weather pattern known now as anticyclones. He later led in the application of statistics to genetics, founded the study of eugenics, and endowed a chair of eugenics at London University; he also devised a way to compare fingerprints. Among psychologists, he is noted for his work on uniting the study of individual differences with the theory of evolution and the development of techniques of psychological measurement, especially correlation. Galton wrote an autobiography, *Memories of My Life* (1908), and in 1909 he was knighted.

Sources

Cowan, Ruth S. 1985. *Sir Francis Galton and the study of heredity in the nineteenth century.* New York: Garland Publishing.

Forrest, Derek W. 1974. *Francis Galton: the life and work of a Victorian genius.* London: Elek.

Gillespie, Charles C., ed. 1973. *Dictionary of scientific biography.* New York: Charles Scribner's Sons.

Grovitz, Herbert. 1970. *Galton's walk: methods for the analysis of thinking, intelligence and creativity.* New York: Harper and Row.

Lee, Sidney, ed. 1920. *Dictionary of national biography: supplement 1901–1911.* London: Oxford University Press.

Pearson, Karl. 1914–30. *The life, letters and labors of Francis Galton.* 3 vols. Cambridge: Cambridge University Press.

Sills, David L., ed. 1968. *International encyclopedia of the social sciences.* New York: Macmillan and Free Press.

Zusne, Leonard. 1984. *Biographical dictionary of psychology.* Westport, Conn.: Greenwood Press.

Zusne, Leonard. 1987. *Eponyms in psychology: a dictionary and sourcebook.* Westport, Conn.: Greenwood Press.

GANDHIAN, GANDHIANISM. Relating to the twentieth-century Indian leader who sought independence for India from the British and used nonviolent political means to achieve reforms. His beliefs melded Western ideas from Leo Tolstoy (1828–1910), John Ruskin (1819–1900), and Henry David Thoreau (1817–62) with Jainism and Vaishnavas from India. These influences were the elements of his religious and political life, a variety of neo-Hinduism, that espoused religious tolerance, condemned conversion, and maintained high-caste values by emphasizing nonviolence, vegetarianism, and celibacy.

Mohandas Karamchand Gandhi (1869–1948) was an Indian leader, born and raised in Porbandar, Kathiawar, where his father was Dewan (prime minister). At age 19 he studied law at University College, London, was admitted to the bar in 1889, and established a legal practice in Bombay. Foregoing an income of £5,000 a year, he left the practice to live on £1 a week in South Africa. Early he was influenced by the Hindu religion, Vaishnavas, and its special worship of its syncretic deity; and by Jainism, a religion close to Buddhism, which purports to deliver one's spirit from the restrictions of the flesh by following knowledge, faith, and virtue. In South Africa Gandhi spent twenty-one years opposing discriminatory legislation against Indians. He returned to India in 1914, and while giving support to the British in World War I, his interest in the Home Rule Movement grew. From 1922 to 1924 he was in jail for conspiracy, and in 1930 he led a 200-mile march to the sea to collect salt in defiance of the government monopoly. He was re-arrested and when released in 1931 attended the London Round Table Conferences on Indian constitutional reform. On his return to India he became known for his fasting as part of a nonviolent political campaign. He was jailed in 1942–44, but in 1946 he negotiated with the British Cabinet Mission, which recommended the new constitutional structure and independence for India (1947). Gandhi was assassinated in Delhi by a Hindu fanatic.

Sources

Erickson, Erik H. 1970. *Gandhi's truth.* London: Faber and Faber.

Kripalani, Krishna. 1968. *Gandhi: a life.* New Delhi: Orient Longmans.

McHenry, Robert, ed. 1992. *The new encyclopedia Britannica.* Chicago: Encyclopedia Britannica, Inc.

Magnussen, Magnus; Goring, Rosemary; and Thorn, John O., eds. 1990. *Chambers biographical dictionary.* Edinburgh: Chambers Ltd.

Ramashray, Roy. 1984. *Gandhi: soundings in political philosophy.* Delhi: Chanakya
    Publications.
Rawding, F. N. 1980. *Gandhi.* Cambridge: Cambridge University Press.
Shirer, William L. 1979. *Gandhi: memoir.* New York: Simon and Schuster.
Woodcock, George. 1972. *Gandhi.* London: Fontana Collins.

GANTT CHART, GANTT TASK AND BONUS PLAN. A graphic aid to
planning and controlling work operations and projects based on the time taken
to complete them. A payment scheme that allowed for workers who were less
than standard in their efficiency to be paid according to a time-rate system, and
those who were at or above the standard to be paid according to a piece-rate
system.

Henry Laurence Gantt (1861–1919) was born into a family ravaged by the
American Civil War. At an early age he acquired the habit of self-discipline.
After graduating in science from Johns Hopkins University (1880), he taught
mechanics and natural science, studied at the Stevens Institute of Technology,
graduated as a mechanical engineer, and joined the Midvale Steel Company in
1887. With Frederick W. Taylor (1856–1915), he worked for a scientific approach to management. After 1901 Gantt became a consulting engineer, wrote
three major books and many papers, lectured at major universities, and was one
of the United States' first highly successful management consultants. He gave
up his work to help the U.S. military in 1917 after poor management practices
had left government agencies with inadequate control of information to coordinate the activities of contractors working for the war effort. To solve the
problem, Gantt produced a bar chart—the Gantt Chart—which showed how
work was scheduled in the course of its completion, identified where projects
were behind schedule, and indicated where corrective action should be taken to
ensure a secure flow to operations.

Sources

Alford, L. P. 1934. *Henry L. Gantt: leader in industry [with bibliography].* New York:
    Harper and Row.
Clark, Wallace. 1924. *The Gantt Chart: a working tool of management.* New York:
    Ronald Press.
Gantt, Henry L. 1916. *Work, wages and profits.* 2d ed. New York: Engineering Magazine
    Co.
Gantt, Henry L. 1919. *Organizing for work.* New York: Harcourt Brace Jovanovich.
Johnson, Allen, and Malone, Dumas, eds. 1931. *Dictionary of American biography.* Vol.
    IV. New York: Charles Scribner's Sons.
Marsh, Arthur. 1979. *Concise encyclopedia of industrial relations.* Westmead, Farnbor-
    ough, Hants: Gower.
Wren, Daniel A. 1987. *The evolution of management thought.* 3d ed. New York: John
    Wiley.

GARBOMANIA. The frenzy aroused during the purchase at public auction in
1990 of Greta Garbo's memorabilia.

Greta Garbo (1905–90) was born in Stockholm, and became a barber's assistant and then a shop girl. In 1921–22 she appeared in two short advertising films, and was noticed in the street and cast as a bathing belle in a comedy short, "Luffar-Peter" (1922). In 1924 she won a scholarship to the Royal Dramatic Theater Drama School in Stockholm, and a year later she assumed the name of "Garbo" to make her first feature film, *Gösta Berlings Saga.* Later she went to Hollywood to work for Metro-Goldwyn-Mayer where she made twenty-four films before retiring in 1941. Frequently rumored to be making a comeback, she never made another film and never married. She became a U.S. citizen in 1951. After her retirement, she lived mostly in New York City, often traveling under an assumed name and refusing interviews or any publicity. She was famous for her line, "I want to be alone" in the film, *Grand Hotel* (1932). On November 16, 1990, six months after her death, hundreds gathered at Sotheby's for the auction of her possessions. They bid in a frenzy to buy a chair that gave them the right to sit where Garbo once sat. Prices were outrageous; items like a pair of flowered candle sticks sold at thirty to forty times their estimated value. In June 1993, among the seventy letters auctioned in London for £26,000 was clear evidence that Garbo hated being alone.

Sources

Cawkwell, Tim, and Smith, John M. 1972. *The world encyclopedia of film.* London: Studio Vista.

Gronowicz, Antonio. 1991. *Garbo: her story.* London: Penguin.

Van Doren, Charles, ed. 1974. *Webster's American biographies.* Springfield, Mass.: G. and C. Merriam.

Walker, Alexander. 1990. *Garbo: a portrait.* London: Weidenfeld and Nicolson.

GARFIELD'S LAW OF CONCENTRATION, GARFIELD CONSTANT.
The law of concentration states that a small group of multidisciplinary and high-impact specialty journals account for a large percentage of references and publications in all fields of science. The constant refers to the average number of citations per cited paper in the annual *Science Citation Index.*

Eugene Garfield (b. 1925) was born in New York, served in the U.S. Army during World War II, and studied at Columbia University and the University of Pennsylvania (Ph.D., 1961) After working as a research chemist (1949–51), he joined the Welch Library machine indexing project (1951–53) at Johns Hopkins University, and in 1954 established himself as an information consultant with his own firm, Eugene Garfield Associates, in Philadelphia. The firm's name was changed to the Institute for Scientific Information in 1960. Garfield is an adjunct professor at the University of Pennsylvania and serves on the council of Rockefeller University. He writes "Current Comments" in *Current Contents,* which he founded in 1957, the *Index of Chemicus* (1960), and *Science Citation Index* (1961), and publishes *Social Sciences Citation Index, Arts and Humanities Citation Index,* and similar indices in neuroscience, biotechnology, biomedical engineering, and materials science. For innovations in information sciences, he has been honored by the American Chemical Society (1977; 1983) and the American Society for Information Science (1975), and his *Essays of an Information Scientist* received the latter society's book of the year award in 1977. The *Essays* have been collected in several volumes beginning in 1971. In addition, he published *Citation Indexing: Its Theory and Application to Science, Technology and the Humanities* (1979). He also publishes the newspaper, *The Scientist* (1986).

Sources

Garfield, Eugene. 1977. Is the ratio between number of citations and publications cited a true constant? *Essays of an information scientist.* Vol 2. Philadelphia: ISI Press, pp. 419–421.

Garfield, Eugene. 1977. The mystery of the transposed journal lists—wherein Bradford's law of scattering is generalized according to Garfield's law of concentration. *Essays of an information scientist.* Vol 1. Philadelphia: ISI Press, pp. 222–223.

Garfield, Eugene. 1981. Bradford's law and related statistical patterns. *Essays of an information scientist.* Vol 4. Philadelphia: ISI Press, pp. 476–483.

May, Hal, ed. 1985. *Contemporary authors.* Vol. 114. Detroit: Gale Research.

Personal Communication.

GARGANTUAN MONUMENTALIS. A pathological compulsion—based on an obsessive concern with buildings—to construct great tombs or memorial statues, for example, architectural trends of the ancient Egyptian rulers and Southern Californians (Peter and Hull, 1969).

King Gargantua was the main figure in François Rabelais' (c. 1490–1553) *Gargantua* (c. 1534). Once a figure in French folklore, Gargantua is noted for his eleven-month gestation, which meant that as a babe he needed milk from over 18,000 cows. For his hair he used a 900-foot comb, once devoured a salad of five or six pilgrims, and lived for centuries. Another of his exploits was to have stolen the bells of Notre Dame Cathedral to hang about his mare's neck.

Sources

Benét, William R. 1990. *The reader's encyclopedia of world literature and arts, with supplement.* New York: Thomas Y. Crowell.

Brewer, Ebenezer Cobham. 1970. *Brewer's dictionary of phrase and fable.* Centenary ed. Rev. by Ivor H. Evans. New York: Harper and Row.

McHenry, Robert, ed. 1992. *The new encyclopedia Britannica.* Chicago: Encyclopedia Britannica, Inc.

Mercatante, Anthony S. 1988. *Encyclopedia of world mythology and legend.* New York: Facts on File.

Peter, Laurence J., and Hull, Raymond. 1969. *The Peter principle: why things always go wrong.* New York: William Morrow.

GARIBALDINI. A democratic Italian political party at the turn of the twentieth century that aimed to realize the ideal of a united Italy.

Giuseppe Garibaldi (1807–82) was born in Nice into a maritime family; he went to sea at age 15 and by 1832 was a ship's master. However, his political activities led to exile from Italy in 1834. He was in Uruguay during 1836–48, and then served the Roman Republic, which was quickly abolished in 1849, and was exiled to the United States in 1850 where he was naturalized. In 1854 he returned to Italy and settled as a farmer on the island of Caprera. In 1859, during the war of Sardinia and France against Austria, Garibaldi commanded his ''Hunters of the Alps,'' an independent army that served Sardinia. To effect the unification of Italy, the Sardinian government secretly supported Garibaldi in an expedition to Sicily, with a thousand volunteers. He became the dictator of Sicily, and crossed to mainland Italy and expelled Francis II from Naples in 1860. On the proclamation of the Two Sicilys and Sardinia, and Victor Emmanuel of Sardinia as Italy's king, Garibaldi retired to the island of Caprera. But in 1862, in an effort to unite Italy, he organized an expedition to Rome and was defeated. In 1870 he fought against Prussia for the French, and on his return to Italy he was elected to the Parliament (1874). After two years he retired to live out his life on Caprera.

Sources

Hibbert, Christopher. 1965. *Garibaldi and his enemies.* London: Longmans.

Jones, Barry, ed. 1989. *The Macmillan dictionary of biography.* Melbourne: Macmillan.

McHenry, Robert, ed. 1992. *The new encyclopedia Britannica.* Chicago: Encyclopedia Britannica, Inc.

Mack Smith, Denis. 1952. *Garibaldi.* London: Hutchinson.

Ridley, Jasper. 1974. *Garibaldi.* London: Constable.

Smith, Benjamin. 1903. *The Century cyclopedia of names.* London: The Times.

GAULLISM, GAULLIST. A political ideology that promotes the national interest of France, seeks to place that interest over party-political and local economic interests, aims to unite the French people to achieve France's common good, and works to establish a technocratic government, one that is efficient, modern, economically sound, and politically stable. A follower of the president of the Fifth Republic of France (1958–69).

Charles André Joseph Marie de Gaulle (1890–1970) was born at Lille, France. During World War I he emerged as a supporter of the air and armor combination that would become the basis of Germany's blitzkrieg in the early 1940s. At the fall of France to Germany in June 1940, de Gaulle went to England to rule the Free French. He entered France in August 1944 leading one of the earliest liberation forces and became head of the Provisional Government (1945–46). He later withdrew from the center of French politics until after the Algerian war for independence when he reintroduced a stable government based on a policy that gave France respect in the European Community. In May 1958 he was called to head a temporary administration, and a later referendum gave him more power as prime minister than any Frenchman had had for years. After he gave up his party leadership, he was elected the first president of the Fifth Republic in December 1958. He remained in this post until April 1969 when he resigned after his proposals for reforms, especially in the Senate, were beaten in a referendum. Followers of de Gaulle may still be found in the right wing of French politics where great support is given to independence in France's foreign policies and national interests.

Sources
Crawley, Aidan. 1969. *De Gaulle: a biography.* London: Collins.
Crozier, Brian. 1973. *De Gaulle.* London: Eyre Methuen.
Lacouture, Jean. 1990–91. *De Gaulle, the ruler (1945–70).* 3 vols. London: Collins Harvill.
Ledwidge, Bernard. 1982. *De Gaulle.* London: Weidenfeld and Nicolson.
McHenry, Robert, ed. 1992. *The new encyclopedia Britannica.* Chicago: Encyclopedia Britannica, Inc.
Magnussen, Magnus; Goring, Rosemary; and Thorn, John O., eds. 1990. *Chambers biographical dictionary.* Edinburgh: Chambers Ltd.
Plano, Jack. 1988. *The international relations dictionary.* 4th ed. Santa Barbara, Calif.: ABC-CLIO.
Riff, Michael A. 1987. *Dictionary of modern political ideology.* Manchester: Manchester University Press.
White, Sam. 1984. *De Gaulle.* London: Harrap.

GEARY ACT. In response to unemployment and labor unrest—caused, it was thought, mainly by the immigration of Chinese—the U.S. Congress extended the Chinese Exclusion Act of 1882 and the Scott Act of 1880 requiring that Chinese show proof of the right to be in the United States. Violators would receive one year's hard labor followed by deportation. In 1893 a further act modified the exclusion law by broadening the scope of the term *laborer,* and in 1894 another act extended the prohibition of Chinese laborer immigration for ten years and precisely defined the classes of admissible Chinese. By 1902 the U.S. immigration policy was determined by "nativism," and ethnic affiliation alone was sufficient to prevent migrants from entering the country.

Thomas J. Geary (1854–1929) was born in Boston and moved to San Francisco with his parents where he attended public schools, studied law at Saint Ignatius College, and was admitted to the bar in 1877. He was elected a candidate of the Democratic and American parties to the Fifty-first Congress to fill the vacancy caused by the resignation of John De Haven. He was reelected to the Fifty-second and Fifty-third congresses, and was an unsuccessful candidate for reelection in 1894, whereafter he resumed his legal practice.

Sources
Commager, Henry S., ed. 1968. *Documents of American history.* 8th ed. New York: Appleton-Century-Crofts.
Greene, Jack P., ed. 1984. *Encyclopedia of American political history.* New York: Charles Scribner's Sons.
Jacob, Kathryn A., and Ragsdale, Bruce A. 1989. *Biographical directory of the United States Congress: 1774–1989.* Bicentennial ed. Washington, D.C.: U.S. Government Printing Office.

GEDDES AXE. The name applied in Britain to the recommendations of a committee of business leaders appointed in 1921 under Sir Eric Geddes, which recommended economies yielding £75 million; £18 million of this sum was to come from education. The Geddes Axe had a profound and lasting effect on education in Britain between 1922 and 1940.

Sir Eric Campbell Geddes (1875–1937), businessman, administrator, and politician, was born in Agra, India, the eldest son of a civil engineer, and educated at Merchiston Castle School, Edinburgh, and the Edinburgh Academy and Oxford Military College, Cowley. In 1906 he joined the North Eastern Railway Company and by 1914 was its deputy general manager. In 1915–16 he became deputy director of munitions, director-general of military railways (War Office), and director-general of transportation to commander-in-chief (France) and inspector-general of transportation for all theaters of war. He was knighted in 1916. In 1916–17 he was made an honorary major general, an honorary vice admiral, and controller of the navy and first lord of the Admiralty (1917–18). Between 1917 and 1922, as a Conservative M.P., he was a member of the War Cabinet in charge of mobilization. He is best remembered as chairman of the Committee on National Expenditure (1921–22), the Geddes Axe Committee. He was chairman of Dunlop Rubber Company and Imperial Airways.

Sources

Blishen, Edward. 1969. *Blond's encyclopaedia of education.* London: Blond Educational.
Clegg, Hugh Armstrong. 1985. *A history of British trade unions since 1889.* Vol. II 1911–1933. Oxford: Clarendon Press.
Legg, L.G. Wickham. 1949. *The dictionary of national biography 1931–1940.* London: Oxford University Press.

GEDDES REPORT. The report of the Shipbuilding Inquiry Committee (1965–66) which recommended appropriate action for employers, trade unions, and government to ensure Britain's shipbuilding was internationally competitive. It suggested using productivity bargaining and joint consultation. In 1971 it was found that the recommendations were not being fully implemented, and it proposed a review of company industrial relations, demarcation rules, the use of further consultation, and company joint councils.

Anthony Reay Mackay Geddes (b. 1912) was educated at Rugby and Cambridge and worked at the Bank of England (1932–35) and at Dunlop Rubber Company from 1935, becoming a director in 1947 and its chairman in 1968–70. During World War II he served in the Royal Air Force. He was deputy chairman of the Midland Bank (1978–84) and became one of its directors (1967–84), and he was also a director of the Shell Transport and Trading Company (1968–82), the Rank Organization (1975–84), and several management associations. In 1965–66 he chaired the Shipbuilding Inquiry Committee. He was appointed governor of the National Institute of Economics and Social Research and the London Graduate School of Business Studies. For his services to the industrial community, he was knighted in 1968 and later received honorary degrees from Aston, Leicester, and Loughborough tertiary education institutions.

Sources

Marsh, Arthur. 1979. *Concise encyclopedia of industrial relations.* Westmead, Farnborough, Hants: Gower.

Who's who, 1971. London: Adam and Charles Black.

Who's who, 1993. London: Adam and Charles Black.

GERONIMO. An exclamation of encouragement in a moment of duress, a battle cry.

Goyathlay (1829–1909)—"one who yawns"—was the original name of Geronimo, an American Chiricahua Apache leader and prophet; he was named Geronimo by the Mexicans after Saint Gerome, who was noted for his austerity and purity. As a youth he fought in many raids, and although he was not Chiricahua, he became their leader. The tribe was moved in 1876, and more raids followed. An enemy to the Mexicans, Geronimo would persistently make nightly terrorist raids and like a shadow disappear into the dark. For this reason his name became a synonym in Spanish for "shadow," and the phrase, "without a Geronimo of a doubt," arose. He led one last bloody campaign against the whites in 1885–86 and was finally captured by General Crook. He escaped and was recaptured for the last time, and put in prison at Fort Sill, Oklahoma. Eventually, Geronimo became a prosperous farmer, raised cattle, joined the Dutch Reformed Church (1903), and was a noted figure at the Saint Louis World's Fair in 1904. In 1905 he attended Theodore Roosevelt's presidential inauguration. He dictated his autobiography to a white writer (1906). "Geronimo" is the battle cry of the U.S. paratroopers, and was screamed out as they leaped from their planes. It was first adopted by the 82nd Airborne, which took it up at Fort Bragg, North Carolina. Some claim that the inspiration for the cry came from a movie that featured Geronimo and was shown at the training base. Another source suggests that the term arose at Fort Sill, Oklahoma, where at Medicine Bluffs, Geronimo is said to have bravely leaped on horseback over a steep cliff down to a river as he escaped the U.S. Cavalry.

Sources

Barrett Stephen M., ed. 1906. *Geronimo: Apache chief 1829–1909.* New York: Duffield.

Davis, Britton. 1929. *The truth about Geronimo.* Edited with an introduction by Milo M. Quaife. New Haven, Conn.: Yale University Press.

Hendrickson, Robert. 1988. *The dictionary of eponyms: names that became words.* New York: Dorset.

Johnson, Allen, and Malone, Dumas eds. 1931. *Dictionary of American biography.* Vol. IV. New York: Charles Scribner's Sons.

GERRYMANDER. To establish electoral districts so that one political party is given an electoral majority in a large number of the districts, while concentrating the voting strength of the opposition in as few districts as possible; a general term for political chicanery and deception.

Elbridge Gerry (1744–1814) was born in Marblehead, Massachusetts, studied at Harvard (1758–62), and went into his father's business. In 1771 and 1773 he was elected to the General Court and thereafter was active in business and politics. He became a notable American statesman who was a prominent patriot in Massachusetts before and during the American Revolution. He signed the Declaration of Independence in 1776 and was among the delegates to the Federal Constitutional Convention in 1789, but he refused to sign the Constitution because of republican principles; that is, taxation was anathema to him. Once it was ratified he supported it and represented his state in Congress. He was elected governor of Massachusetts in 1810 and 1811, but was defeated in 1812; in 1813–14 he was the vice-president of the United States. During his second term as governor, he rearranged the electoral boundaries of Essex County in Massachusetts to benefit his own party; this political practice was neither illegal nor new at the time. A copy of the map was on the wall in the editor's office of the local paper, the *Centinel*. A visitor noticed that the newly drawn district of the state looked like a lizard, and with a crayon added some wings and claws, saying ''That will do for a salamander.'' Overhearing the comment, the *Centinel's* editor said he thought it were best called a ''gerrymander.''

Sources

Funk, Wilfred J. 1950. *Word origins and their romantic stories.* New York: Grossett and Dunlap.

Hendrickson, Robert. 1988. *The dictionary of eponyms: names that became words.* New York: Dorset.

Johnson, Allen, and Malone, Dumas, eds. 1931. *Dictionary of American biography.* Vol. IV. New York: Charles Scribner's Sons.

Smith, Edward C., and Zurcher, Arnold J. 1968. *A dictionary of American politics.* 2d ed. New York: Barnes and Noble.

GIBRAT'S LAW. An economist's law that describes how a process of random growth produces a log-normal distribution of firm sizes. The law assumes that the number of firms is fixed and that the distribution of growth rates for each firm is the same and independent of the firm's growth history and absolute size. So all firms will have the same average proportionate growth rate. This will produce a log-normal distribution of firms whose relative dispersion increases over time. The parameters of such a distribution indicate market concentration because most markets have a few large firms and many little ones.

Robert Pierre Louis Gibrat (1904–80) was born in Lorient, France, studied at Saint Louis, Paris, and in 1922 entered a course in mining engineering. He taught at the School of Mines during 1936–68, became a noted scientist and administrator, and presided over various French scientific societies of civil engineers, statisticians, electricians, and meteorologists in the late 1960s. With a science degree and a doctorate in law from the University of Paris, he was a consultant to industry during the German occupation of France and was in the Ministry of Public Works. Under the Laval government, he served as secretary of state until he resigned when the Allied armies landed in North Africa. After World War II, he was a consulting engineer for French Electric on tidal energy

(1945–68) and director general of atomic energy (1955–74); he also served Central Thermique (1942–80). He wrote reports for the Academy of Sciences, published over 100 professional papers, books on economics and tidal energy, and was made a knight of the Legion of Honor.

Sources

Eatwell, John; Milgate, Murray; and Newman, Peter. 1987. *The new Palgrave: a dictionary of economics.* London: Macmillan.

Gibrat, Robert P.L. 1931. *Les inéqualities économiques.* Paris: Recueil Sirey.

Pearce, David W., ed. 1986. *Macmillan dictionary of modern economics.* New York: Macmillan.

GIDEONS (INTERNATIONAL), GIDEON SOCIETY, GIDEON BIBLE. A Bible distributed by the Christian group, Gideons or the Gideon Society (originally the Christian Commercial Young Men's Association of America), founded by John Nicolson and Samuel Hill, salesmen, in Boscobel, Wisconsin, in 1898. In 1899 with W. J. Knights they organized an association in Janesville, Wisconsin, and later based in Chicago. They named the groups after the Old Testament judge of Israel, and, aiming to have people believe in Christ, they made the Bible freely available by placing a copy in every Pullman car and hotel and motel room in America at no cost. They also distributed the Bible to schools, nurses, prisoners, and soldiers.

Gideon or Gedeon was an Old Testament judge of Israel. He led 300 clansmen of Manesseh in slaying the oppressive Midianites. One legend states that he was influenced by his enemy's cult, and by making an idol led the Israelites to immoral ways. Another tale suggests that he converted the idol to the worship of the God of Israel, and in turn God inspired him to conquer the Midianites. In consequence, Israel developed a monarchy under Abimelech, Gideon's son (Judges 6: 11 and 7: 25).

Sources

Douglas, James D., ed. 1974. *The new international dictionary of the Christian Church.* Exeter: Paternoster Press.

McHenry, Robert, ed. 1992. *The new encyclopedia Britannica.* Chicago: Encyclopedia Britannica, Inc.

GIFFEN GOOD, GIFFEN PARADOX. An economic term that refers to a "good" whose demand tends to fall as its price falls or to rise as its price rises. The paradox, which contradicts the law of demand, was noted in the instance of foodstuffs.

Sir Robert Giffen (1837–1910) was born in Lanarckshire. At age 13 he was apprenticed to a solicitor until 1860 when he turned to journalism and made a reputation in economic circles. He helped published the *Economist* (1868) and was assistant editor before becoming a civil servant. As chief of the Statistical Department of the Board of Trade in 1876 and later, in 1882, its assistant secretary, he served on a number of royal commissions. He edited the *Journal of the Royal Statistical Society* (1876–91); was the society's president (1882–84); and helped found the Royal Economic Society. Alfred Marshall (1842–1924), noted British economist, identified the "Giffen good" when he associated Giffen's name with the observation that the poor bought more bread as its price rose in his *Principles of Economics* (1895:208). Whether or not Giffen himself mentioned the term is not securely known, and the evidence for the paradox is not satisfactory (Stigler, 1947).

Sources

Eatwell, John; Milgate, Murray; and Newman, Peter. 1987. *The new Palgrave: a dictionary of economics.* London: Macmillan.

Rutherford, Donald. 1992. *Dictionary of economics.* London: Routledge.

Stigler, George J. 1947. Notes on the history of Giffen paradox. *Journal of Political Economy* 55:152–156.

GILBERTINES. A Roman Catholic order founded in England in the twelfth century.

Saint Gilbert (c. 1083–1189) was rejected as a youth at home and so turned to learning; after studies in Paris he became a teacher. He worked as a clerk in the house of the bishop of Lincoln and was able to give his private income to the poor. He was ordained in 1123, became a parson at Sempringham, and founded a home for girls, following the ideas of Saint Benedict of Nursia. Later, young men were aligned with the convent to do the heavy labor; lay sisters were associated with the religious work; and finally, clerics and priests joined the organization, which developed its four characteristic spheres of operation. Other similarly organized establishments were founded, and in 1148 Pope Eugenius approved the order. Gilbert was highly esteemed by Henry II and Queen Eleanor who protected him against false and scandalous charges of once trusted servants and officials. He retired from his abbacy long before his death, may have lived to be 100, and was canonized by Pope Innocent III in 1202. Except for one house in Scotland, the order thrived only in England. Henry VIII suppressed it in 1538–40.

Sources

Graham, Rose. 1901. *Saint Gifford and Sempringham and the Gilbertines: a history of the only English monastic order.* London: E. Stock.

McHenry, Robert, ed. 1992. *The new encyclopedia Britannica.* Chicago: Encyclopedia Britannica, Inc.

Stephen, Leslie, and Lee, Sydney, eds. 1917. *The dictionary of national biography.* London: Oxford University Press.

GINI COEFFICIENT. An economist's measure that can show how close a distribution of income is to either absolute inequality or equality. The coefficient could be used to estimate how much change in taxes would affect the distribution of income. If the tax lowered the coefficient, then it would be a progressive tax because the distribution would tend to absolute equality.

Corrado Gini (1884–1965) was born in Motta di Livenza, Italy, and studied at the University of Bologna in 1908. He taught and researched at the universities of Cagliari (1909), Padova (1913), and Rome (1925). His field of interest included sociology, economics, demography, and statistics. In 1909 and 1924 he devised and refined a neo-organicist theory of society that anticipated the essential features of the general systems theory of the 1950s. He also devised a means of evaluating the wealth of nations, wealth distribution, and inequalities. To statistics and economics he contributed the Gini identity (1921), the Gini mean difference (1912), founded scientific journals, and wrote 700 articles and many books. At the University of Rome he established the Institute and Faculty of Statistics, Demography, and Actuarial Sciences in 1926.

Sources

Eatwell, John; Milgate, Murray; and Newman, Peter. 1987. *The new Palgrave: a dictionary of economics.* London: Macmillan.

Greenwald, Douglas. 1973. *The McGraw-Hill dictionary of modern economics.* 2d ed. New York: McGraw-Hill.

Rutherford, Donald. 1992. *Dictionary of economics.* London: Routledge.

Sills, David L., ed. 1968. *International encyclopedia of the social sciences.* New York: Macmillan and Free Press.

GLASSITES. A small religious sect in Scotland in the early eighteenth century.

John Glas or Glass (1695–1773) was born at Auchtermuchty in Fife, Scotland, and educated at the parish school, Kinclaven, and Saint Leonard's College, Saint Andrews, in Edinburgh. He served as minister of Tealing, near Dundee, from 1719. He became so popular a preacher that by 1725 he had formed a society with a hundred followers. He spoke out against the national covenants and the interference of civil authority in religious affairs. On publishing *The Testimony of the King of Martyrs Concerning His Kingdom* (1727), he was immediately suspended from his ministerial work. The General Assembly of the Church of Scotland deposed him in 1730 because of his views on the kingdom of Christ. He had said that all national establishments of religion were unlawful and inconsistent with the spirit of Christianity, and he advanced a system of church government that was essentially Independent or Congregational. After his deposition, a few small churches formed according to his principles in Scotland, England, and America but did not attract a large following. In this he had support from his son-in-law Robert Sandeman (1718–71). A man of great erudition, Glas had his works published in four volumes in 1761 and again in 1872 in five. His ideas survived until the late nineteenth century, but the church doctrine was so rigid that many members left to join other Baptist congregations in Scotland.

Sources

Cross, Frank L. 1974. *The Oxford dictionary of the Christian Church.* 2d ed. New York: Oxford University Press.

McHenry, Robert, ed. 1992. *The new encyclopedia Britannica.* Chicago: Encyclopedia Britannica, Inc.

Stephen, Leslie, and Lee, Sydney, eds. 1917. *The dictionary of national biography.* London: Oxford University Press.

GLEIG'S SCHOOL SERIES. A forty-two volume educational source used to develop routines of study.

George Robert Gleig (1796–1888), a pioneer of army education, was born in Stirling, son of the bishop of Brechin, and educated at Stirling Grammar School and Glasgow University. He served in the army during the Peninsula War (1813), was at Waterloo, and fought in the United States. He was wounded six times in action. He studied at Oxford University, was ordained, and became curate at Kent (1820) and Ash (1821), and rector of Ivy Church (1822), he was made chaplain of the Royal Hospital, Chelsea in 1834 and was chaplain-general to the forces during 1844–75. He served as inspector-general of military schools during 1846–57. Gleig was responsible for the establishment of a Corps of Army Schoolmasters and Inspectors, improvements in school accommodation, and an attempt at grading soldiers by means of intelligence tests. From 1850 he edited for Longmans, a cheap, useful educational library of forty-two volumes that became known as *Gleig's School Series.* He wrote many novels and biographies, *Campaigns of the British Army at Washington and New Orleans* (1820), contributed to *Fraser's Magazine* from 1830, and wrote many histories, all in an effort to support his large family.
Sources
Aldrich, Richard, and Gordon, Peter. 1987. *Dictionary of British educationists.* London: Woburn Press.
Stephen, Leslie, and Lee, Sydney, eds. 1917. *The dictionary of national biography.* London: Oxford University Press.

GLENEAGLES AGREEMENT. An agreement among Commonwealth nations in 1977 to invoke sanctions against South Africa's policy of apartheid.

In London at the Twenty-first Commonwealth Heads of Government Conference on June 8–15, 1977, twenty-six of the thirty-five full members of the Commonwealth were represented. Discussion centered on a threatened boycott of the 1978 Commonwealth Games by African member countries; they had boycotted the 1976 Olympic Games in protest against New Zealand's sporting links with South Africa. The issue was settled amicably on June 11–12 when heads of government visited the Gleneagles Hotel in Scotland for a weekend of informal discussions. A statement on apartheid in sport emerging from discussions between the Canadian prime minister, Mr. Pierre Trudeau, the Nigerian chief of staff, Brigadier Sheu Yar'Adua, Mr. Aboud Jumbue from Tanzania, Mr. Michael Manley from Jamaica, and the New Zealand Prime Minister, Mr. Robert Muldoon, was issued by the heads of government on June 15. The unusual practice of conducting such informal discussions was established at the 1973 Ottowa conference and used again at the 1975 conference in Jamaica.

In Perthshire, Scotland, Gleneagles is a narrow, picturesque glen that runs southward through the Orchil Hills from Stratheran and is much enhanced by the matching outline of its flanking hills. The name is reputedly derived from the Gaelic "Glen Eaglais," meaning "Glen of the church." About two miles northwest of the glen is the Gleneagles Hotel, a spacious railway hotel with renowned golf courses.

Source

Keesings contemporary archives: record of world events. 1977: 28628, 28288, 28503, 28401. London: Keesings Publications.

GLICK EFFECT. The observation that marital instability is greater among high school and college dropouts than among school graduates. It is based on the positive correlation between dropping out of school and marital instability, and it is sometimes known as the "marriage dropout" phenomenon.

Paul Charles Glick (b. 1910) studied at De Pauw University and at the University of Wisconsin (Ph.D., 1938). After teaching sociology and psychology at university, he became a family research analyst and senior demographer in the Bureau of Census, Department of Commerce, in Washington (1939–81). In 1957 he published *American Families,* which stated that "a higher proportion of persons with two or more marriages [is found] among those who dropped out of college before graduation, as compared with college graduates" (p. 147.) The finding was called the Glick effect by Jessie Bernard (1966) and Karl Bauman (1967) and was often reported in sociological studies on relations between education, marriage, and divorce. Glick published *Marriage and Divorce* (1970) and a two-volume work, *The Population of the United States* (1974). Among his many honors are both Silver (1953) and Gold (1970) medals from his department for authorship. He was made a fellow of the American Statistical Association, and a member and president of several professional associations concerned with family, demographic, and sociological research. He joined the Department of Sociology, Arizona State University, in 1982, and continued to publish research on marriage, divorce, and the family life cycle.

Sources

Bernard, Jessie. 1966. Marital stability and patterns of status variables. *Journal of Marriage and the Family* 28:421–439.

Bauman, Karl. 1967. The relationship between age at first marriage, school drop out and marital instability: an analysis of the Glick effect. *Journal of Marriage and the Family* 29:672–680.

Campbell, Robert J., ed. 1989. *Psychiatric dictionary.* 6th ed. New York and Oxford: Oxford University Press.

Glick, Paul C. 1957. *American families.* New York: John Wiley.

Who's who in America, 1982–83. Chicago: Marquis.

Personal Communication.

GOFFMANESQUE. Relating to the American social scientist and his interactionism in social psychology.

Erving Goffman (1922–82) was born in Manville, Atlanta, graduated from

the University of Toronto, and received his M.A. and Ph.D. (1953) from the University of Chicago. He taught at the universities of Edinburgh, Berkeley, and Pennsylvania, and carried out field research in the Shetland Islands and in a public mental hospital in Washington, D.C. He focused attention on a microanalysis of everyday activities in games, public gatherings, stigmatizing behavior, and the interaction of staff and inmates in total institutions. He was often linked to the tradition of social interactionism, but in his later work he appeared to be more interested in the structure of social situations than in their content. Among his many works are *The Presentation of Self in Everyday Life* (1959); *Asylums* (1961); *Encounters: Essays on the Social Situation of Mental Patients and Other Inmates* (1961); *Frame Analysis* (1974); and *Gender Advertisements* (1979).
Sources

Burns, Tom. 1991. *Erving Goffman*. London: Routledge and Kegan Paul.

Devine, Elizabeth; Held, Michael; Vinson, James; and Walsh, George, eds. 1983. *Thinkers of the twentieth century: a biographical, bibliographical and critical dictionary*. London: Macmillan.

Kuper, Adam, and Kuper, Jessica. 1985. *The social science encyclopedia*. London: Routledge and Kegan Paul.

GOG AND MAGOG. Nations represented in the Apocalypse as the forces of Satan and Armageddon.

Gog and Magog appear in the Bible (Revelation, 20: 8) and are names given to the giant figures of Guildhall, London. Magog was the son of Japhet and Gog, a terrible ruler in the far north, who joined with the Persians, Armenians, and Cimmerians against Israel. In the Apocalypse, Gog and Magog appear as the symbol of all future enemies of God's kingdom. Another legend relates to two giant wooden figures at the Guildhall, London. They are images of the last two survivors of a race of giants who lived at Albion. They descended from wicked demons and the thirty-three daughters of Diocletian who, after murdering their husbands, sailed to Albion. Brutus the Trojan destroyed their race and brought the two to be porters at the Royal Palace at Troynovant (New Troy), that is, London. Since the rule of Henry V, the two wooden figures have been standing guard in London. They were replaced once after the 1666 fire and again in 1953 after the Nazi bombing in World War II. Another legend speaks of Gogmagog, a giant chief from Cornwall, who was killed by a companion of Brutus the Trojan. In the Bible Gog is a people—Scythians—who ravaged western Asia (c. 630 B.C.), and Magog is a land (Ezekiel, 38: 2). In rabbinic and apocalyptic literature they are figures who oppose God.
Sources

Cross, Frank L. 1974. *The Oxford dictionary of the Christian Church*. 2d ed. New York: Oxford University Press.

McHenry, Robert, ed. 1992. *The new encyclopedia Britannica*. Chicago: Encyclopedia Britannica, Inc.

GOMARISTS. Followers of the fifteenth-century theologian who favored the severe doctrines of Calvin; they assumed that God, although he accepted the human Fall as a divine command, was not the origin of sin; and they tolerated Jews, Catholics, and other Protestants.

Franciscus Gomarus or Gomar (1563–1641) was born at Bruges, Belgium, and studied at Strasbourg under Johann Sturm. He furthered his theology under Zanchius at Neustadt, and later, in 1583, went to Oxford and Cambridge. He was a pastor of the Dutch Reformed Church (1587–93) at Frankfurt-am-Main, took his doctorate at Heidelberg (1593), and became a professor of theology at Leiden (1594) where he fell into intense conflict with and denounced the Arminians and Jacobus Arminius, who was also a professor there. In 1609 he led a celebrated debate with Arminius before the regional government of Holland. Gomarus became an even more controversial supporter of Calvin when he condemned Arminius's ideas at the Synod of Dort (1618–19), and Gomarus contributed greatly to the divisions in the Dutch church. While Gomarus, the strict Calvinist, asserted that the elect had been chosen from before the Fall, Arminius believed that any one may be chosen to be among the elect. Gomarus's main work was *Opera theologica omnia* (1645). He died at Gröningen in the Netherlands.

Sources

Cross, Frank L. 1974. *The Oxford dictionary of the Christian Church.* 2d ed. New York: Oxford University Press.

Douglas, James D., ed. 1974. *The new international dictionary of the Christian Church.* Exeter: Paternoster Press.

Geddes, Macgregor. 1990. *The Everyman dictionary of religion and philosophy.* London: Dent and Sons.

McHenry, Robert, ed. 1992. *The new encyclopedia Britannica.* Chicago: Encyclopedia Britannica, Inc.

Smith, Benjamin. 1903. *The Century cyclopedia of names.* London: The Times.

GOODHART'S LAW. An economist's law stating that, when a measure of money supply becomes an official target, it will be distorted by the very act of being chosen and will behave differently simply because it has become a center of interest.

Charles Albert Eric Goodhart (b. 1936) was educated at Eton and later Trinity College, Cambridge, and completed national service (1955–57) as a second lieutenant. In 1963 he had the Prize Fellowship in Economics, Trinity College, and attended Harvard Graduate School of Arts and Sciences (Ph.D., 1963). He was appointed an assistant economics lecturer at Cambridge (1963–64) and economic adviser to the government's Department of Economic Affairs (1965–67). In 1967 for two years he was a lecturer in monetary economics at the London School of Economics, and later an adviser on monetary policy (1969–80) to the Bank of England. He studied monetary events and came to his conclusions during 1971–1973. He was the bank's chief adviser in 1980–85. His publications include *The New York Money Market and the Finance of Trade: 1900–1913* (1968); *The Business of Banking: 1891–1914* (1972); *Money, Information and*

Uncertainty (1975); *Monetary Theory and Practice: The U.K. Experience* (1984); and *The Evolution of the Central Bank* (1985). Since 1985 he has been Norman Sosnow Professor of Banking and Finance, London School of Economics and Political Science, and has published in economic journals and books.
Sources
Pearce, David W., ed. 1986. *Macmillan dictionary of modern economics.* New York: Macmillan.
Rutherford, Donald. 1992. *Dictionary of economics.* London: Routledge.
Who's who, 1993. London: Adam and Charles Black.

GOON SQUAD. In industrial relations a group of thugs hired by a trade union or management to create or resist violence during a labor dispute. With an imposing physique and inferior moral and mental qualities, a goon can be relied on to cow the weak and recalcitrant. This use of the term appeared in *American Speech* 13 (1938):178.

Alice the Goon appeared in the comic strip series "Popeye the Sailor" (1929) by Elzie Crisler Segar (1894–1934). The term is probably a portmanteau word that combines "gorilla" with "baboon." In his comic strips Segar introduced the term to refer to subhuman characters. So, in slang, the term came to mean a slugger, bomber, incendiarist, or any person hired by gangsters to terrorize or devastate others. Seger was born at Chester in Illinois and introduced his characters in "Thimble Theater" where the main figures were Ham Gravy, Olive, and Castor Oyl; other characters included Wimpey, who doted on hamburgers, and Eugene the Jeep.
Sources
Marsh, Arthur. 1979. *Concise encyclopedia of industrial relations.* Westmead, Farnborough, Hants: Gower.
Van Doren, Charles, ed. 1974. *Webster's American biographies.* Springfield, Mass.: G. and C. Merriam.

GORBACHEVISM, GORBEUPHORIC, GORBYMANIA. The contribution to Marxism-Leninism under the control of the last communist leader of the USSR. Excitement and astonishment following the Soviet policy changes, which included banning nuclear weapons, sacking the head of the Red Army, free elections, independence of satellites, and a football transfer (1987–89).

Mikhail S. Gorbachev (b. 1931) was born in south Russia and raised by a family deeply committed to the Soviet communist cause. He went to law school at Moscow University (1955–58) where he developed a favorable reputation as a good listener and having a way of never being insulting in discussions or arguments. He established himself on the first rung of the Communist party's career structure. On Stalin's death Gorbachev did not weep, nor did he join in discussions about Russia's future. He accepted Khrushchev's speech of February 1953 on Stalin's atrocities and worked his way up the party ladder from district controller to the upper reaches of the party bureaucracy. In 1961 he was a delegate to the Kremlin. In 1978 he became secretary of the Central Committee of the Communist party. He was elected head of state in 1980, and became executive president with increased authority in 1990, but his attempt to change the USSR into a socialist democracy, open to the world and composed of relatively independent parts, met much internal oppositon. His influence ended in August 1991 in a coup to overcome his authority. The conspirators wanted to ensure no signatures to a treaty that would change the USSR of 1922 into a confederation of distinct and autonomous regions. After the coup, the Communist party was suppressed and suspended, the Soviet Parliament and presidency was abolished, and President Gorbachev resigned (in December 1991).

Sources

Day, Alan J. 1992. *The annual register: a record of world events 1991.* Essex, United Kingdom: Longman.

Doder, Duske, and Bronson, Louise. 1990. *Gorbachev: heretic in the Kremlin.* New York: Viking Press.

Frankland, Mark. 1988. *The sixth continent: Russia and the making of Mikhail Gorbachev.* London: Hamilton.

McHenry, Robert, ed. 1992. *The new encyclopedia Britannica.* Chicago: Encyclopedia Britannica, Inc.

Medvedev, Zhores A. 1986. *Gorbachev.* Oxford: Basil Blackwell.

Miller, John. 1993. *Mikhail Gorbachev and the end of Soviet power.* Sydney: Macmillan.

Sheehy, Gail. 1990. *Gorbachev: the making of the man who shook the world.* London: Heinemann.

Tulloch, Sara. 1991. *The Oxford dictionary of new words.* Oxford: Oxford University Press.

Zemtsov, Ilya, and Farrar, John. 1989. *Gorbachev: the man and the system.* New Brunswick, N.J.: Transaction Books.

GORE-McLEMORE RESOLUTION. A resolution offered in the U.S. Congress in 1916 that opposed Americans traveling on belligerent ships that could be attacked by German U-boats (1915–16). The resolution sought to remove this threat as a pretext for the United States entering World War I. President Woodrow Wilson opposed the resolution.

Thomas Pryor Gore (1870–1949) was born near Embry, Webster County, Mississippi. At age 8 he lost the sight in his left eye and that of his right eye at 11. He attended public schools, graduated in law from Cumberland University, Tennessee, in 1892, and was admitted to the bar. He moved to Oklahoma in 1901 and, on the admission of Oklahoma as a state of the union, was elected to the U.S. Senate for the term ending in 1909. He was reelected and served until 1921, and again in 1930 until 1937. Gore was a pacifist, and although he had supported Woodrow Wilson in his presidential campaign, Gore opposed Wilson's foreign policy, and was an economic conservative and an isolationist. The first totally blind man to sit in the U.S. Senate and a brilliant speaker and debater, Gore was known as the "Blind Orator."

Atkins Jefferson (Jeff) McLemore (1857–1929) was born on a farm in Tennessee and educated in rural schools and by private tutors. He moved to Texas in 1878, and worked as a cowboy, printer, and reporter, and later as a miner in Colorado and Mexico. On returning to Texas he worked on a newspaper. He was elected as a Democrat to the sixty-fourth and sixty-fifth congresses but failed to be reelected in 1918 and returned to newspaper publishing.

Sources

Commager, Henry S., ed. 1968. *Documents of American history.* 8th ed. New York: Appleton-Century-Crofts.

Findling, John E. 1980. *Dictionary of American diplomatic history.* Westport, Conn.: Greenwood Press.

Garraty, John A., and James, Edward T., eds. 1974. *Dictionary of American biography.* Supplement 4. New York: Charles Scribner's Sons.

Jacob, Kathryn A., and Ragsdale, Bruce A. 1989. *Biographical directory of the United States Congress: 1774–1989.* Bicentennial ed. Washington, D.C.: U.S. Government Printing Office.

GRADGRIND. One who regulates people by rule and mechanical application of statistics, allowing nothing for sentiment, feeling, and the natural flaws in human character or individuality.

Thomas Gradgrind, of Charles Dickens's *Hard Times* (1854), was a citizen, merchant of hardware, and retired mill owner in Coketown, a drab center of industry in northern England. He became the local M.P. and lived in Stone Lodge a little way out of town. Essentially a practical man, he thought facts and statistics would bring up his children, Tom and Louisa, better than would their natural spirits and imagination. Although he was not a man of bad heart, his square forehead and square forefinger emphasized all the points he had to make, especially the practical methods of raising his children. He blighted their lives by vigorously suppressing all feelings in their lives. Gradgrind arranged for his daughter to marry a man thirty years her senior, and when the marriage failed and she came back home, Gradgrind saw how foolish he had been.

Sources

Dickens, Charles. 1854. *Hard times: for these times.* London: Bradbury and Evans.

Drabble, Margaret, ed. 1985. *The Oxford companion to English literature.* Oxford: Clarendon Press.

GRAMM-RUDMAN-HOLLINGS ACT. U.S. Balanced Budget and Emergency Deficit Control Act that set a maximum deficit between 1986 and 1991 for the U.S. federal budget and aimed to reduce the deficit to zero: if the deficit exceeded the maximum, then across-the-board cuts had to be made to achieve the required deficit level.

William Philip (''Phil'') Gramm (b. 1942). See GRAMMSTANDING.

Warren Bruce Rudman (b. 1930) was born in Boston and educated at Syracuse University, New York, studied law at Boston College, and was admitted to the bar in New Hampshire in 1960. After serving as legal counsel to the governor of New Hampshire (1960–69), he joined the board of trustees for Daniel Webster

College and became the state's attorney-general (1970–76). He returned to private practice before entering the U.S. Senate as a Republican for New Hampshire, serving from 1980 until his retirement in 1992.

Ernest Frederick Hollings (b. 1922) was born in Charleston, South Carolina, educated at the Citadel, served as a captain in the army during World War II, studied law at the University of South Carolina, and was admitted to the bar in 1947. He was a member of the House of Representatives in South Carolina from 1948 to 1954, the state's lieutenant-governor from 1955 to 1959, and then governor until 1963. During 1954–55 he was a member of the Hoover Commission on Intelligence Activities. Before entering the U.S. Senate in 1966, he practiced in Charleston (1963–66). He chaired many important committees and received awards for leadership in the army, education, and public service, including the Golden Bulldog Award from Watchdog on the Treasury in 1988.

Sources

Plano, Jack C., and Greenberg, Milton. 1989. *The American political dictionary.* New York: Holt, Rinehart and Winston.

Shafritz, Jay M. 1988. *The Dorsey dictionary of American government and politics.* Chicago: Dorsey.

Who's who in America, 1992–93. Chicago: Marquis.

GRAMMSTANDING. "Showboating," or taking credit for achievements one has done nothing to advance.

William Philip Gramm (b. 1942) was born in Fort Benning, Georgia, the youngest of three children. Being a rebellious boy at 15, he was sent to military school in Georgia after taking his mother's Plymouth for a joyride. At the University of Georgia he completed his Ph.D. (1967) and began teaching economics at Texas A&M University, where in 1973 he became a professor. He campaigned successfully as a Democrat for the sixty-fifth congressional seat in 1978 with support of the New Right, and early established a reputation for his strong ego, sometimes to advantage. When he changed his party affiliation from Democrat to Republican following Ronald Reagan's presidential victory in 1980, he was called a spy and traitor. In 1983 he resigned from Congress and ran as a Republican for the Senate, won, and in November 1984 was elected by the largest margin ever given to a Republican in Texas. When Albert Bustamante was about to announce his success in obtaining a federal grant of $297,400 for an impoverished Texan township, he learned Gramm had arranged to delay informing other legislators of the grant, thereby allowing him time to claim the glory for himself by announcing the news. Gramm, who had earlier tried to have the granting agency abolished, readily denied the charge of "showboating."

Sources

The international who's who, 1993. London: Europa Publications.

Moritz, Charles, ed. 1986. *Current biography yearbook.* New York: H. W. Wilson.

Who's who in America, 1993–93. Chicago: Marquis.

GRESHAM'S LAW. A principle regarding the value of different monies and their sources: "bad money drives out good" it is said, because people hoard valuable currency and in doing so withdraw it from circulation.

Sir Thomas Gresham (c. 1519–79), the second son of Sir Richard Gresham, was born between 1518 and 1522, and educated at Cambridge. He was apprenticed to his uncle, Sir John Gresham (c. 1535), from whom he learned about commerce, and he became a successful merchant. He advised royalty, including Henry VIII and Elizabeth I, and founded Gresham College and the Royal Exchange. After 1551 he was the royal finance agent in Antwerp, able and effective, but his methods were not always ethical. After the accession of Elizabeth I, he spent his time in London; on diplomatic and financial missions, he accrued wealth as a mercer, merchant, and banker. In 1560 he asserted that when money of high and low value are circulating together, the inferior coinage remains, while the more valuable is either exported, hoarded, or otherwise driven out of circulation. His observation was made when people were nipping edges from coins made of valuable metal, making it necessary later to introduce tokens and bank notes to overcome this. In 1857 the economist, H. D. MacLeod, gave Gresham's name to the law.

Sources

Eatwell, John; Milgate, Murray; and Newman, Peter. 1987. *The new Palgrave: a dictionary of economics.* London: Macmillan.

Hendrickson, Robert. 1988. *The dictionary of eponyms: names that became words.* New York: Dorset.

Rutherford, Donald. 1992. *Dictionary of economics.* London: Routledge.

Stephen, Leslie, and Lee, Sydney, eds. 1917. *The dictionary of national biography.* London: Oxford University Press.

GROTIAN THEORY. Pertaining to the ideas of the seventeenth-century Dutch founder of the science of international law. The theory assumed a strong opposition to violence, and—if no human authority was sufficiently powerful to prevent war—then the world should be thought of as being ruled by a natural law of immutable moral principles, found in nature, and assumed to operate rationally. So, between sovereign states, relations were assumed to be properly based on a real moral foundation, not the vicissitudes of human desire.

Hugo or Huig De Groot, in Latin "Grotius" (1583–1645), was born into an influential family in Delft, the Netherlands. When his considerable talent became apparent, his education was given over to tutors. He became a jurist, theologian, statesman, and poet who founded the science of international law. At the age of about 11, he attended Leiden University, was influenced by humanism, studied law at Orleans in 1598, and at 18 became historian of the States General and advocate fiscal (attorney-general) of Holland, Zeeland, and West Friesland (1607). In 1609 he published a treatise on free access to the oceans, and in 1613 he went to England to settle trade differences between James I and Holland. He was made pensionary of Rotterdam in 1613, drafted a "Resolution for Peace in the Church,'' and as one of the Remonstrant leaders—so named after the 1610 Remonstrance that presented the Arminian doctrines of salvation—was condemned to life imprisonment at Loevestein Castle. He escaped in 1621 and went to live in Paris. From Paris he was appointed Swedish ambassador to France (1635–45). He wrote *De jure belli ac pacis (On the Law of War and Peace)*, his chief work (1625), and *Deveritate Religionis Christianae* (1627). His theory assumed that the individual is a social being and that the principles of justice are in harmony with human nature and involve perpetual obligation; his theory of atonement states that Christ suffered because of people's sins, and so that God might forgive them, punishment should follow sinful acts. In 1637 he published a *History of the Goths, Vandals and Lombards*. He died of exhaustion after a shipwreck at Rostock, Germany, on his return from Sweden to France.

Sources

Buckle, Stephen. 1991. *Natural law and the theory of property: Grotius to Hume*. Oxford: Clarendon Press.

Bull, Hedley; Kingsbury, Benedict; and Roberts, Adam. 1990. *Hugo Grotius and international relations*. Oxford: Clarendon Press.

Cross, Frank L. 1974. *The Oxford dictionary of the Christian Church*. 2d ed. New York: Oxford University Press.

Eliade, Mircea, ed. 1987. *Encyclopedia of religion*. New York: Macmillan.

Gellinek, Christian. 1983. *Hugo Grotius*. Boston: Twayne Publishers.

McHenry, Robert, ed. 1992. *The new encyclopedia Britannica*. Chicago: Encyclopedia Britannica, Inc.

Pauling, Linus, ed. 1986. *World encyclopedia of peace*. New York: Pergamon Press.

Vreeland, Hamilton, Jr. 1917. *Hugo Grotius: the father of the modern science of international law*. New York: W. D. Gray.

GUILLEBAUD REPORT, GUILLEBAUD FORMULA. Findings of British committees and courts of inquiry known as the Railway Pay Committee of Inquiry (1958–60). It investigated railway workers' pay relative to that of other industries; it established new standards in comparability that became a matter for concern in British incomes policy.

Claude William Guillebaud (1890–1971), an economist and arbitrator on many wage disputes, was educated at Repton School and Saint Johns College, Cambridge, where he taught economics (1925–56), and until retirement was continuously engaged in teaching and in the running of his college. During World War I he worked in the Civil Service, and in 1919 he was with the Supreme Economic Council in Paris. He chaired the Banking Wages Council in 1940, and many other boards, councils, and inquiries into wages in the refreshments, haulage, and agriculture industries. He was also much concerned with the governance of hospitals and chaired the committee that investigated the British National Health Service in 1953. Most of his publications were in labor relations, but he wrote *Economic Recovery of Germany (1933–1938)* (1939), *The Wages Council System in Great Britain* (1962), and on the sisal industry in Tanganyika and arbitration disputes. His main achievement came from successive chairmanships of Guillebaud Committees on the National Health Service and on Railway Wages. In both cases he produced a report that achieved a settlement under most difficult circumstances.

Sources

Marsh, Arthur. 1979. *Concise encyclopedia of industrial relations.* Westmead, Farnborough, Hants: Gower.

Obituaries from the Times, 1971–1975 (August 1971). Reading: Newspaper Archives Developments Ltd.

Who was who, 1971–80. London: Adam and Charles Black.

GUILLOTINE. A term that entered British and American politics late in the nineteenth century. In the British Parliament when time is short for debate, both government and opposition speakers are restricted to a fixed speaking period; often this is done when many bills are due to be passed at the end of a parliamentary session. In the United States the term has been used to indicate the dismissal of government officials when a new president takes office.

Joseph Ignace Guillotin (1738–1814) was born at Saintes and became wrongly known as the inventor of the guillotine, the instrument used to decapitate thousands during the French Revolution. He was a physician. In 1789 as a deputy to the National Assembly, he proposed that all capital punishment should be by decapitation, a privilege that was then reserved for nobility. He suggested that decapitation could be performed quickly and humanely by machine. The machine adopted was prepared by a German mechanic, Tobias Schmidt, under direction from Dr. Antoine Louis, secretary of the Academy of Medicine. It was used first in April 1792 to behead a highwayman, and it was initially known as the ''Louisette.''

Sources

McHenry, Robert, ed. 1992. *The new encyclopedia Britannica.* Chicago: Encyclopedia Britannica, Inc.

Robertson, David. 1985. *The Penguin dictionary of politics.* Harmondsworth: Penguin.

GUTTMAN SCALE. A technique of attitude measurement—scalogram analysis—using a unidimensional scale that gives an arrangement of items such that the agreement with one automatically involves agreement with items of lower rank and disagreement with items of higher rank.

Louis Guttman (1916–87), son of Russian immigrants to the United States, was born in New York. He studied sociology (Ph.D., 1942) at the University of Minnesota and taught there (1936–40). He also taught at Cornell University (1941–50; 1972–78). He served in the U.S. War Department's Division of Education, and in 1947 he went to Israel where he founded the Israel Institute of Applied Social Research and became a professor at the Hebrew University (1958–87). He helped write the renowned study, *The American Soldier* (1949), and won many awards and honors. Among them was the Israel Prize in the Social Sciences (1974) and the Education Testing Award for the Distinguished

Service to Measurement (1984). His approach to scaling is regarded as one of the sixty-two major advances in social science from 1900 to 1965. Realizing that the original scale did not satisfy the need for handling complex data, he developed partial-order scalogram analysis.

Sources

Dancer, L. Suzanne. 1990. Louis Guttman 1916–1987. Obituary. *American Psychologist* 45:773.

Guttman, Louis. 1944. A basis for scaling qualitative data. *American Sociological Review* 9:139–150.

Jaques Cattell Press, ed. 1973. *American men and women of science: the social and behavioral sciences.* New York: Jaques Cattell and R. R. Bowker.

Roth, Cecil E., ed. 1971. *Encyclopedia Judaica.* New York: Macmillan.

Zusne, Leonard. 1987. *Eponyms in psychology: a dictionary and biographical source-book.* Westport, Conn.: Greenwood Press.

H

HADASSAH. A Jewish women's benevolent organization. "Hadassa, the Women's Zionist Organization of America" is the largest Zionist organization in the world and one of the largest women's organizations in the United States. According to its constitution, it is a "voluntary non-profit organization dedicated to the ideals of Judaism, Zionism, American democracy, healing, teaching and medical research." It sponsors medical training, research, and care in Israel, and it pursues Jewish educational activities in the United States.

Esther—the Persian (Esther 2:7) name of the queen after whom one of the Old Testament books takes its name—had the Hebrew name of Hadassah (Myrtle). She is represented in that book as the daughter of Abihail, cousin and adopted daughter of Mordecai of the tribe of Benjamin. A beautiful virgin, she was made queen in place of Vashti by King Ahasuerus (Xerxes 480–65 B.C.), and from this position she was able to protect her people against the hostility of the prime minister, Haman. But she did not reveal that she was a Jewess, so her life was in danger when Haman persuaded the king to exterminate all Jews in the empire. Cleverly, she plotted revenge on Haman, had him condemned to hang, and his edict reversed so that Jews were given permission to avenge themselves against their enemies. A slightly different version of her life appears in the Aggadah. In the arts she represents feminine modesty, courage, and self-sacrifice, and among the biblical heroines she has enjoyed much popularity with writers, artists, and musicians. She is celebrated in the Feast of Purim.
Source
Roth, Cecil, ed. 1971. *Encyclopaedia Judaica.* New York: Macmillan.

HAHN PROBLEM. A problem in economics that examines the dependence of an economy's steady state on relations between natural, warranted, and actual economic growth. The problem concerns the correct expectations affecting the stability of an economy. Economists agree that the aggregated production function put in terms of aggregate capital input is a fable. The question that arose was whether or not the fable was misleading. Hahn's attempt in 1966 to answer the question was named the "Hahn problem," but it was neither new nor problematic.

Frank Horace Hahn (b. 1925) was born in Berlin and educated at the universities of Cambridge and London (Ph.D., 1956). He taught at the University of Birmingham (1948–60), was frequently a visiting professor at the Massachusetts Institute of Technology and the University of California (Berkeley), and successively taught at Cambridge University (1960–66), the London School of Economics (1967–72), Harvard (1973–74), and in Vienna. He was appointed a professor of economics at Cambridge in 1972. His main interest was in general equilibrium theory and microeconomic theory. He published *The Share of Wages in National Income* (1972); co-authored *General Comparative Analysis* (1971); wrote *Money and Inflation* (1982); and *Equilibrium and Macro-economics* (1984).

Sources

Blaug, Mark, ed. 1986. *Who's who in economics: a biographical dictionary of major economists, 1700–1986.* 2d ed. Cambridge, Mass.: MIT Press.

Eatwell, John; Milgate, Murray; and Newman, Peter. 1987. *The new Palgrave: a dictionary of economics.* London: Macmillan.

Sturges, Paul, and Sturges, Claire. 1990. *Who's who in British economics: a directory of economists in higher education, business and government.* Hants, England: Edward Elgar.

HALÉVY THESIS. An explanation of the social and political stability of nineteenth-century England in terms of the value given to Protestantism, especially Wesleyan methodism, as the means by which the artisan became embourgeoised and social conflict in English society was diminished.

Élie Halévy (1870–1937) was born into a family of Protestant intellectuals in Étretat in France, educated in philosophy at the Sorbonne (1900) where he was a brilliant scholar, and later became a professor at l'École Libre de Sciences Politique (Free School of Political Science) in Paris. He taught two famous courses, English History and European Socialism. He published his *The Platonic Theory of Sciences* in 1896 and completed his doctorate in 1901, which was published in three volumes as *The Growth of Philosohical Radicalism* (1901–4) and brought to light the early socialist in *Thomas Hodgskin (1787–1869)* in 1903. In his *History of the English People in the Nineteenth Century* (1912–31), Halévy argued that through Methodism England avoided social changes like the revolution in France. The work appeared in six parts, the first being his *England 1815,* which asked why it was that England alone in Europe was most free of revolution, violence, and sudden change. His view demonstrated the inadequacy of Marxism as a single-minded approach to explanation, and he preferred the sociology of religion to explain stability in Britain. In World War I Halévy was in the medical services; after the war he was offered and refused a position in the League of Nations Secretariat and a professorship at the Sorbonne. He worked for the commission that published the official French documents on World War I. In his *The Era of Tyrannies* (1938), Halévy published one of the first accounts of totalitarianism in both Nazi Germany and Communist Russia.

Sources

Blaug, Mark, ed. 1986. *Who's who in economics: a biographical dictionary of major economists, 1700–1986.* 2d ed. Cambridge, Mass.: MIT Press.

Chase, Myrna. 1980. *É. H. An intellectual biography.* New York: Columbia University Press.

Prevost, M., and Roman-D'Amat, J. . 1986. *Dictionnaire de biographie Francaise.* Paris: Librairie Letouzey et Ané.

Sills, David L., ed. 1968. *International encyclopedia of the social sciences.* New York: Macmillan and Free Press.

Who was who 1929–1940. London: Adam and Charles Black.

HALLIDAYAN. Characteristic of the twentieth-century British neo-Firthian linguist, and the development of a systemic, functional theory of linguistics.

Michael Alexander Kirkwood Halliday (b. 1925) was born in Leeds, completed studies of Chinese language and literature at London University, and studied further in China (Peking and Lingnan universities) and at Cambridge (Ph.D., 1955). He studied with Wang Li (1900–86) and John Rupert Firth (1890–1960). He taught at Cambridge and Edinburgh (1958), and at University College, London (1963), where he directed research into the linguistic properties of scientific English and a Nuffield/Schools Council Program in Linguistics and English Teaching. At the University of London he became a professor of general linguistics (1965–70), taught at the University of Illinois (1973–75), and was appointed foundation professor of linguistics at the University of Sydney (1975–88). He has been honored by academic institutions in France, the United States., Singapore, Canada, the United Kingdom, and Australia. His theory has its origins in post-Saussurean European linguistics, emphasizing a functional and semantic instead of a formal and syntactic approach to language; it takes the text rather than the sentence as its object, and it defines its scope by usage and not grammatically. Language is interpreted as ''social semiotic'': that is, as meaningfull activity by which a culture is constituted. His view opposes that of the American linguist, Noam Chomsky, who saw language as a finite system that produced an infinite body of text. Halliday sees it as an infinite system that produces only a finite body of text. He co-authored *The Linguistic Sciences and Language Teaching* (1964), and among his many books appear *Learning How to Mean* (1975), *Language as Social Semiotic* (1978), *An Introduction to Functional Grammar* (1985), and *Spoken and Written Language* (1989).

Sources
Bullock, Alan, and Woodings, Robert B., eds. 1983. *The Fontana biographical companion to modern thought.* London: Collins.
Halliday, Michael A. K. 1993. Systemic theory. In Ronald E. Asher and J.M.Y. Simpson, eds. *The encyclopedia of language and linguistics.* Oxford: Pergamon Press.
Personal Communication.

HALSEY-WEIR SYSTEM. An incentive payment system—better known as the Halsey Premium Bonus System—that provides a worker with a bonus for time saved.

Frederick Arthur Halsey (1856–1935) was born at Unadilla, New York, and after attending Unadilla Academy he entered Cornell University and graduated in engineering in 1878. In 1880 he joined the Rand Drill Company of New York and designed for the company a slugger drill that he described in "A New Dock Drill," *Transactions of the American Society of Mechanical Engineers, VI, 1885.* The labor troubles of the 1880s directed the attention of industrialists to the problem of harmonizing capital and labor, and during these years Halsey devised a profit-sharing system known as the Halsey Premium Plan of wage payment. He was unable to persuade his New York employers to adopt a system, but in 1880 when he became a general manager of the Canadian Rand Drill Company, he was free to put the plan into operation. His plan was widely adopted in the United States despite the opposition of organized labor, and it received even greater acceptance in Great Britain in the late 1880s. In 1894 Halsey left the company to join the staff of the *American Machinist* as associate editor (1894–1907) and editor in chief (1907–11). He wrote *Slide Valve Gears* (1890); *Handbook for Machine Drivers and Draftsmen* (1913); and *Methods of Machine Shop Work* (1914). He received the 1923 medal of the American Society of Mechanical Engineers for his plan of wage payment. The system was introduced to Britain by Messrs. G. & J. Weir of Cathcart, near Glasgow, known as the Halsey-Weir System.

George and James Weir (fl. 1873–1905) were brothers who established themselves as maritime engineers during a period of rapid development. James was an apprentice with Randolph and Elder, a shipping firm, and became an engineer on vessels plying between Liverpool and the Levant. In 1871 he left life at sea with many patents on which G. & J. Weir flourished, for example, feed heater and pump for steam turbines and evaporators for sea water. In 1886 he and his elder brother George manufactured his inventions in their firm in Cathcart. In 1895 the firm became a public company, and George retired; James retired in 1905 to go on the land.

Sources
American Council of Learned Societies. 1944. *Dictionary of American biography: supplement I.* New York: Charles Scribner's Sons.
Jeremy, David, and Shaw, Christine, eds. 1986. *Dictionary of business biography.* Vol. 5. London: Butterworth.

Marsh, Arthur. 1979. *Concise encyclopaedia of industrial relations.* Westmead, Farm-
    borough, Hants: Gower.

HAMILTONIAN (a). Relating to the nineteenth-century British educationist
and his method of teaching languages without grammar.

   James Hamilton (1769–1829) was born in London, educated in Dublin by
two Jesuits, and became a merchant in France and Germany. In Hamburg he
learned German from General D'Angeli, a French emigré. D'Angeli taught him
word for word and by parsing from a book of German anecdotes. This resembled
the system he had followed in Dublin. In 1815, on a business trip to New York,
he decided to teach languages himself according to D'Angeli's scheme and gave
his first lecture on the Hamiltonian system in Philadelphia in 1816. His philosophy was to teach rather than to order pupils to learn. He toured America and
Canada, and returned to London in 1823. In eighteen months he had 600 students studying languages with seven teachers. Later he taught in Liverpool,
Manchester, Edinburgh, and in the English countryside. His classes usually comprised fifty to sixty adults, and his method put grammar aside and taught according to a word-for-word technique that employed direct translations beneath
the lines of the original text. Among his interlinear translations were parts of
the Bible and Aesop's *Fables.* He wrote *The History, Principles, Practices and
Results of the Hamiltonian System* (1829). Although the method was a success
among many students who found they could control a new language quickly, it
faced considerable controversy and resistance among teachers.
Sources
Preece, Warren E., ed. 1965. *Encyclopedia Britannica.* Chicago: Encyclopedia Britannica,
    Inc., William Benton.
Stephen, Leslie, and Lee, Sydney, eds. 1917. *The dictionary of national biography.* Lon-
    don: Oxford University Press.

HAMILTONIAN (b). Relating to the philosophy of the nineteenth-century
Scottish metaphysician.

   Sir William Hamilton (1788–1856) was born into an academic family in Glasgow. He was educated at the universities of Edinburgh and Glasgow, and at
Balliol College, Oxford and was admitted to the bar in Scotland in 1813. He
was elected a professor of civil history at Edinburgh University in 1821. When
his writings on perception (1830) and logic (1833) appeared in the *Edinburgh
Review,* they established him as a prominent metaphysician and scholar of
German philosophy, and he was elected a professor of logic and metaphysics
in 1836. He was learned in many obscure fields, collected books, and built a
renowned library. His wide reading, dialectical abilities, and strong character
gave him great personal influence; his intellectual contributions owed much to
the Scottish traditions of common sense in philosophy, sharp logic, German
philosophy—especially Kant—and to Aristotle. His students were so influenced
by his ideas that they formed a metaphysics society. He also studied phrenology

and concluded that it made baseless claims. In logic he elaborated the doctrine of the "quantification of the predicate," and in education his writings led to a royal commission (1850) and important reforms. In 1844 he suffered an attack of paralysis from which he never fully recovered.

Sources
Stephen, Leslie, and Lee, Sydney, eds. 1917. *The dictionary of national biography.* London: Oxford University Press.
Zusne, Leonard. 1984. *Biographical dictionary of psychology.* Westport, Conn.: Greenwood Press.

HAMILTONIAN CIRCUIT. Links in a transport network. The network has an unbroken chain through all nodes, and the first and last nodes coincide. The shortest Hamiltonian Circuit solves the problem of the "traveling salesman tour." That is, how can an efficient traveling salesman use a transport network to set out from home, visit customers at different locations, and return home, all by the shortest route?

Charles Horace Hamilton (1901–77) was born in McLennan County, Texas, and educated at Southern Methodist University, Texas University, and North Carolina State University (Ph.D., 1933). He was a rural sociologist at North Carolina State University (1931–36; 1940–77) and associate director, Carolina Population Center, University of North Carolina (1967–71); a member of the advisory committee on population for the 1950 U.S. census; president, Population Association of America, and a specialist in the analysis of internal migration. He published several articles in *Demography* (1965–67) and *Social Forces* (1951), as well as essays in *Selected Studies of Migration since World War II* (1950) and in *North Carolina Population Trends* (1974–75).

Sources
Goodall, Brian. 1987. *The Penguin dictionary of human geography.* Harmondsworth: Penguin.
Jaques Cattell Press, ed. 1973. *American men and women of science: the social and behavioral sciences.* New York: Jaques Cattell and R. R. Bowker.
Petersen, William, and Petersen, Renee. 1985. *Dictionary of demography.* Westport, Conn.: Greenwood Press.

HAMILTONIANISM. A conservative philosophy of government that upholds protection and strong centralized control, and has little faith or trust in the abilities of the common man.

Alexander Hamilton (1757–1804) was born in Nevis, one of the Leeward Islands of the Caribbean, and was subject to an irregular upbringing and a desultory education. His father deserted the family, and when Alexander was 13 his mother died. For four years he worked in a store until his relatives sent him to school in New Jersey. In the Revolution he served George Washington as aide-de-camp and personal secretary (1777). In 1781 he studied law in Albany, New York, and was admitted to the bar in 1782. As a member of Congress (1782–83), he advocated a strong federal government and wrote news articles on the subject. In 1785 he, James Madison (1751–1836), and John Jay (1745–1829) wrote the articles that were collected in two volumes and published as *The Federalist* (1788). As factionalism developed in American politics, Hamilton emerged as leader of the Federalists. In 1795 he left the cabinet but kept much influence in government while he enhanced his reputation as an outstanding lawyer at the New York bar. He died of wounds in a duel.

Sources

Hecht, Marie B. 1982. *Odd destiny, the life of Alexander Hamilton.* New York: Macmillan.

Johnson, Allen, and Malone, Dumas, eds. 1931. *Dictionary of American biography.* Vol. IV. New York: Charles Scribner's Sons.

Morris, Richard B. 1975. *John Jay, the making of a revolutionary.* New York: Harper and Row.

Morris, Richard B. 1985. *Witness at the creation: Hamilton, Madison, Jay and the constitution.* New York: Holt, Rinehart and Winston.

Preece, Warren E., ed. 1965. *Encyclopedia Britannica.* Chicago: Encyclopedia Britannica, Inc., William Benton.

Rutland, Robert A. 1987. *James Madison: the founding father.* New York: Macmillan.

Van Doren, Charles, ed. 1974. *Webster's American biographies.* Springfield, Mass.: G. and C. Merriam.

HAMILTONIANS. The laws of motion for a perfect-foresight economy, competitive or centrally planned. They are described by the Hamiltonian dynamical system and the Hamiltonian function. The differential equations were used as a tool for particle analysis; they used the ideas of autonomy of functioning and the extremization of a problem. Because economic planning involves concepts of maximization and minimization over time, the Hamiltonians appealed to mathematically oriented economists. The Hamiltonians also use duality, another concept useful in economic interpretation. Hamiltonians are also used in descriptive economics. One of the first uses of Hamiltonians appeared in Samuelson and Solow (1956).

William Rowan Hamilton (1805–65) was born and raised in Dublin where he was noted for his outstanding intellect. At 7 he read Hebrew, at 14 he wrote Persian, and at 17 he was recognized as a brilliant young mathematician. He studied at Trinity College, Dublin, and as an undergraduate he was appointed a professor of astronomy and became the royal astronomer for Ireland in 1827. He spent his career at the observatory, Dunsink, near Dublin. In 1834, the Royal Society awarded him a gold medal for his work on general methods of dynamics which resolved difficult problems of bodies in motion. He was knighted in 1835 and became president of the Royal Irish Academy in 1837. Among his notable works was *The Elements of Quaternions* (1866), a new calculus that he devised in 1853.

Sources

Boylan, Henry, ed. 1978. *A dictionary of Irish biography.* New York: Barnes and Noble.

Cass, David, and Shell, Karl. 1976. *The Hamiltonian approach to dynamic economics.* New York: Academic Press.

Eatwell, John; Milgate, Murray; and Newman, Peter. 1987. *The new Palgrave: a dictionary of economics.* London: Macmillan.

Hankins, Thomas. 1980. *Sir William Rowan Hamilton.* Baltimore: Johns Hopkins University Press.

Magill, M.J.P. 1970. *On a general economic theory of motion.* Berlin: Springer-Verlag.

Samuelson, P. A., and Solow, R. M. 1956. A complete model involving heterogeneous capital goods. *Quarterly Journal of Economics* 70:537–562.

Stephen, Leslie, and Lee, Sydney, eds. 1917. *The dictionary of national biography.* London: Oxford University Press.

HAMLET. A political type who makes a tiresome ritual out of deciding whether or not to take action in politics. For example, in November 1991 Mario Cuomo agonized over whether or not to run as a Democratic candidate in the U.S. presidential campaign.

Hamlet, prince of Denmark, is a tragic figure in Shakespeare's *Hamlet* (c. 1600). Hamlet learns that his uncle, Claudius, is responsible for murdering the king, Hamlet's father, and is shocked to see that Claudius reigns with Hamlet's mother Gertrude as the queen. Hamlet considers avenging the murder of his father but cannot bring himself to act. After much vacillation, Hamlet does kill Claudius but dies in a duel from the exchange of poisoned swords. Shakespeare's play showed that the power of action is exhausted by excessive calculation. In time, Hamlet himself became a model for the modern introspective character whose ambivalence and tendency to overthink problems impair important decision making.

Sources

Hoy, Cyrus, ed. 1991. *Hamlet: an authoritative text, from intellectual backgrounds, extracts from sources, essays in criticism/William Shakespeare.* 2d ed. New York: W. W. Norton.

Walker, Martin. 1991. Cuomo road to Camelot. *Guardian Weekly,* November, 145, 18: 9.

HAMPDEN. A defender of popular liberties.

John Hampden (1594–1643) was an English parliamentarian and the eldest son of William Hampden of Hampden, Bucks. In 1621, after his education at Magdalen College, Oxford, and at the Inner Temple, London, he entered Parliament and was given a leading position in the opposition. When King Charles I dissolved Parliament in 1629, Hampden retired to his seat in Buckinghamshire. In both the Short and Long Parliaments, he was a member for Bucks and one of the five members whose attempted seizure by King Charles (1642) precipitated the Civil War. At the outbreak of hostilities, Hampden commanded a regiment for Parliament (1642–43) and was fatally wounded at Chalgrove Field. He is remembered chiefly as the defendant in the case of *The King* v. *John Hampden, Court of Exchequer* (1637–38) for resisting the collection of the obsolete tax of ship-money which Charles I attempted to revive without the authority of Parliament. The case was decided against Hampden, but the House of Lords reversed the decision in 1641.

Sources

Adair, John. 1976. *A life of John Hampden, the patriot (1594–1643)*. London: Macdonald and Janes.

Magnussen, Magnus; Goring, Rosemary; and Thorn, John O., eds. 1990. *Chambers biographical dictionary*. Edinburgh: Chambers Ltd.

HANSARD. Official report of parliamentary proceedings in Britain and the Commonwealth; to confront politicians with their recorded opinions.

Luke Hansard (1752–1828) was born in Norwich and worked for John Hughes, printer to the House of Commons, became a partner in the firm by 1774, and was head of the publishing house named after him by 1800. Luke Hansard printed *Journals of the House of Commons* from 1774 to 1828. He introduced a technique of printing in red and black from the same form. In addition, he greatly impressed many with the speed and accuracy of his printing of parliamentary papers, and found many ways to cut printing costs. His son, Thomas Curson Hansard (1776–1833), began printing the debates in the House of Commons in 1803 for William Cobbett, the political journalist and later a member of Parliament. In time, Thomas Hansard published them himself as *Hansard's Parliamentary Debates* until 1889. In 1909 the series, known as the fifth, became both the official and verbatim record of Parliament. Records of debates are usually available the next day.

Sources

Chisholm, Hugh, ed. 1910–11. *Encyclopedia Britannica*. 11th ed. New York: Encyclopedia Britannica Co.

Myers, Robin, ed. 1991. *An autobiography of Luke Hansard, printer in the house: 1752–1828*. London: Printing Historical Society.

Stephen, Leslie, and Lee, Sydney, eds. 1917. *The dictionary of national biography*. London: Oxford University Press.

HARDMAN REPORT. A British Report of the Committee of Inquiry (1971) into a long dispute between the Post Office and the Union of Post Office Workers. The report, with one dissenter, recommended a pay increase of 9 percent with differential rates in areas of labor shortage outside the London area, productivity measures, and reduction of excessive overtime.

Sir Henry Hardman (b. 1905) was educated at the University of Manchester, lectured the Workers' Educational Association (1927–34), and became an economics tutor at the University of Leeds (1934–45). In 1940 he joined the Ministry of Food, and after World War II he was the deputy head of the British Food Mission to North America (1946–48) and undersecretary of the Ministry of Food (1948–53). He became the deputy secretary in the Ministry of Agriculture, Fisheries and Food (1955–60). He held many other government positions, including permanent undersecretary of state and minister of defense (1964–66), and was a member of the Monopolies Commission (1967–70), chairman of the Covent Gardens Market Authority (1967–75), and the governor and trustee of the Reserve Bank of Rhodesia (1967–79).

Sources
Marsh, Arthur. 1979. *Concise encyclopedia of industrial relations.* Westmead, Farnborough, Hants: Gower.
Who's who, 1992. London: Adams and Charles Black.

HARE VOTING SYSTEM, HARE-CLARK SYSTEM. A system of single transferable votes. The voter indicates his or her preference by ranking the candidates in order, and the counting procedure secures representation of groups of candidates in proportion to their numbers. The system is resisted because it is complex, can produce too many informal votes, and may introduce more than two parties to dominate government. The system is used for election to the lower house in Ireland, Malta, and Tasmania, and has recently replaced the D'Hondt system in the Australian Capital Territory.

Thomas Hare (1806–91) was born in Leigh, Dorset, studied law at the Inner Temple, and was admitted to the bar in 1833. He established a practice, and in 1840 and 1843 with others he published a book on court cases relating to railways and canals. He wrote *Machinery of Representation* (1857) which went through several revisions. Much literature grew around it; societies were formed to promote his ideas and to put them into operation. John Stuart Mill commended it as the only remedy against oppression of political minorities (1860). Hare also wrote on the navigation laws (1826), India's wealth, local government reform and housing in cities, the distribution of seats in Parliament, and essays on the education of apprentices. He retired in 1887.

Andre Inglis Clark (1848–1907) was born in Hobart Town, Tasmania, the youngest son of a successful engineer and builder. After attending Hobart High School, he went into his father's business; later he studied law and was called to the bar (1877). A republican, writer, and debater, he entered the House of Assembly amid great controversy and sought to amend laws on many points. In 1885, after having established a practice in criminal law, he founded the Southern Tasmanian Political Reform Association. On returning from a visit to the United States where he befriended Oliver Wendell Holmes and other academic lawyers, Clark worked enthusiastically for his democratic and republican ideals. When he was attorney-general under Edward Braddon, Clark extended the franchise and introduced voting by proportional representation to Hobart and Launceston (1896). In 1898 he was a puisne judge, Supreme Court, Tasmania, and a senior judge in 1901. In 1907 his Hare-Clark electoral system was adopted in Tasmania.

Sources
Boase, Frederic. 1965. *Modern English biography.* London: Frank Cass.
Bogdanor, Vernon. 1981. *The people and the party in system: the referendum and electoral reform in British politics.* Cambridge: Cambridge University Press.
Doron, Gideon. 1979. Is the Hare voting system representative? *Journal of Politics* 41: 918–922.

Hare, Thomas. 1859. *Treatise on the election of representatives, parliamentary and municipal.* London: Longmans.
Pike, Douglas, et al. 1966–90. *Australian dictionary of biography.* 12 vols. Carlton, Victoria: University of Melbourne Press.

HARKINS, TO PULL A HARKINS. To commit a military act of egregious political stupidity.

Paul Donal Harkins (1904–84) was born in Boston and graduated from the U.S. Military Academy in 1929. He was deputy chief of staff, Western Task Force, in the North African invasion in 1942, and became a protégé of General George S. Patton, Jr. Harkins commanded the cadets at West Point (1948–51), was a commander in Korea (1951–54), served at the Pentagon (1954–57), and commanded forces in the Pacific (1960–62). He was optimistic in his assessment of the Vietnam War, and he strongly supported the Ngo Dinh Diem regime in Vietnam. In the Vietnam War he preceded General William Westmoreland, said confidently that the war would be over in eighteen months, and ordered the bombing of peasant hamlets, killing civilians by the 10,000s. To him the United States' biggest mistake was to withdraw support from Diem. He often differed with the U.S. ambassador, Henry Cabot Lodge. He retired in 1964 and lived in Dallas until he died. Although his appraisal of hostilities was in error, and his conventional tactics were unsuited to guerrilla warfare, others also misjudged the war and used tactics that failed. He has often been used as the military's scapegoat for the U.S. failure to win the Vietnam War.

Sources

Halberstam, David. 1972. *The best and the brightest.* New York: Random House.
Sheehan, Neil; Smith, Hedrick; Kenworthy, E. W.; and Butterfield, Fox. 1971. *The Pentagon papers.* New York: Bantam.
Spiller, Roger J., and Dawson, Joseph G. III, eds. 1984. *Dictionary of American military biography.* Westport, Conn.: Greenwood Press.

HARRIS POLL OR SURVEY. A statistical survey of public opinion used especially during election periods in the United States. The survey results appeared twice weekly in over 250 newspapers and used a policy of balanced questioning in three ways: pro and con questions; answer-in-your-own words questions; and suggestive or projective questions accompanied by the alternative view. All questions and answers were made available to the public. The national sample comprised 1,500 respondents and was accurate to within 3 percent.

Louis Harris (b. 1921) was born in New Haven and spent most of his life at the center of national politics and served business, labor, voluntary organizations, and government agencies as well as the arts. He completed his economics degree at the University of North Carolina, served as an officer in the navy during World War II, and from 1946 to 1956 he worked with Elmo Roper and Associates, and became a partner. In New York from 1956 he headed Louis Harris and Associates, and was a consultant to news corporations; he was also a columnist in most American newspapers including the *Washington Post, Newsweek,* the *Chicago Tribune,* and *Time.* In 1964 he became a professor of political science at the University of North Carolina and director of Donaldson, Lufkin & Jenrette. He wrote many books, including *Is There a Republican Majority* (1954); *The Anguish of Change* (1973); and *Inside America* (1987). He has chaired organizations promoting the arts and sits on many boards of educational institutions and was a member of professional associations related to such activities as sociology, politics, statistics, management, marketing, public opinion, and foreign policy.

Sources

Wheeler, M. 1976. *Lies, damn lies and statistics.* New York: Liveright.
Who's who in America, 1988–89. Wilmette, Ill.: Marquis.

HARRIS-TODARO MODEL. An economic model that explains the high rate of urban-rural migration in developing countries. In the late 1960s it was known as the Harris-Todaro hypothesis.

John Rees Harris (b. 1934) was born in Rockford, Illinois, and studied at Wheaton College and Northwestern University (Ph.D., 1967). He worked with Michael Todaro at the Institute of Development Studies, University College, Nairobi, in 1968. He became a professor of economics at Boston University in 1975.

Michael Todaro (b. 1942) was born in New York City, and educated at Haverford College and Yale (Ph.D., Economics, 1967). He taught at Mararere University in Uganda (1964–65) and the University of Nairobi, Kenya (1968–70; 1974–76). He was at the Rockefeller Foundation (1970–74) and became a professor of economics at New York University in 1978. He wrote on economic theory, and among several books on developing nations are his *Economic Development in the Third World* (1977, 1981) and *The Struggle for Development* (1983). The model was attributed first to Michael Todaro (1968; 1969) and to both Harris and Todaro by 1970.

Sources

Blaug, Mark, ed. 1986. *Who's who in economics: a biographical dictionary of major economists, 1700–1986.* 2d ed. Cambridge, Mass.: MIT Press.
Eatwell, John; Milgate, Murray; and Newman, Peter. 1987. *The new Palgrave: a dictionary of economics.* London: Macmillan.
Harris, John R., and Todaro, Michael. 1970. Migration, employment and development: a two sector analysis. *American Economic Review* 60:126–142.

HARRISON ACT. The control of drugs in the United States originates with the federal tax statute, the Harrison Act (1914), which states that narcotics may be transferred only by individuals or agents who are registered with the Treasury Department. Physicians are exempt, but they must apply to the government for a special tax stamp to exercise this aspect of medical practice. All other acts such as the sale, purchase, importation, or possession of narcotics are illegal and punishable by law. The manufacture or importation of heroin is forbidden.

Byron Patton Harrison (1881–1941), born at Crystal Springs, Mississippi, was descended from the Harrisons of Virginia and distantly related to U.S. presidents William Henry and Benjamin Harrison. His father died when Byron was young, and he helped the family by selling newspapers. After public school, he went to Mississippi State College and later to Louisiana State University where he was a notable baseball player. He was admitted to the bar in 1902 and elected to Congress as a Democrat in 1910 and to the U.S. Senate in 1918 where he served until he died. When the Democrats gained power in 1932, Harrison was appointed chairman of the powerful Finance Committee. He was greatly skilled at pushing early New Deal legislation through Congress. Thus, when the Democrats had legislation they often sent it through the Finance Committee whose membership had been largely selected by Harrison himself. Consequently, Harrison "horse-traded" many acts through the Senate.

Sources

Encyclopedia of sociology. 1974. Guilford, Conn.: Dushkin Publishing.

James, Edward T. 1973. *Dictionary of American biography.* Supplement 3. New York: Charles Scribner's Sons.

Sills, David L., ed. 1968. *International encyclopedia of the social sciences.* New York: Macmillan and Free Press.

HARROD-DOMAR GROWTH MODEL. In economics a one-sector growth model, useful in the short run, which, following Keynes's ideas, assumes a dynamic equilibrium, economic stability, and employment. The model owes much to Keynes and considers the viability of steady-state growth; the probability that such growth occurs in periods of full employment; and how stable that growth might be. Both Domar and Harrod produced similar versions of the theory. The model was outlined in 1939 and expanded into a book by Harrod in *Towards a Dynamic Economics* (1948).

Roy Forbes Harrod (1900–78) was born in Norfolk, England, and educated at Westminster School and New College, Oxford. He lectured at Christ Church College, Oxford, shortly after graduation in 1922. He spent a term at Kings College, Cambridge, where he was much influenced by Keynes, and in time he became his official biographer and a leading promoter of his economics. During World War II Harrod served on Winston Churchill's private statistical staff, later co-edited *The Economic Journal* (1945–61), and was president of the Royal Economic Society (1962–64). He was knighted in 1959. He contributed to imperfect competition theory, international trade, and business cycle theory. Among his works were *The Trade Cycle* (1939), *Life of John Maynard Keynes* (1951), *Economic Essays* (1952), *Foundations of Inductive Logic* (1956), *The British Economy* (1963), *Reforming the World's Money* (1965), *Dollar, Sterling Collaboration* (1968), and *Economic Dynamics* (1973).

Evsey David Domar (b. 1914) was born in Lodz, Russia, grew up in Manchuria, and attended the State Faculty of War in Harbin (1930–31). In 1936 he entered the University of California, Los Angeles, and in 1947 obtained his Ph.D. from Harvard. He was appointed a professor of economics at Massachusetts Institute of Technology and turned his interest to the workings of the Soviet economy, in particular the Soviet collective farm as a producer cooperative. A collection of his essays appeared as *Capitalism, Socialism and Serfdom* (1989).

Sources

Blaug, Mark. 1985. *Great economists since Keynes.* Brighton, England: Harvester Press.

Blaug, Mark, ed. 1986. *Who's who in economics: a biographical dictionary of major economists, 1700–1986.* 2d ed. Cambridge, Mass.: MIT Press.

Domar, Evsey D. 1992. How I tried to become an economist. *Eminent economists.* Cambridge: Cambridge University Press.

Eatwell, John; Milgate, Murray; and Newman, Peter. 1987. *The new Palgrave: a dictionary of economics.* London: Macmillan.

Sills, David L., ed. 1968. *International encyclopedia of the social sciences.* New York: Macmillan and Free Press.

Young, Warren. 1989. *Harrod and his trade cycle group: the origins and development of the growth research programme.* Baskingstoke, England: Macmillan.

HATCH ACTS, LITTLE HATCH ACTS. Acts of the U.S. Congress, 1939 and 1940, intended to regulate the political behavior of U.S federal employees. In 1939 the act restricted service as an alternate or delegate at a political party convention; dealing with political contributions; organizing political clubs; electioneering; running for elected office; and speaking or leading party political meetings. Little Hatch Acts are U.S. state laws that have been passed to regulate party political activities by state employees paid from federal funds.

Carl Atwood Hatch (1889–1963) was born in Kirwin, Kansas. He worked in his father's store in Eldorado while finishing school and then became a reporter for the weekly *Eldorado Courier,* and for a time jointly owned a newspaper. Hatch entered Cumberland University, Lebanon, Tennessee, graduated in law in 1912, and practiced in Eldorado before moving to Clovis, New Mexico, where he served as assistant state attorney-general (1917–18), state district judge (1923–29) and became U.S senator in 1933, 1936, and 1942. While a senator, Hatch was interested in farm and labor legislation, and was concerned that federal relief recipients, especially Works Progress Administration employees, were being asked to contribute to political campaigns. Following Hatch's retirement from the Senate, he was appointed federal district judge in Albuquerque (1959–63). In 1946 Hatch believed his efforts to limit the influence of special interest groups—capital or labor—had failed. Toward the end of his political career he was advocating the full disclosure of all contributions to political parties and individual politicians.

Sources

Commager, Henry S., ed. 1968. *Documents of American history.* 8th ed. New York: Appleton-Century-Crofts.

Garraty, John A., ed. 1981. *Dictionary of American biography*. Supplement 7. New York: Charles Scribner's Sons.
Shafritz, Jay M. 1988. *The Dorsey dictionary of American government and politics*. Chicago: Dorsey.

HAUSSMANNISE. To open out city spaces, and generally to rebuild.

Baron Georges Eugène Haussmann (1809–91) was the French city planner largely responsible for the layout of present-day Paris, where Boulevard Haussmann is named in his honor. He entered public service under Louis Phillipe and completed distinctive work; under Napoleon III he rose to prefect of the Seine in 1853. He began to improve the outward appearance of Paris by widening its streets, laying out boulevards and parks, and building sewers and bridges. For these services he was made baron and senator. But he was dismissed in 1870 because of the heavy costs such projects required of the citizens. "Haussmannizing" became synonymous with reckless destruction of old buildings to make way for roads. He was a Bonapartist member for Corsica in the National Assembly (1877–81) but was rarely active in Parliament. His *Memoires* appeared in three volumes (1890–93).

Sources

Chapman, Joan M., and Chapman, Brian. 1957. *The life and times of Baron Haussmann: Paris in the Second Empire*. London: Weidenfeld and Nicolson.
Haussmann, Georges E. 1979. *Grands travaux de Paris*. [Reprint of volume 3 of *Memoires du Baron Haussmann*.] Paris: G. Durier.
Saalman, Howard. 1971. *Haussmann: Paris transformed*. New York: G. Braziller.

HAWKESPEAK. Political doublespeak; a circumlocutory and often convoluted style of parliamentary or journalistic delivery.

Robert James Lee Hawke (b. 1929) was born at Bordertown, South Australia, raised in his early years on the Yorke Peninsula in Maitland, and on the death of his elder brother in 1939 was brought to be educated in West Australia. He won a scholarship to Perth Modern, an exclusive school for able students. At the University of Western Australia he completed his B.A. and LL.B. degrees and was a Rhodes Scholar (1952). At Oxford University he was awarded a bachelor of letters and was noted in the *Guiness Book of Records* for quaffing 2.5 pints of beer in twelve seconds. On returning to Australia, he undertook research at the Australian National University, and two years later he became a research officer for the Australian Council of Trade Unions for whom he was a successful advocate in wage hearings, and later its president (1969–80). In 1973 he was president of the Australian Labor party (ALP). In Australia's federal Parliament he became shadow minister for industrial relations, and in 1983 Hawke was quickly made ALP federal leader, led the party to electoral success, and became Australia's most popular prime minister. Among his circumlocutions are phrases like "in place" to mean "has happened" or "will be happening"; the turning of nouns into adverbs, as in "Let me say, foundationally,

... ''; often he used the words "address," "in respect of," "consideration," and "position," and used "indicated" for "said," "unfounded" for "untrue," "improper" for "wrong," and "abominable" for anything he did not like. In 1991 he lost the leadership of the Federal ALP and quit Parliament for political journalism.

Sources

Anson, Stan. 1991. *Hawke: an emotional life.* Melbourne: McPhee Gribble.
D'Alpuget, Blanche. 1983. *Robert J. Hawke: a biography.* Rev. ed. East Melbourne: Schwarz/Landsdowne.
Hurst, John. 1979. *Hawke, a definitive biography.* Sydney: Angus and Robertson.

HAWKINS-SIMON CONDITIONS. Economic conditions under which there exists a positive solution to a Leontief system of industrial input-output relationships. In the system, each actor produces a single good, without joint products, and under constant returns to scale; the goods are used in fixed proportion. When these conditions obtain, the balance of demand for and supply of goods in the system may be represented by a set of linear differential equations about the productivity of the system (Eatwell et al., 1987:605). This description shows that the system as a whole is stable or unstable, depending on the eigenvalues of these equations.

David Hawkins (b. 1913) was born in El Paso, Texas, and studied philosophy at Stanford and the University of California (Ph.D., 1940). He taught philosophy at Stanford (1941–43), and he worked on, and wrote a history of, the Manhattan Project, Los Alamos (1943–46). In 1946–47 he became a professor of philosophy at George Washington University and later joined the Department of Philosophy, University of Colorado (1947) and retired emeritus (1982). Much of his time was spent on projects outside university, for example, planning the teaching in physical and in computer sciences, computer sciences, and in early science and mathematics courses for elementary schools. He also taught at various universities in the United States, Canada, Italy, and England, and was a fellow at the Institute of Advanced Study at Princeton (1969–70). He was also a member of the Council of the Smithsonian Institution (1972–78) and of its Advisory Council on Education (1986–88), and served as chairman of the Colorado Endowment of the Humanities (1973–75). He published an historical study of the Manhattan Project (1946; declassified 1962), *Science and Creative Spirit* (1971), *The Language of Nature* (1967), *The Informed Vision* (1974), and *The Science and Ethics of Equality* (1977).

Herbert Alexander Simon (b. 1916) was born in Milwaukee, Wisconsin, educated at public schools, and influenced by an uncle who studied economics and bequeathed a library to him. In 1933 Simon, a vigorous debater on social issues, entered the University of Chicago to study political science and econometrics. He worked for an organization of local government administrators and published *Measurement Standards in City Administration* (1937–38), edited a monthly journal, and the *Annual Municipal Yearbook* (1938). He completed a

Ph.D. at the University of Chicago and published much of it as *Administrative Behavior* (1947). A professor of political science, he taught at Illinois Institute of Technology in 1947, became professor of psychology and administration at Carnegie-Mellon University in 1949, and was drawn to computer science and psychology. He won a Nobel Prize for Economics in 1978 for his studies on organizations. Among his books are *Organizations* (1958), *Models of Thought,* 2 vols. (1979, 1989), and *Scientific Discovery* (1987). He has lectured at many universities around the world and has nineteen honorary degrees. In 1989 he received the Psychological Sciences Gold Medal Award from the American Psychological Association.

Sources

Eatwell, John; Milgate, Murray; and Newman, Peter. 1987. *The new Palgrave: a dictionary of economics.* London: Macmillan.

Editors. 1989. Psychological Sciences Gold Medal Award: Herbert Alexander Simon. *American Psychologist* 44:659–666.

Hawkins, David. 1948. Some conditions of macroeconomic stability. *Econometrica* 16: 309–322.

Hawkins, David, and Simon, Herbert A. 1949. Note: some conditions of microeconomic stability. *Econometrica* 17:245–248.

Jaques Cattell Press, ed. 1989–90. *American men and women of science: the social and behavioral sciences.* 17th ed. New York: Jaques Cattell and R. R. Bowker.

Katz, Bernard S., ed. 1989. *Nobel laureates in economic sciences: a biographical dictionary.* New York: Garland Publishing.

Simon, Herbert A. 1991. *Models of my life.* New York: Basic Books.

Who's who in America, 1992–93. Providence, N.J.: Marquis.

Personal Communication.

HAWTHORNE EXPERIMENTS. A series of field experiments, observations of work groups, and depth interviews with employees undertaken at the Western Electric Company's Hawthorne Plant, Cicero, near Chicago (1924–32). Initiated through the Personnel Department of the company, the program became associated with the Harvard Business School through George Elton Mayo (1880–1949). The results constituted the main evidence used by the Human Relations Movement to create theories of industrial behavior stressing social influences as well as providing impetus to modern trends in personnel management. Controversies over the results of these studies remain in Industrial Sociology and Organization Theory. The results showed that physical and monetary factors alone were insufficient to explain changes in output and employee morale. Special emphasis was given to the impact of informal social organization of work groups. The Hawthorne Experiments had considerable impact on academic and management thinking in the 1940s and 1950s, but today its influence varies, and the interpretations of the work are wide ranging.

The Hawthorne Works, erected in 1902, are located in Hawthorne, one of the earliest settlements in the township of Cicero, near Chicago, and the location of the works of the Western Electric Company. By 1922 nearly all the company's New York shops had been transferred to the Hawthorne site.

See also MAYOISM.

Sources

Finlay, Frank D. 1937. *A survey of the town of Cicero, Illinois.* Department of Statistics and Research, Council of Social Agencies of Chicago.

Gillespie, Richard. 1991. *Manufacturing knowledge: a history of the Hawthorne Experiments.* Cambridge: Cambridge University Press.

Roethlisberger, Fritz J., and Dickson, William J. 1939. *Management and the worker.* Cambridge, Mass.: Harvard University Press.

Spelman, Walter B. 1922. *The town of Cicero, Illinois: history, advantages, and government.* Cicero, Ill.: Morton High School Pamphlet.

Trahair, Richard C. S. 1984. *The humanist temper: the life and work of Elton Mayo.* New Brunswick, N.J.: Transaction Books.

Zusne, Leonard. 1984. *Biographical dictionary of psychology.* Westport, Conn.: Greenwood Press.

HAYEKIANS, HAYEKIAN ECONOMICS. Anticollectivist liberals who formed the Mont Peterin Society in 1947; economic beliefs centering on laissez-faire economics, neoliberalist politics, and economic rationalism. The Hayekian influence spread slowly after 1947 until 1970. It concerned the function of prices in guiding capital accumulation, changes in industry, production, and the economy through a free competitive order, which was assumed to be necessary to sustain humankind. Hayek's early writings criticized government intervention in the economy, advocated freedom of banking to eliminate inflation, advocated no inheritance tax, and recommended a low level of marginal income tax. His ideas converted Margaret Thatcher and her free marketeers.

Friedrick A. von Hayek (1899–1992) was born into a Viennese academic family, served in World War I, and studied law and economics at the University of Vienna (Dr. Juris, 1921: Rev. Pol. 1923). After working briefly with economists in the United States, he formed a circle of economists in Vienna under Ludwig von Mises, became director of the Austrian Institute for Business Cycle Research in 1927, and began teaching at the University of Vienna. His study, *Prices and Production* (1931), led to a secure position at the London School of Economics. He entered an unsuccessful intellectual debate with Keynes, failed to convince many, and published *Profits, Interest and Investment* (1939) and *The Pure Theory of Capital* (1941). He received a D.Sc. at the University of London (1940). Thereafter he turned to the history of political thought and published his *The Road to Serfdom* (1944). He became a professor of social and moral sciences at the University of Chicago and turned to psychology. His *The Constitution of Liberty* (1960) is an exegesis of modern liberalism. He joined the faculty at the University of Freiburg in 1962 and retired to the University of Salzburg in 1968 for the next nine years. His final work was *Law, Legislation and Liberty* (1973–79). He was awarded the Noble Prize jointly in Economics (1974).

Sources
Blaug, Mark. 1985. *Great economists since Keynes.* Brighton, England: Harvester Press.
Blaug, Mark, ed. 1986. *Who's who in economics: a biographical dictionary of major economists, 1700–1986.* 2d ed. Cambridge, Mass.: MIT Press.
Gray, John. 1984. *Hayek on liberty.* Oxford: Basil Blackwell.
The international who's who, 1992–93. London: Europa Publications.
Sills, David L., ed. 1968. *International encyclopedia of the social sciences.* New York: Macmillan and Free Press.

HAYES-BAUTISTA MODEL. A model of the social processes that arise in the patient-practitioner relationship when modifying treatment for the patient. The model is based on common features found in the illness episodes recounted by 200 Chicanos living in the San Francisco Bay area. The model emphasizes the patient's rather than the practitioner's perceptions, and it was offered as an advance on the theory of patient-doctor relationships outlined by Talcott Parsons in 1951.

David E. Hayes-Bautista (b. 1945) was born in San Pedro, California, studied sociology at the University of California, Berkeley, and completed graduate work at the University's Medical Center (Ph.D., 1974). In 1970 he was awarded the Abraham Rosenberg Fellowship in sociology and in 1972 his university Chancellor's Award for Public Service. He served many health agencies in the San Francisco area, including the National Chicano Health Organization, published a resource list of Mexican American services in the city (1970), and wrote several journal articles on the inadequacies of the health services to Chicanos. He continued research in this field and co-authored *The Burden of Support: Young Latinos in an Aging Society* (1988).

See also PARSONIAN THEORY.

Sources
Hayes-Bautista, David. 1976. Modifying the treatment: patient compliance, patient control, and medical care. *Social Science and Medicine* 10:233–238.
Jaques Cattell Press, ed. 1979. *Biographical directory of the American Public Health Association.* New York: Jaques Cattell Press and R. R. Bowker.
Martinez, Julio A., ed. 1979. *Chicano scholars and writers: a bio-bibliographical directory.* Metuchen, N.J.: Scarecrow Press.
Wolinsky, Frederic D. 1988. *The sociology of health.* 2d ed. Belmont, Calif.: Wadsworth.

HAYS CODE. A moral code that influenced the American film industry.

William Harrison (''Will H.'') Hays (1879–1954) was born in Sullivan, Indiana. He was raised to be hard working, cheerful, and optimistic, and to abjure all interest in liquor and the borrowing of money. He studied law at Wabash College, Lincoln Memorial University, was admitted to the bar in 1900, and was an attorney for Sullivan (1910–13). He was chairman of the Republican National Committee (1918–21) and postmaster general (1921–22) under President Warren Harding. In 1922 America citizens were complaining about immorality in movies. Because he was a Republican, influential in politics, worked hard, and negotiated with skill, "Will. H" Hays was chosen to chair the Motion Picture Producers and Distributors of America, Inc. Rather than censor movies, he would try to convince movie-makers to produce wholesome films, that is, without offensive words and scenes and suggestive advertising. He helped formulate the "Hays Code" and administered it from what became known as the "Hays Office." For this he became known as the "Czar" of movies. He published several monographs and talks on the history of the movies and on contemporary problems in the film industry. He was also active in the American Red Cross and the Boy Scouts of America, and was an elder in the Presbyterian Church. Upon retiring from his movie work, he returned to practice law in New York, California, and Indiana.

Sources

Candee, Marjorie D., ed. 1954. *Current biography yearbook.* New York: H. W. Wilson.

Gardner, Gerald. 1987. *The censorship papers: movie censorship letters from the Hays Office, 1934–1968.* New York: Dodd, Mead.

Hays, Will H. 1955. *Memoirs.* Garden City, N.Y.: Doubleday.

Hendrickson, Robert. 1988. *The dictionary of eponyms: names that became words.* New York: Dorset.

Moley, Raymond. 1971. *The Hays Office.* New York: J. S. Ozer.

Roth, Anna, ed. 1943. *Current biography yearbook.* New York: H. W. Wilson.

Who was who in America, 1951–60. Vol. III. Chicago.: Marquis.

HAYTER REPORT. A British report (1961) that argued for the establishment of area studies in the social sciences outside the language departments of tertiary education institutions. American experience supported the policy: efforts toward area studies were strong; area centers could be well organized; and there was a strong emphasis on modern rather than historical studies. British universities were therefore asked to apply for government grants to establish area studies. The University of Hull established South East Asian Studies, while the University of Leeds established a Center for Chinese Studies. Similar centers were established in universities around the world, and have tended to concentrate on Latin American studies, and studies of Russia, the Far East, the Middle East, India, and Muslim countries.

William Goodenough Hayter (b. 1906) was educated at Winchester and New College, Oxford; entered the British Diplomatic Service in 1930; and served the Foreign Office in Vienna (1931), Moscow (1934), China (1938), Washington (1941), and Paris (1948). He was ambassador to Moscow (1953–57), and deputy undersecretary of state in the Foreign Office (1957–58). He wrote the report after inquiries into areas studies (1961). He was also made a fellow of Winchester College (1958–76), a trustee of the British Museum (1960–70), and a warden of New College, Oxford (1958–76). Among his publications are *The Diplomacy of the Great Powers* (1961), *The Kremlin and the Embassy* (1966), *Russia and the World* (1970), *William of Wykeham: Patron of the Arts* (1970), and *Spooner: A Biography* (1977).

Sources
Hayter, William G. 1961. *Report.* London: H.M.S.O.
Hayter, William G. 1974. *A double life: an autobiography.* London: H. Hamilton.
Sills, David L., ed. 1968. *International encyclopedia of the social sciences.* New York:
    Macmillan and Free Press.
Who's who, 1992. London: Adam and Charles Black.

HEARSTISM. Characteristic of the late nineteenth- and early twentieth-century
American newspaper magnate, especially in the pursuit of power by using newspapers to promote rather than report social conflict, and to present propaganda
rather than the truth.

William Randolph Hearst (1863–1951) was born in San Francisco and educated at Saint Paul's School, New Hampshire, and Harvard where he made the
Harvard Lampoon profitable and was expelled for his pranks. His father reluctantly gave him control of the San Francisco *Examiner,* which he also made
profitable with florid crusades against political corruption, real and alleged. On
his father's death he received $7.5 million, bought the New York *Morning
Journal,* and used it to attack the *World* in a contest with Joseph Pulitzer.
Hearst's crude, "yellow" journalism goaded the United States into a war with
Spain over Cuba in 1898. Hearst tended to participate in the hostilities that he
had arranged to have reported. He exploited sensationalism and promoted discord between different social classes—capital against workers and unions. Sur-
rounded by scandal, his attempts to secure a high political post failed (1900–6).
Meanwhile, he acquired many papers and dominated their editorial policy, dictated U.S. foreign policy, promoted scandal, manipulated public opinion, and
set the course for modern newspaper barons. During World War I, he held pro-
German attitudes and later opposed America's entry into the League of Nations.
He had a long-term relationship with a showgirl from the Ziegfield Follies.
Largely to promote her career in the 1920s, Hearst went into the film industry;
he also invested in New York real estate and later helped Roosevelt become
president. In the 1930s his wealth diminished until it reached a mere $60 million
at his death. It is widely held that Hearst's life was depicted in Orson Welles's
film, *Citizen Kane* (1941). When Hearst failed in his final attempt to become a
politician (1906), Richard Croke echoed sentiments of respectable Democrats:
"God help Democracy if Hearstism becomes a guiding principle" (Swanberg,
1961:301).

Sources
Chaney, Lindsay, and Cieply, Michael. 1981. *The Hearsts: family and empire: the later
    years.* New York: Simon and Schuster.
Garraty, John A. 1977. *Dictionary of American biography.* Supplement 5. New York:
    Charles Scribner's Sons.
Robinson, Judith. 1991. *The Hearsts: an American dynasty.* Newark: University of Del-
    aware Press.
Swanberg, William A. 1961. *Citizen Hearst: a biography of William Randolph Hearst.*
    New York: Collier, Macmillan, Scribner Books.

HECKSCHER-OHLIN TRADE THEORY. An explanation of world trade based on differing factor endowments and cost considerations rather than the degree of effort needed to produce goods. The theory assumes that trade originates from differences between nations in the extent to which they own factors of production: this leads to differences in the relative costs of production. Thus, nations rich in capital have the advantage in producing capital-intensive goods, will export them, and import labor-intensive goods.

Eli Filip Heckscher (1870–1952) was born in Sweden and became the first professor of economics and statistics at the new business school, University of Uppsala; in 1929 he became head of the Stockholm Institute for Economic History. He was an orthodox economist and liberal laissez-faire politician who objected to deficit financing and supported the idea of the gold standard. In 1919 he published "The Effect of Foreign Trade on Distribution of Income"; it was later elaborated by Bertil Ohlin and became known as their theorem.

Bertil Gotthard Ohlin (1899–1979) was raised in Klippan, Sweden, son of a lawyer, and studied economics, statistics, and mathematics at the University of Lund (1915) and in 1917 transferred to the Stockholm Institute of Economics and Business Administration where Heckscher was. After completing his early studies, Ohlin reported for government committees on Swedish industry and tariff policies and completed his military service. He attended Cambridge University and Harvard, and was a professor of economics at the University of Copenhagen (1925–30) before returning to Stockholm to succeed Heckscher. Ohlin published *Interregional and International Trade* (1933), which was greatly influenced by Heckscher's 1919 article. It presents the basic mathematical model of trade now known as the Heckscher-Ohlin model. Ohlin anticipated some of Keynes's general theory, contributed to theory of money, employment, and economic fluctuations, and was also a prominent member of Sweden's Parliament (1938–70), leader of the Folkpartiet (1944–67), and won a Nobel Prize for Economics (1977).

Sources

Blaug, Mark, ed. 1986. *Who's who in economics: a biographical dictionary of major economists, 1700–1986.* 2d ed. Cambridge, Mass.: MIT Press.

Eatwell, John; Milgate, Murray; and Newman, Peter. 1987. *The new Palgrave: a dictionary of economics.* London: Macmillan.

Sills, David L., ed. 1968. *International encyclopedia of the social sciences.* New York: Macmillan and Free Press.

Stiegler, Stella E. 1985. *Dictionary of economics and business.* 3d ed. Aldershot: Gower.

HECTOR. To intimidate or dominate in a blustering way, swagger or bully; a bully.

In the *Iliad* Hector was the son of Priam and Hecuba, husband to Andromache and brother of Paris. As prince of Troy he led his followers against the Greeks. He killed Patroculus, friend of Achilles. To avenge his friend's death, Achilles pursued Hector around the walls of Troy, slew him, trampled his corpse, and, with it lashed to his chariot, dragged it in the dust. Hector is the legendary ancestor of the kings of France. In medieval drama, Hector sometimes appears as a boaster and domineering; late-seventeenth-century reports indicate gangs of bullies adopted his name when they frightened Londoners in the street.

Sources

Hendrickson, Robert. 1988. *The dictionary of eponyms: names that became words.* New York: Dorset.

Jobes, Gertrude. 1962. *Dictionary of mythology, folklore and symbols.* New York: Scarecrow Press.

McHenry, Robert, ed. 1992. *The new encyclopedia Britannica.* Chicago: Encyclopedia Britannica, Inc.

HEEP SYNDROME. A subordinate's assertion that they are worthless and undeserving of promotion (Peter and Hull, 1969).

Uriah Heep is a character in *David Copperfield* (1850) by Charles Dickens (1812–70). A fawning and hypocritical clerk in the office of the lawyer Mr. Wickfield, Heep is a detested, sneaky man who ceaselessly reminds people of his humbleness, in an effort to win their sympathy and insinuate himself into their respect. To David he says: ''I am the 'umblest person going . . . my mother is likewise a very 'umble person. We live in a 'umble abode . . . but have much to be thankful for. My father's former calling was 'umble—he was a sexton.''

Sources

Freeman, William. 1973. *Dictionary of fictional characters.* London: J. M. Dent and Sons.

Peter, Laurence J., and Hull, Raymond. 1969. *The Peter principle: why things always go wrong.* New York: William Morrow.

Storey, Graham. 1991. *David Copperfield: interweaving truth and fiction.* Boston: Twayne Publishers.

HEGELIAN, HEGELIANISM. Relating to the nineteenth-century German philosopher of history. His idealistic philosophy, which uses the method of dialectic to produce a systematic and complete account of knowledge and experience by uniting the two in a complete whole. Psychologically, the mind develops from consciousness to self-awareness, and later to reason, spirit, and religion. Finally, it achieves absolute knowledge. This is the highest form of human knowledge and requires that any other form must be critically examined by this idealistic theory. Reality—the absolute—appears as a system of ideas, then as nature, and finally as mind in its most gratifying and satisfying form. The dialectic assumes that a thesis produces an antithesis; the conflict between them is resolved in their synthesis, which in turn is the next thesis, and so on. Social theorists have extended this to the discussion of human interaction.

Georg Wilhem Fredrich Hegel (1770–1831) was born at Stuttgart, studied theology at Tübingen, and became a professor at Jena in 1806. He edited a political journal (1807–8); was head of a high school in Nuremburg (1808–16); and professor of philosophy at Heidelberg (1816–18) and Berlin (1818).

His system, the leading school of metaphysical thought in Germany in the second quarter of the nineteenth century, purported to be a complete philosophy and undertook to explain the whole universe and being. Hegelianism is radically hostile to natural science and especially to the Newtonian philosophy. Hegel's complete works include studies on philosophy of religion, aesthetics, the philosophy of history, and the history of philosophy. Between 1832 and 1841 his works appeared in fourteen volumes.

Sources

Butler, Clark. 1977. *G.W.F. Hegel.* Boston: Twayne Publishers.

Cross, Frank L. 1974. *The Oxford dictionary of the Christian Church.* 2d ed. New York: Oxford University Press.

Inwood, Michael, ed. 1985. *Hegel.* Oxford: Oxford University Press.

McHenry, Robert, ed. 1992. *The new encyclopedia Britannica.* Chicago: Encyclopedia Britannica, Inc.

Miller, David, ed. 1987. *The Blackwell encyclopedia of political thought.* Oxford: Basil Blackwell.

Plant, R. 1983. *Hegel.* London: Allen and Unwin.

Sills, David L., ed. 1968. *International encyclopedia of the social sciences.* New York: Macmillan and Free Press.

Zusne, Leonard, 1984. *Biographical dictionary of psychology.* Westport, Conn.: Greenwood Press.

HEIDER'S P-O-X THEORY OF COGNITIVE BALANCE. In 1958 Fritz Heider established what later became known as attribution theory. He placed a major emphasis on the human need to comprehend and make predictions. Making predictions about other people is vital to the development of interpersonal relationships. By inferring a person's internal dispositions, observers adjust their own behavior to bring about positive outcomes and a balanced state in interacting with that person. The theory had three elements: *P,* the person; *O,* the other person relating to *P;* and *X,* the object that the two had in common.

Fritz Heider (1896–1988) was born in Vienna and spent his childhood in Gratz, receiving a classical education at the official state Gymnasium. Unable to serve in the army during World War I because of a childhood eye injury, he entered the University of Gratz (Ph.D., 1920). In the 1920s he studied at the Psychological Institute in Berlin, where he took classes with eminent scholars such as Wolfgang Köhler (1887–1967), Max Wertheimer (1880–1943), and Kurt Lewin (1890–1947). Heider arrived in the United States in 1930 to work at the Research Department of the Clarke School for the Deaf and to be an assistant professor at Smith College. In 1946 he published his seminal paper on the cognitive oraganization of social attitudes; in 1958 appeared his theory using the same ideas for understanding interpersonal relations. In 1947 he became a professor at the University of Kansas. His personal life, career, and conceptual developments are described in his *The Life of a Psychologist: An Autobiography* (1983).

Sources

Harvey, John H. 1988. Obituary: Fritz Heider (1896–1988). *American Psychologist* 44: 570.

Heider, Fritz. 1946. Attitudes and cognitive organization. *Journal of Psychology* 21:107–112.

Heider, Fritz. 1958. *The psychology of interpersonal relations.* New York: John Wiley.

Sills, David L., ed. 1968. *International encyclopedia of the social sciences.* New York: Macmillan and Free Press.

Wolman, Benjamin, ed. 1989. *Dictionary of behavioral science.* 2d ed. San Diego, Calif.: Academic Press, Inc.

HELLENIC. Relating to the ancient or modern Greeks or Hellenes, or anyone of Greek origin.

Hellen was the chief of a Thessalian tribe in Pthiotis and was reputed to be the ancestor of the Hellenes. He was the son of Pyrrha and Deucalion, descendants of Prometheus, the survivors of the Deluge which Zeus had used to end the wickedness of mortals. The two were the original Stone people, who established an enduring race that was necessary to rescue the earth from the desolation of the deluge. Hellen had a son, Aeolus, who became king of Thessaly.

Sources

Hamilton, Edith. 1940. *Mythology: timeless tales of gods and heroes.* Boston: Little, Brown.

Hammond, Nicholas G.L., and Scullard, Howard H., eds. 1970. *The Oxford classical dictionary.* Oxford: Clarendon Press.

McHenry, Robert, ed. 1992. *The new encyclopedia Britannica.* Chicago: Encyclopedia Britannica, Inc.

HELSINKI ACCORD, HELSINKI PROCESS. The results of an international conference in 1975 on security and cooperation in Europe attended by thirty-five heads of state, including the USSR and the United States. The meeting aimed to advance the policy of detente, that is, agreement on economic and technological cooperation in humanitarian fields, and security and disarmament. The aims were set within the principles of sovereignty and self-determination. The Helsinki Accord or Helsinki Process, officially the Conference on Security and Cooperation in Europe, remains elusive to many people because it is extremely complex and changed its character in the late 1980s.

Helsinki, Finland, is on the Gulf of Finland. It was founded by Gustavus Vasa in 1550 and was declared the capital in 1812. During World War II the city was heavily bombed. It is a center of shipbuilding and the export trade in textiles, engineering, porcelain, metals, and paper.

Sources

Bloed, Arie, and Dijk, Peter van, eds. 1985. *Essays on human rights in the Helsinki Process.* Boston: Martinus Nijhoff.

Crystal, David, ed. 1990. *The Cambridge encyclopedia.* Cambridge: Cambridge University Press.

Lawson, Edward H., ed. 1991. *Encyclopedia of human rights.* New York: Taylor and Francis.

Mastny, Vojtech. 1986. *Helsinki, human rights, and European security: analysis and documentation.* Durham, N.C.: Duke University Press.

Mastny, Vojtech. 1992. *The Helsinki Process and reintegration of Europe: analysis and documentation 1986–1990.* Durham, N.C.: Duke University Press.

Plano, Jack C., and Olton, Roy. 1988. *The international relations dictionary.* 4th ed. Santa Barbara, Calif.: ABC-CLIO.

Shafritz, Jay M. 1988. *The Dorsey dictionary of American government and politics.* Chicago: Dorsey.

Wells, Samuel F., Jr. 1990. *The Helsinki Process and the future of Europe.* Washington, D.C.: Wilson Center Press.

HENRI PRINCIPLE. The rule that espionage is carried out best in groups or cells of five. Members of each group or cell acted independently of other cells so that if one were discovered the others would survive, and the political movement would continue. The principle was applied to the Cambridge Marxists who became Soviet agents for Comintern. Anthony Blunt (1907–83) was a talent spotter and served Guy Burgess (1911–63) who was an associate at one time of Kim Philby (1912–88) and Donald Maclean (1913–83). In the group—the cell-like character of which has been disputed by Philby and celebrated by British newspapermen—the ''Fifth Man'' is not securely known.

Ernst Henri (fl. 1933–85) was born Semyon Nicolayevich Rostovski. He wrote an article for *New Statesman and Nation* (1933) describing how German communists resisted Nazi oppression by forming groups of five. Under the supervision of Guy Burgess at the BBC during World War II, Rostovski broadcast in praise of Russia's military power and intelligence services. In 1951 Rostovski returned to Moscow and was jailed for two years. In 1985 he was living in honorable retirement in Moscow. Although he had always respected Donald Maclean, whom he knew well, Henri claimed to know nothing about spies.
Sources

Henri, Ernst. 1933. Revolutionary movement in Nazi Germany. *Newstatesman and Nation* 6: (August 5): 153–154; (August 19):207–208; (September 16):319–320.

Penrose, Barry, and Freeman, Simon. 1987. *Conspiracy of silence: the secret life of Anthony Blunt.* Revised ed. London: Grafton.

HENRICANS. Followers of a twelfth-century French religious who preached penance, rejected the sacraments, and denied original sin.

Henry of Lausanne, also known as Henry the Monk, the Deacon, the Hermit, and Henry of Clugny (d. c. 1148), was a French itinerant preacher and religious reformer. Rejecting the objective efficacy of the sacraments and the priesthood, he preached and followed the evangelist's life of poverty and penance. On entering Le Mans, he was expelled for his views by the bishop of Hildebert (1101) and went to southern France. In 1119 he was denounced by the Council of Toulouse. For a short period he recanted after his arrest by the bishop of Arles

(1135), but returned to preaching his views. Bernard of Clairvaux was directed to oppose Henry's teachings in 1145, and Henry was again arrested. He died at Toulouse.

Sources

Cross, Frank L. 1974. *The Oxford dictionary of the Christian Church.* 2d ed. New York: Oxford University Press.
Douglas, James D., ed. 1974. *The new international dictionary of the Christian Church.* Exeter: Paternoster Press.
Smith, Benjamin. 1903. *The Century cyclopedia of names.* London: The Times.

HENRY GEORGE LEAGUE, GEORGIST. Followers of economic principles for radical, nonrevolutionary redistribution of wealth through taxation—especially the "single tax"—on land. The modern mixed economy owes much to the Georgist.

Henry George (1839–97) was born in Philadelphia, son of a custom house clerk. He left school at 13 and witnessed mutiny when he was shipped to India as a cabin boy. He became a journeyman printer on newspapers in the Californian and Canadian goldfields. He married and settled in California, and after seven years of hardship became aware of the desperation of poverty. He became a journalist in 1865, was an adviser to the state governor, and briefly had his own newspaper in which he developed ideas of economic reform. By 1870 he believed that every man had the right to something of the Earth's surface. His *Our Land and Policy* (1871) became a classic in economics. His first publication was a eulogy to President Lincoln after his assassination, and his major work was *Progress and Poverty* (1879), which is still regarded as a fine study of economic theory and policy. He opposed poverty, slavery, and land speculation, and advocated a theory of a single tax; he supported free trade, opposed land monopoly, favored trade unions and high wages, but opposed socialism. He went to England and Europe, where his ideas were favorably studied. His influence on Fabianism was early and wide reaching. In 1886 Henry George was an unsuccessful candidate for mayor of New York City, possibly because of electoral fraud; during his second attempt he died suddenly of a stroke.

Sources

Baker, Charles A. 1955. *Henry George.* New York: Oxford University Press.
Cord, Steven B. 1965. *Henry George: dreamer or realist?* Philadelphia: University of Pennsylvania Press.
Eatwell, John; Milgate, Murray; and Newman, Peter. 1987. *The new Palgrave: a dictionary of economics.* London: Macmillan.
George, Henry. c. 1900. *The life of Henry George.* 1960 ed. New York: R. Schalkenbach Foundation.
Miller, David, ed. 1987. *The Blackwell encyclopedia of political thought.* Oxford: Basil Blackwell.
Morris, Dan, and Morris, Inez. 1974. *Who was who in American politics.* New York: Hawthorn Books.
Sills, David L., ed. 1968. *International encyclopedia of the social sciences.* New York: Macmillan and Free Press.

HERBARTIAN. Relating to the nineteenth-century German philosopher and pedagogic psychologist.

Johann Friedrich Herbart (1776–1841) was born at Oldenburg. After studies at Jena, he worked as a tutor at Interlaken in Switzerland (1797–1800). He moved to Göttingen University and in 1805 was appointed professor. In 1808 he became professor at Königsberg where he conducted a seminary of pedagogy; he returned to Göttingen as professor of philosophy in 1833. Herbart is remembered as the founder of a system-embracing logic, metaphysics, and aesthetics, and for his statement: "Every man must have a love for all activities, each must be a virtuoso in one." He is considered the father of the scientific study of education. His pedagogic principles followed five steps: preparation, presentation, comparison and abstraction, generalization, and application. In the United States his followers established the National Society of Education.

Sources

De Garmo, Charles. 1895. *Herbart and the Herbartians.* London: Heinemann.

Deighton, Lee, ed. 1971. *The encyclopedia of education.* New York: Macmillan and Free Press.

Dunkel, Harold B. 1970. *Herbart and Herbartism: an educational ghost story.* Chicago: University of Chicago Press.

Good, Carter V. 1973. *Dictionary of education.* New York: McGraw-Hill.

McHenry, Robert, ed. 1992. *The new encyclopedia Britannica.* Chicago: Encyclopedia Britannica, Inc.

HERCULEAN. Indicative of a person of great strength and courage; of a situation of extreme difficulty and many hazards.

Heracles (the Roman Hercules) was the son of Zeus and Alcmene, wife of Amphitryon. As an infant, he showed his physical potential by strangling two snakes that Hera sent to kill him in his cradle. He was perfectly confident that he could better any living creature; he was a man of deep feeling and sorrow for wrongdoing, but no great intellect. All his famous exploits derive from strength and courage, the most notable being the twelve labors that he had to perform for Eurystheus, king of Mycenae, as an act of expiation after he had killed his own children in a fit of madness sent upon him by Hera, who would never forgive Heracles for being the son of Zeus. First, he had to kill the lion of Nemea, then kill the nine-headed Hydra; third was the capture of the golden-horned stag of Cerynitia, and then the capture of the great boar on Mount Erymanthus; fifth, he had to clean the Augean stables in a day, then drive away the plague of birds threatening Stymphalus; seventh, he had to fetch the Cretan bull, then get the man-eating mares of King Diomedes; in his last four labors he had to bring back the girdle of Queen Hippolyta of the Amazons, the cattle of the monster Geryon, the golden apples of Hesperides, and, finally, the three-headed dog, Cerberus from Hades. But he could not overcome a supernatural force, and he died when Hera used her magic on him.

Sources
Hamilton, Edith. 1940. *Mythology: timeless tales of gods and heroes.* Boston: Little, Brown.
Hammond, Nicholas G.L., and Scullard, Howard H., eds. 1970. *The Oxford classical dictionary.* Oxford: Clarendon Press.
Jobes, Gertrude. 1962. *Dictionary of mythology, folklore and symbols.* New York: Scarecrow Press.
McHenry, Robert, ed. 1992. *The new encyclopedia Britannica.* Chicago: Encyclopedia Britannica, Inc.

HERTER COMMITTEE. A select committee on U.S. foreign aid (1947) which laid the foundation for the Marshall Plan.

Christian Archibald Herter (1895–1966) was born of American parents in the Bohemian world of Parisian artists. He graduated from Harvard University in 1915, was an attaché to the U.S. Embassy in Berlin in 1916, and briefly was in charge of the U.S. legation in Brussels. He served in the State Department in the United States (1917–19), became assistant commissioner and secretary of the diplomatic mission that drew up a prisoner-of-war agreement with Germany, secretary of the American Peace Commission in 1918, and executive secretary of the European Relief Council in 1920. He was the personal assistant to the secretary of commerce, Herbert Hoover, and served as Hoover's press coordinator and investigated food relief for Russia. After six years as a magazine editor (1924), he entered politics, the House of Representatives in Massachusetts (1931–43), and the U.S. Congress (1943–53). In the House of Representatives he was the speaker (1939–43) and later vice-chairman of the House Select Committee—the Herter Committee—on Foreign Aid, which toured eighteen war-ravaged countries in 1947 and reported on the need for U.S. economic assistance in Europe. This work was preliminary to the Marshall Plan for the postwar reconstruction of Europe. He became governor of Massachusetts (1953–57), helped persuade Dwight Eisenhower to run for president (1952), and nominated Richard Nixon for the U.S. vice-presidency (1956). He was also the undersecretary of state to John Foster Dulles (1957–59) and the president's special representative in trade negotiations under John F. Kennedy and Lyndon Johnson in the Kennedy Round of tariff reduction negotiations (1964–66).

Sources
Findling, John E. 1980. *Dictionary of American diplomatic history.* Westport, Conn.: Greenwood Press.
Garraty, John A., and Carnes, Mark C. 1988. *Dictionary of American biography.* Supplement 8, 1966–70. New York: Charles Scribner's Sons.
Morris, Dan, and Morris, Inez. 1974. *Who was who in American politics.* New York: Hawthorn Books.

HERZBERG'S MOTIVATION-HYGIENE THEORY. A humanistic theory of work motivation that assumes two independent reasons for people working: to avoid discomfort and pain and to seek growth and personal fulfillment.

Frederick Herzberg (b. 1923), born in Lynn, Massachusetts, completed his undergraduate studies in New York and his Ph.D. at the University of Pittsburgh in 1950. He researched conditions under which people felt good and bad about work and isolated the factors associated with the job context—"hygiene factors"—supervision, interpersonal relations, physical working conditions, salaries, company policies, administrative practices, and security, which if they fell below an acceptable level were prime sources of work dissatisfaction. Among job content factors or "motivators" were achievement, recognition for work, challenging work, greater job responsibility, advancement, and growth. Herzberg found that hygiene factors could help remove dissatisfaction, while motivators would have a positive effect on work satisfaction. Both sets were required, however, for effective encouragement of people to give their best at work. Since 1952, Herzberg has published five books and hundreds of papers, translated into several languages. He is a distinguished professor of management, University of Utah, and for thirty years has been honored throughout the world for his contributions to the theory and practice of job enrichment in industry and government agencies.

Sources

Clutterbuck, David, and Crainer, Stuart. 1990. *Makers of management: men and women who changed the business world.* London: Macmillan.

Herzberg, Frederick, et al. 1959. *The motivation to work.* New York: John Wiley.

Herzberg, Frederick. 1966. *Work and the nature of man.* New York: Thomas Y. Crowell.

Herzberg, Frederick. 1982. *The managerial choice: to be efficient and to be human.* 2d rev. ed. Salt Lake City, Utah: Olympus.

Herzberg, Frederick. 1991. Happiness and unhappiness: a brief autobiography of Frederick Herzberg. In Arthur Bedeian, ed. *Management laureates: a collection of autobiographical essays.* 3 vols. Greenwich, Conn.: JAI Press.

Wren, Daniel A. 1987. *The evolution of management thought.* 3d ed. New York: John Wiley.

HESSEN THESIS. The general argument that scientific theory is an ideology. Specifically, major contributions in the scientific revolution of the 1600s were due to a bourgeois ideology. For example, under the pressures of capitalism, Newtonian mathematics was merely a response in a commercial society to many problems of technology and industry. The thesis also proposed that in nature God was nothing but a device to reject the materialist ideas of radicals in the English Civil War.

Professor Boris Hessen—"Gessen" in the USSR—(fl. 1931–34) trained in physics under the doyen of Soviet physicists, Abram Feodorovitch Joffe (1880–1960)—"Ioffe" in the USSR—and taught in the Department of the History and Philosophy of the Natural Sciences, Moscow University. As a result of the Deborinate victory over the Mechanists, he rose rapidly in official circles as an approved interpreter of contemporary science. In 1931 he was a member of the Soviet delegation (including other philosophers of science, Ernst Kol'man, B. M. Zavadovsky, and V. F. Mitkevich) to the Second International Congress of the History of Science and Technology in London where he related the scientific revolution of the seventeenth century to the rise of capitalism. J.B.S. Haldane was impressed by his paper. Hessen weathered challenges from Communist party philosophers concerning the status of Einstein's formulas and defended himself until 1934. He vanished, presumably a victim of the purges of the mid-1930s in Stalinist Russia. Kol'man and Zavadovsky were able to change their views readily; for example, Zavadovsky supported the inheritance of acquired characteristics, Lysenkoism.

Source

Hessen, Boris. 1971. The social and economic roots of Newton's Principia. In *Science at the Crossroads.* London: Cass.

HICKSIAN THEORY OF EQUILIBRIUM. A dynamic theory of economic value that uses the concept of temporary equilibrium for the study of current markets. The concept suggests that future markets influence current markets through their agents' expectations and ensuing behavior in current markets. Consequently, the idea of "elasticity of expectations" emerged and contributed a great deal to macroeconomic theory.

John Richard Hicks (1904–89) was born in Leamington Spa and educated at Clifton College. He studied at Balliol, Oxford (1922–25), and, after teaching at the London School of Economics (1926–35), became a fellow at Gonville and Caius College, Cambridge. He was appointed a professor of political economy at Manchèster in 1938 and later returned to Oxford. In 1937 he began analyzing Keynes's theories and established grounds for Keynesian management by government of fiscal and monetary policies that led to changes in employment and output. With his wife, Ursula Kathleen Webb, Hicks collaborated on studies in public finance. In 1951 he was on a royal commission on taxation of profits and income. He was knighted in 1964 and, with Kenneth Arrow, was awarded the Nobel Prize—which cited Hicks's contribution to equilibrium theory—in Economics in 1972. Hicks believed that the award had been made for his *Value and Capital* and the Kaldor-Hicks welfare economics. Among his publications are *The Theory of Wages* (1932; rev. 1963); *Value and Capital* (1939); *The Social Framework* (1942; 4th ed., 1971); *A Revision of Demand Theory* (1956); *A Theory of Economic History* (1969); *The Crisis in Keynesian Economics* (1974); *Causality and Economics* (1979); *Collected Papers* (1981–83); and *Theory of Money* (1989).

Sources

Anon. 1989. The economists' economist. *The New York Times* 23, May:A-27.

Anon. 1989. John Richard Hicks, 85, Shared 1972 Nobel Prize for Economics. *The New York Times Biographical Service,* May:463.

Blaug, Mark. 1985. *Great economists since Keynes.* Brighton, England: Harvester Press.

Devine, Elizabeth; Held, Michael; Vinson, James; and Walsh, George, eds. 1983. *Thinkers of the twentieth century: a biographical, bibliographical and critical dictionary.* London: Macmillan.

Eatwell, John; Milgate, Murray; and Newman, Peter. 1987. *The new Palgrave: a dictionary of economics.* London: Macmillan.

Katz, Bernard S. 1989. *Nobel laureates in economic sciences: a biographical dictionary.* New York: Garland Publishing.

HINDENBURG LINE. A German line of fortification in World War I along the French-Belgium border.

Paul von Beneckendorff und von Hindenburg (1847–1934), an outstanding German soldier, was born at Posen into a Prussian Junker family. He was educated at the cadet school at Wahlstatt and Berlin, fought at the battle of Königgrätz in 1866, in the Franco-Prussian War (1870–71), became a general in 1903, and retired in 1911. He was recalled at the outbreak of World War I, becoming a national hero and father figure to the Germans. A visit to the Western front by the field marshall in 1917 showed the danger at this point. The offensive against Verdun was abandoned, and the German lines were withdrawn to the east of the Hindenburg Line. An Allied offensive failed to penetrate the line. He became president of the German Republic (1925–34). He did not oppose the rise of Hitler, whom he defeated in the presidential election of 1932, but his personal influence during Germany's political crises at that time was so great that Hitler was unable to dominate Germany until von Hindenburg's death.

Sources

McHenry, Robert, ed. 1992. *The new encyclopedia Britannica.* Chicago: Encyclopedia Britannica, Inc.

Magnussen, Magnus; Goring, Rosemary; and Thorn, John O., eds. 1990. *Chambers biographical dictionary.* Edinburgh: Chambers Ltd.

Wheeler-Bennett, John. 1967. *Hindenburg, the wooden Titan.* London: Macmillan.

HIPPOCRATIC OATH, HIPPOCRATIC LOOK. A moral code for the medical profession; the face of a dying person.

Hippocrates (460–377? B.C.) was born on the Greek isle of Cos and became an eminent surgeon and physician, known as the Father of Medicine. Legend holds that his father descended from the Greek god of medicine. The lad studied with his father and the philosopher, Democritus. In his work Hippocrates separated medicine from superstition, and for diagnosis he promoted the value of careful clinical observation. The oath bearing his name is the moral guide to the practice of medicine, sworn to by all medical practitioners. It emphasizes that a doctor's duty is dictated by both the patient's needs and his colleagues' requirements. According to legend, he lived to 110. He wrote medical works known as the *Hippocratic Collection,* and the major source on his life is a biography by Soranus, a Greek physician of the second century A.D.

Sources

McHenry, Robert, ed. 1992. *The new encyclopedia Britannica.* Chicago: Encyclopedia Britannica, Inc.

Walton, John; Beeson, Paul B.; and Scott, Ronald B. 1986. *The Oxford companion to medicine.* Oxford: Oxford University Press.

HIRSCHMAN-HERFINDAHL INDEX. An economics index—the sum of the squared values of all firms' market shares in a given market—popular in the 1980s to indicate the degree of monopoly power of industrial organizations. At first, from the 1950s, it was the Herfindahl index, then the Gia index or Gia coefficient, but later Hirschman's name was used when it became known he had used it to measure patterns in foreign trade.

Albert O. Hirschman (b. 1915) was born in Berlin and studied at the Sorbonne, the London School of Economics, and the University of Trieste, obtaining his Ph.D. in 1938. He was active in fighting European fascism and lived in France during the Nazi occupation, escaping to the United States in 1941. He published *National Power and the Structure of Foreign Trade* (1945), worked as an economist for the Federal Reserve Board, and later taught at Yale, Columbia, and Harvard. In 1964 he wrote an article stating that the index he had devised was attributed to another scholar and reinvented by himself. Economists have thereafter used his name as well as Herfindahl's for the index. With a novel and creative approach to economics he published *A Bias for Hope* (1971), joined the Institute for Advanced Study at Princeton (1974), and later published *The Rhetoric of Reaction: Perversity, Futility, Jeopardy* (1991).

Orris Clemens Herfindahl (1918–72) was born in Parshall, North Dakota, raised in Stanton, Iowa, in a Swedish community, went to the University of Minnesota to study music, but turned to business administration instead. After teaching in Minnesota, he worked for the U.S. Department of Commerce in Washington in 1942 and spent three years in the navy. After the war, he completed his Ph.D. in economics at Columbia University (1951), was hired by the U.S. Department of the Interior (Mines), and in 1957 joined the Resources for the Future in Washington as a research associate. He researched competition between mining firms to improve government policies in that industry, and later he worked for the Planning Commission of the Indian Government (1963) and published *Natural Resource Information for Economic Development* (1969) on his research in Chile (1966–67). His main interests lay in the economics of natural resources, their supply and conservation, the quality of the natural environment, and the economics of the mineral industry.

Sources

Arestis, Philip, and Sawyer, Malcolm. 1992. *A biographical dictionary of dissenting economists.* Brookfield, Vt.: Edward Elgar.

Blaug, Mark, ed. 1986. *Who's who in economics: a biographical dictionary of major economists, 1700–1986.* 2d ed. Cambridge, Mass.: MIT Press.

Eatwell, John; Milgate, Murray; and Newman, Peter. 1987. *The new Palgrave: a dictionary of economics.* London: Macmillan.

Hirschman, Albert O. 1964. The paternity of an index. *American Economic Review* 54: 761–762.

HISS-CHAMBERS AFFAIR. A celebrated espionage case and trial of an alleged communist in high office in the U.S. State Department in the early 1950s.

Whittaker Chambers claimed that Alger Hiss had worked with Chambers for the Communist party in the late 1930s. Hiss denied knowing Chambers and stated that he had never been a communist. After two trials, Hiss was found guilty of perjury for having denied that he had passed secret state documents to Chambers. Within a month the six-year McCarthy era began.

Alger Hiss (b. 1904), born in Baltimore, Maryland, was educated in Massachusetts, and studied at Johns Hopkins University and Harvard Law School (LL.B. 1929). In 1933 he joined the New Deal Agricultural Adjustment Administration, among whose members were several communists. After serving several government agencies, he became secretary of the Dumbarton Oaks conversations (1944). He was appointed a staff adviser at the Yalta Conference, chief organizer of the first United Nations conference in San Francisco (1945), and advised the U.S. delegation of the first meeting of the United Nations. In 1947 he became the president of the Carnegie Endowment for International Peace. In 1951 he was imprisoned for almost four years; afterward he helped reorganize a company (1957–59), and for many years he worked to reopen his case, alleging that conspiracies had put him in prison. He was reinstated as a lawyer, and in 1988 he published his memoirs. In 1992 Hiss claimed to be cleared of spying charges when the chairman of Russia's military intelligence archives, General Dimitri Volkgonov, said the charges were groundless.

Jay Vivian Whittaker Chambers (1901–61) was born in Philadelphia, raised in New York, and attended Columbia College (1920–22). As a writer, he traveled in Europe (1923) and joined the Communist party of America in 1925. After leaving the party (1929–31), he returned as an underground official (1932) and lived under several aliases. As ''George Crosley,'' Chambers met and befriended Alger Hiss (1934), who, allegedly, through Chambers, made government documents available for the Soviets. Chambers defected from communism in 1938 and became an editor with *Time* magazine in 1939. Following Hiss's trials, Chambers published *Witness,* a best-seller, briefly took up farming, traveled to Europe, and returned home to undergraduate studies shortly before he died. In 1984 President Reagan posthumously awarded Chambers the Medal of Freedom for having personified human redemption in the face of evil and suffering.

Sources

Chambers, Whittaker. 1952. *Witness.* New York: Random House.

Frank, Jeffrey A. 1992. General offers latest twist in Hiss Case. *Guardian Weekly,* November 8:18.

Hiss, Alger. 1988. *Recollection of a life.* London: Unwin Hyman.

Weinstein, Allen. 1978. *Perjury: the Hiss-Chambers case.* New York: Alfred A. Knopf.

HITE REPORTS. Best-selling surveys on human sexuality. The first Hite Report (1976), based on mail survey data, centered on women's sexual experiences and practices. Over 75,000 questionnaires were mailed; 3,019 provided adequate data. The report included verbatim statements, conclusions, and recommendations for women on masturbation, orgasm, intercourse, clitoral stimulation, lesbianism, sexual slavery, the sexual revolution, sex among older women, and an essay on the "new attitude" to female sexuality. It became a best-seller, praised for its revelations and frankness by some professional social scientists, and attacked by others because of inadequate sampling, unwarranted generalizations, poor writing, and feminist bias. Hite published two more studies, one on women and love, and the other on men and sex. Her views are still controversial.

Sher Hite (b. 1942) was born Shirley Diana Gregory, in Saint Joseph, Missouri. After her mother divorced and remarried, Shirley took her stepfather's surname, Hite. She lived with her grandparents after her mother's second divorce, and after her grandparents divorced she lived with her uncle's family in Daytona, Florida. She was educated at Seabreeze High School, studied music, and went to the University of Florida. She quit studies at Columbia University, became a high fashion model, and posed for girlie magazines until, repelled by this life, she turned to the feminist movement and joined the National Organization of Women in New York. The publicity received by her studies led to appointments to lecture at Harvard and McGill universities (1977). She married a West German pianist in 1985 and lives in New York.

Sources

Hite, Sher. 1976. *The Hite report: a nationwide study of female sexuality*. London: Talmy, Franklin Ltd.

Hite, Sher. 1987. *The Hite report: women and love: a cultural revolution in progress*. New York: Alfred A. Knopf.

Hite, Sher. 1989. *The Hite report on male sexuality*. New York: Alfred A. Knopf.

Hite, Sher. 1993. *Women as revolutionary agents of change. The Hite reports: 1972–1993*. London: Bloomsbury.

Moritz, Charles, ed. 1988. *Current biography yearbook*. New York: H. W. Wilson.

HITLERISM. Totalitarian policies and practices of the twentieth-century German Nazi dictator, that is, militant anti-Semitic nationalism, subordination of all institutions to the state, unlimited territorial expansion through military invasion, and racial purification through genocide and murder.

Adolf Hitler (1889–1945) was born in Braunau-am-Inn, Austria, son of Alois Hitler (formerly Schickelgruber) and his third wife, Klara Poelz. He first worked in Munich as an architect's draughtsman, joined the German Army in 1914, became a corporal, and was wounded during World War I. While still in the army he joined a socialist group, the German Workers' party, and quickly rose to leadership. Eventually, he changed the name to the National Socialist German Workers' (Nazi) party. As a result of political crises in Germany during the early 1930s, he became chancellor with a coalition government. In March 1933 he had passed the Law for Removing the Distress of the People and Reich, known as the Enabling Law; it gave the Reich cabinet, which Hitler controlled, the power of legislation, control of the budget, approval of foreign treaties, and the power to amend the constitution. The law was to be in effect for only four years. On the death of President von Hindenburg in 1934, Hitler became both president and chancellor; thus, he was finally a totalitarian dictator with control over the German military as well as the German Parliament. All political parties other than the Nazis were forbidden, trade unions were suppressed, free speech was curbed, and the secret police was expanded. Jews, Russians, and communists were declared Germany's enemies. In 1936 Hitler began his campaign to conquer Europe by marching into the Rhineland. Britain was obliged to declare war on Germany in 1939 after the Nazi invasion of Poland. By 1941 Hitler's army occupied most of Western Europe. After the entry of the United States into the war and the Allied invasion of Europe, the German advances were limited. In 1945 Germany was defeated and Hitler committed suicide.

Sources

Bullock, Alan L.G. 1952. *A study in tyranny.* Rev. 1990. Harmondsworth: Penguin.
Bullock, Alan L. 1992. *Hitler and Stalin: parallel lives.* New York: Alfred A. Knopf.
Fest, Joachim C. 1974. *Hitler.* London: Weidenfeld and Nicolson.
Waite, Robert G.L. 1978. *Psychopathic god: Adolf Hitler.* New York: American Library, Inc.

HOARE-LAVAL PLAN. A plan proposed by Britain's foreign secretary and the premier of France in 1935 to end the Italo-Ethiopian War. If implemented, the plan would have given Italy 60,000 square miles of territory in Africa and economic control of the southern half of Ethiopia, including the most fertile areas of the country. Ethiopia would have been compensated with 3,000 square miles of territory elsewhere. Withdrawn after protest from Western powers, the plan demonstrated the weakness of collective security measures through the League of Nations, and both proposers were forced to resign.

Samuel John Gurney Hoare, first Viscount Templewood (1880–1959), was a Conservative M.P. (1901–44) who, as secretary of state for India (1931–35), initiated the act of 1935 by which provincial self-government was granted. Hoare became foreign secretary in 1935 but was forced to resign by the strong protests against the Hoare-Laval Plan. He returned as a minister (1936–40), served as ambassador to Spain (1940–44), and retired with a peerage.

Pierre Laval (1883–1945), born in the Auvergne, was initially self-educated, obtained academic degrees, and practiced as a lawyer in Paris. He was a member of the Chamber of Deputies during 1914–19 and again in 1924. At first, he was a socialist, but he became nonpartisan when he was a senator in 1927. After experience as a minister, he became prime minister (1931–32; 1935–36) and negotiated the Hoare-Laval Pact of 1935. He advocated friendship with Italy and Germany. After the collapse of France in 1940, he took a leading part in the establishment of Marshal Pétain's Vichy regime in 1942 and was prime minister in collaboration with the Germans. After the liberation of France, he fled to Spain but was repatriated, tried, condemned, and executed for treason. His name is an eponym for traitor.

Sources

Cole, Hubert. 1963. *Laval: a biography.* London: Heinemann.

Findling, John E. 1980. *Dictionary of American diplomatic history.* Westport, Conn.: Greenwood Press.

Jones, Barry. 1989. *The Macmillan dictionary of biography.* 3d ed. South Melbourne: Macmillan.

Williams, E. T., and Palmer, Helen M., eds. 1971. *Dictionary of national biography 1951–1960.* London: Oxford University Press.

HOBBESIAN. Pertaining to the ideas of the seventeenth-century English political philosopher.

Thomas Hobbes (1588–1679) was born at Westport, Wiltshire, the second son of the vicar of Westport and Charlton. His father deserted the family after a scandal at the church, and Hobbes was brought up by an uncle. He was educated at Oxford University and entered the service of the first earl of Devonshire, as secretary, and later tutored the future Charles II. Hobbes traveled extensively in Europe and was greatly influenced by Galileo. In philosophy he was a materialistic nominalist with rationalist tendencies; he read Latin and Greek and developed an interest in mathematics, jurisprudence, and political theory. Hobbes was employed by the earls of Devonshire until 1640, when fear of persecution by Parliament for his political opinions drove him to Paris where he stayed until after the Restoration. He is best known for his *Leviathan* (1651) in which he presents humankind as selfish, solitary, and poor; life as nasty, brutish, and short; and the state as a device for peace whose sovereign ought to enjoy absolute authority over his subjects to curb their natural hostility.

Sources

Edwards, Paul, ed. 1967. *The encyclopedia of philosophy.* New York: Macmillan.

Hinnant, Charles H. 1977. *Thomas Hobbes.* Boston: Twayne Publishers.

Miller, David, ed. 1987. *The Blackwell encyclopedia of political thought.* Oxford: Basil Blackwell.

Sills, David L., ed. 1968. *International encyclopedia of the social sciences.* New York: Macmillan and Free Press.

Stephen, Leslie, and Lee, Sydney, eds. 1917. *The dictionary of national biography.* London: Oxford University Press.

Zusne, Leonard. 1984. *Biographical dictionary of psychology.* Westport, Conn.: Greenwood Press.

HOHFELD SYSTEM. A clarification of the concepts of legal right and ownership—ideas too often used imprecisely by lawyers and jurists—which distinguishes four expressions: claim-right, liberty or privilege, power, and immunity.

Wesley Newcomb Hohfeld (1879–1918) was born in Oakland, California. He was a superior student in high school and studied at the University of California, receiving a gold medal for high grades. After studies at Harvard Law School, he began teaching at Stanford University (1905–14). In 1913 he published ''Fundamental Legal Conceptions as Applied to Judicial Reasoning'' in the *Yale Law*

Journal and in 1914 was appointed a professor at Yale. He established what became known as the Hohfeld System, a classification of terms whose meaning had become confused and unclear in legal practice and judgments. His ideas on the correlatives and opposites of the terms *right, privilege, power,* and *immunity* were eventually adopted by the American Law Institute to help restate the law. In addition, the concepts have been adapted for economics. An unpopular but thorough teacher and a severe task master, Hohfeld had a lasting effect on only the elite minority of students. His students found it almost impossible to meet his demands of them and once unsuccessfully petitioned the Yale president to end Hohfeld's appointment.

Sources

Bullock, Alan, and Woodings, Robert B., eds. 1983. *The Fontana biographical companion to modern thought.* London: Collins.

Devine, Elizabeth; Held, Michael; Vinson, James; and Walsh, George, eds. 1983. *Thinkers of the twentieth century: a biographical, bibliographical and critical dictionary.* London: Macmillan.

Hohfeld, Wesley N. 1919. *Fundamental legal conceptions as applied in judicial reasoning.* Ed. Walter Wheeler Cook. Reprinted 1946 and 1984. New Haven, Conn.: Yale University Press.

Malone, Dumas, ed. 1932. *Dictionary of American biography.* Vol. V. New York: Charles Scribner's Sons.

HOLLAND-MARTIN REPORT. An industrial relations report by a British Committee of Inquiry into Trawler Safety (July 1969).

Deric (Douglas Eric) Holland-Martin (1906–77) was educated at the Royal Naval College, Osborne, and Dartmouth. He was a midshipman on the H.M.S. *Iron Duke* (1924–27) and served on various ships until he was made the naval attaché to Argentina, Paraguay, and Uruguay (1947–49). Among the naval positions he later held were commander in chief, Allied Forces, Mediterranean (1961–64) and commandant, Imperial Defence College (1964–66). He became a rear admiral in 1955, a vice-admiral in 1958, and an admiral in 1961. He was knighted in 1960, retired in 1967, and was appointed vice-president and chairman of the Committee of Inquiry into Trawler Safety. In 1968 he became a member of the White Fish Authority and Herring Industry.

Sources

Blake (Lord), and Nicholls, C. S. eds. 1986. *Dictionary of national biography 1971–1980.* Oxford: Oxford University Press.

Who's who, 1977. London: Adam and Charles Black.

HOLLINGSHEAD TWO-FACTOR INDEX OF SOCIAL POSITION. A seven-point scale of status (modified from the Edwards classification) that differentiates among professionals according to the size and wealth of their businesses. The scale gives a value of seven to occupation and four to education.

August de Belmont Hollingshead (1907–80) was born in Lymon, Wyoming, and studied at the universities of California and Nebraska (Ph.D., 1935). After teaching at the universities of Iowa, Alabama, and Indiana, he became a professor of sociology at Yale University (1947–75). As a Fulbright Scholar, he was a visitor to the Psychiatric Institute at the University of London (1957–58); he was also an adviser to the World Health Organization, worked on problems of mental health in Puerto Rico, was a consultant to Planned Parenthood, a member of many boards for mental health, and served academic and professional associations in sociology and psychopathology. He was a consultant to the U.S. surgeon general (1960–69). Among his books are *Principles of Human Ecology* (1938), *Elmtown Youth* (1949), *Principles of Sociology* (1969), and *Elmtown Youth and Elmtown Revisited* (1975).

Sources

Hollingshead, August B. 1971. Commentary on "The indiscriminant state of social class measurement." *Social Forces* 49:563–567.

Hollingshead, August B., and Redlich, Frederick C. 1958. *Social class and mental illness: a community study.* New York: John Wiley.

May, Hal, ed. 1987. *Contemporary authors.* Vol. 120. Detroit: Gale Research.

Miller, Delbert C. 1991. *Handbook of research design and social measurement.* 5th ed. Newbury Park, Calif.: Sage Publications.

Slomczynski, Kazimierz M.; Miller, Joanne; and Kohn, Melvin L. 1981. Stratification, work, and values. *American Sociological Review* 46:720–744.

Who's who in America, 1980–81. Chicago: Marquis.

HOLMES-RAHE SCALE OF STRESS. A general indicator of the level of stress encountered in life changes. Changes are measured in "life change units" from "death of spouse" (100 points) to minor violations of the law (11 points). People who accrue over 200 points in a year tend to become ill with either a new or an old illness.

Thomas Hall Holmes (1918–88) was born in Glasboro, North Carolina, and after studies at the University of North Carolina he completed his M.D. at Cornell in 1943. In various New York hospitals he worked in psychiatry and neurology (1942–44) and served as a major in the U.S. Army Medical Corps (1944–46). After research in psychosomatic medicine at Cornell University and at Bellevue Hospital, he joined the faculty at the University of Washington School of Medicine (1949–85), became a professor of psychiatry and behavioral sciences (1958–85), was on the staff at the Harborview Medical Center (1949–85), and an honorary consultant at the Royal Prince Alfred in Sydney, Australia (1971). He retired in 1985. He co-authored *The Nose* (1950) and *Life Change Events* (1984). He was a member of many professional associations relating to medicine and psychiatry as well as sociology.

Richard Henry Rahe (b. 1936) was born in Seattle, Washington, and studied medicine at the University of Washington (M.D., 1961). He worked at Bellevue Hospital, New York (1961–62), became chief resident psychiatrist at the University of Washington (1962–65), resident psychiatrist at the U.S. Navy Neuropsychiatric Research Unit (1965–68), and headed the Stress Medicine Division

of the U.S. Navy Health Research Center (1970–76). He became a commanding
officer (1976–80) and was in charge of the U.S. Naval hospital in Guam (1981–
84), was appointed a professor of psychiatry at Bethesda Hospital, Maryland
(1984–86), and later became director of the Nevada Stress Center at the
University of Nevada School of Medicine. He researched life changes and illness
in Norway and Sweden and at the University of California (Los Angeles). He
is a fellow of the American Psychiatric Association, the American Psychosomatic Society, the World Psychiatric Association, and the Association of Military Surgeons (U.S.).

Sources

Dohrenwend, Barbara S., and Dohrenwend, Bruce P. 1974. *Stressful life events; their
    nature and effects.* New York: John Wiley.
Gunderson, E.K. Eric, and Rahe, Richard H. 1974. *Life stress and illness.* Springfield,
    Ill.: Charles C. Thomas.
Holmes, Thomas H., and Rahe, Richard H. 1967. The social readjustment rating scale.
    Journal of Psychosomatic Research 11:213–218.
New York Times, January 7, 1989:8.
Who's who in America, 1988–89. Chicago: Marquis.
Wittkower, Eric D., and Warnes, Hector, eds. 1977. *Psychosomatic medicine: its clinical
    applications.* Hagerstown, Md.: Harper and Row.

HOLSTI TYPES. Political characters based on the structure of leaders' beliefs
and preferred operational codes. In particular, Holsti's type B attracted much
interest: such characters see adversaries as highly rational and their goal as the
destruction of one's own nation; they are optimistic in the distant future but see
dangers in the present, which requires one to be vigilant and of strong will and
to advocate deterrence; power-seeking is paramount, as is pragmatism; these
characters are prone to use force when risks are low and gains are great.

Ole Rudolph Holsti (b. 1933), son of a Finnish diplomat in Geneva, was born
in Switzerland and became an American citizen in 1954. He served actively and
on reserve in the U.S. Army (1956–62). After studies at Stanford (Ph.D. 1962)
and Wesleyan University, he taught and researched international studies at Stanford (1962–67) and was professor of political science at the universities of British Columbia (1967–74), California, Davis (1978–79), and at Duke University
(1974–). He received awards and honors from several American foundations
(Ford, Guggenheim, Haynes) and the Canada Council, is a member of several
professional associations for the study of international relations and peace research, and has served on the American Political Science Association Board
(1982–85). The National Science Foundation has supported his research since
1975; he has studied at Harvard, served as editor of several professional journals,
and received the Howard Johnson Distinguished Teaching Award in 1990. Since
1963 he has published regularly on content analysis, international conflict, international leadership, communism, the social psychology of politics and war,
crises in decision making, theories of international relations and foreign policy,

and the domestic and foreign policies of American leaders. He was honored for his study of the Cold War, *The Three-Headed Eagle Revisited,* and received the best published paper award in *International Studies Quarterly* (1981).

Sources

Holsti, Ole R. 1977. The "operational code" as an approach to the analysis of belief systems. Final report, National Science Foundation, Grant SOC 75-15368. Duke University mimeograph.

Holsti, Ole R. 1977. Foreign policy makers viewed psychologically: cognitive process approaches. In G. M. Bonham and M. J. Shapiro, eds. *Thought and action in foreign policy.* Basel: Birkhauser.

Holsti, Ole R. 1979. Theories of crises decision making. In P. G. Lauren, ed. *Diplomacy: new approaches in history, theory and policy.* New York: Free Press.

Holsti, Ole R., and George, A. L. 1975. The effects of stress in the performance of foreign policy makers. In Cornelius Cotter, ed. *Political Science Annual* 6:255–308. Indianapolis, Ind.: Bobbs-Merrill.

May, Hal, and Lezniak, James G., eds. 1990. *Contemporary authors.* Vol. 28. New Revision Series. Detroit: Gale Research.

Personal Communication.

HOMERIC SOCIETY. A society—like most Western societies—in which stories are passed from one generation to the next, especially stories of the calamitous hostility that one social group has for another, and the glorification of war heroes in the ensuing conflict. The phrase was used by Zarko Korac, a child psychologist at Belgrade University, to explain the attitudes to the glorification of war and heroic death held by Bosnian children who witnessed the slaughter of Serbs, Croats, and Muslims in the former Yugoslavia in 1991 [*The Age* (Melbourne) 13, November 1991].

Homer, an unknown poet—or group of poets—is assumed to have written the *Iliad* and the *Odyssey,* the finest monuments of ancient and modern epic poetry. The *Iliad,* a complete catalogue of human calamities, comprises twenty-four books describing the siege of Troy. It caught gods and heroes in a frightening and furious slaughter and focused on an unremitting celebration of heroic exploits. The *Odyssey,* also twenty-four books, recounts the heroic adventures of Ulysses. Homer's name comes from tradition, and the poetry from the period between the ninth and twelfth centuries B.C. Homer hailed from seven cities: Smyrna, Rhodes, Colophon, Salamis, Chios, Argos, and Athens. For centuries the work of Homer was central to education in Western culture.

Sources

Hammond, Nicholas G.L., and Scullard, Howard H., eds. 1970. *The Oxford classical dictionary.* Oxford: Clarendon Press.

McHenry, Robert, ed. 1992. *The new encyclopedia Britannica.* Chicago: Encyclopedia Britannica, Inc.

HOOLIGAN. A street rough; a young, violent, rude person; a prison guard; a hack.

The Hooligan family, an Irish family that lived in England in the 1890s, had their name given to a band of young ruffians who terrorized London's Southwark district. The gang was probably led by Patrick Hooligan, who lived in and used the Lamb and Flag pub as the gang's headquarters. As his followers became known and their network became highly organized, his name attached itself to the gang. Alternatively, in the 1890s a music hall song was written about "Happy Hooligan," a cartoon character from a New York newspaper. The term may also have arisen from other family names, for example, Hulihan or Hooley's gang.

Sources

Hendrickson, Robert. 1988. *The dictionary of eponyms: names that became words.* New York: Dorset.

Partridge, Eric. 1967. *A dictionary of slang and unconventional English.* London: Routledge and Kegan Paul.

HOOPER RATING. A rating of radio listening for a specific program.

Claude E. Hooper (1898–1954), a statistician, was born in Kingsville, Ohio. He graduated from Amherst College and Harvard and was the advertising manager of the *Harvard Business Review* (1924–26) and *Scribner's Magazine* in New York (1926–29). During the 1930s Hooper developed his research techniques and assembled comparative data from random telephone calls made in over thirty metropolitan areas of "equal network opportunity." His organization sold several kinds of information to the radio network and advertisers. A Hooper rating of 20.0—a good rating—meant that one out of every five homes called (including homes in which no one answered the telephone and those in which the radio was not in use) was listening to the program in question. The superiority of Hooper's method, combined with his aggressive salesmanship, promoted a great acceptance of his research findings. He was an executive for many years and president of C. E. Hooper Inc. He published *Radio Audience Measurement* (1944), and in 1946, when Hooper ratings had become the industry's standard of measurement, his company grossed nearly $1 million. The question of what the Hooper ratings measured was controversial. Hooper said he offered merely an index of comparative program popularity in major cities; however, the ratings functioned as a measure of program quality and often became the sole basis of policy decision. In 1950 Hooper sold his national ratings service to Nielsen (A. C. Nielsen Company) and concentrated on local surveys of radio and television in major urban markets.

Source

Garraty, John A., ed. 1977. *Dictionary of American biography.* Supplement 5. New York: Charles Scribner's Sons.

HOOVER MORATORIUM, HOOVERIZE. Presidential moratorium (June 20, 1931) on all intergovernmental payments, including debts and reparations subject to the agreement of other nations (June–July 1931). It aimed to help

Germany out of its Depression-induced financial crisis, and it led to a similar agreement in July 1931 on German short-term debts. Hooverize means to use food economically.

Herbert Clark Hoover (1874–1964), thirty-first president of the United States, was born at West Branch, Iowa, studied mining engineering at Stanford, and worked in the United States, Australia, and China. In London he was chairman of the American Relief Commission in 1914 and arranged for stranded Americans to return home. In 1915–19 he chaired the Commission for Relief in Belgium, and helped to get food and clothing to World War I refugees. When the United States entered the war in 1917, he was U.S. food administrator, sat on the War Trade Council, and chaired the Inter-allied Food Council. At the Paris Peace Conference Hoover was chairman of the Supreme Economic Council and directed the European Relief and Reconstruction Commission and the American Relief Administration which helped feed millions in Russia (1921–23). Under presidents Harding and Coolidge, Hoover was secretary of commerce, and with his popular following defeated Al Smith for president in 1928. But his opposition to direct government assistance for the unemployed after 1929 made him unpopular, and he was defeated for reelection by Franklin D. Roosevelt in 1932. Hoover assisted President Truman with American-European economic relief programs after World War II. He wrote *Problems of Lasting Peace* (1942) and his *Memoirs* (1952–53; 1955).

Sources

Ellis, Lewis E. 1968. *Republican foreign policy, 1921–1933.* New Brunswick, N.J.: Rutgers University Press.

Ferrell, R. 1957. *American diplomacy in the Great Depression.* New Haven, Conn.: Yale University Press.

Findling, John E. 1980. *Dictionary of American diplomatic history.* Westport, Conn.: Greenwood Press.

Magnussen, Magnus; Goring, Rosemary; and Thorn, John O., eds. 1990. *Chambers biographical dictionary.* Edinburgh: Chambers Ltd.

Nash, George H. 1983. *The life of Herbert Hoover.* New York: W.W. Norton.

Robinson, Edgar E., and Bornet, Vaughan D. 1975. *Herbert Hoover, president of the United States.* Stanford, Calif.: Hoover Institution Press, Stanford University.

Smith, Gene. 1970. *The shattered dream.* New York: William Morrow.

HORATIO ALGER STORY. A rags-to-riches success story that celebrates hard work as the key to achievement, and was advanced as a model life for success in business and politics for generations of Americans.

Horatio Alger, Jr. (1832–99). See ALGER COMPLEX.

HOUDINI, TO PULL A HOUDINI. An escaper, one with magical powers in any field, especially in politics. To perform an astounding escape trick. In politics a recent example is Ireland's prime minister, Charles Haughey, who escaped scandals and indictments that would normally end a politician's career, for example, corruption, forced resignation, blackmail, fraud, and natural disasters (Murtagh and Joyce, 1983).

Harry Houdini, the stage-name of Ehrich Weiss (1874–1926), was the son of a rabbi, who brought the family to Appleton, Wisconsin, before Ehrich was born. At age 12 Ehrich ran away to New York. Six years later when his father died the family joined him because he was its main source of support. He worked in the theater during the late 1890s. On returning from Britain, where he had made a sensational escape from Scotland Yard, become a star, and toured the continent, he was taken up by America. He combined theatrical magic, invention, mechanics, personal strength, and dexterity in a range of ingenious escapes with breathtaking showmanship. He took his name from a notable but overrated French magician, Jean Houdin, who would insist that magic performances should not be attributed to supernatural power but to great skill in producing illusion. Houdini wrote his biography, *The Unmasking of Robert-Houdin* (1908). On his mother's death in 1913, Houdini turned to spiritualism and became an expert in exposing fraudulent spiritualists. He was president of the Society of American Magicians. His library is in the U.S. Library of Congress's Houdini Room, and he is celebrated at the Houdini Hall of Fame, Niagara Falls, New York.

Jean Eugene Robert Houdin (1805–71) was born in Blois, worked in Paris making toys and automata, and was noted for his magic and demonstrations at the Palais Royale (1845–55) which made him the Father of Modern Conjuring. To undermine the influence of the dervishes, the French government sent Houdin to Algiers to expose their fake miracles in 1856.

Sources

Brandon, Ruth. 1993. *The life and many deaths of Harry Houdini.* New York: Secker and Warburg.

Epson, D. M. 1988. The case of Harry Houdini. *The New Criterion* 5:25–33.

Fitzsimons, Raymund. 1985. *Death and the magician: the mystery of Houdini.* West Sussex: Atheneum Publications.

Gibson, Walter B. 1930. *Houdin's escapes.* New York: Harcourt, Brace.

Kellock, Harold. 1928. *Houdini: his life story.* London: Heinemann.

Magnussen, Magnus; Goring, Rosemary; and Thorn, John O., eds. 1990. *Chambers biographical dictionary.* Edinburgh: Chambers Ltd.

Malone, Dumas, ed. 1932. *Dictionary of American biography.* Vol. V. New York: Charles Scribner's Sons.

Murtagh, Peter, and Joyce, Joe. 1983. *The boss: Charles J. Haughey in government.* Dublin, Ireland: Poolbeg Press.

HUGHESILIERS. Young men who voluntarily accepted enlistment for military service with Australia in World War I.

William Morris Hughes (1862–1952), the only child of a Welsh carpenter, was born in London and, in 1884 after becoming a successful teacher, immigrated to Australia. He was active in local politics, took up socialism, and, being an able public speaker, organized Australian Labor party (ALP) support and was elected to the New South Wales Parliament (1894) and later the federal Parliament (1901–16). Meanwhile, he qualified as a barrister and organized the union of the Sydney waterfront workers. In October 1915 Hughes became prime minister and held a referendum advocating conscription. Ten thousand troops—Hughesiliers—from the Australian infantry, cadets, and the militia marched in his support. He lost by a small majority of the total vote and in three states. Expelled from the ALP, he formed a cabinet and merged with the National "Win the War" party. In 1917 he held another unsuccessful referendum, offered to resign, but no other leader could form a government. After World War I, he helped secure Australia's interests at several European conferences, but then lost much influence in Australia (1924–39). Prime Minister Robert Gordon Menzies made Hughes attorney-general and his deputy in 1939, and when the ALP was elected to govern, Hughes became deputy leader of the opposition. In 1944 Hughes was expelled from the United Australia party for rejoining the War Advisory Council after all U.A.P. colleagues had left it. He joined Menzies in the new Liberal party in 1949. Until his death, he remained a challenge to both sides of politics, a fiery, witty, and ebullient character.

Sources

Booker, Malcolm. 1980. *The great professional: a study of W. M. Hughes.* Sydney: McGraw-Hill.

Fitzhardinge, L. F. 1964–1979. *William Morris Hughes: a political biography.* 2 vols. Sydney: Angus and Robertson.

Horne, Donald. 1979. *In search of Billy Hughes. (The Little Digger).* South Melbourne: Macmillan.

Pike, Douglas, et al., eds. 1966–91. *Australian dictionary of biography.* Carlton, Victoria: Melbourne University Press.

HULL'S THEOREM. In administration "the combined pull of several patrons is the sum of their separate pulls multiplied by the number of patrons" (Peter and Hull, 1969:42). The multiplication effect occurs because patrons talk with each other about their opinions of subordinates' merits, reinforce them, and demand their subordinates' advancement. The corollary of the theorem is: "many a patron makes a promotion."

Raymond Hull (1919–85) was born in Shaftsbury, Dorset, and worked as cleaner, waiter, artist's model, and civil servant before turning to writing in 1938. He authored twenty-four books—many with others—wrote the television play "Roast Pig," how-to books on making beer and winning elections, and *Man's Best Friend,* a humorous attack on dogs and their owners. His favorite book was *The Peter Principle.* He also became an accomplished translator of Molière's plays and an editor. He died in British Columbia.

Sources

May, Hal, ed. 1986. *Contemporary authors.* Vol. 116. Detroit: Gale Research.

Peter, Laurence J., and Hull, Raymond. 1969. *The Peter principle: why things always go wrong.* New York: William Morrow.

HUMEAN. Relating to the philosophy of the eighteenth-century British philosopher, especially his views on the irreducible elements and principles of human passion and understanding, humanity's response to its environs, the role of history in understanding the basic changes in human nature and behavior, and the methodology of science.

David Hume (1711–76), a moral philosopher, historian, and economist, was born in Edinburgh, the younger son of Joseph Hume, laird of Ninewells. David studied at Edinburgh, went to France (1734–37), and returned to England to become companion to the marquis of Annandale. He was secretary to General St. Clair who appointed him judge-advocate, and he was made keeper of the library at the Faculty of Advocates at Edinburgh in 1752. In 1767–68 he was undersecretary of state. His skeptical views on philosophy have strongly influenced metaphysical ideas since his day. His views on economics were regarded as insightful, especially those on the role of money in an economy. A distinguished writer of his time, Hume was given little recognition, but since his death his work has attracted attention from students in many disciplines. He published *A Treatise on Human Nature* (1739–40), *Essays Moral and Political* (1741–42), *Political Discourses* (1751), and *History of England* (1754–61).

Sources

Flew, Anthony. 1986. *David Hume, philosopher of moral science.* New York: Basil Blackwell.

Gillespie, Charles C., ed. 1973. *Dictionary of scientific biography.* New York: Charles Scribner's Sons.

McHenry, Robert, ed. 1992. *The new encyclopedia Britannica.* Chicago: Encyclopedia Britannica, Inc.

Norton, David F. 1982. *David Hume, common-sense moralist, sceptical metaphysician.* Princeton, N.J.: Princeton University Press.

Sills, David L., ed. 1968. *International encyclopedia of the social sciences.* New York: Macmillan and Free Press.

Stephen, Leslie, and Lee, Sydney, eds. 1917. *The dictionary of national biography.* London: Oxford University Press.

Zusne, Leonard. 1984. *Biographical dictionary of psychology.* Westport, Conn.: Greenwood Press.

HUMPHREY-HAWKINS ACT. The U.S. Full Employment and Balanced Growth Act of 1978, which states that able and willing Americans who seek work have a right to useful, paid employment. It aimed for full employment, balanced growth, and low inflation between 1977 and 1988; specifically, it sought a 3 to 4 percent jobless rate and an inflation rate of 4 percent by 1983 and nil inflation by 1988.

Hubert Horatio Humphrey (1911–78) was born in Wallace, South Dakota, and graduated from the Denver College of Pharmacy, and the universities of Louisiana and Minnesota. He was a pharmacist with Humphrey Drug Company (1933–37), in Huron, South Dakota. After six years he returned to the University of Minnesota (1937) to study political science and later taught political science at the universities of Louisiana (1939) Minnesota (1941) and Macalester College (1943–44). He served the war program in Minnesota (1942–43) and the U.S. Army Air Corps (1944–45). He was mayor of Minneapolis (1945–48), a Democrat in the U.S. Senate (1948–64), a U.S. delegate to the U.N. General Assembly (1956), and U.S. vice-president in 1964. He was the unsuccessful Democratic nominee for the U.S. presidency in 1968. He was elected U.S. senator in 1970, and re-elected in 1976. He chaired the Joint Economic Committee and, when gravely ill (1977), was honored by being made deputy president, pro tem, of the U.S. Senate until his death.

Augustus Freeman Hawkins (b. 1907), a black Democrat from California in the U.S. Congress, was born in Shreveport, Louisiana. He went to Los Angeles with his parents in 1918, attended local schools, and graduated from Jefferson High School and the universities of California and Southern California. He studied economics and went into a real estate firm in Los Angeles in 1945. He was elected to the California Legislative Assembly (1934–62) and the U.S. Congress (1962–89) and chaired the Education and Labor Committee, House Administration, and the Joint Committees on Printing and the Library.

Sources
Berman, Edgar. 1979. *Herbert: the triumph and the tragedy of the Humphrey I knew.* New York: Putnam.

Cohn, Mary, ed. 1988. *Congress A to Z.* Washington, D.C.: Congressional Quarterly Inc.

Englemayer, Sheldon D., and Wagman, Robert J. 1978. *Hubert H: the man and his dream.* New York: Methuen.

Humphrey, Hubert H. 1976. *The education of a public man: my life and politics.* Ed. Norman Sherman. Garden City, New York: Doubleday.

Jacob, Kathryn A., and Ragsdale, Bruce A. 1989. *Biographical directory of the United States Congress: 1774–1989.* Bicentennial edition. Washington D.C.: U.S. Government Printing Office.

Ragsdale, Bruce A., and Treese, Joel D. 1990. *Black Americans in Congress, 1870–1989.* Washington, D.C.: U.S. Government Printing Office.

Ryskind, Allen H. 1968. *Hubert: unauthorized biography of the vice-president.* New Rochelle, New York: Arlington House.

Schantz, Harvey L. 1979. The evolution of Humphrey-Hawkins. *Policy Study Journal* 8: 368–376.

Shafritz, Jay M. 1988. *The Dorsey dictionary of American government and politics.* Chicago: Dorsey.

Solberg, Carl 1984. *Hubert Humphrey: a biography.* New York: W. W. Norton.

Who's who in American politics 1989–90. New York: R. R. Bowker.

HUNTINGDONIAN. A member of a special denomination of Methodists.

Selina Shirley (1707–91) was born near Ashby-de-la-Zouch and married the ninth earl of Huntingdon in 1728. She became known as Lady Bountiful; in 1739 she was converted by Lady Margaret Hastings, her sister-in-law, to Methodism, and when she became a close acquaintance of John and Charles Wesley, helped establish the first Methodist society at Fetter Lane. She also became close to George Whitfield, an itinerant lay preacher, who later broke with the Wesleys. After that separation from Wesley's Methodists, he helped Countess Huntingdon establish her own form of Methodism based on the congregation and Calvinist ideas. In 1743 Methodism consoled Countess Huntingdon for the death of her two sons from smallpox; in 1746 the marriage of her sister-in-law and the death of her husband drew her even closer to the cause of Methodism. On Whitfield's death she became trustee of his foundations in America. She encouraged itinerant lay preaching, built her first chapel at Brighton in 1761, and worked to attract the British upper class to Methodism by establishing chapels at Bath, Tunbridge, and London, which became her center of influence. In North Wales she established a seminary to train ministers whom she chose to work in her chapels, or in any other Protestant denomination. After being disallowed from appointing chaplains as she wished—a privilege of a peeress in most religious matters—she registered her chapels under the Toleration Act as dissenting places of prayer and worship. Her religious sect, a denomination of Calvinist Methodists, was known as the Countess of Huntingdon's Connexion. To perpetuate her work, she bequeathed her chapels, which in 1790 she had formed into an association, to four people upon her death in London.

Sources

Cross, Frank L. 1974. *The Oxford dictionary of the Christian Church.* 2d ed. New York: Oxford University Press.
Figgis, John B. 1891. *The countess of Huntingdon and her connexion.* London: Partridge.
Smith, Benjamin. 1903. *The Century cyclopedia of names.* London: The Times.
Stephen, Leslie, and Lee, Sydney, eds. 1917. *The dictionary of national biography.* London: Oxford University Press.

HUSSERLIAN SOCIAL ETHICS. Social ethics, advanced by the twentieth-century phenomenologist and philosopher, that assumed the properly philosophical life is one of action. The "truth of will" is both an "ought" and an "is," a moral category that permits the good of other people to be part of one's own good. Such a orientation today fits the "Green" policies and some communitarian-anarchist views.

Edmund Husserl (1859–1938), born a Jew in Prossnitz, Moravia (Czechoslovakia), studied in Olmstütz and at the universities of Leipzig, Berlin, and Vienna, obtaining his Ph.D. in 1882. He studied with Franz Brentano in Vienna, turned to the Lutheran faith, and began teaching at the University of Halle (1887–1901). Aiming to solve the difficult task of integrating the formal logic of mathematics with the psychological study of consciousness, Husserl found he needed to examine experience prior to formal thought processes. From this work grew his phenomenology, a fresh orientation to philosophy, that would take a place in psychology and the social sciences after World War II. He published *Logical Investigations* (1890–1901). In seeking to analyze reality as it presented itself immediately to consciousness, he became leader in a phenomenological movement that attracted a wide following. In 1913 he published

Ideas: General Introduction to Pure Phenomenology, and became a professor at the University of Freiberg. He argued that his ideas were the absolute vindication of life—man's ethical autonomy—in his *First Philosophy* (1923–24). In Europe his reputation spread, and he retired in 1928, to be replaced by Martin Heidegger (1889–1976). Although his final years were restricted by Hitler's rise to power, he was able to lecture in public, and published *The Crisis of European Sciences and Transcendental Phenomenology* (1936). At the end, free of church creed, he maintained his views of absolute philosophical self-responsibility.

Sources

Bell, David. 1990. *Husserl.* London: Routledge.

Hart, James G. 1992. *The person and the common life: studies in a Husserlian social ethics.* Dordrecht: Kluwer Academic Publisher.

McHenry, Robert, ed. 1992. *The new encyclopedia Britannica.* Chicago: Encyclopedia Britannica, Inc.

Natanson, Maurice A. 1973. *Edmund Husserl: philosopher of infinite tasks.* Evanston, Ill.: Northwestern University Press.

Zusne, Leonard. 1984. *Biographical dictionary of psychology.* Westport, Conn.: Greenwood Press.

HUSSITE. A follower of the fourteenth-century Bohemian reformer and martyr.

John Hus or Huss (c. 1369–1415), a Bohemian from Husinec, was christened John and given the surname of his birthplace. "John of Husinec" was shortened to John Hus. He graduated and taught at the University of Prague. Under the influence of John Wycliffe's ideas, Hus countered the papal order to burn Wycliffe's books, was deemed a heretic, and forbidden to preach. In 1410 he was excommunicated for opposing papal indulgences in Bohemia, and he retired to write. He was found guilty of heresy before the Council of Constance and burned at the stake after refusing to recant his teachings. Following his death came the Hussite War, a struggle by Bohemians for their own national religion and societal reform. Luther was influenced by Hus's ideas, and Hus became a hero in Czechoslovakia.

See also WYCLIF(F)ITE.

Sources

Cross, Frank L. 1974. *The Oxford dictionary of the Christian Church.* 2d ed. New York: Oxford University Press.

McHenry, Robert, ed. 1992. *The new encyclopedia Britannica.* Chicago: Encyclopedia Britannica, Inc.

Spinka, Matthew. 1968. *John Hus: a biography.* Princeton, N.J.: Princeton University Press.

HUTCHINSONIAN. A follower of the eighteenth-century British philosopher who stated that the Hebrew scriptures included elements of rational philosophy, natural history, and true religion.

John Hutchinson (1674–1737) was born in Yorkshire and educated at home. After serving as steward to the earl of Scarborough and the duke of Somerset,

Hutchinson planned a study of the Mosaic story of the Flood. In his major work *Moses's principia* (1724), he set out a system of biblical philosophy asserting that Hebrew was the primitive language of man and, if correctly interpreted, the key to all secular and religious knowledge. To him the Bible held many symbolic meanings about nature; for example, fire, light, and air corresponded to the Trinity. The work opposed Isaac Newton's *Principia* (1685)—especially the law of gravitation as it involved a vacuum—received support from a circle of "Hutchinsonians," and attracted considerable general interest. His followers included Duncan Forbes (1685–1747) who supported the Hutchinsonians' scriptural symbolism. Hutchinson also invented a timepiece to establish better estimates of longitude and tried to have it patented (1712).

Sources

Cross, Frank L. 1974. *The Oxford dictionary of the Christian Church.* 2d ed. New York: Oxford University Press.

McHenry, Robert, ed. 1992. *The new encyclopedia Britannica.* Chicago: Encyclopedia Britannica, Inc.

Stephen, Leslie, and Lee, Sydney, eds. 1917. *The dictionary of national biography.* London: Oxford University Press.

HUTTERITE. Member of a North American immigrant sect of Moravian Anabaptists. They occupy over one hundred colonies in Canada and the High Plains states, and their number exceeds 25,000. They are self sufficient economically, careful in their purchases outside the community, and have sufficient funds to meet the expectations of their growing population. They use a traditional division of labor—men work on farms, women in the home—and the community members are closely related through religion, the German language, and educational practices (Fogarty, 1980).

Jakob Hutter (d. 1536) was born at Moos, in the South Tyrol; he had little basic education and became a wandering hat-maker. Early in life he joined the Anabaptists and in 1529 became their leader. From 1531 he led the Hutterian Bretheran in Moravia, a haven for the sect. He helped organize a refuge there for his followers and formed communities of them near Auspitz. The pattern of organization was retained, but Hutter was persecuted, and for safety fled for the Tyrol where he was captured, tortured, and put to death at the stake. Communities, which had found asylum in Moravia under his leadership, established settlements based on the communal ownership of property. They were persecuted and wandered extensively; some of their descendants immigrated to the United States.

Sources

Clasen, Claus P. 1972. *Anabaptism: a social history 1525–1618: Switzerland, Moravia, south and central Germany.* Ithaca, N.Y.: Cornell University Press.

Cross, Frank L. 1974. *The Oxford dictionary of the Christian Church.* 2d ed. New York: Oxford University Press.

Fogarty, Robert S. 1980. *Dictionary of American communal and utopian history.* Westport, Conn.: Greenwood Press.

Pickering, William S.F. 1982. *The Hutterites: Christians who practice a communal way of life*. London: Ward Lock Educational.

HYDE AMENDMENT. Following U.S. Republican party policy, an amendment that forbids the use of U.S. federal funds or facilities, especially publicly funded clinics, to help pay for abortions for the poor.

Henry John Hyde (b. 1924) was born in Chicago and graduated from Saint George High School in Evanston, Illinois. He served in the U.S. Navy (1944–46) and retired from the Naval Reserve in 1968. He studied at Georgetown University in Washington and began practicing law after being admitted to the bar in Chicago in 1950. From 1967 to 1974 he sat in the Illinois House of Representatives and served as majority leader (1971–72). Since 1975 he has been a Republican member of the federal Congress.

Sources

Cohn, Mary, ed. 1988. *Congress A to Z*. Washington, D.C.: Congressional Quarterly, Inc.

Jacob, Kathryn A., and Ragsdale, Bruce A. 1989. *Biographical directory of the United States Congress: 1774–1989*. Bicentennial ed. Washington, D.C.: U.S. Government Printing Office.

I

IBSENISM. Dramatic qualities and the kind of social analysis and criticism that appear in the drama of the nineteenth-century Norwegian writer.

Henrik Ibsen (1828–1906), born at Skien, a small coastal town in Norway, received a poor education in European literature. At age 15, after his father's bankruptcy, Henrik moved to Grimstad to work with an apothecary, and there he wrote his play *Catalina* (1850). At age 23, he was appointed director and playwright of the Bergen Theater. In the early 1860s he wrote several poetical satires but did not become an outstanding writer until he left for Rome in 1864, where he wrote all his best known works. His dramas centered on social problems and advocated a critical, radical view of their solution. For example, Ibsen's *The Doll's House* (1879) examines the status of middle-class women and a wife who abandons her family. The audience was scandalized. *Ghosts* (1881) further outraged audiences with its presentation of congenital venereal disease. His *Enemy of the People* (1882) depicted individuals whose venality conflicted with the need to have an uncontaminated water supply in the community. William Archer translated Ibsen's plays into English. George Bernard Shaw (1856–1950) supported their presentation and believed they gave new vigor to English drama. Ibsen's plays raised issues that today are prominent in discussions of community values and welfare.

Sources

Beyer, Edvard. 1978. *Ibsen: the man and his work.* Trans. Marie Wells. London: Souvenir.

Chamberlain, John S. 1982. *Ibsen: the open vison.* London: Athlone.

Clurman, Harold. 1977. *Ibsen.* New York: Macmillan.

Heiberg, Hans. 1969. *Ibsen: a portrait of the artist.* Trans. Joan Tate. Coral Gables, Fla.: University of Miami Press.

McFarlane, James, and Orton, Graham, eds. and trans. 1960–77. *The Oxford Ibsen.* London: Oxford University Press.

McHenry, Robert, ed. 1992. *The new encyclopedia Britannica.* Chicago: Encyclopedia Britannica, Inc.

Meyer, Michael. 1971. *Ibsen: a biography.* 3 vols. 1985 ed. in 1 vol. Harmondsworth: Penguin.

Northam, John. 1973. *Ibsen: a critical study.* Cambridge: Cambridge University Press.

ICARIAN, ICARUS COMPLEX. Presumptuous ambition, ending in ruin or failure; among the young, the obsessive disregard of what elders advise; a set of personality trends, identified by Henry Murray (1955), as a personality poorly integrated by its own history.

Icarus, a mythical character, was the son of Daedalus, who was commissioned by King Minos to build the Labyrinth to house the Minotaur. Later, Minos, believing that the hero Theseus had escaped the Labyrinth with help from Daedalus and his son, imprisoned them there. Daedalus made wings partly of wax for his son and himself, and together they flew from Crete. Daedalus advised Icarus not to fly too high for fear that the sun would melt the wax. Obsessed by the power to fly, Icarus soared too high, the wax melted, and he plunged into that part of the Aegean now known as the Icarian Sea. Hercules found the body and later buried it, while Daedalus landed safely in Sicily.

Sources

Hamilton, Edith. 1940. *Mythology: timeless tales of gods and heroes.* New York: New American Library.

Jobes, Gertrude. 1962. *Dictionary of mythology, folklore and symbols.* New York: Scarecrow Press.

Murray, Henry A. 1955. American Icarus. In Arthur Burton and Robert E. Harris, eds. *Clinical studies in personality.* Vol. 3. New York: Harper, pp. 615–641.

IGNATIAN. Relating to a first-century bishop of Antioch and the epistles attributed to him.

Ignatius Theophoros (c. 35–c. 107) was born in Syria, died a martyr in Rome, and was canonized in 110. He was bishop of Antioch and described himself as "Theophoros" or "bearer of God." He wrote seven letters while traveling under guard from Syria to Asia Minor as a prisoner condemned for heresy and to be eaten in Rome by wild beasts. Representatives from Christian communities came to greet him on the way. The letters provide knowledge of his teachings and personality. The first three thank people for their kindness and sympathy and warn of the dangers of heretical teachings. Letter four, addressed to the church at Rome, asks its members not to interfere to save him, because then he would be deprived of being in a position to die for Christ alone. The letters show Ignatius as a true religious enthusiast and as one much concerned for the spiritual health of all Christians.

Sources

Cross, Frank L. 1974. *The Oxford dictionary of the Christian Church.* 2d ed. New York: Oxford University Press.

Grant, Robert M. 1966. *Ignatius of Antioch.* Camden, N.J.: Thomas Nelson.

Lightfoot, Joseph B. 1891. *The apostolic Fathers.* London: Macmillan.

McHenry, Robert, ed. 1992. *The new encyclopedia Britannica.* Chicago: Encyclopedia Britannica, Inc.

Richardson, Cyril C. 1935. *The Christianity of Saint Ignatius of Antioch.* 1967 reprint. New York: A.M.S. Press.

Schoedel, William R., and Koester, Helmut, ed. 1989. *Ignatius of Antioch: a commentary on letters by Ignatius of Antioch.* Philadelphia: Fortress Press.

INCE PLAN. A British proposal (1954) that, in order to restrain wage demands, industry should make use of arbitration as a final step in the settlement of disputes.

Sir Godfrey Herbert Ince (1891–1960) was born in Surrey, educated at Reigate Grammar School and University College, London, and graduated with first-class honors in mathematics in 1913. During World War I he was wounded in France, and afterward in 1919 he entered the Ministry of Labor as assistant principal. He became principal private secretary to ministers of labor (1930–33) and adviser to the Commonwealth of Australia on Unemployment Insurance (1936–37). He was undersecretary, Ministry of Labor and National Service (1940), and was seconded to offices of the War Cabinet to administer the Production Executive Secretariat (1941). Among his publications are a report on unemployment insurance in Australia (1937) and papers on manpower problems in Great Britain (1945 and 1953). He was knighted in 1943. The Ince Plan was proposed in 1954 when Sir Godfrey was permanent secretary to the Ministry of Labor, following a period when wage awards by arbitration had been small.
Sources
Marsh, Arthur. 1979. *Concise encyclopedia of industrial relations.* Westmead, Farnborough, Hants: Gower.

Who was who, 1961–70. Addenda. London: Adam and Charles Black.

Williams, E. T., and Palmer, Helen M., eds. 1971. *Dictionary of national biography 1951–1960.* London: Oxford University Press.

IRVINGITE. A popular name for a member of the Holy Catholic Apostolic Church which prepared for the Second Coming, 1864.

Edward Irving (1792–1834), born at Annan, Dumfries, in Scotland, was tutored privately and graduated from the University of Edinburgh in 1809. He taught mathematics for two years and became a licensed preacher in the Church of Scotland in 1815. In 1822 Irving was minister of the Caledonian Asylum chapel in Hatton Garden, London, where he became a popular preacher. Many of his eloquent sermons were published in *For the Oracles of God* (1823). His popularity declined when in 1825 he predicted the Second Coming for 1864. Later, he was charged with heresy for his radical views in his *Doctrine of the Incarnation Opened* (1828), and especially on the human nature of Christ. In 1832 he was removed from the pulpit, and by 1833 he was deposed from the ministry and excommunicated by London's presbytery. Irving retired to Scotland

and helped to organize a Christian community that eventually became the Holy Catholic Apostolic Church. Its members became known as Irvingites, a name they did not accept. The church survived, and its chief home, a fine Gothic building in Gordon Square, was built in 1854. The church declined late in the nineteenth century.

Sources

Cross, Frank L. 1974. *The Oxford dictionary of the Christian Church.* 2d ed. New York: Oxford University Press.

Dallimore, Arnold. 1983. *The life of Edward Irving: the forerunner of the Charismatic Movement.* Edinburgh: Banner of Truth Trust.

Douglas, James D., ed. 1974. *The new international dictionary of the Christian Church.* Exeter: Paternoster Press.

Oliphant, Margaret O.W. 1860. *The life of Edward Irving: minister of the National Scotch Church, London: illustrated by his journals and correspondence.* London: Hurst and Blackett.

Stephen, Leslie, and Lee, Sydney, eds. 1917. *The dictionary of national biography.* London: Oxford University Press.

Whitely, Henry C. 1955. *Blinded eagle: an introduction to the life and teaching of Edward Irving.* London: S.C.M. Press.

ISHMAEL. An outcast, one at war with society.

Ishmael was the eldest son of Abraham and Hagar, his handmaid (Genesis 16:15–16). It was predicted that Ishmael would beget twelve princes and found a great nation. This prediction was repeated as a promise to his mother when she and Ishmael were cast out of the house by Sarah, Abraham's wife, who wanted her two-year old son, Isaac, to be Abraham's heir. As outcasts, Ishmael and his mother wandered the desert south of Beersheba, where death by thirst was imminent. When Ishmael was close to death, his prayer was heard by God who made a well gush forth. The well would later refresh the Israelites on their journey through the wilderness. Ishmael died at age 137 having had twelve sons, progenitors of twelve tribes. The Koran calls Ishmael a prophet, and in Hebrew his name means "God hears." While in Judaism he is regarded as a wicked repentant, the Arab peoples see him as their ancestor.

Sources

Bromely, G. W., ed. 1982. *The international standard Bible encyclopedia.* Grand Rapids, Mich.: William B. Eerdman's.

Eliade, Mircea, ed. 1987. *Encyclopedia of religion.* New York: Macmillan.

Roth, Cecil E., ed. 1971. *Encyclopedia Judaica.* New York: Macmillan.

ISIDORIAN. Relating to the seventh-century archbishop of Seville, or to the collection of canons and decretals he adopted, and especially to their forged publications later.

Isidore of Seville (c. 560–636) spread Catholicism by founding schools and convents and by converting Jews. He was an able public speaker and presided at the Councils of Seville (619) and Toledo (633). He wrote historical and ecclesiastical works, including *Etymologies* which is a valuable study for the history of late Latin. He also wrote linguistic studies, works on cosmology and natural science, biographies of eighty-six biblical notables, and a guide to morals and theology. In the Middle Ages his name was given to many published works, especially *Common Law of the Spanish Church,* and in particular to a collection of canons and decretals, and later to an interpolated collection known as the *Pseudo Isidorian* or *False Decretals* (c. 1845) published by Isidore Mercantor and attributed falsely to Isidore of Seville. Famed for his learning, sanctity, and almsgiving, Isidore was made a saint in 1598 and given the title doctor of the church (1722).

Sources

Brehaut, Ernest. 1912. *An encyclopaedist of the Dark Ages; Isidore of Seville.* New York: Longmans, Green.

Cross, Frank L. 1974. *The Oxford dictionary of the Christian Church.* 2d ed. New York: Oxford University Press.

Donini, Guido, and Ford, Gordon B., eds. and trans. 1970. *Isidore of Seville's history of the Goths, Vandals, and Suevi.* Leiden: E. J. Brill.

Douglas, James D., ed. 1974. *The new international dictionary of the Christian Church.* Exeter: Paternoster Press.

Eliade, Mircea, ed. 1987. *Encyclopedia of religion.* New York: Macmillan.

J

JACK REPORT. British reports of courts of inquiry in the 1960s concerned with a national engineering stoppage (1967) at the Ford Motor Company arising out of the dismissal of Kelvin Halpin and other trade union members; reports of an inquiry into the dispute at Spitalfields Borough, Stratford, Brentford, and King's Cross Markets (1964); and reports of inquiries into two air transport disputes, British Overseas Airways Corporation and the Merchant Navy and Airline Officers Association, London Airport (1958), and a steel industry dispute over the lining of furnaces (Steel Company of Wales and the Amalgamated Union of the Building Trades Workers, 1966).

Sir Daniel Thomson Jack (1901–85) was educated at Bellahouston Academy and the University of Glasgow; he taught political economy at the universities of Glasgow (1923–28) and Saint Andrews (1928–35). He was made a professor of economics at the University of Durham (1935–61), and chairman of the Air Transport Licensing Board (1961–70). Among his works are the books *The Economics of the Gold Standard* (1925) and *Studies in Economic Warfare* (1940), and reports on the economies of Sierra Leone (1958) and Tanganyika and Nyasaland (1959). He was awarded a C.B.E. in 1951 and knighted in 1966. When a major strike began at the Ford assembly plant in Dagenham, his court of inquiry faced a conflict of principle—that is, Can management dismiss employees whom it judged to be unsatisfactory, disloyal, or disruptive? The company argued that its control was being undermined by shop stewards who exploited consultative machinery; unions said that the company's problems were due to its preservation of a sacred set of prerogatives. Although the Jack Report found that the company took advantage of the strike to sack seventeen alleged troublemakers, and the union was responsible for poor industrial relations at

Dagenham, it concluded that the existing consultative machinery would be adequate if used properly and loyally.

Sources

Friedman, H. Meredeen S. 1980. *The dynamics of industrial conflict: lessons from Ford.* London: Croom Helm.

Marsh, Arthur. 1979. *Concise encyclopedia of industrial relations.* Westmead, Farnborough, Hants: Gower.

Obituary. *The Times* (London), January 15, 1985.

Who's who, 1985. London: Adam and Charles Black.

JACKSON PHENOMENON. The amazing event in which the black Democratic candidate for the nomination as president of the United States in the 1988 campaign gained almost one-third of the Democratic Convention's delegates; a deeply emotional crusade by black Americans during the 1988 U.S. presidential campaign.

Jesse Jackson (b. 1941), the adopted son of a janitor, was born in Greenville, North Carolina, and won a football scholarship to Illinois University. He entered a Chicago seminary, became a Baptist minister in 1968, and through his charismatic style of preaching and association with Martin Luther King, Jr. (1929–68) became an active politician promoting the economic advancement of Afro-Americans. In 1984 he sought the Democratic presidential nomination by building a "Rainbow Coalition" of radical pressure groups and against Walter Mondale (b. 1928) won a fifth of the delegates. In 1988 he again declared his candidacy, promising "to bring justice to our land, mitigate misery in the world and bring peace to on earth." In the 1988 Democratic Convention, against Michael Dukakis (b. 1933), Jackson doubled his 1984 share of the votes.

Sources

Colton, Elizabeth O. 1989. *The Jackson phenomenon: the man, the power, the message.* New York: Doubleday.

Hatch, Roger D. 1988. *Beyond opportunity: Jesse Jackson's vision for America.* Philadelphia: Fortress Press.

Keesings contemporary archives: record of world events. 1988:35832; 36000. London: Keesings Publications.

Landess, Thomas H., and Quinn, Richard M. 1985. *Jesse Jackson and the politics of race.* Ottawa, Ill.: Jameson Books.

Magnussen, Magnus; Goring, Rosemary; and Thorn, John O., eds. 1990. *Chambers biographical dictionary.* Edinburgh: Chambers Ltd.

Reed, Adolph L. 1986. *The Jesse Jackson phenomenon: the crisis of purpose in Afro-American politics.* New Haven, Conn.: Yale University Press.

Reynolds, Barbara. 1985. *Jesse Jackson, America's David.* Washington, D.C.: JFJ Associates.

JACKSONIAN DEMOCRACY. Political rule that emphasizes the importance of the common person's interests and suppresses aristocratic influences or entitlements.

Andrew Jackson (1767–1845) was born in the backwoods settlement, Waxhaw (North Western Frontier), South Carolina. His parents had migrated from Northern Ireland in 1765, and his father died shortly after Andrew's birth. At age 14 Jackson was an orphan. He studied law and in 1788 went to Nashville with the first party to use the new wagon road. When Tennessee achieved statehood (1796), Jackson was a convention delegate and helped frame its first constitution. Under the new government, Jackson was elected to the only seat allotted to Tennessee in the federal House of Representatives. In 1798 he was elected a judge in Tennessee, and in 1802 he became a general in the local militia. He retired as judge, and after minor political conflicts—including a duel—lived the life of a country gentleman until 1812. In the war against Britain (1812), he served so well that he became a national hero and was called "Old Hickory" for his toughness. At the battle of New Orleans (1815) Jackson led the American destruction of British forces. He was considered a candidate for the U.S. presidency, stood in 1824, but was beaten when his opponents' supporters collaborated against him. He was the first Democratic president and was twice elected to the position (1829–1837). To achieve his ends, he established a strong central government, expanded the franchise by removing property entitlements, made the party system stronger, and used a system of patronage, loyal associates, and the veto.

Sources

Benson, Lee. 1961. *The concept of Jacksonian Democracy.* Princeton, N.J.: Princeton University Press.

Malone, Dumas, ed. 1932. *Dictionary of American biography.* Vol. V. New York: Charles Scribner's Sons.

Meyers, Marvin. 1957. *The Jacksonian persuasion: politics and belief.* Stanford, Calif.: Stanford University Press.

Remini, Robert V. 1966. *Andrew Jackson.* New York: Twayne Publishers.

Schlesinger, Arthur M., Jr. 1945. *The age of Jackson.* Boston: Little, Brown.

Shaw, Ronald, ed. 1969. *Andrew Jackson: 1767–1845.* New York: Ocean Publications.

White, Leonard D. 1954. *The Jacksonians.* New York: Macmillan.

JACOBEAN. Relating to early seventeenth-century (1603–25) British literature and architecture.

James I (1566–1625), king of Great Britain from 1603 to 1625, was the son of Mary Queen of Scots and her second husband, James Stuart, Lord Darnley. He was born in Edinburgh Castle and became king of Scotland the following year when his mother was forced to abdicate. During his minority, a regent ruled Scotland and rival lords fought for the coveted office. James was well educated, especially in theology, and a staunch Protestant. In 1603 when Queen Elizabeth I died, he became England's king, the first of the Stuarts and the first to reign over both countries. He was not popular with either the people or the Parliament, and held fast to the belief in the divine right of the monarchy. The term *Jacobean* refers especially to early English Renaissance architecture and to furniture of this period, later introduced by the first of the great English architects, Inigo Jones (1573–1652), who was engaged by James I to arrange the masques of Ben Jonson and later became surveyor general of royal buildings (1615).

Sources

Bingham, Caroline. 1981. *James I of England*. London: Weidenfeld and Nicolson.
Crystal, David, ed. 1990. *The Cambridge encyclopedia*. Cambridge: Cambridge University Press.
Stephen, Leslie, and Lee, Sydney, eds. 1917. *The dictionary of national biography*. London: Oxford University Press.

JACOBIN. Extremist of the left wing, radical; member of a terrorist group. The toponym is taken from the Dominican convent near Saint Jacques Church, which was the original meeting place of a group of extremists in 1789. The group, the Jacobin Club, was led by Maximilien François-Marie-Isadore de Robespierre (1758–94). Under his Reign of Terror during the French Revolution, 250,000 people were arrested, and 1,500 were guillotined.

Sources

Crystal, David, ed. 1990. *The Cambridge encyclopedia*. Cambridge: Cambridge University Press.
Rudé, George. 1975. *Robespierre: portrait of a revolutionary democrat*. London: Collins.

JACOBITES. Followers of the exiled Stuarts and named for James II (Latin—*Jacobus* for James) after he was overthrown (1688) in the Glorious Revolution. The Jacobites wanted to return the House of Stuart to the British throne. The Jacobite movement opened with the battle of Killiecrankie in 1689. In 1696 a plot to murder the British king William III and restore James II failed because there were too many accomplices, thus making betrayal inevitable, and because there were too few Jacobites in the plan. In 1715 the Jacobites led their first strong rebellion—the Fifteen Rebellion—with the son of James II, James Edward Stuart, at its head, known as the "Old Pretender"; in 1745 his son, the "Young Pretender," Charles Edward Stuart, known romantically as "Bonnie Prince Charlie," led the second rebellion—the Forty-five Rebellion. In April 1746, at the battle of Culloden, the duke of Cumberland defeated the forces of Bonnie Prince Charlie, and the Jacobite Rebellion ended. The last Jacobite to be hanged was Dr. Archibald Cameron in June 1753.

Sources

Crystal, David, ed. 1990. *The Cambridge encyclopedia*. Cambridge: Cambridge University Press.
Findlater, Andrew, ed. 1895. *Chambers encyclopedia*. New ed. London and Edinburgh: William and Robert Chambers Ltd. Philadelphia: J. B. Lippincott Co.
Garrett, Jane. 1980. *The triumphs of providence*. Cambridge: Cambridge University Press.

JACQUERIE. A revolt; the 1358 revolt of North East French peasants.

Guillaume Cale—nicknamed "Jacques Bonhomme" (meaning "Goodman

Jack'' a name now applied in derision to peasants)—was the only leader mentioned in the chronicles of the insurrection against the nobles of France during the Hundred Years' War with England. Alternatively, the name ''Jacquerie'' came from the nobles' scornful reference to peasants as ''Jacques.'' The revolt began after the English victory at Poitiers in 1356 and became a bitter battle between peasants, aggrieved Parisians, and the nobility. During the riots, peasants burned and sacked castles until the nobles joined with the bourgeois of the towns to curb the rebellion in a massacre of 7,000 rebels at Maize and Clermont-en-Beauvaisis (1358).

Sources

Chisholm, Hugh, ed. 1910–1911. *Encyclopedia Britannica.* 11th ed. New York: Encyclopedia Britannica Co.

Crystal, David, ed. 1990. *The Cambridge encyclopedia.* Cambridge: Cambridge University Press.

Neillands, Robin H. 1990. *The Hundred Years War: 1337–1453.* London: Routledge.

Prevost, M., and D'Amat, Roman, eds. 1954. *Dictionniare de biographie Française.* Vol. 6. Paris: Librairie Letouzey et Ané.

JAKOBSONIAN. Pertaining to the twentieth-century American linguist whose work contributed greatly to linguistic and literary thought.

Roman Jakobson (1896–1982), born in Moscow, was educated at the Lazarev Institute of Oriental Languages and the universities of Moscow and Prague, obtaining his Ph.D. in 1930. He founded the Moscow Linguistic Circle before moving to Czechoslovakia in 1920 and establishing the Prague Linguistic Circle. He taught at many universities in Europe and Scandinavia before coming to the United States in 1941. He taught at Columbia University (1943–49), Harvard (1949–67), and the Massachusetts Institute of Technology (1957–67), and for brief periods at other notable universities in the United States and Europe. He received honors and awards from French, English, Swedish, and Slav universities. His interests included children's language, aphasia, and Shakespeare's artistic use of language, and his many publications were translated into fifteen languages. His selected writings were published in eight volumes.

Sources

Crystal, David, ed. 1990. *The Cambridge encyclopedia.* Cambridge: Cambridge University Press.

Gray, Paul E. 1983. *A tribute to Roman Jakobson: 1896–1982* [with bibliography]. Berlin: Mouton.

Locher, Frances C., ed. 1979. *Contemporary authors.* R77-80. Detroit: Gale Research.

May, Hal, ed. 1983. *Contemporary authors.* Vol. 107. Detroit: Gale Research.

JANIS'S GROUPTHINK. An extreme degree of agreement—concurrence seeking—among policymakers of high standing in closely knit groups; each individual values membership more than the outcome of the group decisions, and, in a clublike, oligarchic, and elitist style, free of individual doubt or dissent, they aim to reach consensus in the firm belief that the group is right both morally and technically, and that all opponents are evil and incompetent. Such decision-making tends to be closed-minded, distorts reality, ignores ethical outcomes, and often establishes foolish projects. The concept has been applied to Watergate, the Falkland Islands War, the *Challenger* disaster, and the Iran-Contra Scandal.

Irving Lester Janis (1918–90) was born in Buffalo, New York, the son of a businessman, and studied at the local high school, art museum, and library. He completed undergraduate study at the University of Chicago and began work on his Ph.D. at Columbia University in 1940. During World War II he worked at the Library of Congress analyzing fascist propaganda. After obtaining his Ph.D., he joined the psychology faculty at Yale University (1947–85). His original and extensive research in social psychology owed much to social learning theory, field theory, and psychoanalysis. He edited the *Journal of Abnormal and Social Psychology* and *Sociometry*. Among his early books were *Air War and Emotional Stress* (1951), *Personality and Persuasibility* (1959), and *Psychological Stress* (1958). He was a leader in health psychology with work in weight reduction and smoking clinics. His *Victims of Groupthink* (1972) was revised and enlarged as *Groupthink: Psychological Studies of Policy Decisions and Fiascos* (1982). His last published work was *Crucial Decisions: Leadership in Policy Making and Crisis Management* (1989), and his last book was *Enjoying Art: The Psychology of Gaining Pleasure from Old and Modern Painters*. The American Psychological Association honored him with its William James Fellow award, and he was recognized as a distinguished scientist by the Society for Experimental Psychology. His work was noted for its integration of leadership, cognition in decision and policy-making, and the application of social psychological theory to contemporary issues, for example, peace and social justice.

Sources

Aldag, Ramon J., and Fuller, Sally R. 1993. Beyond fiasco: a reappraisal of the Groupthink phenomenon and a new model of group decision processes. *Psychological Bulletin* 113:533–552.

Russett, Bruce. 1991. In memoriam: Irving L. Janis. *Journal of Conflict Resolution* 35: 179–80.

Singer, Jerome L. 1991. Obituary: Irving L. Janis (1918–1990). *American Psychological Society Observer,* May:31.

Smith, M. Brewster, and Mann, Leon. 1992. Obituary: Irving L. Janis (1918–1990). *American Psychologist* 47:648.

t'Hart, Paul. 1991. Irving L. Janis' victims of Groupthink. *Political Psychology* 12:247–278.

JANSENISM. The doctrine, deduced from Augustine and against the ordinary Catholic dogma of the freedom of the will, that human nature is corrupt and that Christ died only for the elect, all others being condemned to hell. To the Jansenists, it was not possible to meet God's commands without having special grace. They believed that grace is irresistible; that only freedom from compulsion is required for merit, not freedom from necessity; that it is semi-Pelagian to argue that grace is resistible or can be complied with free will, and, similarly, to teach that Christ died for all men. The Jansenists were opposed to the pope and so came into direct conflict with the Jesuits.

Cornelius Otto Jansen (1585–1638) was born at Acquoi near Gorkum, Netherlands, and died at Ypres, Belgium. He was a Dutch Roman Catholic theologian, founder of the sect named after him. After studies at the University of Louvain, he taught theology there. He studied Augustine's writings closely (1612–17) and sought to teach his ideas and with them to put down Protestantism. In this effort he was at loggerheads with the Jesuits, and the conflict would continue well into the eighteenth century. Begun in 1628, his chief work, *Augustinus, of the Doctrine of St. Augustine on the Health, the Sickness and the Cure of Human Nature: Against the Pelagians and Those of Marseilles* (1640), stressed that original justice belongs to human nature. He was bishop of Ypres in Flanders. Because his radical views were in opposition to those of the Jesuits, his ideas were condemned as heretical (1649) and went unknown until the posthumous publication of his work. In practice, Jansenism limited God's grace to the elect, suggesting thereby that the church should ignore those who were never to be converts, people outside the church, and should concentrate on cleansing its own chosen members, by adopting strong discipline and an ascetic way of living.

Sources

Cross, Frank L. 1974. *The Oxford dictionary of the Christian Church.* 2d ed. New York: Oxford University Press.

Douglas, James D., ed. 1974. *The new international dictionary of the Christian Church.* Exeter: Paternoster Press.

Sedgwick, Alexander. 1977. *Jansenism in seventeenth-century France: voices from the wilderness.* Charlottesville: University Press of Virginia.

JAY'S FIRST LAW. A law of human organization, noted by Thomas Martin (1973) and stated by Antony Jay (1967), that many administrators and managers carry in their heads an ideal organization where "the classic hierarchy [comprises] one man at the top with three below him, each of whom has three below him, and so on with fearful symmetry unto the seventh generation, by which stage there is a row of seven hundred and twenty-nine managers and an urgent need for a very large triangular piece of paper" (Jay, 1967).

Sir Antony Rupert Jay (b. 1930), born in London, was educated at Saint Paul's School and Magdalene College, Cambridge. He was a lieutenant in the British Army Signals Corps (1952–54) and afterward became a writer, director, and producer for the BBC in London (1955–64). He edited "Tonight" (1962), was head of Talks for BBC-TV (1963), and since 1964 has been a free-lance writer and chairman of Video Arts Ltd. (1972–89) and served on a government committee examining the future of television (1974–76). He published verse and satirical examinations of the English character. His notable early work *Man-*

agement and Machiavelli (1967; 2d ed., 1987) showed that power was used in corporate life exactly as it had been in government for many years. He maintained his satirical and critical interest in organizations, for example, *The New Oratory* (1971) and *Corporation Man* (1972) and with Jonathan Lynn wrote the acclaimed BBC-TV series, "Yes, Minister" and "Yes, Prime Minister" (2 series and books) which satirized the politics of Britain, and the television documentary and book, *Elizabeth R* (1992). He published two volumes of *The Complete "Yes Minister"* (1981; 1989). He received an honorary M.A. (Sheffield, 1987) and an honorary doctor of business administration (International Management Center, Buckingham, 1988) and was knighted in 1988.

Sources

Jay, Antony R. 1967. *Management and Machiavelli*. New York: Holt, Rinehart and Winston.

Martin, Thomas L., Jr. 1973. *Malice in blunderland*. New York: McGraw-Hill.

Who's who, 1993. London: Adam and Charles Black.

Personal Communication.

JEFFERSONIAN, JEFFERSONIAN BIBLE, JEFFERSONIAN DEMOCRACY. Relating to the third American president; a democrat. A collection of Jesus' teachings compiled from the New Testament and published by Thomas Jefferson. In an agrarian society, democracy that is controlled by a natural aristocracy who follow free trade policies, use strong local government rather than central government, and support freedom of the press, speech, and religion.

Thomas Jefferson (1743–1826) was born at Goochland (Abermarle), Virginia, graduated from the College of William and Mary (1762), studied law, and in 1774 published *A Summary View of the Rights of British America* which argued that the British Parliament had no authority in the colonies and that America's only tie with England was allegiance to the Crown. As a delegate to the Second Continental Congress, 1775–76, he drafted the Declaration of Independence, which was amended only on minor points by Benjamin Franklin (1706–90) and others. Consequently, Jefferson became known as the Father of American Democracy. On returning to Virginia he became governor and endured the British invasion during the American Revolution. Later, he drafted a plan for a decimal coinage and succeeded Franklin as minister to France where he saw the onset of the French Revolution. He was secretary of state (1790), supported state's rights, and opposed centralized government; around him he established a group of "Republicans," the seeds of what would become the Democratic party. In 1796 he became vice-president, and in 1801 he wrote *A Manual of Parliamentary Practice*. In 1801 he was the United States' third president and its first to be inaugurated in Washington. He cut government expenditure, sought to curb powers of the judiciary, and supported the policy of federal government control of foreign matters while states controlled local affairs. In his first term, his government added a million square miles to the U.S. territory with the Louisiana Purchase from the French, and he encouraged expansion westward. After being reelected in 1804, he shepherded the passage of a law forbidding slavery after January 1, 1808. He also encouraged experiments in agriculture and the development of the University of Virginia. In 1809 he retired to Monticello but was ready to advise those who followed him in politics. As a philosopher-statesman, he was always interested in science and the arts, and he believed that education was essential to enlighten people so that democracy would flourish.

Sources

Brodie, Fawn M. 1974. *Thomas Jefferson: an intimate history.* New York: W. W. Norton.

Beard, Charles A. 1943. *The economic origins of Jeffersonian democracy.* New York: Free Press.

Malone, Dumas, ed. 1932. *Dictionary of American biography.* Vol. V. New York: Charles Scribner's Sons.

Malone, Dumas. 1948–81. *Jefferson and his time.* 6 vols. Boston: Little, Brown.

Miller, David, ed. 1987. *The Blackwell encyclopedia of political thought.* Oxford: Basil Blackwell.

Wiltse, Charles M. 1960. *The Jeffersonian tradition in American democracy.* New York: Hill and Wang.

JEHOVAH'S WITNESSES, JEHOVAH COMPLEX. A religious movement founded in 1872, which follows the Bible in its literal sense. Identification of oneself with God in a grandiose delusion of greatness.

The movement is named after Jehovah, God's personal name, which was revealed to be the case by Moses on Mount Horeb (Exodus 3:13–15). The term comes from Hebrew Yahweh, Y H V H. Among the Jews, the word became too sacred to be uttered, so from c. 300 B.C. it was replaced with "Adonai," meaning "Lord" in Hebrew. Later, the vowels A O A were inserted between the four letters of Y H V H and Yaweh became the term for God; later this appeared as "Jehovah," God's personal name. An American movement, it was established by Charles Taze Russell (1852–1916) and Joseph Franklin ("Judge") Rutherford (1869–1942); it rejects the Trinity, the deity of Jesus Christ and the Holy Spirit, and military service and blood transfusion. As the world comes to an end, the movement asserts, there will be 144,000 Jehovah's Witnesses forming the elect in heaven. The active members of the movement are noted for the zeal of their door-to-door proselytizing. With worldwide publishing houses the movement follows an effective propaganda campaign under the name of "Watch Tower Bible and Tract Society."

Sources

Cross, Frank L. 1974. *The Oxford dictionary of the Christian Church.* 2d ed. New York: Oxford University Press.

Douglas, James D., ed. 1974. *The new international dictionary of the Christian Church.* Exeter: Paternoster Press.

Penton, M. James. 1985. *The story of Jehovah's Witnesses.* Toronto: University of Toronto Press.

Stroup, Herbert H. 1945. *The Jehovah's Witnesses.* New York: Columbia University Press.

Zusne, Leonard. 1987. *Eponyms in psychology: a dictionary and sourcebook.* Westport, Conn.: Greenwood Press.

JENSEN CONTROVERSY, JENSENISM. The controversy that arose during the 1970s when evidence was shown that supported a genetic explanation of differences between individuals and demonstrated that IQ differences between American whites and blacks were due partly to genetic factors.

Arthur Robert Jensen (b. 1923) was born in San Diego and studied at the University of California, Berkeley, San Diego State College, and Teachers College, University of Columbia, where he obtained his Ph.D. in 1956. He worked as a medical psychologist (1955–56) at Maryland Psychiatric Institute, in California, and at the Institute of Psychiatry, London University (1956–58). He became a professor of educational psychology at Berkeley in 1958 and a research psychologist at the Institute of Human Learning in 1961. In 1969, in the *Harvard Educational Review,* he published an article that suggested compensatory education programs would fail and waste public money because intelligence is a largely hereditary trait and unequally distributed among ethnic groups and racial groups. Evidence indicated that white Americans were more intelligent than black. Those who supported a sociocultural explanation of differences in school performance were outraged. Jensen was accused of racism, bias, misuse of data, falsely equating intelligence with IQ scores, using a static theory of intelligence, upholding the use of culture-bound tests, and ignoring data on the raising of IQ levels. He was attacked, burned in effigy, had his job put in jeopardy, and colleagues tried to revoke his status in the American Association for the Advancement of Science. His ideas were misrepresented, and he was denounced by the popular press. The attackers spoke of "Jensenism," that is, the ideology that genetic as well as cultural factors may contribute to individual differences and that differences in social class and race may contribute to variations in intelligence and performance in school. He answered the critics in his *Genetics and Education* (1972), *Educability and Group Differences* (1973), *Bias in Mental Tests* (1979), and *Straight Talk about Mental Tests* (1980). He showed that the evidence that contradicted his interpretations was unsound and that his hypothesis required a special methodology to test it.

Sources

Corsini, Raymond J., ed. 1984. *Encyclopedia of psychology.* Vol. 2. New York: John Wiley.

Evory, Ann, ed. 1981. *Contemporary authors.* New Revision Series 2. Detroit: Gale Research.

Harré, Rom, and Lamb, Roger, eds. 1983. *The encyclopedic dictionary of psychology.* Oxford: Basil Blackwell.

JESUIT. A member of the Society of Jesus, which was founded as a Roman Catholic religious order in 1534 by Saint Ignatius Loyola (1491–1556) and confirmed by Paul III in 1540. It originally aimed to resist the Reformation and convert the unbelievers through missionary work. The term comprises the Latin for "Jesus" and "ita" for follower. In the seventeenth century some Jesuits became politically active, and the term *Jesuitical* came to mean politically active in a secretive and underhand way, crafty, and deceptive. Today the Jesuit Society is a powerful educational force; it established the Gregorian University in Rome and nine others in the East. There are many Jesuit schools, colleges, and academies around the world.

Jesus. See CHRISTIAN.

Sources

Aveling, John C.H. 1981. *The Jesuits.* London: Blond and Briggs.

Cross, Frank L. 1974. *The Oxford dictionary of the Christian Church.* 2d ed. New York: Oxford University Press.

Douglas, James D., ed. 1974. *The new international dictionary of the Christian Church.* Exeter: Paternoster Press.

Mitchell, David. 1980. *The Jesuits: a history.* London: Macdonald.

Rawlinson, Peter. 1990. *The Jesuit factor: a personal investigation.* London: Weidenfeld and Nicolson.

JIM CROW, JIM CROW LAWS, JIM CROWISM. A derogatory, generic name for Afro-Americans in the United States. Statutes enacted in the southern states beginning in the 1870s that legalized the segregation of whites and non-whites with regard to transport, schooling, use of parks, theaters, cemeteries, and restaurants. Legal discrimination based on race between the 1870s and the early 1950s.

Jim Crow was a character in a popular minstrel song that had two lines in the refrain: "Wheel about and turn about and do jis so/ And ebery time I wheel about I jump Jim Crow." Thomas Dartmouth ("Daddy") Rice (d. 1860), who copyrighted the song in 1828, portrayed the character on stage; Rice modeled his performance on a worker named Jim Crow whom he had once seen in a field in Kentucky. Later, the book *The History of Jim Crow* appeared, and the term *Jim Crow* became synonymous for nonwhites and the laws that were enacted to segregate nonwhites and whites. In 1954 such laws were declared unconstitutional by the U.S. Supreme Court.

Sources

Christy, Edwin B., comp. 1865. *Jim Crow.* [A song]. Philadelphia: A Winch.

Hendrickson, Robert. 1987. *The Facts on File encyclopedia of words and phrases.* New York: Facts on File.

The Jim Crow song book. 1847. Ithaca, N.Y.: J. E. Barber.

McHenry, Robert, ed. 1992. *The new encyclopedia Britannica.* Chicago: Encyclopedia Britannica, Inc.

Woodward, C. Vann. 1974. *The strange career of Jim Crow.* New York: Oxford University Press.

JOHN LEWIS PARTNERSHIP. A partnership, protected by a trust, which adminsters a large British department store and its branches in the interests of its employees.

John Spedan Lewis (1885–1963), son of John Lewis, the founder of the London department store, Peter Jones, was educated both at Westminster and at home. Disillusioned by his father's commercial success and hearing that he, his father, and his brother received annually far more from the business than the total salary and wages bill, and seeing the repressive and inefficient management practices in the firm, young John considered the value of a business partnership with the employees. While recovering from a riding accident, he had the idea that shares instead of cash should be distributed to those who worked for the firm. When young John succeeded his father and overcame his father's intense opposition, the John Lewis Partnership was organized (1918–20). After his father's death, John worked for twenty-seven years to secure the partnership, which belongs to all who work in the firm and share in its prosperity.

Sources

Flanders, Allen; Pomeranz, Ruth; and Woodward, Joan. 1968. *Experiment in industrial democracy: a study of the John Lewis Partnership.* London: Faber and Faber.

Lewis, John S. 1948. *Partnership for all.* London: Kerr-Cros.

Lewis, John S. 1954. *Fairer shares.* London: Staples.

Marsh, Arthur. 1979. *Concise encyclopedia of industrial relations.* Westmead, Farnborough, Hants: Gower.

Tweedale, Geoffrey. 1985. John Spedan Lewin. In D. J. Jeremy and C. Shaw, eds. *Dictionary of business biography: a biographical dictionary of business leaders active in Britain in the period of 1860–1980.* London: Butterworth.

JOHNNY'S CHILD. A specimen of *homo habilis,* "Handy Man," an ancestor of humankind, found in the Olduvai Gorge originally in the German colony of Tanganyika, Africa (1911). The specimen's cranial capacity was large, the cheek teeth were narrow, the hand bones showed a finely developed precision grip, and the feet bones indicated a full bipedal gait.

Jonathan Leakey (b. 1940) was born in Kenya, the first child of Louis Leakey's second wife, Mary. Both parents were notable archaeologists in Africa, and the lad always traveled with his parents during their fieldwork. Jonathan and his brothers, Richard (b. 1944) and Philip (b. 1948), were educated in Nairobi, Duke of York School, Langata. On leaving school in 1960, Jonathan joined his parents in their work: he liked wandering alone in search of fossil bones. The site where he found enough specimens of a sabre-toothed cat to warrant a dig, FLK site, was known as "Johnny's Site." There in November 1960 Leakey found a piece of lower jaw or mandible as well as cranial fragments from a juvenile hominid. It was named informally after Johnny and formally after the gorge where it was found, that is, OH (Olduvai Hominid) 7. Johnny, unlike his younger brother Richard, did not follow his parents' profession.

Sources

Johanson, David, and Shreeve, James. 1989. *Lucy's Child: the discovery of a human ancestor.* New York: Avon Books.

Leakey, Louis S.B. 1953. *Adam's ancestors: an up to date outline of the Old Stone Age and what is known about man's origin and evolution.* London: Methuen.

Leakey, Louis S.B. 1969. *Fossil vertebrates of Africa.* New York: Academic Press.
Leakey, Mary. 1984. *Disclosing the past.* Garden City, N.Y.: Doubleday.

JONES'S SEVEN LAWS. Seven laws on the social impact of technological change stated by the Australian politician. In summary:

1. In large-scale production, advanced technological innovation reduces aggregate employment relative to market size and increases, at lower wage rates, the employment in technologically related areas.

2. The employment of workers is inversely related to economic efficiency until a chaos point of inefficiency is reached beyond which labor cannot be absorbed.

3. Under conditions of mass production, employment is in inverse relation to demand.

4. In a technologically advanced society, economic viability requires a growing number of small consumers, despite a falling number of large producers.

5. Employment levels rise as demand increases for a diversity of services. The level of complexity of human needs is positively related to levels of employment, and the growth of the services industry is inhibited by overspecialization and economic dependence in single-industry areas.

6. Time spent by generalists in technical decision making is inversely related to the complexity of the topic.

7. Depending on how it is used, all technological change may enhance or degrade human life.

Barry Owen Jones (b. 1932) was born at Geelong, Victoria, in Australia, studied law at the University of Melbourne, and worked as a high school teacher and public servant (1957–67) before practicing as a barrister (1967–) and teaching history at La Trobe University (1968). He earned much publicity as an undefeated quiz champion (1960–69) in Australia and was elected as an Australian Labor party member to Victoria's Legislative Assembly (1972–77) and to the federal Parliament (1977). Under Prime Minister Robert Hawke, Jones was minister for science and technology (1983–84), minister for science (1984–87), and minister for science and small business (1988–90). He is a prominent public figure in Australia; he was on the Anti-Hanging Council of Victoria and the Australian Council for the Arts, and supported Australia's film industry. Among his published works are *The Penalty Is Death: Capital Punishment in the Twentieth Century* (1968), *The Macmillan Dictionary of Biography* (1981), and the work in which the "laws" were stated, *Sleepers, Wake! Technology and the Future of Work* (1982). Today he is no longer a government minister but remains Australia's most prominent spokesman for science and technology, and an analyst of trends and policies in science and its future applications. In October 1991 he was elected to the executive board of the UNESCO Council for a four-year term.

Sources

Jones, Barry O. 1982. *Sleepers, wake! Technology and the future of work.* Melbourne: Oxford University Press.

Jones, Barry O. 1988. Society and the future. *Australian and New Zealand Journal of Psychiatry* 22:358–365.

JONESTOWN. A symbol of the horror of the ritual-suicide-murder in an extreme religious cult. In Guyana at Jonestown over 900 members of the Peoples Temple settlement died when, under the direction of their religious leader, James Jones, they drank poison.

James Warren Jones (1931–1977) was born in Lynn, Indiana. His mother was the center of family life, and she behaved toward the child as if he were destined to be a savior. As a boy, he practiced the skills of an authoritarian preacher with his peers. In the late 1950s he founded the People's Temple in Indiana. He preached racial brotherhood and benevolence toward the poor. In 1965 the growing congregation moved to California. In 1977, in response to newspaper and magazine criticism of Jones' politics, the congregation left the United States and established a compound in the jungle of Guyana. In November a U.S. Congressman, Senator Leo J. Ryan, went to Guyana to investigate charges that Jones was holding people against their will. When attempting to leave, Ryan and others were shot to death. At the same time Jones mustered his followers, announced the killing of Ryan and others, and began the "revolutionary suicide," a ritual that had earlier been rehearsed.

Sources

Chidester, David. 1988. *Salvation and suicide: an interpretation of Jim Jones, the Peoples Temple, and Jonestown.* Bloomington: Indiana University Press.

Feinsod, Ethan, and Rhodes, Odell. 1981. *Awake in a nightmare: Jonestown, the only eyewitness account.* New York: W. W. Norton.

Fogarty, Robert S. 1980. *Dictionary of American communal and utopian history.* Westport, Conn.: Greenwood Press.

Hall, John R. 1987. *Gone from the promised land: Jonestown in American cultural history.* New Brunswick, N.J.: Transaction Books.

Kilduff, Marshal, and Jevers, R. 1978. *Suicide cult: the inside story of the People's Temple sect and the massacre in Guyana.* New York: Bantam Books.

Kroth, Jerry. 1992. *Omens and oracles: collective psychology in the nuclear age.* New York: Praeger Publishers.

Lindsey, Robert. 1978. How Jim Jones gained his power over followers. *New York Times Biographical Service* 9:1052–5 November.

Lindsey, Robert. 1978. Jim Jones—from poverty to power over many lives. *New York Times,* November 26.

Osherow, Neal. 1984. Making sense of the non-sensical: an analysis of Jonestown. In Elliot Aronson, ed. *Readings about the social animal.* New York: W. H. Freeman, pp. 68–86.

Ulman, Richard B., and Abgse, D. Wilfred. 1983. The group psychology of mass madness: Jonestown. *Political Psychology* 4:637–661.

JUDAS, JUDAS TRAP. A traitor, traitorous. The consequence of a self-destructive act that involves people unconsciously sabotaging whatever small measure of happiness they think they might have attained.

Judas Iscariot from Kerioth, or "the zealot," was one of the twelve apostles, treasurer of the group, and the betrayer of Jesus Christ. Judas was tempted by Satan to betray Jesus to the authorities by allowing them to arrest him quietly. Judas plotted the betrayal and waited for the opportunity. During the Passover meal Jesus predicted that he would be betrayed, and Judas left the room. Judas led a band of soldiers and officers of the chief priests and Pharisees to the garden of Gethsemane and identified Jesus for them with a kiss of greeting. For this act of betrayal Judas, who was both greedy and penurious, received thirty pieces of silver, but, later, filled with remorse, he returned the money and hanged himself. His name is associated with a number of expressions: notably, the Judas kiss of betrayal; Judas-colored hair, which is red, because Judas was red-headed; Judas-tree, an elder like that from which he may have hanged himself; Judas hole or slit, the hole through which a prisoner may be spied; and Judas goat which leads unsuspecting goats to their slaughter.

Sources

Cross, Frank L. 1974. *The Oxford dictionary of the Christian Church.* 2d ed. New York: Oxford University Press.

Douglas, James D., ed. 1974. *The new international dictionary of the Christian Church.* Exeter: Paternoster Press.

Myers, Allen C. 1987. Rev. ed. *The Eerdmans Bible dictionary.* Grand Rapids, Mich.: William B. Eerdman's.

Wareham, John. 1983. *Wareham's way: escaping the Judas trap.* New York: Atheneum.

JUGLAR CYCLE. A business cycle of seven to eleven years.

Clément Juglar (1819–1905) was a French physician who noted the relation between France's wealth and fluctuations in human health. This drew him to the study of economic crises. He published *Commercial Crises and Their Periodic Recurrence in France, England and the United States* (1892) and expanded it for publication in 1899. This work made him the first theorist of economic or business cycles. He explained the cycles in three stages: first, he carefully described their history in terms of prices, interest rates, bank balances, and so on; second, he found cycles of an average of six years between 1803 and 1882; and third, he explained cycles in crises and prosperity in terms of the human need to purge the economic system while fear was replacing euphoria. He believed nothing could be done about the crises because it was a necessary part of human nature. However, with statistical data he was able to show that turning points in business cycle could be predicted.

Sources

Blaug, Mark, ed. 1986. *Who's who in economics: a biographical dictionary of major economists, 1700–1986.* 2d ed. Cambridge, Mass.: MIT Press.

Eatwell, John; Milgate, Murray; and Newman, Peter. 1987. *The new Palgrave: a dictionary of economics.* London: Macmillan.

Greenwald, Douglas, ed. 1982. *Encyclopedia of economics.* New York: McGraw-Hill.
Rutherford, Donald, 1992. *Dictionary of economics.* London: Routledge.
Sills, David L., ed. 1968. *International encyclopedia of the social sciences.* New York: Macmillan and Free Press.

JUKES. A family, group, or individual thought to be socially inferior.

Jukes is a fictitious name of a real family studied by Richard Louis Dugdale (1841–83), an American social investigator who was born in Paris. In 1874 he studied county jails for the New York Prison Association and collected data for his book, *The Jukes: A Study in Crime, Pauperism, Disease and Heredity* (1875). He found that through several generations there was a high percentage of familial feeble-mindedness, criminality, and pauperism; he concluded that degeneracy was hereditary. As one of the first reports on this subject, it caused a sensation at the time, but recent work has shown that his conclusion was questionable. In 1911 the original manuscript was found, the actual family was revealed, and a comparative study was made by Arthur Estabrook (1916).
Sources
Estabrook, Arthur H. 1916. *The Jukes in 1915.* Washington, D.C.: Carnegie Institution.
Filler, Louis, ed. 1963. *A dictionary of American social reform.* New York: Philosophical Library.
Hendrickson, Robert. 1988. *The dictionary of eponyms: names that became words.* New York: Dorset.
Pennak, Robert W. 1988. *Collegiate dictionary of zoology.* 2d ed. Malabar, Fla.: Krieger.

JULIAN CALENDAR. The calendar introduced by Julius Caesar (100–44 B.C.) in which the year consisted of 365 days, every fourth year having 366. The calendar is the basis of the civil calendar used worldwide today. It replaced the Republican Calendar, which by 46 B.C. had become so incongruent that the seasons separated the calendar equinox from the astronomical equinox by three months. Following the advice of Sosigenes, Caesar brought the civil and astronomical years into line, and abolished the lunar in favor of the solar calendar. The Julian Calendar was adopted in 45 B.C., with January 1 as the beginning of the year; later refinements made it possible to date civil affairs, religious festivals, and other socially significant and recurrent events at the same time or season each year throughout the world.

See CAESAR.
Source
Preece, Warren E., ed. 1965. *Encyclopedia Britannica.* Chicago: Encyclopedia Britannica, Inc., William Benton.

JUNGIAN. Relating to the ideas, especially the analytical psychology, of the twentieth-century Swiss psychologist.

Carl Gustav Jung (1875–1961) was born at Kesswil (Lake Constance), graduated in medicine at the University of Basel, and became a physician at Burghölzli Mental Hospital (Zurich) before going to Paris (1902–3) to continue his studies. At the time, Freud was expounding psychoanalysis and Jung was drawn into his circle (1907). In 1913, after tense discussions and correspondence with Freud, Jung broke with Freud and psychoanalysis and developed his analytical psychology, which seemed more related to religion and mysticism than was Freud's system. Jung's distinction between introverts and extroverts brought recognition to his work. He wrote many books, studied associations in thinking and reaction times to ideas, and outlined a system of psychological types and a theory of psychological symbols. His life and work have attracted many biographers, and his therapeutic approach and modes of interpretation are gaining acceptance in many cultural studies, literature, and social sciences.

Sources

Brome, Vincent. 1978. *Jung: man and myth.* London: Macmillan.

Devine, Elizabeth; Held, Michael; Vinson, James; and Walsh, George, eds. 1983. *Thinkers of the twentieth century: a biographical, bibliographical and critical dictionary.* London: Macmillan.

Jung, Carl G. 1963. *Memories, dreams and reflections.* New York: Pantheon.

Wehr, Gerhard. 1985. *Jung: a biography.* Boston: Shambhala Publications.

Zusne, Leonard. 1987. *Eponyms in psychology: a dictionary and sourcebook.* Westport, Conn.: Greenwood Press.

JUSTINIAN CODE. The embodiment of Roman Law—*Codex Justinianus* (534)—compiled and annotated at the command of the Emperor Justinian. It consists of the "Pandects" or the condensed opinions of the jurists in fifty volumes: the "Institutiones" and the "Novellai," a collection of ordinances— the whole forms the "Corpus Juris Civilis," or body of civil law, the most important of all monuments of jurisprudence.

Justinian I, Flavius Anicius Justinianus (c. 482–565), was born at Tauresium in Illyria and was emperor of the Eastern Roman Empire from 527 to 565. He was the son of a slavonic peasant and was originally named Sappabbatius. Through his uncle, Justin I, he was educated at Constantinople, was made consul in 521, and in 527 was proclaimed by Justin I to be his colleague in the empire. Justin I died that year, and Justinian, proclaimed the sole emperor, was crowned with his wife Theodora, the actress. His reign was brilliant in the history of the late empire. He had able generals, who helped restore the empire to its ancient limits, and the East and the West were reunited. It was as a legislator that Justinian gained his greatest renown. He and the commissions he established codified the principal imperial constitutional and statutory laws that were in force at his accession.

Sources

Barker, John W. 1966. *Justinian and the later Roman empire.* Madison: University of Wisconsin Press.

Browning, Robert. 1987. *Justinian and Theodora.* Rev. ed. New York: Thames and Hudson.

Douglas, James D., ed. 1974. *The new international dictionary of the Christian Church.* Exeter: Paternoster Press.

Magnussen, Magnus; Goring, Rosemary; and Thorn, John O., eds. 1990. *Chambers biographical dictionary.* Edinburgh: Chambers Ltd.

Smith, Benjamin. 1903. *The Century cyclopedia of names.* London: The Times.

Ure, Percy N. 1951. *Justinian and his age.* Reprinted 1979. Harmondsworth: Penguin.

K

KADARISM. The policies of the modern Hungarian leader who adopted the socialist practices of the Eastern bloc while liberalizing both economic and political life in Hungary.

János Kádár (1912–89) was an active member of the Hungarian Communist party from 1931, holding government posts from 1945. In 1948 he replaced László Rajk as interior minister and contributed much to events leading to Rajk's execution. Kádár was jailed by the Stalinist regime of Mátyás Rákosi in 1951 for "Titoist" tendencies, rehabilitated by Imre Nagy's government in 1954, and elected to the Politburo in July 1956. Siding with Imre Nagy in Hungary's October Revolution led to Kádár becoming first secretary of the Communist party, but he betrayed Nagy in the later nationalist uprising, disappeared from Budapest on the eve of the Soviet intervention in Hungary (November 1956), and returned to head a revolutionary government and see Nagy and the rebels executed. By 1961 he was again prime minister, and in 1962 he began to adopt a policy of working with opposing interest groups in Hungary rather than continuing with Stalinist methods of oppression. Thus, Hungary enjoyed less censorship, and even noncommunists were allowed to offer their expertise in important economic decisions. Under his leadership, Hungary joined in the invasion of Czechoslovakia in 1968. In 1988 he did not respond to pressures for further reform, began losing his power, retired as party leader, and by May 1989 was declared ill and unable to come to terms with Hungary's political changes.

Sources

Candee, Marjorie D., ed. 1957. *Current biography yearbook.* New York: H. W. Wilson.

Dunner, Joseph, ed. 1964. *Dictionary of political science.* New York: Philosophical Library.

Heinrich, Hans-Georg 1956. *Hungary: politics, economics and society.* London: Francis Pinter.

Keesings contemporary archives: record of world events. 1988:36162; 1989:36664, 36830. London: Keesings Publications.
Laqueur, Walter, ed. 1973. *A dictionary of politics.* New York: Free Press.
Moritz, Charles, ed. 1989. *Current biography yearbook.* New York: H. W. Wilson.

KAFKAESQUE. Pertaining to the ideas and writings of the Czech novelist, especially to his imagery of individuals' isolation, bewilderment at their loss of identity in an evil, inhuman world of oppressive red tape and meaningless bureaucracy, and their inner rebellion against such pressures.

Franz Kafka (1883–1924) was born in Prague, graduated in law, but never practiced. He worked in a government insurance office and wrote prolifically but published little. Before he died of tuberculosis—his last years were spent in a sanatorium—he asked a friend, Max Brod, to destroy all his manuscripts. But between 1935 and 1937 Brod published the work. The work reflects Kafka's view of stark tragedy tinged with dark, strange humor and a classic beauty. In the best known of his works, *The Trial* (1925), the hero is arrested without apparently having done anything and never learns why he was arrested. Other important works are *Amerika* (1927) and *The Castle* (1926).

Sources

Brod, Max, ed. 1948. *The diaries of Franz Kafka.* New York: Schocken Books.
Brod, Max. 1960. *Franz Kafka: a biography.* Trans. G. Humphreys Roberts and Richard Winston. New York: Schocken Books.
Glatzer, Nahum N., ed. 1974. *I am a memory come alive: autobiographical writings of Franz Kafka.* New York: Schocken Books.
Hawkins, Joyce M., ed. 1986. *The Oxford reference dictionary.* Oxford: Clarendon Press.
Hayman, Ronald. 1982. *Kafka: a biography.* New York: Oxford University Press.
Pawel, Ernst. 1984. *The nightmare of reason: a life of Franz Kafka.* New York: Harper. 1992 ed.: New York: Noonday, Farrar, Straus and Giroux.

KAHN'S LAW. Any military intelligence policy that emphasizes the offensive tends to neglect intelligence. The law was stated by George O'Toole (1990), who added two corollaries: emphasizing the defensive tends toward an emphasis of intelligence: emphasizing the offensive tends toward an emphasis of counterintelligence.

David Kahn (b. 1930) was born in New York, son of a lawyer, educated at Bucknell University, and became a journalist and reporter for *Newsday* (*Long Island Weekly*) in New York (1955–63), and the *Herald Tribune* in Paris (1965–67). After completing research for his Ph.D. at Oxford University in 1974 he taught journalism at New York University (1975–79) and later returned to *Newsday* (1979). His writings have the ingredients of spy thrillers, but he writes about real personalities rather than fiction. Among his works are *Two Soviet Spy Ciphers* (1960), *The Codebreakers: The Story of Secret Writings* (1967), and *Hitler's Spies: German Military Intelligence in World War II* (1978).

Sources

Metzger, Linda, ed. 1984. *Contemporary authors.* New Revision Series. Vol. 13. Detroit: Gale Research.

O'Toole, George J.A. 1990. Kahn's law: a universal principle of intelligence? *International Journal of Intelligence and Counterintelligence* 4:39–46.

KAISER, KAISER'S WAR. Emperor of Germany. World War I (1914–18).

Friedrich Wilhem Viktor Albert, Wilhelm II (1859–1941), was German emperor when World War I broke out and was widely blamed for its onset. Wilhelm was born at Potsdam, Germany, the eldest child of Crown Prince Frederick, later Emperor Frederick III, and Victoria, eldest child of Britain's Queen Victoria. The child was born with a damaged left arm that never grew fully and was frequently used to explain features of his behavior. In 1888, at age 29, he found himself kaiser and king of Prussia. World War I began as an attempt to save Austria-Hungary from collapse and was transformed into a world conflict by Germany. Wilhelm had encouraged Austria to follow an uncompromising policy, but when he found a great war imminent he was not able to check the mobilization he had advised his generals to undertake. Possibilities for compromise dwindled as he encouraged the grandiose war aims of his politicians and the sophisticated strategies of his military leaders. Although he probably realized Germany would not win the war, he could not see he had to abdicate. Finally, he was forced to step down and seek asylum in Holland in November 1918.
Sources

Cowles, Virginia S. 1963. *The Kaiser.* London: Collins.

Kohut, Thomas A. 1991. *Wilhem II and the Germans: a study in leadership.* New York: Oxford University Press.

Ludwig, Emil. 1926. *Kaiser Wilhem II.* Trans Ethel C. Mayne. Reprinted in 1970 as *Wilhem Hohenzollern: the last of the Kaisers.* London: Putnam.

McHenry, Robert, ed. 1992. *The new encyclopedia Britannica.* Chicago: Encyclopedia Britannica, Inc.

Palmer, Alan W. 1978. *The Kaiser: warlord of the Second Reich.* London: Weidenfeld and Nicolson.

Riche, Norman. 1965. *Friedrich von Holstein: politics and diplomacy in the era of Bismarck and Wilhelm II.* Cambridge: Cambridge University Press.

KALDOR-HICKS TEST, KALDOR-HICKS PRINCIPLE. In welfare economics, a compensation test proposed to differentiate between scientific propositions and value judgments. There was a need to ensure that any proposed change would not make any person or group worse off. Hicks's suggestion was the same as that proposed by Kaldor—a compensation test—stating that a reform should be counted as an improvement if the gainers could afford to compensate the losers and still be better off. The principle asserts that there would be a net gain in social welfare if those who had such gains could compensate losers and still enjoy the net gain.

Nicholas Kaldor (1908–86), born in Budapest, studied and taught at the London School of Economics (1927–47). After two years at the Economic Commission for Europe in Geneva, he went to King's College, Cambridge, and in 1966 he became professor of economics at Cambridge University. He was made a peer in 1974, Baron Kaldor of Newnham. He wrote *An Expenditure Tax* (1955) as well as many papers and reports. His *Collected Economic Essays* (1960; 1964; 1978; 1979) appear in eight volumes and includes his noteworthy "A Model of Economic Growth" and "What Is Wrong with Economic Theory?"

John Richard Hicks (1904–89). See HICKSIAN THEORY OF EQUILIBRIUM.

Sources

Blaug, Mark. 1985. *Great economists since Keynes.* Brighton, England: Harvester Press.

Eatwell, John; Milgate, Murray; and Newman, Peter. 1987. *The new Palgrave: a dictionary of economics.* London: Macmillan.

Hicks, John R. 1939. Foundations of welfare economics. *Economic Journal* 49:696–712.

Kaldor, Nicholas. 1939. Welfare propositions of economics and interpersonal comparisons of utility. *Economic Journal* 49:549–552.

Rutherford, Donald, 1992. *Dictionary of economics.* London: Routledge.

Thirlwail, Anthony P. 1987. *Nicholas Kaldor.* Brighton: Wheatsheaf.

KALLIKAKS. A term for members of a family whose line produces mental deficiency.

Kallikak is the fictitious name of a New Jersey family whose father, Martin Kallikak, had children by a feeble-minded girl. Henry Goddard (1912) studied the family tree and found two lines of descendants; the first line was of respectable citizens, while the second comprised mentally deficient, social misfits. Among the descendants was a high proportion of feeble-minded and criminally inclined children. Hence, this study, like the Jukes study, was used to support the view that unacceptable behavior had a genetic origin.

See also JUKES.

Sources

Goddard, Henry H. 1912. *The Kallikak family: a study in the heredity of feeble-mindedness.* New York: Macmillan. Reprinted in 1931 and 1973. New York: Arno Press.

Pennak, Robert W. 1988. *Collegiate dictionary of zoology.* Malabar, Fla.: Krieger.

KANTIAN. Relating to the eighteenth-century German philosopher. His social theory assumed that society was in a state of progression and that the source of this progress was the antagonism of humankind, its "unsocial sociability." On one hand, humankind socialized its individuals by continuous association with others; on the other, each individual was propelled by antisocial forces. Thus, although humankind sought concord, nature impelled it with its inescapable impulse to discord; the consequent social order would permit, on one hand, a high degree of freedom for each person alone and in competition with others, and, on the other, it would provide sufficient restraint on that freedom whenever oppression or anarchy arose.

Immanuel Kant (1724–1804) was born at Koenigsberg, Prussia (now Kaliningrad), the son of a saddler. His family belonged to a sect of Pietists. His early education was in his home, and later he was prepared for a career in science. Instead, he entered the local university (1740) to study theology. In 1770 he was made a professor of logic and metaphysics. He remained at the University of Koenigsberg until he died, although he had many offers from other universities. According to legend, he never traveled over 30 miles from his home. He taught not only logic and metaphysics but also anthropology, geography, and mathematics. Among his many seminal writings, his first great works were *Critique of Pure Reason* (1781) and *Critique of Practical Reason* (1788).

Sources

Cassirer, Ernst. 1921. *Kant's life and thought.* Trans. James Haden. New Haven, Conn.: Yale University Press.

Miller, David, ed. 1987. *The Blackwell encyclopedia of political thought.* Oxford: Basil Blackwell.

Paulsen, Friedrich. 1902. *Immanuel Kant, his life and doctrine.* Trans. J. E. Creighton and Albert Leferve. London: Nimmo.

Sills, David L., ed. 1968. *International encyclopedia of the social sciences.* New York: Macmillan and Free Press.

Stuckenberg, John H.W. 1986. *The life of Immanuel Kant.* Lanham, Md.: University Press of America.

Zusne, Leonard. 1984. *Biographical dictionary of psychology.* Westport, Conn.: Greenwood Press.

KARDNER'S THEORY OF BASIC PERSONALITY STRUCTURE. Basic personality comprises a set of human characteristics that individuals belonging to a given culture have in common, for example, maternal care, induction of affectivity, early discipline, puberty, marriage, and participation in society. The theory demonstrates that the religious institutions of tribal people are projections of "basic personalty structure" established by observable trauma in child-training practices. The projected system includes magic, art, and religion, and socialization is assumed to be a consequence of economic, political, and social subsystems of society that are involved in the nourishment, shelter, and protection of the child. In this way, the socialization processes affect the personality of the young and provide the means by which culture is integrated.

Abram Kardner (1891–1981) was born in New York, son of a businessman, and educated at City College, now City University of New York, and Cornell (M.D., 1917). He worked at Mount Sinai Hospital (1917–19), Manhattan State Hospital (1919–20), and, after being trained by Sigmund Freud, he practiced as a psychoanalytic psychiatrist (1920–81). He was professor of clinical psychiatry at Cornell (1949–57), directed the Columbia Psychoanalytic Institute (1955–57), helped found the New York Psychoanalytic Institute, and researched at Emory University. He was a member of the American Medical Association, the American Psychoanalytic Association, and a fellow of the Royal Society of Health. He made several studies of the American Negro, and the traumatic neuroses of war, and studied sex and morality. In his noted work, *The Psychological Frontiers of Society* (1945), he combined anthropology and psychoanalysis. Among his publications are *They Studied Man* (1955) and *The Mask of Oppression* (1962).

Sources
Kardner, Abram. 1977. *My analysis with Freud: reminiscences.* New York: W. W. Norton.
Locher, Frances C., ed. 1982. *Contemporary authors.* Vol. 104. Detroit: Gale Research.
May, Hal, ed. 1983. *Contemporary authors.* Vol. 107. New Revision Series. Detroit: Gale Research.
Sills, David L., ed. 1968. *International encyclopedia of the social sciences.* New York: Macmillan and Free Press.
Zusne, Leonard. 1984. *Biographical dictionary of psychology.* Westport, Conn.: Greenwood Press.

KARMATHIAN. A member of the ninth-century pantheistic, socialistic Muslim sect in the Middle East. Also known as Qaramitah, the group left the Ismaili movement, threatened the Abbasid caliphate, and terrorized southern Iraq. The members of the sect were seen as a socialist threat, and the sect was falsely condemned for believing in communal ownership of women and property. They sought a better future and an equitable form of government. Some of their groups experimented with communism, and others resembled an oligarchic state.

Hamdan ben-Ashath Karmat (fl. c. 850–900) was a poor laborer who professed to be a prophet. He was converted to the Ismaili movement and began missionary activities about 873. The rural populace gave him the name Qarmat, meaning ''short-legged'' or ''red-eyed.'' He became a missionary in Kufa and the leading apostle of the Karmathians who saw the Koran as an allegorical book, rejected all revelation, fasting, and prayer, and was communistic in many ways. Between 951 and 1078, the sect fought wars with the Fatimid in Cairo and with Baghdad. The Qaramitah disappeared in 1077–78, and their communities were absorbed by others. Some sources suggest the Druses grew from this sect.

Sources
Brewer, Ebenezer Cobham. 1970. *Brewer's dictionary of phrase and fable.* Centenary ed. Rev. by Ivor H. Evans. New York: Harper and Row.
Eliade, Mircea, ed. 1987. *Encyclopedia of religion.* New York: Macmillan.
Gibb, Hamilton A. R., et al., eds. 1960. *The encyclopedia of Islam.* Leiden: Brill.
McHenry, Robert, ed. 1992. *The new encyclopedia Britannica.* Chicago: Encyclopedia Britannica, Inc.
Smith, Benjamin. 1903. *The century cyclopedia of names.* London: The Times.

KARMEL COMMITTEE. A committee on the Truck Acts which reported in 1961, and recommended their repeal and replacement with more modern laws.

David Karmel (1907–82) was educated at Saint Andrews College and Trinity College, Dublin, and was called to the bar, Grey's Inn, in 1928. He was a master of the Bench, Grey's Inn (1954). He enlisted in the King's Royal Rifle Corps in 1939; served in Tunisia, Italy, and Yugoslavia; and attained the rank of major.

He was a recorder of the Crown Court (1972–79); steward, British Boxing Board of Control; and a member of the Industrial Disputes Tribunal. He chaired many committees, including the Investigation of Agricultural Marketing Act (1958), Truck Acts Committee (1959), and Advisory Committee on Service Candidates (1963), and was deputy chairman of the Central Arbitration Committee (1977) and others.

Sources

Marsh, Arthur. 1979. *Concise encyclopedia of industrial relations.* Westmead, Farnborough, Hants: Gower.

Who's who, 1982. London: Adam and Charles Black.

KATONA EFFECT. The impact of rising inflation on saving. When inflation grows slowly, individuals think real incomes will also rise slowly and that inflation is low enough to ensure the safety of savings; they therefore feel sufficiently secure to invest in fixed interest deposits. But when inflation is rampant, they buy goods in fear of the poverty inflation might bring, and they hoard goods against great leaps in prices (Katona, 1961).

George Katona (1901–81) was born in Budapest, studied law briefly, and studied psychology at the University of Göttingen, obtaining his Ph.D. in 1921. He began work in the research department of a Frankfurt bank, wrote in Berlin on the effects of inflation, and edited the *German Economist* (1926–33). In 1933 he immigrated to the United States where he became an investment counselor in New York City, lectured at the New School of Social Research (1936–42), and was naturalized in 1939. He published *Organizing and Memorizing* (1940) and *War Without Inflation* (1942). With an established reputation as an expert in behavioral economics, he was appointed a professor of economics and psychology at the University of Michigan (1946–72). For the Survey Research Center at the Institute of Social Research, he established the survey of consumer attitudes and the economic behavior program. He was a member of professional associations of psychologists, economists, and statisticians. He retired emeritus and was honored by the universities of Illinois, Berlin, Amsterdam, Dusseldorf, and the American Marketing Association. Among his publications were *The Mass Consumption Society (1964)* which with his *The Powerful Consumer* (1960) established the field of behavioral economics. Later he published *Aspirations and Affluence* (1971), *Psychological Economics* (1975), *A New Economic Era* (1978), and *Essays in Behavioral Economics* (1980).

Sources

Jaques Cattell Press, ed. 1973. *American men and women of science: the social and behavioral sciences.* New York: Jaques Cattell and R. R. Bowker.

Katona, George. 1961. *The powerful consumer: psychological studies of the American economy.* New York: McGraw-Hill.

Locher, Francis, ed. 1982. *Contemporary authors.* Vol. 104. Detroit: Gale Research.

Morgan, James N. 1982. Obituary: George Katona (1901–1981). *American Psychologist* 37:1140–1141.

Rutherford, Donald. 1992. *Dictionary of economics*. London: Routledge.
Who's who in America, 1980–81. Chicago: Marquis.

KEATINGISM. Brutal language, especially colorful insults and personal abuse used in Australia's federal Parliament by the Australian treasurer (1983–89); a form of gutter brawling, consisting of off-color phrases like ''scumbag'' and ''dog's vomit'' and ''pimple on the arse-hole of society,'' all of which referred to people who opposed the treasurer.

Paul John Keating (b. 1944) was born in Bankstown, New South Wales, into a working-class family. He was educated at the Catholic De La Salle College in Bankstown and left at almost 15 years of age. He was on the Sydney County Council, worked towards his school-leaving certificate at Belmore Technical College, and began to study mathematics and electrical engineering part-time at the Sydney Technical College. In 1965 he left his job, worked at several clerical positions, and began research for the Federated Municipal Employees' Union (1968). That year he won preselection for the Australian Labor party (ALP) for Blaxland. He became the youngest New South Wales member of the federal Parliament. When the ALP came to power (1972–75), he was on the back bench, but he became a minister briefly in October 1975. In 1983, when the ALP returned to power, he was made treasurer in the Hawke government, extended his power base, took over as prime minister from Hawke in 1991, and led the ALP to an unexpected win in March 1993.

Sources

Carew, Edna. 1988. *Keating: a biography*. Sydney: Allen and Unwin.
Gordon, Michael. 1993. *A question of leadership: Paul Keating, political fighter*. Saint Lucia, Queensland: University of Queensland Press.
Gratton, Michelle. 1991. Keating's first 100 days will be most crucial. *The Age,* December 21:2.

KELLER PLAN. A self-learning, self-testing personalized system of instruction (PSI) in which the pupils study a unit at their own pace; when they have finished, they discuss the unit with a tutor, and the tutor establishes whether or not they have passed and may go on to the next unit. Since the early 1970s, the Keller Plan had been applied to learning in nearly every discipline worldwide. Its use has also been accompanied by much research on its effectiveness.

Fred Simmons Keller (b. 1899) was born in Rural Grove, New York, and left school to be a telegraph operator for Western Union. He served in France during World War I, and later, on an athletics scholarship he attended Goddard Seminary in Barre, Vermont. He studied at Tufts and Harvard, where he obtained his Ph.D. in 1931, and taught at Harvard until hired by Colgate University in 1931. He wrote *The Definition of Psychology* (1937) and taught at Columbia University from 1938 until his retirement in 1964. Impressed with B. F. Skinner's ideas and the use of reinforcement theory in teaching and research, he applied the theory in World War II to research on training radio operators. On retirement, he went to the Department of Psychology, University of Brasília, and began to develop his PSI. After holding many academic posts, he was made a professor of psychology, Arizona State University (1964–67) and thereafter was a distinguished visitor and teacher at institutes and universities in Maryland, Michigan, Washington, Texas, and North Carolina. Among his writings are *The Keller Handbook* (1974), *Behavior Modification: Applications to Education* (1974), and *History of Psychology: a P.S.I. Companion* (1975).

Sources

Editors. 1977. Distinguished contribution for applications in psychology award: Fred S. Keller. [With bibliography]. *American Psychologist* 32:68–71.

Evory, Ann, and Metzger, Linda, eds. 1984. *Contemporary authors.* Vol. 10. New Revision Series. Detroit: Gale Research.

Keller, Fred S. 1969. Good-bye teacher . . . *Journal of Applied Behavior Analysis* 1:79–89.

Torsten, Husen, and Postlethwaite, T. Neville. 1985. *The international encyclopedia of education.* New York: Pergamon Press.

Zusne, Leonard. 1987. *Eponyms in psychology: a dictionary and sourcebook.* Westport, Conn.: Greenwood Press.

KELLOGG-BRIAND PACT. An international agreement that condemned war as a solution for international conflict. It was first proposed in 1928 by the French foreign minister in regard to Franco-American relations, but to avoid an alliance, the U.S. secretary of state had it changed to a multinational agreement and accepted by the U.S. Senate (1929) and finally accepted by sixty-two nations. It relied on moral force and used no sanctions.

Frank Billings Kellogg (1856–1937) was born in Potsdam, New York, to poor parents who took him to southern Minnesota in 1865. Having had little education, he worked as a janitor and office boy in exchange for instruction in law in Rochester, Minnesota, and was admitted to the bar in 1877. He received an LL.D. from McGill University in 1913. He became a Republican senator in 1916 and lost his seat in 1922. He was made ambassador to Britain (1923) and became secretary of state (1925–29). He was awarded the Nobel Peace Prize for his efforts for the Kellogg-Briand Pact (1929), and at The Hague served on the Permanent Court of International Justice (1930–35), receiving many honors, including the French Legion of Honor (1929), and LL.D.s from the University of Pennsylvania (1926), the George Washington and the New York universities (1927), Harvard (1929), and Brown University (1930).

Aristide Briand (1862–1932), son of an innkeeper, was born in Nantes, educated at Saint Nazaire, studied law in Paris, and entered left-wing political circles. He was a journalist in Paris (1893) and stood unsuccessfully for the Chamber of Deputies (1893; 1895). Although he was successful as a socialist candidate for Saint Etienne (1902), he was expelled from the Socialist party in 1906 for joining the coalition with the Republicans. After holding several ministerial posts, he became prime minister (1909). He was responsible for foreign affairs from 1915 to 1917 and was prime minister from 1921 to 1922 during discussions leading to the Treaty of Versailles. He signed the Locarno Pact (1925) allowing Germany into the Concert of Powers, and in 1926 he received a Nobel Peace Prize for his work in the League of Nations. He failed in his bid for the presidency in 1931.

Sources

Briggs, Asa; Isaacs, Alan; and Martin, Elizabeth. 1985. *Longman dictionary of 20th century biography.* Essex: Longman Group.

Cook, Chris. 1983. *The Macmillan dictionary of historical terms.* London: Macmillan.

Laszlo, Ervin, and Jong Youl Yoo. 1986. *World encyclopedia of peace.* Oxford: Pergamon Press.

Plano, Jack C., and Olton, Roy. 1988. *The international relations dictionary.* 4th ed. Santa Barbara, Calif.: ABC-CLIO.

Schulyer, Robert L., and James, Edward T., eds. 1944. *Dictionary of American biography.* Supplement 2. New York: Charles Scribner's Sons.

KENNEDY ROUND. The sixth round of multilateral trade negotiations (1964–67) in Geneva conducted under the auspices of the General Agreement on Tariffs and Trades (GATT). Unlike the earlier series of trade negotiations, which were designed to encourage multilateral reduction of trade barriers, the Kennedy Round negotiated on specific groups of goods rather than on a single-good basis. By 1973 the Kennedy Round agreements had reduced the average level of world industrial tariffs by approximately one-third. The round was named after the U.S. president whose administration was responsible for the Trade Expansion Act (1962) which initiated the negotiations.

John Fitzgerald Kennedy (1917–63) was born in Brookline, Massachusetts, son of Joseph P. Kennedy, an American multimillionaire, and became the thirty-fifth president of the United States. After studies at Harvard and in London and after service at the U.S. embassy in London (1938), he wrote a thesis on Britain's unpreparedness for war, *Why England Slept* (1940). As a torpedo boat commander in the Pacific, he was awarded the Navy Medal and the Purple Heart. A Democrat, he was elected first representative (1949) and then senator (1952) for Massachusetts, and in 1960 he was the first Catholic and the youngest person to be elected president of the United States. He won on the smallest majority of the popular vote ever recorded. On November 22, 1963, he was assassinated by rifle fire while being driven in an open car through Dallas, Texas. The events leading to his death are still being debated, and he has been the subject of many biographies.

Sources

Longford, Frank P. 1976. *Kennedy.* London: Weidenfeld and Nicolson.

McHenry, Robert, ed. 1992. *The new encyclopedia Britannica.* Chicago: Encyclopedia Britannica, Inc.

Magnussen, Magnus; Goring, Rosemary; and Thorn, John O., eds. 1990. *Chambers biographical dictionary.* Edinburgh: Chambers Ltd.

Martin, Ralph. 1983. *A hero for our times: an intimate story of the Kennedy years.* New York: Macmillan.

Reeves, Thomas. 1991. *A question of character: a life of John F. Kennedy.* London: Bloomsbury.
Snyder, Richard J. 1988. *John F. Kennedy: person, policy, presidency.* Wilmington, Del.: S R Books.
Sorenson, Theodore C. 1965. *Kennedy.* London: Hodder and Stoughton.

KEOGH. A U.S. voluntary retirement fund for the self-employed that emerged from the Keogh Plan/H.R. 10—the Self-Employed Individuals Tax Retirement Act (1962). By way of tax concessions, the act encouraged people to save for retirement pensions rather than rely solely for their retirement on the U.S. Social Security scheme.

Eugene James Keogh (1907–89) was born in Brooklyn, New York, and went to public schools and the Commercial High School in Brooklyn. He graduated in commerce from the New York City University (1927) and in law from Fordham University (1930). He was a teacher for one year and then a clerk in the New York City Board of Transportation (1928–30). After working as a law clerk, he was admitted to the bar in 1932 and began to practice in New York City. He was a New York State assemblyman and as a Democrat was elected to the U.S. Congress (1937–67) where he was the leading sponsor for H.R. 10, the Self-Employed Individuals Tax Retirement Act. Thereafter he resumed his law practice and business interests in New York City. He was chairman of the Franklin D. Roosevelt Memorial Commission in 1980, and director and trustee in several banking and insurance firms.

Sources

Jacob, Kathryn A., and Ragsdale, Bruce A. 1989. *Biographical directory of the United States Congress: 1774–1989.* Bicentennial ed. Washington, D.C.: U.S. Government Printing Office.
Jaques Cattell Press, ed. 1987. *Who's who in American politics, 1985–87.* New York: Jaques Cattell and R. R. Bowker.
New York Times Biography Service. May 1989, 20:494.
Political profiles: the Kennedy years. New York: Facts on File.
Shafritz, Jay M. 1988. *The Dorsey dictionary of American government and politics.* Chicago: Dorsey.
Who's who in America, 1980–81. Chicago: Marquis.

KERNER COMMISSION. In the summer of 1965 in Watts, a section of Los Angeles where primarily African-Americans lived, a 21-year-old man was arrested for a traffic offense near his home. His parents intervened, a crowd gathered, and violence erupted; 34 people were killed, 1,000 were injured, 4,000 were arrested, and the damage covering 46 square miles reached $40 million. Afterward President Lyndon B. Johnson came on television and announced the formation of a National Advisory Commission on Civil Disorder, the Kerner Commission. The commission found that the riots erupted from racism and economic deprivation; that the United States was being sharply divided into two distinct and unequal societies; and there were no quick resolutions for such social problems (1968).

Otto Kerner (1908–76), born in Chicago, was educated at local schools and graduated from Oak Bank High School in 1926. He graduated from Brown University, studied briefly in England, and returned to Northwestern University where he graduated in law and was admitted to the bar in 1934. During World War II he served as a lieutenant colonel and returned in 1954 as a major general. He was elected a judge in Cook County (1954; 1958) and became governor of Illinois in 1960, chaired the Kerner Commission (1965–68), and was made a judge of the U.S. Court of Appeals (1968–74). In 1974 he was jailed for felonious crimes associated with a race-track scandal, paroled a year later, and spent his remaining years clearing his name and promoting prison reform.

Source

Harris, Fred R., and Wilkins, Roger W., eds. 1988. *The Kerner report: twenty years later: or quiet riots: race and poverty in the United States.* New York: Pantheon Books.

Moritz, Charles, ed. 1961; 1976. *Current biography yearbook.* New York: H. W. Wilson.

Shafritz, Jay M. 1988. *The Dorsey dictionary of American government and politics.* Chicago: Dorsey.

KEYNESIAN, KEYNESIAN REVOLUTION. Relating to the twentieth-century British economist and his teaching, especially the argument that within capitalism there is some degree of control over the unrestricted play of national and international forces. The revolution in economic thought following the publication of Keynes' major work in 1936.

John Maynard Keynes (1883–1946), first Baron Keynes of Tilton, a financial expert, was born at Cambridge and died at Tilton. His father lectured at the University, Cambridge. After being educated at Eton and Cambridge, Keynes worked in the India Office (1906–8) before returning to lecture at Cambridge. In 1913–14 he was a member of the Royal Commission on Indian Currency and Finance, and during World War I he served the Treasury, whom he represented at the Paris Peace Conference (1919). From 1921 to 1938 he was chairman of the National Mutual Life Assurance Society and ran an investment company. He was a prominent member of the Bloomsbury group of intellectuals and married the ballerina and actress Lydia Lopokova. The Keynesian Revolution followed the publication of his book *The General Theory of Employment, Interest and Money,* in 1936. Also in 1940 he wrote *How to Pay for the War.* In 1944 he played a central, if not critical, role in the Bretton Woods Conference, which created the International Monetary Fund and the International Bank for Reconstruction and Development. In his approach to economics, Keynes concentrated on microeconomic variables, and three markets—goods, bonds, and labor. He gave most attention to short periods and often put the long run to one side.

Sources

Devine, Elizabeth; Held, Michael; Vinson, James; and Walsh, George, eds. 1983. *Thinkers of the twentieth century: a biographical, bibliographical and critical dictionary.* London: Macmillan.

Hession, Charles H. 1984. *John Maynard Keynes: a personal biography of the man who revolutionized capitalism and the way we live.* New York: Macmillan.

Legg, Leopold G.W., and Williams, E. T., eds. 1959. *Dictionary of national biography 1941–1950.* London: Oxford University Press.

Lekachman, Robert. 1975. *The age of Keynes.* New York: Random House.

Moggridge, Donald E. 1980. *Keynes.* 2d ed. London: Fontana, Collins.

Moggridge, Donald E. 1992. *Maynard Keynes: an economist's biography.* London: Routledge.

Morgan, Brian. 1978. *Monetarists and Keynesians: their contribution to monetary theory.* London: Macmillan.

KHRUSHCHEVISM. The communist vision of 1956 to build a pure society for the early 1960s, as outlined to eighty-one representatives of the Communist party governments meeting in Moscow. It assumed that the Communist party would always direct the future of society; it denounced Stalin's totalitarianism and "cult of the individual," preferring a pure collective leadership; although a peaceful coexistence with capitalism was envisaged, it would be defeated; and a timetable would be set up for the attainment of communism everywhere. It was announced that Russia was completing its goal of building socialism and would continue to lead other communist nations. For many years this vision held the attention of communist-inspired intellectuals and social moralists.

Nikita Sergeyevich Khrushchev (1894–1971) was born in Kalinkova, in Kursk Province, son of a miner and peasant. He was a farm laborer, plumber, and locksmith, and joined the Communist party in 1918; by 1929 he had been trained as a party organizer. He became a member of the Central Committee of the party (1934), secretary of the Moscow District Party Committee (1934–38), was elected to the Politburo (1939), and made general secretary of the Ukraine (1938–46, 1947–53). When the Ukraine was occupied by Germany, he was a lieutenant-general. He was the premier of the Ukraine from 1944 to 1947 and secretary of the Communist party from 1953 to 1964. Meantime, he eliminated the top levels of its leadership and replaced his own nominee, Nikolai A. Bulganin (1895–1975), as premier (1958–64). In October 1965 he was forced out of office and went into political obscurity.

Sources

Frankland, Mark, trans. 1979. *Khrushchev, Nikita: anatomy of terror.* Westport, Conn.: Greenwood Press.

Frankland, Mark. 1966. *Khrushchev.* Harmondsworth: Penguin.

Martin, Kingsley, ed. 1958. *The vital letters of Russell, Khrushchev, Dulles, with an introduction by Kingsley Martin.* London: MacGibbon and Kee.

Medveder, Roy A. 1982. *Khrushchev.* Trans. Brian Pearce. Oxford: Basil Blackwell.

Medveder, Roy A., and Medveder, Zhores A. 1976. *Khruschev: the years in power.* New York: Columbia University Press.

Plano, Jack C., and Olton, Roy. 1988. *The international relations dictionary.* 4th ed.
    Santa Barbara, Calif.: ABC-CLIO.

KINDERSLEY COMMITTEE. A British committee that reviewed medical
doctors' and dentists' remuneration (1962–70) and advised Britain's prime minister on their pay in the National Health Service.

Hugh Kenyon Molesworth Kindersley, second Baron Kindersley (1899–
1976), was educated at Eton, served in World War I in the Scots Guards (1917–
19), and was awarded the Military Cross (1918). He worked in the family's
firms in the United States, Canada, and Europe, and became a leading figure
among businessmen in London. In World War II he again served the Scots
Guards and in the 6th Airborne Division, as temporary brigadier. He became
Lord Kindersley in 1941; was chairman of Rolls-Royce (1956–68); director of
the Bank of England (1947–67); and, being closely associated with the medical
profession, chaired the government's review body on its remuneration.
Sources
Blake (Lord), and Nicholls, C. S., eds. 1986. *Dictionary of national biography 1971–*
    1980. Oxford: Oxford University Press.
Marsh, Arthur. 1979. *Concise encyclopedia of industrial relations.* Westmead, Farnbor-
    ough, Hants: Gower.
Who was who, 1971–80. London: Adam and Charles Black.

KING-BYNG AFFAIR. After a scandal in Canada's Department of Customs,
the minority Liberal party in Parliament lost its support, and the prime minister
asked the governor-general to dissolve Parliament and call an election (1925).
Because the motion of censure was still under debate, the request was refused.
The refusal began the controversy in which the prime minister resigned, the
Conservative leader formed a government and was defeated in a censure motion
itself, and, when asked again, the governor-general granted the dissolution of
Parliament. The Liberals' prime minister won the election, and the governor-
general declined a second term as the king's representative in Canada.

William Lyon Mackenzie King (1874–1950) was born in Berlin, Ontario, son
of a lawyer, and was educated at the University of Toronto in 1895. He studied
economics at Harvard and the University of Chicago. He was Canada's first
deputy minister of labor (1900) and, as a Liberal, became minister of labor
(1909) with a reputation for solving industrial conflict. After defeat in the federal
election (1911) and in the conscription election (1917), he served on the Rockefeller Foundation and wrote *Industry and Humanity* (1918). This work argued
that government, acting on behalf of society, had the task of resolving conflict
between labor and capital. He became leader of the Liberals (1919) and was
prime minister three times (1921–26; 1926–30; 1935–48).

Julian Hedworth George Byng, Viscount Byng of Vimy (1862–1935). See
BING BOYS.

Sources
Dawson, Robert M., and Neatby, H. Blair. 1958–76. *W. L. Mackenzie King 1923–32: 1932–39.* 2 vols. Toronto: University of Toronto Press.
Esberey, Joy E. 1980. *Knight of the Holy Spirit: a study of William Lyon Mackenzie King.* Toronto: University of Toronto Press.
Marsh, James H., ed. 1988. *The Canadian encyclopedia.* 2d ed. Edmonton: Hurtig.
Stacey, Charles P. 1976. *A very double life: the private world of Mackenzie King.* Toronto: Macmillan.
Wallace, W. Stewart, and McKay, William A. 1978. *The Macmillan dictionary of Canadian biography.* 4th ed. Toronto: Macmillan.

KINSEY REPORT. An interview-based study of sexual behavior among 18,500 American adults, the first empirical study in this field. Results showed that so-called sexual perversions—oral sex, for example—were widely practiced.

Alfred Charles Kinsey (1894–1956) was born in Hoboken, New Jersey, and studied zoology at Harvard (Ph.D., 1920). He taught zoology for twenty years at Indiana University and began his research on the sexual behavior of human adults in 1938. He became the director of the Institute for Sex Research at the university, and when his *Sexual Behavior in the Human Male* appeared in 1948, much unexpected interest was aroused in both general and academic circles, and his name became synonymous with the study of sex. Five years later appeared *Sexual Behavior in the Human Female* (1953). Both reports are thought to have been influential in increasing permissiveness in sexual mores during the 1960s. The report also showed that sexual habits were correlated with social class. The work has been analyzed closely and criticized for faults in both sampling and interviewing.

Sources
Christensen, Cornelia V. 1971. *Kinsey: a biography.* Bloomington: Indiana University Press.
Geddes, Donald P., ed. 1954. *An analysis of the Kinsey reports on sexual behavior in the human male and female.* New York: E. P. Dutton.
Kinsey, Alfred C.; Pomeroy, Wardell B.; and Martin, Clyde. 1948. *Sexual behavior in the human male.* Philadelphia: W. B. Saunders.
Kinsey, Alfred C.; Pomeroy, Wardell B.; Martin, Clyde; and Gebhard, Paul H. 1953. *Sexual behavior in the human female.* Philadelphia: W. B. Saunders.
Pomeroy, Wardell B. 1972. *Dr. Kinsey and the Institute for Sex Research.* London: Thomas Nelson.
Sills, David L., ed. 1968. *International encyclopedia of the social sciences.* New York: Macmillan and Free Press.
Zusne, Leonard. 1984. *Biographical dictionary of psychology.* Westport, Conn.: Greenwood Press.

KIRKPATRICK THEORY. A modern political theory which assumes that order is fundamental to all political systems and that absence of order precludes the establishment of other values; that stability rests in traditional and modern society but not in those undergoing change from one to the other; and that unstable states are vulnerable to terrorist rule. The ideas follow from those of the seventeenth-century philosopher, Thomas Hobbes (1588–1679), and were used in advising President Ronald Reagan on White House policy for Central America where authoritarian political structures were recommended.

Jeane Duane Jordan (b. 1926) was born in Duncan, Oklahoma, and was educated at Stephens College in Columbia, Missouri, Barnard College, and Columbia University (Ph.D., 1967). She studied at the Institut de Science Politique in Paris (1952–53), married Evron M. Kirkpatrick, executive director of the American Political Science Association, and later, in 1967, became a professor of government at Georgetown University. She served in many public positions including vice-chairperson of the Democratic National Commission on vice-presidential selection (1972–74), and among her many published works are *Political Woman* (1974), the *New Presidential Elite* (1976), *The Reagan Phenomenon* (1983), and *The Withering Away of the Totalitarian State* (1990). In 1981 she served as U.S. representative at the United Nations and, later, as a syndicated columnist. She has received honorary degrees from many universities in the United States, Europe, and Latin America, and many awards for distinguished political work. She is a member of the International and the American Political Science associations and a fellow of the American Enterprise Institute for Public Policy Research.

Sources

The international who's who, 1992–93. London: Europa Publications.
Kirkpatrick, Jeane. 1981. The Hobbes problem: capital order, capital authority and legitimacy in Central America. In American Enterprise Institute, *Public Policy Week Papers* (1980). Washington, D.C.: American Enterprise Institute.
Moritz, Charles, ed. 1981. *Current biography yearbook.* New York: H. W. Wilson.
Who's who in America, 1992–93. Chicago: Marquis.

KITCHIN CYCLE. A business fluctuation of forty months—known in economics as a minor cycle—named by Joseph Schumpeter (1939) in his theory of three business cycles: the Kondratieff cycle, the Juglar cycle, and the Kitchin cycle.

Joseph Kitchin (1861–1932) was born in England and became a compiler of statistical data on the South African goldfields for the *Financial Times.* In 1897 he began business in South Africa's mining industry. A world authority on statistics about precious metals, he gave evidence at the Currency Commission (1926), the Committee on Finance and Industry (1930), and the Gold Delegation of the Financial Committee, League of Nations (1930). In the *Times Financial Review* (1921), he wrote about trade cycles from 1783 to 1920s. On the U.S. and British trade cycles between 1890 and 1922, he used data on commodity prices, bank clearings, and interest rates. He found minor cycles of forty months, Juglar cycles of seven to eleven years, and trends that relied on moves in the world money supply. He explained the minor cycles as rhythmical movements due to psychological causes, which could be influenced by crop variations that are out of control. The Kitchin cycles appeared regularly after World War II, and recently their major cause seems to lie in inventory investment.

See also JUGLAR CYCLE; KONDRATIEFF CYCLES.

Sources

Eatwell, John; Milgate, Murray; and Newman, Peter. 1987. *The New Palgrave: a dictionary of economics.* London: Macmillan.

Greenwald, D., ed. 1982. *Encyclopedia of economics.* New York: McGraw-Hill.

Kitchin, Joseph. 1923. Cycles and trends in economic factors. *Review of Economics and Statistics* 5:10–16.

Pearce, D. W., ed. 1986. *Macmillan dictionary of modern economics.* New York: Macmillan.

Rutherford, Donald. 1992. *Dictionary of economics.* London: Routledge.

Schumpeter, Joseph. 1939. *Business cycles.* New York: McGraw-Hill.

KLEINIAN. Relating to the woman psychoanalyst in Britain who established her own approach to the study of infants, emphasizing experiences in the first year of life rather than the Oedipal period as many psychoanalysts did before her.

Melanie Klein, née Reizes (1882–1960), was born of Jewish parents in Vienna, the last child of her father's second marriage. Her father qualified as a doctor but eventually went into dentistry. Her mother kept a shop selling plants and animals. She was educated at school and by governesses and studied learned English and French and the humanities at Vienna University. She married at 21. She and her husband lived in small towns in Slovakia and Silesia before settling in Budapest. There she began to read Freud's writings and sought analysis with Sandor Ferenczi (1873–1933), a follower of Freud and a central figure in the International Psychoanalytic Association. With his support, she began to analyze children, and in 1919, after separating from her husband, she moved to Berlin where she began analysis with Karl Abraham (1877–1925), another of Freud's early disciples. In 1925 she was invited to lecture in London and moved there permanently (1926). Freud believed that moral problems as well as technical difficulties related to access to the child's unconscious, but Klein developed a technique of play for psychoanalysis, claiming that it was the major way to the child's unconscious.

Sources

Grosskurth, Phyllis. 1986. *Melanie Klein: her world and her work.* [With bibliography]. New York: Alfred A. Knopf.

Segal, Hanna. 1978. *Introduction to the work of Melanie Klein.* London: Hogarth.

Zusne, Leonard. 1984. *Biographical dictionary of psychology.* Westport, Conn.: Greenwood Press.

KOHLBERG'S THEORY OF MORAL DEVELOPMENT. A cognitive theory of moral development that shows individuals progress along three levels and through two stages at each level. On the first level at stage one, morality is heteronomous, oriented to punishment and obedience; at stage two, morality is naive, egoistic, involves individualism and exchange. On the second level, conventional morality emerges at stage three in interpersonal expectations and conformity; and at stage four comes an orientation toward law and order in a social system, and conscience. On the third level appears principled morality, where at stage five the person orients to sociolegal contracts, while at stage six universal ethical principles emerge.

Lawrence Kohlberg (1927–87), a New Yorker and son of a wealthy businessman, was educated at private schools. While serving in the Merchant Navy, he witnessed the blockade of the Jews from Europe to Palestine and felt conflicted by the issue of moral disobedience versus the law. At the University of Chicago, using Jean Piaget's ideas, he completed a Ph.D. on the moral development of children. For thirty years he refined the theory and procedures for assessing children's moral development. He thought that cognitive development was a better guide to understanding a person's growth than socialization. In the 1960s and 1970s Kohlberg's ideas were very controversial, and civil rights workers from many movements adopted them. In 1973 he fell seriously ill in Latin America and never fully recovered; even so, he began to apply his ideas broadly, for example, to the just community program, moral education in schools and prisons, the sociological analysis of norm formation, and the dynamics of group decision making.

Sources

Bergling, K. 1981. *Moral development: the validity of Kohlberg's theory.* Stockholm: Almqvist and Wiksell.

Fowler, James; Snarey, John; and DeNicola, Karen. 1988. *Remembrances of Lawrence Kohlberg: a compilation of the presentations at the service of remembrance for Lawrence Kohlberg at Memorial Church, Harvard, May 20, 1987.* Atlanta, Ga.: Center for Research in Faith and Development.

Husen, Torsten, and Postlethwaite, T. Neville. 1985. *The international encyclopedia of education research and studies.* Oxford: Pergamon Press.

Kohlberg, L. 1981. *The philosophy of moral development: moral stages and the idea of justice.* San Francisco: Harper and Row.

Kohlberg, L. 1984. *The psychology of moral development: the nature and validity of moral stages.* San Francisco: Harper and Row.

Modgil, S., and Modgil, C. 1986. *Lawrence Kohlberg: consensus and controversy.* London: Falmer.

Rest, James; Power, Clark; and Brabeck, Mary. 1988. Lawrence Kohlberg (1927–87): Obituary. *American Psychologist* 43:399.

KOHN-SCHOOLER MODEL. A sociological theory about the impact of social structure on personality. The general theme of the model states that position in the social structure affects the job conditions individuals experience. In turn, this determines their opportunity for self-direction at work, and affects their personality by way of the value placed on self-direction, intellectual flexibility, sense of well-being, and self-directed orientation to society. The original work began in 1964, and rather than study occupations, it focused on dimensions of work. The work appeared in 1983. Since then the model has been extended and, consequently, generated new knowledge, for example, that the experience of self-direction in realms other than paid employment—particularly schoolwork and housework—has similar effects on personality. The work has also been used in cross-cultural studies, notably Poland and Japan.

Melvin L. Kohn (b. 1928) was born in New York and educated in Deep Springs, California, and at Cornell University (Ph.D., Sociology, 1952). After research in sociology (1952–60), he became chief of the Laboratory of Socio-environmental Studies, National Institute of Mental Health, in Bethesda, Maryland (1960–85). He is a fellow at the American Academy of Arts and Science, has held a Guggenheim Fellowship, is past president of the American Sociological Association, has been an officer of several U.S. and international professional societies, and has served on the editorial boards of several professional journals. He lectured in Norway, Australia, Japan, Poland, Ukraine, and Russia, and in 1992 received the Cooley-Mead Award for his contributions to social psychology. He became a professor of sociology at Johns Hopkins University in 1985.

Carmi Schooler (b. 1933) was born in the Bronx, New York, and educated at Hamilton College and New York University (Ph.D., 1959). In 1959 he became a research psychologist at the Laboratory for Socio-environmental Studies, National Institute of Mental Health, and he is now acting chief of the laboratory. He is a member of the American Psychological and Sociological Associations. His work centers on how social structures affect the psychological functioning of normal individuals and schizophrenics; recently, he completed cross-cultural studies in social psychology in Japan. Among his honors and awards are several from Japan.

Sources

May, Hal, ed. 1985. *Contemporary authors.* Vol. 114. Detroit: Gale Research.

Jaques Cattell Press, ed. 1978. *American men and women of science: the social and behavioral sciences.* 13th ed. New York: Jaques Cattell and R. R. Bowker.

Kohn, Melvin L., and Schooler, Carmi. 1983. *Work and personality: an inquiry into the impact of social stratification.* Norwood, N.J.: Ablex.

Kohn, Melvin L., and Slomczynski, Kazimierz M. 1990. *Social structure and self-direction: a comparative analysis of the United States and Poland.* Oxford: Basil Blackwell.

KOHUTIAN. Pertaining to the American psychoanalyst, whose work on the narcissistic personality contributed much to understanding political behavior and leadership.

Heinz Kohut (1913–81), born in Vienna, completed his M.D. at the University of Vienna in 1938. He claimed that he was at the train to wave goodbye to Sigmund Freud on June 4, 1938. In 1940 Kohut fled to the United States to do further training. After studies at the University of Chicago, he joined Chicago's

Institute of Psychoanalysis (1953). For his work in psychoanalysis, he was honored as president of the American Psychoanalytic Association, awarded the Heinz Hartmann Prize by the New York Psychoanalytic Association, and was vice-president of the Sigmund Freud Archives. His aim was to advance psychoanalysis, both personally and with his ideas. Kohut was an empathic analyst, who, childlike, would playfully think his way into the mind of others. His students found his classes legendary. Using introspection and depth analysis, he established a widely respected theory of self-psychology, an extension of psychoanalysis. His study of narcissism, a state with which he had a personal preoccupation, showed how hurt and rage were prominent in the administration of human life. In recent years his theory has been applied profitably in the psychology of politics (Etheredge, 1979).

Sources

Etheredge, Lloyd. 1979. Hardball politics: a model. *Political Psychology* 1:3–26.

Goldberg, Arnold I. 1982. Obituary: Heinz Kohut (1913–81). *International Journal of Psycho-Analysis* 63:257–258.

Kohut, Heinz. 1966. Forms and transformation of narcissism. *Journal of the American Psychoanalytic Association* 14:243–72.

Kohut, Heinz. 1973. Thoughts on narcissism and narcissistic rage. *The psychoanalytic study of the child.* New York: Quadrangle.

Kohut, Heinz. 1977. *The restoration of the self.* New York: International Universities Press.

KONDRATIEFF CYCLES. Cycles of prices and output over periods of fifty to sixty years. The cycles were identified in 1925 as follows: the first long wave upward was from the 1780s to 1810–17, and then downward from 1810–17 to 1844–51; the second long wave was upward from 1844–51 to 1870–75, and downward from 1870–75 to 1890–96; the third long wave upward went from 1890–96 to 1914–20, and downward from 1914 to 1920. The study is an empirical test for long price and output waves. It fitted ordinary least squares trends to per capita data, and it applied a nine-year moving average of the deviations so that the Juglar trade cycles would be kept out.

Nikolai Dimitrievich Kondratieff (1892–1931?) was born in Russia and studied agricultural and domestic economics; he was appointed deputy minister for food in the Kerensky government in 1917. He founded and was director of the Moscow Business Conditions Institute (1920–28), and collected agricultural data in 1923 in preparation of the first Five-Year Plan. His plan was based on a policy that set targets farmers would be able to meet. In 1928 he was removed from office, apparently for being both wrong and reactionary, and, after serving as a witness at the trials of Stalin's opponents, was probably imprisoned and died. His work, which owes much to the ideas of Mikhail Tugan-Baranovskii (1865–1919), was published in 1925 and translated into English in 1935.

See also TUGAN-BARANOVSKII THEORY OF BUSINESS CYCLES.

Sources

Blaug, Mark, ed. 1986. *Who's who in economics: a biographical dictionary of major economists, 1700–1986.* 2d ed. Cambridge, Mass.: MIT Press.

Eatwell, John; Milgate, Murray; and Newman, Peter. 1987. *The new Palgrave: a dictionary of economics.* London: Macmillan.

Kondratieff, Nikolai D. 1935. The long waves in economic life. *Review of Economic Statistics* 17:105–115.

Mager, Nathan H. 1987. *The Kondratieff waves.* New York: Praeger.

Sills, David L., ed. 1968. *International encyclopedia of the social sciences.* New York: Macmillan and Free Press.

Solomou, Solomos. 1987. *Phases of economic growth, 1850–1973: Kondratieff waves and Kuznet swings.* Cambridge: Cambridge University Press.

KRAUS PLAN. A business plan for participants in the market to use, rationally, the market information indicated by equilibrium prices.

Alan Kraus (b. 1939) was born in Schenectady, New York, and became a professor of economics and finance at the University of British Columbia, Canada. His main contributions appeared in studies on the theory of general and partial equilibrium in financial securities markets under uncertainty; he examined the implications of individual preference functions and security return probability distributions, the conditions for aggregation of individual security demand functions, and the rational use by market participants of information indicated by equilibrium prices. He also studied the effects on stock prices of trading by large financial institutions.

Sources

Blaug, Mark, ed. 1986. *Who's who in economics: a biographical dictionary of major economists, 1700–1986.* 2d ed. Cambridge, Mass.: MIT Press.

Kraus, Alan, and Litzenberger, R. 1975. Market equilibrium in a multi-period state preference model with logarithmic utility. *Journal of Finance* 30:1213–1227.

Kraus, Alan, and Smith, Maxwell. 1989. Market created risk. *Journal of Finance* 44: 557–569.

KURTZ SYNDROME. An anthropological view of how the civilizer becomes the savage that he despises. A pattern of behavior opposite to the Prospero syndrome.

Mr. Kurtz, a central character in Joseph Conrad's tale *Heart of Darkness* (1920), is used by anthropologists to illustrate one way in which Europeans cruelly exploited non-European peoples. Marlowe, the narrator, tells of Mr. Kurtz, a manager of the Inland Station at the heart of the ivory country in Africa. Kurtz, the envy of all other agents, is the most successful agent, apparently because he uses brutal methods in ivory collection. He is ill, has dismissed his assistant, has no help, and will probably die. Marlowe's visit to Kurtz is delayed, probably because of attempts by the envious agents. After a two-month journey upriver through the primitive jungles, Marlowe comes to Kurtz's station where he learns of Kurtz's brilliant achievements in gaining an almost godlike control

over the natives through largely barbarous methods. Once an educated and civ-
ilized man, Kurtz had turned his back on intellect and resorted to the gun to
dominate his native ivory suppliers. He tries to justify going native by arguing
that he has seen the heart of things. On his death bed he cries: ''The horror!
The horror!'' Marlowe leaves with Kurtz's report for the Society for the Suppression of Savage Customs and a letter to his fiancee. Wishing to avoid distressing both himself and the grief-stricken woman, Marlowe lies to her, saying
that Mr. Kurtz's final words indicated he had been thinking of her.

See also PROSPERO SYNDROME

Sources

Drabble, Margaret, ed. 1985. *The Oxford companion to English literature.* Oxford: Clarendon Press.
Obeyesekere, Gananath. 1992. *The apotheosis of Captain Cook: European mythmaking
in the Pacific.* Princeton, N.J.: Princeton University Press.

KUZNETS'S SWINGS OR CYCLES. A fourteen- to twenty-year pattern of
primarily economic fluctuation that centers on variations in growth rate. The
swings appear at certain periods in certain countries, for example, 1856–1913
in Britain. Many explanations have been offered for the cycles, and recent theories give weight to migration, the structure of the world economy, national
economics, the stages of a nation's growth, and complex adjustment mechanisms
relevant to the cycles.

Simon Smith Kuznets (b. 1901) was born in Kharkov, Russia, immigrated to
the United States, and became naturalized. He graduated from Columbia University (Ph.D., 1926) and was on the staff of the National Bureau of Economic
Research in New York (1927–61) while a professor at the University of Pennsylvania (1930–60). During World War II he was associate director of the War
Production Board and afterward an economic adviser to India and China. He
won a Noble Prize in 1971 and has been honored by many universities and
professional bodies for his quantitative studies in economics. He was the main
influence in developing the U.S. national income accounting system, the basis
of much empirical work in economics. He created systematized income and
wealth time series. His study of seasonal variations, cyclical fluctuations, and
secular movements laid the basis of modern research on consumption, saving,
and income. Later, using historical quantitative national income data, he studied
the causes and results of economic growth, incorporating such variables as population size, technology, productivity, business cycles, and income distribution
in a cautiously conceived theory. The first of his many books was *Cyclical
Fluctuations: Retail and Wholesale Trade, United States, 1919–1925* (1926).

Sources

Blaug, Mark, ed. 1986. *Who's who in economics: a biographical dictionary of major
economists, 1700–1986.* 2d ed. Cambridge, Mass.: MIT Press.
Devine, Elizabeth; Held, Michael; Vinson, James; and Walsh, George, eds. 1983. *Thinkers of the twentieth century: a biographical, bibliographical and critical
dictionary.* London: Macmillan.

Eatwell, John; Milgate, Murray; and Newman, Peter. 1987. *The new Palgrave: a dictionary of economics.* London: Macmillan.

Greenwald, D., ed. 1982. *Encyclopedia of economics.* New York: McGraw-Hill.

Lundberg, Erik. 1984. Simon Kuznets' contribution to economics. In Henry W. Spiegel and Warren J. Samuel, eds. *Contemporary economists in perspective.* Greenwich, Conn.: JAI Press.

Pearce, D.W., ed. 1986. *Macmillan dictionary of modern economics.* New York: Macmillan.

Sills, David L., ed. 1968. *International encyclopedia of the social sciences.* New York: Macmillan and Free Press.

L

LACANIAN. A modern French interpretation of psychoanalysis which stresses the importance of real and imaginary symbolic structures into which a child is born, especially language. The interpretation accepts Freud's general principles but redefines many of his concepts, and substitutes an ethics of language for the medical model of analysis, as it had appeared among U.S. ego psychoanalysis. Thus, psychoanalysis becomes a study of the patient's relation to what was true in what the patient said. And the patient's unconscious becomes more a language for the patient than a theory for an analyst to use in treatment and interpretation. In addition, the interpretation considers the position of psychoanalysis in a literary and philosophical culture. On one hand, it appears as a new human science, and on the other, it identifies the limits of a method subject largely to domination by science.

Jacques Lacan (1901–81) was born in Paris and studied at the Collège Stanislas and the Faculté de Médecine de Paris (M.D., 1932) where he became head of the clinic (1932–36). With his training in psychiatry, he later worked at the Médecine des Psychiatriques Hôpitaux de Paris until 1953 and thereafter was a professor at Saint Anne's Hospital in Paris for ten years. In 1963 he was Chargé des Conferences L'école Pratique des Hautes Etudes, Paris, and Director, Editions du Seuil (1963–81). In 1964 he founded L'école Freudienne de Paris and disbanded it in 1980 because its members failed to keep to the principles laid down by Freud. In 1936 he devised a theory of early self–other development using the idea of a growing infant before a mirror learning from its mirror image. In the early 1950s Lacan introduced his distinction between imagery (image-based experience) and the symbolic (language-based experience). In his complex theory of self, he demanded that modern Freudians return to Freud, and appreciate the importance of Lacan's distinction rather than continue to overemphasize the imaginings of their patients. Later, he offered a revision of the Oedipal problem and after the mid-1960s concentrated his work on the real. His teachings appeared in seminars from 1951 to 1980, and since 1976 they have appeared in *Le Séminaire de Jacques Lacan.*

Sources

Benvenuto, Bice, and Kennedy, Roger. 1986. *The works of Jacques Lacan: an introduction.* London: Free Associations.

Borch-Jacobsen, Mikkel. 1991. *Lacan: the absolute master.* Trans. Douglas Brick. Stanford, Calif.: Stanford University Press.

Devine, Elizabeth; Held, Michael; Vinson, James; and Walsh, George, eds. 1983. *Thinkers of the twentieth century: a biographical, bibliographical and critical dictionary.* London: Macmillan.

Grigg, Russell. 1992. Lacan. In Peter Beilharz, ed. *Social theory: a guide to central thinkers.* Sydney: Allen and Unwin.

LAFFER CURVE. Reflecting the view of supply-side economics, a curve that indicates that a tax reduction on incomes and profits will lead people to work harder and invest more. The curve shows that zero tax produces no tax revenue and that increases in tax rates take a growing proportion of income; so as the tax rate increases, the tax base itself decreases in size. There is probably a tax rate at which tax revenue reaches a maximum; thus, a reduction in tax rate will raise tax revenue. Many economists consider actual tax rates are lower than this point, though taxation may affect the incentive to work.

Arthur Betz Laffer (b. 1940), an American economist, was born in Youngstown, Ohio. After graduating from Yale University, Laffer studied economics at Stanford University in California, (Ph.D., International Economics, 1972) and taught at the University of Chicago. In Washington he became the newly created chief economist at the Office of Management and Budget (1970) and gained much attention with his "econometric" formulas based on the assumption that changes in the Federal Reserve Bank's monetary policy may have a marked effect on the gross national product. In 1974 he returned to the University of Chicago, and in 1976 he was appointed a professor of finance, business, and economics at the University of Southern California. He is an adviser to the Taxpayers' Foundation and has received awards for excellent teaching (1980).

Sources

Buchanan, James M., and Lee, Dwight R. 1982. Politics, time and the Laffer Curve. *Journal of Political Economy* 90:816.

Moritz, Charles, ed. 1982. *Current biography yearbook.* New York: H. W. Wilson.

Neil, Edward J., ed. 1984. *Free market conservatism.* London: Allen and Unwin.

Shafritz, Jay M. 1988. *The Dorsey dictionary of American government and politics.* Chicago: Dorsey.

Waud, Roger N. 1985. Politics, deficits, and the Laffer Curve. *Public Choice* 47:509.

Who's who in America, 1992–93. New Providence, N.J.: Marquis.

LAGRANGEAN MULTIPLIER. In economics this "method of undetermined multipliers" is followed when marginalist concepts are being used, as well as the idea of shadow price and imperfect value. It applies to a function of several variables that are subject to constraints, for which a maximum is needed (Pearce, 1986).

Joseph Louis Lagrange (1736–1813) was born of French parents in Turin, Italy. By 16 he had taught himself mathematics, and at age 19 he was appointed a professor of mathematics at Turin's Royal Artillery School. He wrote a paper on isoperimetric problems asking what shape a curve should be to enclose the largest possible area. A circle was the answer. He sent the paper to Leonhard Euler (1707–83) who withheld his own thoughts on the subject, saw the proof was of greater generality than his own, and ensured the younger man was credited with founding a new branch of mathematics, that is, the calculus of variations. His original work on the method of determining minima and maxima appeared in 1762. He contributed to understanding the three-body problem (1764), solutions of equations, theory of numbers, analytic geometry, and the theory of groups. In 1793 he presided over the commission on French weights and measures and advocated the adoption of ten, not twelve, as the base to standard measurement.

Sources

Abbott, David. 1985. *The biographical dictionary of scientists: mathematicians.* London: Blond Educational.

Eatwell, John; Milgate, Murray; and Newman, Peter. 1987. *The new Palgrave: a dictionary of economics.* London: Macmillan.

McHenry, Robert, ed. 1992. *The new encyclopedia Britannica.* Chicago: Encyclopedia Britannica, Inc.

Morris, William, ed. 1965–66. *Grolier universal encyclopedia.* New York: American Book-Stratford Press, Inc.

Pearce, David W., ed. 1986. *Macmillan dictionary of modern economics.* New York: Macmillan.

LAMARCKISM. The theory that species have evolved through the efforts of organisms to adapt to new conditions; for example, giraffes acquired the genetic conditions for a long neck because generations of them fed on leaves high in the trees. This is contrary to the assumption in molecular biology that genetic information flows only from nucleic acid to proteins and other products, not vice versa.

Jean Baptiste Pierre Antoine de Monet Chevalier De Lamarck (1744–1829), a French naturalist, was born at Bazentin, Picardy. He was enrolled at a Jesuit College in Amiens to study theology, but in 1760, on his father's death, the youth left home to serve in the Seven Years' War. Afterward he studied medicine and later was drawn to botany. He became curator of the herbarium of the Jardin du Roi in Paris and was appointed professor of botany in 1788. After the French Revolution, his workplace was named Jardin du Plantes, and he became a professor of invertebrate zoology (1793). Although he was one of the founders of evolutionary thought, his theory was not as well supported by scientific

evidence as that of Charles Darwin (1809–82). The idea that acquired characteristics could be inherited is plausible to social scientists because it seems obvious that people learn generation by generation. It also attracts ideologues who
assert that all humans are born equal because, if so, Lamarckism seems to be
the only course that a theory of social evolution can follow.

Sources

Burkhardt, Richard W. 1977. *The spirit of system: Lamarck and evolutionary biology.*
    Cambridge, Mass.: Harvard University Press.
Cannon, Herbert G. 1959. *Lamarck and modern genetics.* Manchester: Manchester Uni-
    versity Press.
Jordanova, Ludmilla J. 1984. *Lamarck.* Oxford and New York: Oxford University Press.
Zusne, Leonard. 1984. *Biographical dictionary of psychology.* Westport, Conn.: Green-
    wood Press.

LANCASTERIAN. Relating to a teaching method that uses monitors.

Joseph Lancaster (1778–1838), an English educator, was born at Southwark,
London, and died in New York. He opened his own school in Southwark (1798)
and later moved to larger premises (1801). He believed that education should
be available to all children regardless of their ability to pay. Since he could not
afford to hire teachers, he developed the monitorial system, which is based on
a method used by Andrew Bell, a superintendent of Madras Male Orphan Asylum, India (1789). Lancaster traveled in Britain, lecturing and raising funds for
the establishment of new schools, and published a pamphlet describing his
method, *Improvements in Education* (1803). By 1811 there were ninety-five
schools and 30,000 pupils. In 1818 he was bankrupt and immigrated to America
where he carried on his work. The Lancasterian system was widely accepted in
New York State where more than sixty schools were established. Lancaster was
forced out of the organization for financial mismanagement and other personal
reasons, and the schools were taken over by the New York school authorities
in 1853. Although the monitor system lost favor, it was one of the first successful techniques of mass education for the poor in industrial society.

Sources

Aldrich, Richard, and Gordon, Peter. 1987. *Dictionary of British educationists.* London:
    Woburn Press.
Magnussen, Magnus; Goring, Rosemary; and Thorn, John O., eds. 1990. *Chambers bi-
    ographical dictionary.* Edinburgh: Chambers Ltd.
Preece, Warren E., ed. 1965. *Encyclopedia Britannica.* Chicago: Encyclopedia Britannica,
    Inc., William Benton.
Smith, Benjamin. 1903. *The Century cyclopedia of names.* London: The Times.
Stephen, Leslie, and Lee, Sydney, eds. 1917. *The dictionary of national biography.* Lon-
    don: Oxford University Press.

LANDRUM-GRIFFIN ACT. The U.S. Labor-Management Reporting and Disclosure Act, also known as the Labor Reform Act (1959). It provides a ''Bill
of Rights'' for members of labor unions; requires detailed reports to the U.S.

secretary of labor on union finances and the operations of union constitutions and bylaws; and makes misuse of union funds a federal crime. Ex-convicts, communists, and labor officials with conflicting business interests are barred from holding union office. The "Bill of Rights" provisions secured the secret ballot in union elections, freedom of speech in union meetings, hearings in disciplinary cases, and the right of members to sue the union for unfair practices, and they authorized the members' access to union records.

Phillip Mitchell Landrum (b. 1909) was born in Martin, Georgia, studied at public schools and Mercer University in Macon, graduated from Piedmont College and Atlanta Law School (LL.B., 1941), and was admitted to the bar in 1941. In 1942 he enlisted as a private in the U.S. Army Air Corps; he served in Europe and was discharged in 1945 as a first lieutenant. He was assistant attorney-general in Georgia (1946–47), worked for the governor (1947–48), and practiced in Jasper, Georgia, until he entered politics. He was elected a Democrat representative from Georgia to the eighty-third and eleven succeeding U.S. congresses (1953–79).

Robert Paul Griffin (b. 1923) was born in Detroit, Michigan, and attended public schools in Garden City and Dearborn. He served in the 71st infantry in World War II and graduated from Central Michigan College in 1947. He studied law at the University of Michigan, was admitted to the bar in 1950, and was elected as a Republican to the eighty-fifth and four succeeding U.S. congresses (1957–66). Afterward he served in the U.S. Senate (1966–79).

Sources

Bellace, Janice R.; Berkowitz, Alan D.; and Van Dusen, Bruce D. 1979. *The Landrum-Griffin Act: twenty years of federal protection of union members' rights.* Philadelphia: Wharton School, University of Pennsylvania.

Jacob, Kathryn A., and Ragsdale, Bruce A. 1989. *Biographical dictionary of the United States Congress: 1774–1989.* Bicentennial ed. Washington, D.C.: U.S. Government Printing Office.

Lee, Alton R. 1990. *Eisenhower and Landrum-Griffin: a study in labor-management politics.* Lexington: University Press of Kentucky.

McLaughlin, Doris B., and Schoomaker, Anita L. 1978. *The Landrum-Griffin Act and union democracy.* Ann Arbor: University of Michigan Press.

Plano, Jack C., and Greenberg, Milton. 1989. *The American political dictionary.* New York: Holt, Rinehart and Winston.

Shafritz, Jay M. 1988. *The Dorsey dictionary of American government and politics.* Chicago: Dorsey.

LANGE-LERNER MECHANISM. A mechanism of a market-oriented socialist economy which is based on the assumption of an institutional framework in the public ownership of the means of production, but free choice in the area of consumption and employment. To simplify the theory, the private sector is omitted. Consumer preference through "demand prices" is the criterion for allocating production and resource.

Oscar Lange (1904–65) was born near Lodz, Poland, into the family of a

German textile manufacturer. He studied law and economics in Poznan and Cracow, and lectured in economics and statistics at Cracow (1927–37). In 1929 he went to London for further studies, and then to the United States (1934–35) at Harvard and Berkeley. He taught at Chicago (1938–45) and Warsaw (1948–65). The mechanism was devised by Lange and amended after discussion with Lerner in *Review of Economic Studies* (1936–37). Lange was a supporter of Keynes and is credited with helping to establish econometrics as a special field of study. His *Political Economy* (English trans. 1963) is an incomplete but major synthesis of Marxist economics.

Abba Ptachya Lerner (1905–82) was born in Romania, but raised from early childhood in the Jewish immigrant quarter of London's East End. He went to Rabbinical School and, at age 16, began work as a tailor, capmaker, Hebrew schoolteacher, and typesetter. He established his own printing shop; when the business failed, he enrolled in evening classes at the London School of Economics to find the reason why (Ph.D., 1943). He studied at Cambridge with Keynes and was much taken with his ideas. In 1939 a Rockefeller Fellowship took him to the United States where he lived. He was honored with a D.Sc. from Northwestern University and was one of the last of the original, versatile, and prolific nonmathematical economists. Lerner's many papers on market pricing under socialism and on welfare economics appear in his major work, *The Economics of Control Principles of Welfare Economics* (1944).

Sources
Blaug, Mark. 1985. *Great economists since Keynes.* Brighton, England: Harvester Press.
Eatwell, John; Milgate, Murray; and Newman, Peter. 1987. *The new Palgrave: a dictionary of economics.* London: Macmillan.
Pearce, David W., ed. 1986. *Macmillan dictionary of modern economics.* New York: Macmillan.

LASSWELLIAN. Relating to the innovative thought of the modern American political and social scientist. Lasswell invented methods (e.g., content analysis) and concepts for social technology, gave new interpretations of international relations, and devised procedures for large-scale problem solving; he related concepts from diverse fields like psychoanalysis, politics, social science, and psychiatry. His first notable publication, *Psychopathology and Politics* (1930; 1960), is a social science classic; his *Power and Personality* (1948), which centers on the use of power to compensate for personal shortcomings, is also outstanding. Arnold Rogow (1969) published appraisals of his prolific writing.

Harold Dwight Lasswell (1902–78) was born in Donnellson, Illinois, where his father was a Presbyterian minister and his mother a teacher. Always an outstanding student, Harold was educated at a local high school and later by scholarship at the University of Chicago (1918). After completing his Ph.D. in 1926, he traveled in Europe and taught at several universities before becoming a professor of law and political science at Yale (1938). He was one of the earliest major exponents of the behaviorial school of political science and the use of psychoanalytic ideas in the study of politics. He was a consultant to various government agencies, and in 1939 he directed the War Communications Research Commission of the Library of Congress. His intellectual debts were to the philosophical orientation of Alfred North Whitehead (1861–1947), the psychoanalytic method of Freud (1856–1939) and the perspectives of Karl Marx (1818–83). He is known as the founder of the policy sciences.

Sources

Muth, Rodney; Finley, Mary M.; and Muth, Marcia F. 1990. *Harold D. Lasswell: an annotated bibliography.* New Haven, Conn.: Yale University Press.

Rogow, Arnold A., ed. 1969. *Politics, personality and social science in the twentieth century: essays in honor of H. D. Lasswell.* Chicago: University of Chicago Press.

Rothe, Anne, ed. 1947. *Current biography yearbook.* New York: H. W. Wilson.

Shafritz, Jay M. 1988. *The Dorsey dictionary of American government and politics.* Chicago: Dorsey.

Sills, David L., ed. 1968. *International encyclopedia of the social sciences.* New York: Macmillan and Free Press.

Snyder, Richard C. 1979. Harold D. Lasswell, 1902–1978. *Political Psychology* 1:69–72.

Torgerson, Douglas. 1985. Contextual orientation in policy analysis: the contribution of Harold D. Lasswell. *Policy Sciences* 18:241–261.

LAUDIANS. Followers of the seventeenth-century religious beliefs that require uniformity of worship according to the prayer book; the catholicism of the Anglican Church; ritual; and the use of vestments. Their aim was to suppress the Puritans, eliminate Puritanism, and Anglicize the Scottish church in the 1630s.

William Laud (1573–1645) was president of Saint John's College, Oxford (1611), dean of Gloucester (1616), bishop of Saint David's, and through his friend, Buckingham, became influential at court. Under Charles I he advanced quickly to become the archbishop of Canterbury (1633–45). He brought the king's law and order to religious organization; he opposed the Calvinists' views on predestination and supported episcopacy; he planned visits in his province to discipline the clergy; he demanded proper ceremony in the church; and he reformed statutes and discipline in his university, and ordered bishops to reside in their sees. To this he added many other demands, but when he and Charles I imposed a prayerbook on the Scots, Laud's authority collapsed; he was impeached, put in the Tower (1641) for two years without trial, and, because he could not be found a traitor, was condemned by attainder and executed. Laudianism returned with the restoration of the Church of England—especially the liturgy and doctrine—but the social policy of Laudianism was abandoned.

Sources

Carlton, Charles. 1987. *Archbishop William Laud.* London: Routledge and Kegan Paul.

Cross, Frank L. 1974. *The Oxford dictionary of the Christian Church.* 2d ed. New York: Oxford University Press.

Howatt, Gerald M.D. 1973. *Dictionary of world history.* London: Thomas Nelson.

McHenry, Robert, ed. 1992. *The new encyclopedia Britannica.* Chicago: Encyclopedia Britannica, Inc.

Smith, Benjamin. 1903. *The Century cyclopedia of names.* London: The Times.
Trevor-Roper, Hugh R. 1962. *Archbishop Laud.* London: Macmillan.

LAUREANISTAS. Catholic conservatives who aimed to spiritualize Colombia
in the 1930s with the Catholic faith by having the clergy administer social
services and government policy. In rural areas the clergy was to run the local
cooperatives and collectives, and parliamentary democracy was to be put aside.

Laureano Gómez (1889–1965), the eldest son in a middle-class family, was
born in Bogotá and studied at the Jesuit College of Saint Bartholomew and later
for an engineering degree (1909) at the National University. He was elected to
the Congress in 1911 and then the Senate in 1915, became a skilled orator and
staunch conservative, and outraged his colleagues with the announcement that
Colombia could never become cultured because it harbored fanatical Spaniards
and primitive savages. In time, he earned the reputation of a grand inquisitor
(*monstruo,* "the monster"). During the 1920s he denounced conservative policies and the U.S. capitalists who treated Colombian workers badly, and into
the 1930s he appeared to be far from the violent character that he would later
become. Later in the 1930s he opposed totalitarianism in Germany, Italy, and
Russia, and even supported the views of Gandhi. In 1935 he suffered a stroke,
and he appeared to have time during the recovery to reconsider his position. He
established Bogotá's daily *El Siglo* (1936) and, after noting a decline in the
influence of conservatives and a massacre of some (1939), began himself to
threaten public violence. As an extreme right-wing conservative, he denounced
majority rule as "one-half-plus-one," attacked the liberal government he once
supported, and in 1944 was arrested and imprisoned briefly for libel. Between
1948 and 1962 Colombia endured a period of violence—"La Violencia"—
during which over 200,000 people died. As leader of the right wing of the
Colombian Conservative party, he gained from a split among the liberals to win
the presidential election of 1950. During his presidency (1950–53) the violence
grew, and Colombia was a fascist state. He was overthrown in a military coup,
but the military leadership was driven from office in 1957 when world coffee
prices fell. Gómez and the leaders of the conservatives joined the liberals in a
National Front to rule Colombia for the next sixteen years.
Sources:

Braun, Herbert. 1985. *The assassination of Gaitán: public life and urban violence in
    Colombia.* Madison: University of Wisconsin Press.
Cook, Chris. 1983. *Dictionary of historical terms.* London: Macmillan.
Fluharty, Vernon L. 1957. *Dance of the millions: military rule and social revolution in
    Colombia 1930–1956.* Reprinted 1975. Pittsburgh: University of Pittsburgh Press.
Henderson, James D. 1985. *When Colombia bled: a history of the Violencia in Tolana.*
    Tuscaloosa: University of Alabama Press.
Henderson, James D. 1988. *Conservative thought in twentieth-century Latin America:
    the ideas of Laureano Gomez.* Athens, Ohio: Ohio Center for International Stud-
    ies, Center for Latin American Studies.
Howatt, Gerald M.D. 1973. *Dictionary of world history.* London: Thomas Nelson.

McHenry, Robert, ed. 1992. *The new encyclopedia Britannica.* Chicago: Encyclopedia Britannica, Inc.

Molina, Felipe Antonio. 1940. *Laureano Gómez; historia de una rebeldia.* Bogotá: Librería Voluntad.

Oquiet, Paul. 1980. *Violence, conflict and politics in Colombia.* New York: Academic Press.

Socarrás, José. 1942. *Laureano Gómez: psicoanálisis de un residento.* Bogotá: Editorial ABC.

LAVAL. A traitor.

Pierre Laval (1883–1945) was executed for treason at the end of World War II.

See HOARE-LAVAL PLAN.

LAWRENTIAN. Pertaining to the social and political ideas of the British novelist regarding sexual relations; a love for nature rather than technology; preference for tenderness in the place of sophistication; rejection of pornography in the face of frank sexuality. The term also refers to the crypto-fascist political views that the novelist is reputed to have adopted late in life.

David Herbert Lawrence (1885–1930) was born in Nottinghamshire, England, the child of an alcoholic, brutal coal miner, and a puritanical schoolteacher. His childhood was extremely unhappy. He was educated at Nottingham University College, held a teaching certificate (1908), and taught school in Derbyshire (1902–6) and at Davidson Road School in Croydon (1908–11). His first novel was *The White Peacock* (1911). For his novel *The Lost Girl* (1920) he received the Tait Black Memorial Prize from Edinburgh University (1921). He also wrote short stories, plays, nonfiction, and travel sketches. Many of his works were filmed after World War II; several novels were the subject of court cases for obscenity. Among the most notable novels are *Sons and Lovers* (1913) and *Lady Chatterley's Lover* (1928). He suffered a long time from tuberculosis, witnessed the banning of many of his books, and after 1909 traveled to Italy, Australia, Ceylon, France, the Pacific, Mexico, and the United States to find a congenial life and companionship. Some critics objected to his overbearing and hortative style, incessant attacks on institutions, and the tendency to sacrifice character to moralizing in his literary work.

Sources

Buchanan-Brown, John, ed. 1973. *Cassell's encyclopedia of world literature.* London: Cassell.

Burgess, Anthony. 1985. *Flame into being: the life and work of D. H. Lawrence.* London: Heinemann.

Delavenay, Emile. 1972. *D. H. Lawrence: the man and his work, the formative years 1885–1919.* London: Heinemann.

Kermode, Frank. 1973. *Lawrence.* London: Fontana Collins.

McHenry, Robert, ed. 1992. *The new encyclopedia Britannica.* Chicago: Encyclopedia Britannica, Inc.

May, Hal, ed. 1987. *Contemporary authors.* Vol. 121. Detroit: Gale Research.

LAWSONGATE. The scandal in 1988 alleging that Britain's chancellor of the Exchequer in the Thatcher government had deliberately deceived the public about the state of the British economy.

Nigel Lawson (b. 1932) was born in London and educated at Westminster School and Christ Church College, Oxford. He served in the Royal Navy (1954–56) and worked on the *Financial Times* (1956–60), edited the *Sunday Telegraph* (1961–63), was special assistant to the prime minister (1963–64), wrote financial columns, and made broadcasts in 1965. He edited *The Spectator* (1966–70) and wrote regularly for many newspapers. After serving as an adviser to the Conservative party he became M.P. for Blaby, Leicestershire (1974–92), during which time he was opposition whip, spokesman on financial and economic affairs, published *The Power Game* (1976) and *The Coming Confrontation* (1978), and eventually became chancellor of the Exchequer (1983–89) during the Thatcher regime. Since then he has been director, adviser, and counselor for prominent international banks. At the time of the scandal he was named ''Finance Minister of the Year'' in *Euromoney Magazine* (1988).

Sources

The international who's who, 1992–93. London: Europa Publications.

Tulloch, Sara. 1991. *The Oxford dictionary of new words.* Oxford: Oxford University Press.

Who's who, 1992. London: Adam and Charles Black.

LAZARSFELD INDEX, LAZARSFELD MODEL. The index is a continuum along which respondents may be ordered on the basis of their attitudes on a particular subject. In any given study the continuum is divided into classes, the number of classes being one more than the number of attitudes being studied. Each attitude (item) is assigned a probability that a positive response places the respondent in a given latent class: and it is possible to compute the probability that the members of a given latent class will give a positive response to a certain number of items in the study. The model is a system of hypothetical relationships for use in attitude studies.

Paul Felix Lazarsfeld (1901–76) was born in Vienna, became a leader in the socialist student organizations, and created a monthly newspaper for socialist students. His first publication, co-authored with Ludwig Wagner, was published when he was 13, and is a report on a children's summer camp that had been established on socialist principles. He went to the United States in 1933 as a Rockefeller Foundation fellow, remained there and was naturalized. For three decades he was a professor of sociology at Columbia University. Trained as a mathematician, he first thought of himself as a psychologist; only in midlife did he become identified as a sociologist. His major interests lay in the methodology of social research and the development of institutes for training and research in the social sciences. Although stressing the importance of his early socialist involvements, his political activism did not survive in America. During fifty-two years of professional life, Lazarsfeld contributed to four main areas of social

science; the social effects of unemployment, mass communications, voting behavior, and higher education. He was also interested in the history and development of research methods, and the relation between quantitative and
qualitative research. The Bureau of Applied Social Research at Columbia University lists hundreds of published and unpublished reports by Lazarsfeld and
his students (1937–77).

Sources

Garraty, John A., and Sternstein, Jerome L. 1974. *Encyclopedia of American biography.*
    New York: Harper and Row.
Sills, David L., ed. 1968. *International encyclopedia of the social sciences.* New York:
    Macmillan and Free Press.
Theodorson, George A. 1969. *A modern dictionary of sociology.* New York: Thomas Y.
    Crowell.

LE BON'S THEORY OF THE CROWD. An early theory of mass behavior
which assumed a tendency for people in crowds to act emotionally and sometimes do what they would alone condemn. The theory attributes the loss of
personal responsibility to temporary suspension of identity or merging with the
crowd's "unitary consciousness."

Gustav Le Bon (1841–1931) was born in a small village near Chartres, studied
medicine in Paris, and established a private laboratory for scientific experiments.
He applied his ideas on psychopathology to many topical subjects, and he once
claimed to have anticipated Einstein's theory of relativity as well as to have
foreshadowed Nietzche's theory of eternal recurrence. He traveled abroad to
study cultural history. He became famous when he applied Social Darwinian
psychology to political questions. His first best-seller, *The Psychological Laws
of the Evolution of Peoples* (1894: English ed., 1924), discussed the mental
development of "inferior and superior" races in relation to national identity and
colonial conquest. His best known work was *The Crowd* (1895: English ed.,
1896). The book was translated into sixteen languages and reprinted more than
forty-five times in French.

Sources

Goldenson, Robert, ed. 1984. *Longman dictionary of psychology and psychiatry.* New
    York: Longman.
Kuper, Adam, and Kuper, Jessica. 1985. *The social science encyclopedia.* London and
    Boston: Routledge and Kegan Paul.
Nye, Robert. 1975. *The origins of crowd psychology: Gustav Le Bon and the crisis of
    mass democracy in the Third Republic.* London: Sage Publications.
Sills, David L., ed. 1968. *International encyclopedia of the social sciences.* New York:
    Macmillan and Free Press.
Zusne, Leonard. 1984. *Biographical dictionary of psychology.* Westport, Conn.: Green-
    wood Press.

LE CHATELIER PRINCIPLE. A principle, established in 1888, indicating
the tendency of the environment to restore a disturbed system to its stable, static,

or dynamic equilibrium. It requires that the system be in a stable equilibrium at first, and, when some condition is changed, the equilibrium will tend to move so as to restore the original condition. The concept has been used in the study of economic extremum problems (Eatwell et al., 1987) and in modern theories of social organization (Katz and Kahn, 1966).

Henry Louis Le Châtelier (1850–1936) was born in Paris, and after graduation from the École des Mines (1875) he was a mining engineer, and then a professor of chemistry, and eventually taught at the University of Paris (1908). He became an authority on fuels, explosives, metallurgy, and glass; he also studied the properties of alloys, the process of annealing, the setting of cements, firing ceramics, and the combustion of fuels. He was an exacting scientist and teacher, and founded *Revue de Métallurgie,* serving as its editor (1904–14).

Sources

Eatwell, John; Milgate, Murray; and Newman, Peter. 1987. *The new Palgrave: a dictionary of economics.* London: Macmillan.

Katz, Dan, and Kahn, Robert. 1966. *The social psychology of organizations.* New York: John Wiley.

Preece, Warren E., ed. 1965. *Encyclopedia Britannica.* Chicago: Encyclopedia Britannica, Inc., William Benton.

Samuelson, Paul A. 1947. *Foundations of economic analysis.* Cambridge, Mass.: Harvard University Press.

LEIBNIZIAN. Relating to the seventeenth-century German philosopher and mathematician. In philosophical works Leibniz presented a world comprising an hierarchical scheme of simple and self-contained units that mirrored one another, and a universe comprising an organic whole. The logical organization of its elements was evident in both the greatest and the smallest parts of the universe. He wanted to fashion a logical language wherein true propositions would be self-evidently so and false assumptions would be seen clearly to be absurd.

Gottfried Wilhelm Leibniz (1646–1716) was born in Leipzig, where his father was a professor of moral philosophy. He was educated there, and at age 15 he entered the university to study law. In 1666, because he was so young, he was refused permission to graduate so he went to Altdorf and graduated at the university town of Nuremberg in 1667. He was appointed to assist in a project of legal codification by the archbishop of Mainz. Thus, he entered a diplomatic rather than an academic career. At the turn of the century, he was a privy councillor to the electors of Hanover and Brandenburg, Peter the Great of Russia, and the Holy Roman Empire. He is noted for the universality of his genius as well as his special contributions to mathematics and philosophy. He invented the differential and integral calculus—the principle of which was discovered independently by Newton—and advanced the doctrine of monads and preestablished harmony, and basic optimism on the principle of sufficient reason.

Sources

Abbott, David. 1985. *The biographical dictionary of scientists: mathematicians.* London: Blond Educational.

Aiton, E. J. 1985. *Leibniz: a biography.* Bristol: Hilger.

Broad, Charlie D. 1975. *Leibniz: an introduction.* London: Cambridge University Press.

Carr, Herbert W. 1960. *Leibniz.* New York: Dover.

Cross, Frank L. 1974. *The Oxford dictionary of the Christian Church.* 2d ed. New York: Oxford University Press.

MacDonald, Ross. 1984. *Leibniz.* New York: Oxford University Press.

Magnussen, Magnus; Goring, Rosemary; and Thorn, John O., eds. 1990. *Chambers biographical dictionary.* Edinburgh: Chambers Ltd.

Rescher, Nicholas. 1979. *Leibniz: an introduction to his philosophy.* Oxford: Basil Blackwell.

Russell, Bertrand. 1900. *A critical exposition of the philosophy of Leibniz.* Cambridge: Cambridge University Press.

LEICESTER SCHOOL. The school that dominated the approach to the economic history of agriculture in England. A major figure in the school from 1951 was Joan (Irene) Thirsk (b. 1922) whom the University of Leicester honored with a D.Litt. in 1985. The school centered attention on local history and was a creative force in the British Agricultural History Society. Thirsk published *English Peasant Farming* (1957), *Suffolk Farming in the Nineteenth Century* (1958), *Tudor Enclosures* (1959), edited the *Agricultural History Review* (1964–72) in her early days at the University of Leicester, and was made a member of the editorial board of *Past and Present* (1957). She also published *The Rural Economy of England* (1985).

Sources

Chartres, John, and Hey, David. 1990. *English rural society; 1500–1800.* Cambridge: Cambridge University Press.

Finberg, Herbert P.R., with Thirsk, Joan, ed. 1967–1984. *The Agrarian History of England and Wales.* 8 vols. London: Cambridge University Press.

Who's who, 1993. London: Adam and Charles Black.

LENINISM. The major version of Marxism that followed the 1917 revolution in Russia; among other propositions, it held first that capitalism was an international and imperialist force that led to international wars and consequently promoted conditions for a national revolution; second that to overthrow capitalism in any state, a revolutionary political party must rise to power before the proletariat can take over.

Nikolai Vladimir Ilich Lenin was born Vladimir Ilich Ulyanov (1870–1924) at Simbirsk on the Volga River. His father was a provincial inspector of schools, and Lenin was educated at the local secondary school. After being expelled from the University of Kazan for participating in student demonstrations, he studied law at the University of Saint Petersburg and in 1893 joined the growing revolutionary movement. His older brother was executed for plotting against Czar Alexander III. In 1897 he was arrested and exiled to Siberia where he studied and wrote. From 1900 to 1917 he lived mainly in Western Europe and founded the revolutionary newspaper *Iskra,* which was smuggled into Russia by agents. During the food riots of 1917, he returned to Russia and urged that the current "capitalist revolution" be turned into a "socialist revolution." With Bolshevik support, he was able to gain power and establish a dictatorship by gradually eliminating the opposition. His name was legendary in the communist world where he was known as humankind's greatest genius.

Sources

Devine, Elizabeth; Held, Michael; Vinson, James; and Walsh, George, eds. 1983. *Think-ers of the twentieth century: a biographical, bibliographical and critical dictionary.* London: Macmillan.

Harding, Neil. 1977, 1981. *Lenin's political thought.* 2 vols. London: Macmillan.

Meyer, Alfred. 1957. *Leninism.* New York: Praeger.

Miller, David, ed. 1987. *The Blackwell encyclopedia of political thought.* Oxford: Basil Blackwell.

Rice, Christopher. 1990. *Lenin: portrait of a professional revolutionary.* London: Cassell.

LEONTIEF PARADOX. In 1947 U.S. exports were more labor intensive than imports insofar as the capital per person required to produce $1 million of exports was less than the capital per person required to produce $1 million in import substitutes. This fact contrasted with the firm belief that the United States was abundant in capital compared with labor, and was so startling that it was called the Leontief Paradox. It stimulated a search for a new theory of trade that could account for this fact.

Wassily Leontief (b. 1906) was born in Saint Petersburg, the only child in an academic family. He graduated in economics at the University of Leningrad (1925) and then at the University of Berlin (Ph.D., 1928). In 1931 he went to the United States, and was appointed to Harvard University where he remained for the next forty-five years. In 1973 he was awarded the Nobel Prize in Economic Science. His principal scientific contributions appeared in four volumes: *The Structure of the American Economy 1919–1925* (1941); *Studies in the Structure of the American economy* (1953); and *Essays in Economics* (1966; 1977).

Sources

Devine, Elizabeth; Held, Michael; Vinson, James; and Walsh, George, eds. 1983. *Think-ers of the twentieth century: a biographical, bibliographical and critical dictionary.* London: Macmillan.

Eatwell, John; Milgate, Murray; and Newman, Peter. 1987. *The new Palgrave: a dictionary of economics.* London: Macmillan.

The International who's who, 1992. London: Europa Publications.

Magnussen, Magnus; Goring, Rosemary; and Thorn, John O., eds. 1990. *Chambers bi-ographical dictionary.* Edinburgh: Chambers Ltd.

Pearce, David W., ed. 1986. *Macmillan dictionary of modern economics.* New York: Macmillan.

Who's who in America, 1990–91. Chicago: Marquis.

LERNER INDEX. In economics an indicator of monopoly power, defined as price minus marginal cost/price. When perfect competition exists, price equals marginal costs; therefore, the index assumes a value of zero when price exceeds marginal cost. The Lerner Index varies between zero and unity. The closer the index to unity, the greater the degree of monopoly power is said to be possessed by the firm.

Abba Ptachya Lerner (1905–82). See LANGE-LERNER MECHANISM.

Sources

Blaug, Mark. 1985. *Great economists since Keynes.* Brighton, England: Harvester Press.

Eatwell, John; Milgate, Murray; and Newman, Peter. 1987. *The new Palgrave: a dictionary of economics.* London: Macmillan.

Karpman, C., ed. 1972. *Who's who in world Jewry.* New York: Pitman Publishing Corp.

Sills, David L., ed. 1968. *International encyclopedia of the social sciences.* New York: Macmillan and Free Press.

LEVINSON F-SCALE. A modified version of the original F-scale to measure the authoritarian personality. The original scale (T. W. Adorno et al., *The Authoritarian Personality.* New York: Harper, 1950) assessed people for their conventionalism, uncritical submissiveness to ideals, aggression toward the unconventional, opposition to the imaginative, deviations from toughmindedness, superstition, thinking in rigid categories, preoccupation with power and being tough, cynicism and destructiveness, beliefs about dangers all around, and a concern about rampant sexual activities. The modified version is shorter, and the items are worded in the authoritarian direction.

Daniel Jacob Levinson (b. 1920) was born in New York, son of a pharmacist, and educated at the University of California, Los Angeles and Berkeley (Ph.D., Psychology, 1947). He taught psychology at (now Case) Western Reserve University (1947–50), Harvard (1950–60), and Yale (1966–). Among his many works are the notable joint publications *Patienthood in the Mental Hospital* (1964), *The Executive Role Constellation* (1965), and *The Seasons of a Man's Life* (1978).

Sources

American Psychological Association. 1989. *Directory.* Washington, D.C.: APA.

Brewster Smith, M. 1965. An analysis of two measures of "Authoritarianism" among peace corps workers. *Journal of Personality* 33: 573–535.

Jaques Cattell Press, ed. 1978. *American men and women of science: the social and behavioral sciences.* New York: Jaques Cattell and R. R. Bowker.

Locher, Frances C., ed. 1981. *Contemporary authors.* Vol. 102. Detroit: Gale Research.

LEWINIAN FIELD THEORY. Relating to the field theory of the German-American psychologist and its influence in social psychology.

Kurt Lewin (1890–1947) was born in Mogilno (Posen) and studied at the University of Freiberg, Munich, and Berlin (Ph.D., 1909–14). He was a lieutenant in the German Army (1914–18), and later worked as a psychologist at the Psychological Institute, Berlin (1921–26) and taught at the university. He was influenced by Wolfgang Köhler (1887–1967), Max Wertheimer (1880–1943), and Ernst Cassirer (1874–1945). In 1933 he immigrated to the United States and taught first at Cornell, and then at the University of Iowa (1935–41). He also taught at Harvard and was an adviser to the U.S. Department of Agriculture (1944–47) and the Office of Strategic Services (1944–45), and was on the Commission on Community Relations in New York (1944–47). After World War II he became director of the Research Center for Group Dynamics at the Massachusetts Institute of Technology. He founded "field theory" in psychology, which regarded behavior primarily as a function of the person and the present situation. Lewin attempted to formalize this theory by using topology, but this work was less influential than his work in group dynamics. His major works are *A Dynamic Theory of Personality* (1935); *Principles of Topological Psychology* (1936); *Contributions to Psychological Theory* (1938); and *Resolving Social Conflicts* (1948), which was published posthumously.

Sources

Devine, Elizabeth; Held, Michael; Vinson, James; and Walsh, George, eds. 1983. *Thinkers of the twentieth century: a biographical, bibliographical and critical dictionary.* London: Macmillan.

Harre, R., and Lamb, R., eds. 1983. *The encyclopedic dictionary of psychology.* Oxford: Basil Blackwell.

Lewin, K. 1950. *Field theory in social science: selected theoretical papers.* New York: Harper.

Marrow A. J. 1969. *The practical theorist: the life and work of Kurt Lewin.* New York: Basic Books.

Zusne, Leonard. 1984. *Biographical dictionary of psychology.* Westport, Conn.: Greenwood Press.

LIKERT SCALE. A scale of items with the graduations of response along a single dimension; that is, "strongly agree, agree, undecided, disagree, and strongly disagree" with a given statement would form a five-point Likert Scale.

Rensis Likert (1903–81) was born in Cheyenne, Wyoming. He studied economics and sociology at the University of Michigan and psychology at Columbia University (Ph.D., 1932). He taught in the Department of Psychology, New York University (1930–35) and then became director of research for the Life Insurance Agency Management Association in Hartford, Connecticut, where he began a program of research on the effectiveness of different styles of supervision. In 1939 he was appointed director of the Division of Program Surveys in the Bureau of Agricultural Economics, U.S. Department of Agriculture. In 1946 he set up an interdisciplinary Institute of Research in Social Science at the University of Michigan. The institute grew rapidly and became the largest university-based organization for research in the social sciences in the United States. After twenty-five years, Likert retired as director of the Institute for Social Research (1970) but continued to work as a private consultant on problems of organization and management.

Sources

Goldenson, Robert, ed. 1984. *Longman dictionary of psychology and psychiatry.* New York: Longman.

Sills, David L., ed. 1968. *International encyclopedia of the social sciences.* New York: Macmillan and Free Press.

Zusne, Leonard. 1984. *Biographical dictionary of psychology.* Westport, Conn.: Greenwood Press.

Zusne, Leonard. 1987. *Eponyms in psychology: a dictionary and sourcebook.* Westport, Conn.: Greenwood Press.

LINCOLNESQUE. Pertaining to the character of the sixteenth president of the United States and the spirit of his efforts found in American institutions.

Abraham Lincoln (1809–65) was born in Kentucky and raised in poverty with little schooling. In 1837 he settled in Salem, Illinois, worked in a store, and later worked variously as a surveyor, village postmaster, and rail-splitter. Meanwhile, he studied law, practiced, and entered the state legislature (1834–41) and served a term in Congress (1847–49). In opposing the Mexican War, he appeared unpatriotic, and so he avoided politics until 1854 when the slavery issue reemerged. He joined the new Republican cause, and by 1856 he was a likely candidate for the U.S. presidency. In 1858 he was nominated, making the memorable and prescient statement: "A house divided against itself cannot stand." Lincoln lost the election but was elected for the period 1861–65, the years of the Civil War. A vigorous and skilled leader in war, he was deeply affected by its tragedy, as his famous address at the dedication of the soldiers' cemetery at Gettysburg showed (1863). Although at times the war seemed to be going against him, he was reelected, and at its end he uttered his policy to unite America, as he said: "With malice toward none; with charity for all." While watching a performance at Ford's Theater on April 14, 1965, Lincoln was shot by John Wilkes Booth, an actor, and died the next day. He was considered a martyr, an object of adulation, a noble statesman, a skillful politician, and a man of great humanity.

Sources

Anderson, Dwight. 1982. *Abraham Lincoln: the quest for immortality.* New York: Alfred A. Knopf.

Handlin, Oscar, and Handlin, Lillian. 1980. *Abraham Lincoln and the Union.* Boston: Little, Brown.

Magnussen, Magnus; Goring, Rosemary; and Thorn, John O., eds. 1990. *Chambers biographical dictionary.* Edinburgh: Chambers Ltd.

Malone, Dumas, ed. 1933. *Dictionary of American biography.* Vol. VI. New York: Charles Scribner's Sons.

Neeley, Mark E., Jr. 1982. *The Abraham Lincoln encyclopedia.* New York: McGraw-Hill.

LINDAHL EQUILIBRIUM. Equilibrium in Lindahl's model which requires that each individual pay a tax rate equal to his marginal utility from the goods. Every person gains from the provision of public goods; in addition, there is a condition that each person consumes his most preferred (optimal) amount of the public goods given his share of taxes. In applying the model, there are problems in reaching complete agreement, and possibly people will not indicate their true preferences and seek, for example, to get things free (Pearce, 1986).

Erik Robert Lindahl (1891–1960) was born in Stockholm and died in Uppsala, Sweden. He is noted for his work in the famous Stockholm School of Economics. He was the son of a prison officer and grew up in Jönköpine, southern Sweden. He studied at secondary school in Stockholm and at the University of Lund (LL.B., 1914) and wrote his doctorate on public finance (1924). He investigated the national income of Sweden between 1861 and 1930, and researched at the Institute for Social Sciences, Stockholm University, with support from the Rockefeller Foundation. He published his noted *Studies in the Theory of Money and Capital* (1939), was appointed a professor at the University of Uppsala (1942), and retired in 1958.

Sources

Eatwell, John; Milgate, Murray; and Newman, Peter. 1987. *The new Palgrave: a dictionary of economics.* London: Macmillan.

Pearce, David W., ed. 1986. *Macmillan dictionary of modern economics.* New York: Macmillan.

LINDBERGH LAW. An act of the U.S. Congress, passed on May 18, 1934, which, under penalty of death or imprisonment, forbids taking interstate or overseas anyone who has been kidnapped. If the victim is not released within seven days after the kidnapping, the law presumes that person has been taken out of state or abroad. A further act, January 24, 1936, forbade the use of U.S. mails for ransom communications.

Charles Augustus Lindbergh (1902–74) was born in Detroit, attended the University of Wisconsin, but left to study flying in 1922, was commissioned in the U.S. Air Force reserve, and became an airmail pilot in 1925. In his plane, "The Spirit of St. Louis," he flew nonstop from New York to Paris, was appointed a colonel, and toured the country promoting aviation. In 1929 he married Anne Morrow, the daughter of Dwight W. Morrow, the U.S. ambassador in Mexico. Their son was kidnapped in 1932 and died. The trial and capture of the alleged kidnapper, Bruno Richard Hauptmann (1899–1936), was a celebrated criminal case, which caused the family much distress. Today there is doubt that the true killer was caught. Afterward the Lindberghs moved to England (1935), and later Charles worked with Alexis Carrel (1873–1944) on the invention of the artificial heart or profusion pump. He was convinced in 1938 that Germany had the world's superior air power, and on his return to the United States in 1939 made speeches favoring an isolationist policy for America. When falsely declared pro-Nazi, he resigned his reserve commission and quit the National Advisory Commission for Aeronautics. During World War II he flew combat missions in the Pacific. Later he devoted his time to conservation.

Sources

Magnussen, Magnus; Goring, Rosemary; and Thorn, John O., eds. 1990. *Chambers biographical dictionary.* Edinburgh: Chambers Ltd.

Mosley, Leonard. 1976. *Lindbergh: a biography.* New York: Doubleday.

Plano, Jack C., and Greenberg, Milton. 1989. *The American political dictionary.* New York: Holt, Rinehart and Winston.

Smith, Edward, and Zurcher, Arnold. 1968. *Dictionary of American politics.* New York: Barnes and Noble.

LINDLEY MURRAY. An able grammarian.

Lindley Murray (1745–1826) was born into a Quaker merchant's family in Swatara, Pennsylvania, educated there, spent his first twenty years of adult life as a lawyer, and made a personal fortune. In his late thirties he immigrated to York in England (1784). He settled at Holgate and supported philanthropic causes, for example, the mentally ill, and also wrote on religion and biography. In 1795 he wrote a school textbook, *English Grammar, Adapted to the Different Classes of Learners.* This work earned him the title of Father of English Grammar, and he is remembered for his definition: "English grammar is the art of speaking and writing the English language with propriety." Among his works were *English Exercises* (1797), *An English Reader* (1799), and *An English Spelling Book* (1804). All went to more than forty editions.

Sources

Gleason, Henry A., Jr. 1965. *Linguistics and English grammar.* New York: Holt, Rinehart and Winston.

Howatt, Anthony P.R. 1984. *A history of English language teaching.* Oxford: Oxford University Press.

Leonard, Sterling A. 1962. *The doctrine of correctness in English usage: 1700–1800.* New York: Russell and Russell.

Stephen, Leslie, and Lee, Sydney, eds. 1917. *The dictionary of national biography.* London: Oxford University Press.

LOCKEAN. Relating to the seventeenth-century English philosopher whose ideas helped initiate the English and French Enlightenment, advanced the course of modern science, and influence the ideas in the U.S. Constitution.

John Locke (1632–1704) was born at Wrington, Somerset, and educated at Westminster School and Christ Church, Oxford. From 1658 he taught moral philosophy at Oxford. He studied medicine at Oxford and qualified himself (without obtaining a degree) to practice medicine. He also studied chemistry. In 1667 he was adviser and physician to the earl of Shaftesbury, and in 1668 he was made a fellow of the Royal Society. By 1673 he had become secretary to the Council for Trade and Plantations. From 1683 to 1688 he lived in Holland, and on the accession of William of Orange he returned to England and became commissioner of appeals. Central to his philosophical writings were the concepts of civil liberty, religious toleration, the power of reason, and the value of experience. Among his published works are an *Essay Concerning Human Understanding* (1690) and *The Reasonableness of Christianity* (1695). In politics he questioned absolutism and preferred parliamentary government; he invoked the idea of a natural lawfulness that established humankind's reason and social consensus; he separated communal power into legislative, executive, and federative power, and judicial authority. And he assumed it natural that everyone would own their labor as they did property. The function of government was to preserve property, life, and liberty, ideas to which the French and the American revolutionaries owed much. In religion he advanced a theory of toleration that had political implications for persecution in his day. In economics he advanced a labor theory of value.

Sources

Ayers, Michael. 1991. *Locke*. London: Routledge.

Cranston, Maurice W. 1957. *John Locke: a biography*. Reprinted 1985. London: Longmans.

Dunn, John. 1984. *Locke*. Oxford: Oxford University Press.

Magnussen, Magnus; Goring, Rosemary; and Thorn, John O., eds. 1990. *Chambers biographical dictionary*. Edinburgh: Chambers Ltd.

Miller, David, ed. 1987. *The Blackwell encyclopedia of political thought*. Oxford: Basil Blackwell.

Stephen, Leslie, and Lee, Sydney, eds. 1917. *The dictionary of national biography*. London: Oxford University Press.

Woolhouse, Roger S. 1983. *Locke*. Brighton, England: Harvester Press.

Zusne, Leonard. 1984. *Biographical dictionary of psychology*. Westport, Conn.: Greenwood Press.

LOCKWOOD REPORT. A British education report that recommended that a Schools' Council for Curriculum and Examinations should be established (1964).

Sir John Francis Lockwood (1903–65) was a university administrator, born in Preston, Lancashire, son of a stockbroker, and educated at Preston Grammar School and Corpus Christie College, Oxford (1926). He became assistant lecturer in Latin, Manchester University (1927). He lectured in Greek, University College, London (1930–40), and he was a professor of Latin (1945–51) and master of Birkbeck College, University of London (1951–65). He was the vice-chancellor of the University of London (1955–58). With his administrative ability he played an important part on international committees. He is remembered for the Lockwood Report (1964), which led to the establishment of the Schools' Council, as well as the Lockwood Committee on Higher Education in Northern Ireland, which led to the establishment of the New University of Ulster.

Sources

Aldrich, Richard, and Gordon, Peter. 1987. *Dictionary of British educationists*. London: Woburn Press.

Page, G. Terry; Thomas, J. B.; and Marshall, A. R. 1977. *International dictionary of education*. London: Kogan Page.

Williams, E. T., and Nichols, C. S., eds. 1981. *Dictionary of national biography 1961–1970*. Oxford: Oxford University Press.

LODGE COROLLARY. A corollary to the Monroe Doctrine, which arose out of the projected sale of land in lower California, by an American syndicate to a group of Japanese investors. The harbor was deemed to have strategic military value. The corollary resolved that such strategic places could not be sold to a foreign country whose government might make military use of them against the United States. The Senate supported the solution (August 2, 1912), but President Taft (1857–1930) opposed it, and so the sale was never made.

Henry Cabot Lodge, Sr. (1850–1924) was a senator for over thirty years and chairman of the Foreign Relations Committee (1919–24). He is best known for his staunch opposition to President Woodrow Wilson (1856–1924) and the League of Nations. Born in Boston, Lodge graduated from Harvard (LL.B., 1874; Ph.D., 1876) and worked as an assistant editor of the *North American Review* (1873–76). He taught at Harvard (1876–79) before becoming a politician. He helped draft the Sherman Anti-Trust Act (1890). Lodge's political career is more closely tied to U.S. foreign policy: he drafted the Philippine Organic Act, was in charge of the Hay-Pauncefote Treaty (1901), and served on the Alaska Boundary Tribunal (1903). He became a close friend and adviser to President Theodore Roosevelt (1858–1919). As chairman of the Foreign Relations Committee, Lodge was a leading "reservationist" and an opponent to President Wilson. In the Harding administration, Lodge led the debate over the ratification of the German-Austrian Treaties, was delegate to the Washington Conference (1921–22), and introduced the Thomson-Urrutia Treaty which gave $25 million to Colombia.

Sources

Commager, Henry S., ed. 1968. *Documents of American history.* 8th ed. New York: Appleton-Century-Crofts.

Findling, John E. 1980. *Dictionary of American diplomatic history.* Westport, Conn.: Greenwood Press.

Garraty, John A. 1953. *Henry Cabot Lodge: a biography.* New York: Alfred A. Knopf.

Malone, Dumas, ed. 1933. *Dictionary of American biography.* Vol. VI. New York: Charles Scribner's Sons.

LOGAN'S LAMENT. A plea for peace.

John or James Logan (c. 1725–80), or Tahgahjute, was perhaps of full French ancestry or a half-white American Indian or the son of Shikellamy of the Mingo Indians. He may have been born at Shamokin (now Sunbury), Pennsylvania. One legend states that as a boy his father had been captured and raised by the Cayugas. John became known as a friendly Indian and had the respect of the Shawnee tribe who introduced him to his wife. In 1774 he came home to find all his relatives slaughtered, and he attributed their murder to Captain Michael Cresap. Logan declared vengeance on him, and, with the support of the Shawnees, he began fighting what became known as Lord Dunsmore's War. After great losses on both sides, the Indians were overcome. Even though he was avenged for his losses, Logan would not meet in peace with Governor Dunsmore, preferring instead to write a letter to him, known as Logan's Lament. He read it aloud under an elm that is now in Logan's State Park, Circleville. An

368   LOGAN'S LAW

eloquent plea for peace, the lament appeared in newspapers and schoolbooks in
America and is now part of America's popular history. Later, it was shown that
a gang of marauders, and not Cresap, had slaughtered Logan's relatives. So the
vengeance was misplaced, and the war was unnecessary. Further to this misfortune, Logan died in a drunken brawl at the hands of his nephew, who, unknown to Logan, was the last living member of his family.

Sources

Johnson, Thomas H. 1966. *The Oxford companion to American history.* New York:
    Oxford University Press.
Malone, Dumas, ed. 1933. *Dictionary of American biography.* Vol. VI. New York:
    Charles Scribner's Sons.
Matthews, Mitford M. 1966. *A dictionary of Americanisms on historical principles.* Chi-
    cago: University of Chicago Press.
Who was who in America. 1969. Historical volume: 1607–1896. Chicago: Marquis.

LOGAN'S LAW. A law for business success in the theater: All plays should
take their protagonists through experiences that lead to learning or discovering
something about themselves that could have been known all along, but that they
have been blind to. The discovery must be emotionally shattering and change
the course of their life—always for the better. The revelation raises the individual's moral position, the audience becomes excited and healthier-minded, and
the play lives. After his careful study of Aristotle, Shakespeare, and modern
success in theater, Maxwell Anderson (1888–1959), the American playwright,
made these recommendations and told Joshua Logan about them.

Joshua Lockwood Logan (1908–88), theater and film director, producer and
writer, was born in Texarkana, Texas, and was educated at Culver Military
Academy for five years. He studied at Princeton (1927) and there became deeply
interested in theater. In his final year he took a scholarship to the Moscow Art
Theater for eight months learning under Constantin Stanislavsky. Logan worked
on many plays and movies during the 1930s as an actor, stage manager, producer, and director. He became a notable director with the musical *I Married
an Angel* (1938). In the late 1940s he directed two successful Broadway productions, *Mister Roberts* (1948) and the Pulitzer Prize winner, *South Pacific*
(1949). He also directed *Annie Get Your Gun* (1946), *Paint Your Wagon* (1969),
and several films including *Camelot* (1967). During much of his later life he
was subject to manic-depressive illness, and as his career declined he traveled
throughout America offering help to similar sufferers.

Sources

Logan, Joshua L. 1977. *Josh: my up and down, in and out life.* London: Allen and
    Unwin.
Rothe, Anna, ed. 1949. *Current biography yearbook.* New York: H. W. Wilson.
Trotsky, Susan, ed. 1989. *Contemporary authors.* Vol. 126. Detroit: Gale Research.

LOLITA SYNDROME. An unreasoning, self-destructive passion, commonly
found among middle-aged men, for sexual relations with beautiful nymphets.

Lolita is a gorgeous nymphet in Vladimir Nabokov's novel *Lolita* (1955). When Lolita's mother, Charlotte Haze, dies by accident, her stepfather, Humbert Humbert, who had recently married Charlotte merely to be near Lolita and felt so infatuated with her that he even planned to kill Charlotte, takes the nymphet on a cross-country trip intending to seduce her. Instead she seduces him. He becomes ever more infatuated and jealously protective. She escapes, and two years later, married and pregnant, she returns to tell him that while she was his lover she was seeing another man, Clare Quilty, a famous playwright. Insanely jealous, Humbert murders Quilty, is imprisoned, and dies of heart failure before his trial.

Vladimir V. Nabokov (1899–1977) was born in Saint Petersburg into a rich Russian aristocratic family, attended a progressive school, and when the revolution came immigrated to England where he and his brother went to Cambridge on a scholarship and studied Russian and French literature. On graduation he joined his family in Berlin. There his father was murdered. For fifteen years he lived in Berlin, and he later went to Paris (1937–40). He immigrated to the United States and was naturalized in 1945. He became a prominent American poet, novelist, critic, and playwright. He was an entomologist at the Museum of Comparative Zoology, Harvard University, taught Slavic languages at Wellesley College, and became a professor of European literature at Cornell University. From 1959 he lived in Switzerland and became a full-time writer. Among his works are *The Real Life of Sebastian Knight* (1941), *Bend Sinister* (1947), *Pale Fire* (1962), and *Ada* (1969).

Sources

Field, Andrew. 1973. *Nabokov: a bibliography.* New York: McGraw-Hill.

Field, Andrew. 1977. *Nabokov: his life in part.* London: Hamilton.

Hart, James D. 1983. *The Oxford companion to American literature.* New York: Oxford University Press.

Magnussen, Magnus; Goring, Rosemary; and Thorn, John O., eds. 1990. *Chambers biographical dictionary.* Edinburgh: Chambers Ltd.

Nabokov, Vladimir V. 1955. *Lolita.* London: Weidenfeld and Nicolson.

Nabokov, Valdimir V. 1968. *Keys to Lolita.* Bloomington: Indiana University Press.

Nabokov, Valdimir V. 1971. *The annotated Lolita.* With notes by Alfred Appel. London: Weidenfeld and Nicolson.

LOMBARD'S LAW. In organizations, programmed activities (e.g., scheduled meetings) drive out unprogrammed activities (e.g., informal discussions).

George Francis Fabyan Lombard (b. 1911), born in Newton, Massachusetts, was educated at the Rivers School, Milton Academy, and studied economics at Harvard. He became an assistant dean at the Harvard Business School (HBS) in 1936 and later found that his main interest lay in the human problems of administration. He researched with Elton Mayo, taught with F. J. Roethlisberger, and published *Behavior in a Selling Group* (1955). During World War II he was an instructor in Officer Training Courses at HBS. After becoming associate dean at HBS in 1962, Lombard was *ex officio* member of forty-five committees and subcommittees. Although they were seldom scheduled to meet at the same time, he often had pre-breakfast, breakfast, and evening meetings. Consequently, he suggested the Law—a variant on Gresham's Law—at the end of a discussion of how faculty members could spend more time on original work instead of routine activities. Lombard's Law earned currency in HBS classes, and students would drop by Lombard's office simply to find the person behind the Law. Since then, the Law has been overheard in discussions between HBS alumni as far from Boston as the Singapore Airport, and has appeared in a footnote to an article in the *Harvard Business Review*. Lombard's solution to the problems flowing from the Law was to "program the unprogrammed." He made free time in his calendar, and he dropped by colleagues' offices unexpectedly, sometimes to some consternation, for informal discussions. Among the results, he got to know faculty members and their assistants better, and he earned a reputation for being approachable. He and they discovered that they could work together as real people and not just as voices on the telephone. As Louis E. Kirstein Professor of Human Relations, Lombard retired emeritus (1985), and with Charles Savage published a study of factory workers in Colombia, *Sons of the Machine* (1986).

See also GRESHAM'S LAW.

Sources

Barnes, Louis B. 1981. Managing the paradox of organizational trust. *Harvard Business Review* 59:109.

Harvard Business School. 1985. *Course development and research profile*. Soldiers Field, Boston: Harvard Business School, pp. 34–37.

Jaques Cattell Press, ed. 1973. *American men and women of science: the social and behavioral sciences*. New York: Jaques Cattell and R. R. Bowker.

Personal Communication.

LOMBROSIAN THEORY. A deterministic theory in criminology that asserts criminals comprise a biological type—long, low jaw, flat nose, insensitivity to pain—that reverts to a primitive form of man. His theory opposed both the classical theory, which assumed a person chose to act according to the pleasure or pain anticipated, and the social psychological theory, which assumed that individuals' actions result from custom and imitation. Lombrosian ideas were greatly undermined by Charles Goring (1913).

Cesare Lombroso (1836–1909) was born at Verona, Italy, of Jewish parents and educated by the Jesuits; he studied medicine at the University of Pavia (1858) and surgery at the University of Genoa (1859). His major positions at the University of Turin were as a professor of legal medicine and public hygiene (1876); psychiatry (1896); and criminal anthropology (1906). He presented the theories in his books, *The Delinquent Man* (1876) and *The Man of Genius* (1888). He assumed that criminals belonged to a distinct anthropological type and that genius springs from some form of physical or mental illness. His theories have been largely rejected, but his vast collection of anthropometric data on criminals has been valuable to criminologists. His observation, that when in the course of interrogation a person tells a lie, his blood pressure changes significantly, anticipated the modern lie-detector. After much criticism, Lombroso greatly qualified his theory.

Sources

Goring, Charles. 1913. *The English convict: a statistical study.* London: Home Office, Prisons Commission.

Jones, Barry. 1989. *The Macmillan dictionary of biography.* South Melbourne: Macmillan.

Lombroso-Ferraro, Gina. 1911. *Criminal man according to the classification of Cesare Lombroso.* New York: Putnam.

Mannheim, Hermann, ed. 1972. *Pioneers in criminology.* 2d ed. Montclair, N.J.: Patterson Smith.

Sills, David L., ed. 1968. *International encyclopedia of the social sciences.* New York: Macmillan and Free Press.

LORD HAW-HAW. A traitor, after the name given to the British broadcaster in Nazi Germany during World War II.

William Brooke Joyce (1906–46), born in New York and educated at a Jesuit college in Ireland, served briefly in the British Army and later trained as an officer while studying English at London University. He became propaganda director of Oswald Mosley's British Union of Fascists and once was charged with riotous assembly (1934). Joyce began tutoring for a living. Later, he established the National Socialist League, a political party that espoused the abolition of Parliament, compulsory membership for workers in trade unions, and the reconstitution of the English House of Lords as the controlling agency for the British economy. A fascist and anti-Semite, he published *National Socialism Now* (1937), and with dazzling oratory he spoke with much support on the need for an Anglo-German pact to combat Bolshevism and international Jewry. In August 1939 he went to Berlin and became a radio news broadcaster. In Britain his unidentifiable voice earned him the title "Lord Haw-Haw of Zeesen." Beginning with "Germany Calling," initially his broadcasts were amusing, but soon they warned that Germany knew more about Britain's military problems than did most Britons. The German Foreign Office commissioned Joyce to write *Twilight over England* (1940), and in July that year he was identified as the voice of "Lord Haw-Haw." His British passport lapsed, he became a German, and after Hitler died in April 1945, Joyce made his final broadcast. He was captured in May and taken to England where in September he was tried and found guilty of high treason. Unsuccessful appeals were made against the finding on the basis of his citizenship and the status of his British passport. He was hanged in January 1946.

Sources

Cole, John A. 1964. *Lord Haw-Haw and William Joyce: the full story.* New York. Farrar, Straus and Giroux.

Hall, J. W., ed. 1987. *Trial of William Joyce.* (Microreproduction of the original. London: Hodge, 1946.) Aldershot: Gregg.

Roberts, C.E. Bechhofer, ed. 1946. *The trial of William Joyce: with some notes on other recent trials for treason etc.* London: Jarrolds.

Selwyn, Francis. 1987. *Hitler's Englishman: the crime of Lord Haw-Haw.* London: Routledge and Kegan Paul.

West, Rebecca. 1949. *The meaning of treason.* Reprinted 1984 with new introduction. London: Virago.

LORENZ CURVE. In economics, a widely used technique to represent and analyze the size and distribution of income and wealth. The curve plots cumulative proportions of income received as income units and are arranged in ascending order. The curve was proposed in 1905 to compare and analyze inequalities of wealth in a country during different epochs, or in different countries during the same epoch. Since then, the curve has been widely used as a convenient diagram to summarize information on the distribution of income and wealth.

Max Otto Lorenz (1876–1957) was born in Burlington, Iowa. He spent his professional life as a government statistician unconcerned with distributional issues. In 1921 Wesley Clair Mitchell (1874–1948), who followed Lorenz at the University of Wisconsin, and Wilford I. King (1880–1962) and others, drew what was called "the well-known Lorenz curve" in various conceivable ways. But widespread familiarity with the curve did not become evident until the publication of economics textbooks after World War II. Prewar texts, including one co-authored by Lorenz, devoted little space to income or wealth inequality and none to the Lorenz curve because it was not until then that sufficient data were available to make a chapter on inequality interesting, or the presentation of the curve worthwhile. The concept was promoted by Mitchell.

Sources

Eatwell, John; Milgate, Murray; and Newman, Peter. 1987. *The new Palgrave: a dictionary of economics.* London: Macmillan.

Greenwald, Douglas, ed. 1982. *Encyclopedia of economics.* New York: McGraw-Hill.

Lorenz, Max O. 1905. Methods of measuring the concentration of wealth. *Journal of the American Statistical Association* 9:209–219.

Pearce, David W., ed. 1986. *Macmillan dictionary of modern economics.* New York: Macmillan.

LOUIS QUATORZE. Characteristic of the period 1643–1715 in France, especially its architecture and decoration.

Louis XIV (1638–1715) was called "Le roi Soleil" because of the splendor of his court and his adoption of the rising sun as his emblem. His reign was the longest of any European monarch and marked the peak of French absolutism. The son of Louis XIII and Anne of Austria, he ascended the throne at 5 years of age, not assuming personal rule until 1661. He was able to assess ability and talent in others, and he encouraged great artists to celebrate and enhance the magnificence of his reign, for example, Molière, Bossuet, Le Nôtre, Mansart, and Le Brun. Because of the influence of his minister of war, François-Michel Le Tellier Louvois, Louis XIV pursued a bellicose policy toward the Protestant states and the French Huguenots. Admitting he had loved war too much, he died in a bankrupt nation. Louis Quatorze style may be contrasted with Louis Treize style, after Louis XIII (1610–43) with its changes from rich and free Renaissance forms to classicism; and the Louis Quinze style after Louis XV (1750–74) with its fantasy and lightness of the Rococo period; and the Louis Seize style after Louis XVI (1774–93) with its return to the classic ideals of ornamentation.

Sources

Carsten, F. L., ed. 1961. *The new Cambridge modern history.* The ascendancy of France 1648–88. Cambridge: University Press.

Cronin, Vincent. 1990. *Louis XIV.* London: Collins and Harvill.

Magnussen, Magnus; Goring, Rosemary; and Thorn, John O., eds. 1990. *Chambers biographical dictionary.* Edinburgh: Chambers Ltd.

McHenry, Robert, ed. 1992. *The new encyclopedia Britannica.* Chicago: Encyclopedia Britannica, Inc.

LOVESTONEITE. An anti-Stalinist supporter of one of the strong leadership groups in the internal conflict within the Communist party of America in the late 1920s.

Jacob Leibstein (1898–1985) was born in Lithuania and immigrated to the United States in 1908. He changed his name to Jay Lovestone, attended public schools in New York City, and studied at City College of New York. He became a committed socialist and helped found the American Communist party in 1919. He was its general secretary, edited its journal, and found in the factional struggles within the party in the 1920s that he did not have enough support. At the Communist International Congress in 1928 he was removed from office. Thereafter he led a small group of anti-Stalinist supporters, or ''Lovestoneites.'' Because he was so capable a tactician, he became the director of international affairs in the International Ladies Garment Workers Union in 1943. Later, he became director of the International Confederation of Free Trade Unions (1949–63) and was director of Department of International Affairs for the American Federation of Labor-Congress of Industrial Organizations (1963–74).

Sources

Fink, Gary M., ed. 1984. *Biographical dictionary of American labor.* Westport, Conn.: Greenwood Press.

Who's who in America, 1984–85. Chicago: Marquis.

LOWRY MODEL. A model of the generation and spatial allocation of urban activities and land uses developed in 1964 for the Pittsburgh urban region. The urban activities were total population, basic (manufacturing and primary) employment, and service employment; the corresponding land uses were residential, industrial, and service. The model uses economic theory to establish the overall activity levels. In 1966 the model was reformulated by R. A. Garin and is known as the Garin-Lowry model.

Ira South Lowry (b. 1930) was born in Laredo, Texas, and educated at the University of Texas. He studied economics at the University of California, Berkeley (Ph.D., Economics, 1959). As a noted American urban economist and demographer, he began work in 1963 at the Rand Corporation in Santa Monica, California, where he was a senior economist in the management science department. He was also a consultant on regional planning, highway development, and urban problems, generally using computer modeling to establish solutions to his research problems. Among his many publications are *Portrait of a Region* [Pittsburgh] (1963); *Metropolitan Populations to 1985: Trial Projections* (1964); *A Model of Metropolis* (1964); *Migration and Metropolitan Growth: Two Analytical Models* (1966); and *The Science and Politics of Ethnic Enumeration* (1980).

Sources

Jaques Cattell Press, ed. 1978. *American men and women of science: the social and behavioral sciences.* New York: Jaques Cattell and R. R. Bowker.

Johnston, Ronald J. 1981. *The dictionary of human geography.* Oxford: Basil Blackwell.

Petersen, William, and Petersen, Renee. 1985. *Dictionary of demography.* Westport, Conn.: Greenwood Press.

LUCY, LUCY'S CHILD. The oldest, most complete, and best preserved skeleton of any erect walking human ancestor ever found; *Homo habilis,* the ancestor of *Homo erectus* and *Homo sapiens*—the ancestors of today's humans. Lucy's child is the name given by Donald Johanson and James Shreeve (1989) to a hominid found by Louis S. B. Leakey (1903–72). It had a body like Lucy's but a brain empowered far beyond her reach, and may have been a specimen of *Homo habilis,* "Handy Man," from which *Homo erectus* could have descended, an ancestor of *Homo sapiens* to whom present-day humankind turns for its origins.

Lucy, approximately 3.5 million years old, was found on November 30, 1974 by Donald C. Johanson, an American paleoanthropologist, and Tom Gray, a graduate student, near Hadar on the Awash River, Ethiopia. Lucy's official name is AL 288-1 in the Hadar collection. Fully grown, Lucy would have been about 3'6" when she died, and aged between 25 and 30. She appears to have died quietly, from either illness or accidental drowning. Her body was buried deeper and deeper under sand and mud for several millennia, until the rains of Hadar exposed her remains by chance to Johanson and Gray. For five years Johanson kept her in his office at the Cleveland Museum of Natural History, and in 1979 her discovery was made official. Her name was taken from a popular song composed by John Lennon and performed by the Beatles, "Lucy in the Sky with Diamonds." On the day of her discovery, the song was being played at the camp where the find was being celebrated. The original Lucy in the song was thought to be no particular person, and it was thought that the key words in the title referred to Lennon's alleged use of LSD, a psychedelic drug which had a reputation for stimulating creativity, as in composing music. According to another account, the song title came from the name of a little girl who attended the same nursery school as John Lennon's three-year-old son, Julian. Shortly before February 28, 1967, when the Beatles first rehearsed the song, Julian came home from his nursery school with a painting. When asked by his father what it was, Julian said, "Lucy, in the sky with diamonds."

Sources

Johanson, Donald C., and Edey, Maitland A. 1981. *Lucy: the beginnings of humankind.* New York: Simon and Schuster.

Johanson, Donald C., and Shreeve, James. 1989. *Lucy's child: the discovery of a human ancestor.* New York: Avon Books.

Lewisohn, Mark. 1989. *The complete Beatles recording sessions.* London: Hamlyn.

LUCY STONE LEAGUE. A league of woman who wished to maintain their identity and individual rights and refused to change their form of identification from their unmarried name to their married name. They were sometimes known as "Lucy Stoners."

Lucy Stone (1818–93) was born in West Brookfield, Massachusetts, and as a child was aghast at the Bible for upholding men's domination of women. Because her father refused to provide the funds, she put herself through college and graduated from the only college that accepted women at the time, Oberlin (1847), and immediately began her vigorous career by supporting women's political rights and by opposing slavery. She called for a Women's Rights Convention to be held in Worcester, Massachusetts, and at her own expense published the proceedings. She helped establish the National American Women's Association, was its president, and founded the *Women's Journal* (1870), the Association's official publication for fifty years. Lucy Stone spoke eloquently and often for women's rights throughout the United States and in 1855 married Henry Brown Blackwell, an anti-slavery advocate. To draw attention to the inequality of the marriage laws, Mrs. Lucy Stone—as she became known—and her husband refused to have her adopt her husband's surname. The Lucy Stone League was formed in 1921 to defend the right of all married women to use their own name and not to be forced to adopt the name of their spouses.

Sources

Hendrickson, Robert. 1988. *The dictionary of eponyms: names that became words.* New York: Dorset.

Magnussen, Magnus; Goring, Rosemary; and Thorn, John O., eds. 1990. *Chambers biographical dictionary.* Edinburgh: Chambers Ltd.

Malone, Dumas, ed. 1935. *Dictionary of American biography.* Vol. IX. New York: Charles Scribner's Sons.

Uglow, Jennifer S. 1982. *The Macmillan dictionary of women's biography.* London: Macmillan.

LUDDITE. A person who opposes technological innovation and may destroy machinery for fear it could reduce employment, impair work conditions, lower the quality of life, and advance the techniques of war.

Ned Ludd (fl. 1779), a Leicestershire youth reputed to have been mentally impaired, destroyed two or more stocking-frames or knitting-machines in a local factory sometime between 1782 and 1799. From him the term *Luddite* was taken to denote rioters and their leaders—''King Ludds''—who deliberately destroyed machinery to protect their employment and pay levels in the factories of northern England (1812–18). The legend has not been adequately confirmed, and it remains speculative.

Sources

Brewer, Ebenezer Cobham. 1970. *Brewer's dictionary of phrase and fable.* Centenary ed. Rev. by Ivor H. Evans. New York: Harper and Row.

Hendrickson, Robert. 1988. *The dictionary of eponyms: names that became words.* New York: Dorset.

Magnussen, Magnus; Goring, Rosemary; and Thorn, John O., eds. 1990. *Chambers biographical dictionary.* Edinburgh: Chambers Ltd.

Peel, Frank. 1968. *The risings of the Luddites, Chartists and Plug-Drawers.* London: Cass.

Reid, Robert. 1986. *Land of lost content: the Luddite revolt.* London: Heinemann.

Thomis, Malcolm I. 1972. *The Luddites: machine-breaking in Regency England.* New York: Schocken Books.

LUTHERAN, LUTHERANISM. Relating to the sixteenth-century German Protestant reformer and to his doctrines; a traditional Christian belief centering on the conviction that only through having faith in God's grace can a person be made righteous, and that the sermon alone proclaims God's grace. In 1947 the Lutheran World Federation was formed in Germany, the United States, and Scandinavia, flourished elsewhere, and in the 1980s attracted a following of 60 to 70 million.

Martin Luther (1483–1546), the son of a slate cutter, was born and died at Eisleben, in Prussian Saxony. His early education was at Magdeburg and Eisenach; in 1505 he graduated from the University of Erfurt and taught physics and the ethics of Aristotle. At Erfurt he became a monk and entered the Augustine monastery; he was a priest in 1507 and then appointed a professor of philosophy at the University of Wittenberg. His first important reform was to publish ninety-five theses against the sale of indulgences. The theses were condemned as heresy, and he was violently attacked. In 1520 he was excommunicated, and his works were burned. In 1522 he completed his translation of the New Testament, and shortly afterward the book of Moses and Psalms and a hymn book. His works of over sixty volumes provide the basis for the Lutheran Church and its religious beliefs. He also wrote hymns, for example, ''Away in a Manger'' and he introduced the Lutheran chorale to the Reformation church service.

Sources

Atkinson, James. 1983. *Martin Luther: prophet to the Church Catholic.* Grand Rapids, Mich.: William B. Eerdman's.

Brecht, Martin. 1985. *Martin Luther: his road to Reformation 1483–1521*. Philadelphia: Fortress Press.

Brendler, Gerhard. 1990. *Martin Luther: theology and revolution*. Trans. Claude R. Foster. New York: Oxford University Press.

Erikson, Erik H. 1959. *Young man Luther: a study in psychoanalysis and history*. London: Faber.

Miller, David, ed. 1987. *The Blackwell encyclopedia of political thought*. Oxford: Basil Blackwell.

O'Neill, Judith. 1975. *Martin Luther*. London: Cambridge University Press.

Pelikan, Jaroslav. 1968. *Spirit versus structure: Luther and the institutions of the church*. London: Collins.

Rupp, E. G. 1968. Luther and the German Reformation to 1529. In G. R. Elton. *The new Cambridge modern history*. Vol. II. Cambridge: Cambridge University Press, pp. 70–95.

Siggins, Ian D.K., ed. 1972. *Luther*. Edinburgh: Oliver and Boyd.

LYCURGUS. A severe or harsh lawmaker; characteristic of the constitutional innovations attributed to the Spartan lawgiver.

Lycurgus (seventh century B.C.) was a Spartan, and the traditional author of the laws and institutions of Sparta, the rigid social code by which Sparta's aristocracy was kept apart from the other inhabitants, and of the system of military education by which between the ages of 6 and 20 the strictest obedience, self-discipline, and rigorous training were imposed on all Spartan boys. Lycurgus's origins are obscure; some say he may have been a hero or a god; others believe that he belonged to the Eurypontid house and was a regent for Charillus, the Eurypontid King.

Sources

Jones, Barry. 1989. *The Macmillan dictionary of biography*. Melbourne: Macmillan.

McHenry, Robert, ed. 1992. *The new encyclopedia Britannica*. Chicago: Encyclopedia Britannica, Inc.

Magnussen, Magnus; Goring, Rosemary; and Thorn, John O., eds. 1990. *Chambers biographical dictionary*. Edinburgh: Chambers Ltd.

LYNCH. To execute for a crime without the proper trial or judgment. The origin of the term is not securely known.

Charles Lynch (1736–96) was born at Chestnut Hill, the family estate, Lynchburg, Virginia. He married, settled in Bedford County, became a wealthy planter, and was made a justice of the peace (1766). The American Revolution disrupted the normal operations of the courts so that an extralegal court was established to punish lawlessness, and Lynch presided. Frequent convictions were dealt with by summary whippings. When a loyalist conspiracy was discovered in 1780, Lynch's extralegal court tried and sentenced the conspirators. Lynch had to explain, but was exonerated two years later because, although his actions were not legal, they were justified by the imminent danger at the time. From this came the term *lynch law,* that is, the putting of suspects to death without adequate recourse to law.

William Lynch (1742–1820) of Pittsylvania in Virginia, created a judicial tribunal in Virginia in about 1776. According to Edgar Allan Poe (1809–49), William Lynch led citizens to curb public disorder by using corporal punishment adequate to the crime (1780). So "lynch law" came to mean mob justice without using the law. Sometimes alleged criminals were hanged.

James Lynch FitzStephen (fl. 1493 or 1526) was mayor or warden of Galway. He tried, found guilty, condemned, and executed his own son for murder.

Other legends suggest the term comes from the meetings of self-appointed lawmen at Lynch's Creek, South Carolina, in 1786.

Sources

Cutler, James E. 1905. *Lynch law: an investigation into the history of lynching in the United States.* New York: Longman, Green.

Malone, Dumas, ed. 1933. *Dictionary of American biography.* Vol. VI. New York: Charles Scribner's Sons.

Partridge, Eric. 1950. *Name into word.* New York: Books for Librarians Press.

LYNSKEY TRIBUNAL. A British inquiry into the Board of Trade (1948), which centered on the alleged bribery and corruption of John Belcher and other officials by Sidney Stanley, an undischarged bankrupt, during the Labor government shortly after World War II. The Labor party was embarrassed by charges that government members received rewards and payments for the granting of licenses and permission, and the withdrawal of any proceedings.

George Justin Lynskey (1888–1957) was born in West Derby, Liverpool, son of a solicitor. He was educated at Saint Francis Xavier's College and the University of Liverpool and was awarded the LL.D. in 1951. He entered his father's firm of solicitors, was called to the bar in 1920, and became a King's Counsel in 1930. On the Northern Circuit he was most successful, and he also enjoyed a high reputation in London. He was made a judge of Salford Hundred Court of Record, and in 1944 he was raised to the King's Bench and knighted. In 1948 he chaired judicial inquiries into the Board of Trade—Lynskey Tribunal— and later declined promotion to the Court of Appeal.

See also SIDNEY STANLEY PRINCIPLE OF FINANCE.

Sources

Keesings contemporary archives: weekly diary of world events. 1949:9810. London: Keesings Publications.

Robinton, Madeline R. 1953. The Lynskey tribunal: the British method of dealing with political corruption. *Political Science Quarterly* 68, 1:109–124. Reprinted in Arnold J. Heidenheimer, ed. *Political corruption: readings in comparative analysis.* New York: Holt, Rinehart and Winston, pp. 249–258.

Who was who, 1951–60. Vol. V. London: Adam and Charles Black.

Williams, E. T., and Palmer, Helen M., eds. 1971. *Dictionary of national biography 1951–1960.* London: Oxford University Press.

LYSENKOISM. The political doctrine of a chief Soviet geneticist stating that acquired characteristics are heritable, that is, Lamarckism.

Trofim Denisovich Lysenko (1898–1976) was an agronomist and geneticist. He was born at Karlovka, Ukraine, and reputedly taught good crop husbandry to peasants during the famines of the early 1930s. In the belief that the phases of plant growth can be accelerated by short doses of low temperatures, he constructed a quasiscientific "theory" that good husbandry can alter heredity. In 1949 he received the Order of Lenin, and he was awarded the Stalin prize for his *Agrobiology* (1948). From 1938 to 1956 and from 1958 to 1962, he controlled the Academy of Agricultural Sciences; he held his post in the Institute of Genetics until 1965 when he resigned due to ill-health. When Khrushchev came to power and introduced new agrarian policies, Lysenko was put aside. He was reinstated in 1958 but today his theory is discounted.

See also LAMARCKISM.

Sources

Devine, Elizabeth; Held, Michael; Vinson, James; and Walsh, George, eds. 1983. *Thinkers of the twentieth century: a biographical, bibliographical and critical dictionary.* London: Macmillan.

Magnussen, Magnus; Goring, Rosemary; and Thorn, John O., eds. 1990. *Chambers biographical dictionary.* Edinburgh: Chambers Ltd.

Medvedev, Zhores A. 1969. *The rise and fall of T. D. Lysenko.* New York: Columbia University Press.

M

MAASTRICHT TREATY. A treaty to promote economic and political unity and cooperation among twelve member states of Europe: United Kingdom, Belgium, France, Germany, Italy, Luxembourg, Netherlands, Denmark, Ireland, Greece, Spain, and Portugal. Among its many provisions are new security and defense arrangements. After years of discussion, the Maastricht Treaty on European Unity was agreed to in December 1991 and formally signed on February 7, 1992. Denmark did not sign it, and the Danish electorate voted against signing it as it was then constituted on June 2, 1992. When the ratification timetable was revised, so that Denmark would not have to use a European currency or take part in a common defense policy, the Danish electorate agreed to join the Treaty in May 1993. Those elsewhere who opposed the treaty saw it as a product of ambitious European bureaucrats imposing unity on Europeans without adequate consultation with the people. Others queried it because of the implications it might have for currency values and industrial relations. Still others objected on nationalistic grounds.

Maastricht, Netherlands, is the capital of Limburg Province on the Maas (Meuse) River and was originally a Roman fortress near the Belgian frontier. It has the oldest church in the Netherlands. In 1284 it was controlled by the dukes of Brabant and the prince-bishop of Liege. In 1579, 8,000 inhabitants were murdered by the invading Spanish who took the city from Dutch rebels. It was returned to the Dutch in 1632, and in the next 180 years it was lost twice to the French. The Nazis took it in 1940, and it was recaptured by the Americans in 1944.

Sources

An analysis of the Maastricht Treaty. 1992. London: International Currency Review.
Blanpain, Roger. 1992. *Labor law and industrial relations of the European union: Maas-*

tricht and beyond, from a community to a union. Deventer, Netherlands: Kluwer
Academic Publisher.

Canby, Courtlandt. 1984. *The encyclopedia of historic places.* London: Mansell Publishing.

Keesings contemporary archives: record of world events. 1991:38504; 1992:39205, 39244. London: Keesings Publications.

Treaty on European union. 1992. Luxembourg: Office of Official Publications of the European Communities.

MABO DECISION. A decision in the Australian High Court, June 3 1992, that the Meriam, the indigenous inhabitants of the Murray Islands, Torres Strait (90 miles northeast of Cape York, Queensland, Australia), possess rights to land on those islands (see *Mabo and Others* v. *the State of Queensland*). This court decision has wider significance for indigenous people in Australia: it revokes the legal assumption of Australia as *terra nullius,* that is, that Australia belonged to no one at the time of settlement.

Eddie Koiki Mabo (1937–92) was born on Mer, one of the Murray Islands, and had no formal education beyond primary school. His adoptive father, Benny Mabo, whose name Eddie took, helped him, and he found work cutting sugarcane. Eddie Mabo, an independently minded person, became politically active in the 1970s and moved for self-rule in the Torres Islands. But nothing was done until 1981 when he attended a conference on land rights at James Cook University, Townsville, and took an active part in a meeting in which a move for a land case was made. On May 20, 1982, Mabo and four other Murray Islanders issued a writ claiming land that they had inherited in accordance with their system of law. After playing a leading role for ten years in the case, Eddie Mabo died of cancer in January 1992, a hero of the land rights movement among indigenous and other Australians.

Sources

Eddie Mabo and Others v. *the State of Queensland.* High Court of Australia (Full Court) No. 92/104 1992 66 ALJR 408.

Keon-Cohen, Bryan. 1992. *Eddie Mabo and Ors* v. *the State of Queensland. Aboriginal Law Bulletin* 2:22–23.

Sharp, Nonie. 1992. Scales from the eyes of justice. *Arena* 99/100:56–61.

Sharp, Nonie. 1993. *Stars of Tagai: the Torres Strait islanders.* Canberra: Aboriginal Studies Press.

Walker, Jamie. 1993. Eddie Mabo—Australian of the Year. *The Australian,* January 26: 1, 7.

MACHIAVELLIAN, MACHIAVELLIAN DIPLOMACY, MACHIAVELLIAN PERSONALITY. Politically amoral, ruled by expediency only, crafty, perfidious; one who imitates the statesman and writer of Florence; any cunning and unprincipled statesman. The principles taught by the statesman, or conduct regulated by them. In modern sociopolitical research, Richard Christie and F. Geis (1970) devised a scale of Machiavellianism (Mach Scale) and established a political personality or type with the following characteristics: cool and independent interpersonal relations; little moral or ethical restraint; and a passion for winning, combined with an excessively rational approach to winning strategies. Their work was taken up by many social scientists in the 1970s.

Niccolò Machiavelli (1469–1527) was born and died in Florence. His father was a poor noble; Niccolò had a desultory education unsuited to his talents and may have studied under Marcello Virgilio Adriani. At age 29 he was appointed head of the second chancery and dealt with the internal affairs of Florence, but being also secretary of the magistrate he saw much travel and in 1500 went on a mission to the French court. On returning to Florence, he witnessed the vicious and bloody rise of Cesare Borgia on whom he would later model his "Prince." From Rome Machiavelli saw Borgia's eventual decline, and on later travels he witnessed further political turbulence between the Italian republics, Germany, and France. In 1512 when the Medici returned to power, he was imprisoned for plotting against Giovanni de' Medici (1513). Released later that year, he retired to a country estate and devoted himself to writing based on his observations of political life. He established a secure reputation for political writing. He also wrote a comedy, *The Mandrake* (1518), and he was elected to the University of Florence as the republic's historiographer. His advice was sought by various popes on reorganizing government. In 1525 he completed an official history of Florence for Pope Clement VII. His most noted work, *The Prince* (1513), gives advice on how to acquire, justify, and keep power without recourse to conventional moral standards. Blunt axioms in his work gave the impression of immorality, and later *Machiavellianism* became a term of bitter criticism by the French who used him as a scapegoat to express their hatred for all matters Italian.

Sources

Christie, Richard and Geis, F. 1970. *Studies in Machiavellianism.* New York: Academic Press.

McHenry, Robert, ed. 1992. *The new encyclopedia Britannica.* Chicago: Encyclopedia Britannica, Inc.

Meagher, Paul K.; O'Brien, Thomas C.; and Aherne, Marie, eds. 1979. *Encyclopedic dictionary of religion.* Washington, D.C.: Corpus Publications.

Miller, David, ed. 1987. *The Blackwell encyclopedia of political thought.* Oxford: Basil Blackwell.

Sills, David L., ed. 1968. *International encyclopedia of the social sciences.* New York: Macmillan and Free Press.

Skinner, Quentin. 1981. *Machiavelli.* Oxford: Oxford University Press.

MACKENZIE REPORT. Report of a British court of inquiry (1922) into the dispute between the Engineering and National Employer's Federation and the Amalgamated Engineering Union. The dispute is known as the "Overtime and Managerial Functions" dispute and gave rise to the 1922 Engineering Procedure Management Agreement, Manual Workers. The inquiry concluded that management alone was in a position to judge whether or not overtime was necessary.

William Warrender MacKenzie, first Baron Amulree (1860–1942), was born at Scone in Perthshire, son of a farmer, and educated at Perth Academy and Edinburgh University. He was called to the bar in 1886, Lincoln's Inn, and on the Northern circuit he specialized in matters relating to rights, duties, and responsibilities. He edited editions of *Pratt's Law of Highways,* and he helped edit *Laws of England,* the *Overseer's Handbook,* and *Licensing Acts.* He was knighted in 1918, and during World War I he arbitrated in many industrial disputes; was a chairman of the Committee on Production (1917–19); and was first president, Industrial Court (1919–26); chairman of Railway National Wages Board (1920–26) and of Royal Commissions on Licensing (1929–31) and Newfoundland (1933). He chaired many other industrial relations committees. He published *Industrial Relations in Great Britain* (1929) and was raised to the peerage that year, was made a privy councillor in 1930, and briefly became secretary of state for air (1930–31). He was also chairman of the Royal Society of Arts (1937–38). In the House of Lords his main interests lay in the debates on government, housing, and licensing.

Sources

Legg, Leopold G. W., and Williams, E. T., eds. 1959. *Dictionary of national biography 1941–1950.* London: Oxford University Press.

Marsh, Arthur. 1979. *Concise encyclopedia of industrial relations.* Westmead, Farnborough, Hants: Gower.

MACMILLANITE. A Cameronian or Reformed Presbyterian, a member of a small group of Scottish Presbyterians who did not accept the Settlement of 1690 that established the Church of Scotland. The Reformed Presbytery was formed in 1743; in 1876 most members joined the Free Church of Scotland, and few remained part of an independent body (Livingstone, 1977).

John Macmillan (1670–1753) was born at Barncachla, Kirkcudbrightshire, Scotland, graduated from Edinburgh University in 1697, and was ordained in 1701. Early in his ministry he dissented against corruption and against errors in church government, and was deposed in 1703 for divisive practices. Nevertheless, his popularity was so great that he could keep both the church and the manse, and his successor had to officiate from a nearby barn. He was a minister to the "remnant," commonly called Cameronians, who would not swear to support king and government because they rescinded the covenants and acts of the Reformation period. In 1706 Macmillan's call by this remnant, the "Macmillanites" as they were called, was signed, and remained in force until 1743. The Reformed Presbyterians found Macmillan's accession important, and he was the first ordained minister associated with them. He toured the country for converts and was joined by Thomas Nairn, minister for Abbotshall, Fifeshire. They erected the Reformed Presbytery, which remained undivided until 1753.

Sources

Livingstone, Elizabeth A., ed. 1977. *The concise Oxford dictionary of the Christian church.* Oxford: Oxford University Press.

Stephen, Leslie, and Lee, Sydney, eds. 1917. *The dictionary of national biography.* London: Oxford University Press.

MADISON MODEL. An intellectual framework for government which is characteristic of the U.S. Constitution in its emphasis on checks and balances between sources of power.

James Madison (1751–1836) was born in Virginia, son of a rich landowner, was educated at New Jersey College (now Princeton University), and in 1766 helped to draft the constitution of Virginia. He was in the Continental Congress (1778–83) and the Virginia legislature (1784–86). With Alexander Hamilton (1755–1804) and John Jay (1745–1829), Madison contributed to the *Federalist Papers* (1788–89) and was in the U.S. House of Representatives (1789–97). Madison opposed Hamilton's financial policies and supported adoption of a Bill of Rights. Under Thomas Jefferson, Madison was secretary of state (1801–9) and became leader of the Democrat Republicans. He was elected the fourth president of the United States in 1808. During his second term, hostilities with Britain became known as "Madison's War," during which Washington was captured and the White House burned. In the last ten years of his life, Madison was rector of the University of Virginia. As a political theorist who insisted on the structure of the present U.S. Constitution, Madison is known as the Father of the Constitution.

Sources

Brandt, Irving. 1941–61. *James Madison.* 6 vols. Indianapolis: Bobbs-Merrill.

Burns, James MacGregor. 1963. *The deadlock of democracy: four party politics in America.* Englewood Cliffs, N.J.: Prentice-Hall.

Johnson, Allen, and Malone, Dumas, eds. 1931. *Dictionary of American biography.* Vol. VI. New York: Charles Scribner's Sons.

Jones, Barry. 1989. *The Macmillan dictionary of biography.* Melbourne: Macmillan.

Riemer, Neil. 1986. *James Madison: creating the American Constitution.* Washington, D.C.: Congressional Quarterly.

Shafritz, Jay M. 1988. *The Dorsey dictionary of American government and politics.* Chicago: Dorsey.

MADONNA CONNECTION. Ways in which the postmodern cultural icon of the late 1980s and early 1990s "broaches divisions and underscores the extent of her cultural power." This is achieved by linking "total strangers in dialogue and highlight[ing] the ephemerality of all boundaries" (Schwichtenberg, 1993: 20) The dialogue centers on enablement and constraint for modern woman, and the issues involve virginity, materialism, gender games, chains on women, vampirish whores, bad daughters, brattish behavior of strong and financially successful woman, dressing with underwear on the outside, breast-slit jackets, garish sadomasochism, and scandalizing of Roman Catholic idols.

Madonna Louise Veronica Ciccone (b. 1958) was born in Bay City, Michigan, into a family of six. Her father was design engineer for Chrysler/General Dynamics, and her mother was French-Canadian. In 1965 her mother died, the family moved to Pontiac, and her father married the housekeeper. Madonna felt displaced by her stepmother and as an adolescent escaped into the local night life. She won a dance scholarship to the University of Michigan in 1976 but dropped out; destitute, she went to New York in 1978, modeled, and made soft-core movies for a living. She learned to dance, turned to rock and roll music, became a minor disco star, briefly performed in Paris, and later became a singer and drummer for a rock group in New York. When she could not get the group to perform her songs, she left, was employed by a new manager, and began her own band, "Madonna." In post-punk fashion she achieved success in New York, and by the middle of 1984 was a star and a popular culture icon. With outrageous costumes, overt sexuality, and the image of a tramplike indolent goddess in a movie *Desperately Seeking Susan* (1985), she reached for the top of the entertainment world. In countless ways she changed her image from brat to demure virgin, from controlling bimbo to spokeswoman for oppressed women, and she personified a range of roles many women admired but were too frightened to play themselves. Since the late 1980s her fame has become secure, and she has attracted a vast range of fashionable comment from intellectuals and academics as well as those in popular journalism.

Sources

Anderson, Christopher. 1991. *Madonna: unauthorized.* New York: Simon and Schuster.

Mackie, Fiona. 1992. The meanings of Madonna. *Arena Magazine,* December 1992– January 1993:32–34.

Moritz, Charles, ed. 1986. *Current biography yearbook.* New York: H. W. Wilson.

Schwichtenberg, Cathy. 1993. *The Madonna connection: representational politics, subcultural identities and cultural; theory.* London: Allen and Unwin.

Van Buren, Jane. 1989. *The modernist Madonna: semiotics and the maternal metaphor.* London: Karnac.

Welldon, Estella V. 1986. *Mother, Madonna, whore: the idealizations and denigration of motherhood.* London: Free Associations Press.

MADONNA FACTOR. The Madonna Factor or Madonna Operation refers to the surge of political activism in Japan in mid-1989, largely involving women, that sent both left and right parties scrambling to find women candidates to put before the voters. In July 1989 20 percent of the candidates in the election for the House of Councillors (Upper House) of the Diet in Japan were women. The head of the Japanese Socialist party, Takako Doi (b. 1928), who was the first woman to lead a major Japanese political party, campaigned for women candidates. In the campaign, her charisma together with the large number of women candidates and the corruption in the Liberal Democratic party combined to raise anger among many voters. In addition, Liberal politicians foolishly referred to women in politics as useless and said they were wrong to be political leaders. They also suggested Takako Doi was unfit to be prime minister because she was unmarried and had no children. In the July 1989 election, the Japanese Socialist party (JSP) under Takako Doi's leadership won enough seats to deny the Liberal Democratic party an overall majority. In the February 1990 election, the JSP increased its share of the vote by a further 7 percent and won another 53 seats to hold 136 of the 512 seats in the House of Representatives.

Madonna. See MADONNA CONNECTION.

Sources

The Europa world yearbook, 1989. London: Europa Publications.

Graham, Judith, ed. 1992. *Current biography yearbook.* New York: H. W. Wilson.

Keesings contemporary archives: record of world events. 1989:36800-36801; 1990: 37237, 37278, 37714.

Kodanshua. 1993. *Encyclopedia of Japan.* Tokyo: Kodanshua.

MAE WEST FACTOR. A political pollster's concept that explains why un-committed voters tend to choose the opposition party candidate rather than the candidate for the party in power. The pollster assumes that when in doubt the voter expects that the opposition party could be no worse in office than the incumbent party, and chooses the lesser of the two evils. Mae West's name attaches to the idea because of her quip in the movie *Klondike Annie* (1936): "Between two evils I always pick the one I never tried" (West, 1959: 186).

Mae West (1892–1980) was born in Brooklyn, New York. Her father was a private detective of English-Irish origins, and her Bavarian mother modelled corsets. At age 7 Mae began tap dancing, a year later was on the stage profes-sionally, and at 14 years entered vaudeville, secretly married Frank Wallace, her song and dance partner, and separated immediately. In 1935, the marriage was revealed when a court action for alimony payable to Wallace was made public. Her Broadway debut was in 1911 and in 1918 she made the "shimmy" dance popular in New York. During the 1920s she began to shape her reputation for making witty quips and portraying alluring characters. In 1932 she made her first film, *Night after Night.* She took the lead in a successful play that she wrote, *Diamond Lil,* and filmed it in 1933 as *She Done Him Wrong.* She became very wealthy, and in 1935 her annual salary of $480,000 was five times that of the U.S. president, and only $20,000 short of America's highest paid man, Wil-liam Randolph Hearst. In 1940 she made what critics agree was her best film—*My Little Chickadee*—with W. C. Fields.

Sources

Ransley, John, ed. 1991. *Chambers dictionary of political biography.* Edinburgh: W. and R. Chambers.

West, Mae. 1959. *Goodness had nothing to do with it: the autobiography of Mae West.* Englewood Cliffs, N.J.: Prentice-Hall Inc.

MAGDALENE. A repentant prostitute; an institute for receiving such persons (abbreviation for Magdalene Hospital Asylum); names of Oxford and Cambridge colleges.

Mary was born at Magdala, a prosperous, infamous fishing village on the western shore of the Sea of Galilee. According to the Bible, she was possessed by seven devils. When Jesus freed her of this demonic possession, she gave her services and money to support the material needs of Jesus and his followers (Luke 8:2–3). At Christ's crucifixion she stood beside the cross and witnessed his burial (Mark 15:40). When she and some other women came to anoint Jesus' corpse on Easter morning, she learned that he had risen. She was commissioned to take this news to the Apostles. She actually saw the risen Lord, who told her to report his resurrection to those close to him (Mark 16). Legend also holds that she was the repentant woman, a sinner who anointed the feet of Jesus in Simon's house (Luke 7:36–50), and was also Mary of Bethany (John 11).

Sources

Cross, Frank L. 1974. *The Oxford dictionary of the Christian Church.* 2d ed. New York: Oxford University Press.

Hastings, James, ed. 1909. *Dictionary of Christ and the gospels.* Edinburgh: T. and T. Clark.

McDonald, William, ed. 1967. *New Catholic encyclopedia.* New York: McGraw-Hill.

MAGINOT LINE, MAGINOT-MINDED. The abortive French fortifications constructed in the 1930s along the German border. Overconcerned with the defensive in military terms, static in ideas.

Andre Maginot (1877–1932) was born in Paris and after studying political science became assistant to the governor-general of Algeria in 1907. In 1910 he went into politics, was elected to the Chamber of Deputies, and became undersecretary of state for war. In World War I he saw the importance of old fortifications in the defense of Verdun. The war crippled him for life. In 1916 he returned to politics and served in six successive governments; in his last term of office he served as minister for war (1929–31). He directed the building of the 200-mile fortifications from Switzerland to Belgium that were named after him and completed in 1938. The Maginot Line was intended to fortify France against any future German military advances; it failed to do so in World War II largely because the Nazis used aerial attacks and partly because the line had not been extended to the French-Belgian frontier. The Germans invaded Belgium in May 1940 and then marched through Belgium and crossed the Somme River. The Maginot Line has been used to refer to many fortifications, hopeless or otherwise unfounded, that appear to limit a real or an imagined enemy (Connell, 1986; Lens, 1982).

Sources

Connell, John, 1986. *The new Maginot Line.* London: Secker and Warburg.

Hughes, Judith M. 1971. *To the Maginot Line: the politics of French miliary preparation in the 1920s.* Cambridge, Mass.: Harvard University Press.

Lens, Sidney. 1982. *The Maginot Line syndrome: America's hopeless foreign policy.* Cambridge, Mass.: Ballinger.

McHenry, Robert, ed. 1992. *The new encyclopedia Britannica.* Chicago: Encyclopedia Britannica, Inc.

MAJORISM. ''Rising unemployment and deep recession provide the most accurate definition of Majorism'' (attributed to Neil Kinnock, *Guardian Weekly,* June 23, 1991:3).

John Major (b. 1943) was born in Merton (London), England, son of a vaude-ville company manager, acrobat, and tightrope walker. John was educated at Cheam Common Primary School, Rutlish Grammar, and studied accountancy. Work in Nigeria taught him to hate racism. In 1979 he entered politics for Huntingdon, and by 1987 he had a place on the front bench. In July 1989 Prime Minister Margaret Thatcher promoted Major to foreign secretary; in October 1989 he became chancellor of the Exchequer at a time when Britain's economy was ailing. In November 1990 he replaced Mrs. Thatcher as prime minister.
Sources
Anderson, Bruce. 1991. *John Major: the making of a prime minister.* London: Fourth Estate.
Deming, A. 1991. Basking in the Gulf glow. *Newsweek* 117:42.
Ellis, Nesta Wyn. 1991. *John Major: a personal biography.* London: Futura.
Garcia, G. 1990. A victory of major proportions. *Time* 136:51.
Moritz, Charles, ed. 1990. *Current biography yearbook.* New York: H. W. Wilson.
Who's who, 1991. London: Adam and Charles Black.

MALTHUSIAN, MALTHUS'S LAW OF POPULATION, MALTHUSIAN-ISM. A Malthusian upheld a ''natural'' law of population which stated that the increase in population tends to outstrip the increase in the means of living. Mathusianism was a theory of population that advocated positive and preven-tative checks on the rate of population growth. That is, positive checks were disease, famine, and war, while preventative checks were moral restraint (late marriages and premarital chastity) and celibacy. The positive checks were em-phasized and closely associated with Malthus; consequently, Malthusianism was thought to be a prescription for disaster.

Thomas Robert Malthus (1766–1834), an English political economist, was born near Guilford in Surrey and died at Saint Catharines near Bath. In 1788 he graduated from Cambridge, and in 1793 he became a fellow of Jesus College. In 1798 after taking holy orders, he became curate of Albury in Surrey; he also published *Principle of Population,* an essay that asserted that population in-creases geometrically, while the means of subsistence increases arithmetically; that two necessary checks on the population increase are crime and vice. He advocated the view that it was the duty of the upper classes to learn the principle of population and with this knowledge help reduce the unfortunate consequences of population increase by encouraging the poor to use moral restraint in their intimate relations. In politics he was a Whig, and he supported Catholic eman-cipation. In 1805 he was a professor of history and political economy at Hail-eybury.
Sources
Eatwell, John; Milgate, Murray; and Newman, Peter. 1987. *The new Palgrave: a dictionary of economics.* London: Macmillan.
Sills, David L., ed. 1968. *International encyclopedia of the social sciences.* New York: Macmillan and Free Press.
Soloway, Richard A. 1982. *Birth control and the population question in England, 1877–1930.* London: University of North Carolina.

Stephen, Leslie, and Lee, Sydney, eds. 1917. *The dictionary of national biography.* London: Oxford University Press.

Winch, Donald. 1987. *Malthus.* Oxford: Oxford University Press.

Wingley, Edward A., and Souden, David, eds. 1986. *The works of Thomas Robert Malthus.* 8 Vols. London: William Pickering.

Zusne, Leonard. 1984. *Biographical dictionary of psychology.* Westport, Conn.: Greenwood Press.

MANCHESTER SCHOOL. A school of economic and political thought founded in 1820 at meetings of the Manchester Chamber of Commerce and given the name mainly by German socialists. The school supported laissez-faire economics, free trade, free competition, and freedom of contracts in business. Their economic policy tended to individualism, and their politics upheld isolationism in foreign affairs and pacifism. Many members were Lancashire mill owners and some unusually humanitarian men of business. They were led by Richard Cobden and John Bright, and they dominated the Liberal party in the nineteenth century, especially during the period when the Anti-Corn Law League flourished (1838–46). The group was also named the "Cobden and Bright School" by Benjamin Disraeli (1845).

John Bright (1811–88) was born at Greenbank, near Rochdale, and became a partner in John Bright and Bros., cotton spinners and manufacturers. He entered Parliament for Durham City (1843–47), Manchester (1847–57), and Birmingham (1857–88). He was liberal, opposed Gladstone's Home Rule policy, and was active in the Anti-Corn Law League in the 1840s. He became president of the Board of Trade (1868–70) and chancellor of the Duchy of Lancaster (1873–74; 1880–82).

Richard Cobden (1804–65) was born in Midhurst, Sussex, and became a cotton printer in Lancashire. He was director of the Manchester Chamber of Commerce and a leading figure in the Anti-Corn Law League. He was a member of Parliament (1841–57; 1859–65).

See also COBDENISM.

Sources

Cook, Chris. 1983. *The Macmillan dictionary of historical terms.* London: Macmillan.

Eatwell, John; Milgate, Murray; and Newman, Peter. 1987. *The new Palgrave: a dictionary of economics.* London: Macmillan.

Grampp, William D. 1960. *The Manchester school of economics.* Stanford, Calif.: University of Stanford Press.

Rutherford, Donald. 1992. *Dictionary of economics.* London: Routledge.

Stenton, Michael, ed. 1976–81. *Who's who of British members of Parliament.* Vol. 1. 1832–85. Atlantic Highlands, N.J.: Humanities Press.

MANICHAEAN. Relating to the belief that the world is a fusion of spirit and matter, the basic principles of good and evil, and that everything is a product of light or good, and evil or dark.

Mani, Manes, or Manichaeus (c. 215–77), born near Seleucia-Ctesiphon, cap-

ital of the Persian Empire, was the founder of Manichaeanism. He is thought to
have had a careful education in Ctesiphon from his father, Futak. Futak was a
member of the Moghtasilah sect, the Baptists, of southern Babylonia. They had
accepted some Christian ideas. At the court of Sapor I, Mani, at about age 25,
proclaimed his new religion and attracted some followers. The Magians, on
whom the king depended, arranged for Mani's imprisonment. Hormus, who
succeeded Sapor I, was more in favor of Mani's views, but Bahram I put Mani
to death and banished his disciples. Mani's publications were known to Muslim
historians, but they are now lost. He taught that all things originated from one
of two principles: good or evil, light or darkness. He revealed a previously
hidden truth that the purpose of religion was to release the light that Satan had
stolen from the world of light and kept in humankind's brain. Jesus—known as
"Jesus, the brilliant light"—and other renowned prophets were to sent to help
in effecting this release. Furthermore, the whole universe was set to this task,
so it was asserted that everyone's actions resonated throughout the universe in
working for this great release. The release was to be achieved through asceti-
cism, celibacy, and vegetarianism. Although Saint Augustine had raised no objection to Manichaean practices, they were often regarded as abominations. The
sect spread through Egypt, Rome, Africa, and China, but later died out largely
because the followers were bitterly persecuted. Today the influence of Manichaeanism is still debated.

Sources

Cross, Frank L. 1974. *The Oxford dictionary of the Christian Church.* 2d ed. New York:
    Oxford University Press.
Ferguson, Everett, ed. 1990. *The encyclopedia of early Christianity.* New York: Garland
    Publishing.
McHenry, Robert, ed. 1992. *The new encyclopedia Britannica.* Chicago: Encyclopedia
    Britannica, Inc.

MANN ACT. U.S. "White Slave" Traffic Act (1910) which outlawed the transportation of women across state lines for immoral purposes, especially prostitution. Because the Federal Bureau of Investigation abused the application of
the act, the U.S. Justice Department limited its use to instances when commercial
interests were clear (1940).

James Robert Mann (1856–1922) was born near Bloomington, Illinois. He
attended public schools and graduated from the University of Illinois at Urbana
and from the Union College of Law, Chicago (1881). He was admitted to the
bar, commenced practice in Chicago, and later became attorney for Hyde Park
Commissioners of Chicago; he was secretary of the Citizens Association which
secured the adoption of Jackson Park as the site for the World's Fair. He entered
Congress in 1897, remaining there until his death, and his name was attached
to much important legislation of the period. Measures bearing his name are the
Mann-Elkins Act (1910; railroad rate regulations, antirebate law), the Pure Food
and Drugs Act (1906), and the Bureau of Corporations Act (1903). Mann be-

came leader of the Republican party (1912) when the party lost power to the Democrats, and he was a formidable antagonist to anyone trying to enact loose or unwise Democratic legislation.

Sources

Connelly, Mark T. 1980. *The response to prostitution in the Progressive Era.* Chapel Hill: University of North Carolina Press.

Jacob, Kathryn A., and Ragsdale, Bruce A. 1989. *Biographical directory of the United States Congress: 1774–1989.* Bicentennial ed. Washington, D.C.: U.S. Government Printing Office.

Malone, Dumas, ed. 1933. *Dictionary of American biography.* Vol. VI. New York: Charles Scribner's Sons.

Preston, Wheeler. 1974. *American biographies.* Detroit: Gale Research.

MANNERHEIM LINE. A fortified line of defense built during 1931–39 across the Karelian Isthmus. It was taken by the Russians in 1940 and dismantled.

Carl Gustav Emil von Mannerheim (1867–1951), a Finnish soldier and statesman, was born at Villnäs and became an officer in the Russo-Japanese War (1904–5) and in World War I. In 1918 Finland declared its independence after the Russian Revolution, and Mannerheim became supreme commander and regent. After being defeated in the presidential election of 1919, he retired, but in 1931 he became chairman of the Finnish Defence Council and commander in chief against the Russians in the Winter War (1939–40). During his chairmanship, the line of fortification was built. He commanded the Finnish forces until he became president of the Finnish republic (1944–46).

Sources

Borenius, Tancred. 1940. *Field-Marshall Mannerheim.* London: Hutchinson.

Bridgewater, W., ed. 1960. *The Columbia Viking desk encyclopedia.* 2d ed. New York: Viking Press.

Canby, Courtlandt. 1984. *The encyclopedia of historic places.* London: Mansell Publishing.

McHenry, Robert, ed. 1992. *The new encyclopedia Britannica.* Chicago: Encyclopedia Britannica, Inc.

Magnussen, Magnus; Goring, Rosemary; and Thorn, John O., eds. 1990. *Chambers biographical dictionary.* Edinburgh: Chambers Ltd.

Mannerheim, Carl G.E. 1954. *Memoirs.* Trans. from Swedish by Count Eric Lewenhaupt. New York: E. P. Dutton.

MAOISM, MAOIST. A form of Marxist-Leninist political philosophy suited to China and opposed to pure Marxism in regard to the role of the socialist revolution in an agrarian society, the use of guerrilla war practices, the definition of the bourgeoisie, the peasantry, and the elements of contradictions in a society. One who supports modern Chinese communism.

Mao Tse-tung (1893–1976) was born in Shoashan in Hunan Province, son of a poor peasant who had become affluent in the grain trade. He was taught to value education only for recordkeeping. At 13 he left school to work on the family farm. He rebelled against his parents' authority, left home, and went to study, eventually, at Beijing University. He was converted to the ideas of Marx and Engels and helped establish the Chinese Communist party; in 1929 he became its president in Hunan Province. He followed Lenin's *Theory of Imperialism* (1919) but changed it to suit the conditions of an agrarian society in China. He was president of the first Chinese Peasants Union (1927), joined the "Long March" (1934–36), and after World War II was chairman of the Central People's government. In 1958 he established people's communes. In 1959 he stepped down from his position as head of state in China, but remained chairman of the Communist party and could still use his personal authority to rule Communist China.

Sources
McHenry, Robert, ed. 1992. *The new encyclopedia Britannica.* Chicago: Encyclopedia Britannica, Inc.
Miller, David, ed. 1987. *The Blackwell encyclopedia of political thought.* Oxford: Basil Blackwell.
Wenxian, Zhong, ed. 1986. *Mao Zedong: biography, assessment, reminiscences.* Beijing: China International Book Trading and Foreign Language Press.
Wilson, Dick, ed. 1977. *Mao Tse-Tung in the scales of history.* Cambridge: Cambridge University Press.

MARCIONITE. An adherent of the second-century ethico-dualistic philosophy of religion that assumed there was a radical split between the Old and the New Testament, and between the law and the Gospel.

Marcion (d. 165), a gnostic and teacher of religion, was son of the bishop of Sinope in Pontus. He founded the Marcionite sect in Rome; it remained until the seventh century and extended into Northern Africa, Gaul, Asia Minor, and Egypt. He believed in the eternity of matter, a principle that was taken up and taught by Hermogenes, another second-century gnostic. Marcion immersed bodies three times during baptism, allowed women to minister, and kept the wine from the Eucharist.

Sources
Cross, Frank L. 1974. *The Oxford dictionary of the Christian Church.* 2d ed. New York: Oxford University Press.
Ferguson, Everett, ed. 1990. *The encyclopedia of early Christianity.* New York: Garland Publishing.
Harnack, Adolf von. 1990. *Marcion: the gospel of the alien God.* Trans. John E. Steely and Lyle D. Bierma. Durham, N.C.: Labyrinth Press.
McDonald, William, ed. 1967. *New Catholic encyclopedia.* New York: McGraw-Hill.
McHenry, Robert, ed. 1992. *The new encyclopedia Britannica.* Chicago: Encyclopedia Britannica, Inc.

MARCUSEAN. Relating to or a follower of the twentieth-century psychologist and humanist philosopher, whose Hegelian-Freudian-Marxist ideas helped justify resistance to established order, and asserted that Western society was spiritually and intellectually unfree because it oppressed its masses with the materialistic benefits of advanced technology and the complacency that ensued. The ideas attracted popular support among intellectuals after the 1968 student demonstrations in West Berlin, Paris, and New York.

Herbert Marcuse (1898–1979) was born in Berlin and educated at the University of Freiburg (Ph.D., 1922), researched at Freiburg (1922–32), and in 1933 fled from the Nazis to Geneva and to the United States. He taught at Columbia University and was naturalized in 1940. During World War II he was an intelligence analyst, and taught at Harvard and Columbia until 1954, Brandeis University (1954–65), and at the University of California, San Diego, until he retired in 1976 and was made emeritus. Among his more popular writings were *Eros and Civilization* (1955), *One Dimensional Man* (1964), *Counter-revolution and Revolution* (1972), and *Studies in Critical Philosophy* (1972).

Sources

MacIntyre, Alasdair C. 1970. *Marcuse.* London: Fontana.

McHenry, Robert, ed. 1992. *The new encyclopedia Britannica.* Chicago: Encyclopedia Britannica, Inc.

Miller, David, ed. 1987. *The Blackwell encyclopedia of political thought.* Oxford: Basil Blackwell.

Nordquist, Joan 1988. *Herbert Marcuse: a bibliography.* Social Theory, a bibliographic series, No. 9. Santa Cruz, Calif.: Reference and Research Services.

MARKOV OR MARKOVIAN PROCESSES, MARKOV CHAIN. The process is a sequence of dependent states in which the probability of any one is independent of all others, with the exception of the state immediately beforehand. Under certain conditions the process may be stationary, and then it is known as a Markov chain. The idea is suited to use in atomic physics, genetics, and quantum theory. It has also been used in economic, political, and social psychological studies where theorizing is predictive and concerns the probability of events taking place. One of the first uses of Markov chains was in a study of voting intentions (Anderson, 1954). Recently, the process has been employed in relation to dynamic programming and to migration between countries and its relation to past population movements.

Andrei Andreevich Markov (1856–1922) was born in Ryazan, and although he was ill in his youth, he was able to study mathematics at the University of Petersburg (1874–78). He won a gold medal for his dissertation on the integration of differential equations. He worked as a tutor and completed his Ph.D. in 1884. Markov taught mathematics until 1893 at Saint Petersburg and then became active as a liberal in politics, questioning the czar's repressive moves against the Russian Parliament (1907). In the 1890s his interest turned to probability calculus, and after 1900 he worked on probability theory, published his *Probability Calculus* (1906), and developed the idea of a Markov chain, a chance process with the special feature so that its future may be predicted from what is known in the present as accurately as if all its past were known. He illustrated his idea by calculating the alteration of vowels and consonants in Pushkin's *Eugene Onegin* (1823). For political reasons in 1917 he worked for no pay teaching mathematics in a secondary school in the interior of Russia.

Sources

Abbott, David, 1985. *The biographical dictionary of scientists: mathematicians.* London: Blond Educational.

Anderson, T. W. 1954. Probability models for analysing time changes in attitudes. In Paul F. Lazarsfeld, ed. *Mathematical thinking in the social sciences.* Glencoe, Ill.: Free Press.

Bartholomew, David J. 1982. *Stochastic models for the social processes.* New York: John Wiley.

Eatwell, John; Milgate, Murray; and Newman, Peter. 1987. *The New Palgrave: a dictionary of economics.* London: Macmillan.

Gillespie, Charles C., ed. 1973. *Dictionary of scientific biography.* New York: Charles Scribner's Sons.

Preece, Warren E., ed. 1965. *Encyclopedia Britannica.* Chicago: Encyclopedia Britannica Inc., William Benton.

Rutherford, Donald. 1992. *Dictionary of economics.* London: Routledge.

Zusne, Leonard. 1987. *Eponyms in psychology: a dictionary and sourcebook.* Westport, Conn.: Greenwood Press.

MARONITE. A member of the seventh-century Monothelite sect, now Uniats, living near Lebanon. The church is one of the largest Eastern-rite religious communities of the Roman Catholic Church in modern Lebanon; it has no non-Catholic counterpart. Its founder and origins are not definitively known. At the end of the nineteenth century, many Maronites from Lebanon immigrated to the United States and settled in the larger cities. In 1961 a seminary was founded in Washington, and in 1972 the Diocese of Saint Maro was established in Detroit. Other dioceses may be found in Syria, Egypt, Brazil, and Australia; followers are in Argentina, France, Canada, Central America, and Africa.

Saint Maron or Maro of Cyr (d. 433) was born in Syria and lived in the late fourth and early fifth centuries. He became a monk, and as a hermit on a mountain near Apamea, prayed, mortified himself, and attracted masses for his spiritual wisdom. He trained hermits and monks and founded three monasteries. Another source of the sect is said to be Saint John Maron or Joannes Maro, a patriarch of Antioch (685–707), who led the defeat of invading Byzantine armies in 684 and established the independence of the Maronite people. The Maronites were first accepted as a distinct community by Caliph Marwan II (744–48).

Sources

Cross, Frank L. 1974. *The Oxford dictionary of the Christian Church.* 2d ed. New York: Oxford University Press.

McHenry, Robert, ed. 1992. *The new encyclopedia Britannica.* Chicago: Encyclopedia Britannica, Inc.

Meagher, Paul K.; O'Brien, Thomas C.; and Aherne, Marie, eds. 1979. *Encyclopedic dictionary of religion.* Washington, D.C.: Corpus Publications.

MARPRELATE. To inveigh like Puritans against the church.

Martin Marprelate was the name under which pamphlets were published during an attack by the Puritans in about 1589 against those who supported the English church. To avoid government intervention, the press that published the pamphlets was continually moved; eventually, it was seized near Manchester. Even so the pamphlets still appeared. Some people believed that Martin Marprelate may have been a layman at court. The campaign was put down with the execution of John Penry (1563–93) and Henry Barrow(e) (1550–93), two of many people thought to have written the pamphlets.

Sources

Brewer, Ebenezer Cobham. 1970. *Brewer's dictionary of phrase and fable.* Centenary ed. Rev. by Ivor H. Evans. New York: Harper and Row.

Carlson, Leland H. 1981. *Martin Marprelate, gentleman: master Job Throkmorton laid open in his colors.* San Marino: Huntington Library.

Cross, Frank L. 1974. *The Oxford dictionary of the Christian Church.* 2d ed. New York: Oxford University Press.

McGinn, Donald J. 1966. *John Penry and the Marprelate controversy.* New Brunswick, N.J.: Rutgers University Press.

Stephen, Leslie, and Lee, Sydney, eds. 1917. *The dictionary of national biography.* London: Oxford University Press.

MARSHALL PLAN. Announced by George Marshall, U.S. secretary of state, June 5, 1947, at Harvard University, the European Recovery Plan sought to ensure that West Germany, Italy, and France did not come under Soviet domination after World War II. The plan offered financial aid in postwar reconstruction, providing the European powers first indicated a genuine interest in collaboration rather than in competing among themselves. Warmly welcomed by France and Britain, the plan was seen by the Soviet Union as an attempt to extend American influence in Europe.

George Catlett Marshall (1880–1959) was born at Uniontown, Pennsylvania, and educated at the Virginia Military Institute. As a second lieutenant he served in the Philippines, 1902–3, and was advanced through the ranks to general by 1944. As a five-star general, he was still on active duty when he died. Marshall resigned as chief of staff in 1945 and was appointed special representative of President Truman to China with the rank of ambassador, but failed to mediate the Chinese civil war. He was appointed secretary of state by President Truman in 1947 and secretary of defense in 1950. He represented President Eisenhower at the coronation of Elizabeth II in 1953 and in that year was awarded the Nobel Peace Prize for his contribution to the economic rehabilitation of Europe.

Sources

Commager, Henry S., ed. 1968. *Documents of American history.* 8th ed. New York: Appleton-Century-Crofts.

Cray, Ed. 1991. *General of the army: George C. Marshall, soldier and statesman.* New York: W. W. Norton.

Hoffmann, Stanley, and Maier, Charles, 1984. *The Marshall Plan: a retrospective.* Boulder, Colo.: Westview Press.

Hogan, Michael J. 1989. *The Marshall Plan: America, Britain and the reconstruction of Europe.* Cambridge: Cambridge University Press.
Kindleberger, Charles P. 1987. *The Marshall Plan days.* London: Allen and Unwin.
McHenry, Robert, ed. 1992. *The new encyclopedia Britannica.* Chicago: Encyclopedia Britannica, Inc.
Robertson, David. 1985. *A dictionary of modern politics.* London: Europa Publications.

MARSHALL-LERNER CONDITIONS. Those conditions in an economy that indicate whether or not a currency devaluation will improve or worsen the balance-of-payments deficit.

Alfred Marshall (1842–1924) was born in London and graduated in mathematics at Saint John's College, Cambridge in 1865. He was made a professor of political economy at the University of Cambridge (1885–1908), and he published his influential *Principles of Economics* (1890), which studied the economics of the stationary state. He claims that he discovered the theory of marginal utility and that his decision to study economics was a moral one, and had a clear impact on his economics of welfare. He concluded that redistribution of income from the wealthy to the impoverished would lead to greater satisfaction for all. Much of John M. Keynes's thinking was influenced by Marshall.

Abba Ptachya Lerner (1905–82). See LANGE-LERNER MECHANISM.

Sources

Blaug, Mark. 1985. *Great economists since Keynes.* Brighton, England: Harvester Press.
Blaug, Mark, ed. 1986. *Who's who in economics: a biographical dictionary of major economists, 1700–1986.* 2d ed. Cambridge, Mass.: MIT Press.
Eatwell, John; Milgate, Murray; and Newman, Peter. 1987. *The new Palgrave: a dictionary of economics.* London: Macmillan.
Reisman, David A. 1987. *Alfred Marshall: progress and politics.* Basingstoke: Macmillan.
Sills, David L., ed. 1968. *International encyclopedia of the social sciences.* New York: Macmillan and Free Press.
Weaver, John R.H., ed. 1937. *Dictionary of national biography 1922–1930.* London: Oxford University Press.
Wood, John C. 1982. *Alfred Marshall: critical assessments.* London: Croom Helm.

MARTIN'S LAWS. Amusing laws of administration which are often applied to universities.

Martin's Laws of Academia: (1) The faculty expands its activity to fit whatever space is available, so that more space is always required. (2) Faculty purchases of equipment and supplies always increase to match the funds available, so these funds are never adequate. (3) The professional quality of the faculty tends to be inversely proportional to the importance it attaches to space and equipment.

Martin's Laws of Academic Status: (1) A faculty member's true national academic stature as a scholar tends to be inversely proportional to his degree of involvement in the affairs of the American Association of University Professors. (2) A faculty member's professional productivity tends to be inversely proportional to his wife's involvement in the Faculty Women's Club. (3) Departmental prestige on campus is directly proportional to its physical distance from the plants and grounds building; corollary buildings in the College of Engineering are always located immediately adjacent to the power plant.

Martin's Law of Committees: All committee reports conclude that it is not prudent to change the policy or procedure or organization or whatever at this time.

Martin's Law of Exclusion Regarding Committee Reports: Committee reports dealing with wages, salary, fringe benefits, facilities, computers, employee parking, libraries, coffee breaks, and secretarial support always call for dramatic expenditure increases.

Martin's Law of Communication: The inevitable result of improved and enlarged communication between different levels in a hierarchy is a vastly increased area of misunderstanding.

Thomas Lyle Martin, Jr. (b. 1921) was born in Memphis, Tennessee, and studied electrical engineering at Rensselaer Polytechnical Institute. In World War II he was a captain in the U.S. Army Signals Corps, and later, in 1951, he completed his Ph.D. at Stanford. He taught at the universities of New Mexico (1948–53) and Arizona. His professional interests lay in electrical circuitry and the ionization of the lower atmosphere. He turned to administration and became an academic dean of engineering at Arizona (1958–63), Florida (1963–66), the Institute of Technology at the Southern Methodist University (1966–74), and the Illinois Institute of Technology in Chicago (president, 1974–87). He was on the board of many companies as well as the Dallas-Forth Worth Regional Airport (1970–74) and the Museum of Science and Industry (1975–87).

Sources

Ethridge, James M., and Kapala, Barbara, eds. 1965. *Contemporary authors.* 11–12 First Revision Series. Detroit: Gale Research.

Jaques Cattell Press, ed. 1973. *American men and women of science: the social and behavioral sciences.* New York: Jaques Cattell and R. R. Bowker.

Martin, Thomas L., Jr. 1973. *Malice in Blunderland.* New York: McGraw-Hill.

Who's who in America, 1992–93. New Providence, N.J.: Marquis.

MARTINET. A French military drilling system; a person who insists on strict discipline and obedience.

Jean, marquis de Martinet (d. 1672), was an officer in the regular army created by Louis XIV and the marquis de Louvis from 1660 to 1670. During this period, the self-trained and self-equipped soldier of fortune gave over to the enlisted man, who had to be trained from the moment he was recruited. Methods of drill and training became standard. Lieutenant-colonel and, later, Inspector-general Martinet trained the infantry using a strict discipline and even gave his name to one of the drills. Consequently, the French Army became a mighty power in Europe at the time. Martinet was accidentally killed by his own troops.

Sources

Barnhart, Robert K., ed. 1988. *The Barnhart dictionary of etymology.* New York: H. W. Wilson.

Brewer, Ebenezer Cobham. 1970. *Brewer's dictionary of phrase and fable.* Centenary ed. Rev. by Ivor H. Evans. New York: Harper and Row.

Hendrickson, Robert. 1988. *The dictionary of eponyms: names that became words.* New York: Dorset.

MARXIAN, MARXIAN ANTHROPOLOGY, MARXIAN ECONOMICS, MARXIAN POLITICS, MARXIAN SOCIOLOGY. Relating to socialism, particularly Russian socialism and its economic consequences.

In anthropology it is the view that private areas of human concern—family, code of sexuality—were tied to a society's politico-economic system, largely because humankind had evolved through five stages: primitive communism, slavery, feudalism, capitalism, and communism. Because Marxist anthropology invoked other stages (modes of production) for India and China, this field of social science has been subject to much controversy.

In economics, Marxist thought tended to center on the stages of capitalism dominated by monopolies rather than on competition between economic units. It considered the internal division or type of capital—land versus industry, or large units versus small units—which, although they have general capital functions in common, also support unique economic interest. Marxist economics also recognizes the pursuit of markets in developing countries, and attempts to transform them into economic colonies of large international corporations.

In politics, the Marxist assumption that the ruling classes use the state as their instrument has been put aside in favor of the view that the state is independent of the ruling classes, and that, through Parliament, the state responds to working-class interests; even so, the view is held that the state tends to favor capitalist concerns.

In sociology, there are several points at which it has been necessary to revise Marx's theory on the impact of the collapse of capitalism for class structure, especially the conflict between capital and labor, changes in patterns of ownership, and the rise of the middle class and the idea that class consciousness is a necessary condition for the class struggle. Marxist sociology has also developed considerable interest in the study of ideology, how it is used to maintain the dominance of ruling classes. Modern Marxist social science has turned from the strict scientific view that it should concern itself only with what can be known or what propositions can be tested to the view that what can be understood of human life is important.

Karl Marx (1818–83), a German economist and revolutionary socialist, was born at Trier. His family was middle class and gave him a sound education and other advantages. He studied history and philosophy at the University of Bonn and at the University of Berlin. He received his doctorate from the University of Jena in 1842 and began journalism. After a year, he went to Paris and joined political radicals; his own radicalism attracted the attention of the Prussian government which demanded his expulsion from Paris. He went to Brussels and organized the German Communist League with help from Friedrich Engels. In 1847–48 he wrote the *Communist Manifesto,* a powerful revolutionary call on workers to unite and attack capitalists. In 1848 he was expelled from Europe and lived in England until his death. Toward the end of his life, Marx read widely in anthropology and followed the ideas of Lewis Henry Morgan (1818–81). His work was written by Engels from Marx's notes and published as *The Origins of the Family, Private Property and the State.* Since then developments in social thought owe much to his ideas.

Sources

Carver, Terrell. 1988. *A Marx dictionary.* Cambridge: Polity.

Carver, Terrell, ed. 1991. *The Cambridge companion to Marx.* Cambridge: Cambridge University Press.

McLellan, David. 1975. *Marx.* London: Fontana.

Miller, David, ed. 1987. *The Blackwell encyclopedia of political thought.* Oxford: Basil Blackwell.

Seymour-Smith, Charlotte. 1988. *Macmillan dictionary of anthropology.* London: Macmillan.

Sills, David L., ed. 1968. *International encyclopedia of the social sciences.* New York: Macmillan and Free Press.

Singer, Peter. 1980. *Marx.* Oxford: Oxford University Press.

Zusne, Leonard. 1984. *Biographical dictionary of psychology.* Westport, Conn.: Greenwood Press.

MARXISM, MARXIST-LENINISM. A social philosophy—the meaning of which is much in debate—that centers first on the view that economic factors (forces and relations of production) are the prime conditions for political and cultural change. The process by which the change occurs involves stages of social revolution, a class struggle between those who have variable access to economic production, and the formation of economic institutions and an ideology to maintain them. Second, the philosophy argues for a society where, through common ownership of economic production, bitter conflict is prevented, for example, as in a socialist or communist society. Third, the philosophy outlines how a capitalist society, which is transitory, may become a socialist or communist society through revolution or liberal reformation. Variations on these themes appear as Marxist-Leninism, neo-Marxism, Stalinism, and Maoism.

See also MARXIAN.

Sources

Kolakowski, Leszek. 1978. *Main currents of Marxism: its rise, growth and dissolution.* Trans. P. S. Falb. 3 vols. Oxford: Clarendon Press.

Lichtheim, George. 1961. *Marxism: an historical and critical study.* Rev. ed. 1967. London: Routledge and Kegan Paul.

McLellan, David. 1980. *Marxism after Marx: an introduction.* London: Macmillan.

Schapiro, Leonard B. 1960. *The Communist party of the Soviet Union.* 2d rev. ed., 1970. London: Eyre and Spottiswood.

MARY FACTOR. The impact of Ireland's first woman president on the politics of Ireland in the early 1990s; a symbol of Ireland's aspirations to be a European nation, its self-confidence, and national pride. At the time she became president, Ireland was bedeviled by the split between north and south, persistent terrorism, divisiveness over birth control and abortion, and embarrassed by the scandals surrounding the thirteen-year prime ministership of Charles Haughey.

Mary Terese Winifred Bourke (b. 1944) was born into the Catholic gentry in Ballina, County Mayo. At age 17 she spent a year at finishing school in Paris where she learned that a country's culture is enriched by diversity, which she still believes, and that Ireland could be liberated from British domination by aligning with Europe. After Paris she entered Trinity College, Dublin, to study law, and went on to Harvard for a master's degree in law (1967). On her return to Ireland, she married the son of a Protestant banker, Nicholas Robinson, and worked to legalize birth control and divorce, served the Labor party, and spent twenty years in the Senate. She failed to win election to the lower house, the powerful Dáil. She broke with the party on its Northern Ireland policy and helped establish the Irish Center for European Law in Dublin. Her policy was that legal change would bring social change. She dressed plainly and presented herself clearly as a bluestocking; but for the election she changed her image to dress smartly. Late in 1990 she was elected for seven years as nonexecutive president of Ireland and became a most popular figure, although at election time she won by only a narrow margin. In March 1992 she proved her strength as leader in the abortion-rape case of a 14 year old; she brought into question the Irish people's views on whether their constitution, which recognized equal rights of mother and unborn child, should be altered to accommodate such a case. In the November 1992 referendum on the constitution, two-thirds of the Irish people wanted the right to receive information about abortion services and to be free to travel to other nations in the European community to seek abortions. Also in June 1993, Mary Robinson shook hands with leaders of Sein Féin, the political arm of the Irish Republican Army; and in May 1993, she visited London as the first Irish head of state to be received by British royalty since Irish independence in 1921.

Sources

Duffy, Martha. 1992. Symbol of the new Ireland. *Time,* June 29:62–64.

The international who's who, 1992–93. London: Europa Publications.

Keesings contemporary archives: record of world events. 1990:37868; 1991:38480; 1992:R111, 38780, 38942, 39065, 39160; 1993:R113, 39480, 39526.

MARYA SYNDROME. Maternally inspired preoccupation with moral justification among political leaders, especially revolutionaries (McIntyre, 1985).

Marya Nikolayevna Volkonsky (1790–1830) was the daughter of Prince Volkonsky and raised in good Russian society. She learned German, English, and Italian, played the piano, studied the history of art, and from her father learned algebra and geometry. An emotional girl and a daydreamer, she also learned to hide her feelings. She was plain and did not expect to marry; but she became engaged to a cousin who died before their marriage. Afterward, while living in Moscow, she was introduced to the young and impecunious Count Nicholas Ilich Tolstoy, and they were married shortly afterward. Her fourth son was Leo Tolstoy (1828–1910), the great Russian novelist. Not long after the birth of her fifth child, she died, and although the 3-year-old Leo could not remember her, as an adult he conjured a view of her from the talk of others, his imagination, and his deep longing for her love. She was good, gentle, upright, proud, intelligent, and an excellent storyteller. Tolstoy was driven by his need for her love and the strong feeling he had of her as an ideal of saintliness, his highest image of love.

Sources

McIntyre, Angus. 1985. Book review: Revolutionary morality, a psychosexual analysis
   of twelve reactionaries, by William Blanchard. *Political Psychology* 6:529–533.
Troyat, Henri. 1980. *Tolstoy.* Harmondsworth, England: Penguin.

MASADA, MASADA COMPLEX. A symbol of Jewish nationalism, especially in the protection of Israel against Arab aggression; an Arab symbol for Israel's diplomatic inflexibility, especially relating to its policy on occupied areas around Israel. The Masada Complex is a set of deep feelings that Arab leaders refer to pejoratively to indicate and explain the fervor of Jews for the welfare of Israel.

   Masada, a fortress on the top of an isolated rock, close to the Dead Sea Valley and the Judean Desert, is in southeast Israel where the Jews last fought against the Romans after the fall of Jerusalem in A.D. 70. Herod built most of Masada, although it was fortified by the Hasomonean king Alexander Jannaeus, who reigned 103–76 B.C. After Herod died (48 B.C.), the Romans captured Masada, but a Jewish force took it suddenly in A.D. 66. In A.D. 72–73 a Roman force of 15,000 fought fewer than 1,000 Jewish zealots, who finally chose death to surrender and becoming slaves. Two women and five children lived to tell the story. In the second century, the Jews occupied Masada briefly, and it was the site of a Byzantine church in the fifth and sixth centuries. Abandoned until the twentieth century, it was excavated in 1963–65, and since then it has been a symbol of Jewish nationalism. Climbing up to the fortress is difficult, but Jewish youths do it regularly to demonstrate their commitment to being prepared for attack from outsiders. It is also a tourist attraction.

Sources

Canby, Courtlandt. 1984. *The encyclopedia of historic places.* London: Mansell Publish-
   ing.
Cowley, Robert, ed. 1992. *Experience of war.* New York: W. W. Norton.
McHenry, Robert, ed. 1992. *The new encyclopedia Britannica.* Chicago: Encyclopedia
   Britannica, Inc.
Pearlman, Moshe. 1980. *Digging up the Bible: the stories behind the great archeological
   discoveries in the Holy land.* New York: William Morrow.
Roth, Cecil E., ed. 1971. *Encyclopedia Judaica.* New York: Macmillan.

Yadin, Yigael. 1966. *Masada: Herod's fortress and the Zealot's last stand.* Trans from Hebrew by Moshe Pearlman. New York: Random Press.

MASLOW'S NEED HIERARCHY. A theory of personal motivation which proposes that human needs may function at different levels, such that lower level needs have to be satisfied before motivation shifts to higher level needs. The hierarchy comprises physiological needs; the need for safety; the need for love and a sense of belonging; the need for esteem; and the need for self-actualization.

Abraham Harold Maslow (1908–70) was born in Brooklyn, New York, and attended New York City College, Cornell University, and the University of Wisconsin (Ph.D., 1934). He taught at Wisconsin (1930–35) and was a Carnegie fellow at Teachers College, Columbia University (1935–37). He taught psychology at Brooklyn College (1935–51) and Brandeis University (1951–69) and later accepted a fellowship at the Laughlin Foundation in Menlo Park, California. A leader in humanistic psychology, he departed from Freudian and behaviorist psychologies, and was greatly interested in creative people and their self-actualization at the highest stage in his hierarchy of needs. He believed that education should encourage children to be creative and responsibly free, and he wrote many articles on creativity and education. Among his publications are *Towards a Psychology of Being* (1962), *Religion Values and Peak Experiences* (1964), and *Farther Reaches of Human Nature* (1971).

Sources

Devine, Elizabeth; Held, Michael; Vinson, James; and Walsh, George, eds. 1983. *Thinkers of the twentieth century: a biographical, bibliographical and critical dictionary.* London: Macmillan.

Garraty, John A., and Carnes, Mark C. 1988. *Dictionary of American biography.* Supplement 8. New York: Charles Scribner's Sons.

Goble, Frank G. 1970. *The third force: the psychology of Abraham Maslow.* New York: Grossman.

Hoffman, Edward. 1988. *The right to be human: a biography of Abraham Maslow.* Los Angeles: J. P. Tarcher; New York: St. Martin's Press.

McHenry, Robert, ed. 1992. *The new encyclopedia Britannica.* Chicago: Encyclopedia Britannica, Inc.

Ohles, John F., ed. 1978. *Biographical dictionary of American educators.* Westport, Conn.: Greenwood Press.

Zusne, Leonard. 1984. *Biographical dictionary of psychology.* Westport, Conn.: Greenwood Press.

MASOCHISM. Sexual pleasure from cruel treatment usually administered by the other sex; excessive gratification in physical or mental suffering.

Leopold Ritter von Sacher-Masoch (1836–95) was born in Lemberg in Lindheim, Austria. His childhood was dominated by terror, bewildering cruelty, and savage parenting. He studied at Graz and was awarded a law degree from the University of Prague in 1855. For brief periods he was a professor in Lemberg and then gave his time fully to writing. He wrote history and short novels devoted largely to perversion. He was also an actor. Among his many novels were *Das Vermachtnis Kains* (1870), *Die Messalinen Wiens* (1874), and *Polnische Judengeshicten* (1886). His most popular novel was *Venus in Furs* (1870), which reflects his childhood fears and abnormal fantasies and interests. He died in an asylum, where his wife had committed him for his frequent attempts to murder her. Ten years before his death, his wife announced that he had died and mourned his passing. The term *masochism* was coined by Baron Richard Krafft-Ebing (1840–1902), the German neurologist and psychiatrist who noted the writer's obsession with sexually gratifying domination by the opposite sex, and its connection with self-inflicted pain. Sadomasochism is a variety of masochism related to cruel sexual perversion.

Sources

Barnhart, Robert K., ed. 1988. *The Barnhart dictionary of etymology.* New York: H. W. Wilson.

Cleugh, James. 1967. *The first masochist: a biography of Leopold von Sacher-Masoch.* New York: Stein and Day.

Deleuze, Gilles, and von Sacher-Masoch, Leopold. 1971. *Masochism: Coldness and cruelty, and Venus in furs.* English trans., 1989. New York: Zone.

Garland, Henry, and Garland, Mary. 1986. *The Oxford companion to German literature.* Oxford: Clarendon Press.

McHenry, Robert, ed. 1992. *The new encyclopedia Britannica.* Chicago: Encyclopedia Britannica, Inc.

MASON-DIXON LINE. The boundary between Pennsylvania and Maryland, which has been used as a political symbol separating the free Northern American states from the slave states of the South.

Charles Mason (1730–87) assisted at the Greenwich Observatory (1756–60) and with Jeremiah Dixon was chosen by the Royal Society to observe the transit of Venus in Bencoolen, Sumatra. Because of delays caused by a naval conflict with the French, they had to observe the transit from the Cape of Good Hope; in December 1761 he collected tidal data at Saint Helena before being employed by William Penn and Lord Baltimore to survey the boundary between Maryland and Pennsylvania. They went 244 miles west of the Delaware River and were stopped about 36 miles short of the goal by Indians in November 1767. Mason and Dixon made many complicated measurements and computations, and fixed the border between Maryland and Pennsylvania at parallel 39° 43' 17.6" N, beginning at the eastern boundary of Maryland with Delaware. They completed other observations and returned in 1768. Mason made more observations for the Royal Society, worked on experiments on gravity, and collected further astronomical observations before returning to Philadelphia where he died. During debates in Congress over the Missouri Compromise in 1819, the phrase "Mason-Dixon line" was used to include the Ohio River from Pennsylvania to its mouth at the Mississippi. In time, the line came to symbolize the boundary between the North and the slave states of the South.

Jeremiah Dixon (1733–79) was born in Durham, son of a Quaker coal miner, and educated at John Kipling's School, Barnard Castle. When Charles Mason was chosen to observe the transit of Venus in Sumatra in 1761, Dixon went with him. In 1763 he and Mason signed an agreement with the hereditary proprietors of Pennsylvania and Maryland to visit North America to survey the disputed boundary between the two provinces. In 1768 he returned to England and observed the transit of Venus from Norway on behalf of the Royal Society. On returning to England he continued his work as a surveyor; he died in County Durham.

Sources

Dudley, Lavinia P. 1963. *The encyclopedia Americana.* International ed. New York: Americana Corp.

McHenry, Robert, ed. 1992. *The new encyclopedia Britannica.* Chicago: Encyclopedia Britannica, Inc.

Malone, Dumas, ed. 1934. *Dictionary of American biography.* Vol. VII. New York: Charles Scribner's Sons.

Mason, A. Hughlett, ed. 1969. *The journal of Charles Mason and Jeremiah Dixon.* Philadelphia: American Philosophical Society.

Nicholls, C. S., ed. 1993. *Dictionary of national biography: missing persons.* New York: Oxford University Press.

Stephen, Leslie, and Lee, Sydney, eds. 1917. *The dictionary of national biography.* London: Oxford University Press.

MASTERMAN LINE. A line separating industrial and manipulative grades of employees in the British Civil Service from higher grades; those below the line were permitted to enter party politics but those above were not. Trade unions objected to the arbitrariness of the line. Discussions continued until March 1953, when the government published a White Paper, "Political Activities of Civil Servants," which introduced the idea of an "intermediate group" between the "politically free" and the "politically restricted."

Sir John Cecil Masterman (1891–1977) was born in Kingston-on-Thames, educated at Evelyns, and became a naval cadet. In 1913 he quit the navy to study modern history and became a lecturer at Oxford University. He was interned in Germany during World War I. Afterward he returned to academe, excelled in cricket and tennis, and wrote a novel, a play, and a detective story (1933–37). In World War II he served in MI5 and was responsible for the XX System of double agents. He returned to university and in 1947–48 chaired the committee on the Political Activities of Civil Servants, which recommended that the industrial and minor manipulative grades of civil servants, but no others, be free to embark on party politics. In retirement, he consulted for industry and wrote *The Double Cross System in the War of 1939 to 1945* (1972) and *On the Chariot Wheel: An Autobiography* (1975).

Sources

Blake (Lord), and Nicholls, C. S., eds. 1986. *Dictionary of national biography, 1971–1980.* Oxford: Oxford University Press.

Drewry, G., and Butcher, Tony. 1988. *The civil service today.* Oxford: Basil Blackwell.
    Report of the Committee on the Political Activities of Civil Servants; under the chair-
    manship of J. C. Masterman Cmd 7718. London: HMSO.

MASTERS AND JOHNSON STUDY. A modern study in human sexual behavior and gender research of the anatomy, physiology, and activity of human
sexual behavior under laboratory conditions (1966). The work described all
phases of sexual response in men and women, the problems and reasons for the
study, and laboratory procedures, and examined myths and folklore about sexual
behavior.

William Howell Masters (b. 1915) was educated at Hamilton College, Clinton,
New York and the University of Rochester (M.D., 1943), specializing in gy-
necology. He joined the medical faculty, University of Washington, Saint Louis
in 1947 and began his noted sex research in 1954. He became director of the
Reproductive Biology Research Foundation (1964–73), later named the Masters
and Johnson Institute. He was its co-director (1973–80) and chairman of the
board (1981–). In 1966, with Virginia Johnson, he published *Human Sexual
Response* and has seen it appear in at least ten languages.

Virginia Eshelman Johnson (b. 1925) was born in Springfield, Missouri. She
studied at Drury College, Springfield, and the University of Missouri (Kansas)
Conservatory of Music (1944–46). She trained in psychology, and in 1957 she
began as Masters' research associate, and together, in 1964, they established the
Reproductive Biology Research Foundation. She became the co-director with
Masters of the Masters and Johnson Institute in 1974. She was awarded a D.Sc.,
University of Missouri, in 1964. Masters and Johnson also conducted clinical
marriage counseling to help those with difficulties in sexual performance. They
published *Human Sexual Inadequacy* (1970), *The Pleasure Bond* (1975), *Homosexuality in Perspective* (1979), and *Human Sexuality* (1982). They married
in 1971 and were recently divorced.

Sources

Brecher, Ruth, and Brecher, Edward. 1967. *An analysis of "Human sexual response."*
    London: Routledge and Kegan Paul.
Kay, Ernest, ed. 1978. *The world who's who of women.* Cambridge: International Bio-
    graphical Center.
Masters, William H.; Johnson, Virginia E.; and Kolodny, Robert C. 1986. *Masters and
    Johnson on sex and human learning.* Boston: Little, Brown.
Moritz, Charles, ed. 1968. *Current biography yearbook.* New York: H. W. Wilson.
Vernoff, Edward, and Shore, Rima, eds. 1987. *International dictionary of 20th century
    biography.* New York: New American Library.

MATA HARI. A woman spy or secret agent.

Mata Hari (1876–1917) was born Gertrud Margarete Zelle (Margaretha Geer-
truida Zelle) in Leeuwarden, Holland. At age 17, in answer to a lonely hearts
advertisement, she married an officer of the Dutch East Indies, John Macleod.
They went to Java where she became interested in the local dancing; the mar-

riage failed, and by 1902 she was divorced, penniless, and living in Holland. In 1904 in a Paris circus she performed as an exotic dancer billed as "Mata Hari," meaning "Eye of the Dawn." Later she became a courtesan among upper class men. At the outbreak of World War I, she was close to the chief of police in Berlin and was reluctantly led into the Secret Service. While dallying with a German intelligence officer in Madrid, she had an affair with Captain Ladoux of the French Secret Service. In 1916 her relationship with German agents was discovered in London, the French arrested her in 1917, and she was shot for espionage in October of that year. In fact, she was an incompetent spy, untrustworthy, and gave Germany no useful intelligence, and her death sentence was unexpected. For this reason it was probably an attempt to raise flagging French morale in wartime. With Greta Garbo's film *Mata Hari,* the name became a legend; but not until 1991 did her hometown acknowledge her and establish a permanent exhibition in her honor.

Sources

Howe, Russell W. 1986. *Mata Hari: the true story.* New York: Dodd, Mead and Co.

Knightly, Phillip. 1986. *The second oldest profession: the spy as bureaucrat, patriot, fantasist and whore.* London: Andre Deutsch.

McHenry, Robert, ed. 1992. *The new encyclopedia Britannica.* Chicago: Encyclopedia Britannica, Inc.

Newman, Bernard. 1956. *Inquest on Mata Hari.* London: Robert Hale.

Waagenaar, Sam. 1964. *The murder of Mata Hari.* London: Barker.

MATTHEW EFFECT. A pattern of credit given to scientific work, which indicates that the degree of recognition among scientists has a tendency to be self-reinforcing, positively and negatively, and that the career lines of scientists tend to logistic curves rather than to straight lines. The effect was based on a statement by Saint Matthew in his account of "The parable of the talents" (Matthew 25:14–30). Verse 29 says: "For unto everyone that hath shall be given, and he shall have abundance; but from him that hath not shall be taken away even that which he hath." Robert K. Merton (b. 1910), the American sociologist, chose this verse to express the accruing of great increments in recognition for certain contributions to scientists of repute, and the withholding of recognition from those who were hardly known, for example, Nobel laureates (1968). Recent study indicates that significant work tends to be recognized regardless of who produces it, but the speed of its diffusion is influenced by the author's reputation (Cole, 1970).

Saint Matthew, or Levi, was one of Jesus' twelve apostles. He was once a publican or a collector of tolls payable on goods and by travelers crossing the Sea of Galilee to land at Capernaum. In Jesus' parable of the talents, a rich man gives three servants different amounts of money, according to their ability, while he is absent. On returning, he is pleased to reward the two who used the money to earn a profit but angry with the one who, fearing his master's hard nature and rapacious ways, did not trade but merely returned the amount he had been given. The master accused the fellow of sloth and ordered that the money he had been left be given to the man who had made the most profit. Furthermore, the fellow was to quit service and be sent to "outer darkness" where there were many similar individuals "weeping and gnashing teeth." Legend states that Matthew was killed in Parthia; September 27 is his feast day.

Sources

Cole, Stephen. 1970. Professional standing and the reception of scientific discoveries. *American Journal of Sociology* 76:286–306.

Eliade, Mircea, ed. 1987. *Encyclopedia of religion.* New York: Macmillan.

Meagher, Paul K.; O'Brien, Thomas C.; and Aherne, Marie, eds. 1979. *Encyclopedic dictionary of religion.* Washington, D.C.: Corpus Publications.

Merton, Robert K. 1968. The Matthew effect in science. *Science* 159, 3810 (January 5): 56–63. In Robert K. Merton and Norman W. Storer, eds. 1973. *The sociology of science: theoretical and empirical investigations.* Chicago: University of Chicago Press, pp. 441–459.

Ziman, John. 1987. *Science in a "steady state": the research system in transition.* London: Science Policy Support Group.

MAUD COMMITTEE. A British committee within the Ministry of Aircraft production, which was given the camouflaged name MAUD in April 1940. The committee's aim was to determine whether it was possible to produce power or explosion from nuclear fission. The original members met at the Royal Society in secret; they were professors George Thomson, James Chadwick, John Cockroft, Marcus Oliphant, and Dr. P. B. Moon. In July 1941 George Thomson, the chairman, reported to the British cabinet that it was possible to produce a uranium fission bomb before the end of World War II.

When Denmark was invaded by Nazi Germany in April 1940, Niels Bohr, noted physicist, sent a telegram that included several personal messages to Dr. Otto Frisch in England. The final message was TELL COCKROFT AND MAUD RAY KENT. By substituting "i" for "y" in the word *Ray,* it was thought the message said "radium taken," meaning, in code, the Germans are well on the way to making an atom bomb. So Maud was chosen for the committee's name—a code-name with no meaning—but later it was said that "Maud" was an acronym and stood for Military Applications of Uranium Detonation, or perhaps Ministry of Air: Uranium Development. Late in 1943, when Niels Bohr reached London, he asked if the personal message ever reached the governess of his children, Miss Maud Ray, living in Kent.

Sources

Clark, Ronald W. 1961. *The birth of the bomb: the untold story of Britain's part in the weapon that changed the world.* London: Phoenix House.

Gowing, Margaret. 1964. *Britain and atomic energy, 1939–1945.* New York: St. Martin's Press.

MAVERICK INDEPENDENT. A type of politician who enters Parliament without the support of a major party. Alone or with other independents, the maverick independent may hold the balance of power in government and push for interests opposed to the policy of the government in office, for example, environmental issues and anticorruption policies. Political commentators often present such politicians as holding a government to ransom while pretending to keep it honest, and seeking the advantages of office that regular ministers enjoy, for example, information and perks.

Samuel Augustus Maverick (1803–70) was a Texas cattle-raiser, pioneer, and politician who fought for the independence of the state of Texas. In about 1855, Maverick put some cattle under the supervision of an employee who did not brand the calves, and later let them wander. Neighbors called any unbranded, wandering cattle, "one of Maverick's," and the term gradually came to mean anyone's unbranded stock. According to legend, Maverick deliberately did not brand his own cattle and would claim that all stock without a brand were his. He employed stock detectives to ensure that no other cattlemen ran off his stock and branded them. After the American Civil War, maverick cattle belonged to any person who could brand them. Later, "maverick" came to mean a noncon-formist.

Sources

Dudley, Lavinia P. 1963. *The encyclopedia Americana.* International ed. New York: Americana Corp.

Malone, Dumas, ed. 1933. *Dictionary of American biography.* Vol. VI. New York: Charles Scribner's Sons.

Schapsmeier, Edward L., and Schapsmeier, Frederick H. 1975. *Encyclopedia of American agricultural history.* Westport, Conn.: Greenwood Press.

Van Doren, Charles, ed. 1974. *Webster's American biographies.* Springfield, Mass.: G. and C. Merriam.

MAYOISM, MAYO SCHOOL OF INDUSTRIAL ANTHROPOLOGY. A managerial ideology that advocates raising levels of employee performance and cooperation by improving the managers' interpersonal skills and changing in-formally organized work groups. The ideology prefers cooperation over conflict and competition, group relations over individual action, social over material rewards of work, and participative and even manipulative styles of influence over autocratic management style. Little attention is paid to trade unions and to occupational interests and associations outside work. Mayoism was based on some ideas of Elton Mayo but was not of his making. The ideology arose from criticisms of the efforts of those who applied Mayo's ideas manipulatively to raise management control over subordinates at work. The Mayo School of In-dustrial Anthropology focused on the human aspects of labor, the inner expe-riences of work rather than its objective constraints, and the wide social context in which it was done; and conflict was considered pathological.

George Elton Mayo (1880–1949), an Australian academic philosopher and psychologist, was born in Adelaide, taught philosophy at the University of Queensland (1912–20), and after a short period at the University of Pennsylvania's Wharton Business School joined the Harvard Business School as a director of Industrial Research (1927–47). Funded by the Rockefeller Foundation, he studied the human, social, and political problems of industrial civilization. He was associated with and publicist for the classical American research in industrial sociology, the Hawthorne Studies (1902), at the Western Electric Company in the township of Cicero, near Chicago. It found that the employees' personal background and the social relations they had developed at work were important to their work behavior.

See also HAWTHORNE EXPERIMENTS.

Sources

Child, John. 1969. *British management thought: a critical analysis.* London: Allen and Unwin.

Gillespie, Richard. 1992. *Manufacturing knowledge: a history of the Hawthorne experiment.* Cambridge: Cambridge University Press.

Roethlisberger, F. J., and Dickson, W. J. 1939. *Management and the worker.* Cambridge, Mass.: Harvard University Press.

Sills, David L., ed. 1968. *International encyclopedia of the social sciences.* New York: Macmillan and Free Press.

Trahair, Richard C.S. 1984. *The humanist temper: the life and work of Elton Mayo [with bibliography].* New Brunswick, N.J.: Transaction Books.

MAZARINADE. A satire or pamphlet hostile to the seventeenth-century French cardinal.

Jules Mazarin (1602–61) was born in Italy and assumed French nationality when he entered the service of Louis XIII in 1639. He was made a cardinal in 1641, although he had taken only minor orders. In 1642, after Richelieu's death, Mazarin succeeded him as chief minister. He gained the confidence of the queen mother and regent, Anne of Austria, after the death of Louis XIII and supervised the upbringing of Louis XIV who was only 5 when he assumed the throne. Mazarin wanted to extend French power at the expense of both Spain and Austria. He prosecuted the Thirty Years' War, and in 1648 at the Treaty of Westphalia secured favorable terms. Nevertheless, his policy of centralizing power and upholding royal absolutism met hostility among the nobility and the law courts and led to civil war in the Fronde (1648–53). At this time, leading Parisians circulated the pamphlets in response to Mazarin's attempts to recoup the costs of the war. The opposition to his policies spread among the higher nobility, and in the provinces opposition to him found popular support, again largely because of the pamphlets. Twice he was forced to quit the court, but he could return because he had enough backing from the boy King Louis XIV and Anne of Austria.

Sources

Bailly, Auguste. 1935. *Mazarin.* Paris: A. Fayard.

Brewer, Ebenezer Cobham. 1970. *Brewer's dictionary of phrase and fable.* Centenary ed. Rev. by Ivor H. Evans. New York: Harper and Row.

Goubert, Pierre. 1990. *Mazarin.* Paris: Fayard.

Guth, Paul 1972. *Mazarin*. Paris: Flammarion.
McHenry, Robert, ed. 1992. *The new encyclopedia Britannica*. Chicago: Encyclopedia Britannica, Inc.

MAZLISH'S REVOLUTIONARY ASCETIC. A political character who withdraws love from his interpersonal relations and imposes it onto an ideal vision that he creates, and then fully identifies it with himself. He is independent, cold, hostile, without pity or sympathy, masterful, and has a godlike sense of his own superiority. Ruthless in his control of himself and self-punishing in regard to wickedness in himself, he attracts followers by his apparent lack of self-interest.

Bruce Mazlish (b. 1923) was born in New York and educated at Columbia College and Columbia University (Ph.D., 1955). After graduation, he taught history at the University of Maine (1946–48), Columbia University (1949–50), and thereafter at the Massachusetts Institute of Technology (MIT). He directed the American School, Madrid (1953–55), headed the Humanities Department and History Section at MIT, and as professor of history occupies the Meloy Chair of Rhetoric. Among his many honors and awards are the Toynbee Prize in Social Science (1986–87); he has long been a fellow of the American Academy of Arts and Sciences and the Social Science Research Council; and he has edited various international journals of history and political psychology and psychohistory, as well as advising and consulting special committees on related matters. Among his works are *In Search of Nixon* (1972), *Psychoanalysis and History* (1963; 1971), *The Western Intellectual Tradition* (1960), *James and John Stuart Mill: Father and Son* (1975; 1988), *A New Science: The Breakdown of Connections and the Birth of Sociology* (1989), and *The Leader, the Led, and the Psyche: Essays in Psychohistory* (1990).

Sources

Mazlish, Bruce. 1976. *The revolutionary ascetic: evolution of a political type*. New York: Basic Books.
Personal Communication.

McCARRAN ACT. The U.S. Internal Security Act (1950) that aimed to control the Communist party and other groups that represented totalitarian interests; the act outlawed those groups controlled from abroad that conspired to establish a dictatorship, peacefully or otherwise, in the United States. The Subversive Activities Control Board (later abolished) would identify the communist fronts, groups, and infiltrators; such organizations and people would have to be registered with the attorney-general, their publications would be labeled as communist; and trade unions infiltrated by them would no longer have rights under the nation's labor laws. Passport and employment restrictions would be put on people who belonged to such fronts. Most major provisions of the act were subject to judicial rejection. For example, the Supreme Court declared invalid the requirement that individual communist leaders be registered because it violated the right against self-incrimination.

Patrick Anthony McCarran (1876–1954) was born in Reno, Nevada, and became a farmer, stockman, lawyer, and Nevada Democrat. He was educated at the local schools and graduated from the University of Nevada, became a farmer and raised stock, and entered the state legislature in 1903. He represented Nevada in an irrigation congress in 1903, studied law, and was admitted to the bar in 1905. He practiced in Nevada and became district attorney in 1907–9, associate justice of the Supreme Court of Nevada (1913–17), and chief justice (1917–18). He was elected as a Democrat to the United States Senate in 1932 and served until his death. His name was given to two acts—one regarding internal security (1950) and another which restricted immigration to the United States (1952). Both had strong anticommunist overtones.

Sources

Blevins, Leon W. 1974. *The young voters' manual, dictionary of American government and politics.* Totowa, N.J.: Rowman and Littlefield.

Filler, Louis. 1987. *Dictionary of American conservatism.* New York: Philosophical Library.

Jacob, Kathryn A., and Ragsdale, Bruce A. 1989. *Biographical directory of the United States Congress: 1774–1989.* Bicentennial ed. Washington, D.C.: U.S. Government Printing Office.

Keesings contemporary archives: weekly diary of world events. 1950:10976. London: Keesings Publications.

Morris, Dan, and Morris Inez, eds. 1974. *Who was who in American politics.* New York: Hawthorn Books.

Plano, Jack C., and Greenberg, Milton, 1989. *The American political dictionary.* New York: Holt, Rinehart and Winston.

McCARRAN-WALTER ACT. The U.S. Immigration and Nationality Act (1952) which restated the U.S. policy on immigration and was especially harsh in its anticommunist tone. It set small quotas for Asians, Africans, and those from Southern and Eastern Europe. Communists and those who wanted to overthrow the U.S. government by violence were not to be admitted, such people already living in the United States could not be naturalized, and some could, if necessary, have their naturalization revoked.

Patrick Anthony McCarran (1876–1954). See McCARRAN ACT.

Francis Eugene Walter (1894–1963) was born in Easton, Pennsylvania, and was educated at public schools and at Princeton, Leigh, and Georgetown universities. He was admitted to the bar in 1919, was a Northampton County solicitor, Eastern Hospital trustee (1928–33), and served in the U.S. Congress from 1933 until his death. He served in the U.S. Navy in both world wars and became a banker. As a Democrat from Pennsylvania, he chaired the House Un-American Activities Committee, which many have described as a witch-hunting body. As chairman of the Immigration Naturalization Sub-committee, he became what has been described as the czar of immigration legislation. Among his actions was the co-authorship of the McCarran-Walter Act which, in his *New York Times* obituary, was called the fundamental restriction on immigration. Although he opposed both Truman and Kennedy on questions of internal security and immigration, he supported Kennedy's economic and social legislation.

Sources

Garraty, John A., ed. 1981. *Dictionary of American biography.* Supplement 7. New York: Charles Scribner's Sons.

Jacob, Kathryn A., and Ragsdale, Bruce A. 1989 *Biographical directory of the United States Congress: 1774–1989.* Bicentennial ed. Washington, D.C.: U.S. Government Printing Office.

Keesings contemporary archives: weekly diary of world events. 1952:11046. London: Keesings Publications.

Malone, Dumas, ed. 1932. *Dictionary of American biography.* Vol. V. New York: Charles Scribner's Sons.

Plano, Jack C., and Greenberg, Milton. 1989. *The American political dictionary.* New York: Holt, Rinehart and Winston.

McCARTHYISM, McCARTHYITE. Searching for and removing from public employment of all suspected of communism between 1950 and 1954. Relating to this kind of purge especially persecution without reliable evidence, attribution of guilt without proper recourse to law.

Joseph Raymond McCarthy (1908–57) was born at Grand Chute, Wisconsin, and at age 16 left school to work on his father's farm; he went to night school and graduated from Marquette University (LL.B., 1935). He was elected circuit judge in Wisconsin, and during World War II he took temporary leave from judicial duties, was commissioned as a lieutenant, and served in the Marines as an intelligence officer, returning home in 1944. Relieved from active service he resigned in March 1945, and later claimed falsely that he had risen from buck private to captain, won a Distinguished Flying Cross and Air Medal, and been wounded in action. In 1946 he was elected to the U.S. Senate. In February 1950 he made his celebrated speech in Wheeling, West Virginia, in which he expressed outrage at the U.S. State Department's harboring of communists. In 1953, as chairman of the Permanent Subcommittee on Investigations, he began inquiries into the Voice of America and the Army Signal Corps at Fort Monmouth. After his search for subversive and un-American and communist activities had led to the destruction of many careers, it was criticized for its violation of democratic procedures. His name is now associated only with witch-hunting practices.

Sources

Caute, David. 1978. *The great fear: the anti-communism purge under Truman and Eisenhower.* New York: Simon and Schuster.

Garraty, John A., ed. 1980. *Dictionary of American biography.* Supplement 6. New York: Charles Scribner's Sons.

Latham, Earl. 1973. *The meaning of McCarthyism.* 2d ed. Lexington, Mass.: D. C. Heath.

Oshinsky, David M. 1983. *A conspiracy so immense: the world of Joe McCarthy.* New York: Free Press.

Reeves, Thomas C. 1982. *The life and times of Joe McCarthy.* New York: Stein and
     Day.
Riff, Michael A. 1987. *Dictionary of modern political ideologies.* Manchester: Man-
     chester University Press.
Rovere, Richard H. 1959. *Senator Joe McCarthy.* Cleveland: World.

McGREGOR'S THEORY X AND THEORY Y. Two aspects of modern
management practices that differ in the human response to and motivation for
work.

Douglas McGregor (1906–64) completed his Ph.D. at Harvard University
where he taught from 1935 to 1937. Thereafter he was at the Massachusetts
Institute of Technology as a psychology professor and as Antioch's president,
1948–54. While at Antioch he learned to exercise authority and carry a leader's
responsibility, and in *The Human Side of Enterprise* (1960) he set down two
sets of antithetical assumptions about people at work. "Theory X" assumed
people disliked work, acted accordingly, had to be coerced to behave appropriately, and preferred life that way. "Theory Y" assumed people had a natural
liking for work, exercised self-direction in doing it, were committed to work,
and found it satisfying under conditions conducive to that commitment. The
humanistic assumptions of "Theory Y" guided modern management in the late
1960s and early 1970s, but were later refined to include the differing needs of
people at work and variations in the demands of organizations.
Sources

Bedeian, Arthur. 1986. *Management.* New York: Dryden Press.
Bennis, Warren G.; Schein, Edgar H.; and McGregor, Caroline, eds. 1966. *Leadership
     and motivation: essays of Douglas McGregor.* Cambridge, Mass.: MIT Press.
McGregor, Douglas. 1960. *The human side of enterprise.* New York: McGraw-Hill.
Morse, John J., and Lorsch, Jay W. 1970. Beyond Theory Y. *Harvard Business Review*
     48:61–68.
Wren, Daniel A. 1979. *The evolution of management thought.* 2d ed. New York: John
     Wiley.

McGUFFEY'S READER. A school reader with moral guidance.

William Holmes McGuffey (1800–73) was born in Pennsylvania and was
taken to Ohio in 1802, educated at homes and occasionally in rural schools, and
at Greersberg Academy in Pennsylvania. He graduated from Washington College in 1826 and taught ancient languages and mental philosophy at Miami
University in Oxford, Ohio (1926–36), Woodward College, Cincinnati, and the
University of Virginia. He was president of Cincinnati College (1836–39) and
of the University of Ohio, Athens (1839–43), and he helped to found the Common School system for Ohio. He was professor of mental and moral philosophy
at the University of Virginia from 1845 until his death. In 1836 he published
McGuffey's First Eclectic Reader. For two generations the readers were con-
stantly revised, and they sold more than 120 million copies for use among
schoolchildren. The last version appeared in 1857. As late as 1960 the reader

was still selling well. The readers were appreciated for their examples of fine English literature as well as their morally sound essays.

Sources

Crawford, Benjamin F. 1963. *William Holmes McGuffey: the schoolmaster to a nation.* Delaware, Ohio: Carnegie Church Press.

Malone, Dumas, ed. 1933. *Dictionary of American biography.* Vol. VI. New York: Charles Scribner's Sons.

Ohles, John F., ed. 1978. *Biographical dictionary of American educators.* Westport, Conn.: Greenwood Press.

McHUGH DISPUTE. A serious British industrial dispute at Austin, Longbridge (1952–53), over the dismissal of the secretary of the Austin Motor Company Joint Shop Stewards Committee, as part of a redundancy program at the end of the production of the A90 Atlantic Model automobile. The issue led to a long and important strike in February 1953 and to a court of inquiry in May 1953.

John McHugh (fl. 1928–53) worked at Austin for over twelve years, though not continuously; after 1928 he was discharged five times owing to trade circumstances, and once left on his own accord. His last period of employment began in 1948; shortly afterward he became a shop steward. By 1952 he was regarded as the union chief at the works, though not by management. He was president of his union branch, secretary of the Austin Motor Company Joint Shop Stewards Committee, and chairman of the Austin-Morris Stewards Merger Committee, and held other union offices. The company had announced that model (A90) was being discontinued and that it would discharge 700 hourly paid men and 100 staff on the "last in, first out" principle. When McHugh received his notice, the NUVB claimed that McHugh was being victimized for his union activities. The court of inquiry concluded that McHugh's dismissal could not be attributed to victimization because of his previous union activities. The strike involved 23,000 strike-days; McHugh was not re-engaged.

Sources

Marsh, Arthur. 1979. *Concise encyclopedia of industrial relations.* Westmead, Farnborough, Hants: Gower.

Turner, Herbert A.; Clack, Garfield; and Roberts, Geoffrey. 1967. *Labor relations in the motor industry: a study of industrial unrest and an international comparison.* London: Allen and Unwin.

McKENZIE, McKENZIE FRIEND, McKENZIE MAN. In Britain a person who goes to court to help another. The term derives from the case, *McKenzie* vs. *McKenzie* (1970), in which an Australian barrister was in court in the non-professional role of friend to help the defendant. Three judges found that any person, whether or not a professional lawyer, could attend a trial as a friend of either party, take notes, and quietly make suggestions and give advice.

Leveine McKenzie and Maizie McKenzie (fl. 1954–70) were born in Jamaica, married in 1954, and had many children. Leveine came to London in 1956, and Maizie followed him a year later. In 1964 their marriage began to break down, and by September 1965 each had complained in court about the cruelty of the other. After psychiatric examination, pregnancy, and a hysterectomy, Maizie sought a divorce on grounds of cruelty, while Leveine sought divorce on grounds of adultery. At the trial in 1969 Leveine's legal aid ceased, and seeing him in much trouble, Mr. Hanger, an Australian barrister, who had been working at the solicitor's that Leveine had earlier retained, volunteered to help. But the judge, noting that the solicitor's firm that Leveine had been using was no longer on record, decided that it was improper for Mr. Hanger to take part in proceedings, and he did not appear. In June 1970 a court of appeal decided unanimously that the judge had erred.

Sources

Niekirk, Paul H. 1970. *The all England law reports.* Vol 3. London: Butterworth.

Tulloch, Sara. 1991 *The Oxford dictionary of new words.* Oxford: Oxford University Press.

McMAHON ACT. A bill that established the U.S. Atomic Energy Commission (1946) and forbade the transmission of any information on atomic energy to a foreign power. The bill ended the agreement made between Roosevelt and Churchill (1944) to cooperate in the development of atomic energy for military and civil purposes after World War II. The act promoted rivalry between Britain and the United States in the development of larger nuclear bombs and weapons.

James O'Brien McMahon (1903–52) was born in Norwalk, Connecticut, was educated at public schools, at Fordham University (1924), and at Yale Law School (1927). After graduation, he changed his name to Brien McMahon and commenced a law practice in Norwalk. In 1944 he was elected to the U.S. Congress, and served until his death. He chaired the U.S. Congress Joint-Committee on Atomic Energy and argued for greater public access to atomic information at hearings on security issues. He also encouraged public debate on Soviet-American arms control, and warned President Truman (1949) that if the United States did not win the race for supremacy in nuclear arms, then catastrophe would ensue.

Sources

Jacob, Kathryn A., and Ragsdale, Bruce A. 1989. *Biographical directory of the United States Congress: 1774–1989.* Bicentennial ed. Washington, D.C.: U.S. Government Printing Office.

Gowing, Margaret. 1964. *Britain and atomic energy: 1939–1945.* New York: St. Martin's Press.

Williams, Robert Chadwell. 1987. *Klaus Fuchs: atom spy.* Cambridge, Mass.: Harvard University Press.

McNAIR REPORT. A British educational report on teachers (1944) that recommended longer training courses and a wider field of recruitment; it also ended the ban on married women teachers, established areas of training and training organizations, a central council, and supported increases in teaching salaries.

Arnold Duncan McNair, first Baron McNair (1885–1975), was educated at

Aldenham School and the University at Cambridge. He studied law and after being a solicitor and lecturer in law was appointed a reader of international law at London University (1926–27), and later Whewell Professor of International Law at Cambridge (1935–37), and vice-chancellor of the University of Liverpool (1937–45). He served on many commissions and committees and was president of the European Court of Human Rights (1959–65). He chaired the committee on the Supply and Training of Teachers (1944), and its proposals became known as the McNair Report. He was knighted in 1943 and raised to the peerage in 1955. Among his published works are *The Legal Effects of War* (1920); *Doctor Johnson and the Law* (1943); *International Law Options* (1956); and *Lord McNair: Selected Papers and Bibliography* (1974).

Sources

Aldrich, Richard, and Gordon, Peter. 1987. *Dictionary of British educationists.* London: Woburn Press.

Blake (Lord), and Nicholls, C. S., eds. 1986. *Dictionary of national biography 1971–1980.* Oxford: Oxford University Press.

McNAUGHTEN RULES. Rules under which mental abnormality relieves a defendant from criminal responsibility.

Daniel McNaughten (1813–65) was born in Glasgow, apprenticed to a wood carver, and went into business for five years. In about 1841 he sold the business, telling people that spies were threatening to kill him. For peace of mind he went to lectures on anatomy, but concluded his suffering was due to the leader of the Tories, Sir Robert Peel, the prime minister, whom he decided to kill. In error, he shot to death the popular private secretary to the prime minister, Edward Drummond (1792–1843). McNaughten was tried for the murder, found not guilty owing to paranoid delusions, was put in Bethlem Hospital, and diagnosed as a monomaniac. Always believing his life was under threat he read and knitted, and in 1864 he was transferred to Broadmore Criminal Lunatic Asylum where he died of anemia, brain disease, and heart failure. He was buried in an unmarked grave. The law of England as to the criminal responsibility of the insane was embodied in the McNaughten Rule: an accused person is presumed sane until it is clearly proved that, at the time of committing the act, the accused was laboring under such a defect of reason as not to know the nature of the act, or that he was doing wrong. In 1957 the McNaughten Rules were superseded in English law.

Sources

Boase, Frederic. 1965. *Modern English biography.* London: Frank Cass.

Clyne, Peter. 1973. *Guilty but insane: Anglo-American attitudes to insanity and criminal guilt.* London: Thomas Nelson.

McHenry, Robert, ed. 1992. *The new encyclopedia Britannica.* Chicago: Encyclopedia Britannica, Inc.

Maeder, Thomas. 1985. *Crime and madness: the origins and evolution of the insanity defense.* New York: Harper and Row.

MEADIAN. Relating to the ideas, especially of the "generalized other" and "self" and the distinction between "I" and "me," in the work of the twentieth-century American social psychologist.

George Herbert Mead (1863–1931) was born in South Hadley, Massachusetts, graduated from Oberlin College, Ohio, and worked as a schoolteacher and surveyor (1883–87). He continued his studies at Harvard (1887–88), and the universities of Berlin and Leipzig (1888–91). After teaching philosophy at the University of Michigan, Ann Arbor (1891–94), Mead was invited by John Dewey (1859–1952) to the Department of Philosophy, University of Chicago (1894), and he worked there until he died. His writing dealt with philosophical, psychological ideas and with some social and educational reforms. In the 1920s Mead developed a social psychology that was popular among his students and was especially suited to sociology. His influential ideas were the *generalized other*—society's representative in the individual, a generalized set of attitudes— and the *self*—the "I" and the "me" of a person, parts that roughly indicated the impassioned self and the controlling self. He also developed the concept of "role" and discussed the social significance of time, especially in work and organizations. His ideas were useful in criticisms of the biological conceptions of human behavior, acted as counter to the ideas of Freud and individualistic psychology, were used in theories of socialization and of the internalization of cultural norms, and showed how personal control related to social control. His students published his work as *Mind, Self and Society,* apparently because he was not aware of the value of his original thoughts.

Sources

Devine, Elizabeth; Held, Michael; Vinson, James; and Walsh, George, eds. 1983. *Thinkers of the twentieth century: a biographical, bibliographical and critical dictionary.* London: Macmillan.

Joas, Hans. 1980. *G. H. Mead: a contemporary re-examination of his thought.* Cambridge: Polity Press.

Morris, Charles W., ed. 1934. *Mind, self and society.* Chicago: University of Chicago Press.

Natanson, Maurice A. 1973. *The social dynamics of George H. Mead.* The Hague: Martinus Nijhoff.

Sills, David L., ed. 1968. *International encyclopedia of the social sciences.* New York: Macmillan and Free Press.

Strauss, Anselm. 1956. *George Herbert Mead on social psychology.* Phoenix Books. Chicago: University of Chicago Press.

Zusne, Leonard. 1984. *Biographical dictionary of psychology.* Westport, Conn.: Greenwood Press.

MECHITARIST, MEKHITARIST. An Armenian Uniat monk who devoted his life to mission work, study, and education.

Peter Mekhitar (1676–1749), an Armenian religious reformer, was born at Sebaste in Armenia and died at San Lazzaro near Venice. He founded an order of Roman Catholic Armenian monks at Constantinople in 1701. They were driven from Constantinople in 1703, were confirmed by the pope in 1712, and finally settled on the island of San Lazzaro near Venice (1717). The Mekhitarists are devoted to the religious and literary interests of the Armenian people and have published many ancient Armenian manuscripts as well as original works. The society is organized as a literary academy that confers honorary membership without regard to race or religion. It is known for the support given to Armenian philology, culture, and especially literature in the early part of the nineteenth century.

Sources

Cross, Frank L. 1974. *The Oxford dictionary of the Christian Church.* 2d ed. New York: Oxford University Press.

Douglas, James D., ed. 1974. *The new international dictionary of the Christian Church.* Exeter: Paternoster Press.

McHenry, Robert, ed. 1992. *The new encyclopedia Britannica.* Chicago: Encyclopedia Britannica, Inc.

MEDICEAN. Pertaining to a Florentine family with sovereign power in the fifteenth century.

The Medici, a distinguished Italian Renaissance family, acquired enormous wealth in commerce and banking beginning in the thirteenth century. By the fifteenth century, the family was the richest banker in Italy and dominated Florentine politics. In 1478 the family survived the ''Pazzi Conspiracy'' and became, in name if not fact, the rulers of Italy. Some prominent members were Giovanni di Bicci de' Medici (1360–1429), Cosimo de' Medici (1389–1464) and his grandson Lorenzo de' Medici (1449–92). In politics and art ''Lorenzo the Magnificent'' was the model Renaissance prince. He aimed to preserve peace in Italy by maintaining a balance of power among Italian states. The family produced two popes, Leo X (1513–21) and Clement VII (1523–34), a military leader, Giovanni de' Medici (1498–1526) and two queens of France, Marie de' Medici (1573–1624) and Catherine (1519–89). In 1737 the last of the Medici grand dukes died without heirs.

See also PAZZI CONSPIRACY.

Sources

Acton, Harold M.M. 1979. *The Pazzi conspiracy: the plot against the Medici.* London: Thames and Hudson.

McHenry, Robert, ed. 1992. *The new encyclopedia Britannica.* Chicago: Encyclopedia Britannica, Inc.

Magnussen, Magnus; Goring, Rosemary; and Thorn, John O., eds. 1990. *Chambers biographical dictionary.* Edinburgh: Chambers Ltd.

Paxton, John. 1991. *The Penguin dictionary of proper names.* London: Penguin.

Schevill, Ferdinand. 1960. *The Medici.* New York: Harper and Row.

MENCKEN'S LAW. An amusing law, uttered by one of America's most sagacious journalists, about interpersonal relations: When A annoys or injures B on the pretense of saving or improving X, A is a scoundrel.

Henry Louis Mencken (1880–1956), born in Baltimore, was educated at a school for middle-class German Americans, Knapp's Institute, and at Baltimore Polytechnic. At an early age he used the Enoch Pratt Free Library, he wrote essays, plays, and verse in high school, and afterward he went to work in his father's cigar firm. On his father's death in 1899, Mencken entered journalism and was city editor of the *Evening Herald* (1904), and later worked for the *Baltimore Sun* (1906–48). Among his works are *A Book of Prefaces* (1917), *A Book of Burlesque* (1916), *In Defense of Women* (1918), *Treatise on the Gods* (1930), and *Treatise on Right and Wrong* (1934). An archive of his papers and memorabilia is in the Enoch Pratt Free Library.

Sources

Bode, Carl. 1969. *Mencken.* Carbondale: Southern Illinois University Press.

Dorsey, John. 1980. *On Mencken: essays.* New York: Alfred A. Knopf.

Garraty, John A., ed. 1980. *Dictionary of American biography.* Supplement 6. New York: Charles Scribner's Sons.

Manchester, William. 1952. *The sage of Baltimore: the life and riotous times of H. L. Mencken.* London: A. Melrose. Also reprinted in 1986 as *Disturber of the peace: the life of H. L. Mencken.* Amherst: University of Massachusetts Press.

Winokur, Jon, ed. 1987. *The portable curmudgeon.* New York: New American Library.

MENNONITE. Member of a Protestant sect combining some of the characteristics of the Baptists and Friends.

Menno Simons or Symons (1496–1561) was born at Witmarsum, Friesland, in Holland. He was a preacher and reformer, and chief founder of the Mennonites. They believed that baptism should be administered only upon confession of faith, and therefore they did not baptize infants; they refused to take oaths to bear arms, and they condemned divorce and every kind of revenge. The first congregation formed in Zurich (1525); the sect spread through Switzerland and the south of Germany and Austria; and it had a large following at Augsburg and Strasburg. There were many divisions within the sect; the more fanatical were repressed. Menno Simons organized congregations throughout Holland and north Germany. Many Mennonites migrated to America and built their first churches in Pennsylvania in the late 1680s.

Sources

Cross, Frank L. 1974. *The Oxford dictionary of the Christian Church.* 2d ed. New York: Oxford University Press.

McHenry, Robert, ed. 1992. *The new encyclopedia Britannica.* Chicago: Encyclopedia Britannica, Inc.

MacMaster, Richard K. 1983. *Land, piety, peoplehood: the establishment of Mennonite communities in America 1683–1790.* Scottdale, Penn.: Herald Press.

Redekop, Calvin. 1989. *Mennonite society.* Baltimore: Johns Hopkins University Press.

MEROVINGIAN. Relating to the first dynasty of Frankish kings in Gaul, founded by Clovis.

Merovaeus (or Merovech, or Merovingi) is Latin for the king of the Salian

Franks, grandfather of Clovis (c. 465–511) who established the Merovingian rule. The dynasty rose to power when he defeated the Roman governor Syagrius (486), adopted the Roman faith (496), and died after becoming the sole ruler of the Franks. Clovis, the grandson of the half-legendary Merovaeus, became king (448–57) and may have supported the Roman general, Flavius Aëtius, at the defeat of Attila (c. 451). The last of the Merovingians, Childeric III, was deposed in 750 by Pepin III.

Sources

Bachrach, Bernard. 1972. *Merovingian military organization, 481–751.* Minneapolis: University of Minnesota Press.

Brewer, Ebenezer Cobham. 1970. *Brewer's dictionary of phrase and fable.* Centenary edition. Rev. by Ivor H. Evans. New York: Harper and Row.

Dill, Samuel. 1966. *Roman society in Gaul in the Merovingian age.* New York: Barnes and Noble.

McHenry, Robert, ed. 1992. *The new encyclopedia Britannica.* Chicago: Encyclopedia Britannica, Inc.

MERTON'S SELF-FULFILLING PROPHECY, MERTONIAN THESIS. The prophecy showed an aggregation effect that arises from the coincidence of preferences of individuals; for example, fearing their bank will fail, depositors who draw out funds contribute to the bank's bankruptcy. The Mertonian Thesis showed that the scientific developments of the seventeenth century were determined more by the rise of Protestant religious ideas than by purely socioeconomic pressures. Personal experience and careful experiments arose from the rejection of overbearing authority in Protestant theology. The thesis follows Max Weber's view that ideas shape the economy as much as vice versa, and comprises subtheses, which have led to valuable studies on relations between religion and modern science.

Robert King Merton (b. 1910) was born in Philadelphia and educated at Temple University and Harvard (Ph.D., 1936). For three years he taught at Harvard, after which he was appointed a professor of sociology at Tulane University (1939–41) and thereafter at Columbia University until 1974, when he became emeritus. During his career he taught at many universities in the United States; served on many advisory, educational, editorial, and foundation boards; was honored by many professional bodies, associations, and councils; and received fellowships and honorary degrees from universities around the world. He published and edited many books and became one of America's leading social scientists. He is noted as the founder of the sociology of science. He identified the norms that scientists upheld, followed, and violated in a paradigm and argued that a major motive for scientists was to become eponymous. Later, he distinguished the usual or normal pursuit of science from the rare scientific revolution when a new form is given to a scientific theory and practice.

Sources

Coser, Lewis A. 1975. *The ideas of social structure: papers in honor of Robert K. Merton.* New York: Harcourt Brace.

Crothers, C. 1987. *Robert K. Merton.* London: Tavistock.

Devine, Elizabeth; Held, Michael; Vinson, James; and Walsh, George, eds. 1983. *Thinkers of the twentieth century: a biographical, bibliographical and critical dictionary.* London: Macmillan.

Merton, Robert K. 1938. *Science, technology and society in seventeenth-century England.* 1970 ed. New York: H. Fertig.

Merton, Robert K. 1957. *Social theory and social structure.* Rev. ed. Glencoe, Ill.: Free Press.

Merton, Robert K. 1987. Three fragments from a sociologist's notebooks: establishing the phenomena, specified ignorance, and strategic research materials. *Annual Review of Sociology* 13:1–28. Palo Alto, Calif.: Annual Reviews Inc.

Sztompka, Pietr. 1986. *Robert K. Merton, an intellectual profile.* New York: St. Martin's Press.

Turner, Bryan S. 1990. The anatomy lesson: a note on the Merton thesis. *The Sociological Review* 38:1–18.

Who's who in America, 1992–93. New Providence, N.J.: Marquis.

MICHELS' IRON LAW OF OLIGARCHY. In organizations committed to democratic values, strong oligarchic tendencies inevitably arise. Leaders tend to take advantage of their followers' incompetence and irrationality, hold onto their elected positions, become unwilling to submit to the wishes of those whom they originally represented, and seek to choose the leaders they want to follow them. In this way the elected dominate the electors.

Robert Michels (1876–1936), a German sociologist and economist, was born in Cologne into a bourgeois-patrician family with a German-French-Belgian background. He was educated in Berlin and later served in the army. He studied in England and at the Sorbonne. He was interested in understanding the Anglo-Saxon culture, and wrote on nationalism, socialism, and fascism as well as the role of intellectuals, social mobility, and elites. He is best known for *Political Parties* (1911) in which he stated the iron law of oligarchy in democratic organizations. The law of oligarchy was identified when he observed that the new socialist parties of his day appeared to be as undemocratic in their functioning as the traditional parties. Later, it became clear to him that in principle, because of the structural characteristics of organizations, any organization will tend to be dominated by the few individuals in the top positions. As he observed: "Who says organization says oligarchy." He refused to support Germany in World War I, and in 1914 he moved to Basel where he became a professor of economics. In 1926 he taught political sociology at the University of Rome; the following year he was a visiting professor in the United States and then professor of economics at the University of Perugia. He died in Rome.

Sources

Borgatta, Edgar F. 1992. *Encyclopedia of sociology.* New York: Macmillan.

Michels, Robert. 1911. *Political parties: a sociological study of the oligarchical tendencies of modern democracy.* 1966 ed. Trans. Eden and Cevar Paul. New York: Free Press.

Miller, David, ed. 1987. *The Blackwell encyclopedia of political thought.* Oxford: Basil Blackwell.

Nye, Robert A. 1977. *The anti-democratic sources of elite theory: Pareto, Mosca, Michels.* London: Sage Publications.

Sills, David L., ed. 1968. *International encyclopedia of the social sciences.* New York: Macmillan and Free Press.

MICKEY MOUSE. In social science discussion, the phrase is used to describe inept administration based on heavy effort, foolish government policies and practices, and trite education courses that lead nowhere.

Mickey Mouse (b. 1923), named Mortimer Mouse, was born in a garage—Walt Disney's (1901–66) Laugh O'Gram Studio—in Kansas City. Originally, he was an animated cartoon character, quick, bright, confident, and capable. In a parody on Charles Lindbergh (1907–74), who had recently flown the Atlantic, Mortimer first appeared in *Plane Crazy* (1928), and shortly afterward, with his name changed to Mickey he played in *Steamboat Willie* (1928), an instant success. Within three years he was an international star, Mary Pickford's (1893–1979) sweetheart, and India's leading American hero. Disney received an award from the Academy of Motion Pictures in 1932 for Mickey Mouse, who had been drawn by Ub Iwerks and whose words were spoken by Disney himself. Mickey's woman companion was Minnie Mouse, and together they had many successful adventures. Mickey Mouse was attached to countless commercial items. During World War II his name was given to maps for the invasion of Normandy, and in the Korean War it was given to boots and childish acts of discipline. With the spread of popular American culture, especially through a children's television program, "The Mickey Mouse Show," which depicted adults and growing children as having motives like those of animated cartoon characters, the image of Mickey Mouse changed. His enthusiasm seemed shallow, his optimism misplaced, and his behavior superficial and slick. Gradually, an overactive, aimless, and foolish looking adult took the place of the original quick-witted cartoon character.

Sources

Hollis, Richard, and Sibley, Brian. 1981. *The Disney studio story.* New York: Crown.

Leebron, Elizabeth, and Gartley, Lynn. 1979. *Walt Disney: a guide to references and resources.* Boston: G. K. Hall.

Mosley, Leonard. 1986. *The real Walt Disney: a biography.* London: Grafton.

Shafritz, Jay M. 1988. *The Dorsey dictionary of American government and politics.* Chicago: Dorsey.

MIDAS, MIDAS TOUCH. One greedy for wealth, or one fooled by the value of sudden wealth. The ability to make money very easily.

Midas (fl. 700 B.C.) was a Phrygian king and father of King Gordius whose Gordian knot Alexander the Great (356–323 B.C.) cut decisively. But in Greek legend, as king of Phrygia, the grateful Dionysus granted Midas a wish that everything Midas touched would turn to gold. As even his food turned to gold,

Midas begged for release from this cursed power. Dionysus therefore instructed Midas to bathe in the Pactolus River, which from then on had gold-bearing sand. Another myth about Midas's foolishness concerns his declaration that Pan (or Marsyas) was a better flautist than Apollo, whereupon Apollo gave Midas the ears of an ass. In shame, Midas hid his ears beneath his cap, but his barber discovered the secret. So as to relieve himself of keeping it, Midas whispered his secret into a hole in the ground. Immediately, Apollo had reeds grow on the spot and in the wind whisper to the world of Midas's shameful secret. Once Midas foolishly implored the satyr, Silenus—sometimes known as the Greek god of wine and of fertility and noted for his great powers as a prophet—to teach him Silenus's wisdom. Appropriately, Silenus advised Midas not to have been born in the first place, and if he were, then to die as soon as he could!
Sources

Brewer, Ebenezer Cobham. 1970. *Brewer's dictionary of phrase and fable.* Centenary ed. Rev. by Ivor H. Evans. New York: Harper and Row.

McHenry, Robert, ed. 1992. *The new encyclopedia Britannica.* Chicago: Encyclopedia Britannica, Inc.

MILGRAM EXPERIMENT. An experiment in the social psychology of obedience that involved cruelty and deception, and provoked much debate on the ethics of human experimentation.

Stanley Milgram (1933–84) was born in New York, educated at Queen's College and Harvard (Ph.D., 1960), and after teaching at Yale and Harvard, became a distinguished professor of psychology at the City University of New York Graduate Center. His real interest lay in problems drawn from common experience rather than in academic disciplines. In 1963 Milgram published experimental research that illustrated what ordinary people did when ordered to give electric shock to innocent victims. Under instruction, experimental subjects shocked "victims"—people who had been previously instructed to feign being shocked—with up to what appeared to be 450 volts, and continued to obey experimenters even when the "victims" demanded release, screamed in pain, and finally failed to respond. The American Association for the Advancement of Science gave Milgram its Sociobiology award for his work. His *Obedience to Authority* (1974) was translated into many languages and was nominated for a U.S. National Book Award. Milgram's research, issues of deception, and the realistic study of distress in social science were debated for many years. They contributed to establishing a code of ethics for human experimentation.
Sources

Milgram, S. 1963. Behavioral study of obedience. *Journal of Abnormal and Social Psychology* 67:371–378.

Milgram, Stanley. 1974. *Obedience to authority: an experimental view.* London: Tavistock Publications.

Sabini, John. 1986. Stanley Milgram (1933–84), *American Psychologist* 41:1378.

MILL'S CANONS. Five principles that govern inductive reasoning about the relation of cause to effect and that are central to the logic of social scientific inquiry. First, the law of agreement states that if a large number of observed events all have a factor in common, then that factor is a probable cause of those events; second, the law of differences states that differences appearing between effects that are otherwise similar are due to their antecedent conditions; third, the law of joint agreement and disagreement asserts that if A always leads to B and non-A always leads to non-B, then A is a cause, or part cause of B; fourth, the law of residues states that if an unexplained factor remains in effect, then it is owing to an unexplained remainder in antecedent conditions; and fifth, the law of concomitant variation says that variables that change together are connected as cause and effect, or they have a single cause. The principles, especially the third, have been used to guide the use of control groups in social psychological experiments.

John Stuart Mill (1806–73) was born in London, the son of James Mill, a Scottish philosopher (1773–1836), who taught John Greek, Latin, arithmetic, and logic when he was very young. John's recreation was a daily walk with his father, who continuously held the lad to oral examinations. In 1820 John visited France, and on his return he read history, law, and philosophy. His father molded him into a future leader of the Benthamite movement, and in 1823 John became a member of a small Utilitarian Society. A devout Malthusian, he was arrested in 1824 for helping to distribute birth control literature among London's poor. In 1843 he published his famous system of logic with its celebrated canons of induction that are effective if Mill's law of the uniformity of nature is assumed. Mill also helped to change the intellectual climate and exerted a profound, lasting influence on the political reformers of his day. On election to Westminster (1865), he gave over three years to support of women's suffrage. He was one of the major English supporters of the social and political philosophy of utilitarianism. One of Mill's major works was *Utilitarianism* (1836); in this work he emphasized that the greatest happiness for the greatest number comes primarily when humankind is least hampered by arbitrary social rules.

Sources

Magnussen, Magnus; Goring, Rosemary; and Thorn, John O., eds. 1990. *Chambers biographical dictionary.* Edinburgh: Chambers Ltd.

Mazlish, Bruce. 1975. *James and John Stuart Mill: father and son in the nineteenth century.* London: Hutchinson.

Pace, Michael St J. 1954. *The life of John Stuart Mill.* 1970 ed. New York: Capricorn.

Sills, David L., ed. 1968. *International encyclopedia of the social sciences.* New York: Macmillan and Free Press.

Skorupski, John. 1989. *John Stuart Mill.* London: Routledge.

Zusne, Leonard. 1987. *Eponyms in psychology: a dictionary and sourcebook.* Westport, Conn.: Greenwood Press.

MILLER'S SCALE OF INTERNATIONAL PATTERNS AND NORMS. A set of twenty rating scales for measuring norms in different cultures, for example, social acceptance, health standards, trust for others, security of the person and property, family solidarity, independence of children, moral codes, religion, class structure and consciousness, and democratic orientation.

Delbert Charles Miller (b. 1913) was born in Findlay, Ohio, and educated at Miami University and the University of Minnesota (Ph.D., 1940). He taught high school in Ohio (1934–36) and sociology at the University of Minnesota (1937–40) and at Washington State University (1940–42). During World War II he worked briefly for Sperry Gyroscope in New York (1942–43) and for the War Labor Board in Washington, D.C. (1943–44). For three years he taught at Kent State University, Ohio, and later at the University of Washington (1947–57), and at Pennsylvania State (1957–59) before joining the business faculty at the University of Indiana in 1961. He completed research for the U.S. Air Force (1951–53) and in Bristol, England (1954–55) and for the Wage Stabilization Board (1951–53), and lectured in Peru and Argentina. His main interests include industrial sociology, international community and power, complex organizations, and urban and regional sociology. He is a member of several professional associations for social research in the United States and Latin America. His notable, encyclopedic text on research design and social measurement had gone through five editions to 1991.

Sources

Jaques Cattell Press, ed. 1978. *American men and women of science: the social and behavioral sciences.* New York: Jaques Cattell and R. R. Bowker.

Miller, Delbert. 1968. The measurement of international patterns and norms: a tool for comparative research. *Southwestern Social Science Quarterly* 48:531–547.

Miller, Delbert M. 1991. *Handbook of social research methods and research design.* 5th ed. New York: David McKay.

MILLERITE. An American nineteenth-century religious sect that believed in the Second Coming, precursors of the Seventh Day Adventists.

William Miller (1782–1849) had little education, farmed in upstate New York, and served in the War of 1812 as a captain. A religious skeptic, he underwent a conversion in 1816, studied the Bible—especially Revelations—and by 1818 concluded that in twenty-five years the world would end. In 1831 he started preaching that in 1843 Christ would reappear on earth. With the Boston preacher, Joshua V. Haines (1805–95), Miller toured northeastern America. Eventually, 700 ministers joined the Adventist movement and carried the idea of a Second Coming to the American West. As a preacher in the Baptist Church, Miller troubled the conventional churchmen by urging his followers to join the Adventist movement. When Christ did not appear as predicted, Miller recalculated the date of his coming to March and later October 1844. Disillusioned, 50,000 to 100,000 followers returned to their original churches. In 1860 his remaining followers changed their name from Millerites to Seventh Day Adventists, and now they have almost 2 million followers around the world. Miller maintained his belief in the Second Coming, did not work for the Adventist churches, became blind, and died in obscurity.

Sources
Bowden, Henry W. 1977. *Dictionary of American religious biography.* Westport, Conn.:
   Greenwood Press.
Brewer, Ebenezer Cobham. 1970. *Brewer's dictionary of phrase and fable.* Centenary
   ed. Rev. by Ivor H. Evans. New York: Harper and Row.
Gale, Robert. 1975. *The urgent voice: the story of William Miller.* Washington, D.C.:
   Review and Herald Publishing Association.
McHenry, Robert, ed. 1992. *The new encyclopedia Britannica.* Chicago: Encyclopedia
   Britannica, Inc.
Malone, Dumas, ed. 1933. *Dictionary of American biography.* Vol. VI. New York:
   Charles Scribner's Sons.

MILNER'S KINDERGARTEN. A sometimes derisive name given to a group of Oxford graduates—Leopold C.M.S. Amery (1873–1955), Robert H. Brand (1878–1963), John Buchan (1875–1940), Lionel G. Curtis (1872–1955), Patrick Duncan (1870–1943), Geoffrey Robinson [Dawson] (1874–1944), and Philip Kerr (1882–1940)—who held the main positions in the administration of the high commissioner of South Africa and governor of the Cape Colony, and followed his ideas regarding the continued functioning of the British Empire after its faltering in the Boer War. In 1910 the group returned to Britain and founded the *Round Table,* a journal that supported the political system of a federal empire with a parliament of representatives from each of Britain's colonies and dominions. The term was first used in derision by Sir William Marriott (1834–1903) who saw at first hand what was being attempted in South Africa after the Boer War and considered puerile the ideas supported by the group.

Alfred George Milner (1854–1925), first Viscount Milner, was born in Hesse-Darmstadt, Germany, and educated at Tübingen, and afterward at Kings College, London, and Balliol College, Oxford. He was a journalist before entering public life. He was appointed British high commissioner for South Africa (1897–1905) and the governor of the Cape Colony. His efforts on behalf of the Uitlanders, British residents of the Transvaal and Orange Free State who had come for gold and had no citizenship rights, were thought to have provoked the Boer War. He was an intransigent negotiator, and the two Boer republics declared war on Britain. After the war, he administered the two republics Britain had annexed and negotiated a peace (1902). For this he was made a baron and a viscount (1901, 1902). His scheme was generally to settle and educate the Boers in English ways. For this he gathered a group around him, his "kindergarten," but his plan attracted inadequate support in the British government and he resigned and returned to Britain (1905). Later, he was in Lloyd George's War Cabinet (1916–21). After World War I, he advocated imperial trade preferences with protective tariffs, and he led a mission recommending the recognition of Egyptian independence (1919).

Sources
Curtis, Lionel G. 1951. *With Milner in South Africa.* Oxford: Basil Blackwell.
Halperin, Vladimir. 1952. *Lord Milner and the empire: evolution of British imperialism.*
   London: Odham Press.

Jones, Barry. 1989. *The Macmillan dictionary of biography.* Melbourne: Macmillan.

Lee, Sidney, ed. 1920. *Dictionary of national biography: supplement 1901–1911.* London: Oxford University Press.

Legg, Leopold G.W., ed. 1949. *Dictionary of national biography 1931–1940.* London: Oxford University Press.

Legg, Leopold G.W., and Williams, E. T., eds. 1959. *Dictionary of national biography 1941–1950.* London: Oxford University Press.

McHenry, Robert, ed. 1992. *The new encyclopedia Britannica.* Chicago: Encyclopedia Britannica, Inc.

Marlowe, John. 1976. *Milner: apostle of empire: a life of Alfred George, the Right Honorable Viscount Milner of St. James's and Cape Town, 1854–1925.* London: Hamish Hamilton.

O'Brien, Terence H. 1979. *Milner: Viscount Milner of St. James's and Cape Town, 1854– 1925.* London: Constable.

Preece, Warren E., ed. 1965. *Encyclopedia Britannica.* Chicago: Encyclopedia Britannica Inc., William Benton.

Weaver, J.B.H., ed. 1937. *Dictionary of national biography 1921–1930.* London: Oxford University Press.

Williams, E. T., and Nichols, C. S., eds. 1981. *Dictionary of national biography 1961– 1970.* Oxford: Oxford University Press.

Williams, E. T., and Palmer, Helen M., eds. 1971. *Dictionary of national biography 1951–1960.* London: Oxford University Press.

MIRANDA, MIRANDIZE. A U.S. legal case in which the accused was denied his constitutional rights during interrogation while under arrest. To warn a suspect under arrest that any statements he makes may be used against him, that he has the right to remain silent, that he has the right to an attorney being present, that one will be appointed if he is indigent, and that any waiver of these rights is voluntarily and intelligently done.

Ernesto A. Miranda (b. 1940), a convicted robber and an indigent Mexican, had little education, appeared emotionally ill, and was possibly schizophrenic with pronounced sexual fantasies. But he was intelligent within normal limits, legally sane, and competent enough to stand trial. On March 13, 1963, he was arrested for the kidnapping and rape of an 18-year-old woman in Phoenix, Arizona. The woman identified Miranda in a police lineup. The police officers did not advise Miranda that he had the right to an attorney and interrogated him. At first, he denied the charges but later signed a confession. Against his counsel's objection, Miranda's confession was admitted as evidence at his trial where he was found guilty. He lost on appeal, but when his case went, with others, to the Supreme Court on *certiorari,* the finding was reversed. The reasons were that Miranda's confession was inadmissible at his trial because he had not been apprised of his right to counsel, or justly protected against self-incrimination. Today Miranda means that the Fifth Amendment to the U.S. Constitution vests a right in the individual to remain silent and lays down a code of procedure for law enforcement officers.

Sources

Baker, Liva. 1983. *Miranda: crime, law and politics.* New York: Atheneum.

Chandler, Ralph; Enslen, Richard; and Renstrom, Peter. 1987. *The constitutional law dictionary.* Oxford: Clio Press.

Levy, Leonard W., et al. 1986. *Encyclopedia of the American Constitution.* New York: Macmillan, pp. 1263–1265.

Milner, Neal A. 1971. *The court and local law enforcement: the impact of Miranda.* Beverly Hills, Calif.: Sage Publications.

Schopter, Ernest H., et al. 1967. *U.S. Supreme Court reports.* Lawyer's ed. Second series, vol. 16. Rochester, N.Y.: Lawyers Cooperative Publishing Co., pp. 694–764.

MOHAMMEDAN. A follower of the seventh-century Arabic prophet.

Mohammed, Muhammad, or Mahomet (c. 570–632), an Arabic religious and political leader, founded the Islamic religion and empire. Born after his father's death, he grew up an orphan in Mecca and was raised by his grandfather, the head of a local clan and a prominent leader in Meccan town affairs. Marriage to a rich widow in 595 gave Mohammed sufficient money to enter trade in the town. In 610 he felt that God was calling him to be a prophet and wanted him to proclaim God's word and have the people worship Him, to tell them to be generous with their wealth, and to believe that they would appear before God on the Last Day when they would be rewarded or punished for earthly deeds. He began preaching in 613. The messages that Mohammed had from God until his death were later collected to form a book, the Koran. Despite early opposition from the merchants and many clans in Mecca, by the time he died, Mohammed left a well-established, growing religion.

Sources

Cook, Michael. 1983. *Muhammad.* Oxford: Oxford University Press.

Cross, Frank L. 1974. *The Oxford dictionary of the Christian Church.* 2d ed. New York: Oxford University Press.

McHenry, Robert, ed. 1992. *The new encyclopedia Britannica.* Chicago: Encyclopedia Britannica, Inc.

Magnussen, Magnus; Goring, Rosemary; and Thorn, John O., eds. 1990. *Chambers biographical dictionary.* Edinburgh: Chambers Ltd.

Rodinson, Maxine. 1971. *Mohammed.* Trans. Anne Carter. London: Allen Lane.

MOLINISM. A religious doctrine that takes the name of Luis Molina and that reconciles predestination and free will through God's foreknowledge, and assumes that the cooperation of the will ensures the efficacy of grace. A religious doctrine that takes the name of Miguel de Molinos and that emphasizes quiet spiritual passivity.

Luis Molina (1535–1600), a Spanish Jesuit, was born at Cuenca, New Castille, and died in Madrid. At age 17 he entered the Jesuit Society, studied at Coimbra (1554–62), and was appointed professor of theology at Evora (1563–67) where he taught (1568–83). His major works were a commentary on the *Summa* of Saint Thomas Aquinas (1593), *De Justitia et Jure* (1592), and the treatise on the reconciliation of free will and grace, *Liberi Arbitrii cum Gratiae Donis* . . . *Concordia* (1588). His ideas are commonly taught in the Jesuit schools.

Miguel de Molinos (1628–96), a Spanish Catholic priest ordained in 1652, was the mystic who founded Quietism. His *Guida spirituale* (1675) taught that a spiritual passivity—a prayer of the "Quiet"—was a superior form of spirituality, and that external actions do not affect the soul. In 1685 he was condemned as a heretic and imprisoned for life.

Sources

Costello, Frank B. 1974. *The political philosophy of Luis de Molina, S.J. (1535–1600).* Spokane, Wash.: Gonzaga University Press.
Cross, Frank L. 1974. *The Oxford dictionary of the Christian Church.* 2d ed. New York: Oxford University Press.
Ferguson, Everett, ed. 1990. *The encyclopedia of early Christianity.* New York: Garland Publishing.
McHenry, Robert, ed. 1992. *The new encyclopedia Britannica.* Chicago: Encyclopedia Britannica, Inc.

MOLLY MAGUIRES. Members of an Irish society established in 1843 to fight government evictions and the landlords whom the government supported; in the United States, members of a Pennsylvanian secret society, crushed in 1877, that was formed to resist oppressive conditions in the coal mining industry.

Molly Maguire was a Irish widow who in the 1840s led agitators seeking leniency from their landlords. The name was adopted by a branch of the Irish Ribbonmen who formed a society and dressed as women and, under cover of darkness, resisted their government's decisions on evictions. The name is also the familiar form of "Mary Maguire," a common Irish name for women. In the United States, the "Mollies" was the name given to those who murdered and committed sabotage over working conditions in the coal mines in Pennsylvania (1862–76). Mine owners hired James McParlan to join their group, allegedly protected by the Ancient Order of Hibernians, and to spy on them. Later, the trials of 1875–77 led to the hanging of ten men for murder, and fourteen went to prison. With improvements in the economy, terrorism on the mine fields diminished.

Sources

Bimba, Anthony. 1932. *The Molly Maguires.* New York: International.
Brewer, Ebenezer Cobham. 1970. *Brewer's dictionary of phrase and fable.* Centenary ed. Rev. by Ivor H. Evans. New York: Harper and Row.
Coleman, J. Walter. 1936. *The Molly Maguire riots.* Richmond, Va.: Garrett and Marnie.
McHenry, Robert, ed. 1992. *The new encyclopedia Britannica.* Chicago: Encyclopedia Britannica, Inc.
Roberts, Harold S. 1966. *Roberts' dictionary of industrial relations.* Washington, D.C.: BNA.

MOLOTOV COCKTAIL, MOLOTOV BASKET, MOLOTOV-RIB-BENTROP PACT. Hand grenade made from a bottle of inflammable liquid and a burning wick, used by urban terrorists and revolutionaries. A basket used for carrying high explosives and scattering incendiary bombs. A secret nonaggression pact between Nazi Germany and the Soviet Union (August 1939), also known as the Hitler-Stalin pact, which prepared the way for the Nazi invasion of Poland in September 1939 and outlined how Eastern Europe would be divided under Nazi and Russian rule. Nazi Germany violated the pact in June 1941.

Vyacheslav Mikhaylovich Molotov (1890–1986) whose original surname was Skriabin or Skyrabin, was born in Kukarka, Viatka Gouvt, son of a shop clerk. He was educated at Kazan High School and became a Bolshevik in 1906. He was exiled to north Russia where he formed a Bolshevik group in 1909. In 1911 he began studying economics in Saint Petersburg Polytechnic, organized student revolutionaries, and established the newspaper *Pravda*. In 1912 he changed his surname to Molotov, ''son of the hammer.'' After further exile, he served on the military-revolutionary committee of the Petrograd soviet which took over from the provisional government in 1917. He was elected to the political bureau of the Communist party (1926), became premier (1930–41), and was succeeded by Stalin. He was Russia's foreign minister during 1939–49 and 1953–56. In 1939 he negotiated the Soviet-Nazi nonaggression pact. In hostilities with Russia (1940), the Finnish underground gave his name to their home-made hand grenades which they dropped into the ventilators of invading Russian tanks. Similar ''Molotov cocktails'' were used in Russia's invasion of Hungary in 1956. Molotov was disgraced in 1957 when he failed to unseat Nikita S. Khrushchev (1894–1971), was banished to an ambassadorship in Mongolia, and expelled from the Communist party (1964). Although reinstated in 1984 when he supported Mikhail S. Gorbachov, Molotov was not honored with a state funeral when he died in Moscow.

Joachim von Ribbentrop (1893–1946), son of a military officer, was born in Wesel, educated at Metz and Grenoble, and spent four years as a businessman in Canada. He served in World War I and became a lieutenant, later married the daughter of a famous champagne manufacturer, and became a success in the export of fine wines. In 1932 he joined the Nazi party and was Hitler's adviser on foreign affairs. His haughter attracted loathing from top Nazis, but Hitler likened him to Bismarck. As the ambassador to London he offended many Britons, and he concluded Britain was a danger to Nazi Germany's plans. Appointed the Third Reich's foreign minister in 1938, he topped his career with the nonaggression pact of August 23, 1939, and paved the way for the invasion of Poland in September 1939. He personally believed that Britain would not oppose the German invasion. He lost influence, survived a putsch by his senior minister, Martin Luther (1895–1945), was arrested in June 1945, and was hanged for war crimes in October 1946 at Nuremberg prison.

Sources
Brewer, Ebenezer Cobham. 1970. *Brewer's dictionary of phrase and fable*. Centenary ed. Rev. by Ivor H. Evans. New York: Harper and Row.

Leonhard, Wolfgang. 1989. *Betrayal: the Hitler-Stalin pact of 1939.* Trans. Richard D. Bosley. New York: St. Martin's Press.
McHenry, Robert, ed. 1992. *The new encyclopedia Britannica.* Chicago: Encyclopedia Britannica, Inc.
Magnussen, Magnus; Goring, Rosemary; and Thorn, John O., eds. 1990. *Chambers biographical dictionary.* Edinburgh: Chambers Ltd.
Snyder, Louis L. 1976. *Encyclopedia of the Third Reich.* New York: McGraw-Hill.
Vronskaya, Jeanne. 1989. *A biographical directory of the Soviet Union 1917–1988.* London: S. G. Saur.
Vizulis, Izidors. 1990. *The Molotov-Ribbentrop pact: the Baltic case.* New York: Praeger.
Waxman, Maron L., ed. 1977. *Great Soviet encyclopedia.* New York: Macmillan.
Wistrich, Robert. 1982. *Who's who in Nazi Germany.* New York: Macmillan.

MOND-TURNER CONFERENCES. Conferences on industrial reorganization and industrial relations (1928–29) between British industrial and trade union leaders. The conferences sought to improve the climate of industrial relations in Great Britain.

Alfred Moritz Mond, first Baron Melchett (1868–1930) was a British industrialist and politician, son of Ludwig Mond, a German-English chemist and industrialist who had settled in England in 1867. After experience in industry, Mond became a Liberal M.P. in 1906, was first commissioner of works during 1916–21, and minister of health in 1922. He helped to form the Imperial Chemical Industries, of which he became chairman; a conference he organized in 1928 with the Trades Union Congress suggested the formation of a national industrial council. He was raised to the peerage in 1928.

Ben Turner (1863–1942) was educated at dame and at church schools and learned to be a weaver. In 1911 he was chairman of Britain's Labor party and in 1928 chairman of the Trades Union Congress. He entered Parliament (1922–24; 1929–31) and was secretary for mines (1929–30). He became the general president of the National Union of Textile Workers and joint chairman of the Industrial Council for the Woollen Trade. He published his autobiography, *About Myself* (1930), two histories of the Yorkshire textile unions, and *Collected Rhymes and Verses* (1934). He was knighted in 1931.

Sources
Jones, Barry, and Dixon, Meredith V. 1989. *The Macmillan dictionary of biography.* 3d ed. South Melbourne: Macmillan.
Legg, L.G.W., and Williams, E. T., eds. 1959. *Dictionary of national biography 1941–1950.* London: Oxford University Press.
Magnussen, Magnus; Goring, Rosemary; and Thorn, John O., eds. 1990. *Chambers biographical dictionary* Edinburgh: Chambers Ltd.
Marsh, Arthur. 1979. *Concise encyclopedia of industrial relations.* Westmead, Farnborough, Hants: Gower.
Weaver, J.B.H., ed. 1937. *Dictionary of national biography 1921–1930.* London: Oxford University Press.
Who was who, 1941–50. Vol. IV. London: Adam and Charles Black.

MONROE DOCTRINE. The political principle that Europe must not intervene in the affairs of nations on the American continents. It arose when John Quincy Adams (1767–1848), secretary of state, saw a threat from the Concert of Europe and the Holy Alliance, and formulated the principle to resist attempts to re-establish European hegemony in the Americas. Adams preferred diplomatic means, but the views of the secretary of war led the president to state the doctrine in his State of the Union address on December 2, 1823. He said that the American continents could not be annexed by European nations, and any interference would be seen as a threat to American security. In addition, the United States would not interfere with existing European colonies on the American continents or enter wars between European nations. The last statement was violated in 1917 when the United States entered World War I, but the doctrine is used to support U.S. policies in Central and Southern America and is seen as representing its domination of countries on the South American continent.

James Monroe (1758–1831), fifth U.S. president, was born in Westmoreland County, Virginia, the descendant of Scots who had immigrated a century earlier. At 18 he entered William and Mary College but soon left to join Washington's army. As a lieutenant-colonel Monroe served with Jefferson. In 1782 he was elected to the Assembly of Virginia and appointed to the Executive Council. In 1785 he was chairman of a committee whose report led to the conventions of Annapolis and Philadelphia in 1786 and 1787 where the American Constitution was framed. In 1816 he was elected president and served two terms. His popular acts were the recognition of the independence of the Spanish American republics and the Monroe Doctrine.

Sources

Ammon, Harry. 1991. *James Monroe: a bibliography.* Westport, Conn.: Meckler.

Commager, Henry S., ed. 1968. *Documents of American history.* 8th ed. New York: Appleton-Century-Crofts.

DeConde, A. 1968. *A history of American foreign policy.* Vol. 1. New York: Charles Scribner's Sons.

Levy, Leonard, ed. 1986. *Encyclopedia of the American Constitution.* New York: Macmillan.

Malone, Dumas, ed. 1934. *Dictionary of American biography.* Vol. VII. New York: Charles Scribner's Sons.

Plano, Jack C. 1988. *The international relations dictionary.* 4th ed. Santa Barbara, Calif.: ABC-CLIO.

MONTAGUE GRAMMAR. A theory from the study of formal languages—semantics—that was applied to studies of language.

Richard Merett Montague (1930–71) was born in Stockton, California, and did his undergraduate and postgraduate studies at the University of California at Berkeley, moving to the university campus at Los Angeles in 1955, where he worked until his murder. In the Philosophy Department where he taught, Montague established a new system of logic for application to natural language. It was elaborate and highly technical, but nevertheless it gained a considerable following in the 1970s from those interested in natural language. His collected papers were published in 1974.

Sources

Dowty, David R. 1979. *Word meaning and Montague grammar.* Dordrecht: D. Reidel.

Dowty, David R.; Wall, Robert E.; and Peters, Stanley. 1981. *Introduction to Montague semantics.* Dordrecht, Holland: D. Reidel.

Thomason, Richmond H. 1974. *Formal philosophy: selected papers of Richard Montague.* New Haven, Conn.: Yale University Press.

MONTE CARLO METHODS. In economics two different but related methods of evaluation: the first involves the evaluation of definite integrals by using random variables, and the second refers to the repeated simulation of a stochastic process to study the properties of statistical techniques applied to it (Eatwell, 1987). The methods depend on the computer to provide pseudorandom numbers to initiate the random processes that are assumed to provide economic data.

Monte Carlo is the capital of the tiny principality of Monaco on the Mediterranean coast. In 1858 a giant casino was built for gamblers, and it has become the symbol of wealth acquired by gambling, and a playground for the very rich. The term is also synonymous with chance, or events that are determined apparently by random. In the Monte Carlo methods, the term relates to the pseudorandom numbers involved.

Sources

Courtlandt, Canby. 1984. *The encyclopedia of historic places.* London: Mansell Publishing.

Eatwell, John; Milgate, Murray; and Newman, Peter. 1987. *The new Palgrave: a dictionary of economics.* London: Macmillan.

Hammersley, John M., and Handscombe, David C. 1964. *Monte Carlo methods.* London: Methuen.

Pearce, David W., ed. 1986. *Macmillan dictionary of modern economics.* New York: Macmillan.

Smith, Vincent K. 1973. *Monte Carlo methods: their role for econometrics.* Lexington, Mass.: Lexington Books.

MONTESSORI METHOD. An educational method that values spontaneity and freedom from restraint in learning.

Maria Montessori (1870–1952) studied at the University of Rome and was the first woman in Italy to graduate in medicine (1894). In 1898 she opened the Orthophrenic School, a special school for mentally retarded children, and in 1907 she established her first "Casa dei Bambini" (Children's House), a school for normal children 3 to 7 years of age. In the school the teacher was more of a leader than a controlling instructor. In Italy and other countries many schools used what came to be called the Montessori Method. In 1933 she left Italy for Spain, and later she founded training schools in the Netherlands and India before returning to the University of Rome in 1947. She wrote *The Montessori Method* (1912) and *The Advanced Montessori Method* (1917).

Sources
Deighton, Lee C., ed. 1971. *The encyclopedia of education.* New York: Macmillan and Free Press.
Devine, Elizabeth; Held, Michael; Vinson, James; and Walsh, George, eds. 1983. *Thinkers of the twentieth century: a biographical, bibliographical and critical dictionary.* London: Macmillan.
Husen, Torsten, and Postlethwaite, T. Neville. 1985. *The international encyclopedia of education research and studies.* Oxford: Pergamon Press.
Kramer, Rita. 1976. *Maria Montessori: a biography.* New York: Putnam.
Montessori, M. 1964. *Montessori method.* New York: Schocken Books.
Zusne, Leonard. 1984. *Biographical dictionary of psychology.* Westport, Conn.: Greenwood Press.

MONTEZUMA'S REVENGE. Slang for the diarrhoea that sometimes affects travelers eating in Mexico; an amusing political term symbolic of the longstanding Mexican attitude of hostility toward the United States.

Montezuma II (1466–1520) Xocoyotzin, "The Younger," ruled the Aztecs. In 1503 he succeeded his uncle, Ahuitzotl, as ruler of the Mexican Empire, and under his regime the city of Tenochtilán achieved great fame and splendor. However, the Zapotecs and other dissenting tribes freed themselves from Aztec rule. Montezuma was devoted to his god Huitzilopochtli who appears to have induced in him a fatalistic attitude when he heard rumors of the Spaniards' landing in the Caribbean. When Cortés arrived on the mainland (1519), he quickly contacted several tribes who were willing to ally themselves with him against Aztec domination. Cortés was asked to quit the region but ignored the requests. So Montezuma, hoping to appease both his god and the Spaniards, welcomed Cortés. But while Cortés was absent, his lieutenant, Alvarado, lost control of hostilities and to regain it started to massacre all Aztecs. Montezuma was murdered when he tried to warn the Aztecs. In time diarrhoea among visitors to Mexico became regarded with amusement as compensation for the Aztec massacre.

Sources
Burland, Cottie A. 1973. *Montezuma, lord of the Aztecs.* London: Weidenfeld and Nicolson.
McHenry, Robert, ed. 1992. *The new encyclopedia Britannica.* Chicago: Encyclopedia Britannica, Inc.
Magnussen, Magnus; Goring, Rosemary; and Thorn, John O., eds. 1990. *Chambers biographical dictionary.* Edinburgh: Chambers Ltd.

MONTFORTIANS. Supporters, especially among the barons, of the thirteenth-century reforms for royal government in England.

Simon de Montfort, earl of Leicester (c. 1208–65), was an Anglo-French baron and son of Simon IV of Montfort l'Amaury (Normandy) and Alice of Montmorency. In 1238 he married a sister of the English king Henry III whom he would later oppose in a revolt of the English barons. He was Henry's deputy in Gascony (1248–63), but when his actions were questioned, he sided with English barons who had Provisions for the reform of the government of England. The Provisions of Oxford (1253) and Westminster (1259) stated that the king should rule through a council of fifteen magnates. But Montfort believed that the barons should also be subject to the council's authority. When a split appeared in their ranks, the king had the chance to repudiate the Provisions. Montfort returned to England in 1263 and rallied the barons to civil war in 1264. His victory put him in charge of the country, and he made the king and Prince Edward his prisoners. He called a parliament in 1265 to regularize matters, but one of his supporters, the duke of Gloucester, defected. Prince Edward then escaped, rallied the king's followers, and won the decisive battle at Eversham where Montfort was killed. The civil war ended in 1267, and the barons surrendered.

Sources

Jones, Barry. 1989. *The Macmillan dictionary of biography.* Melbourne: Macmillan.

Labarge, Margaret W. 1962. *Simon de Montfort.* London: Eyre and Spottiswoode.

Stephen, Leslie, and Lee, Sydney, eds. 1917. *The dictionary of national biography.* London: Oxford University Press.

MONTT-VARISTAS. Reactionary wing of the Pelucones in nineteenth-century Chile who took their name from the president and his secretary of state.

Manuel Francisco Antonio Julian Montt Torres (1809–80) was born in Petorca, Chile; he studied law and became a rector (1835–40) but quit when elected to the Chilean Congress (1840). He served as minister for the interior until elected president. He survived armed revolt and remained in office for ten years (1851–61). Although he was an autocrat and led a conservative oligarchy, his administration made progressive changes; codifying the laws, reforming commercial and banking practices, improving public education, and changing immigration rules. During his regime, Chile became a haven for exiled intellectuals from other Latin American countries. He reformed the tax system and decreased Chile's dependence on regressive taxation. Chilean industry was protected with tariffs, and it grew rapidly during his rule. But as his successor he tried to appoint the minister of the interior, Antonio Varas. In response, the liberals led another armed uprising. He brought them under control by shifting his support to a moderate. In retirement, Montt was a senator, diplomat, and president of the Chilean Supreme Court. He died in Santiago.

Antonio Varas (1817–86) was born at Cauquenes, studied law, and served as minister for justice under President Manuel Bulnes (1799–1866), the Chilean statesman. Varas was the principal minister under President Montt (1851–56) and again briefly in 1861. He founded the Montt-Varistas party and had a reputation as one of the country's greatest conservatives.

Sources

Cook, Chris. 1983. *Dictionary of historical terms.* 2d ed., 1990. London: Macmillan.

Howatt, Gerald, M.D. 1973. *Dictionary of world history.* London: Thomas Nelson.

McHenry, Robert, ed. 1992. *The new encyclopedia Britannica.* Chicago: Encyclopedia Britannica, Inc.

Nunn, Frederich M. 1976. *The military in Chilean history: essays on the civilian-military relations, 1810–1973.* Albuquerque: University of New Mexico.

Talbot, Robert D. 1974. *A history of Chilean boundaries.* Ames: Iowa State University Press.

MOONIES. A collective, and now sometimes derogatory, term for members of the Unification Church.

Sun Myung Moon (b. 1920) was born in northwest Korea. His family joined the Presbyterian Church, rejecting the Shinto faith of the Japanese invaders (1930). A sensitive boy, Sun Myung Moon was educated in Seoul, trained at the Pentecostal Church, and in 1936, Jesus came to him. He studied Western and Eastern religious figures and the principles of religion in the universe. In 1938 he studied electrical engineering briefly in Tokyo. His interests then turned to undermining Japanese domination of Korea. After World War II he returned to Korea, but his spiritual work was crushed by the new communist regime, and he was imprisoned until 1950 when the United Nations forces liberated him. He fled south, attracted followers, and began writing his *Divine Principle* (1957; 1973) on God's unchanging truths and on integrating Christian and Oriental religious principles. He entered business, which later provided for the church; he also started an international mission, which by 1959 had established itself in the United States as the Freedom Leadership Foundation (1969). In 1971 Moon brought his ''Day of Hope'' message to America; in 1973 he returned, attracting large audiences and supporting President Nixon, arguing he should be forgiven for Watergate. Moon's proselytizing led to an investigation, with parents suing him for alienating their children. His Unification Church and its business practices became the subject of scandal and were investigated, and Moon's name was linked with the autocratic rule of South Korea, Koreagate (1977–78). By 1976 he had ended his personal ministry in America. In 1982, Moon was found guilty of tax evasion, fined $25,000 and sentenced to eighteen months in prison; in September 1983 his conviction was upheld by a federal court of appeal in New York City. In 1988, he was still officiating at the mass weddings of his followers in South Korea and claiming to be fighting communism and restoring moral virtues to the world. For almost ten years Moon gave no interviews. But in late 1989 he broke his silence with an interview in Seoul, South Korea. In 1990 he visited Gorbachev in Moscow and gave a speech titled ''True Unification and One World'' that stated that he and the companies of the Unification Church in thirty-five countries were planning to make vast commercial investments in Russia as they had already done fifty miles from Hong Kong inside southern China. The companies dealt in weapons, soft drinks, car parts, computers, and fish.

Sources

Bethell, T. 1990. Moon over Moscow. *The American spectator,* June 23:9–11.

Clift E., and Miller, M. 1988. Rev. Moon's political moves. *Newsweek* February 15:31.

Cooper, N. 1989. Rev. Moon's rising son. *Newsweek* April 11: 39.

Holt, T. H. 1989. A view of the Moonrise. *Conservative Digest* January-February, 15: 36–37.

Judis, John B. 1989. Rev. Moon's rising political influence. *U.S. News and World Report,* March 27: 27–29.

Green, M. L. 1993. Moonstruck in Connecticut. *Christianity Today* June 21:54.

Mass, Peter. 1990. Moon over Moscow. *The New Republic,* November 19, 203:7–8.

Moritz, Charles, ed. 1983. *Current biography yearbook.* New York: H. W. Wilson.

Owen, Roger J. 1982. *The Moonies: a critical look at a controversial group.* London: Ward Lock Educational.

Sandars, S. W. 1991. Moon over Moscow. *National Review,* April 15, 43:39–41.

MORENO'S SOCIOMETRY. A technique for measuring social relations in which the interpersonal structure and dynamics of groups are determined and plotted by asking each member to choose one or more individuals with whom he or she would like to work, eat, study, or share an apartment. This method reveals members who are popular (''stars'') and those who are rejected (''isolates''), and the best leaders. Sociometry shows cliques, pairs, triangles and other patterns of group structure.

Jacob Levy Moreno (1889–1974), a Romanian-American psychiatrist, was born in Bucharest, Romania, and lived in the United States after 1927. In 1917 he graduated with an M.D. from the University of Vienna. Following years in private practice in Vienna and Vöslav, he went to the United States (1927) and began private practice in New York (1928). He was the founder and director of Beacon Hill Sanatorium (1936–68) and an adjunct professor of sociology at New York University (1951–66). He founded and edited the *International Journal of Sociometry* (1937) and *Group Psychotherapy and Psychodrama* (1947) and was the editor of *Group Psychiatry.* His principal contribution to psychiatry and psychology was his introduction of a new therapeutic technique, psychodrama. He demonstrated that when acting in a dramatic situation the patient reveals his personality, motivations, and conflicts. His books include *Who Shall Survive?* (1934), *Psychodrama* (1946), *Group Psychotheraphy* (1947), *Sociometry and the Science of Man* (1956), and *Discovery of Spontaneous Man* (1965).

Sources

Goldenson, Robert, ed. 1984. *Longman dictionary of psychology and psychiatry.* New York: Longman.

Marineau, Rene F. 1989. *Jacob Levy Moreno: 1889–1974. Father of psychodrama, sociometry and group psychotherapy.* London: Tavistock and Routledge.

Moreno, Jacob L. 1934. *Who shall survive?* Washington, D.C.: Nervous and Mental Diseases Monograph, 58.

Moreno, Jacob L. 1937. Sociometry in relation to other social sciences. *Sociometry* 1: 206–219.

Zusne, Leonard. 1984. *Biographical dictionary of psychology.* Westport, Conn.: Greenwood Press.

MORGAN'S LAWS OF POLITICS, MORGAN'S SECRET LAW OF JOURNALISM.

Morgan's Laws of Politics state that (1) Anyone who wants to be a politician would have to be one short of a quorum; and (2) In order to gain support, all politicians must behave and speak in ways that make them totally unfit to govern. The Secret Law of Journalism states that the degree of frankness with which the dark side of politics, the police and the law, business, and unionism can be reported in the media varies is the square of the distance between the point of origin and the publication point. The first two laws were based on newspapermen's observations of the activities associated with U.S. presidential campaigns since World War II. The last comes from personal experience at all levels of the news world.

John Arnold Timothy Morgan (b. 1928) was born in Wales and educated at Kettering Grammar School, Northamptonshire, the Royal Liberty School, Essex, and Royd's Hall Grammar School in Yorkshire. He was a journalist on the Huddersfield *Examiner* (1948–51) and the Manchester *Evening News* (1951–54) before immigrating to Australia, where he worked as a journalist and later as features editor on the *Sun-New Pictorial* in Melbourne (1954–68). He became the editor of the books and magazine division of that newspaper, and then its editor (1974–78); executive editor of The Herald and Weekly Times Ltd. (1978–84); and a director of the Argus and Australasian (1980–86). In 1977 he led the first delegation of Australian newspaper editors to China; in 1985 he was awarded the Officer's Cross of the Order of Merit by the Federal Republic of Germany. He was invited to lecture at the Chinese School of Journalism in Beijing (1988) and was a consultant to the Suva *Daily Post* (1989). Since 1981 he has been a member of the Australian Press Council, and was a committee member of the Communication Media Law Association (1989–90).

Sources

Draper, William J., ed. 1985. *Who's who in Australia.* Melbourne: Herald and Weekly Times.

Howie, Ann C., ed. 1992. *Who's who in Australia.* Melbourne: Information Australia.

Morgan, John. 1992. The odd declarations of independents. *The Age* (Melbourne), September 8:15.

Personal Communication.

MORGENTHAU PLAN.

A plan drawn up in August 1944 by the secretary of the U.S. Treasury to dismantle Germany's industrial facilities, close its mines, and transform the nation into an agricultural and pastoral society. The plan also suggested closing the Ruhr District, which would also remove a major competitor to British industry. President Roosevelt and British prime minister Winston Churchill discussed the plan; Roosevelt was initially in favor but adverse public reaction soon turned him against the plan. The plan was referred to occasionally, until the secretary of state, James Byrnes, officially dispensed with it in his September 1946 speech at Stuttgart, owing to growing U.S.-Soviet conflict over Germany's future.

Henry Morgenthau, Jr. (1891–1967), was born in New York, studied architecture at Cornell University, but turned to agriculture. He was the son of a banker and diplomat, and became a gentleman farmer and close friend of Franklin D. Roosevelt. He served in the U.S. Navy in World War I, worked with the Hoover Food Commission, and bought the *American Agriculturalist,* which he edited until 1933. He helped Roosevelt become New York's governor, and when he became president, Morgenthau was appointed chairman of the Federal Farm Board. He was undersecretary of Treasury (1933–34) and later secretary of Treasury (1934–45). During World War II he coordinated aid to the Allies and helped in the sale of War Bonds. He took a leading role at the Bretton Woods Conference (1944), which established the International Monetary Fund and the World Bank. In 1945 he wrote *Germany Is Our Problem,* and when the plan to dismantle Germany's economy was rejected, he resigned from government and worked for Jewish philanthropies. He was the general chairman of the United Jewish Appeal (1947–50) and its honorary chairman (1951–53); he chaired the board of governors of the Hebrew Union (1950–51) and worked for the American Financial and Development Corporation for Israel (1951–54).

Sources

Blum, John M. 1959–67. *From the Morgenthau diaries.* 3 vols. Boston: Houghton Mifflin.

Blum, John M. 1970. *Roosevelt and Morgenthau: a revision and condensation of "From the Morgenthau diaries."* Boston: Houghton Mifflin.

Everest, Alan S. 1973. *Morgenthau, the New Deal and Silver: a story of pressure politics.* New York: Da Capo Press.

Gaddis, John L. 1972. *The United States and the origins of the cold war.* New York: Columbia University Press.

Garraty, John A., and Sternstein, Jerome L. 1974. *Encyclopedia of American biography.* New York: Harper and Row.

Kimball, Warren. 1976. *Swords or ploughshares? The Morgenthau plan for defeated Nazi Germany, 1943–1946.* Philadelphia: Lippincott.

Who was who in America, 1961–68. Vol. IV. Chicago: Marquis.

MORISONIAN. Member of the Evangelical Union.

Reverend James Morison (1816–93) was born at Bathgate, Linlithgowshire, studied at Edinburgh University, and began training for the ministry at the United Secession Church under John Brown, D.D. (1834). In 1839 he had charge of Cabrach church, and in 1840 of Kilmarnock church. Morison believed that the Lord made atonement not simply for the elect but for all humankind; he published his views in his tract, *The Question, "What Must I Do to Be Saved?" Answered by Philanthropos* (1840). These views led to his suspension from the ministry in 1841. With his father and other suspended ministers, Morison formed the Evangelical Union in 1843. The Union was an advisory body, not adjudicative, and it included congregations of both Presbyterian and Congregational orders, thus reproducing the policy of the "happy union" and improving on it by admitting lay delegates.

Sources
Cross, Frank L. 1974. *The Oxford dictionary of the Christian Church.* 2d ed. New York: Oxford University Press.
Douglas, James D., ed. 1974. *The new international dictionary of the Christian Church.* Exeter: Paternoster Press.
Stephen, Leslie, and Lee, Sydney, eds. 1917. *The dictionary of national biography.* London: Oxford University Press.

MOSAIC LAW. God's laws for the Jews given to Moses and appearing in the first five books of the Old Testament.

Moses (thirteenth century B.C.) was born to Amram and Joachebed of the Levi tribe of Israelites at a time in Egypt when all newborn Hebrew boys were being killed at pharaoh's command. For three months Moses was hidden and then placed by his parents in a floating basket in the reeds along the Nile until he was found by the daughter of the pharaoh. She named him Moses, and he was raised as an Egyptian of high caste. As a young man he slew a cruel Egyptian, was sought by pharaoh, and fled to Midian where he married and tended the flocks of his father-in-law. One day God came to him and commanded Moses to deliver the Israelites from bondage in Egypt to Canaan, a land of milk and honey. Moses undertook the task. God gave Moses commandments, laws, and ordinances for the governance of the Jews.

Sources
Cross, Frank L. 1974. *The Oxford dictionary of the Christian Church.* 2d ed. New York: Oxford University Press.
Eliade, Mircea, ed. 1987. *Encyclopedia of religion.* New York: Macmillan.
Roth, Cecil E., ed. 1971. *Encyclopedia Judaica.* New York: Macmillan.

MOTHER SHIPTON. A woman who professes to foretell the future.

Ursula Shipton, née Southill or Southiel (c. 1488–1561), was born so ugly she earned the reputation of the Devil's child. Her mother was reputed to be a witch. The young woman was born and lived in Knaresborough, Yorkshire, and married a builder, Tobias or Tony Shipton. Legends grew around her name and were published by Richard Head in his *Life of Mother Shipton* (1667). According to tradition, she was the child of Agatha Shipton and the Devil. As "Mother Shipton" she accurately predicted the death of Oliver Cromwell and the fire of London (1666). According to folklore she predicted the steam engine, amazing advances in telecommunications, and even the end of the world! The last prediction drove people into the fields to pray all night. This folklore was explained in 1873 when Charles Hindley confessed to having forged a publication of Ursula's biography and added to it the necessary modern predictions. Few people had noted the confession. Meanwhile, Mother Shipton had become the female version of Nostradamus.

See also NOSTRADAMUS.

Sources
Hendrickson, Robert. 1988. *The dictionary of eponyms: names that became words.* New York: Dorset.
Magnussen, Magnus; Goring, Rosemary; and Thorn, John O., eds. 1990. *Chambers biographical dictionary.* Edinburgh: Chambers Ltd.
Smith, Benjamin. 1903. *The Century cyclopedia of names.* London: The Times.

MUGGLETONIAN. Member of a Puritan sect formed in England.

Lodowicke Muggleton (1609–98) was a journeyman tailor who, with his cousin John Reeve (1608–58), founded the Muggletons (c. 1651). Before the English Civil War, Muggleton was deeply influenced by the Puritans and the beliefs of the Ranters. His sect believed in the personal inspiration of the founders who claimed to be the two witnesses in Revelations 11:3–6. Muggleton was Aaron while Reeve was Moses. Their *Transcendent Spiritual Treatise* was published in 1652. They were condemned as blasphemous, and Muggleton was pilloried, put in prison and fined, but he carried forward their work after Reeves's death. The sect flourished for 200 years.

Sources
Cross, Frank L. 1974. *The Oxford dictionary of the Christian Church.* 2d ed. New York: Oxford University Press.
Douglas, James D., ed. 1974. *The new international dictionary of the Christian Church.* Exeter: Paternoster Press.
Magnussen, Magnus; Goring, Rosemary; and Thorn, John O., eds. 1990. *Chambers biographical dictionary.* Edinburgh: Chambers Ltd.
Powell, Nathaniel. 1983. *A true account of the trial and sufferings of Lodowick Muggleton: one of the two last prophets and witnesses of the spirit: left by our friend Powell, who witnessed the trial and all his sufferings.* Facsimile of 1808 publication. York: Michael Cole.

MULDERGATE. A political scandal in South Africa (1978) in which the Information Ministry was found to have channeled public money to support a secret fund for dubious activities and propaganda. A commission of inquiry found President John Vorster responsible, and he had to resign in June 1979.

Cornelius ("Connie") P. Mulder (1925–88) was born Warmbaths in the Transvaal, youngest of ten, and educated at Krugersdorp and Potchefstroom University. Trained as a teacher, he worked at Randgate (1946–55) and for three years at Riebeeck secondary school, Randfontein. For a thesis on the influence of the Bible on the Afrikaners' character, he received a doctorate from the University of Witwatersrand in 1957. Elected to Parliament in the National party (1958), he was appointed the party's chief information officer (1967), became a cabinet member in 1968, and was minister of Bantu Administration and Development and of Information by 1978. In the Transvaal he was leader of the National party, but he was forced to resign the leadership and ministry when the scandal broke in 1978. He retired from political life following the inquiries, repeatedly claiming that he had not been guilty of misconduct, that he had acted in the interests of his country, and that he had done so in the firm belief that no rules apply when the continued existence of one's country is threatened. In 1979 he founded the National Conservative party.

Sources

Keesing's Record of World Events 1979:28850; 28864; 28925; 29333. London: Longman.

Rees, Mervyn, and Day, Chris. 1980. *Muldergate: the story of the info scandal.* Johannesburg: Macmillan.

Uwechue, Ralph. 1991. *Makers of modern Africa.* London: Africa Books.

MUNDELLA CODE. A British educational code that encouraged enlightened teaching methods in class and a wide range of optional subjects in school courses.

Anthony John Mundella (1825–97) was a British politician born in Leicester, son of an Italian political refugee. Educated at Saint Nicholas National School, Leicester, he left at age 9 to be a hosiery manufacturer's apprentice. He became the firm's manager and a partner in a Nottingham hosiery business (1848). From this business he made enough money to devote his time to politics, his two main interests being factory legislation and popular education. Mundella studied the German system of instruction and advanced technical education in England. As vice-president of the Committee of Council on Education (1880–85), he was, with Lord Spencer, responsible for the Education Act of 1880 which introduced universal elementary education in England. Mundella was president of the Board of Trade in the last two Gladstone ministries (1886; 1892–94).

Sources

Aldrich, Richard, and Gordon, Peter. 1987. *Dictionary of British educationists.* London: Woburn Press.

Armytage, Walter H.G. 1951. *A. J. Mundella, 1825–1897: the liberal background to the labor movement.* London: Benn.

Stephen, Leslie, and Lee, Sydney, eds. 1917. *The dictionary of national biography.* Supplement. London: Oxford University Press.

MURDOCK FUNCTIONS. The functions or tasks performed in a family such that it is recognized as a nuclear family: socializing children, regulating sexual access to adults, reproducing children, and distributing economic resources to its members (Faris, 1964).

George Peter Murdock (1897–1985) was born in Meriden, Connecticut, and studied at Harvard Law School (1919–20) and Yale University (Ph.D., 1925). In World War I he served in the U.S. Army. He taught at the University of Maryland (1925–27), Yale (1928–60), and the University of Pittsburgh (1960–85). He became one of the United States' leading cultural anthropologists and did fieldwork among Indians in British Columbia and Oregon in the 1930s. In World War II he served in the U.S. Navy Reserve. He began the Human Relations Area Files, a cross-cultural survey to establish generalizations for sociology and anthropology. He was awarded several medals for outstanding work in his field; was fellow of the American Academy of Arts and Sciences and the American Sociological Association; and was president of the American Anthropological Association. In his *Social Structure* (1949) he focused on kinship, in order to present functionally related characteristics of families in many societies. Among his many publications was *Our Primitive Contemporaries* (1934), *Ethnographic Bibliography of North America* (1941), *Africa* (1959), and *Culture and Society* (1965).

Sources

Faris, Robert E.L. 1964. *Handbook of modern sociology.* Chicago: Rand McNally.

Jaques Cattell Press, ed. 1973. *American men and women of science: the social and behavioral sciences.* New York: Jaques Cattell and R. R. Bowker.

Magnussen, Magnus; Goring, Rosemary; and Thorn, John O., eds. 1990. *Chambers biographical dictionary.* Edinburgh: Chambers Ltd.

Murdock, George P. 1949. *Social structure.* New ed., 1965. New York: Macmillan.

Sills, David L., ed. 1968. *International encyclopedia of the social sciences.* New York: Macmillan and Free Press.

Who was who in America, 1982–85. Vol. 8. Chicago: Marquis.

MURRAY'S THEMATIC APPERCEPTION TEST. A projective test developed by H. A. Murray and Christiana D. Morgan for assessing attitudes, complexes of emotions, conflicts, drives, and sentiments. It comprises twenty cards depicting ambiguous images and scenes. The individual is expected to tell stories about each card, and from the stories assessment can be made of the person's level of emotional maturity, imagination, psychological insight, creativity, and family dynamics.

Henry Alexander Murray (1893–1988) was born in New York, studied history at Harvard, and completed both an M.D. (1919) and an M.A. in Biology (1920) at Columbia. He was a surgeon (1924–26) and, after being deeply influenced by his visit to Carl Jung (1875–1961) in 1926, Murray returned to Harvard where he completed his Ph.D. in biochemistry. In 1929 Murray became a clinical psychologist, succeeded Morton Prince (1854–1929) at Harvard, and developed a theory of human needs in his *Explorations in Personality* (1938). He was a lieutenant colonel at the center for the selection of agents for the Office of Strategic Services (1942–46), and director of the Harvard Psychological Clinic (1929–62). He became professor of clinical psychology (1948) at Harvard and was a lifelong scholar of the American novelist Herman Melville. In his name the Henry A. Murray Research Center for the Study of Lives of American women was founded at Radcliffe College in 1976; influenced by his work, it supports an in-depth, multidisciplinary study of individual lives.

Sources

Bales, Robert, et al. 1989. Faculty of Arts and Sciences: Memorial Minute. *Harvard Gazette,* December 15.

Corsini, Raymond J. 1984. *Encyclopedia of psychology.* 4 vols. New York: John Wiley.

Robinson, Forrest G. 1992. *Love's story told: a life of Henry A. Murray.* Cambridge, Mass.: Harvard University Press.

Schneidman, Edwin, ed. 1981. *Endeavors in psychology: selections from the personology of Henry A. Murray.* New York: Harper and Row.

Smith, M. Brewster, and Anderson, James William. 1989. Henry A. Murray (1893–1988): Obituary. *American Psychologist* 44:1153.

Sweetland, Richard C., and Keyser, Daniel J., eds. 1986. *Tests: a comprehensive reference for assessments in psychology, education and business.* Kansas City: Test Corp. of America.

Triplet, Rodney. 1992. Henry A. Murray: the making of a psychologist. *American Psychologist* 47:299–307.

Wolman, Benjamin. 1989. *Dictionary of behavioral science.* 2d ed. San Diego, Calif.: Academic Press.

N

NADERIST, NADER'S RAIDERS, NADERISM. A supporter and follower of the American representative of consumer interests. Nader's Raiders work for Ralph Nader's reform organizations, for example, Public Citizens, Center for Auto Safety, and the Study of Responsive Law. Naderism is public agitation for greater safety and higher quality in consumer goods and services (*Britannica Book of the Year 1969*).

Ralph Nader (b. 1934), consumer advocate, lawyer, and author, was born in Winstead, Connecticut, son of Lebanese immigrants who ran a small restaurant and bakery. He graduated from Princeton University in 1955. At Harvard Law School he edited the *Harvard Law Record,* which he used for discussion of social reform. His first article on unsafe vehicle design, ''American Cars: Designed for Death,'' appeared in the *Record* (1958). After graduation, he established a legal practice in Connecticut. In the early 1960s he traveled in the Soviet Union, Africa, and South America as a free-lance journalist for the *Atlantic Monthly* and the *Christian Science Monitor.* Distressed by the indifference of American corporations to the global consequences of their actions, he decided to carry his fight to Washington. In 1964–65 he produced a legislative background paper on highway safety and published his book *Unsafe at Any Speed* (1965; rev. 1972), emphasizing the automobile industry's drive for style over safety. His campaign for the public interest led to improved safety standards in the construction of natural gas pipelines and in underground coal mining. By 1971 a Harris Poll found that Nader was the sixth most popular figure in the United States; but by the early 1980s his popularity had waned and a feeling emerged that Naderism results in overregulation of industry. His books cover topics on the relation between consumers and atomic energy, pensions, giant corporations, defective goods (lemons), insurance, whistleblowing, corporate power, lawyers, and chemical poisons.

Sources

Buckhorn, Robert F. 1972. *Nader: the people's lawyer.* Englewood Cliffs, N.J.: Prentice-Hall.

Gorey, Hayes. 1975. *Nader and the power of everyman.* New York: Grosset and Dunlap.

Locher, Francis C., ed. 1979. *Contemporary authors.* Vols. 77–80. Detroit: Gale Research.

Magnussen, Magnus; Goring, Rosemary; and Thorn, John O., eds. 1990. *Chambers biographical dictionary.* Edinburgh: Chambers Ltd.

Moritz, Charles, ed. 1986. *Current biography.* New York: H. W. Wilson.

Who's who in America, 1992–93. New Providence, N.J.: Marquis.

NAKASONE'S REFORMS. Reforms in Japan after 1982, which were partly successful and centered on deregulating finance, reducing import restrictions, making tax reforms, privatizing the Japanese national rail network, reforming an education system that appeared to lack adequate creativity and discipline, increasing military security, and generally reducing public sector activities.

Yasuhiro Nakasone (b. 1917) was born in Takasaki, Japan, and graduated in law at Tokyo Imperial University. In 1941 he became minister for Home Affairs and was a lieutenant in wartime. After World War II, he was elected to the House of Representatives on the first of sixteen consecutive occasions (1947). In 1967 he was president of Takushoku University. As a member of the Liberal Democratic party, he became Japan's prime minister in 1982, serving for six years. Using presidential-style leadership, he led a movement for reform in public administration, which symbolized a shift from the center of bureaucratic power in the Japanese government to increased influence for members of the Diet and to more popular representation. In 1986 his government extended military expenditure beyond the 1 percent limit of gross national product in the face of public disapproval. In 1987 his proposal to introduce a sales tax met with so much resistance he had to withdraw it. Gradually, his attempt to increase the power of Japan's prime ministership by favoring parts of the government bureaucracy and alliances with businessmen lost him the support of the traditional supporters of the party. Among his publications are *The Ideal of Youth* (1947), *Japan Speaks* (1954), and *The New Conservatism (New Conservative Logic)* (1978). In 1984 he received an honorary doctorate from Johns Hopkins University. Recent studies of his policies and practices argue that Nakasone's reforms were inconsistent and more rhetorical than real.

Sources

Butcher, Diane, ed. 1989. *Who's who in Australasia and the Far East.* Cambridge: Melrose Press for the International Biographical Center.

Eccleston, Bernard. 1989. *State and society in post-war Japan.* Cambridge: Polity.

McCormack, Gavan, and Sugimoto, Yoshio. 1986. *Democracy in contemporary Japan.* New York: Armonk.

NANSEN PASSPORT. League of Nations passport for stateless people.

Fridtjof Nansen (1861–1930) was born at Store-Frøen near Christiania (now Oslo) and, intending to live an outdoor life, studied zoology at the university (1880). He became an explorer, outdoor sportsman, scientist and Norwegian statesman. He led an expedition to the Arctic between 1888 and 1896 and an oceanographic expedition to the North Atlantic in 1900 and again between 1910 and 1914. He invented an ocean-water sampler to be used at varying depths. He published *Eskimo Life* (1891), *Farthest North* (1897), and *Northern Mists* (1911). As a statesman, he took part in discussions about dissolving the union of Sweden and Norway, and when Norway became a monarchy, Nansen was made ministerial representative in London (1906–8). He was appointed chairman of the Norwegian Association for the League of Nations (1918) and headed the Norwegian delegation of the first assembly of the League of Nations (1920). His first job as High Commissioner for Refugees was to help repatriate from Russia a half-million prisoners of war of the German and Austro-Hungarian armies. Also, he directed relief efforts to reduce starvation in Russia and raised funds for the International Russian Relief Executive when the League of Nations was unable to provide financial aid. In July 1922 his efforts to provide identification for displaced persons resulted in the creation of the Nansen passport, which was intended to help people whose nation, state, or community of origin had been destroyed or otherwise lost during World War I. He received the Nobel Peace Prize (1922) and represented Norway on the Disarmament Committee at the League of Nations (1927). After his death, the Nansen International Office for Refugees was established in Geneva to care mainly for White Russians and Armenians from Turkey, and later for Jews from Germany.

Sources

Gillespie, Charles C., ed. 1973. *Dictionary of scientific biography.* Vol. 15. Supplement I, 1978. New York: Charles Scribner's Sons.

McHenry, Robert, ed. 1992. *The new encyclopedia Britannica.* Chicago: Encyclopedia Britannica, Inc.

Magnussen, Magnus; Goring, Rosemary; and Thorn, John O., eds. 1990. *Chambers biographical dictionary.* Edinburgh: Chambers Ltd.

Reynolds, Ernest E. 1949. *Nansen.* Harmondsworth: Penguin.

NAPOLEONIC. Relating either to Napoleon I, "The Great" Napoleon Bonaparte and his autocratic, frightening power over Europe in the nineteenth century, or to Napoleon III, "The Little" Emperor of the French and his dictatorship of the Second Empire.

Napoleon Bonaparte I (1769–1821). See BONAPARTEAN.

Napoleon II (1811–32) was the son of Napoleon I and Marie Louise of Austria. Raised in Austria, he lived a sad, dissolute life and died of tuberculosis. He had the title "King of Rome" until his father abdicated in 1814. Later, he was known as the prince of Parma, then duke of Reichstadt.

Napoleon III (1808–73) was the second son of Louis Bonaparte and Hortense de Beaubarnais, and a nephew to Napoleon I. In 1848 he was elected president of France with three votes to his opposition's one. He became a dictator in 1851 and converted the French Republic into the Second Empire. He became emperor of the French (1852–70). The empire fell in the Franco-Prussian War (1870–71), Napoleon III was captured (1870), and after the war he was released and died in exile.

Sources

Bury, John P.T. 1968. *Napoleon III and the Second Empire.* New York: Harper and Row.

Gerard, Albert L. 1956. *Napoleon I: a great life in brief.* New York: Alfred A. Knopf.

Gooch, Brison D. 1969. *The reign of Napoleon III.* Chicago: Rand McNally.

Mackenzie, Norman I. 1982. *The escape from Elba: the fall and flight of Napoleon.* Oxford: Oxford University press.

Magnussen, Magnus; Goring, Rosemary; and Thorn, John O., eds. 1990. *Chambers biographical dictionary.* Edinburgh: Chambers Ltd.

Preece, Warren E., ed. 1965. *Encyclopedia Britannica.* Chicago: Encyclopedia Britannica, Inc., William Benton.

NARCISSISM. Sensual gratification from one's own body, whether at a normal or pathological stage of growth. Narcissism refers to a fixation on an inflated sense of oneself and is accompanied by little interest in any restraints on one's actions or concern for others. In psychoanalytic theory the term relates to two levels of self-love; in primary narcissism, sexual energy attaches to the self and may be seen among the very young; secondary narcissism involves emotions like pride when the self and one's ideals are felt to be at one. Recent psychoanalytic extensions of the theory by Heinz Kohut (1913–81) have received much attention from psychoanalysts, as well as political and social scientists.

In Greek mythology Narcissus was the beautiful son of a nymph. He fell in love with his own reflection in a pool. He took no notice of Echo who died for love of him. He pined away for love of his own image and was transformed into a flower, named the Narcissus, a daffodil of the Amaryssis family.

Sources

Jobes, Gertrude. 1962. *Dictionary of mythology, folklore and symbols.* New York: Scarecrow Press.

Lasch, Christopher. 1979. *The culture of narcissism.* New York: W. W. Norton.

McHenry, Robert, ed. 1992. *The new encyclopedia Britannica.* Chicago: Encyclopedia Britannica, Inc.

Partridge, Eric. 1970. *Name into word: proper names that have become common property: a discursive dictionary.* 2d rev. ed. Freeport, N.J.: Books for Libraries.

NASSERISM, NASSERITE. Pan-Arabism, the political principles and policy of the twentieth-century Egyptian leader of the United Arab Republic. A supporter of Nasser.

Gamal Abdel Nasser (1918–70), the Egyptian political leader and president of the United Arab Republic, was born in Alexandria, the eldest of four sons of an Upper Egypt middle-class family. His father, an Arab, was a civil servant.

At age 16 Nasser organized and led the students of Cairo's Al Nandan Al Misria School in a demonstration against British domination in Egypt. In 1939 he entered the Royal Military Academy, one of 40 chosen from 400 applicants. He spoke out against colonialism, and aware of the Egyptians' opposition to British influences, he began to plan revolution. From the men he met in the army he picked his followers. In 1948 Nasser was determined to overthrow the monarchy; the coup he had been planning for ten years was staged on July 23, 1952, and forced King Farouk to abdicate. In 1953 Egypt was proclaimed a republic, Nasser became an Egyptian hero, influential among most Arabs and the enemy of Israel. He preferred nonalignment and turned to the Soviet camp when the United States denied him economic and military aid. President Nasser ruled Egypt for fourteen years—the Republic of Egypt from 1956 and the United Arab Republic from 1958 until his death.

Sources

Candee, Marjorie D. 1954. *Current biography yearbook.* New York: H. W. Wilson.

Dutton, Anthony. 1972. *Nasser.* New York: E. P. Dutton.

McHenry, Robert, ed. 1992. *The new encyclopedia Britannica.* Chicago: Encyclopedia Britannica, Inc.

Magnussen, Magnus; Goring, Rosemary; and Thorn, John O., eds. 1990. *Chambers biographical dictionary.* Edinburgh: Chambers Ltd.

Nasser, Gamal. 1955. *Egypt's liberation: the philosophy of revolution.* Washington, D.C.: Public Affairs Press.

Stephens, Robert H. 1971. *Nasser: a political biography.* London: Allen Lane.

Vatikiotis, P. J. 1978. *Nasser and his generation.* London: Croom Helm.

NEEDHAM THESIS. A Marxist thesis that explains why science in China ceased to develop at the critical periods of growth in Western science. The thesis argues that in China the emperor's autocratic control over intellectual traditions did not put enough value on innovation and instead focused on maintaining the already established systems of thought and knowledge. Meanwhile, in the West revolutionary social change promoted a capitalist economy, which in turn led to technical and scientific changes.

Joseph Needham (b. 1900) was born into an English medical family and was strongly influenced by his father's views on religion and philosophy as well as by the well-stocked family library. His father, a Harley Street specialist, had been active in the Oxford Movement and studied various forms of philosophical theology. Needham attended Oundle School in Northampton and Caius College, Cambridge, to study medicine. He researched in chemistry (Ph.D., 1924), and later came to believe Christian doctrine could be integrated with the historical materialism of Marxism, and that the class struggle could be a manifestation of ways God worked in the evolution of society. In the 1930s he became an active member of the Cambridge branch of the Socialist League and edited *Christianity and the Social Revolution* (1935). In 1942 the British government asked him to lecture to scientists in China, and there he turned to planning research on the history of science and technology in China and environs. On returning to England, he started the project in 1950. He was director of the East Asian History of Science Library at the Needham Research Institute in Cambridge (1976–89).

Sources

The international who's who, 1992–93. London: Europa Publications.

Needham, Joseph. 1961–84. *Science and civilization in China*. Cambridge: University Press.

Needham, Joseph. 1981. *Science in traditional China*. Hong Kong: Chinese University Press.

Teich, Mikulas, and Young, Robert, eds. 1972. *Changing perspectives in the history of science: essays in honor of Joseph Needham*. Boston: D. Reidel.

Who's who, 1992. London: Adam and Charles Black.

NEMESIS. Retributive justice; an avenger.

In Greek mythology, Nemesis was the name of two divine conceptions. The first was a minor goddess or nymph who was worshiped by Rhamnus in Attica. She was similar to Artemis, goddess of wild animals, vegetation, childbirth, and the hunt. The second was an abstraction in Greek religion referring to feelings of indigent disapproval of wrongdoing, particularly the disapproval of the gods at human aspirations, ambitions, and violations of sacred law. Eventually, she became the personification of that disapproval. In this sense she was goddess of retribution; in other accounts she is the goddess of ill and good fortune.

Sources

Brewer, Ebenezer Cobham. 1970. *Brewer's dictionary of phrase and fable*. Centenary ed. Rev. by Ivor H. Evans. New York: Harper and Row.

Jobes, Gertrude. 1962. *Dictionary of mythology, folklore and symbols*. New York: Scarecrow Press.

Partridge, Eric. 1970. *Name into word: proper names that have become common property: a discursive dictionary*. 2d rev. ed. Freeport, N.J.: Books for Libraries.

NEO-DARWINISM. The reformulation of Darwinism to incorporate Gregor Mendel's findings for genetics; that is, the rearranging of genetic contributions helps explain inherited differences, while natural selection becomes a general term for the unequal contribution that different organisms can make to the origins of the next generation. This new view of Darwinism helps overcome the original and poor explanation for evolving differences between organisms by involving simple natural selection of favorable variations. In addition, the effect of random origins and mutations is still available in the theory.

See DARWINIAN.

Sources

Berry, Robert J. 1982. *Neo-Darwinism*. London: Edward Arnold.

Mae-Wan Ho and Saunders, Peter T, eds. 1984. *Beyond neo-Darwinism: an introduction to the new evolutionary paradigm*. London: Academic Press.

NEO-FIRTHIAN. A development of Firth's linguistics led by Michael A.K. Halliday, University College, London (1965–70).

See also FIRTHIAN; HALLIDAYAN.

Source

Monaghan, James. (1979). *The neo-Firthian tradition and its contribution to general linguistics.* Tübingen: Niemeyer.

NEO-FORDISM. Two strategies in response to the worldwide crisis that followed the outcome of Fordism: (1) intensification of mass-production principles, internationalization of markets, demand for high protection of industry, reorganization of corporations, and extensive use of computers in all aspects of corporate operations; (2) innovation and specialization using the basic Fordist structures for organizing work but abandoning mass for specialty production.

See also FORDISM.

Source

Zeitlin, Jonathan. 1986. *The automobile industry and its workers: between Fordism and flexibility.* Cambridge: Polity and Blackwell.

NEO-FREUDIAN. A modern view in psychoanalysis that avoids libidinal forces as the prime human motives, and emphasizes the development and growth of individuals in their environs. It relates primarily to the American school of psychoanalytic thinking that stressed the social and interpersonal circumstances of an individual's neurotic behavior, adjustments, and feelings of anxiety, for example, Erik H. Erikson (b. 1902); Erich Fromm (1900–80); Heinz Hartmann (1874–1970); Karen Horney (1885–1952); and Harry Stack Sullivan (1892–1949).

See also ERIKSONIAN; FREUDIAN.

Sources

Devine, Elizabeth; Held, Michael; Vinson, James; and Walsh, George, eds. 1983. *Thinkers of the twentieth century: a biographical, bibliographical and critical dictionary.* London: Macmillan.

Guntrip, Harry. 1971. *Psychoanalytic theory, therapy, and the self: a basic guide to the human personality in Freud, Erikson, Klein, Sullivan, Fairbairn, Hartmann, Jacobson and Winnicott.* New York: Basic Books.

Knapp, Gerhard P. 1989. *The art of living: Erich Fromm's life and work.* New York: P. Lang.

Kurzweil, Edith. 1989. *The Freudians: a comparative perspective.* New Haven, Conn.: Yale University Press.

Loewenstein, Rudolph M. 1970. Obituary: Heinz Hartmann 1894–1970. *International Journal of Psychoanalysis* 51:417–419.

Monte, Christopher. 1980. *Beneath the mask: an introduction to theories of personality.* New York: Holt, Rinehart and Winston.

Perry, Helen S. 1982. *Psychiatrist of America: the life of Harry Stack Sullivan.* Cambridge, Mass.: Belknap Press.

Quinn, Susan. 1988. *A mind of her own: the life of Karen Horney.* Reading, Mass.: Addison-Wesley.

Roazen, Paul. 1985. *Helene Deutsch: a psychoanalyst's life.* New York: Doubleday.
Rubins, Jack. 1978. *Karen Horney: gentle rebel of psychoanalysis.* London: Weidenfeld and Nicolson.
Schafer, Roy. 1970. An overview of Heinz Hartmann's contributions to psychoanalysis. *International Journal of Psychoanalysis* 51:425–446.
Zusne, Leonard. 1984. *Biographical dictionary of psychology.* Westport, Conn.: Greenwood Press.

NEO-HEGELIANISM. The idealism of Hegel as advanced and examined by Thomas Hill Green (1836–92); Francis Herbert Bradley (1846–1924); Bernard Bosanquet (1848–1923); John Ellis McTaggart (1866–1925); Robin George Collingwood (1889–1943); Léon Brunschvicg (1869–1944); and Bendetto Croce (1866–1952). For Hegel the rational whole was more real than any of its parts; thus, a group enjoyed more reality than the individuals who were members of it. Such a view has been used to justify extreme authoritarian beliefs from the right to the left. Until logical positivism began to establish itself at the turn of the century, a modified form of Hegel's views was prominent in Britain among idealist philosophers Bradley, Bosanquet, Green, and McTaggart.

See HEGELIAN.

Sources
Devine, Elizabeth; Held, Michael; Vinson, James; and Walsh, George, eds. 1983. *Thinkers of the twentieth century: a biographical, bibliographical and critical dictionary.* London: Macmillan.
Edwards, Paul. 1967. *The encyclopedia of philosophy.* New York: Macmillan.
Magnussen, Magnus; Goring, Rosemary; and Thorn, John O., eds. 1990. *Chambers biographical dictionary.* Edinburgh: Chambers Ltd.

NEO-KANTISM. A late-nineteenth-century revival in Germany of interest in pure principles of understanding and a priorism to manage the developments in natural sciences and mathematics. Some of the major philosophers were Friederich Albert Lange (1828–75), Hermann Cohen (1842–1914), Paul G. Natorp (1854–1924), Ernst Cassirer (1874–1945), and in France Charles Renouvier (1815–1903).

See also KANTIAN.

Sources
Guyer, Paul E., ed. 1992. *The Cambridge companion to Kant.* Cambridge: Cambridge University Press.
Scruton, Roger. 1982. *Kant.* Oxford: Oxford University Press.
Willey, Thomas E. 1978. *Back to Kant.* Detroit: Wayne State University Press.

NEO-LAMARCKISM. A belief, popular at the turn of the century, that acquired characteristics could be inherited. The belief opposed Darwin's theory that new species may arise by accident or random mutation, and it was supported by the opinion that adaptation to the environment would surely involve purposive changes.

See also LAMARCKISM.

Source
Bowler, Peter J. 1983. *The eclipse of Darwinism.* Baltimore: Johns Hopkins University
    Press.

NEO-MALTHUSIANISM. A nineteenth-century British ideology, contrary to Malthus's original view, that advocated induced abortion and contraception to control population. The Malthusian League—actually neo-Malthusian—was founded in 1861, and supported contraception and eugenics in Britain and the United States.
    See also MALTHUSIAN.

Source
Soloway, Richard A. 1982. *Birth control and the population question in England, 1887–
    1930.* Chapel Hill: University of North Carolina Press.

NEO-MARXISM. Revisions of Marxism after World War II that centered on Hegel's ideas in Karl Marx's theory, the functions of intellectuals in politics, how the proletariat would replace the bourgeoisie in the domination of capitalism, subjective apects of Marxist thought, and Marxism as science. Among prominent neo-Marxists were Louis Althusser (1918–90), Antonio Gramsci (1891–1937), Georg Lukás (1885–1971), Jean-Paul Sartre (1905–80), and members of the Frankfurt School.
    See MARXIAN.

Sources
Gorman, Robert A. 1982. *Neo-Marxism, the meanings of modern radicalism.* Westport,
    Conn.: Greenwood Press.
Gorman, Robert A., ed. 1986. *Biographical dictionary of neo-Marxism.* Westport, Conn.:
    Greenwood Press.
Rockmore, Tom, et al. 1981. *Marxism and alternatives: towards the conceptual inter-
    action among Soviet philosophy, neo-Thomism, pragmatism, and phenomenology.*
    Boston: D. Reidel.
Stanfield, Ron. 1973. *The economic surplus and neo-Marxism.* Lexington, Mass.: Lex-
    ington Books.

NEO-RICARDIANISM. A term used in the 1970s to describe the beliefs underlying the work of the Italian-born economist who lived in England, Piero Sraffa (1898–1983) in *Production of Commodities by Means of Commodities: Prelude to a Critique of Economic Theory* (1960; 1975). The term could be traced to modern Marxists who sought to distinguish their views from those of Sraffa. Sraffa said that his views originated from the classical economists, Adam Smith and David Ricardo. Sraffa reexamined classical theories of value and income distribution, and led others to reconsider or drop their support for marginalist economic theory.
    See also RICARDIAN.

Sources

Blaug, Mark, ed. 1986. *Who's who in economics: a biographical dictionary of major economists, 1700–1986.* 2d ed. Cambridge, Mass.: MIT Press.

Eatwell, John; Milgate, Murray; and Newman, Peter. 1987. *The new Palgrave: a dictionary of economics.* London: Macmillan.

Sills, David L., ed. 1979. *International encyclopedia of the social sciences.* Biographical Supplement. New York: Macmillan and Free Press.

Who's who, 1974. London: Adam and Charles Black.

NEO-THOMISM. A new study and extension of the ideas of Saint Thomas Aquinas (1226–74) in the Roman Catholic religion. In 1875 Pope Leo XII turned many scholars to modern Thomism, and later Jacques Maritain (1882–1973) advanced Thomism by considering crises in theology and existentialism in Christianity. The revival was intended to help answer modern problems in the philosophy of science that consider naturalism, modern psychiatric issues, and recent psychological theories of the self that concern being and becoming.

See also THOMISM.

Sources

Brennan, Robert E. 1969. *Thomist psychology.* New York: Macmillan.

Brown, Barry F. 1985. *Accidental being: a study in metaphysics of St. Thomas Aquinas.* Lanham, Md.: University of America Press.

Burrell, David B. 1979. *Aquinas: God and action.* London: Routledge and Kegan Paul.

Gilson, Etienne H. 1957. *The Christian philosophy of St. Thomas Aquinas.* Trans. L. K. Shook. New York: Random House.

Maritain, Jacques. 1968. *Bergsonian philosophy and Thomism.* Trans. M. and J. G. Andison. Westport, Conn.: Greenwood Press.

Maritain, Jacques. 1970. *True humanism.* Trans. M. R. Adamson. Westport, Conn.: Greenwood Press.

Maurer, Armand A., ed. 1974. *Saint Thomas Aquinas 1274–1974: commemorative studies.* 2 vols. Toronto: Pontifical Institute of Mediaeval Studies.

NERONIAN, NERONIC. Pertaining to the first-century Roman emperor; extremely cruel and tyrannical domination.

Nero Claudius Caesar (37–68) was born Lucius Domitius Ahenobarbus, son of Agrippina II, great grand-daughter of Augustus. Agrippina married Claudius I and persuaded him to adopt Nero and make him the guardian of Brittanicus, Claudius's son; Octavia, Claudius's daughter, was made Nero's wife. Nero became emperor on the death of Claudius in A.D. 54. Under the tuition and advice of Seneca and Burrus, his rule began well. But as Agrippina lost her influence over Nero, she plotted in Brittanicus's favor, and Nero poisoned him. Nero took Poppae Sabina, wife of Otho, his friend, as a mistress, and under her influence, legend states, Nero's evil was established and grew. In A.D. 59 he murdered his mother, and in 62 his wife. Nero lost his best advisers, and in 64 when Rome burned—arranged, according to rumors, as the backdrop to his recitation on the fall of Troy—Nero blamed the Christians. He began their Roman persecution and, according to Christian belief, included Saint Peter and Saint Paul among his victims. He rebuilt Rome, erected a great palace, and laid out broad and regular streets. Even so he was hated by all, and when a plot to oust him failed in 65, he murdered with vengeance. Always aspiring to be an artist and actor, he visited Greece in A.D. 67, a culture he much admired. After several unsuccessful attempts, the Praetorian guard revolted against him in 68, and this last of Julius Caesar's family committed suicide, uttering: ''What an artist the world is losing in me!''

Sources

Brewer, Ebenezer Cobham. 1970. *Brewer's dictionary of phrase and fable.* Centenary ed. Rev. by Ivor H. Evans. New York: Harper and Row.

Grant, Michael. 1970. *Nero: emperor in revolt.* New York: Heritage Press.

McHenry, Robert, ed. 1992. *The new encyclopedia Britannica.* Chicago: Encyclopedia Britannica, Inc.

NESTOR. A wise, old counselor; an old man; a senior in a company; a fine political orator.

In Greek mythology Nestor was king of Pylos in the Peloponnese. In Homer's *Iliad* he is the old and respected man, father of Antilochus who is full of advice and reminiscences. He was a hero at Troy and showed remarkable eloquence and wisdom and lived a long life. In the *Odyssey* he is back in his palace and entertaining Telemachus. He seldom appears in post–Homeric literature.

Sources

Brewer, Ebenezer Cobham. 1970. *Brewer's dictionary of phrase and fable.* Centenary ed. Rev. by Ivor H. Evans. New York: Harper and Row.

Jobes, Gertrude. 1962. *Dictionary of mythology, folklore and symbols.* New York: Scarecrow Press.

Preece, Warren E., ed. 1965. *Encyclopedia Britannica.* Chicago: Encyclopedia Britannica, Inc., William Benton.

NESTORIAN. Relating to the fourth-century patriarch of Constantinople and his teaching that the divinity and humanity of Christ are not one, but that Christ embodied distinct divine and human persons.

Nestorius (d. c. 451) was born of Persian parents in Germanicia, a city of northern Syria. He was probably trained by Theodore, bishop of Mopsuestia. After receiving his priest's orders at Antioch, Nestorius entered the monastery of Saint Euprepius and became so eminent for his zeal, ascetic life, and eloquent preaching that he was selected by the emperor to be patriarch of Constantinople in 428. In 431 after being condemned as a heretic, deposed, and witnessing the burning of his writings, he was confined to a monastery. Four years later he was banished to Petra, Arabia. A refugee, he was sheltered in the Greater Oasis in Upper Egypt and later died in obscurity. Mere fragments of his writings have been preserved, but in 1895 his ''Bazaar of Heraclides'' was found in a Syrian translation. It is an autobiographical argument that defends his ideas, and pleads for charity and forgiveness; subsequently, his heretical views were reconsidered, and his guilt was questioned. Today opinion is divided as to what Nestorius's doctrine was and to what extent it was heretical. What he actually advocated was that a person's existence may be extended by reference to other things; in Christ's case he used manhood to manifest himself, and consequently manhood was included in the presentation of his identity. In the Roman Empire, Nestorianism was suppressed, but it survives today among a few people in North and South America, India, Russia, and the Middle East.

Sources

Cross, Frank L. 1974. *The Oxford dictionary of the Christian Church.* 2d ed. New York: Oxford University Press.

Ferguson, Everett, ed. 1990. *The encyclopedia of early Christianity.* New York: Garland Publishing.

Grant, Asahel. 1841. *The Nestorians.* New York: Harper and Bros.

Joseph, John. 1961. *The Nestorians and their Muslim neighbours.* Princeton, N.J.: Princeton University Press.

Loofs, Friedrich. 1914. *Nestorius and his place in the history of Christian doctrine.* Cambridge: Cambridge University Press.

McDonald, William J., ed. 1967. *New Catholic encyclopedia.* New York: McGraw-Hill.

McHenry, Robert, ed. 1992. *The new encyclopedia Britannica.* Chicago: Encyclopedia Britannica, Inc.

NEWCASTLE COMMISSION. A British education inquiry (1858–61) which showed that, despite the extent of elementary instruction, over 120,000 children were without schooling. Doubts were raised about the quality of the report.

Henry Pelham Fiennes, Pelham-Clinton, fifth duke of Newcastle (1811–64), was born in London, educated at Eton, and graduated from Oxford University in 1832. He established Newcastle scholarships at Eton College in 1829. In Parliament he represented South Nottinghamshire (1832–46) and was a lord of the Treasury in Robert Peel's first government (1834–35), first commissioner of woods and forests (1841–46) and briefly chief secretary to the lord lieutenant of Ireland. When his father died in 1851, he succeeded to the title of the fifth duke of Newcastle. (He had previously been earl of Lincoln and was entitled to a seat in the House of Lords.) He became secretary of state for the colonies (1852–54), secretary of war (1854–55), and colonial secretary (1859–64). Between 1858 and 1861 he was chairman of a royal commission appointed to inquire into elementary education. The commissioner's major recommendation, the establishment of county and borough education boards with power to assist other schools, was not taken up.

Sources

Aldrich, Richard, and Gordon, Peter. 1987. *Dictionary of British educationists.* London: Woburn Press.

Boase, Frederic. 1965. *Modern English biography.* London: Frank Cass and Co. Ltd.

Magnussen, Magnus; Goring, Rosemary; and Thorn, John O., eds. 1990. *Chambers biographical dictionary.* Edinburgh: Chambers Ltd.

Munsell, F. Darrell. 1985. *The unfortunate duke: Henry Pelham, duke of Newcastle 1811–64.* Columbia: University of Missouri Press.

Stephen, Leslie, and Lee, Sydney, eds. 1917. *The dictionary of national biography.* London: Oxford University Press.

NIELSEN RATINGS. A television rating system based on weekly sampling of over 1,000 households and used by television networks since 1950 to establish prime-time schedules for advertising.

Arthur Charles Nielsen (1897–1980) was born in Chicago, educated in Berwyd and Cicero, and worked as an office boy in the local fish market. He graduated in electrical engineering from the University of Wisconsin, served in the U.S. Navy Reserve, and after World War I worked briefly as an electrical engineer and in publishing. In 1923 he founded A. C. Nielsen and Company to make performance surveys for industrial manufacturers. In the 1930s he devised the Nielsen Food and Drug Index to record the flow of consumer goods. Later, his firm invented mechanical meters to measure the listening habits of radio audiences; by 1942 he was offering the radio networks the Nielsen Radio Index to assess the impact of advertising. His firm overcame competition from Crossley Ratings (1946), bought Hooper Ratings (1950), and flourished to become America's largest firm in the television ratings business. He established his firm in Britain (1939), Canada (1944), Australia (1948), and in most European countries and South Africa. He was honored by most marketing organizations and received an honorary D.Sc. from his university in 1974.

Sources
Moritz, Charles, ed. 1980. *Current biography yearbook.* New York: H. W. Wilson.
Obituary. *New York Times,* June 4, 1980:A 26.
Who's who in America, 1980. Chicago: Marquis.

NIETZSCHEAN. Relating to the ideas of the nineteenth-century German philosopher who argued that no single morality can be appropriate to all people.

Friedrich Nietzsche (1844–1900) was born at Roecken Saxony-Anhalt. His father was a Protestant minister. Friedrich studied classical philology at the universities at Bonn and Leipzig; in 1869 he became a professor at the University of Basel in Switzerland. In 1872 he published his first book, *The Birth of Tragedy from the Spirit of Music,* which considers Wagner's music dramas and the prospects of rebirth of tragedy. In 1879 he resigned from the university; his health was poor, and he lacked the energy to teach and write. From that time he usually published one volume each year, living frugally and spending his summers in Switzerland and his winters in Italy. In 1889 he collapsed on a street in Turin, Italy. Until his death eleven years later he was insane and lived in an asylum. Most twentieth-century philosophers were influenced by him. The Nazis made use of his doctrines, especially those relating to the embodiment of perfection in humankind, the Ubermensch or superman, who dominated others without pity and with extreme efficiency.

Sources

Hayman, Ronald. 1980. *Nietzsche: a critical life.* London: Weidenfeld and Nicolson.

Magnussen, Magnus; Goring, Rosemary and Thorn, John O. eds. 1990. *Chambers biographical dictionary.* Edinburgh: Chambers Ltd.

McHenry, Robert, ed. 1992. *The new encyclopedia Britannica.* Chicago: Encyclopedia Britannica, Inc.

Miller, David, ed. 1987. *The Blackwell encyclopedia of political thought.* Oxford: Blackwell.

Kaufmann, Walter A., ed. 1971. *The portable Nietzsche.* London: Chatto and Windus.

Pletsch, Carl. 1991. *Young genius: becoming a genius.* New York: Free Press.

Zusne, Leonard. 1984. *Biographical dictionary of psychology.* Westport, Conn.: Greenwood Press.

NIMROD. A great hunter.

Nimrod (fl. 2450 B.C.) was a mighty hunter (Genesis 10:8). He was a son of Cush, and as a Cushite, he established a kingdom in Shinar, the classic Babylonia, and along the Tigris he extended his rule over Assyria and established the capitals Babel, Accad, Ninevah, and Calah. In the Chaldean epic of the deluge, Nimrod was identified with the hero, Gilgamesh (c. 2200 B.C.), who is represented as fighting with a beast.

Sources

Cross, Frank L. 1974. *The Oxford dictionary of the Christian Church.* 2d ed. New York: Oxford University Press.

Partridge, Eric. 1970. *Name into word: proper names that have become common property: a discursive dictionary.* 2d rev. ed. Freeport, N.J.: Books for Libraries.

Preece, Warren E., ed. 1965. *Encyclopedia Britannica.* Chicago: Encyclopedia Britannica, Inc., William Benton.

NIOBE. An inconsolable, bereaved woman; a symbol of grief.

Niobe was the daughter of Tantalus, king of Sipylus in Lydia, and the wife of Amphion, king of Thebes, by whom she had an equal number of sons and daughters. (Some legends say six, others nine or ten.) Niobe boasted that she was superior to Leto, who had only two children, Apollo and Artemis. In response, Leto sent her divine pair to kill all of Niobe's children. Niobe wept for nine days and nights, before the Olympians buried the bodies; then, still dripping with tears, she turned to stone on Mount Sipylus. Niobe's story is told as common knowledge in the *Iliad,* and the death of her children was the subject for many Hellenistic sculptors.

Sources

Brewer, Ebenezer Cobham. 1970. *Brewer's dictionary of phrase and fable.* Centenary ed. Rev. by Ivor H. Evans. New York: Harper and Row.

Partridge, Eric. 1970. *Name into word: proper names that have become common property: a discursive dictionary.* 2d rev. ed. Freeport, N.J.: Books for Libraries.

Preece, Warren E., ed. 1965. *Encyclopedia Britannica.* Chicago: Encyclopedia Britannica, Inc., William Benton.

NIXON DOCTRINE, NIXON-KENNEDY DEBATES, NIXONLAND. The Nixon Doctrine was elucidated in a speech on November 3, 1969. In this speech

President Nixon stated that the United States should not be involved in a land war for the sake of its allies; America would keep its treaties and shield its allies against nuclear threat and give economic and military aid short of battle troops for them. Consequently, small states were expected to follow America's anticommunist policy, and their political systems were not questioned, providing their policies were anticommunist. The Nixon-Kennedy debates were the first televised debates ever between two presidential candidates in the United States, beginning September 26, 1960. ''In one direction lies a land of slander and scare, the land of sly innuendos, the poison pen, the anonymous phone call, and hustling, pushing, shoving; the land of smash and grab and anything to win. This is Nixon land'' (Stevenson, 1977).

Richard Milhous Nixon (1913–94) was born in Yorba Linda, California. After five years in a law practice, he served in the U.S. Navy, prior to his election to the House of Representatives in 1946. In 1950 he became a senator and in 1952 vice-president. His swift climb in political circles was the result of fearless outspokenness and brilliant political tactics. He was particularly prominent as a member of the House Un-American Activities Committee, and on a visit to Moscow in 1957, he achieved notoriety by his outspoken exchanges with Khrushchev. In 1968 he won the presidential election by a small margin and was reelected in 1972 by a large majority. During an official investigation into a break-in attempt at the Democratic National Committee's headquarters at Watergate in Washington, Nixon lost the support of the American people and his political allies, and resigned in August 1974 under threat of impeachment.

John F. Kennedy. See KENNEDY ROUND.

Sources

Aitken, Jonathan. 1993. *Nixon: a life.* London: Wiedenfeld and Nicolson.

Ambrose, Stephen E. 1987. *Nixon: the education of a politician 1913–1962.* New York: Simon and Schuster.

Ambrose, Stephen E. 1989. *Nixon: the triumph of a politician 1962–1972.* New York: Simon and Schuster.

Ambrose, Stephen E. 1991. *Nixon: ruin and recovery, 1973–1990.* New York: Simon and Schuster.

Brodie, Fawn. 1981. *Richard Nixon: the shaping of his character.* New York: W. W. Norton.

Colodny, Len, and Gettlin, Robert. 1991. *Silent coup: the removal of Richard Nixon.* London: Victor Gollancz.

Hoffmann, Stanley. 1980. *Primacy or world order.* New York: McGraw-Hill.

Magnussen, Magnus; Goring, Rosemary; and Thorn, John O., eds. 1990. *Chambers biographical dictionary.* Edinburgh: Chambers Ltd.

Stevenson, Adlai E. 1977. *Papers,* Vol. 6, November 5, 1956, October 27, 1956:316, 306.

Szulc, Tad. 1978. *The illusion of peace.* New York: Viking Press.

NOACHIAN, NOACHIC. Of the time when the Lord wanted to begin life on earth again.

In biblical legend the Lord saw the world plagued by evil and violent men, except for the 600-year-old Noah. The Lord told Noah to build an ark—"Noah's Ark"—of gopher wood, sealed with pitch, 300 cubits long, 50 cubits wide, and 30 cubits high, with a window, a side door, and three levels inside. Into the ark Noah was ordered to bring his family and a male and female of all living things, and enough food. While the Lord flooded the earth, Noah protected his family and the contents of the floating ark. It rained continuously for forty days, flooded the earth for 150 days, and all living things died. When the flood subsided, the ark settled on Mount Ararat, and life on earth began again.

Sources

Brewer, Ebenezer Cobham. 1970. *Brewer's dictionary of phrase and fable.* Centenary ed. Rev. by Ivor H. Evans. New York: Harper and Row.

Cross, Frank L. 1974. *The Oxford dictionary of the Christian Church.* 2d ed. New York: Oxford University Press.

Preece, Warren E., ed. 1965. *Encyclopedia Britannica.* Chicago: Encyclopedia Britannica, Inc., William Benton.

NOBEL PRIZE. One of the five annual prizes for achievement: for invention or discovery in physics; for chemical discovery or improvement; for discovery in physiology or other branches of medicine; for literary work with an idealistic tendency; and for the greatest contribution to the peace of the world. Except for the peace prize, the winner is selected by appropriate learned academics in Sweden. The peace prize is determined by a committee elected by the Parliament of Norway. In 1968 Sweden's central bank financed an economics prize in memory of Nobel.

Alfred Bernhard Nobel (1833–96) was born in Stockholm, son of an engineer and inventor who spent much of his life in Russia. Nobel was privately educated and traveled widely in Europe and the United States. In 1850 on his return to Russia from studies in America, he found his father manufacturing explosives. Nobel had a vision of peaceful uses for explosives, and on his return to Sweden in 1859 he began to manufacture nitroglycerine. When his factory exploded in 1864, killing his brother, the Swedish government refused to allow the factory to be rebuilt; Nobel was thought to be a mad scientist who manufactured destruction. In 1866 Nobel invented dynamite and blasting gelatine, and became rich from producing explosives and operating the Baku oil wells in Russia. At his death, Nobel left a fund of over $9 million for the establishment of annual prizes in the five fields of Peace, Literature, Physics, Chemistry, and Medicine.

Sources

McHenry, Robert, ed. 1992. *The new encyclopedia Britannica.* Chicago: Encyclopedia Britannica, Inc.

Magnussen, Magnus; Goring, Rosemary; and Thorn, John O., eds. 1990. *Chambers biographical dictionary.* Edinburgh: Chambers Ltd.

Schuck, Henrik, et al. 1962. *Nobel: the man and the prizes.* Amsterdam: Elsevier.

NORBERTINES. Premonstratensians, followers of Saint Norbert.

Saint Norbert (c. 1085–1134) was the younger son in the Xanten family,

Duchy of Cleves, at Wesel, Prussia. After becoming a priest, he led a noble-man's self-indulgent life, until, struck by lightning, he reformed himself and was ordained (1115). He sold his estates, gave all his money and possessions to the poor, and Pope Gelasius allowed him to be a wandering preacher. With support from the bishop of Laon, he established the Premonstratensians in the Premontre Valley. Following the rule of Saint Augustine, he lived austerely, reformed the clergy, and recovered alienated church property. In 1126 he was consecrated archbishop of Magdeburg. Although attempts on his life were made by those who lost their possessions, he had support from Emperor Lothair II who made him chancellor for Italy in 1133. He was canonized by Gregory XIII in 1582.
Sources

Cross, Frank L. 1974. *The Oxford dictionary of the Christian Church.* 2d ed. New York: Oxford University Press.
Delaney, John, and Tobin, James Edward. 1961. *Dictionary of Catholic biography.* Garden City, N.Y.: Doubleday.
McHenry, Robert, ed. 1992. *The new encyclopedia Britannica.* Chicago: Encyclopedia Britannica, Inc.

NORRIS-LA GUARDIA ANTI-INJUNCTION ACT. A U.S. federal act (1932) that helped unions pressure employers by removing from federal juris-diction the power to prevent unions from acting coercively, providing that the action was not violent or fraudulent. As a result, U.S. labor was free to establish economic goals legally. The act was followed by the Wagner Act, which guar-anteed U.S. labor the right to organize and enter collective bargaining. The Anti-injunction Act made agreements by workers not to join unions—yellow dog contracts—no longer enforceable.

George William Norris (1861–1944) was a progressive, and later disaffected, Republican from Nebraska who was elected to the U.S. House of Representa-tives (1903–13) where he led the revolt against the speaker, Joseph Cannon, in 1910 to limit the speaker's autocratic authority to determine which legislation came before the House. He entered the Senate (1913–43) and authored the Twentieth Amendment—the "lame duck" amendment of 1933 that moved the inauguration of the president from March to January—supported the policies of the New Deal, and was a critic of Supreme Court decisions that argued that the New Deal legislation was unconstitutional. His autobiography, *Fighting Liber-als,* appeared in 1945.

Fiorello Henry La Guardia (1882–1947), son of an enlisted bandmaster, was born in Greenwich Village, New York City, and educated in Prescott, Arizona. In Budapest and Trieste he served the American consular service (1901–4), was an interpreter on Ellis Island for the immigration service (1907–10), and grad-uated from the New York University Law School (1910). He became deputy state attorney-general in 1915. As a Republican, he entered the U.S. Congress (1917–19), resigned to join the air service, rose to major, and commanded the U.S. Air Force on the Italian-Austrian front, receiving the Italian War Cross.

After the war, he was reelected to the U.S. Congress (1923–32). In 1932 he helped defeat President Hoover's sales tax and agitated successfully for the Anti-injunction Act. He endorsed the presidency of Franklin D. Roosevelt. In 1929 he had failed to be elected mayor of New York, but he won in 1933 and 1937. With a policy of "a government with a heart" to New York, he brought social reforms and many public improvements. One of New York's airports was given his name. After retirement he served the United Nations (1946).

Sources

Elliot, Laurence. 1983. *Little flower: the life and times of Fiorello La Guardia.* New York: William Morrow.

Garraty, John A., and James, Edward T., eds. 1974. *Dictionary of American biography.* Supplement 4. New York: Charles Scribner's Sons.

James, Edward T. 1973. *Dictionary of American biography.* Supplement 3. New York: Charles Scribner's Sons.

Kersner, Thomas. 1989. *Fiorello H. La Guardia and the making of modern New York.* New York: McGraw-Hill.

Zucker, Norman L. 1966. *George W. Norris: gentle knight of democracy.* Urbana: University of Illinois Press.

NORTH-HATT OR NORC SCALE. The North-Hatt-NORC scale, a landmark in the assessment of occupational status in the United States, came from a study of occupational prestige (1947) which was sponsored by President Harry S Truman's Scientific Research Board, the Ohio State University, and the National Opinion Research Center (NORC). North and Hatt, two sociologists, carefully prepared the scale in 1947 and asked a quota sample of the adult population to assess occupations. Results showed that the top occupations were U.S. Supreme Court justice, physician, and state governor, while the least prestigious were garbage collector, street sweeper, and shoe shiner. When the occupations were classified, the highest were government officials, professional and semiprofessional workers, and proprietors, managers, and nonfarming officials; the lowest categories were farm laborers, nonprotective, nondomestic service workers, and nonfarm laborers.

Cecil Clare North (1878–1961) was born in Taylor County, Iowa, and studied at the universities of Nebraska, Yale, and Chicago (Ph.D., 1905). He was a professor of sociology and economics at Miami University (1907–8) and De Pauw University (1908–16) before joining the faculty at Ohio State University in 1916 where he remained until retirement. He was emeritus in 1948. He published *Sociological Implications of Ricardo's Economics* (1915); *Social Differentiation* (1927); *The Community and Social Welfare* (1931); and *Social Problems and Social Planning* (1932). North's retirement and the death of Paul K. Hatt prevented them from completing a monograph on their work.

Paul Kitchener Hatt (1914–53) was born in Vancouver, went to the United States in 1937, and was naturalized in 1941. He studied at Linfield College and the University of Washington (Ph.D., 1945). He taught at the University of

Indiana (1941–42) and worked with the American Red Cross (1942–44). After teaching for a year at the University of Miami, he went to Ohio State University and then to Wayne State University. He also taught at Princeton (1947–49) and in Puerto Rico (1947), and worked at the Columbia University Bureau of Applied Social Research (1948–49). He became a professor of sociology at Northwestern, published in professional journals, and was a member of several sociological and social research associations in the United States. Bendix and Lipset (1953) dedicated their book to Hatt.

Sources

North, Cecil C., and Hatt, Paul K. 1947. Jobs and occupations: a popular evaluation. *Opinion News* 9, September 1:3–13. Reprinted in Reinhard Bendix and Seymour M. Lipset, eds. 1953. *Class, status and power: a reader in social stratification.* Glencoe, Ill.: Free Press, pp. 411–426.

Reiss, Albert J., Jr. 1955. Occupational mobility of professional workers. *American Sociological Review* 20:693–700.

Reiss, Albert J., Jr. 1961. *Occupations and social status.* New York: Free Press of Glencoe.

Who was who in America, 1963. Vol. 3. Chicago: Marquis.

Who was who in America, 1968. Vol. 4. Chicago: Marquis.

NOSBINOR RULE. The reverse of the Robinson Rule—that is, "coefficients of correlation based on individuals cannot be projected into generalizations pertaining to populations" (Dodge and Martin, 1970:312).

William S. Robinson. See ROBINSON RULE.

Sources

Dodge, David L., and Martin, Walter T. 1970. *Social stress and illness: mortality patterns in industrial society.* Notre Dame, Ind.: University of Notre Dame Press.

Robinson, William S. 1950. Ecological correlations and the behavior of individuals. *American Sociological Review* 15:351–357.

NOSTRADAMUS. One who professes to foretell the future.

Nostradamus (1503–66), the astrologer, was born Michel de Notredame or Nostredame at Saint Rémy, France. He studied medicine in Agen (1529), went to Salon (1544), and by 1546–47 was treating victims of the plague at Aix and Lyon. At this stage he began making prophecies. They were published in 1555, and a special enlarged edition was dedicated to the king in 1588. His claims to esoteric knowledge and his prophecies made him famous, especially when he foretold the death through tournament wounds of Henri II. Nostradamus came to the notice of Catherine de' Medici and her son, King Charles IX, who appointed him court physician. His writings, *The Centuries,* drawn from the whole body of late medieval prophetic literature, have often enjoyed popularity since his death. In 1781 the Congregation of the Index, the Roman Catholic organization for evaluating books and manuscripts, condemned Nostradamus's prophecies. Because they are in several languages and cryptic, they tend to support more controversy than belief. Today people who make vague and evasive predictions bear his name.

Sources

McHenry, Robert, ed. 1992. *The new encyclopedia Britannica.* Chicago: Encyclopedia Britannica, Inc.

Magnussen, Magnus; Goring, Rosemary; and Thorn, John O., eds. 1990. *Chambers biographical dictionary.* Edinburgh: Chambers Ltd.

NUFFIELD APPROACH. An approach to British education, especially the natural sciences, sponsored by the Nuffield Foundation, which involved the use of university and high school staff to test modern proposals for new teaching styles and curriculae. Nuffield projects were found in most natural sciences as well as languages, social science, and classical studies. The preferred teaching technique centered on an active rather than a passive role for students and pupils.

William Richard Morris, Viscount Nuffield (1877–1963), wanted to study medicine, but his family could not afford university education and so at 16 the lad began work in a bicycle shop. After nine months, with a small loan he opened a shop himself, made money, and in 1912 bought a factory near Oxford and began to make cars. His works were turned to military purposes in World War I. By 1926 he owned acres of factories and produced 1,000 cars per week. Created a baronet in 1929, he was raised to the peerage in 1934 and was viscount in 1938. He was known as the Henry Ford of Britain for his manufacturing of the Morris Oxford automobile. He became one of the nation's greatest benefactors in the twentieth century.

Sources

Andrews, Philip W.S., and Brunner, Elisabeth. 1958. *The life of Lord Nuffield: a study of enterprise and benevolence.* Oxford: Basil Blackwell.

Jackson, Robert. 1964. *The Nuffield story.* London: Muller.

Overy, R. J. 1976. *William Morris, Viscount Nuffield.* London: Europa Publications.

NUREMBERG LAWS, NUREMBERG RALLIES, NUREMBERG TRIALS. The Laws refer to Hitler's anti-Semitic decrees of September 15, 1935, which made Jews second-class citizens; the laws defined Jews, denied them rights of citizenship, marriage, and sexual relations between "Jews" and "non-Jews," and excluded them from public office and most occupations. The Rallies comprised vast crowds at Nazi party congresses (1933–38) where oratory and dramatic propaganda were perfected technically to appeal to both participants and observers. The Trials were of twenty-four Nazi leaders, and there were twelve trials for major war crimes committed during and after World War II. Altogether 177 were tried; 25 were acquitted, 20 imprisoned for life, and 25 sentenced to death, and the remainder were sentenced to 10 to 20 years in prison.

Nuremberg (German: Nürnberg) is on the Pegnitz River, 92 miles northwest of Munich, Bavaria. It was founded in the mid-eleventh century, chartered in 1219, and flourished after the twelfth century as a commercial link with Italy;

it became the cultural center of the German Renaissance and was noted for early printing. The artist Albrecht Dürer (1471–1528) was born there; the city was also a center for science, and the Peace of Nuremberg, signed in 1532, gave tolerance to Lutherans. After the Thirty Years' War (1618–48), the city declined and in 1803 was eclipsed by Bavaria. In the 1930s it was the headquarters of the Nazi movement under Adolf Hitler. Anti-Semitic propaganda was produced in Nuremberg, and it became the focus for Hitler's industrial and political efforts. The city was damaged by Allied bombings during World War II, and 6,716 people died in January and February 1945; it was used as the site for judicial hearings of the Nazi war crimes. Recently, the old interior of the city was restored, and today the Hohenzollern Castle, medieval churches, and parts of the old city wall remain.

Sources

Canby, Courtlandt. 1984. *The encyclopedia of historic places.* London: Mansell Publishing Ltd.

McHenry, Robert, ed. 1992. *The new encyclopedia Britannica.* Chicago: Encyclopedia Britannica, Inc.

Shaw, Warren, and Taylor, James. 1989. *A dictionary of the Third Reich.* London: Grafton Books.

Smith, B. F. 1977. *Reaching a judgement at Nuremberg.* London: Andre Deutsch.

O

OCCAMISM. The doctrine that entities are not to be multiplied without necessity. It originated with the principles of the fourteenth-century nominalist schoolman, especially (in Latin) *entia non sunt multiplicanda*—entities are not to be multiplied—and *pluralites non est ponenda sine necessitate*—excess cannot exist without necessity.

William of Occam (c. 1290–1350), an English philosopher, was born at Ockham, Surrey. He joined the Franciscan order as a young man and was educated at Oxford. Subsequently, he allied himself with the Franciscans who opposed Pope John XXII on the question of monastic poverty. Excommunicated, the group fled to Pisa and later Munich where Occam wrote his political treatises against subordination of civil authority to the papacy as well as many of his philosophical and theological works. He may have died in Munich. Occam popularized the principle of economy widely known as ''Occam's razor.'' He also asserted that groups of people have no objective reality but are merely names that exist only in the mind. He was known as the first of the Protestants because he was opposed to subtleties and to the primary tenets of Scholastic philosophy. Developing the thought of Duns Scotus (c. 1265–1308), he taught that God does not will something because it is good; rather, he said, the thing is good because God wills it.

Sources

Cross, Frank L. 1974. *The Oxford dictionary of the Christian Church.* 2d ed. New York: Oxford University Press.

McHenry, Robert, ed. 1992. *The new encyclopedia Britannica.* Chicago: Encyclopedia Britannica, Inc.

Magnussen, Magnus; Goring, Rosemary; and Thorn, John O., eds. 1990. *Chambers biographical dictionary.* Edinburgh: Chambers Ltd.

Zusne, Leonard. 1987. *Eponyms in psychology: a dictionary and sourcebook.* Westport, Conn.: Greenwood Press.

OEDIPUS COMPLEX. In classical psychoanalysis, the unconscious pattern of feelings in family life that center on a son's strong love for his mother and his equally strong hostility toward his father whom the son regards as his rival for his mother's love.

In Greek legend, Oedipus, the banished son of Laius and Jocasta, king and queen of Thebes, unwittingly slayed his father who had left home to find an answer to the riddle of the Sphinx. Oedipus answers the Sphinx's riddle, and she dies; as a reward for ridding Thebes of the Sphinx, Oedipus was offered and accepted the throne and the hand of the widowed queen, Jocasta. When she learned of her incest, Jocasta hanged herself in remorse; Oedipus blinded himself on discovering what had happened. During his self-analysis, Freud chose the legend as a metaphor for the problem he was recalling (Gay, 1988); later he used it as a theoretical model in dream analysis—for understanding the emotional problems that psychoanalysts would find in their patients' memories of family life, and for the major pattern of feelings shared in social life. The complex of feelings is like that in the Theban plays, and Freud argued that it was universal among boys between three and six; the parallel complex of feelings attributed to girls is sometimes known as the Electra complex, originally suggested by Carl Jung but rejected by Freud. The term has been used widely, and has attracted both support and criticism (Macmillan, 1991).

See also FREUDIAN.

Sources

Gay, Peter. 1988. *Freud: a life for our time.* New York: Doubleday.
Hamilton, Edith. 1940. *Mythology: timeless tales of gods and heroes.* Boston: Little, Brown.
Jobes, Gertrude. 1962. *Dictionary of mythology, folklore and symbols.* New York: Scarecrow Press.
McHenry, Robert, ed. 1992. *The new encyclopedia Britannica.* Chicago: Encyclopedia Britannica, Inc.
Macmillan, Malcolm. 1991. *Freud evaluated: the completed arc.* Amsterdam: Elsevier.
Zusne, Leonard. 1987. *Eponyms in psychology: a dictionary and sourcebook.* Westport, Conn.: Greenwood Press.

OKUN'S LAW. A generalization developed in the 1960s that potential gross national product (defined as total output of the economy when all resources are fully employed) grows in the United States at an annual rate of 4 percent in real terms. Therefore, a 4 percent annual rate of growth in gross national product is needed to keep the unemployment rate stable. If real gross national product grows at a rate higher than 4 percent per year, the unemployment rate will decrease in the proportion of one percentage point for each percentage point increase in the annual growth rate of the real gross national product, with growth cutting the unemployment faster than this ratio, the higher the unemployment rate.

Arthur Okun (1928–80), an American economist, was born in Jersey City and educated at Columbia University (Ph.D., 1956). He began teaching at Yale University in 1960 and became professor of economics in 1963. He was a staff economist for President Kennedy's Council of Economic Advisers in Washington (1961–62) and under President Johnson (1964–69). He joined the Brookings Institution as a senior fellow in 1969 and remained there until 1980. Among his works are *The Political Economy of Prosperity, Equality and Efficiency: The Big Trade Off* (1975); thirty-one of his papers have been reprinted under the title, *The Economics of Policy Making* (1953).

Sources

Blaug, Mark. 1985. *Great economists since Keynes.* Brighton: Harvester Press.

Nemmers, E. E. 1978. *Dictionary of economics and business.* Totowa, N.J.: Rowman and Littlefield.

Pearce, David W., ed. 1986. *Macmillan dictionary of modern economics.* New York: Macmillan.

Pechman, J. A., ed. 1983. *The economics of policy making.* Cambridge, Mass.: MIT Press.

OLIVERIAN. An adherent of the Protector, during the English Civil War in the 1640s.

See also CROMWELLIAN.

OLLIEMANIA. The sympathetic and otherwise favorable public response to a central military figure in the Iran-Contra hearings in the United States during the summer of 1987.

Colonel Oliver Laurence North (b. 1943) was born at Fort Sam Houston into a military family and was taken to Ghent during World War II, where the family had long owned a wool-combing mill. After World War II, the Norths settled in Philmont, New York. Larry studied at the Ockawamick High School (1961) and trained at a teacher's college near Rochester. Two years later he entered Annapolis Naval Academy, where graduation was delayed until 1968 because of a serious automobile accident. He became a Marine second lieutenant and served in Vietnam where he was an admired platoon commander and decorated for exceptional bravery. He was posted to Okinawa for training troops but later spent three weeks back in Bethesda Hospital for emotional distress (1974). He worked at Marine headquarters in Washington in 1975, and in 1980 he was chosen to attend the Naval War College. After graduation he was appointed to the National Security Council, where he quickly became deputy director of the council's political-military affairs division and took over the council's seat in the Central American Restricted Interagency Group. This placed him at the center of daily policy-making, increasing his influence to the point where he became, in effect, a Contra commander in chief. From this post he was able to use money sent by Saudi Arabia to support the Contra interests. He was put on trial for having lied to Congress about the deal for America to sell arms to Iran and then diverted the money to the Contra rebels in Nicaragua. Earlier, the Congress had decided not to allow President Reagan to continue military support for the Contras. In March 1988, North was indicted on sixteen counts of conspiring to defraud the government and other charges. In January 1989, the special prosecutor, Lawrence E. Walsh, was obliged to dismiss four charges. The trial of North began in the early spring of 1989; his defense was that he did not believe he was acting illegally in telling Congress what he had said and that what he did was to follow what he understood were the legal orders of his superiors who had decided to cover their tracks. The cover was thought to be well known by all concerned, including President Reagan and Vice-president Bush, both of whom either denied any involvement or said they forgot whatever involvement was theirs. He was found guilty of obstructing the U.S. Congress, destroying classified documents, and accepting an illegal gratuity. In July 1990, a federal appeals court reversed the conviction for destroying documents and set aside the other two. When, in September 1991, National Security Adviser Robert C. McFarlane said his testimony had been colored by North's earlier account of his actions before Congress, frustrated prosecutor Walsh dropped all charges. Immediately North claimed he had been fully vindicated.

Sources

Bradlee, Ben. 1988. *Guts and glory: the rise and fall of Oliver North.* New York: D. I. Fine.

Graham, Judith, ed. 1992. *Current biography yearbook.* New York: H. W. Wilson.

Toobin, Jeffrey. 1991. *Opening arguments: young lawyer's first case, United States* v. *Oliver North.* New York: Viking Press.

ONASSIS PRIZE. The Alexander Onassis Foundation was established to promote welfare, religious, artistic, and educational activities, mainly in Greece, and to make annual awards based on the Swedish Nobel Prize.

Aristotle Socrates Onassis (1906–75) was born in Turkey, which he left in 1922 when the Turkish troops defeated the Greek forces at Smyrna. In Argentina he restored the family's tobacco business, and in 1925 he became a citizen of both Argentina and Greece. Early in the 1930s he began to acquire ships, and later he became the first Greek to own tankers. His financial ambitions were bolstered in 1946 by his marriage to the daughter of Stavros Livanos, the powerful Greek shipowner. Onassis, Livanos, and Onassis's brother-in-law together helped form the world's most influential shipping cartel. In 1961 Onassis divorced his wife, having had a long liaison with the opera singer Maria Callas (1923–77). When he remarried, instead of marrying Callas he chose the widow of John F. Kennedy, Jacqueline (née Bouvier) (1929–94). Onassis was always a controversial figure in international finance and once was principal owner of the Monte Carlo casino. In 1957 he founded Olympic Airways of Greece. In 1957, two years after the death in an air crash of his playboy son, twenty-four year-old Alexander, Onassis established the Alexander S. Onassis Public Benefit Foundation in memory of the young man. It was established in Vaduz, Lichtenstein, and aimed to ensure that the Onassis empire would live through two holding companies, Alpha and Beta.

Sources

Evans, Peter. 1986. *Ari: the life and times of Aristotle Socrates Onassis.* London: Jonathan Cape.

McHenry, Robert, ed. 1992. *The new encyclopedia Britannica.* Chicago: Encyclopedia Britannica, Inc.

Moritz, Charles, ed. 1963. *Current biography yearbook.* New York: H. W. Wilson.

ORBILIUS, THE ORBILIUS STICK. A schoolmaster who has a sadistic interest in capital punishment by flogging; a cane or birch rod used to punish pupils in class.

Orbilius Pupillus, a Roman schoolmaster from 63 B.C. who died at nearly 100 years of age, is described by Horace in his poem, *Orbilium.* Horace was not sent to the local school near his father's farm at Venusia, but to a school kept by L. Orbilius Pupillus of Beneventum. From this teacher Horace learned Homer's *Iliad* and of the early Roman poet, Livius Andronicus, translator of the *Odyssey.* A vigorous, stern character, Orbilius had once been a calvary officer, and although he gave up the barracks for the schoolroom, he retained his military attitude to discipline. His statue appears at Beneveto, but he is better known from Horace's epithet "plagosus," the flogger.

Source

Dilke, Oswald A.W., ed. 1982. Horace: *Epistles book I.* Letchworth, Hertfordshire: Bradda Books.

ORIGENIST. One who uses allegorical methods of interpreting scriptures or theology.

Origen (c. 185–251) was born a Christian in Alexandria. As a young man, Origen instructed converts in the catechism and studied philosophy with Ammonius Saccas and other intellectuals of Alexandria. He broadened his knowledge of the church through travels to Rome, Athens, Asia Minor, and Arabia. Soon, by combining Christian belief with the Platonic principles of eternal reality, he became widely known as the leading Christian teacher of the age. He was a prolific writer, producing comments on nearly all books in the Bible, for example, "Commentary on John," and on the Psalms. Among his works were *On First Principles* and *Against Celsus,* a reply to an attack on Christianity. He died after being jailed and tortured in the Decian persecution.

Sources

Cross, Frank L. 1974. *The Oxford dictionary of the Christian Church.* 2d ed. New York: Oxford University Press.

Douglas, James D., ed. 1974. *The new international dictionary of the Christian Church.* Exeter: Paternoster Press.

Ferguson, Everett, ed. 1990. *The encyclopedia of early Christianity.* New York: Garland Publishing.

McHenry, Robert, ed. 1992. *The new encyclopedia Britannica.* Chicago: Encyclopedia Britannica, Inc.

Magnussen, Magnus; Goring, Rosemary; and Thorn, John O., eds. 1990. *Chambers biographical dictionary.* Edinburgh: Chambers Ltd.

ORWELLIAN. Relating to the description in *1984* (1949) of three totalitarian states, especially Oceania, with its endless night of war, paranoid domination by Big Brother, the thought police and the language of Newspeak, and the ideology of Ingsoc; also, the belief in authority illustrated in the fable of Soviet communism in *Animal Farm* (1945).

George Orwell (1903–50) is the pseudonym of Eric Arthur Blair, British novelist and essayist. He was born in Bengal, brought to England, and sent to Eton. He served in the Indian Imperial Police in Burma (1922–27), but his loathing of imperialism and a desire to write led him to resign. These experiences appear in his first novel, *Burmese Days* (1934). *Down and Out in Paris and London* (1933) tells of his years of poverty that followed. Four novels published in the next five years were all marked by strong socialist convictions. He was a democratic socialist who hated totalitarianism; he was disillusioned with the aims and methods of communists, and in the Spanish Civil War he fought for the loyalists. He recorded the hardships of war in *Homage to Catalonia* (1938). In 1945 he published *Animal Farm,* a satire on Stalinism, and in 1949 he published *1984,* a dreadful view of a totalitarian future ruled by Big Brother.

Sources

Crick, Bernard. 1981. *George Orwell: a life.* London: Secker and Warburg.

Crick, Bernard, and Coppard, Audrey. 1984. *Orwell remembered.* London: British Broadcasting Corp.

Devine, Elizabeth; Held, Michael; Vinson, James; and Walsh, George, eds. 1983. *Thinkers of the twentieth century: a biographical, bibliographical and critical dictionary.* London: Macmillan.

Fleischmann, Wolfgang B. 1971. *Encyclopedia of world literature in the 20th century.* New York: Frederick Ungar.

McHenry, Robert, ed. 1992. *The new encyclopedia Britannica.* Chicago: Encyclopedia Britannica, Inc.

Sheldon, Michael. 1991. *Orwell: the authorized biography.* London: Heinemann.

OSLERIZE. To end the life of all men over 40 years for utilitarian reasons.

Sir William Osler (1849–1919) was a Canadian physician educated at McGill University. In his day he was a renowned physician, medical historian, and brilliant teacher. He was appointed professor of medicine at McGill (1875–84), the University of Pennsylvania (1884–89), Johns Hopkins (1889–1904), and Oxford University from 1905. He was knighted in 1911. He specialized in the study of the blood, wrote a frequently revised and reprinted textbook on medicine and a concise history of medicine, and his life attracted two biographies. In February 1905 at Johns Hopkins University, he made an address stating that men ought to be stopped from working at age 60. He was widely misquoted as saying that men over the age of 40 should be put to death as useless, or "oslerized." After he himself turned 60, he made some of his most valuable contributions to science.

Sources

Cushing, Harvey W. 1940. *The life of Sir William Osler.* Originally 1925, 2 vols. London: Oxford University Press.

Hendrickson, Robert. 1988. *The dictionary of eponyms: names that became words.* New York: Dorset.

Kingsbury, Mary. 1987. Congenial associates: the biographical essays of William Osler. *Biography* 10:225–240.

OSMANLI, OTTOMAN. Pertaining to the founder of the Turkish Empire in Asia, the empire itself, and its branches and language. A Turk.

Osmanli, Othman, Osman I (1258–1324) was founder of the Ottoman Empire. He became chief of his tribe in 1288 and assumed the title of emir in 1299. His greatest success in the war with the Byzantines was the conquest of Burra. The Ottoman Turks originally lived in central Asia, but under Osman I they founded a realm in Asia Minor which was soon extended to Europe. With the capture of Constantinople in 1453, they succeeded to the Byzantine Empire and, at its height, their rule in the sixteenth century extended over most of southeastern Europe and much of western Asia and northern Africa. The Ottoman Turks are Sunnite Mohammedans and regarded the sultans as representative of the former caliphs.

Sources

Karpat, Kemal H. 1974. *The Ottoman state and its place in world history.* Leiden: E. J. Brill.

Itzkowitz, Norman, ed. 1980. *Ottoman empire and Islamic tradition.* Chicago: University of Chicago Press.

McHenry, Robert, ed. 1992. *The new encyclopedia Britannica.* Chicago: Encyclopedia Britannica, Inc.

Magnussen, Magnus; Goring, Rosemary; and Thorn, John O., eds. 1990. *Chambers biographical dictionary.* Edinburgh: Chambers Ltd.

Shaw, Stanford J., and Shaw, Ezel K. 1976–1977. *History of the Ottoman empire and modern Turkey.* 2 vols. Cambridge: Cambridge University Press.

OTHELLO ERROR, OTHELLO SYNDROME. The Othello error occurs when an interviewer is trying to discover whether or not an interviewee is lying. If the interviewer assumes that an emotional outburst from the interviewee always indicates lying, then the interviewer will commit the Othello error whenever the interviewee is actually truthful, and becomes emotional in response to being suspected of lying. The Othello syndrome arises in a situation where a husband attacks, beats, or murders his wife out of passionate and possessive jealousy that is unfounded. Some women see the aggression favorably at first, believing it indicates they are passionately desired. Killing seems to occur in the belief that, "if I can't have you, no one else will"; the husband continuously checks on his wife's movements or restricts her movements by preventing her from leaving their house for the day.

Othello, the main character in Shakespeare's play *Othello* (1604), is a Moor who commands the forces of Venice and elopes with Desdemona. Othello wins a decisive victory over the Turks in Cyprus, and on his return Iago, the Moor's envious lieutenant, leads Othello to believe that his bride might have deceived him in an affair with Cassio. Iago encourages Othello's growing jealousy; maddened by the thought of her presumed infidelity, Othello murders Desdemona, and, when he finds he has been misled by Iago, he commits suicide. The plot of Shakespeare's play originated with Cinthio's *Hecatommithi* (1565), and it has also been the subject of Verdi's operatic tragedy.

Sources

Adamson, Jane. 1980. *Othello as tragedy: some problems of judgement and feeling.* Cambridge: Cambridge University Press.

Ekman, Paul. 1985. *Telling lies: clues to deceit in the market place, politics and marriage.* New York: W. W. Norton.

Elliot, Martin. 1988. *Shakespeare's invention of Othello.* London: Macmillan.

Rosenberg, Marvin. 1971. *The masks of Othello.* Berkeley: University of California Press.

OUT-HEROD HEROD. To outdo other rulers in tyranny, violence, evil, and wickedness.

Herod the Great (c. 73–4 B.C.) ruled Judea. According to the Bible, upon being told that the king of the Jews would be born in Bethlehem, Herod consulted with his religious advisers who confirmed the imminent birth. Herod then sent three wise men to Bethlehem to note when the birth occurred and to report it to him. They found the child, rejoiced, and departed to their own country, having been warned by God not to return to Herod. Joseph was instructed to take the child and mother to Egypt. Furious when he realized that he had been mocked by the wise men, King Herod promptly had all children under two years in Bethlehem slaughtered (Matthew 2:3–16). The phrase "out-Herod Herod" comes from *Hamlet,* Act III, Scene 2, when Hamlet is advising the players on how to perform: "I would have such a fellow whipped for o'verdoing Termagant: it out-Herods Herod: pray you, avoid it."

Sources

McDonald, William J., ed. 1967. *New Catholic encyclopedia.* New York: McGraw-Hill.

McHenry, Robert, ed. 1992. *The new encyclopedia Britannica.* Chicago: Encyclopedia Britannica, Inc.

O'Brien, Conor C. 1978. *Herod: reflections on political violence.* London: Hutchinson.

OWENITE, OWEN'S SILENT MONITOR. A follower of socialistic cooperation advocated by the early nineteenth-century British industrialist. A wooden indicator with four painted sides—black, blue, yellow, and white—each indicating a level of merit among factory workers from bad to good.

Robert Owen (1771–1858) was born at Newtown, Montgomeryshire, Wales. At 18 he founded and managed a cotton mill in Manchester, and after the firm became profitable he sold it and became its salaried manager. By 1800 Owen had become manager and part owner of the cotton mills at New Lanark in Scotland. He employed young people, introduced extensive reforms to improve conditions for his operators, and sought to improve all of village life, sanitation, education, and streets. He was a careful observer of work in the factory. To manage problems of discipline, he devised a monitor with four sides, each denoting a level of merit at work the previous day. Every operative had a monitor beside them, and it could readily be seen how satisfactorily they had been working. He turned to the enormous task of overcoming the misery of industrialization in Britain through moral education of capitalists. He failed in this attempt and so went to America and by 1825 had founded a socialistic community—a "village of cooperation"—at New Harmony, Indiana. It too, failed. He later devoted himself to propagating socialism, and in 1834 he led the trade union movement in Britain to the collective control of the means of production. Again he failed; nevertheless, his efforts did help establish concern about the human factor in work organization.

See also RAPPIST.

Sources

Cole, G.D.H. 1966. *The life of Robert Owen.* 3d ed. Hamden, Conn.: Archon Books.

Fogarty, Robert S. 1980. *Dictionary of American communal and utopian history.* Westport, Conn.: Greenwood Press.

Miller, David, ed. 1987. *The Blackwell encyclopedia of political thought.* Oxford: Basil Blackwell.

Owen, Robert. 1857. *The life of Robert Owen.* London: Effingham Wilson. Reprinted, 1967, Augustus M. Kelley.

Sills, David L., ed. 1968. *International encyclopedia of the social sciences.* New York: Macmillan and Free Press.

Wren, Daniel A. 1987. *The evolution of management thought.* 3d ed. New York: John Wiley.

P

PACKWOOD CASE. A recent case against a U.S. Republican senator from Oregon charged with sexually harassing many women between 1970 and 1992. In 1992 he denied the charge, alleging it was a political lie given to the press to prevent his reelection in November 1992. Therefore, the press withheld the story; after he won the election narrowly, he admitted to the charge but refused to step down. A poll conducted after the election showed that only 34 percent of voters would have supported him had they known of the charges. Two hundred and fifty Oregonians petitioned to have him sacked, a U.S. Senate committee was convened in May 1993 to see whether or not it had the authority to deny Packwood his seat.

Robert Packwood (b. 1932) was born in Portland, Oregon, graduated from Willamette University in Salem, Oregon, studied law at New York University, and was admitted to the bar in 1957. He practiced law in Portland and entered the state legislature (1963–68); he has been a Republican senator from 1969 to the present. While a senator, he was chairman of the Republican senatorial committee, the Republican Conference, the Committe of Commerce, Science, and Transportation, and the Committee on Finance.

Sources

Clark, Pilita. 1993. Political campaign lies under fire. *The Age (Melbourne)*, May 12:8.

The international who's who, 1992–93. London: Europa Publications.

Jacob, Kathryn A., and Ragsdale, Bruce A. 1989. *Biographical directory of the United States Congress: 1774–1989.* Bicentennial ed. Washington, D.C.: U.S. Government Printing Office.

Moritz, Charles, ed. 1981. *Current biography yearbook.* New York: H. W. Wilson.

Smolowe, Jill. 1993. No thanks for the memories: senator's diary prompts questions of crime, proprietry and privacy. *Time* (Australia) 8 November:30–31.

Who's who in America, 1992–93. New Providence, N.J.: Marquis.

PAISLEYISM, PAISLEYITE. A movement led by the Ulster clergymen in opposition to cooperation with the Republic of Ireland. A supporter of the Irish clergyman and his advocacy of Protestant interests in Northern Ireland, and especially the independence of Northern Ireland from the Republic of Ireland.

Ian Richard Kyle Paisley (b. 1926) was born in Armagh, North Ireland, the younger son of the Reverend J. Kyle Paisley, the "hell fire and brimstone" preacher who broke away from his denomination and started his own church. Ian Paisley started his preaching at age 16, obtained a diploma from the Theological Hall of the Reformed Presbyterian Church in Belfast, and was ordained into the ministry of his father (1946) in a ceremony viewed as untraditional by some Presbyterians. Ian Paisley founded the dissident Free Presbyterian Church of Ulster (1951) and took the title of moderator. In 1969 he established the Martyrs Memorial Free Presbyterian Official Church named in honor of the Protestant reformers John Calvin and John Knox. The official Presbyterian Church has repeatedly sought to dissociate itself from Paisley's anti-Catholic rhetoric, but his message has found a receptive audience. Although he often denied that he is bigoted toward individual Catholics, he clearly considers the Roman Catholic Church to be his enemy. Campaigning on a platform to end the moderate reforms benefiting Catholics, Paisley was elected member of Parliament for North Antrum beginning in 1970. He is the only leader of the working-class Democratic Unionist party of Northern Ireland, and has been a representative to the European Parliament since 1979. In 1983 he was reelected to the British Parliament, and again to the European Parliament in 1984. Among his publications are *History of the 1859 Revival* (1959), *United Ireland—Never!* (1972), *No Pope Here* (1982), and *Union with Rome* (1989).

Sources

Clark, Sylvia, 1988. *Paisley: a history.* Edinburgh: Mainstream.

Delury, G., ed. 1987. *World encyclopedia of political systems and parties.* Oxford: Facts on File Publications.

The international who's who, 1992–93. London: Europa Publications.

Moritz, Charles, ed. 1986. *Current biography yearbook.* New York: H. W. Wilson.

O Maolain, Ciaran. 1987. *The radical right: a world directory.* London: Keesings Reference Publications, and Longman.

Who's who, 1993. London: Adam and Charles Black.

PALMER RAIDS. Raids by the agents of the U.S. attorney-general, 1917–20, which led to the arrest or deportation of thousands of U.S. citizens and aliens without due process of law and in violation of their basic liberties. The arrests were driven by the fear that anarchists, communists, radicals, "reds," and subversives would take over U.S. government agencies. In addition, after the United States entered World War I, the attorney-general was made alien property custodian, and between October 1917 and March 1919 sequestered $600 million of property from enemy aliens. He was authorized to sell it to American citizens, and the management of these sequestrations led him into controversy.

Alexander Mitchell Palmer (1872–1936) was born near White Haven, Pennsylvania, was educated at public schools and the Moravian Parochial College in Bethlehem, and graduated from Swarthmore College. He was official stenographer for the forty-third judicial district in Pennsylvania (1892), graduated in law, and was admitted to the bar in 1893. A Democrat, he was elected to Congress (1909–15), but failed as a candidate for the Senate (1914). He became U.S. attorney-general (1919–21), and later he practiced law in Washington, D.C. He seemed to have a great fear of radicalism, and he sought to promote legislation against sedition in peacetime, offering nearly seventy bills in Congress (1919–20), but few were passed.

Sources

Coben, Stanley. 1972. *A. Mitchell Palmer: politician.* New York: Da Capo Press.

Murray, Robert K. 1955. *Red Scare: a study in national hysteria, 1919–20.* 1964 ed. New York: McGraw-Hill.

Schulyer, Robert L., and James, Edward T., eds. 1944. *Dictionary of American biography.* Supplement 2. New York: Charles Scribner's Sons.

PANDORA'S BOX. Source of great and unexpected troubles.

According to legend, Pandora was the first woman whom Zeus created. She was intended as a punishment for humankind after Prometheus had stolen fire from heaven to help the human race. She came with a box in which all evils and diseases were stored. When Prometheus's brother, Epimetheus, married Pandora and opened the box, all those troubles escaped, leaving only hope at the bottom to alleviate some of the world's problems. Pandora was probably a pre-Greek goddess, and her name meant "giving all."

Sources

Evans, Ivor H. 1989. *Brewer's dictionary of phrase and fable.* 14th ed. London: Cassell.

Jobes, Gertrude, 1962. *Dictionary of mythology, folklore and symbols.* New York: Scarecrow Press.

Leach, Maria. 1975. *Funk and Wagnall's standard dictionary of folklore, mythology and legend.* London: New English Library.

PAPARAZZO. An intrusive journalist.

Paparazzo (fl. 1959) appears in Federico Fellini's film *La Dolce Vita* (1959). The central character, played by Marcello Mastroianni, is an opportunistic gossip columnist, and the plot is a dreamlike sequence of disconnected masques showing him in pursuit of venal pleasures, all of which elude him. He is accompanied by Paparazzo, who intrudes into the personal lives of others in a sleazy and alarming way. His name is given to any photographer who snaps members of the fast set to get some unflattering pictures of them off guard.

Sources

Fava, Claudio G., and Vigano, Aldo. 1984. *The films of Federico Fellini.* Secaucus, N.J.: Citadel Press.

PARETIAN, PARETIAN OPTIMALITY, PARETO'S LAW. Relating to ideas of the early twentieth-century Italian economist, for example, Pareto's law,

Paretian optimality; Pareto conditions, Pareto improvement; Pareto noncomparability. Paretian optimality is a condition in which no further improvement of one individual's total utility can be achieved without taking utility away from someone else. It is a concept in normative economics and microeconomic theory that considers that point of equilibrium or circumstances wherein economic efficiency is highest. Although the optimum upholds efficiency, it is not necessarily the case that incomes are distributed as desired, and social welfare levels are satisfactory. With regard to Pareto's law, in all countries, regardless of taxation or political circumstances, a frequency distribution of incomes at different times and places will show a high degree of stability; the distribution of income sizes would be highly skewed toward low incomes. So to raise the income of the poor, overall production must rise.

Vilfredo Pareto (1848–1923) was born in Paris (his father having been exiled from Italy) and educated in France and Italy. He specialized in mathematics and classical literature. After graduation from the Polytechnic Institute in Turin, he spent over twenty years as an engineer and director of two Italian railway companies. In 1890 he began to study economics, which he taught at Lausanne for seven years, resigning in 1900 when he inherited a fortune. He lived in Switzerland the rest of his life studying and writing. In 1923 he was appointed to the Italian Senate by Mussolini's government. Pareto was noted for his early use of mathematics in political and social analysis; for the view that all societies would establish elites and masses; and for the influence of his ideas on the rise of Italian fascism. His major works are *Cours D'Economie Politique* (1896–97), *Manual of Political Economy* (1911), and a massive work in four volumes, *The Mind and Society: A Treatise on General Sociology* (1916). Here he argued that elites would perpetuate themselves by forbidding the masses entry to their membership: then the mass leaders would organize a mass revolt, overthrow the elite, and replace it with a new elite. His critique of sociologist thought, including Marxism, appeared in three volumes, *Les Sytemes Socialistes*. His books were not translated into English until 1963 (*Mind and Society*), and 1971 (*The Manual*).

Sources

Blaug, Mark. 1986. *Great economists before Keynes*. Brighton, England: Harvester Press.

Devine, Elizabeth; Held, Michael; Vinson, James; and Walsh, George, eds. 1983. *Thinkers of the twentieth century: a biographical, bibliographical and critical dictionary*. London: Macmillan.

Lopreato, Joseph. 1972. Notes on the work of Vilfredo Pareto. *Social Science Quarterly* 54:451–468.

Lopreato, Sally C. 1973. Toward a formal restatement to Vilfredo Pareto's theory of the circulation of elites. *Social Science Quarterly* 54:491–507.

Sills, David L., ed. 1968. *International encyclopedia of the social sciences*. New York: Macmillan and Free Press.

PARKINSON'S LAW (OR THE RISING PYRAMID). Any regular inefficiency in officialdom, but originally Parkinson's first law: work expands so as to fill the time available for its completion, as can be seen from the observation that the busiest person has time to spare.

Parkinson's laws: (1) Work expands to fill the time available for its completion; Corollary 1: an official wants to multiply subordinates, not rivals, and Corollary 2: officials make work for each other. (2) Expenditure rises to meet income.

Parkinson's laws of committee size: (1) A membership of three is too small because a quorum is impossible to collect. (2) The ideal size of a committee usually appears to be five. With that number, two members can be absent or sick at any one time. Five members are easy to collect and, when collected, can act with competence, secrecy, and speed. (3) The point of complete ineffectiveness in a committee occurs when the total membership exceeds twenty.

Parkinson's law of triviality: In a discussion of high finance, time spent on any item of the agenda will be in inverse proportion to the sum of money involved.

Cyril Northcote Parkinson (1909–93) attended Emmanual College, Cambridge and became a fellow (1935–38). He taught history at Blundell's school in Devon (1938–39) and at the Royal Naval College, Dartmouth (1939–40). During World War II he was a major in the army (1940–46) and afterward taught at the University of Liverpool until he was made Raffles Professor of History, University of Malaya (1950–58). After the publication of his book on officialdom, he lectured at Harvard, the universities of Illinois and California, and was honored with an LL.D. (University of Maryland) and a D.Litt. (Troy State University). He published many works on historical, political, and economic subjects but achieved wider renown with his satire on bureaucracy and his parody on malpractices in administration, with his law that was first stated in *The Economist* (1955). He wrote sixty books, and retired to the Channel Islands to paint and write naval histories.

Sources

Evory, Ann, ed. 1982. *Contemporary authors.* New Revision Series. Vol. 5. Detroit: Gale Research.

The international who's who, 1992–93. London: Europa Publications.

Magnussen, Magnus; Goring, Rosemary; and Thorn, John O., eds. 1990. *Chambers biographical dictionary.* Edinburgh: Chambers Ltd.

Parkinson, C. Northcote. 1957. *Parkinson's law or the pursuit of progress.* Boston: Houghton-Mifflin.

PARNELLISM, PARNELLITES, ANTI-PARNELLITES. The principles and policy of Home Rule for Ireland that included a Parliament in Ireland which would be responsible for Ireland's internal affairs rather than direct rule from London. Those who supported the Home Rule policy before 1880–90. Those who opposed the leadership of Parnell and, later, those who opposed Home Rule for Ireland.

Charles Stewart Parnell (1846–91), a Protestant landowner in Ireland, united the many political factions of predominantly Catholic Ireland and became a force in British politics. In Parliament he led sixty-eight members of the Home Rule party with iron discipline. In 1881 the Land League that he had a founded was suppressed; Parnell was jailed for encouraging agrarian violence, but was soon released to prevent even greater violence. He brought down the Gladstone government in 1885 on the issue of Home Rule. The Conservatives returned to power in 1886, and the Home Rule Bill failed. Several years later Parnell's influence eroded when he was named correspondent in the celebrated O'Shea divorce case (1890). The Home Rule party split; forty-five Irish Nationalists demanded his resignation, whereas twenty-six supported him. Justin McCarthy (1830–1912) led Irish Nationalist members of Parliament who refused to support Parnell, and they were called anti-Parnellites; later, this term was occasionally used to refer to any person opposing Home Rule for Ireland. In 1892 seventy-one anti-Parnellites led by McCarthy were elected, while only nine Parnellites gained office.

Sources

Abels, Jules. 1966. *The Parnell tragedy.* London: Bodley Head.

Bew, Paul. 1980. *C. S. Parnell.* Dublin: Gill and Macmillan.

Bew, Paul. 1987. *Conflict and conciliation in Ireland, 1890–1910: Parnellites and radical agrarians.* New York: Oxford University Press.

Lyons, Francis S.L. 1960. *The fall of Parnell, 1890–91.* Toronto: University of Toronto Press.

Lyons, Francis S.L. 1977. *Charles Stewart Parnell.* London: Collins.

Magnussen, Magnus; Goring, Rosemary; and Thorn, John O., eds. 1990. *Chambers biographical dictionary.* Edinburgh: Chambers Ltd.

O'Day, Alan. 1986. *Parnell and the first Home Rule episode, 1884–87.* Dublin: Gill and Macmillan.

O'Day, Alan, ed. 1991. *Parnell in perspective.* London: Routledge.

Stephen, Leslie, and Lee, Sydney, eds. 1917. *The dictionary of national biography.* London: Oxford University Press.

PARSONIAN THEORY. A form of sociological theory that is concerned with the limitations and universals of social life. The theory states systematically the dynamic relation between society's most important variables; establishes a social paradigm for sociological theories in the middle range; and develops a language for social theories that is sufficiently abstract to encompass other theoretical positions. The theory was popular and influential in the 1950s until its critics showed that the theory was merely a classification system rather than a propositional theory, and that it described stability and dealt inadequately with change. Nevertheless, it led to much social research.

Talcott Parsons (1902–79), son of a congregational minister, was born in Colorado Springs, educated at an experimental school at Columbia University, and at first planned a medical career while studying at Amherst. However, in 1924–25 he studied at the London School of Economics with B. Malinowski (1889–1942), and later with Alfred Weber (1868–1958), brother of Max Weber

(1864–1920), at Heidelberg, where Max Weber had taught. Parsons translated into English two of Max Weber's more important works. After returning to America, Parsons taught at Amherst, and in 1927 he went to Harvard to teach economics; in 1931 he changed to sociology and continued in this area until retirement in 1973. He became one of the United States' leading social theorists, chaired Harvard's Department of Social Relations for ten years, and was active in professional associations related to social sciences. His reputation grew in 1937 with the publication of *The Structure of Social Action,* which presented his philosophical viewpoint; in 1951 his *The Social System* and *Toward a General Theory of Action* presented the shape of his theorizing. In 1953 his *Working Papers in the Theory of Action* and in 1956 *Economy and Society* gave more definition to his position. In 1979 the University at Heidelberg honored him, and later that year he died in Munich. His ideas were influenced largely by Freud (1856–1939), Durkheim (1858–1917) and Max Weber.

Sources

Cubbon, H. Alan. 1992. Talcott Parsons. In Peter Beilharz, ed. *Social theory: a guide to central thinkers.* Sydney: Allen and Unwin.

Devine, Elizabeth; Held, Michael; Vinson, James; and Walsh, George, eds. 1983. *Thinkers of the twentieth century: a biographical, bibliographical and critical dictionary.* London: Macmillan.

Lackey, Pat N. 1987. *Invitation to Talcott Parsons' theory.* Houston: Cap and Gown Press.

Loubser, Jan C., et al. 1976. *Explorations in general theory in social science: essays in honor of Talcott Parsons.* New York: Free Press.

Parsons, Talcott. 1954. A short account of my intellectual development. *Alpha Kappa Delta* 29:3–12.

Sills, David L., ed. 1968. *International encyclopedia of the social sciences.* New York: Macmillan and Free Press.

PASQUINADES. Political lampoons.

Pasquino (fl. late 1400s) was an Italian tailor, cobbler, or barber in Rome who was remembered for a caustic wit. Shortly after he died, a mutilated statue was dug up opposite his business; on the statue were posted anonymous lampoons. Pasquino's name was given to them. A statue of Mars, known by the populace as "Marfario," stood at the far end of the city; when witty and rude remarks were posted on Pasquino, like-minded responses were posted on Marfario. Serious political issues were expressed, and these were parried between the two statues; in time, living political figures took the place of the statues, and were defended and attacked in a similar way. In 1736, Henry Fielding published a dramatic satire entitled *Pasquin.*

Source

Smith, Benjamin. 1903. *The Century cyclopedia of names.* London: The Times.

PAULIAN. A follower of the third-century Monarchian Unitarian of Antioch.

Paul of Samosata (fl. third century), the Socinus of the third century, was born at Samosata on the Euphrates, capital of a district of Syria, and became bishop or patriarch of Antioch (260), the most important see of the East. Antioch then belonged to the Palmyrene kingdom, and Paul was the vice-regent of Queen Zenobia from whom he received support in maintaining his heresy. This was monoarchianism, that is, the doctrine that Father, Son, and Holy Ghost are the one God, and that the Father has from all eternity produced the Logos, his Son, who is an attribute rather than a person. Antioch was recaptured by Aurelian in 272 and Paul was deposed, but his doctrines survived and he had followers, Paulinists, until the fourth century.

Sources

Cross, Frank L. 1974. *The Oxford dictionary of the Christian Church.* 2d ed. New York: Oxford University Press.

McHenry, Robert, ed. 1992. *The new encyclopedia Britannica.* Chicago: Encyclopedia Britannica, Inc.

PAULICIAN, PAULIANIST. A dualistic sect of obscure origin in Asia Minor (c. 750–800) that reacted against the hierarchical organization of the church. They were first noted at the Synod of Dwin (719). Their first leader was Constantine who founded a Paulician community at Kibossa in Armenia during the reign of Emperor Constantine. Their name was taken either from Paul of Samosata of the Paulians or Saul of Tarsus of the Paulines whose doctrines were similar to those of the Paulicians.

   See also PAULIAN; PAULINE.

Sources

Cross, Frank L. 1974. *The Oxford dictionary of the Christian Church.* 2d ed. New York: Oxford University Press.

McDonald, William, ed. 1967. *New Catholic encyclopedia.* New York: McGraw-Hill.

McHenry, Robert, ed. 1992. *The new encyclopedia Britannica.* Chicago: Encyclopedia Britannica, Inc.

PAULINE, PAULINE CONVERSION. Relating to the first-century apostle or his teaching and theology, a member of any religious order following the Apostle, or a pupil of Saint Paul's School (London) named after the apostle; a sudden reversal of belief often used to explain an abrupt change in a politician who one day proposes a policy and the next its opposite.

   Saul (c. 5 to 10–66), later Paul, was born at Tarsus; he was an embittered persecutor of the early Christians, until one day on the road to Damascus he had a vision and was converted to Christianity. Thereafter his journeys were subject to the perils of thieves, the sea, rivers, and false brethren. Shortly after converting one of Nero's concubines, he was beheaded, and, legend continues, milk, not blood, flowed from his wound. He was proclaimed a martyr, elevated to sainthood, and is commemorated on June 30. His symbols are the sword, the instrument of his death, and the open book, an indicator of his new law that he spread as the apostle of the Gentiles. His name was changed to Paul in honor of one of his converts, Sergius Paulus. He is author of the Epistles in the New Testament.

Sources

Cross, Frank L. 1974. *The Oxford dictionary of the Christian Church.* 2d ed. New York: Oxford University Press.

Eliade, Mircea, ed. 1987. *Encyclopedia of religion.* New York: Macmillan.

Ferguson, Everett, ed. 1990. *The encyclopedia of early Christianity.* New York: Garland Publishing.

McDonald, William J., ed. 1967. *New Catholic encyclopedia.* New York: McGraw-Hill.

McHenry, Robert, ed. 1992. *The new encyclopedia Britannica.* Chicago: Encyclopedia Britannica, Inc.

PAVLOVIAN. Relating to the work of the Russian physiologist on conditioned and unconditioned stimuli, reflexes, reactions, and responses; among social scientists it means automatic, unthinking and is often used as a pejorative term.

Ivan Petrovich Pavlov (1849–1936) was born near Ryazan, the son of a village priest. He studied medicine at Saint Petersburg and conducted research at Breslau and Leipzig. He became a professor at Saint Petersburg in 1891 and in 1904 was the first Russian to win the Nobel Prize for Physiology and Medicine. As director of the Institute of Experimental Medicine in 1913, he studied the physiology of circulation and digestion, but he is most renowned for his study of the "conditioned" or acquired reflexes associated with a part of the brain's cortex and basic to learning theories in psychology. He thought of the brain's function as being the coupling of neurones to produce reflexes.

Sources

Babkin, Boris P. 1951. *Pavlov: a biography.* London: Gollancz.

Gillespie, Charles C., ed. 1973 *Dictionary of scientific biography.* New York: Charles Scribner's Sons.

Gray, Jeffrey A. 1979. *Pavlov.* London: Fontana.

McHenry, Robert, ed. 1992. *The new encyclopedia Britannica.* Chicago: Encyclopedia Britannica, Inc.

Schultz, Heinrich E.; Urban, Paul K.; and Lebed, Andrew I. 1972. *Who was who in the U.S.S.R.* Metuchen, N.J.: Scarecrow Press.

Zusne, Leonard. 1984. *Biographical dictionary of psychology.* Westport, Conn.: Greenwood Press.

PAZZI CONSPIRACY. Hostilities between the de' Medici family of Florence and the papacy reached their peak in the plot of 1478 to kill the grandsons of the late Cosimo de' Medici (1389–1464) who had established the family's rule in Florence. The Pazzi family, with papal support, planned the details of the assassination.

The Pazzi family, old Florentine patricians, saw the Medicis' power increase under Cosimo de' Medici (1389–1464) and his son, Pero (d. 1469), and become well established in the hands of Pero's sons Guiliano (1454–78) and Lorenzo (1449–92). At the same time the Pazzi family fortunes were dwindling. The two families were commercial rivals in Florence, and, although they intermarried, their rivalry did not abate. In the plot, whose leading sponsor was Girolomo Riario (d. 1488), Francesco de Pazzi agreed to kill Guiliano de' Medici; old Jacopo de Pazzi, the laird of the Pazzi family, would prepare the public outcry that would follow the killings and justify them to the Florentines. Because Lorenzo's killer in the Pazzi family backed out at the last moment, two priests agreed to take his place. Renato de Pazzi opposed the conspiracy. Guiliano was murdered in the cathedral as planned, but his brother Lorenzo escaped. Immediately, Lorenzo sought revenge. He hanged old Jacopo, Renato, and Francesco from the windows of public places; beside them he hanged the archbishop of Pisa and altogether killed over 100 suspects. The pope immediately excommunicated Lorenzo, in a fury put the city under interdict, and declared war on the de' Medici. The crisis was solved with Lorenzo's apology to the pope. Riario was not murdered until ten years later (1488).

See also MEDICEAN.

Sources

Acton, Harold M.M. 1979. *The Pazzi conspiracy: the plot against the Medici.* London: Thames and Hudson.

Howatt, Gerald, M.D. 1973. *Dictionary of world history.* London: Thomas Nelson.

McHenry, Robert, ed. 1992. *The new encyclopedia Britannica.* Chicago: Encyclopedia Britannica, Inc.

PEARSON REPORT. Reports of British Courts of Inquiry on the Electricity Industry (1964); a dispute between British Overseas Airways Corporation and the British Airline Pilots Association (1968); and the final report on the shipping industry (1967).

Colin Hargreaves Pearson, Baron Pearson (1899–1980), was born in Canada, the youngest child of Ernest Pearson, a lawyer. The family moved to London when Pearson was 7. He was educated at Saint Paul's School and after military service in the 5th Guards Machine Gun Regiment, he studied classics at Balliol College, Oxford University. He was admitted to the bar in 1924, was appointed junior counsel to the Office of Works in 1930, and during World War II worked in the Treasury Solicitor's Office. He took silk in 1949 and was appointed a judge, Kings Bench Division of the High Court. Pearson was a valued committee man and conducted inquiries into many industrial disputes; electricity supply (1964), shipping (1966–67), civil air transport (1967–68), steel (1968), the docks (1970), and teacher's pay (1971–72).

Sources

Blake (Lord), and Nicholls, C. S., eds. 1986. *Dictionary of national biography 1971–1980.* Oxford: Oxford University Press.

Marsh, Arthur. 1979. *Concise encyclopedia of industrial relations.* Westmead, Farnborough, Hants: Gower.

Who was who, 1971–80. Vol. VII. London: Adam and Charles Black.

PECKSNIFF. A hypocrite.

Mr. Pecksniff is a character in Charles Dickens's novel *Martin Chuzzelwit*

(1843–44). Pecksniff, an architect and land surveyor at Salisbury, preaches to others on the duty of forgiveness and the beauty of charity. He is best at sleek smiles and drawling hypocrisy, and he appears as mild as a lamb and gentle as a dove, but underneath he is more like a crocodile. He exposes his meanness and treachery by trying to bully Martin Chuzzelwit's sweetheart, Mary, into marrying him. Martin's grandfather exposes the hypocrite and blesses Mary's marriage to his grandson. Eventually, Pecksniff becomes a begging drunkard, squalid, obviously impoverished by his own life of hypocrisy.

Sources

Evans, Ivor H. 1989. *Brewer's dictionary of phrase and fable.* 14th ed. London: Cassell.

Freeman, William. 1973. *Everyman's dictionary of fictional characters.* 3d rev. ed. London: J. M. Dent and sons.

Hammond, Nicholas G.L., and Scullard, Howard H., eds. 1985. *The Oxford companion to English literature.* Oxford: Clarendon Press.

Patridge, Eric. 1970. *Name into word: proper names that have become common property: a discursive dictionary.* 2d rev. ed. Freeport, N.J.: Books for Libraries.

Pringle, David. 1987. *Imaginary people: a who's who of modern fictional characters.* London: Grafton.

PEELITE. A follower of a reform policy for the Corn Laws, which in 1815 and 1822 had totally prohibited the importing of corn until the local price had risen. In 1825, when Robert Peel was a minister, the prohibition was abolished, and a duty on a sliding scale was introduced. By 1845 the famine in Ireland and the propaganda of the Anti-Corn Law League led Peel to change his belief in protection for agriculture, and by 1846 the Corn Laws were repealed.

Sir Robert Peel (1788–1850). See BOBBY.

PEIRCE'S LAW. "Ideas tend to spread continuously and to affect certain others which stand to them in a peculiar relation of affectability. In this spreading they lose intensity, and especially the power of affecting others, but gain generally and become welded with other ideas" (Potter, 1967:133).

Charles "Santiago" Sanders Peirce (1839–1914) was born in Cambridge, Massachusetts, son of a prominent Harvard mathematician who trained him in formal logic and mathematics. Charles was educated at local schools, graduated from Harvard and the Lawrence Scientific School, and worked for the U.S. Coastal Survey staff (1861–91) until retirement. He taught at Harvard (1864–65) and at the Harvard Observatory (1872–75), and he published *Photometric Researches* (1878). In 1878 he set down a theory in *Popular Science Monthly,* which he called "Pragmatism" (1901), and he taught again at Harvard (1903–4). To avoid confusion with the ideas of others, he later called it "Pragmaticism." Most of his work centered on logic, and he is now recognized as the greatest formal logician of his time for his original work, emendations to Boolean algebra, and contributions to probability theory, induction, and the logic of methodology. He could never find a book publisher for his ideas. From his lifelong friend, William James, Peirce, took his middle name, meaning "Saint James."

Sources

Brent, Joseph. 1993. *C. S. Peirce: a life.* Bloomington: University of Indiana Press.

Hartshorne, Charles, and Weiss, Paul, ed. 1960–66. *Collected papers of Charles Sanders Peirce.* Cambridge, Mass.: Belknap/Harvard University Press.

Hookway, Christopher, 1985. *Peirce.* London: Routledge and Kegan Paul.

Knight, T. S. 1965. *Peirce.* New York: Washington Square Press.

Malone, Dumas, ed. 1934. *Dictionary of American biography.* Vol. VII. New York: Charles Scribner's Sons.

Potter, Vincent G. 1967. *Charles S. Peirce on norms and ideals.* Worcester: University of Massachusetts Press.

Preece, Warren E., ed. 1965. *Encyclopedia Britannica.* Chicago: Encyclopedia Britannica Inc., William Benton.

Zusne, Leonard. 1984. *Biographical dictionary of psychology.* Westport, Conn.: Greenwood Press.

PELAGIAN. A follower of the fourth-century British monk who did not accept original sin and advocated the heresy that humankind can choose good because it has a God-given nature and therefore can take the first steps toward salvation without Divine Grace.

Pelagius (c. 360–420) was born in Britain; he wrote *The Doctrine Known as Pelagianism* and was condemned as a heretic. He went to Rome in about 400 and began to spread his teachings on free will as opposed to what he considered was a too passive reliance on the grace of God and too pessimistic a view of human nature. In 409–410, when the Goths menaced Rome, Pelagius left for Africa and later Palestine. In Africa his doctrine was attacked by Saint Augustine. In 415 he was accused of heresy by a Spanish priest but managed to clear himself of the charge. In 418 Pope Zosimus formally condemned Pelagius and Pelagianism. One of Pelagius's works, "Commentary on the Epistles of St. Paul," has been preserved in the works of his opponent, Saint Jerome. The term *pelagianism* is commonly used for any teaching that lays more emphasis on free will than on the power of divine love.

Sources

Cross, Frank L. 1974. *The Oxford dictionary of the Christian Church.* 2d ed. New York: Oxford University Press.

Evans, Ivor H. 1989. *Brewer's dictionary of phrase and fable.* 14th ed. London: Cassell.

Eliade, Mircea, ed. 1987. *Encyclopedia of religion.* New York: Macmillan.

Meagher, Paul K.; O'Brien, Thomas C.; and Aherne, Marie, eds. 1979. *Encyclopedic dictionary of religion.* Washington, D.C.: Corpus Publications.

PERCY REPORT. A special British committee (1944) to consider the needs of higher technological education in England and Wales. The committee's recommendations changed postwar technical education in Britain.

Eustace Sutherland Campbell Percy, Baron Percy of Newcastle, later duke of

Northumberland (1887–1958), was born in London, educated at Eton and Christ-church, Oxford, entered the diplomatic service in 1909, and served at the Washington Embassy (1910–14). He stood unsuccessfully for Parliament in 1915 but was elected for Hastings (1921) which he represented until 1937. He was president of the Board of Education (1924–29) where he advocated raising the school age in technical education. He was a minister without portfolio in 1935 but resigned the following year in protest at Britain's failure to react to German militarism. He became rector of King's College, Newcastle (1937–52), and in 1944 chairman of the special committee set up by the minister of education. Among his publications are *The Responsibilities of the League* (1920), *Education at the Crossroads* (1930), *Democracy on Trial* (1931), and *The Heresy of Democracy* (1954).

Sources

Aldrich, R., and Gordon, P. 1989. *Dictionary of British educationists.* London: Woburn Press.

Magnussen, Magnus; Goring, Rosemary; and Thorn, John O., eds. 1990. *Chambers biographical dictionary* Edinburgh: Chambers Ltd.

Williams, E. T., and Palmer, Helen M., eds. 1971. *Dictionary of national biography 1951–1960.* London: Oxford University Press.

PERICLEAN. Pertaining to the Golden Age of politics, arts, and letters in Athens.

Pericles (c. 495–429 B.C.), an Athenian statesman, represented the ideal Athenian, a man of fine character, sober, incorruptible, and reserved. He was the son of Xanthippes, entered public life in about 469 B.C., became the leader of the democratic party, and in 444 B.C. was the principal minister in Athens. He helped the military and naval development of the state, encouraged art and literature, completed the fortification of Athens and Piraeus, and caused the building of the Parthenon. He died a victim of the plague.

Sources

Benét, William R. 1988. *The reader's encyclopedia.* London: Adam and Charles Black.

McHenry, Robert, ed. 1992. *The new encyclopedia Britannica.* Chicago: Encyclopedia Britannica, Inc.

Magnussen, Magnus; Goring, Rosemary; and Thorn, John O., eds. 1990. *Chambers biographical dictionary.* Edinburgh: Chambers Ltd.

PERONISTS, PERONISM. Followers of the popular twentieth-century president of Argentina. An Argentinian political ideology—between the extremes of American capitalism and Russian communism—which led to mass organization of workers against middle-class elites in the interests of nationalism, social progress, and Argentina's leadership of Latin America.

Juan Domingo Perón Sosa (1895–1974) was born in Lobos and grew up on the fringe of the rural middle class in an atmosphere of insecurity and resentment against the established order. He graduated from Argentina's Military Academy (1913), rose to captain, and in a coup helped topple the democratically elected president Hipolito Irigoyen (1930). From 1930 to 1936 Perón was a professor of military history at the Escuela Superior de Guerra, while serving as private secretary to the minister of war and as an aide-de-camp to senior officers. He wrote several books on military history and strategy. Perón's rapid rise to power began in 1943 when he supported the coup that deposed President Ramon Castillo. He became undersecretary of war and chief of staff of the first Army Division, and director of the National Department of Labor, which he transformed into the powerful Secretariat of Welfare and Labor. He used his positions to win a large, devoted following among the workers. In 1946 Perón was formally elected president, but chaos followed as government spending led to inflation, corruption flourished, the treasury was depleted, and nationalized industries stagnated. For national security, Perón controlled the judiciary, censored the press, jailed dissenters, and smothered opposition in trade unions, political parties, and universities. In 1955 a military revolt forced him to resign and flee to Paraguay. In 1972 Perón's Justicialist party was officially recognized as a legal political party, and he returned. He did not try to regain power until 1973 when he became president.

Sources

McHenry, Robert, ed. 1992. *The new encyclopedia Britannica.* Chicago: Encyclopedia Britannica, Inc.

Moritz, Charles, ed. 1974. *Current biography yearbook.* New York: H. W. Wilson.

Owen, Frank. 1957. *Peron: his rise and fall.* London: Cresset Press.

Page, Joseph A. 1983. *Peron: a biography.* New York: Random House.

PEROT FACTOR, PEROTIANS. An explanation for the remarkable surge in popularity of a third candidate in the 1992 U.S. presidential campaign; after he had withdrawn in June, and then returned to the campaign in October, the Perot factor came to mean the fears relating to the third candidate and their impact on the election in November. The impact was difficult to predict, and in the last weeks of campaigning there was much speculation not only about how many votes he might get from the electorate, but also from which of the other two candidates—George Bush and Bill Clinton—he might draw them, and in which state he might receive them. Some political commentators saw the early interest as revolutionary, and Perot's followers were dubbed Perotians. In the campaign's early stages for many weeks, the third candidate held more support than either of the other major party candidates.

Henry Ray Perot (b. 1930) was named after his mother's brother, and in fifth grade he was given his father's and deceased brother's middle name, Ross. His early childhood is a mixture of his own legends and investigative journalism. He was an outstanding boy scout, and after high school he attended the U.S. Naval Academy at Annapolis. After four years in the navy, he became an IBM salesman and founded his own company, Electronic Data Systems, which he eventually sold to IBM. This made him very rich. In recent years he has worked to rescue prisoners of war held in Vietnam and pursued charitable aims. A confident business leader who treated people as his instruments—sometimes kindly, sometimes without feeling—Perot created an image of being pro-people, pro-business, and he seemed to impress many Republican supporters who were planning to desert Bush and vote for Perot because they did not like the U.S. political system and its politicians. Unlike previous third-party contenders for the presidency, Perot himself had enough money to continue the campaign.

Sources

Chiu, Tony. 1992. *Ross Perot in his own words.* New York: Warner.

Gillespie, J. David, 1993. *Politics at the periphery: third parties in a two-party America.* Columbia: University of Southern Carolina Press.

Gross, Ken. 1992. *Ross Perot: the man behind the myth.* New York: Random House.

Ingham, John N., and Feldman, Lynne B. 1990. *Contemporary American business leaders: a biographical dictionary.* Westport, Conn.: Greenwood Press.

Levin, Doron P. 1989. *Irreconcilable differences: Ross Perot versus General Motors.* Boston: Little, Brown.

Mason, Todd. 1990. *Perot: an unauthorized biography.* Homewood, Ill.: Dow Jones-Irwin.

Moritz, Charles, ed. 1971. *Current biography yearbook.* New York: H. W. Wilson.

Walker, Martin. 1992. Running scared of Perot. *Guardian Weekly,* June 14:11.

PESTALOZZIAN, PESTALOZZI METHODS. Pertaining to a system of education reforms; a follower of such reforms. Principles of education emphasizing the role of mother, sensory experience, and the immediate environment in the development of ideas and coherence of thinking. The ideas were used in Russia as well as by the German philosopher, Johann Gottlieb Fichte (1762–1814), and later in England by the Reverend Charles Mayo (1792–1846) who opened a boarding school at Epsom (1822–26) and Cheam (1826–46) with help from his sister Elizabeth Mayo (1793–1865).

Johann Heinrich Pestalozzi (1746–1827) was born into a wealthy family at Zurich, studied theology and law, and later turned his attention to agriculture. He was devoted to the education of the people, and in 1775 he established a school on his estate. At his school pupils were encouraged to observe and reason and to develop an interest in their studies. Jean Jacques Rousseau's (1712–78) ideas contributed much to the system. It failed to draw financial support by popular subscription so that Pestalozzi was obliged to give up the plan in 1780. The first account of his method of instruction was published at about this time, but his principal literary work was *Lienhardt and Gertrude: A Book for the People,* which was written between 1781 and 1785. In 1798, with support from the government, he founded an educational institution for poor people at Stanz. It was abandoned in 1799. He then took charge of a school at Burgdorf during 1804–25. His collected works were published in sixteen volumes between 1869 and 1872.

Sources

Dudley, Lavinia P. 1963. *The encyclopedia Americana.* International ed. New York: Americana Corp.

McHenry, Robert, ed. 1992. *The new encyclopedia Britannica.* Chicago: Encyclopedia
    Britannica, Inc.
Magnussen, Magnus; Goring, Rosemary; and Thorn, John O., eds. 1990. *Chambers bi-
    ographical dictionary.* Edinburgh: Chambers Ltd.
Silber, Kate, 1960. *Pestalozzi.* London: Routledge and Kegan Paul.
Zusne, Leonard. 1984. *Biographical dictionary of psychology.* Westport, Conn.: Green-
    wood Press.

PÉTAIN. A traitor.

Henri Philippe Pétain (1856–1951), a peasant's son born at Cauchy-La-Tour,
France, was raised by his stepmother, and, reputedly starved of affection, became reticent and shy. He was sent to Saint Bertin's College, a Dominican
institution in Saint Omer, and later went to military school in Nancy (1873) and
the military academy of Saint Cyr (1876). Although his training record shows
that he was not an able commissioned officer, he rose to brigadier in 1914 and
commanded the army in France in 1916. The defense of Verdun made him a
hero. He was promoted to marshall of France in 1918 and became France's
minister of war in 1934. When France fell to the Germans in 1940, Pétain, 84,
succeeded Paul Reynaud as head of the government, and sought terms with Nazi
Germany in the belief that France would be regenerated only through suffering.
When France was liberated, he was tried, and the death sentence for treason was
commuted to life in prison, where he died.

Sources

Bolton, Glorney. 1957. *Petain.* London: Allen and Unwin.
Ferro, Marc. 1987. *Petain.* Paris: Fayard.
McHenry, Robert, ed. 1992. *The new encyclopedia Britannica.* Chicago: Encyclopedia
    Britannica, Inc.
Magnussen, Magnus; Goring, Rosemary; and Thorn, John O., eds. 1990. *Chambers bi-
    ographical dictionary.* Edinburgh: Chambers Ltd.

PETER PAN, PETER PAN SYNDROME. An immature man, usually charm-
ingly childlike, who refuses to relinquish the comforts and lack of responsibility
he had as a child.

Peter Pan was a character in the poetical play *Peter Pan or the Boy Who
Wouldn't Grow Up* (1904) by Sir James Matthew Barrie (1860–1937). In 1902
Barrie had presented the fantasy world of Peter Pan in *The Little White Bird.*
The play was an immediate and lasting success, and a statue of Peter Pan is in
London's Kensington Gardens. Peter was named after one of Barrie's nephews
for whom the story was written, and after Pan, Greek god of the woodlands. In
the play Peter Pan befriends Wendy, and together they build a house small
enough for only children to use. It was called the "Wendy House." Wendy
herself was named by Barrie after the nickname, "Friendly-wendy," given to
him by Margaret Henley, daughter of Barrie's close friend, W. E. Henley.

Sources

Benét, William R. 1990. *The reader's encyclopedia of world literature and arts, with
    supplement.* New York: Thomas Y. Crowell.

Evans, Ivor H. 1989. *Brewer's dictionary of phrase and fable.* 14th ed. London: Cassell.
Hammond, Nicholas G.L., and Scullard, Howard H., eds. 1985. *The Oxford companion to English literature.* Oxford: Clarendon Press.
Kiley, Dan. 1983. *The Peter Pan syndrome: men who have never grown up.* New York: Dodd, Mead.
McHenry, Robert, ed. 1992. *The new encyclopedia Britannica.* Chicago: Encyclopedia Britannica, Inc.

PETER PRINCIPLE. In a hierarchy individuals tend to rise to their levels of incompetence. Corollary one states that, given enough time and enough ranks in the hierarchy, each employee rises to and remains at his or her level of incompetence; corollary two states that in time every post tends to be occupied by an employee who is incompetent to carry out its duties; corollary three states that work is accomplished by those employees who have not yet reached their level of incompetence; and corollary four states that supercompetence is more objectionable to a hierarchical superior than incompetence. Relating to this principle are many others: Peter's bridge, circumambulation, circumbendibus, corollary, inversion, invert, nuance, palliatives, paradox, parry, placebo, plateau, prescriptions, pretty pass, prognosis, prophylactics, remedies, spiral, and interpretation.

Laurence Johnston Peter (1919–90) was born in Vancouver, educated at the University of British Columbia, Western Washington University, and Washington State University (Ed.D., 1963). He taught industrial arts in British Columbia (1941–47) and became a mental health coordinator and counselor (1948–64). He joined the education faculty of the University of British Columbia and taught at the University of Southern California (1966–69) and the University of California (1975–79). Written in 1964, his book was rejected for publication until 1969, and then sold 8 million copies and was translated in thirty-eight languages. He followed it with *The Peter Prescription and How to Make Things Go Right* (1972), *The Peter Plan: A Proposal for Survival* (1975), and *Peter's People and Their Marvellous Ideas* (1979). The authors claimed that the Peter Principle and hierachiology—a "new science" of the study of organizations whose members are arranged in order of grade, rank, or class—provide the unifying factor for all social science.

Sources

Martin, Thomas L., Jr. 1973. *Malice in Blunderland.* New York: McGraw-Hill.
Metzger, Linda, and Straub, Deborah A., eds. 1986. *Contemporary authors.* New Rev. Series 17. Detroit: Gale Research.
Peter, Laurence J., and Hull, Raymond. 1969. *The Peter principle: why things go wrong.* New York: William Morrow.
Trotsky, Susan M. 1990. *Contemporary authors.* Vol. 130. Detroit: Gale Research.

PETRINE, PETRINISM. Relating to the apostle Peter; a theory of Ferdinand Christian Baur (1792–1860) and his Tübingen school which noted a trend in primitive Christianity toward Judaism, ascribed to Peter and his party, and opposed to Paulinism. Baur, influenced by Hegel (1770–1831), was a prominent New Testament critic and helped establish modern studies of church history with his *History of the Christian Church* (1853–63).

Peter, originally called Simon, was one of the twelve apostles. He was a fisherman and later became one of Christ's favored disciples, and was a prominent leader of the church after the ascension. According to tradition, he founded the church at Rome and was martyred there in the reign of Nero.

See also NERONIAN.

Sources

Cross, Frank L. 1974. *The Oxford dictionary of the Christian Church.* 2d ed. New York: Oxford University Press.

McHenry, Robert, ed. 1992. *The new encyclopedia Britannica.* Chicago: Encyclopedia Britannica, Inc.

Magnussen, Magnus; Goring, Rosemary; and Thorn, John O., eds. 1990. *Chambers biographical dictionary.* Edinburgh: Chambers Ltd.

PETROBUSIANS. Those who reject all external forms of worship.

Peter of Bruis (d. 1126) was a French priest from Embrun who preached in southwest France during the religious ferment of the first half of the twelfth century. By abolishing such practices as baptism and the mass, he hoped to return the church to its original purity. Legend states that he was sacked, and he retaliated by preaching in Dauphine and Provence, and attracting many followers, "Petrobusians," who harassed priests and even tried to have them find wives. At Saint Gilles, near Nîmes, the angry people threw Peter into the flames because he was burning crosses.

Sources

Cross, Frank L. 1974. *The Oxford dictionary of the Christian Church.* 2d ed. New York: Oxford University Press.

McDonald, William, ed. 1967. *New Catholic encyclopedia.* New York: McGraw-Hill.

Meagher, Paul K.; O'Brien, Thomas C.; and Aherne, Marie, eds. 1979. *Encyclopedic dictionary of religion.* Washington, D.C.: Corpus Publications.

PETROV AFFAIR. The last of the main Soviet spy dramas of the cold war (1945–54) involving the dramatic defection in Australia of a colonel and his wife in Soviet intelligence. It became a political event when it was alleged that Australia's prime minister, Robert G. Menzies (1894–1978), and the Australian Security Intelligence Organization (ASIO) conspired to use the defection against the Australian Labor party (ALP) and its leader Dr. Herbert V. Evatt (1894–1965). The affair split the ALP and kept it out of office until 1972.

Vladimir Petrov (1907–91) was born Anafasy Mikhailovich Shorokhov in Siberia and worked as a blacksmith's apprentice until a Bolshevik agitator encouraged him to establish a Komsomol cell in his village. In 1927 he became a member of the Communist party and was educated in Sverdlovsk. Two years later, renamed Protelarsky, he organized young factory workers in northern Siberia and later served three years in the navy where he learned cipher operations.

By 1933 he was recruited to the Moscow State Security Service where he became a cipher expert for the NKVD under diplomatic cover. Later, he attended the Moscow show trials. As a major in the NKVD, he maintained communications between concentration camps and the NKVD. When Germany invaded Russia, he was renamed Petrov and sent to Sweden (1941). In 1947 he and his wife returned to Moscow and three years later were sent to Australia where he controlled the MGB (Ministry of State Security) matters and was promoted to colonel. His cover was an embassy official to the third secretary concerned with cultural and consular matters. Immediately, he was befriended and cultivated by what he thought was a pro-Soviet Pole, Dr. Michael Bialoguski, but who was, in fact, an ASIO agent. Together they became friends, each one trying to engage the other as a double agent. On April 3, 1954, Petrov was induced to defect in Sydney; two weeks later his wife followed amid much drama and an unsuccessful attempt by Russian agents to abduct her in Darwin. The defection provided information on Soviet penetration of British intelligence agencies as well as the conspiracy theory, which now has little to support it. Petrov died in secrecy in Melbourne.

Evdokia Petrov, neé Kartsev (b. 1914), was 5 years old when she and her family quit their village, Lipky, near Moscow, in search for food. In 1924 they settled in Moscow where she studied English, and at 19 she was encouraged to join the OGPU (United State Political Directorate). By 1934 she was a codebreaker and a student of Japanese. In eight years she became a specialist in these activities and was promoted. She married in 1936, but her husband fell immediately under suspicion and was banished to a labor camp. In 1938 she married Protelarsky and traveled with him as an intelligence officer and cipher expert in her own right.

Sources

Manne, Robert. 1987. *The Petrov affair: politics and espionage.* Sydney: Pergamon Press.

Petrov, Vladimir, and Petrov, Evdokia. 1956. *Empire of fear.* London: André Deutsch.

Whitlam, Nicholas, and Stubbs, John. 1974. *Nest of traitors: the Petrov affair.* Brisbane: Jacaranda.

PHAEDRA COMPLEX. Pattern of emotional problems that may arise in a new stepparent and the teenage child of the original marriage.

In Greek legend, Phaedra was the daughter of Minos and Pasiphae, sister of Ariadne and wife of Theseus. She was noted for her love of her stepson, Hippolytus. He repulsed her, and she slandered him to Theseus, thus securing his death. When his innocence became known, she committed suicide. She is the subject of tragedies by Euripides, Seneca, and Racine.

Sources

Howatson, M. C., ed. 1989. *The Oxford companion to classical literature.* 2d ed. Oxford: Oxford University Press.

Jobes, Gertrude. 1962. *Dictionary of mythology, folklore and symbols.* New York: Scarecrow Press.

Smith, Benjamin. 1903. *The Century cyclopedia of names.* London: The Times.

PHAETON COMPLEX. In reviewing a study of British prime ministers, Hugh Berrington (1974) expanded on Lucy Iremonger's (1970) work and found they were not as sociable, flexible, and tolerant as expected, but instead were ambitious, vain, highly sensitive, disliked close relations, lonely, and shy. He concluded they suffered from a ''Phaeton complex.''

According to Ovid, Phaeton was the son of a mortal woman, Clymene, and the Sun-god, Helios [or Phoebus]. Phaeton was troubled by his origins and searched for his father. When he found his father in the Palace of the Sun, the Sun-god proudly offered the youth anything he wanted to prove that he was the youth's father and that he loved him. The youth wanted to drive the Sun's chariot across the sky, bringing light to the world. Regretfully, the father reminded the youth that because he was mortal he would be incapable of driving the fiery chariot due to hazards on the way across the sky and the intractable behavior of the horses. Obsessed by the glory of the task, Phaeton ignored his father's advice and insisted that he be allowed to take his father's place. Phaeton mounted the chariot and momentarily felt he was Lord of the Sky. Immediately, however, the horses took control, and Phaeton collapsed in terror as they careered recklessly across the heavens, plunging to the earth and setting it on fire. To save Mother Earth, Jove struck Phaeton dead with lightning, shattered the chariot, and drove the maddened horses into the sea. The youth's burning corpse was submerged in the unseen river Eridanus, cooled, and buried by the Naiads. Although Phaeton had failed greatly, he was admired for daring so greatly.

Sources

Berrington, Hugh B. 1974. The fiery chariot: British prime ministers and the search for love. *British Journal of Political Science* 4:345–369.

Hamilton, Edith. 1940. *Mythology: timeless tales of gods and heroes.* Boston: Little, Brown.

Iremonger, Lucille. 1970. *The fiery chariot: a study of British prime ministers and the search for love.* London: Secker and Warburg.

PHELPS-BROWN REPORT. The report of one of two committees of inquiry into the pay and conditions of London busmen (1963–64) and building and civil engineering (1968).

Sir Ernest Henry Phelps-Brown (b. 1906) was born in Calme, Wiltshire, educated at Taunton School, Wadham College, Oxford, and served with the Royal Artillery in World War II. Later he was a member of the Council on Crisis, Productivity Incomes (1959); the National Economic Development Council (1962); and the Royal Commission on the Distribution of Incoming Wealth (1974–78). He was a professor of economics and labor at the University of London (1947–68). Among his publications are *The Framework of the Pricing*

System (1936); *A Course in Applied Economics* (1951); *The Balloon* (1953), a novel; *The Growth of British Industrial Relations* (1959); and *The Economics of Labor* (1963).

Sources

Eatwell, John; Milgate, Murray; and Newman, Peter. 1987. *The new Palgrave: a dictionary of economics.* London: Macmillan.
The international who's who, 1992–93. London: Europa Publications.

PHELPS-FRIEDMAN THEORY. In any economy, there is a "natural" or "real" rate of employment at which people's expectations of wage and price changes are fully realized by the actual rate of wage and price changes. Attempts by governments to lower the level of unemployment below that rate by expansionary, fiscal, and monetary policies generates expectations of rising wages and prices, which in turn induces behavior that accelerates inflation. The entire process halts only when unemployment rises once again and returns to the natural rate at a permanently higher level of inflation.

Edmund S. Phelps (b. 1933) was born in Evanston, Illinois, and graduated from Amherst College and Yale University (Ph.D., 1959). After a year with the Rand Corporation he worked at the Massachusetts Institute of Technology and three years at Yale before moving to the University of Pennsylvania as professor of economics. Later he taught at New York University and at Columbia University. Phelps invented the "natural-rate" hypothesis in 1967, at much the same time the idea occurred to Milton Friedman. Earlier, Phelps wrote repeatedly on growth theory and in particular on the "golden rules" of economic growth. In his first published work, "The Golden Rule of Accumulation: A Fable for Growthmen," *American Economic Review* (1961), he both expounded and ridiculed the principle of the "golden rule." In *Inflation Policy and Unemployment Theory: A Cost-Benefit Approach to Monetary Planning* (1972), Phelps and others wrote on the problem of the simultaneous occurrence of inflation and unemployment. That is, stagflation.

Milton Friedman (b. 1912) was born in New York City, the son of poor Jewish immigrants. He studied at Rutgers University, the University of Chicago, and Columbia University (Ph.D., 1946). After a long spell at Columbia, he joined the University of Chicago in 1948 and remained there until he retired in 1979. He was adviser to Barry Goldwater, the unsuccessful presidential candidate in 1964, and subsequently advised President Nixon. He was president of the American Economic Association (1969). Friedman's early training and publications were in statistics, but he made his name in 1946 with his doctoral dissertation on the income of independent professional practice (National Bureau of Economic Research, 1946). It was in his *Studies in the Quantity Theory of Money* that Friedman turned toward monetary economics (1956) and became influential in shaping the economic policies of Britain under Prime Minister Thatcher in her early years (1979–85) and of the United States when Ronald Reagan was the president (1981–88).

Sources

Blaug, Mark. 1985. *Great economists since Keynes.* Brighton, England: Harvester Press.
The international who's who, 1992–93. London: Europa Publications.
Magnussen, Magnus; Goring, Rosemary; and Thorn, John O., eds. 1990. *Chambers biographical dictionary.* Edinburgh: Chambers Ltd.
Straub, Deborah A., ed. 1988. *Contemporary authors.* New Revision Series. Vol. 22. Detroit: Gale Research.

PHILIPPIC. Invective-laden discourse or bitter, hostile political statement.

Philip II (382–336 B.C.) was born at Macedon, the youngest son of Amyntas II. He spent his youth as a hostage at Thebes, which was then the major city-state. On the death of his brother, Perdiccas III, he returned to Macedon to claim the Crown (359 B.C.). In support of his claims, Philip established an infantry and cavalry, and in less then a year defeated all rivals to the throne. Then he planned to unify the kingdom by abolishing semi-independent principalities and extending his empire through conquest and thereby making Macedon a supreme state in the Balkans. After many decisive victories, he planned to lead an invasion force to Persia, Greece's traditional enemy. During preparations for the invasion, he was assassinated by a young nobleman with a personal grievance against him. The term *Philippic* takes its origin from one of three speeches made by Demosthenes against Philip.

Sources

McHenry, Robert, ed. 1992. *The new encyclopedia Britannica.* Chicago: Encyclopedia Britannica, Inc.
Magnussen, Magnus; Goring, Rosemary; and Thorn, John O., eds. 1990. *Chambers biographical dictionary.* Edinburgh: Chambers Ltd.
Smith, Benjamin. 1903. *The Century cyclopedia of names.* London: The Times.

PHILLIPS CURVE. In economics the strong inverse relation normally existing between percent unemployment and the percent price-level increase illustrates graphically that as unemployment declines, wages and prices—inflation—rises. The usual negative slope of the curve shifts to a positive slope in times of stagflation. In the 1960s the curve was central in the economic models used in government policies that traded unemployment for inflation; but in the mid-1960s its empirical soundness was questioned. An alternative explanation offered for the convex curve involved the inflexibility of wages when excess demand reached a low level, and the flexibility of wages when excess demand reached a high level.

A. William Phillips (1914–75) was born in Te Rehunga, New Zealand. At age 16 he left school to begin work for the Australian Mining Camp and began to study electrical engineering in the evenings. He went to London in 1937, passed the examinations of London's Institute for Electrical Engineers (1938), and worked for the London Electricity Board. He joined the army, was taken prisoner of war in the Far East, and after World War II, at age 32, he enrolled at the London School of Economics as a sociology student. His first article,

"Mechanical Models and Economic Dynamics," *Economica* (1950) led to a teaching post at the school, and he rose quickly to become a professor of statistics. In 1958 he published his ideas on the Phillips Curve, and in 1969 he left Britain to become a professor at Australian National University in Canberra. After suffering a severe stroke in 1970, he returned to his native New Zealand where he taught part-time.

Sources

Blaug, Mark. 1985. *Great economists since Keynes.* Brighton, England: Harvester Press.

Hines, A. G. 1972. The Phillips curve and the distribution of unemployment. *American Economic Review* 62:155–160.

Nemmers, Erwin E. 1978. *Dictionary of economics and business.* Totowa, N.J.: Rowman and Littlefield.

Phillips, William A. 1958. The relation between unemployment and the rate of exchange of money wage rates in the United Kingdom, 1861–1957, *Economica,* November: 283–299.

Sills, David L., ed. 1968. *International encyclopedia of the social sciences.* New York: Macmillan and Free Press.

PIAGETIAN. Relating to twentieth-century theories of cognitive and moral development in children. The cognitive theory covers six stages from the sensory-motor stage in infancy to the formal, operational stage of adolescence and adulthood. The development is characterized by forecasting and feedback, and by adapting through the dual processes of selective assimilation of new material and accommodation of what is known to what is new. The theory of moral development of the child goes from an amoral stage to a stage of respect for rules and the internalization of moral norms according to a principle of moral justice based on mutual respect, reciprocity, and equality. The moral development runs in tandem with the cognitive and owes much to the child's peer group as the source of moral role taking.

Jean Piaget (1896–1980) was born in Neuchâtel, Switzerland, and studied zoology. He made very close studies of his own children and turned to psychology with a strong interest in many aspects of children's growth, especially their cognitive development. He was a professor of psychology at Geneva (1929–54) and head of an institute for the study of education. He postulated stages of cognitive growth and moral development. Among his works are *The Child's Conception of the World* (1926), *The Origin of Intelligence in Children* (1936), and *The Early Growth of Logic in the Child* (1958).

Sources

Boden, Margaret A. 1985. *Piaget.* London: Fontana.

Devine, Elizabeth; Held, Michael; Vinson, James; and Walsh, George, eds. 1983. *Thinkers of the twentieth century: a biographical, bibliographical and critical dictionary.* London: Macmillan.

Magnussen, Magnus; Goring, Rosemary; and Thorn, John O., eds. 1990. *Chambers biographical dictionary* Edinburgh: Chambers Ltd.

Piaget, Jean. 1932. *The moral judgment of the child.* 1965 ed. New York: Free Press.

Sills, David L., ed. 1968. *International encyclopedia of the social sciences.* New York: Macmillan and Free Press.
Zusne, Leonard. 1984. *Biographical dictionary of psychology.* Westport, Conn.: Greenwood Press.

PICKWICKIAN. Pertaining to a popular fictional hero of nineteenth-century London, or the special sense in which epithets are used in describing others; a member of the Pickwick Club.

Samuel Pickwick is a character in *The Posthumous Papers of the Pickwick Club,* a novel by Charles Dickens (1812–70), first issued in twenty parts (1836–37). Pickwick, an elderly, overweight gentleman, naive and benevolent, is the chairman of the Pickwick Club which he founded to investigate the source of the Hampstead ponds. With three companions he has many misadventures to this purpose and one sad experience with Mrs. Bardell, which leads to a trial. The Pickwickian sense refers to the insulting use of epithets that are not understood to have the same meaning that they would have in usual or natural usage. Consequently, people with a high regard for each other may use insults and offensive epithets in a "Pickwickian sense," and their respect for one another is undiminished. Dickens's aim was to amuse the public every month with an episode on the activities of the club's members; people of all classes and ages bought copies of the work, and by the fifteenth installment 40,000 were on sale. Pickwick is one of the more amusing burlesques of London life in the nineteenth century.

Sources

Evans, Ivor H. 1989. *Brewer's dictionary of phrase and fable.* 14th ed. London: Cassell.
Hammond, Nicholas G.L., and Scullard, Howard H., eds. 1985. *The Oxford companion to English literature.* Oxford: Clarendon Press.

PIGOU EFFECT, PIGOVIAN TAX. The Pigou Effect is the impact on consumption of a change in the real value of cash balances caused by a change in the money supply; for example, if an increase in the money supply leads prices to rise, purchasing power falls and consumption is lowered. The Pigovian tax is a tax levied on producers for the external costs that productive activities attract.

Arthur Cecil Pigou (1877–1959) was born at Ryde, the Isle of Wight, son of a retired army officer. He won a scholarship to Harrow, and at King's College, Cambridge, he won a medal for poetry, the Burney Prize (1900). He graduated with a thesis on Robert Browning as a religious teacher (1901). Pigou began lecturing in economics at Cambridge and was appointed a professor of political economy (1908–44). He was a prolific writer, and among his major works are *Principles and Methods of Industrial Peace* (1905), *Wealth and Welfare* (1912), *Unemployment* (1914), *Economics of Welfare* (1920), and his notable *Theory of Unemployment* (1933).

Sources
Blaug, Mark. 1985. *Great economists since Keynes.* Brighton, England: Harvester Press.
Blaug, Mark, ed. 1992. *Arthur Pigou.* London: Elgar.
Eatwell, John; Milgate, Murray; and Newman, Peter. 1987. *The new Palgrave: a dictionary of economics.* London: Macmillan.
Rutherford, Donald. 1992. *Dictionary of economics.* London: Routledge.
Williams, E. T., and Palmer, Helen M., eds. 1971. *Dictionary of national biography 1951–1960.* London: Oxford University Press.

PILGER. To confront, investigate, reveal, castigate; or to polemicize, manipulate, orchestrate, infuriate. The term was used by Oberon Waugh, the British writer, when he described a prominent Australian investigative journalist.

John Pilger (b. 1939) was born and raised in Bondi, Sydney, Australia, and worked in a post office, was a union member, and belonged to the Australian Labor party. He became a journalist and worked on the London *Daily Mirror,* writing in the style of journalistic investigation which exploited the human interest story, defended humanitarian causes, and exposed injustices and poverty. Recent among his many honors were a British Academy Award (1991), the George Foster Peabody Award (1990), News Reporter of the Year (1974), Journalist of the Year (1979), Campaigning Journalist of the year (1977), and a United Nations peace award (1991). His many critics maintain that his work is based on elusive evidence and poorly supported conclusions. His credibility was undermined in the Sunee affair in which he was tricked into buying a Thai girl as a slave (1982) when she was being properly cared for by her mother. He has helped produce over thirty books and television documentaries, the most memorable of which was an account of ''TV Cambodia: The Betrayal,'' which claimed that United Nations aid was being used to store U.S. arms for use against Cambodians by the Khmer Rouge. Among his works are *Heroes* (1986), a caustic exposé of Australian Labor party politics and the role of the U.S. Central Intelligence Agency in the downfall of Australia's prime minister Gough Whitlam (1975), *A Secret Country* (1989), and *Distant Voices* (1992). His recent film, *Return to Year Zero* (1993), critically examines the United Nations' role in the return to power of the Khmer Rouge in Cambodia before the United Nations sponsored elections in May 1993.

Sources
McDonald, John. 1993. The martyrdom of St John. *The Independent Monthly,* February 4:4–6.
Sing, Raylee; Alexander, Kirsten; and Arnold, John, eds. 1991. *Who's who of Australian writers.* Port Melbourne, Victoria: David W. Thorpe and National Center for Australian Studies.
Wilkinson, Michael, ed. 1993. *Who's who in Australia: 1993.* Melbourne: Information Australia Group.

PILKINGTON COMMITTEE. A British committee that examined aspects of agricultural education (1960). Although it was required to report on the education at the diploma level, the committee ranged more widely to indicate how agricultural and technical education should be related in Britain.

William Henry Pilkington, Baron Pilkington of Saint Helens (1905–83), the eldest son of Richard Austin Pilkington, was educated at Rugby and Magdalene College, Cambridge. He was knighted in 1953. He was chairman of Pilkington Brothers Ltd. (1949–73) and was appointed a nonexecutive director in 1973. He was also a director of the Bank of England (1955–72) and was created a life peer in 1968. He became chancellor of Loughborough University of Technology in 1966 and vice lord-lieutenant, Merseyside in 1974. He was president of British Industries (1953–55), the Council of European Industrial Federations (1954–57), and the Court of British Shippers Council (1971–74). He also chaired the royal commission to consider the pay of doctors and dentists (1957–60); the Committee on Broadcasting (1960–62); the National Advisory Council for Education for Industry and Commerce (1956–66); the Economic Development Committee for the Chemical Industry (1976–72); and many other royal commissions.
Sources

Blake (Lord), and Nicholls, C. S., eds. 1990. *Dictionary of national biography 1981–1985.* New York: Oxford University Press.

Blishen, Edward. 1969. *Blond's encyclopedia of education.* London: Blond Educational.

PINKERTON. American private detective.
Allan Pinkerton (1819–84). See FINK.

PITTITE. Follower of the young eighteenth-century British politician and statesman.

William Pitt (1759–1806) was the second son of William Pitt, first earl of Chatham, and Hester, daughter of Richard Greville. Pitt, the younger, was born at Hayes near Bromley in Kent. As a child he was precocious, and at age 7 he planned to follow his father's career. His health was delicate, and he was educated at home where his father took a great interest in his studies. At 14 the boy matriculated and entered Pembroke Hall, Cambridge, to study Latin and Greek, was called to the bar in 1780, and in 1781 was elected to Parliament, where he aligned himself with Lord Shelbourne in opposition to Lord North's administration. On the fall of North's government, Pitt was offered some minor offices including vice-treasurer of Ireland, a post once held by his father. At 23 he became chancellor of the Exchequer and before reaching 25, he was prime minister. His administration ended with his resignation in 1801 after the king opposed Pitt's efforts to relieve Roman Catholic disabilities.
Sources

Harvey, Arnold D. 1989. *William Pitt the younger.* Westport, Conn.: Meckler Corp.

Jarret, Derek. 1974. *Pitt the younger.* London: Weidenfeld and Nicolson.

Magnussen, Magnus; Goring, Rosemary; and Thorn, John O., eds. 1990. *Chambers biographical dictionary.* Edinburgh: Chambers Ltd.

Stephen, Leslie, and Lee, Sydney, eds. 1917. *The dictionary of national biography*. London: Oxford University Press.
Watson, John S. 1960. *The reign of George III, 1760–1815*. Oxford: Clarendon Press.

PLATONIC, PLATONISM. Relating to the Greek philosopher, to his philosophy and politics, and to love between people with no sensual desire; a belief in the existence of universals and abstract entities, a belief that time was essential, ideas or Forms were all that wholly existed because only they provide absolutely certain knowledge, as in mathematics.

Plato (c. 427–348 B.C.), originally Aristocles, was born into an ancient Athenian family; he studied under Socrates whom he admired, and in 399 B.C. on Socrates's death Plato retired to Megora. In about 386 B.C. in the Academy, an olive grove near Athens, Plato began teaching philosophy. Twice he tried to enter politics but each time was repelled by the iniquities he witnessed. The rest of his life was occupied mainly with instruction and composition of the "Dialogues," in which Socrates figures as though he is conducting discussions. One of Plato's principal contributions to philosophical thought is his "theory of ideas." Platonic love, a Renaissance phrase, denoting love of spiritual character completely free from sensuality, was first used by Ficino (1433–99) synonymously with Amor Socraticus to denote the kind interest in young men that was imputed to Socrates.

Sources

Ross, William D. 1951. *Plato's theory of ideas*. Oxford: Clarendon Press.
Russell, Bertrand. 1946. *The problem of philosophy*. London: Oxford University Press.
Shafritz, Jay M. 1988. *The Dorsey dictionary of American government and politics*. Chicago: Dorsey.
Sills, David L., ed. 1968. *International encyclopedia of the social sciences*. New York: Macmillan and Free Press.
Zusne, Leonard. 1984. *Biographical dictionary of psychology*. Westport, Conn.: Greenwood Press.

PLOWDEN REPORT. A comprehensive two-volume British educational report, *Children and Their Primary Schools* (1967), on the primary education system in Britain and its relation to secondary education. It made 197 recommendations on such topics as school organization, children's development, and independent schools.

Lady Bridget Horatia Plowden, Née Richmond (b. 1910), was educated at Downe House. She was a director of Trust House Forte Ltd. (1961–72) and became the first woman to chair the Central Advisory Council for Education (1963–66). She established a career as an administrator and was on the board of governors of the Phillippa Fawcett College of Education (1967–76) and of the Robert Montefiore Comprehensive School (1968–79). In 1976 she was honored with a D.Litt. at the University of Loughborough. She also chaired the Independent Broadcasting Authority in 1975–80 and was president of the National Institute of Adult Continuing Education (1980–88).

Sources

The international who's who, 1992–93. London: Europa Publications.

Magnussen, Magnus; Goring, Rosemary; and Thorn, John O., eds. 1990. *Chambers biographical dictionary.* Edinburgh: Chambers Ltd.

Peaker, Gilbert F. 1971. *The Plowden children four years later.* Slough: National Foundation for Educational Research in England and Wales.

Peters, Richard S., ed. 1969. *Perspectives on Plowden.* London: Routledge and Kegan Paul.

Who's who, 1993. London: Adam and Charles Black.

PLUTOCRAT, PLUTOCRACY, PLUTOLOGY, OR PLUTONOMY. A wealthy and powerful person. A body of people who rule only because of their wealth. Political economy.

In Greek mythology Plutus was the son of Demeter and Iasion, the god of wealth and originally the god of agricultural riches. Plutus was blinded by Zeus so that he would distribute his wealth without favor or discrimination or prejudice. Greeks represented him as blind for this reason; as lame because riches come slowly; and with wings because riches disappear more quickly than they come. In time, Plutus recovered his sight and spread his bounty to only honest men.

Sources

Evans, Ivor H. 1989. *Brewer's dictionary of phrase and fable.* 14th ed. London: Cassell.

Hammond, Nicholas G.L., and Scullard, Howard H., eds. 1970. *The Oxford classical dictionary.* Oxford: Clarendon Press.

Higgs, Henry, ed. 1963. *Palgrave's dictionary of political economy.* Reprints of Economic Classics. New York: Augustus M. Kelly, Bookseller.

Jobes, Gertrude. 1962. *Dictionary of mythology, folklore and symbols.* New York: Scarecrow Press.

Leach, Maria, ed. 1950. *Dictionary of folklore, mythology and legend.* New York: Funk and Wagnalls.

McHenry, Robert, ed. 1992. *The new encyclopedia Britannica.* Chicago: Encyclopedia Britannica, Inc.

PODSNAPPERY. English philistinism; a term alluding to insular complacency, self-satisfaction, and a refusal to face what is unpleasant.

Mr. Podsnap is a character in Charles Dickens's *Our Mutual Friend,* a novel published in monthly episodes, 1864–65. Podsnap is a smiling, pompous, and self-satisfied soul, eminently respectable, and one who always knows exactly what Providence means, thus providing comfort and a sense of wonder to those who follow and thoughtlessly accept all he says. His wife had the neck and nostrils of a rocking horse, while his daughter, Georgiana, "the young person," as he called her, was always trying to hide her elbows.

Sources

Evans, Ivor H. 1989. *Brewer's dictionary of phrase and fable.* 14th ed. London: Cassell.

Hammond, Nicholas G.L., and Scullard, Howard H., eds. 1985. *The Oxford companion to English literature.* Oxford: Clarendon Press.

PONTRYAGIN'S PRINCIPLE OF OPTIMALITY. In the practice of economics, for the optimal control process to occur, there are shadow prices; if certain conditions obtain, then the optimal value of control at any time will maximize profit flow in accordance with those shadow prices (Eatwell et al., 1987, vol. 3:910–912).

Lev Semyonovich Pontryagin (1908–88) was born in Moscow. At age 14 he lost his sight but was able to study mathematics and became a professor (1935) at the University of Moscow. He was a topologist and contributed to algebraic topology, and differential equations to optimal control. His *Topological Groups* (1939) became a standard work in this field.

Sources

Eatwell, John; Milgate, Murray; and Newman, Peter. 1987. *The new Palgrave: a dictionary of economics*. London: Macmillan.

Gamkrelidze, R. V. 1986. *L. S. Pontryagin: selected works*. New York: Gordon and Breach Science Publishers.

Morris, Sydney A. 1977. *Pontryagin duality and the structure of locally compact abelian groups*. Cambridge: Cambridge University Press.

PONZI SCHEME. Illegal method of raising money from investors.

Carlo Ponzi (1878–1949) was born in Italy and went to live in Boston in the 1890s. At first he worked as a waiter, a translator, smuggled in aliens, and lived from forgery. In 1919 he devised the plan in whereby he could turn a profit from buying abroad International Postal Reply Coupons and redeeming them in the United States. He and his associates invested $1,250 and in ninety days made $750 profit. He quickly established the Boston Financial Exchange Company, and in the nine months to August 1920 small investors gave him millions. The scheme succeeded, and investors eventually made a 50 percent return in forty-five days. He paid his early customers—and himself—with money from the later ones. When accused of financial malpractice, Ponzi silenced his critics by suing for $500,000. Ponzi used the profits to buy a firm of importers and exporters for whom he once worked; he went on a spending spree and bought a controlling interest in the Hanover Trust Company. In August 1920, when he was reported to the authorities for shady operations, the scheme collapsed. In eight months he had collected $20 million and paid out $15 million. He tried to use $2 million to recoup losses at roulette, failed, and his investors rioted. He was found guilty of mail fraud and jailed for four years. On his release he was found guilty again of fraud and jailed for nine years, but his appeal succeeded and he fled to Florida, where, this time for land swindling, he was again jailed. On his release he was brought back north to serve nine years in jail, and in 1934 he was deported to Italy. He worked, again fraudulently, for Mussolini until he had to escape for his life to South America. He died in Rio de Janiero.

Sources

Deeson, Arthur F.L. 1971. *Great swindlers*. London: Foulsham.

Dunn, Donald H. 1975. *Ponzi! The Boston swindler*. New York: McGraw-Hill.

Green, Jonathan. 1980. *The directory of infamy: the best of the worst.* London: Mills and
    Boon.
Preece, Warren E., ed. 1965. *Encyclopedia Britannica.* Chicago: Encyclopedia Britannica,
    Inc., William Benton.

POPPERIAN. Relating to the twentieth-century philosopher of science, particularly his approach to scientific method and philosophy of social reform. Science establishes reliable knowledge through the falsifiability of hypotheses, not their illustration or verification; social theories tend to authoritarian domination when they espouse a blueprint for change and fail to put the conceptions and experiences of the individual before those of the collectivity. To this end, Popper prefers the use of small-scale social plans rather than great schemes for social reform. Such plans should represent individual interests—sometimes in conflict—and be continually monitored for their adequacy and manageable refinements.

Karl Raimund Popper (b. 1902) was born in Vienna and became a naturalized British citizen in 1945. The son of a cultivated Viennese lawyer, Karl was given a broad and varied education, despite the distressing conditions of life in Vienna after World War I. He wrote a dissertation in psychology and taught at school for some years before leaving for New Zealand (1937). He returned to Britain to teach at the London School of Economics (1946) where he was a professor of logic and scientific method, and retired in 1969. His critique of Marxism is *The Open Society and Its Enemies* (1945); he also criticizes historical prediction in *The Poverty of Historicism* and other works. In 1977 he co-authored *The Self and Its Brain.*

Sources
Devine, Elizabeth; Held, Michael; Vinson, James; and Walsh, George, eds. 1983. *Thinkers of the twentieth century: a biographical, bibliographical and critical dictionary.* London: Macmillan.
Hear, Anthony. 1980. *Karl Popper.* London: Routledge and Kegan Paul.
The international who's who, 1992–93. London: Europa Publications.
Magee, Brian. 1973. *Popper.* 1985 ed. London: Fontana.
Magnussen, Magnus; Goring, Rosemary; and Thorn, John O., eds. 1990. *Chambers biographical dictionary.* Edinburgh: Chambers Ltd.
Popper, Karl 1966. Autobiography. In C. Alec Mace, ed. *British philosophy in the mid-century: a Cambridge symposium.* London: Allen and Unwin.

POST-FORDISM. In some modern industries, an important departure from the dominant managerial pattern of Fordism and neo-Fordism. The change includes new concepts of industrial production, individual-centered manufacturing, flexibility in technical organization and specialization, and diversity in quality production.

See also FORDISM; NEO-FORDISM.

Sources
Lipietz, Alain. 1993. *Towards a new economic order: Postfordism, ecology and democracy.* Cambridge: Polity Press.

Matthews, John. 1989. *Age of democracy: the politics of post-Fordism.* Melbourne: Oxford University Press.

POST-FREUDIAN. Relating to the British School of Psychoanalysis in the generation after Freud. It includes Anna Freud (1895–1982) who spent her life as her father's companion, was analyzed by him, and concentrated her interest on children and adolescents; Melanie Klein (1882–1960); Susan Isaacs (1885–1948); Joan Rivière (1883–1962); Donald W. Winnicott (1896–1971); Geza Roheim (1891–1953); Roger Ernle Money-Kyrle (1898–1980); John Carl Flugel (1884–1955); and William R.D. Fairbairn (1889–1965).

See also FREUDIAN.

Sources

Devine, Elizabeth; Held, Michael; Vinson, James; and Walsh, George, eds. 1983. *Thinkers of the twentieth century: a biographical, bibliographical and critical dictionary.* London: Macmillan.

Gardner, Dorothy E.M. 1969. *Susan Isaacs.* London: Methuen.

Grosskurth, Phyllis. 1986. *Melanie Klein: her world and her work.* New York: Alfred A. Knopf.

Guntrip, Harry. 1971. *Psychoanalytic theory, therapy, and the self: a basic guide to the human personality in Freud, Erikson, Klein, Sullivan, Fairbairn, Hartmann, Jacobson and Winnicott.* New York: Basic Books.

Hughes, Athol, ed. 1991. *The inner world and Joanne Riviere.* Collected papers: 1928–1958. London: Karnac Books.

Khan, M.; Masud, R.; Tizard, Jack P.M.; and Gillespie, W. H. 1971. Obituaries: Donald W. Winnicott (1896–1971). *International Journal of Psychoanalysis* 52:225–228.

Kurzweil, Edith. 1989. *The Freudians: a comparative perspective.* New Haven, Conn.: Yale University Press.

Muensterberger, Warner, and Wilbur, George B., eds. 1951. *Psychoanalysis and culture: essays in honor of Geza Roheim.* New York: International Universities Press.

Obituary: Roger E. Money-Kyrle. 1980. *The Times (London),* August 8:12g.

Peters, Uwe H. 1985. *Anna Freud: a life dedicated to children.* English trans. London: Weidenfeld and Nicolson.

Sutherland, John D. 1989. *Fairbairn's journey into the interior.* London: Free Association Books.

Young-Breuhl, Elisabeth. 1988. *Anna Freud: a biography.* New York: Summit.

Zusne, Leonard. 1984. *Biographical dictionary of psychology.* Westport, Conn.: Greenwood Press.

POTEMKIN VILLAGES. Village facades, especially used to conceal the poverty of the subjects of Catherine the Great.

Grigori Aleksandrovich Potemkin (1739–91) was born near Smolensk into a noble, impoverished family. He joined the Russian Horse Guard in 1755 and became the lover of Catherine II of Russia (1729–96). He was outstanding in Catherine's first Turkish War (1768–74), after which he was her publicly accepted paramour and was influential in determining Russia's domestic and foreign policy. He may have been married to her secretly. He controlled vast landholdings in the south and directed construction of the Russian fleet in the Black Sea. In the second Turkish War (1787–92), he controlled the army, and he was given credit for magnificent victories, even those that were the work of others. An unscrupulous character, politically astute, extremely wealthy, and excessively extravagant, Potemkin is reputed to be the man who won the Crimea for Russia, and the founder of Sebastopol. The villages are so named after his orders that as Catherine II toured by impoverished and destitute villages she would see specially erected facades that would lead her and others to believe the community was well off and that her subjects were happy and loyal.

Sources

Magnussen, Magnus; Goring, Rosemary; and Thorn, John O., eds. 1990. *Chambers biographical dictionary.* Edinburgh: Chambers Ltd.

Soloveytchik, George. 1938. *Potemkin: a picture of Catherine's Russia.* London: Butterworth.

Troyat, Henri. 1980. *Catherine the Great.* Trans. Joan Pinkham. New York: E.P. Dutton.

POTSDAM CONFERENCE. A conference between U.S. President Harry S Truman (1884–1972), British Prime Minister Clement Richard Attlee (1883–1967), and the Russian leader Joseph Stalin (1879–1953) which laid down the Allied plans for central and southeast Europe (July–August 1945). The document was intended to convince all Germans that they were totally defenseless, entirely responsible for the outcome of the ruthless war they had conducted in Europe, had ruined the German economy, that their National-Socialist party, its associations, and laws were destroyed, and that all war criminals were to be brought to justice. It was the last meeting of the leaders of the three great powers. It was followed by the Potsdam Declaration which demanded Japan's surrender; Japan's resistance met with the bombing of Hiroshima a few days later.

In East Germany, Potsdam is an industrial city, capital of the Potsdam district 16 miles southwest of Berlin on the Havel River. A Slav settlement in the tenth century, it was chartered in the fourteenth century and became the residence of Prussian royalty beginning with Frederick the Great who built the palace, Sans Souci (1745–47). Other palaces were erected there, and for two centuries Potsdam became a center for the military. Still standing are the Garrison church (1731) and part of the German Empires archives. The city was badly damaged during World War II.

Sources

Canby, Courtlandt. 1984. *The encyclopedia of historic places.* London: Mansell Publishing.

Feiss, Herbert. 1960. *Between war and peace: the Potsdam conference.* Reprint 1969. Princeton, N.J.: Princeton University Press.

McHenry, Robert, ed. 1992. *The new encyclopedia Britannica.* Chicago: Encyclopedia Britannica, Inc.

Mee, Charles L. 1975. *Meeting at Potsdam.* New York: M. Evans.

POUJADIST, POUJADISM. One who supports antiparliamentary beliefs in France, the aims of the little man, and wants taxes reduced. Lower middle-class dissatisfaction with state interference—especially state tax schemes—in an individual's pursuit of economic self-interest. The state should concern itself only with law and order, and big business and powerful unions should not dominate an economy. In 1956 the Poujadist Association for the Defense of Shop Keepers and Artisans received 3 million votes and secured fifty-two seats in the French Parliament, but in 1958 their influence was swept aside by the ideology of Gaullism.

Pierre Poujade (b. 1920) was born in Saint Cere and was an executive on a French newspaper. During World War II he served in the Royal Air Force in Britain; later he became a publisher and bookseller (1954–58) and was active in French politics. In 1953 he organized a strike of shopkeepers against the French government's tax policy. He headed an independent conservative movement, a union for the defense of traders and artisans, in France. It won fifty-two seats in the 1956 elections on a platform of anti-intellectualism, covert anti-Semitism, antisocialism, and anti-European slogans. It based its strength on the protest of France's small shopkeepers and lower middle-class and self-employed manual workers. The party opposed taxation, inflation, and central government. When De Gaulle rose to power after 1958, the movement and its leaders no longer held public attention. Poujade continued his work at local government levels. He led an economic and social mission to Romania (1990), and founded a French center for tourists and gastronomes (La Vallée Heureuse, La Bastide-l' Evéque).

Sources

The international who's who, 1992–93. London: Europa Publications.

Magnussen, Magnus; Goring, Rosemary; and Thorn, John O., eds. 1990. *Chambers biographical dictionary.* Edinburgh: Chambers Ltd.

McHenry, Robert, ed. 1992. *The new encyclopedia Britannica.* Chicago: Encyclopedia Britannica, Inc.

POWELLISM, POWELLITE. Views advanced in Britain in the 1960s that had support in the right wing of the Conservative party; among the views were those that advocated individualism in politics and espoused the strengths of the British Constitution; monetarism in economics and opposition to Britain's entry into the European Economic Community; consideration of race as a sensible criterion for Britain's immigration policy. A follower of such views.

(John) Enoch Powell (b. 1912) was born at Stechford, Birmingham, and educated at King Edward's School, Birmingham, and Trinity College, Cambridge. In 1937–39 he was a professor of Greek at the University of Sydney; in World War II he enlisted as a private in 1939, was commissioned in 1940, and rose to brigadier. In 1946 he joined the Conservative party and in 1950 was elected the member for Wolverhampton. He was parliamentary secretary, Ministry of Housing (1955–57), financial secretary to the Treasury in 1957 and minister for health in 1960. In 1963 he refused to serve in the cabinet of Sir Alec Douglas-Home, the British prime minister. He was dismissed from the shadow cabinet of the Conservative party in 1968. Because of his opposition to Britain's entry into the common market, he did not stand for reelection in February 1974, but was returned in October as an Ulster Unionist. His outspoken attitude on social problems allegedly due to uncontrolled immigration of colored people has made him the center of controversy and charges of racial prejudice and bigotry. He lost his seat in South Devon in 1987.

Sources

Abse, Leo. 1973. *Private member*. London: MacDonald.

Abse, Leo. 1989. *Margaret, daughter of Beatrice: a politician's psychobiography of Margaret Thatcher*. London: Jonathan Cape.

The international who's who, 1992–93. London: Europa Publications.

Magnussen, Magnus; Goring, Rosemary; and Thorn, John O., eds. 1990. *Chambers biographical dictionary*. Edinburgh: Chambers Ltd.

Moritz, Charles, ed. 1964. *Current biography yearbook*. New York: H. W. Wilson.

Pilkington, Edward. 1992. Enoch the sceptic. *Guardian Weekly,* June 21:21.

Robbins, Keith. 1990. *British political life in the twentieth century*. Oxford: Basil Blackwell.

PRESLEYMANIA. A resurgence of public interest in the 1950s U.S. rock and roll singer, particularly during the U.S. presidential election campaign of 1992 when several candidates used his name to attract voters.

Elvis Aaron Presley (1935–77) was born in Tupelo, Mississippi, and was taken to Memphis in 1948 where he attended Humes High School and played guitar. He became a truck driver (1953) and in 1954 made a record with a group, The Blue Moon Boys, "That's Alright Mama," which was an instant success. Colonel Tom Parker promoted Elvis, became his manager (1955), and in 1956 Elvis made his first great hit, "Heartbreak Hotel." He scandalized the musical public with his hip-swivelling style, and he became a household name, especially among the young. By 1957 Elvis Presley was a rich star and bought Graceland, his home, near Memphis. He served in the U.S. Army in Germany for two years and in 1960, on returning to America, made popular films for ten years. He resumed concert tours in 1970 and was renowned for his outrageous costumes. He died at Graceland, allegedly a victim of drugs; the day after his death 80,000 came to pay their respects. His career afforded him ninety-four gold single records, included thirty-two feature films that grossed over $200 million, and in 1992 the U.S. Post Office honored him with a 29 cent stamp. To many, Elvis is still alive—at least in spirit.

Sources

Hammontree, Patsy G. 1985. *Elvis, a bio-bibliography*. Westport, Conn.: Greenwood Press.

Hopkins, Jerry. 1971. *Elvis: a biography*. New York: Warner Books.

Hopkins, Jerry. 1981. *Elvis: the final years*. New York: Playboy Publishers.

Marcus, Greil. 1991. *Dead Elvis: a chronicle of a cultural obsession*. London: Viking Press, Penguin.

Vellega, Dick. 1989. *Elvis and the colonel*. London: Grafton.

Wark, McKenzie. 1989. Elvis listen to the loss. *Art & Text*. December–February:24–28.

PRIDE'S PURGE. The expulsion on December 6, 1648, of about 140 members from the Long Parliament in England.

Thomas Pride (d. 1658) commanded a regiment at Naseby (1645) and was with Oliver Cromwell at Preston (1648), Dunbar (1650), and Worcester (1651). On Army Council orders, Colonel Pride stood at the entrance of the House of Commons and either arrested or excluded most members, hence the name "Pride's Purge." Most of those excluded had continued to negotiate with King Charles I after the second Civil War, which was in defiance of the Army Council. They had also opposed the trial of the king. The army did not believe the king could be trusted. After the purge, what remained of the Long Parliament was known as the "Rump," comprised of only fifty to sixty members. The purge made it possible for the army and its supporters to have Parliament push through matters relating to the execution of the king and establishment of the Commonwealth. Pride was one of the judges who signed the king's death warrant (1649). He did not support Cromwell becoming a king, and he took a place in Cromwell's upper house.

Sources

Howatt, Gerald M.D. 1973. *Dictionary of world history.* London: Thomas Nelson.

McHenry, Robert, ed. 1992. *The new encyclopedia Britannica.* Chicago: Encyclopedia Britannica, Inc.

Stephen, Leslie, and Lee, Sydney, eds. 1917. *The dictionary of national biography.* London: Oxford University Press.

PRIESTLEY FORMULA. A formula for the remuneration of Britain's civil servants that was introduced in a Royal Commission on the Civil Service (1955). The formula was based on fair comparisons with the current pay of outside staff on broadly comparable work, taking into account differences in other conditions of service.

Sir Edmund Raymond Priestley (1886–1974), a scientist and educationist, was born in Tewkesbury, Gloucestershire, the second of eight children of the headmaster of Tewkesbury Grammar School. He was educated in his father's school and taught there for a year before reading geology at Bristol University College (1905–7) and took part in the British Antarctic expedition (1907–9). On his return to England, he contributed to Ernest Shackleton's *The Heart of the Antarctic* (1909). He later returned to the Antarctic with Captain R. F. Scott, and his experiences are told in Priestley's *Antarctic Adventure* (1914). On returning to England, Priestley served in World War I and was awarded the Military Cross. He then turned to academic administration, and after various positions in England he became a vice-chancellor of Melbourne University, Australia (1935–38), and afterward of Birmingham University (1938–52). After retirement, he continued his public service, first as chairman of the Royal Commission on the Civil Service (1953–55). The Priestley Commission accepted the principle and set out guidelines to link pay throughout the civil service with equivalent positions in industry. Priestley's last public office was as president of the Royal

Geographical Society (1961–63). He was knighted in 1949 and held the Polar
Medal and Bar and Founders Medal of the Royal Geographical Society.
Sources
Blake (Lord), and Nicholls, C. S., eds. 1986. *Dictionary of national biography 1971–
     1980.* Oxford: Oxford University Press.
Marsh, Arthur. 1979. *Concise encyclopedia of industrial relations.* Westmead, Farnbor-
     ough, Hants: Gower.

PROCRUSTEAN, PROCRUSTEAN BED. Relating to the production of conformity by violent means and inflexibility in outlook. An arbitrary and brutally
applied standard.

Procrustes (or Polpemon, or Damastes) was a fabulous Greek giant, a highwayman and robber who ensnared passing travelers near Eleusis. He would force
the tall captives onto his short bed and the short victims onto his long bed. Then
he stretched and cut the unfortunates to size. A Procrustean bed is therefore a
term for a predetermined standard or system that tolerates no deviation or change
and into which a person is forced to fit. Procrustes died by his own methods at
the hand of the Attic hero, Theseus.
Sources
Bell, Robert E. 1982. *Dictionary of classical mythology.* Santa Barbara, Calif.: ABC-
     CLIO.
Grimal, Pierre. 1990. *A concise dictionary of classical mythology.* Oxford: Basil Black-
     well.
Hammond, Nicholas G.L., and Scullard, Howard H., eds. 1970. *The Oxford classical
     dictionary.* Oxford: Clarendon Press.
McHenry, Robert, ed. 1992. *The new encyclopedia Britannica.* Chicago: Encyclopedia
     Britannica, Inc.

PROSPERO SYNDROME. The belief that the European is the harbinger of
civilization, remaining immune to the ways of the savage; the opposite to the
Kurtz syndrome (Obeyesekere, 1992).

In Shakespeare's *The Tempest* (1611) Prospero, the banished duke of Milan,
deposed by his brother, rules a desert island with his daughter, Miranda, and
two ethereal beings, Ariel and Caliban. Prospero uses magic to control others,
and he extends his knowledge through sorcery. In an atmosphere of forgiveness,
he uses his powers on his enemies, whom chance has thrown in his path, and
eventually he leads his daughter to fall in love with Ferdinand, son of the king
of Naples. Prospero returns to Milan, gives up magic, brings social justice to
society, and again accepts his moral obligations, albeit in melancholy style. As
the central character, he is part of several themes in the play: philosopher-
magician, selfish father, embittered and tyrannical exile, a clear failure and a
partial success. An unpleasant character, he harasses, threatens, and complains
as a matter of course. A dramatic character but unconflicted, he had already
resolved his own problems before being exiled, and he decides that with his
magic he can, should, and will control the destiny of others. In this regard, he

treats Ariel and Caliban deplorably. Consequently, to many *The Tempest* is an allegory of colonial exploitation and inhuman treatment of local, original inhabitants by remaining distant from and superior to their individual needs and culture. Prospero is possibly taken from Prospero Adorno (fl. 1460–1588), a deposed duke of Genoa.

See also KURTZ SYNDROME.

Sources

Boyce, Charles. 1990. *Shakespeare A to Z.* New York: Facts on File.

Campbell, Oscar J., and Quinn, Edward. 1966. *The reader's encyclopedia of Shakespeare.* New York: Thomas Y. Crowell.

Obeyesekere, Gananath. 1992. *The apotheosis of Captain Cook: European mythmaking in the Pacific.* Princeton, N.J.: Princeton University Press.

Quennell, Peter, and Johnson, Hamish. 1973. *Who was who in Shakespeare.* London: Weidenfeld and Nicolson.

PULITZER PRIZE. Annual monetary prizes for outstanding work in American journalism, letters, and music, established in 1917 from a fund Pulitzer left to Columbia University.

Joseph Pulitzer (1847–1911) was born in Mako, Hungary, raised in Budapest, and at 17 left home to make his fortune as a soldier. He was rejected by the Austrian, French, and British military because of his defective eyesight. He went to America in 1864 as a recruit for the Union Army in the Civil War (1861–65) and was discharged in 1865. Penniless, he went to Saint Louis and became a reporter. He was naturalized in 1867 and began to acquire defunct newspapers. After buying the bankrupt *St. Louis Dispatch,* Pulitzer combined it with the *Post,* and created the *St. Louis Post Dispatch,* which, under his editorship, gained a national reputation for the good sense in its editorials. In 1883 he also published and edited the *New York World.* He pursued human interest stories, undertook crusades on social and political issues, and followed a liberal policy in editorials. In 1887 he established the *Evening World* in New York. His fame was secured when he established the School of Journalism at Columbia University (1903) and the fund for the prizes.

Sources

Garraty, John A., ed. 1977. *Dictionary of American biography.* Supplement 5. New York: Charles Scribner's Sons.

Malone, Dumas, ed. 1935. *Dictionary of American biography.* Vol. VIII. New York: Charles Scribner's Sons.

Morris, William, ed. 1965–66. *Grolier universal encyclopedia.* New York: American Book-Stratford Press, Inc.

Seitz, Don Carlos. 1924. *Joseph Pulitzer, his life and letters.* New York: Simon and Schuster.

Stuckey, William J. 1981. *The Pulitzer Prize novels: a critical backward look.* 2d ed. Norman: University of Oklahoma Press.

Swanberg, William A. 1967. *Pulitzer.* New York: Charles Scribner's Sons.

Van Doren, Charles, ed. 1974. *Webster's American biographies.* Springfield, Mass.: G. and C. Merriam.

PUSEYISM. A nineteenth-century term—often used opprobriously—for the ideas of the Tractarian Movement that originated from the name of E. B. Pusey, taken from an essay he wrote in *Tracts for the Times,* in December 1833.

Edward Bouverie Pusey (1800–1882) was born near Oxford. Originally, his name was Edward Bouverie. His family was of Huguenot origin; they became lords of the Manor at Pusey, near Oxford, and from it took their new name. In 1818 he entered Christ Church Oxford and in 1823 became a fellow of Oriel. In 1828 he was ordained deacon and priest and appointed Regius professor of Hebrew at Oxford and canon of Christ Church. In 1833 he joined the Oxford Movement and published his tract "Thoughts on the Benefits of the System of Fasting Enjoined by Our Church." Earlier writings had been anonymous, but Pusey's initials were appended to this essay, and the ideas of the movement became known as "Puseyism." He published regularly and became a notable among members of the Oxford Movement and eventually became its leader in 1841. He was suspended from preaching at the university for two years in 1843 after delivering the sermon "The Holy Eucharist a Comfort of the Penitent." The sermon was considered a teaching error by several influential academic divines. Consequently, the distribution of his tracts grew rapidly. His thoughts on the Real Presence became widely discussed, as were his ideas on the reality of priestly absolutism. The practice of private confession dates from his work. He championed the High Church movement and defended its doctrines, upheld the principle of revelation as laid down by the early church, and rejected the use of philosophy as the basis of theological thought. Also he led a controversy over the university's old tutorial system. On his death, Pusey House, Oxford, was founded in his name. He published *The Doctrine of the Real Presence* (1855), *The Real Presence* (1857), *The Minor Prophets, with a Commentary* (1860), and *Daniel the Prophet* (1864).

Sources

Butler, Perry. 1983. *Pusey rediscovered.* London: S.P.C.K.

Cross, Frank L. 1974. *The Oxford dictionary of the Christian Church.* 2d ed. New York: Oxford University Press.

Forrester, David. 1989. *Young Doctor Pusey: a study in development.* London: Mowbray.

Lough, Arthur G. 1981. *Dr. Pusey—restorer of the church.* Newton Abbot: A. G. Lough.

Magnussen, Magnus; Goring, Rosemary; and Thorn, John O., eds. 1990. *Chambers biographical dictionary.* Edinburgh: Chambers Ltd.

Stephen, Leslie, and Lee, Sydney, eds. 1917. *The dictionary of national biography.* London: Oxford University Press.

PUSSYFOOT. In a political campaign moving with caution, guile and cunning.

William Eugene Johnson (1862–1945) was born in Coventry, New York. He worked as a journalist and later was a special officer in the U.S. Indian Service (1908–11), where his nickname "Pussyfoot" was given to him for the methods he used in raiding gambling saloons in Indian Territory. In the United States and Europe he lectured vigorously for the cause of prohibition. He lost an eye in a struggle when dragged by medical students from a lecture platform in London.

Sources

Evans, Ivor H. 1989. *Brewer's dictionary of phrase and fable.* 14th ed. London: Cassell.

Magnussen, Magnus; Goring, Rosemary; and Thorn, John O., eds. 1990. *Chambers biographical dictionary.* Edinburgh: Chambers Ltd.

Matthews, Mitford M. 1966. *Americanisms: a dictionary of selected Americanisms on historical principles.* Chicago: University of Chicago Press.

PYGMALION EFFECT. The raising of managers' expectations of subordinates boosts productivity; a cost saving approach to increasing motivation in work organization (Eden, 1990).

In Greek legend, Pygmalion, the misogynist King of Cyprus, fell in love with the ivory statue he sculpted of Aphrodite. He prayed that it would come to life, the gods obliged, and the couple were married (Ovid's *Metamorphoses,* x). The modern version appears in Shaw's comedy *Pygmalion* (1913). It tells of a London flower girl, Eliza Doolittle, and her "Pygmalion," a professor of phonetics, Henry Higgins. She asks him to help her improve her speech; but he goes further and flatters, cajoles, and threatens her until she agrees to let him transform her from a flower girl into a lady fit to grace any London drawing room—providing that conversation extends no further than the weather and health. She rises to many occasions brilliantly, but not without an occasional faux pas that provide grounds for much of the play's humor. In an amusing subsidiary plot, her father, Alfred Doolittle, a rascal of a dustman, is made respectable by a legacy from a philanthropist while his daughter is elevated into London society. In his preface to the play Shaw tells that Higgins and Eliza do not marry, even though the play itself leaves the impression that the two will never part.

Sources

Benét, William R. 1990. *The reader's encyclopedia of world literature and arts, with supplement.* New York: Thomas Crowell.

Eden, Dov. 1990. *Pygmalion effect in management: productivity as a self-fulfilling prophecy.* New York: Free Press, Lexington Books.

PYRRHIC VICTORY. Any victory gained at too great an expense.

Pyrrhus, king of Epirus (318–272 B.C.), was a great military adventurer who carried out campaigns against Rome in Sicily during 280–275 B.C. He was one of the great generals of antiquity. Tarentum invited Pyrrhus to assist it against Rome in 280 B.C. He defeated the Romans at Heracleria on the Siris, but did so at great cost, after which he was said to exclaim: "Another such victory and we are lost!" In 279 B.C. he won again at Asculum. He remained in Sicily until 276 B.C. and was defeated by the Romans at Beneventum in 275 B.C. That year he returned to Epirus with 9,000 men and seized most of Macedonia. While attempting to wrest Greece from Antigonus in a night attack on Argos, Pyrrhus was killed by a roof tile thrown down on him by an old woman.

Sources
McHenry, Robert, ed. 1992. *The new encyclopedia Britannica.* Chicago: Encyclopedia
    Britannica, Inc.
Magnussen, Magnus; Goring, Rosemary; and Thorn, John O., eds. 1990. *Chambers bi-
    ographical dictionary.* Edinburgh: Chambers Ltd.
Smith, Benjamin. 1903. *The Century cyclopedia of names.* London: The Times.

PYRRHONISM. Skepticism in philosophy.

Pyrrho(n) (c. 365–275 B.C.), a native of Elis in the Peloponnese, lived in the time of Alexander the Great and joined his expedition in Persia and India. He was the founder of the Skeptical Pyrrhonian School of Philosophy, which maintained that certain knowledge on any matter was unattainable and that suspension of judgment was true wisdom and the source of happiness. He wrote nothing himself, but his views were recorded by a disciple, Timon the Sillographer. Pyrrhonism influenced the Middle and New Academy of Athens, and philosophers in seventeenth-century Europe with the republication of works on Greek skepticism from the third century. Much of Pyrrhon's teaching has been preserved in the poems of Timon of Philus.

Sources
McHenry, Robert, ed. 1992. *The new encyclopedia Britannica.* Chicago: Encyclopedia
    Britannica, Inc.
Magnussen, Magnus; Goring, Rosemary; and Thorn, John O., eds. 1990. *Chambers bi-
    ographical dictionary.* Edinburgh: Chambers Ltd.

PYTHAGOREAN. A philosophical school that asserts that reality is mathematical in nature, that philosophy can purify the spirit, and that the human soul can unite with the divine. Followers of the school were to keep their membership secret and be loyal to each other and accept that certain symbols were of great mystical importance. The brotherhood was suppressed when it pursued politics, and by the middle of the fourth century was extinct. Nevertheless, it influenced the development of classical Greek and medieval philosophy, and its doctrines were applied to the theory of music, acoustics, astronomy, and geometry. It was one of the first schools to suggest that the brain was vital to the soul and that the planets revolved around the sun.

Pythagoras (c. 580–500 B.C.) was a native of Samos and settled at Crotona in Italy where he founded a brotherhood that followed his ascetic practices and vegetarianism, and studied his philosophical teachings. In 532 B.C. he fled the tyranny of Samos and established an academy at Croton. The brotherhood was suppressed, but the Pythagorean doctrines survived. It was he who assigned a mathematical basis to the universe and used musical principles in his system. He supposed the heavenly bodies to be divided by intervals according to the law of musical harmony. This gave rise to the idea of the harmony of the spheres. As a mathematician, Pythagoras is credited with the discovery known as the Pythagorean Theorem, that the square on the hypotenuse of a right angled triangle is equal to the sum of the squares on the other two sides. The Pythagorean Letter, or the Samian letter, is the twentieth in the Greek alphabet, known as epsilon, and was regarded by Pythagoras a symbol of vice and virtue going their own ways. None of his writings is extant.

Sources

Benét, William R. 1990. *The reader's encyclopedia of world literature and arts, with supplement.* New York: Thomas Crowell.

McHenry, Robert, ed. 1992. *The new encyclopedia Britannica.* Chicago: Encyclopedia Britannica, Inc.

Magnussen, Magnus; Goring, Rosemary; and Thorn, John O., eds. 1990. *Chambers biographical dictionary.* Edinburgh: Chambers Ltd.

Smith, Benjamin. 1903. *The Century cyclopedia of names.* London: The Times.

Q

QUEEN ANNE'S WAR, QUEEN ANNE'S BOUNTY. The second series of wars (1702–13) fought between France and Britain for control of the American continent; it was largely a naval war conducted off the West Indies, Carolina, and the coast of New England. The British supported the colonists along the border of Canada and elsewhere. At the war's end, Britain gained possession of Nova Scotia, Newfoundland, and the Hudson Bay area from France. On the European continent, the war was known as the War of the Spanish Succession, which ended in the Treaty of Utrecht and gave Britain recognition of its Protestant succession to the throne. Queen Anne's Bounty was a perpetual grant of the first fruits and tithes that Henry VIII had long before confiscated for the Crown (1534). It was to augment the costs of maintaining the clergy.

Queen Anne (1665–1714), the second daughter of England's James II, was raised in the Church of England and married the prince of Denmark (1683). After her father's flight from the throne (1688), Anne attended the coronation of William and his wife, her sister, Mary (1689). On Mary's death (1694) Anne was much favored by King William, and she showed much loyalty to him. When he died, she ascended the throne (1702), her own father having died six months beforehand. She was a popular queen at first, and especially so for the establishment in November 1704 of the bounty named after her. She worked for the union of Scotland and England (1707), which became the great political success of her reign. But during the later part of her rule she was troubled by conflict among her favorites at court and lost much of the popularity she had once enjoyed.

Sources

Howatt, Gerald M.D. 1973. *Dictionary of world history.* London: Thomas Nelson.
Langer, William L. 1968. *An encyclopedia of world history.* 4th ed. Boston: Houghton Mifflin.

McHenry, Robert, ed. 1992. *The new encyclopedia Britannica.* Chicago: Encyclopedia
    Britannica, Inc.
Stephen, Leslie, and Lee, Sydney, eds. 1917. *The dictionary of national biography.* Lon-
    don: Oxford University Press.

QUEENSBERRY RULES. Rules applied originally to boxing, but later to standards of proper behavior in a conflict, physical or verbal.

John Sholto Douglas, eighth marquis of Queensberry (1844–1900), was born
in London and served in the navy from 1859 to 1864. He helped found the
Amateur Athletics Club in 1860 and was an authority on boxing. With John
Graham Chambers, a prominent athlete, Queensberry was part author in framing
the prize-ring rules that carry only his name. Among other conditions, the
Queensberry Rules insisted on boxing gloves, three-minute rounds, no seconds
in the ring, no wrestling or hugging, and no shoes or boots with sprigs (1867).
He sat in the House of Lords as a Scottish representative peer (1872–80). In
1881 he published *The Spirit of the Matterhorn,* a meditation in blank verse.
He was the father of Lord Alfred Douglas (1870–1945), the poet and associate
of Oscar Wilde (1854–1900). Queensberry's intense disapproval of their intimate
relationship led to the trial and imprisonment of Wilde in 1895.
Sources
McHenry, Robert, ed. 1992. *The new encyclopedia Britannica.* Chicago: Encyclopedia
    Britannica, Inc.
Magnussen, Magnus; Goring, Rosemary; and Thorn, John O., eds. 1990. *Chambers bi-
    ographical dictionary.* Edinburgh: Chambers Ltd.
Stephen, Leslie, and Lee, Sydney, eds. 1917. *The dictionary of national biography.* Sup-
    plement. London: Oxford University Press.

QUIRINAL. The Italian government as distinct from the Vatican; one of the
hills of Rome.

Quirinus, an Italian divinity like Mars or Jupiter, is associated with the ancient
Sabine settlement, part of which formed the original Rome. The site itself corresponds to the Quirinal. Quirinus was so like Mars that some myths assert he
is another form of that deity. Also, in Roman legend he is identified with Romulus, founder of Rome (753 B.C.) and its first king (753–716 B.C.). He was the
son of Mars and the vestal, Rhea Silvia. When Romulus disappeared mysteri-
ously in a storm, the Romans, who believed he had been changed into a god,
worshiped him as Quirinus and ranked him next in importance to Jupiter and
Mars.
Sources
Graves, Robert. 1968. *New Larousse encyclopedia of mythology.* London: Hamlyn.
McHenry, Robert, ed. 1992. *The new encyclopedia Britannica.* Chicago: Encyclopedia
    Britannica, Inc.
Mercatante, Anthony S. 1988. *Encyclopedia of world mythology and legend.* New York:
    Facts on File.

QUISLING. A supporter of, and particularly an official aid to, the enemy after its occupation of one's native land.

Vidkun Quisling (1887–1945) was born at Fyresdal, Norway; he was trained at Norway's military academy (1911) and by 1931 had reached major in the field artillery. He served as military attaché at Leningrad (1918–19) and Helsinki (1919–21) and was employed by the League of Nations for work with its high commissioner for refugees, Fridtjof Nansen (1861–1930), to save refugees in Russia (1922–1927). Quisling represented British interests at the Norwegian legation in Moscow (1927–29). He entered the Norwegian Parliament and became minister of defense (1931–33). He resigned his seat to form the National Unity party patterned on the Nazis in Germany, but he was never reelected to Parliament. At the outbreak of World War II, he urged Hitler to occupy Norway and assisted the Germans in their subsequent invasion. He declared himself head of the Norwegian government, but it collapsed, and instead he was appointed minister-president in 1942 under the authority of the Nazi Reich commissioner. At the end of World War II when the Germans were expelled, Quisling was arrested, tried, found guilty of high treason against Norway, and shot by firing squad.

Sources

Hayes, Paul M. 1971. *Quisling: the career and political ideas of Vidkun Quisling, 1887–1945.* Newton Abbot: David and Charles.

Hoidal, Oddvar K. 1989. *Quisling: a study in treason.* Oslo: Norwegian University Press.

Langer, William L. 1968. *An encyclopedia of world history.* 4th ed. Boston: Houghton Mifflin.

McHenry, Robert, ed. 1992. *The new encyclopedia Britannica.* Chicago: Encyclopedia Britannica, Inc.

Magnussen, Magnus; Goring, Rosemary; and Thorn, John O., eds. 1990. *Chambers biographical dictionary.* Edinburgh: Chambers Ltd.

R

RACHMANISM. Conduct of a landlord who charges extortionate rents for property where squalor and slum conditions prevail.

Peter Rachman (1920–62) was a Polish Jew who endured the Nazi and Russian regimes. After Hitler's invasion of Russia (1941), he was sent to fight beside the British in the Middle East, and after World War II he lived in Britain (1946) at refugee camps. He worked in factories and as a tailor, and began to rent and sublet flats (1950). He demanded rapacious rents, paid in cash, in Paddington, a slum area of postwar London. In time he had properties all over London. In 1957 the Rent Act lifted rent restrictions, and Rachman raised the rents of his properties, particularly those of prostitutes. Thugs were used to beat the rent from recalcitrant tenants. Eventually, the problem attracted a parliamentary debate, and a new Rent Act was passed in 1965 to curb the practice. After his death in 1962, Rachman's reputation grew as a gross and gluttonous man with an insatiable lust for prostitutes, gambling, and the upper classes. In 1989 the British play, *Singer,* was loosely based on Rachman's life, and in Jacobin style critically presented contemporary British politics as riddled by the same policies that Rachman had followed.

Sources

Magnussen, Magnus; Goring, Rosemary; and Thorn, John O., eds. 1990. *Chambers biographical dictionary.* Edinburgh: Chambers Ltd.

Radford, Edwin, and Smith, Alan, eds. 1981. *To coin a phrase.* London: Macmillan.

RADCLIFF REPORT. A government report (April 1962) on the British security services. The Radcliffe Committee, established in May 1961, recommended that for entry into the British secret service all applicants should be positively vetted, that the "need to know" principle should be upheld, and that members of the security services should be properly trained and indoctrinated so as to prevent further cases like those of the recently jailed spy, George Blake (b. 1922). The committee comprised Sir Gerald Templer (1898–1979), director of military intelligence, Sir David (Ronald) Milne (1904–82), and Sir Kenneth Gilmour Younger (1908–76).

Cyril John Radcliffe, viscount (1899–1978), was educated at Haileybury and New College, Oxford, and studied law. He was director general of the Ministry of Information (1941–43). He was made a lord of appeal in 1949 and a life peer, and created a viscount in 1962. He chaired many commissions on taxation, profits, and income, and the border between India and Pakistan; drew up a constitution for Cyprus (1956); and investigated Britain's security services (1961–63). After retirement from judicial work, he became the chancellor of the new University of Warwick (1966).

Sources

Blake (Lord), and Nicholls, C. S., eds. 1986. *Dictionary of national biography 1971–1980*. Oxford: Oxford University Press.

Magnussen, Magnus; Goring, Rosemary; and Thorn, John O., eds. 1990. *Chambers biographical dictionary*. Edinburgh: Chambers Ltd.

Pincher, Chapman. 1984. *Too secret too long*. London: Sidgwick and Jackson.

West, Rebecca. 1982. *The meaning of treason*. London: Virago.

RAMBO. A macho-type man who practices survival techniques and prefers the life of a loner; a political advocate of violent retribution.

Rambo is a hulking Vietnam veteran whose violent expressions of anger and frustration clearly indicate the sense of failure and confusion felt by U.S. soldiers who fought in Vietnam. He was created by Professor David Morrell in his novels *First Blood* (1972) and made famous in the films by Sylvester Stallone, *Rambo* (1982) and *Rambo: First Blood II* (1985). President Ronald Reagan, once referred to Rambo as an inspiring figure, but Morrell said Rambo illustrated only escapism. Many condemned the violence of his action because it set an example for young criminals; however, only ten actual criminal cases have been attributed to this influence. Morrell wrote the book as an antiwar novel about a man who was programmed as a war machine. It was based on the material given him in English literature classes by Vietnam veterans, especially by those who were troubled by Morrell as an authority figure (Tulloch, 1991).

Sources

Tulloch, Sara. 1991. *The Oxford dictionary of new words*. Oxford: Oxford University Press.

Zoglin, R. 1985. An outbreak of Rambomania. *Time,* 125:72–73.

RAMSEY PRICES, RAMSEY SAVING RULE, RAMSEY TAXES. In economics, prices—Pareto optimal prices—that attain a set profit level and maximize the total of an industry's prices and producers' surplus. A rate of saving, multiplied by the marginal utility of money. (This should always be the same as the amount by which the total net rate of enjoyment of a utility falls short of the highest rate of enjoyment.) Ramsey taxes are those that raise a set revenue from proportionate taxes on commodities, while the decrease in utility is minimized (Rutherford, 1992).

Frank Plumpton Ramsey (1903–30) was born in Cambridge, England; his father, a mathematician, was president of Magdelene College, and his brother was archbishop of Canterbury. He was educated at Winchester and Trinity College, Cambridge, and became a fellow of King's College (1924) and a university lecturer in mathematics. He drafted a translation of Ludwig Wittgenstein's *Tractus logicophilosophicus* (1922). His main contributions to economics were in his theories of taxation and saving.

Sources

Eatwell, John; Milgate, Murray; and Newman, Peter. 1987. *The new Palgrave: a dictionary of economics.* London: Macmillan.

Ramsey, Frank P. 1927. A contribution to the theory of taxation. *Economic Journal* 37: 47–61.

Ramsey, Frank P. 1928. A mathematical theory of saving. *Economic Journal* 38:543–559.

Rutherford, Donald. 1992. *Dictionary of economics.* London: Routledge.

RAPACKI PLAN. A plan (1957) to have no nuclear weapons in Poland, Czechoslovakia, East or West Germany. The monitors of the plan were to come from North Atlantic Treaty Organization and Warsaw Pact countries, and the plan itself was to be a model for other zones to be free of nuclear weapons; it was also to be the basis for a policy to reduce all conventional forces. The Soviets approved the plan when it was presented to the United Nations General Assembly on October 2, 1957; but the United States and Britain did not support it because the plan favored the USSR troop establishment and would have involved future talks on East and West Germany which Britain rejected at the time.

Adam Rapacki (1909–70) was born in Zwierzyniec in eastern Poland, and his father was a prominent leader of the cooperative movement. Adam was educated in Warsaw at the Higher School of Economics and joined the Young Workers' Association. From graduation in 1932 until World War II, he worked at the Institute for Social Research and the Scientific Institute of the Study of Economic Cycles. As a prisoner of war during 1939–45, he worked for the underground resistance. On returning to Poland he joined the Socialist party, and when it was reconstructed as part of the Communist party he achieved considerable influence and was elected to the Central Committee (1947) and the Political Committee (1948). He was minister for marine affairs (1949–50), minister for higher education (1950–51), and minister for foreign affairs (1956–58). He opposed the Polish participation in the invasion of Czechoslovakia and would not support the anti-Zionist campaign that purged liberals and Jews from the ministry. For this he lost his position in 1969.

Sources
Candee, Marjorie D., ed. 1958. *Current biography yearbook.* New York: H. W. Wilson.
Cook, Chris. 1983. *Macmillan dictionary of historical terms.* London: Macmillan.
Howatt, Gerald M.D. 1973. *Dictionary of world history.* London: Thomas Nelson.
Moritz, Charles, ed. 1970. *Current biography yearbook.* New York: H. W. Wilson.

RAPPIST, RAPPITE. A member of the Harmonist community. It sought a speedy second coming of Jesus Christ and amassed much wealth for the Lord's use; members practiced self-denial, celibacy, and tight economy, and held all things in common. With assets worth millions, it owned farms, vineyards, dairies, and shares in banks and the railways. With time, however, numbers fell, and by 1906 the community had gone.

George Rapp (1770–1847) was born at Würtemberg, Germany. He studied at the village school and became a linen weaver. His religious beliefs so favored socialism that he and his followers were persecuted by the government. Consequently, he and 300 followers migrated to America and settled in Pennsylvania (1803). In 1814, the Harmonists moved to Indiana and established the Harmony community. By 1824, their property was worth $150,000; they sold the holdings to Robert Owen (1771–1858) who used the site and the buildings to establish the community of New Harmony. During this time, Rapp, an autocratic leader, urged celibacy on his followers, a practice that was not accepted by many of the younger people. In the early 1830s, a group of 250 of them seceded from the Harmony Society and went to Pennsylvania to establish themselves as the New Philadelphia Society. They settled near Economy. Rapp remained the spiritual leader of the community until his death.

See also OWENITE.

Sources
Arndt, Karl J.R. 1972. *George Rapp's successors and material heirs, 1847–1916.* Rutherford, N.J.: Fairleigh Dickinson Press.
Bowden, Henry W. 1977. *Dictionary of American religious biography.* Westport, Conn.: Greenwood Press.
Cross, Frank L. 1974. *The Oxford dictionary of the Christian Church.* 2d ed. New York: Oxford University Press.
Dudley, Lavinia P. 1963. *The encyclopedia Americana.* International ed. New York: Americana Corp.
Fogarty, Robert S. 1980. *Dictionary of American communal and utopian history.* Westport, Conn.: Greenwood Press.
Magnussen, Magnus; Goring, Rosemary; and Thorn, John O., eds. 1990. *Chambers biographical dictionary.* Edinburgh: Chambers Ltd.
Melton, Gordon J. 1989. *The encyclopedia of American religions.* Detroit: Gale Research Inc.

RASPUTINISM. Libertine principles and practices relating to corrupting influence over government.

Grigory Efimovitch Novikh (1871?–1916) was a Russian peasant, born at

Pokrovskoe, Tobolsk Province, Siberia, and, after coming to Saint Petersburg in 1907 wielded a malign, magnetic power over the Tsarina and others at the Russian Court, causing the dismissal of Prime Minister Kokovstev. He took the name of Rasputin; he thought God had inspired him and believed one should sin in order to be forgiven. He was a mystic and a favorite at the court of the Russian emperor, Nicholas II. Rasputin means literally "debauchee" and is used elusively of one who resembles Rasputin in having an insidious, corruptive influence over the governing class in particular. The secret of his popularity at court was due to an alleged miracle he had performed in restoring the health of the young Grand Duke Alexis. Both Nicholas II and his consort were frequently exhorted to dismiss him, but all such efforts failed. In 1916 he was assassinated at the Yusupov Palace by a party of noblemen.

Sources

De Jonge, Alex. 1982. *The life and times of Grigorii Rasputin.* London: Collins.

Magnussen, Magnus; Goring, Rosemary; and Thorn, John O., eds. 1990. *Chambers biographical dictionary.* Edinburgh: Chambers Ltd.

McHenry, Robert, ed. 1992. *The new encyclopedia Britannica.* Chicago: Encyclopedia Britannica, Inc.

Rasputin, Maria, and Barham, Pate. 1977. *Rasputin, the man behind the myth: a personal memoir.* London: W. A. Allen.

RASTAFARIAN OR RAS TAFARIAN. In Jamaica those who reject Western culture, assert blacks are the chosen people, claim the former emperor of Ethiopia, Haile Selassie, is God Incarnate, the Messiah of the black people, and believe he will return to ensure safe passage to the African homeland. They believe they are the reincarnation of the Israelites, whom God punished for their sins by placing them beneath the inferior race of white peoples. Their true homeland is Africa, heaven on earth, where eventually the black people will have whites as servants. These ideas were evident in 1953 when groups of Jamaicans formed and rejected Christianity and the Jamaican-European culture they had endured for so long. Returning to Africa is not as important to them as it once was; in recent years they have turned more to black militancy, religious mysticism, smoking of marijuana (ganja), and wearing their hair uncombed in "dreadlocks."

Makonnen, Tafari, later Ras (Prince) Tafari, Prince Haile Selassie (1891–1975) was the emperor of Ethiopia from 1930 to 1974. He was educated by French missionaries and was made governor of Sidamo and later Harer Province. A political progressive, he helped break the feudal practices of the nobles and establish a competent civil service. In 1923 he got his country admitted to the League of Nations. He was crowned emperor in 1930, but when Mussolini invaded Abyssinia in 1935, Haile Selassie fled to England, returning in 1941 when the British liberated his people. He helped form the Organization of African Unity (1960s), but in the mid-1970s was strongly opposed and charged with corruption, especially after the 1973 famine and ensuing economic and political chaos, and the mutiny among his militia. He lived as a prisoner in his palace and may have been murdered. After he died, he was made spiritual leader of his followers, the Ras Tafarians.

Sources

Barrett, Leonard E., Sr. 1989. *The Rastafarians.* Boston: Beacon.

McHenry, Robert, ed. 1992. *The new encyclopedia Britannica.* Chicago: Encyclopedia Britannica, Inc.

Magnussen, Magnus; Goring, Rosemary; and Thorn, John O., eds. 1990. *Chambers biographical dictionary.* Edinburgh: Chambers Ltd.

RAWLSIAN JUSTICE. A normative theory of justice with three practical features: first, everyone should have the same right to the broadest range of basic liberties that is compatible with a similar system of liberty for all; second, socioeconomic inequalities should be arranged to give the greatest benefit to those who are least advantaged, and be available freely and fairly to all persons; and third, justice should provide its own motivational supports, such that everyone has a sense of what is just and always desires it.

John Bordley Rawls (b. 1921) was born in Baltimore, Maryland, graduated from Kent School (1939), and completed his postgraduate studies at Princeton and Cornell universities. He served with the U.S. armed forces (1943–46); was a Fulbright fellow at Oxford (1952–53); and after being a professor of philosophy he became the James Bryant Conant University professor at Harvard (1979–91) and is now emeritus. He wrote many articles for professional journals, and his ideas led to many extensions, refinements, and alternative theories. He helped edit *Philosophical Review* (1956–59). His *A Theory of Justice* (1971), one of the most discussed texts in social and political philosophy since World War II, is an alternative to the utilitarian view of justice, and it seems most suited to a constitutional democracy and an economy that espouses competition.

Sources

Devine, Elizabeth; Held, Michael; Vinson, James; and Walsh, George, eds. 1983. *Thinkers of the twentieth century: a biographical, bibliographical and critical dictionary.* London: Macmillan.

Green, Philip. 1985. Equality since Rawls: objective philosophers, subjective citizens and rational choice. *Journal of Politics* 47:970–997.

The international who's who, 1992–93. London: Europa Publications.

Miller, David, ed. 1987. *The Blackwell encyclopedia of political thought.* Oxford: Basil Blackwell.

Peltit, Philip. 1980. *Judging justice.* London: Routledge.

Rawls, John. 1971. *A theory of justice.* Cambridge, Mass.: Belknap Press of Harvard University Press.

Turner, Ronald. 1987. *Thinkers of the twentieth century.* Chicago: St. James Press.

Who's who in America. 1993. Chicago: Marquis.

Wolf, Robert. 1977. *Understanding Rawls: a reconstruction and critique of "A theory of justice."* Princeton, N.J.: Princeton University Press.

REAGANOMICS, REAGANISM, REAGAN DOCTRINE, REAGAN REV-OLUTION. Reaganomics was an economic policy—a variety of supply-side economics—that appeared to dominate the United States during the presidency of Ronald Reagan (1980–88). The policy argued that lower taxation rates would lead new capital into greater investment; then jobs would be created, the economy would grow, and revenue from taxes would rise. The policy appears to have been driven by a belief in market supremacy and the need to cut government spending and taxes, and it seems to have advantaged the rich and disadvantaged the poor. It was overoptimistic in predictions for the U.S. economy. At the end of the period, the United States' current account deficit was so great that it led the next president to change completely the budget strategy of the Reagan period. Reaganism included the economic policy, and a set of conservative values about the family, religion, and feminist movements. The Reagan Doctrine was a U.S. foreign policy, so named in *Time,* in April 1985, that emphasized threats to the Western world from the Soviets and promoted regimes that sought to suppress communism by permitting limited intervention in local conflicts by U.S. forces. The Reagan Revolution, another consequence of Reaganomics, asserted that a nation's well-being grew with the extended economic benefits that only tax cuts would induce, rather than from greater spending on welfare programs.

Ronald W. Reagan (b. 1911) was a movie actor who helped introduce labor unions to Hollywood in the late 1930s, served in World War II, and later promoted General Electric and members of the Republican party who were up for reelection. His standing in the party rose in 1964 during the presidential campaign of Barry Goldwater (b. 1909); consequently, Reagan became governor of California (1967–75) and U.S. president (1980). His regime was noted for Reaganomics, record budget deficits, the invasion of Grenada, and the Iran-Contra affair.

Sources

Boskin, Michael J. 1985. *Reaganomics examined: successes, failures, unfinished agendas.* San Francisco: Institute for Contemporary Studies.

Cannon, Lou. 1982. *Reagan.* New York: Putnam.

Evans, Rowland, and Novak, Robert. 1981. *The Reagan revolution.* New York: E. P. Dutton.

Greenstein, Fred I., ed. 1983. *The Reagan presidency: an early assessment.* Baltimore: Johns Hopkins University Press.

Halliday, Fred. 1986. *The making of the second cold war.* 1989 ed. London: Verso.

Kymlicka, B. B., and Matthews, Jean. 1988. *The Reagan revolution.* Chicago: Dorsey.

Reagan, Ronald W. 1965. *Where's the rest of me?* New York: Duell, Sloan and Pearce. Reprinted 1984, London: Sidgwick and Jackson.

Wills, Garry. 1987. *Reagan's America: innocents at home.* Garden City, N.Y.: Doubleday.

RECHABITE. Descendant of Jonadab whose father would not drink wine or dwell in houses; a total abstainer from intoxicating drinks, especially a member of the Independent Order of Rechabites founded in 1835; a tent-dweller. The original Rechabites were a reactionary group of Israelites, who retained their nomadic ways, for religious reasons, well after others had settled in Canaan. They vowed to live in tents as did their ancestors, and not to till the soil, build houses, or grow grapes and drink wine. Their origins are obscure; some say they came from the Cinites (or Kenites), and others from Jonadab. They represent a protest against contemporary civilization and a preference for simplicity in life.

The founder of the Rechabites was Jehonadab (or Jonadab, fl. 842 B.C.), son of Re'chab (fl. before 842 B.C.) who encouraged Jehu (842–815 B.C.), a king of Israel, to abolish the Tyrian Baal worship (Jeremiah 35: 6,8,7,14,16,19). The house of Rechab fled for protection into Jerusalem at the approach of Nebuchadnezzar, who ruled from 604 to 562 B.C. As a reward for their adherence to the ordinance of Jehonadab, Jeremiah (fl. 7th–6th centuries B.C.) promised them that they should never lack a man to represent them before Yahweh. Later Jewish tradition states that the Rechabites intermarried with the Levites.

Sources

Cross, Frank L. 1974. *The Oxford dictionary of the Christian Church.* 2d ed. New York: Oxford University Press.

Evans, Ivor H. 1989. *Brewer's dictionary of phrase and fable.* 14th ed. London: Cassell.

Harrison, Roland K., ed. 1988. *The new Ungar's Bible dictionary.* Chicago: Moody Press.

McDonald, William, ed. 1967. *New Catholic encyclopedia.* New York: McGraw-Hill.

McHenry, Robert, ed. 1992. *The new encyclopedia Britannica.* Chicago: Encyclopedia Britannica, Inc.

Roth, Cecil E., ed. 1971. *Encyclopedia Judaica.* New York: Macmillan.

REICHIAN. A discredited branch of psychoanalytic theory that emphasized sexual frustration at the failure to reach orgasm as the origin of most neuroses, and advocated the use of bio-energetics, character analysis, and the belief in the value of orgone, a blue life force, as therapeutics.

Wilhelm Reich (1897–1957) was born in Austria and practiced psychoanalysis while a medical student in Vienna. Early he was convinced that the orgasm was essential to good mental health, as he wrote in *The Function of the Orgasm* (1927). He invented the "orgone accumulator," which was reputed to collect particles of energy without any mass, and transferred them to the user of the device with remarkable consequences for their sexual satisfaction. He was a communist, but the German Communist party expelled him in 1933, after which he went to Scandinavia and immigrated to America (1939). He founded the Orgone Institute, and in 1955 he was imprisoned in the United States for selling, as medical equipment, his Orgone Energy Accumulator. He became a cult figure during the sexual revolution of the 1960s in the United States.

Sources

Cattier, Michael. 1971. *The life and work of Wilhelm Reich.* Trans. Ghislaine Boulanger. New York: Horizon.

Devine, Elizabeth; Held, Michael; Vinson, James; and Walsh, George, eds. 1983. *Think-*

ers of the twentieth century: a biographical, bibliographical and critical dictionary. London: Macmillan.

Miller, David, ed. 1987. The Blackwell encyclopedia of political thought. Oxford: Basil Blackwell.

Reich, Wilhelm. 1988. Passion of youth: an autobiography, 1897–1922. Eds. Mary Boyd Higgins and Chester M. Raphael and trans. Philip Schmitz and Jerii Tompkins. New York: Farrar, Straus and Giroux.

Rycroft, Charles. 1971. Reich. London: Fontana, Collins.

Shraf, Myron. 1983. Fury on earth: a biography of Wilhelm Reich. London: Andre Deutsch.

Zusne, Leonard. 1984. Biographical dictionary of psychology. Westport, Conn.: Greenwood Press.

REILLY'S LAW. The Law of Retail Gravitation, a method designed to establish the relative amount of retail trade that two cities attract from an intermediate point at the vicinity of the breaking point, that is the point up to which one center dominates retail trade influence and beyond which the other tends to dominate. The attraction is almost proportional to the population of the two cities, and in inverse proportion to the distance of the cities from the intermediate town. The law does not seem to apply where the difference between populations is very great.

William John Reilly (1899–1970) was born in Pittsburgh, Pennsylvania, and studied at the Carnegie Institute of Technology and the University of Chicago (Ph.D., 1927). After developing small-sampling theory and scientific techniques for marketing research (1927), he taught market research at the University of Texas (1927–29), directed research at Erickson Company (1929–32), and founded and directed the National Institute for Straight Thinking (1932). He published several books on advertising, including What Place Has the Advertising Agency in Market Research? (1929), Marketing Investigation (1929), Sales Quota Procedure (1930), and How to Avoid Work (1949). He wrote many popular how-to-be-successful books on work careers, human relations, and clear thinking in business—for example, The Law of Intelligent Action Applied in Business Relations (1945). He applied a theory of social roles to the analysis of the marketplace and was concerned to see a scientific approach taken to marketing through the use of valid and reliable techniques of data collection, basic surveys, organization of a clearinghouse on marketing data, and the effective training of detached and impartial scholars in marketing research. For over twenty years he was a business consultant, and in 1959 many professional institutions honored him for his efforts to bring scientific research principles to marketing.

Sources

Bartels, Robert. 1961. The development of marketing thought. Homewood, Ill.: Irwin.

Goodall, Brian. 1987. The Penguin dictionary of human geography. Harmondsworth, Middlesex: Penguin.

Johnston, Ronald J. 1981. The dictionary of human geography. Oxford: Basil Blackwell.

Nemmwers, Erwin E. 1978. *Dictionary of economics and business.* Totowa, N.J.: Rowman and Littlefield.
New York Times. Obituary. November 18, 1970:50.
Reilly, William J. 1931. *The law of retail gravitation.* New York: Knickerbocker Press.
Who was who in America, 1969–73. Vol. 5. Chicago: Marquis.

REUTERS. An authority on information, a reliable source for news, as in "according to Reuters."

Israel Beer (1816–99), a Jew, was baptized in 1844 in Berlin where he took the name of Paul Julius Reuter. At age 13, while working in a bank, he apparently developed an interest in the telegraph in Göttingen. In 1845 he married, and with his father-in-law's capital, Beer became a shareholder in a Berlin bookshop and publisher, Reuter and Startgardt. In the late 1840s he immigrated to Paris where he established a news firm. It failed, but in Aachen (1850), after acquiring forty pigeons, he and his wife had them carry late news of stock prices printed on thin tissue paper in a silken bag under their wings. When the telegraph wire from Berlin reached him, Reuter used a relay of horses to carry news. Later, he turned to news collecting and distribution, but because others firmly controlled the German wire services he went to Britain (Christmas 1850). He established offices in London and collected news from agents on the continent. By 1857 he had become a British subject. Although at first he failed to secure the interest of *The Times* in his political news gathering, he had much support from other papers. After establishing news links in America, his services extended throughout the world. He was created a baron, and his name became synonymous for authoritative news and reliable journalism.

Sources

Jones, Roderick. 1951. *A life in Reuters.* London: Hodder and Stoughton.
Lawrenson, John, and Barber, Lionel. 1985. *The price of truth: the story of the Reuters millions.* Edinburgh: Mainstream.
Storey, Graham. 1951. *Reuters' century, 1851–1951.* London: Parrish.

RHODES SCHOLAR. An outstanding all-round young scholar.

Cecil John Rhodes (1853–1902) was born at Bishop's Stortford, Hertfordshire, England. He was educated at the local grammar school and because of his poor health went to South Africa where he worked a moderately prosperous claim in the newly discovered diamond fields of the Orange Free State. In 1873 he returned to England to complete his education at Oxford University (1881). During this period he increased his holdings in the Kimberley diamond fields and by 1888 dominated gold mining in the Transvaal. Rhodes won election to the Cape House of Assembly and served as prime minister of Cape Colony (1890–96). Using his vast wealth, he attempted to extend the British Empire in Africa from the Cape to Cairo, but in 1896 after one of his expansionist ventures failed, he resigned and devoted himself to the growth of Rhodesia. At his death he left a large endowment for the international scholarships that bear his name.

Sources

Flint, John. 1971. *Cecil Rhodes.* Boston: Little, Brown.

Lee, Sidney, ed. 1920. *Dictionary of national biography: supplement 1901–1911.* London: Oxford University Press.

McHenry, Robert, ed. 1992. *The new encyclopedia Britannica.* Chicago: Encyclopedia Britannica, Inc.

Magnussen, Magnus; Goring, Rosemary; and Thorn, John O., eds. 1990. *Chambers biographical dictionary.* Edinburgh: Chambers Ltd.

Millin, Sarah G.L. 1933. *Rhodes.* London: Chatto and Windus.

Williams, Basil. 1968. *Cecil Rhodes.* Westport, Conn.: Greenwood Press.

RICARDIAN, RICARDO'S IRON LAW OF WAGES, RICARDO'S LAW OF COMPARATIVE COSTS. Relating to the ideas of the English political economist. The iron law of wages is a pessimistic law of economic development that argues that if the market wage rises above the "natural" level, this will encourage people to have larger families (or attain a higher survival rate), which in time gradually expands the labor supply and will depress the market wage rate; if the market wage rate falls below the subsistence level, then families will delay having children (or fewer of the children would attain adulthood) and the market wage will rise again to its "natural" level. The law of comparative costs states that under certain conditions of international trade, a nation will benefit from importing some goods, even though it can produce them cheaper itself.

David Ricardo (1772–1823) was the son of a Dutch Sephardic Jew who had become wealthy as a London stockbroker. After a short education at a Jewish school in Amsterdam, at age 14 Ricardo entered the family business, but he quit and left the Jewish faith when he married a Quaker and became a Christian. In 1799 he became interested in political economy and in 1809 published "The High Price of Bullion, a Proof of the Depreciation of Banknotes." By 1814 success on the stock exchange enabled him to retire. In 1817 he published his major work, *On the Principles of Political Economy and Taxation,* which includes a discussion of values, wages, and rent. The work was noted for the attention it gave to laws governing the division of wealth between participants and production. From 1819 until his death he was a radical M.P. for Portarlington, and in his few but influential speeches he foreshadowed the policy of free trade—the hallmark of the Anti-Corn Law League—that would become so popular in Britain's economic policy. Other aspects of his theorizing have become eponymous, for example, Ricardo Equivalence Theorem, Ricardo Law of Comparative Costs, Ricardo Socialists, and Ricardo-Hayek effect.

Sources

Blaug, Mark. 1986. *Great economists before Keynes.* Brighton, England: Harvester Press.

Eatwell, John; Milgate, Murray; and Newman, Peter. 1987. *The new Palgrave: a dictionary of economics.* London: Macmillan.

Magnussen, Magnus; Goring, Rosemary; and Thorn, John O., eds. 1990. *Chambers biographical dictionary.* Edinburgh: Chambers Ltd.

Sills, David L., ed. 1968. *International encyclopedia of the social sciences.* New York: Macmillan and Free Press.

Weatherall, David. 1976. *David Ricardo: a biography.* The Hague: Martinus Nijoff.
Wood, John C., ed. 1985. *David Ricardo: critical assessments.* London: Croom Helm.

RIESMAN'S TRADITION-, INNER-, AND OTHER-DIRECTED TYPES.
Three types of character which refer primarily to mechanisms of conformity.
The mechanisms may be found in characters, individuals, and societies. In tra-
dition-directed types, social change is minimal, and obedience to tradition is
near-automatic; inner-directed types tend to obey according to internalized
controls instilled in childhood; and other-directed types tend to conform with a
sensitive attention to the requirements of one's contemporaries.

David Riesman (b. 1909), born into a medical family, attended Harvard where
he worked on the *Crimson,* studied law, and held a postgraduate scholarship
while helping to prepare Carl J. Friedrich's *Constitutional Government and Politics* (1937). After working briefly with a Boston law firm, he taught law at the
University of Buffalo and entered psychoanalysis with Erich Fromm (1939). In
a search for a new vocation, he studied at Columbia Law School but was drawn
to anthropology and sociology and went to study the social sciences at the
University of Chicago (1946). He worked on community studies, researched
education, and by 1957 had moved into sociology at Harvard's Department of
Social Relations where he worked until retirement.

Sources

Devine, Elizabeth; Held, Michael; Vinson, James; and Walsh, George, eds. 1983. *Think-
    ers of the twentieth century: a biographical, bibliographical and critical
    dictionary.* London: Macmillan.
Gans, Herbert, et al. 1979. *On the making of Americans: essays in honor of David
    Riesman* [with bibliography to 1978]. Philadelphia: University of Pennsylvania
    Press, pp. 319–346.
Riesman, David, with Glazer, Nathan. 1952. *Faces in the crowd: individual studies in
    character and politics.* New Haven, Conn.: Yale University Press.
Riesman, David. 1960. *The lonely crowd: a study of changing American character.* New
    Haven, Conn.: Yale University Press.
Riesman, David. 1988. On discovering and teaching sociology: a memoir. *Annual Review
    of Sociology* 14:1–24. Palo Alto, Calif.: Annual Reviews Inc.
Riesman, David. 1990. Becoming an academic man. In Bennett M. Berger, ed. 1990.
    *Authors of their own lives: intellectual autobiographies by twenty American so-
    ciologists.* Berkeley: University of California Press, pp. 22–74.
Weiland, S. 1988. An interview with David Riesman. *Michigan Quarterly Review* 27:
    373–387.
Who's who in America, 1992–93. Chicago: Marquis.

ROBENS REPORT. British report by the Committee on Safety and Health at
Work (1970–72) which recommended the Health and Safety at Work Act (1974)
and the establishment of the Health and Safety Commission. The report referred
to the poor safety and health arrangements at work, recommended more self-
regulation, and brought together both management and unions in a system of

unified legislation. The report is the first comprehensive study of occupational safety in the United Kingdom.

Alfred Robens (b. 1910) was born in Manchester and educated at the Council School. A trades unionist, he was elected a Labor M.P. for the Wansbeck Division of Northumberland (1945–50) and Blyth (1950–60), and was made minister for labor (1951). He sat on a Royal Commission on Trade Unions and Employers' Association (1965–68) and chaired the Safety and Health at Work inquiry (1970–72). He was made a life peer, Lord Robens of Woldingham, and appointed chancellor of the University of Surrey (1966–77). He published various articles for journals and magazines, and *Engineering and Economic Progress* (1965), *Industry and the Government* (1979), and *Ten Year Stint* (1972).

Sources

Howells, Richard W.L. 1972. The Robens report. *Industrial Law Journal* 4:185–196.

The international who's who, 1992–93. London: Europa Publications.

Magnussen, Magnus; Goring, Rosemary; and Thorn, John O., eds. 1990. *Chambers biographical dictionary* Edinburgh: Chambers Ltd.

Marsh, Arthur. 1979. *Concise encyclopedia of industrial relations*. Westmead, Farnborough, Hants: Gower.

ROBERT'S RULES OF ORDER. An authority on parliamentary procedures.

Henry Martyn Robert (1837–1923) was born in Robertville, South Carolina, son of a pastor. He attended the United States Military Academy (1853–57), and taught natural and experimental philosophy, and military engineering. He became the officer in charge of San Juan Island, Washington Territory, and in the U.S. Civil War he rose to major. As an engineer, he was responsible for defending the New England coastline, Washington, and Philadelphia. Until 1901 he worked on improving America's rivers, coasts, and harbors, and he retired as a brigadier-general and chief of Army Engineers. In response to events at an unruly church meeting, Roberts set down procedures for the orderly conduct of a meeting. They were published as *Pocket Manual of Rules of Order for Deliberative Assemblies* (1876). The book was one of several works, which included *The Water Jet as an Aid to Engineering Construction* (1881) and a topical index of army engineering reports (1881). The book on rules of order was revised in 1915; in 1921 it was entitled *Parliamentary Practice* and in 1923 it became *Parliamentary Law*. It was revised again in 1943.

Sources

Robert, Henry M. 1967. *Robert's rules of order.* With a guide and commentary by Rachel Vixman. Old Tappan N.J.: F. H. Revell.

Starr, Harris E., ed. 1944. *Dictionary of American biography*. Supplement 1. New York: Charles Scribner's Sons.

ROBERTSON REPORT. Reports of several British courts of inquiry (Comnd 3692 and Comnd 3855) into the steel industry in Wales (1966), industrial relations in the motor industry, Rootes Motors, Lindwood (1968) and Girling Ltd.,

Bromborough (1968), and the work of railway guards and shunters (1967) and airport firemen (1970).

Donald James Robertson (1926–70) was born in Glasgow and educated at Hutcheson's Boys' Grammar School in Glasgow and the University of Glasgow. He taught political economy (1945–50), was a research officer at the Oxford Institute of Statistics (1950–51), and lectured at the University of Glasgow (1951–61), where he became a professor of applied economics (1961–69) and industrial relations (1969–70). He chaired the Wages Council (1955–69) and many courts of inquiry into industrial disputes. He published contributions to scholarly and professional journals, and *Factory Wage Structures and National Agreements* (1960), *Economics and Wages* (1961) and *Labor Market Issues of the 1970s* (1970).

Sources

Evory, Ann, ed. 1983. *Contemporary authors.* New Revision Series. Vol. 10. Detroit: Gale Research.

Marsh, Arthur. 1979. *Concise encyclopedia of industrial relations.* Westmead, Farnborough, Hants: Gower.

ROBINSON CRUSOE ECONOMY. A type of economy referred to in late nineteenth-century discussions of economic thought to show the principles of supply and demand. The term *Crusoe* came to mean a rational economic individual who would deploy his available resources to maximize his satisfaction in the present and the foreseeable or immediate future.

Robinson Crusoe is the central character in the book *The Life and Strange Surprizing Adventures of Robinson Crusoe of York, Mariner* (1719). The book purported to be a true narrative by the central character himself. There was no indication that it had been written by Daniel Defoe (1660–1731). The story was based on the published account of the experiences of Alexander Selkirk (1676–1721), a shoemaker's son from Scotland, who went to sea on the Cinque Ports galley, argued with Captain Stradling, and at his own request was left on the desert island, Juan Fernandez, off the Chilean coast (1704–19) until rescued by Captain Woodes Rogers. Selkirk built two huts on the island, became skilled at catching wild goats and making clothes from their skins. Also he made knives from old iron hoops. Rogers published the original account after Selkirk's arrival in England in 1711. In his fictionalized account, Defoe describes how Crusoe made a life for himself, found the footprint of a human savage, befriended him, named him Friday, and attempted to educate him and make him a Christian. In 1712, Selkirk returned to the life of a recluse in Largo, Fifeshire; later he married but found he could not settle down, went back to life as a sailor, and died at sea.

Sources

Benét, William R. 1990. *The reader's encyclopedia of world literature and arts, with supplement.* New York: Thomas Y. Crowell.

Carpenter, Humphrey, and Pritchard, Mari. 1984. *The Oxford companion to children's literature.* New York: Oxford University Press.

Eatwell, John; Milgate, Murray; and Newman, Peter. 1987. *The new Palgrave: a dictionary of economics.* London: Macmillan.

Hammond, Nicholas G.L., and Scullard, Howard H., eds. 1985. *The Oxford companion to English literature.* Oxford: Clarendon Press.

Stephen, Leslie, and Lee, Sydney, eds. 1917. *The dictionary of national biography.* London: Oxford University Press.

ROBINSON RULE. Opposite to the Nosbinor Rule, that is, "We cannot use coefficients of correlations based on aggregates of data—the so-called 'ecological correlation'—to make statements about relationships involving individual members of that population" (Dodge and Martin, 1970:312).

William S. Robinson (b. 1913) was born in Los Angeles, educated in philosophy at the University of California, Los Angeles, and on a scholarship went to Columbia University where he studied statistics and sociology (Ph.D., 1940) and later taught (1938–46). He was also chief statistician at the Bureau of Applied Social Research (1940–46). At the University of California he was appointed a professor of sociology (1946–62) in the Department of Anthropology and Sociology, published the rule bearing his name (1950), and afterward joined the Department of Sociology, University of Oregon (1962), specializing in statistics, sociological theory, and research methods. He was a member of professional associations of statisticians, psychologists, and sociologists, and was a director of the National Institute of Mental Health Research Training Program. In 1970 he resigned from the Department in 1970 in protest over the departmental policy regarding the training of research sociologists. An inspiring, charismatic teacher, he was honored by former students at the Pacific Sociological society meeting in May 1973. Until 1985, when he became ill, he worked on the application of principal components analysis to problems in archaeology.

See also NOSBINOR RULE.

Sources

Dodge, David L., and Martin, Walter T. 1970. *Social stress and illness: mortality patterns in industrial society.* Notre Dame, Ind.: University of Notre Dame Press.

Jaques Cattell Press, ed. 1968. *American men and women of science: the social and behavioral sciences.* New York: Jaques Cattell Press and R. R. Bowker.

Robinson, William S. 1950. Ecological correlations and the behavior of individuals. *American Sociological Review* 15:351–357.

Personal Communication.

ROBINSON-PATMAN ACT. An antitrust measure, the Anti-Chain Store Act (1936), which sought to curb transactions in which large purchasers received discounts and rate rebates, and tended to injure competitors and reduce competition. The act was pushed through Congress by pressure from small independent retail merchants who claimed that the big chain stores were being given favored treatment by manufacturers and wholesalers.

James William Robinson (1878–1964) was born in Coalville Summit County, Utah, attended public schools, and graduated from Brigham Young University and Law School at the University of Chicago (1912). He practiced in Utah (1912–33) and was then elected as a Democrat from Utah to the Seventy-third and six succeeding congresses (1933–47). He chaired the Committee on Public Lands and Committee on Roads, and was an unsuccessful candidate for reelection in 1946.

John William Wright Patman (1893–1976) came from Texas where he attended public schools and studied at Hughes Springs High School and graduated in law from Cumberland University in Lebanon, Tennessee (1916). After being admitted to the bar, he began practice in Hughes Springs, and in World War I he was first a private and later a machine-gun officer. He was elected as a Democrat to the Seventy-first Congress and served from 1929 until 1976. He was chairman of the Select Committee on Small Business; the Joint Economic Committee; the Joint Committee on Defense Production; and the Committee on Banking and Currency.

Sources

Jacob, Kathryn A., and Ragsdale, Bruce A. 1989. *Biographical directory of the United States Congress: 1774–1989.* Bicentennial ed. Washington, D.C.: U.S. Government Printing Office.

Plano, Jack C., and Greenberg, Milton. 1989. *The American political dictionary.* New York: Holt, Rinehart and Winston.

ROCHDALE REPORT. The report of a British committee (1970) that reviewed the organization and structure of the shipping industry. The committee made recommendations about manpower and the training of seafarers and shore staff, approved the development of interunion cooperation through the British Seafarers Joint Council, advocated a merger between the Merchant Marine Service and Association, the Merchant Navy Airline Officers Association, and the Radio Electronics Officer's Union, and recommended that all naval ratings be members of the National Union of Seamen.

John Durival Kemp, first Viscount Rochdale (b. 1906), was created Viscount Rochdale of Rochdale, co-palatine of Lancaster (1960). He was educated at Eton and studied at Trinity College, Cambridge. He became chairman of Kelsall and Kemp Ltd. of Rochdale (1950–71), deputy chairman of W. Riding Worsted and Woollen Company Ltd. (1969–72), and of Williams and Glyn Bank Ltd. and held many other positions of prestige in the United Kingdom. He was an honorary colonel in the 851st Field Battery, Westmorland and Cumberland, Royal Artillery (1959–67); and president of the National Union of Manufacturers (1953–56). In 1961–62 he chaired a Committee of Inquiry into Major Ports of Great Britain and of National Ports Council (1964–67); he was chairman of the Committee of Inquiry into Shipping Industry (1967–70) and a director of National and Commercial Banking Group Ltd. (1971–77).

Sources

The international who's who, 1992–93. London: Europa Publications.

Marsh, Arthur. 1979. *Concise encyclopedia of industrial relations.* Westmead, Farnborough, Hants: Gower.

Montague-Smith, Patrick, ed. 1980. *Debretts Peerage and Baronetage 1980.* London: Debrett's Peerage Ltd.

ROCKEFELLER, RICH AS ROCKEFELLER. The American equivalent of Croesus, sometimes referred to as a "Regular Rockefeller." To be exceedingly wealthy.

John Davison Rockefeller (1839–1937) was born in Richford, New York, and was educated at Moravia, New York, and later in an academy when the family moved to Owega. He also went to Cleveland High School (1853), and although he wanted further education, his father insisted he be a businessman. After three years as a commission agent, he went into business in Cleveland with a partner, and, dealing in meat, grain, and miscellany, they enjoyed the boom in foodstuffs during the Civil War. After the war, Rockefeller bought out his partner, and his career in oil expanded rapidly. In 1870 he established Standard Oil Company with his brother William (1841–1922), and used it to get control of America's oil trade. He amassed a fortune from oil before his Standard Oil trust was dissolved by the Supreme Court (1911) after years of legal wrangling. The firm was the largest trust in the world. He distributed over $500 million to medical research, universities, and the Baptist Church, and he established the Rockefeller Foundation (1913) to promote the well-being of humankind. His philanthropies included the University of Chicago and the Rockefeller Institute for Medical Research (1901).

Sources

Collier, Peter, and Horowitz, David. 1976. *The Rockefellers: an American dynasty.* New York: Holt, Rinehart and Winston.

Fosdick, Raymond B. 1952. *The story of the Rockefeller Foundation.* New York: Harper.

Latham, Earl. 1949. *John D. Rockefeller: robber baron or industrial statesman?* Boston: D. C. Heath.

McHenry, Robert, ed. 1992. *The new encyclopedia Britannica.* Chicago: Encyclopedia Britannica, Inc.

Magnussen, Magnus; Goring, Rosemary; and Thorn, John O., eds. 1990. *Chambers biographical dictionary.* Edinburgh: Chambers Ltd.

Nevins, Allan. 1940. *John D. Rockefeller: the heroic age of American enterprise.* New York: Charles Scribner's Sons.

Partridge, Eric. 1970. *Name into word: proper names that have become common property: a discursive dictionary.* 2d rev. ed. Freeport, N.J.: Books for Libraries.

Schulyer, Robert L., and James, Edward T., eds. 1944. *Dictionary of American biography.* Supplement 2. New York: Charles Scribner's Sons.

RODHAMISM. The growing influence during the early months of 1993— attributable more to nepotism than to feminism—of U.S. President Clinton's wife in the White House and in American public life.

Hillary Diane Clinton, née Rodham (b. 1947), was born in Chicago, where her father was a clothing store owner and a Republican. As a teenager, she was deeply impressed at meeting Martin Luther King, Jr. She was religious and became a devout Methodist, aiming to relieve the suffering of others; she upholds personal salvation and applied Christianity, and always has a Bible with her. She attended Maine East and later Maine South high schools, studied at Wellesley College (1965–69), and was initially a Young Republican, but by 1968 had become a Democrat and supported Eugene McCarthy. In 1969 she was chosen to make the graduation speech for her class, and later she studied law at Yale University, where she edited a left-wing magazine, led demonstrations against the Vietnam War, worked for the Children's Defense Fund, and helped to investigate Richard Nixon. She joined a leading U.S. law firm in Arkansas, earned a high salary, and twice was placed among the top 100 U.S. lawyers. Within eight weeks of her husband being inaugurated as U.S. president in January 1993, Hillary Clinton, who insisted she be known as Hillary Rodham, was more popular than her husband with the U.S. people and saw her influence grow as she became a regular member of conferences attended by her husband, and especially when she was appointed to head the health care committee.

Sources

Carlson, Margaret. 1993. At the center of power: the First Lady wants more than clout. She wants to have a life too. Can she find a formula? *Time* (Australia), May 10: 23–27.

Kaus, Mickey. 1993. Thinking of Hillary: the perils of creeping Rodhamism. *The New Republic,* February 15, 4074:6.

Kay, Ernest, ed. 1991. *The world's who's who of women: 1990–91.* 10th. ed. Cambridge: International Biographical Center.

Warner, Judith. 1993. *Hillary Clinton: the inside story.* Sydney, Australia: Pan Macmillan.

Who's who in American law, 1985. Chicago: Marquis.

Who's who in emerging leaders of America: 1987. 1st ed. Wilmette, Ill.: Marquis Who's Who.

ROE V. WADE. A U.S. Supreme Court decision (1973) that made abortion legal in the United States and became a symbol of any U.S. woman's right to choose to have an abortion before viability and to obtain it without undue interference by the state.

Norma "Pixie" McCorvey (b. 1948?), raised in an unstable family, left school in tenth grade. She married at 16, became pregnant, left her young husband, returned to her mother, and lost the custody of the daughter to her mother and stepfather. She claimed that one night in August 1969 she was raped outside Augusta, Georgia. On returning to Dallas and finding herself pregnant, she failed to get an illegal abortion, and was found by Linda Coffee and Sarah Weddington, two lawyers looking for a woman plaintiff for a suit to change the Texas abortion laws. Norma agreed, providing her name not be used. They decided on Jane Roe because at the time the lawyers had another couple helping them, Mary and John "Doe." On March 3, 1970, Coffee filed two suits, *Roe* v. *Wade* and *Does* v. *Wade.* The issue was fought up to the U.S. Supreme Court and, in Norma's case, on January 22 1973, the decision was made in favor of a woman's right to abortion. For ten years Norma maintained her anonymity. In the 1980s she hired an entertainment agent in Dallas and would be interviewed only if paid. In 1987 she denied that she had been raped in 1969.

Henry Wade (b. 1915) was a self-made man and a conservative Democrat, who became district attorney of Dallas County (1950–86). Early in his career, a campaign against drunk-driving established Wade's reputation for extreme strictness. In 1964 he prosecuted Jack Ruby, the killer of Lee Harvey Oswald, and was district attorney in the notorious *Lenell Geter* case (1984) where a black engineer was eventually freed from a life sentence for robbery that the prosecutors admitted later he did not commit. Wade's office was known as one of the most relentless in the United States, with a reputation for preferring Draconian sentences to justice. Beneath a folksy manner Henry Wade hid a keen, competitive legal mind and a strong belief in the efficacy of punishment. He secured the death sentence in twenty-nine of his thirty demands for it, and in his last case he won prison terms of over 5,000 years for two kidnappers.

Sources

Applebombe, Peter. 1986. Henry Wade. Dallas prosecutor: 36 years as Law-and-Order Icon. *The New York Times Biographical Service*, July:919.

Cooper, James, ed. 1974. *United States Supreme Court reports: October Term, 1972.* Vol. 35. Lawyers edition 2d:147–200.

Faux, Marian. 1988. *Roe v. Wade: the untold story of the landmark Supreme Court decision that made abortion legal.* New York: Macmillan.

Hall, Kermit L. 1992. *The Oxford companion to the Supreme Court of the United States.* New York: Oxford University Press.

ROGERENE. A member of a nonconformist religious sect, originally Baptist, and influenced greatly by the Society of Friends (Quakers), founded in Connecticut. The sect's doctrines and practices were opposed to some of the formal usages of church participation in the military. The church declined in the twentieth century, and a small group remained in the 1940s in Mystic, Connecticut, and in California.

John Rogers (1648?–1721) was raised in Connecticut, son of a wealthy resident, James Rogers. John and his wife left the Congregational Church and joined the Seventh-Day Baptists in Newport, Connecticut. After his wife left him, John and his family began a Baptist congregation in New London, and he was its pastor. He objected both to the Congregational Church having support from the state through taxes and to the practice of infant baptism. In about 1677 his congregation broke its ties with the Baptists in Newport. Because his group was so vehemently persecuted for not paying church taxes, traveling on Sundays, and demonstrating publicly against alleged idolatry, John Rogers spent many years in jail. On his death his religious practices were continued by his son, John Rogers, Jr.

Sources

Matthews, Mitford. 1966. *A dictionary of Americanisms: on historic principles.* Chicago: University of Chicago Press.

Melton, Gordon J. 1989. *The encyclopedia of American religions.* 3d ed. Detroit: Gale
    Research.

ROGERNOMICS. An economic strategy used in New Zealand during the
1980s and later sought by Eastern European countries, Brazil, and Australia to
improve the national economy. It aims for a high consumption tax (12.5 percent)
without exemptions and cuts in income tax from 66 percent to 33 percent.

Roger Owen Douglas (b. 1937), born in Auckland, educated at Auckland
Grammar School, the University of Auckland, and Canterbury University, was
first elected Labor politician for Manakau (1969). He was a Labor party maverick, who accurately predicted the decline of New Zealand's economy and
advocated its deregulation. When the Labor party came to power under Prime
Minister David Lange in 1980, Douglas became finance minister until 1988.
Under Rogernomics the NZ dollar was devalued 20 percent and floated; controls
on exchange and interest rates were removed; import duties were reduced; government agencies borrowed at commercial rates, and paid taxes and dividends;
electricity costs were cut 20 percent; NZ Telecom was privatized; and the waterfront and railways were reformed. At first, the scheme worked because its
opponents were disoriented and the Organization for Economic Cooperation and
Development (OECD) was impressed, but in 1990 New Zealand's debts and
unemployment were high, and economic growth was low. These free market
policies eventually contributed to the Labor party's defeat in 1990. After quitting
politics, Douglas became an international economic adviser and continually recommended his crash formula of economic rationalism. To some he lost power
because he failed to keep the people's support, showed he cared little about
whether he got elected, and appeared a zealot.

Sources

Douglas, Roger. 1987. *Roger Douglas: towards prosperity. [Towards prosperity: people
    and politics in the 1980s—a personal view.]* Auckland, New Zealand: David
    Bateman.
Duke, Suzanne, ed. 1982. *Debrett's handbook of Australia and New Zealand.* Sydney:
    Debrett's Peerage Ltd.
Keesings contemporary archives: record of world events. 1988:36293, 35681, 36192,
    36380. London: Keesings Publications.
Notable New Zealanders: the pictorial who's who (1979). Auckland: Paul Hamlyn.

ROGERS'S NONDIRECTIVE THERAPY, ROGERS'S INTERVIEW. A
style of psychotherapy or interviewing in which the patient or interviewee is
kept at the center of influence and directs the course of the relationship with the
therapist/interviewer. The therapist's task is to listen carefully and reflect his or
her understanding to the speaker.

Carl Ransom Rogers (1902–87) was born in Chicago, studied with Frederick
Allen and perhaps Jesse Taft, taught at the universities of Wisconsin, Chicago,

and Ohio State, and directed the Child Guidance Center in Rochester. The person rather than the role, status, position, or class of the individual was important to him. In the 1940s he developed his nondirective therapy in opposition to prevailing authoritarian therapy. It is now a widely accepted approach in psychotherapy. In time he renamed nondirective therapy client-centered therapy and later renamed that person-centered therapy. Experience showed him that academic degrees were not necessary for training in therapy, and he recommended training any person in the helping occupations for the task. He wrote on marriage, encounter groups, and education. From 1972 he applied his method to politics, leader training, group-conflict resolution, and policy-making in Hungary, Brazil, the Soviet Union, and South Africa.

Sources

Devine, Elizabeth; Held, Michael; Vinson, James; and Walsh, George, eds. 1983. *Thinkers of the twentieth century: a biographical, bibliographical and critical dictionary.* London: Macmillan.

Evans, Richard I. 1975. *Carl Rogers: the man and his ideas.* New York: E. P. Dutton.

Frick, William B. 1971. *Humanistic psychology: interviews with Maslow, Murphy and Rogers.* Columbus, Ohio: Merrill.

Gendlin, Eugene T. 1988. Carl Rogers (1902–87). *American Psychologist* 43:127.

Kirschenbaum, Howard, and Henderson, Valerie, L., eds. 1989. *Carl Rogers—dialogues.* Boston: Houghton Mifflin.

Rogers, Carl R. 1951. *Client-centered therapy: its current practice, implications and theory.* Boston: Houghton Mifflin.

Rogers, Carl R. 1974. In retrospect: forty-six years. *American Psychologist* 29:115–123.

ROGERS PLAN. A peace plan for the Middle East (1969) which combined proposals for an Israeli-Egyptian and Israeli-Jordanian peace. The Rogers Plan called for Arab consent to a permanent peace based on the assurance to Israel of territorial integrity under the provisions of the Security Council Resolution, following which Israel would withdraw from territory occupied since the Six-Day War of June 1967. Neither Israel nor the Arab States accepted the plan.

William Pierce Rogers (b. 1913) was born in Norfolk, New York, graduated from Colgate University and Cornell Law School, and was admitted to the bar in 1937. From 1938 to 1942 he served as assistant district attorney under Thomas E. Dewey (1902–71). After four years in the U.S. Navy during World War II, Rogers worked for the U.S. Senate as special counsel (1947–48) and as chief counsel for a subcommittee of the Senate Investigations Committee (1948–50). He worked for Richard Nixon's campaign for the vice-presidency in 1952 and as a result was named deputy attorney-general in the Eisenhower administration (1953). Four years later he rose to attorney-general, and his main concern was enforcing civil rights legislation. In the Nixon administration (1968–75), he served as secretary of state until, at Nixon's request, he resigned in 1973 to allow Kissinger to hold the position.

Sources
Brandon, Henry. 1973. *The retreat of American power.* London: Bodley Head.
Commager, Henry S., ed. 1968. *Documents of American history.* 8th ed. New York:
    Appleton-Century-Crofts.
The international who's who, 1992–93. London: Europa Publications.
Magnussen, Magnus; Goring, Rosemary; and Thorn, John O., eds. 1990. *Chambers bi-
    ographical dictionary.* Edinburgh: Chambers Ltd.
Stookey, Robert. 1975. *America and the Arab states.* New York: John Wiley.
Szulc, Tad. 1978. *The illusion of peace.* New York: Viking Press.

RÖHM PURGE, RÖHM PUTSCH. Between June 29 and July 2, 1934, leaders of the Nazi SA Brownshirts were slaughtered by the Nazi SS Blackshirts under
the control of Heinrich Himmler (1889–1945) and Hermann Goering (1893–
1946). Some were murdered at Stadelheim Prison, Munich, and others at the Cadet School, Lichtenfelde, Berlin. Non-Nazis were also slaughtered. On July 13
Adolf Hitler (1889–1945) described the murders as the "Night of the Long
Knives" and announced that sixty-one had been shot as part of a conspiracy; thirteen died resisting arrest and three committed suicide. In fact, over 1,000 died. The
aim was to crush the political influence of the SA. It was a turning point in the
Nazi regime which allowed Hitler to succeed German Chancellor von Hindenburg
(1847–1934) as head of state and commander in chief of Germany's army. It also
showed the ruthless exercise of power by the Nazi SS.

Ernst Röhm (1877–1943) was born in Munich. His father came from a family
of Bavarian civil servants. Ernst became a soldier in 1906, and during World
War I he was wounded three times and attained the rank of major. Before Hitler
rose to power, Röhm helped establish the National Socialist Workers' party. He
supported Hitler's efforts to win over the army in Bavaria, and he helped Hitler
establish his powerful personal military force, the Brownshirts, in October 1921.
Röhm became the organizer and commander of the Stormtroopers, that is, a
combined force of Brownshirts and Blackshirts, in 1931. He was made state
commissioner of Bavaria, but in 1934 he was charged with a conspiracy to
overthrow Hitler and was executed without trial.

Sources
Fest, Joachim C. 1970. *The face of the Third Reich.* London: Wiedenfeld and Nicolson.
Fest, Joachim C. 1974. *Hitler.* London: Weidenfeld and Nicolson.
Gallo, Max. 1973. *The night of the long knives.* London: Souvenir.
McHenry, Robert, ed. 1992. *The new encyclopedia Britannica.* Chicago: Encyclopedia
    Britannica, Inc.
Magnussen, Magnus; Goring, Rosemary; and Thorn, John O., eds. 1990. *Chambers bi-
    ographical dictionary.* Edinburgh: Chambers Ltd.
Zentner, Christian, and Friedmann, Bedurftig. 1991. *The encyclopedia of the Third Reich.*
    New York: Macmillan.

ROKEACH'S DOGMATISM SCALE. A measure of open–closed mindedness
or more generally, cognitive structure. The scale includes measures of ambi-

tiousness, self-adoration, severe suspiciousness, and a deep lack of trust, punitive thinking styles, idealized attitudes to authority, strong identification with noble causes, hatred of disbelievers, and a strong sense of aloneness. In the 1960s the scale was used in social psychological research on the cognitive organizing principles that are behind attitudes individuals use in interpersonal relations.

Milton Rokeach (1918–88) was born in Hrubishow, Poland. He became a naturalized U.S. citizen and studied at Brooklyn College, New York and the University of California at Berkeley (Ph.D., 1947). He became known for his studies on attitudes and belief systems. His long professional association with the academic community included positions at Michigan State University, Western Ontario University (Canada), and Washington State University. He was professor of communication and psychology at the University of Southern California, Los Angeles. Among his many publications were *The Open and Closed Mind* (1960); *The Three Christs of Ypsilanti: A Psychological Study* (1964); and *The Nature of Human Values* (1973). He contributed more than 100 articles to professional journals.

Sources

Ahrlich, H. J. 1978. Dogmatism. In Harvey London, J. R. Exner, and E. John, eds. *Dimensions of personality.* New York: John Wiley, pp. 127–164.

Christie, Richard. 1990. Milton Rokeach (1918–88). *American Psychologist* April:547.

Evory, Ann, ed. 1982. *Contemporary authors.* New Revision Series 5. Detroit: Gale Research.

Rokeach, Milton. 1960. *The open and closed mind: investigation into the nature of belief systems and personality systems.* New York: Basic Books.

Trosky, Susan, ed. 1989. *Contemporary Authors.* Vol. 127. Detroit: Gale Research.

ROOSEVELT'S FOUR FREEDOMS. The four conditions for which Americans were prepared to fight. In a speech on January 6, 1941, President Franklin D. Roosevelt said

> freedom of speech and expression—everywhere in the world . . . freedom of every person to worship god in his own way—everywhere in the world . . . freedom from want—which, translated into world terms, means economic understandings which will secure to every nation a healthy peace time life for its inhabitants—everywhere in the world . . . freedom from fear—which, translated into world terms, means a worldwide reduction of armaments to such a point and in such a thorough fashion that no nation will be in a position to commit an act of physical aggression against any neighbour—anywhere in the world.

Franklin Delano Roosevelt (1882–1945) was born in Hyde Park, New York, into a wealthy family; he was educated at home by a Swiss governess and in Europe at Bad Nauheim. At age 14 he attended Groton School in Massachusetts before going to Harvard and Columbia Law School. He went to the bar in 1907. He was state senator (1910–13), assistant secretary of the U.S. Navy (1913–20), and a Democratic candidate for the U.S. vice-presidency in 1920. Despite being stricken with paralysis in the early 1920s, he was elected New York's governor

(1928–32). In 1932 he became the thirty-second U.S. president, and, facing the Great Depression of the 1930s, he led his country in a New Deal policy. He was reelected in 1936, 1940, and 1944. He died a few weeks before the Nazi surrender that ended World War II in Europe.

Sources

Commager, Henry S., ed. 1968. *Documents of American history.* 8th ed. New York: Appleton-Century-Crofts.

Freidel, Frank B. 1952. *Franklin D. Roosevelt.* Boston: Little, Brown.

Freidel, Frank B. 1990. *Franklin D. Roosevelt: a rendezvous with destiny.* Boston: Little, Brown.

James, Edward T. 1973. *Dictionary of American biography.* Supplement 3. New York: Charles Scribner's Sons.

Magnussen, Magnus; Goring, Rosemary; and Thorn, John O., eds. 1990. *Chambers biographical dictionary.* Edinburgh: Chambers Ltd.

The public papers and addresses of Franklin D. Roosevelt. New York: Russell and Russell. Vol. 9:663.

Rosendbaum, Herbert D., and Bartelme, Elizabeth, eds. 1987. *Franklin D. Roosevelt: the man, the myth, the era 1882–1945.* Westport, Conn.: Greenwood Press.

Simpson, Michael. 1989. *Franklin D. Roosevelt.* New York: Basil Blackwell.

RORSCHACH TEST. An ink-blot test of intelligence, personality, and mental state.

Hermann Rorschach (1884–1922), a Swiss psychiatrist with both scientific and artistic interests, had to make a choice of career in 1904. He completed a medical doctorate on the study of hallucination in 1912 under the supervision of the Swiss psychiatrist Eugene Bleuler (1857–1939). For a year Rorschach worked in an asylum near Moscow (1913) and thereafter spent his working life in Swiss mental hospitals. He was much impressed by the German poet Julius Kerner (1786–1862) and his use of ink-blots for poetic inspiration. Rorschach was drawn to the ideas of Freud and Jung, and Binet's uses of an ink-blot test for children. Beginning in 1911, he combined the association technique of Jung and bilaterally symmetrical cards with the ink-blot in tests with psychiatric patients and children. He wanted to see how people transferred sensory experiences from one modality to another, and to assess imaginative mental processes. In 1921, after much difficulty, his work was published. The test enjoyed repeated vogue in clinical psychology and social psychology, and is accepted as a revealing method for studying creativity and the personal and social features of human personality. He was the vice-president of the Swiss Psychoanalytic Society.

Sources

Ellenberger, Henri. 1970. *The discovery of the unconscious.* New York: Basic Books.

McHenry, Robert, ed. 1992. *The new encyclopedia Britannica.* Chicago: Encyclopedia Britannica, Inc.

Sills, David L., ed. 1968. *International encyclopedia of the social sciences.* New York: Macmillan and Free Press.

Zusne, Leonard. 1984. *Biographical dictionary of psychology.* Westport, Conn.: Greenwood Press.

ROSENTHAL EFFECT. A self-fulfilling prophecy held among pupils that
high expectations of their aptitudes—real or imagined—lead to an increase in
classroom performance.

Robert Rosenthal (b. 1933) was born in Giessen, Germany, and came to the
United States in 1940 where he was naturalized in 1946. He graduated from the
University of California, Los Angeles (Ph.D., 1956), completed postdoctoral
training at the Wadsworth Veterans Administration Hospital (1956–57), and
taught psychology at the University of North Dakota (1957–58) where he coordinated clinical training (1958–62). He taught clinical psychology (1962–67)
at Harvard and Boston universities and was appointed a professor of social
psychology at Harvard (1967). He received the Distinguished Lecture Award
from the American Psychological Association in 1982. He has written many
books and articles, including *Experimenter Effects in Behavioral Research*
(1966), *Essentials of Behavioral Research* (1991), and several works on meta-
analyses.

Sources

Deighton, Lee C. 1971. *The encyclopedia of education.* New York: Macmillan.
Metzger, Linda, and Straub, Deborah A., eds. 1986. *Contemporary authors.* Vol. 16.
    Detroit: Gale Research.
Rosenthal, Robert, and Jacobson, Lenore. 1968. *Pygmalion in the classroom.* New York:
    Holt, Rinehart and Winston.

ROSICRUCIAN. A member of an alleged secret society whose origins are
obscure and whose members made great pretensions to knowledge of the secrets
of nature, transmutation of metals, elemental spirits, and magical signatures.

Christian Rosenkreuz (1378–1484?) was the name allegedly taken by Johan
Valentin Andreä (1586–1654). He was born near Tübingen and became a noted
German (Lutheran) theologian and mystic. In 1614 he published *Fama fraternitas* and in 1615, *Confessio rosae crucis. Fama fraternitas* tells of the journey
of Christian Rosenkreuz, a man who lived for 106 years. Many regard him as
a legendary figure rather than a real person. He is reputed to have founded the
Rosicrucian Society or to have restored the teachings it upheld. Later, Andreä
stated that the history of the society was utter fabrication. He died in Stuttgart.
On publication, the books caused much excitement in Europe. They describe
how the society developed from eastern and Arabian origins, but some scholars
believe that the name of the society was used simply to get attention. Some of
the society's members claim their order existed from Egyptian times. They use
occult symbols—rose, cross, swastika, pyramid—and base their work on mystical writing. Some ties with Freemasonry exist with the society. When the
Thirty Years' War (1618–48) began, Rosicrucianism was associated with her-

esies and Protestantism. Another account suggests that the Swiss alchemist, Paracelus (d. 1541), founded Rosicrucianism.

Sources

Eliade, Mircea, ed. 1987. *Encyclopedia of religion.* New York: Macmillan.

Evans, Ivor H. 1989. *Brewer's dictionary of phrase and fable.* 14th ed. London: Cassell.

McHenry, Robert, ed. 1992. *The new encyclopedia Britannica.* Chicago: Encyclopedia Britannica, Inc.

Magnussen, Magnus; Goring, Rosemary; and Thorn, John O., eds. 1990. *Chambers biographical dictionary.* Edinburgh: Chambers Ltd.

ROSS AWARD. A British industrial relations award, the result of a decision by the Board of Arbitration on January 23, 1952. As a result, the Fire Brigades Union lost its claim to traditional parity of pay and conditions with those of the police; it was a parity that the union insisted had existed until the application of the Industrial Court Award of 1950.

William Ross, Lord Ross of Marnock (1911–88), was born in Ayr, Scotland, son of a train driver. He studied at Ayr Academy and Glasgow University, and taught school before World War II. In 1946 he became a Labor member of Parliament for Kilmarnock in a by-election and served until 1979 when he was created a peer. In 1952 he chaired the Board of Arbitration. He was the longest serving secretary of state for Scotland (1964–70; 1974–76).

Sources

Magnussen, Magnus; Goring, Rosemary; and Thorn, John O., eds. 1990. *Chambers biographical dictionary.* Edinburgh: Chambers Ltd.

Marsh, Arthur. 1979. *Concise encyclopedia of industrial relations.* Westmead, Farnborough, Hants: Gower.

Who's who, 1987. London: Adam and Charles Black.

ROTTER'S THEORY OF SOCIAL LEARNING, ROTTER'S INTERNAL-EXTERNAL LOCUS OF CONTROL SCALE. A theory that draws together a wide range of ideas and evidence from social psychology and clinical psychology. It assumes that the interaction of individuals with their meaningful environs is the proper unit of observation in social science; that human behavior has direction and from the individual's viewpoint meets his internal reinforcement or needs, and from the viewpoint of others in his environment meets his external reinforcement or goals; that behavior is best understood as varying at stages of an individual's development; and that the function of behavior is related to its direction of the individual's goals and needs. The psychological principles in the theory were validated from laboratory as well as clinical data. The theory draws its concepts from the work of Alfred Adler (1870–1937), Kurt Lewin (1890–1947), Jacob R. Kantor (1888–1984), Edward L. Thorndike (1874–1949), Edward C. Tolman (1886–1959), and Clark L. Hull (1884–1952). The scale measures the extent to which individuals feel they have a degree of control over their lives (internal) or how far they believe their life is in the hands of fate, powerful others, or chance (external).

Julian Bernard Rotter (b. 1916) was born in New York City, studied chemistry at Brooklyn College, and did postgraduate studies at the University of Iowa and clinical psychology at the University of Indiana (Ph.D., 1941). He worked briefly at the Worcester State Hospital (1938–39), taught at the University of Indiana (1939–40), and became a psychologist at the Norwich State Hospital in Connecticut (1941–42) before serving in the U.S. Army (1942–46). Thereafter he was a consultant to the U.S. Veterans' Administration and helped select people for the Peace Corps. Later, he directed clinical training at Ohio State University (1946–63) and the University of Connecticut (1963–). He specialized in personality theory and assessment, and among his contributions was an Interpersonal Trust Scale and the Internal-External Scale (1966). In 1989 he was honored by the American Psychological Association for pioneering the social learning framework that changed the behavioral sciences approach to personality and clinical psychology and integrated expectancy and reinforcement in a social psychological learning theory.

Sources

Editors. 1989. Julian B. Rotter. *American Psychologist* 44:625–626.

Jaques Cattell Press, ed. 1978. *American men and women of science: the social and behavioral sciences.* New York: Jaques Cattell and R. R. Bowker.

Rotter, Julian B. 1954. *Social learning and clinical psychology.* Englewood Cliffs, N.J.: Prentice-Hall.

Rotter Julian B. 1966. Generalized expectancies for internal versus external control of reinforcement. *Psychological Monographs* 80: whole no. 609.

RUCKER PLAN. A plantwide bonus system used in industry and involving productivity sharing. It takes account only of value that is added by manufacture, omitting the cost of raw materials and supplies. The scheme assumes a direct and proportional relationship between annual production value per worker and annual pay per worker in every company, the former being taken to be the value added by the manufacturer, less cost of materials and supplies. A ratio of wages to production value can therefore be set and employees guaranteed a fixed percentage of any improvement above that ratio.

Allen Willis Rucker (1887–1964) was born in Bristol, Virginia, and educated in Tennessee. After holding various managerial positions in the city of Bristol (1919–27), Rucker was a staff member of the University in Cambridge, Massachusetts, and later between 1929 and 1960 he was a partner of Eddy-Rucker-Nickels, a consulting firm, in Cambridge, Massachusetts, where he developed the "pay-as-you-produce" wage plan (1934). He studied data published in the U.S. Census and surveyed manufacturers in 1932–33, and found that the economic productivity of the U.S. factory employment had been stable from 1899 to 1929. The plan developed thereafter was widely publicized by Rucker in America and in Britain by F. R. Bentley Company Ltd. By 1979 it was operating in forty British companies. Rucker was a regular speaker to the American business community, and most of his speeches were published as pamphlets (1928–60), many of them by the Eddy-Rucker-Nickels Company.

Sources

Bentley, F. R. 1964. *People, productivity, and progress.* London: Business Publications
    Ltd.
Heyel, Carl. 1973. *The encyclopedia of management.* New York: Van Nostrand Reinhold
    Co.
Marsh, Arthur I. 1979. *Concise encyclopedia of industrial relations.* Westmead, Farn-
    borough, Hants: Gower.
Rucker, Allen W. 1962. *Gearing wages to productivity.* Cambridge, Mass.: Eddy-Rucker-
    Nichols Co.
Who was who in America, 1961–68. Vol. IV. Chicago: Marquis.

RUDOLF STEINER SCHOOL. Children's school with a strong spiritual and
humanistic outlook on education and special educational methods, known in
America as the Waldorf method. The first Rudolf Steiner School was established
as the Waldorf School in 1919 for the children of employees of the Waldorf-
Astoria cigarette factory in Stuttgart. Closed by the Nazis, the school reopened
in 1945, and the movement spread to most European countries, the United
States, Canada, Australia, New Zealand, South Africa, and South America.

Rudolf Steiner (1861–1925), an Austrian social philosopher, scientist, and
artist, was the son of a railway station master. He was educated in Vienna, much
of it through his own efforts; he edited Goethe's scientific writings and published
his Ph.D. thesis, *Truth and Science,* and *The Philosophy of Freedom* (1894). He
edited a journal in Berlin, lectured at a workingman's college, and studied an-
throposophy, the knowledge produced by the higher self. In 1912–13 he founded
the Anthroposophical Society, and in 1913 he began to build his first school of
spiritual science. From his ideas developed the Waldorf School movement,
homes for defective and maladjusted children, a form of therapy, biodynamic
agriculture, centers of scientific and mathematical research, eurythmy, and
schools of most cultural arts. He emphasized the educational value of play acting, art, and mythmaking for children. The Waldorf schools taught children to
find their own outlook for adulthood, to realize their full potential, and to make
fruitful relationships. Steiner's main contribution was to give a detailed account
of child development—later confirmed by prominent child psychologists—and
a curriculum designed to support the development of the child, with strong
emphasis on the physical as well as psychological aspects of maturation. Each
class has a teacher who moves forward with the group, thereby helping the
children with problems of authority as well as schoolroom subjects.

Sources

Babel, Ulrich, and Giddens, Craig, comps. 1977–79. *Bibliographical reference list of the
    published works of Rudolf Steiner.* English trans. London: Rudolf Steiner Press.
Blisher, Edward, ed. 1969. *Blond's encyclopedia of education.* London: Blond Educa-
    tional.
Davy, John, ed. 1975. *Work arising from the life of Rudolf Steiner.* London: Rudolf
    Steiner Press.
McDermott, Robert A., ed. 1984. *The essential Steiner: basic writings of Rudolf Steiner.*
    San Francisco: Harper and Row.

Richards, Mary C. 1980. *Towards wholeness: Rudolf Steiner education in America.* Middletown, Conn.: Wesleyan University Press.

Wilson, Colin. 1985. *Steiner: the man and his vision [with bibliography].* Wellingborough: Aquarian Press.

RUSH-BAGOT AGREEMENT. An Anglo-American treaty that established limits to naval armaments on the Great Lakes (1817). It was drawn up by the American secretary of state and the British minister in Washington. Both Britain and the United States agreed to limit their warships to 100 tons, one each on Lake Champlain and Ontario, and two on the Upper Lakes above Niagara Falls. The treaty was ratified in 1818.

Richard Rush (1780–1859) was born in Philadelphia, studied at the College of New Jersey (now Princeton), and was admitted to the bar in 1800. He was appointed attorney-general of Pennsylvania (1811) and spoke in Washington in support of the war with Britain (1812). In 1814 he accepted the offer of attorney-general at the invitation of President Monroe (1758–1831). Later, he became secretary of state, and in this post he negotiated the famous treaty with Britain.

Charles Bagot (1781–1843) was born in Blithfield, Staffordshire, and was educated at Rugby and Christ Church, Oxford. He was M.P. for Castle Rising (1807) and became undersecretary of state for foreign affairs (1808) and minister to France (1814), an envoy to the United States (1815–19), and ambassador to Saint Petersburg (1820–23), The Hague (1824), and Vienna (1835). In 1842 he became governor-general of the Canadas. Upper and Lower Canada had had their first united parliament in 1841, and his task was to ensure that the harmonious unison of executive members—some nominated by the Crown and others elected by the two sets of provinces, French and English. He died in Kingston shortly after resigning due to ill-health (1843).

Sources

Commager, Henry S., ed. 1968. *Documents of American history.* 8th ed. New York: Appleton-Century-Crofts.

Johnson, Allen, and Malone, Dumas, eds. 1930. *Dictionary of American biography.* Vol. III. New York: Charles Scribner's Sons.

Lee, Sidney, ed. 1920. *Dictionary of national biography: supplement 1901–1911.* London: Oxford University Press.

Plano, Jack. 1988. *The international relations dictionary.* 4th ed. Santa Barbara, Calif.: ABC-CLIO.

Smith, Benjamin. 1903. *The Century cyclopedia of names.* London: The Times.

Taylor, A.J.P., and Howat, Gerald M.P. 1973 *Dictionary of world history.* London: Thomas Nelson.

RUSSELLITE. A member of the International Bible Students' Association or Jehovah's Witnesses.

Charles Taze Russell (1852–1916), an American religious leader known as "Pastor Russell," was born at Pittsburgh to parents of Scotch-Irish descent. Educated in local schools, he had his learning augmented with private tutoring.

As a youth, he was taken into the Congregational Church of his parents, but he rebelled against the doctrine of eternal punishment. Several years of Bible study convinced him that Christ's Second Coming would occur in 1874. His conclusions were published in *The Object and Manner of Our Lord's Return* (1874) which had a wide circulation. In 1878 he began publishing a magazine, *The Watch Tower and Herald of Christ's Presence,* which attracted a circulation of 45,000, semimonthly, and was translated into fifteen languages. In 1879 he married and in 1909 was divorced for immoral conduct with women members of the church. Five appeals against the finding were disallowed. Through extensive travel in America in his later years, he gradually established branches of his church and more than 1,200 congregations. He died of heart failure on a train in Texas.

Sources

Cross, Frank L. 1974. *The Oxford dictionary of the Christian Church.* 2d ed. New York: Oxford University Press.

McHenry, Robert, ed. 1992. *The new encyclopedia Britannica.* Chicago: Encyclopedia Britannica, Inc.

Malone, Dumas, ed. 1935. *Dictionary of American biography.* Vol. VIII. New York: Charles Scribner's Sons.

Stroup, Henry H. 1945. *The Jehovah's witnesses.* New York: Columbia University Press.

S

SADAT INITIATIVE. The preparedness of an Arab leader to explain directly to the Israeli legislature (Knesset) the Arab policy on the Middle East and how that policy had caused the crippling cost to Egypt of military defense. Egypt's Sadat visited Israel on November 19–21, 1977, and this was the first tacit recognition of Israeli sovereignty in the Middle East. The initiative was rejected by the Palestine Liberation Organization, Syria, Algeria, and Libya.

Mohamed Anwar al-Sadat (1918–81) was born into an Egyptian Sudanese family in the Tala district. He joined the army and was commissioned in 1938. For making contact with the Germans during World War II he was imprisoned in 1942. He worked to overthrow the British-dominated Egyptian monarchy, and in 1952 he was one of a group of officers who deposed King Farouk. Under Gamal Abdel Nasser, Sadat held several posts and was one of four vice-presidents (1964–67) and later sole vice-president (1969–70). On Nasser's death Sadat became Egypt's president and favored the West instead of the Soviets; he went to war against Israel in 1973, but followed this move with a major peace initiative and went to Jerusalem in 1977 for the talks that led to the Egyptian-Israeli Peace Treaty in 1979. With the Israeli prime minister, Menachem Begin, Sadat shared the Nobel Peace Prize in 1978. He published his life story in 1978, *In Search of Identity; An Autobiography.* Sadat was assassinated by Egyptian soldiers while watching a military parade in Cairo.

Sources
Fernandez-Armesto, Felipe. 1983. *Sadat and his statecraft.* London: Kensal.
Jones, Barry. 1989. *The Macmillan dictionary of biography.* Melbourne: Macmillan.
Magnussen, Magnus; Goring, Rosemary; and Thorn, John O., eds. 1990. *Chambers biographical dictionary.* Edinburgh: Chambers Ltd.
Moritz, Charles, ed. 1981. *Current biography yearbook.* New York: H. W. Wilson.

Shoukri, Ghali. 1981. *Egypt: portrait of a president 1971–81: the counter revolution in Egypt, Sadat's road to Jerusalem.* London: Zed.

SADDAMIZED. Newspapers around the world used "Saddam" as a pejorative term during the Gulf War (1991)—for example, to ensure that how things are made to seem is more important than how they actually are. Here the term was used to describe the propaganda from Baghdad radio and television reporting the defeat of the Iraqi forces, especially during the ground war in Kuwait in February 1991. In the Middle East journalists found that illusion and reality got confused, and one headline stated; "Iraq Gets a Saddamized Version of the Truth" (*The Age,* February 26, 1991). In this case, Iraqi radio would deny that thousands of Iraqi soldiers were taken prisoner, even though pictures of lines of them appeared on CNN TV. Another meaning is to portray another person, especially a leader of one's opposition group, as a dangerous ogre. As Claude Forell, in *The Age* of March 13, 1991, wrote "the opposition's main problem in trying to saddamize [leading trade unionist in Australia] Mr. Halfpenny is . . ."

Saddam Hussein (b. 1937) was born in Tikrit, son of an impoverished peasant who died before the boy was born. His mother, Sabha, left the child to be raised by his maternal uncle, Khairallah Talfah. His name, Saddam, means "one who conflicts." The uncle, an Arab nationalist, was jailed for participating in a failed uprising (1941), and the boy had to live with his mother and endure beatings by his stepfather, the brother of his natural father. At age 10 the lad returned to live with his maternal uncle and to begin school. He graduated from primary school (1955) and that year began secondary school in Baghdad. He was more interested in politics than in schooling, however, and joined the Ba'th party in 1957. In 1958 he participated in the murder of a government official, was imprisoned, and released six months later for lack of adequate evidence. He helped in the attempted assassination of General Abol al-Karin Qassem, Iraq's leader, and with the party was forced underground and then into exile. He graduated from high school in Cairo (1961), studied law briefly, later enrolled at Baghdad University, and in 1976 was awarded an M.A. in law. He rose quickly to power in the party and became the totalitarian leader of Iraq in 1979. He built a personality cult around him, used the Ba'th party to control the nation, abrogated Iraq's treaty with Iran in 1980, and thereafter developed both a cruel and benign image.

Sources

Aragno, Anna. 1991. Master of his universe. *Journal of Psychohistory* 19:97–108.

Karsh, Efrain, and Rautsi, Inari. 1991. *Saddam Hussein: a political biography.* New York: Free Press.

Miller, Judith, and Mylorie, Laurie. 1990. *Saddam Hussein and the crisis in the Gulf.* New York: Times Books.

Moritz, Charles, ed. 1981. *Current biography yearbook.* New York: H. W. Wilson.

Post, Jerold M. 1991. Saddam Hussein of Iraq: a political psychology profile. *Political Psychology* 12:279–289, 723–725.

Sciolino, Elaine. 1991. *The outlaw state: Saddam Hussein's quest for power and the Gulf crisis.* New York: John Wiley.

SADDUCEE. Zadokites, a party of traditionalist, reactionary, aristocratic, and conservative Jewish priests who rejected beliefs that others adopted, such as life after death.

Zadok I, the father of Ahimaaz and Jerushah, was a priest in the time of David and Solomon (c. 961–922 B.C.), and was of the same status as Abiathar, the priest whom Saul (c. 1020–1000 B.C.) slew. During the rebellion of Absalom, Zadok and Abiathar guarded the Ark at Jerusalem, and, under orders from David, were to spread favorable propaganda in David's support. Absalom died in the ensuing struggle for the throne, and Zadok gave his support to Solomon; on anointing him, Zadok was made chief of priests. The Old Testament reveals that Zadok founded a prominent priestly family, was the grandfather of Jotham, Sealer of the Covenant, a high priest, scribe, and builder of the wall.

Sources

Hastings, James. 1920. *Encyclopedia of religion and ethics.* Edinburgh: T. and T. Clark.
MacGregor, Geddes. 1990. *The Everyman dictionary of religion and philosophy.* London: Dent and Sons.
Miller, Madelene S., and Miller, J. Lane, eds. 1973. *Harpers Bible dictionary.* New York: Harper and Row.
Roth, Cecil E. 1962. *The standard Jewish encyclopedia.* Garden City, N.Y.: Doubleday.
Roth, Cecil E., ed. 1971. *Encyclopedia Judaica.* New York: Macmillan.

SADISM. A desire for sexual pleasure by cruelly inflicting pain on another.

Comte Donatien Alphonse Francois de Sade, known as the marquis de Sade (1740–1814), was born in Paris and served in the military (1754–66) before returning to Paris. He was noted for his immorality and was sentenced to die at Aix (1772) for an unnatural crime and for murder by poisoning. He escaped to Italy. When he returned to Paris in 1777, he was imprisoned again but escaped once more. Again he was caught, and again he was put in prison, the Bastille. There he began a career as a novelist and playwright, with *Justine* (1791), *Juliette* (1798), and *Les Crimes de l'Amour* (1800). Later, he was found to be mentally unbalanced and was put in Charenton Lunatic Asylum where he lived his final years.

Sources

Hayman, Ronald. 1978. *De Sade: a critical biography.* London: Constable.
McHenry, Robert, ed. 1992. *The new encyclopedia Britannica.* Chicago: Encyclopedia Britannica, Inc.
Magnussen, Magnus; Goring, Rosemary; and Thorn, John O., eds. 1990. *Chambers biographical dictionary.* Edinburgh: Chambers Ltd.
Selzer, Michael. 1979. *Terrorist chic: an exploration of violence in the seventies.* New York: Hawthorn Books.
Thomas, David. 1979. *The marquis de Sade.* Boston: Little, Brown.

SAINT-SIMONISM. A state socialistic system; the founding policy of French socialism.

Claude Henri de Rouvroy, Comte de Saint-Simon (1760–1825), was born at Paris into an ancient, noble, but impoverished family. He served as a volunteer in the American Revolution, but his aristocratic birth prevented him from playing a prominent part in the French Revolution. After making a fortune by speculating in confiscated lands, he devoted his time to the study of philosophy. The later years of his life were spent in poverty because he wasted his fortune in costly experiments. The major exposition of his ideas appears in his *Nouveau Christianisme* (1825). These views were developed by his followers into Saint-Simonism, which held that the state should possess all property, inheritance should be abolished, distribution of the products of labor should not be equal but each person should be rewarded according to the service rendered the state, and the active and able people should receive a larger share than the slow and dull.

Sources

Ansart, Pierre. 1969. *Saint-Simon.* Paris: Presses Universitaires de France.

Coser, Lewis A. 1977. *Masters of sociological thought.* New York: Harcourt Brace Jovanovich.

Cross, Frank L. 1974. *The Oxford dictionary of the Christian Church.* 2d ed. New York: Oxford University Press.

McHenry, Robert, ed. 1992. *The new encyclopedia Britannica.* Chicago: Encyclopedia Britannica, Inc.

Miller, David. 1987. *The Blackwell encyclopedia of political thought.* Oxford: Basil Blackwell.

Sills, David L., ed. 1968. *International encyclopedia of the social sciences.* New York: Macmillan and Free Press.

SALESIAN. Relating to Saint Francis of Sales or members of his order, the Visitants; there are two Roman Catholic congregations with this name, one for women and the other for men, and both concern the education of the young, especially those who are poor.

Francis de Sales (1567–1622) was born at Thorens, Savoy, in the castle of his family, and studied in Paris at the Jesuit College of Clermont (1580–88) and afterward went to the University of Padua to study law and theology. He was ordained and appointed provost of Geneva in 1593, and he became the bishop of Geneva in 1602. In the Counter-Reformation he was a noted administrator, intellectual leader, teacher, and founder of several schools. He was canonized in 1665 and made patron saint of the Catholic press in 1923. John Bosco (1815–88) founded the Salesians (formerly the Society of Saint Francis de Sales) in Turin, Italy (1859), and by the time he died the group had expanded through Europe to England and South America.

Sources

Cross, Frank L. 1974. *The Oxford dictionary of the Christian Church.* 2d ed. New York: Oxford University Press.

Delaney, John. 1982. *Dictionary of saints.* Surrey: Kay and Ward Ltd.
McHenry, Robert, ed. 1992. *The new encyclopedia Britannica.* Chicago: Encyclopedia
    Britannica, Inc.
Magnussen, Magnus; Goring, Rosemary; and Thorn, John O., eds. 1990. *Chambers bi-
    ographical dictionary.* Edinburgh: Chambers Ltd.

SAM HILL. One who always runs for political office, as in the phrase "to run [or go] like Sam Hill"; a euphemism for "Hell."

Colonel Sam Hill of Guilford, Connecticut, apparently was a perpetual candidate for office and in reference to his political obsession the phrase, "to run like Sam Hill," appeared in the Havana, New York, *Republican* (1839).

Sources

Hendrickson, Robert. 1988. *The dictionary of eponyms: names that became words.* New
    York: Dorset.
Mitchell, Edwin V. 1946. *Encyclopedia of American politics.* Garden City, N.Y.: Dou-
    bleday.
Partridge, Eric. 1984. *A dictionary of slang and unconventional English.* Completely rev.
    8th ed. London: Routledge and Kegan Paul.
Wentworth, Harvey, and Flexner, Stuart B. 1975. *Dictionary of American slang.* New
    York: Thomas Y. Crowell.

SAMUELSON REPORT. A British report of the Royal Commission on Technical Instruction (1881–84) which compared the instruction given to the working classes in England with that in other countries, and outlined a program to develop technical education at all social levels.

Sir Bernhard Samuelson (1820–95) was born in Hamburg, son of a merchant, and educated at a private school at Hull, East Yorkshire. From the age of 14 he gained wide experience in industrial fields, eventually establishing a railway works at Tours and a reaping-machine factory at Orleans. His main achievement was the building of an iron works at Middleborough, Yorkshire (1870), which was then the largest and most modern plant of its kind. He was the member of Parliament for Banbury (1859, 1865–85) and for North Oxfordshire (1885–95), and he was created a baronet (1884). He was a strong supporter of technical instruction, and served on a Select Committee on the provision of technical instruction (1868) and a Royal Commission on Scientific Instruction (1870–75). He also chaired the Royal Commission on Technical Instruction.

Sources

Aldrich, Richard, and Gordon, Peter. 1987. *Dictionary of British educationists.* London:
    Woburn Press.
Blishen, Edward. 1969. *Blond's encyclopaedia of education.* London: Blond Educational.
Lee, Sidney, ed. 1912. *Dictionary of national biography: Supplement 1901–1911.* Lon-
    don: Oxford University Press.

SANDEMANIAN. A Glasite, or follower of the American religious sect.

Robert Sandeman (1718–71) was born at Perth, Scotland, and died at Danbury, Connecticut. He was a Scottish elder, and son-in-law and zealous disciple of John Glas (1695–1773), the founder of the Glasites. Sandeman was also a promoter of the American colonies and of the sect that came to bear his name from 1764 to 1771. He and his followers were strongly opposed by the prominent New England ministers for rejecting the Covenant of Grace and the doctrine of justification by faith as an act of regeneration. The sect flourished from 1725 to about 1900. Sandeman established churches that were managed by several co-equal presbyters and followed decisions that were based on agreement rather than majority votes. They upheld the Glasite practices of infant baptism, foot-washing, and excommunication; the sect's distinctive practices were observance of the community of goods, abstinence from eating the flesh of creatures that had been strangled, love-feasts, and weekly celebration of communion. Conditions of membership were strict—the church could control the use of a member's private funds—and membership was low. Sandeman published *Some Thoughts on Christianity* (1762), and his biography appears in the 1857 edition of his *Discourses on Passages in Scriptures.*

Sources

Cross, Frank L. 1974. *The Oxford dictionary of the Christian Church.* 2d ed. New York: Oxford University Press.

Douglas, James D., ed. 1974. *The new international dictionary of the Christian Church.* Exeter: Paternoster Press.

Hastings, James. 1913. *Encyclopedia of religion and ethics.* New York: Charles Scribner's Sons.

Magnussen, Magnus; Goring, Rosemary; and Thorn, John O., eds. 1990. *Chambers biographical dictionary.* Edinburgh: Chambers Ltd.

Smith, Benjamin. 1903. *The Century cyclopedia of names.* London: The Times.

SAPIR-WHORF HYPOTHESIS. A theory of the relationship between language and thought—the theory of linguistic relativity—which assumes that individuals analyze nature along the lines laid down by their native languages and by the linguistic systems in their minds. Today, in its strongest form most linguists do not accept this hypothesis.

Edward Sapir (1884–1939) was born in Pomerania, Germany, and arrived in the United States with his family when he was 5. He first made his reputation as an expert on the languages of the American Indian. He taught at the University of Chicago and later at Yale, and was one of the first to explore the relationship between language studies and anthropology. His book, *Language* (1921), is his major publication for the general reader. In addition, he published many articles and some verse in periodicals.

Benjamin Lee Whorf (1897–1941) was born in Winthrop, Massachusetts, and after graduation from Winthrop High School, entered the Massachusetts Institute of Technology and majored in chemical engineering. After graduation, he worked as a fire prevention officer with an insurance company. His interest in linguistics did not appear until 1924 when he was concerned about the supposed conflict between science and religion. He felt that the answer lay in a penetrating linguistic exegesis of the Old Testament. For this reason in 1924 he began to study Hebrew. Then he studied Aztec and other Mexican languages. After several years of study in Mexico, Whorf enrolled in Sapir's first course at Yale in American Indian language. Whorf became known for his studies of the Hopi, and he developed the idea that the strange grammar of Hopi might provide a different way for the native speaker to perceive things.

Sources

Crystal, David. 1980. *A first dictionary of phonetics.* London: Andre Deutsch.

Devine, Elizabeth; Held, Michael; Vinson, James; and Walsh, George, eds. 1983. *Thinkers of the twentieth century: a biographical, bibliographical and critical dictionary.* London: Macmillan.

Darnell, Regna. 1990. *Edward Sapir: linguist, anthropologist, humanist.* Berkeley: University of California Press.

Sapir, Edward. 1921. *Language.* New York: Harvest/HBJ Book.

Sebeok, Thomas A., ed. 1966. *Portraits of linguists.* Bloomington: University of Indiana Press.

Zusne, Leonard. 1984. *Biographical dictionary of psychology.* Westport, Conn.: Greenwood Press.

SARTRIAN. Relating to the twentieth-century French novelist, dramatist, and social philosopher, as well as his followers and admirers.

Jean-Paul Sartre (1905–80) was born and educated in Paris, and began his career in 1929 as a teacher in secondary schools in the provinces and later in Paris. Before World War II, he wrote several psychological studies, *Imagination* (1936), *Emotions; Outline of a Theory* (1939) and *The Psychology of Imagination* (1940). In 1938 he published his novel *Nausea,* and the next year *The Wall,* both of which dramatized the discovery of the meaninglessness of life, which was a precondition for the philosophy of existentialism, as Sartre would develop it. He joined the French Army in 1939 and became a prisoner in Alsace in 1940. After nine months, he escaped and resumed teaching in Paris, taking an active part in the underground resistance to Nazi rule. After the liberation of France, he left teaching and organized the politico-literary review, *Les temps modernes.* He became known internationally as the leader of a group of intellectuals described in many of the works of Simone de Beauvior (1908–86), a lifelong woman friend. He was a prolific writer of plays and novels.

Sources

Barnes, Hazel E. 1973. *Sartre.* Philadelphia: Lippincott.

Cohen-Sola, Annie. 1987. *Sartre: a life.* London: Heinemann.

Colombel, Jeannette. 1981. *Sartre: ou, le parti de vivre.* Paris: Grasset.

Dante, Arthur C. 1975. *Jean-Paul Sartre.* 2d ed. 1991. Hammersmith: Fontana.

McHenry, Robert, ed. 1992. *The new encyclopedia Britannica.* Chicago: Encyclopedia Britannica, Inc.

Magnussen, Magnus; Goring, Rosemary; and Thorn, John O., eds. 1990. *Chambers biographical dictionary.* Edinburgh: Chambers Ltd.

Zusne, Leonard. 1984. *Biographical dictionary of psychology.* Westport, Conn.: Greenwood Press.

SASANID, SASSANID. A member of a first-century Persian dynasty, which was later overthrown by the Arabs of Nehavend.

Sasan (fl. first century) was probably a prince in the province of Persisi and a vassal of the chief petty king in Persis. His descendant, Babak, was the father of Ardashir I, who founded the Sasanian Empire. The dynasty lasted from 224 to about 651. It was established by conquest (208–24) under Ardashir I, who then ruled from 224 to 241. The Sasanians conquered the Parthians, established an empire, and saw its territories change in response to the efforts of Rome and Byzantium in the West and to pressures from the Kushans and Hephthalites in the East. Under Sasanian rule Iranian nationalism emerged, Zoroastrianism was established as the official religion; government was centralized and helped finance city building and agriculture; literature was recorded; chess, music, and polo became popular; and for those close to royalty it was an age of luxury. Under Khusrau I and II the dynasty was at its height; it disintegrated under the Muslim onslaught (637–51).

See also ZOROASTRIANISM.

Sources

Howatt, Gerald, M.D. 1973. *Dictionary of world history.* London: Thomas Nelson.

McHenry, Robert, ed. 1992. *The new encyclopedia Britannica.* Chicago: Encyclopedia Britannica, Inc.

Smith, Benjamin. 1903. *The Century cyclopedia of names.* London: The Times.

SAUSSURIAN. The view that language comprises mutually defining entities that are systematically related; this view contributed largely to modern theories of linguistic structure.

Ferdinand de Saussure (1857–1913) was born in Geneva, son of an eminent naturalist. As a lad he was introduced to linguistic studies by a philologist and family friend, Adolphe Pictet. At age 15, after studies in Greek, which added to his work in French, German, English, and Latin, he undertook Sanskrit. In 1875 he attended the University of Geneva and, following family tradition, studied chemistry and physics. He continued to study Greek and Latin grammar. Deciding that his career lay in the study of languages, he was sent to the University of Leipzig to study Indo-European languages. When he was only 21, he published a study on the primitive systems of vowels in these languages, *Mémoire sur le systéme primitif des voyelles dans les Langues indo-européennes,* which was judged at the time to be the most splendid work in comparative philology. After teaching in France and Germany, he returned to Geneva (1891) to give lectures on Sanskrit and historical linguistics which were published in Paris as *Cours de linguistique générale* (1916).

Sources

Bright, William, ed. 1992. *International encyclopedia of linguistics.* New York: Oxford University Press.

Culler, Jonathan. 1976. *Saussure.* Rev. ed. 1986. Ithaca, N.Y.: Cornell University Press.

Devine, Elizabeth; Held, Michael; Vinson, James; and Walsh, George, eds. 1983. *Thinkers of the twentieth century: a biographical, bibliographical and critical dictionary.* London: Macmillan.

Gadet, Francoise. 1989. *Saussure and contemporary culture.* Trans. Gregory Elliot. London: Radius/Century Hutchinson.

Sills, David L., ed. 1968. *International encyclopedia of the social sciences.* New York: Macmillan and Free Press.

SAY'S LAW. A controversial law of markets based on the belief that supply creates its own demand (or the quantity of products demanded is determined by the quantity produced) and that products are exchanged for products. Consequently, it appears that money is secondary; that all parties to economic exchange are interested in one another's prosperity; and that it is false to assume that as one party gains in the marketplace another loses. It also suggests that the imbalances between high production and low consumption are transitory.

Jean-Baptiste Say (1767–1832) was born in Lyon, France, and established himself as a cotton manufacturer. He was also an editor of *La De/cade* (1793–99), and in 1817 he became a professor of industrial economics in Paris. Among his many books was a *Treatise on Political Economy* (1803) which was often reprinted. Guided by Adam Smith's (1723–90) ideas, Say developed the role of the entrepreneur and his famous law on markets. In nineteenth-century France, most teaching of economics, particularly political economy, was dominated by his ideas, especially those that clearly separated the functions of the capitalist and the entrepreneur. He advocated the systematic study of problems rather than simple empirical observations, deplored David Ricardo's (1772–1823) abstractions, and always preferred facts to ideas. He supported the ideas behind the French Revolution, but not the regime of Napoleon; he tended to make economic policy rather than contribute to economics itself. Nevertheless, his innovative ideas contributed to marginalist thought, for example, Carl von Menger (1840–1921), William S. Jevons (1835–82), Leon Walras (1834–1910), and later, Alfred Marshall (1842–1924).

Sources

Blaug, Mark, ed. 1986. *Who's who in economics: a biographical dictionary of major economists, 1700–1986.* 2d ed. Cambridge, Mass.: MIT Press.

Eatwell, John; Milgate, Murray; and Newman, Peter. 1987. *The new Palgrave: a dictionary of economics.* London: Macmillan.

Magnussen, Magnus; Goring, Rosemary; and Thorn, John O., eds. 1990. *Chambers biographical dictionary.* Edinburgh: Chambers Ltd.

Sills, David L., ed. 1968. *International encyclopedia of the social sciences.* New York: Macmillan and Free Press.

SCAMP REPORT. Reports of several British inquiries into the work of the Motor Industry Joint Labor Council, for example, Motor Vehicle Collections

Ltd. and Avon Car Transporters (1966), Ford Motor Company (1968), British Rail (1965), British Airline Pilots (1967), and ''The Dustman's Strike'' of 1970.

Athelstan Jack Scamp (1913–77) was born in Birmingham, son of a house decorator, and at 14 left school and worked for ten years with the Great Western Railway as a clerk. He worked briefly in insurance, served in the Royal Artillery during World War II, and then turned to industrial relations for over twenty years. He was personnel manager for the Rover Car Company, Butlers of Birmingham, Rugby Portland Cement, Plessey Company, and Massey-Ferguson (U.K.), and then, in 1962, he joined the General Electric Company as personnel director. His direct and friendly manner and fine sense of humor with union leaders quickly helped reduce the tensions characteristically found in industrial relations. Intending to improve Britain's industrial relations, the British government in the 1960s appointed Scamp to head committees of inquiry. For his work he was knighted (1968), and he was frequently recalled from retirement to act as a peacemaker in many disputes in different industries.

Sources

Blake (Lord), and Nicholls, C. S., eds. 1986. *Dictionary of national biography 1971–1980.* Oxford: Oxford University Press.

Marsh, Arthur. 1979. *Concise encyclopedia of industrial relations.* Westmead, Farnborough, Hants: Gower.

SCANLON PLAN. A suggestion plan in U.S. industry that sought to reduce operating costs and benefit workers as a group for their suggestions.

Joseph Norbett Scanlon (1899?–1956) was a cost accountant, a professional boxer, a steelworker, and later a union official. In 1936 he unionized steelworkers and became president of the local union. In 1938 after consulting with steelworkers at the near-bankrupt La Pointe Machine Tool Company, Scanlon outlined a productivity plan that gave workers, as a group rather than as individuals, rewards for suggestions they might make to improve the efficiency of operations. Stressing cooperation rather than competition, the plan helped save the firm and encouraged further union–management cooperation in cost reduction. Participation in decisions to help the firm gave the workers a sense of belonging to the organization. Because work in the steel industry had damaged his health, Scanlon accepted a professorship at the Massachusetts Institute of Technology in 1946 to further develop his scheme in the hope that it would improve industrial relations in the United States. The Scanlon plan differed from similar schemes in that it rewarded groups, not individuals, used management–union committees to suggest changes, and had workers share not in greater profits but in reduced operating costs.

Sources

Lesieur, Frederick G., ed. 1958. *The Scanlon plan: a frontier in labor–management cooperation.* New York: John Wiley and Cambridge, Mass.: MIT Press.

Obituary: Joseph Scanlon. *New York Times,* February 11, 1956:11.

Wren, Daniel A. 1987. *The evolution of management thought.* 3d ed. New York: John Wiley.

SCARMAN REPORT. A British report on the disorders of April 10–12, 1981 in Brixton. On British television, viewers witnessed violence and disorder; when the police arrived, they saw a few hundred people, mainly blacks, stone policemen and hurl bricks and petrol bombs, and produce chaos and damage similar to that experienced by the British from a Nazi air raid in World War II. The causes were thought to be, first, oppressive police methods and harassment of blacks over many years; and second, a protest against a society of deeply divided and frustrated people who saw violence as a chance to draw atention to their distress.

Leslie George Scarman (b. 1911) was educated at Radley College and Brasenese College, Oxford, and was admitted to the bar in 1936. He received an O.B.E. in 1944 and was knighted in 1961. He became queen's counsel and was appointed a judge of the High Court of Justice, Probate, Divorce and Admiralty Division and Family Division (1961–73). He was lord justice of appeal (1973–77), and thereafter lord of appeal. In 1973 he became a privy councillor.

Sources

Benyon, John, ed. 1984. *Scarman and after.* Oxford: Pergamon Press.

The international who's who, 1992–93. London: Europa Publications.

McHenry, Robert, ed. 1992. *The new encyclopedia Britannica.* Chicago: Encyclopedia Britannica, Inc.

Marsh, Arthur. 1979. *Concise encyclopedia of industrial relations.* Westmead, Farnborough, Hants: Gower.

Scarman, Leslie G. 1982. *The Scarman report: the Brixton disorders 10–12 April 1981: report of an inquiry by the Rt. Hon. the Lord Scarman O.B.E.* Harmondsworth: Penguin Books.

SCHAFIITE. Member of one of four major sects of the Sunnites, or orthodox Muslims.

Abu Abdallah Mohammed Ibn Idris (c. 767–820) was called ''al-Shafii'' from the name of one of his ancestors who descended from Mohammed's grandfather, Abdul Muttalib. Al-Shafii was a member of the Koraish tribe, taught in Cairo, and died there. As an orthodox religious leader, al-Shafii followed the traditions of his teacher, Malik ibn Anas (715–795), who had gathered from the Koran and local traditions of Mohammed his ''Muwattaa'' or Beaten Path—that is, a complete body of law and religion.

Sources

Eliade, Mircea, ed. 1987. *Encyclopedia of religion.* New York: Macmillan.

Gibb, H.A.A., and Kramers, J. H., eds. 1965. *Shorter encyclopedia of Islam.* Ithaca, N.Y.: Cornell University Press.

Heravi, Mehdi, 1973. *Concise encyclopedia of the Middle East.* Washington, D.C.: Public Affairs Press.

Rahim, Abdur. 1981. *The principles of Muhammaden jurisprudence according to the Hanafi, Maliki, Shafii and Hanbali schools.* Westport, Conn.: Hyperion Press.

SCHLIEFFEN PLAN. A politico-military plan for the attack on the West by Germany in August 1914. The plan was devised in 1895, modified several times, and at first was a success until manpower shortages halted its effect; it was also the basis of the Nazi blitzkrieg in 1940.

General Count Alfred von Schlieffen (1833–1913) was born in Berlin and became a staff officer in the Prussian Wars (1866–70). Later, he was chief of the general staff (1891–1905). The aim of the plan was to attack France through Belgium, while fighting only a holding operation on the Russian front. In World War I the plan was the basis of the unsuccessful German strategy. Von Schlieffen advocated the training of general staff officers in how armies should be led and he pushed hard for the advanced use of technical equipment and the army's use of mobile heavy artillery.

Sources

Bucholz, Arden. 1991. *Moltke, Schlieffen, and Prussian war planning.* New York: Berg/ St. Martin's Press.

Cook, Chris, 1983. *Macmillan dictionary of historical terms.* London: Macmillan.

Crystal, David, ed. 1990. *The Cambridge encyclopedia.* Cambridge: Cambridge University Press.

Preece, Warren E., ed. 1965. *Encyclopedia Britannica.* Chicago: Encyclopedia Britannica, Inc., William Benton.

Ritter, Gerhard. 1958. *The Schlieffen Plan: a critique of a myth.* London: O. Wolff.

SCHUMAN PLAN. A plan for the European Coal and Steel Community (1950), which sought to achieve economic and military unity in Europe and a rapprochement between France and Germany so that the two would not go to war again. The community was realized in 1952 on an economic basis when six nations of Europe established the European economic union. This was the beginning of a set of economic agreements on which the European Common Market was formed in 1958.

Robert Schuman (1886–1963) was born in Luxembourg into a well-to-do family and was educated at German-language schools. He studied at the universities of Bonn, Berlin, and Munich, and graduated in law from the University of Strasbourg. He practiced law in Metz. He spent World War I in prison, having refused to enter combat. Afterward he was elected to the French Chamber of Deputies and for seventeen years was head of the Assembly Finance Division. In 1940 he was arrested by the Gestapo, escaped, and worked for the French underground resistance. In 1946 he was France's finance minister and introduced an austerity campaign. He became a prime minister in 1947, and in 1950 he advanced the plan to pool the coal and steel resources that had been in dispute in Europe. He successfully weathered the electoral reforms of Charles de Gaulle, and in November 1958 he was reelected to the French National Assembly. He was elected president of the Strasbourg European Assembly (1958–60) and awarded the Charlemagne Prize.

Sources

Bullen, Roger, and Pelley, M. E., et al., eds. 1986. *The Schuman Plan, the Council of Europe and Western European integration: May 1950–December 1952.* London: H.M.S.O.

Diebold, William. 1959. *The Schuman plan: a study in economic cooperation, 1950–59.* New York: Praeger.

McHenry, Robert, ed. 1992. *The new encyclopedia Britannica.* Chicago: Encyclopedia Britannica, Inc.

Magnussen, Magnus; Goring, Rosemary; and Thorn, John O., eds. 1990. *Chambers biographical dictionary.* Edinburgh: Chambers Ltd.

Moritz, Charles, ed. 1963. *Current biography yearbook.* New York: H. W. Wilson.

Rothe, Anna, ed. 1948. *Current biography yearbook.* New York: H. W. Wilson.

SCHUTZIAN. Relating to the modern German social philosopher and his descriptive sociology that holds that sociologists are important in whatever they investigate.

Alfred Schutz (1899–1959) was born in Austria-Hungary (now Austria), studied at the University of Vienna, and became a banker. His main work, *The Phenomenology of the Social World* (1932), was translated in 1967. He immigrated to the United States in 1939 where he continued to work in the banking profession in New York. In 1952 he became a professor of philosophy and sociology at the New School of Social Research where his phenomenological approach to social investigation enjoyed much support during the 1960s and early 1970s and he had a strong influence on ethnomethodology and critical theory in sociology, especially on Jürgen Habermas (b. 1929).

Sources

Bullock, Alan, and Woodings, R. B. 1983. *The Fontana biographical companion to modern thought.* London: Collins.

McHenry, Robert, ed. 1992. *The new encyclopedia Britannica.* Chicago: Encyclopedia Britannica, Inc.

Magnussen, Magnus; Goring, Rosemary; and Thorn, John O., eds. 1990. *Chambers biographical dictionary.* Edinburgh: Chambers Ltd.

Natanson, Maurice A. 1986. *Anonymity: a study in the philosophy of Alfred Schutz.* Bloomington: Indiana University Press.

Schutz, Alfred. 1970. *On phenomenology and social relations.* Chicago: Chicago University Press.

Schutz, Alfred. 1982. *Life forms and meaning structure.* London: Routledge and Kegan Paul.

SCHWENCKFELDER. Member of the sixteenth-century Protestant sect that upheld the deification of the humanity of Christ—that is, that he was begotten, not created—and the belief that God is apart from all creatures and therefore is the Father of Christ's humanity and deity.

C(K)aspar von Schwenckfeld (1490–1561) was born into a noble family near Liegnitz, Lower Silesia. For two years he studied in Cologne, and then he served at different courts with Duke Charles of Münsterberg and as a counselor to Duke Frederick II of Liegnitz. In 1521 Schwenckfeld retired to study the scriptures. He followed the beliefs of Martin Luther at Worms and in 1525, identifying his interests with those of the reformer, went to Wittenberg to see him, where he found that their views differed widely. Schwenckfeld's religious views brought him rejection and extreme dislike from both Lutherans and Catholics. Emperor Ferdinand forced the duke of Liegnitz to banish him in 1529, and he traveled through Europe attracting bands of followers as well as persecutors, and died at Ulm. His beliefs made him a religious outlaw at a convention of evangelical theologians in 1540. After he died, a small group, "Confessors of the Glory of Christ," spread his ideas, published his writings, and established themselves in Silesia until 1826. In 1734 forty families of his followers immigrated to England and later to Pennsylvania and established their community. A small group of 2,000–3,000 might still be found there.

Sources

Cross, Frank L. 1974. *The Oxford dictionary of the Christian Church.* 2ed. New York: Oxford University Press.

Douglas, James D., ed. 1974. *The new international dictionary of the Christian Church.* Exeter: Paternoster Press.

McHenry, Robert, ed. 1992. *The new encyclopedia Britannica.* Chicago: Encyclopedia Britannica, Inc.

Magnussen, Magnus; Goring, Rosemary; and Thorn, John O., eds. 1990. *Chambers biographical dictionary.* Edinburgh: Chambers Ltd.

Hastings, James, 1920. *Encyclopedia of religion and ethics.* Edinburgh: T. and T. Clark.

Smith, Benjamin. 1903. *The Century cyclopedia of names.* London: The Times.

SCOPES TRIAL. A trial in July 1925 that discredited religious fundamentalism in the United States.

John Thomas Scopes (1900–1970) was born in Paducah, Kentucky, educated at public schools and, after graduating from the University of Kentucky in 1924, was appointed to a teaching position at Central High School, Dayton, Tennessee. In March 1925 the state legislature passed a law against teaching evolution in the public schools of Tennessee; in May the American Civil Liberties Union sought someone willing to test the constitutionality of the law. Scopes, who had substituted for his school principle in teaching biology, agreed to be defendant in the test case because he believed that religion and politics should not interfere with the acquisition of knowledge. William Jennings Bryan (1860–1925) a notable U.S. political figure, lawyer, and fundamentalist and Clarence Seward Darrow (1857–1938), a prominent U.S. criminal lawyer, volunteered to oppose each other in the case, thereby ensuring that the trial would become an international event, which it did. The trial began July 10. The judge would not allow the law to be tested by reference to Darwin's theory of evolution, so the trial itself, distinct from the enormous publicity it received, focussed on whether or not Scopes had taught evolution. He said he had, was found guilty, and fined $100. On appeal the state supreme court upheld the law, but acquitted Scopes on the argument that the fine had been excessive. Afterward, Scopes left teaching and became a geologist with Gulf Oil Company and later the United Gas Corporation. In 1960 he helped to promoted a film version of the play *Inherit the Wind* that was based on his trial. He retired in 1964. The law was repealed in 1967, the year he published his memoirs.

Sources

Colletta, Paola E. 1964–69. *William Jennings Bryan: a political biography.* 3 vols. Lincoln: University of Nebraska Press.

Darrow, Clarence S. 1932. *The story of my life.* New York: Charles Scribner's Sons.

De Camp, L. Sprague. 1968. *The great monkey trial.* Garden City, New York: Doubleday.

Douglas, James D., ed. 1974. *The new international dictionary of the Christian Church.* Exeter: Paternoster Press.

Garraty, John A., and Carnes, Mark C., eds. 1988. *Dictionary of American biography.* Supplement 8. New York: Charles Scribner's Sons and Collier Macmillan.

Ginger, Ray. 1958. *Six days or forever? Tennessee v. John Thomas Scopes.* 1968 edition. Chicago: Quadrangle Books.

Koenig, Louis W. 1971. *Bryan: a political biography.* New York: Putnam.

Scopes, John T. 1925. *The world's most famous court trial: State of Tennessee v. John Thomas Scopes. Complete stenographic report of the court test of the Tennessee anti-evolution act at Dayton, July 10–21, 1925 including speeches and arguments of attorneys.* Reprint 1971. New York: Da Capo Press.

Scopes, John T., and Presley, James. 1967. *Center of the storm: memoirs of John T. Scopes.* New York: Holt, Rinehart and Winston.

Weinberg, Arthur, and Weinberg, Lila. 1980. *Clarence Darrow: a sentimental rebel.* New York: Putnam.

SCOTISM, SCOTIST. The metaphysical system of the thirteenth-century theologian which assumed that distinctions drawn by the mind were real, even though their existence depended on their relation to the mind. Such distinctions were the basis of formal thought. The system also assumed the principle of Haecceity, that is, that human existence is a peculiar element of being and cannot be described, conceived of, or given any qualities or attributes. In 1535 universities were forbidden to teach Scotism by royal injunction.

Johannes Duns Scotus (c. 1265–1308). See DUNCE.

SCOTT BADER COMMONWEALTH. A British collaborative management–worker organization designed to reduce industrial conflict and enhance working life for all.

Annie Eliza Dora Scott (1884–1979), born in England, cared for babies while her mother took in student boarders. In 1912 Ernest Bader took a room in the Scott house, they married (1915), and she became a nurse. They pursued business interests in the Scott Bader Company, and she became a director. In addition to the traditional work of a wife, she helped Ernest, traveled with him, and took part in the many of his humanistic causes.

Ernest Bader (1890–1982) was born in Switzerland, son of a Protestant farmer, and, from his father's bitter experience with moneylenders, learned to equate interest with usury. After completing military service he went to England, married, and worked for a bank in London. In 1917 he and his wife moved to the countryside to join a community of conscientious objectors. In 1920 he established an importing agency, Scott Bader Ltd., which became a flourishing chemical, plastics, and resin manufacturer. The bombing of London in 1940 led Bader to move to Wollaston Hall, where their firm prospered during World War II. In 1945 a committed pacifist, he believed that business should serve society and that social conflict could be resolved through common ownership of industry. He established the Scott Bader Commonwealth Ltd., a charity that held 90 percent of the capital of Scott Barder Ltd., and decided how the firm's profits were to be distributed. Bader's patriarchal control of Commonwealth lasted until 1963 when a Quaker sociologist, F. Blum, completed an action research study of the organization, and power was moved from Bader to a self-governing work community. In 1970 Bader took up other humanitarian causes and toured the world in search of solutions to human distress and conflict.

Sources

Blum, Fred H. 1968. *Work and community: the Scott Bader Commonwealth and the quest for a new order.* London: Routledge and Kegan Paul.

Hoe, Susanna. 1978. *The man who gave his company away: a biography of Ernest Scott Bader, founder of Scott Bader Commonwealth.* London: Heinemann.

Jeremy, David J. 1984. Ernest Bader. In D. J. Jeremy and C. Shaw, eds. *Dictionary of business biography: a biographical dictionary of business leaders in Britain in the period of 1860–1980.* London: Butterworth.

SCOTTISH ENLIGHTENMENT. A founding school of thought in political economy.

The inspiration and economic growth of eighteenth-century Scotland was partly encouraged by the union of Scotland and England (1707) which gave Scotland free trade with England in exchange for its independent parliament. This union drew much attention to economic development and to the ways institutions were related, and, from the intellectual discussions that ensued, political economy as a field of inquiry and research was founded. Between 1740 and 1790 the intellectual activity that centered in Scotland and England involved the ideas of David Hume (1711–76) and Adam Smith (1723–90); other notables were Adam Ferguson (1723–1816), Francis Hutcheson (1694–1746), William Robertson (1721–93), Lord Kames (1696–1782), Thomas Reid (1710–96), John Millar (1735–1801), and Sir James Stuart (1712–80). Their interests were wide, but in time they concentrated on problems of progress in society and, to advance this idea, turned to history, political and moral philosophy, and issues of politics and the economy.

Sources

Campbell, Ray H., and Skinner, Andrew S. 1982. *The origins and nature of Scottish Enlightenment.* Edinburgh: John Donald.

Eatwell, John; Milgate, Murray; and Newman, Peter. 1987. *The new Palgrave: a dictionary of economics.* London: Macmillan.

Miller, David. 1987. *The Blackwell encyclopedia of political thought.* Oxford: Basil Blackwell.

SEASHORE'S GROUP COHESIVENESS INDEX. A measure of group cohesiveness defined as attraction to the group, or resistance to leaving. Group members are asked how much they feel part of their group; how they would feel about moving to another group to work under similar conditions; and to compare their group with others (Miller, 1991:375).

Stanley E. Seashore (b. 1915) was born in Wahoo, Nebraska, and studied at the universities of Iowa, Minnesota, and Michigan (Ph.D., 1954). He worked as a personnel manager for U.S. Steel (1939–45), a staff consultant for Kearney and Company (1945–50), and in 1956 began teaching and conducting research at the University of Michigan at Ann Arbor, and directing research at the Institute for Social Research. A professional psychologist, he was on the committee for the certification of psychologists in Michigan. He is a member of several professional associations in the social sciences, a specialist in organizational psychology and industrial psychology, and has been honored by the Guggenheim Foundation (1965–66) and the Academy of Management (1984). He published on organizational performance and change and on general social issues, and with his colleagues at the Institute of Social Research contributed to many books and monographs in his specialty.

Sources

Miller, Delbert C. 1991. *Handbook of research design and social measurement.* 5th ed. Newbury Park, Calif.: Sage Publications.

Seashore, Stanley E. 1954. *Group cohesiveness in the industrial work group.* Ann Arbor: University of Michigan, Institute for Social Research and Survey Research Center.

Straub, Deborah, ed. 1988. *Contemporary authors.* New Revision Series 24. Detroit: Gale Research.

SELEUCID. Member of an early Syrian dynasty.

Seleucus I, surnamed Nicator (c. 358–281 B.C.), was a general in the Macedonian Army of Alexander the Great (356–323 B.C.). After Alexander's death he became satrap of Babylonia, fought Antigonus, captured Babylon (312 B.C), and conquered areas of central Asia and India. He ascended the throne in about 306 B.C. In 301 B.C. he led his allies, Cassander and Lysimachus, in the defeat of Antigonus at Ipsus, a port of Asia Minor which he came to control. In 285 B.C. he took Demetrius prisoner, defeated Lysimachus at Corupedium (281 B.C.), and briefly ruled the lands that once were Alexander's. The Seleucidae dynasty ruled Syria until 65 B.C.

Sources

Bevan, Edwin R. 1966. *The house of Seleucus.* London: Routledge and Kegan Paul.

Downey, Glanville. 1961. *A history of Antioch in Syria: from Seleucus to the Arab conquest.* Princeton, N.J.: Princeton University Press.

McHenry, Robert, ed. 1992. *The new encyclopedia Britannica.* Chicago: Encyclopedia Britannica, Inc.

Magnussen, Magnus; Goring, Rosemary; and Thorn, John O., eds. 1990. *Chambers biographical dictionary.* Edinburgh: Chambers Ltd.

SELJUK. Member of Turkish dynasties in the twelfth and thirteenth centuries whose conquests extended from the Mediterranean to the western borders of China.

Seljuk (fl. tenth century) was leader—a Ghuzz or Oghuz chieftain—of a nomadic tribe during the migration of Turkish peoples from central Asia and southeast Russia to the lower Syr Darya River. They fought the Samanids and later Mahmud of Ghanza. In time, they were converted to the Sunnite form of Islam, and Seljuk's two grandsons, Chagri Beg and Toghril Beg (d. c. 1063), reigned in central and western Asia from the eleventh through the thirteenth centuries. After conquering Persia, Toghril Beg, a Sunnite, rescued the Abbassid caliph at Baghdad from his Shiite lieutenant and was nominated "Commander of the Faithful." In 1063 he was succeeded by his nephew, Alp Arslan, who took Syria and Palestine from the Fatimite caliph of Egypt, and in 1071 he defeated and captured the Byzantine emperor, Romanus Diogenes, who later bought his release by the cession of much of Asia Minor. Alp Arslan was followed by his son, Malik Shah, on whose death in 1092 succession was disputed. Civil war ensued and resulted in the partition of the empire among four branches of the Seljukian family. Although the dynasty was superseded by the Ottomans at the end of the thirteenth century, it had established a model of land tenure for oriental feudalism and many forms of enduring administration.

Sources

McHenry, Robert, ed. 1992. *The new encyclopedia Britannica.* Chicago: Encyclopedia Britannica, Inc.

Morris, William, ed. 1965–66. *Grolier universal encyclopedia.* New York: American Book-Stratford Press, Inc.

Roth, Cecil E., ed. 1971. *Encyclopedia Judaica.* New York: Macmillan.

SENECAN. In the style of the Stoic philosopher and writer of declamatory tragedies.

Lucius Annaeus Seneca (c. 4 B.C.–A.D. 65) was born at Corduba, Spain, and as a child was brought to Rome with his parents. He studied rhetoric and philosophy and became a noted pleader of causes, and a senator under Caligula. In the first year of the reign of Caligula's successor, Claudius, Seneca was banished to Corsica for the alleged seduction of the princess, Julia Livilla, the emperor's niece (41). Through the influence of Agrippina, Claudius's new wife, Seneca was recalled (49) and given the task of educating her son, Nero. On the accession of Nero (54), Seneca enjoyed much control of government. However, his attempts to restrain the emperor led to Seneca's retirement from the court (62) and to charges of complicity in the conspiracy of Piso. Seneca was ordered to commit suicide. His writings consist of many prose works and tragedies such as *Hercules, Medea,* and *Oedipus.*

See also NERONIAN.

Sources

McHenry, Robert, ed. 1992. *The new encyclopedia Britannica.* Chicago: Encyclopedia Britannica, Inc.

Magnussen, Magnus; Goring, Rosemary; and Thorn, John O., eds. 1990. *Chambers biographical dictionary*. Edinburgh: Chambers Ltd.
Motto, Anna L. 1973. *Seneca*. New York: Twayne Publishers.
Seneca, Lucius A. 1968. *The Stoic philosophy of Seneca: essays and letters of Seneca*. New York: W. W. Norton.

SENUSSI, SANUSI, SANUSIY(Y)AH. A member of a North African Muslim mystic sect or brotherhood sometimes noted for fanaticism and belligerence.

Sidi Muhammad ibn 'Ali as-Sanusi (c. 1791–c. 1859) founded the sect in 1837. He was born sometime before 1806, migrated with his father to Fez (1814), and in 1829 went on a pilgrimage to Mecca after being initiated into various sects in Africa. In Mecca he joined the Khidri, which split in two in 1835. He established his new order, and the brotherhood became a reformist missionary movement seeking a return to the life of early Islam, especially by reforming the Bedouins and converting non-Muslims in Central Africa. He lived on Mount Abu Oubais (Mecca) until 1843, and he returned to Africa where his sect's influence spread. Most Sanusi were personal followers of as-Sanusi al-Kabir, the Grand Sanusi and family. Because it united religious and tribal institutions, the order was so powerful in Cyrenaica that during World War I it effectively challenged the Italians. Between the world wars, the Sanusis continued to be a strong political force for the Cyrenaicans in their negotiations, especially with the Italians and the British. In 1951 the head of the Senussi—or Sanusiyah as they are now known—was made king of the independent and united nation of Libya. In 1969 the kingdom was overthrown by a military junta.

Sources

Evans-Pritchard, Edward E. 1954. *The Sanusi of Cyrenaica*. Oxford: Clarendon Press.
Hastings, James. 1920. *Encyclopedia of religion and ethics*. Edinburgh: T. and T. Clark.
Hinnells, John, ed. 1984. *The Facts on File dictionary of religions*. New York: Facts on File.
Macgregor, Geddes. 1990. *The Everyman dictionary of religion and philosophy*. London: J. M. Dent.
McHenry, Robert, ed. 1992. *The new encyclopedia Britannica*. Chicago: Encyclopedia Britannica, Inc.

SEWARD'S FOLLY, SEWARD'S ICE BOX. The decision by the United States to purchase Alaska. Alaska.

William Henry Seward (1801–71) was born at Florida, Orange County, New York, graduated from Union College and was admitted to the bar in 1822. An anti-Masonic candidate in the New York State Senate (1830), he was elected and served until 1834 and became state governor in 1838. He was elected a Republican senator (1849–61) and was a candidate for the Republican nomination for president in 1860. He was stabbed in the throat by Lewis Powell, fellow conspirator in the assassination of Abraham Lincoln (April 1865), and after recovering was President Andrew Jackson's secretary of state (1861–69). He handled the Trent Affair (1861)—an international dispute with Britain—

under Lincoln, and during Jackson's administration Seward oversaw the purchase of Alaska from Russia for $7.2 million (1867). He also advocated the purchase of the Virgin Islands at the time, but resistance of the purchase of the "icebox wasteland," as Alaska was called, became too strong to gain support for the plan.

Sources

Jacob, Kathryn A., and Ragsdale, Bruce A. 1989. *Biographical dictionary of the United States Congress: 1774–1989.* Bicentennial ed. Washington, D.C.: U.S. Government Printing Office.

McHenry, Robert, ed. 1992. *The new encyclopedia Britannica.* Chicago: Encyclopedia Britannica, Inc.

Magnussen, Magnus; Goring, Rosemary; and Thorn, John O., eds. 1990. *Chambers biographical dictionary.* Edinburgh: Chambers Ltd.

Malone, Dumas, ed. 1935. *Dictionary of American biography.* Vol. VIII. New York: Charles Scribner's Sons.

SHAPLEY VALUE. In economics the assessment of what a person expects when they gamble or enter a lottery, and the value they put on the outcome for any other participants.

Lloyd Stowell Shapley (b. 1932) was born in Cambridge, Massachussetts, educated at Harvard, and studied mathematics at Princeton (Ph.D., 1953). He became a professor of mathematics at the University of California, Los Angeles (1981–), and specialized in game theory and its application to mathematical economics and political science. He is a member of the National Academy of Science, the American Mathematical Society, and a fellow of the American Academy of Arts and Sciences.

Sources

Adcock, Edgar H., Jr., ed. 1992. *American men and women of science 1992–93.* Physical, biological and related sciences. 18th ed. New Providence, N.J.: R. R. Bowker.

Eatwell, John; Milgate, Murray; and Newman, Peter. 1987. *The new Palgrave: a dictionary of economics.* London: Macmillan.

Hazelwinkel, Michiel, ed. 1992. *Encyclopedia of mathematics.* Dordrecht: Kluwer Academic Publishers.

McHenry, Robert, ed. 1992. *The new encyclopedia Britannica.* Chicago: Encyclopedia Britannica, Inc.

SHARPEVILLE. A political symbol, as in "Remember Sharpeville!," the catch-phrase for the international movement against South Africa's apartheid policy. In Sharpeville, March 20–21, 1960, police fired on Africans, led by the militant Pan-Africanist Congress which was seeking, in a nonviolent campaign, to demonstrate against South Africa's Pass Laws and have them abolished. The laws required that black people carry passes to travel within South Africa. Among the 67 killed and the 186 wounded were 48 women and children. The African National party called for a national day of mourning, and the government, wavering at first, announced the suspension of Pass Laws. So many people burned their passes that a state of national emergency was declared a week later, the African National Congress was banned, and Nelson Mandela and 1,800 political activists were imprisoned. International leaders condemned South Africa's apartheid policy. The ban was lifted at the end of August, and the prisoners were released. The Pass Laws were extended to women over 16, and police were no longer allowed to arrest anyone unable to produce their passbook on demand.

Sharpeville, in southcentral Transvaal, South Africa, is a black township, a suburb of Vereeniging.

Sources

Davies, Rob; O'Meara, Dan; and D'Lamini, Sipho. 1988. *The struggle for South Africa.* London: Zed Books.

Keesings contemporary archives: weekly diary of world events. 1959–60:17449, 17469, 17528, 17684. London: Keesings Publications.

McHenry, Robert, ed. 1992. *The new encyclopedia Britannica.* Chicago: Encyclopedia Britannica, Inc.

Mandela, Nelson. 1963. *No easy walk to freedom.* London: Heinemann.

SHAVIAN. Relating to the English dramatist and his social commentary and witty remarks on humankind; a follower or admirer of the dramatist; like the style of writing Shaw used, that is, Shavian wit, Shavian insouciance, irreverence, paradox, ebullience.

George Bernard Shaw (1856–1950) was born in Dublin, Ireland, had a desultory education, learned music from his mother, a singing teacher, and, by reading and visiting the National Gallery of Dublin, taught himself about literature and art. He worked as an office boy and later as a cashier for an estate agent, and went to London. He published five novels (1879–83) with little success, and he joined the socialist Fabian Society. His plays were performed with great success (1904–7) at London's Court Theater, his reputation grew, and in 1925 he was awarded the Nobel Prize for Literature. His social satires on the English character and British institutions amused his countrymen immensely. He was regarded as a crank for his vegetarianism and abstinence from alcohol; conservatives where shocked by his free thought, socialism, views on the war production industry, medical profession, and liberal attitudes to sexual relations (e.g., *Mrs. Warren's Profession*). Few social institutions escaped his witty analysis and criticism.

Sources

Devine, Elizabeth; Held, Michael; Vinson, James; and Walsh, George, eds. 1983. *Thinkers of the twentieth century: a biographical, bibliographical and critical dictionary.* London: Macmillan.

Ganz, Arthur. 1983. *George Bernard Shaw.* New York: Grove.

Hammond, Nicholas G.L., and Scullard, Howard H., eds. 1985. *The Oxford companion to English literature.* Oxford: Clarendon Press.

Holroyd, Michael. 1979. *The genius of Shaw: a symposium.* London: Hodder and Stoughton.

Holroyd, Michael. 1988. *Bernard Shaw*. London: Chatto and Windus.
McHenry, Robert, ed. 1992. *The new encyclopedia Britannica*. Chicago: Encyclopedia Britannica, Inc.
Mathews, John F. 1969. *George Bernard Shaw*. New York: Columbia University Press.
Ousby, Ian, ed. 1988. *The Cambridge guide to literature in English*. Cambridge: Cambridge University Press.

SHAWCROSS REPORT. A royal commission report on Britain's newspaper industry (1961–62) which criticized manning standards and demarcation of work. It was based on a survey by Personnel Administration Ltd. but had little direct effect. Eventually, however, it led to the establishment of the Joint Board for the Newspaper Industry, another survey by the National Newspaper Industry (1966), and major changes in Fleet Street.

Hartley William Shawcross, Baron Shawcross (b. 1902), was born in Gniessen, Germany, educated at Dulwich College and abroad, and was called to the bar in 1925. He was elected Labor M.P. for Saint Helens (1945–58), and was made attorney-general (1945–51) and chief prosecutor at the Nuremberg Trials (1945–46). As such, he became a noted international jurist, especially when he led investigations relating to the Lynskey Tribunal (1948) and to the prosecution of the second atom spy, Klaus Fuchs (1911–88) in 1950. Because of his dislike of the narrow political approach and tactics of the Labour party, he resigned from Parliament in 1953 and from the party in 1958. He was created a life peer in 1959 and was the chairman of the Royal Commission on the Press in 1961–62.

See also SIDNEY STANLEY PRINCIPLE OF FINANCE.

Sources

The international who's who, 1992–93. London: Europa Publications.
Magnussen, Magnus; Goring, Rosemary; and Thorn, John O., eds. 1990. *Chambers biographical dictionary*. Edinburgh: Chambers Ltd.
Marsh, Arthur. 1979. *Concise encyclopedia of industrial relations*. Westmead, Farnborough, Hants: Gower.

SHAYS REBELLION. An armed revolt (1786–87) in Massachusetts that involved farmers who were distressed by the amount of their debts and taxes and the cost of their judiciary. In September 1786 they attacked the courts; the local militia would not fight against the farmers, and if the militia of eastern Massachusetts had not come to its defense, the Springfield arsenal might have been taken. The rebels were beaten by an army raised by the state government and commanded by Major General Benjamin Lincoln. The rebellion showed how inadequately the Articles of Confederation could deal with internal conflict.

Daniel Shays (1747–1825) may have been born in Hopkinton, Massachusetts; he was poorly educated and raised in rural poverty. He was a laborer and may have served as a drill sergeant in the local militia. He did serve courageously and with distinction in the Patriot Army against the British until 1780, and he rose to captain in the 5th Massachusetts regiment. In 1780 he retired and became a local civic leader. He chaired a committee that drafted a resolution concerning the attempts of debt-ridden farmers who were intent on preventing the local judiciary from performing its duties, and who wanted to stop the Supreme Court in Springfield from sitting. Shays became leader of the rebels in January 1787 when General Lincoln was sent to put down the rebellion. No shots were fired. Shays died in Sparta, New York.

Sources

Magnussen, Magnus; Goring, Rosemary; and Thorn, John O., eds. 1990. *Chambers biographical dictionary.* Edinburgh: Chambers Ltd.

Malone, Dumas, ed. 1935. *Dictionary of American biography.* Vol. IX. New York: Charles Scribner's Sons.

Shays' Rebellion. 1987. Microfilm. Alexandria Va.: Chadwyck-Healey, Inc.

Spiller, Roger J. 1984. *Dictionary of American military biography.* Westport, Conn.: Greenwood Press.

SHERMAN ANTI-TRUST ACT. The U.S. antimonopoly law (1890) which forbids "every contract, combination . . . or conspiracy in the restraint of trade or commerce." Enforcement of the act is provided through criminal penalties, civil suit action, injunction, and seizure of property. The U.S. Congress saw that to maintain competition in business it was important to intervene in the economy to prevent powerful monopolies from eliminating competitors. The act failed two tests in the Supreme Court but was strengthened by two further acts in 1914.

John Sherman (1823–1900) was born at Lancaster, Ohio, and he left school at 14 to work on canal maintenance. Later, he began studying law (1840), was admitted to the bar (1844), and became president of the first Ohio Republican State Convention (1855). He was elected as a Republican to the Thirty-fourth and three succeeding congresses (1855–61). He resigned but was reelected in 1866, and was chairman of financial committees in both houses. He authored bills for the reconstruction of the seceded states and the resumption of specie payment in 1879. In 1877 he was appointed secretary of the Treasury, and in 1878 he had prepared a redemption fund in gold that raised the legal tender notes to par value. In 1887 and 1888, he was returned to the Senate, became its president, and afterward chaired the Committee on Foreign Relations. In 1897 he was secretary of state and retired in 1898. The Sherman Act (1890; repealed in 1893) sanctioned large purchases of silver by the Treasury. Sherman published many speeches on finance, currency, and taxation, and an autobiography, *Recollections of John Sherman,* in two large volumes covering his life to 1895.

Sources

Commager, Henry S., ed. 1968. *Documents of American history.* 8th ed. New York: Appleton-Century-Crofts.

Jacob, Kathryn A., and Ragsdale, Bruce A. 1989. *Biographical directory of the United States Congress: 1774–1989.* Bicentennial ed. Washington, D.C.: U.S. Government Printing Office.

Magnussen, Magnus; Goring, Rosemary; and Thorn, John O., eds. 1990. *Chambers biographical dictionary*. Edinburgh: Chambers Ltd.

Malone, Dumas, ed. 1935. *Dictionary of American biography*. Vol. IX. New York: Charles Scribner's Sons.

Plano, Jack C., and Greenberg, Milton. 1989. *The American political dictionary*. New York: Holt, Rinehart and Winston.

Who was who, 1897–1942. Vol. 1. Chicago: Marquis.

SHYLOCK. A creditor with no compassion for his debtors.

In Shakespeare's *Merchant of Venice* (1595), Shylock is a Jewish money-lender who decides to kill Antonio by exacting his due—a pound of flesh—from a contract made with the merchant. In court Shylock loses and falls into disgrace for taking such a pitiless attitude to debt collection. With comic intentions, Shakespeare made the character a stereotypical image of the Jew in those days, that is, a person with a vicious hatred of Christians, a miser obsessed with money. The name of the character may have come from Shallack, Hebrew for cormorant; Shiloh, for the coming of the Messiah in association with Salah or Selah, father of Eber from whom Hebrews took their name; the word for a contemptible English idler, Shullock or Shallock of the sixteenth century; or from Roderigo Lopez (d. 1594), a Jew, who was born in Portugal and practiced medicine in London at Saint Bartholomew's Hospital. In 1586 he became a physician at the court of Elizabeth I. In this period of anti-Semitism, he was accused of attempting to poison the queen, found guilty, and executed. In 1595 Shakespeare's creation of Shylock was a response to popular anti-Jewish feeling at the time, and perhaps he used as his immediate source the play at the Rose Theater, *The Venesyan Comedy* (1594); or he may have reversed a tale about the well-liked Roman Jew, Samson Cesena, victim of a Christian usurper, Paolo Secchi.

Sources

Boyce, Charles. 1990. *Shakespeare A to Z*. New York: Facts on File.

Campbell, Oscar J., and Quinn, Edward. 1966. *The reader's encyclopedia of Shakespeare*. New York: Thomas Y. Crowell.

Evans, Gareth L., and Evans, Barbara L. 1978. *The Shakespeare companion*. New York: Charles Scribner's Sons.

Gross, John. 1992. *Shylock*. London: Chatto and Windus.

Halliday, Frank E. 1964. *A Shakespeare companion*. London: Duckworth.

Kirkpatrick, D. L. 1991. *Reference guide to English literature*. 2d ed. London: St. James Press.

Wesker, Arnold. 1990. *Shylock and other plays*. Harmondsworth: Penguin.

SIDNEY STANLEY PRINCIPLE OF FINANCE. A fraudulent principle of financing operations without money (Aitken, 1991).

Sidney Stanley (fl. 1933–49) was to be deported from Britain in 1933 with his brother Marcus on grounds of fraud. He used five different names, but the one he became known by, Sidney Stanley, revealed him as a comic little fixer who flourished with the austerity and rationing in Britain after World War II by persuading others that he was wealthy. He gave new suits and strings of sausages to junior ministers in Attlee's government (1945–51). His fraud ended with the Lynskey Tribunal (1948–49). At this investigation, it was learned that he had three bank accounts at different banks and moved money between them so rapidly that the banks had no time to see that there was in fact no money. He became a close associate of John Belcher and others at the Board of Trade, and he was involved in the acquisition and distribution of amusement machines, licenses for buildings in London, exporting cement to France and Belgium, gifts to public officials, and money paid to government members. The truth about his activities was said by Sir Hartley William Shawcross (b. 1902), who cross-examined Stanley, to be concealed by falsehoods, no memory for facts, and imagination.

See also LYNSKEY TRIBUNAL.

Source

Aitken, Ian. 1991. The high tragi-comedy of high finance. *The Guardian Weekly,* December 15.

SIMEONITE. Low-churchman.

Charles Simeon (1759–1836) was born at Reading, Berkshire, educated at Eton and King's College, Cambridge, and elected fellow at his college (1782). In that year he took Holy Orders and was immediately appointed perpetual curate of Trinity Church, Cambridge. As a preacher, he was noted for his impassioned evangelicalism that at first aroused much deep opposition. At the university his followers became known as "Simeonites." By 1822 they became the butt of undergraduate humor for their purity and their unsophisticated attitude to wine and women. He made many converts and became enormously influential throughout England. He took a controlling part in the work of the Church Missionary Society, which he founded (1797), and his influence survived long after his death. His *Horae Homileticae* in seventeen volumes (1819–28) includes over 2,500 sermon outlines.

Sources

Hopkins, Hugh A.E. 1977. *Charles Simeon of Cambridge.* Grand Rapids, Mich.: William B. Eerdman's.

McHenry, Robert, ed. 1992. *The new encyclopedia Britannica.* Chicago: Encyclopedia Britannica, Inc.

Pollard, Arthur, and Hennell, Michael. 1959. *Charles Simeon: essays written in commemoration of his centenary by members of the Evangelical Fellowship of Theological Literature.* London: SPCK.

SIMON LEGREE. A slave driver at work, a brutal master.

Simon Legree is a character in *Uncle Tom's Cabin* (1852) by Harriet Elizabeth Beecher Stowe (1811–96). It was a very popular antislavery novel in America. The author presented Uncle Tom as a man who was willing to tolerate anything, a simple, easygoing person with a noble mind and deeply drawn to Christianity. When he refuses bravely to tell where two women slaves are hiding, Simon Legree flogs him to death. Thereafter Legree's name became a synonym for a brutal master who drove his employees as if they were slaves.

Sources

Hart, James D. 1983. *The Oxford companion to American literature.* New York: Oxford University Press.

Herzberg, Max J. 1962. *The reader's encyclopedia of American literature.* New York: Thomas Y. Crowell.

Perkins, George; Perkins Barbara; and Leininger, Phillip, eds. 1991. *Benet's reader's encyclopedia of American literature.* New York: HarperCollins.

SKINNERIAN, SKINNER BOX. A follower of the ideas of the American behavioral psychologist; an experimenter's box with a lever or bar at one end and into which a laboratory animal can be placed and learn to operate the bar so as to receive rewards or avoid punishment. Skinner introduced the box in the 1950s, and it was variously modified by others for their learning experiments.

Burrhus Frederic Skinner (1904–90) was born in Susquehanna, Pennsylvania, and studied English at Hamilton College and scientific experimental psychology (Harvard, Ph.D., 1931). Until 1936 he was a research fellow at Harvard, and then he joined the faculty at the University of Minnesota. His first paper (1932) was on schedules of reinforcement, and his research studies appeared in *The Behavior of Organisms* (1938). He chaired the Psychology Department at the University of Indiana (1945–48) and returned to Harvard until 1974 when he retired, emeritus. His ideas greatly influenced modern scientific psychology, and he received many awards and honors from associations of psychologists around the world. He dispensed with theories of mind and brain; he argued that an adequate science of psychology should center on three types of variations and selection outside the individual, that is, natural selection; the evolution of operant conditioning that enabled an individual's environment to select behavior with contingencies not stable enough to function by way of natural selection; and the evolution of culture. To Skinner, culture was a rich series of circumstances affecting reinforcement and largely responsible for the behavioral repertoire that individuals learn. The mind and other ideas about cognitive structures were unnecessary because they could be explained by contingences of selection that explain behavior; the brain was merely a part of the organism and thus only part of what was to be explained.

Sources

Devine, Elizabeth; Held, Michael; Vinson, James; and Walsh, George, eds. 1983. *Thinkers of the twentieth century: a biographical, bibliographical and critical dictionary.* London: Macmillan.

Holland, James G. 1992. B. F. Skinner (1904–90). *American Psychologist* 47:665–667.

Lattal, Kennon A., ed. 1992. Reflections on B. F. Skinner and psychology. *American Psychologist* (Special Issue) 47:1269–1533.

Moritz, Charles, ed. 1990. *Current biography yearbook.* New York: H. W. Wilson.

Skinner, B. F. 1976. *Particulars of my life.* London: Jonathan Cape.
Skinner, B. F. 1983. *A matter of consequences.* New York: Alfred A. Knopf.
Skinner, B. F. 1983. *The shaping of a behaviorist.* New York: Alfred A. Knopf.

SLOANE RANGER. A London middle-class character (1970s) whose clothing, work, leisure pursuits, and speech reflected a fresh elitism and a sense of social class in Britain. As a woman, the Sloane Ranger was a personal assistant to an executive in advertising, hospitality, and expanding industries, and she wore a classic semi-uniform dress, a head scarf, jacket, and Italian shoes; the man tended to be in law, finance, the wine industry, real estate, and dressed like a gentleman.

Sloane Square is ringed with chimney-turreted Victorian facades in London's fashionable Chelsea, has plane trees, a fountain, and Holy Trinity Church, Royal Court Theater, Royal Court Hotel, and into it pour cosmopolitan shoppers. From Knightsbridge Station, Chelsea is bounded by Sloane Street, Chelsea Bridge Road, the Chelsea Embankment, Old Church Street, Fulham Road, Brompton Road, and Harrods Store back to the Station. This area of London blossomed under the Stuarts and the Georges, and during this period flourished Sir Hans Sloane (c. 1660–1753), a moneyed court physician, lord of Chelsea manor, who owned much property in the area. His names attached to the Square and the Street.

The Lone Ranger was devised by a committee and was first heard on George W. Trendle's WXYZ radio station, Detroit, when the 1930s Depression had forced him to the wall. The Lone Ranger, like Robin Hood, a law-and-order figure, was a mysterious stranger from places unknown and would disappear immediately after justice had been done. With hoof-beats to the strains of the *William Tell Overture* the "Masked Rider of the Plains," astride his horse Silver and accompanied by his loyal Indian companion, Tonto, championed justice in America's West. The radio serial was heard nightly on 224 stations for a half-hour. For the cinema, Republic produced a serial (1938) based on the radio series; five men played the masked rider, and later on television the most frequently used of the men, Clayton Moore, played in 130 films known around the Western world as "The Lone Ranger and Tonto" (1948–61).

Sources

Barr, Ann, and York, Peter. 1982. *The Sloane Ranger official handbook.* London: Ebury Press.
Barr, Ann, and York, Peter. 1983. *The official Sloane Ranger diary.* London: Ebury Press.
Dorfman, Ariel. 1983. *The Empire's old clothes: what the Lone Ranger, Babar and other innocent heroes do to our minds.* London: Pluto.
Parks, Rita. 1982. *The western hero in film and television: mass media mythology.* Ann Arbor, Mich.: UMI Press.
Stephen, Leslie, and Lee, Sydney, eds. 1917. *The dictionary of national biography.* London: Oxford University Press.
Tulloch, Sara. 1991. *The Oxford dictionary of new words.* Oxford: Oxford University Press.

SLUTSKY EQUATION. An economic equation in the modern theory of utility discovered by Slutsky in 1915 and by Hicks and Allen in *Value and Capital* (1934). "A price effect is equal to the sum of the income and substitution effects" (Greenwald, 1982:424). This equation of price theory splits the effect of a price change into an income effect and a substitution effect. The effect can also be applied to the effect on the labor supply of a lump sum.

Eugeny Slutsky (1880–1948) was born in Yaroslavl, Russia, and graduated in law and political economy at the University of Kiev where he taught law and became a professor of political economy at the Kiev Institute of Commerce (1918–26), and later at the Moscow Institute of Business Cycles (1926–31) and the Mathematics Institute, Academy of Sciences (1934–48). Afterward he worked with mathematical statistics and probability theory on stochastic processes that helped in the study of fluctuations and cycles in economic data.

Sources

Afriat, Sydney N. 1980. *Demand functions and the Slutsky matrix.* Princeton, N.J.: Princeton University Press.

Allen, R.D.G. 1950. The work of Eugen Slutsky. *Econometrica* 18:209–216.

Blaug, Mark, ed. 1986. *Who's who in economics: a biographical dictionary of major economists, 1700–1986.* 2d ed. Cambridge, Mass.: MIT Press.

Greenwald, Douglas, ed. 1982. *Encyclopedia of economics.* New York: McGraw-Hill.

Rutherford, Donald. 1992. *Dictionary of economics.* London: Routledge.

Sills, David L., ed. 1968. *International encyclopedia of the social sciences.* New York: Macmillan and Free Press.

SMITH ACT. A U.S. Alien Registration Act (1940) that required annual registration of aliens and forbade advocating the forcible overthrow of the U.S. government. Aimed at organizations as well as individuals, it specifically forbade undermining the loyalty of the armed forces, assassinations of public officials, and all violent political activities. It was the first peacetime law against sedition in the United States since 1798. In mentioning but not naming organizations, the act intended to outlaw communist, Nazi, and other fascist groups.

Howard Worth Smith (1883–1976) was born in Broad Run, Fauquier, Virginia, educated at public schools, and graduated from Bethel Military Academy in Warrenton. He studied law at the University of Virginia, was admitted to the bar in 1904, and began to practice in Alexandria, Virginia. He was also a banker and a farmer. He was made assistant general counsel and alien property custodian (1917–18) and was commonwealth attorney of Alexandria (1918–22) and a judge (1922–30). From 1931 to 1967 he served as a Democrat in seventeen succeeding U.S. congresses, and, when unsuccessful for renomination in 1966, he resumed his law practice. In 1940 he sponsored the Aliens Act that was given his name, and during his political career he chaired the Committee on Rules in two congresses.

Sources

Dierenfield, Bruce J. 1987. *Keeper of the rules: Congressman Howard W. Smith of Virginia.* Charlottesville: University Press of Virginia.

Jacob, Kathryn A., and Ragsdale, Bruce A. 1989. *Biographical directory of the United States Congress: 1774–1989.* Bicentennial ed. Washington, D.C.: U.S. Government Printing Office.

SMITHSONIAN AGREEMENT. An agreement of 1971 by the "Group of Ten" (composed of financial ministers of the industrialized nations of the free world); a stage in the transition of the International Monetary Fund from the fixed exchange rate, dominated by the U.S. dollar for many years, to the current system whereby exchange rates float. Its name comes from the place where the agreement was made, the Smithsonian Institution, in Washington. After it was agreed that the dollar would be devalued, other nations shortly followed and set their exchange rates according to their own interests.

The Smithsonian Institution was created by an act of the U.S. Congress in 1846 to carry out the terms of the will of James Smithson (1765–1829) of England, who in 1829 bequeathed his entire estate to the United States, "to found Washington, under the name of the Smithsonian Institution, an establishment for the increase in diffusion of knowledge among men." To carry out Smithson's mandate, the institution, as an independent trust establishment, performs fundamental research; publishes the results of studies, explorations, and investigations; preserves for study and reference over 70 million items of scientific cultural and historical interest; maintains exhibits representative of the arts, U.S. history, technology, aeronautics and space exploration, and natural history; participates in the eternal exchange of learned publications; and engages in programs of educational research. It is supported by its trust endowments and gifts, grants, and contracts and funds appropriated to it by the Congress.

James Macey Smithson (1765–1829) was born in France and known in early life as James Lewis (or Louis) Macie, an illegitimate son of Hugh Smithson Percy, duke of Northumberland. James was a noted mineralogist and chemist who spent much time abroad, and among his correspondents were many eminent men of science. He discovered the zinc mineral calamine which bears his name. In his will he left over 100,000 pounds to the United States to establish an institution for the increase and spread of knowledge. In 1846 the Smithsonian Institute was inaugurated. In 1865 nearly all of Smithson's papers were destroyed by fire at the institute.

Sources

Greenwald, Douglas, ed. 1982. *Encyclopedia of economics.* New York: McGraw-Hill.

Magnussen, Magnus; Goring, Rosemary; and Thorn, John O., eds. 1990. *Chambers biographical dictionary.* Edinburgh: Chambers Ltd.

Shafritz, Jay M. 1988. *The Dorsey dictionary of American government and politics.* Chicago: Dorsey.

Stephen, Leslie, and Lee, Sydney, eds. 1917. *The dictionary of national biography.* London: Oxford University Press.

SMOOT-HAWLEY TARIFF ACT. A U.S. act that reduced foreign trade by authorizing President Herbert Hoover to alter duties, up or down, by 50 percent without discriminating between the nations involved. The act, supported by many Democrats and objected to by Republicans for its effect on trade, met broad foreign retaliation and allegedly exacerbated the breakdown in international trade and the economic Depression of the 1930s. The effect was to raise tariff levels to the highest they had ever been.

Reed Smoot (1862–1941) was born in Salt Lake City, Utah, educated at Mormon schools, and graduated from Brigham Young Academy (1879). He worked in banking, livestock, and mining industries, and made woollen goods. He was a Republican senator (1902–33) and chaired many influential committees. On retirement from business in 1933, he became one of the twelve apostles of the Mormon Church, and before he died he was close to succeeding the church's president.

Willis Chatman Hawley (1864–1941) was born in the old Belknap settlement, Munroe-Benton County, Oregon, educated at country schools, and graduated in law from Willamette University in Salem, Oregon (1888). After being admitted to the bar in 1893, he was a professor of history at the university for sixteen years before being elected to Congress as a Republican (1907–33). Afterward he returned to Salem to practice law.

Sources

De Conde, Alexander. 1978. *Encyclopedia of American foreign policy.* New York: Charles Scribner's Sons.

Jacob, Kathryn A., and Ragsdale, Bruce A. 1989. *Biographical directory of the United States Congress: 1774–1989.* Bicentennial ed. Washington, D.C.: U.S. Government Printing Office.

James, Edward T. 1973. *Dictionary of American biography.* Supplement 3. New York: Charles Scribner's Sons.

Plano, Jack. 1988. *The international relations dictionary.* 4th ed. Santa Barbara, Calif.: ABC-CLIO.

SOCIAL DARWINISM. An ideology that applies biological evolution, especially natural selection, to historical change, and identifies the changes as development in a human society. The ideology stresses that the development arose because, in the struggle to exist, only the fittest survived. The ideology appeared before Charles Darwin's work was published, and it became popular because it gave pseudoscientific and biological support to the outcome of social conflict, for example, problems of social stratification, international politics, imperialism, and war. In England it stemmed from the work of Herbert Spencer (1820–1903) and Walter Bagehot (1826–77) and was taken up in the United States by William Graham Sumner (1840–1910). It was a feature of Nazism and the belief in competition among business interests worldwide. Despite its role today in businesspeople's ideology of "success," the ideology has been severely discredited with the growth of reliable knowledge in biology, social science, and the study of culture.

See also DARWINIAN.

Sources

Hofstadter, Richard. 1955. *Social Darwinism in American thought.* Rev. ed. Boston: Beacon.

Holbrook, David. 1987. *Evolution and the humanities.* Aldershot: Gower.

Jones, Greta. 1980. *Social Darwinism and English thought: and interaction between biological and social theory.* Brighton, England: Harvester Press.

Kaufmann, Herbert. 1985. *Time, chance, and organizations: natural selection in a perilous environment.* Chatham, N.J.: Chatham House.

Kaye, Howard L. 1986. *The social meaning of modern biology: from Social Darwinism to sociobiology.* New Haven, Conn.: Yale University Press.

McHenry, Robert, ed. 1992. *The new encyclopedia Britannica.* Chicago: Encyclopedia Britannica, Inc.

Miller, David, ed. 1987. *The Blackwell encyclopedia of political thought.* Oxford: Basil Blackwell.

Oldroyd, David, and Langham, Ian, eds. 1983. *The wider domain of evolutionary thought.* Dordrecht, Holland: D. Reidel.

Sills, David L., ed. 1968. *International encyclopedia of the social sciences.* New York: Macmillan and Free Press.

SOCINIAN. Relating to the sixteenth-century Italian Unitarians, a religious sect founded in 1560. The sect believed in the divinity of Jesus Christ, but not that he was supernatural; the Socinians also believed that baptism is a rite of declaration of faith, that the Last Supper is merely a commemorative occasion, that the Holy Spirit is a form of divine energy rather than a separate entity, and that the soul is naturally pure and imbued with evil only by early experiences.

Lælius Socinus, or Lelio Sozzini (1525–62), and Faustus Socinus (1539–1604) were uncle and nephew, respectively. Lælius was born at Sienna in Tuscany into a family notable for its cultivation of literature and science. His father was a lawyer and wished his son to follow him, but Lælius had a strong preference for theological inquiry. To help his Bible studies he learned Greek, Hebrew, and Arabic. He was a Protestant thinker, but unlike many heretics he was a modest and reticent man. He died in Zurich. His nephew, Faustus Socinus (Fauste Sozzini), was born at Sienna; his parents died when he was young, and his education was neglected. In his teens he became a heretic, and on the death of his uncle took charge of his papers. He lived in Italy and Basel, visited Transylvania (1578–79), and afterward lived in Poland. Among his works is *De Jesu Christo Servatore.* He and his uncle are said to be important precursors of the spirit of rationalism in modern thought. In 1658 the Diet of Warsaw limited their influence, and they gradually declined. Their beliefs lay at a point between the idea that Jesus was divine and the view that denied his existence was altogether beyond nature.

Sources

Cross, Frank L. 1974. *The Oxford dictionary of the Christian Church.* 2d ed. New York: Oxford University Press.

McHenry, Robert, ed. 1992. *The new encyclopedia Britannica.* Chicago: Encyclopedia
      Britannica, Inc.
Smith, Benjamin. 1903. *The Century cyclopedia of names.* London: The Times.

SOCRATIC, SOCRATES COMPLEX. Relating to the philosophy of the great
Greek teacher and to a teaching method that raises and clarifies group discussion
by putting questions and pursuing the reasoning behind answers that members
offer; in administration, meddlesome didactism that is evident from persistent
questioning that aims solely to reveal how little the listener understands (Peter
and Hull, 1969).

Socrates (c. 470–399 B.C.) was born in Athens, son of a sculptor. Before
joining the army, he worked at his father's craft. As a soldier, he showed much
courage in saving the lives of Alcibiades and Xenophon. They became his pupils
later and with Plato helped him establish the method of teaching named after
him. Socrates was accused of impiety and corrupting youth by suggesting there
were new gods, and he was sentenced to poison himself with hemlock. His ideas
and work were preserved in the writings of Plato, Euclid, the Megaric, Aristippus, Antisthenes, and the Cynic. His method of teaching was to develop an
argument and provide information by questions and answers. The method is
commonly used in tertiary education. He could demolish opponents by gradually
establishing their ignorance and having them appear to be fools.

Sources

Brun, Jean. 1962. *Socrates.* Trans. Douglas Scott. New York: Walker.
Magnussen, Magnus; Goring, Rosemary; and Thorn, John O., eds. 1990. *Chambers bi-
      ographical dictionary.* Edinburgh: Chambers Ltd.
Miller, David, ed. 1987. *The Blackwell encyclopedia of political thought.* Oxford: Basil
      Blackwell.
Peter, Laurence J., and Hull, Raymond. 1969. *The Peter principle: why things always
      go wrong.* New York: William Morrow.
Stone, Isidor F. 1988. *The trial of Socrates.* Boston: Little, Brown.
Zusne, Leonard. 1984. *Biographical dictionary of psychology.* Westport, Conn.: Green-
      wood Press.

SOLON. A lawmaker.

Solon (638–559 B.C.), one of the Seven Wise Men of Greece, was a noted
Athenian lawgiver who was appointed to reform the constitution of Athens. His
legislation is known only from fragments set down by Greek historians. Before
Solon became archon (chief magistrate) in 594 B.C., Athenians were in economic
and civil conflict largely because the poor were enslaved by the rich. First, he
canceled debts, and then he enacted laws that made it illegal to take loans on
the person of the debtor. He ordered the population into four classes according
to their property; set down rules for the election of magistrates; prohibited dow-
ries; changed inheritance regulations so that citizens with no children could leave
their property to any one they chose, whereas earlier the property had to remain
within the family; he made a law that a son whose father had denied them the

opportunity to learn a craft had no obligation to support his father; and he also forbade exporting all farm products except olive oil. Afterward Solon went into voluntary exile, returning in 580 B.C. He induced the Athenians to resume the war in which they had lost the island Salamis. Eventually they won it back.

Sources

Ehrenberg, Victor. 1968. *From Solon to Socrates: Greek history and civilization during the sixth and fifth centuries B.C.* London: Methuen. 1991 ed. London: Routledge.

McHenry, Robert, ed. 1992. *The new encyclopedia Britannica.* Chicago: Encyclopedia Britannica, Inc.

Magnussen, Magnus; Goring, Rosemary; and Thorn, John O., eds. 1990. *Chambers biographical dictionary.* Edinburgh: Chambers Ltd.

Smith, Benjamin. 1903. *The Century cyclopedia of names.* London: The Times.

Woodhouse, William J. 1965. *Solon the liberator: a study of the agrarian problem in Attika in the seventh century.* New York: Octagon.

SOUTHCOTTIANS. A nineteenth-century religious community who followed a woman who claimed she would give birth to a prince of peace.

Joanna Southcott (1750–1814) was an English domestic servant who became a Methodist, and, assuming that supernatural powers dictated prophecies in rhyme, she proclaimed herself to be the woman mentioned in the Apocalypse (ch. xii). Although she was 64, she declared that she would be delivered of "Shiloh," the prince of peace. She died of dropsy ten days later. At that time she had thousands of followers and had published *The Strange Effects of Faith* (1801), *A Warning* (1803), and the *Book of Wonders* (1813–14).

Sources

Cross, Frank L. 1974. *The Oxford dictionary of the Christian Church.* 2d ed. New York: Oxford University Press.

Hastings, James. 1920. *Encyclopedia of religion and ethics.* Edinburgh: T. and J. Clark.

Magnussen, Magnus; Goring, Rosemary; and Thorn, John O., eds. 1990. *Chambers biographical dictionary.* Edinburgh: Chambers Ltd.

Stephen, Leslie, and Lee, Sydney, eds. 1917. *The dictionary of national biography.* London: Oxford University Press.

SPARTACISTS. Left-wing revolutionaries and other extremists active in Germany from the summer of 1915 who supported the communist revolution of 1918 when the German Communist party was established. They were led by Rosa Luxembourg (1871–1919) and Karl Liebknecht (1871–1919) who parted from the Social Democrats in Germany in 1917, called for the end of World War I, supported the Bolsheviks in the Russian Revolution, and advocated the toppling of Germany's government in favor of the workers' and soldiers' soviets. The Spartacists, or Spartacus League, were the extreme left of German Social Democracy and reorganized in 1919 as the Communist party of Germany. They violently attacked the Republican government of Ebert after the kaiser had abdicated (November 1918). Both Luxembourg and Liebknecht were murdered by the German Freikorps in 1919.

Spartacus (d. 71 B.C.) was a Roman gladiator born in Thrace, who led a revolt against the Romans in Capua in 73 B.C. He was joined by slaves, army deserters, and renegades numbering almost 90,000. For two years he withstood the Roman Army but found it ever more difficult to control his own followers. His forces were beaten by those of Marcus Licinius Crassus. Spartacus may have been killed in action, or caught and crucified with many of the rebels, their crosses lining the Appian Way. Pompey killed the survivors in 70 B.C. From Plutarch's account in his *Lives of Crassus and Pompey* Spartacus became a legend in his lifetime.

Sources

Geras, Norman. 1976. *The legacy of Rosa Luxembourg.* London: N.L.B.

Howard, Dick, ed. 1971. *Selected political writings of Rosa Luxembourg.* New York: Monthly Review Press.

Nettl, J. Peter. 1966. *Rosa Luxembourg.* 2 vols. London: Oxford University Press.

Wieczynski, Joseph, ed. 1984. *The modern encyclopedia of Russian and Soviet history.* Gulf Breeze, Fla.: Academic International Press.

SPENCERIAN. Relating to or follower of the synthetic philosophy, psychology, or sociology of the nineteenth-century English thinker.

Herbert Spencer (1820–1903) was born at Derby, the only surviving child of a schoolteacher. His father and his uncle, rector of Hinton, educated the boy. He was articled to a civil engineer in 1837, but in 1845 he left engineering to devote his time to literature. He was assistant editor of *The Economist* during 1845–53; and in 1855, four years before Darwin published *The Origin of the Species,* Spencer published his *Principles of Psychology* which centers on the principle of evolution. In 1860 Spencer published his *System of Synthetic Philosophy* in which, beginning with the first principles of knowledge he proposed to trace the progress of evolution in life, mind, society, and morality. Among his diverse publications are *The Principles of Biology* (1863), *Ceremonial Institutions* (1879), and *Negative Beneficence and Positive Beneficence* (1893).

See also DARWINIAN.

Sources

Eatwell, John; Milgate, Murray; and Newman, Peter. 1987. *The new Palgrave: a dictionary of economics.* London: Macmillan.

Kennedy, James G. 1978. *Herbert Spencer.* Boston: Twayne Publishers.

Lee, Sydney, ed. 1920. *The dictionary of national biography.* Supplement 1901–1911. London: Oxford University Press.

McHenry, Robert, ed. 1992. *The new encyclopedia Britannica.* Chicago: Encyclopedia Britannica, Inc.

Magnussen, Magnus; Goring, Rosemary; and Thorn, John O., eds. 1990. *Chambers biographical dictionary.* Edinburgh: Chambers Ltd.

Peel, John David Y. 1971. *Herbert Spencer: the evolution of a sociologist.* London: Heinemann.

Sills, David L., ed. 1968. *International encyclopedia of the social sciences.* New York: Macmillan and Free Press.

Turner, Jonathan H. 1985. *Herbert Spencer: a renewed appreciation.* Beverly Hills, Calif.: Sage Publications.

Zusne, Leonard. 1984. *Biographical dictionary of psychology.* Westport, Conn.: Greenwood Press.

SPINELLI INITIATIVE. A plan, or movement—Movimento Federalista Europeo—for a Federal European Community that proposed more power for European rather than nation-based institutions in Europe, for example, the European Parliament and the European Economic Commission. The plan was basic to the Draft Treaty on European Union that the European Parliament endorsed in February 1984; the plan led in January 1986 to the Single European Act.

Altiero Spinelli (1907–86) was born in Rome and became a strong opponent of Mussolini. An intellectual and political activist, Spinelli spent much time in prison and was confined to an island off the coast of Rome and Naples (1927–43). On his release he was active in the Italian underground resistance. He advocated following the precise thinking of British federalists, and he helped in secret to draft a plan with resistance workers from eight countries of Europe, including Germany. He founded the European Federalist Movement (1943), was elected to the Italian Parliament (1946), and from 1961 to 1964 was at the Center for Advanced International Studies. He also founded the Institute of International Affairs (Rome) which he directed in 1966. He was a member of the European Commission (1970–76) and a member of the European Parliament from 1976. In Brussels he was appointed commissioner for European Communities (1976–79), was elected a deputy on the communist list, and became a member of the Foreign Affairs Commission. The Single European Act (1986) was not as comprehensive as his original plan and met with his criticism. Among the books he published were *The Eurocrats* (1966) and *The European Adventure* (1973). In 1984 he published his autobiography.

Sources

Coppa, Frank J. 1985. *Dictionary of modern Italian history.* Westport, Conn.: Greenwood Press.

Groeg, Otto J. 1980. *Who's who in Italy.* 3d ed. Milan: Who's who in Italy.

Keesings contemporary archives: record of world events. 1986:34629. London: Keesings Publications.

McHenry, Robert, ed. 1992. *The new encyclopedia Britannica.* Chicago: Encyclopedia Britannica, Inc.

Who's who, 1986. London: Adam and Charles Black.

SPINOZISM. Pantheistic monism of the seventeenth-century philosopher; the ideas combine anthropology, ethics, metaphysics, political theory, and religion in a view that identifies nature with God and argues for the unity of reality.

Benedict Spinoza (1632–77) was born at Amsterdam into a family of wealthy Spanish or Portuguese Jews. Spinoza was educated privately and devoted himself to a life of scholarship. He criticized the Jewish heritage, and, as a heretic, in 1656 he left Amsterdam's Jewish community to live most of his life in The

Hague. Subsequently, philosophy became his prime interest, and to support himself he learned the skill of polishing lenses. Declining financial help from friends, he lived close to poverty. His outstanding personal features were simplicity, great forbearance, stoicism, and a childlike warmth. After his death, both Jews and Christians forbade his teachings, and it was not until the end of the eighteenth century that his views were studied and he became a significant contributor to modern philosophy. Literature on his philosophy is extensive, especially in Germany, and his life has been the subject of a romance, *Spinoza: A Novel,* by Berthold Auerbach (1812–82).

Sources

Auerbach, Berthold. 1837. *Spinoza: a novel.* Translated by E. Nicholoson. London: S. Low.

Delahunty, R. J. 1985. *Spinoza.* London: Routledge and Kegan Paul.

Donagan, Alan. 1988. *Spinoza.* Brighton, England: Harvester Press.

McHenry, Robert, ed. 1992. *The new encyclopedia Britannica.* Chicago: Encyclopedia Britannica, Inc.

Sills, David L., ed. 1968. *International encyclopedia of the social sciences.* New York: Macmillan and Free Press.

Wigoder, Geoffrey. 1989. *The encyclopedia of Judaism.* New York: Macmillan.

Zusne, Leonard. 1984. *Biographical dictionary of psychology.* Westport, Conn.: Greenwood Press.

SROLE'S ANOMIE SCALE. A five-item scale of eunomia–anomia that measures self-to-other sense of belongingness versus distance and alienation.

Leo Srole (b. 1908) was born in Chicago and studied at Harvard and the University of Chicago (Ph.D., 1940). During World War II he taught at New York University and at Hobart and William Smith College (1941–42), and was a military psychologist for the U.S. Air Force (1943–45). Afterward he became a welfare director for the United Nations in Germany (1945–46), a member of the Bureau of Applied Social Research at Columbia University (1947–48), and a research director for B'nai B'rith (1948–52). He was appointed a professor of sociology at Cornell University Medical College (1952–59), a research professor at Albert Einstein Medical College (1959–61), and a professor of sociology at the State University of New York Downtown Medical Center (1951–65). For twenty years he has conducted research into social aspects of psychiatry, edited several journals in sociology and psychiatry, and been honored by many professional associations.

Sources

Jaques Cattell Press, ed. 1973. *American men and women of science: the social and behavioral sciences.* 13th ed. New York: Jaques Cattell and R. R. Bowker.

Miller, Delbert C. 1991. *Handbook of research design and social measurement.* 5th ed. Newbury Park, Calif.: Sage Publications.

Srole, Leo. 1956. Social integration and certain corollaries. *American Sociological Review* 21:709–716.

Who's who in America, 1992–93. Chicago: Marquis.

STAHLIAN, STAHLIANISM. Relating to the eighteenth-century German physician and his animistic philosophy.

Georg Ernst Stahl (c. 1660–1734) was born at Ansbach, Franconia, studied medicine at the University of Jena, and after graduation (1684) lectured and researched in chemistry where he attained a high reputation as a scientist. In 1687 he became court physician at Weimar for seven years before being made a professor of medicine at Halle University. In 1715 Stahl left Halle to be physician to the king of Prussia, Frederick William I. Although Stahl's personality often seemed antagonistic and his writing style obscure and difficult, he was a major force in medicine. He was a prolific writer but his greatest work, *Theoria Medica Vera* (1737), with its doctrinal details on physiology and pathology, presents his animistic philosophy as incidental to its argument.

Sources

Gillespie, Charles C., ed. 1973. *Dictionary of scientific biography.* New York: Charles Scribner's Sons.

McHenry, Robert, ed. 1992. *The new encyclopedia Britannica.* Chicago: Encyclopedia Britannica, Inc.

STAKHANOVISM, STAKHANOVITE, STAKHANOVITE MOVEMENT.
An efficient and productive worker in Russia; a movement upholding efficiency and high productivity in work.

Alexei Grigorievich Stakhanov (c. 1905–77) was born in Lugovaia, Orel Province. As a brakeman, he worked at the Tsentral'naia-Irmino Mine, Kadievka (Donbas) in 1927, and later he became a pneumatic-drill operator, or cutter, in a coal mine (1933). In 1935, after completing a course for cutters at the mine, he set a record on August 30–31 by extracting 102 tons of coal in a six-hour night shift. This was fourteen times the quota of seven tons. He and his timberman achieved this by efficient division of their labor. Stalin is alleged to have praised his efforts, and this recognition ensured that his achievements attracted enough support throughout the Soviet Union to provide a basis for the Stakhanovite movement. After becoming a member of the Communist party, he studied at Moscow's Industrial Academy (1936–41); was a mine chief for two years; and worked at the Ministry of Coal Industry (1943–57). From 1957 to 1959 he was deputy director of the Chistiakovan-tratsil Trust, and in 1959 he was assistant chief engineer of the Mine Administration. In 1970 he was made a Hero of Soviet Organiz and retired in 1974.

The movement that bears Stakhanov's name comprised workers, engineers, and technicians who aimed to raise the productivity of labor. It was organized into brigades, sections, and units—not unlike shock troops—and achieved remarkably high levels of productivity during the Second Five-Year Plan (1933–1937) and World War II. It followed principles of one man to two machines, a combination of functions allocated to one position, and accelerated production and construction rates.

Sources
Magnussen, Magnus; Goring, Rosemary; and Thorn, John O., eds. 1990. *Chambers biographical dictionary.* Edinburgh: Chambers Ltd.
Prokhorov, A. M., ed. 1980. *Great Soviet encyclopedia.* New York: Macmillan.
Wieczynski, Joseph, ed. 1984. *The modern encyclopedia of Russian and Soviet history.* Gulf Breeze, Fla.: Academic International Press.

STALINISM, STALIN'S LAW. The totalitarian policy of twentieth-century Russia, that is, collectivization of agriculture and the industrialization of Russia by the use of purges and forced labor camps; secret policy-making and other forms of bureaucratic terrorism; the development of a personality cult favoring Stalin as hero; a foreign policy of hostility to all capitalism, and the revision of all history and literature to this end. The reversal of Stalinism began with de-Stalinization (February 1956) in Khrushchev's "secret" speech against Stalin's personal reign of terror and the separation of Stalinism from earlier conceptions of Marxist ideology. Stalin's Law states that, as opportunities for treachery increase, the Soviets will expand their assets to exploit them. For example, of the 800 Russians assigned to United Nations duties as international civil servants, almost 25 percent of the United Nations Secretariat, most are espionage agents (Pincher, 1987:43).

Joseph Stalin, pseudonym of Iosif Vissarionovich Dzhugashvili (1879–1953), was born near Tiflis, Georgia, the son of a shoemaker. He attended a theological seminary near Tiflis but was expelled for expressing Marxist propaganda. In 1896 he joined the Social Democratic party and sided with the Bolsheviks after the party split in 1903. He was often exiled to Siberia for political activity (1904–13) but always managed to escape. He took the name, Stalin, "Man of Steel," from his activities before the Russian Revolution. A close associate of Lenin, Stalin took part in the 1917 Revolution and became a member of its military council (1920–23). Following Lenin's death (1924), Stalin established himself as Russia's dictator and is now held fully responsible for murderous purges in most aspects of Russian life during his rule. Following the Nazi invasion of Russia in 1941, he became commissar for defense and chairman of the Council of People's Commissars, thus taking over supreme direction of military operations. In 1943 he was created marshal of the Soviet Union. Until his death he held personal power over all Russia.

See also LENINISM.

Sources
Bullock, Alan. 1991. *Hitler and Stalin: parallel lives.* London: HarperCollins.
Cohen, Stephen F. 1985. *Rethinking the Soviet experience.* New York: Oxford University Press.
De Jonge, Alex. 1986. *Stalin.* London: Collins.
Franklin, Bruce, ed. 1973. *The essential Stalin.* London: Croom Helm.
Laquer, Walter. 1990. *Stalin: the Glasnost revelations.* London: Unwin Hyman.
McHenry, Robert, ed. 1992. *The new encyclopedia Britannica.* Chicago: Encyclopedia Britannica, Inc.

Magnussen, Magnus; Goring, Rosemary; and Thorn, John O., eds. 1990. *Chambers biographical dictionary.* Edinburgh: Chambers Ltd.
Pincher, Chapman. 1987. *Traitors.* New York: St. Martin's Press.

STALKERGATE. The British scandal (1986) surrounding the charges that the deputy chief constable of Greater Manchester had improper associations with criminals when he was the chairman of an inquiry into the Royal Ulster Constabulary's "shoot-to-kill" policy in Northern Ireland (1982). After the investigation all allegations were rejected.

John Stalker (fl. 1982–86) was appointed in May 1984 to head an inquiry into the "shoot-to-kill" policy that allegedly led to the killing of six suspected terrorists by security forces in Northern Ireland in November–December 1982. But on May 30, 1986, Stalker was sent on enforced leave while allegations against him of disciplinary offenses, unrelated to the earlier killings, were investigated. At the time the M.P. for the constituency in which the killings had occurred, Seamus Mallon, stated that sinister forces were preventing Stalker from continuing the inquiry. Ten accusations were made against Stalker, one of which suggested he had close associations with a businessman who was known to consort with criminals. Stalker was reinstated and, in response, proposed that an inquiry be held into the way the investigation into his activities had been conducted. In addition, at the time, Amnesty International and twenty members of the U.S. Congress urged the British government to inquire further into the 1982 killings.
Sources

Keesings contemporary archives: weekly diary of world events. 1984:32195, 32809, 33180, 33181; 1985:33940; 1986:343182, 34761. London: Keesings Publications.
Tulloch, Sara. 1991. *The Oxford dictionary of new words.* Oxford: Oxford University Press.

STAR OF DAVID. A Jewish emblem, Magen David, "Shield of David," a six-pointed star comprising two interlocking triangles. Commonly known as the "Star of David," the emblem is found in Jewish designs and appears on gravestones and pendants. It also appears on Kabbalistic amulets and in Jewish magical drawings of the Middle Ages, and is reputed to have protective powers. The Nazis used Magen David to mark the places where Jews lived and worked, and required that Jews wear the sign on their clothes. Magen David is on the flag of Israel. Although it appeared on some synagogues in Germany in the late Middle Ages, as well as in medieval Hebrew manuscripts, the emblem seemed to have no definite meaning.

David, Israel's second king (1055–1015 B.C.), was born at Bethlehem, youngest of seven sons of Jesse, of the tribe of Judah. At age 18, while tending his father's flock, David was secretly anointed king of Israel by Samuel the prophet. David slew a philistine giant of a man, Goliath, with a sling shot, and, after the death in battle of King Saul, David, aged 30, became the king of Judah and

later ruled all Israel's tribes. During his thirty-year rule, he was idealized and became the model for all succeeding rulers of Israelites.
Sources
Eliade, Mircea, ed. 1987. *Encyclopedia of religion.* New York: Macmillan.
Unterman, Alan. 1991. *Dictionary of Jewish lore and legend.* London: Thames and Hudson.
Wigoder, Geoffrey. 1989. *The encyclopedia of Judaism.* New York: Macmillan.

STEPHENSON'S Q-METHODOLOGY, STEPHENSON'S Q-SORT, STEPHENSON'S Q-TECHNIQUE. A procedure for putting a sample of objects in an order that is significant for one individual. For example, a Q-sample could be a set of opinion statements, and an individual has the task of ranking them from the least to the most acceptable; they are sorted in a Q-sort. When the Q-sorts of several people are factor analyzed, then clusters of people who rank items similarly comprise a clear type or group. The factors are explained by referring to common viewpoints. Q-methodology comprises the theory and principles of the Q-sort techniques, methods of sampling, and explanation. Since Q-techniques involve the subjective facts of a person, they contrast with R-techniques in social science, which are concerned with objective data on a sample of people drawn from a defined population.

William Stephenson (1902–89), born in Northumberland, England, studied physics at Durham University (Ph.D., 1926) and psychology at the University of London (Ph.D., 1929). Later he worked with Sir Cyril Burt (1883–1971). The idea of using Q-methodology first appeared in Thomson (1935). However, Stephenson published a letter in *Nature,* August 24, 1935, indicating the value of person correlations independently of Thomson. Since Stephenson's letter was posted June 28, 1935, his name and not Thomson's attaches first to the Q-methodology and related procedures. Stephenson published his *Testing School Children* (1949) after immigrating to America in 1948 to join the psychology faculty, University of Chicago, where he wrote *The Study of Behavior: Q-technique and Its Methodology* (1953). Following work in the advertising industry (1955–58), Stephenson became a professor of advertising research at the University of Missouri's School of Journalism. In 1967 he published *The Play Theory of Mass Communication* which made a significant contribution to the field of communication. On retiring in 1972, Stephenson was honored with a festschrift, *Science, Psychology and Communication.* Thereafter Stephenson worked on establishing the conditions for a science of subjectivity, wrote on connections between physics and psychology, and contributed to the thirty-year debate over the technicalities and general value of the Q-approach.
Sources
Brown, Steven R. 1980. *Political subjectivity: applications of Q methodology in political science.* New Haven, Conn.: Yale University Press.
Brown, Steven R. 1986. Q technique and method: principles and procedures. In W. D. Berry and M. S. Lewis-Beck, eds. *New tools for the social scientist.* Beverly Hills, Calif.: Sage Publications, pp. 57–76.

Brown, Steven R. 1991. William Stephenson. 1902–89. *American Psychologist* 46:244.

Thomson, G. H. 1935. On complete families of correlation co-efficients, and their tendency to zero tetrad differences: including a statement of the sampling theory of abilities. *British Journal of Psychology (General Section)* 26:63–92.

STERN GANG. A notorious band of Jews, sometimes condemned as terrorists, who fought for the freedom of Israel.

Avraham Stern (1906–42) was born in Suvalki, Russian Poland, was educated at the Hebrew High School, studied classics, and in 1925 attended the Hebrew University in Jerusalem. He wrote poetry of a messianic character and left the Irgun group of political activists to form the Fighters for Freedom in Israel. He was more interested in the militant struggle of Zionists against Britain and the Arabs than in the war against Germany. Most Jews did not accept Stern's ideology: in fact, the Jewish militia believed he sought a tactical alliance with Germany in 1940 to help remove Jews from Europe. In November 1941 the gang killed a Jewish policeman, and in January 1942 they shot a pedestrian during a bank robbery. Local Jews plotted to get rid of Stern, and he was shot and killed shortly after capture by British officers in Tel Aviv and buried there. The question of justifiable homicide has never been satisfactorily settled. A pariah in his day, he became a Jewish hero, and a commemorative stamp was issued in celebration of the fiftieth anniversary of the group's founding. Stern's martyrdom spurred the gang to further terrorism, for example, the murder of Lord Moyne in Cairo (1944) and the assassination of the United Nations mediator, Count Bernadotte, in Jerusalem (1948). Winston Churchill likened the killers to the Nazi gangsters. After Stern's death the gang was jointly led by Yitzah Shamir, code-name "Michael," until the gang was outlawed by Israel's first government.

Sources

Black, Ian. 1992. Terrorist or martyr? *The Guardian Weekly,* March 1:21–22.

McHenry, Robert, ed. 1992. *The new encyclopedia Britannica.* Chicago: Encyclopedia Britannica, Inc.

Morton, Geoffrey. 1957. *Just the job.* London: Hodder and Stoughton.

Shimoni, Yaacov, and Levine, Evyatar, eds. 1972. *Political dictionary of the Middle East in the twentieth century.* Jerusalem, Israel: Jerusalem Publishing House.

STIGLER'S LAW OF EPONYMY. Eponyms are never named after their original discoverer. The main reason for this seeming contradiction is that too often those who bestow the eponym are poorly informed as to its origin or are concerned more with rewarding a person's merit than establishing a particular achievement.

Stephen Mac Stigler (b. 1941) was born in Minneapolis and educated at Carlton College and studied statistics at the University of California at Berkeley (Ph.D., 1967). Before becoming a professor of statistics at the University of Chicago (1979–), he taught and researched at the University of Wisconsin.

Among his publications is *The History of Statistics: The Measurement of Uncertainty Before 1900* (1986).

Sources

Stigler, Stephen M. 1980. Stigler's law of eponymy. In Thomas F. Gieryn, ed. *Science and social structure: a festschrift for Robert K. Merton.* New York: New York Academy of Sciences, pp. 147–157.

Who's who in America, 1992–93. New Providence, N.J.: Reed Reference Publishing.

STIMSON DOCTRINE. A U.S. diplomatic statement (1932) sent to China and Japan indicating that the United States could not recognize any treaty or any de facto government that impaired U.S. treaty rights with China, or the provisions of the Nine-Power Treaty, or any situation that violated the Kellogg-Briand Pact (1929). The statement was aimed specifically at Japanese action in Manchuria and was approved by the League of Nations. Most member nations refused to recognize the puppet state of Manchukuo, created that month by Japan in what had been Manchuria.

Henry Lewis Stimson (1867–1950), an American lawyer and administrator, was born in New York City. He graduated from Yale and Harvard (LL.B., 1890) and was admitted to the New York bar in 1891. A Republican, he served as U.S. secretary of war under President Taft (1911–13). He was governor-general of the Philippines (1927–29), and as President Hoover's secretary of state (1929–33) he proposed the doctrine in opposition to Japan's aggression in Manchuria. He claimed the doctrine was original, but it had precedent in U.S. diplomatic history. In 1940 President Roosevelt made him secretary of war (1940–45). He took the ultimate responsibility in recommending the use of the atomic bomb against Japan in August 1945 and soon afterward decided to retire from a life-time of government service.

Sources

Current, Richard N. 1970. *Secretary Stimson: a study in statecraft.* 2d ed. With new Introduction. Hamden, Conn.: Archon.

Findling, John E. 1980. *Dictionary of American diplomatic history.* Westport, Conn.: Greenwood Press.

Garraty, John A., and James, Edward T., eds. 1974. *Dictionary of American biography.* Supplement 4. New York: Charles Scribner's Sons.

Hodgson, Godfrey. 1990. *The colonel: the life and wars of Henry Stimson, 1867–1950.* New York: Alfred A. Knopf/Random House.

McHenry, Robert, ed. 1992. *The new encyclopedia Britannica.* Chicago: Encyclopedia Britannica, Inc.

Magnussen, Magnus; Goring, Rosemary; and Thorn, John O., eds. 1990. *Chambers biographical dictionary.* Edinburgh: Chambers Ltd.

Morrison, Elting E. 1963. *Turmoil and tradition: a study of the life and times of Henry L. Stimson.* New York: Atheneum.

STOCKHOLM SCHOOL. A school of economics that established the discipline in Sweden over two generations. The first generation included Gustav

Cassel (1866–1944) and David Davidson (1854–1942) who helped establish a respectable reputation for economics, and the second generation was established in the 1920s and 1930s. Davidson was a professor at Uppsala from 1889 to 1921; among other notables were Erik Lindahl (1891–1960), Gunnar Myrdal (1898–1987), and Erik Lundberg (b. 1907). In the 1920s the younger generation of economists was challenged by Sweden's sudden rise in unemployment. Because old theories did not answer the economists' questions on this subject, new theories of business cycles were developed in the 1930s. For such fields of study, Lindahl introduced the term *microeconomics,* and the ideas of Knut Wicksell (1851–1926) became prominent. The school was funded by the Rockefeller Foundation. Because the school did not attract students or followers after World War II and because Swedish economics turned to Keynes's ideas, the school did not survive.

Stockholm, the capital of Sweden, is a picturesque city on the east coast where Lake Mälaren meets the Baltic Sea. Founded in 1252 when a fortified castle was built on the island of Stadsholmen, the town grew to become Sweden's major commercial center and fortress by 1300. The city was one of Europe's great cultural centers in the seventeenth century. In 1750 the Royal Palace was completed, and in 1786 the Concert House of the Swedish Academy was built, which is now where the Nobel Prizes are awarded. Today Stockholm is a modern center of communication and travel in Europe.

Sources

Eatwell, John; Milgate, Murray; and Newman, Peter. 1987. *The new Palgrave: a dictionary of economics.* London: Macmillan.

Jonung, Lars. 1991. *The Stockholm School of economics revisited.* Cambridge: Cambridge University Press.

Morris, William, ed. 1965–66. *Grolier universal encyclopedia.* New York: American Book-Stratford Press, Inc.

SWEDENBORGIAN. A follower of the eighteenth-century Swedish religious teacher and founder of the New Jerusalem Church.

Emanuel Swedenborg (1688–1772) was the son of Jesper Swedenborg (originally Swedberg), who later became professor of theology at Uppsala and bishop of Skara. After studies at Uppsala and extended travels in England and elsewhere, Swedenborg was appointed by Charles II of Sweden to a post on the Swedish Board of Mines (1716). With his mathematical ability he anticipated many subsequent hypotheses and discoveries, for example, nebular theory, magnetic theory, the machine gun, and aeroplane. Some claim he founded crystallography. After feeling he was in direct contact with the angels and the spirit world, through dreams and visions and in his conscious life (1743–45), he decided God was calling him to spread his ideas among humankind through the New Church. In 1747 he resigned from the Board of Mines to make a comprehensive study of the scriptures. His best work is reputed to be *Divine Love and Wisdom* (1763).

Sources

Cross, Frank L. 1974. *The Oxford dictionary of the Christian Church.* 2d ed. New York: Oxford University Press.

Jonsson, Inge. 1971. *Emanuel Swedenborg.* New York: Twayne Publishers.

McHenry, Robert, ed. 1992. *The new encyclopedia Britannica.* Chicago: Encyclopedia Britannica, Inc.

Trobridge, George. 1974. *Swedenborg: life and teaching.* London: Swedenborg Society.

Zusne, Leonard. 1984. *Biographical dictionary of psychology.* Westport, Conn.: Greenwood Press.

T

TADPOLE AND TAPER. Time-serving and vote-seeking politicians; political tools serving powerful interest groups to realize petty and underhand schemes.

Tadpole and Taper are characters in Benjamin Disraeli's (1804–81) political novels *Coningsby* (1844) and *Sybil, or the Two Nations* (1845). They are depicted as unprincipled office-seekers and party managers: one worshiped organization, and the other favored a ''cry'' or an attractive policy in the pursuit of office. In *Coningsby* some say that the characters were based on political figures of the day and that Tadpole was based on Charles Ross and Taper on Alexander Pringle.

Taper was based on Alexander Pringle (fl. 1830–45), who was a representative of the Pringles of Whytbank, an old family in the county of Selkirk. He was a lord of the Treasury, an advocate, and a vice-lieutenant of Selkirkshire. In 1830 he sat as a Conservative for Selkirkshire; he was defeated by R. Pringle (1831), a Reform Bill supporter of Clifton (1832). He regained his seat (1835–45) and was then appointed clerk of sessions.

Tadpole was based on Charles Ross (d. 1860), married the daughter of Charles, second marquis of Cornwallis, and was made lord of the Admiralty. He was also a lord of the Treasury (December 1834–April 1835). He held the Conservative seat for Saint Germains (1826–32) when he was elected for Northampton until 1837.

Sources

Briggs, Asa. 1962. Foreword. In Benjamin Disraeli. 1844. *Coningsby.* Signet classic ed. New American Library.

Ousby, Ian, ed. 1988. *The Cambridge guide to literature in English.* Cambridge: Cambridge University Press.

Stenton, Michael, ed. 1976. *Who's who of British members of Parliament.* Vol 1. 1832–85. Brighton, England: Harvester Press.

TAFOYA LAW. A U.S. federal law stating that it is an offense to use an interstate or foreign commerce utility—phone, airline, or rental car—to commit murder-for-hire.

Eugene A. Tafoya (b. 1934) was born in New Mexico, and at age 14 joined the New Mexico National Guard by lying about his age. After two years' service he was discharged, and in the Korean War he joined the Marines (1953). He left after three years, worked in an aircraft factory, married, returned to New Mexico, and worked briefly as a deputy sheriff. He entered the U.S. Army Special Forces which valued his aggressive manner and his command of Spanish (1963). He was on five tours in Vietnam and operated clandestine missions behind Viet Cong lines. In 1976 he retired with a Bronze Star and a Combat Infantryman's Badge. On returning to New Mexico, he worked as a mercenary with Edwin Wilson (b. 1928), a contract employee of the Central Intelligence Agency and Office of Naval Intelligence. Tafoya worked in Libya, believing the work was a CIA operation. He was given the task of murdering a Libyan dissenter in Fort Collins, Colorado; before a witness he wounded the man badly and fled the country. Police traced the gun to Tafoya in 1981 when he returned to the United States, and he was arrested on a charge of unlawful flight to avoid prosecution. Admitting to attempted murder, he received two prison terms, one for the murder attempt and another for violating income tax laws. In Tafoya's case, federal law did not cover the situation.

Sources

Goulden, Joseph C. 1984. *The death merchant.* New York: Simon and Schuster.
Goulden, Joseph C. 1986. The rogue of rogues. *The International Journal of Intelligence and Counterintelligence* 1:76–82.

TAFT COMMISSION. A U.S. Commission on Economy and Efficiency (1912) that required a national budgeting system for the United States and whose recommendations were put in the Budget and Accounting Act of 1921.

William Howard Taft (1857–1930) was born in Cincinnati and graduated from Yale (1878) and Cincinnati Law School (1880). He practiced law in that city and held minor positions in civic life. He was appointed judge of the superior court in Ohio (1887) and was named solicitor-general by President Benjamin Harrison (1833–1901) in 1892. In 1904 he was appointed secretary of war by President Theodore Roosevelt (1858–1919), became a close friend of the president, won the Republican nomination with Roosevelt's help, and became president himself in 1908. He chaired the commission during his presidency, but his presidency was put in jeopardy by a growing split within the Republican party, and in 1912 he lost the election to Woodrow Wilson. In 1913 he was appointed a professor of constitutional law at Yale, held a vital position on the War Labor Board during World War I and, under President Harding (1865–1923), became chief justice of the United States Supreme Court (1921–30).

Sources

Burton, David. 1988. *The learned presidency: Theodore Roosevelt, William Howard Taft, Woodrow Wilson.* Rutherford, N.J.: Fairleigh Dickinson University Press.

Coletta, Paolo E. 1973. *The presidency of William Howard Taft.* Lawrence: University Press of Kansas.

Coletta, Paolo E. 1989. *William Howard Taft: a bibliography.* Westport, Conn.: Meckler Corp.

Malone, Dumas, ed. 1935. *Dictionary of American biography.* Vol. IX. New York: Charles Scribner's Sons.

Pringle, Henry F. 1964. *The life and times of William Howard Taft: a biography.* Hamden, Conn.: Archon Books.

TAFT-HARTLEY ACT. U.S. Public Law 101, a major revision of the Wagner Act (1935), that sought to equalize the power of employers and labor unions. In general, the Taft-Hartley Act limits labor union practices, regulates certain internal arrangements of unions, and strengthens the position of the individual worker. Specifically, it outlaws the closed shop but permits the union shop; bans jurisdictional strikes, secondary boycotts, political expenditures and excessive dues; and permits unions and employers to sue each other for contract violations and allows use of the injunction and other "cooling off" procedures in strikes that threaten national welfare. The internal affairs of unions are regulated by requiring them to file reports on the use of union funds and organizational procedures. The act was a reaction to growing union strength, to allegations that the Wagner Act favored unions, and to revelations of communism and corruption in some unions. President Truman vetoed the act, but it was later passed. After 1947 the union movement campaigned to repeal or amend the law.

Robert Alphonso Taft (1889–1953), born in Cincinnati, was educated in public schools, in Manila in the Philippines, and at Taft School in Watertown, Connecticut. He was the son of President William Howard Taft (1857–1930). Robert graduated from Yale University (1910) and Harvard Law School (1913). In 1913 he was admitted to the bar in Ohio, entered a legal practice, and conducted several businesses in Cincinnati. He was elected to represent Ohio (1921–26), and was speaker and majority house leader. He served the Ohio Senate (1931–32), and in 1938 he was elected to the U.S Senate as a Republican and reelected in 1944 and 1950. In 1952 he was an unsuccessful candidate for the Republican nomination for the presidency.

Fred Allan Hartley, Jr. (1902–69) was born in Harrison, Hudson County, New Jersey, and attended public schools and Rutgers University. He became the library commissioner for New Jersey (1923–24) and Kearny fire commissioner (1924–28). He was the Republican representative from New Jersey, and was elected to the Seventy-first and to nine succeeding congresses (1929–49). He co-sponsored the act bearing his name. He did not stand as a candidate for renomination in 1948, and afterward he became a business consultant.

See also WAGNER-CONNERY ACT.

Sources

Commager, Henry S., ed. 1968. *Documents of American history.* 8th ed. New York: Appleton-Century-Crofts.

Jacob, Kathryn A., and Ragsdale, Bruce A. 1989. *Biographical directory of the United*

States Congress: 1774–1989. Bicentennial ed. Washington, D.C.: U.S. Government Printing Office.

Millis, Harry A., and Brown, Emily C. 1950. *From the Wagner Act to Taft-Hartley.* Chicago: University of Chicago Press.

Plano, Jack C., and Greenberg, Milton. 1989. *The American political dictionary.* New York: Holt, Rinehart and Winston.

TAMMANY SOCIETY, TAMMANY HALL. Notoriously corrupt political society in New York City politics in the nineteenth century. The building it leased to the local Democratic party.

The first Tammany Society was formed in Philadelphia on May 1, 1772. Thereafter, several societies with this name, and patterned on the original, appeared in the United States, the most notable in New York. In New York City, William Moody (1756–1831) founded a Tammany Society (1786) and celebrated it on May 12, 1789. Republicanism and patriotism were Moody's interests in establishing the society; its first members were bound by an oath to support state institutions and to resist centralization of power in general government. They were also to uphold the values of charity and benevolence, nonpartisanship, and fraternalism. Representing the thirteen American states, the society formed thirteen tribes, headed by a sachem, and named after a totem animal, for example, Otter and Rattlesnake. From the thirteen sachems was chosen the grand sachem as its head, and the U.S. president held the office of great grand sachem. In time, several U.S. presidents enjoyed political support from the Tammany Society. By 1811 the society had split into a social and a political club, Tammany No. I, or the "Tammany Hall Political Party." The title referred to the hall purchased by the social group and rented to the political group for its meetings in New York. Aaron Burr, who gained much control of the organization in 1798, is credited with turning the society into a political club by the mid-1830s, and thereafter most of his followers benefited from becoming highly influential in Tammany Hall's corrupt politics. Today, Tammany Hall probably wields less power than it once held, but the phrase is still used in local and federal politics to denigrate politicians by the suggestion they have gained and extended their power through corrupt deals.

Tammanend or Tammany (fl. 1685), a Leni-Lenape (Delaware) Indian chief, whose name means "affable" or "deserving," probably signed one of William Penn's treaties, and other documents, for the purchase of Philadelphia (1683) and may well have been a friend of George Washington. To the colonial army during the Revolutionary War, Tammanend became a great hero, his name a symbol of the liberty for which the war was fought. After the American Revolution he was patron saint of several political organizations, for example, Sons of King Tammany, later Sons of Saint Tammany in Philadelphia (1772), and the Society of Tammany in New York.

Sources
McHenry, Robert, ed. 1992. *The new encyclopedia Britannica.* Chicago: Encyclopedia Britannica, Inc.

Malone, Dumas, ed. 1935. *Dictionary of American biography*. Vol. IX. New York: Charles Scribner's Sons.

TARSKI'S THEORY OF TRUTH. The modern theory of truth—on a meta-linguistic level of discussion—that requires strict conditions under which "truth language" is to be applied to problems, and that tends to support philosophical realism.

Alfred Tarski (1902–83) was born, educated, and taught in Warsaw. In 1939 he went to the United States, and he taught at the University of California at Berkeley (1942–68). His main contributions were to pure mathematics and mathematical logic, and he is noted for his definition of "truth" in formal logical languages in his work, *The Concept of Truth in Formalized Languages* (1933).

Sources

Etchemendy, John. 1990. *The concept of logical consequence*. Cambridge, Mass.: Harvard University Press.

Harré, Romano. 1972. *The philosophies of science*. Oxford: Oxford University Press.

Magnussen, Magnus; Goring, Rosemary; and Thorn, John O., eds. 1990. *Chambers biographical dictionary*. Edinburgh: Chambers Ltd.

Simons, Peter. 1992. *Philosophy and logic in Central Europe from Belzano to Tarski*. Dordrecht: Kluwer Academic Publishers.

TARTUFFE, TARTUFFIAN. A hypocrite who pretends to be religious.

Le Tartuffe is a character in a witty play, *Tartuffe* (1664), by Molière (1622–1673). A religious hypocrite, Tartuffe, worms his way into the household of Orgon, a credulous fool who deeds all his property to the impostor and intends to marry his daughter to him. Orgon's wife, Elmire, tricks Tartuffe, who is unaware that Orgon is watching, into trying to seduce her. Finally understanding Tartuffe's true nature, Orgon orders him from the house. But Tartuffe, owning the house, evicts the family instead and arranges Orgon's arrest. The king intervenes at the last moment, and Tartuffe is dispatched to prison. In time, the word *tartuffe* came to mean religious hypocrite, and the play was adapted as political parody (Ouzounian, 1987).

Sources

Drabble, Margaret, ed. 1985. *The Oxford companion to English literature*. London: Oxford University Press.

Gray, Simon. 1990. *The holy terror: Tartuffe*. London: Faber.

Hampton, Christopher, trans. 1984. *Moliere's Tartuffe: or the impostor*. London: Faber and Faber.

Ouzounian, Richard. 1987. *Moliere's Tartuffe: what happens at the NO Nancy Summit*. Toronto: Ms Fit Press.

TAYLORISM. A philosophy of modern management that assumes scientific facts provide the soundest base for management, administration, and the resolution of industrial conflict.

Frederick Winslow Taylor (1856–1915), the Father of Scientific Management, had a liberal education, but after high school ill-health prevented him from studying law. He was first an apprentice pattern-maker and afterward a laborer at Midvale Steel in Pennsylvania (1878). He began to note the inefficiencies in the factory where he worked, and he saw the need for careful observation of activities on the job, the physical conditions under which they were done, the systematic use of correctly designed tools, the establishment of efficient procedures through scientific attitude to their description and definition, and the training of supervisors in this approach to managing work. He believed the results would be greater profits and higher wages. In time, he proved that his ideas worked well at various American steel works, and he made a successful career from consulting with manufacturers on the best way to plan their works and job routines. His influence was seen in the efficient techniques of the U.S. Army in France during World War I and in Russia where Lenin advocated Taylorism for efficiency in Russia's industries. It assumes there is only one best way of doing a job, and that way can be established scientifically by measuring the time and observing the motions employed by a first-class worker to do his job effectively. Taylorism met much resistance from unions, and recently Taylor's role in applying scientific thinking to management has been questioned (Wrege and Greenwood, 1991).

Sources

Copely, Frank B. 1923. *Frederick Winslow Taylor: father of scientific management.* New York: Harper and Row.

Gillespie, Charles C. 1970–80. *Dictionary of scientific biography.* Vol. 12. New York: Charles Scribner's Sons.

Kakar, Sudhir. 1970. *Frederick Taylor: a study in personality and innovation.* Cambridge, Mass.: MIT Press.

Malone, Dumas, ed. 1935. *Dictionary of American biography.* Vol. IX. New York: Charles Scribner's Sons.

Nelson, David. 1980. *Frederick Winslow Taylor and the rise of scientific management.* Madison: University of Wisconsin Press.

Schacter, Hindy L. 1989. *Frederick Taylor and the public administration community: a revaluation.* Albany: State University of New York Press.

Taylor, Frederick W. 1911. *The principles of scientific management.* 1947 ed. New York: Harper and Row.

Wrege, Charles D., and Greenwood, Ronald G. 1991. *Frederick Winslow Taylor, the father of scientific management: myth and reality.* Homewood, Ill.: Business One Irwin.

TEAPOT DOME SCANDAL. An American scandal in the 1920s that linked U.S. politics with the oil industry during the administration (1921–23) of President Warren G. Harding (1865–1923). Harding transferred the control of naval oil reserves at Teapot Dome, Wyoming, from the secretary of the navy to Albert Bacon Fall (1861–1944), a lawyer and senator from New Mexico, secretary of the interior, and old friend of Harding. In 1920 Fall had been chairman of the

Senate subcommittee on Mexican affairs, and it was alleged he had invested in the counterrevolution after having established financial interests in Mexico. When, in 1922, Fall leased further reserves of oil at Elk Hill, California, to a different oil developer, further corruption was rumored. A Senate investigation of alleged bribery led to Fall's eleven-month imprisonment in the New Mexico penitentiary (June 1931), the cancellation of the leases, and criticism of Harding's part in the affair.

Teapot Dome is an area near Casper, in northcentral Wyoming; its name comes from a sandstone formation, vaguely resembling a teapot, that rises above the sagebrush. Below the rock outcrop is a reservoir of oil that was naturally formed in the shape of a dome. The oil and the ground above it make up a small part of the federal holdings of oil in America's West. In 1915 President Woodrow Wilson assigned control of Teapot Dome to the U.S. Navy Department to supply U.S. warships. Today much of the rock once shaped like a teapot is weathered away.

Sources

Bates, James L. 1963. *The origins of Teapot Dome.* Urbana: University of Illinois Press.
James, Edward T. 1973. *Dictionary of American biography.* Supplement 3. New York: Charles Scribner's Sons.
Stewart, George. 1978. *American place names.* New York: Oxford University Press.
Werner, Morris R., and Starr, John. 1959. *Teapot Dome.* New York: Viking Press.

TEDDY BOY, TEDDY GIRL. An unruly British adolescent of the 1950s who wore dandy clothes, "teddy suits," with fitted, stove-pipe trousers and coats or short jackets like those in fashion during the reign of Edward VII (1901–10). A Teddy girl was a teddy boy's woman companion and partner-counterpart in such conduct and dress.

See also EDWARDIAN.

Sources

Hendrickson, Robert. 1988. *The dictionary of eponyms: names that became words.* New York: Dorset.
Hudson, Kenneth. 1983. *A dictionary of the teenage revolution and its aftermath.* London: Macmillan.
Partridge, Eric. 1961. *A dictionary of slang.* New ed. 1974. London: Routledge and Kegan Paul.
Partridge, Eric. 1984. *A dictionary of slang and unconventional English.* Completely revised. 8th ed. London: Routledge and Kegan Paul.

THATCHERISM, THATCHERITE. A New Right ideology that upholds market forces, weakens trade unions, and values corporatism, monetarism, centralized political authority, law and order; the economic strategy of Margaret Thatcher, Britain's prime minister (1979–90). A follower of hers who assumes a nation prospers from only policies of free enterprise, hard work, and competition.

Margaret Thatcher (b. 1925), the second daughter of a grocer, Methodist lay preacher, and mayor of a small English town, was educated at Grantham Girl's School and Oxford University. After working as a research chemist and taxation barrister, she was elected Conservative member of Parliament for Finchley (1959), becoming education minister in the Heath government during 1970–74. She won leadership of the Conservative party (1975), and became the first woman prime minister of Britain (1979–90). She aimed for a free, open, class-less Britain based on individual self-reliance and hard work. She used restrictive legislation to weaken trade unions; tightly controlled the money supply; dereg-ulated industry; encouraged foreign investment; built a free market economy; cut the income tax; and privatized many industries. Subsequently, unemploy-ment reached 6 percent and inflation 11 percent; social welfare was slashed; roads and railways were neglected; the homeless were seen on the streets; self-ishness and greed seemed to dominate business. She strengthened Britain's in-fluence in Europe and kept close relations with the United States; Moscow named her "The Iron Lady" for her implacable attitude toward Russian policies, but at an early date she saw that Gorbachev's policies favored unity in a divided Europe. In 1989 she opposed Britain's joining the European monetary system and introduced an unpopular poll tax to replace the property tax as a source of community funds in Britain. Dissent within her party and loss of her colleagues' support led her to resign the prime ministership on November 22, 1990. She now sits in the House of Lords.

Sources

Abse, Leo. 1989. *Margaret, daughter of Beatrice: a politician's psychobiography of Margaret Thatcher.* London: Jonathan Cape.

Bosanquet, Nick. 1983. *After the New Right.* London: Heinemann.

Drucker, H., et al. 1986. *Developments in British politics 2.* Basingstoke: Macmillan.

Geelhoed, E. Bruce. 1992. *Margaret Thatcher in victory and downfall, 1987 and 1990.* Westport, Conn.: Greenwood Press.

MacInnes, John. 1987. *Thatcherism at work: industrial relations and economic change.* Buckingham: Open University Press.

Magnussen, Magnus; Goring, Rosemary; and Thorn, John O., eds. 1990. *Chambers bi-ographical dictionary.* Edinburgh: Chambers Ltd.

Mikadadi, Faysal. 1993. *Margaret Thatcher: a bibliography.* Westport, Conn.: Green-wood Press.

Thatcher, Margaret. 1993. *Margaret Thatcher: the Downing Street years: 1979–1990.* London: Collins.

Time Magazine, December 3, 1990.

Tulloch, Sara. 1991. *The Oxford dictionary of new words.* Oxford: Oxford University Press.

Young, Hugo. 1989. *One of us: biography of Margaret Thatcher.* London: Macmillan.

THEIL'S ENTROPY INDEX. A measure of spatial inequality used to distin-guish the contribution of between-region and within-region inequality to areal differentiation (Goodall, 1987:469).

Henri Theil (b. 1924) was born in Amsterdam and studied economics at the

University of Amsterdam (Ph.D., 1951). He worked for the Central Planning Bureau at The Hague (1952–55), was a professor of economics at the Netherlands School of Economics at Rotterdam (1953–66), and directed the school's Econometrics Institute (1956–66). He visited the universities of Chicago, Harvard, Southern California, and Western Australia (1956–82) and was a professor at the University of Chicago (1965–81) where he directed the Center for Mathematical Studies in Business and Economics. Since 1981 he has been professor of econometrics and decision sciences at the University of Florida. He has published many books on economic forecasting, operations research, econometrics, decision making, and the application of statistics to administration and management sciences. Universities in America and Europe have awarded him honorary degrees; he is a fellow of the American Academy of Arts and Sciences and a member of professional associations of economists and statisticians; and he was editor of *Mathematical and Managerial Economics*.

Sources

Balder, Raj, and Koerts, Johan, eds. 1992. *Henri Theil's contribution to economics and econometrics*. Dordrecht: Kluwer Academic Publishers.

Bewley, Ronald A.; Tran, Van Hoa; and Theil, Henry. 1991. *Contributions to consumer demand and econometrics: essays in honour of Henri Theil*. London: Macmillan.

Blaug, Mark, ed. 1986. *Who's who in economics: a biographical dictionary of major economists, 1700–1986*. 2d ed. Cambridge, Mass.: MIT Press.

Goodall, Brian. 1987. *The Penguin dictionary of human geography*. Harmondsworth, Middlesex: Penguin.

Who's who in America, 1992–93. New Providence, N.J.: Marquis.

THERBLIG. In the management of time and motion study, a distinct unit of work, or absence of work, into which an industrial operation may be divided; a symbol representing such a unit.

Frank Bunker Gilbreth (1868–1924) was born in Fairfield, Maine; graduated from the English High School, Boston (1885); and studied at Brown University (Ph.D., 1904). He was a contracting engineer in Boston (1895–1904) and a consulting engineer from 1911. He lectured at many American and European universities and was the director of the Summer School of Management for professors of engineering, and psychology and economics. Among his publications are *Field System* (1908); *Concrete System* (1908); *Bricklaying System* (1909); *Motion Study* (1911); and *Primer of Scientific Management* (1911). Therblig is a reversal of his surname, and emerged from time and motion work during World War I.

Lillian Moller Gilbreth (1878–1972) married Frank Gilbreth in 1904, and together they established Gilbreth Inc. and specialized in time and motion studies. She received her first Ph.D. in psychology from Brown University (1915) and her second in engineering from Rutgers College (1929). She published *Psychology of Management* (1914) and with Frank wrote three books on industrial efficiency. Their children wrote a sketch of Frank's life, *Cheaper by the Dozen* (1949).

Sources
Gilbreth, Frank B., Jr., and Carey, Ernestine M. 1949. *Cheaper by the dozen.* London: Heinemann.
Who was who in America, 1897–1942. Vol. 1. Chicago: Marquis.
Wren, Daniel A. 1987. *The evolution of management thought.* 3d ed. New York: John Wiley.
Zusne, Leonard. 1987. *Eponyms in psychology: a dictionary and sourcebook.* Westport, Conn.: Greenwood Press.

THOMAS'S THEOREM. If humankind defines situations as real, they are real in their consequences.

William Isaac Thomas (1863–1947) was born into a rural Protestant family in Virginia. In 1880 he studied literature and classics at the University of Tennessee, and became an effective orator and a captain in the officer training unit. He received his first doctorate (English and Classics) from the university in 1886 and began teaching Greek and natural history. In 1889 he studied at Göttingen and Berlin, and returned to Oberlin College to teach English until 1895 when he went to the University of Chicago to study sociology as one of Albion Small's (1854–1926) first graduate students. From 1895 to 1918 Thomas taught sociology at the university. In 1908, on a substantial research grant, he toured Europe collecting data for what would become a famous study, *The Polish Peasant in Europe and America,* in collaboration with Florian Znaniecki (1882–1958). After being forced to leave his university in a scandal, Thomas spent the remainder of his professional life in social research, occasionally lecturing and organizing meetings of social science scientists. When he was elected president of the American Sociological Association (1927), he used his address to extend the idea expressed in the Thomas theorem, which appeared in his study of children in America (1928). He traveled to Sweden to foster social research in Europe, published much social research in the United States, and his last teaching post was at Harvard (1936–37) before he retired.

Sources
Janowitz, Morris, ed. 1966. *W. I. Thomas on social organization and social personality* [with bibliography]. Chicago: Phoenix Book, University of Chicago Press.
Sills, David L., ed. 1968. *International encyclopedia of the social sciences.* New York: Macmillan and Free Press.
Thomas, W. I. 1927. Situational analysis: the behavior pattern and situation. Presidential address. *Proceedings,* 22nd Annual Meeting of the American Sociological Society, Publications 22:1–13.
Thomas, William I., and Thomas, D. S. 1928. *The child in America: behavior problems and programs.* New York: Alfred A. Knopf.

THOMISM, THOMIST. Doctrines of the thirteenth-century Italian philosopher and scholar. One who follows those doctrines. Aquinas adapted Aristotle's ideas to fit his own ideas on Christian theology, with a belief in the unity of body and soul, and a classification of the soul into the rational, sensitive, and vegetative categories.

Saint Thomas Aquinas, also Thomas of Aquino (c. 1225–74), was born in the family castle at Roccasecca near Aquino and educated by Benedictine monks at Monte Cassino and then at the University of Naples. In 1243 he entered the Dominican order and founded a theological school at Cologne where he taught until 1252. Later he went to the Dominican monastery of Saint Jacques, in Paris. He was canonized by Pope John XXII in 1323, proclaimed doctor of the church by Pious V in 1567, and declared patron of Catholic schools in 1880. He is especially remembered for his systematization of Catholic theology and for the philosophical system now known as Thomism. In 1897 the Roman Catholic Church accepted the Thomist philosophy as its official philosphical position. He is sometimes known as the ''Angelic Doctor,'' or ''Prince of Scholastics,'' or ''Father of Moral Philosophy.''

Sources

Hastings, James. 1921. *Encyclopedia of religion and ethics.* Vol. 12. New York: Charles Scribner's Sons.

Miller, David, ed. 1987. *The Blackwell encyclopedia of political thought.* Oxford: Basil Blackwell.

Zusne, Leonard. 1984. *Biographical dictionary of psychology.* Westport, Conn.: Greenwood Press.

THOMSON COLONY. A communal farming settlement in Salina, Kansas, established in 1880 with funds from a twentieth-century philanthropist and formed by the Co-operative Colony Aid Association of New York City. Each colonist was allotted a home and land, large tracts were worked cooperatively, time was allocated to the colony work and maintenance, and the profits were distributed on a pro rata basis.

Elizabeth Rowell Thomson (1821–99) was born in New England and employed as a housemaid until she married a patron of the arts, Thomas Thomson (1843). They lived in Boston until 1860, moved to New York City, and became known for their philanthropic work. When Thomson died, his wife was left $50,000 a year, which she used partly to further women's suffrage and the temperance movement. In 1871 she provided funds for the Co-operative Colony Aid Association. She also supported scientific research and was the first patron of the American Association for the Advancement of Science.

Sources

Fogarty, Robert S. 1980. *Dictionary of American communal and utopian history.* Westport, Conn.: Greenwood Press.

James, Edward T. 1971. *Notable American women 1607–1950.* Cambridge, Mass.: Belknap Press/Harvard University Press.

THURSTONE SCALE. Thurstone attitude scales comprise a series of statements, each selected according to the method of equal-appearing intervals and each assigned a scale value on the basis of the judgments of at last 100 raters on such subjects as capital punishment, communism, the church, and censorship.

Louis Leon Thurstone (1887–1955) was born in Chicago and graduated in psychology from the University of Chicago (Ph.D., 1917). He contributed to the theory of factor analysis and undertook major studies of human intelligence in search for primary mental abilities. He identified seven such abilities and constructed tests to measure them. He joined the faculty of the Carnegie Institute of Technology (1917–23) and was at the University of Chicago (1924–52) and, after retirement, at the University of North Carolina. He wrote twenty-three books and monographs, 165 articles, 95 laboratory reports, and constructed 47 tests. In psychophysics, Thurstone considered the law of comparative judgments to be his best. His main works were *Measurement of Attitudes* (1929); *Primary Mental Abilities* (1938); *Factorial Studies of Intelligence* (1941); and *Multiple Factor Analysis* (1947).

Sources

Garraty, John A., ed. 1977. *Dictionary of American biography.* Supplement 5. New York: Charles Scribner's Sons.

Goldenson, R., ed. 1984. *Longman dictionary of psychology and psychiatry.* New York: Longman.

Wolman, Benjamin, ed. 1989. *Dictionary of behavioral science.* San Diego, Calif.: Academic Press.

Zusne, Leonard. 1984. *Biographical dictionary of psychology.* Westport, Conn.: Greenwood Press.

TIEBOUT HYPOTHESIS. A hypothesis that assumes a mechanism for revealing preferences for publicly available goods if their consumers can choose among "jurisdictions." The primary application of the hypothesis may occur when a large number of autonomous suburban jurisdictions provide goods that are generally available from local governments, for example, primary and secondary education, police protection, provision of sewer and water services, and fire protection. In its application, the hypothesis has both normative and positive aspects. Normative aspects are clear when the provision of public goods locally is desired, and positive aspects are evident in predicting that individuals will respond to local taxes and services to pay for them.

Charles Mill Tiebout (1924–68) was born in Norwalk, Connecticut, and was educated at Wesleyan University and the University of Michigan (Ph.D., 1959). He taught at Northwestern University (1954–58) and the University of California, Los Angeles (1968–62), and was appointed a professor of economics and business administration at the University of Washington, Seattle (1962). His major work was "Pure Theory of Local Expenditure," *Journal of Political Economy* (1956) from which the hypothesis was derived.

Sources

Eatwell, John; Milgate, Murray; and Newman, Peter. 1987. *The new Palgrave: a dictionary of economics.* London: Macmillan.

Pearce, David W., ed. 1986. *Macmillan dictionary of modern economics.* New York: Macmillan.

Tiebout, Charles M. 1962. *The community economic base study.* New York: Committee for Economic Development.

TIMONISE. To play the misanthrope.

Timon of Athens (fifth century B.C.), a noted misanthrope, lived during the Peloponnesian War. In Shakespeare's play, *Timon of Athens* (1608), which was probably based on Plutarch's account, Timon gives away money with excessive generosity until he learns that he is penniless. When asked to help him, his friends, who had enjoyed his generosity, refuse and he becomes furious. With unremitting hostility to all humankind, he refuses to live in anything but the lowest poverty and suffering until he dies, disillusioned with fellow humans and filled with hatred for the world. Aristophanes alludes to him often, as do other comedians of the Attic stage. Plutarch gives a short account of his life in the biography of Mark Antony, and he gives his name to Lucian's dialogues.

Sources

Campbell, Oscar J., and Quinn, Edward. 1966. *The reader's encyclopedia of Shakespeare.* New York: Thomas Y. Crowell.

Evans, Gareth L., and Evans, Barbara L. 1978. *The Shakespeare companion.* New York: Charles Scribner's Sons.

Halliday, Frank E. 1964. *A Shakespeare companion.* London: Duckworth.

Shadwell, Thomas. 1969. *The history of Timon of Athens, the man hater: an adaptation of Shakespeare's play.* London: Cornmarket.

TINDALE'S MAP.

A map of Australian tribes where the name of each one is set out systematically according to evidence from field trips (1920s–60s) and available literature. The maps summarize the distribution and nomenclature of all tribal groupings on the Australian continent; show that the Australian black inhabitants are the largest and most widely spread of the hunter-gatherer groups still on earth; and reveal that they occupied the whole continent. The maps are especially valuable because they give the most concise and complete account of the distribution of all tribes before white settlement.

Norman Barnett Tindale (b. 1900) was born in Perth, Western Australia (W.A.), educated at the Tokyo Grammar School, and studied science at the University of Adelaide. In 1917 he joined the scientific staff of the South Australian Museum, and later became assistant entomologist. In 1920–21 he began zoological fieldwork at Groote Eylandt and continued it at Cape York (1926–27). In 1921–22 Tindale learned from a wandering Ngandi tribe songmaker the existence of tribal boundaries beyond which danger might well be found. This view contradicted the popular belief that all Australian aboriginals wandered freely over the whole continent. From 1927 to 1965, while he was the curator of the museum, Tindale continued his research into the territoriality of Australia's original black inhabitants throughout W.A., South Australia, New South Wales, and the Northern Territory. His ideas and work received help and guidance from Alfred L. Kroeber (1876–1960), University of California, and Earnest A. Hooton (1887–1954) of Harvard and support from the Carnegie Corporation. He completed the first part of the fieldwork in 1938–39. He was also a visiting professor to California on a regular basis between 1936 and 1959. During World War II he was a Wing commander in the Royal Australian Air Force. The anthropological mapping work was continued in the 1950s and 1960s and was finally published in 1974. He published *Distribution of Australian Aboriginal Tribes* (1940) as well as 160 papers on ethnology, entomology, and geology. Although today there are some disputes about the boundaries he had superimposed on the maps, his work remains a baseline for understanding Australian aboriginal territorial organization and contemporary land rights and land claims.

Sources

Alexander, Joseph A. 1962. *Who's who in Australia.* Melbourne: Herald.

Fifth international directory of anthropologists. 1975. Chicago: University of Chicago Press.

Tindale, Norman B. 1974. *Aboriginal tribes of Australia: their terrain, environmental controls, distribution, limits and proper names.* 2 vols. with maps. Canberra: Australian National University Press.

TITOISM. The domestic and foreign policies of the former Yugoslavia after 1948. The ideology is a revision of communism—market socialism—that permitted more contact with foreign nations than Stalin would allow, a growing tourist industry, the reverse of collectivization with support for small farms, and worker self-government in industry. The foreign policy was possible because the independent Yugoslavia took advantage of its position between Russia and the West, and at the same time developed sound foreign relations with other communist bloc countries.

Josip Broz or Brizovich Tito (1892–1980) was born at Kumrovac, a village near Zagreb, Croatia. In 1914 he was conscripted into the Austro-Hungarian Army, and the following year he was imprisoned by the Russians. He was freed in 1917 during the Russian Revolution and fought with the Bolsheviks during the Russian civil war. He underwent training as a communist agent and in 1924 returned to his homeland, now the former Yugoslavia, as a union organizer among the metal workers of Zagreb. Following the Nazi invasion of Russia in 1941, he emerged as Tito, the underground leader of partisan guerrilla forces. In May 1943 he began to receive military aid from the Allies; he revealed his identity as Josip Broz and was awarded the title of marshal of the People's Army. In 1945 he became premier of Yugoslavia. Suppressing all elements hostile to his regime, Tito firmly led Yugoslavia toward international sovietization and industrialization in cooperation with Russia.

Sources

Bilainkin, Georgo. 1950. *Tito.* New York: Philosophical Library.

Christman, Henry M., ed. 1970. *The essential Tito.* Newton Abbot, Devon: David and Charles.

McHenry, Robert, ed. 1992. *The new encyclopedia Britannica.* Chicago: Encyclopedia Britannica, Inc.

Maclean, Fitzroy. 1957. *Disputed barricade: the life and times of Josip Broz Tito, Marshal of Yugoslavia.* London: Jonathan Cape.

Pavlowitch, Stephen K. 1971. *Yugoslavia.* New York: Praeger.

Plano, Jack. 1988. *The international relations dictionary.* 4th ed. Santa Barbara, Calif.: ABC-CLIO.

Rusinow, Dennison. 1977. *The Yugoslav experiment 1948–74.* London: C. Hurst for Royal Institute of International Affairs.

TOJO. One or more Japanese soldiers during World War II.

Hideki Tojo (1884–1948) was born in Tokyo, the eldest in a family of ten children, and was raised in the simple home of a military man of the old samurai class. A quarrelsome, spirited, and aggressive adolescent, he entered a Tokyo military preparatory school in 1899, and owing to the Boxer rising, the school was put on a military footing. He graduated from a central military school (1905) and was decorated in a successful war that aimed for peace in the Orient (1906), the same reason given for Japan's attack on the United States in 1941. He married and lived with his family (1911), and in 1912 he entered an army war college. In 1915, after Japan had invaded China, he graduated as captain, a member of Japan's military elite. In 1919 he was sent to Europe to study its culture, language, and history, and returned in 1922 to a nation in crisis; the general opinion was that Japan's domestic affairs were subject to excessive American intervention and that the Japanese military elites were in decline. The answer lay in a policy of Japanese expansion into East Asia. After 1927 the threat to this policy centered on China and Russia, and later the United States. By 1937 Tojo was head of Japan's army in Manchuria, vice-president of the War Cabinet in 1938–39, and in 1940–41 was Japan's minister for war. By October 1941 he was Japan's military dictator and fully responsible for the Pearl Harbor attack in December. Japan's policy for a "New Order in Asia" failed after it lost the Mariana Islands in 1944. Tojo was forced to resign; after Japan surrendered he was found guilty of war crimes and hanged by an international tribunal with six other wartime leaders by the American Army at Sugamo Prison in Tokyo.

Sources

Butow, Robert J. 1969. *Tojo and the coming of the War.* 2d ed. Stanford, Calif.: Stanford University Press.

Itaska, Gen, ed. 1983. *Kodansha encyclopedia of Japan.* Tokyo: Kodansha International.

McHenry, Robert, ed. 1992. *The new encyclopedia Britannica.* Chicago: Encyclopedia Britannica, Inc.

TOKYO ROSE. A woman traitor and the name given by U.S. soldiers to many English-speaking women who broadcast propaganda on shortwave radio during World War II in the Pacific. Their allegedly sirenlike voices and messages were sent to undermine the U.S. soldiers' morale and were often accompanied by the music soldiers from America liked to hear.

The myth that there was only one "Tokyo Rose" centered on Iva Togori D'Aquino (fl. 1941–76) who was born in the United States of Japanese parents and graduated from the University of California, Los Angeles. She was caught in Japan after the Japanese attacked Pearl Harbor (December 1941). She worked as a typist with three Allied prisoners of war on "Zero Hour," which was described as a program of light music and allegedly humorous light banter (Itaska, 1983). She was identified in 1945, arrested, and released in 1946. In 1948 she was arrested again and was found guilty of treason in 1949, fined $10,000, and sentenced to ten years in prison. She was paroled in 1956. In 1976 the prosecution witnesses admitted to giving false evidence at her trial. She was pardoned by President Ford in 1976 and allowed to reclaim her citizenship. The verdict against her was surrounded by political pressure, harassment, distorted accounts of the war, intimidation, false evidence, and newspaper sensationalism. The other women said to be Tokyo Rose included Ruth Hayakawa, born in the United States of Japanese parents, Mieko Furuya Oki, and Katherine Morooka Reyes. In 1950 their American citizenship was reinstated.

Sources

Duus, Masayo. 1983. *Tokyo Rose: orphan of the Pacific.* Trans Peter Duus. Tokyo: Kodansha International.

Howe, Russell W. 1990. *The hunt for "Tokyo Rose."* Lanham, Md.: Madison Books.

Itaska, Gen, ed. 1983. *Kodansha encyclopedia of Japan.* Tokyo: Kodansha International.

TOLPUDDLE MARTYRS. Six agricultural laborers of Tolpuddle—George Loveless (1797–1874), Henry Loveless, his brother, their brother-in-law Thomas Stanfield, their nephew Thomas Stanfield, James Hammett, and James Brine— who were sentenced in 1834 to seven years' transportation to Australia for sedition.

In 1833 laborers in Tolpuddle received seven shillings per week; when they thought this sum should be raised to ten, their employers threatened to cut their wages to six instead. In response, George Loveless, a ploughman and Wesleyan preacher, married with three children, and familiar with the writings of Robert Owen (1771–1858) and the establishment of trades unions, advised the threatened laborers on forming the Friendly Society of Agricultural Laborers. Since the Combination Laws had been repealed (1824), forming a union was not illegal, but witnesses testified that the men had bound their members by "unlawful oaths." The local magistrate was alarmed and wrote to Viscount Melbourne, who drew attention to the legislation, the Unlawful Oaths Act of 1797, directed against sedition. The six men were arrested and tried by Sir John, later Baron, Williams, a friend of Lord Melbourne, who was said to have concluded his address to the jury with the words: "If these men had been allowed to go on with their wicked plans they would have destroyed property. If you do not find them guilty you will forget the good will and confidence of the Grand

Jury.'' In Tasmania, George Loveless learned that a public protest forced a pardon by Lord Russell in March 1836. On returning to England Hammett settled in Tolpuddle; in time the others became Chartists and immigrated to Canada. George Loveless published his story in *The Victims of Whiggery* (1837).

Near Dorchester, Tolpuddle is one of a group of villages that lie along the length of the River Puddle in south England. At Dorchester the courthouse in which the martyrs were sentenced was purchased by the Trades Union Congress in 1956 and returned to the Rural District Council in 1967 to serve as their memorial.

Sources

Citrine, W. M., et al., eds. 1934. *The book of the martyrs of Tolpuddle, 1843–1934.* London: Victoria House Printing Co.

Grolier Society of Australia. 1965. *The Australian encyclopedia.* Sydney: Grolier.

Pike, Douglas, et al. 1966–90. *Australian dictionary of biography.* 12 vols. Carlton, Victoria: University of Melbourne Press.

TOMKINS'S SCRIPT THEORY. A modern social psychological theory of personality that places individuals in the role of playwright constructing their life dramas. Life drama comprises affect-laden scenes of events that include at least one affect and one object of that affect; scripts are formed as the scenes are subject to the individuals' own rules of interpreting scenes relative to one another.

Silvan S. Tomkins (1911–91) was born in Philadelphia and studied playwriting at the University of Pennsylvania. After completing a Ph.D. in psychology (1934), he studied at the Harvard Psychological Clinic. In the early 1940s he devised the Tomkins-Horn Picture Arrangement Test (PAT) for the study of worker absenteeism, edited *Contemporary Psychopathology* (1943), and published a definitive manual on Murray's Thematic Apperception Test (1946). He became a professor of psychology at Princeton (1947–68), directed clinical training, and in 1966 received one of the first Career Scientist Awards from the National Institute of Mental Health. He became director of the Center for Research in Cognition and Affect in New York (1964–68) and formed a new department at Livingstone College, Rutgers University (1970). After retirement (1975), he was emeritus at the Wharton School, University of Pennsylvania, until 1991. He published widely, received many professional awards, and consulted for several U.S. government agencies. His noted works include *Affect, Images and Consciousness* (1962), *Affect, Cognition and Personality* (1966), and *Affect, Imagery and Consciousness* (1991). His studies of ideology and personality have drawn him to the attention of political scientists who are interested in his ''Script Theory.''

Sources

Alexander, Irving, 1992. Obituary: Silvan Samuel Tomkins (1911–1991). *American Psychologist* 47:1674–1675.

Carlson, Rae, and Brinka, Julie, 1987. Studies in script theory: III ideology and political imagination. *Political Psychology* 8:563–574.

Jaques Cattell Press, ed. 1973. *American men and women of science: the social and behavioral sciences.* New York: Jaques Cattell and R. R. Bowker.

Tomkins, Silvan S. 1987. Script theory. In Joel Arnoff, Albert. I. Rabin, and Robert E. Zucker, eds. *The emergence of personality.* New York: Springer, pp. 147–216.

Who's who in American Jewry, 1980. Los Angeles: Standard Who's Who.

Personal Communication.

TOMLIN FORMULA. A formula for comparing classes inside the British Civil Service with occupation levels outside. It was introduced by a Royal (Tomlin) Commission on the Civil Service, 1930–50. The final report was based on the assumption that Civil Service remuneration ought to reflect the long-term trends in the nation's wage changes and its economy.

Thomas James Cheshire Tomlin, Baron Tomlin of Ash (1867–1935), was educated at Harrow and New College, Oxford, studied law, and was called to the bar in 1891. He served many government agencies. He was counsel to the boards of Trade, Inland Revenue, and Education. He took silk (1913), became counsel to the Royal College of Physicians (1922), chaired the lord chancellor's committee on reorganizing aspects of the courts (1919–20), and was appointed a high court judge (1923–29). He chaired several important government committees on awards to inventors, child adoption, cruelty to animals, and served the University of London's commissioners. He chaired the Royal Commission on the Civil Service in 1929. For his public services he was knighted in 1923, was made a baron in 1929, and was honored by London, Toronto, and Columbia universities.

Sources

Ford, P., and Ford, G., eds. 1969. *A breviate of parliamentary papers 1917–1939.* Shannon, Ireland: Irish University Press.

Marsh, Arthur. 1979. *Concise encyclopedia of industrial relations.* Westmead, Farnborough, Hants: Gower.

Who was who, 1929–40. Vol. III. London: Adam and Charles Black.

TONTINE. Life annuity scheme.

Lorenzo Tonti (1620–90) was a Neapolitan banker who settled in Paris in the time of Cardinal Mazarin. Tonti invented the life annuity in 1653. The financial scheme had subscribers, each of whom received an annuity that increased as the number of subscribers died. The last subscriber received all the income. Tonti submitted his idea to the cardinal as a device for raising funds by the state; the members of the association were to subscribe the sum of money needed by the French government and were to receive shares in the society. The original fund was to return to the government after the death of the last member. In 1689 Louis XIV, who needed funds, began a tontine that lasted over forty years, the last survivor drawing $367,500 from his original investment of $1,500.

Sources

McHenry, Robert, ed. 1992. *The new encyclopedia Britannica.* Chicago: Encyclopedia Britannica, Inc.

Magnussen, Magnus; Goring, Rosemary; and Thorn, John O., eds. 1990. *Chambers biographical dictionary.* Edinburgh: Chambers Ltd.

Smith, Benjamin. 1903. *The Century cyclopedia of names.* London: The Times.

TORQUEMADA. A cruel persecutor, a torturer.

Tomás de Torquemada (c. 1420–98), of Jewish descent, was born in Valladolid, Spain, and entered San Pablo Dominica, the local convent, graduated in theology, and was appointed a prior of Santa Cruz convent in Segovia in 1452. Later, he was made confessor to the Royal Treasurer and to Queen Isabella I and King Ferdinand V (1474). Despite his Jewish origins, he helped prepare the first royal demand for an inquisition into the crypto-Jews, those who were insincere in their Christianity or had been forcibly converted (1478). The queen persuaded Pope Sixtus IV to organize the whole Inquisition under Torquemada's control as Spanish Grand Inquisitor (1483). Pope Alexander VI appointed four more inquisitors to restrain Torquemada; nevertheless, he remained in control until after his retirement. While he was in power over 2,000 crypto-Jews were executed, and many others were cruelly tortured with methods Torquemada had devised. He never believed in the sincerity of the Maranos and Moriscos, who were Jewish converts to Catholicism, and in 1492 he was probably responsible for the royal decree that expelled 200,000 Jews from Spain. His methods were used as a model for ensuing inquisitors, especially in dealings with heretics who were eventually burned at the stake.

Sources

Cross, Frank L. 1974. *The Oxford dictionary of the Christian Church.* 2d ed. New York: Oxford University Press.

McDonald, William, ed. 1967. *New Catholic encyclopedia.* New York: McGraw-Hill.

McHenry, Robert, ed. 1992. *The new encyclopedia Britannica.* Chicago: Encyclopedia Britannica, Inc.

TORRENS SYSTEM. A statutory system for the transfer of real property.

Sir Robert Torrens (1814–84) was born in Ireland and educated at Trinity College, Dublin. In about 1835 his interest in a problem of a friend who had suffered misfortune in a land transfer drew his attention to the law on this subject. He immigrated to South Australia in 1839 and became collector of customs at Adelaide. In 1851 Torrens was nominated by the governor as a member of the House of Assembly in the new Parliament of South Australia and became treasurer in the Ministry (1856). In 1857 he was premier, but his government lasted less than a month. That year he passed his property transfer bill through the assembly. In Adelaide some attempts were made to minimize Torrens's credit for the ideas involved in his plan for land transfer. The system meant that property was transferred by registration of title rather than by deeds, and it has since been widely adopted in the world. In 1863 Torrens left Australia and settled in England and was a member of the House of Commons for Cambridge (1868–74). He was made a knight in 1872.

Sources

Chisholm, Alec H., ed. 1963. *The Australian encyclopedia.* Sydney: Grolier Society of Australia.

Elder, Bruce, ed. 1987. *The A to Z of who's who in Australian history.* Brookvale, N.S.W.: Childs and Associates.

McHenry, Robert, ed. 1992. *The new encyclopedia Britannica.* Chicago: Encyclopedia Britannica, Inc.

Pike, Douglas, et al. 1966–90. *Australian dictionary of biography.* 12 vols. Carlton, Victoria: University of Melbourne Press.

Simpson, Brian 1984. *Biographical dictionary of the common law.* London: Butterworth.

Stephen, Leslie, and Lee, Sydney, eds. 1917. *The dictionary of national biography.* London: Oxford University Press.

TOWNSEND MOVEMENT, TOWNSEND PLAN. An American social movement (1934) with the motto "Youth for work, age for leisure." It arose from a plan to reduce poverty for the elderly with a $200 government pension for those over 60, and, to turn around the depressed economy, with a proviso that the money should be spent in thirty days. The movement declined after the Social Security Act (1935) was passed.

Francis Everett Townsend (1867–1960) was born near Fairbury, Illinois, and after little schooling tried his luck in the Los Angeles land boom (1887), failed, took up farming in Kansas, quit, and worked in the Colorado mines. While a drifter, he saved enough to enter medical college in Omaha (1899–1903) and practiced in the Black Hills of South Dakota until World War I. He moved his family to Long Beach, California in 1919 and struggled to earn a living in medicine. Old and poor in the 1930s Depression, he began to campaign to free those like him from poverty by proposing his pension plan (September 1933) which would expand the economy and eliminate the Depression. In ninety days a social movement was evident; Townsend Clubs were formed, and the *Townsend National Weekly* appeared. With support from millions of people, Townsend, feeling he was on God's mission, joined with others, including Huey Long's "Share the Wealth" society, and became a political force with the Townsend National Recovery Plan. After the Social Security Act was passed, his political influence diminished, he placed himself in contempt of Congress— President Roosevelt commuted the jail sentence—and spent his life addressing the elderly on his schemes.

Sources

Garraty, John A., ed. 1980. *Dictionary of American biography.* Supplement 6. New York: Charles Scribner's Sons.

Holtzman, Abraham. 1963. *The Townsend Movement: a political study.* New York: Bookman Associates.

Messinger, Sheldon L. 1955. Organizational transformation: a case study of a declining social movement. *American Sociological Review* 20:3–10.

Pinner, F. A., Jacobs, P., and Selznick, P. 1959. *Old age and political behavior: a case study.* Berkeley: University of California Press.

Townsend, Francis E. 1943. *New horizons: an autobiography*. Ed. Jesse G. Murray. Chicago: J. L. Stewart.

TOZER, TOZERISM. To remove a person from office in response to pressure from another; an untrue or inaccurate statement.

Horace Tozer (1844–1916) was born at Port Macquarie, New South Wales, educated at Collegiate School, Newcastle, and became a Brisbane solicitor in 1866. He settled at Gympie, Queensland, and became alderman of the town's first council in 1880. In 1888 he was elected to the Legislative Assembly; from 1890 to 1893 he was colonial secretary, and in 1898 home secretary. At an early date his authority on mining law established his reputation. Although he had an impressive and fluent style, he was not an able speechmaker, but distinguished himself for capable administration. In 1895 he introduced legislation that, though initially resisted, laid the ground for the regulation of hours and conditions of work in shops and factories in Queensland. He also helped establish the public library and art gallery in Brisbane. From 1898 to 1909 he was Queensland's agent-general in London, from which he retired owing to ill-health. He was knighted in 1897. In June 1896 George Reid (1845–1918), a prominent New South Wales politician, coined this new word *tozer* to indicate what happens when one person is shunted by a second in deference to the influence of a third. A *tozerism* was invented by John Macrossan (1832–1891), a Queensland politician, to indicate something that was probably not true; it takes its origin from the late 1890s when Tozer became notorious for his unreliable statements under close questioning in Parliament.

Sources

Chisholm, Alec H., ed. 1963. *The Australian encyclopedia*. Sydney: Grolier Society of Australia.

Pike, Douglas, et al. 1966–90. *Australian dictionary of biography*. 12 vols. Carlton, Victoria: University of Melbourne Press.

Ramson, William S. 1988. *The Australian national dictionary: a dictionary of Australianisms on historical principles*. Melbourne: Oxford University Press.

TROTSKYISM, TROTSKYITES, TROTSKYISTS. A Marxist ideology of 1906 that supported Marx's "permanent revolution" (1850): that is, if national socialist revolutions became internationalized quickly, then in Russia it was conceivable that socialism could be reached directly and it could lead the world in this regard. The ideology assumed that economically underdeveloped nations could have a socialist revolution. At the Soviet show-trials (1937–38), Trotskyites were those who had followed Trotsky; it only became a derogatory term when introduced to American politics and scholarship. In the 1960s Trotskyists revived the ideology with a strong emphasis on internationalism, the original tenets of Bolshevism, and the use of revolution by the workers—not parliamentary legislation—to achieve the socialist state.

Leon Trotsky, pseudonym for Lev Davidovich Bronstein (1879–1940), was the son of a prosperous Jew in the Ukraine. As a student, he was influenced by the revolutionary movement in Russia, and in 1898 he was arrested for political agitation and exiled to Siberia. There he joined the new Russian Social Democratic Worker's party, and in 1902 he escaped to join the party's leaders in Switzerland. During the revolution of 1905 he returned to Russia, was arrested when the revolution failed, and was again exiled to Siberia but again managed to escape abroad. After the 1917 revolution, Trotsky returned to Russia, joined the Bolsheviks, and quickly became Lenin's second in command. During the civil war of 1918–20, Trotsky was in charge of military operations and distinguished himself with energetic leadership. His actions aroused the hostility of other communist leaders, particularly Stalin. In 1924 Trotsky was publicly attacked for the heresy of worldwide revolution, or ''Trotskyism,'' and in 1928 he was exiled to soviet central Asia. He settled in Mexico in 1937 and was murdered by a communist agent in 1940.

Sources

Beilharz, Peter. 1987. *The social and political thought of Leon Trotsky.* Oxford: Clarendon Press.

Callinicos, Alex. 1991. *Trotskyism.* Buckingham: Open University Press.

Devine, Elizabeth; Held, Michael; Vinson, James; and Walsh, George, eds. 1983 *Thinkers of the twentieth century: a biographical, bibliographical and critical dictionary.* London: Macmillan.

King, D., and Wyndham, J. 1972. *Trotsky.* Harmondsworth: Penguin.

Kuci-Paz, B. 1978. *Trotsky, Trotskyism and the transition to socialism.* London: Croom Helm.

Lowy, M. 1981. *The politics of combined and uneven development.* London: Verso.

Mandel, E. 1979. *Revolutionary Marxism today.* London: New Left Books.

Trotsky, Leon. 1930. *My life.* 1975 ed. Harmondsworth: Penguin.

TRUDEAUMANIA. The emotional public response to the succession to the prime ministership of Canada in mid-1968 (Marsh 1988).

Pierre Elliot Trudeau (b. 1919), born into a wealthy family and raised in an affluent suburb of Montreal, was educated at an elite French-Canadian Jesuit School in Montreal, studied law (1943), and was admitted to the bar in Quebec. He campaigned against military conscription during World War II, completed his M.A. (Harvard, 1945), and studied economics and political science in London and Paris. He was elected to the House of Commons for Mont-Royal (1965), became minister of justice and attorney-general of Canada (1967), and in 1968 was the leader of the Liberal party and was elected Canada's prime minister with the largest majority in ten years. He was reelected in 1972. He published articles and papers on social, political, and economic issues, was awarded the Albert Einstein international peace prize (1984), and was made a Companion of Honor (1984) and a Companion of the Order of Canada (1985).

Sources

Marsh, James A., ed. 1988. *The Canadian encyclopedia.* 2d ed. Edmonton: Hurtog.

Moritz, Charles, ed. 1968. *Current biography yearbook.* New York: H. W. Wilson.

Radwanski, George. 1978. *Trudeau.* Toronto: Macmillan.
Simpson, Kiernan, ed. 1987. *Who's who in Canada.* Vol. XXII. Toronto: University of
    Toronto Press.
Trudeau, Pierre E. 1993. *Memoirs.* Willowdale, Ontario: McClelland and Stewart.
Vastel, Michel. 1989. *Trudeau, le Quebecois.* Montreal: Editions de l'homme.

**TRUMAN COMMITTEE, TRUMAN DOCTRINE, TRUMAN LOYALTY
ORDER.** The Truman Committee, the Committee for the Investigation of the
Defense Program (1941–44), was given Truman's name and noted for its saving
of federal funds in defense spending.

The Truman Doctrine, announced on March 12, 1947, marked a change in
traditional American foreign policy. With the departure of British troops from
Greece during a civil war, there appeared evidence of communist-inspired political instability that extended to other Mediterranean areas. Recognizing the
reality of the cold war, Truman called for an immediate $100 million aid pro-
gram for Greece and Turkey to prevent the threat of internal subversion or
external aggression. Although the doctrine referred specifically to Greece and
Turkey, the principle of protecting friendly nations from subversion or aggression was open-ended and extended to all Western Europe with the Marshall Plan
and North Atlantic Treaty Organization.

With regard to the Loyalty Order, In March 1947 Truman required that "there
shall be a loyalty investigation of every person entering the civilian employment
of any department or agency of the Executive Branch of the Federal Government." The oath was aimed at protecting the United States from, primarily,
communism, and also at protecting individuals from unfounded accusations of
disloyalty. The Federal Bureau of Investigation would investigate, give the information to a loyalty board, and the board would decide if there were grounds
for a charge of disloyalty.

Harry S Truman (1884–1972) was born at Lamar, Missouri, and educated at
Independence, Missouri. He served as an artillery captain on the western front
in World War I and after the war returned to his farm and went into partnership
in a men's clothing store. The business venture failed, but he insisted on paying
the creditors in full, which took fifteen years. Truman studied law but did not
qualify as a lawyer, and he entered politics as a Democrat. As a senator (1935–
45), he became well known through his chairmanship (1941–44) of the Committee for the Investigation of the Defense Program. Elected vice-president in
1944, he succeeded to the presidency upon Franklin Roosevelt's death in 1945.
Truman was responsible for dropping the atomic bombs on Japan in August
1945. Despite predictions to the contrary, he won a comfortable victory in the
presidential campaign of 1948; he made the decision that initiated the Korean
War in 1950 and showed courage in dismissing General Douglas MacArthur for
his political intervention. To counter Soviet influence and expansion in Europe,
he devised a policy of economic and military aid, which came to be called the
Truman Doctrine. He declined to stand for reelection in 1952.

Sources

Barth, Alan. 1952. *The loyalty of free men.* New York: Pocket Books.

Commager, Henry S., ed. 1968. *Documents of American history.* 8th ed. New York: Appleton-Century-Crofts.

Donovan, Robert J. 1983. *Tumultous years: the presidency of Harry S. Truman, 1948–1953.* New York: W. W. Norton.

Gaddis, John L. 1972. *The United States and the origins of the Cold War.* New York: Columbia University Press.

Jenkins, Roy. 1986. *Truman.* London: Collins.

McCullough, David. 1992. *Truman.* New York: Simon and Schuster.

Messer, Robert L. 1985. *The end of an alliance: James F. Byrnes, Roosevelt, Truman, and the origins of the cold war.* Chapel Hill: University of North Carolina Press.

Messer, Robert L. 1985. New evidence on Truman's Doctrine. *Bulletin of the Atomic Scientists* 41:50–56.

Truman, Harry S. 1955. *Years of decision.* New York: Doubleday.

Truman, Harry S. 1956. *Trial and hope.* New York: Doubleday.

TUCHMAN'S LAW. If power corrupts, weakness in the seat of power, with its constant necessity of deals and bribes and compromising arrangements, corrupts even more.

Barbara Wertheim Tuchman (1912–89) was born in New York City; her father was an international banker, publisher, and philanthropist, and her mother came from the Morgenthau family. Barbara was educated at Walden School, New York, spent summers in Europe, and studied at Radcliffe. After working briefly for the Institute of Pacific Relations in Tokyo, she became a reporter for *Nation,* covered the Spanish Civil War, and published the first of many books, *The Lost British Policy: Britain and Spain since 1700* (1938). During World War II she worked for the Office of War Information (Far East) and published *Bible and Sword* (1956) and *The Zimmerman Telegram* (1958). She won her first Pulitzer Prize for *The Guns of August* (1958), which was acclaimed as a brilliant diplomatic and military history of the outbreak of World War I. She advocated that history be written as it occurred and that the historian stay close to the evidence. Among her other works was a second Pulitzer Prize winner, *Stilwell and the American Experience in China* (1971). Frequently, she wrote for newspapers and contributed to the foreign affairs section of the *New York Times.* Among her many honors was a gold medal from the American Association of Arts and Letters and the Order of Leopold from the Belgian government. In her final years she published *A Distant Mirror* (1987), *The March of Folly: From Troy to Vietnam* (1984), and *The First Salute* (1988).

Sources

Moritz, Charles, ed. 1963. *Current biography yearbook.* New York: H. W. Wilson.

Moritz, Charles, ed. 1989. *Current biography yearbook.* New York: H. W. Wilson.

Tuchman, Barbara. 1970. If Asia were clay in the hands of the West—the Stilwell Mission to China, 1942–44. *The Atlantic Monthly,* September:80.

Who's who in America, 1988–89. Wilmette, Ill.: Marquis.

TUCKER ACT. Thirty-two years after establishing the Court of Claims, Congress enacted the Tucker Act (1887), which extends that court's jurisdiction to decide on claims made against the U.S. government based on the U.S. Constitution. The act supports the view that the federal government has no immunity from the law (24 Stat 505 [1887]).

John Randolph Tucker (1823–97), born at Winchester, Virginia, was educated at private schools in Winchester and Richmond, and studied mathematics, physical sciences, and moral and political philosophy at the University of Virginia (1839–43). In 1843 he received his law degree and practiced in Winchester (1845–57). He became attorney-general of Virginia (1857–65) and entered the U.S. Congress (1875–87). As a Democratic leader, he strongly supported the U.S. Constitution and the rights of states. He advocated tariff and tax reforms and favored the Chinese exclusion policies and the policy of "sound money." Meanwhile, he was a professor of law at Washington and Lee University (1870–74; 1889–97). He was also president of the American Bar Association. After retiring from Congress, he returned to university teaching, became dean of the Law School, and wrote *The Constitution and the United States* (1899).

Sources

Dudley, Lavina, ed. 1963. *Encyclopedia Americana.* New York: Americana Corp.

Jacob, Kathryn A., and Ragsdale, Bruce A. 1989. *Biographical directory of the United States Congress: 1774–1989.* Bicentennial ed. Washington, D.C.: U.S. Government Printing Office.

Levy, Leonard W., ed. 1986. *Encyclopedia of the American Constitution.* New York: Macmillan.

Malone, Dumas, ed. 1936. *Dictionary of American biography.* Vol. X. New York: Charles Scribner's Sons.

Plano, Jack C., and Greenberg, Milton. 1989. *The American political dictionary.* New York: Holt, Rinehart and Winston.

TUCKER'S "WARFARE PERSONALITY." Based on the theory of neurosis outlined by Karen Horney (1885–1952), this political type, a "warfare personality," is driven by basic anxiety, isolated, lonely, and powerless in a threatening world; he seeks to make up for all he lacks by establishing a super being and then identifying with it. To those who unsettle him and hurt his pride, he becomes vindictive and arrogant, and wants to triumph over them; to this end, he may provoke opposition, show he can overcome it, and consequently be a winner once again.

Robert Charles Tucker (b. 1918) was born in Kansas City, Missouri, and educated at the University of Michigan and Harvard (Ph.D., 1958). During World War II he was on the staff of the Office of Strategic Services (1942–44) and the U.S. Foreign Service at the embassy in Moscow (1944–53). After four years in the Social Science Division of the Rand Corporation (1954–58), he was appointed a professor of government, Indiana University (1958–69) and of politics at Princeton (1962–). In 1974 he received a National Book Award nomination for his study of Stalin, and in 1975 he was made a fellow of the Academy of Arts and Sciences and the National Endowment for the Humanities. Among his publications are *Politics as Leadership* (1981), *The Soviet Political Mid: Studies in Stalinism and Post Stalin Change* (1963), and *Political Culture and Leadership in Soviet Union: from Lenin to Gorbachev* (1989).

Sources

Evory, Ann, ed. 1981. *Contemporary authors.* New Revision Series, Vol. 3. Detroit: Gale Research.

Tucker, Robert C. 1973. *Stalin as revolutionary, 1879–1929: a study in history and personality.* New York: W. W. Norton.

Tucker, Robert C. 1977. "The Georges" Wilson re-examined: an essay on psychobiography. *American Political Science Review* 71:605–618.

TUDOR, TUDORESQUE, TUDOR ROSE. Pertaining to the Welsh family and to the period it occupied the English throne (1485–1603). The architecture with its Late Perpendicular, the Tudor arch with its flattened form, and the Tudor flower, with its upright stalk used in long rows on cornices. The Tudor rose, red and white, a conventional emblem that Henry VII used as a badge and a political symbol to indicate the uniting of the Houses of Lancaster and York which had been at war for so long.

The Tudors, a Welsh family, produced five sovereigns for England. They originated in the thirteenth century, but the family's dynastic fortunes started with Owen Tudor—Owen ap Meredydd—(c. 1400–61), an adventurer who served Henry V. After Henry's death in 1422, Owen lived with and probably married the king's widow, Catherine of Valois (1401–37). Of the five children born to them three were sons; the eldest, Edmund (c. 1430–1456), was created earl of Richmond by Henry VI, the second, Jasper (c. 1431–1495), was made earl of Pembroke and later duke of Bedford. Jasper headed the Lancastrian party in Wales, fought for Henry VI against the Yorkists, and after the final Lancastrian defeat in 1471 withdrew to Brittany where he groomed his nephew Henry, Edmund's only child, for the throne. In 1485 Henry led the invasion against the last of the Yorkist kings, Richard III, and claimed the throne. Henry VII established a dynasty that ruled until 1603 and included Henry VIII (1491–1547) who ruled from 1509, and finally Elizabeth I (1533–1603) who ruled from 1558.

Sources

Howatt, Gerald M.D. 1973. *Dictionary of world history.* London: Thomas Nelson.

McHenry, Robert, ed. 1992. *The new encyclopedia Britannica.* Chicago: Encyclopedia Britannica, Inc.

TUGAN-BARANOVSKII THEORY OF BUSINESS CYCLES. A theory of business cycles according to which the level of wages in a capitalist society depends on, first, the productivity of social labor, which determines the amount of the aggregate product, and, second, the social strength of the working class, which determines the share of the social product that comes under the worker's control.

Mikhail Ivanovich Tugan-Baranovskii (1865–1919) was born in Kharkov Province. He graduated from the University of Kharkov (1888) and completed a master's degree in political economy on the industrial crises in modern England and its effect on the people (1894). He began to consider a new way to conceptualize business cycles, and taught political economy in the University of Saint Petersburg (1895–99). Studies of Russian industry were published in his work, *The Russian Factory, Past and Present* (1898). He joined the constitutional Democrats in the Russian Revolution (1905–7) and became a professor at the Saint Petersberg Polytechnic Institute (1913). His important work was *The Social Basis of Cooperation* (1916). He became minister of finance of the counterrevolutionary Central Rada (1917–18).

Sources

Eatwell, John; Milgate, Murray; and Newman, Peter. 1987. *The new Palgrave: a dictionary of economics.* London: Macmillan.

Tugan-Baranovskii, Mikhail I. 1966. *Modern socialism in its historical development.* Trans by M. I. Redmount. New York: Russell and Russell.

Tugan-Baranovskii, Mikhail I. 1970. *The Russian factory in the nineteenth century.* Trans. Arthur Levin and Claora Levin. Homewood, Ill.: American Economic Association.

Waxman, Maron, ed. 1983. *Great Soviet encyclopedia.* New York: Macmillan.

TUPAMAROS. A band of up to 10,000 left-wing urban guerrillas, founded in about 1963 and led by Rául Sendic, a labor organizer in Uruguay. Their aim was a Marxist revolution, and they were noted for their Robin Hood-like approach to getting resources. At the height of their influence in 1969, they robbed banks, blew up radio stations, raided government arms supplies, and abducted, kidnapped, and held to ransom notable foreigners in Uruguay. In 1972 police right-wing paramilitary groups began to crush the Tupamaros, and they were beaten by 1974.

Túpac Amarú II was an eighteenth-century Inca leader who led a revolt against the Spaniards. The name was assumed by José Gabriel Condorcanqui (1742–81) who was born at Tinta, near Cuzco in Peru. Because he descended on his mother's side from the Incas, he came to be known as ''the last of the Incas.'' The original Inca, Túpac Amarú, had been killed by the Spanish in 1571. Condorcanqui's aim was to better the lot of Indians rather than get rid of the Spanish overlords. When he failed in this ambition, he led a rebellion that spread widely and soon dominated large regions of the interior. He won a great victory at Sangarará (1780) but was caught by the Spaniards in 1781; he and his family were tortured to death at Cuzco.

Sources

Cook, Chris. 1983. *Macmillan dictionary of historical terms.* London: Macmillan.

Dudley, Lavinia P. 1963. *The encyclopedia Americana.* International ed. New York: Americana Corp.

Howatt, Gerald M.D. 1973. *Dictionary of world history.* London: Thomas Nelson.
McHenry, Robert, ed. 1992. *The new encyclopedia Britannica.* Chicago: Encyclopedia Britannica, Inc.

TUPPERISM. A trite and moralistic philosophy.

Martin Farquhar Tupper (1810–89), a poet and inventor, was born at Marylebone, son of an eminent London surgeon who twice refused a baronetcy. Martin Tupper was educated at the Charter House (1821–26) and with private tutors, and at age 19 went to Christ Church, Oxford (M.A., 1835). A stammer hindered him from taking religious orders, so, after graduating in 1831, he entered Lincoln's Inn and was called to the bar (1835) but did not practice. He became a successful writer, was elected to the Royal Society (1845), and made two tours in America to read from his own works (1851 and 1876). Among his writings was *Proverbial Philosophy (1838–67)* which sold 5,000 copies annually for twenty-five years, was translated into German, Danish, and French, and sold 1 million copies in America. His work was read enthusiastically by the middle classes who revered his wisdom. His *Rides and Reveries of Mr. Aesop Smith* (1857) denounced dull parsons, hypocrites, poor servants, and wicked wives, and advocated changes in divorce laws. Other works like *War Ballads* (1854), which advocated close Anglo-American relations, and *Rifle Ballads* (1859), which supported the volunteer movement, were not as popular as his philosophical moralism. Critics and parodists so ridiculed his ideas and their popularity that ''Martin Tupper'' became synonymous with all that was contemptible and commonplace. His inventions were not as successful as his writing—for example, safety horse shoes, glass screwtops to bottles, steam vessels with the paddles inside—but in 1886 from his own huge archives he compiled *My Life as an Author, a Curious Self Study of a Poet.*

Sources
Law, M. D., and Dixon, M. Vibart. 1966. *Chambers encyclopedia.* New rev. ed. London: Pergamon Press.
Magnussen, Magnus; Goring, Rosemary; and Thorn, John O., eds. 1990. *Chambers biographical dictionary.* Edinburgh: Chambers Ltd.
Stephen, Leslie, and Lee, Sydney, eds. 1917. *The dictionary of national biography.* London: Oxford University Press.

TYCHISM. A theory of wealth and prosperity that accepts pure chance.

In Greek mythology Tyche is the goddess of fortune, a divinity whose protection was believed to assure prosperity, wealth, and good luck; ''Agethe Tyche'' means good fortune. She was a daughter of Zeus and believed to be the divinity who guided and conducted the affairs of the world with a rudder. Holding in her hand a ball, she represented the unsteadiness of fortune.

Sources
Benét, William R. 1990. *The reader's encyclopedia of world literature and arts, with supplement.* New York: Thomas Y. Crowell.
Graves, Robert. 1960. *The Greek myths.* Revised ed. Harmondsworth: Penguin.

McHenry, Robert, ed. 1992. *The new encyclopedia Britannica.* Chicago: Encyclopedia
    Britannica, Inc.
Pinset, John. 1969. *Greek mythology.* London: Hamlyn.

TYLERIZE. A few weeks after assuming the U.S. presidency, John Tyler was
at loggerheads with other members of the Whig party because of his support
for certain Democratic policies. During his term (1840–44), the breach widened
and many no longer regarded him as a Whig. Thus, "to Tylerize" became a
term meaning to forsake the party to which one has allegiance or office. (1851
Oregon Statesmen 6th June: "It will be seen from our telegraphic dispatch that
the president has Tylerized at last and in earnest.")

John Tyler (1790–1862), the tenth president of the United States, was born
in Greenway, Virginia. He was a former Virginia Democrat elected vice-
president on a Whig ticket (1841–45). After graduating from William and Mary
College in 1807, Tyler studied law and was admitted to the bar in 1809. He
was a member of the Virginia Legislature (1811–16; 1823–25; 1839–40). He
was a U.S. representative (1817–21), governor of Virginia (1825–27), U.S. senator (1827–36), and president of the Senate (1835). He was defeated in 1836.
In the election of 1840, he ran for U.S. vice-president and was swept into office
with William Henry Harrison. When President Harrison died one month after
his inauguration, Tyler became president. Tyler did not seek renomination in
1844. He was elected to the Confederate House of Representatives but died
before he could occupy his seat.

Sources

Durfee, David A., ed. 1970. *William Henry Harrison, 1773–1841: John Tyler, 1790–
    1862: chronology, documents, bibliographical aids.* Dobbs Ferry, N.Y.: Oceana
    Publications.
Malone, Dumas, ed. 1936. *Dictionary of American biography.* Vol. X. New York:
    Charles Scribner's Sons.
Morris, Dan, and Morris, Inez. 1974. *Who was who in American politics.* New York:
    Hawthorn Books.
Peterson, Norma L. 1989. *The presidencies of William Henry Harrison and John Tyler.*
    Lawrence: University of Kansas Press.
Sperber, Hans, and Trittschuh, Travis. 1962. *American political terms.* Detroit: Wayne
    State University Press.

TYLORISM, NEO-TYLORISM. Both Tylorism and neo-Tylorism comprise
an intellectual school of anthropology of religion that opposes the functional-
sociological explanation of religious events. The latter view was espoused by
Robin Horton (1967) who argued that African traditional thought may be seen
best as a theoretical activity similar to that used in science.

Edward Burnett Tylor (1832–1917), son of a Quaker brass founder, entered
the family business, but consumption forced his withdrawal (1855) and he left
England to tour America. In Havana a chance meeting with a Quaker antiquarian
and ethnologist, Henry Christie (d. 1865), led Tylor to a four-month trip through

Mexico and the publication of his *Anahuac: Mexico and the Mexicans, Ancient and Modern* (1861?). In 1865 he published *Researchers into the Early History of Mankind* and in 1871 his two-volume masterpiece, *Primitive Cultures*. He was recognized as the father of British anthropology and founder of American cultural anthropology largely for his application of science to the study of culture. He is remembered for his comparative method, theory of survival and animism, and application of evolutionary theory to the study of civilization. In 1883 he was made keeper of the University Museum, Oxford, and supervised the Pitt-Rivers collection. In 1889–91 he gave the Gifford lectures. In 1881 he published a popular introductory book, *Anthropology*. He was influenced by the humanitarianism of the Quakers, Darwin, Comte, and John Stuart Mill. In 1884 he was the first president of the Anthropological Section of the British Association for the Advancement of Science. From 1896 to 1906 he was the first professor of anthropology at Oxford.

Sources

Horton, Robin. 1967. African traditional thought and Western science. *Africa* 37:155–187.

Sills, David L., ed. 1968. *International encyclopedia of the social sciences.* New York: Macmillan and Free Press.

Zusne, Leonard. 1984. *Biographical dictionary of psychology.* Westport, Conn.: Greenwood Press.

U

ULLMAN'S BASES FOR INTERACTION. A theory of commodity flow using concepts of complementarity, intervening opportunities, and transferability, and relating them to empirical studies of commodity flow in the United States. Although no working operational model of the whole theory has been developed, the concepts are evident in other operational models of commodity and passenger flows.

Edward Louis Ullman (1912–76) was born in Chicago and studied at Harvard and the University of Chicago (Ph.D., 1942, Geography). He taught at Washington State College (1935–37), in Indiana (1941), and was chief of the transport section in the Office of Strategic Services (1942–43) during World War II. He taught at Harvard (1946–51) and became a professor of geography at Seattle's University of Washington (1951–76). He was a Fulbright scholar in Rome (1956–57) and lectured at University College in London and in Vienna (1957), as well as a visiting professor at Washington University in Saint Louis (1959–61), and in Moscow and Austria (1965). He directed the Meramec Basin Reserve Project (1959–62) and was president of the Washington Center Metropolitan Studies, D.C. (1965–66). He published widely on commodity flow and rail traffic, water and economic development in the Meramec Basin, and problems of human geography in cities.

Sources

Jaques Cattell Press, ed. 1973. *American men and women of science: the social and behavioral sciences.* New York: Jaques Cattell and R. R. Bowker.

Johnston, Ronald J. 1981. *The dictionary of human geography.* Oxford: Basil Blackwell.

Ullman, Edward L. 1941. A theory for the location of cities. *American Journal of Sociology* 46:853–864.

Ullman, Edward L. 1956. The role of transportation and the bases for interaction. In

William L. Thomas, Jr., ed. *Man's role in changing the face of the earth.* Chicago: University of Chicago Press, pp. 862–880.
Who was who in America, 1977–81. Vol. 7. Chicago: Marquis.

UNCLE SAM. Personification of the U.S. government or its people.

Samuel Wilson (1766–1854) was born in Menotomy (later Arlington), Massachusetts, and at age 14 joined the army to fight in the American Revolution. In 1789 he moved to Troy, New York, and opened a meatpacking business. For his friendly manner and honesty in business he was known as "Uncle Sam" by Troy's townsfolk, and consequently in the war of 1812 was contracted by the government to provide meat for troops stationed nearby. The initials of his nickname, which were the same as those of his country, would be stamped on the meat barrels in the rendering room. On October 1, 1812, the first allusion to the United States as "Uncle Sam" appeared when a soldier, Pheododorus Bailey, noticed a worker assert the "U.S." stamped on meat barrels stood for "Uncle Sam" rather than the "United States." Wilson eventually entered politics, and his name, as America's national symbol, was formally recognized by an act of the Eighty-seventh Congress.

Source
Panati, Charles. 1987. *Extraordinary origins of everyday things.* New York: Harper and Row.

URSULINES. The oldest and largest teaching order in the Roman Catholic Church; religious congregations of women in Europe, the United States, Canada, Cuba, Brazil, Australia, India, Southeast Asia, Africa.

Saint Ursula was, according to legend, martyred in Cologne in the third century. She was a princess of Cornwall who had agreed to marry the English king's son if he became a Christian and said she would wait three years until she returned from a pilgrimage to Rome with her 11,000 virgins. On the return journey they were met by the Huns and all were put to death. Many human bones, thought to be the bones of the virgin martyrs, were found in Cologne when foundations were being dug in the twelfth century. There is no mention of Saint Ursula before the tenth century, several hundred years after her martyrdom. Details of the story itself do not appear until the twelfth century and were given by Geoffrey of Monmouth. Other sources trace her to the Swabian moon goddess, Hoersel, the wandering Isis. In 1535 Saint Angela Merici (1470–1540) of Brescia founded a congregation of Ursulines, a women's order for the education and care of the sick.

Sources
Cross, Frank L. 1974. *The Oxford dictionary of the Christian Church.* 2d ed. New York: Oxford University Press.
McHenry, Robert, ed. 1992. *The new encyclopedia Britannica.* Chicago: Encyclopedia Britannica, Inc.
Meagher, Paul K.; O'Brien, Thomas C.; and Aherne, Marie, eds. 1979. *Encyclopedia dictionary of religion.* Washington, D.C.: Corpus Publications.

V

VANCE-OWEN PROPOSAL OR PARTITION. The proposal (1992–93) advanced by the major mediators—one for the United Nations, the other for the European Community—to partition Bosnia-Herzegovina into ten ethnic groups, or autonomous republics, to create a country that could live without civil war between Croats, Serbs, and Muslims. Nine of the groups would be ruled by either Serbs, Muslims, or Croats, and one, the area around Sarajevo, would be shared. A federal government with limited powers would also be shared between the three groups. In mid-1993 the proposal was rejected.

Cyrus Roberts Vance (b. 1917) was born in Clarksburg, West Virginia, educated at Kent School, and studied at Yale (LL.D., 1942). In World War II he was a lieutenant in the U.S. Navy (1942–46). He has worked as a lawyer since and has frequently been a member of politically significant committees worldwide. He served under presidents Kennedy, Johnson, and Carter, and was frequently involved in U.S. foreign relations, especially as a mediator and negotiator, with South American states, the Middle East, Southeast Asia, and Russia. He attended the Paris Peace Talks on Vietnam (1968–69) and was awarded a Medal of Freedom in 1969. He was appointed to the Supreme Court and to the Council of Foreign Relations; he was on the committee that investigated police corruption in New York (1970–72); he became chairman of the U.S. Development Corporation; and he was chairman of the Rockefeller Foundation (1975–77). In 1989 he was chairman of the Board of Governors, Federal Reserve Bank, New York.

David Anthony Llewellyn Owen (b. 1938) was born in Plymouth, England, son of a doctor. He was educated at Mudd House, Plymouth, and boarded at Bradfield School, Berkshire. He studied at Cambridge and at Saint Thomas Hospital, London, and completed his medical studies (1962–63). In 1966 he was elected to Parliament and was made undersecretary of state for defense (Royal Navy) and secretary of state for defense. In 1976 he was created a privy councillor, and he became foreign secretary in the Labor government (1977–79). In 1981 he helped found the Social Democratic party. He was chairman of the European Community-sponsored peace process, and with Vance, the co-chairman of the United Nations–European Community peace initiative, in attempts to reduce military conflict in Bosnia-Herzogovina.

Sources

Carroll, Jane, ed. 1991. *The economist dictionary of political biography.* London: Business Books.

Dolling, Yolanda, ed. 1990. *Who's who in European politics.* London: Bowker-Saur.

The international who's who, 1992–93. London: Europa Publications.

Krauthammer, Charles. 1993. The doves are right about Bosnia. *Time,* February 8:64.

Malcolm, Noel. 1993. Lord fraud: the real story of David Owen, diplomat du jour. *The New Republic,* June 14:19–20.

Moritz, Charles, ed. 1977. *Current biography yearbook.* New York: H. W. Wilson.

VANSITTARTISM. Extreme anti-German beliefs and attitudes.

Sir Robert Gilbert Vansittart, first Baron Vansittart of Denham (1881–1957), was born at Wilton House, Farnham, into a military family and spent seven years at Eton. He entered the diplomatic service and went to Paris (1903), Tehran (1907), and Cairo (1909). Established at the Foreign Office, he jointly headed departments concerned with contraband and later the prisoners of war during World War I. He was made secretary (1920–24) to Britain's foreign secretary, George Nathaniel Curzon (1859–1924). He also served as private secretary (1928) to Prime Minister Stanley Baldwin (1867–1947) and then became permanent undersecretary at the Foreign Office (1930–38) and chief diplomatic adviser to the foreign secretary (1938–41). Although many politicians did not agree with him at the time, he saw Germany as the greatest threat to peace in Europe during the 1920s and 1930s. He published the *Collected Poems of Robert Vansittart* (1934) and wrote about the national characteristics of Germans in *Black Record: German Past and Present* (1941). He also published his personal views in *Lessons of My Life* (1943) and *Even Now* (1949), and wrote novels and plays, including *Les Pariah's* (1902) and *Dead Heat* (1939).

Sources

Vansittart, Robert G. 1958. *The mist procession: the autobiography of Lord Vansittart.* London: Hutchinson.

Williams, E. T., and Palmer, Helen M., eds. 1971. *Dictionary of national biography 1951–1960.* London: Oxford University Press.

VERDOORN'S LAW. A law in economics that states there is a close relation between the long-run growth of manufacturing productivity and output (Eatwell et al., 1987:804). The faster the growth rate in output, the faster the growth rate of labor productivity (Goodall, 1987:494). Such a relation indicates that a large part of productivity growth is due to factors within the growth process itself, and is determined by the expansion rate of output through economies of scale and the effects of technological progress.

Petrus Johannes Verdoorn (fl. 1949–80) was a Dutch economist at Erasmus University, Rotterdam (1979), and at the Central Planning Bureau in The Hague. He co-authored *Research Method in Economics and Business* (1962) and was a member of the American Economics Association (1974). The idea attaching to his name was raised in 1949 and, because it was initially published in Italian, escaped attention until 1969 when it was used to explain why most industrial countries had grown faster than the United Kingdom since World War II.

Sources

Eatwell, John; Milgate, Murray; and Newman, Peter. 1987. *The new Palgrave: a dictionary of economics.* London: Macmillan.

Goodall, Brian. 1987. *The Penguin dictionary of human geography.* Harmondsworth, Middlesex: Penguin.

Verdoorn, Petrus J. 1980. Verdoorn's law in retrospect: a comment. *Economic Journal* 90:382–385.

VICAR OF BRAY. A turncoat, one who changes sides in a conflict to suit the times.

Simon Aleyn (fl. 1540–88) was vicar of Bray in Berkshire between 1540 and 1588. During the reigns of Henry VIII, Edward VI, Mary I, and Elizabeth I, he saw extreme religious conflict in England but managed to survive as power moved from papist to Protestant. He denied any treachery and maintained that his only purpose and major religious interest lay in holding the position of vicar of Bray. Some sources suggest his origins are more obscure, that is, in a song on this theme the Vicar of Bray is thought to be Simon Symonds, a seventeenth-century vicar of Bray in Berkshire; another source suggests the song was written by a British Army officer during the reign of George I.

Sources

Hendrickson, Robert. 1988. *The dictionary of eponyms: names that became words.* New York: Dorset.

Radford, Edwin, and Smith, Alan. 1981. *To coin a phrase.* London: Macmillan.

Smith, Benjamin. 1903. *The Century cyclopedia of names.* London: The Times.

VICHY GOVERNMENT. The French government that ruled while the Germans occupied France during World War II. It was an autocratic, antirepublican regime (1940–44) that collaborated with the Germans who occupied Vichy France in November 1942.

Vichy (ancient: Vicus Calidus) is a town in the French Allier Department on the Allier River in the Auvergne, 227 miles south-southeast of Paris. It was established in Roman times, and in the seventeenth century it became a famous spa, visited often by European royalty. After the Franco-German armistice (1940), Vichy was made the seat of the collaborationist government of Marshal Henri Philippe Pétain (1856–1951). As the war came to an end, the Vichy government withdrew to Sigmaringen, Germany, and collapsed in 1945. In 1944 when France was liberated, 5,000 collaborators were summarily executed, and another 15,000 were put to death. Vichy leaders were tried for treason; Laval, for example, was executed and Pétain imprisoned for life.

See also LAVAL; PÉTAIN.

Sources

Canby, Courtlandt. 1984. *The encyclopedia of historic places.* London: Mansell Publishing.

Rousso, Henry. 1991. *The Vichy syndrome: history and memory in France since 1944.* Trans. Arthur Goldhammer. Cambridge, Mass.: Harvard University Press.

Taylor, James, and Shaw, Warren. 1987. *A dictionary of the Third Reich.* London: Grafton.

VICTORIAN. Relating to a period during the reign of the nineteenth-century queen of England, 1837–1901; representative of the art, letters, industrial expansion, scientific discovery, religious conflict, and the strict, conventional, narrow-minded, smug, prudish, moralistic standards of those times.

Alexandrina Victoria (1819–1901) was born in London, the only child of the duke of Kent, fourth son of George III. She was educated under the direction of her mother and the duchess of Northumberland. On the death of William IV, the third son of George III, she succeeded to the British throne (1837). In 1840 she married Albert, prince of Saxe-Coburg-Gotha. In 1877 she became empress of India, celebrated the jubilee of her reign in 1887, and her diamond jubilee in 1897. Among the many things named in her honor were a colony in Australia, a large water-lily in Brazil, a low four-wheeled carriage with a foldaway hood, a large red plum, and a military cross for bravery, founded in 1856 and made from the metal of a Russian canon captured at Sebastopol in the Crimean War, as well as an age of history. Queen Victoria reigned for over sixty-three years, four years longer than the longest reign of any English monarch.

Sources

Benson, Edward F. 1935. *Queen Victoria.* London: Longmans.

Ford, Boris. 1982. *From Dickens to Hardy.* Harmondsworth: Penguin.

Houghton, Walter E. 1957. *The Victorian frame of mind: 1830–1870.* New Haven, Conn.: Yale University Press.

McHenry, Robert, ed. 1992. *The new encyclopedia Britannica.* Chicago: Encyclopedia Britannica, Inc.

Mitchell, Sally, ed. 1988. *Victorian Britain: an encyclopedia.* New York: Garland Publishing.

Stephen, Leslie, and Lee, Sydney, eds. 1917. *The dictionary of national biography.* Vol. 22, Supplement. London: Oxford University Press.

Strachey, G. Lytton. 1921. *Queen Victoria.* London: Chatto and Windus.

Young, George M. 1977. *Portrait of an age: Victorian England.* London: Oxford University Press.

VINCENTIAN. Relating to the seventeenth-century saint and the charitable associations he established.

Saint Vincent de Paul (c. 1575/80–1660), canonized in 1737, was born into a peasant family in Gascony, France, studied theology at Toulouse, and was ordained in 1600. In 1605 he was taken into slavery for two years in Tunisia before escaping to Avignon. Under the influence of Pierre de Bérulle (1575–1629) in Paris, he decided to dedicate himself to charitable works (1609). He helped prisoners while he tutored in the house of the count de Gondi (1613–25); at this time he founded the Congregation of the Mission (Lazarists or Vincentians) for the giving of missions and training in theology. In 1633 he founded the Sisters of Charity, which was devoted to caring for the sick and the poor. During the minority of King Louis XIV, the Queen Regent (Anne of Austria) appointed Vincent de Paul to the Council of Conscience (1643). In the Wars of the Fronde (1648–53), during the minority of Louis XIV, he organized relief to those who suffered. He opposed Jansenism. He died at Saint Lazare, Paris, and in 1833 Antoine Frederic Ozanam (1813–53) founded the Society of Saint Vincent de Paul to defend Catholic truth against freethinkers.

Sources

Cross, Frank L. 1974. *The Oxford dictionary of the Christian Church.* 2d ed. New York: Oxford University Press.

Farmer, David H. 1978. *The Oxford dictionary of saints.* Oxford: Clarendon Press.

McHenry, Robert, ed. 1992. *The new encyclopedia Britannica.* Chicago: Encyclopedia Britannica, Inc.

Whalen, John, ed. 1966. *New Catholic encyclopedia.* Washington, D.C.: Catholic University of America.

VOLSTEADISM. A policy prohibiting the production and sale of alcoholic beverages in the United States. Prohibition was enacted in 1919 with the Eighteenth Amendment to the U.S. Constitution and ended with the Twenty-First Amendment (1933).

Andrew John Volstead (1860–1947) was born near Kenyon, Goodhue County, Minnesota, educated at the local public schools, and graduated from Decorah Institute, Iowa, in 1881. He studied law, was admitted to the bar in 1883, and moved to Granite Falls, Minnesota, where he was mayor (1900–2). Elected as a Republican to the Fifty-eighth and nine succeeding congresses (March 4, 1903–March 3, 1923), Volstead was an unsuccessful candidate in 1922. He resumed his law practice and lived in Granite Falls until he died. While in Congress, he authored the Farmers Cooperative Marketing Act (1923), but he is best known for the Prohibition Act of 1919, named after him. The Volstead Act, passed over President Wilson's veto, was in force until 1933.

Sources

Cashman, Sean D. 1981. *Prohibition: the lie of the land.* New York: Free Press.

Coffey, Thomas M. 1975. *The long thirst: Prohibition in America 1920–1933.* New York: W. W. Norton.

Commager, Henry S., ed. 1968. *Documents of American history.* 8th ed. New York: Appleton-Century-Crofts.

Jacob, Kathryn A., and Ragsdale, Bruce A. 1989. *Biographical directory of the United*

States Congress: 1774–1989. Bicentennial ed. Washington, D.C.: U.S. Government Printing Office.
Kobler, John. 1973. *Ardent spirits: the rise and fall of Prohibition.* New York: Putnam.
Magnussen, Magnus; Goring, Rosemary; and Thorn, John O., eds. 1990. *Chambers biographical dictionary.* Edinburgh: Chambers Ltd.
Whipple, Sidney B. 1934. *Noble experiment: a portrait of America under Prohibition.* London: Methuen.

VOLTAIREAN. One who supports and follows the views, doctrines, spirit, and principles of the eighteenth-century French poet, dramatist, historian, and skeptic; a skeptical, sarcastic attitude, especially toward Christianity.

Voltaire, pen-name of François Marie Arouet (1694–1778), was educated in Paris at the Jesuit College Louis-le-Grand and early showed a talent for verse and a skeptical, satirical temperament. He established himself as the leading spirit of the Enlightenment in opposing the ancient regime, pursuing justice, religious tolerance, and liberal social reforms. In 1717 he was sent to the Bastille because of satirical verses against the regent, and meanwhile he began his epic *La Ligue* (1728) appearing as *La Henriade.* Voltaire lived for many years in exile in England after publishing his *Letters Concerning the English Nation,* a skillfully veiled attack on autocratic and religious abuses in France. Through the intercession of Madame Pompadour, Voltaire was recalled to the French court and elected to the French Academy (1746). Nevertheless, publication of his satires again forced him to quit Paris for Lorraine and later Geneva, where he published a stream of pamphlets directed against the credibility of the Bible.
Sources
Ayer, Alfred J. 1986. *Voltaire.* London: Weidenfeld and Nicolson.
McHenry, Robert, ed. 1992. *The new encyclopedia Britannica.* Chicago: Encyclopedia Britannica, Inc.
Richter, Reyton, and Ricardo, Ilona. 1980. *Voltaire.* Boston: Twayne Publishers.
Wayne, Andreas. 1981. *Voltaire.* New York: New Directions.
Zusne, Leonard. 1984. *Biographical dictionary of psychology.* Westport, Conn.: Greenwood Press.

VOLUMNIA SYNDROME. The subtle undercutting of the father-as-hero in family life by an imperious mother, who demands superior and public attainment of her son to compensate for the waste and frustration of her unused gifts (Davies, 1980).

Volumnia, a legendary figure, was the mother of Coriolanus in Shakespeare's play of that name. She was an aristocratic Roman matron who raised her son to be a proud, inflexible, and victorious warrior. Her maternal love was pathological, driven by a warped need for glory; she equated Coriolanus's birth with his fighting and her breast with his head wounds. Coriolanus was so bound to Volumnia that her values were his, and he became so dependent on her judgment and approval that he brought on his own ruin. To have him become a Roman consul, she bullied Coriolanus into sacrificing his pride to get the approval of the commoners (*Coriolanus* III, 2:41–86). But the mother-induced pride was too infexible to prevent him from displaying his contempt for the people, and he was banished from Rome. In vengeance he joined and led Rome's enemies, the Volscians. When he was on the verge of sacking Rome, Volumnia persuaded him to withdraw the Volscian forces, even though it meant his death as a traitor to them (*Coriolanus* V, 3:87–182).

Sources

Boyce, Charles. 1990. *Shakespeare A to Z.* New York: Facts on File.
Davies, Alan F. 1980. *Skills, outlooks and passions: a psychoanalytic contribution to the study of politics.* Cambridge: Cambridge University Press.

VON NEUMANN RATIO, VON NEUMANN TECHNOLOGY. In economic theory, the ratio determines the proportion of maximal balanced growth in a non-Neumann technology; the technology is a way to describe and analyze economic systems (Eatwell et al., 1987).

John Von Neumann (1903–57) was born in Budapest. His intellectual ability was recognized at an early age, and he was tutored and encouraged in his mathematics. At 19 he published his first paper, and he studied mathematics at the University of Budapest (Ph.D., 1926) and in Zurich. In 1928 he published the axiomatics of set theory. He taught at the universities of Berlin (1927–29) and Hamburg (1930–33) before going to the United States and becoming a professor at Princeton University (1933–55). He worked on the Manhattan Project for development of the atom and hydrogen bombs, and thereafter he was a member of the U.S. Atomic Energy Commission and a member of the Institute for Advanced Study at Princeton. He received many honors for his work and ideas from several universities, and he is known as one of the first to make significant contributions to the application of mathematics to the social sciences through devising game theory, published in 1944. Among his publications are *The Logic of Quantum Mechanics* (1936), *Probabilistic Logics* (1956), and *Theory of Self-producing Automata* (1966). His work was honored in a special issue of the *Bulletin of the American Mathematical Society,* May 1958.

Sources

Eatwell, John; Milgate, Murray; and Newman, Peter. 1987. *The new Palgrave: a dictionary of economics.* London: Macmillan.
Gillespie, Charles C., ed. 1973. *Dictionary of scientific biography.* New York: Charles Scribner's Sons.
Sills, David L., ed. 1968. *International encyclopedia of the social sciences.* New York: Macmillan and Free Press.
Von Neumann, John, and Morgenstern, Oskar. 1944. *The theory of games and economic behavior.* Princeton, N.J.: Princeton University Press.
Zusne, Leonard. 1984. *Biographical dictionary of psychology.* Westport, Conn.: Greenwood Press.

VON THÜNEN MODEL. A form of analysis of agricultural location that is based on the work of the nineteenth-century German economist (1826). The aim of the model was to explain the type of agricultural production that would best be carried out at a given location. The model assumes a single market center that sets the price for all agricultural commodities, surrounded by farm land for fertility. Transport costs are assumed to increase with a distance at the same rate in all directions. Locations are therefore given, and the problem is to calculate the optimum crop and cropping system in response to market price and cost of transport to market.

Johann Heinrich von Thünen (1783–1850) was born on the family estate, in the Grand Duchy of Oldenburg, Germany. He studied mathematics and was taught the practicalities of agriculture, and he attended an agricultural college near Hamburg, and the University of Göttingen. He completed many experiments and collected data systematically on an estate that he had purchased in 1810 in Mecklenburg. On the basis of this research, he published his notable *Der Isolierte Staat* in three volumes (1826–63), which made him one of the most original and significant economists of his time.

Sources

Blaug, Mark, ed. 1992. *Johann von Thunen (1783–1850), Augustin Cournot (1801–1877), Jules Dupiut (1804–1866)*. Aldershot, England: E. Elgar.
Goodall, Brian. 1987. *The Penguin dictionary of human geography*. Harmondsworth: Penguin.
Johnston, Ronald J. 1981. *The dictionary of human geography*. Oxford: Basil Blackwell.
Sills, David L., ed. 1968. *International encyclopedia of the social sciences*. New York: Macmillan and Free Press.

VOODOO. A religion from the West Indies that was introduced to the West in the seventeenth century; it was practiced in Haiti and was noted for its use of black magic, mystery, and cannibalism. It was brought to the West Indies from Africa.

Peter Waldo, Valdo or Valdez (d. 1217), had his name given to the Waldenses, who were accused of sorcery by the French. In the West Indies, French missionaries likened the witch doctors and their preaching of black magic to the heretical activities of the Waldenses, and named them *Vaudois* which was later corrupted to *Voodoo*. Alternatively, *voodoo* is derived from *vodun*, a god or spirit of the Fon people of Benin (once Dahomey); or from *vodun*, a variant on the Ashanti *obosum*, a fetish or guardian of the spirit.

See also WALDENSES.

Sources

Hendrickson, Robert. 1988. *The dictionary of eponyms: names that became words*. New York: Dorset.
McHenry, Robert, ed. 1992. *The new encyclopedia Britannica*. Chicago: Encyclopedia Britannica, Inc.
Smith, Benjamin. 1903. *The Century cyclopedia of names*. London: The Times.
Weekley, Ernest. 1924. *Concise etymological dictionary of modern English*. New York: E. P. Dutton.
Weekley, Ernest. 1961. *The romance of words*. New York: Dover.

W

WAGNER-CONNERY ACT. A U.S. National Labor Relations Act, also known as the Wagner-Connery Act, or more widely as the Wagner Act. It was passed in July 1935, two months after the National Industrial Recovery Act, which protected the rights of employees to organize without employer interference, was declared unconstitutional. The act established the employees' right to organize themselves, the means for holding elections, and exclusive bargaining rights for a union. The law aimed to cut industrial strife by encouraging collective bargaining. Major changes were made to the act in 1947, called the Taft-Hartley Act.

Robert Ferdinand Wagner (1877–1953) was born in Nastätten, Hessen-Nassau, Germany, and immigrated to America with his parents, settling in New York in 1885. After attending public schools, he graduated from the College of the City of New York (1898) and New York Law School (1900). With help from Tammany Hall, he got his beginning in politics (1898), entered the New York State Assembly and later the Senate, and became a leading legislator. A friend of the poor, he campaigned for humane working conditions. In 1918 he was elected to the First District Supreme Court. As a Democrat, he was elected to the U.S. Senate (1926–49), where he was a noted supporter of President Franklin D. Roosevelt's policies for a welfare state.

William Patrick Connery, Jr. (1888–1937) was born in Lynn, Massachusetts, was educated at the local schools in Lynn, Mandrel College in Canada, and Holy Cross College in Worcester, Massachusetts. He was an actor and theater manager from 1908 until World War I when he served as an infantryman. In 1923 he was elected to the U.S. Congress, and he served on the Committee of Labor until he died.

See also TAFT-HARTLEY ACT.

Sources

Commager, Henry S., ed. 1968. *Documents of American history*. 8th ed. New York: Appleton-Century-Crofts.

Jacob, Kathryn A., and Ragsdale, Bruce A. 1989. *Biographical directory of the United States Congress: 1774–1989*. Bicentennial ed. Washington, D.C.: U.S. Government Printing Office.

Garraty, John A., ed. 1977. *Dictionary of American biography*. Supplement 5, 1951–55. New York: Charles Scribner's Sons.

Huthmacher, J. Joseph. 1968. *Senator Robert F. Wagner and the rise of urban liberalism*. New York: Atheneum.

Marsh, Arthur. 1979. *Concise encyclopedia of industrial relations*. Westmead, Farnborough, Hants: Gower.

Morris, Dan, and Morris, Inez. 1974. *Who was who in American politics*. New York: Hawthorn Books.

Roberts, Harold S. 1966. *Roberts' dictionary of industrial relations*. Washington, D.C.: BNA.

WAHABI OR WAHABEE. A member of a Muslim sect established in central Arabia (c. 1760) which condemned other Muslims as idolators for visiting the tombs of their saints to get help in emergencies, and sought to restore Islam to its original purity as taught by Mohammed and practiced by his followers.

Muhammad Ibn 'Abd-al-Wahhab (c. 1703–92) was born in Central Africa, traveled as a student and merchant, and with the chief of Dirai'yyah was determined to restore Islam to its original purity. They opposed all practices that were not sanctioned in the Koran and worked to restore primitive Islam. The Wahabis controlled all provinces between Hijaz and the Persian Gulf, and under the son of Wahhabi attacked the outposts of the Ottoman Empire and massacred the inhabitants of Imam Husain (1801). In ensuing wars with the Egyptian government, Wahhabi power was diminished, most of the lands were recovered, and the leaders executed (1818). Wahhabism was brought to India in 1824, and the followers gained some of their former power in the 1830s in central Arabia.

Sources

Crim, Keith, ed. 1981. *Abingdon dictionary of living religions*. Nashville, Tenn.: Abingdon Press.

Eliade, Mircea, ed. 1987. *Encyclopedia of religion*. New York: Macmillan.

Gibb, Hamilton A.R. 1960–. *Encyclopedia of Islam*. Leiden: E. J. Brill.

Hastings, James, ed. 1921. *Encyclopedia of religion and ethics*. Vol. XII. Edinburgh: T. and T. Clark.

Hinnells, John R. 1984. *The Penguin dictionary of religions*. London: Allen Lane Penguin books.

WAKEFIELD SYSTEM. A doctrine of colonization advocating that colonial land should be sold at a fixed price and the money used to encourage immigration to the colony and its economic development.

Edward Gibbon Wakefield (1796–1862) was born into a large family in London, educated at Westminster School and Edinburgh High School, and admitted to Gray's Inn. In 1816 he eloped with a ward of chancery, had the marriage approved by Parliament, and he fathered two children before his young wife died in 1820, leaving him a comfortable income. In 1826 he abducted a young heiress, was caught, tried, and jailed (1827). He then studied and published on crime, emigration, and colonization. He argued that the proper sale of colonial lands could produce sufficient funds to encourage young people to immigrate to Australia and thereby relieve the pressure of population in Britain and expand the British Empire with productive colonies. Land price should be set high enough to dissuade laborers from purchasing land they could not effectively use and to encourage those with capital to buy land on which they could employ the young colonists as laborers. His ideas influenced the colonization of South Australia, West Australia, Canada, and New Zealand. In 1853 he settled in New Zealand and was elected to the first New Zealand General Assembly. His criminal record prevented him from holding significant political posts, however, forcing him to be a promoter rather than an administrator of colonial policy.

Sources

Pike, Douglas, et al. 1966–90. *Australian dictionary of biography.* 12 vols. Carlton, Victoria: Melbourne University Press.

Preece, Warren E., ed. 1965. *Encyclopedia Britannica.* Chicago: Encyclopedia Britannica, Inc., William Benton.

Stephen, Leslie, and Lee, Sydney, eds. 1917. *The dictionary of national biography.* London: Oxford University Press.

WALDENSES. A community of austere Christians devoted to a simple interpretation of the gospel.

Peter Waldo (d. 1217) was a wealthy merchant of Lyons who heard the call to Christ's teaching and to give away his fortune (1176). A brotherhood devoted to apostolic poverty soon grew around him, and he began to preach in the streets. Pope Alexander III tolerated Waldo, but in 1179 the Third Lateran Council condemned his "Poor Men of Lyon," as they became known. Forbidden to preach and excommunicated for disobedience by Pope Lucius III in 1184, the Waldenses formed a separate church and allied themselves with other dissident groups. During the thirteenth century, they established themselves in the mountain valleys of southeastern France and Piedmont. The modern Waldensian church belongs to the alliance of Presbyterian churches.

Sources

Cross, Frank L. 1974. *The Oxford dictionary of the Christian Church.* 2d ed. New York: Oxford University Press.

Douglas, James D., ed. 1974. *The new international dictionary of the Christian Church.* Exeter: Paternoster Press.

Douglas, James D.; Elwell, Walter A.; and Toon, Peter. 1989. *The concise dictionary of Christian tradition.* London: Marshall Pickering.

Eliade, Mircea, ed. 1987. *Encyclopedia of religion.* New York: Macmillan.

Ferguson, Sinclair B., and Wright, David F. 1988. *New dictionary of theology.* Leicester, U.K.: Inter-Varsity Press.

McDonald, William J., ed. 1967. *New Catholic encyclopedia.* New York: McGraw-Hill.

WALRAS'S LAW, WALRAS'S THEORY OF CAPITAL. Whether or not an economy is in equilibrium, the sum of demand minus the supply of each good and service multiplied by its price should be zero. The law is true by definition in a barter economy, but it is not true for all demand when a difference appears, as Keynes indicated, between effective and notional demand. For notional demand the law does not hold. And in models with continuous rather than discrete times there is another such law. The theory of capital is an extension of the theory of noncapital production, including four added variables: rate of net income, prices of capital goods, quantities of capital goods in demand, and total value of saving (Eatwell et al., 1987).

Marie-Esprit Leon Walras (1834–1910) was born in Evreaux, France, son of the noted amateur economist Antoine A. Walras (1801–66). He completed a bachelor of letters (1851) and science degree (1853) and turned his interest to the social sciences (1858). In Paris he was a journalist (1859–62), and worked in a railways cooperative (1865). He gave lectures on cooperatives and helped edit *Le Travail,* with a view to advancing compromise and harmony among social classes. Until 1870 he was unable to get an academic post, and he was appointed a professor of economics at the University of Lausanne, Switzerland. At first he followed his father's ideas, but later he made original contributions to economic theory, especially marginal utility theory (1873) and a multiequational model of general equilibrium theory (1874–79). Among other topics he wrote on monetary reform; however, his contributions were not recognized until the 1930s. The law was named as such by Oscar Lange in 1942.

Sources

Blaug, Mark, ed. 1986. *Who's who in economics: a biographical dictionary of major economists, 1700–1986.* 2d ed. Cambridge, Mass.: MIT Press.

Eatwell, John; Milgate, Murray; and Newman, Peter. 1987. *The new Palgrave: a dictionary of economics.* London: Macmillan.

Lange, Oscar. 1942. Say's law: a restatement and criticism. In Oscar Lange, ed. *Studies in mathematical economics and econometrics.* Chicago: University of Chicago Press.

Levacic, Rosalind, and Rebmann, Alexander. 1982. *Macro economics: an introduction to Keynesian-neoclassical controversies.* 2d ed. London: Macmillan.

Pearce, David W., ed. 1986. *Macmillan dictionary of modern economics.* 3d ed. New York: Macmillan.

Sills, David L., ed. 1968. *International encyclopedia of the social sciences.* New York: Macmillan and Free Press.

WANNSEE CONFERENCE. A conference summoned in November 1941 for December 9 but postponed until January 20, 1942, at the villa Am Grossen Wannsee overlooking Berlin's pleasant lake in the suburb of Grossen-Wannsee. Led by Reinhard Heydrich (1904–42), it was attended by fifteen top Nazi bureaucrats, including Karl Adolf Eichmann (1906–62). Eight of the fifteen invitees had a Ph.D. The aim of the conference was to implement Adolf Hitler's policy to exterminate Europe's Jews, or, as it was stated at the time, to reach a "final solution" to the "Jewish question." The conference decided to round up the Jews of Europe, put them in labor camps, and treat them so inhumanely that eventually most would die; those who survived would be "treated accordingly." Subsequently, poison-gas chambers were established in Poland's extermination camps under the control of Heinrich Himmler (1900–45), his Gestapo, and the SS. Six million Jews died. The villa is now a memorial museum.

Sources

Gutman, Israel, ed. 1990. *Encyclopedia of the Holocaust.* New York: Macmillan.

McHenry, Robert, ed. 1992. *The new encyclopedia Britannica.* Chicago: Encyclopedia Britannica, Inc.

WARNOCK REPORT. A British report (1984) from the Committee of Inquiry into Human Fertilization and Embryology, 1982, that recommended reforms on social, legal, and ethical procedures and regulations concerning artificial insemination, the treatment of infertility, the legitimacy of children conceived by parents other than their own, questions of inheritance, confidentiality of parenthood, selection of donors, surrogacy agreements, and the status at law of embryos and research on them.

Helen Mary Warnock, baroness of Weeke in the city of Winchester (b. 1924), was educated at Saint Swithin's, Winchester, and Lady Margaret Hall, Oxford; was a fellow and tutor in philosophy at Saint Hugh's College, Oxford (1949–66); headmistress of Oxford High School (1966–72); and a research fellow at Lady Margaret Hall, Oxford (1972–76). She married Sir Geoffrey Warnock (1945) and has two sons and three daughters. After the Committee of Inquiry, she became mistress of Girton College, Cambridge, and was made a life peer (1985). Among her many publications are *Ethics Since 1900* (1960), *Existential Ethics* (1966), *Existentialism* (1970), *A Question of Life* (1985), and *Universities: Knowing Our Minds* (1989).

Source

Ernest, Kay. 1993. *The world's who's who of women: 1992–93.* Cambridge, England: International Biographical Center.

WARREN COMMISSION. A commission appointed by President Lyndon B. Johnson to investigate the assassination of John F. Kennedy in 1963. The commission consisted of the chief justice, members of the Senate, members of the House of Representatives and private citizens retired from previous government service. In 1964 it issued a controversial report, *Report of the President's Commission on the Assassination of President John F. Kennedy* (RPCAP). It found that Lee Harvey Oswald (1939–63) had acted alone in assassinating the president. The commission was discredited when it became clear to many that Kennedy may have died at the hands of several killers. By then, it was too late to remedy the failures of the commission, and whoever murdered Kennedy is not known with certainty. Many books have appeared on the conspiracy, and a strong case advances that the conspiracy theories are unsound and that Oswald alone assassinated Kennedy (Cohen, 1992).

Earl Warren (1891–1974), attorney-general of California, Republican party governor of California, and fourteenth chief justice of the U.S. Supreme Court (1953–69), is best remembered for his outspoken defense of individual rights. The most famous decision in which he wrote the majority opinion was the case of *Brown* v. *Board of Education of Topeka* (1954), a decision that held radically segregated public schools to be unconstitutional. A leading judicial activist, Warren regularly voted in favor of civil liberties, protections under due process of law. He opposed racism, political abuses, intolerance, and legal oppression. Some believe that Warren presided over the Supreme Court during the period of its greatest influence when it was a genuine agency of social change. He also chaired the commission that investigated Kennedy's assassination.

Sources

Blevins, Leon W. 1974. *Dictionary of American government and politics.* Totowa, N.J.: Rowman and Littlefield.

Cohen, Jacob 1992. Yes, Oswald alone killed Kennedy. *Commentary* 93, June:32–40.

Commager, Henry S., ed. 1968. *Documents of American history.* 8th ed. New York: Appleton-Century-Crofts.

Editor. 1992. The Kennedy assassination. A discussion of the June 1992 article "Yes, Oswald alone killed Kennedy." *Commentary* 94, November:10–21.

Lurtz, Michael L. 1982. *Crime of the century: the Kennedy assassination from an historian's perspective.* Knoxville: University of Tennessee Press.

Meagher, Sylvia. 1980. *Master index to the JFK assassination investigations: the reports and supporting volumes of the House Select Committee on Assassinations and the Warren Commission.* Metuchen, N.J.: Scarecrow Press.

Moritz, Charles, ed. 1974. *Current biography yearbook.* New York: H. W. Wilson.

Schwarz, Bernard. 1983. *Super Chief: Earl Warren and his Supreme Court—a judicial biography.* New York: New York University Press.

White, G. Edward. 1982. *Earl Warren: paradoxes of a public life.* New York: Oxford University Press.

WARSAW PACT. On May 14, 1955, the communist bloc—Albania, Bulgaria, Czechoslovakia, the German Democratic Republic, Hungary, Poland, Romania, and the Soviet Union—became members of a twenty-year Eastern European Mutual Assistance Treaty of friendship, cooperation, and mutual assistance. The eight members had a unified military command with headquarters in Moscow. Each signatory was expected to give immediate armed support to any other should there be an attack on Eastern Europe. After 1962 Albania did not join in military activities. In January 1991 Czechoslovakia, Hungary, and Poland announced their withdrawal of cooperation from the Warsaw Treaty organization, effective July 1991.

Warsaw is on the river Vistula, the capital of Poland, and a city of world heritage. It was established in the thirteenth century and became Poland's capital in 1596. During both world wars, Germany occupied Warsaw. By 1943 most residents in the city's Jewish ghetto had died. After the city's near destruction in World War II, it was rebuilt following the medieval town's streets. In the Polish Academy of Science, two universities, the Cathedral of Saint John, a royal castle, and a museum of literature are located in Warsaw. Every five years the city hosts the international Chopin competition.

Sources

Clawson, Robert W., and Kaplan, Laurence S., eds. 1986. *The Warsaw Pact: political purpose and military means.* Wilmington, Del.: Scholarly Resources.

Crystal, David, ed. 1990. *The Cambridge encyclopedia.* Cambridge: Cambridge University Press.

Holloway, David, and Sharp, Jane M.O., eds. 1984. *The Warsaw Pact: alliance in transition.* Ithaca, N.Y.: Cornell University Press.

McHenry, Robert, ed. 1992. *The new encyclopedia Britannica.* Chicago: Encyclopedia Britannica, Inc.

Nelson, David N., ed. 1984. *Soviet allies: the Warsaw Pact and the issue of reliability.* Boulder, Colo.: Westview Press.

Plano, Jack C., and Greenberg, Milton. 1989. *The American political dictionary.* New York: Holt, Rinehart and Winston.

WASHINGTON MODEL. The form of federal government used in the United States at Washington that contrasts with the Westminster system in Britain. In the Washington model the executive and legislative functions of government are separated, and, unlike the Westminster system, both branches derive their authority directly from election. The upper house of the legislature, the Senate, has an equal number of members from each state. Appointment to high office in the public service departments is based on an individual's political interests and connections, as well as on previous service to the party in power. In contrast, in the Westminster system public servants are appointed solely on merit and make themselves a career of service to the nation no matter what party wins at the elections. The Washington model usually requires a political appointee to offer his or her resignation should there be a change in the party in power; an alternative is to limit appointments of public servants to five years. A blend of the Washington model and the Westminster system may be found in some of Britain's former colonies, notably Australia (Thompson, 1980).

Washington, the federal capital of the United States, is a city covering the District of Columbia between Virginia and Maryland on the east coast of the United States. A spacious imperial city, it has wide avenues, fine government architecture, and large, impressive museums and monuments. The White House, where U.S. presidents live, was started in 1792, and in 1800 when the government moved to Washington, John Adams was the first president to live there. In 1814 the British captured Washington during the War of 1812 and burned the city; the White House was slowly rebuilt, and by 1856 the city was substantial again. In the 1920s and 1930s Washington was the center of political interest in the United States, a city of mass demonstrations and vast cultural exhibitions. Today all major U.S. institutions relating to international affairs, diplomacy, business, finance, and commerce are found there.

See also WESTMINSTER SYSTEM.

Sources

Canby, Courtlandt. 1984. *The encyclopedia of historic places.* London: Mansell Publishing.

Curtis, Michael. 1968. *Comparative government and politics: and introductory essay in political sciences.* New York: Harper and Row.

Robertson, David. 1985. *The Penguin dictionary of politics.* Harmondsworth: Penguin.

Shaw, Malcolm. 1968. *Anglo-American Democracy.* London: Routledge and Kegan Paul.

Thompson, Elaine. 1980. Washminster mutation. In Patrick D. Weller and Dean Jaensch, eds. *Responsible government in Australia.* Richmond, Victoria: Drummond Publishing for the Australasian Political Studies Association.

Wheare, Kenneth C. 1968. *Legislatures.* 2d ed. London: Oxford University Press.

WATERGATE. A political scandal involving bureaucratic corruption at the highest level that destroys confidence in government and its agents. The term originally referred to a political scandal that began on the night of June 17, 1972, when employees of the Campaign to Re-elect the President (Richard Nixon) were caught when they broke into the Democratic party's National Committee headquarters. The burglars were Bernard L. Barker (b. 1917 in Cuba, a CIA member); Virgilio R. Gonzalez, a locksmith; Eugenio R. Martinez, a Cuban exile; James W. McCord (b. 1924), an ex-C.I.A. member; and Frank A. Sturgis, a former marine. The committee's headquarters were in the Watergate office-hotel-apartment building in Washington, D.C. The president's staff kept the affair from the public, but a reporter from the *Washington Post* had attended the court when the five were arraigned, and by January 1973 when they appeared in court the White House was accused of a coverup.

Watergate, as this event was named, unfolded over more than two years and implicated the U.S. president Nixon and his advisers, leading to his resignation and to the imprisonment of several close associates. The term *Watergate* became synonymous with political disgrace and spawned other terms like *Irangate* to indicate political scandals in other places. In the United States Watergate symbolizes crimes involving the abuses of power, especially as they relate to the Federal Bureau of Investigation, the Central Intelligence Agency, and the president. Faith in the U.S. government declined when its agents lied, law enforcement agencies concocted evidence, forged letters, faked death threats, planted information as agent provocateurs, and kidnapped. The original scandal raised many ethical issues, questions about Nixon's morality and about illegalities centering on the White House, and provoked political outrage at vast deceptions regarding political judgments, as well as indicating how adaptive the American presidential system was.

Sources

Friedman, Leon, and Levantrosser, William F., eds. 1992. *Watergate and afterward: the legacy of Richard M. Nixon.* Westport, Conn.: Greenwood Press.

Shafritz, Jay M. 1988. *The Dorsey dictionary of American government and politics.* Chicago: Dorsey.

White, Theodore H. 1975. *Breach of faith: the fall of Richard Nixon.* New York: Atheneum.

WEBERIAN. Referring to the twentieth-century German sociologist and theorist in social sciences and to his ideas on bureaucracy, the Protestant ethic, charisma in politics, value-free social research, and his general aim to explain the unique development of Western civilization, especially its emphasis on rationalism.

Max Weber (1864–1920) was the son of a lawyer and was encouraged in his interests by the intellectual life in his home. He studied at the universities of Heidelberg and Göttingen, took his bar exam, and completed academic training in law, economics, history, and philosophy (1891). He taught at university, but in 1897 he suffered a mental breakdown and did not resume his work until 1903. In 1904 he began publishing his works as a private scholar and returned to university life only a few years before he died. His work was marked by intellectual tensions and strong opposition to Marx's writings. A founder of sociology, he assumed the study began with the individual in action, and he held the view that inner feelings and self-perception were important in the explanation of social action. His noted sociological work was *The Protestant Ethic and the Spirit of Capitalism* which depicted a close relation between the way heavenly salvation could be cultivated and the techniques used to further capitalist economies. In politics he suggested that political changes were the result of charisma being routinized by way of traditional and then rational-legal forms of authority. His thoughts on bureaucracy were seminal, as were his studies in the sociology of religion.

Sources

Bendix, Reinhard. 1960. *Max Weber: an intellectual portrait.* Garden City, N.Y.: Doubleday.

Coser, Lewis A. 1977. *Masters of sociological thought.* New York: Harcourt Brace Jovanovich.

Devine, Elizabeth; Held, Michael; Vinson, James; and Walsh, George, eds. 1983. *Thinkers of the twentieth century: a biographical, bibliographical and critical dictionary.* London: Macmillan.

Gerth, H. H., and Mills, C. Wright, eds. 1946. *From Max Weber: essays in sociology.* New York: Oxford University Press.

Mitzman, Arthur. 1970. *The iron cage: an historical interpretation of Max Weber.* New York: Alfred A. Knopf.

Parkin, Frank. 1982. *Max Weber.* London: Methuen.

Sica, Alan. 1991. *Weberian social theory.* Oxford: Basil Blackwell.

Sills, David L., ed. 1968. *International encyclopedia of the social sciences.* New York: Macmillan and Free Press.

Weber, Marianne. 1988. *Max Weber; a biography.* Trans. and ed. Harry Zohn. New Brunswick, N.J.: Transaction Books.

Zusne, Leonard. 1984. *Biographical dictionary of psychology.* Westport, Conn.: Greenwood Press.

WEIMAR REPUBLIC. Germany's first democratic parliament after World War I. After Kaiser Wilhem II abdicated on November 9, 1918, the Republic was established and its constitution drawn up and promulgated, August 11, 1919. But the Republic fell in 1930 when the global recession hit Germany. For ten years the Republic had failed to get unified support from the German people; it suffered from the resentment of those who wanted a monarchy; the ill-will of the conservatives who opposed the terms of the Treaty of Versailles; the discontent of left-wing radicals who sought a revolution in Germany; and the extreme pressures of French foreign policy. Weimar symbolized the failure of Germans to accept democracy in the first half of the twentieth century; however, during its tenure unusual and lasting developments occurred in German art, theater, music, and cinema. The Republic was led by Friedrich Ebert (1919–25) and von Hindenburg (1925–34); it disappeared in 1933 when Adolf Hitler became chancellor and instituted the Third Reich by passing an Enabling Act suspending the Weimar Republic.

Weimar is the Thuringian city in the southwest of what was East Germany on the River Ilm. It has colleges of technology, music, and architecture and the Weimar Castle, and is recalled fondly for its associations with the German literary figures, Goethe and Schiller, and the musician, Franz Liszt. Nearby was the Nazi concentration camp, Buchenwald.

Sources

Cerci, Ian, ed. 1990. *Weimar: why did German democracy fail?* New York: St. Martin's Press.

Canby, Courtlandt. 1984. *The encyclopedia of historic places.* London: Mansell Publishing.

Crystal, David, ed. 1990. *The Cambridge encyclopedia.* Cambridge: Cambridge University Press.

Gay, Peter. 1969. *Weimar culture: the outsider as insider.* London: Secker and Warburg.

Laquer, Walter. 1974. *Weimar: a cultural history, 1918–1933.* London: Weidenfeld and Nicolson.

WEISMANNISM. A theory of heredity that assumes continuity of germ plasm and nontransmission of acquired characteristics.

August Friedrich Leopold Weismann (1834–1914) was born at Frankfurt am Main, and when young developed a deep interest in natural history from his collecting of insects and plants. He studied at the University of Göttingen (1852–56), worked as a chemist, became an army doctor, and was appointed physician to Archduke Stephen of Austria. In 1863 he joined the medical faculty, University of Freiburg, and directed its zoological institute and museum until retirement (1912). Failing eyesight making him unable to use a microscope in his later years, he turned to theory and asserted that germ cells contained an hereditary substance vital to the continuation of a species. Today it is known by chromosomes, genes, and DNA. He also predicted the possibility of nuclear division. Although he opposed the idea that acquired characteristics could be inherited, he supported Darwin's theory. A deeply patriotic German, he backed Bismarck's policy of a unified nation in World War I and refused to be honored by the British.

Sources

Gaupp, Ernst. 1917. *August Weismann sein Leben und sein Werk.* Jena: G. Fischer.

Gillespie, Charles C., ed. 1976. *Dictionary of scientific biography.* New York: Charles Scribner's Sons.

McHenry, Robert, ed. 1992. *The new encyclopedia Britannica.* Chicago: Encyclopedia Britannica, Inc.

Weismann, August F.L. 1893. *The germ plasm: a theory of heredity.* Trans. W. Newton Parker and Harriet Ronnfeldt, 1974. London: W. Scott.

WELLSIAN. Mind-boggling but realizable, especially relating to science and social science fiction; the suggestion that humankind could easily lead a rational life in a humane civilization; also relating to a shabby but genteel world inhabited by some of Wells's characters.

Herbert George Wells (1866–1946) was born at Bromley, Kent, son of a professional cricketer, and educated at Midhurst Grammar, Sussex. He was apprenticed to a chemist, and at age 18 he became a pupil-teacher and attended the Royal College of Science. He graduated in science at London University and then taught in a private school; he turned to professional writing with the first of his popular imaginative fantasies, *The Time Machine* (1895), a social allegory about a two-class society. It was quickly followed by many other fantasies, including *A Modern Utopia* (1905). He was at the height of his fame during World War I, and his novel *Mr. Brittling Sees It Through* presented war from the homefront. His *The Outline of History* was first published in serial parts during 1919–20. He also became a novelist and scientific visionary. From his fantastic imagination came the invisible man, time warps, tanks, air warfare, the atomic bomb, and interplanetary war and much else that occupies science fiction buffs. His more enduring literature can be found in *Kipps, Tono-Bungay,* and *The History of Mr. Polly;* his bias for this form of social realism has been attributed to his lower middle-class upbringing. Wells, a prolific writer until he died, was disabused of his views on the rationality of humankind by World War I and II, as indicated by his autobiographies *Experiments in Autobiography* (1934) and *Mind at the End of Its Tether* (1945).

Sources

Coren, Michael. 1992. *The invisible man: the life and liberties of H. G. Wells.* London: Bloomsbury.

Hammond, Nicholas G.L., and Scullard, Howard H., eds. 1985. *The Oxford companion to English literature.* Oxford: Clarendon Press.

Legg, Leopold G.W., and Williams, E. T., eds. 1959. *Dictionary of national biography 1941–1950.* London: Oxford University Press.

McHenry, Robert, ed. 1992. *The new encyclopedia Britannica.* Chicago: Encyclopedia
    Britannica, Inc.
Ousby, Ian, ed. 1988. *The Cambridge guide to literature in English.* Cambridge: Cam-
    bridge University Press.
Vinson, James. 1979. *Novelists and prose writers.* London: Macmillan.
West, Anthony. 1984. *H. G. Wells: aspects of a life.* London: Hutchinson.

WESLEYAN. Relating to the system or doctrine in particular of the Methodist
Church and its eighteenth-century leader, an evangelist, educator, and social
reformer, who formed a religion based on the prayerbook, a book of homilies,
and the Bible, and directed primarily to England's working class.

John Wesley (1703–91), the British evangelist, was born at Epworth in England, the son of Samuel Wesley. He was educated at Charterhouse School and
at Christ Church Oxford, and became a fellow of Lincoln College (1726). From
1727 to 1729 he was curate to his father. Then he settled in Oxford where he
became leader of a band of young men noted for their religious earnestness,
regularity, and strictness in their lives and studies. His brother, Charles, wrote
thousands of Methodist hymns, and it was his lifestyle, so regular and method-
ical as a student at Oxford, that gave rise to the term *Methodism.* Wesley went
to Georgia as a missionary in 1735 and returned in 1738. At first he was allied
with the Moravians, but he soon abandoned all ecclesiastical traditions and established the Methodist Church. In 1739 he began open-air preaching, and tens
of thousands would wait to hear him; he would visit the poor, the sick, and
those in prison, practice self-discipline, and examine the self for ways to improve. Most of his converts were colliers, miners, weavers, and laborers, and
his earnestness angered the parish clergy who refused to open their pulpits to
him. The first Methodist conference was held in 1744. Wesley's literary work
was extensive.

Sources

Cross, Frank L. 1974. *The Oxford dictionary of the Christian Church.* 2d ed. New York:
    Oxford University Press.
Green, Richard. 1882. *John Wesley.* London: Cassell, Petter, Galpin.
Pollock, John. 1989. *John Wesley.* London: Hodder and Stoughton.
Stacey, John. 1988. *John Wesley: contemporary perspectives.* London: Epworth.
Stephen, Leslie, and Lee, Sydney, eds. 1917. *The dictionary of national biography.* Lon-
    don: Oxford University Press.

WESTERMARCK EFFECT. In children's early experiences of incest, constant contact leads to aversion, and in turn this aversion leads to brother-sister
avoidance. This explanation of the taboo against incest opposes that attributed
to Freud, which states early separation of brother from sister leads to repression
of mutual sexual desire, which in turn leads to great horror at the thought of
having sexual desires for one's sibling and strong taboos against incest (Faris,
1964:715).

Edward Alexander Westermarck (1862–1939) was born in Helsinki, Finland,

and received his Ph.D. from the local university (1890). His main interest lay in marriage, ethics, and religion, and his first book, *The History of Marriage* (1891), was so successful that it was translated into many languages and revised in 1921. For his studies he completed fieldwork in Morocco, examined records in the British Museum, and sent questionnaires to informants working among primitive peoples. Westermarck assumed that moral life was based more on conscious feelings than on intellect, and wrote on this aspect in *The Origin and Development of Moral Ideas* (1906–8). He published *A Short History of Marriage* (1926) in which he outlined his aversion theory to explain the incest taboo and exogamy. The work was augmented by his *Three Essays on Sex and Marriage* (1934), which opposed Freud's concept of the Oedipus Complex.

See also OEDIPUS COMPLEX.

Sources
De Mause, Lloyd. 1991. The universality of incest. *The Journal of Psychohistory* 19: 123–164.
Faris, Robert E.L. 1964. *Handbook of modern sociology.* Chicago: Rand McNally.
Sills, David L., ed. 1968. *International encyclopedia of the social sciences.* New York: Macmillan and Free Press.
Westermarck, Edward A. 1929. *Memories of my life.* New York: Macaulay.

WESTMINSTER SYSTEM. The British system of government in Westminster, London, and one favored by most of its colonies of settlement and some other members of the Commonwealth. In the system, executive power of government is exercised by ministers who are responsible to the lower house of Parliament. Their responsibility is both collective and individual; the government as a whole resigns or calls elections if it loses the support of the lower house: individual ministers answer to the house and, in theory, should resign if they mislead it or administer their departments incompetently; and the head of state is a monarch or president whose functions are largely ceremonial and who almost always acts on the advice of ministers. The system follows these principles: real power lies with the elected Parliament; Parliament makes the laws; judges and courts have powers separate from those of lawmakers; the political and administrative functions of government are separate; ministers are selected from Parliament; and ministers receive advice from civil servants in a neutral permanent public service and may act on its advice if they see fit.

Westminster, a city in inner London, is on the Thames River and is known as the center of British government. Whitehall, Downing Street, Buckingham Palace, the home of royalty, and the national shrine, Westminster Abbey, are found in Westminster. The Abbey was established in the tenth century, and since the fourteenth century the Palace of Westminster has been the home of the British Parliament. The palace was rebuilt in 1852 after the fire of 1834. Westminster has become synonymous with the British system of government.

See also WASHINGTON MODEL.

Source

Canby, Courtlandt. 1984. *The encyclopedia of historic places.* London: Mansell Publishing.

WHITLAMESQUE. Relating to the political imagery in Australia in 1972 that was associated with vision, confidence, initiative, challenge, faith in radical change, and the charisma of a leader who led the people to accept the slogan "It's time" (for change).

Gough Edward Whitlam (b. 1916) was born in Kew, Victoria, and was taken to live first in Sydney and later to Canberra where his father was deputy Crown solicitor. Gough was educated at Knox Grammar School, Telopea High School, Canberra Grammar, and the University of Sydney. Whitlam became an associate to Mr. Justice Allan Maxwell until World War II when he served in the Royal Australian Air Force. In 1945 he returned to university studies and completed a law degree (1946). In 1945 he had joined the Australian Labor party (ALP), and in 1952 he represented the ALP in the federal election and won the seat of Werriwa. In 1960 Whitlam became deputy leader of the ALP, and leader in 1967. In December 1962 he led the ALP to victory after over twenty years in opposition. Despite his demonstrative, witty, and charismatic leadership style, his government could survive only three years before being dismissed by the governor-general, Sir John Kerr.

Sources

Freudenberg, Graham. 1977. *A certain grandeur.* South Melbourne: Macmillan Australia.
Kelly, Paul. 1976. *The unmaking of Gough.* Sydney: Angus and Robertson.
Oakes, Laurie. 1973. *Whitlam PM.* Sydney: Angus and Robertson.
Reid, Alan. 1976. *The Whitlam venture.* Melbourne: Hill of Content.
Walter, James A. 1980. *The leader: a political biography of Gough Whitlam.* Saint Lucia, Queensland: University of Queensland Press.

WHITLEY COUNCIL, WHITLEYISM. A joint standing industrial council, national or local, composed of representatives of employers and workers in an organized trade to consider and settle conditions of employment; recommended in the report by the Reconstruction Subcommittee (1917, 1918).

John Henry Whitley (1866–1935) was born in Halifax and educated at Clifton and London University. He worked for his father, a cotton spinner of Halifax, and, with a strong interest in planning, architecture, youth, and social work, he became a member of the local town council (1893–1900). Elected a Liberal MP for Halifax (1900–28), he was chosen to be Liberal whip (1907–10) and chairman of ways and means. He made speeches on education and was elected speaker in 1921, having been deputy speaker for ten years. In the difficult industrial relations climate following the World War I reconstruction of British industry, Whitley's name attached to the joint consultation machinery (national joint councils, district councils, works committees) that was recommended by the committee of inquiry that he chaired (1917, 1918). The reports aimed for conciliation and cooperation in industrial relations. The ideas had wide support at the time. Whitley was also chairman of a royal commission on labor in India (1929–31), and he was appointed to chair the board of governors of the British Broadcasting Corporation (1930).

Sources

Legg, Leopold G.W., ed. 1949. *Dictionary of national biography 1931–1940.* London: Oxford University Press.

Marsh, Arthur. 1979. *Concise encyclopedia of industrial relations.* Westmead, Farnborough, Hants: Gower.

WICKSELL'S EFFECTS, WICKSELL'S THEORY OF CAPITAL. The values given to capital stock in realistic economic models with different types of capital goods; the term, introduced in Carl Uhr (1951), refers to the change in value of capital stock from one steady state to another. The overall Wicksell effect is the sum of the price and the real Wicksell effects, that is, the revaluation of the inventory of capital goods due to new prices plus the price-weighted sum of changes in the physical amount of different capital goods. Wicksell's theory of capital assumes that capital and interest may exist without money or credit, and can later be modified and refined as money appears and as an economy moves toward positive equilibrium.

Johan Gustav Knut Wicksell (1851–1926) was born in Stockholm, Sweden, orphaned early, and in 1869 entered Uppsala University to study mathematics. After an emotional crisis, he became a religious freethinker, taught secondary school (1873–74), and turned to student activism. In 1879 he studied social sciences, and following the work of the neo-Malthusian, George Drysdale, he became a popular lecturer on the origin of social ills. In the 1880s he lectured in Sweden and studied economics in London, and later he studied under Brentano in Strasbourg (1887) and went to Vienna (1888) and Paris (1889). In the 1890s he wrote about the marginal productivity theory of distribution, completed a treatise on taxes and a law degree, and secured a university appointment in 1900. He advocated market socialism, and his views on political economy together with his religious beliefs led to a prison sentence. He was found guilty of disturbing the religious peace with a satire on the Immaculate Conception and was put in a gaol of his own choosing for two months. After retirement from the university, he became an influential adviser to young economists, was active in his profession, and in the 1930s his followers were part of the Stockholm School of Economics. It drew on his ideas on value, capital, rent, gold standards, progressive taxation, and the theory of money.

Sources

Blaug, Mark, ed. 1986. *Who's who in economics: a biographical dictionary of major economists, 1700–1986.* 2d ed. Cambridge, Mass.: MIT Press.

Eatwell, John; Milgate, Murray; and Newman, Peter. 1987. *The new Palgrave: a dictionary of economics.* London: Macmillan.

Sills, David L., ed. 1968. *International encyclopedia of the social sciences.* New York: Macmillan and Free Press.

Uhr, Carl G. 1951. Knut Wicksell, a centennial evaluation. *American Economic Review* 41:829–860.

Uhr, Carl G. 1960. *Economic doctrines of Knut Wicksell.* Berkeley: University of California Press.

WIENER PROCESS. Economists' term for Brownian Motion, the first stochastic process, observed by the British botanist Robert Brown (1773–1858) in 1827. He observed particles suspended in a fluid. They were clearly moving; from this he concluded that motion arose from the particles themselves and that such unceasing and irregular motion is a property of all particles suspended in fluid. The idea was extended by other scientists into the kineteic theory of gases, and was, eventually, applied to economics.

Norbert Wiener (1894–1964) was born in Columbia, Missouri, graduated from Ayr Public High School in Massachusetts at 12 years of age, and at 15 entered Harvard Graduate School to study zoology, but turned to philosophy and completed a Ph.D. (1913) on the relations between philosophy and mathematics. His major understanding of mathematics began in 1918, and he joined the Mathematics Department at the Massachusetts Institute of Technology in 1919 where he remained until retirement. In 1921 Wiener gave Brownian Motion a mathematically rigorous formulation (Wiener, 1964). He made his name with *Cybernetics: or the Control and Communication in the Mind and the Machine* (1948). He helped design systems for World War II antiaircraft guns, and at the time he saw that a control system required a feedback loop that gave information on the results of its actions.

Sources

Blaug, Mark, ed. 1986. *Who's who in economics: a biographical dictionary of major economists, 1700–1986.* 2d ed. Cambridge, Mass.: MIT Press.

Gillespie, Charles C. ed. 1973. *Dictionary of scientific biography.* New York: Charles Scribner's Sons.

Levinson, N., et al. 1966. Norbert Wiener. *Bulletin of the American Mathematical Society.* Special Issue: 72. [With bibliography.]

Moritz, Charles, ed. 1964 and 1950. *Current biography yearbook.* New York: H. W. Wilson.

Nelson, Edward. 1967. *Dynamical theories of Brownian Motion.* Princeton, N.J.: Princeton University Press.

Wiener, Norbert. 1953. *Ex-prodigy: my childhood and youth.* Garden City, N.Y.: Doubleday.

Wiener, Nobert. 1956. *I am a mathematician: the later life of a prodigy.* Garden City, N.Y.: Doubleday.

Wiener, Norman. 1964. *Selected papers.* Cambridge, Mass.: MIT Press.

Zusne, Leonard. 1984. *Biographical dictionary of psychology.* Westport, Conn.: Greenwood Press.

WILBERFORCE REPORT. One of two British reports of courts of inquiry into a dispute between parties represented on the National Joint Industrial Council for the electricity supply industry.

Richard Orme Wilberforce, baron (b. 1907), was educated at Winchester College and Oxford University, and was called to the bar and made a fellow of All Soul's College (1932). He became a high court judge (1961–64), was created a life peer in 1964, and appointed lord of appeal (1964–82) and a member of the Permanent Court of Arbitration (1964–). In 1970–71 he was the chairman of the court of inquiry into the electricity workers dispute, and the mineworkers' dispute (1972). Since then, he has held many important public offices and became chancellor of the Hull University in 1978.

Sources

The international who's who, 1992–93. London: Europa Publications.

Marsh, Arthur. 1979. *Concise encyclopedia of industrial relations*. Westmead, Farnborough, Hants: Gower.

WILL ROGERS EFFECT, WILL ROGERS ILLUSION. The modern American humorist is reported to have said that one consequence of Oklahomans moving to California in the 1930s was to raise the average intelligence level in both states. This assumes a set of scores that has been divided in two may be divided again so that both subgroup means increase or decrease. For this to happen, the means of the two subgroups must be different. When the score falls between the two means, moving it from the group with the lower mean to the group with the higher mean will lower the mean of both groups, and vice versa. This is the Will Rogers effect. If both subgroup means are decreased, the illusion is created that the mean of the aggregate group has fallen. This is the Will Rogers illusion (Messick and Ascuncion, 1993). The consequences of the Will Rogers illusion could lead, for example, to the belief that overall quality of education declines when better students from disadvantaged schools transfer to good schools.

William Penn Adair (''Will'') Rogers (1879–1935) was born near Claremont in Indian Territory (later Oklahoma), son of a prosperous father of Indian origin, and went to various schools until 1898 before working as a cowboy in Texas. While traveling in South Africa, he joined a circus as a rope artist, calling himself ''The Cherokee Kid'' (1902). He toured Australia and brought his act home (1904) for the Saint Louis Exhibition, and with his southwestern drawl and his offhand, diffident, and amusing personality, he developed a career as an entertainer in New York (1905). Between 1916 and 1925 he was often in the Ziegfield Follies where he uttered his famous statement: ''Well, all I know is what I read in the papers.'' Beneath the wry and good-natured humor lay sharp satire, reserved especially for social and political issues. He wrote a column for the *New York Times* (1922) and toured Europe as President Calvin Coolidge's ambassador of goodwill. Among his publications were *The Illiterate Digest* (1924) and *There's not a Bathing-Suit in Russia* (1927). He became a popular movie star with *A Connecticut Yankee* (1931) and *State Fair* (1933). He died in an airplane crash.

Sources
Collins, Peter C. 1984. *Will Rogers: a bio-bibliography.* Westport, Conn.: Greenwood
    Press.
Croy, Homer. 1953. *Our Will Rogers.* New York: Duell, Sloan and Pearce.
Ketchum, Richard M. 1973. *Will Rogers, his life and times.* New York: American Her-
    itage/McGraw-Hill.
Messick, David M., and Ascuncion, Arlene G. 1993. The Will Rogers Illusion in
    judgements about social groups. *Psychological Science* 4:46–48.
O'Brien, Patrick J. 1935. *Will Rogers: ambassador of good will.* London: Hutchinson.
Starr, Harris E., ed. 1944. *Dictionary of American biography.* Supplement 1. New York:
    Charles Scribner's Sons.
Van Doren, Charles, ed. 1974. *Webster's American biographies.* Springfield, Mass.: G.
    and C. Merriam.

WILLINK COMMISSION. A British Royal Commission on the Police (1960)
with broad terms of reference on the constitution and functions of the local
police authorities, relations between the public and the police, and principle that
should determine police wages. It recommended that police pay rates be related
to selected skilled occupations.

Henry Urmston Willink (1894–1973) was educated at Eton and Trinity College, Cambridge, and rose to major during World War I. He was awarded the
French Croix de Guerre and the British Military Cross. In 1920 he was called
to the bar and entered Parliament (1940–48), becoming minister for health
(1943–45). He chaired several royal commissions, including one on betting
(1949) and another on problems of minorities in Nigeria (1957). He was
knighted in 1957.

Sources
Marsh, Arthur. 1979. *Concise encyclopedia of industrial relations.* Westmead, Farnbor-
    ough, Hants: Gower.
Who's who, 1972. London: Adam and Charles Black.

WILSON'S FOURTEEN POINTS. President Woodrow Wilson made fourteen
points that were the working basis of the armistice with Germany after World
War I (1918). They included (1) covenants of peace openly arrived at instead
of secret diplomacy; (2) absolute freedom in navigation on the seas in peace
and war; (3) the removal of all trade barriers; (4) general disarmament; (5)
impartial settlement of all colonial claims; (6,7,8) evacuation and restoration of
territory in Russia, Belgium, and France, including the return of Alsace-
Lorraine; (9) readjustment of Italian frontiers; (10 and 12) self-determination for
people of the Hapsburg and Ottoman empires; (11) restoration of the territory
of Romania, Montenegro, and Serbia; (13) creation of an independent Poland
with access to the Baltic; and (14) the establishment of the League of the
Nations.

Thomas Woodrow Wilson (1856–1924) was born in Staunton, Virginia, and
educated at Princeton and Johns Hopkins universities. He practiced law in At-

lanta, lectured at Bryn Mawr and Princeton, and became president of Princeton (1902) and governor of New Jersey (1911). A Democrat, he was elected the twenty-eighth president of the United States in 1912, serving two terms. His administration ended in his physical breakdown and is remembered for international problems with Mexico involving the Zimmermann Telegram and America's entry into World War I, his support of the League of Nations, and the U.S. Senate's rejection of the Treaty of Versailles. On the domestic front he was associated with the Volstead Act and the women's suffrage amendments to the U.S. Constitution. Among his many publications was *History of the American People* (1902).

See also ZIMMERMANN NOTE OR TELEGRAM.

Sources

Commager, Henry S., ed. 1968. *Documents of American history.* 8th ed. New York: Appleton-Century-Crofts.

Freud, Sigmund, and Bullitt, William C. 1967. *Thomas Woodrow Wilson: a psychological study.* London: Weidenfeld and Nicolson.

George, Alexander, and George Juliette. 1956. *Woodrow Wilson and Colonel House: a personality study.* New York: John Day. 1964 ed. New York: Dover.

Magnussen, Magnus; Goring, Rosemary; and Thorn, John O., eds. 1990. *Chambers biographical dictionary.* Edinburgh: Chambers Ltd.

Malone, Dumas, ed. 1936. *Dictionary of American biography.* Vol. X. New York: Charles Scribner's Sons.

Tucker, Robert C. 1977. "The Georges" Wilson re-examined: an essay on psychobiography. *American Political Science Review* 71:606–618.

Walworth, Arthur C. 1969. *Woodrow Wilson.* Baltimore: Penguin.

WILSONIAN STEALTH. The approach taken by the twentieth-century British prime minister (1964–70) to the policy of Britain's entry into the European Community. "A long recurring pretence to Euro-scepticism while he pursued an application for membership simply (in his deliberately ambiguous phrase) to 'find what the terms would be' " (Aitken, 1992:28). He had a reputation—imagined or real—for evasiveness and deviousness, and he became a controversial figure. Some even say his 1976 resignation was forced by British secret service officers.

(James) Harold Wilson, Baron Wilson of Rievaulx (b. 1916), was born in Yorkshire and educated at Wirral Grammar School and Oxford University, where he later lectured in economics. During World War II he worked in the Ministry of Fuel and was elected a Labor member of Parliament (1945). He served in Clement Atlee's postwar governments, and was president of the Board of Trade. He resigned in 1951 in protest against the government's arms policy. Under Hugh Gaitskill, Wilson became principal spokesperson on financial matters, and in 1963 on Gaitskill's death, Wilson was chosen to be leader of the opposition. He led the Labor party to victory in 1964 and became prime minister. He was defeated in 1970, reelected to power in 1974, resigned in 1976, was knighted (1976), and made a peer (1983).

Sources
Aitken, Ian. 1992. A labor leader quite out of the ordinary. *Guardian Weekly,* December
    6:28.
Leigh, David. 1988. *The Wilson plot.* London: Heinemann.
McHenry, Robert, ed. 1992. *The new encyclopedia Britannica.* Chicago: Encyclopedia
    Britannica, Inc.
Pimlott, Ben. 1992. *Harold Wilson.* London: HarperCollins.
Ziegler, Phillip. 1993. *Harold Wilson: the authorized life.* London: Weidenfeld and Nic-
    olson.

WINTER'S *n*-POWER SCORING SYSTEM. A scoring system using Murray's Thematic Apperception Test pictures to measure power motivation or the
need (*n*) for power. Research showed a distinction between the Hope for Power
and the Fear of Power and how the two relate in small groups. Results also
indicate that the private pursuit of power tends to be compensatory, while the
social pursuit of power is an expression of a stable personality (Winter, 1973).

David Garrett Winter (b. 1939) was born in Grand Rapids, Michigan. He
studied at Harvard, was a Rhodes Scholar at Saint Johns College, Oxford, and
completed a Ph.D. in social psychology (Harvard, 1967). He taught and researched at Wesleyan University (1967–87), was a Guggenheim fellow at the
University of Amsterdam (1971–72), and since 1988 has been at the Psychology
Department, University of Michigan, Ann Arbor. Among his publications are
Motivating Economic Achievement [with D. C. McClelland] (1969) and *A Case
for the Liberal Arts* [with others] (1981). He has published widely on human
motivation in professional journals and currently works in political psychology
on problems of power motivation.

Sources
Jaques Cattell Press, ed. 1978. *American men and women of science: the social and
    behavioral sciences.* 13th ed. New York: Jaques Cattell and R. R. Bowker.
Winter, David G. 1973. *The power motive.* New York: Free Press.
Winter, David G., and Stewart, A. J. 1978. The power motive. In Harvey London and
    John E. Exner, Jr., eds. *Dimensions of personality.* New York: John Wiley, pp.
    391–447.
Winter, David G. 1992. Power motivation revisited. In C. P. Smith, ed. *Motivation and
    personality: handbook of thematic content analysis.* New York: Cambridge Uni-
    versity Press, pp. 301–310.
Personal Communication.

WOLFENDEN REPORT. A British report that revolutionized attitudes to homosexuality and prostitution. It stated that prostitution was a social fact deplor-
able in the eyes of moralists, sociologists, and the majority of ordinary people.
It recommended against making prostitution illegal, even though prostitution
violated traditional efforts to stabilize societies through its three main disinte-
grating features: payment for, promiscuity of, and emotional indifference in

sexual relations. The report was followed by invoking penalties for street solic-itation, brothel keeping, and taking rent from the proceeds of prostitution.

Sir John Frederick Wolfenden, baron (1906–85), was an educationist and chairman of public inquiries. He was born in Halifax, son of a chief clerk in the education office, and was educated at Wakefield Grammar School and Queens College, Oxford. He was appointed a tutor at Magdalen College (1929), and was later headmaster of Uppingham School (1933) and vice-chancellor of the University of Reading (1950–63). He served on academic committees and charitable trusts and was chairman of the Youth Advisory Council at the Ministry of Education. Between 1954 and 1957 he chaired the Committee on Homosexual Offences and Prostitution. The Wolfenden Report and its recom-mendations made him a public figure. He was knighted in 1956 and was created a life peer in 1974.

Sources

Aldrich, Richard, and Gordon, Peter. 1987. *Dictionary of British educationists.* London: Woburn Press.

Blake (Lord), and Nicholls, C. S., eds. 1990. *Dictionary of national biography 1981–1985.* New York: Oxford University Press.

Report of the Committee on Homosexual Offences and Prostitution. London: HMSO. Cmnd. 247.

Wolfenden, John F. 1976. *Turning points.* London: Bodley Head.

WOLF(F)IAN. Relating to the eighteenth-century philosopher who systema-tized and popularized Leibniz's philosophy and worked for the growth of natural theology and rationalism.

Christian Wolf(f) (1679–1754) was born in Breslau and studied theology at the University of Jena. His main interest lay in mathematics, and he graduated from the University of Leibzig. He was made a professor of mathematics at Halle, and he was elected to the Berlin Academy (1711). After being exiled by Frederick I of Prussia, who was much influenced by the Pietists (1723), Wolf was made a professor of mathematics and philosophy at the University of Mar-burg Hesse (1723–40). He returned to Halle when Frederick II became Prussia's ruler (1740), was appointed the university's chancellor (1741–54), and was eventually made a baron of the Holy Roman Empire (1745). He assumed all propositions and facts to be derived from the principle of identity and Leibniz's principle of sufficient reason. His system contained nothing that did not follow from self-evident axioms or established truths. To him philosophy was, as he stated, the ''science of all possible things in so far as they are possible.'' He published works on logic, ethics, psychology, and empirical psychology.

Sources

Edwards, Paul, ed. 1967. *The encyclopedia of philosophy.* New York: Macmillan.

McHenry, Robert, ed. 1992. *The new encyclopedia Britannica.* Chicago: Encyclopedia Britannica, Inc.

Reese, William. 1980. *Dictionary of philosophy and religion: Eastern and Western thought.* Atlantic Highlands, N.J.: Humanities Press.
Runes, Dagobert, ed. 1953. *Dictionary of philosophy.* London: Peter Owen, Vision Press.

WYCLIF(F)ITE. Relating to the fourteenth-century English reformer and translator of the Bible and to his followers.

John Wyclif or Wycliffe (c. 1329–84) was born in Yorkshire, educated at Oxford, was briefly master of Balliol (1360–61), and became a doctor of divinity (1372). He turned to politics in 1374, and with royal approval he discussed with representatives of the pope the differences between Rome and England, especially on taxes and appointments to religious posts. He wrote a political treatise on divine claims to authority, and he recommended that since ownership of property was sinful the church might better give it away and live in poverty. He preached a modest disendowment of the church in London, thereby angering his superiors. While they were at odds among themselves, he became popular for his views and influential. When he argued that it was legal to retain the treasure usually associated with Rome, the pope sought his arrest. His attack on the church was based on a belief in predestination and the presence of an invisible church of the elect. He was first to translate the Bible into English, and was taken up by the Lollards who spread his views. His social and religious reforms were supportive of the Peasants' Revolt (1381), and many believe he was the forerunner of the Protestant Reformation.

Sources

Cross, Frank L. 1974. *The Oxford dictionary of the Christian Church.* 2d ed. New York: Oxford University Press.
Fountain, David. 1984. *John Wycliffe; the dawn of the Reformation.* Southampton: Mayflower Christian Books.
Kenny, Anthony. 1985. *Wyclif.* New York: Oxford University Press.
McHenry, Robert, ed. 1992. *The new encyclopedia Britannica.* Chicago: Encyclopedia Britannica, Inc.
Robertson, Edwin. 1984. *Wycliffe: morning star of the Reformation.* Hants: Marshall, Morgan and Scott.
Stephen, Leslie, and Lee, Sydney, eds. 1917. *The dictionary of national biography.* London: Oxford University Press.
Workman, Herbert B. 1926. *John Wyclif: a study of the English medieval church.* Oxford: Clarendon Press.

WYKEHAMIST. Present or past pupil of Winchester College, Britain's oldest public school, on the River Itchen 60 miles southwest of London.

William of Wykeham or Wickham (1324–1404) was born at Wykeham in Hampshire and rose from obscure origins to much wealth and influence through politics. He was a typical worldly religious of the Middle Ages. A noted English statesman, he became bishop of Winchester in 1367 and chancellor of England (1367–71; 1389–91). A charitable administrator and generous patron of learning, he endowed a grammar school at Winchester (1382) and New College, Oxford

(1379). In 1404 he finished rebuilding the nave of Winchester Cathedral and was buried in the chantry. Among leading Wykehamists were Dr. Thomas Arnold of Rugby, Anthony Trollope, Sir Stafford Cripps, Arnold Toynbee, and Hugh Gaitskell.

Sources

Hayter, William G. 1970. *William of Wykeham: patron of the arts.* London: Chatto and Windus.

Law, M. D., and Dixon, M. Vibart, eds. 1966. *Chambers encyclopedia.* London: Pergamon Press.

McHenry, Robert, ed. 1992. *The new encyclopedia Britannica.* Chicago: Encyclopedia Britannica, Inc.

Stephen, Leslie, and Lee, Sydney, eds. 1917. *The dictionary of national biography.* London: Oxford University Press.

X

XANT(H)IPPE. A shrew; a shrewish wife who nags and quarrels.

Xant(h)ippe (fifth century B.C.) was the wife of Socrates. According to gossip from later sources, she had a shrewish temper. Apparently, Socrates bore it patiently, and even told his son, Lamprocles, that he must be dutiful to his mother in spite of her temper. According to legend, perhaps Socrates was so ugly, uncouth, and difficult that he would test the goodwill of any woman who had the misfortune to be his wife. A recent blasphemous satire reconstructs her character in discussions of her views on domestic politics and the fitness of philosophers to rule (Scruton, 1993).

Sources

Brewer, Ebenezer Cobham. 1970. *Brewer's dictionary of phrase and fable.* Centenary ed. Rev. by Ivor H. Evans. New York: Harper and Row.

Hendrickson, Robert. 1988. *The dictionary of eponyms: names that became words.* New York: Dorset.

Scruton, Roger. 1993. *Xanthippic dialogues.* Trafalgar Square, London: Sinclair Stevenson.

XAVERIAN. Relating to the sixteenth-century Jesuit, the "Apostle of the Indies," and his work as a missionary.

Saint Francis Xavier (1506–52) was born at Xavier Castle, Sangüesa, Navarre, in northern Spain. He studied at the University of Paris, lectured there, and became acquainted with Ignatius Loyola. Xavier is reputed to be the most notable of modern Roman Catholic missionaries. He helped establish Christianity in Japan, India, and the Malay archipelago. He took his vows as one of the first of the Society of Jesus (Jesuits) led by Ignatius of Loyola (1534). The vows were to live in poverty and celibacy, as did Christ, and to go on a pilgrimage to the Holy Land. He spent his life saving both believers and unbelievers. Xavier's life is surrounded by legends and criticism, but recent studies confirm his saintly efforts. The Catholic Church canonized him and Ignatius of Loyola in 1622, and in 1927 Xavier became patron of all missions. December 3 is his feast day.

Sources

McHenry, Robert, ed. 1992. *The new encyclopedia Britannica*. Chicago: Encyclopedia Britannica, Inc.

Magnussen, Magnus; Goring, Rosemary; and Thorn, John O., eds. 1990. *Chambers biographical dictionary*. Edinburgh: Chambers Ltd.

Smith, Benjamin. 1903. *The Century cyclopedia of names*. London: The Times.

XENOCRATIC. Relating to the Greek philosopher whose ideas owed much to Plato: all reality derives from the interaction of two principles, the "one" and the "indeterminate dyad," such that the dyad accounts for diversity, wickedness, and motion while the one accounts for unity, rest, and peace. He differentiated mind, body, and soul; although he tended to reject earthly pleasure, he admitted that external circumstances were important to happiness.

Xenocrates (396–314 B.C.) went to Athens as a youth to study under Plato, accompanied him to Sicily (361), and when Plato died (347) Xenocrates went with Aristotle to Arteneus. In 339, because Aristotle was in Macedonia, Xenocrates succeeded Speusippus, Plato's nephew, as the Academy's principal, winning by merely a few votes from Menedemus and Heracleides. Three times he was a member of the Athenian legation, once to Philip and twice to Antipater. In 322, after the death of Demosthenes, Xenocrates refused to be a citizen of Athens because of the prevailing Macedonian influence, and would have been forced into slavery because he was unable to pay the alien resident's tax had it not been for the oratory of Lycurgus.

Sources

Brewer, Ebenezer Cobham. 1970. *Brewer's dictionary of phrase and fable*. Centenary ed. Rev. by Ivor H. Evans. New York: Harper and Row.

McHenry, Robert, ed. 1992. *The new encyclopedia Britannica*. Chicago: Encyclopedia Britannica, Inc.

Magnussen, Magnus; Goring, Rosemary; and Thorn, John O., eds. 1990. *Chambers biographical dictionary*. Edinburgh: Chambers Ltd.

Preece, Warren E., ed. 1965. *Encyclopedia Britannica*. Chicago: Encyclopedia Britannica, Inc., William Benton.

Y

YALTA AGREEMENT. The controversial Crimean conference, code-named "Argonaut," between Winston Churchill, Joseph Stalin, and Franklin Roosevelt (February 4–11, 1945) to agree on disarmament after World War II, the partition of Germany, and the Russo-Polish frontier, and to establish the United Nations Organization as planned at Dumbarton Oaks (1944). It was also agreed secretly that Russia would declare war on Japan after the defeat of Germany.

Yalta, originally the Greek colony, Yalita, passed to the Turks in the fifteenth century and later became a lumber and shipbuilding center on the Black Sea. In the late eighteenth century, after the Russians deported the population, the settlement was revived and became a principal spa in the Soviet Union. Several resorts were established along the subtropical coast, and many hotels and sanatoria were built with Yalta at their center. Wine-making, orchards, tobacco growing, and fish canning flourished, too. The Yalta Conference was held at the luxurious resort of Livadiya.

See also DUMBARTON OAKS.

Sources

Baudot, Marcel; Bernard, Henri; Brugmans, Hendrik; Foot, Michael; and Jacobsen, Hans A., eds. 1980. *The historical encyclopedia of World War II.* New York: Facts on file.

Canby, Courtlandt. 1984. *The encyclopedia of historic places.* London: Mansell Publishing.

de Senarclens, Pierre. 1988. *Yalta.* Trans. Jasmer Singh. New Brunswick, N.J.: Transaction Books.

Laloy, Jean. 1988. *Yalta: yesterday, today, tomorrow.* Trans. William R. Tylor. 1990. New York: Harper and Row.

Plano, Jack C., and Olton, Roy. 1988. *The international relations dictionary.* 4th ed. Santa Barbara, Calif.: ABC-CLIO.

Seltzer, Leon E. 1962. *The Columbia Lippincott gazetteer of the world.* New York: Columbia University Press and Lippincott Co.
Snyder, Louis S. 1982. *Louis S. Snyder's historical guide to World War II.* Westport, Conn.: Greenwood Press.
Sulzberger, Cyrus L. 1982. *Such a peace: the roots and ashes of Yalta.* New York: Continuum.
Thacharis, Athan G. 1970. *The Yalta myths: an issue in U.S. politics, 1945–55.* Columbia: University of Missouri Press.

YEZHOVSHCHINA. A reign of terror, lasting from September 1936 to December 1938, in Russia.

Nikolai Yezhov or Ezhov (1895–c. 1940) was born in Saint Petersburg. He was lame and stood five feet tall, and so was known as the "Dwarf." He became a member of the Communist party in 1917, and during the civil war was a commissar in the Red Army. He made a career through the Party Central Committee to became a favorite of Stalin (1927). He was put on Stalin's central Purge Commission that rid the party of over a million members, and in 1937 he was appointed general commissar of state security (NKVD). He organized the great purges at their most severe stage. The period "Yezhov time" that was given his name included the second and third Moscow Trials, during which half the Communist party membership was either executed or put into forced labor camps. Yezhov received the Order of Lenin in 1937. In all, about 7 million Russians were arrested, and most of them perished. Then for some unknown reason, Stalin began to suspect him. Yezhov was dismissed in January 1939, presumably executed, was never heard of thereafter, and was succeeded by Lavrenty Beria.

Sources

Conquest, Robert. 1990. *The great terror.* Revised ed. London: Hutchinson.
McHenry, Robert, ed. 1992. *The new encyclopedia Britannica.* Chicago: Encyclopedia Britannica, Inc.
Schultz, Heinrich E.; Urban, Paul, K.; and Lebed, Andrew I., eds. 1972. *Who was who in the U.S.S.R.* Metuchen, N.J.: Scarecrow Press.

YOUNG PLAN. A suggestion to reduce by 75 percent Germany's World War I reparations payments which had been agreed to in the Dawes Plan: the remaining payments were to be made as annuities to the international bank until 1988. The plan was proposed on June 7, 1929, and accepted in August 1929. In 1933 when Hitler became chancellor of Germany and refused to make the payments, the plan collapsed.

Owen D. Young (1874–1962) was born at Van Hornesville, New York, graduated from Saint Lawrence University (1894) and the Law School at Boston University (1896), and practiced until 1913. Thereafter he served the community, especially in industrial matters. He was the founder and first chairman of Radio Corporation of America (1919–33) and was chairman of the board of General Electric Company (1922–39). In 1919 he was a member of President

Wilson's first Industrial Conference; in 1921 he served at President Harding's Conference on Unemployment; in 1924 he was an unofficial adviser to the London Conference of Premiers. He was a member of the first and the second Committee of Experts appointed by the Reparations Commission, and he helped frame the plan under which Germany paid reparations to the Allies, until August 31, 1929. The committee sat in Paris, and since Young was chairman, its report was known as the Young Plan. He held many similar posts and was honored by the French and the Belgians for his work.

Sources

Cook, Chris. 1983. *Macmillan dictionary of historical terms.* London: Macmillan.

Howatt, Gerald M.D. 1973. *Dictionary of world history.* London: Thomas Nelson.

Moritz, Charles, ed. 1945, 1962. *Current biography yearbook.* New York: H. W. Wilson.

Tarbell, Ida M. 1932. *Owen D. Young: a new type of industrial leader.* New York: Macmillan.

Z

ZHDANOVSHCHINA. From 1946 to 1948—the "Zhdanov time"—when the Russian Communist party demanded ideological conformity from its writers.

Andrei Zhdanov (1896–1948) was born in Mariupol, Ukraine, and, from 1915, when he became a member of the Bolsheviks, progressed through the ranks to become a party boss in Leningrad (now Saint Petersburg); he led the city's defense forces against the Nazis (1941–44). Close to Stalin, Zhdanov was a member of the Politburo (1939) and enjoyed much influence after World War II. As secretary of the Central Committee, he directed Russian ideology, and, as he tightened the guidelines for postwar cultural activities, he attacked such writers as Boris L. Pasternak (1890–1960), Anna Akhmatova (pseudonym of the poet, Anna Gorenko) (1889–1966) and Mikhail Zoshchenko (1895–1958). Under his domination, Russian culture (1946–53) is thought to have reached its most impoverished stage. His death is a mystery; it preceded the "Leningrad affair" when almost 2,000 people died in a purge, many of whom were his associates.

Sources

McHenry, Robert, ed. 1992. *The new encyclopedia Britannica.* Chicago: Encyclopedia Britannica, Inc.

Schultz, Heinrich E.; Urban, Paul K.; and Lebed, Andrew I., eds. 1972. *Who was who in the U.S.S.R.* Metuchen, N.J.: Scarecrow Press.

Swayze, Harold 1962. *Political control of literature in USSR, 1946–1959.* Cambridge, Mass.: Harvard University Press.

Waxman, Maron, ed. 1983. *Great Soviet encyclopedia.* New York: Macmillan.

ZIMBARDO EXPERIMENT. The Stanford Prison Experiment, a social psychological study of mock imprisonment in which young men played the roles of prisoner and guard. It was conducted by its director at Stanford University, August 14–20, 1972. Originally planned for two weeks, the study was ended after six days because for the majority of participants the experiment became an evil reality. That is, they temporarily undid a lifetime of learning decent behavior—the "guards" were corrupted by the power of their roles and cruelly broke the "prisoners'" spirit so that each one lost his sense of solidarity, abandoned the others, and looked after himself alone.

Philip George Zimbardo (b. 1933) was born in New York City and educated at Brooklyn College, now the City University of New York, and at Yale (Ph.D., 1959). He taught at Yale (1959–60), New York University (1960–67), and Columbia University (1968), and has been a professor of psychology at Stanford University since 1968. He received distinguished awards from the American Psychological Foundation (1975) for his teaching and for research from the California State Psychological Association (1978). He has published over 100 articles and books, notably *Influencing Attitudes and Changing Behavior* (1969), *Psychology and Life* (1971), which has gone through thirteen editions, and studies in shyness, *Shy Child* (1980). The Zimbardo Experiment is on a television tape, *Quiet Rage: The Stanford Prison Study,* and is used for teaching in criminal justice courses. His interest centers on evil, the subtle control of feelings, and how normal people succumb to the pathology of thought and feeling.

Sources

Locher, Frances, ed. 1980. *Contemporary authors.* New Revision Series 85–88. Detroit: Gale Research.

Zimbardo, Philip G. 1972. Pathology of imprisonment. *Society* 9:4–8.

Personal Communication.

ZIMMERMANN NOTE OR TELEGRAM. A secret telegram from the German foreign secretary to the German ambassador in the United States, Count Johann von Bernstorff, January 16, 1917. It was intercepted and decoded by the British Intelligence Service. In the note, Von Bernstorff was told that Germany would resume unrestricted submarine warfare on February 1, 1917; he was directed not to tell the United States about this date until the very day itself; he was also directed to make a secret proposal to Mexico that if it were to side with Germany and declare war on the United States in the event America sided with England in World War I, then Germany would reward Mexico with the return of Texas, New Mexico, and Arizona, which had been lost sixty years before. Also, Japan should be encouraged to join Mexico in attacking America. President Woodrow Wilson made the telegram public on March 1, 1917, and thereby helped turn U.S. public opinion in support of those who sought America's entry in World War I.

Arthur Zimmermann (1864–1940) was born in Marggrabowa, East Prussia (now Olecko in Poland), son of a merchant. He studied at Königsberg and Leipzig, and became a clerk in Germany's consular service (1893). Zimmermann served in Shanghai, Canton, and Tientsin, and in 1896 he returned to Germany from China through America. He was promoted to legation counselor in 1902 in the German Foreign Office and directed the diplomatic service from 1904; was promoted to department director in 1910; and became undersecretary in the Foreign Office in 1911. Americans favored his appointment in 1916 as state secretary of Germany's Foreign Office. He was the first commoner to be appointed to the position. After the "Zimmermann note" was discovered, he resigned his position and disappeared from world politics. He died in Berlin.

Sources

Commager, Henry S., ed. 1968. *Documents of American history.* 8th ed. New York: Appleton-Century-Crofts.

Herwig, Holger, and Heyman, Neil M. 1982. *Biographical dictionary of World War I.* Westport, Conn.: Greenwood Press.

McHenry, Robert, ed. 1992. *The new encyclopedia Britannica.* Chicago: Encyclopedia Britannica, Inc.

Magnussen, Magnus; Goring, Rosemary; and Thorn, John O., eds. 1990. *Chambers biographical dictionary.* Edinburgh: Chambers Ltd.

Neilson, W. A., ed. 1964. *Webster's biographical dictionary.* Springfield, Mass.: G. and C. Merriam.

Tuchman, Barbara. 1958. *The Zimmermann telegram.* 2d ed., 1966. New York: Macmillan.

ZINOVIEV LETTER. A letter of September 15, 1924, and published shortly before the British election, October 29, apparently written by the head of the Communist International to the British Communist party. Party members were told to work for a revolution in Britain's militia. Political commentators thought the letter turned voters from the Labor party to the Conservatives, and ruined economic and political relations with Russia until World War II. The Soviet Union insisted the letter was a forgery by Russian émigrés in Berlin that had been planted in the European intelligence community and brought to the attention of the British secret service and the press by the British secret agent, Sidney Reilly (1874–1925). The British Foreign Office thought the letter was genuine.

Grigori Zinoviev—whose real name was Radomyslskiy—(1883–1936) was born in Elisavetgrad, Ukraine, and educated at Berne University. He joined the Russian Social Democratic party (1901), sided with the Bolsheviks in 1902, attended socialists' meetings in Europe, and helped edit periodicals, including *Pravda.* He immigrated to Switzerland and then returned to Russia (1902–5). He was Lenin's companion in exile and believed that England could never be reconciled to Russia. In World War I he was an internationalist, and with Lenin returned to Moscow from Switzerland (1917). After the October revolt, he was elected chairman of the Petrograd Soviet and later became chairman of the Comintern (1919–26). He made up the powerful "troyka" with Stalin and Kamenev during Lenin's decline (1924). Zinoviev campaigned against Trotsky and was elected to the Politburo in 1925, but later headed the "Leningrad opposition" and joined Trotsky. This action led to his expulsion from the Politburo (1926) and the party (1927). After recanting, he was readmitted and became a

Presidium member, but by 1932 he was again expelled from the party for counterrevolutionary actions. After again recanting, he was reinstated (1933). In 1935
he was sentenced to prison but executed a year later for alleged assassination
plans against Soviet leaders and for support of Trotsky. He published *War and
Crises of Socialism* (1920), and his *Collected Works* covered nine volumes. His
show trial of 1936 was annulled by the Soviet Supreme court (1988), and he
was cleared of wrongdoing.

Sources

Andrew, Christopher. 1977. The British secret service and Anglo-soviet relations in the
     1920s. *Historical Journal* 20, 3:637–706.
Chester, Lewis; Fay, Stephen; and Young, Hugo. 1965. *The Zinoviev letter*. London:
     Heinemann.
Knightley, Phillip. 1986. *The second oldest profession: the spy as bureaucrat, patriot,
     fantasist and whore*. London: Andre Deutsch.
Lockhart, Robin B. 1967. *Reilly: ace of spies*. New York: Stein and Day.
Magnussen, Magnus; Goring, Rosemary; and Thorn, John O., eds. 1990, *Chambers bi-
     ographical dictionary*. Edinburgh: Chambers Ltd.
Schultz, Heinrich E.; Urban, Paul, K.; and Lebed, Andrew I., eds. 1972. *Who was who
     in the U.S.S.R.* Metuchen, N.J.: Scarecrow Press.

ZIPF'S LAWS, ZIPF'S CURVE. From a statistical analysis of languages and
literary genres, the following appeared (1932): In a language, the more often
words are used the shorter they become; the most frequently used words are the
shortest, oldest, have the simplest structure, and the greatest semantic extension.
The law applies to other phenomena, for example, cities according to their population, and books according to their number of pages. The Zipf curve expresses
either the relation between frequency of occurrence of an event and the number
of different events occurring with that frequency; or the relation between the
frequency of occurrence of an event and its rank when events are ordered in
regard to the frequency of occurrence. Such curves have a remarkably uniform
shape under various circumstances, for example, different topics, authors, and
languages.

George Kingsley Zipf (1902–50) was born in Freeport, Illinois, graduated
from Harvard, and studied for a year in Germany. He earned his Ph.D. from
Harvard (1930) and taught German until 1950. The research for his Ph.D. concerned the relative frequency of use as a determinant of phonetic change in the
evolution of language. The laws and curve appeared from the statistical analysis
of language and genres (1932), and Zipf extended the theory to nonlinguistic
topics. He applied the theory and statistical methods to city size and population
movement in *National Unity and Disunity* (1941). Further extensions of the
work to semantics, psychology, sociology, and geography appeared in his *Human Behavior and the Principle of Least Effort* (1949).

Sources

Hartmann, Reinhard R.K., and Stork, F. C. 1972. *Dictionary of language and linguistics.*
     London: Applied Science Publishers.

Miller, George A. 1965. Introduction. In George K. Zipf. *The psycho-biology of language: and introduction to dynamic philology*. Cambridge, Mass.: MIT Press.

Sills, David L., ed. 1968. *International encyclopedia of the social sciences*. New York: Macmillan and Free Press.

Zipf, George K. 1965. *The psycho-biology of language*. Cambridge, Mass.: MIT Press.

ZOILISM, ZOILEAN. Unjustifiable, carping criticism.

Zoïlus (c. 400–c. 320 B.C.), a pupil of Polycrates and Isocrates, was a critic, grammarian, and rhetorician of Amphipolis during the reign of Philip of Macedonia. Zoilus was a Cynic philosopher and perhaps a Sophist. His name became proverbial because of his carping, malignant, critical statements about Homer, Plato, and Isocrates. He was called "Homeromastix," meaning "Scourge of Homer," for his sadistic criticism in nine books on Homer, for example, in Homer's grammar and imagery.

Sources

Brewer, Ebenezer Cobham. 1970. *Brewer's dictionary of phrase and fable*. Centenary ed. Rev. by Ivor H. Evans. New York: Harper and Row.

Howatson, M. C., ed. 1989. *The Oxford companion to classical literature*. 2d ed. Oxford: Oxford University Press.

Preece, Warren E., ed. 1965. *Encyclopedia Britannica*. Chicago: Encyclopedia Britannica, Inc., William Benton.

ZOLAISM, ZOLAESQUE. Literary manner and realistic orientation of the nineteenth-century French novelist who aimed for naturalism in his accounts of social life.

Emile Zola (1840–1902) was born in Paris, the only child of a French mother and an Italian father. In 1842 his father's death left the family in hardship. Emile studied at the Lycée Saint-Louis, failed to graduate, and struggled to find work. He became a clerk in a publishing house and then turned to journalism. He was the leading figure in the French school of naturalistic fiction, of which *Therese Raquin* (1867) is his first example. He was influenced by Jules Michelet and H. A. Taine, who advanced a scientific approach to literary history by stressing the value of theories of heredity. Zola planned a novel-cycle that turned on the fortunes of a single family during the Second Empire, so he studied that period and its common experiences. The series, called the "Rougan-Macquart," began with *La Fortune des Rougon* (1871) and continued until the twentieth novel, *La Debacle* (1892). The novels are realistic, but they have epic qualities that set them above mere realism. Zola supported Dreyfus's cause in an open letter against the French military, was tried for libel, and eventually sentenced to prison (1898), but escaped to England, and returned to Paris a hero (1899). He was accidentally suffocated by charcoal fumes in his Paris home.

Sources

Drabble, Margaret. 1985. *The Oxford companion to English literature*. London: Oxford University Press.

McHenry, Robert, ed. 1992. *The new encyclopedia Britannica.* Chicago: Encyclopedia Britannica, Inc.
Magnussen, Magnus; Goring, Rosemary; and Thorn, John O., eds. 1990. *Chambers biographical dictionary.* Edinburgh: Chambers Ltd
Richardson, Joanna. 1978. *Zola.* London: Weidenfeld and Nicolson.
Walker, Philip 1985. *Zola.* Boston: Routledge and Kegan Paul.

***ZORACH* CASE.** The Fourteenth Amendment to the U.S. Constitution ensured that religious speech was safe from interference by local authorities. In public education the Supreme Court insisted on separation of church and state, and extended this to outlawing release of time for religious instruction on school premises even if the parents asked for it. In the *Zorach* case the Court reconsidered the issues of "release of time" and approved of the New York City rule of allowing students to attend a religious center that was not on school property for their religious instruction during class times (*Zorach v. Clauson* 343 U.S. 306 [1952]).

Tessim Zorach (b. 1915) was born in New York, son of William Zorach, the sculptor. In 1949 the American Civil Liberties Union chose Tessim to become the first plaintiff after noting that he was well informed on the implications of a "release time" program and had several personal reasons for objections to issues it raised. He was thought to be a suitable citizen who would give a high standing to the litigation.

Sources

Alley, Robert S., ed. 1988. *The Supreme Court on church and state.* New York: Oxford University Press.
Grant, Daniel, and Nixon, H. C. 1975. *State and local government in America.* Boston: Allyn and Bacon.
Krinsky, Fred, ed. 1968. *The politics of religion in America.* Beverly Hills, Calif.: Glencoe Press.
Marks, Claude. 1984. *World artists 1950–1980.* New York: H. W. Wilson.
Pfeiffer, Leo. 1967. *Church, state and freedom.* Boston: Beacon Press.
Shafritz, Jay M. 1988. *The Dorsey dictionary of American government and politics.* Chicago: Dorsey.
Sorauf, J. Frank. 1976. *The wall of separation.* Princeton, N.J.: Princeton University Press.
Yinger, J. Milton. 1970. *The scientific study of religion.* New York: Macmillan.

ZOROASTRIANISM. A national religion of Persia from the sixth century B.C. to the seventh century A.D., and now found among only Guebres and Parsees in India. Its doctrines on the conflict between good and evil entered Judaism, and, through Gnosticism, Christianity.

Zoroaster (the grecized form of Zarathustra) was a Persian prophet who founded the religion. Legend states that he probably lived in the sixth century B.C. and was the prophet of Ormuzd, a spirit of light and good. According to the religion he taught, good and light spirits would overcome Ahriman, the spirit of darkness and evil, and, depending on one's earthly practices, one's own spirit would find life after death or eternal pain.

Sources

Cross, Frank L. 1974. *The Oxford dictionary of the Christian Church.* 2d ed. New York: Oxford University Press.

McHenry, Robert, ed. 1992. *The new encyclopedia Britannica.* Chicago: Encyclopedia Britannica, Inc.

Magnussen, Magnus; Goring, Rosemary; and Thorn, John O., eds. 1990. *Chambers biographical dictionary.* Edinburgh: Chambers Ltd.

Pauling, Linus, ed. 1986. *Word encyclopedia of peace.* New York: Pergamon Press.

Smith, Benjamin. 1903. *The Century cyclopedia of names.* London: The Times.

ZUKOR'S LAW. The public is never wrong.

Adolph Zukor (1873–1976) was born at Ricse in the Hungarian countryside and was orphaned at 8 years of age. His maternal uncle, a rabbi, raised him, and he was educated at the local school until he was 12. Then he was apprenticed to a storekeeper, doing chores while he learned to be a clerk and attended night school. He immigrated to the United States in 1888 where he studied in night school and worked in the fur trade. In 1902 he ventured into films as a partner in kinetoscope and phonograph machines, and two years later he built Crystal Hall, his first movie theater. In 1916 he signed up Mary Pickford (1893–1979) for Hollywood, and with the Jessie L. Lansky Feature Play Company formed the Famous Players-Lasky Corporation to make and distribute films directed by Edwin S. Porter (1870–1941). Later, Zukor worked with Cecil B. De Mille (1881–1959) (who said, "The public is always right") and Samuel Goldwyn (1882–1974). From 1917 he headed Paramount Pictures and was its chairman into his nineties. For his service to the film industry over a forty-year period, he was given a special Academy Award in 1948.

Sources

Cawkwell, Tim, and Smith, John. 1972. *The world encyclopedia of film.* London: November Books.

Halliwell, Leslie. 1984. *Filmgoer's book of quotes.* London: Granada.

Thomson, David. 1980. *A biographical dictionary of cinema.* London: Secker and Warburg.

Wakeman, John, ed. 1987. *World film directors: I, 1890–1945.* New York: H. W. Wilson.

Zukor, Adolph. 1953. *The public is never wrong: the autobiography of Adolph Zukor.* New York: Putnam.

ZWINGLIAN. Relating to the sixteenth-century Swiss reformer and his religious doctrines concerning the Eucharist.

Huldreich or Ulrich Zwingli (1484–1531) was born at Wildhaus, Saint Gall, in Switzerland. He was initially educated at home and then studied Latin at Berne, at the University of Basel, and in Vienna. He became parish priest in Glarus (1506–16) and Einsiedeln (1516–18). He turned to humanism, and, in the belief that one cannot overcome sin in this earthly existence, he insisted that life was best seen as penance or as a war to be fought against sinning, and primarily a challenge to follow the example of Jesus for one's salvation. He wanted to preach the gospel in Zurich (1519) and to replace the traditional mass with a daily sermon and prayer. In addition, he changed the Grossmunster chapel, where he had become parish priest, into a seminary for evangelical ministers. Zwingli's New Testament lectures are regarded as an important origin of the ideas of the Swiss Reformation. His attacks on Roman doctrine and practice resulted in the establishment of ecclesiastical independence. But the Reformation divided Switzerland, civil war erupted in 1531, and, at the battle of Kappel, Zwingli was killed while serving as chaplain and standard-bearer with Swiss Protestant forces. Among his works are *De vera et falsa religione (Of True and False Religion)* and *Fidei ratio.*

Sources

Bietenholz, Peter G., and Deutscher, Thomas B. 1985. *Contemporaries of Erasmus: a biographical register of the Renaissance and Reformation.* Toronto: University of Toronto Press.

Cross, Frank L. 1974. *The Oxford dictionary of the Christian Church.* 2d ed. New York: Oxford University Press.

McHenry, Robert, ed. 1992. *The new encyclopedia Britannica.* Chicago: Encyclopedia Britannica, Inc.

Smith, Benjamin. 1903. *The Century cyclopedia of names.* London: The Times.

Appendix: Classification of Social Science Eponyms

Anthropology and Archaeology

Benedict's Patterns of Culture

Benjamin

Binfordian Thesis

Cicerone, Ciceronian

Cochise

Dionysian and Apollonian Temperaments

Frazerian Hero

Galton's Problem

Johnny's Child

Kurtz Syndrome

Lucy, Lucy's Child

Mabo Decision

Marxian Anthropology

Mayo School of Anthropology

Prospero Syndrome

Tindale's Map

Tylorism, Neo-Tylorism

Economics

Ackerman Formula

Adam Smith's Invisible Hand

Almon Lag

Arrow-Debreu Model of General Equilibrium

Arrow's Theorem

Austrian School of Economics

Averch-Johnson Model and the Averch-Johnson Effect

Barlow Report, 1940

Bayesian Inference, Bayesian Methods

Behrens-Fisher Problem, Behrens-Fisher Distribution

Bernoulli Hypothesis

Bertrand's Duopoly Model

Birmingham School of Economics

Bland-Allison Act

Bolívar

Brady Commission, Brady Plan

Brandt Report

Chicago School of Economics

Coase Theorem

Cobb-Douglas Production Function

Cobdenism

Sherman Anti-Trust Act

Slutsky Equation

Smoot-Hawley Tariff Act

Stakhanovism, Stakhanovite, Stakhanovite
  Movement

Stockholm School

Taft Commission

Tiebout Hypothesis

Tontine

Tugan-Baranovskii Theory of Business
  Cycles

Tychism

Verdoorn's Law

Von Neumann Ratio, von Neumann
  Technology

Wakefield System

Walras's Law, Walras's Theory of
  Capital

Wicksell's Effects, Wicksell's Theory of
  Capital

Wiener Process

Education

Barlow Report, 1946

Birrelism, Birreligion

Bloom's Taxonomy

Bone Up on, to

Bryce Report (1895)

Bullock Reports

Burnham Committees

Burt Affair

Cowper-Temple clause

Devonshire Commission

Deweyan

Diggleism

Dunce

Feldenkrais Method

Flexner Report

Froebelian

Fulbright, Fulbright Act

Garfield's Law of Concentration, Garfield
  Constant

Geddes Axe

Gleig's School Series

Hamiltonian (a)

Hayter Report

Herbartian

Keller Plan

Lancasterian

Lindley Murray

Lockwood Report

McGuffey's Reader

McNair Report

Montague Grammar

Montessori Method

Mundella code

Newcastle Commission

Nuffield Approach

Orbilius, The Orbilius Stick

Percy Report

Pestalozzian, Pestallozzi Methods

Pilkington Committee

Plowden Report

Rhodes Scholar

Rosenthal Effect

Rudolph Steiner School

Samuelson Report

Wykehamist

Gender and Sexuality

Eonism

Hite Reports

Kinsey Report

Lolita Syndrome

Masochism

Masters and Johnson study

Packwood Case

Human Geography

Alonso Model
Berkeley School of Geography
Clawson Method
Colby Hypothesis
Hamiltonian Circuit
Haussmannise
Le Chatelier Principle
Lowry Model
Reilly's Law
Theil's Entropy Index
Ullman's Bases for Interaction
Von Thünen Model

Journalism

Burchett Interview, Burchett Declaration
Hearstism
Morgan's Secret Law of Journalism
Paparazzo
Pilger
Pulitzer Prize
Reuters

Language and Linguistics

Bloomfieldian
Chomskyan
Donat or Donet
Esperanto
Firthian
Hallidayan
Jakobsonian
Neo-Firthian
Sapir-Whorf Hypothesis
Saussurian
Zipf's Laws, Zipf's Curve

Legal Studies

Aristides
Austinian
Bakke Decision

Bertillonage, Bertillon System
Black Maria
Bobby, Peeler
Campbell's Act
Church Committee
Code of Hammurabi
Code Napoleon
Coke upon Littleton
Connally Amendment
Diddle
Dillon's Rule
Draconian
Durham Rule
Durham-McDonald Test
Fagin
Grotian Theory
Hohfeld System
Jim Crow, Jim Crow Laws, Jim Crowism
Justinian Code
Lindbergh Law
Lombrosian Theory
Lycurgus
Lynch
Lynskey Tribunal
Mann Act
McKenzie, McKenzie Friend, McKenzie Man
McNaughten Rules
Miranda, Mirandize
Mosaic Law
Nuremberg Laws, Nuremberg Rallies, Nuremberg Trials
Peelite
Pinkerton
Ponzi Scheme
Queensberry Rules
Rawlsian Justice
Scopes Trial

Sidney Stanley Principle of Finance

Solon

Tafoya Law

Torrens System

Tucker Act

Wolfenden Report

Management, Administration, Industry, and Business

Ackoff's Fables

Aldington-Jones Report

Alger Complex

Amulree Report

Ardrey's Laws

Ashby's Law

Attilaisms

Babbitt

Barnard's Executive Functions, Barnard's Zone of Indifference

Barzun's Law

Bedaux System

Bennis's Principle

Bergoff Technique

Blackett's Circus

Blake and Mouton's Managerial Grid

Boulwarism

Bumbledom

Butterworth Report

Caesarean Transference

Cameron Report

Carr Report

Cockburn Commission

Davis-Bacon Act

De Jonge Case

Diogenes Complex

Donovan Commission

Edsel

Fayol's Gangplank

Fink, Ratfink

Follett's Circular Response

Fordization

Gantt Chart, Gantt Task and Bonus Plan

Geddes Report

Goon Squad

Guillebaud Report, Guillebaud Formula

Halsey-Weir System

Hardman Report

Herzberg's Motivation-Hygiene theory

Holland-Martin Report

Hooper Rating

Hull's Theorem

Ince Plan

Jack Report

Jay's First Law

John Lewis Partnership

Karmel Committee

Kindersley Committee

Landrum-Griffin Act

Logan's Law

Lombard's Law

Mackenzie Report

Martin's Laws

Mayoism

McHugh Dispute

Mond-Turner Conferences

Nielsen Ratings

Norris-La Guardia Anti-Injunction Act

Owen's Silent Monitor

Parkinson's Law (or The Rising Pyramid)

Pearson Report

Peter Principle

Phelps-Brown Report

Priestley Formula

Pygmalion Effect

Robens Report

Robertson Report

Robinson-Patman Act

Rochdale Report

Ross Award

Rucker Plan

Scamp Report

Scanlon Plan

Scarman Report

Scott Bader Commonwealth

Shawcross Report

Socrates Complex

Stakhanovite, Stakhanovite Movement

Taft-Hartley Act

Taylorism

Therblig

Tolpuddle Martyrs

Tomlin Formula

Wagner-Connery Act

Whitley Council, Whitleyism

Wilberforce Report

Willink Commission

Zukor's Law

Philosophy and Early Social Theory

Althusserianism

Andersonian

Aristotelian and Galilean Modes of
    Thought

Aristotelian, Aristotelianism

Baconian (a)

Baconian (b)

Benthamism

Bergsonism

Berkeleian

Bradleyan

Buridan's Ass

Cartesian, Cartesian Linguistics

Christian Existentialism

Cliometrics

Cyrenaic

Diogenic

Euhemerism

Gaia Hypothesis, Gaia Theory

Hamiltonian (b)

Hegelian, Hegelianism

Hobbesian

Humean

Husserlian Social Ethics

Kantian

Leibnizian

Lockean

Mill's Canons

Neo-Hegelianism

Neo-Kantism

Nietzschean

Occamism

Peirce's Law

Platonic, Platonism

Popperian

Pyrrhonism

Pythagorean

Sartrian

Schutzian

Scotism, Scotist

Senecan

Socratic

Spinozism

Stahlian, Stahlianism

Tarski's Theory of Truth

Thomism, Thomist

Tupperism

Voltairean

Wellsian

Xenocratic

Politics and Political Science

Acheson-Lilienthal Report

Acton's law

Agnewism

Ananias, Ananias Club

Armagnacs

Augustan

Baader-Meinhof Group

Babouvism

Baconists

Balfour Declaration

Ballinger-Pinchot Controversy

Barbarossa

Barber's Model

Barebones Parliament

Baruch Plan

Benedict Arnold

Bennite

Berry Blight, Berryism, Berryite

Bevanite

Bevin Boys

Big Brother

Bing Boys

Bircher

Bismarckian

Blimp, Blimpish

Bob's Your Uncle

Bolo

Bonapartean, Bonapartism, Bonapartist

Borda Count

Boulangism

Bourbon

Boycott

Braddon's Blot

Brady Bill

Bretton Woods System

Brezhnev Doctrine

Brother Jonathan

Brownlow Committee

Brutus

Bryce Report (1915)

Burke Model

Burke's Peerage

Bush Plan, Bushspeak, Bushusuru

Butskellism

Cabal

Cabochiens

Cadmean victory

Caesar, Caesaresque, Caesar Cipher, Caesaropapism

Caesar's Wife Principle

Camp David Accords, Camp David Spirit

Cannonism

Capetian

Carlist

Carlylism (also Carlylese, Carlylesque, Carlylean)

Caroline, Carolean

Carolingian, Carlovingian

Carry Nation

Carter Doctrine

Castroism, Fidelism

Catiline, Catilinarian

Chamberlain Letter

Chicago School of Politics

Chomskyan

Christian Democracy, Christian Socialism

Churchillian

Clausewitz

Clifford-Elsey Report

Clinton, Clinton Republicans, Clintonism, Clinton Doctrine

Cobbett's Parliamentary Debates

Cobdenite, Cobden Treaty

Condorcet's Paradox

Creanspeak

Cromwellian

Crowe Memorandum

Curiel Apparatus

Jacobites

Jacquerie

Jeffersonian, Jeffersonian Democracy

Judas

Kadarism

Kahn's Law

Kaiser, Kaiser's War

Keatingism

Kellogg-Briand Pact

Khruschevism

King-Byng Affair

Kirkpatrick Theory

Lasswellian

Laureanistas

Laval

Lawsongate

Leninism

Lincolnesque

Lodge Corollary

Logan's Lament

Lord Haw-Haw

Louis Quatorze

Lovestoneite

Lynskey Tribunal

Maastricht Treaty

Machiavellian, Machiavellian Diplomacy, Machiavellian Personality

Madison Model

Mae West Factor

Maginot Line, Maginot-minded

Majorism

Mannerheim Line

Maoist, Maoism

Marshall Plan

Martinet

Marxian Politics

Marxism, Marxist-Leninism

Mary Factor

Marya Syndrome

Masada, Masada Complex

Mason-Dixon Line

Masterman Line

Mata Hari

Maud Committee

Maverick Independent

Mazarinade

Mazlish's Revolutionary Ascetic

McCarran Act

McCarran-Walter Act

McCarthyism, McCarthyite

McMahon Act

Medicean

Merovingian

Michels' Iron Law of Oligarchy

Milner's Kindergarten

Molly Maguires

Molotov Cocktail, Molotov Basket, Molotov-Ribbentrop Pact

Monroe Doctrine

Montezuma's Revenge

Montfortians

Montt-Varistas

Morgan's Laws of Politics

Morgenthau Plan

Muldergate

Naderist, Nader's Raiders, Naderism

Nakasone's Reforms

Nansen Passport

Napoleonic

Nasserism, Nasserite

Neronian, Neronic

Nestor

Nimrod

Nixon Doctrine, Nixon-Kennedy Debates, Nixonland

Oliverian

Orwellian

Osmanli, Ottoman

Out-Herod Herod

Paisleyism, Paisleyite

Palmer Raids

Parnellism Parnellites, Anti-Parnellites

Pasquinades

Pazzi Conspiracy

Peelite

Periclean

Peronists, Peronism

Perot Factor, Perotians

Pétain

Petrov Affair

Pittite

Plutocrat, Plutocracy

Potemkin Villages

Potsdam Conference

Poujadist, Poujadism

Powellism, Powellite

Pride's Purge

Pussyfoot

Pyrrhic Victory

Queen Anne's War, Queen Anne's
   Bounty

Quirinal

Quisling

Radcliff Report

Rapacki Plan

Rasputinism

Reaganism, Reagan Doctrine, Reagan
   Revolution

Robert's Rules of Order

Rodhamism

Rogers Plan

Röhm Purge, Röhm Putsch

Roosevelt's Four Freedoms

Rush-Bagot Agreement

Sadat Initiative

Saddamized

Sam Hill

Sasanid, Sassanid

Schlieffen Plan

Seleucid

Seljuk

Seward's Folly, Seward's Ice Box

Sharpeville

Shays Rebellion

Smith Act

Spartacists

Spinelli Initiative

Stalinism, Stalin's Law

Stalkergate

Star of David

Stern Gang

Stimson Doctrine

Tadpole and Taper

Tammany Society, Tammany Hall

Teapot Dome Scandal

Thatcherism, Thatcherite

Titoism

Tojo

Tokyo Rose

Tozer, Tozerism

Trotskyism, Trotskyites, Trotskyists

Truman Committee, Truman Doctrine,
   Truman Loyalty Order

Tuchman's Law

Tudor, Tudoresque, Tudor Rose

Tupamaros

Tylerize

Uncle Sam

Vance-Owen Proposal or Partition

Vansittartism

Vicar of Bray

Vichy Government

Victorian

Volsteadism

Wannsee Conference

Warren Commission

Warsaw Pact

Washington Model

Watergate

Weimar Republic

Westminster System

Whitlamesque

Wilson's Fourteen Points

Wilsonian Stealth

Yalta Agreement

Yezhovshchina

Young Plan

Zhdanovshchina

Zimmermann Note or Telegram

Zinoviev Letter

Popular Culture and Mass Behavior

Batmania

Bondomania

Campbellmania

Capra-esque

Chauvinism

Coxey's Army

Disneyism, Disney Pioneers, Disney
  Experience

Garbomania

Gorbeuphoric, Gorbymania

Madonna Connection

Madonna Factor

Olliemania

Presleymania

Rambo

Trudeaumania

Psychology and Social Psychology

Adlerian

Asch Experiment

Bernreuter Personality or Personal
  Adjustment Inventory

Bowlby Child

Electra Complex

Eriksonian

Erotic

Freudian

Icarus Complex

Jehovah Complex

Judas Trap

Jungian

Kleinian

Kohutian

Lacanian

Marcusean

Maslow's Need Hierarchy

McGregor's Theory X and Theory Y

Murray's Thematic Apperception Test

Narcissism

Neo-Freudian

Oedipus Complex

Othello Syndrome

Pavlovian

Peter Pan, Peter Pan Syndrome

Phaedra Complex

Phaeton Complex

Piagetian

Post-Freudian

Reichian

Rogers's Nondirective Therapy, Rogers's
  Interview

Rokeach's Dogmatism Scale

Rorschach Test

Sadism

Skinnerian, Skinner Box

Tomkins's Script Theory

Tucker's ''Warfare Personality''

Will Rogers Effect, Will Rogers Illusion

Winter's *n*-Power Scoring System

Zimbardo Experiment

Religion

Abraham's Bosom, Abrahamic Covenant, Abraham-Man

Arian Doctrine

Arnoldists

Athanasian Creed

Augustine

Barrowists

Barthian

Basilian

Benedictine

Bernardine

Bollandist

Bourignonist

Brocard

Brownist

Buchmanism

Buddhism

Cainite

Calixtin(e)

Calvinism

Cameronian

Campbellite

Celestine

Christian, Christianity

Christian Science

Clarendon Code

Clementine

Cocceians

Confucian

Constantinian

Crockford

Darbyite

Dominican

Donatist

Druze

Eddyism

Erastianism

Erostratus or Herostratus

Eutychian

Father Damien

Father Mathew

Febronianism

Franciscan

Gideons (International), Gideon Society, Gideon Bible

Gilbertines

Glassites

Gomarists

Huntingdonian

Hussite

Hutchinsonian

Hutterite

Ignatian

Irvingite

Isidorian

Jansenism

Jeffersonian Bible

Jehovah's Witness

Jesuit

Karmathian

Laudians

Lutheran, Lutheranism

Macmillanite

Manichaean

Marcionite

Maronite

Marprelate

Mechitarist, Mekhitarist

Mennonite

Millerite

Mohammedan

Molinism

Moonies

Morisonian

Muggletonian

Neo-Thomism

Nestorian

Noachian, Noachic

Norbertines

Origenist

Paulian

Paulician, Paulianist

Pauline, Pauline Conversion

Pelagian

Petrine, Petrinism

Petrobusians

Puseyism

Rappist or Rappite

Rastafarian or Ras Tafarian

Rogerene

Rosicrucian

Russellite

Sadducee

Salesian

Sandemanian

Schafiite

Schwenckfelder

Senussi, Sanusi, Sanusiy(y)ah

Simeonite

Socinian

Southcottians

Swedenborgian

Tartuffe, Tartuffian

Ursulines

Vincentian

Voodoo

Wahabi or Wahabee

Waldenses

Wesleyan

Wolf(f)ian

Wyclif(f)ite

Xaverian

Zorach Case

Zoroastrianism

Zwinglian

Sociology

Allport-Vernon-Lindzey Scale of Values

Bakhtinian

Bales's Interaction Process Analysis

Barnardos, Barnardo Boy, Barnardo's
    Children, Barnado's Home

Bavelas Experiment

Bennington Study

Beveridge Report, Beveridge System

Bion-type Group

Bogardus Scale of Social Distance

Boswellian

Brokaw Hazard

Burgess Marriage Adjustment Scale

Carry Nation

Ceausesca Orphan

Chapin's Living Room Scale

Cheshire Homes

Chicago School of Sociology

Comstockery

Comtism

Darling Case

Darwinian

Dickensian

Dix-Mann Formula

Dodge-Martin Thesis

Durkheimian, Durkheim's Law of
    Suicide, Durkheim's Law of Social
    Development

Edwards Social-economic Groupings of
    Occupations

Ferrer Movement, Ferrer Colony

Festinger's Theory of Cognitive
    Dissonance

Fiedler's Contingency Model

Neo-Lamarckism

Neo-Malthusianism

Neo-Marxism

Nestor

Nimrod

Niobe

Nobel Prize

North-Hatt or NORC Scale

Nosbinor Rule

Nostradamus

Onassis Prize

Oslerize

Othello Error

Owenite

Pandora's Box

Parsonian Theory

Pecksniff

Philippic

Pickwickian

Podsnappery

Post-Fordism

Procrustean, Procrustean Bed

Queensberry Rules

Rachmanism

Rechabite

Riesman's Tradition-, Inner-, and Other-Directed Types

Robinson Rule

Rockefeller, Rich as Rockefeller

Roe v. *Wade*

Rotter's Theory of Social Learning, Rotter's Internal-External Locus of Control Scale

Saint-Simonism

Seashore's Group Cohesiveness Index

Shavian

Shylock

Simon Legree

Sloane Ranger

Smithsonian Agreement

Social Darwinism

Spencerian

Srole's Anomie Scale

Stephenson's Q-Methodology, Stephenson's Q-Sort, Stephenson's Q-Technique

Stigler's Law of Eponymy

Teddy Boy, Teddy Girl

Thomas's Theorem

Thomson Colony

Thurstone Scale

Timonise

Torquemada

Townsend Plan, Townsend Movement

Volsteadism

Volumnia Syndrome

Warnock Report

Weberian

Weismannism

Wellsian

Westermarck Effect

Xant(h)ippe

Zimbardo Experiment

Zoilism, Zoilean

Zolaism, Zolaesque

Select Bibliography

Bayer, Alan E. 1987. The "Biglan Model" and the smart messenger: a case study of eponym diffusion. *Research in Higher Education* 26:212–223.

Beaver, Donald de B. 1976. Reflections on the natural history of eponymy and scientific law. *Social Studies of Science* 6:89–98.

Beeching, Cyril L. 1983. *Dictionary of eponyms.* 2d rev. London: Bingley.

Boycott, Rosie. 1982. *Batty, bloomers and boycott: a little etymology of eponymous words.* London: Hutchinson.

Coon, Deborah J. 1982. Eponymy, obscurity, Twitmyer, and Pavlov. *Journal of the History of the Behavioral Sciences* 18:255–262.

De Sola, Ralph. 1978. *Abbreviations dictionary: abbreviations, acronyms, anonyms, and eponyms, appellations, contractions, geographical equivalents, historical and mythological characters, initials and nicknames, short forms and slang short cuts, signs and symbols.* New international 5th ed. New York: Elsevier North-Holland.

Douglas, Auriel. 1990. *Webster's New World dictionary of eponyms: common words from proper names.* New York: Webster's New World.

Garfield, Eugene. 1981. Bradford's law and related statistical patterns. *Essays of an information scientist.* Vol 4. Philadelphia: ISI Press, pp. 476–483.

Garfield, Eugene. 1984. Current comments: what's in a name? The eponymic route to immortality. *Essays of an information scientist* 7:384–395.

Hendrickson, Robert. 1972. *The dictionary of eponyms: names that became words.* Reprinted 1985. New York: Stein and Day.

Leavy, Stanley A. 1985. Demythologizing Oedipus. *Psychoanalytic Quarterly* 54:444–454.

Manser, Martin H. 1988. *Dictionary of eponyms.* London: Sphere.

Merton, Robert K. 1973. *The sociology of science: theoretical and empirical investigations.* Chicago: University of Chicago Press.

Ruffner, James A., et al., eds. 1977. *Eponyms dictionaries index: a reference guide to persons, both real and imaginary, and the terms derived from their names.* Detroit: Gale Research.

Simonton, Dean K. 1984. Leaders as eponyms: individual and situational determinants of ruler eminence. *Journal of Personality* 52:1–21.

Stigler, George J. 1947. Notes on the history of the Giffen paradox. *Journal of Political Economy* 55:152–156.

Stigler, Stephen M. 1980. Stigler's law of eponymy. In Thomas F. Gieryn, ed. *Science and social structure: a festschrift for Robert K. Merton.* New York: New York Academy of Sciences, pp. 147–157.

Terban, Marvin. 1988. *Guppies in tuxedos: funny eponyms.* New York: Clarion Books.

Trahair, Richard C.S. 1990. *An Australian dictionary of eponyms.* Melbourne: Oxford University Press.

Valsrub, S. 1972. Mythologic eponyms updated. *Journal of the American Medical Association* 220:724.

Zusne, Leonard. 1987. *Eponyms in psychology: a dictionary and sourcebook.* Westport, Conn.: Greenwood Press.

Index

Main entries are indicated in bold.

Burgess, Ernest Watson, 123
Burgess, Guy, 272
Burgess Marriage Adjustment Scale, 94–95
Burgundians, 17-18, 103
Buridan's Ass, 95–96
Burke Model, 96
Burke's Peerage, 96–97
Burnham Committees, 97
Burr, Aaron, 602
Burrus, 456
Burt, Sir Cyril, 594
Burt Affair, 97–98
Bush, George Herbert Walker, 84, 85, 108, 124, 126, 132, 472, 492
Bush Plan, Bushspeak, Bushusuru, 98–99
Bustamante, Albert, 242
Butler, Richard Austen "RAB," 99
Butskellism, 60, 99–100
Butterworth Report, 100
Byng, Julian Hedworth George, 63, 336
Byrd, William, 192
Byrnes, James, 439

Cabal, 101–2
Cabochiens, 102–3
Cadmean Victory, 103
Cadmus, 103
Caesar, Gaius Julius, 23, 90, 127, 151, 320, 457
Caesar, Caesaresque, Caesar Cipher, Caesaropapism, 103–4
Caesar's Wife Principle, 104–5
Caesarean Transference, 105
Cainite, 105
Calandrini, Giovanni, 146
Cale, Guillaume, 308
Caliban, 515
Caligula, 572
Calixtin(e), 106
Callas, Maria, 472
Calvin, John, 237, 480
Calvinism, 106
Calvo, Carlos, 178
Cameron, Archibald, 308
Cameron Report, 106–7
Cameronian, 107

Cameronians, 384
Camp David Accords, Camp David Spirit, 107–8
Campbell, John, 109
Campbell, Alexander, 109
Campbell, Avril (Kim), 110
Campbell-Bannerman, Sir Henry, 35
Campbellite, 109–10
Campbellmania, 110–11
Campbell's Act, 108–9
Cannon, Joseph Gurney, 463
Cannonism, 111
Capetian, 112
Capraesque, 112–13
Condorcet, Caritat Marie Jean Antoine Nicolas de Marquis de, 141-42
Carlist, 113
Carlomen, 115
Carlylism (Also Carlylese, Carlylesque, Carlylean), 113–14
Caroline, Carolean, 114–15
Carolingian, Carlovingian, 115
Carpenter, Edward, 125
Carr Report, 115–16
Carrel, Alexis, 364
Carry Nation, 116
Carter, James Earl "Jimmy," 108, 132, 159, 631
Carter Doctrine, 116–17
Cartesian, Cartesian Linguistics, 117
Cassandra of Macedonia, 196
Cassel, Gustav, 597
Cassio, 476
Cassirer, Ernst, 361, 454
Cassius, 105
Castroism, Fidelism, 118
Catherine of Valois, 624
Catherine the Great, 510
Catiline, Catilinarian, 118–19
Cavendish, William, 162
Ceausesca Orphan, 119
Celestine, 119–20
Cesena, Samson, 578
Chadwick, James, 408
Chamberlain, Arthur Neville, 127
Chamberlain Letter, 120–21
Chambers, Jay Vivian Whittaker, 280
Chaos, 195, 220

Minos, King, 300
Miranda, 514
Miranda, Mirandize, 428–29
Mitchell, Wesley Clair, 372
Mitkevich, V. F., 276
Mohammed (Muhammad or Mahomet)
  201, 565, 640
Mohammedan, 429
Molinism, 429–30
Molinos, Miguel de, 429, 430
Molly Maguires, 207, 430
**Molotov Cocktail, Molotov Basket, Mo-
  lotov-Ribbentrop Pact**, 430
Molotov-Ribbentrop pact, 37
Mond-Turner Conferences, 432
Mondale, Walter, 306
Money-Kyrle, Roger Ernle, 509
Monroe Doctrine, 433
Montague Grammar, 433–34
Montague-Barlow, Sir Clement Anderson,
  39
Monte Carlo Methods, 434
Montessori Method, 434–35
Montezuma's Revenge, 435
Montfortians, 435–36
Montt-Varistas, 436–37
Moody, William, 602
Moon, P. B., 408
Moonies, 437–38
Moore, Clayton, 581
Mordecai, 247
Moreno's Sociometry, 438
Morgan, Christiana D., 444
Morgan, Lewis Henry, 400
Morgan, M. J. de, 137
**Morgan's Laws of Politics, Morgan's
  Secret Law of Journalism**, 439
Morgenthau Plan, 439–40
Morisonian, 440–41
Morrell, David, 526
Morris, William Richard, 466
Morrow, Anne, 364
Morrow, Dwight W., 364
Mortimer Mouse, 423
Mosaic Law, 441
Moses, 101, 441
Mosley, Oswald, 371
Mother Shipton, 441–42

Mouton, Jane Srygley, 68-69
Moyner, Lord, 595
Muggletonian, 442
Muhammad ibn Isma-'i-al Darazi-, 179
Muldergate, 442–43
Muldoon, Robert, 235
Mulroney, Brian, 110
Mundella Code, 443
Murdock Functions, 443–44
Murray, Henry Alexander, 34, 194, 300,
  444
Murray, Lindley, 365
Murray's Thematic Apperception Test,
  444–45
Mussolini, Benito, 482, 507, 529, 589
Myrdal, Gunnar, 597

Nabokov, Vladimir, 369
Naderist, Nader's Raiders, Naderism,
  447–48
Nagy, Imre, 323
Naiads, 498
Nairn, Thomas, 384
Nakasone's Reforms, 448
Nansen, Fridtjof, 523
Nansen Passport, 449
Napier, Jack, 45
Napoleon I, 121, 128, 137
Napoleon III, 261
Napoleonic, 449–50
Narcissism, 450
Nasser, Garmel Agdel, 555
Nasserism, Nasserite, 450–51
Nation, Carry Amelia, 116
Nation, David, 116
Natorp, Paul G., 454
Needham Thesis, 451–52
Nemesis, 452
Neo-Darwinism, 452
Neo-Firthian, 452–53
Neo-Fordism, 453
Neo-Freudian, 453–54
Neo-Hegelianism, 454
Neo-Kantism, 454
Neo-Lamarckism, 454–55
Neo-Malthusianism, 455, 653
Neo-Marxism, 455
Neo-Ricardianism, 455–56

Parnellism, Parnellites, Anti-Parnellites, 483–84
Parsonian Theory, 484–85
Parsons, Elsie C., 49
Parsons, Talcott, 184
Pasiphae, 497
Pasquinades, 485
Pass Laws, 574
Pasternak, Boris L., 669
Patman, John William Wright, 540
Patroculus, 268
Paul III, Pope, 314
Paul, Saint, 457
Paulian, 485–86
Paulician, Paulianist, 486
Pauline, Pauline Conversion, 486–87
Pavlovian, 487
Pazzi Conspiracy, 487–88
Pearson Report, 488
Pecksniff, 488–89
Pedrarias (Pedro Arias de Avila), 144
Peel, Sir Robert, 417, 458, 489
Peelers, 73
Peelite, 73
Peirce's Law, 489–90
Pelagian, 490
Pelham-Clinton, Henry Pelham Fiennes, 458
Penn, William, 602
Penry, John, 396
Pepin III, 115, 421
Percy Report, 490–91
Perdiccas III, 500
Periclean, 491
Peronists, Peronism, 491–92
Perot Factor, Perotians, 492–93
Pestalozzian, Pestalozzi Methods, 493–94
Pétain, Marshal Henri-Philippe, 282, 633
Pétain, 494
Peter, Laurence Johnston, 495
Peter, Saint, 12, 457
Peter of Bruis, 496
Peter Pan, Peter Pan Syndrome, 494–95
Peter Porcupine, 134
Peter Principle, 495

Peter the Great, 358
Petrine, Petrinism, 495–96
Petrobusians, 496
Petrov Affair, 496–97
Phaedra Complex, 497–98
Phaeton Complex, 498
Phelps-Brown Report, 498–99
Phelps-Friedman Theory, 499–500
Philby, Kim, 272
Philip II, 500
Philip II Augustus, 112
Philip of Macedonia, 162, 673
Philippic, 500
Phillips Curve, 500–501
Piaget, Jean, 340
Piagetian, 501–2
Pickford, Mary, 423, 675
Pickwickian, 502
Pictet, Adolphe, 562
Pierce, Franklin, 170
Pierus, 132
Pigou Effect, Pigovian Tax, 502–3
Pilger, 503
Pilkington Committee, 503–4
Pinchot, Gifford, 36
Pinkerton, Allan, 207
Pinkerton men, 207
Pinkerton, 504
Pious XII, Pope, 57
Pittite, 504–5
Plato, 17, 586, 664, 673
Platonic, Platonism, 505
Plowden Report, 505–6
Plutocrat, Plutocracy, Plutology or Plutonomy, 506
Podsnappery, 506
Poe, Edgar Allan, 378
Poiret, Peter, 81
Polycrates, 673
Pompadour, Madame, 636
Pompeia, 104
Pompey, 127, 588
Pontryagin's Principle of Optimality, 507
Ponzi Scheme, 507–8
Pope, Alexander, 55
Poppae Sabina, 456

About the Author

RICHARD C. S. TRAHAIR conducts social research in the Faculty of Social Sciences at La Trobe University in Australia. His publications include *The Humanist Temper: Life and Work of Elton Mayo* (1984) and *What's in a Name?: An Australian Dictionary of Eponyms* (1990), along with several bibliographies and journal articles.

ISBN 0-313-27961-6

90000>

EAN

9 780313 279614

HARDCOVER BAR CODE